KF 1849 H44 1983b

37793

DATE DUE

North Hennepin Community College Library
7411 85th Avenue North
Brooklyn Park, MN 55445

American Casebook Series
Hornbook Series and Basic Legal Texts
Nutshell Series

of

WEST PUBLISHING COMPANY
P.O. Box 3526
St. Paul, Minnesota 55165
May, 1983

ACCOUNTING

Fiflis and Kripke's Teaching Materials on Accounting for Business Lawyers, 2nd Ed., 684 pages, 1977 (Casebook)

Siegel and Siegel's Accounting and Financial Disclosure: A Guide to Basic Concepts, approximately 250 pages, 1983 (Text)

ADMINISTRATIVE LAW

Davis' Cases, Text and Problems on Administrative Law, 6th Ed., 683 pages, 1977 (Casebook)

Davis' Basic Text on Administrative Law, 3rd Ed., 617 pages, 1972 (Text)

Davis' Police Discretion, 176 pages, 1975 (Text)

Gellhorn and Boyer's Administrative Law and Process in a Nutshell, 2nd Ed., 445 pages, 1981 (Text)

Mashaw and Merrill's Introduction to the American Public Law System, 1095 pages, 1975, with 1980 Supplement (Casebook)

Robinson, Gellhorn and Bruff's The Administrative Process, 2nd Ed., 959 pages, 1980, with 1983 Supplement (Casebook)

ADMIRALTY

Healy and Sharpe's Cases and Materials on Admiralty, 875 pages, 1974 (Casebook)

Maraist's Admiralty in a Nutshell, approximately 325 pages, 1983 (Text)

AGENCY—PARTNERSHIP

Fessler's Alternatives to Incorporation for Persons in Quest of Profit, 258 pages, 1980 (Casebook)

AGENCY—PARTNERSHIP—Continued

Henn's Cases and Materials on Agency, Partnership and Other Unincorporated Business Enterprises, 396 pages, 1972 (Casebook)

Reuschlein and Gregory's Hornbook on the Law of Agency and Partnership, 625 pages, 1979, with 1981 pocket part (Text)

Seavey's Hornbook on Agency, 329 pages, 1964 (Text)

Seavey and Hall's Cases on Agency, 431 pages, 1956 (Casebook)

Seavey, Reuschlein and Hall's Cases on Agency and Partnership, 599 pages, 1962 (Casebook)

Selected Corporation and Partnership Statutes and Forms, 556 pages, 1982

Steffen and Kerr's Cases and Materials on Agency-Partnership, 4th Ed., 859 pages, 1980 (Casebook)

Steffen's Agency-Partnership in a Nutshell, 364 pages, 1977 (Text)

AMERICAN INDIAN LAW

Canby's American Indian Law in a Nutshell, 288 pages, 1981 (Text)

Getches, Rosenfelt and Wilkinson's Cases on Federal Indian Law, 660 pages, 1979, with 1983 Supplement (Casebook)

ANTITRUST LAW

Gellhorn's Antitrust Law and Economics in a Nutshell, 2nd Ed., 425 pages, 1981 (Text)

Gifford and Raskind's Cases and Materials on Antitrust, approximately 625 pages, 1983 (Casebook)

LAW SCHOOL PUBLICATIONS—Continued

ANTITRUST LAW—Continued

Oppenheim, Weston and McCarthy's Cases and Comments on Federal Antitrust Laws, 4th Ed., 1168 pages, 1981 (Casebook)

Posner and Easterbrook's Cases and Economic Notes on Antitrust, 2nd Ed., 1077 pages, 1981, with 1982–83 Supplement (Casebook)

Sullivan's Hornbook of the Law of Antitrust, 886 pages, 1977 (Text)

See also Regulated Industries, Trade Regulation

BANKING LAW

White's Teaching Materials on Banking Law, 1058 pages, 1976, with Case and Statutory Supplement (Casebook)

BUSINESS PLANNING

Epstein and Scheinfeld's Teaching Materials on Business Reorganization Under the Bankruptcy Code, 216 pages, 1980 (Casebook)

Painter's Problems and Materials in Business Planning, 791 pages, 1975, with 1982 Supplement (Casebook)

Selected Securities and Business Planning Statutes, Rules and Forms, 485 pages, 1982

CIVIL PROCEDURE

Casad's Res Judicata in a Nutshell, 310 pages, 1976 (text)

Cound, Friedenthal and Miller's Cases and Materials on Civil Procedure, 3rd Ed., 1147 pages, 1980 with 1982 Supplement (Casebook)

Ehrenzweig, Louisell and Hazard's Jurisdiction in a Nutshell, 4th Ed., 232 pages, 1980 (Text)

Federal Rules of Civil-Appellate-Criminal Procedure—West Law School Edition, 343 pages, 1983

Hodges, Jones and Elliott's Cases and Materials on Texas Trial and Appellate Procedure, 2nd Ed., 745 pages, 1974 (Casebook)

Hodges, Jones and Elliott's Cases and Materials on the Judicial Process Prior to Trial in Texas, 2nd Ed., 871 pages, 1977 (Casebook)

Kane's Civil Procedure in a Nutshell, 271 pages, 1979 (Text)

Karlen's Procedure Before Trial in a Nutshell, 258 pages, 1972 (Text)

Karlen, Meisenholder, Stevens and Vestal's Cases on Civil Procedure, 923 pages, 1975 (Casebook)

Koffler and Reppy's Hornbook on Common Law Pleading, 663 pages, 1969 (Text)

CIVIL PROCEDURE—Continued

McBaine's Cases on Introduction to Civil Procedure, 399 pages, 1950 (Casebook)

Park's Computer-Aided Exercises on Civil Procedure, 118 pages, 1976 (Coursebook)

Shipman's Hornbook on Common-Law Pleading, 3rd Ed., 644 pages, 1923 (Text)

Siegel's Hornbook on New York Practice, 1011 pages, 1978 with 1981–82 Pocket Part (Text)

See also Federal Jurisdiction and Procedure

CIVIL RIGHTS

Abernathy's Cases and Materials on Civil Rights, 660 pages, 1980 (Casebook)

Cohen's Cases on the Law of Deprivation of Liberty: A Study in Social Control, 755 pages, 1980 (Casebook)

Lockhart, Kamisar and Choper's Cases on Constitutional Rights and Liberties, 5th Ed., 1298 pages plus Appendix, 1981, with 1983 Supplement (Casebook)—reprint from Lockhart, et al. Cases on Constitutional Law, 5th Ed., 1980

Vieira's Civil Rights in a Nutshell, 279 pages, 1978 (Text)

COMMERCIAL LAW

Bailey's Secured Transactions in a Nutshell, 2nd Ed., 391 pages, 1981 (Text)

Epstein and Martin's Basic Uniform Commercial Code Teaching Materials, 2nd Ed., 667 pages, 1983 (Casebook)

Henson's Hornbook on Secured Transactions Under the U.C.C., 2nd Ed., 504 pages, 1979 with 1979 P.P. (Text)

Murray's Commercial Law, Problems and Materials, 366 pages, 1975 (Coursebook)

Nordstrom and Clovis' Problems and Materials on Commercial Paper, 458 pages, 1972 (Casebook)

Nordstrom and Lattin's Problems and Materials on Sales and Secured Transactions, 809 pages, 1968 (Casebook)

Nordstrom, Murray and Clovis' Problems and Materials on Sales, 515 pages, 1982 (Casebook)

Nordstrom's Hornbook on Sales, 600 pages, 1970 (Text)

Selected Commercial Statutes, approximately 1360 pages, 1983

Speidel, Summers and White's Teaching Materials on Commercial and Consumer Law, 3rd Ed., 1490 pages, 1981 (Casebook)

Stockton's Sales in a Nutshell, 2nd Ed., 370 pages, 1981 (Text)

Stone's Uniform Commercial Code in a Nutshell, 507 pages, 1975 (Text)

LAW SCHOOL PUBLICATIONS—Continued

COMMERCIAL LAW—Continued

Uniform Commercial Code, Official Text with Comments, 994 pages, 1978

UCC Article 8, 1977 Amendments, 249 pages, 1978

UCC Article 9, Reprint from 1962 Code, 128 pages, 1976

UCC Article 9, 1972 Amendments, 304 pages, 1978

Weber and Speidel's Commercial Paper in a Nutshell, 3rd Ed., 404 pages, 1982 (Text)

White and Summers' Hornbook on the Uniform Commercial Code, 2nd Ed., 1250 pages, 1980 (Text)

COMMUNITY PROPERTY

Mennell's Community Property in a Nutshell, 447 pages, 1982 (Text)

Verrall and Bird's Cases and Materials on California Community Property, 4th Ed., approximately 550 pages, 1983 (Casebook)

COMPARATIVE LAW

Barton, Gibbs, Li and Merryman's Law in Radically Different Cultures, 960 pages, 1983 (Casebook)

Glendon, Gordon, and Osakwe's Comparative Legal Traditions in a Nutshell, 402 pages, 1982 (Text)

Langbein's Comparative Criminal Procedure: Germany, 172 pages, 1977 (Casebook)

CONFLICT OF LAWS

Cramton, Currie and Kay's Cases-Comments-Questions on Conflict of Laws, 3rd Ed., 1026 pages, 1981 (Casebook)

Scoles and Hay's Hornbook on Conflict of Laws, Student Ed., 1085 pages, 1982 (Text)

Scoles and Weintraub's Cases and Materials on Conflict of Laws, 2nd Ed., 966 pages, 1972, with 1978 Supplement (Casebook)

Siegel's Conflicts in a Nutshell, 469 pages, 1982 (Text)

CONSTITUTIONAL LAW

Engdahl's Constitutional Power in a Nutshell: Federal and State, 411 pages, 1974 (Text)

Lockhart, Kamisar and Choper's Cases-Comments-Questions on Constitutional Law, 5th Ed., 1705 pages plus Appendix, 1980, with 1983 Supplement (Casebook)

CONSTITUTIONAL LAW—Continued

Lockhart, Kamisar and Choper's Cases-Comments-Questions on the American Constitution, 5th Ed., 1185 pages plus Appendix, 1981, with 1983 Supplement (Casebook)—reprint from Lockhart, et al. Cases on Constitutional Law, 5th Ed., 1980

Manning's The Law of Church-State Relations in a Nutshell, 305 pages, 1981 (Text)

Miller's Presidential Power in a Nutshell, 328 pages, 1977 (Text)

Nowak, Rotunda and Young's Hornbook on Constitutional Law, 2nd Ed., Student Ed., approximately 1000 pages, 1983 (Text)

Rotunda's Modern Constitutional Law: Cases and Notes, 1034 pages, 1981, with 1983 Supplement (Casebook)

Williams' Constitutional Analysis in a Nutshell, 388 pages, 1979 (Text)

See also Civil Rights

CONSUMER LAW

Epstein and Nickles' Consumer Law in a Nutshell, 2nd Ed., 418 pages, 1981 (Text)

McCall's Consumer Protection, Cases, Notes and Materials, 594 pages, 1977, with 1977 Statutory Supplement (Casebook)

Selected Commercial Statutes, approximately 1360 pages, 1983

Spanogle and Rohner's Cases and Materials on Consumer Law, 693 pages, 1979, with 1982 Supplement (Casebook)

See also Commercial Law

CONTRACTS

Calamari & Perillo's Cases and Problems on Contracts, 1061 pages, 1978 (Casebook)

Calamari and Perillo's Hornbook on Contracts, 2nd Ed., 878 pages, 1977 (Text)

Corbin's Text on Contracts, One Volume Student Edition, 1224 pages, 1952 (Text)

Fessler and Loiseaux's Cases and Materials on Contracts, 837 pages, 1982 (Casebook)

Freedman's Cases and Materials on Contracts, 658 pages, 1973 (Casebook)

Friedman's Contract Remedies in a Nutshell, 323 pages, 1981 (Text)

Fuller and Eisenberg's Cases on Basic Contract Law, 4th Ed., 1203 pages, 1981 (Casebook)

Jackson and Bollinger's Cases on Contract Law in Modern Society, 2nd Ed., 1329 pages, 1980 (Casebook)

Keyes' Government Contracts in a Nutshell, 423 pages, 1979 (Text)

LAW SCHOOL PUBLICATIONS—Continued

CONTRACTS—Continued

Reitz's Cases on Contracts as Basic Commercial Law, 763 pages, 1975 (Casebook)

Schaber and Rohwer's Contracts in a Nutshell, 307 pages, 1975 (Text)

Simpson's Hornbook on Contracts, 2nd Ed., 510 pages, 1965 (Text)

COPYRIGHT

See Patent and Copyright Law

CORPORATIONS

Hamilton's Cases on Corporations—Including Partnerships and Limited Partnerships, 2nd Ed., 1108 pages, 1981, with 1981 Statutory Supplement (Casebook)

Hamilton's Law of Corporations in a Nutshell, 379 pages, 1980 (Text)

Henn's Cases on Corporations, 1279 pages, 1974, with 1980 Supplement (Casebook)

Henn's Hornbook on Corporations, 3rd Ed., Student Ed., approximately 1170 pages, 1983 (Text)

Jennings and Buxbaum's Cases and Materials on Corporations, 5th Ed., 1180 pages, 1979 (Casebook)

Selected Corporation and Partnership Statutes, Regulations and Forms, 556 pages, 1982

Solomon, Stevenson and Schwartz' Materials and Problems on the Law and Policies on Corporations, 1172 pages, 1982 (Casebook)

CORRECTIONS

Krantz's Cases and Materials on the Law of Corrections and Prisoners' Rights, 2nd Ed., 735 pages, 1981, with 1982 Supplement (Casebook)

Krantz's Law of Corrections and Prisoners' Rights in a Nutshell, 2nd Ed., approximately 365 pages, 1983 (Text)

Popper's Post-Conviction Remedies in a Nutshell, 360 pages, 1978 (Text)

Robbins' Cases and Materials on Post Conviction Remedies, 506 pages, 1982 (Casebook)

Rubin's Law of Criminal Corrections, 2nd Ed., 873 pages, 1973, with 1978 Supplement (Text)

CREDITOR'S RIGHTS

Epstein's Debtor-Creditor Law in a Nutshell, 2nd Ed., 324 pages, 1980 (Text)

Epstein and Landers' Debtors and Creditors: Cases and Materials, 2nd Ed., 689 pages, 1982 (Casebook)

Epstein and Sheinfeld's Teaching Materials on Business Reorganization Under the Bankruptcy Code, 216 pages, 1980 (Casebook)

CREDITOR'S RIGHTS—Continued

Riesenfeld's Cases and Materials on Creditors' Remedies and Debtors' Protection, 3rd Ed., 810 pages, 1979 with 1979 Statutory Supplement and 1981 Case Supplement (Casebook)

Selected Bankruptcy Statutes, 351 pages, 1979

CRIMINAL LAW AND CRIMINAL PROCEDURE

Cohen and Gobert's Problems in Criminal Law, 297 pages, 1976 (Problem book)

Davis' Police Discretion, 176 pages, 1975 (Text)

Dix and Sharlot's Cases and Materials on Criminal Law, 2nd Ed., 771 pages, 1979 (Casebook)

Federal Rules of Civil-Appellate-Criminal Procedure—West Law School Edition, 343 pages, 1983

Grano's Problems in Criminal Procedure, 2nd Ed., 176 pages, 1981 (Problem book)

Israel and LaFave's Criminal Procedure in a Nutshell, 3rd Ed., 438 pages, 1980 (Text)

Johnson's Cases, Materials and Text on Substantive Criminal Law in its Procedural Context, 2nd Ed., 956 pages, 1980 (Casebook)

Kamisar, LaFave and Israel's Cases, Comments and Questions on Modern Criminal Procedure, 5th ed., 1635 pages plus Appendix, 1980 with 1983 Supplement (Casebook)

Kamisar, LaFave and Israel's Cases, Comments and Questions on Basic Criminal Procedure, 5th Ed., 869 pages, 1980 with 1983 Supplement (Casebook)—reprint from Kamisar, et al. Modern Criminal Procedure, 5th ed., 1980

LaFave's Modern Criminal Law: Cases, Comments and Questions, 789 pages, 1978 (Casebook)

LaFave and Scott's Hornbook on Criminal Law, 763 pages, 1972 (Text)

Langbein's Comparative Criminal Procedure: Germany, 172 pages, 1977 (Casebook)

Loewy's Criminal Law in a Nutshell, 302 pages, 1975 (Text)

Saltzburg's American Criminal Procedure, Cases and Commentary, 1253 pages, 1980 with 1983 Supplement (Casebook)

Saltzburg's Introduction to American Criminal Procedure, 702 pages, 1980 with 1983 Supplement (Casebook)—reprint from Saltzburg's American Criminal Procedure, 1980

LAW SCHOOL PUBLICATIONS—Continued

CRIMINAL LAW AND CRIMINAL PROCEDURE—Continued

Uviller's The Processes of Criminal Justice: Investigation and Adjudication, 2nd Ed., 1384 pages, 1979 with 1979 Statutory Supplement and 1980 Update (Casebook)

Uviller's The Processes of Criminal Justice: Adjudication, 2nd Ed., 730 pages, 1979. Soft-cover reprint from Uviller's The Processes of Criminal Justice: Investigation and Adjudication, 2nd Ed. (Casebook)

Uviller's The Processes of Criminal Justice: Investigation, 2nd Ed., 655 pages, 1979. Soft-cover reprint from Uviller's The Processes of Criminal Justice: Investigation and Adjudication, 2nd Ed. (Casebook)

Vorenberg's Cases on Criminal Law and Procedure, 2nd Ed., 1088 pages, 1981 (Casebook)

See also Corrections, Juvenile Justice

DECEDENTS ESTATES

See Trusts and Estates

DOMESTIC RELATIONS

Clark's Cases and Problems on Domestic Relations, 3rd Ed., 1153 pages, 1980 (Casebook)

Clark's Hornbook on Domestic Relations, 754 pages, 1968 (Text)

Krause's Cases and Materials on Family Law, 2nd Ed., approximately 1150 pages, 1983 (Casebook)

Krause's Family Law in a Nutshell, 400 pages, 1977 (Text)

EDUCATION LAW

Morris' The Constitution and American Education, 2nd Ed., 992 pages, 1980 (Casebook)

EMPLOYMENT DISCRIMINATION

Player's Cases and Materials on Employment Discrimination Law, 878 pages, 1980 with 1982 Supplement (Casebook)

Player's Federal Law of Employment Discrimination in a Nutshell, 2nd Ed., 402 pages, 1981 (Text)

See also Women and the Law

ENERGY AND NATURAL RESOURCES LAW

Rodgers' Cases and Materials on Energy and Natural Resources Law, 2nd Ed., approximately 870 pages, 1983 (Casebook)

Selected Environmental Law Statutes, 768 pages, 1983

Tomain's Energy Law in a Nutshell, 338 pages, 1981 (Text)

ENERGY AND NATURAL RESOURCES—Continued

See also Environmental Law, Oil and Gas, Water Law

ENVIRONMENTAL LAW

Findley and Farber's Cases and Materials on Environmental Law, 738 pages, 1981, with 1983 Supplement (Casebook)

Findley and Farber's Environmental Law in a Nutshell, approximately 332 pages, 1983 (Text)

Hanks, Tarlock and Hanks' Cases on Environmental Law and Policy, 1242 pages, 1974, with 1976 Supplement (Casebook)

Rodgers' Hornbook on Environmental Law, 956 pages, 1977 (Text)

Selected Environmental Law Statutes, 768 pages, 1983

See also Energy and Natural Resources Law, Water Law

EQUITY

See Remedies

ESTATES

See Trusts and Estates

ESTATE PLANNING

Kurtz' Cases, Materials and Problems on Family Estate Planning, 853 pages, 1983 (Casebook)

Lynn's Introduction to Estate Planning, in a Nutshell, 3rd Ed., 370 pages, 1983 (Text)

See also Taxation

EVIDENCE

Broun and Meisenholder's Problems in Evidence, 2nd Ed., 304 pages, 1981 (Problem book)

Cleary and Strong's Cases, Materials and Problems on Evidence, 3rd Ed., 1143 pages, 1981 (Casebook)

Federal Rules of Evidence for United States Courts and Magistrates, 327 pages, 1983

Graham's Federal Rules of Evidence in a Nutshell, 429 pages, 1981 (Text)

Kimball's Programmed Materials on Problems in Evidence, 380 pages, 1978 (Problem book)

Lempert and Saltzburg's A Modern Approach to Evidence: Text, Problems, Transcripts and Cases, 2nd Ed., 1296 pages, 1983 (Casebook)

Lilly's Introduction to the Law of Evidence, 486 pages, 1978 (Text)

McCormick, Elliott and Sutton's Cases and Materials on Evidence, 5th Ed., 1212 pages, 1981 (Casebook)

LAW SCHOOL PUBLICATIONS—Continued

EVIDENCE—Continued

McCormick's Hornbook on Evidence, 2nd Ed., 938 pages, 1972, with 1978 pocket part (Text)

Rothstein's Evidence, State and Federal Rules in a Nutshell, 2nd Ed., 514 pages, 1981 (Text)

Saltzburg's Evidence Supplement: Rules, Statutes, Commentary, 245 pages, 1980 (Casebook Supplement)

FEDERAL JURISDICTION AND PROCEDURE

Currie's Cases and Materials on Federal Courts, 3rd Ed., 1042 pages, 1982 (Casebook)

Currie's Federal Jurisdiction in a Nutshell, 2nd Ed., 258 pages, 1981 (Text)

Federal Rules of Civil-Appellate-Criminal Procedure—West Law School Edition, 343 pages, 1983

Forrester and Moye's Cases and Materials on Federal Jurisdiction and Procedure, 3rd Ed., 917 pages, 1977 with 1981 Supplement (Casebook)

Merrill and Vetri's Problems on Federal Courts and Civil Procedure, 460 pages, 1974 (Problem book)

Redish's Cases, Comments and Questions on Federal Courts, 878 pages, 1983 (Casebook)

Wright's Hornbook on Federal Courts, 4th Ed., Student Ed., 870 pages, 1983 (Text)

FUTURE INTERESTS

See Trusts and Estates

HOUSING AND URBAN DEVELOPMENT

Berger's Cases and Materials on Housing, 2nd Ed., 254 pages, 1973 (Casebook)—reprint from Cooper et al. Cases on Law and Poverty, 2nd Ed., 1973

See also Land Use

INDIAN LAW

See American Indian Law

INSURANCE

Dobbyn's Insurance Law in a Nutshell, 281 pages, 1981 (Text)

Keeton's Cases on Basic Insurance Law, 2nd Ed., 1086 pages, 1977

Keeton's Basic Text on Insurance Law, 712 pages, 1971 (Text)

Keeton's Case Supplement to Keeton's Basic Text on Insurance Law, 334 pages, 1978 (Casebook)

Keeton's Programmed Problems in Insurance Law, 243 pages, 1972 (Text Supplement)

INSURANCE—Continued

York and Whelan's Cases, Materials and Problems on Insurance Law, 715 pages, 1982 (Casebook)

INTERNATIONAL LAW

Henkin, Pugh, Schachter and Smit's Cases and Materials on International Law, 2nd Ed., 1152 pages, 1980, with Documents Supplement (Casebook)

Jackson's Legal Problems of International Economic Relations, 1097 pages, 1977, with Documents Supplement (Casebook)

Kirgis' International Organizations in Their Legal Setting, 1016 pages, 1977, with 1981 Supplement (Casebook)

Weston, Falk and D'Amato's International Law and World Order—A Problem Oriented Coursebook, 1195 pages, 1980, with Documents Supplement (Casebook)

Wilson's International Business Transactions in a Nutshell, 393 pages, 1981 (Text)

INTERVIEWING AND COUNSELING

Binder and Price's Interviewing and Counseling, 232 pages, 1977 (Text)

Shaffer's Interviewing and Counseling in a Nutshell, 353 pages, 1976 (Text)

INTRODUCTION TO LAW

Dobbyn's So You Want to go to Law School, Revised First Edition, 206 pages, 1976 (Text)

Hegland's Introduction to the Study and Practice of Law in a Nutshell, approximately 400 pages, 1983 (Text)

Kinyon's Introduction to Law Study and Law Examinations in a Nutshell, 389 pages, 1971 (Text)

See also Legal Method and Legal System

JUDICIAL ADMINISTRATION

Carrington, Meador and Rosenberg's Justice on Appeal, 263 pages, 1976 (Casebook)

Nelson's Cases and Materials on Judicial Administration and the Administration of Justice, 1032 pages, 1974 (Casebook)

JURISPRUDENCE

Christie's Text and Readings on Jurisprudence—The Philosophy of Law, 1056 pages, 1973 (Casebook)

JUVENILE JUSTICE

Fox's Cases and Materials on Modern Juvenile Justice, 2nd Ed., 960 pages, 1981 (Casebook)

Fox's Juvenile Courts in a Nutshell, 2nd Ed., 275 pages, 1977 (Text)

LAW SCHOOL PUBLICATIONS—Continued

LABOR LAW

Gorman's Basic Text on Labor Law—Unionization and Collective Bargaining, 914 pages, 1976 (Text)

Leslie's Labor Law in a Nutshell, 403 pages, 1979 (Text)

Nolan's Labor Arbitration Law and Practice in a Nutshell, 358 pages, 1979 (Text)

Oberer, Hanslowe and Andersen's Cases and Materials on Labor Law—Collective Bargaining in a Free Society, 2nd Ed., 1168 pages, 1979, with 1979 Statutory Supplement and 1982 Case Supplement (Casebook)

See also Employment Discrimination, Social Legislation

LAND FINANCE

See Real Estate Transactions

LAND USE

Hagman's Cases on Public Planning and Control of Urban and Land Development, 2nd Ed., 1301 pages, 1980 (Casebook)

Hagman's Hornbook on Urban Planning and Land Development Control Law, 706 pages, 1971 (Text)

Wright and Gitelman's Cases and Materials on Land Use, 3rd Ed., 1300 pages, 1982 (Casebook)

Wright and Webber's Land Use in a Nutshell, 316 pages, 1978 (Text)

See also Housing and Urban Development

LAW AND ECONOMICS

Manne's The Economics of Legal Relationships—Readings in the Theory of Property Rights, 660 pages, 1975 (Text)

See also Antitrust, Regulated Industries

LAW AND MEDICINE—PSYCHIATRY

Cohen's Cases and Materials on the Law of Deprivation of Liberty: A Study in Social Control, 755 pages, 1980 (Casebook)

King's The Law of Medical Malpractice in a Nutshell, 340 pages, 1977 (Text)

Shapiro and Spece's Problems, Cases and Materials on Bioethics and Law, 892 pages, 1981 (Casebook)

Sharpe, Fiscina and Head's Cases on Law and Medicine, 882 pages, 1978 (Casebook)

LEGAL HISTORY

Presser and Zainaldin's Cases on Law and American History, 855 pages, 1980 (Casebook)

See also Legal Method and Legal System

LEGAL METHOD AND LEGAL SYSTEM

Aldisert's Readings, Materials and Cases in the Judicial Process, 948 pages, 1976 (Casebook)

Bodenheimer, Oakley and Love's Readings and Cases on an Introduction to the Anglo-American Legal System, 161 pages, 1980 (Casebook)

Davies and Lawry's Institutions and Methods of the Law—Introductory Teaching Materials, 547 pages, 1982 (Casebook)

Dvorkin, Himmelstein and Lesnick's Becoming a Lawyer: A Humanistic Perspective on Legal Education and Professionalism, 211 pages, 1981 (Text)

Fryer and Orentlicher's Cases and Materials on Legal Method and Legal System, 1043 pages, 1967 (Casebook)

Greenberg's Judicial Process and Social Change, 666 pages, 1977 (Coursebook)

Kempin's Historical Introduction to Anglo-American Law in a Nutshell, 2nd Ed., 280 pages, 1973 (Text)

Kimball's Historical Introduction to the Legal System, 610 pages, 1966 (Casebook)

Mashaw and Merrill's Introduction to the American Public Law System, 1095 pages, 1975, with 1980 Supplement (Casebook)

Murphy's Cases and Materials on Introduction to Law—Legal Process and Procedure, 772 pages, 1977 (Casebook)

Reynolds' Judicial Process in a Nutshell, 292 pages, 1980 (Text)

See also Legal Research and Writing

LEGAL NEGOTIATION

Edwards and White's Problems, Readings and Materials on the Lawyer as a Negotiator, 484 pages, 1977 (Casebook)

Williams' Legal Negotiation and Settlement, 207 pages, 1983 (Coursebook)

LEGAL PROFESSION

Aronson's Problems in Professional Responsibility, 280 pages, 1978 (Problem book)

Aronson and Weckstein's Professional Responsibility in a Nutshell, 399 pages, 1980 (Text)

Mellinkoff's The Conscience of a Lawyer, 304 pages, 1973 (Text)

Mellinkoff's Lawyers and the System of Justice, 983 pages, 1976 (Casebook)

Pirsig and Kirwin's Cases and Materials on Professional Responsibility, 3rd Ed., 667 pages, 1976, with 1981 Supplement (Casebook)

Schwartz and Wydick's Problems in Legal Ethics, approximately 300 pages, 1983 (Casebook)

LAW SCHOOL PUBLICATIONS—Continued

LEGAL PROFESSION—Continued

Smith's Preventing Legal Malpractice, 142 pages, 1981 (Text)

LEGAL RESEARCH AND WRITING

Cohen's Legal Research in a Nutshell, 3rd Ed., 415 pages, 1978 (Text)

Cohen and Berring's How to Find the Law, 8th Ed., approximately 600 pages, 1983. Problem book available (Casebook)

Dickerson's Materials on Legal Drafting, 425 pages, 1981 (Casebook)

Felsenfeld and Siegel's Writing Contracts in Plain English, 290 pages, 1981 (Text)

Gopen's Writing From a Legal Perspective, 225 pages, 1981 (Text)

Mellinkoff's Legal Writing—Sense and Nonsense, 242 pages, 1982 (Text)

Rombauer's Legal Problem Solving—Analysis, Research and Writing, 4th Ed., approximately 350 pages, 1983 (Coursebook)

Squires and Rombauer's Legal Writing in a Nutshell, 294 pages, 1982 (Text)

Statsky's Legal Research, Writing and Analysis, 2nd Ed., 167 pages, 1982 (Coursebook)

Statsky's Legislative Analysis: How to Use Statutes and Regulations, 216 pages, 1975 (Text)

Statsky and Wernet's Case Analysis and Fundamentals of Legal Writing, 576 pages, 1977 (Text)

Teply's Programmed Materials on Legal Research and Citation, 334 pages, 1982. Student Library Exercises available (Coursebook)

Weihofen's Legal Writing Style, 2nd Ed., 332 pages, 1980 (Text)

LEGISLATION

Davies' Legislative Law and Process in a Nutshell, 279 pages, 1975 (Text)

Nutting and Dickerson's Cases and Materials on Legislation, 5th Ed., 744 pages, 1978 (Casebook)

Statsky's Legislative Analysis: How to Use Statutes and Regulations, 216 pages, 1975 (Text)

LOCAL GOVERNMENT

McCarthy's Local Government Law in a Nutshell, 2nd Ed., approximately 350 pages, 1983 (Text)

Michelman and Sandalow's Cases-Comments-Questions on Government in Urban Areas, 1216 pages, 1970, with 1972 Supplement (Casebook)

Reynolds' Hornbook on Local Government Law, 860 pages, 1982 (Text)

Stason and Kauper's Cases and Materials on Municipal Corporations, 3rd Ed., 692 pages, 1959 (Casebook)

LOCAL GOVERNMENT—Continued

Valente's Cases and Materials on Local Government Law, 2nd Ed., 980 pages, 1980 with 1982 Supplement (Casebook)

MASS COMMUNICATION LAW

Gillmor and Barron's Cases and Comment on Mass Communication Law, 3rd Ed., 1008 pages, 1979 (Casebook)

Ginsburg's Regulation of Broadcasting: Law and Policy Towards Radio, Television and Cable Communications, 741 pages, 1979, with 1983 Supplement (Casebook)

Zuckman and Gayne's Mass Communications Law in a Nutshell, 2nd Ed., 473 pages, 1983 (Text)

MILITARY LAW

Shanor and Terrell's Military Law in a Nutshell, 378 pages, 1980 (Text)

MORTGAGES

See Real Estate Transactions

NATURAL RESOURCES LAW

See Energy and Natural Resources Law, Environmental Law, Oil and Gas, Water Law

OFFICE PRACTICE

Hegland's Trial and Practice Skills in a Nutshell, 346 pages, 1978 (Text)

Strong and Clark's Law Office Management, 424 pages, 1974 (Casebook)

See also Legal Interviewing and Counseling, Legal Negotiation

OIL AND GAS

Hemingway's Hornbook on Oil and Gas, 2nd Ed., Student Ed., approximately 535 pages, 1983 (Text)

Huie, Woodward and Smith's Cases and Materials on Oil and Gas, 2nd Ed., 955 pages, 1972 (Casebook)

Lowe's Oil and Gas Law in a Nutshell, approximately 365 pages, 1983 (Text)

See also Energy and Natural Resources Law

PARTNERSHIP

See Agency—Partnership

PATENT AND COPYRIGHT LAW

Choate and Francis' Cases and Materials on Patent Law, 2nd Ed., 1110 pages, 1981 (Casebook)

Miller and Davis' Intellectual Property—Patents, Trademarks and Copyright in a Nutshell, approximately 400 pages, 1983 (Text)

LAW SCHOOL PUBLICATIONS—Continued

PATENT AND COPYRIGHT LAW—Continued

Nimmer's Cases on Copyright and Other Aspects of Law Pertaining to Literary, Musical and Artistic Works, 2nd Ed., 1023 pages, 1979 (Casebook)

POVERTY LAW

Brudno's Poverty, Inequality, and the Law: Cases-Commentary-Analysis, 934 pages, 1976 (Casebook)

LaFrance, Schroeder, Bennett and Boyd's Hornbook on Law of the Poor, 558 pages, 1973 (Text)

See also Social Legislation

PRODUCTS LIABILITY

Noel and Phillips' Cases on Products Liability, 2nd Ed., 821 pages, 1982 (Casebook)

Noel and Phillips' Products Liability in a Nutshell, 2nd Ed., 341 pages, 1981 (Text)

PROPERTY

Aigler, Smith and Tefft's Cases on Property, 2 volumes, 1339 pages, 1960 (Casebook)

Bernhardt's Real Property in a Nutshell, 2nd Ed., 448 pages, 1981 (Text)

Boyer's Survey of the Law of Property, 766 pages, 1981 (Text)

Browder, Cunningham, Julin and Smith's Cases on Basic Property Law, 3rd Ed., 1447 pages, 1979 (Casebook)

Burby's Hornbook on Real Property, 3rd Ed., 490 pages, 1965 (Text)

Burke's Personal Property in a Nutshell, approximately 318 pages, 1983 (Text)

Chused's A Modern Approach to Property: Cases-Notes-Materials, 1069 pages, 1978 with 1980 Supplement (Casebook)

Cohen's Materials for a Basic Course in Property, 526 pages, 1978 (Casebook)

Donahue, Kauper and Martin's Cases on Property, 2nd Ed., approximately 1350 pages, 1983 (Casebook)

Hill's Landlord and Tenant Law in a Nutshell, 319 pages, 1979 (Text)

Moynihan's Introduction to Real Property, 254 pages, 1962 (Text)

Phipps' Titles in a Nutshell, 277 pages, 1968 (Text)

Uniform Land Transactions Act, Uniform Simplification of Land Transfers Act, Uniform Condominium Act, 1977 Official Text with Comments, 462 pages, 1978

See also Housing and Urban Development, Real Estate Transactions, Land Use

REAL ESTATE TRANSACTIONS

Bruce's Real Estate Finance in a Nutshell, 292 pages, 1979 (Text)

Maxwell, Riesenfeld, Hetland and Warren's Cases on California Security Transactions in Land, 2nd Ed., 584 pages, 1975 (Casebook)

Nelson and Whitman's Cases on Real Estate Transfer, Finance and Development, 2nd Ed., 1114 pages, 1981, with 1983 Supplement (Casebook)

Osborne's Cases and Materials on Secured Transactions, 559 pages, 1967 (Casebook)

Osborne, Nelson and Whitman's Hornbook on Real Estate Finance Law, 3rd Ed., 885 pages, 1979 (Text)

REGULATED INDUSTRIES

Gellhorn and Pierce's Regulated Industries in a Nutshell, 394 pages, 1982 (Text)

Morgan's Cases and Materials on Economic Regulation of Business, 830 pages, 1976, with 1978 Supplement (Casebook)

Pozen's Financial Institutions: Cases, Materials and Problems on Investment Management, 844 pages, 1978 (Casebook)

See also Mass Communication Law, Banking Law

REMEDIES

Dobbs' Hornbook on Remedies, 1067 pages, 1973 (Text)

Dobbs' Problems in Remedies, 137 pages, 1974 (Problem book)

Dobbyn's Injunctions in a Nutshell, 264 pages, 1974 (Text)

Friedman's Contract Remedies in a Nutshell, 323 pages, 1981 (Text)

Leavell, Love and Nelson's Cases and Materials on Equitable Remedies and Restitution, 3rd Ed., 704 pages, 1980 (Casebook)

McCormick's Hornbook on Damages, 811 pages, 1935 (Text)

O'Connell's Remedies in a Nutshell, 364 pages, 1977 (Text)

York and Bauman's Cases and Materials on Remedies, 3rd Ed., 1250 pages, 1979 (Casebook)

REVIEW MATERIALS

Ballantine's Problems
Black Letter Series
Smith's Review Series
West's Review Covering Multistate Subjects

LAW SCHOOL PUBLICATIONS—Continued

SECURITIES REGULATION

Ratner's Securities Regulation: Materials for a Basic Course, 2nd Ed., 1050 pages, 1980 with 1982 Supplement (Casebook)

Ratner's Securities Regulation in a Nutshell, 300 pages, 1978 (Text)

Selected Securities and Business Planning Statutes, Rules and Forms, 485 pages, 1982

SOCIAL LEGISLATION

Brudno's Income Redistribution Theories and Programs: Cases-Commentary-Analyses, 480 pages, 1977 (Casebook)—reprint from Brudno's Poverty, Inequality and the Law, 1976

LaFrance's Welfare Law: Structure and Entitlement in a Nutshell, 455 pages, 1979 (Text)

Malone, Plant and Little's Cases on Workers' Compensation and Employment Rights, 2nd Ed., 951 pages, 1980 (Casebook)

See also Poverty Law

TAXATION

Chommie's Hornbook on Federal Income Taxation, 2nd Ed., 1051 pages, 1973 (Text)

Dodge's Federal Taxation of Estates, Trusts and Gifts: Principles and Planning, 771 pages, 1981 with 1982 Supplement (Casebook)

Garbis and Struntz' Cases and Materials on Tax Procedure and Tax Fraud, 829 pages, 1982 (Casebook)

Gunn's Cases and Materials on Federal Income Taxation of Individuals, 785 pages, 1981 (Casebook)

Hellerstein and Hellerstein's Cases on State and Local Taxation, 4th Ed., 1041 pages, 1978 with 1982 Supplement (Casebook)

Kahn's Handbook on Basic Corporate Taxation, 3rd Ed., Student Ed., 614 pages, 1981 with 1983 Supplement (Text)

Kahn and Gann's Corporate Taxation and Taxation of Partnerships and Partners, 1107 pages, 1979, with 1981 Supplement (Casebook)

Kragen and McNulty's Cases and Materials on Federal Income Taxation, Vol. I: Taxation of Individuals, 3rd Ed., 1283 pages, 1979 with 1983 Supplement (Casebook)

Kragen and McNulty's Cases and Materials on Federal Income Taxation, Vol. II: Taxation of Corporations, Shareholders, Partnerships and Partners, 3rd Ed., 989 pages, 1981 with 1983 Supplement (Casebook)

TAXATION—Continued

Lowndes, Kramer and McCord's Hornbook on Federal Estate and Gift Taxes, 3rd Ed., 1099 pages, 1974 (Text)

McNulty's Federal Estate and Gift Taxation in a Nutshell, 3rd Ed., 509 pages, 1983 (Text)

McNulty's Federal Income Taxation of Individuals in a Nutshell, 3rd Ed., approximately 425 pages, 1983 (Text)

Posin's Hornbook on Federal Income Taxation of Individuals, Student Ed., approximately 425 pages, 1983 (Text)

Rice's Problems and Materials in Federal Estate and Gift Taxation, 3rd Ed., 474 pages, 1978 (Casebook)

Rice and Solomon's Problems and Materials in Federal Income Taxation, 3rd Ed., 670 pages, 1979 (Casebook)

Rose and Raskind's Advanced Federal Income Taxation: Corporate Transactions—Cases, Materials and Problems, 955 pages, 1978 (Casebook)

Selected Federal Taxation Statutes and Regulations, 1218 pages, 1982

Soboloff and Weidenbruch's Federal Income Taxation of Corporations and Stockholders in a Nutshell, 362 pages, 1981 (Text)

TORTS

Christie's Cases and Materials on the Law of Torts, 1264 pages, 1983 (Casebook)

Green, Pedrick, Rahl, Thode, Hawkins, Smith and Treece's Cases and Materials on Torts, 2nd Ed., 1360 pages, 1977 (Casebook)

Green, Pedrick, Rahl, Thode, Hawkins, Smith, and Treece's Advanced Torts: Injuries to Business, Political and Family Interests, 2nd Ed., 544 pages, 1977 (Casebook)—reprint from Green, et al. Cases and Materials on Torts, 2nd Ed., 1977

Keeton's Computer-Aided and Workbook Exercises on Tort Law, 164 pages, 1976 (Coursebook)

Keeton, Keeton, Sargentich and Steiner's Cases and Materials on Torts, and Accident Law, approximately 1344 pages, 1983 (Casebook)

Kionka's Torts in a Nutshell: Injuries to Persons and Property, 434 pages, 1977 (Text)

Malone's Torts in a Nutshell: Injuries to Family, Social and Trade Relations, 358 pages, 1979 (Text)

Prosser's Hornbook on Torts, 4th Ed., 1208 pages, 1971 (Text)

Shapo's Cases on Tort and Compensation Law, 1244 pages, 1976 (Casebook)

See also Products Liability

LAW SCHOOL PUBLICATIONS—Continued

TRADE REGULATION

McManis' Unfair Trade Practices in a Nutshell, 444 pages, 1982 (Text)

Oppenheim, Weston, Maggs and Schechter's Cases and Materials on Unfair Trade Practices and Consumer Protection, 4th Ed., approximately 1000 pages, 1983 (Casebook)

See also Antitrust, Regulated Industries

TRIAL AND APPELLATE ADVOCACY

Appellate Advocacy, Handbook of, 249 pages, 1980 (Text)

Bergman's Trial Advocacy in a Nutshell, 402 pages, 1979 (Text)

Goldberg's The First Trial (Where Do I Sit?) (What Do I Say?) in a Nutshell, 396 pages, 1982 (Text)

Hegland's Trial and Practice Skills in a Nutshell, 346 pages, 1978 (Text)

Jeans' Handbook on Trial Advocacy, Student Ed., 473 pages, 1975 (Text)

McElhaney's Effective Litigation, 457 pages, 1974 (Casebook)

Nolan's Cases and Materials on Trial Practice, 518 pages, 1981 (Casebook)

Parnell and Shellhaas' Cases, Exercises and Problems for Trial Advocacy, 171 pages, 1982 (Coursebook)

TRUSTS AND ESTATES

Atkinson's Hornbook on Wills, 2nd Ed., 975 pages, 1953 (Text)

Averill's Uniform Probate Code in a Nutshell, 425 pages, 1978 (Text)

Bogert's Hornbook on Trusts, 5th Ed., 726 pages, 1973 (Text)

Clark, Lusky and Murphy's Cases and Materials on Gratuitous Transfers, 2nd Ed., 1102 pages, 1977 (Casebook)

Gulliver's Cases and Materials on Future Interests, 624 pages, 1959 (Casebook)

Gulliver's Introduction to the Law of Future Interests, 87 pages, 1959 (Casebook)—reprint from Gulliver's Cases and Materials on Future Interests, 1959

TRUSTS AND ESTATES—Continued

McGovern's Cases and Materials on Wills, Trusts and Future Interests: An Introduction to Estate Planning, 750 pages, 1983 (Casebook)

Mennell's Cases and Materials on California Decedent's Estates, 566 pages, 1973 (Casebook)

Mennell's Wills and Trusts in a Nutshell, 392 pages, 1979 (Text)

Powell's The Law of Future Interests in California, 91 pages, 1980 (Text)

Simes' Hornbook on Future Interests, 2nd Ed., 355 pages, 1966 (Text)

Turrentine's Cases and Text on Wills and Administration, 2nd Ed., 483 pages, 1962 (Casebook)

Uniform Probate Code, 5th Ed., Official Text With Comments, 384 pages, 1977

Waggoner's Future Interests in a Nutshell, 361 pages, 1981 (Text)

WATER LAW

Trelease's Cases and Materials on Water Law, 3rd Ed., 833 pages, 1979 (Casebook)

See also Energy and Natural Resources Law, Environmental Law

WILLS

See Trusts and Estates

WOMEN AND THE LAW

Kay's Text, Cases and Materials on Sex-Based Discrimination, 2nd Ed., 1045 pages, 1981, with 1983 Supplement (Casebook)

Thomas' Sex Discrimination in a Nutshell, 399 pages, 1982 (Text)

See also Employment Discrimination

WORKMEN'S COMPENSATION

See Social Legislation

ADVISORY BOARD
AMERICAN CASEBOOK SERIES
HORNBOOK SERIES AND BASIC LEGAL TEXTS
NUTSHELL SERIES

CURTIS J. BERGER
Professor of Law
Columbia University School of Law

JESSE H. CHOPER
Dean and Professor of Law
University of California, Berkeley

DAVID P. CURRIE
Professor of Law
University of Chicago

DAVID G. EPSTEIN
Professor of Law
University of Texas

ERNEST GELLHORN
Dean and Professor of Law
Case Western Reserve University

YALE KAMISAR
Professor of Law
University of Michigan

WAYNE R. LaFAVE
Professor of Law
University of Illinois

RICHARD C. MAXWELL
Professor of Law
Duke University

ARTHUR R. MILLER
Professor of Law
Harvard University

JAMES J. WHITE
Professor of Law
University of Michigan

CHARLES ALAN WRIGHT
Professor of Law
University of Texas

THE LAW

OF

OIL AND GAS

SECOND EDITION

By

RICHARD W. HEMINGWAY

Eugene Kuntz Professor of Oil and Gas and
Natural Resources Law University of Oklahoma

HORNBOOK SERIES

STUDENT EDITION

ST. PAUL, MINN.
WEST PUBLISHING CO.
1983

COPYRIGHT © 1971 By WEST PUBLISHING CO.
COPYRIGHT © 1983 By WEST PUBLISHING CO.
50 West Kellogg Boulevard
P.O. Box 3526
St. Paul, Minnesota 55165

All rights reserved
Printed in the United States of America

Library of Congress Cataloging in Publication Data

Hemingway, Richard W.
  The law of oil & gas.

  (Hornbook series student edition)
  Includes index.
  1. Petroleum law and legislation—United States.
2. Gas, Natural—Law and legislation—United States. I.
Title. II. Title: Handbook of the law of oil and gas. III.
Series.
KF1849.H435   1983B 346.7304'6823   83-1201
                    347.3064'6823

ISBN 0-314-71558-4

Hemingway Law of Oil & Gas 2nd Ed. HB

To:
Stephanie, Evan, and Michael, Jr.

PREFACE

At the time the first edition was prepared, I was hopeful that a one-volume work covering the basic principles and cases on the law of oil and gas would be helpful to the law student and lawyer, as well as to those in the oil and gas industry. As seven printings have been made of the first edition, I feel that it, indeed, was well received. However, as more than ten years have passed since the publication of the first edition, it is now time to bring the work up to date with the inclusion of the major decisions and developments that have occurred since 1971. Again, the areas on pooling and unitization, government regulation of oil and gas, federal taxation of oil and gas, and sharing agreements have been only briefly touched on. Also, I have not extensively cited the major encyclopedic works. However, I would like to point out that in addition to the multi-volume treatise by Summers, *Oil and Gas Law*, published by West Publishing Company, two other multi-volume works are available for those who need to delve deeper into specific subjects. These are *The Law of Oil and Gas*, by Dean Emeritus Eugene Kuntz and *Oil and Gas Law*, by Professors Williams and Meyers. All are excellent works.

I would like to express my thanks and my special appreciation to Mrs. Marian Pfenning for the untold hours that she spent in helping with basic research, and in reading, clarifying, and correcting the manuscript.

Along with the love, support, and assistance of my wife and children, I have had new helpers this time who "aided" me. These are my grandchildren, to whom this second edition is dedicated.

RICHARD W. HEMINGWAY

Norman, Oklahoma
March, 1983

SUMMARY OF CONTENTS

Chapter	Page
1. Mineral Estate: Definition	1
2. Creation of Interests in the Oil and Gas Mineral Estate by the Landowner	32
3. Conveyances, Partition, and Adverse Possession of the Mineral Estate	101
4. Trespass, Surface and Sub-Surface, and Third Party Claims	152
5. The Oil and Gas Lease—Leases From Owners of Concurrent, Successive, or Restricted Interests	185
6. The Oil and Gas Lease—Duration	239
7. The Oil and Gas Lease—Royalty and Other Particular Lease Clauses	335
8. Covenants of the Lessee to Protect, Develop, and Administer the Lease	410
9. Transfers by the Lessor and by the Lessee	454
Table of Cases	507
Index	533

*

TABLE OF CONTENTS

CHAPTER 1. MINERAL ESTATE: DEFINITION

Sec.		Page
1.1	"Minerals" As Including Oil, Gas and Petroleum Products	1
1.2	"Minerals" and "Oil, Gas and Other Minerals" As Including Substances Other Than Petroleum Products	8
1.3	Nature of Ownership of the Mineral Estate	23

CHAPTER 2. CREATION OF INTERESTS IN THE OIL AND GAS MINERAL ESTATE BY THE LANDOWNER

2.1	Introduction	33
2.2	Attributes of the Mineral Estate—The Power to Lease	34
	(A) Alienability of the Power to Lease	36
	(B) Revocability of the Power to Lease	38
	(C) Duration of Ownership of the Power to Lease	39
	(D) Standard of Exercise of the Power	42
2.3	—— The Right to Delay Rentals	48
2.4	—— The Right to Bonus	50
2.5	—— The Right to Royalty	52
	(A) Nature of Royalty Interests Prior to Lease	53
	(B) Nature of Royalty Interests After Lease	53
	(C) Separation of Royalty Interests From the Mineral Estate—Nature and Duration of Such Interests	56
	(D) Nature of Production Accruing to a Royalty Interest—Federal Income Taxation and Separate-Community Property Status	60
	(E) Minimum Royalty and Shut-In Royalty	60
2.6	—— The Problem of Whether Payments Out of Production Constitute Bonus or Royalty	61
2.7	—— Interests Created When Fractional Interests Are Conveyed or Reserved	65
	(A) Interests Created—Mineral or Royalty?	66
	(B) Conveyances of "Oil and Gas In, Under, and That May Be Produced From . . ."	68
	(C) Conveyances of "Royalty"	70
	(D) Conveyances of "Oil and Gas Produced and Saved"	78

TABLE OF CONTENTS

Sec.		Page
2.7	—— Interests Created When Fractional Interests Are Conveyed or Reserved—Continued	
(E)	Conveyances of "Royalty" Coupled With Language Inconsistent With a Royalty Interest	81
(1)	"Royalty," Plus "Oil and Gas, In, Under, and That May Be Produced"	81
(2)	"Royalty" Together With Express Rights of Ingress and Egress	85
(3)	Conveyances of "Royalty Rights," "Royalty and the Rights Thereto," etc.	86
(F)	Miscellaneous Words and Phrases	86
(1)	Profits	86
(2)	"Landowner's Interest" and "Landowner's Rights"	87
(G)	The Effect of the Quantum of the Interest Conveyed or Reserved on the Mineral-Royalty Distinction, and Problems Occurring as to the Quantum of Production to Which a Mineral or Royalty Owner May Be Entitled	88
(1)	Royalty Conveyances	89
(2)	Mineral Conveyances	92
(H)	Effect of a Conveyance or Reservation of a Mineral Interest, Less the Right to Bonus, Delay Rentals and the Power to Lease	93
(I)	Effect of a Conveyance or Reservation of a Mineral Interest, Less the Right to Bonus and Delay Rentals	96
(J)	Effect of Recitals to Other Instruments	99
2.8	—— Conveyances of Royalty and Mineral Interests for a Limited Term	100

CHAPTER 3. CONVEYANCES, PARTITION, AND ADVERSE POSSESSION OF THE MINERAL ESTATE

3.1	Conveyances of the Mineral Estate—Description of Fractional Interests	102
(A)	General	102
(B)	Description of Quantum of Interest—Undivided Interests	102
(C)	Description of Quantum of Interest—Percentage Interests and Mineral or Royalty Acre Interests	104

TABLE OF CONTENTS

Sec.		Page
3.2	Problems Commonly Encountered in Conveyances or Reservations of Fractional Interests in the Mineral Estate	108
	(A) General—Use of Parol Evidence	109
	(B) Reservations and Exceptions—Effect of False Recitals of Fact, and Effect of Those Made in Favor of Third Parties	110
	(C) Reservations and Exceptions of Fractional Mineral or Royalty Interests From Conveyances of Undivided Mineral or Royalty Interests	112
	(D) The Effect of an Exception or Reservation in an Instrument in Which Grantor Has Breached His Covenant of Warranty by Overconveyance—After Acquired Title and the Doctrine of Duhig v. Peavy-Moore Lumber Co.	116
	(E) Estoppel by Deed as to a Reserved Interest Contained in a Deed Executed by One Without Title to One With Title	126
3.3	Partition of the Mineral Estate	126
	(A) Basis for Judicial Partition of Concurrently Owned Interests in the Minerals	127
	(B) Elements Necessary for Partition of the Mineral Estate	129
	(1) Necessity of a Possessory Interest	130
	(2) The Concept of Estates of Equal Dignity or of Right to Possession	131
	(3) Necessity of Ownership Throughout the Entire Tract to Be Partitioned	136
	(4) Method of Partition	137
	(C) Equitable Partition	139
3.4	Adverse Possessors—Effect of Surface Possession	140
	(A) Non-user	141
	(B) No Severance of Surface and Minerals	142
	(C) Prior Severance of Surface and Minerals	143
	(D) Tacking of Possession Between Successive Possessors	146
	(E) Merger of Severed Estate	147
3.5	Adverse Possession—Actual Possession of the Minerals	148
	(A) Acts of Actual Possession	149
	(B) Rights Acquired—Claiming Under Color of Title	150
	(C) Rights Acquired—Not Claiming Under Color of Title	151

TABLE OF CONTENTS

CHAPTER 4. TRESPASS, SURFACE AND SUB-SURFACE, AND THIRD PARTY CLAIMS

Sec.		Page
4.1	The Geophysical Surface Trespasser	152
	(A) The Right to Explore	153
	(B) Surface Geophysical Exploration Where a Trespass Is Involved	155
	(C) Surface Geophysical Exploration With No Physical Entry	158
	(D) Surface Geophysical Exploration That Causes Physical Damage	158
4.2	The Geophysical Sub-Surface Trespasser	161
	(A) Sub-Surface Trespass That Results in No Production	161
	(B) Sub-Surface Trespass That Results in Production or Drainage	164
	(1) Recovery and Remedy	164
	(2) The Good-Faith Trespasser	169
	(3) Directional Underground Trespass	173
	(4) Discovery and Limitations	174
	(C) Trespass Caused by Underground Intrusion of Injected Substances	175
	(D) Conversion Caused by Negligent Sub-Surface Operations	176
4.3	Slander of Title Affecting Oil and Gas Interests	177

CHAPTER 5. THE OIL AND GAS LEASE—LEASES FROM OWNERS OF CONCURRENT, SUCCESSIVE, OR RESTRICTED INTERESTS

5.1	Co-tenants	185
	(A) Right of a Co-tenant to Develop and Produce	186
	(B) Accounting to a Non-joined Co-tenant by a Producing Co-tenant	187
	(C) Co-tenant Leasing	191
	(D) Ratification by a Non-joined Co-tenant	194
5.2	Life Tenant and Remainderman	196
	(A) Leases From a Life Tenant or a Remainderman	197
	(B) Joint Leases by Life Tenant and Remainderman	199
	(C) Leases Preceding the Life Estate—The Open Mine Doctrine	202
	(D) Application of the Uniform Trust Act and the Uniform Principal and Income Act	207

TABLE OF CONTENTS

Sec.		Page
5.3	The Determinable Fee Estate, Estates Subject to a Power of Termination, and Fee Estates Subject to Executory Interests	210
5.4	Lands Subject to Servitudes and Restrictions	213
5.5	Landlord and Tenant	214
5.6	Lands Subject to Security Interests	218
5.7	Leases From Persons Acting in a Representative Capacity	223
	(A) Attorneys-in-Fact	225
	(B) Trustees	225
	(C) Administrators, Executors, and Guardians	231
	(D) Business Entities	235
	(E) Governmental Entities	235
	(F) Unascertainable or Unknown Owners	237

CHAPTER 6. THE OIL AND GAS LEASE—DURATION

6.1	The Nature of an Oil and Gas Lease	239
6.2	Classification of Oil and Gas Leases by Duration	246
6.3	Keeping the Lease Alive During the Primary Term—The Delay Rental	249
	(A) The Delay Rental—Payment Date	253
	(B) —— Tender	255
	(C) —— Notice of Assignment by the Mineral Owner	260
	(D) —— Effect of Operations During the Primary Term	263
	(E) —— Effect of Improper Payment	267
	(F) —— Estoppel, Waiver, and Ratification of an Improper Payment by the Mineral Owner	272
6.4	Propelling the Lease Past the Primary Term and Keeping It Alive During the Secondary Term by Production of Oil or Gas—Definition of "Production"	277
	(A) Production—Quantum of Production, i.e., Paying Quantities	282
	(B) —— Sporadic Production and Temporary Cessation of Production	291
6.5	Propelling the Lease Past the Primary Term and Keeping It Alive During the Secondary Term—Contractual Substitutes for Production—The Nature of Shut-In Royalties	304
	(A) Shut-In Royalties—Time of Payment	308
6.6	Propelling the Lease Past the Primary Term by Operations —Completing the Well Drilling at the End of the Primary Term	316

Sec.		Page
6.7	—— Commencement of Drilling Operations	321
6.8	Keeping the Lease Alive by Operations During the Secondary Term—The Dry Hole Clause	324
6.9	—— The Continuous Operations Clause	327

CHAPTER 7. THE OIL AND GAS LEASE—ROYALTY AND OTHER PARTICULAR LEASE CLAUSES

Sec.		Page
7.1	Products Covered by the Royalty Clauses—Introduction	336
7.2	Royalty on Gas Produced From an Oil Well—Casinghead Gas and Gasoline	342
	(A) Where No Clause Provision	342
	(B) Express Clause Provision	346
7.3	Royalty on Liquid Components Produced From a Gas Well—Condensate and Distillate	348
7.4	Compensation for Royalty Based Upon "Market Value," "Market Price," and "Proceeds"	351
	(A) General	351
	(B) Market Price	352
	(C) Market Value	354
	(D) Proceeds	355
	(E) Market Price or Value Royalty Clauses and the Long-Term Gas Sales Contract Problem	356
	(F) Expenses of Transportation and Preparation for Market	361
	(G) "FERC-Out" and "Market-Out" Clauses	362
7.5	Division and Transfer Orders	362
	(A) Nature of the Division Order	363
	(B) Effect of the Division Order	365
	(C) Modification or Termination of Division Orders	369
7.6	Minimum Royalty Clause	370
7.7	Description and Mother-Hubbard Clause	371
7.8	The Proportionate Reduction and Warranty Clauses	377
7.9	The Surrender Clause	383
7.10	Lessee's Right to Remove Fixtures From the Lease	385
7.11	The Force Majeure Clause	387
7.12	The Free Gas Clause	391
7.13	Pooling and the Pooling Clause	395
	(A) Formation of Units	396
	(B) Basis and Authority of the Lessee to Pool	399
	(C) Designation of Pooling	405
	(D) The Effect of Production and Operations Within the Unit Upon Acreage Within and Outside of the Unit	406
	(E) Allocation of Production	408
7.14	The Entirety and Assignment Clauses	409
7.15	Lessor's Special Inspection Clause	409

TABLE OF CONTENTS

CHAPTER 8. COVENANTS OF THE LESSEE TO PROTECT, DEVELOP, AND ADMINISTER THE LEASE

Sec.		Page
8.1	The Basis and Nature of Covenants Implied in Oil and Gas Leases	410
8.2	Implied Covenants to Develop the Lease—To Drill an Initial Well	413
8.3	—— After Production Is Acquired	414
	(A) Profitability to the Lessee	416
	(B) Reasonable Diligence of the Lessee	417
	(C) Exploration and Development of Other Areas and Formations Where Profitability Cannot Be Shown	421
8.4	—— Effect of Express Provisions in the Lease	425
8.5	Implied Covenant of Protection—Duty to Protect Against Drainage	429
8.6	The Effect of an Express Offset Clause on the Implied Covenant to Protect Against Drainage	431
8.7	Implied Covenant of Protection—Not to Depreciate the Lessor's Interest	433
8.8	The Implied Covenant to Protect Against Drainage as Affected by Operations to Stimulate Production and Statutory Enactments	438
8.9	Implied Covenants—Other Miscellaneous Covenants	439
	(A) The Covenant to Use Reasonable Care in Operations	439
	(B) The Covenant to Produce	441
	(C) The Covenant to Market	442
	(D) The Covenant to Seek Favorable Administrative Action	444
8.10	Remedies for Breach of Implied Covenants—Damages	445
8.11	—— Cancellation of Lease	449
8.12	Breach of Implied Covenants—Effect of Release	451
8.13	Breach of an Express Clause to Drill	452

CHAPTER 9. TRANSFERS BY THE LESSOR AND BY THE LESSEE

9.1	Post-Lease Conveyances by the Lessor That Are Expressly "Subject to" an Outstanding Lease—Effect Upon the Quantum of Interests Conveyed	455
9.2	—— Effect as to the Land Covered by the Conveyance	463
9.3	—— Effect Upon the Lease to Which the Reference Is Made and Upon the Duration of the Deed in Which the Recitation Is Contained	464

TABLE OF CONTENTS

Sec.		Page
9.4	Post-Lease Conveyances of the Lessor—Apportionment or Non-apportionment of Rentals and Royalties	466
9.5	The Entirety Clause	472
9.6	Transfers by the Lessee	480
9.7	Contracts to Assign Oil and Gas Leases	480
9.8	Assignment of Oil and Gas Leases	483
9.9	Creation of Non-Cost-Bearing Interests From the Lessee's Interest	487
	(A) Definition of Fraction	488
	(B) Costs to Be Borne	490
	(C) Extent of Production From Which Paid and Minerals Covered	490
	(D) Graduated, Sliding Scale, or Conversion Provisions	490
	(E) Implied Covenants	491
	(F) Effective Date	491
	(G) Mortgage Upon Oil and Gas Interests	492
9.10	Divisibility of Covenants	494
	(A) Habendum Clause and Modifying Clauses	495
	(B) Delay Rentals	497
	(C) Divisibility of Implied Covenants	498
9.11	Relationship of Lessor, Lessee, and Owners of Non-Cost-Bearing Interests	500
	(A) Creation of a Fiduciary Relationship	500
	(B) Assignment of Leases as Affecting Liability Upon Express and Implied Covenants	503
Table of Cases		507
Index		533

THE LAW

OF

OIL AND GAS

SECOND EDITION

*

CHAPTER 1

MINERAL ESTATE: DEFINITION

Analysis

Sec.
1.1 "Minerals" As Including Oil, Gas and Petroleum Products.
1.2 "Minerals" and "Oil, Gas and Other Minerals" As Including Substances Other than Petroleum Products.
1.3 Nature of Ownership of the Mineral Estate.

§ 1.1 "Minerals" As Including Oil, Gas and Petroleum Products

In perhaps a majority of the states, a conveyance or reservation of the "minerals" will include oil, gas and petroleum products, unless a contrary intent is manifested on the face of the instrument. If not treated as ambiguous, parol evidence is excluded. Contrary intent may be found in any part of the instrument, such as in restrictive wording of the habendum clause or in clauses defining rights of surface usage appropriate only to hard mineral mining. Constructional rules such as *ejusdem generis* are generally rejected.

In a substantial number of states, the term "mineral" has an uncertain meaning, and is examined with reference to the facts and circumstances existing at the time of the transaction, in an effort to determine actual intent of the parties.

In Pennsylvania a reservation or conveyance of the "minerals" is presumed not to include oil, gas and petroleum products. This presumption, which was originally stated as a rule of property, may be rebutted only by clear and convincing evidence.

From early times man has recognized that land was valuable for the extraction of substances to be found therein, as well as for agriculture and farming. In order to convey the right to all such substances underlying a tract of land, the generic term "mineral" has evolved. However, the meaning and understanding of the term has constantly changed. As technology has advanced, new uses and more efficient methods of extraction have led to sharply increased demand and market value for erstwhile common materials, and to discovery of new substances. Whether such newly discovered or used substances are included in prior conveyances or reservations of "minerals" has led to extensive litigation.

The development of the internal combustion engine created such a demand for oil and other petroleum products, as the construction of interstate pipeline distribution systems did for gas. In the late 1800's cases began to be decided by the courts dealing with the question of whether oil, gas and petroleum products were to be included within the definition of the term "mineral" when not specifically mentioned by the parties.

Courts early recognized that if all matter were divided into the three classes of animal, vegetable and mineral, a broad definition of the term "mineral" would include the soil itself as well as all substances contained therein.[1] To embrace such a broad definition would remove any distinction between the minerals in Blackacre and the land itself, and courts have generally rejected such a supposed intent of the parties as being unreasonable.[2] On the other hand, the courts have also rejected an undue restriction of the term, as including only metallic ores or precious metals.[3] In determining whether the parties intended to include oil, gas and petroleum products within the term "mineral," when not specifically mentioned, the courts have taken three approaches: (1) that petroleum products were not included;[4] (2) that the parties used the term as commonly understood in the vicinity at the time of the conveyance or reservation, allowing free use of parol evidence to determine such understanding;[5] and (3) that the term includes oil, gas and petroleum products,[6] restricting

---

1. Northern Pacific Railway Co. v. Soderberg, 188 U.S. 526, 23 S.Ct. 365, 47 L.Ed. 575; Silver v. Bush, 213 Pa. 195, 62 A. 832; Puget Mill Co. v. Duecy, 1 Wash. 2d 421, 96 P.2d 571; Sult v. A. Hochstetter Oil Co., 63 W.Va. 317, 61 S.E. 307.

2. Elkhorn City Land Co. v. Elkhorn City, Ky.App., 459 S.W.2d 762; Fisher v. Keweenaw Land Association, 371 Mich. 575, 124 N.W.2d 784; MacMaster v. Onstad, N.D., 86 N.W.2d 36; Campbell v. Tennessee Coal, Iron & Railroad Co., 150 Tenn. 423, 265 S.W. 674; Atwood v. Rodman, Tex.Civ.App., 355 S.W.2d 206, refused n.r.e.; State Land Board v. State Department of Fish and Game, 17 Utah 2d 237, 408 P.2d 707.

3. Northern Pacific Railway Co. v. Soderberg, 188 U.S. 526, 23 S.Ct. 365, 47 L.Ed. 575; Dunham v. Kirkpatrick, 101 Pa. 36; Gibson v. Tyson, 5 Watts (Pa.) 37; Sult v. A. Hochstetter Oil Co., 63 W.Va. 317, 61 S.E. 307; But cf. Doster v. Friedensville Zinc Co., 140 Pa. 147, 21 A. 251; Fisher v. Keweenaw Land Association, 371 Mich. 575, 124 N.W.2d 784.

4. Detlor v. Holland, 57 Ohio St. 492, 49 N.E. 690; Dunham v. Kirkpatrick, 101 Pa. 36; Silver v. Bush, 213 Pa. 195, 62 A. 832; Highland v. Commonwealth of Pennsylvania, 400 Pa. 261, 161 A.2d 390, cert. denied 364 U.S. 901, 81 S.Ct. 234, 5 L.Ed.2d 194, and 364 U.S. 630, 81 S.Ct. 357, 5 L.Ed.2d 363; New York State Natural Gas Corp. v. Swan-Finch Gas Development Corp., C.A.3d, 278 F.2d 577, criticized in 62 W.Va.L.Rev. 84; Avery v. Moore, 150 W.Va. 136, 144 S.E.2d 434.

5. Missouri Pacific Railroad Co. v. Strohacker, 202 Ark. 645, 152 S.W.2d 557; Stegall v. Bugh, 228 Ark. 632, 310 S.W.2d 251; Mining Corp. of Arkansas v. International Paper Co., D.C.Ark., 324 F.Supp. 705; Monon Coal Co. v. Riggs, 115 Ind.App. 236, 56 N.E.2d 672, rehearing denied 115 Ind.App. 236, 57 N.E.2d 598; Ambarann Corp. v. Old Ben Coal Corp., 395 Ill. 154, 69 N.E.2d 835; Huie Hodge Lumber Co. v. Railroad Lands Co., 151 La. 197, 91 So. 676; McKinney's Heirs v. Central Kentucky Natural Gas Co., 134 Ky. 239, 120 S.W. 314; Barker v. Campbell-Ratcliff Land Co., 64 Okl. 249, 167 P. 468; Dingess v. Huntington Development & Gas Co., C.C.A. 4th, 271 F. 864; Burdette v. Bruen, 118 W.Va. 624, 191 S.E. 360.

6. Burke v. Southern Pacific Railway Co., 234 U.S. 669, 34 S.Ct. 907, 58 L.Ed. 1527; Wall v. Shell Oil Co., 209 Cal.App. 2d 504, 25 Cal.Rptr. 908; Kentucky-West Virginia Gas Co. v. Browning, Ky.App., 521 S.W.2d 516; Weaver v. Richards, 156 Mich. 320, 120 N.W. 818. Stocker & Sitler, Inc. v. Metzger, 19 Ohio App. 135, 250 N.E.2d 269; Anderson & Kerr Drilling Co. v. Bruhlmeyer, 134 Tex. 574, 136 S.W.2d 800, 127 A.L.R. 1217, answers conformed to 138 S.W.2d 1118; Western Development Co. v. Nell, 4 Utah 2d 112, 288 P.2d 452 (ambiguous); Warren v. Clinchfield Coal Corp., 166 Va. 524, 186 S.E. 20; Amoco Production Co. v. Guild Trust, D.C.Wyo., 461 F.Supp. 279, affirmed, C.A.10th, 636 F.2d 261 (citing text).

the search for a contrary intent to the four corners of the instrument,[7] unless found ambiguous. These cases have involved a variety of situations: conveyances,[8] reservations and exceptions from conveyances,[9] tax statutes,[10] statutes reserving mineral interests to the sovereignty upon severance of federal or state-owned lands,[11] condemnation statutes,[12] lien statutes,[13] etc.

In the early case of Dunham v. Kirkpatrick,[14] the court laid down what has become known as the "Pennsylvania" rule, i.e., a reservation or conveyance of "minerals" does not include oil or gas. Recognizing that oil, gas and petroleum products come within the broad definition of "mineral," the court limited the term to substances so understood by the mass of mankind at the time of the transaction, viz., that petroleum was no more understood to be a mineral than animal or vegetable oil. The court further stated that even if the parties intended to include oil and gas, they were mistaken in using a word in a manner not sanctioned by the common understanding of mankind. It is apparent that the court was laying down a rule of property rather than one of construction; however, later cases have restated the rule in the form of a presumption, rebuttable only by clear and convincing evidence.[15] Although sometimes cited in other jurisdictions, it is believed application of the Pennsylvania rule is limited to its birthplace.[16]

7. Federal Gas, Oil & Coal Co. v. Moore, 290 Ky. 284, 161 S.W.2d 46; Gibson v. Sellers, Ky., 252 S.W.2d 911; Bulger v. McCourt, 179 Neb. 316, 138 N.W.2d 18; Maynard v. McHenry, 271 Ky. 642, 113 S.W.2d 13; Anderson & Kerr Drilling Co. v. Bruhlmeyer, 134 Tex. 574, 136 S.W.2d 800, 127 A.L.R. 1217; Warren v. Clinchfield Coal Corp., 166 Va. 524, 186 S.E. 20.

8. Detlor v. Holland, 57 Ohio St. 492, 49 N.E. 690; Monon Coal Co. v. Riggs, 115 Ind.App. 236, 56 N.E.2d 672; McKinney's Heirs v. Central Kentucky Natural Gas Co., 134 Ky. 239, 120 S.W. 314.

9. Missouri Pacific Railway Co. v. Strohacker, 202 Ark. 645, 152 S.W.2d 557; Murray v. Allard, 100 Tenn. 100, 43 S.W. 355; Maynard v. McHenry, 271 Ky. 642, 113 S.W.2d 13; Western Development Co. v. Nell, 4 Utah 2d 112, 288 P.2d 452.

10. Brizzolara v. Powell, 214 Ark. 870, 218 S.W.2d 728, noted in 4 Ark.L.Rev. 249; Mid-Northern Oil Co. v. Walker, 65 Mont. 414, 211 P. 353; Wilson v. A. Cook Sons Co., 298 Pa. 85, 148 A. 63; Stephens County v. Mid-Kansas Oil & Gas Co., 113 Tex. 160, 254 S.W. 290, 29 A.L.R. 566.

11. Burke v. Southern Pacific Railroad Co., 234 U.S. 669, 34 S.Ct. 907, 58 L.Ed. 1527; Missouri Pacific Railroad Co. v. Strohacker, 202 Ark. 645, 152 S.W.2d 557; Monon Coal Co. v. Riggs, 115 Ind.App. 236, 56 N.E.2d 672.

12. Right of Way Oil Co. v. Gladys City Oil, Gas & Manufacturing Co., 106 Tex. 94, 157 S.W. 737.

13. Barton v. Wichita River Oil Co., Tex.Civ.App., 187 S.W. 1043.

14. 101 Pa. 36.

15. Bundy v. Myers, 372 Pa. 583, 94 A.2d 724; Highland v. Commonwealth of Pennsylvania, 400 Pa. 261, 161 A.2d 390, cert. denied 364 U.S. 901, 81 S.Ct. 234, 5 L.Ed.2d 194, and 364 U.S. 630, 81 S.Ct. 357, 5 L.Ed.2d 363. But cf. Bannard v. New York State Natural Gas Corp., 448 Pa. 239, 293 A.2d 41 (1972), which rejects the Dunham rule as to tax deeds which include all substances properly included in the assessment.

16. Monon Coal Co. v. Riggs, 115 Ind.App. 236, 56 N.E.2d 672; McKinney's Heirs v. Central Kentucky Natural Gas Co., 134 Ky. 239, 120 S.W. 314; Huie Hodge Lumber Co. v. Railroad Lands Co., Ltd., 151 La. 197, 91 So. 676. Expressly rejecting the Pennsylvania rule, see Barker v. Campbell-Ratcliff Land Co., 64 Okl. 249, 167 P. 468; Luse v. Boatman, Tex.Civ.App., 217 S.W. 1096; Dingess v. Huntington Development & Gas Co., C.C.A.4th, 271 F. 864.

Jurisdictions not following the Pennsylvania rule are divided into two substantial groups: those that treat the term "mineral" as being uncertain in meaning and allow consideration of evidence of the facts and circumstances existing at the time of the transaction to determine if usage included oil and gas,[17] and those that treat the term as being of sufficient definitional context so as to include oil and gas.[18]

In jurisdictions that follow the latter approach, parol evidence of the facts and circumstances existing at the time of the transaction is generally inadmissible unless the instrument is treated as being ambiguous.[19] In this view, knowledge and understanding of the parties is immaterial.[20] However, not all courts agree on the definition of the term "ambiguous." Some allow parol evidence only when the instrument is so uncertain or obscure in meaning as to defy interpretation,[21] while others allow evidence of facts and circumstances when meaning is doubtful or capable of more than one construction.[22]

In construction of unambiguous instruments these courts, for the most part, have given effect to all parts of the instrument in order to determine the intent of the parties, rather than follow the older and more formal rules of construction.[23]

An intent not to include oil, gas and petroleum products has been found from the enumeration of specific substances in a grant or reservation. When the terms "mineral" or "mineral rights" are coupled with an enumeration of specific substances, not including oil and gas, two rules of construction have been repeatedly urged as limiting the term "mineral," viz., *ejusdem generis*, that general words following a specific enumeration will be limited to things of a like class;[24] and,

17. See note 5, supra.

18. See note 6, supra.

19. Wall v. Shell Oil Co., 198 Cal.App. 2d 504, 25 Cal.Rptr. 908; Ambarann Corp. v. Old Ben Coal Corp., 395 Ill. 154, 69 N.E.2d 835; Gibson v. Sellars, Ky., 252 S.W.2d 911; Federal Gas, Oil & Coal Co. v. Moore, 290 Ky. 284, 161 S.W.2d 46; Kentucky-West Virginia Gas Co. v. Browning, Ky.App., 521 S.W.2d 516; Bulger v. McCourt, 179 Neb. 316, 138 N.W.2d 18; Stocker & Sitler, Inc. v. Metzger, 19 Ohio App. 135, 250 N.E.2d 269; Anderson & Kerr Drilling Co. v. Bruhlmeyer, 134 Tex. 574, 136 S.W.2d 800, 127 A.L.R. 1217, answers conformed to 138 S.W.2d 1118; Western Development Co. v. Nell, 4 Utah 2d 112, 288 P.2d 452; Warren v. Clinchfield Coal Corp., 166 Va. 524, 186 S.E. 20; Burdette v. Bruen, 118 W.Va. 624, 191 S.E. 360; Amoco Production Co. v. Guild Trust, D.C.Wyo., 461 F.Supp. 279, affirmed C.A.10th, 636 F.2d 261.

20. Maynard v. McHenry, 271 Ky. 642, 113 S.W.2d 13; Kentucky-West Virginia Gas Co. v. Browning, Ky.App., 521 S.W.2d 516.

21. Gibson v. Sellars, Ky., 252 S.W.2d 911.

22. Hudson & Collins v. McGuire, 188 Ky. 712, 223 S.W. 1101, 17 A.L.R. 148; Anderson & Kerr Drilling Co. v. Bruhlmeyer, 134 Tex. 574, 136 S.W.2d 800, 127 A.L.R. 1217; Western Development Co. v. Nell, 4 Utah 2d 112, 288 P.2d 452.

23. See note 19, supra.

24. Huie Hodge Lumber Co. v. Railroad Lands Co., 151 La. 197, 91 So. 676; Highland v. Commonwealth of Pennsylvania, 400 Pa. 261, 161 A.2d 390; Cronkhite v. Falkenstein, Okl., 352 P.2d 396; Panhandle Co-operative Royalty Co. v. Cunningham, Okl., 495 P.2d 108; Allen v. Farmers' Union Co-operative Royalty Co., Okl., 538 P.2d 204; West v. Aetna Life Insurance Co., Okl.App., 536 P.2d 393; Sloan v. Peabody Coal Co., C.A.10th, 547 F.2d 115; Right of Way Oil Co. v. Gladys City Oil, Gas & Manufacturing Co., 106 Tex. 94, 157 S.W. 737.

§ 1.1 MINERAL ESTATE: DEFINITION

expressio unius est exclusio alterius, the expression of one thing is the exclusion of another.[25] Like most rules of construction when evidence of actual intent is lacking, they are used for the convenience of the courts in arriving at a result in terms of supposedly observed human behavior, rather than an attempt to determine the actual intent of the parties. The rules have had little application in cases dealing with oil and gas,[26] and the prevailing view seems to be that the term "mineral" will not be so limited, whether preceded or followed by a specific enumeration.[27] However, it is sometimes held such an enumeration raises sufficient doubt as to the meaning of the instrument to allow the use of parol evidence.[28]

In the Texas case of Southland Royalty Company v. Pan American Petroleum Corporation,[29] the Texas Supreme Court stated that in the phrase, "potash and other minerals," the term "mineral" was not limited to hard minerals of like character to potash, and that the doctrine of *ejusdem generis* had never been recognized in Texas. This later statement seems erroneous as to earlier case law,[30] but there is no doubt that it is not followed in Texas at the present time.

In the later Texas case of Acker v. Guinn,[31] dealing with the question of whether lignite is included in a grant of "oil, gas and other minerals," the court specifically rejected the *ejusdem generis* rule, citing Southland. However, if the rule is dead in Texas, it is followed in other jurisdictions.[32]

In Oklahoma the leading case applying the rule of *ejusdem generis* is that of Cronkhite v. Falkenstein.[33] It has been followed generally. The history of the rule is well summarized in the case of West v. Aetna Life Insurance Co.[34]

---

25. Bulger v. McCourt, 179 Neb. 316, 138 N.W.2d 18.

26. See note 24, supra.

27. Federal Gas, Oil & Coal Co. v. Moore, 290 Ky. 284, 161 S.W.2d 46; Bulger v. McCourt, 179 Neb. 316, 138 N.W.2d 18; Watkins v. Certain-Teed Products Corp., Tex.Civ.App., 231 S.W.2d 981; Anderson & Kerr Drilling Co. v. Bruhlmeyer, 134 Tex. 574, 136 S.W.2d 800, 127 A.L.R. 1217; Southland Royalty Co. v. Pan American Petroleum Corp., Tex., 378 S.W.2d 50; Burdette v. Bruen, 118 W.Va. 624, 191 S.E. 360. But, cf. Right of Way Oil Co. v. Gladys City Oil, Gas & Manufacturing Co., 106 Tex. 94, 157 S.W. 737 (applying *ejusdem generis*)

28. Western Development Co. v. Nell, 4 Utah 2d 112, 288 P.2d 452. But cf. Nance v. Donk Brothers Coal & Coke Co., 13 Ill.2d 399, 151 N.E.2d 97.

29. Tex., 378 S.W.2d 50.

30. See for instance: Fleming Foundation v. Texaco, Inc., Tex.Civ.App., 337 S.W.2d 846, refused n.r.e.

31. Tex., 464 S.W.2d 348.

32. See note 24, supra, and: Panhandle Co-operative Royalty Co. v. Cunningham, Okl., 495 P.2d 108; Allen v. Farmers' Union Co-operative Royalty Co., Okl., 538 P.2d 204; West v. Aetna Life Insurance Co., Okl.App., 536 P.2d 393; Sloan v. Peabody Coal Co., C.A.10th, 547 F.2d 115; State Land Board v. State Department of Game and Fish, 17 Utah 2d 237, 408 P.2d 707 (But cf. Western Development Co. v. Nell, 4 Utah 2d 112, 288 P.2d 452); Dawson v. Meike, Wyo., 508 P.2d 15.

33. Okl., 352 P.2d 396.

34. Okl.App., 536 P.2d 393. Also see Haynes v. Board of Commissioners, 66 Colo. 397, 182 P. 897; Wolf v. Blackwell Oil & Gas Co., 77 Okl. 81, 186 P. 484; Panhandle Co-operative Royalty Co. v. Cunningham, Okl., 495 P.2d 108; Allen v. Farmers' Union Co-operative Royalty Co., Okl., 538 P.2d 204; Sloan v. Peabody Coal Co., C.A.10th, 547 F.2d 115.

When construing an unambiguous instrument, limiting intent may also be found in the habendum clause and in language defining the scope and nature of surface use for extraction purposes. Language restricted to methods and structures appropriate to hard mineral mining or open pit extraction may demontrate an intent not to include oil and gas.[35] For instance, the granting of a right to "mine" has been held not to include the sinking of an oil and gas well.[36] Such limiting intent is found most frequently in jurisdictions having an extensive history of hard mineral mining.[37] In Texas, however, a mine is a generic term including the whole mode of obtaining metals and minerals from beneath the ground.[38]

Many jurisdictions, in determining whether an intent exists to exclude oil and gas from a conveyance or reservation of the minerals, have treated the term "mineral" as being of uncertain meaning, and have been liberal in allowing consideration of parol evidence,[39] in addition to the language of the instrument, to determine intent. This position was taken in the early case of Detlor v. Holland,[40] and is well stated in the later case of Dingess v. Huntington Development and Gas Co.: "[T]he word mineral is not capable of a definition of universal application but is susceptible of limitation according to the intention of the parties using it to be ascertained from the language of the deed, the relative position of the parties, and the nature of the transaction."[41] Under this view, primary importance is attached to the knowledge and understanding of the parties to the instrument concerning the existence and commerical usage of petroleum products at the time of the transaction. It is often stated that the parties will have been understood to have used the term "mineral" in its common and ordinary sense at the time of the conveyance.[42] However, courts

---

35. Huie Hodge Lumber Co. v. Railroad Lands Co., Ltd., 151 La. 197, 91 So. 676; Detlor v. Holland, 57 Ohio St. 492, 49 N.E. 690; McKinney's Heirs v. Central Kentucky Natural Gas Co., 134 Ky. 239, 120 S.W. 314; Western Development Co. v. Nell, 4 Utah 2d 112, 288 P.2d 452.

36. Lambert v. Pritchett, Ky., 284 S.W.2d 90; Barton v. Wichita River Oil Co., Tex.Civ.App., 187 S.W. 1043.

37. Davis v. Plunkett, 187 Kan. 121, 353 P.2d 514; Federal Gas, Oil & Coal Co. v. Moore, 290 Ky. 284, 161 S.W.2d 46; Sellars v. Ohio Valley Trust Co., Ky., 248 S.W.2d 897; Williams v. South Penn. Oil Co., 52 W.Va. 181, 43 S.E. 214; and see note 35, supra.

38. Luse v. Boatman, Tex.Civ.App., 217 S.W. 1096. In those jurisdictions, which have rejected application of constructional limitations such as the *ejusdem generis* rule and which treat most enumerations of surface usage for mining purposes generically, conveyances and reservations of the "minerals" will include oil and gas unless excluded by precise language.

39. Missouri Pacific Railroad Co. v. Strohacker, 202 Ark. 645, 152 S.W.2d 557; Stegall v. Bugh, 228 Ark. 632, 310 S.W.2d 251; United States v. 1,253.14 Acres of Land, C.A.10th, 455 F.2d 1177; McKinney's Heirs v. Central Kentucky Natural Gas Co., 134 Ky. 239, 120 S.W. 314; Besing v. Ohio Valley Coal Co., Inc. of Kentucky, 155 Ind.App. 527, 293 N.E.2d 510; Kentucky-West Virginia Gas Co. v. Browning, Ky., 521 S.W.2d 516; Huie Hodge Lumber Co. v. Railroad Lands Co., Ltd., 151 La. 197, 91 So. 676; Vang v. Mount, 300 Minn. 393, 220 N.W.2d 498; Weyerhaeuser Co. v. Burlington Northern, Inc., 15 Wn.App. 314, 549 P.2d 54; Dingess v. Huntington Development & Gas Co., C.C.A.4th, 271 F. 864.

40. 57 Ohio St. 492, 29 N.E. 690.

41. C.C.A.4th, 271 F. 864.

42. Marvel v. Merritt, 116 U.S. 11, 6 S.Ct. 207, 29 L.Ed. 550; Mining Corp. of

have differed greatly on the question of whose knowledge and understanding will be employed, i.e., that of a particular grantor,[43] general knowledge in the vicinity,[44] general knowledge in the state,[45] general knowledge in the state when it is shown that it was not so known by a particular grantor,[46] or knowledge of the mass of mankind.[47] Other relevant facts considered include the type of business in which the recipient of the mineral interest was then or thereafter engaged, claims and extraction of oil and gas by third parties,[48] etc.

Obviously, an *ad hoc* determination of definitional context engenders uncertainty in titles until laid to rest by litigation or agreement of the parties involved. Some lessees, in an effort to acquire the mineral interest, will take multiple leases from all persons they feel may have a legitimate claim to ownership of the minerals. It seems highly unrealistic to attempt to determine, at a later date, whether, in an early conveyance, the parties intended to include or to exclude oil and gas from their usage of the term "minerals," where such intent is purportedly determined by reference to "facts and circumstances then existing" and of which adequate proof has long since vanished. All too often this "intent," as determined, results from application of the rules of evidence concerning burden of proof and presumptions, which have little relevance to the actual intent of the parties. This was apparently recognized by the dissenting justice in the Arkansas cases of Stegall v. Bugh,[49] and Ahne v. Reinhart and Donovan Co.,[50] who, despairing of case-to-case determination of common knowledge and understanding, concluded that the court should hold that oil and gas became generally known throughout the state on January 1, 1900, in effect, converting the Arkansas rule to one of property as to transactions occurring after such date. However, to the despair of lessees, the "Strohacker Doctrine" is a rule of property in Arkansas, requiring a factual determination whether oil and gas (or other substance) was commonly known in legal and commercial usage in the area where the instrument was executed at the time of its execution.[51]

Arkansas v. International Paper Co. D.C. W.D.Ark., 324 F.Supp. 705; Cronkhite v. Falkenstein, Okl., 352 P.2d 396; Gibson v. Tyson, 5 Watts (Pa.) 34; Pfister v. Brown, Wyo., 498 P.2d 1243; Dawson v. Meike, Wyo., 508 P.2d 15.

43. Detlor v. Holland, 57 Ohio St. 492, 29 N.E. 690.

44. Ahne v. Reinhart and Donovan Co., 240 Ark. 691, 401 S.W.2d 565; Armstrong v. Lake Champlain Granite Co., 147 N.Y. 495, 42 N.E. 186.

45. Missouri Pacific Railroad Co. v. Strohacker, 202 Ark. 645, 152 S.W.2d 557; Ahne v. Reinhart & Donovan Co., 240 Ark. 691, 401 S.W.2d 565.

46. Stegall v. Bugh, 228 Ark. 632, 310 S.W.2d 251.

47. Dunham v. Kirkpatrick, 101 Pa. 36; Murray v. Allard, 100 Tenn. 100, 43 S.W. 355; Carothers v. Mills, Tex.Civ. App., 233 S.W. 155; As to the present Texas view, see Heinatz v. Allen, 147 Tex. 512, 217 S.W.2d 994.

48. Monon Coal Co. v. Riggs, 115 Ind. App. 236, 56 N.E.2d 672.

49. 228 Ark. 632, 310 S.W.2d 251, at page 254.

50. 240 Ark. 691, 401 S.W.2d 565, at page 570.

51. Missouri Pacific Railroad Co. v. Strohacker, 202 Ark. 645, 152 S.W.2d 557, and see cases note 39, supra. Strohacker is apparently based on the "contemporaneous construction" rule set forth in Boyd v. United States, 116 U.S.

§ 1.2 "Minerals" and "Oil, Gas and Other Minerals" As Including Substances Other than Petroleum Products

A conveyance or reservation of "minerals" or "oil, gas and other minerals" will generally include substances having a special value apart from the land itself, whose removal will not substantially interfere with surface usage, and which are traditionally not associated with surface ownership.

The jurisdictions are divided in application of constructional rules such as *ejusdem generis* and the consideration of parol evidence.

The question is often presented as to what substances, other than oil, gas, and petroleum products, will be included in ownership[1] of the mineral estate, apart from the surface. When A conveys to B "all of the minerals" or "the oil, gas and other minerals," controversies have arisen as to ownership of gravel, clay, granite, sandstone, coal, lignite, surplus salt water, iron ore, and, more recently, uranium, fissionable materials, subterranean water,[2] helium, carbon dioxide, and

616, 6 S.Ct. 524, 29 L.Ed. 746, and will be applied to determine whether specific substances are intended to be included in the term "minerals," when not specifically set forth. The rule may be a delight of logic to some, but it has proven a rule of torment to oil and gas lessees through the years.

1. The owner of the oil and gas or rights thereto usually has the right to use so much of the surface estate as may be reasonably necessary for the exploration, development and production of oil and gas. Maxwell, The Meaning of Minerals—The Relationship of Interpretation and Surface Burden, 8 Tex.Tech.L.R. 255; Patterson, The Ownership of Other Minerals, 25 Rocky Mt.Min.L.Inst., 21–1; Emery, What Surface is Mineral and What Mineral is Surface, 12 Okla.L.R. 499; Reeves, The Meaning of the word "Minerals," 54 N.D.L.R. 419; and see comment, 12 St. Marys L.J. 580 (1980).

2. Weyerhaeuser Co. v. Burlington Northern, Inc., 15 Wn.App. 314, 549 P.2d 54 (basaltic rock); Carson v. Missouri Pacific Railroad Co., 212 Ark. 963, 209 S.W.2d 97, 1 A.L.R.2d 784 (bauxite); Cole v. McDonald, 236 Miss. 168, 109 So.2d 628 (bentonite); Hans v. Great Bend Brick & Tile Co., 172 Kan. 478, 241 P.2d 475 (clay); Atwood v. Rodman, Tex.Civ. App., 355 S.W.2d 206, refused n.r.e. (caliche); Mining Corp. of Arkansas v. International Paper Co., D.C.Ark., 324 F.Supp. 705 (cinnabar ore and mercury); Besing v. Ohio Valley Coal Co., Inc. of Kentucky, 155 Ind.App. 527, 293 N.E.2d 510 (coal); River Rouge Minerals, Inc. v. Energy Resources of Minnesota, La. App., 331 So.2d 878, cert. denied La., 337 So.2d 221 (coal and lignite); Christman v. Emineth, N.D., 212 N.W. 543 (coal and lignite); Olson v. Dillerud, N.D., 226 N.W.2d 363 (coal and lignite); Sloan v. Peabody Coal Co., C.A.10th, 547 F.2d 115 (coal); Doochin v. Rackley, Tenn., 610 S.W.2d 715 (coal); Reed v. Wylie, Tex., 597 S.W.2d 743 (coal and lignite); Adams County v. Smith, 74 N.D. 621, 23 N.W.2d 873 (coal); Gibson v. Tyson, 5 Watts (Pa.) 34 (chromate of Iron); Panhandle Co-operative Royalty Co. v. Cunningham, Okl., 495 P.2d 108 (copper, silver, gold); Christman v. Emineth, N.D., 212 N.W. 543 (copper, silver, gold, lead); West v. Aetna Life Insurance Co., Okl.App., 536 P.2d 393 (metallic ores); Kentucky Diamond Mining & Developing Co. v. Kentucky Transvaal Diamond Co., 141 Ky. 97, 132 S.W. 397 (diamond); McMullin v. Magnuson, 102 Colo. 230, 78 P.2d 964 (feldspar); Armstrong v. Lake Champlain Granite Co., 147 N.Y. 495, 42 N.E. 186 (granite); Morrison v. Socolofsky, 43 Colo.App. 212, 600 P.2d 121 (gravel); United States v. 1,253.14 Acres of Land, C.A.10th, 455 F.2d 1177 (gravel); Rickelton v. Universal Constructors, Inc., 91 N.M. 479, 576 P.2d 285 (gravel and sand); Western Nuclear, Inc. v. Andrus, D.C. Wyo., 475 F.Supp. 654 (gravel); Kinder v. LaSalle County Carbon Coal Co., 310 Ill. 126, 141 N.E. 537 (gravel); Cronkhite v. Falkenstein, Okl., 352 P.2d 396 (gypsum); White v. Miller, 200 N.Y. 29, 92 N.E. 1065 (gypsum); Certain-Teed Products Corp. v. Comly, 54 Wyo. 79, 87 P.2d 21 (gypsite); Guinn v. Acker, Tex.Civ.App., 451 S.W.2d 549, affirmed Tex., 464 S.W.2d 348 (iron); Wulf v. Shultz, 211 Kan. 724, 508 P.2d 896 (limestone, clay, gypsum); Vang v. Mount, 300 Minn. 393, 220 N.W.2d 498 (limestone and gravel);

geothermic matter such as hot water and steam used for power purposes.³

From early times the term "minerals" has been used in legal instruments to refer to something other than to the soil or to the land itself. Where minerals have been conveyed or reserved, the residuary rights or ownership in the land have been referred to as the "surface." Together, the mineral-surface dichotomy is descriptive of the ownership of all substances that comprise any particular tract of land.

The courts generally have not considered the mineral estate as being definite or certain of meaning.⁴ From time to time the mineral

Holland v. Dolese Co., Okl., 540 P.2d 549 (limestone); Heinatz v. Allen, 147 Tex. 512, 217 S.W.2d 994 (limestone); Gibson v. Tyson, 5 Watts (Pa.) 34 (magnesia); Deer Lake Co. v. Michigan Land & Iron Co., Ltd., 89 Mich. 180, 50 N.W. 807 (marble); Singer v. Tatum, 251 Miss. 661, 171 So.2d 134, cert. denied 382 U.S. 845, 86 S.Ct. 46, 15 L.Ed.2d 85 (salt); Ambassador Oil Corp. v. Robertson, Tex.Civ.App., 384 S.W.2d 752, refused n.r.e., Tex., 390 S.W.2d 472 (salt water); Blythe v. Hines, Okl., 577 P.2d 1268 (sand, gravel, limestone); Hendler v. Lehigh Valley Railroad Co., 209 Pa. 256, 58 A. 486 (sand); Kalberer v. Grassham, 282 Ky. 430, 138 S.W.2d 940 (sandstone); Cumberland Mineral Co. v. United States, Ct.Cl., 513 F.2d 1399 (sandstone and clay); McCombs v. Stephenson, 154 Ala. 109, 44 So. 867 (shale); Elkhorn City Land Co., Inc. v. Elkhorn City, Ky.App., 459 S.W.2d 762 (shale and clay); State v. Evans, 46 Wash. 219, 89 P. 565 (silica); Newell, Inc. v. Randall, Ala., 373 So.2d 1068 (soil); Singer v. Tatum, 251 Miss. 661, 171 So.2d 134, cert. denied 382 U.S. 845, 86 S.Ct. 46, 15 L.Ed.2d 85 (sulphur), see Summers, Legal Relations Respecting Sulphur, 9 Tex.L.Rev. 465; MacMaster v. Onstad, N.D., 86 N.W.2d 36: New Mexico & Arizona Land Co. v. Elkins, D.C.N.M., 137 F.Supp. 767, noted in 4 Ark.L.Rev. 249, and 3 U.C.L.A.L.Rev. 612; Reiss v. Rummel, N.D., 232 N.W.2d 40 (uranium and coal); Moser v. United States Steel Corp., Tex.Civ.App., 601 S.W.2d 731 (uranium); Pfister v. Brown, Wyo., 498 P.2d 1243 (uranium); Dawson v. Meike, Wyo., 508 P.2d 15 (uranium); Cain v. Neumann, Tex.Civ.App., 316 S.W.2d 915 (uranium); See Adoue, Howell & Simmons, Mineral Laws of the State of Texas in Relation to Fissionable Materials, 7 Baylor L.Rev. 247; Vogel v. Cobb, 193 Okl. 64, 141 P.2d 276, 148 A.L.R. 774 (surface water); Fleming Foundation v. Texaco, Inc., Tex.Civ.App., 337 S.W.2d 846, refused n.r.e. (subterranean water).

3. See: Navajo Tribe of Indians v. United States, 176 Ct.Cl. 502, 364 F.2d 320 (helium, as included in lease of "all the oil and gas deposits"); Ashland Oil, Inc. v. Phillips Petroleum Co., C.A.10th, 554 F.2d 381, cert. denied 434 U.S. 921, 98 S.Ct. 396, 54 L.Ed.2d 278, and 434 U.S. 968, 98 S.Ct. 513, 54 L.Ed.2d 456, rehearing denied 434 U.S. 977, 98 S.Ct. 540, 54 L.Ed.2d 471; Northern Natural Gas Co. v. Grounds, C.A.10th, 441 F.2d 704; Phillips Petroleum Co. v. Texaco, Inc., 415 U.S. 125, 94 S.Ct. 1002, 39 L.Ed.2d 209; McCombe, Helium and Its Place in the Petroleum and Natural Gas Lease, 2 Alberta L.Rev. 9; Holland, Is Helium Covered by Oil and Gas Leases? 41 Tex.L.Rev. 409; New Values Under Old Oil and Gas Leases: Helium, Who Owns It? 62 Mich.L.Rev. 1158; Geothermal Kinetics, Inc. v. Union Oil Co. of California, 75 Cal.App.3d 56, 141 Cal.Rptr. 879; Pariani v. State, 1st Dist., 105 Cal.App.3d 923, 164 Cal.Rptr. 683; United States v. Union Oil Co. of California, C.A.9th, 549 F.2d 1271, cert. denied 434 U.S. 930, 98 S.Ct. 418, 54 L.Ed.2d 291, rehearing denied 435 U.S. 911, 98 S.Ct. 1462, 55 L.Ed.2d 502; Acquisition of Geothermal Rights, Proposed Methods, 1 Idaho L.Rev. 49; Legislation: West's Ann.Cal.Pub.Res.Code, § 3700 et seq., Geothermal Energy: Wells for Discovery and Production of Geothermal Energy—Power and Jurisdiction of State Oil and Gas Supervisor.

4. For instance see: United States v. 1,253.14 Acres of Land, C.A.10th, 455 F.2d 1177; Vang v. Mount, 300 Minn. 393, 220 N.W.2d 498; Rickelton v. Universal Constructors, Inc., 91 N.M. 479, 576 P.2d 285; Weyerhaeuser Co. v. Burlington Northern, Inc., 15 Wn.App. 314, 549 P.2d 54; Western Nuclear, Inc. v. Andrus, D.C.Wyo., 475 F.Supp. 654. Also see cases listed, note 2, supra.

estate has been expanded or narrowed as to the substances included. This rather elastic definition is a result of the courts accommodating substances that rather recently have acquired greatly increased economic value; substances that were unknown to the parties at the time of the execution of the instruments being construed; or, substances whose removal would occasion substantial damage or disruption to the surface of the land. Of course, to the extent to which the mineral or surface estate is expanded, the other is correspondingly contracted.

The courts generally have refused to classify all substances associated with the soil as mineral,[5] although English cases and some early American cases[6] classified as mineral everything in the soil not used for agricultural purposes. Other early decisions included only metallic ores,[7] or tried to distinguish a mineral from a non-mineral on the basis of whether it could be extracted by mining, as distinguished from quarrying.[8]

The courts have followed a variety of approaches in determining whether a particular substance, not named in an instrument, should be classified as a "mineral:"[9]

(1) Whether the substance possesses an exceptional characteristic or peculiar property, giving it a special value apart from the

---

5. Kinder v. LaSalle County Carbon Coal Co., 310 Ill. 126, 141 N.E. 537 (limestone); Hendler v. Lehigh Valley Railroad Co., 209 Pa. 256, 58 A. 486 (sand).

6. McCombs v. Stephenson, 154 Ala. 109, 44 So. 867 (shale); See Northern Pacific Railway Co. v. Soderberg, 188 U.S. 526, 23 S.Ct. 365, 47 L.Ed. 575; Brady v. Smith, 181 N.Y. 178, 73 N.E. 963; Sult v. A. Hochstetter Oil Co., 63 W.Va. 317, 61 S.E. 307; and Psencik v. Wessels, Tex. Civ.App., 205 S.W.2d 658, for a discussion of English precedents.

7. Doster v. Friedensville Zinc Co., 140 Pa. 147, 21 A. 251. But cf. Northern Pacific Railway Co. v. Soderberg, 188 U.S. 526, 23 S.Ct. 365, 47 L.Ed. 575; Nephi Plaster & Manufacturing Co. v. Juab County, 33 Utah 114, 93 P. 53.

8. Brady v. Smith, 181 N.Y. 178, 73 N.E. 963 (limestone); White v. Miller, 200 N.Y. 29, 92 N.E. 1065 (gypsum); Beury v. Shelton, 151 Va. 28, 144 S.E. 629 (limestone). But cf. Northern Pacific Railway Co. v. Soderberg, 188 U.S. 526, 23 S.Ct. 365, 47 L.Ed. 575 (granite).

9. Of the substances listed in note 2, supra, the following have been held to be minerals: (geothermal), Geothermal Kinetics, Inc. v. Union Oil Co. of California, 75 Cal.App.3d 56, 141 Cal.Rptr. 879, and Pariani v. State, 1st Dist., 105 Cal.App.3d 923, 164 Cal.Rptr. 683, and United States v. Union Oil Co. of California, C.A.9th, 549 F.2d 1271, certiorari denied 434 U.S. 930, 98 S.Ct. 418, 54 L.Ed.2d 291, rehearing denied 435 U.S. 911, 98 S.Ct. 1462, 55 L.Ed.2d 502; (gravel), United States v. 1,253.14 Acres of Land, C.A.10th, 455 F.2d 1177; (bentonite), Cole v. Berry, 245 Miss. 359, 147 So.2d 306, but cf. Cole v. McDonald, 236 Miss. 168, 109 So.2d 628; (clay), State v. Evans, 46 Wash. 219, 89 P. 565; however, clay normally is classified as a non-mineral, see Hans v. Great Bend Brick & Tile Co., 172 Kan. 478, 241 P.2d 475; Rock House Fork Land Co. v. Raleigh Brick & Tile Co., 83 W.Va. 20, 97 S.E. 684, 17 A.L.R. 144; Atwood v. Rodman, Tex.Civ.App., 355 S.W.2d 206, refused n.r.e.; (coal) Adams County v. Smith, 74 N.D. 621, 23 N.W.2d 873; (chromate of iron) Gibson v. Tyson, 5 Watts (Pa.) 34; (diamond) Kentucky Diamond Mining & Developing Co. v. Kentucky Transvaal Diamond Co., 141 Ky. 97, 132 S.W. 397; (feldspar) McMullin v. Magnuson, 102 Colo. 230, 78 P.2d 964; (granite) Northern Pacific Railway Co. v. Soderberg, 188 U.S. 526, 23 S.Ct. 365, 47 L.Ed. 575, but cf. Armstrong v. Lake Champlain Granite Co., 147 N.Y. 495, 42 N.E. 186; (gypsite) Certain-Teed Products Corp. v. Comly, 54 Wyo. 79, 87 P.2d 21; (gypsum) White v. Miller, 200 N.Y. 29, 92 N.E. 1065, but cf. Cronkhite v.

§ 1.2   **MINERAL ESTATE: DEFINITION**   11

land itself.[10] Whether the substance is traditionally associated with surface ownership, or is considered essential or beneficial to the utilization of the surface of the land.

(2) Whether there existed local knowledge of the substance as an extractable mineral at the time of the execution of the instrument.[11]

Falkenstein, Okl., 352 P.2d 396; (salt) Deseret Livestock Co. v. State, 110 Utah 239, 171 P.2d 401; Singer v. Tatum, 251 Miss. 661, 171 So.2d 134, certiorari denied 382 U.S. 845, 86 S.Ct. 46, 15 L.Ed.2d 85; (salt water) Ambassador Oil Corp. v. Robertson, Tex.Civ.App., 384 S.W.2d 752, refused n.r.e., Tex., 390 S.W.2d 472; (sandstone) Kalberer v. Grassham, 282 Ky. 430, 138 S.W.2d 940; (clay and sandstone) Cumberland Mineral Co. v. United States, Ct.Cl., 513 F.2d 1399; (shale) McCombs v. Stephenson, 154 Ala. 109, 44 So. 867; (silica) State v. Evans, 46 Wash. 219, 89 P. 565; (sulphur) Singer v. Tatum, 251 Miss. 661, 171 So.2d 134, certiorari denied 382 U.S. 845, 86 S.Ct. 46, 15 L.Ed.2d 85; (uranium) Cain v. Neumann, Tex.Civ.App., 316 S.W.2d 915, New Mexico & Arizona Land Co. v. Elkins, D.C.N.M., 137 F.Supp. 767, noted in 3 UCLA L.Rev. 612; but cf. MacMaster v. Onstad, N.D., 86 N.W.2d 36. Water occurring on the surface of the ground, whether in lakes, ponds, watercourses, or in a diffused state, is normally excluded from a conveyance or reservation of the "minerals." Vogel v. Cobb, 193 Okl. 64, 141 P.2d 276, 148 A.L.R. 774; Stephen Hays Estate, Inc. v. Togliatti, 85 Utah 137, 38 P.2d 1066. But cf. Hathorn v. Natural Carbonic Gas Co., 194 N.Y. 326, 87 N.E. 504 (high mineral content). However, water also occurs in large quantities as migrating subterranean water which is removed only by the drilling of wells similar to those used in the production of oil and gas. In Mack Oil Co. v. Laurence, Okl., 389 P.2d 955, and Fleming Foundation v. Texaco, Inc., Tex. Civ.App., 337 S.W.2d 846, refused n. r. e., subterranean water was held to be nonmineral; criticized in 49 Calif.L.Rev. 763, approved in 40 Tex.L.Rev. 163. But cf. Goodloe v. City of Richmond, 272 Ky. 100, 113 S.W.2d 834 (involving statute of frauds); Adams v. Grigsby, La.App., 152 So.2d 619, writ refused 244 La. 662, 153 So.2d 880 (use of underground water for secondary recovery operations). After extensive litigation it has been held in Texas that, unless expressly limited in the oil and gas lease (or the instrument severing the mineral estate from the surface), the lessee has the right to use underground fresh water for secondary recovery operations. Such operations must be reasonably necessary for production of oil and gas, and the fresh water usage must benefit the land under lease. Sun Oil Co. v. Whitaker, Tex., 483 S.W.2d 808, 4 Tex.Tech L.Rev. 341 (1973); Robinson v. Robbins Petroleum Corp., Inc., Tex., 501 S.W.2d 865. Also see Dunn v. Southwest Ardmore Tulip Creek Sand Unit, Okl.App., 548 P.2d 685; Greyhound Leasing & Financial Corp. v. Joiner City Unit, C.A.10th, 444 F.2d 439.

10. Northern Pacific Railway Co. v. Soderberg, 188 U.S. 526, 23 S.Ct. 365, 47 L.Ed. 575 (granite); Newell, Inc. v. Randall, Ala., 373 So.2d 1068 (fill dirt); United States v. 1,253.14 Acres of Land, C.A. 10th, 455 F.2d 1177 (gravel); Elkhorn City Land Co., Inc. v. Elkhorn City, Ky. App., 459 S.W.2d 762 (clay and shale); Vang v. Mount, 300 Minn. 393, 220 N.W.2d 498 (limestone and gravel); State ex rel. State Highway Commission v. Trujillo, 82 N.M. 694, 487 P.2d 122 (gravel); Rickelton v. Universal Constructors, Inc., 91 N.M. 479, 576 P.2d 285 (gravel); Holland v. Dolese Co., Okl., 540 P.2d 549 (limestone); Hendler v. Lehigh Valley Railroad Co., 209 Pa. 256, 58 A. 486 (sand); Heinatz v. Allen, 147 Tex. 512, 217 S.W.2d 994 (limestone). The suggestion in the Heinatz case that a common substance might be classified as a mineral at such time following a conveyance as it acquired an exceptional character or value was rejected by a lower appellate court in Atwood v. Rodman, Tex.Civ.App., 355 S.W.2d 206, refused n. r. e., restricting the finding of value to the time of the transaction (limestone); Weyerhaeuser Co. v. Burlington Northern, Inc., 15 Wn.App. 314, 549 P.2d 54 (basaltic andesite rock); Western Nuclear, Inc. v. Andrus, D.C.Wyo., 475 F.Supp. 654 (gravel). Also see: Salzeider v. Brunsdale, N.D., 94 N.W.2d 502 (gravel); Puget Mill Co. v. Duecy, 1 Wn.2d 421, 96 P.2d 571 (mixed sand).

11. Mining Corp. of Arkansas v. International Paper Co., D.C.Ark., 324 F.Supp. 705; Morrison v. Socolofsky, 43 Colo.App. 212, 600 P.2d 121; Christman v. Emineth, N.D., 212 N.W. 543; Olson v.

(3) That the term "mineral" is inherently ambiguous, allowing consideration of parol evidence, including facts and circumstances relating to the transaction.[12]

(4) That constructional aids such as the doctrine of *ejusdem generis* will be applied.[13]

(5) Whether the methods of extraction of the substance will so detrimentally affect the surface use of the land as to be presumed not to have been within the intent of the parties.[14]

Dillerud, N.D., 226 N.W.2d 363; Doochin v. Rackley, Tenn., 610 S.W.2d 715; Pfister v. Brown, Wyo., 498 P.2d 1243.

12. Newell, Inc. v. Randall, Ala., 373 So.2d 1068; Morrison v. Socolofsky, 43 Colo.App. 212, 600 P.2d 121; United States v. 1,253.14 Acres of Land, C.A.10th Colo., 455 F.2d 1177; Besing v. Ohio Valley Coal Co., Inc. of Kentucky, 155 Ind.App. 527, 293 N.E.2d 510; Wulf v. Shultz, 211 Kan. 724, 508 P.2d 896; Cumberland Mineral Co. v. United States, Ct.Cl., 513 F.2d 1399; River Rouge Minerals, Inc. v. Energy Resources of Minnesota, La.App., 331 So.2d 878, cert. denied La., 337 So.2d 221; Vang v. Mount, 300 Minn. 393, 220 N.W.2d 498; Rickelton v. Universal Constructors, Inc., 91 N.M. 479, 576 P.2d 285; Panhandle Co-operative Royalty Co. v. Cunningham, Okl., 495 P.2d 108; Riedt v. Rock Island Improvement Co., Okl., 521 P.2d 79; Allen v. Farmer's Union Co-operative Royalty Co., Okl., 538 P.2d 204; Blythe v. Hines, Okl., 577 P.2d 1268; Weyerhaeuser Co. v. Burlington Northern, Inc., 15 Wn.App. 314, 549 P.2d 54; Western Nuclear, Inc. v. Andrus, D.C.Wyo., 475 F.Supp. 654.

13. Besing v. Ohio Valley Coal Co., Inc. of Kentucky, 155 Ind.App. 527, 293 N.E.2d 510; Wulf v. Shultz, 211 Kan. 724, 508 P.2d 896; River Rouge Minerals, Inc. v. Energy Resources of Minnesota, La.App., 331 So.2d 878, cert. denied La., 337 So.2d 221; Cronkhite v. Falkenstein, Okl., 352 P.2d 396; cf. Panhandle Co-operative Royalty Co. v. Cunningham, Okl., 495 P.2d 108; Allen v. Farmer's Union Co-operative Royalty Co., Okl., 538 P.2d 204; West v. Aetna Life Insurance Co., Okl.App., 536 P.2d 393; Sloan v. Peabody Coal Co., C.A.10th, 547 F.2d 115; Pfister v. Brown, Wyo., 498 P.2d 1243; Dawson v. Meike, Wyo., 508 P.2d 15.

Within the phrase "oil, gas and other minerals" the following have been included in the term "minerals": Pariani v. State, 1st Dist., 105 Cal.App.3d 923, 164 Cal.Rptr. 683 (geothermal resources); Christman v. Emineth, N.D., 212 N.W. 543 (lignite); Olson v. Dillerud, N.D., 226 N.W.2d 363 (lignite); Weyerhaeuser Co. v. Burlington Northern, Inc., 15 Wn.App. 314, 549 P.2d 54 (uranium). However, the following have been excluded from the term "minerals": Newell, Inc. v. Randall, Ala., 373 So.2d 1068 (soil); Morrison v. Socolofsky, 43 Colo.App. 212, 600 P.2d 121 (gravel); Besing v. Ohio Valley Coal Co., Inc. of Kentucky, 155 Ind.App. 527, 293 N.E.2d 510 (coal); Wulf v. Shultz, 211 Kan. 724, 508 P.2d 896 (limestone); Elkhorn City Land Co., Inc. v. Elkhorn City, Ky.App., 459 S.W.2d 762 (clay and shale); Reiss v. Rummel, N.D., 232 N.W.2d 40 (lignite); Cronkhite v. Falkenstein, Okl., 352 P.2d 396 (gypsum); Panhandle Co-operative Royalty Co. v. Cunningham, Okl., 495 P.2d 108, and Riedt v. Rock Island Improvement Co., Okl., 521 P.2d 79 (copper, silver, gold); West v. Aetna Life Insurance Co., Okl.App., 536 P.2d 393 (metallic ores); Sloan v. Peabody Coal Co., C.A.10th, 547 F.2d 115 (coal); Doochin v. Rackley, Tenn., 610 S.W.2d 715 (coal); Acker v. Guinn, Tex., 464 S.W.2d 348, (iron ore); Reed v. Wylie, Tex., 554 S.W.2d 169, and Reed v. Wylie, Tex., 597 S.W.2d 743 (lignite), 18 Houst. L. R. 201 (1980); Pfister v. Brown, Wyo., 498 P.2d 1243 (uranium); Dawson v. Meike, Wyo., 508 P.2d 15 (uranium).

14. Geothermal Kinetics, Inc. v. Union Oil Co. of California, 75 Cal.App.3d 56, 141 Cal.Rptr. 879 (geothermal resources); Farrell v. Sayre, 129 Colo. 368, 270 P.2d 190 (sand and gravel); Morrison v. Socolofsky, 43 Colo.App. 212, 600 P.2d 121 (gravel); United States v. 1,253.14 Acres of Land, C.A.10th, 455 F.2d 1177 (gravel); Peabody Coal Co. v. Erwin, C.A.6th, 453 F.2d 398 (strip mine); Cumberland Mineral Co. v. United States, Ct. Cl., 513 F.2d 1399 (clay and sandstone); River Rouge Minerals, Inc. v. Energy Resources of Minnesota, La.App., 331 So.2d 878, cert. denied La., 337 So.2d 221 (coal and lignite); cf. Continental Group, Inc. v. Allison, La.App., 379 So.2d 1117, reversed La., 404 So.2d 428 (strip mining of solids); Fisher v. Keweenaw Land Asso-

§ 1.2   MINERAL ESTATE: DEFINITION

(6) That a statutory context will affect the meaning of minerals or mineral estate.[15]

As mentioned above, the first cases dealing with the definition of a mineral tried to find attributes of a substance that would differentiate it from the land itself. One of the more recent cases refusing to classify a substance as a mineral, as it could not be distinguished from the land itself, is the case of Newell v. Randall.[16] In this Alabama case the question was the classification of some 530,000 cubic yards of fill dirt which was used for construction of Interstate 10. It was held that it was not included within a reservation of "gas, oil, sulphur, clay, gravel, or other minerals," for to hold otherwise would be to include the land itself. This is similar to the result in Cumberland Mineral Co. v. U. S.[17] dealing with the question of whether clay and sandstone were included within a reservation of "mineral, oil and gas." The surface of the land was some 75% sandstone and was used for forestry purposes. The court held that clay and sandstone could not be included within the reservation, for to do so would defeat the purpose of the grant.

Assuming that the substance was not so associated with the land as to constitute part of the soil itself, the courts then addressed themselves to the question of relative values,[18] if any, between a mineral substance and a non-mineral substance. For instance, is a relatively small pocket of gravel a mineral? It does have some economic value; it may be used for road building purposes. Does ownership of such gravel belong to the grantor or grantee in a deed of Blackacre containing a reservation to the grantor of "all the minerals?"

---

ciation, 371 Mich. 575, 124 N.W.2d 784 (sand and gravel); Resler v. Rogers, 272 Minn. 502, 139 N.W.2d 379 (sand, gravel and clay); Vang v. Mount, 300 Minn. 393, 220 N.W.2d 498 (limestone and gravel); cf. Christman v. Emineth, N.D., 212 N.W. 543 (lignite); Olson v. Dillerud, N.D., 226 N.W.2d 363; Panhandle Co-operative Royalty Co. v. Cunningham, Okl., 495 P.2d 108 (copper, silver, gold); Holland v. Dolese Co., Okl., 540 P.2d 549 (limestone); Blythe v. Hines, Okl., 577 P.2d 1268 (sand, gravel, limestone, rock); Campbell v. Tennessee Coal, Iron & Railroad Co., 150 Tenn. 423, 265 S.W. 674 (limestone); Doochin v. Rackley, Tenn., 610 S.W.2d 715 (coal); Acker v. Guinn, Tex., 464 S.W.2d 348, (iron ore); Reed v. Wylie, Tex., 554 S.W.2d 169, and Reed v. Wylie, Tex., 597 S.W.2d 743 (lignite); Williford v. Spies, Tex.Civ.App., 530 S.W. 2d 127 (lignite); Riddlesperger v. Creslenn Ranch Co., Tex.Civ.App., 595 S.W.2d 193 (coal and lignite); Sheffield v. Gibbs Brothers and Co., Tex.Civ.App., 596 S.W. 2d 227 (coal and lignite); Moser v. United States Steel Co., Tex. Civ.App., 601 S.W.2d 731, error granted (uranium); Beury v. Shelton, 151 Va. 28, 144 S.E. 629 (limestone); Rock House Fork Land Co. v. Raleigh Brick & Tile Co., 83 W.Va. 20, 97 S.E. 684, 17 A.L.R. 144 (clay).

15. Aleut Corp. v. Arctic Slope Regional Corp., D.C.Alaska, 421 F.Supp. 862; State ex rel. State Highway Commission v. Trujillo, 82 N.M. 694, 487 P.2d 122; Christman v. Emineth, N.D., 212 N.W. 543; Olson v. Dillerud, N.D., 226 N.W.2d 363; Riedt v. Rock Island Improvement Co., Okl., 521 P.2d 79; Jones v. Rock Island Improvement Co., Okl. App., 510 P.2d 1405; Doochin v. Rackley, Tenn., 610 S.W.2d 715; Western Nuclear, Inc. v. Andrus, D.C.Wyo., 475 F.Supp. 654.

16. Ala., 373 So.2d 1068.

17. Ct.Cl., 513 F.2d 1399.

18. See cases note 10, supra.

Although gravel often may have value sufficient to justify separation of it from the soil, it is normally not classified as a mineral.[19] It may be removed at a profit; however, it is not usually of exceptional value, it has been traditionally associated with ownership of the soil, and its removal, especially where widely distributed, would tend to destroy the surface for agricultural purposes.

The Texas case of Heinatz v. Allen[20] is typical of this approach. In this case the question was whether commercial limestone came within the "mineral rights" in a tract of land. In holding that it did not, the court stated: "In our opinion substances such as sand, gravel and limestone are not minerals within the ordinary and natural meaning of the word unless they are rare and exceptional in character or possess a peculiar property giving them special value, as for example sand that is valuable for making glass and limestone of such quality that it may profitably be manufactured into cement. Such substances, when they are useful only for building and road-making purposes, are not regarded as minerals."

The prevailing view seems to be that the term "minerals" is considered of uncertain meaning and that parol evidence will be examined to determine whether a substance is part of the mineral estate.[21] This is expressly stated in many opinions and in others such evidence is examined without comment. For example, in an Indiana case[22] the court felt that it could interpret "oil, gas and all other minerals" as meaning (1) minerals produced from an oil well, (2) some, but not all minerals, or (3) all minerals. One court's rationale[23] for treating the term "mineral" as ambiguous has been stated that "it is a flexible entity which expands with the development of arts and sciences to include more minerals" such as heated water, etc.

A basic consideration in interpreting the term "minerals" is a definition of what meaning should be accorded it, i.e., scientific, popular, etc. In Heinatz v. Allen[24] the court stated: "The words 'the mineral

---

19. See case note 9, supra.

20. 147 Tex. 512, 217 S.W.2d 994.

21. Morrison v. Socolofsky, 43 Colo. App. 212, 600 P.2d 121; Besing v. Ohio Valley Coal Co., Inc. of Kentucky, 155 Ind.App. 527, 293 N.E.2d 510; Wulf v. Shultz, 211 Kan. 724, 508 P.2d 896; Cumberland Mineral Co. v. United States, Ct. Cl., 513 F.2d 1399; Vang v. Mount, 300 Minn. 393, 220 N.W.2d 498; Singer v. Tatum, 251 Miss. 661, 171 So.2d 134, cert. denied 382 U.S. 845, 86 S.Ct. 46, 15 L.Ed. 2d 85; Rickelton v. Universal Constructors, Inc., 91 N.M. 479, 576 P.2d 285; Panhandle Co-operative Royalty Co. v. Cunningham, Okl., 495 P.2d 108; Allen v. Farmer's Union Co-operative Royalty Co., Okl., 538 P.2d 204; Weyerhaeuser Co. v. Burlington Northern, Inc., 15 Wn. App. 314, 549 P.2d 54; Western Nuclear, Inc. v. Andrus, D.C.Wyo., 475 F.Supp. 654. But cf. Northern Pacific Railway Co. v. Soderberg, 188 U.S. 526, 23 S.Ct. 365, 47 L.Ed. 575; State v. Evans, 46 Wash. 219, 89 P. 565. Texas apparently has treated the term as unambiguous in older cases, Anderson and Kerr Drilling Co. v. Bruhlmeyer, 134 Tex. 574, 136 S.W.2d 800.

22. Besing v. Ohio Valley Coal Co., Inc. of Kentucky, 155 Ind.App. 527, 293 N.E.2d 510.

23. Western Nuclear, Inc. v. Andrus, D.C.Wyo., 475 F.Supp. 654.

24. See note 20, supra; also see Cronkhite v. Falkenstein, Okl., 352 P.2d 396. Also see Psencik v. Wessels, Tex. Civ.App., 205 S.W.2d 658, error refused.

rights' used in the will are to be interpreted according to their ordinary and natural meaning, there being nothing in the will manifesting an intention on the part of the testatrix to use them in a scientific or technical sense." However, in a Colorado case[25] considering whether gravel was included in a reservation of "oil, gas and other minerals," the court stated the test to be "what the words mean in the vernacular of the mining world, the commercial world and landowners at time of the grant, and whether the particular substance was so regarded as a mineral." In dealing with a similar situation in a statutory context the Supreme Court of North Dakota[26] stated that "words and phrases shall be construed according to the context and rules of grammar and the approved usage of the language. Technical words and phrases and such others as have acquired a peculiar and appropriate meaning in law, or as are defined by statute, shall be construed according to such peculiar and appropriate meaning or definition." As may be seen, no uniform definition has been applied.

Evidence examined includes facts and circumstances existing at the time of execution of the instrument,[27] or at the time suit is brought,[28] testimony of experts,[29] knowledge of the parties,[30] effect on the surface,[31] value of the substance,[32] and intentions of the parties.[33]

Several courts have strongly emphasized the element of the knowledge of the parties at the time of execution of the instrument.[34] This, of course, is the basis of the Strohacker doctrine in Arkansas, concerning the question of whether oil and gas are included within the meaning of minerals.[35] This doctrine has caused extreme difficul-

25. Morrison v. Socolofsky, 43 Colo. App. 212, 600 P.2d 121; also see Holland v. Dolese Co., Okl., 540 P.2d 549, citing Mack Oil Co. v. Laurence, Okl., 389 P.2d 955.

26. Christman v. Emineth, N.D., 212 N.W. 543.

27. Besing v. Ohio Valley Coal Co., Inc. of Kentucky, 155 Ind.App. 527, 293 N.E.2d 510; Vang v. Mount, 300 Minn. 393, 220 N.W.2d 498 (a case of first impression).

28. Reed v. Wylie, Tex., 597 S.W.2d 743.

29. Morrison v. Socolofsky, 43 Colo. App. 212, 600 P.2d 121.

30. Besing v. Ohio Valley Coal Co., Inc. of Kentucky, 155 Ind.App. 527, 293 N.E.2d 510; Vang v. Mount, 300 Minn. 393, 220 N.W.2d 498.

31. Acker v. Guinn, Tex., 464 S.W. 2d 348; Reed v. Wylie, Tex., 597 S.W.2d 743.

32. See cases note 10, supra.

33. Besing v. Ohio Valley Coal Co., Inc. of Kentucky, 155 Ind.App. 527, 293 N.E.2d 510; Vang v. Mount, 300 Minn. 393, 220 N.W.2d 498.

34. Mining Corp. of Arkansas v. International Paper Co., D.C.Ark., 324 F.Supp. 705 (also see cases at notes 48–50, supra); Morrison v. Socolofsky, 43 Colo.App. 212, 600 P.2d 121; Christman v. Emineth, N.D., 212 N.W. 543; Olson v. Dillerud, N.D., 226 N.W.2d 363 (statute presumes method of extraction as being only in the principal manner and method prevailing in Tennessee at time instrument was executed, where method not expressly set forth in instrument); Pfister v. Brown, Wyo., 498 P.2d 1243.

35. See discussion at note 48 et seq., § 1.1, supra. Mining Corp. of Arkansas v. International Paper Co., D.C.Ark., 324 F.Supp. 705 would apparently apply the Strohacker doctrine to hard minerals such as cinnabar and mercury and exclude them from a reservation of "minerals, coal, oil and gas" where the instrument was executed in 1911 and the substances were not known in the area until 1932. The actual holding in the case appears to hold the reservation void for indefiniteness.

ty in Arkansas in oil and gas cases. Although it may be appealing to couch the test of what constitutes a mineral in terms of the intent of the parties, it would seem to serve neither the cause of accuracy in interpretation nor certainty in titles. Intent resting on extrinsic evidence existing at the time of the execution of an instrument should be discarded as a touchstone in determining the scope of the term "minerals" in an instrument. At least one state has changed its intent test from the date of the instrument to the date of trial.[36]

Where a grant or reservation is in the form of "oil, gas and other minerals" the rule of construction known as *ejusdem generis* may be applied. As discussed earlier, the rule would limit other minerals to those "of like kind" with oil and gas.[37] Although the rule is expressly rejected by some courts,[38] in other cases it seemingly has been applied by a court which states that it is not applying the rule.[39]

The constructional rule seems to be followed by the courts of Indiana,[40] Kansas,[41] Louisiana,[42] Oklahoma,[43] and Wyoming.[44] An ex-

---

36. Reed v. Wylie, Tex., 597 S.W.2d 743.

37. People ex rel. Carrell v. Bell, 237 Ill. 332, 86 N.E. 593; Besing v. Ohio Valley Coal Co., Inc. of Kentucky, 155 Ind. App. 527, 293 N.E.2d 510; Wulf v. Shultz, 211 Kan. 724, 508 P.2d 896; River Rouge Minerals, Inc. v. Energy Resources of Minnesota, La.App., 331 So.2d 878, certiorari denied La., 337 So.2d 221; Cronkhite v. Falkenstein, Okl., 352 P.2d 396; Panhandle Co-operative Royalty Co. v. Cunningham, Okl., 495 P.2d 108; Allen v. Farmer's Union Co-operative Royalty Co., Okl., 538 P.2d 204; West v. Aetna Life Insurance Co., Okl.App., 536 P.2d 393; Sloan v. Peabody Coal Co., C.A. 10th, 547 F.2d 115; Dawson v. Meike, Wyo., 508 P.2d 15; Western Nuclear, Inc. v. Andrus, D.C.Wyo., 475 F.Supp. 654. Cf. Acker v. Guinn, Tex., 464 S.W.2d 348; Fleming Foundation v. Texaco, Inc., Tex. Civ.App., 337 S.W.2d 846; State Land Board v. State Department of Fish and Game, 17 Utah 2d 237, 408 P.2d 707.

The view of the Texas courts is somewhat uncertain. In the case of Southland Royalty Co. v. Pan American Petroleum Co., Tex., 378 S.W.2d 50, the court flatly stated that the *ejusdem generis* rule had not been applied in Texas. In Acker v. Guinn, Tex., 464 S.W.2d 348, the court merely stated they would not apply the rule, but did not indicate that it was not part of the jurisprudence of the state. However, it would appear that in all probability it will not be applied by the Texas courts. See: Simms, Has *Ejusdem Generis* as Applied to Mineral Deeds Been Accepted in Texas, 2 Tex. Tech L.R. 164.

Also see discussion at notes 24–34, § 1.1, supra.

38. See Southland Royalty Co. v. Pan American Petroleum Co., and Acker v. Guinn, supra, note 37.

39. See Besing v. Ohio Valley Coal Co., Inc. of Kentucky, 155 Ind.App. 527, 293 N.E.2d 510 (would include only component or constituent substances); Panhandle Co-operative Royalty Co. v. Cunningham, Okl., 495 P.2d 108 (would include only component or constituent substances).

40. Besing v. Ohio Valley Coal Co., Inc. of Kentucky, 155 Ind.App. 527, 293 N.E.2d 510 (coal).

41. Wulf v. Shultz, 211 Kan. 724, 508 P.2d 896 (limestone).

42. River Rouge Minerals, Inc. v. Energy Resources of Minnesota, La.App., 331 So.2d 878, certiorari denied La., 337 So.2d 221 (applies *ejusdem generis* as to physical characteristics, not chemical, and would not include coal and lignite as other minerals in "oil, gas and mineral" leases).

43. Cronkhite v. Falkenstein, Okl., 352 P.2d 396 (gypsum); Allen v. Farmer's Union Co-operative Royalty Co., Okl., 538 P.2d 204 (copper, gold, silver); West v. Aetna Life Insurance Co., Okl.App., 536 P.2d 393 (metallic ores) (case distinguishes Panhandle Co-operative Royalty Co. v. Cunningham, Okl., 495 P.2d 108, copper, gold, silver); Sloan

44. See note 44 on page 17.

cellent discussion of the application of the rule, as it applies to various substances, as well as its history in Oklahoma, is found in the case of West v. Aetna Life Insurance Co.[45]

The cornerstone cases in Oklahoma are those of Cronkhite v. Falkenstein,[46] Allen v. Farmer's Union Co-operative Royalty Co.,[47] and the West case.

In 1960 the Oklahoma court in the Cronkhite case[48] decided that gypsum was not included in a deed of oil, gas and other minerals. It expressly applied the *ejusdem generis* rule, that gypsum was not of like kind with oil and gas. Following the Cronkhite case, in 1971 the Oklahoma court decided in Panhandle Co-operative Royalty Co.[49] that copper, silver and gold were not included in a grant of "oil, gas and other minerals" (the Farmer's Flagg deed). The basis of the decision was that only minerals produced as a component or constituent of oil and gas would be included, whether a hydrocarbon or not. The court expressly stated that it was not applying the rule of *ejusdem generis*.

The constituent element construction would exclude any hydrocarbon substance on the land not produced with oil or gas. Coal and lignite would be excluded. However, although Panhandle was not expressly overruled by the West case[50] in 1974 and the Allen case[51] in 1975, the latter two cases would seem to have firmly established *ejusdem generis* as the constructional rule of preference in Oklahoma.

As in cases dealing with oil and gas, the courts often look to all parts of an instrument in order to determine the intent of the parties whether certain substances should be included. Language restricting methods of recovery[52] or easements provided for entry and removal of products[53] may aid the courts in interpreting the language in an instrument.

v. Peabody Coal Co., C.A.10th, 547 F.2d 115 (coal).

44. Dawson v. Meike, Wyo., 508 P.2d 15 (uranium); Western Nuclear, Inc. v. Andrus, D.C.Wyo., 475 F.Supp. 654 (gravel).

45. Okl.App., 536 P.2d 393. (Not include metallic ores in reservation of "all oil, gas and/or minerals")

46. Okl., 352 P.2d 396. An earlier case in Oklahoma apparently applying the rule is that of Kansas City Southern Railway Co. v. Reinman, 63 Okl. 69, 162 P. 726, decided in 1917.

47. Okl., 538 P.2d 204 (not include copper, gold, silver in reservation of "all of the oil, gas and mineral rights").

48. See note 45, supra.

49. Okl., 495 P.2d 108 (not include copper, silver and gold in deed of "oil, gas and other minerals"). This case was cited and followed in Besing v. Ohio Valley Coal Co., Inc. of Kentucky, 155 Ind. App. 527, 293 N.E.2d 510.

50. See note 45, supra.

51. See note 47, supra.

52. See discussion § 1.1, at note 35, supra. Also see Praetorian Diamond Oil Association v. Garvey, Tex.Civ.App., 15 S.W.2d 698.

53. Easements for removal: Armstrong v. Lake Champlain Granite Co., 147 N.Y. 495, 42 N.E. 186; Singer v. Tatum, 251 Miss. 661, 171 So.2d 134, cert. denied 382 U.S. 845, 86 S.Ct. 46, 15 L.Ed. 2d 85; State Land Board v. State Department of Fish and Game, 17 Utah 2d 237, 408 P.2d 707; Rock House Fork Land Co. v. Raleigh Brick & Tile Co., 83 W.Va. 20, 97 S.E. 684, 17 A.L.R. 144; royalty clause: Doster v. Friedensville Zinc Co., 140 Pa. 147, 21 A. 251; habendum clause: Waugh v. Thompson Land & Coal Co., 103 W.Va. 567, 137 S.E. 895; Easley v. Melten, Ky., 262 S.W.2d 686; Wulf v. Shultz, 211 Kan. 724, 508 P.2d 896; River Rouge Minerals, Inc. v. Energy Re-

This shift in emphasis is illustrated by the Texas case of Acker v. Guinn.⁵⁴ The case involved a declaratory judgment action to determine whether low grade iron ore was included in a conveyance of "an undivided ½ interest in and to all of the oil, gas and other minerals in and under" a tract of land. Knowledge of the iron ore as a commercially removable substance had existed in the area since the Civil War.

The lower court held iron ore was not included, applying the doctrine of *ejusdem generis*, as "other minerals" would only include substances of like kind with oil and gas.

The Texas Supreme Court affirmed the decision of the lower court, but upon a different rationale. The court refused to apply the *ejusdem generis* rule. The court specifically held that the iron ore had commercial value (satisfying the value test), but pointed out that it must be mined by open pit or strip mining methods. Such methods of removal would destroy or greatly diminish the utility of the surface for farming, ranching and timber production.

The court stated that the essential question was whether the parties to a grant or reservation of "all the minerals" intended to include substances not specifically mentioned, whose removal would substantially damage or destroy the utility of the surface estate. The court quoted Professor Kuntz:

> " 'The contradiction and conflict between the cases on the point arise from the very fact that the courts are seeking to give effect to an intention to include or exclude a specific substance, when, as a matter of fact, the parties had nothing specific in mind on the matter at all. It is submitted that an intention test is the proper one, but not as applied heretofore. The intention sought should be the general intent rather than any supposed but unexpressed *specific intent*, and, further, that general intent should be arrived at, not by defining and redefining the terms used, but by considering the *purposes* of the grant or reservation in terms of manner of enjoyment intended in the ensuring interests.
>
> "When a general grant or reservation is made of all minerals without qualifying language, it should be reasonably assumed that the parties intended to sever the entire mineral estate from the surface estate, leaving the owner of each with definite incidents of ownership enjoyable in distinctly different manners. The manner of enjoyment of the mineral estate is through extraction of valuable substances, and the enjoyment of the surface is through retention of such substances as are necessary for the use of the surface, and these respective modes of enjoyment must be considered in arriving at the proper subject matter for each es-

---

sources of Minnesota, 331 So.2d 878, cert. denied La., 337 So.2d 221.

54. Tex., 464 S.W.2d 348.

§ 1.2 MINERAL ESTATE: DEFINITION 19

tate.' Kuntz, The Law Relating to Oil and Gas in Wyoming, 3 Wyo.L.J. 107, 112.

"In our opinion the basic approach there suggested is entirely sound."

and the court in Acker continues and holds:

"The parties to a mineral lease or deed usually think of the mineral estate as including valuable substances that are removed from the ground by means of wells or mine shafts. This estate is dominant, of course, and its owner is entitled to make reasonable use of the surface for the production of his minerals. It is not ordinarily contemplated, however, that the utility of the surface for agricultural or grazing purposes will be destroyed or substantially impaired. Unless the contrary intention is affirmatively and fairly expressed, therefore, a grant or reservation of 'minerals' or 'mineral rights' should not be construed to include a substance that *must* be removed by methods that will, in effect, consume or deplete the surface estate." (emphasis supplied)

The Acker case has been followed in Texas[55] and has been cited with approval in other jurisdictions.[56] Some form of surface destruction test and application of Professor Kuntz's presumed intent test appears to have been applied in the majority of cases dealing with the classification of substances as mineral or surface.[57]

55. Reed v. Wylie, Tex., 554 S.W.2d 169; Reed v. Wylie, Tex., 597 S.W.2d 743, 18 Houst.L.R. 201 (1980); Williford v. Spies, Tex.Civ.App., 530 S.W.2d 127; DuBois v. Jacobs, Tex.Civ.App., 551 S.W.2d 147; Riddlesperger v. Creslenn Ranch Co., Tex.Civ.App., 595 S.W.2d 193; Sheffield v. Gibbs Brothers and Co., Tex.Civ.App., 596 S.W.2d 227.

56. Besing v. Ohio Valley Coal Co., Inc. of Kentucky, 155 Ind.App. 527, 293 N.E.2d 510; Wulf v. Shultz, 211 Kan. 724, 508 P.2d 896; River Rouge Minerals, Inc. v. Energy Resources of Minnesota, La.App., 331 So.2d 878, cert. denied La., 337 So.2d 221; Reiss v. Rummel, N.D., 232 N.W.2d 40; West Virginia Department of Highways v. Farmer, W.Va., 226 S.E.2d 717. In Panhandle Co-operative Royalty Co. v. Cunningham, Okl., 495 P.2d 108, the court cites the Acker case and is critical that the Acker court would not consider that surface destruction might be recompensed by payment of damages.

57. Morrison v. Socolofsky, 43 Colo. App. 212, 600 P.2d 121 (gravel); United States v. 1,253.14 Acres of Land, C.A.10th, 455 F.2d 1177 (gravel); Peabody Coal Co. v. Erwin, C.A.6th, 453 F.2d 398 (right to strip mine); Cumberland Mineral Co. v. United States, Ct.Cl., 513 F.2d 1399 (clay and sandstone); River Rouge Minerals, Inc. v. Energy Resources of Minnesota, La.App., 331 So.2d 878, certiorari denied La., 337 So.2d 221 (coal and lignite), cf. Continental Group, Inc. v. Allison, La.App., 379 So.2d 1117, reversed La., 404 So.2d 428 (lignite); Vang v. Mount, 300 Minn. 393, 220 N.W.2d 498 (limestone), cf. Christman v. Emineth, N.D., 212 N.W. 543 (lignite); Panhandle Co-operative Royalty Co. v. Cummingham, Okl., 495 P.2d 108 (copper, silver, gold); Holland v. Dolese Co., Okl., 540 P.2d 549 (limestone); Blythe v. Hines, Okl., 577 P.2d 1268 (sand, gravel); Acker v. Guinn, Tex., 464 S.W.2d 348, (iron ore); Reed v. Wylie, Tex., 554 S.W.2d 169 (lignite); Reed v. Wylie, Tex., 597 S.W.2d 743 (lignite); Williford v. Spies, Tex.Civ.App., 530 S.W.2d 127 (lignite), Riddlesperger v. Creslenn Ranch Co., Tex.Civ.App., 595 S.W.2d 193 (gravel); Sheffield v. Gibbs Brothers and Co., Tex.Civ.App., 596 S.W.2d 227 (sand, gravel; cf. Moser v. United States Steel Co., Tex.Civ.App., 601 S.W.2d 731, error granted (uranium).

The two Texas decisions in the case of Reed v. Wylie[58] have further defined the holding in the Acker case. Here the parties tried to avoid the effect of the Acker case on the ground that evidence should be admissible to show that lignite did not *have* to be removed by methods injurious to the utilization of the surface estate. The Court of Appeals refused to remand due to other evidence of intent in the case. Upon appeal the holding of the lower court was affirmed by the Texas Supreme Court in the Reed I case.

Reed I involved a deed containing the following reservation:

"In addition to the above and foregoing exception there is hereby excepted and reserved to the Grantors herein a one-fourth ($1/4$) undivided interest in and to all *oil, gas and other minerals on and under the land* and premises herein described and conveyed; and it is hereby expressly agreed and understood that Grantors herein, their heirs and assigns shall have, and they hereby have the right of ingress and egress *for the sole and only purpose of mining and operating for oil, gas and all other minerals, on and under said land,* and to produce, mine, save and take care of said products, and to take all usual, necessary and convenient means for *working, preparing and removing said minerals* from under and away from said land and premises." (emphasis supplied)

The issue involved ownership of coal and lignite underlying the land, i.e., was it owned by the owner of the reserved mineral interest, or the owner of the surface estate. It was argued by the owner of the reserved mineral interest that the rule in the Acker case gives to the owner of the mineral estate all of the coal and lignite except that which *must* be produced by strip or pit mining. The court, in rejecting this contention, pointed out that, as in the Acker case, the language in question did not specifically include the substance being contested. The court then restated and affirmed the Acker rule as follows:

"Furthermore, mineral ores and coal and lignite would ordinarily be reserved to the mineral interest owner by the terms of the Wylie to Baker instrument. That is not true, however, under Acker v. Guinn, *if any part* of the substance lies so near the surface and '*must be removed by methods that will, in effect, consume or deplete the surface estate.*' (emphasis supplied) Because it is not expected that the parties to the instrument would have intended the destruction of the surface by the mineral owner in the absence of an expression of that intention, their use of 'mineral' in the instrument is not construed to include the near surface substance. Once the instrument is construed to that effect, this particular substance—*at whatever depth*—is not a 'mineral' for all purposes of the instrument.

58. Tex., 554 S.W.2d 169, commonly referred to as "Reed I"; Reed v. Wylie, Tex., 597 S.W.2d 743, commonly referred to as "Reed II," 18 Houst.L.R. 201 (1980).

"Acker v. Guinn stands for the rule that a substance *is not a 'mineral'* if substantial quantities of that substance lie so near the surface that the production will entail the stripping away and substantial destruction of the surface." (emphasis supplied)

"It is improper therefore to declare that the surface owner is entitled to only so much of the substance as may be produced by strip mining or pit mining. We are not dividing the right to produce the substance; we are construing the instrument of conveyance to ascertain the ownership of the substance. * * * Instead, the surface estate owner must prove that, as of the date of the instrument being construed, if the substance near the surface had been extracted, that extraction would necessarily have consumed or depleted the land surface.

"If the method of production required the removal of surface soil, it is immaterial that devices of restoration or reclamation were available."

The case was remanded for proof as to depth of the lignite and whether extraction would remove or destroy the surface of the land.

Apparent guidelines that may be gleaned from Reed I are:

(1) Acker will not apply to a conveyance or reservation of any substance specifically included in the grant or reservation, even if removal would cause damage or destruction of the surface estate.[59]

(2) "Minerals", unless intention is otherwise shown, will not include substances that are found at the surface (as contrasted to substances "near the surface"). The method of extraction is immaterial.

(3) The burden of proof is on the surface owner to show that, *as of the date of the instrument*, the removal of a particular near surface substance would *necessarily* consume or deplete the land. This would seem to leave open the situation where alternative methods of removal would not cause such damage.

(4) If a substance is not a mineral due to the Acker test, *the entire deposit at whatever depth* is not a mineral but part of the surface estate.

(5) If, due to the Acker test, a substance is not a mineral, methods of restoration, *value*, unexpressed knowledge or intent, are all immaterial.[60]

---

59. For other cases finding a specific intent to include substances whose removal would cause surface destruction: Continental Group, Inc. v. Allison, La. App., 379 So.2d 1117, reversed La., 404 So.2d 428; Christman v. Emineth, N.D., 212 N.W. 543. Also see: Moser v. United States Steel Co., Tex.Civ.App., 601 S.W.2d 731, error granted, uranium, where no surface damage contemplated.

60. Cf. Christman v. Emineth, N.D., 212 N.W. 543.

Reed I raised a number of questions that would not be easy to answer by the large number of persons leasing for coal and lignite in Texas:

(a) What methods of extraction were available in a particular area *at the date of the instrument*?[61] Of those, did a surface-destructive method *have* to be used?

(b) What is a "near surface" substance?

(c) What is a "surface" substance?

Reed II[62] modified guideline (3), above, of Reed I. It changed the date of examination in (a), above, and attempted to answer questions (b) and (c), and changed the surface estate owner's burden of proof as to types of extraction to be proven. Guidelines (1), (2), (4) and (5) still apply under Reed II.

As mentioned above, no further proof is necessary by the surface owner than to prove the substance is found "at the surface" of the land. First, the court pointed out that "at the surface" did not mean merely on the top of the ground, but that it would have some depth. This was defined as a depth shallow enough that it must have been contemplated by the parties that its removal would be by a surface-destructive method.

Secondly, the court would find a substance "at the surface" if it outcropped or was at the surface on the land or within the "reasonable immediate vicinity" of the tract. Factually, lignite appears to have outcropped on the tract of land involved as well as others within half a mile and two miles from the Reed tract. It was held that lignite "was at the surface" as a matter of law.

When the test of a substance "at the surface" cannot be factually satisfied, the surface owner may prevail as to a particular substance if it is proven (1) the substance is at the "near surface", and (2) *any* "reasonable method of removal of * * * (the substance) * * * will consume, deplete, or destroy the surface, including such a method *as of the date of this opinion*."[63] (emphasis supplied)

The court also stated that if a substance is within 200 feet of the surface it is a "near surface" substance as a matter of law. Probably the most significant change in the surface owner's burden of proof was from showing that the method of extraction "must" be surface destructive to being able to show that "any reasonable method of removal" would be surface destructive. The date of such method of extraction was changed from that of the instrument to the time of trial. A vigorous concurring opinion[64] was filed taking the point of

---

61. This raises problems similar to those under the Strohacker rule in Arkansas; see notes 39 and 50, § 1.1, supra.

62. Reed v. Wylie, Tex., 597 S.W.2d 743.

63. Id., note 62, supra.

64. Reed v. Wylie, Tex., 597 S.W.2d 743, concurring opinion by Justice Spears.

view that parties should be able to tell from the instrument itself whether a substance is part of the mineral or surface estate.

The Reed decisions have been set forth at some length as they are typical of the interpretive problems arising in this area. Rather than treat possible surface destruction as a factor to be taken into account, it is given overriding weight. Why should methods of restoration and the ability of the mineral estate owner to respond in damages be ignored? Substances treated as minerals from early times may well be held to be part of the surface estate if surface destructive methods of extraction are deemed a reasonable method of removal, and this would be true of the substance at all depths.

Reed I and II would seem to do little to resolve the title dilemma of persons attempting to lease and develop substances whose removal might be surface destructive. At best they have merely removed the burden of developing proof from ancient facts. Cases involving the same substance from different tracts will remain *ad hoc*. Litigation in Texas continues[65] and will do so until the Texas courts adopt a more pragmatic, definitive approach.

§ 1.3 Nature of Ownership of the Mineral Estate

Around the year 1900 litigation began reaching the courts in the United States dealing with the rights of the landowner in oil and gas in the ground, prior to discovery and development. Recognizing the fugitive nature of oil and gas and limited by inexact knowledge of its occurrence and nature, courts analogized to the law dealing with wild animals and water in an attempt to define the landowner's interest. Such analogies generally led to a concept that, like wild animals, the landowner had title only to such products as he actually reduced to possession. With fuller understanding of reservoir mechanics these analogies have been rejected. From the early cases have evolved two divergent concepts regarding rights to the oil and gas in the ground:

(a) **The ownership-in-place concept.** Jurisdictions following the ownership-in-place concept recognize ownership of the oil and gas in the ground as a part of the land, similar to ownership of hard minerals. In such jurisdictions a corporeal estate in realty may be created in the oil and gas apart from the rest of the land. Such a severed mineral interest is subject to the same laws and rules as affect other corporeal interests in real property.

65. See note 63, supra. In both Reed I and II the court would include surface destructive substances in the mineral estate if expressly mentioned in the instrument. In Riddlesperger v. Creslenn Ranch Co., Tex.Civ.App., 595 S.W.2d 193, a reservation of "all of the oil, gas, uranium and other minerals, and gravel, in and under * * * " did not by implication (due to specific mention of gravel, a surface destructive substance) include other types of surface destructive substances such as coal and lignite, on the ground that the instrument must affirmatively and fairly express an intent to include a surface destructive substance in the mineral estate. Also see: Sheffield v. Gibbs Brothers and Co., Tex.Civ.App., 596 S.W.2d 227 (implication also denied). Cf. Moser v. United States Steel Co., Tex. Civ.App., 601 S.W.2d 731, error granted, where uranium, removable by a solvent method, not surface destructive, held to be part of the mineral estate.

(b) Non-ownership concept. The theory of ownership-in-place has been rejected in many jurisdictions as illogical. Such jurisdictions generally recognize no ownership in the oil and gas while in the ground, only of a right to search for and reduce the oil and gas to possession. However, in a few of the non-ownership jurisdictions a sufficient interest is recognized as existing in the oil and gas in place so that the landowner may have standing to prevent injurious or wasteful operations to the reservoir. Such jurisdictions are sometimes referred to as qualified ownership states.

When the right to search for oil and gas is owned apart from the land, it is usually classified as a profit à prendre, an incorporeal interest in the land, although it has also been classified as a license, a servitude, or a chattel real.

In many non-ownership jurisdictions remedial legislation has been required in the areas of conveyancing, security interests, recording and taxation statutes, etc., to provide a framework necessary for convenient commerce in oil and gas.

The Kentucky case of Hail v. Reed,[1] decided in 1854, holding that the owner of land could maintain trover for conversion of oil and gas, ushered in a new area of litigation in the property field. The case is considered the first case in the United States dealing with the nature of a landowner's interest in oil and gas. Following the Reed case, the courts were soon confronted with cases dealing with fundamental problems such as injuries to the common reservoir,[2] waste and spoilage of products,[3] and the right of each owner to produce from the common reservoir.[4]

In formulating juridical relationships with reference to petroleum ownership and production, the courts were disturbed by lack of precise knowledge concerning occurrence and movement of oil and gas, which, unlike hard minerals, were recognized as being capable of migration from one tract of land to another.[5] In Barnard v. Monongahela Natural Gas Co.,[6] decided in 1907, an injunction to prohibit drilling, by a landowner on adjacent land, was denied partly on the ground that the court was unable to determine the extent or nature of drainage from plaintiff's land: "Exact knowledge on this subject is not at present attainable, but the vagrant character of the mineral and the porous sand rock * * * fully justify the conclusion we have stated above." It was found hard to perceive of ownership of a substance that moved of its own volition to and fro beneath the ground. At common law only water and wild animals had the proper-

---

1. 54 Ky. 479. An examination of the arguments presented in the case shows an anticipation of most of the areas of litigation as to the nature of ownership of oil and gas that have continually plagued the courts to the present time.

2. Ohio Oil Co. v. Indiana, 177 U.S. 190, 20 S.Ct. 576, 44 L.Ed. 729; Manufacturers Gas & Oil Co. v. Indiana Natural Gas & Oil Co., 155 Ind. 461, 57 N.E. 912.

3. Townsend v. State, 147 Ind. 624, 47 N.E. 19; Hague v. Wheeler, 157 Pa. 324, 27 A. 714.

4. Barnard v. Monongahela Natural Gas Co., 216 Pa. 362, 65 A. 801.

5. Brown v. Spilman, 155 U.S. 665, 15 S.Ct. 245, 39 L.Ed. 304.

6. See Note 4 supra.

ty of transmigration, and the early courts were quick to draw analogies to the law concerning such things.[7] Such analogies generally led to the result that the landowner was treated as having no ownership in the oil and gas in place beneath his tract of land, owning only such products as were actually produced and reduced to possession.[8] This proved a convenient support for early regulatory statutes, for regulation could not constitute a "taking" for which the landowner might claim compensation,[9] but also removed a protectable property interest in the landowner who found his products being drained or his ability to produce being destroyed by wasteful and injurious methods of production by operators on other lands over the common reservoir.[10]

Neither analogy was particularly apt. Unlike migrating underground water, oil and gas occur in essentially closed systems with possible ownership restricted to the owners of lands overlying the reservoir. Although capable of transmigration, oil and gas are not free-moving but amenable to the laws of physics. Until the reservoir is pierced by drilling or disturbed by natural occurrences the system is essentially static. Insofar as the early cases relied upon analogies to water or wild animals, they have been rejected,[11] but they left a heavy imprint upon subsequent development of concepts relating to ownership and development of oil and gas.

Today the states having commercial production of petroleum are primarily divided into (a) those that recognize ownership of oil and gas in place beneath the surface of the ground as though a part of the land itself, similar to ownership of hard minerals;[12] and (b) those

---

7. *Ferae naturae*: Townsend v. State, 147 Ind. 624, 47 N.E. 19; State v. Ohio Oil Co., 150 Ind. 21, 49 N.E. 809; Barnard v. Monongahela Natural Gas Co., 216 Pa. 362, 65 A. 801; Hammonds v. Central Kentucky Natural Gas Co., 255 Ky. 685, 75 S.W.2d 204; water: People's Gas Co. v. Tyner, 131 Ind. 277, 31 N.E. 59; Higgins Oil & Fuel Co. v. Guaranty Oil Co., 145 La. 233, 82 So. 206, 5 A.L.R. 411; Westmoreland & Cambria Natural Gas Co. v. De Witt, 130 Pa. 235, 18 A. 724; Jones v. Forest Oil Co., 194 Pa. 379, 44 A. 1074. Also see Merrill, Evolution of Oil and Gas Law, 13 Miss.L.J. 281; Walker, Fee Simple Ownership of Oil and Gas in Texas, 6 Tex.L.Rev. 125; and Summers, Property in Oil and Gas, 9 Ky. L.J. 1.

8. Townsend v. State, 147 Ind. 624, 47 N.E. 19; Hammonds v. Central Kentucky Natural Gas Co., 255 Ky. 685, 75 S.W.2d 204; Jones v. Forest Oil Co., 194 Pa. 379, 44 A. 1074.

9. State v. Ohio Oil Co., 150 Ind. 21, 49 N.E. 809.

10. People's Gas Co. v. Tyner, 131 Ind. 277, 31 N.E. 59 (shooting well with nitroglycerin); Jones v. Forest Oil Co., 194 Pa. 379, 44 A. 1074 (suction pump).

11. White v. New York State Natural Gas Corp., D.C.Pa., 190 F.Supp. 342; Manufacturers Gas & Oil Co. v. Indiana Natural Gas & Oil Co., 155 Ind. 461, 57 N.E. 912; Lone Star Gas Co. v. Murchison, Tex.Civ.App., 353 S.W.2d 870, 94 A.L.R.2d 529.

12. Adams v. Riddle, 233 Ala. 96, 170 So. 343; Sun Oil Co. v. Oswell, 258 Ala. 326, 62 So.2d 783 (Alabama); Bodcaw Lumber Co. v. Goode, 160 Ark. 48, 254 S.W. 345, 29 A.L.R. 578 (Arkansas); Simson v. Langholf, 133 Colo. 208, 293 P.2d 302; Matheson, Colorado Oil and Gas Law, 33 Rocky Mt.L.Rev. 331; also see March, Interest of Landowner and Lessee in Oil and Gas in Colorado, 25 Rocky Mt.L.Rev. 117 (Colorado); Froelich v. United Royalty Co., 178 Kan. 503, 290 P.2d 93, modified 179 Kan. 652, 297 P.2d 1106 (Kansas); Kiser v. Eberly, 200 Md. 242, 88 A.2d 570 (Maryland); Rathbun v. State, 284 Mich. 521, 280 N.W. 35 (Michigan); Phillips Petroleum Co. v. Millette, 221 Miss. 1, 72 So.2d 176 (Mississippi); Homestake Exploration Corp. v.

that recognize no ownership of oil and gas in place, only of a right to search for and reduce them to possession.[13]

Typical of the states recognizing the ownership of the oil and gas in place is Texas, whose Supreme Court in 1915 stated " * * * they (oil and gas) lie within the strata of the earth, and necessarily are a part of the realty. Being a part of the realty while in place, it would seem to logically follow that, whenever they are conveyed while in that condition or possessing that status, a conveyance of an interest in the realty results. * * * If the oil and gas, the subject of the conveyance, are in fact not beneath or within the land, and are therefore not capable of being reduced to possession, the conveyance is of no effect. But if they have not departed and are beneath it, they are there as a part of the realty; and their conveyance while in place, if the instrument be given any effect, is consequently the conveyance of an interest in the realty."[14] This concept of ownership of oil and gas *in situ* is an adaptation of the common law maxim *cujus est solum, ejus est usque ad coelum et ad inferos*.[15]

Schoregge, 81 Mont. 604, 264 P. 388; Gas Products Co. v. Rankin, 63 Mont. 372, 207 P. 993, 24 A.L.R. 294 (Montana); Sachs v. Board of Trustees, 89 N.M. 712, 557 P.2d 209, appeal after remand 92 N.M. 615, 592 P.2d 961; Kelly v. Ohio Oil Co., 57 Ohio St. 317, 49 N.E. 399; Pure Oil Co. v. Kindall, 116 Ohio St. 188, 156 N.E. 119. But cf. Back v. Ohio Fuel Gas Co., 160 Ohio St. 81, 113 N.E.2d 865 (Ohio); Hamilton v. Foster, 272 Pa. 95, 116 A. 50 (cf. earlier view, Westmoreland & Cambria Natural Gas Co. v. De Witt, 130 Pa. 235, 18 A. 724). Sawyer, Interests Created by Oil and Gas Leases in Pennsylvania, 4 U.Pittsburgh L.Rev. 274 (Pennsylvania); Murray v. Allard, 100 Tenn. 100, 43 S.W. 355; Stephens County v. Mid-Kansas Oil & Gas Co., 113 Tex. 160, 254 S.W. 290, 29 A.L.R. 566 (Texas); Boggess v. Milam, 127 W.Va. 654, 34 S.E.2d 267 (W.Va.). Also see Mineral Interests and the Executive Right in West Virginia, 66 W.Va.L. Rev. 221.

13. Callahan v. Martin, 3 Cal.2d 110, 43 P.2d 788, 101 A.L.R. 871; Gerhard v. Stephens, 68 Cal.2d 864, 69 Cal.Rptr. 612, 442 P.2d 692. Also see Walker, Nature of Land-Owner's Interest in California, Rights of Covenants, Nature of Oil Royalties, 25 Calif.L.Rev. 220; Adsit, Oil Estates, 9 So.Calif.L.Rev. 299 (California); Transcontinental Oil Co. v. Emmerson, 298 Ill. 394, 131 N.E. 645, 16 A.L.R. 507; Miller v. Ridgley, 2 Ill.2d 223, 117 N.E.2d 759 (Illinois); Manufacturers' Gas & Oil Co. v. Indiana Natural Gas & Oil Co., 155 Ind. 461, 57 N.E. 912 (Indiana); Frost-Johnson Lumber Co. v. Nabors Oil & Gas Co., 149 La. 100, 88 So. 723. Also see Classifying Mineral Interests—Mineral Servitude v. Mineral Royalty, 23 La.L. Rev. 106 (Louisiana); Louisville Gas Co. v. Kentucky Heating Co., 132 Ky. 435, 111 S.W. 374; Gray-Mellon Oil Co. v. Fairchild, 219 Ky. 143, 292 S.W. 743. But cf. Scott v. Laws, 185 Ky. 440, 215 S.W. 81, 13 A.L.R. 369, and see Gardner, Comparison of Results Under Ownership and Non-Ownership Views, 29 Ky.L.J. 116 (Kentucky); Rich v. Doneghey, 71 Okl. 204, 177 P. 86 (Oklahoma). Some writers include a third category, qualified ownership: That oil and gas are a part of the land and belong to the owner thereof as long as they remain in or on the land; upon migration to another tract the title of the former owner is lost. This is essentially a theory of non-ownership, although it may produce a property right that is protected under the doctrine of correlative rights. At least one writer believes it is the product of misconstruction of the case of Westmoreland & Cambria Natural Gas Co. v. De Witt, 130 Pa. 235, 18 A. 724. See Summers Oil & Gas, § 62, p. 167. Other cases purported to expound this theory are Ohio Oil Co. v. Indiana, 177 U.S. 190, 20 S.Ct. 576, 44 L.Ed. 729; Rich v. Doneghey, 71 Okl. 204, 177 P. 86.

14. Texas Co. v. Daugherty, 107 Tex. 226, 176 S.W. 717.

15. "To whomever the soil belongs, he owns also to the sky and to the depths." Co.Litt. 4.

In such jurisdictions not only does the landowner have a possessory estate in the oil and gas, but he may create, either in himself or a third party, a similar estate in the oil and gas in place, separate from the rest of the land.[16] The separation of the oil and gas mineral estate (hereinafter for convenience referred to as the mineral estate) from the rest of the land may be accomplished by a grant to a third party or retention of the mineral estate by the landowner in a conveyance of the rest of the land.[17] At common law a distinction was made between an exception and a reservation to the grantor.[18] The former withdrew from the operation of the conveyance a part of the thing granted (a corporeal interest), whereas the latter was treated as the rendition to the grantor of something that issued out of the thing granted, such as a rent (an incorporeal interest). By strict application of this distinction the landowner in an ownership-in-place jurisdiction would be unable to retain the mineral estate by way of reservation; however, the courts have disregarded the distinction and have given effect to the intent to retain the mineral estate whether expressed as a reservation or an exception.[19]

Language indicating an intent to except or reserve the mineral estate to the grantor will be given effect if found in the habendum clause or elsewhere in the instrument. The attitude of the present day courts is to give effect to the intent of the parties wherever expressed in the instrument. This is done without regard to older rules of construction which would declare void, as repugnant to the grant of a fee simple estate in the land, expressions of limiting intent following the granting clause.[20]

In the ownership-in-place jurisdictions, such a grant or reservation is said to have "severed" the mineral estate from the rest of the land.[21] Such severed mineral estate is a corporeal estate in real property, and, if not limited by the instrument creating the severance, will constitute a fee simple absolute.[22] Such lesser estates and interests may be created in the severed mineral estate as in any other corporeal realty.

When the mineral estate has been "severed," the remaining aggregate of rights in the land has become generically termed as the

---

16. Stephens County v. Mid-Kansas Oil & Gas Co., 113 Tex. 160, 254 S.W. 290, 29 A.L.R. 566.

17. Bodcaw Lumber Co. v. Goode, 160 Ark. 48, 254 S.W. 345, 29 A.L.R. 578.

18. Proctor v. Graham, 32 Colo.App. 102, 506 P.2d 1236; also see discussion in Summers, Oil and Gas, § 137.

19. Proctor v. Graham, 32 Colo.App. 102, 506 P.2d 1236; Silvis v. Peoples Natural Gas Co., 386 Pa. 453, 126 A.2d 706.

20. See discussion in Townsend v. Cable, Ky., 378 S.W.2d 806, and cf. Fry v. Hurst, Okl., 293 P.2d 552.

21. Sun Oil Co. v. Oswell, 258 Ala. 326, 62 So.2d 783; Mitchell v. Espinosa, 125 Colo. 267, 243 P.2d 412; Rathbun v. State, 284 Mich. 521, 280 N.W. 35; Pure Oil Co. v. Kindall, 116 Ohio St. 188, 156 N.E. 119.

22. Humphreys-Mexia Co. v. Gammon, 113 Tex. 247, 254 S.W. 296, 29 A.L.R. 607. In some jurisdictions it may be necessary to include words of inheritance in order to create a fee simple estate. Cf. Kirby Lumber Corp. v. Claypool, Tex.Civ.App., 438 S.W.2d 655.

"surface" rights. Some cases speak of the "surface estate" and the "mineral estate." [23] As discussed elsewhere,[24] such graphic nomenclature is greatly misleading, and has tended to lead to a mechanical approach to the problems involving the conflict of interests between the owners of the mineral estate and the owners of the remaining interests in the land.[25]

The great advantage of the ownership-in-place theory is a property interest whose attributes are more or less predictable and which fits into the pre-existing rules and laws applying to other corporeal interests in realty.[26]

A substantial number, if not a majority, of the petroleum producing states have rejected the ownership-in-place theory as being illogical.[27] Not only was it found difficult to equate the concept of title to substances over which the landowner has neither possession nor control, serious criticism was leveled at the so-called "rule of capture," [28] a corollary to the ownership-in-place theory, which states that a landowner's title is lost as to oil and gas drained from his lands by legitimate operations upon adjoining tracts of land.[29] It was argued that this result was contrary to the essential characteristic of ownership, viz., the right of an owner to follow and to re-acquire his property from one who has removed it without permission, and concluded that oil and gas are incapable of being owned apart from the rest of the land until actually reduced to possession, the right of the landowner being one to search for and produce such products. This right or interest of the landowner, however, is treated as being sufficiently connected with the land so as to pass with a conveyance of the land as an appurtenance thereto, where no mention is made of the mineral estate.[30]

23. Rathbun v. State, 284 Mich. 521, 280 N.W. 35, and see note 21, supra, which holds a mineral severance creates two separate fee simple estates, one in the minerals and the other in the surface.

24. See Chapter 2, § 2.2, and Chapter 3, § 3.4.

25. See Fleming Foundation v. Texaco, Inc., Tex.Civ.App., 337 S.W.2d 846, refused n. r. e., subterranean water; Hammonds v. Central Kentucky Natural Gas Co., 255 Ky. 685, 75 S.W.2d 204, and Lone Star Gas Co. v. Murchison, Tex.Civ.App., 353 S.W.2d 870, 94 A.L.R.2d 529, refused n. r. e.; Humble Oil & Refining Co. v. West, Tex., 508 S.W.2d 812, appeal after remand Tex.Civ.App., 543 S.W.2d 667, cert. denied 434 U.S. 875, 98 S.Ct. 224, 54 L.Ed.2d 154, underground storage of gas.

Also see discussion § 4.2, note 72 infra.

26. Kiser v. Eberly, 200 Md. 242, 88 A.2d 570 (statute of frauds); Caswell v. Llano Oil Co., 120 Tex. 139, 36 S.W.2d 208 (recording acts); Watkins v. Certain-Teed Products Co., Tex.Civ.App., 231 S.W.2d 981 (forms of action—ejectment); Stephens County v. Mid-Kansas Oil & Gas Co., 113 Tex. 160, 254 S.W. 290, 29 A.L.R. 566 (ad valorem tax).

27. See note 13, supra.

28. See Chapter 2.

29. See Adams, The Right of a Landowner to Oil and Gas in His Land, 63 U.Pa.L.Rev. 471; Greer, The Ownership of Petroleum Oil and Natural Gas in Place, 1 Tex.L.Rev. 162; and Roberts, Inconsistencies Under the "Ownership in Place" Theory of Oil and Gas, 29 Ky.L.J. 3.

30. Murbarger v. Franklin, 18 Ill.2d 344, 163 N.E.2d 818; Gray-Mellon Oil Co. v. Fairchild, 219 Ky. 143, 292 S.W. 743; Rives v. Gulf Refining Co., 133 La. 178, 62 So. 623; Back v. Ohio Fuel Gas Co., 160 Ohio St. 81, 113 N.E.2d 865.

§ 1.3   MINERAL ESTATE: DEFINITION   29

In a non-ownership jurisdiction, the landowner may grant to a third party or retain to himself the right to search for and produce the oil and gas, apart from the ownership of the land. However, little uniformity exists as to the nature of the right, and rarely have the courts attempted to define this right or interest with any particularity.[31]

It would seem improper to speak of the grant or retention of this right as a "severance" of the minerals from the surface,[32] although some cases seem to do so.[33] Rather than effecting a severance or removal of a corporeal interest from the rest of the land, such grant or reservation has subjected the land to the burden of an outstanding right to enter and remove oil and gas, which is usually spoken of as a profit à prendre.[34] Where the benefit runs to an individual, and not other lands, it would be classified as a profit in gross. This proprietary right to search for and remove oil and gas from the lands of another has also been classified as a license,[35] a servitude,[36] a real right,[37] and a chattel real.[38]

Although superficially similar, in that none equate to ownership of a corporeal interest in realty, each has different attributes. The profit à prendre is an incorporeal hereditament, a non-possessory interest in the land.[39] In this context, non-possessory signifies that the holder of a profit at common law did not have seisen, not that the holder did not have the right to use and occupy the land for the purposes indicated. Where perpetual, the profit constitutes a fee interest, an interest in realty, such designation referring to the duration of the interest rather than its quality. If of lesser duration it has been classified as a chattel real, an interest in personalty.[40] A license, on

---

31. However, see discussion in Callahan v. Martin, 3 Cal.2d 110, 43 P.2d 788, 101 A.L.R. 871; Gerhard v. Stephens, 68 Cal.2d 864, 69 Cal.Rptr. 612, 442 P.2d 692 (1968); Radke v. Union Pacific Railroad Co., 138 Colo. 189, 334 P.2d 1077; Transcontinental Oil Co. v. Emmerson, 298 Ill. 394, 131 N.E. 645, 16 A.L.R. 507; Miller v. Ridgley, 2 Ill.2d 223, 117 N.E.2d 759; and Heller v. Dailey, 28 Ind.App. 555, 63 N.E. 490.

32. Updike v. Smith, 378 Ill. 600, 39 N.E.2d 325.

33. See Miller v. Ridgley, 2 Ill.2d 223, 117 N.E.2d 759.

34. The majority of non ownership jurisdictions so classify the interest. See Greenshields v. Warren Petroleum Corp., C.A.10th, 248 F.2d 61, cert. denied, 355 U.S. 907, 78 S.Ct. 334, 2 L.Ed.2d 262; Gerhard v. Stephens, 68 Cal.2d 864, 69 Cal.Rptr. 612, 442 P.2d 692 (1968).

35. Kansas Natural Gas Co. v. Board of Commissioners of Neosho County, 75 Kan. 335, 89 P. 750 (lease).

36. Frost-Johnson Lumber Co. v. Nabors Oil & Gas Co., 149 La. 100, 88 So. 723; and see Classifying Mineral Interests—Mineral Servitude v. Mineral Royalty, 23 La.L.Rev. 106.

37. Shaw v. Watson, 151 La. 893, 92 So. 375.

38. Callahan v. Martin, 3 Cal.2d 110, 43 P.2d 788, 101 A.L.R. 871; Gerhard v. Stephens, 68 Cal.2d 864, 69 Cal.Rptr. 612, 442 P.2d 692; Burden v. Gypsy Oil Co., 141 Kan. 147, 40 P.2d 463; but cf. Dabney-Johnston Oil Corp. v. Walden, 4 Cal.2d 637, 52 P.2d 237, which indicates the interest is one in real property.

39. Gerhard v. Stephens, 68 Cal.2d 864, 69 Cal.Rptr. 612, 442 P.2d 692; Miller v. Ridgley, 2 Ill.2d 223, 117 N.E.2d 759; Halbert v. Hendrix, 121 Ind.App. 43, 95 N.E.2d 221.

40. See Gerhard v. Stephens, 68 Cal.2d 864, 69 Cal.Rptr. 612, 442 P.2d 692 (1968); Rich v. Doneghey, 71 Okl. 204, 177 P. 86; and see note 33, supra.

the other hand, when not irrevocable, is generally treated as a mere privilege to do an act on another's land, a personal right.[41] In Louisiana, the right to search for oil and gas is classified as a servitude, an interest in land, but subject to prescription after ten years non-user.[42] Such differences in basic concept may, but do not always, produce differing results as the nature of the interests that may be created in the oil and gas in non-ownership jurisdictions.

Although to some, non-ownership may be a satisfying theoretical approach, unlike the jurisdictions adapting the ownership-in-place concept, the non-ownership jurisdictions many times have found the resulting interests were not included within the existing legal structures dealing with conveyancing,[43] lien and security interests,[44] recording statutes,[45] taxation statutes,[46] etc., which were thought necessary for safe and convenient commerce in the oil and gas field. As a result, remedial legislation was often passed placing such interests in substantially the same position as if they had been corporeal interests in realty.

The diversity existing as to the nature of the landowner's interest in the oil and gas and of the interests that may be created in the minerals, apart from ownership of the remainder of the land, is largely the result of haphazard development of the law in the oil and gas area. Initial decisions adjudicated narrow questions [47] upon an *ad hoc* basis rather than with regard to the development of a realistic and consistent body of law well adapted to the search for, development and production of petroleum resources. Once adopted, the con-

---

41. See Radke v. Union Pacific Railroad Co., 138 Colo. 189, 334 P.2d 1077; Heller v. Dailey, 28 Ind.App. 555, 63 N.E. 490.

42. See note 36, supra.

43. Heller v. Dailey, 28 Ind.App. 555, 63 N.E. 490.

44. Phillips v. Springfield Crude Oil Co., 76 Kan. 783, 92 P. 1119; Southport Petroleum Co. of Delaware v. Fithian, 203 La. 49, 13 So.2d 382 (not within mechanics' and materialmen's lien statutes).

45. Back v. Ohio Fuel Gas Co., 160 Ohio St. 81, 113 N.E.2d 865.

46. Mississippi River Fuel Corp. v. Fontenot, C.A.5th, 234 F.2d 898, cert. denied 352 U.S. 916, 77 S.Ct. 213, 1 L.Ed.2d 122; Transcontinental Oil Co. v. Emmerson, 298 Ill. 394, 131 N.E. 645, 16 A.L.R. 507.

47. Halbert v. Hendrix, 121 Ind.App. 43, 95 N.E.2d 221 (statutory interpretation); Mitchell v. Espinosa, 125 Colo. 267, 243 P.2d 412 (taxation); Heller v. Dailey, 28 Ind.App. 555, 63 N.E. 490 (formalities for transfer); Triger v. Carter Oil Co., 372 Ill. 182, 23 N.E.2d 55 (right of participation); Stoughten's Appeal, 88 Pa. 198 (powers of a guardian to lease or otherwise deal with the oil and gas); Louisville Gas Co. v. Kentucky Heating Co., 132 Ky. 435, 111 S.W. 374 (liability for conversion); Elliff v. Texon Drilling Co., 146 Tex. 575, 210 S.W.2d 558, 4 A.L.R. 191 (measure of damages); Moorer v. Bethlehem Baptist Church, 272 Ala. 259, 130 So.2d 367 (forms and nature of actions); Gerkins v. Kentucky Salt Co., 100 Ky. 734, 39 S.W. 444 (passing of title under laws of descent and distribution); Trimble v. Kentucky River Coal Corp., 235 Ky. 301, 31 S.W.2d 367 (dower rights); People v. Associated Oil Co., 211 Cal. 93, 294 P. 717 (condemnation); Watford Oil & Gas Co. v. Shipman, 233 Ill. 9, 84 N.E. 53; Rupel v. Ohio Oil Co., 176 Ind. 4, 95 N.E. 225 (waste); Poe v. Ulrey, 233 Ill. 56, 84 N.E. 46 (homestead laws); Back v. Ohio Fuel Gas Co., 160 Ohio St. 81, 113 N.E.2d 865 (application of recording statutes); Phillips v. Springfield Crude Oil Co., 76 Kan. 783, 92 P. 1119; National Supply Co. v. McLeod, 116 Kan. 477, 227 P. 350 (application of lien statutes); Stokes v. Tutvet, 134 Mont. 250, 328 P.2d 1096 (right of specific performance).

cepts of the initial decisions were perpetuated into many other areas involving oil and gas without critical re-examination.[48]

48. In the newer producing areas a serious look is being given to the effect of adoption of the various theories and concepts in light of judicial and economic effectiveness. See Cohen, Property Theories Affecting the Landowner in a New Oil and Gas Producing State, 10 Ala.L. Rev. 323.

CHAPTER 2

CREATION OF INTERESTS IN THE OIL AND GAS MINERAL ESTATE BY THE LANDOWNER

Analysis

Sec.
2.1 Introduction.
2.2 Attributes of the Mineral Estate—The Power to Lease.
 (A) Alienability of the Power to Lease.
 (B) Revocability of the Power to Lease.
 (C) Duration of Ownership of the Power to Lease.
 (D) Standard of Exercise of the Power.
2.3 ——— The Right to Delay Rentals.
2.4 ——— The Right to Bonus.
2.5 ——— The Right to Royalty.
 (A) Nature of Royalty Interests Prior to Lease.
 (B) Nature of Royalty Interests After Lease.
 (C) Separation of Royalty Interests from the Mineral Estate—Nature and Duration of Such Interests.
 (D) Nature of Production Accruing to a Royalty Interest—Federal Income Taxation and Separate-Community Property Status.
 (E) Minimum Royalty and Shut-In Royalty.
2.6 ——— The Problem of Whether Payments Out of Production Constitute Bonus or Royalty.
2.7 ——— Interests Created When Fractional Interests Are Conveyed or Reserved.
 (A) Interests created—Mineral or Royalty?
 (B) Conveyances of "Oil and Gas in, under, and that may be Produced from."
 (C) Conveyances of "Royalty."
 (D) Conveyances of "Oil and Gas Produced and Saved."
 (E) Conveyances of "Royalty" Coupled with Language Inconsistent with a Royalty Interest.
  (1) "Royalty," plus "Oil and gas, in, under, and that may be produced."
  (2) "Royalty" together with express rights of ingress and egress.
  (3) Conveyances of "Royalty Rights," "Royalty and the Rights Thereto," etc.
 (F) Miscellaneous Words and Phrases.
  (1) Profits.
  (2) "Landowner's Interest" and "Landowner's Rights."
 (G) The Effect of the Quantum of the Interest Conveyed or Reserved on the Mineral-Royalty Distinction, and Problems Occurring as to the Quantum of Production to Which a Mineral or Royalty Owner May be Entitled.
  (1) Royalty Conveyances.
  (2) Mineral Conveyances.

Sec.
2.7 ____ Interests Created When Fractional Interests Are Conveyed or Reserved—Continued
   (H) Effect of a Conveyance or Reservation of a Mineral Interest, Less the Right to Bonus, Delay Rentals and the Power to Lease.
   (I) Effect of a Conveyance or Reservation of a Mineral Interest, Less the Right to Bonus and Delay Rentals.
   (J) Effect of Recitals to Other Instruments.
2.8 ____ Conveyances of Royalty and Mineral Interests for a Limited Term.

§ 2.1 Introduction

Words are merely symbols of thoughts to be communicated, and, as stated by Judge Learned Hand, "Words are utterly inadequate to deal with the multiform occasions which come up in human life." The term "ownership" is a rather inadequate symbol designating a particular complex of rights, duties, privileges, benefits, and obligations with regard to the use, possession, and enjoyment of specific property, which are borne or enjoyed by one termed an "owner." Such rights and duties vary in accordance with the nature of the property to which they relate and the duration of time during which ownership may last. Generally speaking, the extent of the rights and privileges of use and enjoyment will vary directly, and the duties and obligations of care will vary indirectly, with the duration of possible ownership.

The relative rights of use, possession, and enjoyment of real property have evolved within rather fixed frameworks. These frameworks, which are collectively referred to as the estate system, are derived from our common law heritage. Each particular designation, such as fee simple absolute, life estate, estate for years, etc., not only indicated the possible duration of the interest but also became a shorthand designation of the owners rights, duties, and obligations. To understand the meaning of ownership of each such interest, it is necessary to understand the totality of rights, duties, and obligations as they relate to such interest. This is no less true as to interests created in oil and gas. To understand the meaning of ownership of the oil and gas mineral estate, it is necessary to be aware of the complex of rights, obligations, and duties that are enjoyed or borne by the owner of each interest.

Depending upon the jurisdiction, the owner of the mineral estate has either a possessory corporeal estate in the minerals or the right to use and occupy the surface of the land for the exploration, development and production of the oil and gas. In any event, the owner of the minerals has the inherent right to enter the land and conduct his own operations in developing the mineral estate. However, due to the high cost of development, the mineral owner usually conveys the development rights to another by use of an instrument with a defeasible term, usually referred to as an oil and gas lease, under which the mineral owner lessor and the lessee share together in the benefits of the enterprise.[1]

Under the usual oil and gas lease, the costs of exploration, development, and production, with minor exceptions, are borne entirely by the lessee, the grantee of the development rights. The economic benefits enjoyed or reserved by the lessor depend upon the agreement of the parties. Such benefits usually include a cash payment for the execution of the lease, certain payments made by the lessee to maintain the development rights in effect prior to the time that oil or gas is discovered and produced, and, upon production, a share in the production from the land. They may be tabulated as follows:

(a) the power to lease;

(b) the right to bonus;

(c) the right to delay rentals;

(d) the right to royalty;

(e) the right to shut-in-royalty, and other rights.

The nature of these rights will be discussed in the following sections.

§ 2.2 Attributes of the Mineral Estate—The Power to Lease

The power to lease is the right to transfer the development rights of the mineral estate to another. Such rights may relate to the interest in the mineral estate owned by the holder of the power, or to an interest in the mineral estate owned by a third party.

If an intent is sufficiently manifested in the creation of the power to lease, it will be irrevocable, alienable by deed, will, or operation of the statutes of descent, and will survive the death of either the owner of the mineral interest to which it relates or the holder of the power.

Although it has been argued that the power to lease, when owned apart from other interests in the mineral estate, should be treated as sufficiently connected with the land so as not to violate the rule against perpetuities, it is believed most jurisdictions will treat the power when so owned, as analogous to a power to sell or to a power of appointment so as to violate the rule.

The power to lease, sometimes referred to as the executive right, is the right to transfer the development rights of the mineral estate to another. Such power may be exercised as an incident of the ownership of the mineral estate owned by the holder of the power to

---

1. However, the fact that the owner himself of the mineral estate may choose to develop must be borne in mind by persons receiving grants of interests from the mineral owner, as it will affect the form of instruments by which such rights are created.

In some instances the patentee of land from the sovereign may not be granted the mineral estate, although he may have the power to execute oil and gas leases. In this event, the landowner would have no power of self development. This is true as to land in Texas subject to the Texas Relinquishment Act of 1919. As to such lands the mineral estate has been reserved to the State of Texas, and the landowner under such act is designated as the agent of the State for the leasing of such lands.

§ 2.2   IN THE OIL AND GAS MINERAL ESTATE   35

lease. For example, O, the owner of Blackacre may transfer to Rex Oil Company, by way of an oil and gas lease, the exclusive right to develop the mineral estate.

Such power may also relate to a mineral interest not owned by the holder of the power to lease. O may sell Blackacre to A and retain to himself only an undivided interest in the mineral estate. If O desires to control the leasing of the entire mineral estate, he will also reserve to himself the power to lease that portion of the mineral estate that he conveyed to A.[1] To this extent O has a right to deal with A's mineral estate in Blackacre for a limited purpose, which right is not an incident of O's retained mineral interest.

The validity of the power to lease the land of another has been generally recognized, or assumed without comment.[2] However, the precise nature of this right has not been defined by the courts which have found themselves confronted with problems concerning the alienability and duration of the right: (1) Is the power to lease another's property merely personal to the holder of the power, or may it be alienated by the holder of the power;[3] (2) will the power to lease another's property survive the death of the holder of the power to lease or the death of the owner of the mineral estate to which it relates;[4] (3) may the power to lease be revoked by the owner of the mineral estate to which it relates;[5] and (4) may ownership of the power to lease, apart from the interest in the mineral estate to which it relates, last in perpetuity?[6]

In attempting to reach a solution to these and other questions, the courts, as in other areas of basic property concepts in the oil and gas field, have attempted to fit the power to lease into pre-existing concepts. At one time or another the power has been classified as a power coupled with an interest,[7] a power of appointment,[8] a power in trust,[9] an assignable personal right,[10] an unassignable personal

1. Kilfoyle v. Wright, C.A.5th, 300 F.2d 626.

2. Kilfoyle v. Wright, C.A.5th, 300 F.2d 626; Mountain Forest Fur Farms of America, Inc., v. Cockrell, 179 La. 795, 155 So. 228; Federal Land Bank of Wichita, Kan. v. Nicholson, 207 Okl. 512, 251 P.2d 490; Superior Oil Co. v. Stanolind Oil & Gas Co., 150 Tex. 317, 240 S.W.2d 281, affirming Tex.Civ.App., 230 S.W.2d 346.

3. Keville v. Hollister Co., 29 Cal.App. 3d 203, 105 Cal.Rptr. 238; Howard v. Dillard, 198 Okl. 116, 176 P.2d 500; Pan American Petroleum Corp. v. Cain, 163 Tex. 323, 355 S.W.2d 506.

4. Bonzo v. Nowlin, Ky., 285 S.W.2d 153; Howard v. Dillard, 198 Okl. 116, 176 P.2d 500; Pan American Petroleum Corp. v. Cain, 163 Tex. 323, 355 S.W.2d 506.

5. Bonzo v. Nowlin, Ky., 285 S.W.2d 153; Odstrcil v. McGlaun, Tex.Civ.App., 230 S.W.2d 353.

6. Dallapi v. Campbell, 45 Cal.App.2d 541, 114 P.2d 646; Keville v. Hollister Co., 29 Cal.App.3d 203, 105 Cal.Rptr. 238.

7. Bonzo v. Nowlin, Ky., 285 S.W.2d 153; Allison v. Smith, Tex.Civ.App., 278 S.W.2d 940.

8. See discussion in Dallapi v. Campbell, 45 Cal.App.2d 541, 114 P.2d 646; and Keville v. Hollister Co., 29 Cal.App. 3d 203, 105 Cal.Rptr. 238.

9. See discussion in Howard v. Dillard, 198 Okl. 116, 176 P.2d 500; and Hollister Co. v. Cal-L Exploration Corp., 26 Cal.App.3d 713, 102 Cal.Rptr. 919.

10. Dallapi v. Campbell, 45 Cal.App. 2d 541, 114 P.2d 646; Skelly Oil Co. v. Butner, 201 Okl. 372, 205 P.2d 1153.

right,[11] a security or administrative power,[12] and a right exercisable as the owner of the property leased;[13] and courts have denied that it is a covenant real,[14] an estate in land,[15] an agency,[16] or a covenant running with the land.[17] It has also been argued that it is analogous to an option to sell, or a vested property right in itself.

(A) Alienability of the Power to Lease

Although the majority of cases hold that the power to lease is assignable, in some cases it has been held that the power to lease is personal to the holder and will not run to his heirs or devisees. In the Oklahoma case of Howard v. Dillard,[18] grantor reserved, among other rights, "* * * management and control of the minerals * * * and that he shall have the sole and exclusive right to lease said lands to any person to whom he may choose and upon such terms and conditions suitable to him * * *." The court held that the reserved right to lease was personal to grantor and constituted a power in trust, which power terminated upon the death of the grantor. However, in the later case of Skelly Oil Co. v. Butner,[19] grantor of an undivided interest in the mineral estate reserved, "* * * that said grantors or their heirs or assigns shall have the exclusive right at all times to execute leases without the consent of the grantee herein." The court distinguished the Howard case and stated that the holding there was not predicated upon the theory that the reservation of the power to lease the interest granted was of itself a power in trust, but that the reservation there merely reflected an intent to create a power personal to grantor concerning rights that were incident to the estate granted. Thus, such intent negated the existence in the grantor of any assignable right in the power. It was emphasized in the Butner case that the power to lease was expressly reserved not only to the grantor but also to his assigns, which affirm-

---

11. Howard v. Dillard, 198 Okl. 116, 176 P.2d 500.

12. Pan American Petroleum Corp. v. Cain, 163 Tex. 323, 355 S.W.2d 506.

13. Hightower v. Marktzky, 194 La. 998, 195 So. 518; Stone v. Texoma Production Co., Okl., 336 P.2d 1099, noted in 13 Okl.L.Rev. 341.

14. Rawling v. Fisher, 101 W.Va. 253, 132 S.E. 489.

15. Dallapi v. Campbell, 45 Cal.App.2d 541, 114 P.2d 646; Pan American Petroleum Corp. v. Cain, 163 Tex. 323, 355 S.W.2d 506.

16. Hightower v. Marktzky, 194 La. 998, 195 So. 518.

17. Dallapi v. Campbell, 45 Cal.App.2d 541, 114 P.2d 646.

18. 198 Okl. 116, 176 P.2d 500.

19. 201 Okl. 372, 205 P.2d 1153. This case involved a contest between the grantee and subsequent holders of the grantor's reserved interest, wherein the court stated that the power to lease would pass, as an incident to real property, to the subsequent holders of the reserved interest unless the power to lease was severed from the grantor's land and became non-assignable. In the Butner case the court makes no holding whether the interest conveyed by the grantor, when there is an outstanding lease, is a mineral or royalty interest. It should be noted that the terms are treated as being somewhat ambiguous in Oklahoma, see Section 2.7, infra. If classified as royalty, the grantee would not have received the right to lease as an incident to the royalty interest in any event.

atively indicated an intent that grantor remain vested with the right to lease and that such right be assignable.

There is, of course, a considerable difference whether the court in the Howard case conceived of the power to lease as a power in trust, or applied a different concept. If, in fact, the court in the Howard case treated the right to lease as a power in trust, it is correct that the donee of the power does not have the ability to convey the right to exercise the power. Such donee would, in fact, be a trustee, and the office of trustee is not assignable. It has been stated that the court in the Howard case was not referring to a mandatory power of appointment, but to a statutory power in trust, a remnant from the Field Code as originally enacted in that jurisdiction and carried forward into present Oklahoma statutes.[20]

A result similar to that in Howard v. Dillard was reached in the recent Texas case of Pan American Petroleum Corp. v. Cain,[21] where grantor of an undivided interest in the mineral estate provided in the deed, "It is also agreed and understood that the Grantor herein reserves the right to lease said land without the joinder of the grantee * * *." Upon the death of the grantor, it was held that the right to lease did not descend to his daughters under the statutes of descent, but terminated at his death. The Texas Supreme Court classified the right to lease as a security or administrative power. It rejected the theory asserted in earlier Texas cases that the right to lease constituted a power coupled with an interest, as the power did not relate to the interest in the minerals owned by the holder of the power.[22] It was further stated that such power would not necessarily be revoked by the death of the holder, but that it would so terminate

---

20. Kuntz, The Rule Against Perpetuities and Mineral Interests, 8 Okl.L.R. 183, 190. However, if this view is followed, it would seem the Howard court was incorrect in holding that the right to lease was a non-assignable interest. It is doubtful whether the intent to reserve a power to lease is in fact a manifestation of an intent to create a true trust relationship. Drake v. O'Brien, 99 W.Va. 582, 130 S.E. 276; and see Skelly Oil Co. v. Butner, 201 Okl. 372, 205 P.2d 1153.

21. 163 Tex. 323, 355 S.W.2d 506.

In Keville v. Hollister Co., 29 Cal.App. 3d 203, 105 Cal.Rptr. 238, where the reservation was:

"* * * the sole and exclusive right and power to enter into and execute leases and agreements for the purpose of prospecting, exploring and mining for minerals thereon, and for the purpose of extracting and transporting minerals; and the right to do any and all things on said real property necessary or proper for mining purposes, or for the purpose of mining, or boring or exploring for oil or other minerals thereon." The court expressly held the power to lease was transferable, as it was specifically reserved "unto Grantor and its successors and assigns."

22. Superior Oil Co. v. Stanolind Oil & Gas Co., 150 Tex. 317, 240 S.W.2d 281; Odstrcil v. McGlaun, Tex.Civ.App., 230 S.W.2d 353; DeBusk v. Cosden Petroleum Corp., Tex.Civ.App., 262 S.W.2d 767; Allison v. Smith, Tex.Civ.App., 278 S.W.2d 940. However, see Hightower v. Marktzky, 194 La. 998, 195 So. 518; Drake v. O'Brien, 99 W.Va. 582, 130 S.E. 276; and dissenting opinion in Pan American Petroleum Corp. v. Cain, 163 Tex. 323, 355 S.W.2d 506, to the effect that as a co-tenant owns an undivided interest in all of the property, the power of necessity must relate to the holder's interest as well as that of the non-participating interest owner.

"unless there is something to indicate that the parties intended that the power should survive and be exercised by others."

In keeping with the modern view of free alienability of interests, it is believed that unless the instrument creating the power evidences an intent that personal trust and confidence is being placed in the holder of the power, the power to lease should be treated as being freely alienable by deed, will, or under statutes of descent, without regard to the conceptualism of a particular jurisdiction. Statutes eliminating the necessity of using words of inheritance in order to create an assignable interest have not been applied in cases dealing with the right to lease, on the ground that such statutes apply only to estates in land.[23] Inclusion of words of inheritance will probably be necessary to effectively manifest such intention[24] in creating or reserving a power to lease.

(B) Revocability of the Power to Lease

It has been held that the power to lease is irrevocable[25] in the few cases dealing expressly with the right of the owner of the mineral estate to revoke the power to lease held by another. This result has been based upon a consideration that the power is one coupled with an interest in the land. But, this result should also follow if it is treated as a pure contractual right or as a power of appointment.[26] The power should likewise survive the death of the holder of the power.

The right of partition between owners of undivided interests in the mineral estate has been denied where one owner also was the holder of the power to lease the other's interest, where the result of such partition would be to effectively revoke such power to lease the resulting segregated interests.[27]

---

23. Pan American Petroleum Corp. v. Cain, 163 Tex. 323, 355 S.W.2d 506, and see dissenting opinion in Howard v. Dillard, 198 Okl. 116, 176 P.2d 500.

24. Skelly Oil Co. v. Butner, 201 Okl. 372, 205 P.2d 1153; Stone v. Texoma Production Co., Okl., 336 P.2d 1099, noted in 13 Okl.L.Rev. 341; Pan American Petroleum Corp. v. Cain, 163 Tex. 323, 355 S.W.2d 506; Rawling v. Fisher, 101 W.Va. 253, 132 S.E. 489.

25. Bonzo v. Nowlin, Ky., 285 S.W.2d 153; Odstrcil v. McGlaun, Tex.Civ.App., 230 S.W.2d 353; Allison v. Smith, Tex. Civ.App., 278 S.W.2d 940. In the Bonzo case the court indicates that the parties may create an interest that will not terminate at the death of the holder if they so desire and manifest such intent. The court criticizes the necessity of classifying the power to lease as a power coupled with an interest to reach such results. See Mechem, Agency, 4th Ed., page 269.

26. In Pan American Petroleum Corp. v. Cain, 163 Tex. 323, 355 S.W.2d 506, the court classifies the power as less than one coupled with an interest, but more than a naked power, i.e., a power in the nature of a security right, and apparently conforms to the suggestion made in the Bonzo case, supra note 25, that it may be made irrevocable if intended. Also see Restatement of the Law of Agency, Second, §§ 138, 139, which abolishes the distinction between a power coupled with an interest and a security power, both of which would be treated as irrevocable unless otherwise indicated by the parties.

27. Odstrcil v. McGlaun, Tex.Civ. App., 230 S.W.2d 353.

(C) Duration of Ownership of the Power to Lease

Assuming that a power to lease may extend beyond the lifetime of the holder of the power, if the possible duration of the power is perpetual, will it violate the rule against perpetuities?

As pointed out above, the power to lease, if properly drafted, may extend beyond the life of the original holder of the power and pass to his heirs, successors and assigns. Although it has been argued that the power to lease should be treated as a sufficiently connected interest in real property, i.e., an incorporeal hereditament, so as to escape the rule, it is believed most jurisdictions will classify the right as analogous to a power to sell or power to appoint. It has been traditionally held that a power does not constitute an interest in the land to which it relates, and, like an executory interest, will violate the rule against perpetuities unless exercise is expressly limited to the period of the rule.[28]

Apparently, where the holder of the power to lease another's interest in the mineral estate also owns a vested interest in the mineral estate, the power is treated as being sufficiently connected with a vested interest so as not to violate the rule against perpetuities.[29] This is true even where the power to lease does not relate to the interest that is vested in the owner of the power.[30] However, where the holder of the power to lease owns no other interest in the mineral estate it has been held to violate the rule.[31] In the California case of Dallapi v. Campbell,[32] a corporate developer of realty reserved "The exclusive right * * *, as against the grantee, to lease and contract for, drilling for and to market * * * oil and gas * * *" The developer did not own any interests in the mineral estate. The court upheld a contention that the reservation violated the rule against perpetuities, in that it allowed the creation of interests in real property to vest in the indefinite future. The court classified the power to lease merely as a contractual right, and denied an argument that the power was a presently exercisable general power of appoint-

---

28. Bundy v. United States Trust Co. of New York, 257 Mass. 72, 153 N.E. 337, Camden Safe Deposit & Trust Co. v. Scott, 121 N.J.Eq. 366, 189 A. 653, 110 A.L.R. 1442, noted in 36 Mich.L.R. 146 (1937). Also see Stone v. Texoma Production Co., Okl., 336 P.2d 1099, noted in 13 Okl.L.Rev. 341, which has been interpreted as classifying the power to lease as a property right.

29. Keville v. Hollister Co., 29 Cal. App.3d 203, 105 Cal.Rptr. 238; Mountain Forest Fur Farms of America, Inc., v. Cockrell, 179 La. 795, 155 So. 228; Federal Land Bank of Wichita, Kansas v. Nicholson, 207 Okl. 512, 251 P.2d 490; Odstrcil v. McGlaun, Tex.Civ.App., 230 S.W.2d 353; DeBusk v. Cosden Petroleum Corp., Tex.Civ.App., 262 S.W.2d 767, error refused.

30. Dallapi v. Campbell, 45 Cal.App. 2d 541, 114 P.2d 646; Pan American Petroleum Corp. v. Cain, 163 Tex. 323, 355 S.W.2d 506; but see note 22, supra.

31. Dallapi v. Campbell, 45 Cal.App. 2d 541, 114 P.2d 646. Also see Meyers, The Effect of the Rule Against Perpetuities on Perpetual Non-Participating Royalty and Kindred Interests, 32 Tex.L.Rev. 369.

32. Note 31, supra, and see Keville v. Hollister Co., 29 Cal.App.3d 203, 105 Cal. Rptr. 238.

ment as the power could not be exercised for the benefit of the donee of the power.

Treating the power to lease as a general power of appointment would remove the power from the onus of the "Rule," in that it is generally held that if the donee of a power has the right to acquire the property subject to the power within his lifetime (including a testamentary exercise) that the power does not violate the rule.[33]

In the Dallapi case, the grounds for denial of the general power of appointment are not immediately apparent, as the language of the reservation is not so restrictive. However, in fact, the power could not be exercised for the benefit of the owner of the power, as he owned no interest in the minerals.

However, in the Dallapi case, it may be argued that, as the language creating the power to lease does not restrict the owner of the power in his designation of lessee, the holder has the right to acquire the development rights himself. The right to acquire property has been equated to ownership of the property itself. In applying this analogy, the development rights would be treated as being vested in the holder of the power to lease, and the execution of a lease would constitute, in reality, the transfer of a vested interest.

The California case of Keville v. Hollister Co.[34] indicates a movement by the California courts away from the position of Dallapi v. Campbell, that a reservation of the right to lease may violate the rule against perpetuities. In the Keville case, defendant conveyed an undivided 50% interest in the minerals to plaintiff, reserving the right to lease in the following language:

> "The sole and exclusive right and power to enter into and execute leases and agreements for the purpose of prospecting, exploring and mining for minerals thereon, and for the purpose of extracting and transporting minerals; and the right to do any and all things on said real property necessary or proper for mining purposes, or for the purpose of mining, or boring or exploring for oil or other minerals thereon."

Plaintiff asserted that the reserved interest violated the rule against perpetuities, citing Dallapi v. Campbell. It was held that the reserved power to lease did not violate the rule on three grounds:

(1) The court distinguished the Dallapi case on the basis that the power to lease had there been classified as a special power of appointment, not being exercisable into the holder of the power, as he had no interest in the mineral estate, thereby violating the rule as a nonvested interest. In the present case it was held that, as the power was exercisable into the holder and was a vested interest, it did not violate the rule.

---

33. Simes, Future Interests, Sec. 135.   34. 29 Cal.App.3d 203, 105 Cal.Rptr. 238.

§ 2.2   IN THE OIL AND GAS MINERAL ESTATE   41

(2) The court discussed the power to lease as a collection of rights, all of which are vested:

"An alternative to the classification of an executive interest as a power of appointment views a mineral estate as a collective bundle of rights, which includes the right to go on the land to extract minerals, the right to a share of the minerals or their proceeds, and the right to designate who may exercise these first two rights. At bench, defendants' grantor retained all rights in the mineral estate except the share in the income of the mineral proceeds it conveyed to plaintiffs. That share, a right to receive income from the mineral estate, is an incorporeal hereditament in the nature of rent carved out of the mineral estate. As such it is an interest in land. (Callahan v. Martin, 3 Cal.2d 110, 119–124.) Although the receipt of income may be uncertain in fact, the right to receive that income is present and established at law, and as such it is a vested right. The bundle of rights retained by defendants' grantor, i.e. the remaining mineral rights, is likewise present, established, and vested, subject only to the incorporeal burden of plaintiffs' non-executive mineral interest. Since all interests in the mineral estate are vested, the rule against perpetuities has not been violated. (Accord, Hanson v. Ware (Ark.1955) 274 S.W.2d 359, 46 A.L.R.2d 1262) Like any other owner of property defendants possess the right to lease the property, now or sometime in the future."

(3) The power to lease does not violate the rule, as it does not constitute inconvenient fettering of the mineral estate.

This is further discussed in the related case of Hollister Co. v. Cal-L Exploration Corp.,[35] cited in the Keville case:

"This method of holding the leasing power in a single party is a practical and legally unobjectionable means of simplifying the les-

---

35. Hollister Co. v. Cal-L Exploration Corp., 26 Cal.App.3d 713, 102 Cal.Rptr. 919. The reservation of the power to lease in this case was quite extensive:

"Excepting And Reserving unto Grantor and its successors and assigns, the sole and exclusive right and power to enter into and execute leases and agreements for the purpose of prospecting, exploring and mining for minerals thereon, and for the purpose of extracting and transporting minerals; and the right to do any and all things on said real property necessary or proper for mining purposes, or for the purpose of mining, or boring or exploring for oil or other minerals thereon.

"The exclusive leasing power reserved herein by Grantor (which power is sometimes referred to as an executive right) shall not be construed as a general power of appointment, but, on the contrary, is expressly intended to be an incorporeal hereditament, carved out of the total mineral estate, and constituting a burden thereon, as an incident to Grantor's own retained mineral estate.

"The herein reserved exclusive leasing power shall be exercisable by Grantor for the mutual benefit of Grantor and the respective Grantees of the fractional mineral interest conveyed hereby.

"The herein reserved leasing power shall survive the death of the respective Grantees hereunder, and said exclusive leasing power shall be an alienable, descendable and devisable estate in the real property.

"It is the intention of the Grantor that the undivided mineral interests transferred to the Grantees by this

sor-lessee relationship. The parties found it convenient and agreeable when they were dealing with each other, and there appears to be no reason why the courts should not recognize and apply it as the parties intended."

The question here, as in many other areas of basic property concepts in the oil and gas field, is not what common law concept will fit best, but whether the right to execute leases for oil and gas exploration upon another's interest in the mineral estate is to be considered as such a separation of the power of use and possession apart from the land to which it relates as to be severely restricted in its duration by public policy.

(D) Standard of Exercise of the Power

If O holds the power to lease A's interest in the mineral estate, the exercise of the power by O must fall within some standard of conduct toward A. When, as in the usual case, the instrument is bare of language concerning the exercise of the power, the courts will re-construct, from the circumstances of the transaction, what they believe the parties would have intended as a standard for the exercise.[36] Present case law is of little help in formulating such standards, other than enunciating that O's conduct must be "of utmost fair dealing" and "in good faith".[37] But, what is "fair" and what constitutes "good faith"? Depending upon the relationship of parties, courts have found standards of duty *inter se* that run the gamut of requiring the very highest duties of care and loyalty[38] to merely requiring an absence of fraud.[39]

Actions condoned within the standard of either extreme would be "fair" and "in good faith" in relation to the applicable standard; how-

Deed, which do not carry any right in the individual grantees to execute leases for development of said oil, gas and minerals (and which are sometimes referred to as 'non-executive interests') shall be presently vested and alienable estates and not contingent interests in the real property. Said interests shall carry not only the right to share in royalties, but also the right to share in any bonuses and/or lease rentals obtained in the development of the mineral estates."

36. See Elliott, Executive Right, 42 Tex.L.Rev. 865, and Jones, Non-Participating Royalty, 26 Tex.L.Rev. 569.

37. Hudgins v. Lincoln National Life Insurance Co., D.C.Tex., 144 F.Supp. 192; Union Producing Co. v. Scott, D.C.Tex., 173 F.Supp. 361, affirmed C.A.5th, 267 F.2d 469, cert. denied 363 U.S. 842, 80 S.Ct. 1607, 4 L.Ed.2d 1726, rehearing denied 364 U.S. 855, 81 S.Ct. 32, 5 L.Ed.2d 78; Archer County v. Webb, 161 Tex. 210, 338 S.W.2d 435; Wintermann v. McDonald, 129 Tex. 275, 102 S.W.2d 167, rehearing denied 129 Tex. 275, 104 S.W.2d 4; Allison v. Smith, Tex.Civ.App., 278 S.W.2d 940, refused n. r. e.; Schlittler v. Smith, 128 Tex. 628, 101 S.W.2d 543; Portwood v. Buckalew, Tex.Civ.App., 521 S.W.2d 904, refused n. r. e.; Kimsey v. Fore, Tex.Civ.App., 593 S.W.2d 107, refused n. r. e.

38. Hollister Co. v. Cal-L Exploration Corp., 26 Cal.App.3d 713, 102 Cal.Rptr. 919; Teas v. Twentieth Century-Fox Film Corp., D.C.Tex., 178 F.Supp. 742, reversed C.A.5th, 286 F.2d 373, cert. denied 368 U.S. 818, 82 S.Ct. 33, 7 L.Ed.2d 24; Portwood v. Buckalew, Tex.Civ.App., 521 S.W.2d 904; Kimsey v. Fore, Tex.Civ. App., 593 S.W.2d 107, refused n. r. e.

39. Hanson v. Ware, 224 Ark. 430, 274 S.W.2d 359, 46 A.L.R.2d 1262; Warren v. Amerada Pet. Corp., Tex.Civ.App., 211 S.W.2d 314.

ever, those acceptable in an arm's length transaction may be grossly variant in relation to a transaction requiring the conduct of a fiduciary. It is obvious that the statements of the courts requiring conduct of fair dealing and good faith dealing are useless without first characterizing the severity of the standards of care and loyalty to be imposed upon the parties.

Many times the standard of conduct follows as a consequence of the characterization of the relationship of the parties, viz., ownership, principal-agent, trustee-beneficiary, bailor-bailee, etc. However, as pointed out above, the courts have been less than unanimous in their classification of the power to lease.[40] Variations in classification may lead to variations in the standard of duty required. If the power to lease is regarded as the exercise of a power akin to the exercise of a power of appointment, the donee of the power may be free to exercise the power in any manner so long as the exercise is not regarded as a fraud upon the power.[41] If treated as a presently exercisable general power of appointment, exercise would be unrestricted.[42] When the power to lease is conceived to be in the nature of a power delegated by a principal to an agent, the exercise of the power by the agent must fall within the actual, implied or incidental authority of the agent. The scope of this authority also may follow from the classification of the nature of the agency relationship.[43] If the power to lease is thought to be one creating a trustee-beneficiary relationship, the holder of the power would be bound to the highest of fiduciary duties and loyalty in its exercise.[44]

However, deriving the standards of duty of the holder of the power from conceptual classification of the relationship has been criticized as not representing the actual basis of court decisions, and that basic rationale is to be found, partly at least, in generalizations to be drawn from what is considered to be normal conduct of business as to a particular transaction.[45]

In the case of Hollister Co. v. Cal-L Exploration Corp.,[46] the California court further discussed the nature of the relationship of the holder of the power to lease and others owning property subject to the power. In this case a question was raised concerning the right of the holder of the power to lease to give notice of default to a lessee. In upholding the right of the holder to act exclusively for the owners

40. See § 2.2, supra.
41. See Simes, Future Interests, § 73.
42. See Simes, Future Interests, § 71 and 3 Restatement of Property (1940) § 356(a), (b).
43. Mechem, Outline of Agency (Fourth Ed.) §§ 61–63.
44. See Bogert, Law of Trusts (4th Ed.) §§ 95, 96; also see Hollister Co. v. Cal-L Exploration Corp., 26 Cal.App.3d 713, 102 Cal.Rptr. 919.
45. Note 43, supra.
46. 26 Cal.App.3d 713, 102 Cal.Rptr. 919. Also see note 35, supra, setting forth the reservation of the power to lease, which was quite extensive. In the Texas case of Andretta v. West, Tex., 415 S.W.2d 638, it was held that the owner of the power to lease had the right, without the joinder of the non-participating interest owners, to execute a lease amendment providing for payment of a cash-in-lieu royalty by the lessee until such time as lessee drilled to offset a well lessee had on an adjoining tract of land.

of interests subject to the right to lease (and further deciding that acceptance of delay rentals by the other co-tenants did not waive the right of the holder to so act) the court discussed the relationship of the parties:

> "This method of holding the leasing power in a single party is a practical and legally unobjectionable means of simplifying the lessor-lessee relationship. The parties found it convenient and agreeable when they were dealing with each other, and there appears to be no reason why the courts should not recognize and apply it as the parties intended. Estate entered into the lease as sole lessor, under its executive right, and Estate's successor in interest, Hollister, was equally qualified to act alone in giving notice of default. The rule of the Jameson case, supra, is not applicable, because here there was only one lessor, and that party is enforcing the lease."

> "For the purpose of an action such as this one the position of the holder of the executive right is analogous to that of a trustee of an express trust, who is authorized by Code of Civil Procedure section 369 to sue without joining the persons for whose benefit the action is prosecuted. Since the holders of the non-executive mineral rights look to the holder of the executive right to protect their interest, both in making leases and enforcing them, they will be bound by the judgment, insofar as it decides that the lease has been terminated. No one will be prejudiced by their non-joinder. The holders of the mineral interest are thus not indispensable parties."

The court indicated that the owner of the power to lease is analogous to that of a trustee of an express trust. Although this has been indicated by some courts in an attempt to state the standard of conduct of the trustee, the Hollister case extends the analogy by placing in the owner of the power to lease the operative and administrative actions. It further states, "the same reasoning precludes treating the acceptance of rent by the mineral holders as a waiver of default. The executive right would be unworkable if holders of non-executive interests had power to *countermand* the action taken by the executive" (emphasis supplied). Would the California courts also hold that only the holder of the power to lease can give notice of default or file suit for termination?

The Texas courts,[47] on the other hand, appear to treat the relationship as implying a covenant of utmost fair dealing and would require,

---

47. Portwood v. Buckalew, Tex.Civ. App., 521 S.W.2d 904; Kimsey v. Fore, Tex.Civ.App., 593 S.W.2d 107. In both Portwood v. Buckalew, Tex.Civ.App., 521 S.W.2d 904, and Andretta v. West, Tex., 415 S.W.2d 638, however, the courts also talk in terms of a confidential relationship. In the former case, it is in connection with the rights created under a family partition agreement; and, in the latter, monies collected for the benefit of all interest owners.

where reasonable, the owner of the power to lease to acquire for the non-participating interests every benefit he exacts for himself.[48]

In the exercise of the power to lease, the holder of the power is faced with decisions concerning when the power should be exercised, the general terms and conditions to be included in the transaction, and whether he may reserve economic benefits in a form in which the owner of the non-participating interest will not share.

It would seem obvious that a duty to lease exists within a reasonable time after discovery that the land is being drained by production from adjacent lands.[49] Although no case is found regarding the right to lease where no drainage exists, it could be strongly argued that failure to lease, although not occasioning an ultimate loss of products, will cause loss of interest for the use of money that would be received by the royalty owner upon timely development. In certain cases a non-participating interest has been granted for a limited term that will not continue unless production is acquired by a certain expiration date.[50] Must the holder of the power lease, so that production may be acquired prior to the expiration of the term's interest? Furthermore, is he derelict in his duty if he does not include in the lease an express obligation to drill a test well prior to the expiration date of the term interest?

In the case of Federal Land Bank of Houston v. United States,[51] plaintiff, owner of a 1/16th non-participating 20 year term royalty interest, recovered for an alleged taking of such interest by the Department of Interior. The Department, the holder of both the power to lease and the reversionary interest in the minerals, had delayed leasing for a two-month period of time, which delay, plaintiff alleged, caused production to come after termination of the term royalty interest, resulting in its acquisition by the Department.[52]

The court characterized the standard of conduct of the holder of the power as being one "of diligence and discretion on the part of the mineral fee holder as would be expected of the average landowner who because of self interest is normally willing to take affirmative

---

48. Portwood v. Buckalew, Tex.Civ. App., 521 S.W.2d 904.

49. Federal Land Bank of Houston v. United States, 144 Ct.Cl. 173, 168 F.Supp. 788, and see Hudgins v. Lincoln National Life Insurance Co., D.C.Tex., 144 F.Supp. 192.

50. In Kimsey v. Fore, Tex.Civ.App., 593 S.W.2d 107, the court found that a 5-year term interest terminated when drilling was not done timely and that such delay was deliberate. Damages were awarded; however, it would seem reinstatement of the term interest could have been awarded. Also see: Midwest Oil Corp. v. Winsauer, Tex.Civ.App., 315 S.W.2d 608, and Holchak v. Clark, Tex. Civ.App., 284 S.W.2d 399, error refused.

51. 144 Ct.Cl. 173, 168 F.Supp. 788, noted in 11 Baylor L.Rev. 474, and U.C. L.A.L.Rev. 395. Dissenting Justice Whitaker maintained that the holder of the power to lease does not have a duty to protect the interests of the royalty owner to the disadvantage of the interests of the holder of the power. He also may not impair, for his own advantage, the interest of the royalty owner.

52. The lands in question were part of an Air Force base. Production was obtained upon lands adjoining the base in August, 1955. The first offer to lease was made in July, 1956, as a single tract, but was withdrawn about a month later. In October, 1956, the tract was included in an offering including other lands.

steps to cooperate with a prospective lessee." The court further stated that a more stringent rule would be imposed where the non-participating interest was for a limited term. It was recognized that an individual would act more speedily than a body politic, but that in this case the delay of two months did not comply with the above standard.

The dissenting Justice objected that the standard imposed by the court was a fiduciary standard, and that the landowner was under no duty to protect a non-participating interest to the disadvantage of the interests of the holder of the power to lease. It was urged that the Department had the right to withdraw the land in question so as to include it in a package of other lands if this would be advantageous to the Department. It was further pointed out that there was no evidence that the delay was done for the purpose of impairing the royalty interest of the plaintiff.

A reading of the majority opinion strongly leads to the impression that the court is of the opinion that not only is the holder of the power to lease under a duty to execute the power within a reasonable time before the expiration of a non-participating term interest, but he may also be under a duty to include in the lease an express obligation to drill prior to the expiration of the term. Much, however, can be said for the dissent. In weighing the interest of the term interest owner against the interest of the holder of the power to lease, it would seem that the dissenting Justice was correct in stating that the holder of the power is under no duty to prematurely lease, merely to extend the term interest, where delay would in all probability lead to substantially increased benefits. Such a situation might exist where land, although leasable, is not being drained at the end of the term of the non-participating interest, but development is being begun in the area. To require leasing immediately upon discovery of production in the close vicinity, to protect the term interest from expiration, would be unreasonable and will place the holder of the power in a disadvantageous position in negotiating for development. However, in the Federal Land Bank case, it would seem that a reasonable length of time existed in which the Department could have negotiated without disadvantage.

In exercising the power to lease, the holder of the power has a duty to execute a lease with the most advantageous terms available and containing the usual and normal provisions in connection with a particular transaction.[53] In Portwood v. Buckalew[54] the court stated that holder of the power has an implied covenant to acquire for all

---

53. Union Producing Co. v. Scott, D.C.Tex., 173 F.Supp. 361, affirmed C.A.5th, 267 F.2d 469, cert. denied 363 U.S. 842, 80 S.Ct. 1607, 4 L.Ed.2d 1726, rehearing denied 364 U.S. 855, 81 S.Ct. 32, 5 L.Ed.2d 78; Wintermann v. McDonald, 129 Tex. 275, 102 S.W.2d 167; Warren v. Amerada Petroleum Corp., Tex. Civ.App., 211 S.W.2d 314.

54. Tex.Civ.App., 521 S.W.2d 904. Here surface of land was partitioned into lots and the mineral estate was left undivided. The surface owners were granted the power to lease the minerals under their lots. Most took a large cash payment and payments out of production as "surface damages." The court held the non-participating owners could share in

§ 2.2 IN THE OIL AND GAS MINERAL ESTATE   47

owners "every benefit he exacts for himself." It has been held that the inclusion of a shut-in-royalty clause would increase the marketability of the lease, although inclusion of the clause would also allow the continuance of the lease beyond the primary term without necessity of actual production.[55] Likewise, the holder of the power to lease did not violate his duty where he leased in consideration of the drilling of an obligation well in lieu of a cash bonus, where the jury found that a lease could not be otherwise obtained.[56] However, generally it has been held that the holder of the power to lease does not have the right to pool or unitize the interest of the non-participating interest owner with owners of other mineral interests in the same area, as this would dilute the share of the non-participating owner in production while removing his interest from the market for the indefinite future.[57]

When the owner of the non-participating interest has a right to share only in royalty payments made out of actual production, may the holder of the power to lease, in addition to a normal royalty, reserve an increased cash bonus or further payments out of production of a nature (such as deferred bonus payments) that the royalty owner will not share? At least one case has held that the duty of the holder of the power to lease is satisfied where there is reserved to the owner of the non-participating interest the normal or usual royalty.[58] However, it seems to be recognized that the holder of the power to lease is bound to create an interest in a form in which the non-participating owner may share.[59] In the case of Morris v. First National Bank of Mission,[60] it was stated that the question whether the lessor did create a royalty is not so important as whether the lessor could create a royalty different from the usual royalty. This view was followed in

---

the "bonus payments," as they had no reasonable relationship to actual damages to the surface. Interest was also allowed at highest rate allowed by law (10%).

55. Union Producing Co. v. Scott, D.C.Tex., 173 F.Supp. 361, affirmed C.A.5th, 267 F.2d 469, cert. denied 363 U.S. 842, 80 S.Ct. 1607, 4 L.Ed.2d 1726, rehearing denied 364 U.S. 855, 81 S.Ct. 32, 5 L.Ed.2d 78.

56. Allison v. Smith, Tex.Civ.App., 278 S.W.2d 940.

57. Brown v. Smith, 141 Tex. 425, 174 S.W.2d 43, but cf. LeBlanc v. Haynesville Mercantile Co., 230 La. 299, 88 So.2d 377.

58. The Federal Land Bank of Houston v. United States, 144 Ct.Cl. 173, 168 F.Supp. 788, noted in 11 Baylor L.Rev. 474, and 7 U.C.L.A.L.Rev. 395; Warren v. Amerada Petroleum Corp., Tex.Civ.App., 211 S.W.2d 314.

59. Portwood v. Buckalew, Tex. Civ.App., 521 S.W.2d 904; Teas v. Twentieth Century-Fox Film Corp., D.C.Tex., 178 F.Supp. 742, reversed C.A.5th, 286 F.2d 373, and see Hudgins v. Lincoln National Life Insurance Co., D.C.Tex., 144 F.Supp. 192; Schlittler v. Smith, 128 Tex. 628, 101 S.W.2d 543; Morriss v. First National Bank of Mission, Tex.Civ.App., 249 S.W.2d 269, refused n. r. e.; Allison v. Smith, Tex.Civ.App., 278 S.W.2d 940, refused n. r. e. See discussion at note 54, supra.

Also see Houston v. Moore Investment Co., Tex.Civ.App., 559 S.W.2d 850, where grantee acquired right to lease a one-half undivided mineral interest reserved to grantor. The instrument required the holder of the power to lease for 1/8 royalty, and stated that grantor was entitled to "one-half of the royalties." It was held that omission of mention of right to grantor to 1/2 of the rentals or bonus in the language creating the right to lease did not, by implication, modify the one-half mineral interest reserved.

60. Tex.Civ.App., 249 S.W.2d 269.

the case of Teas v. Twentieth Century-Fox Film Corporation.[61] In this case the non-participating owner had a right to receive 50% of bonus and rental payments, as well as $8\frac{1}{3}\%$ royalty. Among other payments reserved, the holder of the power to lease reserved a substantial interest out of production characterized as a "variable participating royalty". The court applied the principle that equity considers done that which ought to be done, and characterized the payment out of production as a bonus in which the owner of the non-participating interest could share.

Basic to any discussion of the duty of the holder of the power to lease is a consideration of the position of the parties. It is obvious that, except as may be required by the courts, the holder of the power may freely submit or withhold the land subject to the power from mineral exploration and development, and, to a great extent, also determine the form and amount of economic benefits to be derived from the transaction. When O is the holder of the power to lease the interest of A, what A may not do for himself, O must do for him. Toward this end, the law will imply an obligation upon O to protect A's interest against loss, as well as to acquire a full and complete development of the property. A minimum obligation upon O should include a duty to timely lease so as to obtain maximum benefits for himself and A, the owner of the non-participating interest, insofar as may be considered reasonable in connection with the circumstances existing at the time, and giving due regard for the interests of O as well as A. Such obligation would also seem to forbid the use by O of the power to lease A's land so as to obtain benefits for O that would not also be shared by A. Such result may be justified by considering such use of the power to lease as constituting a fraud upon the power.

§ 2.3 Attributes of the Mineral Estate—The Right to Delay Rentals

Delay rentals are payments made by the lessee for the purpose of delaying the commencement of operations during the primary term of a lease. Under the better view, delay rentals constitute an interest in real property and are an incident of the mineral estate.

Delay rentals may be generally defined as payments made by the lessee to the lessor, from year to year, during the primary term of an "unless" or "drill or pay"[1] form lease, for the purpose of delaying the commencement of development operations on the leased land.[2] The right to such payments may be of substantial value where large

---

61. D.C.Tex., 178 F.Supp. 742, C.A.5th, 286 F.2d 373.

1. See Chapter 6, infra, for a discussion of the "unless" and "drill or pay" forms of oil and gas leases.

2. Commissioner v. Wilson, C.A.5th, 76 F.2d 766; State ex rel. Fatzer v. Board of Regents, 176 Kan. 179, 269 P.2d 425; Carroll v. Bowen, 180 Okl. 215, 68 P.2d 773; Davis v. Hardman, 146 W.Va. 82, 133 S.E.2d 77; Caruthers v. Leonard, Tex.Com.App., 254 S.W. 779; State v. Magnolia Petroleum Co., Tex.Civ.App., 173 S.W.2d 186; Texas Co. v. Parks, Tex. Civ.App., 247 S.W.2d 179.

§ 2.3   IN THE OIL AND GAS MINERAL ESTATE

tracts of land are involved, as the amount of the delay rental is generally computed on a per acre basis. Where no production is obtained, the right to delay rentals may well be the most valuable right of the owner of the mineral estate.

Authority is meager concerning the nature of delay rentals. Early cases sometimes indicated that, as the payments related to the use of the surface of the land, such payments were an incident of the surface estate and would not pass to the grantee of a mineral interest.[3]

Under the present state of the laws it clearly appears that the right to delay rentals is an incident of the mineral estate, and, upon severance of the mineral estate from the surface estate, delay rentals are to be paid to the owner of the mineral estate.[4] Upon conveyance of the mineral estate, either before or after the execution of an oil and gas lease, the right to delay rentals will pass to the grantee. The right to delay rentals may also be conveyed apart from the rest of the mineral estate.[5] Under the better view, that the right to delay rentals constitutes a vested interest in the realty, such conveyance should not be subject to the rule against perpetuities. Delay rentals which have accrued at the time of such conveyance constitute personal property and do not pass under such conveyance [6] unless expressly included therein.

In attempting to define the nature of delay rentals, many courts have assumed they are analogous to common law rent,[7] constitute incorporeal interests in the land,[8] and as such pass with a conveyance of the land. In jurisdictions which classify an oil and gas lease as creating a corporeal interest in the mineral estate, delay rentals may properly be classified as common law rents. However, in those jurisdictions in which the oil and gas lease constitutes a profit-à-prendre,[9] this classification would seemingly be precluded by the common law rule that an incorporeal interest may only be created out of a corpore-

---

3. Caruthers v. Leonard, Tex.Com. App., 254 S.W. 779. It was held that a conveyance of land "subject to" a prior oil and gas lease passed only the reversionary right to execute future leases and none of the rentals under the existing lease. Although the court recognized delay rentals as being in the nature of common law rents, it stated they did not arise from oil and gas in the ground and were not connected with the mineral estate.

4. Wright v. Carter Oil Co., 97 Okl. 46, 223 P. 835; Harris v. Currie, 142 Tex. 93, 176 S.W.2d 302; Theo Oil Co. v. Thomas, Tex.Civ.App., 108 S.W.2d 555; Cates v. Greene, Tex.Civ.App., 114 S.W. 2d 592. In Texas, Harris v. Currie is thought of as overruling Caruthers v. Leonard, Tex.Com.App., 254 S.W. 779, although the Harris case did not involve a "subject to" conveyance. Also see Currie v. Harris, Tex.Civ.App., 172 S.W.2d 404.

5. Holifield v. Perkins, 233 Miss. 876, 103 So.2d 433.

6. Cates v. Greene, Tex.Civ.App., 114 S.W.2d 592.

7. Commissioner v. Wilson, C.A.5th, 76 F.2d 766; Caruthers v. Leonard, Tex. Com.App., 254 S.W. 779; Texas Co. v. Parks, Tex.Civ.App., 247 S.W.2d 179.

8. Cates v. Greene, Tex.Civ.App., 114 S.W.2d 592; Currie v. Harris, Tex.Civ. App., 172 S.W.2d 404; but cf. Abney v. Lewis, 213 Miss. 105, 56 So.2d 48. See Sheffield v. Hogg, 124 Tex. 290, 77 S.W.2d 1021, rehearing denied 124 Tex. 290, 80 S.W.2d 741.

9. State ex rel. Fatzer v. Board of Regents, 176 Kan. 179, 269 P.2d 425.

al interest.¹⁰ In such jurisdictions the delay rental would not constitute an interest in land, but only chose in action, unassignable at common law, and, where assignable today, would not follow a conveyance of the mineral estate or reversion therein, unless expressly included. It would seem a better view, however, to apply a broader concept of rent as including any "income, return, or profit" arising out of the land.¹¹ Under this view delay rentals would constitute rent.

Delay rentals do not constitute a return of the mineral estate itself.¹² In community property states, delay rentals paid incident to the development of the separate property of one spouse constitute income rather than a return of corpus, and are classified as community property of the marital unit.¹³ Likewise, delay rentals constitute ordinary income to the recipient,¹⁴ are not subject to depletion, and are deductible by the lessee.¹⁵

§ 2.4 Attributes of the Mineral Estate—The Right to Bonus

Bonus is a sum paid to the owner of the mineral estate for the execution of an oil and gas lease. Such sum may be paid in cash or on a deferred basis out of future production.

Bonus may be defined as a payment made for the execution of an oil and gas lease. It more or less represents the market value for a "sale" of the minerals to the lessee¹ for a limited term, for development purposes. The amount of bonus paid, usually referred to as a per acre amount, may fluctuate widely between properties. The amount paid depends upon the nature of the development activity in the vicinity. If the land is located in a semi-proven area, or in a logical extension of a proven field, the bonus paid may be substantial.

---

10. See 3 Tiffany, The Law of Real Property (3rd Ed.), § 879.

11. See Bearden v. Knight, 149 Tex. 108, 228 S.W.2d 837.

12. Commissioner v. Wilson, C.A.5th, 76 F.2d 766; Bennett v. Scofield, 170 F.2d 887; Caruthers v. Leonard, Tex. Com.App., 254 S.W. 779; Texas Co. v. Parks, Tex.Civ.App., 247 S.W.2d 179.

13. Commissioner v. Wilson, C.A.5th, 76 F.2d 766; Bennett v. Scofield, C.A.5th, 170 F.2d 887; McGarraugh v. McGanaugh, Tex.Civ.App., 177 S.W.2d 296.

14. See Houston Farms Development Co. v. United States, C.C.A.5th, 131 F.2d 577, rehearing denied 132 F.2d 861; Jefferson Lake Sulphur Co. v. Lambert, D.C.La., 133 F.Supp. 197, affirmed C.A.5th, 236 F.2d 542; Bennett v. Scofield, C.A.5th, 170 F.2d 887. The depletion allowance is technically in recognition of production from a wasting asset, including partial return of principal, and, as delay rentals are not treated as return of mineral production, they are not subject to depletion. Compare royalty Sec. 2.5, infra. See Burnet v. Harmel, 287 U.S. 103, 53 S.Ct. 74, 77 L.Ed. 199, and United States v. Dougan, C.A.10th, 214 F.2d 511.

15. Normal delay rentals may be either deducted by the lessee as an expense, as a carrying charge on non-productive property, or capitalized. They normally are expensed. However, if the payments cannot be avoided by the lessee, they may be treated as installments of bonus, and must be capitalized. See Bennett v. Scofield, supra, note 14.

1. Geller v. Smith, 130 Cal.App. 485, 20 P.2d 102. The term "sale" is not entirely inappropriate as an oil and gas lease generally constitutes a defeasible conveyance of an interest in land. The concept of bonus may be compared with royalty, which represents the landowner's share in the profits of a joint enterprise, the landowner putting up the land, and the lessee contributing the capital and skill.

On the other hand, if located in a wildcat area, i.e., a new area of development, or one which has been partially condemned by the drilling of dry holes, the sum may be quite small.² Where a lease is abandoned before the end of the first year of the primary term, bonus may constitute the entire return to the landowner.

Although bonus is usually paid in cash, when the amount of bonus is large, a portion may be paid on a deferred basis, out of future production.³ This may be advantageous to the landowner, as it will prevent bunching of income into any particular taxable year. The right to bonus, to be paid in cash or out of future production, is properly viewed as an incorporeal interest in land, and will pass with a conveyance of the reversionary mineral estate.⁴

In community property estates, bonus paid incident to leases on the separate property of a spouse is generally treated in the same manner as royalty.⁵ For income tax purposes, cash bonus is considered as ordinary income not subject to percentage depletion.⁶

Where the right to bonus is of limited duration, such as incident to a term mineral interest, litigation has occurred as to the right to participate in bonus payments, where the term interest has terminated prior to production on the lease for which the bonus was paid. In the case of Parmelee v. Nueces Royalty Co.,⁷ O conveyed to A a right to receive one-half of royalties and bonus for five years and as long thereafter as production continued, O retaining the power to lease. O executed a lease in the last year of the term of A's deed, which then expired, as there was no production from the lease at the end of the term of A's interest. The question was raised whether the cash bonus should be prorated over the life of A's term interest, so that A would be entitled only to one-fifth of one-half of the bonus paid. It was held that cash bonus was not apportionable over the term. However, a contrary result was reached where the bonus was to be paid out of future production. In the case of Minchen v. Fields the term interest expired at a time when production was then not sufficient to

---

2. In any event, the amount of bonus paid should be sufficient to qualify the lessee as a purchaser for value under the recording statutes and under the equitable doctrine of bona fide purchaser, so as to cut off prior equities. In Louisiana such consideration must be more than a nominal amount. See Greer v. Carter Oil Co., 373 Ill. 168, 25 N.E.2d 805; Noxon v. Union Oil Co. of California, 210 La. 1074, 29 So.2d 67; Strong v. Strong, 128 Tex. 470, 98 S.W.2d 346, 109 A.L.R. 739.

3. Probst v. Ingram, Okl., 373 P.2d 58; State National Bank of Corpus Christi v. Morgan, 135 Tex. 509, 143 S.W.2d 757.

4. Geller v. Smith, 130 Cal.App. 485, 20 P.2d 102; Texas Co. v. Fontenot, 200 La. 753, 8 So.2d 689; Sykes v. Dillingham, Okl., 318 P.2d 416, noted in 11 Okl. L.Rev. 225; State National Bank of Corpus Christi v. Morgan, 135 Tex. 509, 143 S.W.2d 757; Morriss v. First National Bank of Mission, Tex.Civ.App., 249 S.W.2d 269.

5. See § 2.5(D), infra.

6. Tax Reduction Act of 1975, I.R.C., Section 613A, (a), (b), (c); Rev.Rul. 81-44. The latter ruling states that under the independent producers and royalty owners' exemption, percentage production is available only with respect to production. Cost depletion is available with respect to bonus payments. See Murphy Oil Co. v. Burnet, 287 U.S. 299, 53 S.Ct. 161, 77 L.Ed. 318.

7. Tex.Civ.App., 361 S.W.2d 585.

pay out the entire amount of bonus to which the term interest owner was entitled. It was held that the right to share in the unpaid bonus expired at the time the mineral interest expired.[8]

§ 2.5 Attributes of the Mineral Estate—The Right to Royalty

The landowner's royalty is a right to a fractional portion of the minerals, as compensation, where the land is developed by one other than the owner of the mineral estate. In most jurisdictions, a royalty interest is an incorporeal real property interest which may be separated from the remainder of the mineral estate by grant or reservation. Such separate interest is termed a "non-participating" royalty interest and will not share in the right to lease, or in the other economic benefits from an oil and gas lease. A non-participating royalty may have a duration in fee or for some lesser period, and should not violate the rule against perpetuities.

In Kansas it appears that a royalty interest constitutes personal property, being only the obligation of the lessee to pay during the existence of a particular lease. A conveyance of royalty of unlimited duration will violate the rule against perpetuities.

A "royalty" interest may be broadly defined as a right to a fractional share of production of petroleum products, free of cost or expense incident to exploration, development, or production. Although a royalty interest may be paid out of the lessee's interest in production under an oil and gas lease to one not the owner of the mineral estate,[1] the royalty interest discussed here is that portion of production returned to the owner of the mineral estate as compensation for an oil and gas lease.[2] It is sometimes referred to as the "landowner's royalty", and will exist where the landowner does not develop the mineral estate himself.[3]

---

8. Minchen v. Fields, 162 Tex. 73, 345 S.W.2d 282.

1. Twentieth Century-Fox Film Corp. v. Teas, C.A.5th, 286 F.2d 373, cert. denied 368 U.S. 818, 82 S.Ct. 33, 7 L.Ed.2d 24; Wright v. Brush, C.C.A.10th, 115 F.2d 265; Maynard v. Ratliff, 297 Ky. 127, 179 S.W.2d 200; Sykes v. Dillingham, Okl., 318 P.2d 416, noted in 11 Okl. L.Rev. 225; Griffith v. Taylor, 156 Tex. 1, 291 S.W.2d 673, noted in 35 Tex.L.Rev. 459. Where O leases to Rex Oil Corporation for a $1/8$th landowner's royalty, and Rex later assigns to B a $1/16$th royalty interest payable out of Rex's $7/8$th interest in production, such royalty is termed an "overriding royalty". This term is sometimes applied to a royalty payable to the lessor in addition to his normal landowner's royalty.

2. Depending upon the jurisdiction and the bargaining power of the parties, the amount of the landowner's royalty provided in an oil and gas lease will vary. In the past, a $1/8$th royalty was customarily provided in leases in Texas, whereas in California it was a $1/6$th. Due to the current high interest in developing oil and gas, landowner's royalty may well exceed $1/8$th and $1/6$th. Leases are frequently executed with landowner's royalty ranging from $3/16$ to $3/8$. Since cash bonus is no longer subject to percentage depletion, many landowners would prefer a larger royalty on leases that show a probability of successful production.

3. In the somewhat rare instances where the owner of the mineral estate engages in developing the property himself, his net return, after payment of all costs and expenses of development and production, would be in the nature of a profit, not a royalty.

(A) Nature of Royalty Interests Prior to Lease

Prior to the execution of an oil and gas lease, the right to a royalty return from production is one of the constituents of the mineral estate, and of like character with the mineral estate of which it is a part. It may be conveyed apart from other incidents of the mineral estate prior to lease.[4] However, following the execution of an oil and gas lease, the royalty to which the landowner is entitled is determined from the provisions of the lease. This gives rise to the question of whether royalty payable under the lease is a real property interest or constitutes personal property in the nature of a contractual obligation of the lessee, a chose in action.

(B) Nature of Royalty Interests After Lease

The courts are unanimous that royalty which has accrued from production and severance of petroleum products, constitutes personal property.[5]

The decisions have been inconsistent in their definition of the lessor's interest in unaccrued royalty, i.e., royalty to be paid from future production under the lease. It may be stated, however, that, with the exception of Kansas and perhaps one or two other jurisdictions, the lessor's interest in unaccrued royalty is held to be a real property interest.[6] In those jurisdictions that follow the ownership-in-place doctrine, where an oil and gas lease vests a corporeal interest in the mineral estate lessee, the landowner's royalty constitutes an incorporeal hereditament, analogous to rent, which will pass with a conveyance of the reversion to the mineral estate.[7] The same result has

---

4. See discussion at § 2.5(C), infra.

5. Kentucky Bank & Trust Co. v. Ashland Oil & Transportation Co., Ky., 310 S.W.2d 287; Lone Star Gas v. Murchison, Tex.Civ.App., 353 S.W.2d 870, 94 A.L.R.2d 529.

6. (a) *Personal property*: Lathrop v. Eyestone, 170 Kan. 419, 227 P.2d 136; Pure Oil Co. v. Kindall, 116 Ohio St. 188, 156 N.E. 119. Also see: Hardy v. Greathouse, 406 Ill. 365, 94 N.E.2d 134, and Logue v. Marsh, 50 Ill.App.3d 493, 8 Ill.Dec. 773, 365 N.E.2d 1159, royalty interest of less than perpetual duration is personal property. (b) *Real property*: Arrington v. United Royalty Co., 188 Ark. 270, 65 S.W.2d 36, 90 A.L.R. 765; Callahan v. Martin, 3 Cal.2d 110, 43 P.2d 788, 101 A.L.R. 871; Dabney-Johnston Oil Corp. v. Walden, 4 Cal.2d 637, 52 P.2d 237; Gerhard v. Stephens, 68 Cal.2d 864, 69 Cal.Rptr. 612, 442 P.2d 692; Williams' v. Union Bank & Trust Co., 283 Ky. 644, 143 S.W.2d 297, 131 A.L.R. 1364; Kentucky Bank & Trust Co. v. Ashland Oil & Transportation Co., Ky., 310 S.W.2d 287; Melancon v. Texas Co., 230 La. 593, 89 So.2d 135; White v. McVey, 168 Okl. 19, 31 P.2d 850, 94 A.L.R. 656; Duquesne Natural Gas Co. v. Fefolt, 203 Pa.Super. 102, 198 A.2d 608; Sheffield v. Hogg, 124 Tex. 290, 77 S.W.2d 1021. For an extensive collection of cases see Summers, Oil and Gas, §§ 572–585.

7. Arrington v. United Royalty Co., 188 Ark. 270, 65 S.W.2d 36, 90 A.L.R. 765; Hanson v. Ware, 224 Ark. 430, 274 S.W.2d 359, 46 A.L.R. 1262; Kentucky Bank & Trust Co. v. Ashland Oil & Transportation Co., Ky., 310 S.W.2d 287; Merrill Engineering Co. v. Capitol National Bank, 192 Miss. 378, 5 So.2d 666; Duquesne Natural Gas Co. v. Fefolt, 203 Pa.Super. 102, 198 A.2d 608; Sheffield v. Hogg, 124 Tex. 290, 77 S.W.2d 1021; State v. Quintana Petroleum Co., 134 Tex. 179, 133 S.W.2d 112, 128 A.L.R. 843. In the Hogg case the court characterizes the royalty interest as remaining in the landowner upon execution of the lease, which might lead to a conclusion that the royalty interest in Texas is a corporeal in-

been reached in the jurisdictions which view the oil and gas lease as placing in the lessee a profit à prendre, i.e., a right to search, where the lease may continue in fee, or for life.[8] This conclusion may be questioned on technical grounds. At common law, an incorporeal interest could only be created out of a corporeal interest, and thus under a lease in a non-ownership jurisdiction the landowner's royalty would be classified as a chose in action.[9] Although a chose in action is assignable today, the right to royalty under such classification would not be an incident to the landowner's reversion in the mineral estate nor pass with a conveyance thereof.[10] It appears that in the non-ownership states the classification of the landowner's royalty as a real property interest is a desirable result of public policy.

In the rare instance that an oil or gas lease is executed for a duration of a term of years or some lesser estate, in both ownership and non-ownership jurisdictions the landowner's right to unaccrued royalty would constitue personal property. This would seem to follow from the definition of an incorporeal hereditament with a duration of less than freehold as constituting a chattel real.[11]

terest. It is believed that the statements of the court in the Quintana case represent the prevailing view in Texas, as the oil and gas lease is viewed as severing and placing the entire possessory estate to the minerals in the lessee. See McBride v. Hutson, 157 Tex. 632, 306 S.W.2d 888.

8. Callahan v. Martin, 3 Cal.2d 110, 43 P.2d 788, 101 A.L.R. 871; Dabney-Johnston Oil Corp. v. Walden, 4 Cal.2d 637, 52 P.2d 237; Gerhard v. Stephens, 68 Cal.2d 864, 69 Cal.Rptr. 612, 442 P.2d 692; Williams' Administrator v. Union Bank & Trust Co., 283 Ky. 644, 143 S.W.2d 297, 131 A.L.R. 1364; White v. McVey, 168 Okl. 19, 31 P.2d 850, 94 A.L.R. 656. The Callahan and Gerhard cases contain an excellent discussion of the nature of the oil and gas lease and the landowner's royalty in a non-ownership jurisdiction. The landowner's royalty is incident to and will pass with a conveyance of the reversionary interest in the mineral estate: United States v. Noble, 237 U.S. 74, 35 S.Ct. 532, 59 L.Ed. 844; Agajanian v. Cuccio, 141 Cal.2d 828, 297 P.2d 755; Hardcastle v. McCluskey, 139 Kan. 757, 33 P.2d 127, mortgage of reversion; Williams' Administration v. Union Bank & Trust Co., 283 Ky. 644, 143 S.W.2d 297, 131 A.L.R. 1364; Merrill Engineering Co. v. Capital National Bank of Jackson, 192 Miss. 378, 5 So.2d 666; White v. McVey, 168 Okl. 19, 31 P.2d 850, 94 A.L.R. 656, mortgage of reversion. The use of the word "reversion" here is somewhat of a misnomer, as a reversion may be defined as a future interest left in the grantor upon the conveyance of less than the entire estate. Restatement of Property, Sec. 154(1)(a). In those jurisdictions in which an oil and gas lease is deemed to be in the nature of a profit or license to explore, the interest left in the landowner would be classified as a fee subject to the profit or license. As the oil and gas lease in such jurisdictions does not effect a severance of the mineral estate, unless the landowner's royalty interest were classified as a chose in action arising from the lease, it would remain a part of the landowner's fee estate in the minerals and pass under a conveyance thereof. See In re Randolph's Estate, 175 Kan. 685, 266 P.2d 315; William's Administrator v. Union Bank & Trust Co., 283 Ky. 644, 143 S.W.2d 297, 131 A.L.R. 1364; White v. McVey, 168 Okl. 19, 31 P.2d 850, 94 A.L.R. 656.

9. See discussion in Atlantic Oil Co. v. County of Los Angeles, 69 Cal.2d 585, 72 Cal.Rptr. 886, 446 P.2d 1006; Callahan v. Martin, 3 Cal.2d 110, 43 P.2d 788; and, Gerhard v. Stephens, 68 Cal.2d 864, 69 Cal.Rptr. 612, 442 P.2d 692.

10. Leydig v. Commissioner, C.A.10th, 43 F.2d 494; Lathrop v. Eyestone, 170 Kan. 419, 227 P.2d 136.

11. Callahan v. Martin, 3 Cal.2d 110, 43 P.2d 788, 101 A.L.R. 871; Dabney-Johnston Oil Corp. v. Walden, 4 Cal.2d 637, 52 P.2d 237; Gerhard v. Stephens, 68 Cal.2d 864, 69 Cal.Rptr. 612, 442 P.2d 692; Arrington v. United Royalty Co., 188 Ark. 270, 65 S.W.2d 36, 90 A.L.R.

§ 2.5   IN THE OIL AND GAS MINERAL ESTATE   55

The characterization of royalty payable to the landowner under a lease, as above discussed, has been affected by the difference in the form of the royalty clause as it pertains to oil or to gas production. The oil royalty clause customarily will provide that the lessor's share of the oil will be delivered to the lessor in his tanks or to his credit in the pipeline to which the wells are attached.[12] This form of clause contemplates the delivery of royalty "in kind." As lessor is considered to have retained an interest in the "royalty oil" under this form of clause, little difficulty has been encountered in characterizing such royalty as a real property interest.

However, the provision for royalty on gas production usually states that lessee will pay to the lessor a fraction of the "market value" or "market price" or "proceeds" of the gas production.[13] It is generally held that under this type clause title to the gas passes to the lessee under the lease.[14] Although some decisions have held that the right of the lessor to gas royalty is in the nature of a chose in action to enforce the contractual obligation of the lessee,[15] such decisions are seldom encountered today. The weight of authority would treat royalty payable in money as a real property interest.[16]

As indicated above, Kansas courts have held that the landowner's royalty reserved in an oil and gas lease is not a real property interest.[17] This position is somewhat anomalous, for Kansas entertains the view that the owner of the mineral estate has a corporeal interest in the minerals in place.[18] In the case of Lathrop v. Eyestone,[19] the Supreme Court of Kansas defined royalty as that part of the oil and

---

765. The Callahan and Gerhard cases contain an excellent discussion.

12. E. g., "The royalties to be paid by Lessee are: (a) on oil, one-eighth of that produced and saved from said land, the same to be delivered at the wells or to the credit of Lessor into the pipe line to which the wells may be connected; Lessee may from time to time purchase any royalty oil in its possession, paying the market price therefor prevailing for the field where produced on the date of purchase; * * * ".

13. e.g., " * * * (b) on gas, including casinghead gas or other gaseous substance, produced from said land and sold or used off the premises or for the extraction of gasoline or other product therefrom, the market value at the well of one-eighth of the gas so sold or used * * * ".

14. Greenshields v. Warren Petroleum Corp., C.A.10th, 248 F.2d 61, cert. denied 355 U.S. 907, 78 S.Ct. 334, 2 L.Ed.2d 262.

15. Hager v. Stakes, 116 Tex. 453, 294 S.W. 835, discussed 7 Tex.L.Rev. 1, pp. 32–49; Continental Supply Co. v. Texas Co., Tex.Civ.App., 7 S.W.2d 174, aff'd Tex.Com.App., 18 S.W.2d 602.

16. United States v. Noble, 237 U.S. 74, 35 S.Ct. 532, 59 L.Ed. 844; Sheffield v. Hogg, 124 Tex. 290, 77 S.W.2d 1021; State v. Quintana Petroleum Co., 134 Tex. 179, 133 S.W.2d 112, 128 A.L.R. 843.

17. Leydig v. Commissioner, C.A.10th, 43 F.2d 494; Miller v. Sooy, 120 Kan. 81, 242 P. 140; Bellport v. Harrison, 123 Kan. 310, 255 P. 52; Lathrop v. Eyestone, 170 Kan. 419, 227 P.2d 136; Shepard v. John Hancock Mutual Life Insurance Co., 189 Kan. 125, 368 P.2d 19; Stratmann v. Stratmann, 204 Kan. 658, 465 P.2d 938.

18. This also is apparently the situation in Ohio, an "ownership" theory state which held unaccrued royalty to be personal property in Pure Oil Co. v. Kindall, 116 Ohio St. 188, 156 N.E. 119. Also see: Hardy v. Greathouse, 406 Ill. 365, 94 N.E.2d 134; and, Logue v. Marsh, 50 Ill. App.3d 493, 8 Ill.Dec. 773, 365 N.E.2d 1159 holding that a royalty interest with a duration less than perpetual is an interest in personal property.

19. 170 Kan. 419, 227 P.2d 136.

gas payable to the lessor by the lessee out of oil and gas actually produced and saved, as compensation for the lease, which interest does not include a perpetual interest in the oil and gas in place. It was held that the landowner's royalty was personal property which would expire upon the termination of the then existing lease.

Although the view that the landowner's royalty interest constitutes personal property appears to be the prevailing attitude of the Kansas courts, this view has been repudiated in one case [20] which held that such royalty constituted real property within the application of statutes relating to passage of property by devise or descent.

(C) Separation of Royalty Interests from the Mineral Estate—Nature and Duration of Such Interests

In those jurisdictions which view royalty as a real property interest, an interest in royalty may be conveyed or reserved apart from the mineral estate.[21] Such conveyance may be made prior to the execution of an oil and gas lease, or at a time when a lease is presently outstanding. In the latter event, the conveyance would usually include a right to royalty under the present lease as well as the right to royalty out of future production. Where the grant passes only a royalty interest, the grantee acquires no right to participate in the right to lease, bonuses, delay rentals, or other benefits under future leases, and the interest is therefore called a "non-participating royalty interest." [22]

A non-participating royalty interest may be created in fee or for some lesser duration. However, the ability of the landowner to create a royalty interest of perpetual duration apart from the mineral estate may be limited (a) by the conceptual nature of royalty in a particular jurisdiction, (b) by the nature of the rights reserved at the time the land is severed from the sovereignty of the soil, or (c) by the rule against perpetuities. Such result may also occur due to deliberate intent or by inadvertence or mistake.

It appears that in Kansas it is not possible to create a royalty interest apart from the mineral estate, except as to royalty payable under an existing lease.[23] The Kansas courts have held that the right

---

20. In re Randolph's Estate, 175 Kan. 685, 266 P.2d 315; in this case the court attempted to distinguish prior cases on the basis that in none of them did the court deal with the unaccrued royalty. Also see Hardcastle v. McCluskey, 139 Kan. 757, 33 P.2d 127.

21. Hanson v. Ware, 224 Ark. 430, 274 S.W.2d 359, 49 A.L.R.2d 1262; Callahan v. Martin, 3 Cal.2d 110, 43 P.2d 788, 101 A.L.R. 871; Humble Oil & Refining Co. v. Guillory, 212 La. 646, 33 So.2d 182; Gulf Refining Co. v. Stanford, 202 Miss. 602, 30 So.2d 516, 173 A.L.R. 1099; Schlittler v. Smith, 128 Tex. 628, 101 S.W.2d 543; Picard v. Richards, Wyo., 366 P.2d 119.

22. Schlittler v. Smith, 128 Tex. 628, 101 S.W.2d 543; and see Jones, Non-Participating Royalty, 26 Tex.L.R. 569. See Humble Oil & Refining Co. v. Guillory, 212 La. 646, 33 So.2d 182.

23. Leydig v. Commissioner, C.A.10th, 43 F.2d 494; Miller v. Sooy, 120 Kan. 81, 242 P. 140; Bellport v. Harrison, 123 Kan. 310, 255 P. 52; Lathrop v. Eyestone, 170 Kan. 419, 227 P.2d 136; Shepard v. John Hancock Mutual Life Insurance Co., 189 Kan. 125, 368 P.2d 19.

to royalty is in the nature of a contractual obligation enforceable against the lessee, which obligation will terminate when the respective lease terminates.[24] However, even in those jurisdictions that consider a royalty interest in the nature of real property, a party may cast the instrument in such form as to create merely a personal covenant where it is not in form to run with the land.[25]

Royalty may also be limited in duration to that of an existing lease due to the nature of the rights acquired in the land by the landowner at the time of the severance of the land from the sovereignty of the soil. For instance, the State of Texas has reserved the oil and gas in all lands which were classified as "mineral lands" and which were patented between September 1, 1895, and August 1, 1931, the effective date of the Sales Act of 1931.[26] Such lands are subject to the Relinquishment Act of 1919, which constitutes the landowner the agent of the State in leasing the lands. The landowner has the right to one-half of the economic benefits which are limited to the life of the particular lease. Any assignment of royalty will be so limited in duration, and the landowner has no power to create a perpetual royalty interest in such lands.[27] By 1942 the State of Texas had reserved the minerals underlying some 7,485,000 acres of land, and, of these, 7,400,000 are subject to the Act.

Under the Act the "owner of the soil" is the agent of the State of Texas for the purpose of leasing lands subject to the Act. In Glass v. Skelly Oil Co.,[28] the owner of the surface in fee, subject to the Act, devised the land to A for life, with the express right to lease. Remaindermen brought suit against the life tenant and the surviving spouse to determine the validity of a lease executed by defendants on behalf of the State, and also of plaintiff's right to participate in economic benefits under the lease. The court, in a decision of first im-

---

24. Bellport v. Harrison, 123 Kan. 310, 255 P. 52; Lathrop v. Eyestone, 170 Kan. 419, 227 P.2d 136. In the Bellport case all parties approved an instruction to the jury which defined royalty as "the compensation provided in oil and gas leases for the privilege of drilling for oil and gas, and consists of a share in the oil and gas produced under existing leases, but a royalty interest does not consist of a perpetual interest in the oil and gas as they lie in the ground. On the expiration of the existing leases the right of the owner of the royalty expires." The question in the case was whether a memorandum of a contract of sale concerned a royalty or mineral interest. The above statement was cited with approval in the Lathrop case.

25. See Callahan v. Martin, 3 Cal.2d 110, 43 P.2d 788, 101 A.L.R.2d 1262; In re Broome's Estate, 166 Cal.App.2d 488, 333 P.2d 273; and McIntosh v. Vail, 126 W.Va. 395, 28 S.E.2d 607, 151 A.L.R. 804.

26. Greene v. Robison, 117 Tex. 516, 8 S.W.2d 655.

27. Lewis v. Oates, 145 Tex. 77, 195 S.W.2d 123. Limitation of the landowner's rights may occur where the reservation of the mineral estate was made by a prior sovereign. This is true throughout the Southwest, where such reservations were made by prior Spanish and Mexican decrees. Such reservation by Mexico led directly to relinquishment provisions of the Texas Constitution of 1866. For a brief but splendid discussion of the era, see Hawkins, El Sal del Rey, Texas State Historical Association (1947).

28. Tex.Civ.App., 469 S.W.2d 237. Also the landowner has no standing to represent the State of Texas in an attempt to set aside a force pooling order of the Texas Railroad Commission involving in part lands covered by the Relinquishment Act, Exxon Corp. v. First National Bank of Midland, Tex.Civ.App., 529 S.W.2d 110, refused n. r. e.

pression, upheld the lease, in effect holding that the life tenant was the "owner of the soil" for purposes of the Act. The court stated that as the determination of the ultimate fee owners of the land was speculative, the intention of the testator would be carried out. No opinion was expressed on the situation where a testator created a life estate but did not expressly mention the right to lease.

As mentioned above, the third limitation upon the creation of a perpetual non-participating royalty interest is the possible application of the rule against perpetuities. Since the rule operates only against interests that are contingent in nature, in jurisdictions where royalty is considered to be real property in the nature of an incorporeal hereditament, a vested perpetual interest in royalty should not violate the rule.[29] Although the cases are few, this view is apparently followed in most jurisdictions. Kansas is an exception. In the case of Miller v. Sooy,[30] the Kansas Supreme Court viewed a deed granting "one-half of royalties, rentals, and bonuses to accrue under present or future leases" as creating a binding obligation in equity to convey royalty in the future. In the later case of Lathrop v. Eyestone,[31] the same court followed the Miller case and stated: "Moreover there is no limitation of time within which a future lease would be required to be executed. It is, therefore, wholly problematical when, if ever, such an interest would vest. Such a grant violates the rule against perpetuities, a rule against too remote vesting."

It may be questioned to what extent Kansas will follow this view. At least two cases [32] have treated the right to royalty as a real property interest, and in the case of Shepard v. John Hancock Mutual Life Insurance Co.,[33] the court avoided the perpetuity question by construing the deed involved as passing a mineral rather than a royalty interest.

---

29. Union Oil Co. of California v. Ogden, Tex.Civ.App., 278 S.W.2d 246. The court distinguishes the prior Kansas decisions by stating: "Unlike the situation in Kansas, it is settled in Arkansas that "royalties in gas or oil, until brought to the surface and reduced to possession are interests in real estate and not personal property."

Rousselot v. Spanier, 60 Cal.App.3d 238, 131 Cal.Rptr. 438. However, where the incident vesting the interest may occur in the indefinite future it has been held to violate the rule. See Cities Service Oil Co. v. Sohio Petroleum Co., W.D. Okl., 345 F.Supp. 28, containing the following provision:

"Any renewal, extension or new lease or leases covering the lands assigned herein acquired by Assignee or a third person wholly or partly for Assignee's benefit on said land shall be deemed to continue and preserve Assignor's rights reserved."

"The reservations, conditions and covenants of this conveyance shall run with the real estate herein described and shall be binding upon and enjoyed by the said Assignor and the said Assignee and their respective heirs, administrators, executors, devisees, successors and assigns."

The rule was violated as no limitation was placed upon the time period in which new leases could be executed upon which the overriding royalty would attach.

30. 120 Kan. 81, 242 P. 140.

31. 170 Kan. 419, 227 P.2d 136.

32. Hardcastle v. McCluskey, 139 Kan. 757, 33 P.2d 127; In re Randolph's Estate, 175 Kan. 685, 266 P.2d 315.

33. 189 Kan. 125, 368 P.2d 19.

§ 2.5 IN THE OIL AND GAS MINERAL ESTATE   59

Where a royalty interest is granted at a time when an oil and gas lease is outstanding, the grantor may expressly limit the royalty conveyed to production from the present lease.[34] Limitation of royalty to a presently outstanding lease at the time of the conveyance may also occur through inadvertence.[35] In the case of Keaton v. Murphy,[36] grantor did "grant, sell and convey an undivided ½ of ⅛th royalty held by Grantor in and to all of the oil and gas in, under the (described land) * * * subject to (description of outstanding lease) * * * and for such consideration does hereby grant and convey to grantee * * * ½ of ⅛ interest in all oil royalty * * * due us or may become due as under the aforesaid lease." The court held that the royalty interest conveyed was limited in duration to the outstanding lease. However, it was held to the contrary in the Texas case of Kaiser v. Love,[37] where the reservation was of "all the oil and gas rights in the above tract of land hereby conveyed, in the full terms set forth in an oil and gas lease executed to Breeding in 1915." In the Keaton case the draftsman apparently made the common mistake of trying to make everything crystal clear by doing the same thing twice. The reward of redundancy is often ambiguity. In Kaiser the draftsman apparently didn't see the problem.

The draftsman should pay particular attention to the form of the deed where it is desired to convey a perpetual non-participating royalty interest at a time when there is an outstanding lease on the property. As it is generally necessary to refer to the existing lease, care must be used that the reference will not limit the duration of the royalty conveyed.[38] If the language of limitation is ambiguous or vague, the limitation will probably be denied, by application of constructional rules that a deed be construed against the grantor so as to pass the greatest estate possible to the grantee.[39] Parol evidence may also be considered to determine intent of the parties.[40]

---

34. McNabb v. South Eastern Gas Co. of West Virginia, 268 Ky. 532, 105 S.W.2d 622; McWilliams v. Standard Oil Co., 205 Ark. 625, 170 S.W.2d 367; Morgan v. Farr, Ark., 614 S.W.2d 233; Iskian v. Consolidated Gas Utilities Corp., 207 Okl. 615, 251 P.2d 1073.

35. Keaton v. Murphy, 198 Ark. 799, 131 S.W.2d 625; Longino v. Machen, 217 Ark. 641, 232 S.W.2d 826; Kaiser v. Love, Tex.Civ.App., 352 S.W.2d 885, reversed 163 Tex. 558, 358 S.W.2d 586.

36. 198 Ark. 799, 131 S.W.2d 625.

37. Tex.Civ.App., 352 S.W.2d 885, reversed 163 Tex. 558, 358 S.W.2d 586.

38. Crowder v. James, 110 Okl. 214, 236 P. 891.

39. Dabney-Johnston Oil Corp. v. Walden, 4 Cal.2d 637, 52 P.2d 237; Kaiser v. Love, Tex.Civ.App., 352 S.W.2d 885, reversed 163 Tex. 558, 358 S.W.2d 586. In the Dabney case the court stated that the royalty grant would not be limited to the existing lease unless such intent was clearly and unequivocally indicated.

40. Crowder v. James, 110 Okl. 214, 236 P. 891.

(D) Nature of Production Accruing to a Royalty Interest—Federal Income Taxation and Separate-Community Property Status

For federal income tax purposes royalties from production are ordinary income subject to depletion in the year of receipt, being considered as a return of corpus from a wasting asset activity.[41]

In those jurisdictions which recognize ownership of community as well as separate property,[42] the problem is encountered whether royalty received during marriage produced from lands owned as separate property of one spouse will be treated as separate or community property. The community property states are not uniform in their treatment of such royalty. The status of royalty received from separately owned lands will depend upon the statutory and judicial treatment of profits, increase and produce from separate lands.[43] The conceptual treatment of such returns varies; in Texas[44] royalty from separate property is treated as corpus and partakes of the nature of the property from which it is produced, i.e., separate. In Louisiana, however, all income and returns from a lease of separate property are treated as community income.[45]

(E) Minimum Royalty and Shut-In Royalty

Minimum royalties and shut-in royalties are contractual rights to certain payments in lieu of actual production.[46] The minimum royalty is generally a minimum dollar amount stated in the oil and gas lease to be paid as royalty, although royalty payments from actual production may be less.[47] Shut-in royalties are dollar amounts stated in the oil and gas lease to be paid as royalty where a gas well has been completed capable of producing gas in paying quantities, but which has been shut in due to a lack of a pipe line connection.[48]

---

41. Sections 61, and 611, Internal Revenue Code of 1954 (26 U.S.C.A.), as amended, and see Alexander v. King, C.C.A.10th, 46 F.2d 235, cert. denied 283 U.S. 845, 51 S.Ct. 492, 75 L.Ed. 1455.

42. States that presently recognize separate and community property are: Arizona, California, Idaho, Louisiana, Nevada, New Mexaco, Texas, and Washington.

43. It is felt that more than a brief mention of the problem is outside the scope of this book.

44. Norris v. Vaughan, 152 Tex. 491, 260 S.W.2d 676.

45. Milling v. Collector of Revenue, 220 La. 773, 57 So.2d 679.

46. See Chapter 7.

47. See Producers Pipe & Supply Co. v. James, Okl., 332 P.2d 958; Morriss v. First National Bank of Mission, Tex.Civ. App., 249 S.W.2d 269.

48. As it is impractical to store gas in any quantity above the surface of the ground, where gas is discovered at a time when there is no gathering line in the vicinity, and in those jurisdictions that require marketing within the definition of production, the shut in royalty is paid to keep the lease alive after the expiration of the primary term until actual production is commenced. Texas is the prime example of such a jurisdiction.

In the few cases dealing with the nature of minimum and shut in royalties such, although usually payable as a fixed sum, payments have been classified as royalties, not bonus or rentals.[49]

§ 2.6 Attributes of the Mineral Estate—The Problem of Whether Payments Out of Production Constitute Bonus or Royalty

In those situations where the right to bonus is owned by one person and a right to royalty by another, or by several persons in non-equal amounts, a problem has arisen as to the nature of payments to be made out of production by the lessee. Although case law is meager, it is apparent that if a payment is an interest in production, not chargeable with expenses of development, operations, or production, and is payable throughout the life of a lease, it will be considered to be a royalty payment.

On the other hand, where the payment is limited in amount and is certain to pay out, or for which there exists an absolute obligation to pay, it will be considered as bonus. A limited payment out of production that will never pay out will probably be considered to be royalty.

In some instances the terms "royalty" and "bonus" have been considered sufficiently ambiguous to allow the consideration of parol evidence.

As stated above,[1] bonus may be defined as a sum paid for the execution of an oil and gas lease, whereas royalty represents the landowner's share in the fruits of any oil and gas development activity. Broadly defined both may be said to be a return or consideration to the landowner for an oil and gas lease.[2] In those instances where payment of bonus is to be paid out of future production, the line between bonus and royalty grows dim insofar as the form of payment is concerned.[3] It is not surprising that an area of litigation has developed whether payments made by the lessee to the landowner constitute bonus or royalty.[4] Problems as to the nature of such payments

---

49. Carlisle v. United Producing Co., C.A.10th, 278 F.2d 893 (shut in royalty); Producers Pipe & Supply Co. v. James, Okl., 332 P.2d 958; Morriss v. First National Bank of Mission, Tex.Civ.App., 249 S.W.2d 269 (minimum royalty).

1. See supra, §§ 2.4, and 2.5. See argument of appellant in Masterson v. Gulf Oil Corp., Tex.Civ.App., 301 S.W.2d 486, to the effect that bonus, royalty, and rentals are all of the same basic nature, but made in lieu of each other.

2. Geller v. Smith, 130 Cal.App. 485, 20 P.2d 102; State National Bank of Corpus Christi v. Morgan, 135 Tex. 509, 143 S.W.2d 757; Sykes v. Dillingham, Okl., 318 P.2d 416, noted in 11 Okl.L.Rev. 225; Probst v. Ingram, Okl., 373 P.2d 58; Griffith v. Taylor, 156 Tex. 1, 291 S.W.2d 673, noted in 35 Tex.L.Rev. 459.

3. See Twentieth Century-Fox Film Corp. v. Teas, C.A.5th, 286 F.2d 373, cert. denied 368 U.S. 818, 82 S.Ct. 32, 7 L.Ed. 2d 24; Texas Co. v. Fontenot, 200 La. 753, 8 So.2d 689.

4. Some litigation has occurred in other areas such as whether a payment is a delay rental or a royalty. See Morriss v. First National Bank of Mission, Tex.Civ. App., 249 S.W.2d 269; and Carlisle v. United Producing Co., C.A.10th, 278 F.2d 893, the latter holding that a shut in royalty payment, in the same amount as delay rentals payable under a lease, is a royalty interest and not a delay rental. From the landowner's standpoint, bonus payable out of production and royalty are ordinary income subject to either cost or percentage depletion, whichever is greater. However, if classified as bonus, the payments must be capitalized by the lessee as cost of the lease, and recovered through depletion. Royalty, on the other hand, is deducted from the lessee's gross income and passed through to the lessor.

have arisen in connection with determining the burden of severance and production taxes,[5] operation of the proportionate reduction clause under an oil and gas lease,[6] the nature of a salesman's commission,[7] and the right of various persons to share, where the right to royalty and bonus are held by persons in different proportions.[8]

A common situation may occur somewhat as follows: O, the owner of Blackacre in fee, executes and delivers to A a deed conveying a non-participating royalty interest equal to one-half of royalty payable under future leases. At the time there is no lease outstanding. Under this conveyance A has a right to share in the production of oil and gas if, as and when produced, and usually [9] has no right to lease, or share in bonus or delay rental payments. Assuming that the property is located in a "hot" producing area, O desires to lease but does not desire to receive all of the rather substantial bonus money in the year of lease, as this would have a detrimental effect on his tax situation.[10] Lessee therefore provides that most of the bonus is to be paid out of future production and includes a clause in the lease: "Lessor shall receive, as deferred bonus, $1/16$th of $7/8$th of all of the oil, gas and other minerals produced under this lease, free of cost and expense, until he shall have received the amount of $120,000.00." Is A entitled to one-half of these payments?

Little consistency is found in the cases. It should be observed that parties to a deed conveying limited rights to the mineral estate have full freedom to define the economic benefits in which each will share from existing and future leases. A's understanding of the "royalty" he may participate in through his deed may be entirely different from O's understanding of the nature of certain payments to be made under the lease. The problem here is one of adequate defini-

---

5. Texas Co. v. Fontenot, 200 La. 753, 8 So.2d 689; Sheppard v. Stanolind Oil & Gas Co., Tex.Civ.App., 125 S.W.2d 643.

6. Probst v. Ingram, Okl., 373 P.2d 58; McMahon v. Christmann, 157 Tex. 403, 303 S.W.2d 341.

7. Geller v. Smith, 130 Cal.App. 485, 20 P.2d 102.

8. Twentieth Century-Fox Film Corp. v. Teas, C.A.5th, 286 F.2d 373, cert. denied 368 U.S. 818, 82 S.Ct. 33, 7 L.Ed.2d 24; Wright v. Brush, C.C.A.10th, 115 F.2d 265; Patterson v. Texas Co., C.C.A. 5th, 131 F.2d 998, cert. denied 319 U.S. 761, 63 S.Ct. 1318, 87 L.Ed. 1712; State ex rel. Fatzer v. Board of Regents, 176 Kan. 179, 269 P.2d 425; Sykes v. Dillingham, Okl., 318 P.2d 416, noted in 11 Okl. L.Rev. 225; State National Bank of Corpus Christi v. Morgan, 135 Tex. 509, 143 S.W.2d 757; Griffith v. Taylor, 156 Tex. 1, 291 S.W.2d 673, noted in 35 Tex.L. Rev. 459; Morriss v. First National Bank of Mission, Tex.Civ.App., 249 S.W.2d 269.

9. The further assumption is made here that the term "royalty" as used only designates an interest in production, see § 2.5 supra.

10. The situation may also arise where the lessor tries to increase the benefits to himself in a situation where he has considerable bargaining power by placing them in the form of deferred bonus rather than royalty. See § 2.2(D), supra. May A rely upon the statement of the Texas court in the case of Schlittler v. Smith: "There is nothing whatever to indicate that the royalty to be reserved was the usual one-eighth, although very likely neither of the parties thought it would be less. We think that self-interest on the part of the grantee (who had the power to lease) may be trusted to protect the grantor (the holder of a reserved non-participating royalty) as to the amount of royalty reserved."?

tion in the deed. For instance, in the above example, if A's attorney had defined in the deed the term "royalty" to include "any payments to be made to lessor out of production under future leases, whether or not limited in amount," A would share in O's reserved payment without regard to the label placed upon it by the parties to the lease. Unfortunately, in many of the cases the terms, "royalty," "overriding royalty," "bonus," etc., are used without further definition.[11]

In attempting to distinguish between bonus paid out of future production and royalty, an early approach was to classify all payments to be received by the lessor over his "normal royalty." In Sheppard v. Stanolind Oil & Gas Co.,[12] lessor was paid a $1/6$th royalty, a cash bonus, and additional sums "to be paid out of $1/6$ of $5/6$ of first oil and gas produced." The issue involved was whether, for gross production tax purposes, the additional payment out of production stood on the same footing as royalty. In answering the question in the affirmative, the court stated that "bonus was merely a convenient term applied indiscriminately to consideration for leases received over and above the usual royalty," and further defined bonus as involving an absolute liability to pay. The later case of State National Bank of Corpus Christi v. Morgan[13] followed the Sheppard case and classified as bonus payments to be made out of production in excess of the normal royalty. The court said: "The usual royalty is $1/8$. Applying this definition the difference between $1/8$ and $1/6$ would come within this definition of bonus. * * * The fact stated in the foregoing quotation that the usual royalty in oil and gas leases is $1/8$, is in our opinion one so generally known that judicial knowledge may be taken of it. * * * The quotation illustrates, however, the difficulty of drawing a distinct line of demarcation between bonus and royalty, for it shows that the difference between the usual $1/8$ royalty and the $1/6$ royalty comes within the definition of bonus and may be properly termed a *royalty bonus*." (emphasis supplied)

To treat all sums payable in excess of the "normal" royalty as bonus is unsound. For the court to take judicial knowledge of a particular "normal" royalty will deprive parties of contractual freedom to create a royalty in excess of this amount. Although the usual royalty provided in oil and gas leases in Texas is $1/8$, this amount is not sacrosanct. In the last analysis the amount of royalty to be paid by a lessee depends upon the bargaining power of the parties.

---

11. The secret, if any, of good draftsmanship, is first the definitive understanding by the draftsman of his subject matter, and second the stating of his understanding in clear and concise language. The first is essential for the second. In the oil and gas field a lack of understanding of the essential nature of basic interests dealt with is probably the most common cause of litigation.

12. Tex.Civ.App., 125 S.W.2d 643.

13. 135 Tex. 509, 143 S.W.2d 757. It is unfortunate that the court chose to call a bonus payable out of production a "royalty bonus."

The approach of the Morgan case has been rejected by the Texas Supreme Court in the case of Griffith v. Taylor,[14] which classified as royalty an additional payment of $1/16$th of production to be made to lessor as "additional consideration and bonus royalty." The court correctly held that parties to a deed may designate the economic benefits or returns in which they might share. Recognizing the fact that bonus to be paid out of future production and royalty were overlapping concepts, the court distinguished between them on the basis that royalty is a sum continuing throughout the life of the lease, and that bonus is a sum certain to be paid out of cash or production.

In Texas, therefore, a payment out of production will constitute bonus if there exists an absolute obligation to pay, or the sum is certain to be paid out of production. It will constitute royalty, however, if the sum is payable throughout the life of the lease. In fact, a limited payment out of production is properly considered royalty if it may be shown that the sum is so large that the reserves are insufficient for it ever to pay out.[15]

In some instances the terms "royalty" and "bonus" have been found sufficiently ambiguous so as to allow the use of parol evidence in an attempt to determine intent.[16] In the Oklahoma case of Sykes v. Dillingham,[17] grantee was conveyed an undivided $1/4$ mineral interest, with the provision that grantor should have "one-half of the bonus money derived from the sale of an oil and gas lease or extension of the same on the above land." Under a later extension lease a provision was made for the payment of a royalty equal to $46/256$. As the normal $1/8$ royalty equals $32/256$, the lease royalty exceeded the custom-

---

14. 156 Tex. 1, 291 S.W.2d 673, noted in 35 Tex.L.Rev. 459. Here the draftsman had apparently read the Morgan case and tried to follow it in the preparation of the deed! Also see: Delta Drilling Co. v. Simmons, 161 Tex. 122, 338 S.W.2d 143, and Lane v. Elkins, Tex.Civ. App., 441 S.W.2d 871, refused n. r. e.

15. Ample authority for such result exists in the field of federal income taxation in distinguishing between a "sale" and a "lease" of an oil and gas property on the basis of whether, upon transfer of the property a continuing interest in production is retained. The transaction will constitute a lease where a continuing interest is reserved or where the reserved interest is in the form of a limited production payment, but which, in fact, will never pay out. If the reserved interest will actually have a duration less than the life of the oil and gas lease out of which it is reserved, a sale will result. If holding period requirements are satisfied, the transaction may be taxed as a long term capital gain rather than ordinary income. The distinction was the basis of the so-called "ABC transaction." In order to insure such termination it may be provided that, in any event, the reserved interest terminates when reserves are reduced to a stated minimum figure, whether or not the interest has then paid out. Although no case has been found applying this technique to a reserved interest by the lessor, it might be advantageous in jurisdictions following the approach stated in Griffith v. Taylor.

16. Some jurisdictions follow the so-called "four corner rule" of construction, whereby monumental efforts are made to harmonize all parts of a written instrument without consideration of parol evidence, on the premise that no ambiguity exists. In such jurisdictions, if royalty and bonus are thought to have judicially definable meanings, parol evidence would probably be excluded. See Murphy v. Dilworth, 137 Tex. 32, 151 S.W.2d 1004; Garrett v. Dils Co., 157 Tex. 92, 299 S.W.2d 904.

17. Okl., 318 P.2d 416, noted in 11 Okl.L.Rev. 225.

ary royalty by $^{14}/_{256}$. In holding this excess to be bonus in which the grantor could participate, the court considered parol evidence of the conduct of the parties, the surrounding circumstances, and the customs of the area. It was concluded that such evidence established that the parties to the deed contemplated royalty to mean that which was ordinary and customary in the area.

Parol evidence was also allowed in the recent case of Twentieth Century Fox Film Corp. v. Teas.[18] Landowner contracted that plaintiff would receive $8^1/_3\%$ of future production, together with 50% of future bonus or rental payments. Subsequently, landowner executed a lease providing (1) for a basic royalty of 20% of production, which included plaintiff's $8^1/_3\%$ royalty to be paid directly to plaintiff, and (2) for a "variable participating royalty" equal to one-half of lessee's net profits. The question involved was the extent to which plaintiff could participate in the basic royalty over $8^1/_3\%$ and in the variable royalty. Upon trial it was held that plaintiff could share to the extent of one-half of both the 20% basic royalty and the variable royalty. On appeal the court held that the term "royalty" as used by the parties to the contract referred to the character, rather than the quantity, of payments in which the plaintiff would not share, and that under the contract plaintiff would not share in royalty payments in excess of $8^1/_3\%$. Although the 20% basic royalty exceeds the normal royalty,[19] it was clearly royalty payment, as it constituted an interest measured by gross production; would bear no part of the cost of development, operations, or production; and would last throughout the life of the lease. As to basic royalty, the approach of the court is consistent with that of Griffith v. Taylor.

The court reversed, however, as to the variable royalty, on the grounds that such payments were bonus. The court observed that the variable royalty was only payable out of net profits, would not necessarily be payable out of each and every barrel of oil produced, and was only payable after deduction of all operating and development costs. Parol evidence was allowed of a custom that all incidental benefits received by the lessor as consideration for the lease, other than royalty, are considered bonus.

§ 2.7 Attributes of the Mineral Estate—Interests Created When Fractional Interests Are Conveyed or Reserved

In most jurisdictions, bonus, delay rentals, and royalty may be severed and sold, in various combinations and variations, apart from the remainder of the mineral estate. Questions constantly arise concerning construction of instruments encountered during an historical title search and language to be used in instrument preparation. Such

---

18. C.A.5th, 286 F.2d 373, cert. denied 368 U.S. 818, 82 S.Ct. 33, 7 L.Ed.2d 24.

19. The normal or customary landowner's royalty provided in leases executed in California is $^1/_6$th or $16^2/_3\%$ of gross production.

constructional problems relate to the nature of the rights involved as well as to the quantum of production to which the holder of a particular interest may be entitled.

Unfortunately, a great lack of uniformity exists in verbiage which has been used to convey or reserve interests in the mineral estate. Such lack of uniformity may have been caused by uncertainty as to language necessary to create desired interests, or, where certainty of language exists, may be due to inability to use such language, by reason of heedlessness or ignorance. At any rate, the variations in form of conveyances of interests in the landowner's mineral estate are legion.

It is impossible, within the scope of this book, to attempt to catalogue all of the variations that may exist. To one engaged in an historical title search, any particular instrument encountered will have to be studied in relation to the law of the jurisdiction involved to determine the course to be taken in interpretation of the interests created, as well as any steps that may be necessary to cure the title. However, certain broad patterns have emerged, which, when recognized, should aid the draftsman in creating the desired interests, as well as providing an approach to interpretations of an existing instrument.

(A) Interests Created—Mineral or Royalty?

Due to separate alienability of the various rights that compose the mineral estate, and the fact that conveyances and reservations of such rights are found in varying combinations, difficult problems of construction have arisen as to the nature of fractional interests created. Some broad patterns have emerged.

At the outset, it may be asked which is the more valuable interest: a fractional $1/8$ interest in the minerals, fully participating in all economic benefits, or a fractional $1/8$ interest in gross production? The owner of the mineral interest will participate in a number of economic benefits derived from the mineral estate. For instance, if O conveys to A an undivided $1/8$ fully participating interest in the minerals, A will be entitled, upon lease, to the bonus and delay rentals which he may negotiate for the leasing of such interest, as well as $1/8$ of the landowner's royalty customarily provided. If the customary royalty is $1/8$ of gross production, A will receive $1/8$ of $1/8$, or $1/64$, of production, free of costs of development and production. On the other hand, the owner of a $1/8$ interest in gross production only, will receive such fraction of gross production, free of costs, but will not share in other economic benefits to be derived from the lease or leasing transaction.

Obviously, no categorical answer can be given to the question posed, as the benefits to be derived depend upon the geophysical nature of the area in which such interest may be located. In a highly productive area, the right to $1/8$ of gross production would be highly desirable. On the other hand, in an unproved area the fully partici-

§ 2.7   IN THE OIL AND GAS MINERAL ESTATE

pating interest may provide the more valuable economic benefits. Although the right to gross production may be eight times smaller, i.e., $1/64$ as compared to $1/8$, the further right to a cash bonus for the execution of a lease and entitlement to delay rentals, paid after lease and prior to production, may well offset decreased royalty income (if any). This, of course, may occur where development is delayed, where the land is leased several times (specially if of large acreage), or where production is marginal or non-existent.

Apart from the question of the economic value of an interest, the problem to be considered is whether a grant or reservation creates a fully participating mineral interest or a right limited to a fractional share of gross production.

The cases usually involve the following typical clauses in grants and reservations:

(1) "an undivided _____ interest in and to all of the oil, gas and other minerals in, under, and that may be produced from the described land together with the right of ingress and egress for the purpose of entering, developing and producing same."

(2) same as (1) above, without the right of ingress and egress.

(3) "an undivided _____ interest in and to all of the oil, gas and other minerals that may be produced from the described land."

(4) same as (3), above, with a right of ingress and egress.

(5) "an undivided _____ royalty interest in and to the oil, gas, and other minerals in, under, and that may be produced from the land described."

(6) "an undivided _____ royalty interest in and to all of the oil, gas and other minerals produced and saved from the land described."

(7) same as (5) and (6), above, with rights of ingress and egress.

(8) "an undivided _____ interest in and to all of the oil royalty and gas royalty that may be produced from the described land."

(9) "an undivided _____ interest in and to all of the oil royalty and gas royalty, and the rights thereto, that may be produced from the described lands."

(10) "an undivided _____ interest in all of the oil, gas and other minerals, in and under the land, with grantor reserving the right to lease, bonus moneys and delay rentals."

As a background to an understanding of the cases, it will be helpful to survey the various approaches to interpretation applied by the courts in the oil and gas producing states:

(1) Whether, looking at the instrument as a whole, it expresses an intent that the interest be cost bearing or free of costs. This

can be found from direct language in the instrument or implied from the presence or omission of statements relating to the right to discover or produce, to lease, rentals, and bonus.

(2) Whether the language of the instrument indicates an interest in place in the ground (mineral) or only after produced (royalty), a mechanical approach.

(3) That the term "royalty" has a definite meaning, indicating only an interest in gross production equal to the fraction stated, or to the percentage of royalty provided for in later leases. This interest would not share in bonus, delay rentals or the right to lease.

(4) A lingering construction of the terms "royalty" and "profits" as indicating a mineral interest. This conclusion follows the common law concept that a conveyance of the profits of the land is a conveyance of the land itself.

(5) Treat the words as ambiguous and allow parol evidence to determine intent.

(6) Any combination of the above.

(B) Conveyances of "Oil and Gas in, under, and that may be Produced from * * * "

It is generally held that a conveyance of the "minerals" or "mineral rights" will designate a fully participating mineral interest, whether or not express rights of ingress and egress are included. Some courts, especially in ownership jurisdictions, have given weight to words indicating that an interest in the ground has been created.

It appears that in all jurisdictions a grant or reservation in the form of "a fractional undivided interest in and to all of the oil, gas and other minerals in, under, and that may be produced from the following described land," will grant or reserve a fractional fully participating mineral interest.[1] In reaching this conclusion, ownership-in-place jurisdictions have placed emphasis on the presence of language indicating that the grant or reservation is of minerals "in or under"

---

1. Little v. Mountain View Dairies, 35 Cal.2d 232, 217 P.2d 416; Simson v. Langholf, 133 Colo. 208, 293 P.2d 302; Gallin v. Combs, Ky., 341 S.W.2d 778; Horn v. Skelly Oil Co., 224 La. 709, 70 So.2d 657; Phillips Petroleum Co. v. Richard, La.App., 127 So.2d 816; Stokes v. Tutvet, 134 Mont. 250, 328 P.2d 1096; Smith v. County of Musselshell, 155 Mont. 376, 472 P.2d 878; Manley v. Boling, 186 Okl. 59, 96 P.2d 30; Coker v. Hudspeth, Okl. 308 P.2d 291; Murphy v. Dilworth, 137 Tex. 32, 151 S.W.2d 1004. However, see: Extraction Resources, Inc. v. Freeman, Tex.Civ.App., 555 S.W.2d 156, refused n.r.e. It was held that where the only interest owned by the grantor was a non-participating royalty interest, conveyances in this form conveyed a royalty interest. Interestingly, the grantor here owned a $1/16$th royalty interest and executed 366 deeds, each of which purported to convey a $1/64$ royalty!

A variation on the "in and under" language that has been universally held to denote a mineral interest is a grant or reservation of "oil and gas deposits." In Hinkle v. Gauntt, 201 Okl. 432, 206 P.2d 1001, this was held to indicate an intention to reserve a mineral interest, and the court applied "an interest in place in the ground" rationale.

§ 2.7 IN THE OIL AND GAS MINERAL ESTATE

the ground,[2] or similar language, which indicates that the conveyance is of minerals in place. On the other hand, in non-ownership states,[3] where it is not possible to own minerals in place, such language is given little weight as a factor to be considered in determining whether a grant or reservation creates less than a fully participating mineral interest. Notwithstanding the absence of such language, in both ownership and non-ownership jurisdictions a grant or reservation in descriptive terms of the mineral estate, such as "minerals," "mineral estate," or "mineral rights," will usually be construed as indicating an intent that a fully participating mineral interest is being dealt with.[4]

As a fully participating mineral interest creates rights of occupancy and use of the mineral estate, it is customary to include in the instrument, in addition to the above language, an express grant of easement rights across the surface for development purposes.[5] However, the omission of an express grant of easement rights should not cause the interest to be construed as being less than a fully participating mineral interest, unless specific intent to so limit the grant or reservation otherwise appears in the instrument.[6] As a mineral inter-

2. See Stokes v. Tutvet, 134 Mont. 250, 328 P.2d 1096; Smith v. County of Musselshell, 155 Mont. 376, 472 P.2d 878; Murphy v. Dilworth, 137 Tex. 32, 151 S.W.2d 1004; but cf. Miller v. Speed, Tex. Civ.App., 248 S.W.2d 250.

3. Little v. Mountain View Dairies, 35 Cal.2d 232, 217 P.2d 416. But see Jolly v. Wilson, Okl., 478 P.2d 886; Swearingen v. Oldham, 195 Okl. 532, 159 P.2d 247 (1945); and Hinkle v. Gauntt, 201 Okl. 432, 206 P.2d 1001 ("oil and gas deposits").

4. Amundson v. Gordon, 134 Mont. 142, 328 P.2d 630; Klein v. Humble Oil & Refining Co., 126 Tex. 450, 86 S.W.2d 1077. Also see: Smith v. Anisman, La. App., 85 So.2d 351 ("mineral acres"); Starling v. Preston, Tex.Civ.App., 144 S.W.2d 1009 ("oil and gas rights"); Amundson v. Gordon, 134 Mont. 142, 328 P.2d 630, and Martin v. Snuggs, Tex.Civ. App., 302 S.W.2d 676 ("oil and mineral rights"); but see Voyta v. Clonts, 134 Mont. 156, 328 P.2d 655 ("mineral rights" held to denote a royalty interest in reservation in deed executed when oil and gas lease outstanding). However, modifying intent may be found in other parts of the instrument, see Picard v. Richards, Wyo., 366 P.2d 119. Such general language is uncertain at best, and conformity to judicially accepted verbiage is strongly recommended, see Barnett v. Morris, 207 Ark. 761, 182 S.W.2d 765.

5. Such clause is often found in simple form following the description of the property: " * * * , together with the right of ingress and egress for the purpose of prospecting, mining, developing and producing the same." It may be observed that the scope of this clause is much less than that customarily found in an oil and gas lease: " * * * for the purpose of testing, by any method or methods, for formations or structures investigating, exploring, prospecting, drilling and mining for and producing the gas, and other minerals, laying pipe lines, and other structures thereon, to produce, save, take care of, treat, transport, and own said products, and housing its employees, and for dredging and maintaining canals, constructing and maintaining roads and bridges, and, in general, for all appliances or structures, equipment, servitudes and privileges which may be necessary, useful or convenient in connection with any such operations conducted by lessee, * * * ." See Summers, Oil and Gas, § 1302. The suggestion has been made that the prudent person acquiring a fully participating mineral interest from the owner of the fee title should include such grant of rights as may be described in oil and gas leases to be executed. However, such clause may cause some initial difficulties in negotiations with landowners who do not understand the purpose for its inclusion.

6. Early Oklahoma cases drew a sharp distinction between grants and reservations of mineral interests. Where rights of ingress and egress were omit-

est carries with it rights to possession and development, in the event that express rights of entry are omitted, such rights as are reasonably necessary for the exploration, development, and production of the petroleum products will be implied by law.[7]

(C) Conveyances of "Royalty"

In many jurisdictions a grant or reservation of a "royalty" interest will be interpreted as creating a non-cost bearing interest that will share only in a fractional portion of gross production, and will not participate in bonus, delay rentals, or the power to lease.

In a few jurisdictions, notably Oklahoma, the term "royalty" is treated as being uncertain in meaning. Circumstances surrounding the transaction will bear on the supposed intent of the parties. Generally speaking, a grant of a "royalty" interest made at a time when no lease is in existence will be construed as denoting a fully participating mineral interest. However, if a lease is outstanding at the time intent will be construed in the narrow sense as indicating an interest that will share only in gross production. It is submitted that a treatment of the term "royalty" as uncertain in meaning is unsound.

To reserve or convey an interest limited only to sharing in a fractional part of gross production, an intention to grant or reserve less than a full mineral interest must appear in the instrument. As mentioned above, merely omitting the express right of ingress and egress from a grant or reservation of what otherwise is a fully participating mineral interest is generally not sufficient to accomplish this result. As an interest limited to sharing only in a part of gross production is commonly referred to as a royalty interest, many instruments are found which convey or reserve an interest which is designated as a "royalty interest." For example, O may convey to A "an undivided $1/16$ royalty interest" or "an undivided one-half of royalty" in the oil and gas. What is the extent of A's interest?

In many jurisdictions the word "royalty" has a definite and unambiguous meaning denoting a fractional interest in production, free of costs and expense, which will not share or participate in bonus, delay rentals, or the power to lease.[8] Such view is typified by the Texas

---

ted from a grant of a mineral interest, it was held that the grant was void. However, if the rights of ingress and egress were omitted from a reservation of a mineral interest, the reservation was treated as valid, and the rights would be implied. Newbern v. Gould, 162 Okl. 82, 19 P.2d 157 and Morgan v. Mc Gee, 117 Okl. 212, 245 P. 888. This distinction is no longer followed, and whether a mineral interest is granted or reserved, the rights of ingress and egress for development will be implied. Melton v. Sneed, 188 Okl. 388, 109 P.2d 509 and Burns v. Bastien, 174 Okl. 40, 50 P.2d 377.

7. Such implied rights are akin to easements by necessity implied to one acquiring property surrounded by property of the grantor and to which there is no entry way. See Hurley v. Northern Pacific Railway Co., 153 Mont. 199, 455 P.2d 321; Gulf Pipe Line Co. v. Pawnee Tulsa Petroleum Co., 34 Okl. 775, 127 P. 252; Gulf Production Co. v. Continental Oil Co., 139 Tex. 183, 132 S.W.2d 553, and cf. Getty Oil Co. v. Royal, Tex.Civ.App., 422 S.W.2d 591, weighing relative inconvenience to the parties.

8. *Arkansas:* Longino v. Machen, 217 Ark. 641, 232 S.W.2d 826; *California:*

case of Schlittler v. Smith,[9] where, in holding that a reservation of an undivided one-half interest in "royalty rights" did not include the right to bonus or delay rentals, the court stated: "The words 'royalty,' 'bonus,' and 'rentals' have a well-understood meaning in the oil and gas business. Likewise, 'minerals' and 'mineral rights' have a well-recognized meaning. Broadly speaking, a reservation of minerals or mineral rights without limitation would include royalties, bonuses, and rentals. A conveyance of land without reservations would include all minerals or mineral rights. However, it is well settled that a grantor may reserve minerals or mineral rights and he may also reserve royalties, bonuses, and rentals, either one, more or all. Here we have a reservation of only 'royalty rights.' It is obvious, it seems to us, that this does not include a reservation of bonuses or rentals, but only of an interest in oil, gas, or minerals paid, received, or realized as 'royalty' under any lease existing on the land at the time of the reservation, or thereafter executed by the grantee, his heirs, or assigns. A reservation of 'royalty' on all oil, gas, and minerals which may be produced necessarily implies that the grantor contemplated the leasing of the land for production. He reserved no right of leasing to himself, and consequently the grantee possesses such right."

In Kansas, the term "royalty" also has a definite meaning as including only a portion of gross production. However, in Kansas the royalty is restricted to royalty payable under an existing lease.[10] This view was established in the landmark Kansas case of Bellport v. Harrison.[11] In this case the plaintiff attempted to enlarge his rights

---

Callahan v. Martin, 3 Cal.2d 110, 43 P.2d 788, 101 A.L.R. 871; Dabney-Johnston Oil Corp. v. Walden, 4 Cal.2d 637, 52 P.2d 237, however, the exact nature of the royalty interest is somewhat uncertain as the courts tend to speak of the royalty owner as a "cotenant" with the other owners of the mineral estate, which may imply broader rights than normally attributed to such interest; *Kansas*: Bellport v. Harrison, 123 Kan. 310, 255 P. 52; *Kentucky*: Texas Co. v. Bowen, 292 Ky. 676, 167 S.W.2d 822; Lively v. Federal Land Bank of Louisville, 296 Ky. 133, 176 S.W.2d 264; *Louisiana*: Gulf Refining Co. v. Goode, 212 La. 502, 32 So.2d 904; and see, Cormier v. Ferguson, La.App., 92 So.2d 507; *Mississippi*: Palmer v. Crews, 203 Miss. 806, 35 So.2d 430, 4 A.L.R.2d 483; and see Payne v. Campbell, 250 Miss. 227, 164 So.2d 780; *Montana*: see Stokes v. Tutvet, 134 Mont. 250, 328 P.2d 1096, but some uncertainty appears in the cases; *North Dakota*: Corbett v. LaBere, N.D., 68 N.W.2d 211; *New Mexico*: Duval v. Stone, 54 N.M. 27, 213 P.2d 212; *Texas*: Schlittler v. Smith, 128 Tex. 628, 101 S.W.2d 543; Watkins v. Slaughter, 144 Tex. 179, 189 S.W.2d 699; Arnold v. Ashbel Smith Land Co., Tex.Civ.App., 307 S.W.2d 818; *West Virginia*: Davis v. Hardman, 148 W.Va. 82, 133 S.E.2d 77; *Wyoming*: It is hard to tell the position of the Wyoming courts from the case of Picard v. Richards, Wyo., 366 P.2d 119. However, it is placed here with the hope that this is an accurate prediction. The court cites cases from jurisdictions in which royalty has a definite meaning and those in which it does not, in equal measure. It may be that the tone of the decision is to the latter, which the author considers unsound.

9. 128 Tex. 628, 101 S.W.2d 543.

10. Bellport v. Harrison, 123 Kan. 310, 255 P. 52; Lathrop v. Eyestone, 170 Kan. 419, 227 P.2d 136; Davis v. Hurst, 150 Kan. 130, 90 P.2d 1100, 122 A.L.R. 957; Shepard v. John Hancock Mutual Life Insurance Co., 189 Kan. 125, 368 P.2d 19; Corbin v. Moser, 195 Kan. 252, 403 P.2d 800.

11. 123 Kan. 310, 255 P. 52. However, see Shepard v. John Hancock Mutual

under a conveyance of a "$^1/_{16}$ royalty" to that of a mineral interest, on the ground that the term "royalty" was definite and unambiguous and related only to production under a specific lease which had expired. Apparently, it is not possible to create a perpetual non-participating royalty interest in Kansas.

Other jurisdictions, however, have treated the terms "mineral" and "royalty" as being ambiguous or uncertain of meaning [12] and will consider the surrounding circumstances and the acts of the parties in determining intent.

As mentioned above, in Oklahoma, as in most jurisdictions, a grant or reservation in the form of,

> "an undivided ½ interest in and to all of the oil, gas and other minerals, in, under, and that may be produced from the described land, together with the right of ingress and egress for the purpose of entering, developing and producing same,"

will pass a mineral interest whether or not a lease is outstanding at the time. This is true whether or not the right of ingress and egress is included.

However, Oklahoma also has followed the West Virginia rule equating profits to a mineral interest in certain circumstances, where not restricted by the wording of the instrument. The court in Burns v. Bastien,[13] quoted from the West Virginia case of Toothman v. Courtney.[14]

> his reservation of all the rental or royalty to be derived from it compels the court to hold, by construction of the instrument, that it vests in him the title to that thing, the beneficial use whereof has been reserved, namely, the oil in place. Jarman on Wills, * * * says: A devise of rents and profits or of the income of land passes the land itself both at law and in equity—a rule, it is said founded on the feudal law, according to which the whole ben-

Life Insurance Co., 189 Kan. 125, 368 P.2d 19, where the court in effect reformed a conveyance of a royalty interest to a mineral interest to avoid the effect of the rule against perpetuities.

12. Simson v. Langholf, 133 Colo. 208, 293 P.2d 302; Corlett v. Cox, 138 Colo. 325, 333 P.2d 619; Carroll v. Bowen, 180 Okl. 215, 68 P.2d 773. This view is apparently based on early West Virginia cases such as Paxton v. Benedum-Trees Oil Co., 80 W.Va. 187, 94 S.E. 472, and Toothman v. Courtney, 62 W.Va. 167, 58 S.E. 915, which followed the common law rule equating ownership of profits from land to ownership of land itself. This view appears to be overruled by the case of Davis v. Hardman, 148 W.Va. 82, 133 S.E.2d 77. The viewpoint of the Colorado courts is uncertain, but the rationale of the Cox case seems strongly oriented to the Oklahoma approach, which is unfortunate. Also see: Burns v. Bastien, 174 Okl. 40, 50 P.2d 377.

13. 174 Okl. 40, 50 P.2d 377. Also see discussion at § 2.7(F)(1), infra.

Note: The material from here to footnote 85 is an excerpt from Hemingway, The Mineral-Royalty Distinction in Oklahoma, 52 O.B.J. 2791 (Nov. 28, 1981), reprinted with permission of the Oklahoma Bar Association.

The author would also like to acknowledge the assistance of Mrs. Marian G. Pfenning in the preparation of this material.

14. 62 W.Va. 167, 58 S.E. 915.

eficial interest in land consisted of the right to take the rents and profits * * *.

> * * * if there had been no lease on the land, I would be of the same opinion, for a reservation of all possible benefit of the oil is tantamount to a reservation of the corpus thereof * * *.

The landmark case in Oklahoma applying the above principle appears to be Melton v. Sneed.[15] At the time that the deed in question was executed, there was no oil and gas lease outstanding on the land. The deed contained the following grant,

> " * * * one-third (⅓) of all royalties, from oil, gas, or other minerals arising from or out of or produced upon the said above described lands."

The court construed the grant as an undivided ⅓ mineral interest, which entitled the grantee to one-third of the royalty, rentals and bonus. In explaining the holding, the court stated:

> * * * upon examination of the conveyance it is readily apparent that the word was not used in its strict sense, but in the broader sense * * * as denoting an interest in the minerals. That the word (royalty) is frequently used in this State to denote an interest in the mineral rights is a matter of common knowledge. The conveyance in question here employed it in that sense. There is no reference therein to any lease, or to the royalty reserved thereunder, and the grant is expressly made perpetual * * *.

The court relied upon the case of Carroll v. Bowen.[16] In Carroll the court stated:

> * * * if the reservation of "royalty" **does not specify the percentage of production** meant to be included therein, and where it is **not made with reference to any existing lease establishing the amount**, the term is ambiguous and extrinsic evidence may be examined to determine the intent of the parties * * * (emphasis supplied).

The Melton court held that the deed was ambiguous. Parol evidence was deemed to be admissible, including the presence or absence of an oil and gas lease at the time of execution of the deed. The Melton case established a rule of construction that has been consistently followed in Oklahoma, viz., that a conveyance of a fractional interest "of royalty," [17] where no reference is made in the deed to any

---

15. 188 Okl. 388, 109 P.2d 509; also see, Murphy v. Athans, Okl., 265 P.2d 461; Burns v. Bastien, 174 Okl. 40, 50 P.2d 377; Carroll v. Bowen, 180 Okl. 215, 68 P.2d 773; Gardner v. Jones, 198 Okl. 691, 181 P.2d 838; Meeks v. Harmon, 207 Okl. 459, 250 P.2d 203; Colonial Royalties Co. v. Keener, Okl., 266 P.2d 467; Cook v. McClellan, Okl., 311 P.2d 244; Jolly v. Wilson, Okl., 478 P.2d 886; Sanders v. Bell, Okl., 350 P.2d 293; Simpson v. Burris, Okl., 365 P.2d 134; Wilson v. Hecht, Okl., 370 P.2d 28; Hays v. Phoenix Mutual Life Insurance Co., Okl., 391 P.2d 214.

16. 180 Okl. 215, 68 P.2d 773, see discussion at note 22, infra.

17. Grants or reservations of "a 1/16 royalty interest" will entitle the owner to

lease, or to the royalty reserved thereunder, and the deed is executed at a time when no oil or gas lease is outstanding, will be construed to convey a mineral interest in the amount of the stated fraction.

The case of Federal Land Bank of Wichita v. Nicholson[18] is typical of the cases following Carroll. In it the following reservation was construed:

> * * * it is understood that the grantors herein retain a one-half interest in all royalties received from any oil and gas leases the party of the second part may give on the above described land, but the grantee is to receive all rentals from said lease * * *.

Following the rationale that under Carroll, the instrument was ambiguous, the court reached the conclusion that the interest reserved was an undivided one-half mineral interest. As no lease was on the property at the time the deed was executed, the court felt that it would make no sense to tie royalty to any lease that might be executed in the future.

There exists a second line of cases in Oklahoma where the conveyance of a royalty interest will be construed as passing an interest in the minerals. These are cases where the term "rights" has been coupled with "royalty." Several cases have held that a grant or reservation of an interest of "royalty rights" is the indication of an intent to convey a mineral interest.[19] In the case of Meyers v. Central National Bank of Okmulgee,[20] the rationale was that in Oklahoma it was not possible to create a corporeal mineral interest in the land, only the "right" to enter and explore. Since the only interests other than the right to explore that could be created were an interest in the land itself or a royalty interest, "rights" must refer to something more than royalty and less than the land itself, i.e., the right to enter and explore, a mineral interest.

At times, a grant or reservation will state a fraction of gross production not dependent upon the terms of a lease. Where no lease is outstanding and no mention of a lease is made in the deed, and the conveyance of royalty refers to a fraction of gross production, the Oklahoma cases are consistent in construing the conveyance as creating a royalty interest in the amount of the stated fraction. A typical case is Sykes v. Austin,[21] where the interest was, " * * * one-half

---

$1/16$ of gross production independent of the royalty provided in any oil and gas lease. Where the interest is "of royalty", i.e., "one-half of royalty," the amount of gross production received by the owner of the interest will depend upon the royalty payable under oil and gas leases. Where additional payments out of production are provided for, difficult questions of construction arise whether such other payments out of production are "royalty." Also see discussion at footnote 72, § 2.7(G), infra.

18. 207 Okl. 512, 251 P.2d 490.

19. Wilson v. Olsen, 167 Okl. 527, 30 P.2d 710; Meyers v. Central National Bank of Okmulgee, 183 Okl. 231, 80 P.2d 584; Cook v. McCellan, Okl., 311 P.2d 244.

Also see § 2.7(E), (3), infra.

20. 183 Okl. 231, 80 P.2d 584.

21. 182 Okl. 299, 77 P.2d 719; and also see: Colonial Royalties v. Keener, Okl., 266 P.2d 467.

of the one-eighth royalty of the oil and gas arising from the land * * * ." Restated, this is (one-half x one-eighth) royalty interest, or a $1/16$ royalty interest. In Sykes it was held that, as the fraction was stated, the instrument was not ambiguous, and that a $1/16$ royalty interest was created.

In the landmark case of Carroll v. Bowen,[22] which involved the question of ownership of bonus, the court construed the following clause, " * * * an undivided one-half ($1/2$) interest in and to the Royalty (the ordinary $1/8$ ordinarily left the grantor in oil and gas leases being the royalty above referred to)."

The court stated:

> * * * where the reservation of "royalty" **specified the exact amount of the production thereby contemplated,** it is not ambiguous and must be construed in its strict sense, without introduction of parol testimony * * * it entitles the owner thereof to only that portion of the production definitely specified. It does not carry with it the right to bonus and rentals unless so stipulated * * * (emphasis supplied).

The court held that, due to the language within the parentheses, the clause was not ambiguous, and that a royalty interest in the amount of $1/16$ was created.

This royalty result, then, is reached when no lease is outstanding, and the fraction stated refers to a definite portion of production rather than to a portion of the "royalty." Unless other factors are present, the provision should be considered unambiguous.

From an examination of the cases in which no mention is made of an existing lease and the fractional interest is determined to be ambiguous, it appears that the principal extrinsic fact the courts look to in determining intent is the presence or absence of an oil and gas lease outstanding at the time of execution of the instrument.

Meeks v. Harmon[23] is typical of the cases reaching a result that a royalty interest has been created. In this case the second conveyance provided:

> * * * and for and in consideration of the sum above set out * * * the ($2/3$) Two-Thirds of all royalties on oil, gas and other minerals, produced and saved from said real estate at any time, whether under the terms and conditions of the above mentioned lease, or under the terms and conditions of any other subsequent lease made by said party of the first part * * * .

The court held that a royalty interest was created. The court found that an intent existed to create a royalty interest, as there was a lease outstanding at the time of the assignment, and that reference was made to such lease. It also was held that the royalty was not limited to royalty under the lease referred to.

22. 180 Okl. 215, 68 P.2d 773 and see discussion at note 16, supra.

23. 207 Okl. 459, 250 P.2d 203.

The Oklahoma courts have been consistent in following the approach that the existence of a lease on the property at the time of execution of a deed indicates an intent that a royalty interest was created, and that the word "royalty" in those cases should be construed in a narrow sense. Where no lease was outstanding at the time, the broader construction of mineral interest has been applied.

A major line of cases [24] in Oklahoma would construe a grant or reservation in the form of a stated fraction of oil and gas "produced" as creating a royalty interest. The courts in these cases have emphasized language indicating an interest in the oil and gas after it has reached the surface.

The case of Gardner v. Jones [25] involved the construction of a "future lease" clause in a deed. Here the deed was made subject to an outstanding lease, and then stated the ownership of the economic benefits if a future lease were to be executed after the expiration of the present lease.

> " * * * it is expressly agreed that the grantee shall have an undivided one-sixteenth ($1/16$) interest in and to all oil, gas or other mineral produced from said premises under and by virtue of the new lease so executed."

Grantee expressly had no right to lease, bonus or delay rentals. The court held that the instrument was clear on its face and showed a clear intent that grantee was entitled to $1/16$ of gross production. Although a basis for the result can be found other than in the language of oil and gas "produced," the Gardner case has been repeatedly cited for this proposition.

A following case, which is also well cited for the same proposition, is that of Armstrong v. McCraken.[26] This case involved a provision very similar to that in Gardner. The stated rationale is of interest in understanding the scope of these decisions:

> The Armstrongs retained only one-sixteenth of the oil and gas produced. They were to get nothing if oil and gas were not produced; but if they were produced, they were to get a full one-sixteenth and not one-sixteenth of one-eighth. It is clearly apparent that the Armstrongs did not intend to produce the oil and gas themselves and retained no right to contract with anyone else to produce it for them. They simply retained for themselves one-sixteenth of all oil and gas that might be produced. We think this view is strengthened by the fact that the grantors retained no

---

24. Gardner v. Jones, 198 Okl. 691, 181 P.2d 838; Armstrong v. McCraken, 204 Okl. 319, 229 P.2d 590 (1951); Fry v. Smith, 205 Okl. 222, 236 P.2d 699; Elliott v. Berry, 206 Okl. 594, 245 P.2d 726; Casteel v. Crigler, Okl., 266 P.2d 643; and Lawsen v. Earp, Okl., 309 Okl. 721. However, on the effect of an ingress and egress clause in a "produced" case see Pease v. Dolezal, 206 Okl. 696, 246 P.2d 757, where the court relied upon the clause in construing what would otherwise have been a royalty interest, as a mineral interest.

Also see § 2.7(D), infra.

25. 198 Okl. 691, 181 P.2d 838.

26. 204 Okl. 319, 229 P.2d 590.

claim to the rentals or bonus money which clearly indicates that they were taking simply what the words of the reservation said.

Two cases reached the same result where no lease was outstanding at the time of the execution of the deed.[27] In one of those cases the instrument did not reserve the right to lease, bonus or rentals from the grant.[28] From the rationale of the Armstrong case it would seem that a royalty construction would result in this type of case whether or not a lease was outstanding at the time of the execution of the deed. Many of the cases emphasize the fact that the clause does not refer to an interest in oil and gas "in and under" the ground.[29]

One variation on the conclusion that a royalty interest is created is found in two cases [30] with the following language,

" * * * in *all* oil, gas and other minerals produced from the following described lands * * * " (emphasis supplied)

In both the cases the courts emphasized the word "all" as indicating an intent to transfer ownership of all of the rights making up a mineral interest. Accordingly, it was held that a mineral interest was created. However, both cases also stressed that an oil and gas lease was not outstanding at the time the deeds were executed. The value of these cases as precedent is questionable, if cited for the effect of the inclusion of the word "all." If anything, the word is redundant.

In another case the court found a reservation in this form ambiguous and allowed consideration of parol evidence to determine the intent of the parties.[31]

The approach of the Oklahoma courts in attempting to determine the intent of the parties as to the meaning of the term "royalty" by reference to the circumstances outside the instrument is unsound. To treat the term "royalty" as being ambiguous is subject to criticism on the ground that it will produce uncertainty in titles and ensuing clarifying litigation. It appears sufficiently difficult for the average lawyer to understand the distinction between a royalty and mineral interest, without the further complicating factor of having to determine which of several meanings a term may have. The inevitable end result would be that of producing a specialized bar consisting of a small group of lawyers who are competent to deal with such mat-

---

27. Casteel v. Crigler, Okl., 266 P.2d 643; and, Fry v. Smith, 205 Okl. 222, 236 P.2d 699.

28. Casteel v. Crigler, Okl., 266 P.2d 643.

29. Many of the cases distinguished Swearingen v. Oldham, 195 Okl. 532, 159 P.2d 247 on the ground it emphasized "in and under" language, and upon the court's reliance in that case on parol evidence.

30. Sanders v. Bell, Okl., 350 P.2d 107; and, Wilson v. Hecht, Okl., 370 P.2d 28.

31. Kraker v. Unknown Heirs, etc., Okl., 434 P.2d 282. Here the reservation was of a " * * * $1/16$ royalty from oil and gas produced from * * * " The case seems clearly incorrect in treating the reservation as ambiguous.

(D) Consequences of "Oil and Gas Produced and Saved"

Uncertainty exists whether a grant or reservation of "oil, gas and other minerals produced, saved and made available for market" will create a royalty or mineral interest. In probably a majority of jurisdictions it has been construed as passing a non-cost bearing royalty interest. An opposite conclusion has been reached in at least two jurisdictions on the ground that the phraseology indicates no intent that the interest be cost free.

Instruments providing for conveyances or reservations of fractional interests in "oil and gas produced, saved, and made available for market," or containing similar phrases, have not been uniformly interpreted. One line of authority tends to the constructional preference that the phrase has reference to petroleum products only after they have been severed from the ground. This construction then leads to the inference that it was the intent of the parties to convey a cost-free interest in such production, i.e., a royalty interest, and not a fully participating mineral interest.[32] On the other hand it has been held that such phraseology should not be controlling.[33]

However, this also does not appear to be the view of the Colorado courts, which treat such wording as unambiguous. In the two major cases [34] reaching the conclusion that a mineral interest has been created, the courts have rationalized that a conveyance of a perpetual royalty interest will be treated as passing the "profits" of the land and, hence, the land itself.[35] Upon this reasoning in Corlett v. Cox [36] it was held that a reservation of "6¼% of all gas, oil and minerals that may be produced on any of the above land, or other words reserves ½ of the usual ⅛ royalty" reserved a mineral interest.

A like result, upon a different rationale, has been reached in Mississippi in the case of Mounger v. Pittman,[37] where it was held that a reservation of "⅛ of all oil and gas that may be produced from said land" was a mineral interest. In reaching this result the court emphasized the necessity of looking at the instrument as a whole. The court stated: "It must be conceded that the reservation retained in the grantors an interest in real estate pertaining to oil and gas. It

---

32. Mitchell v. Hannah, 123 Mont. 152, 208 P.2d 812; Casteel v. Crigler, Okl., 266 P.2d 643; Miller v. Speed, Tex. Civ.App., 248 S.W.2d 250; Barker v. Levy, Tex.Civ.App., 507 S.W.2d 613, refused n.r.e. This case contains a good review of cases showing the different constructional preferences; Davis v. Hardman, 148 W.Va. 82, 133 S.E.2d 77. For a discussion of the Oklahoma cases, see discussion at footnote 24, supra.

33. Simson v. Langholf, 133 Colo. 208, 293 P.2d 302; Mounger v. Pittman, 235 Miss. 85, 108 So.2d 565; McNeese v. Renner, 197 Miss. 203, 21 So.2d 7; Sanders v. Bell, Okl., 350 P.2d 293; Wilson v. Hecht, Okl., 370 P.2d 28.

34. Simson v. Langholf, 133 Colo. 208, 293 P.2d 302; Corlett v. Cox, 138 Colo. 325, 333 P.2d 619.

35. Also see discussion § 2.7(F), infra.

36. 138 Colo. 325, 333 P.2d 619.

37. 235 Miss. 85, 108 So.2d 565.

does not provide, either expressly or by implication, that grantors' share of production is to be free of cost of discovery and production, * * * . The deed containing the reservation did not specifically grant to the grantee any right to discover and produce the one-eighth of the oil and gas, or to grant leases, or to receive bonuses and delay rentals; therefore, all these rights were retained by the grantors. * * * The inescapable conclusion is that the interest reserved by the grantors was an estate in the oil and gas in place. The estate created by the reservation has all the characteristics of an estate in the oil and gas, or minerals, in place. It has none of the characteristics of a non-participating royalty interest." In a vigorous dissent it was maintained that characterizing the provision as reserving only a share in gross production resulted in all other rights passing to the grantee. In the dissent it is pointed out that the acts of the grantors following the conveyance were more consistent with an intent to reserve a royalty interest rather than a mineral interest, as was the size of the interest conveyed. The case is illustrative of the constructional problems in this area.[38]

Cases continue to differ in approach and conclusion. In a recent Texas case it was reemphasized that such language denotes a royalty interest, and the approach of Mounger v. Pittman and Simson v. Langholf, was expressly rejected.[39]

On the other hand, several cases have applied the approach in Mounger v. Pittman that the entire instrument will be looked to for a determination whether the interest granted or reserved is a royalty or mineral interest.[40] In Gardner v. Pan American Petroleum Corp.,[41] which construed the following devise:

" * * * Shall Shear EQUIL [sic], One Third Each (⅓) between them, in all Gas and Oil and other minerals and Royalties that is

---

38. A similar result has been reached in Oklahoma. See Sanders v. Bell, Okl., 350 P.2d 293, and Wilson v. Hecht, Okl., 370 P.2d 28. However this does not appear to be the majority view in Oklahoma. See discussion at footnote 24, supra, and cf. Casteel v. Crigler, Okl., 266 P.2d 643. Several cases have indicated that a conveyance of what would otherwise be a mineral interest will not be converted into a royalty interest by the addition of "produced, saved, and marketed," "when discovered," etc.: Little v. Mountain View Dairies, 35 Cal.2d 232, 217 P.2d 416; Marias River Syndicate v. Big West Oil Co., 98 Mont. 254, 38 P.2d 599; McNeese v. Renner, 197 Miss. 203, 21 So. 2d 7; Miller v. Speed, Tex.Civ.App., 248 S.W.2d 250; and see Stokes v. Tutvet, 134 Mont. 250, 328 P.2d 1096.

39. Barker v. Levy, Tex.Civ.App., 507 S.W.2d 613, where the grant was:

" * * * have granted, sold, conveyed, transferred and assigned, and by these presents do bargain, grant, sell, convey, transfer and assign unto the said Adrian F. Levy a One/one hundred and sixtieth (1/160th) part of all oil, gas, petroleum, sulphur and all other minerals that may be produced and saved from the following described lands, to wit: * * *. It is intended by this instrument to convey unto the said Adrian F. Levy a 1/160th part of all the oil, gas, sulphur and other minerals that may be produced and saved from all lands in the State of Texas, the title to which is now owned in whole or in part by me, as well as such lands in the State of Texas which I have heretofore sold but in which I have retained an interest in minerals."

40, 41. See notes 40 and 41 on page 80.

or May be PROUDEOSED [sic] from any Well or Wells or Mines, etc. From the Land Above Described to them, Over the ENTIRE Six Hundred, Thirty (630) Acres of Land."

the court concluded only a royalty interest was created, as no possessory right was granted the devisee in the land. It should be noted the devise is virtually identical with that in Mounger v. Pittman, which held the interest created was a mineral interest.

Perhaps of help in this uncertain situation in Mississippi is the later case of Lockey v. Corley.[42] The case involved the construction of the following reservation:

"The grantors herein reserve unto themselves all oil, gas and minerals in and upon the hereinabove described lands, together with rights-of-way over, through and across the said lands for the purpose of developing and removing the same, less and except an undivided one-half interest in an undivided one-sixteenth interest in and to said oil, gas, and minerals that may hereafter be produced from the said lands."

The court cited the following characteristics of royalty and mineral interests from the Mounger case:

"The distinguishing characteristics of a non-participating royalty interest are: (1) Such share of production is not chargeable with any of the costs of discovery and production; (2) the owner has no right to do any act or thing to discover and produce the oil and gas; (3) the owner has no right to grant leases; and (4) the owner has no right to receive bonuses or delay rentals. Conversely, the distinguishing characteristics of an interest in minerals in place are: (1) Such interest is not free of costs of discovery and production; (2) the owner has the right to do any and all acts necessary to discover and produce oil and gas; (3) the owner has the right to grant leases; and (4) the owner has the right to receive bonuses and delay rentals. (235 Miss. at 86, 108 So.2d at 566.)"

It was held that a royalty interest was created, as three of the four royalty characteristics were present. Here no mention was made in the instrument whether the interest would bear costs or be cost free. Mounger was distinguished, and the royalty construction was upheld where three of the four royalty characteristics were present and no express provision was set forth that the interest would be cost bearing. The court additionally emphasized "may hereafter be produced" is an indication of a royalty construction. These cases coupled with Mounger illustrate the difficult problems of construction faced in Mississippi in determining whether an interest is a mineral or royalty.

---

40. Gardner v. Pan American Petroleum Corp., Miss., 243 So.2d 399; Lackey v. Corley, Miss., 295 So.2d 762.

41. See note 40, supra.

42. See note 40, supra. Cf. Smith v. County of Musselshell, note 47, infra.

It is submitted that undue emphasis should not be given to the mechanical aspect of words such as "when produced," "produced, saved, and marketed" or those of similar import in determining intent of the parties. As mentioned in a foregoing paragraph, the distinction implied between an interest in petroleum in the ground compared to an interest in petroleum after it is produced has not been deemed of particular significance in states in which no ownership is recognized in petroleum products prior to production. In ownership-in-place states, such phraseology might be susceptible of the interpretation that it designates an interest in personal property rather than realty. In either jurisdiction it would seem proper to treat such verbiage as ambiguous and allow parol evidence to determine the intent of the parties.

(E) Conveyances of "Royalty" Coupled with Language Inconsistent with a Royalty Interest

Grants of a "royalty" interest coupled with additional language may be treated as creating royalty or mineral interests, depending upon the approach of the courts in either treating the term "royalty" as merely one of the indicia of intent of the grantor to be construed in a manner so as to give effect to all operative words of the instrument, or in treating the term "royalty" as adequately defining the interest as a non-cost bearing interest.

From the above discussion it may be seen that conveyances of an undivided fractional "royalty" interest in most jurisdictions will pass to the recipient a cost-free interest in gross production equal to the stated fraction, but will pass no rights to delay rentals, bonus or the power to lease. Where the term "royalty" is coupled with other terms, the result is not always clear. Although other combinations of wording may be found, the following examples are encountered sufficiently often to merit discussion:

(1) Conveyances of "the oil and gas, in, under, and that may be produced from the land" characterized as a royalty.

(2) Conveyances of a royalty interest together with express rights of ingress and egress.

(3) Conveyances of "royalty rights" or royalty "and the rights thereto."

(1) "Royalty," Plus "Oil and Gas, in, Under, and That May Be Produced"

In jurisdictions in which the term "royalty" has a definite meaning, the presence of the term "royalty" may convert what is otherwise a mineral interest to one of royalty only.[43] Probably the landmark case to this effect is the Texas case of Watkins v. Slaugh-

---

43. Texas Co. v. Bowen, 292 Ky. 676, 167 S.W.2d 822; Payne v. Campbell, 250 Miss. 227, 164 So.2d 780; Watkins v. Slaughter, 144 Tex. 179, 189 S.W.2d 699; Arnold v. Ashbel Smith Land Co., Tex. Civ.App., 307 S.W.2d 818.

ter,[44] which was concerned with the following reservation: " * * * a $1/16$ interest in and to all of the oil, gas and other minerals in and under and that may be produced from said land * * * and the grantor, his heirs, or assigns, shall receive the royalty retained herein only from actual production of oil, gas or other minerals on said land." In construing the reserved interest as a cost-free interest the court stated: "Had the word 'royalty' appeared in the first clause, above quoted * * * then there could be no contention that the interest reserved was only a mineral fee interest. Certainly the reservation should not be given a different meaning merely because the description of the reserved interest as a royalty interest appears in the last clause of the sentence rather than in the first clause."

In Texas and jurisdictions following Watkins, either of the following clauses would reserve or convey a right to $1/16$ of gross production, i.e., a $1/16$ royalty interest:[45]

(a) "an undivided one-sixteenth ($1/16$th) royalty interest in and to all of the oil, gas and other minerals in, under, and that may be produced from the following described land * * * ."

(b) "an undivided one-sixteenth ($1/16$th) interest in and to all of the oil, gas and other minerals in, under, and that may be produced from the following described land, payable as a royalty. * * * ."

In those states where the term "royalty" is not given such definitive significance as to the intent of the parties, the courts will attempt to construe the instrument as a whole to determine intent and will give weight to that portion of the clause which would otherwise convey or reserve a mineral interest. It appears to be the viewpoint in Louisiana that a mineral interest is a "superior" interest to a royalty interest, and that the characterization as a royalty interest of what would otherwise be a mineral interest, is ineffectual. This was the result in Phillips Petroleum Co. v. Richard,[46] in which it was held that grantor reserved a mineral interest in a deed which passed to the grantee the power to lease, bonus and delay rentals and reserved to the grantor "an undivided one-fourth of the oil, gas and other minerals under and produced and saved from said land, which reservation is equal to a one-thirty-second royalty interest under the said existing lease and as well a like royalty interest under future mineral leases * * * ."

A like conclusion (but different reasoning) is found in the early Montana case of Marias River Syndicate v. Big West Oil Co.,[47] where it was held that a reservation of " * * * a $12^{1}/_{2}$ per cent. interest

---

44. 144 Tex. 179, 189 S.W.2d 699. It should be noted that in this case an alternative ground for decision was that the power to lease, and the rights to bonus and delay rentals were expressly passed to the grantee. See discussion in subparagraph (I) of this section, infra.

45. See Arnold v. Ashbel Smith Land Co., Tex.Civ.App., 307 S.W.2d 818.

46. La.App., 127 So.2d 816.

47. 98 Mont. 254, 38 P.2d 599. See Smith v. County of Musselshell, 155 Mont. 376, 472 P.2d 878 (expressly following Marias, although the language as

and royalty in and to all oil and gas and other minerals of whatsoever nature, found in or located upon or under said land or premises above described, or that may be produced therefrom," contained in a conveyance executed at a time when no lease was outstanding on the land in question, reserved a mineral and not a royalty interest to the grantor. In determining intent the court limited the definition of "royalty" as denoting only an interest in gross production under an outstanding lease. As no lease was outstanding at the time, the term "royalty" was ignored. The court also felt the fact that the grantors had later made conveyances of portions of their reserved interests containing express rights of ingress and egress was consistent with the court's conclusion that the parties' intent was to create a mineral interest by the reservation.

The case has been subject to some criticism. The fact of whether or not a lease is outstanding seems a fragile basis upon which to formulate presumptions as to intent. It would seem that the use of the term "royalty" when taken in connection with the fraction of production designated, i.e., $12\frac{1}{2}\%$ or $\frac{1}{8}$, would have sufficed to support a conclusion of an intent to create a non-cost bearing interest.

However, the question was again presented to the Montana court in the case of Stokes v. Tutvet,[48] which concerned an action for specific performance of a contract of sale which provided that the deed to be executed would contain a reservation: " * * * excepting and reserving unto the said first parties all except two per cent (2%) of the landowner's royalty rights in and to all oil, gas and other minerals in, under or upon said premises, * * * ." Again, no lease was outstanding upon the property. Each party prepared a deed for execution which was unacceptable to the other. Seller's deed provided for a reservation of " * * * all of the oil and gas and other minerals, in, under and that may be produced from said land," i.e., reserving all of the mineral estate, plus a separate assignment to buyer of 2% of the landowner's royalty of oil and gas produced. Buyer's deed provided only for a reservation of $10\frac{1}{2}\%$ of the landowner's royalty, i.e., the usual $12\frac{1}{2}\%$ royalty minus 2% transferred to buyer. The seller contended that the word "all" in the contract clause would include all of the mineral estate except 2% of gross production to be paid to buyer, whereas buyer contended the term "all" only had reference to royalty and did not include the underlying mineral estate. The question here concerned the ownership of the underlying mineral estate, not the amount of royalty to be paid to buyer.[49] Although the court remanded the case as it found the instrument ambiguous, the court indicated that if it could decide the case on its merits it would reject

construed did not contain the term "royalty." Touchstone for the court was that no clear expression was contained that the interest was free and clear of expense, hence a mineral interest. The court also disregarded as not determinative the phrase "that may be *produced* from" as it was only one-half of the common language "produced and saved" which indicates a royalty intent). (Cf. Lockey v. Corley, note 42, supra.)

48. 134 Mont. 250, 328 P.2d 1096.

49. See footnote 33, § 2.5, supra. Also see the Kansas case of Lathrop v. Eyestone, 170 Kan. 419, 227 P.2d 136, for a similar situation.

the temptation to give the term "royalty" a controlling meaning, and applying the Marias decision, construed "royalty * * * in, on, under or upon said premises" as designating a fully participating mineral interest.[50]

It is interesting to note that had the court been able to decide the case on its merits it would have concluded that buyer would have received a 2% mineral interest, which would entitle him to 2% of royalty, or under the customary royalty of $12\frac{1}{2}\%$ in Montana, a share equal to $\frac{1}{4}$ of 1% of gross production. Both parties rejected the court's conclusion and agreed that in any event buyer was entitled to 2% of gross production.[51]

Typical of the cases where the term "royalty" is not given controlling effect is the case of Wynn v. Sklar & Phillips Oil Co.[52] The disputed language in the case was:

"a one eight (being all the Royalty retained by us) undivided interest of, in and to all the oil, gas and minerals on, in and under the

---

50. The court distinguished the situation where the term "royalty" is followed by the words "produced and saved from" which it would construe as a royalty interest. It was also stated that the absence or presence of an oil and gas lease at the time of the execution of a conveyance or reservation would not be treated as immaterial. However, the application of the Stokes case will be modified in Montana where sufficiently specific language is included to indicate an overall intent to create a non-cost bearing interest. See Amundson v. Gordon, 134 Mont. 142, 328 P.2d 630, where the reservation read, "$6\frac{1}{4}\%$ of all oil, gas and minerals underlying the surface thereof. Such reservation is what is commonly referred to as landowner's interest and in case of production is to be deducted from the share grantee would otherwise receive, without deduction of any kind." It was treated as reserving a royalty interest.

---

51. Seller's contention:

Seller's Interest
All rights to mineral estate, i.e., right to lease, bonus and royalty, subject only to buyer's interest.

Buyer's Interest
2% of gross production, non-cost bearing interest.

Buyer's contention:

Seller's Interest
$10\frac{1}{2}\%$ of gross production, non-cost bearing interest.

Buyer's Interest
All rights to mineral estate, i.e., right to lease, bonus and delay rental, subject only to Seller's interest.

Court's contention:

Seller's Interest
98% of the mineral estate, i.e., right to lease, bonus and delay rentals.

Buyer's Interest
2% of the mineral estate, i.e., right to lease, bonus and delay rentals.

---

52. 254 Ark. 332, 493 S.W.2d 439 (1973). Also see: Extraction Resources, Inc. v. Freeman, Tex.Civ.App., 555 S.W.2d 156, refused n.r.e., where grantor executed some 366 deeds entitled "Royalty Deed," each of which conveyed a fractional interest "in and to all of the oil, gas and other minerals in and under and that may be produced from the (described lands) together with the right of ingress and egress (for drilling and exploring)." The deeds were held to convey royalty interests, as the grantors owned only a royalty interest prior to the execution of the conveyances.

* * * lands * * * granting to the said J. M. Talley, his heirs and assigns, the right of ingress to and upon said lands for the purposes of securing, storing and removing oil and gas, and the right of occupancy of said lands for and only for the purposes of storing, securing and removing oil and gas."

The court followed the Marias case in that intent should be determined from a reading of the instrument as a whole and held that a mineral interest was created. The court discussed the various alternative interpretations the deed might have if the term "Royalty" were to be treated as controlling:

"If we consider the various meanings which have been accorded the word "royalty," and treated the parenthetical clause as controlling, the deed might be taken to have conveyed any of the following: (1) The "royalty" payable under the lease described in Item 2, which was then only slightly more than two years old; (2) fee title to $1/8$ of the minerals in place, with all attendant incidents, with the parties considering the $1/8$ interest and "royalty" as synonymous and inserting the parenthetical clause in an effort to clarify the interest conveyed; (3) a perpetual royalty either "participating" or "nonparticipating," which constitutes a beneficial interest in future oil and gas production; (4) a beneficial interest in future production together with an interest in oil and gas in place; and (5) an interest that enabled the grantee to grant an oil and gas lease and collect the entire royalty paid thereunder."

Without the parenthetical clause the interest clearly was a mineral interest. It was held that the parenthetical clause could not control over the otherwise clear meaning of the deed.

(2) "Royalty" Together With Express Rights of Ingress and Egress

In jurisdictions where the term "royalty" is treated as ambiguous or being of uncertain meaning, the presence or absence of express rights of entry is a factor considered along with other circumstances to determine the nature of the interest intended. In jurisdictions which consider "royalty" as having a precise meaning, the presence of express rights of entry following a conveyance or reservation of a royalty interest is given no particular significance in determining the nature of the interest.[53] Such rights of ingress and egress may be held void as being repugnant to the grant of a royalty interest,[54] or construed as entitling the holder of the interest to access to the lease for purposes of information as to royalty production.[55]

53. Kilfoyle v. Wright, C.A.5th, 300 F.2d 626; Hickey v. Dirks, 156 Kan. 326, 133 P.2d 107; Hays v. Phoenix Mutual Life Insurance Co., Okl., 391 P.2d 214.

54. Kilfoyle v. Wright, C.A.5th, 300 F.2d 626.

55. Hays v. Phoenix Mutual Life Insurance Co., Okl., 391 P.2d 214. However, cf. Pease v. Dolezal, 206 Okl. 696, 246 P.2d 757, where the court concluded that broader easement rights existed, including rights of development and production, on the ground that no lease was outstanding at the time of the conveyance. Also see footnote 24, § 2.7(C), supra.

A royalty interest is normally considered a non-possessory interest. To prevent ambiguity a grant or reservation of a royalty interest should not be coupled with express easement rights, unless limited to access for informational purposes. Surprisingly, printed forms commonly used for conveyance of royalty interests often contain such clauses. These provisions should be struck from the form or modified before use.

(3) Conveyances of "Royalty Rights," "Royalty and the Rights Thereto," etc.

Coupling of the term "rights" or "interest" with a conveyance of "royalty" has been construed as creating a mineral interest.[56] This construction is questionable. Words such as "rights" and "interest" have no independent meaning, and normal construction would be to treat such terms as merely being redundant of the rights created.

(F) Miscellaneous Words and Phrases

(1) Profits

It would appear that a conveyance or reservation of a "profits" interest will be construed as exhibiting an intent to grant or reserve a royalty interest. However, a few courts have reached a conclusion that a mineral interest was intended, by application of the common law concept that a conveyance of the profits of the land is a conveyance of the land itself. This concept, as to oil and gas, has been abandoned in virtually all jurisdictions, but may be presently applied by the Colorado and Oklahoma courts.

At common law it was considered that the ownership of the economic benefits from a tract of land was ownership of the land itself. Beginning with early West Virginia cases,[57] which were later adopted by the Oklahoma and Colorado courts, this concept was introduced into oil and gas jurisprudence. As royalty in these jurisdictions was classified as a profit from the land, ownership of royalty was equated to ownership of the mineral estate.

This concept has apparently been abandoned in its parent state of West Virginia,[58] but has left its imprint on the approach of the Oklahoma courts, which treat a conveyance of "royalty" when no lease is outstanding as a conveyance of the mineral estate itself, and is being

---

56. Wilson v. Olsen, 167 Okl. 527, 30 P.2d 710 (⅓ interest in and to all of the royalty of the gas, oil and mineral and the rights thereto, at a time when no lease was outstanding, held to be a mineral interest; Meeks v. Harmon, 207 Okl. 459, 250 P.2d 203; Marias River Syndicate v. Big West Oil Co., 98 Mont. 254, 38 P.2d 599; Stokes v. Tutvet, 134 Mont. 250, 328 P.2d 1096; but see Riffel v. Dieter, 159 Kan. 628, 157 P.2d 831; and Schlittler v. Smith, 128 Tex. 628, 101 S.W.2d 543. Also see footnotes 19 and 20, § 2.7(C), supra.

57. Toothman v. Courtney, 62 W.Va. 167, 58 S.E. 915; Paxton v. Benedum Trees Oil Co., 80 W.Va. 187, 94 S.E. 472. Also see discussion at footnotes 13 and 14, § 2.7(C),supra.

58. Davis v. Hardman, 148 W.Va. 82, 133 S.E.2d 77.

mulled over at the present time by the Colorado courts.[59] Although an application of the rule is sometimes used as a starting place to unravel cases where a mineral estate has been hopelessly carved up by inept draftsmen,[60] in the great majority of jurisdictions the rule has little application. The landmark case rejecting the West Virginia approach is Gulf Refining Co. v. Stanford,[61] where it was concluded that a provision by the parties to a conveyance "to share the profits equally" reserved to the grantor one-half of the royalties only. The court viewed the term "profits" as elastic in meaning but construed it as the share of the grantor in production after it was brought to the surface and reduced to possession. It is interesting to note that the court had three alternative solutions: (1) that profits meant royalty, (2) that profits carried with it the land itself, as was argued by the dissent, or (3) that the term indicated "net" profits, or one-half of the residue of production after payment of all costs and expenses, but not including the right to lease, bonus, or delay rentals.[62]

(2) "Landowner's Interest" and "Landowner's Rights"

An attempt has been made to find meaningful intent in terms such as "landowner's interest" or "landowner's rights." It is submitted that the terms are undefinable and should be disregarded. Montana cases appearing to find significance in such terminology are in confusion.

O conveys to A an undivided $1/16$ "landowner's interest," or "landowner's royalty rights," or "landowner's mineral interest." Mineral or royalty? The question presented, of course, is whether the terms "landowner," "rights," or "interest," should have any significance. Does "landowner" denote the interest of the landowner before or after a lease? Any person owning an interest in land generically can be called a landowner; technically, however, in a non-ownership state the word would have no application to the mineral estate. The terms "rights" or "interest" being merely redundant, it would seem that the better view is that the words have no special significance at all, and particular grants should be interpreted without consideration of them.

This may be demonstrated by a consideration of a trilogy of cases from Montana, which illustrate the pitfalls of both the courts and practitioners in dealing with the mineral-royalty distinction.

In the case of Stokes v. Tutvet,[63] it was proclaimed as constructional law in Montana that a conveyance of a "landowner's royalty

---

59. See discussion in Simson v. Langholf, 133 Colo. 208, 293 P.2d 302; Corlett v. Cox, 138 Colo. 325, 333 P.2d 619.

60. See discussion in Chapter 9, § 9.1, infra, as further examples of inept draftsmanship.

61. 202 Miss. 602, 30 So.2d 516, 173 A.L.R. 1099; but see Gallin v. Combs, Ky., 341 S.W.2d 778.

62. The term "net proceeds" is sometimes used, which would seem to indicate a similar meaning. See Rogers v. Morgan, 250 Miss. 9, 164 So.2d 480, also see Chapter 7, § 7.4(D), infra, for a discussion of the meaning of the term "proceeds" as used in the royalty clause in an oil and gas lease.

63. 134 Mont. 250, 328 P.2d 1096 (August 11, 1956).

rights" in the oil and gas "in, under, or upon the premises" would be considered as creating a mineral interest. But in the contemporary case of Amundson v. Gordon,[64] it was apparently concluded that a reservation of, " * * * $6\frac{1}{4}$ per cent of all oil, gas and minerals underlying the surface thereof. Such reservation is what is commonly referred to as landowner's interest and in case of production, is to be deducted from the share grantee would otherwise receive, without deduction of any kind," reserved a royalty and not a mineral interest. The difference in result apparently stems from the court's giving no weight to the phrase "landowner's royalty rights" in the Stokes case, while finding the second sentence in the reservation in the Amundson case controlling as to intent. Even so, it would seem that the result would be unchanged had the phrase "landowner's interest" been omitted.

Interestingly, in the case of Voyta v. Clonts,[65] decided a month after the Amundson case, and two days after the Stokes case, the court apparently considered as ambiguous a clause in a contract of sale whereby seller would retain "4.6875% of landowner's mineral rights." The court held that the interest to be retained was a royalty interest, not a mineral interest, as it was determined from extrinsic evidence that if considered as denoting a mineral interest it would provide a much smaller share of gross production to the seller than the parties had contemplated.

The presence of words such as "rights," "interest," and "landowner's," modifying "royalty" or "mineral" cannot be considered constructionally clarifying and should be omitted by the draftsman or, if used, ignored.

(G) The Effect of the Quantum of the Interest Conveyed or Reserved on the Mineral-Royalty Distinction, and Problems Occurring as to the Quantum of Production to Which a Mineral or Royalty Owner May be Entitled

A grant of a fractional royalty or mineral interest may be considered as ambiguous when compared to the fraction designated. Such ambiguity has been found where a royalty interest has been granted in a larger than customary amount, but only rarely from a grant of a mineral interest in a small fractional amount.

Constructional problems have been presented where the draftsman has failed to distinguish whether the fraction is to apply to a mineral or royalty interest, or has failed to appreciate the distinction between a grant of a "fractional royalty interest" and "a fractional interest of royalty."

The wording of a grant or reservation, if considered alone, may indicate a mineral or royalty interest; however, if the size of the fractional interest is unusual, i.e., an uncustomarily large royalty interest

---

64. 134 Mont. 142, 328 P.2d 630 (July 11, 1958, rehearing denied August 7, 1958).

65. 134 Mont. 156, 328 P.2d 655.

§ 2.7   IN THE OIL AND GAS MINERAL ESTATE   89

or small mineral interest, the grant or reservation may be considered ambiguous.[66] For example, it is highly improbable that parties might create a $1/2$ royalty interest.[67] Without further manifestation of intent, is it feasible to conclude that fifty per cent of production will not bear any part of the cost or expense of exploration and development? Can a lessee normally be found to drill a 50% working interest? On the other hand, is it reasonable to suppose that the actual intent of parties granting a $1/32$ interest in and to all of the oil, gas, and other minerals is to create a fully participating mineral interest, where the recipient will be entitled to only a $1/256$ royalty, and $1/32$ of bonuses and delay rentals?[68]

The question is not whether such interests can be created, for they can, but whether a conclusion should be reached that they were. In probably no other area of oil and gas law, than in cases involving the mineral-royalty distinction, can examples be found of courts, on behalf of befuddled litigants, benevolently and improperly granting reformation in the guise of a judgment for title.[69]

(1) Royalty Conveyances

In those jurisdictions in which the term "royalty" denotes a non-cost bearing interest in gross production, not sharing in bonus, delay rentals, or the power to lease, it is possible, but not generally economically feasible, to create a large non-cost bearing interest by characterizing the interest as royalty. For instance, in the Texas case of Arnold v. Ashbel Smith & Co.,[70] a reservation was made of a one-fourth royalty in all oil, gas and other minerals, which the court held to entitle the holder to 25% of gross production without deduction of costs. Although the instrument contained further language upon which the court could conclude that a royalty interest was reserved, it is clear that the result would have been the same if the additional language had been omitted.

Obviously the intent of the parties is questionable where a royalty interest is created larger than is customarily provided for in oil and gas leases. In the Mississippi case of Payne v. Campbell,[71] the court refused to characterize a grant as conveying a royalty interest in an instrument prepared on a form entitled a "non-participating royalty" and providing that there was granted "$1/2$ of the whole of any oil, gas or other minerals, on, under, or that may be produced * * * (the) royalty herein described shall be delivered or paid to purchaser out of

---

66. Lathrop v. Eyestone, 170 Kan. 419, 227 P.2d 136; Melancon v. Cheramie, La.App., 138 So.2d 138; Rogers v. Morgan, 250 Miss. 9, 164 So.2d 480; Payne v. Campbell, 250 Miss. 227, 164 So.2d 780; Harriss v. Ritter, 154 Tex. 474, 279 S.W.2d 845; Arnold v. Ashbel Smith Land Co., Tex.Civ.App., 307 S.W.2d 818.

67. See Payne v. Campbell, 250 Miss. 227, 164 So.2d 780.

68. See Melancon v. Cheramie, La. App., 138 So.2d 138; Mounger v. Pittman, 235 Miss. 85, 108 So.2d 565.

69. See, for example, Garrett v. Dils Co., 157 Tex. 92, 299 S.W.2d 904.

70. Tex.Civ.App., 307 S.W.2d 818.

71. 250 Miss. 227, 164 So.2d 780.

and deducted from royalty reserved to lessor in said lease." It was held that the instrument although being plain on its face was latently ambiguous when applied to the subject matter to which it was to operate. The court emphasized that such conveyances could not be considered in a vacuum apart from the nature of the business, and concluded that restricting the interest to $1/2$ of $1/8$ royalty (or $1/2$ of royalty) was reasonable in the circumstances. As the deed referred to an outstanding lease in which only a $1/8$ royalty interest was provided, the case reaches a correct result.

In both of the above cases other provisions materially aided the courts in reaching the respective results. Although the Payne case may have been decided without the consideration of parol evidence, it raises the question whether an instrument conveying a "royalty" in excess of that normally or customarily provided should be treated as being latently ambiguous, thus allowing the use of parol evidence. Aside from the fact that in states like Texas, where the term "royalty" has a legally definable meaning, the practitioner in such cases must treat such interests as ambiguous, or at the least as questionable. O, the owner of Blackacre in fee, conveys a $1/2$ royalty interest to A. O then executes an oil and gas lease to Humble Oil and Refining Co., providing for a $1/8$ landowner's royalty. Can the attorney for Humble be certain that the lease from O constitutes a lease on all the fee? If so, what is the obligation for royalty by Humble?[72] As a practical matter Humble, in all probability, will not drill what is in effect a $1/2$ interest lease. If attempts at negotiations with A fail, i.e., to convince A that his interest is $1/2$ of royalty, i.e., a $1/16$, or if the same result cannot be obtained in an action to construe the deed, the lease may be abandoned. The approach of the court in the Payne case has merit, that a conveyance or reservation of a royalty interest may become ambiguous where the amount is substantially in excess of the customary royalty in oil and gas leases in the area.

A sharp distinction must be made between a conveyance or reservation of royalty in the form of a "'$1/16$th royalty interest" and "an interest being $1/16$th of royalty." For instance, under the better view, a conveyance or reservation of "a $1/16$th royalty interest in and to all of the oil, gas and other minerals, in, under and that may be produced and saved from the following described land" should be interpreted as passing a definite quality of estate, i.e., a non-cost bearing interest limited to gross production, with the quantum of such estate fixed as $1/16$. Where properly executed and recorded, persons subsequently dealing with the mineral estate are bound by a fixed outstanding interest. In contrast, where the conveyance or reservation is a $1/16$ of royalty, the quality of the estate is likewise determined as being limited to a non-cost bearing interest in gross production; however, the quantum of such estate is dependent upon the royalty reserved in

---

72. See Chapter 7, § 7.8, infra, for a discussion of warranty problems in this connection.

future leases and is calculated as a fractional portion of that amount. Hence, following a conveyance by O to A of "$1/16$th of royalty," O then executes an oil and gas lease reserving a landowner's royalty of $1/8$. A will receive $1/16$ of $1/8$, or a $1/128$, share of gross production, whereas if the conveyance was in the form of a "$1/16$ royalty" A would receive $1/16$ of gross production. This is well illustrated in the case of Harriss v. Ritter,[73] involving a reservation of "$1/2$ of $1/8$ of the oil, gas and other mineral royalty that may be produced from said land." In finding that the reservation was of a perpetual royalty interest, it was held that the quantum of gross production to which the grantor was entitled was $1/16$ of the royalty provided in the lease, i.e., $1/128$ ($1/2$ of $1/8$ of $1/8$), rather than $1/16$ ($1/2$ of $1/8$).

Differences between the "fractional royalty" grant and the "of royalty" grant can be illustrated by the following examples:

O executes to A a deed of $1/16$ royalty interest. Following this, O executes a deed of $1/2$ of royalty to B. O then executes a lease with a $1/8$ royalty reserved to the lessor.

In this example, A will receive $1/16$ of gross production. B will receive $1/2$ of $1/8$ royalty, or $1/16$ of gross production. O will receive nothing, as he had previously granted away royalty in this amount.

However, if the lease that O executed provided for a $3/16$ royalty, the results would be different. A would still receive $1/16$ of gross production, as this is the fraction provided for in the deed to A. B would receive $1/2$ of $3/16$, or $3/32$ of gross production. This leaves $1/32$ royalty left over, which would go to O.

If the deeds to A and B were both of $1/2$ of royalty, with a $3/16$ landowner's royalty in the lease, O again would have no royalty in which to share. However, if both deeds were of a $1/16$ fractional royalty interest, O would share in $1/16$ of gross production.

Ambiguities sometimes arise when a conveyance or reservation is made in the "of royalty" form, and the interest is restated as a fraction of gross production. Two Texas cases, decided about a year apart, reached opposite results.

In one case,[74] grantor reserved "1/2 of the 1/8 royalty (same being a 1/16 of the total production)". When a lease was later executed providing for more than a 1/8 royalty, the court held that grantor had reserved a fractional royalty of 1/16th of the total production, and did not reserve a fraction of royalty determinable upon the execution of some future lease.

In the other case,[75] the granting clause of the deed provided that the grantee receive "an undivided one-fourth (1/4th) interest in and to

---

73. 154 Tex. 474, 279 S.W.2d 845. Also see Palmer v. Lide, 263 Ark. 731, 567 S.W.2d 295 (1978), Corbin v. Mosser, 195 Kan. 252, 403 P.2d 800, and, Canter v. Lindsey, Tex.Civ.App., 575 S.W.2d 331, refused n.r.e.

74. Helms v. Guthrie, Tex.Civ.App., 573 S.W.2d 855, refused n.r.e.

75. Farmers Canal Co. v. Potthast, Tex.Civ.App., 587 S.W.2d 805, refused n.r.e.

all of the sulphur royalty, oil royalty, gas royalty, and royalty in all other minerals." In a later provision of the deed it was provided that "Grantee shall only receive * * * one fourth (1/4th) of the one-eighth (1/8th) royalty on oil, gas and all other minerals provided for in such lease or leases." It was held that the deed clearly provided for a 1/4 of royalty, and as such would participate in one-fourth of the 1/6 royalty provided in a later lease. The rationale of the court was that any later clauses that conflicted with the granting clause were void. Here the court could not find that the later restriction was meant to limit the granting clause. It would seem that this case is contrary to the usual application of the four corners rule as applied in Texas.

(2) Mineral Conveyances

As indicated above, not all ambiguities and doubtful intent due to the size of the interest granted or reserved occur in the guise of royalty interests larger than royalty customarily provided in oil and gas leases. Such ambiguity may also occur where the grant or reservation is of a mineral interest of an abnormally small amount. Such small interests may occur naturally when mineral interests are successively fractured by passing through several estates. Fractional mineral interests of a magnitude of $1/3000$ are far from rare. However, it is where mineral interests are of a size of $1/16$, $1/32$, or $1/64$ that trouble occurs, as the size of the interest is in the range of normal royalty conveyances.

Consider the situation where Jones, the owner of the Jolly Green Ranch, has executed an oil and gas lease which now may be in existence or may have expired. Under such lease Jones has received, or should receive, 1/8 of production. Smith comes along and, after some discussion, persuades Jones to sell half of his "minerals", using the term generically. Without technical knowledge of the distinction between a mineral interest, as a cost-bearing and fully participating interest in the oil and gas, and a royalty interest, as indicating only a share in gross production, Jones considers that he owns 1/8 of the minerals. For, after all, that is the fraction of products to which he is entitled to upon production. Jones, of course, is mistaken, for he owns 100% of the minerals, which will entitle him to 100% of the customary royalty paid in his area, in this hypothetical case being 1/8. Jones, avoiding lawyers, goes to the stationery store and buys a "Mineral Deed" which he promptly executes, inserting in the blank in the granting clause: " * * * does hereby grant, bargain, sell and convey unto Smith an undivided _____ of all of the oil, gas, and other minerals, in, under and that may be produced from the following described land * * *" the fraction "1/16"! Jones has thereby granted to Smith a 1/16 mineral interest rather than a "1/2" mineral interest by reason of confusion in understanding the difference between a royalty and a mineral interest.[76] Since a mineral interest may be conveyed in any fractional amount, and there is no normal or customary fraction, as in the case of royalty, no latent ambiguity can be said to exist solely by reason of the small fractional interest. In a suit for title, where no latent or patent ambiguity exists, parol evidence will be excluded, and the only proper result would be to construe the instrument as passing a mineral interest in the quantum stated. Although it would seem the general view that no latent ambiguity occurs, one case has tended to treat a conveyance in form of a mineral conveyance with a small fractional share as ambiguous.[77] Other provisions in the instrument were deemed pertinent to the decision.

(H) Effect of a Conveyance or Reservation of a Mineral Interest, Less the Right to Bonus, Delay Rentals and the Power to Lease

The trend of authority appears to support a conclusion that a grant in the form of a mineral interest, where the fractional interest is equal to or less than royalty customarily provided, but reserving all economic benefits except a right to share in production, will be interpreted as a royalty interest equal to the stated fractional interest. However, in jurisdictions which follow a mechanical construction of the grant, the share of production to which the holder of such interest is entitled will be the proportion of royalty customarily attributed to such fractional mineral interest. Under this latter view the interest would be classified as a "non-participating mineral interest."

Heretofore the question examined has been whether certain phraseology would serve to convey or reserve a mineral interest, a fully participating interest, or a royalty interest, a non-cost bearing interest that participates only in a fraction of gross production. This section and the one following consider the situation where a grant (or reservation) is made in the form of a mineral interest, but some or all of the rights and economic benefits attributable to a fully participating mineral interest, other than a right to share in production, are reserved by the grantor. For example, Rancher Jones conveys Blackacre to Smith in the following form: "* * * does hereby grant, bargain, sell and convey the following described land (described); there is excepted and reserved, however, unto Grantor, his heirs and assigns, an undivided 1/16 interest in and to all of the oil, gas, and other minerals in, under and that may be produced from the above described land, it being further provided that Grantor, his heirs and assigns, shall not participate in bonus, delay rentals, or the power to lease." What is the nature of Jones' interest?

---

76. Rancher Jones is not the only one confused. See comments of the court directed to counsel as to the quantum of Hall's interest under the "first" instrument, considered in Lathrop v. Eyestone, 170 Kan. 419, 227 P.2d 136.

77. Melancon v. Cheramie, La.App., 138 So.2d 138.

In the form considered in this section, there is little question that Rancher Jones has only a right to participate in a share of production. It is expressly stated that this is his only right or benefit to be obtained from the mineral estate. However, what is his share? Should the reservation of a mineral estate when shorn of all rights and economic benefits save a right to production, be classified as a royalty interest? If so, Jones would be entitled to 1/16 of gross production without deduction of costs. On the other hand, does the reserved interest constitute, for want of a better term, a "non-participating mineral interest"? In this event Jones would be entitled only to that proportion of royalty attributable to a mineral interest, viz., 1/16 x 1/8, or 1/128 of gross production.

In some jurisdictions the distinction may involve more than the interest in production to which a party is entitled. The Louisiana courts distinguish rather sharply between a royalty and mineral interest. It appears to be the law of that jurisdiction that in the event leased interests are pooled with other lands, production from the unit well is sufficient to constitute an interruption of prescription as to interests classified as mineral in unit tracts but upon which the unit well is not located; however, actual production upon the tract is necessary to interrupt prescription as to interests therein classified as royalty.[78] Therefore the classification as a royalty or non-participating mineral interest may affect the duration of the interest in Louisiana as well as the portion of production to which the owner is entitled.

Although it would appear that the trend of authority is toward the conclusion that a royalty interest is created, little uniformity is found in the cases.[79] Supportive argument may be made for each position. Sustaining the conclusion that the interest retained is a royalty, it may be argued with some force that no matter what the form of the reservation, that it must be looked at as a whole to determine the intent of the parties. Since all other rights and economic benefits have been passed to the grantee, the only reasonable conclusion is that the parties' manifest intent is to reserve a 1/16th royalty interest. On the other hand, support for a non-participating conclusion

78. This was, in fact, the issue in the Phillips case, note 80 infra. It is interesting to note that the court apparently construed the phrase, "which is equal to a one-thirty-second royalty interest" as relating to the quantum but not the quality of the reserved interest.

79. To the effect that a "non-participating" mineral interest is created see: Skelly Oil Co. v. Cities Service Oil Co., 160 Kan. 226, 160 P.2d 246; Hightower v. Maritzky, 194 La. 998, 195 So. 518; Phillips Petroleum Co. v. Richard, La.App., 127 So.2d 816; Rogers v. Morgan, 250 Miss. 9, 164 So.2d 480; Howard v. Dillard, 198 Okl. 116, 176 P.2d 500; Swearingen v. Oldham, 195 Okl. 532, 159 P.2d 247; Jolly v. Wilson, Okl., 478 P.2d 886; that a royalty is created see: Gardner v. Jones, 198 Okl. 691, 181 P.2d 838; Armstrong v. McCracken, 204 Okl. 319, 229 P.2d 590; Lawson v. Earp, Okl., 309 P.2d 721; Murphy v. Earp, Okl., 382 P.2d 731 (however, as to the last four cases, the interest was in "oil and gas produced," an interest in royalty in Oklahoma); Watkins v. Slaughter, 144 Tex. 179, 189 S.W.2d 699; Klein v. Humble Oil & Refining Co., 126 Tex. 450, 86 S.W.2d 1077.

may be derived from a rather mechanical approach that all economic benefits and rights pertaining to the mineral estate being alienable, a $1/16$th mineral interest would entitle its holder to 1/128th of production in the event that the right to delay rentals were in another, and no difference should result if all rights other than to a share of production were in another. In other words, a conveyance in the form of a mineral interest will entitle the owner only to a proportionate part of production equal to royalty customarily attributable to such mineral interest, whether or not the other rights and economic benefits are owned by the holder of the interest.

A statement of the rationale of the courts in determining that a non-participating mineral interest has been created is found in the Louisiana case of Phillips Petroleum Co. v. Richard.[80] In this case the grant was in the form of a mineral conveyance, with the reservation to the grantor of the right to lease, bonus, and delay rentals. The court cited a former case [81] and stated: "In both of these cases, our Supreme Court held that the grant or reservation of an undivided interest in the minerals in or under the tracts created a mineral right, despite the retention by the landowner of the right to grant subsequent mineral leases without joinder of the mineral interest owner. In the Futral case, as in the present, the landowner was to receive the entire amounts received for rentals or renewals on an existing or on subsequent leases."

However, jurisdictions which would classify the interest created as a royalty are not consistent where the fraction involved is in excess of the royalty customarily provided under a lease. For instance it has been held that a grant or reservation of "an undivided $1/2$ interest in and to all of the oil, gas, and other minerals in, under and that may be produced from * * * ," less the power to lease, bonus and delay rentals creates a royalty interest but entitles the holder of the interest only to one-half of royalty or $1/16$ of gross production.[82] In effect, this is a holding that the interest created is a non-participating mineral interest. If treated as a royalty interest the holder of the $1/2$ royalty would be entitled to 50% of gross production without deduction of costs.[83]

It appears Oklahoma follows the "non-participating mineral interest" approach. This was established in the case of Swearingen v. Oldham, [84] which concerned a deed reserving to the grantor a "$1/16$ of all oil, gas or other minerals in and under said land" but passing to

---

80. La.App., 127 So.2d 816.

81. Cormier v. Ferguson, La.App., 92 So.2d 507, and see Standard Oil Co. of Louisiana v. Futral, 204 La. 215, 15 So.2d 65.

82. Skelly Oil Co. v. Cities Service Oil Co., 160 Kan. 226, 160 P.2d 246; Rogers v. Morgan, 250 Miss. 9, 164 So.2d 480.

83. Klein v. Humble Oil & Refining Co., 126 Tex. 450, 86 S.W.2d 1077.

84. Swearingen v. Oldham, 195 Okl 532, 159 P.2d 247. Same result in Howard v. Dillard, 198 Okl. 116, 176 P.2d 500, although Swearingen not cited; and in Jolly v. Wilson, Okl., 478 P.2d 886. In both Swearingen and Jolly the court emphasized the presence of "in and under the land" type language.

the grantee the power to lease, bonus and rentals. In a suit for reformation it was held that the reservation was not ambiguous and would reserve a mineral interest. Under this construction grantor or his successors would be entitled to $1/16 \times 1/8$, or a $1/128$ interest in gross production. Parol evidence was properly admitted in the reformation action, not to determine the meaning of the clause, but to determine if the clause as so construed reflected the true intent of the parties.

Other Oklahoma cases have reached the result that a royalty interest was created, but in these cases it seems that this would have been the result without the express language reserving all rights except the right to royalty. The grants or reservations were of interests "produced" from the ground.[85]

(I) Effect of a Conveyance or Reservation of a Mineral Interest, Less the Right to Bonus and Delay Rentals

In those instances where a grant is originally in the form of a mineral interest, and several, but not all, of the rights to bonus, delay rentals, and power to lease, are reserved in addition to reservation of a right to share in production, the courts have not been consistent in interpretation of the ownership of interests not specifically mentioned. The preferable approach would be to view all interests not specifically excluded from a mineral grant or reservation as being respectively granted or reserved, as the case may be.

In section (H), above, there was considered the nature of interests created where a conveyance or reservation was made in the form of a mineral interest, but where all economic benefits and rights except the right to share in production passed to the other party. In this section essentially the same question is presented, but with the additional twist that less rights and benefits are passed to the other party. Combinations occurring are found in the form of a conveyance of Blackacre containing a reservation of a mineral interest, with (1) the right to bonus and rentals passing to the grantee;[86] (2) the right to lease such interest passing to the grantee;[87] or (3) where the grantor reserved the rents and royalties, with the remainder of Blackacre

---

85. Gardner v. Jones, 198 Okl. 691, 181 P.2d 838; Armstrong v. McCracken, 204 Okl. 319, 229 P.2d 590; Lawson v. Earp, Okl., 309 P.2d 721; Murphy v. Earp, Okl., 382 P.2d 731.

86. Hudgins v. Lincoln National Life Insurance Co., D.C.Tex., 144 F.Supp. 192; Shepard v. John Hancock Mutual Life Insurance Co., 189 Kan. 125, 368 P.2d 19; Westbrook v. Ball, 222 Miss. 788, 77 So.2d 274; Martin v. Snuggs, Tex.Civ.App., 302 S.W.2d 676; Grissom v. Guetersloh, Tex.Civ.App., 391 S.W.2d 167. And see Jolly v. Wilson, Okl., 478 P.2d 886.

87. Hern v. Skelly Oil Co., 224 La. 709, 70 So.2d 657; Burns v. Audes, Tex.Civ.App., 312 S.W.2d 417. In the latter case it was held that the right to lease another's mineral interest does not impliedly carry with it the right to bonus and delay rentals. Who has the possessory right? It is also indicated in this case that the holder of the power to lease may charge the holder of the interest subject to the power with reasonable costs for exercise. Also see to same effect: Houston v. Moore Investment Co., Tex.Civ.App., 559 S.W.2d 850.

passing to the grantee.[88] The question of construction presented, of course, is who owns the omitted interest, being the right to lease in the first instance, the bonus and rentals in the second, and right to lease and bonus in the third.

The bulk of litigation has occurred in that category of cases where O, the owner of Blackacre, conveys the land to A, but reserves "an undivided $1/16$th interest in and to all of the oil, gas and other minerals in, under or that may be produced from said land, it being expressly provided, however, that the grantor shall have no right to bonuses or rentals under present or future leases." The primary concern here is who holds the power to lease, with a secondary question arising as to the amount of production to which the holder of the reserved interest is entitled.

The few cases extant have resolved the questions by applying two differing approaches to the constructional problem. One line of cases, (however, there is hardly sufficient case law to dignify by referring to it as a "line") looks at the overall intent of the parties and appears to conclude that the right to lease should be vested in the person who is the holder of the right to bonus and delay rentals.[89] This is typified by the case of Hudgins v. Lincoln Nat. Life Ins. Co.,[90] which involved a reservation similar to the hypothetical case above.[91] It was there contended by defendant grantor that leases executed by his grantee and the grantee's successor (plaintiff) did not cover grantor's interest in the minerals. Grantor thereupon refused to ratify the leases unless he would be entitled therefrom to a $1/4$ royalty or some type of net-profits interest. Plaintiff deemed this to be unreasonable, and, as the lessee threatened to withhold one-half of the bonus money until the controversy was settled, plaintiff brought suit to declare rights under the leases and for damages. The resulting decision construed grantor's reserved interest as a one-half non-participating mineral interest, limiting grantor to only one-half of royalty paid under future leases, with the exclusive right to lease passing to the grantee under the deed. The holding of the court was based in part upon the constructional principle that a deed would be construed to pass the greatest possible estate to the grantee, where there exists any doubt as to the construction of the language. It was also thought that a basic inconsistency existed if the person entitled to the entire bonus on the property had only a right to lease one-half of the property. The practical effect of such limitation would have been to restrict the

88. Mounger v. Pittman, 235 Miss. 85, 108 So.2d 565.

89. Hudgins v. Lincoln National Life Insurance Co., D.C.Tex., 144 Supp. 192; Grissom v. Guetersloh, Tex.Civ.App., 391 S.W.2d 167.

90. D.C.Tex., 144 F.Supp. 192.

91. "There is reserved unto Grantor an undivided one-half ($1/2$) interest in the oil, gas and other minerals in, under and on said property but shall not be entitled to receive any part of any bonuses paid by leases or any part of the rentals that may be paid for the privilege of deferring the commencement of a well or drilling operations."

plaintiff's interest to a one-half interest in the property in circumstances where the owner of the reserved interest refused to lease.

A similar result is found in the recent Texas case of Grissom v. Guetersloh,[92] which did not cite the Hudgins case as authority. The court held that the reservation of an interest in the form of a mineral interest, but without the right to bonus or delay rentals, did not convert the mineral interest into a royalty interest.[93] Again, in reasoning similar to that found in the Hudgins case, it was held that the right to lease passed to the grantee.[94] The holding as to right to lease would impliedly include the right to possession and development.

Contrasted with the above is the conclusion that all interests not specifically granted should be treated as not passing under the conveyance, that only the specific rights granted would be treated as being vested in the grantee.[95] The Mississippi Court has clearly stated this rationale in the case of Westbrook v. Ball:[96] "The owner of minerals has the right to execute oil, gas and mineral leases, selecting the lessee and fixing the terms of the lease, and to receive therefrom the bonuses, delay rentals and royalties. All these rights are transferable and a grantor can transfer all of them, or only part of them, but in reserving the minerals, all are retained that are not specifically granted. Appellee reserved the minerals and it was only specified that the bonuses and rentals from any lease executed would go to appellant."[97]

The difference in conclusions reached appears to be a result of courts such as in the Hudgins case treating the reservation as being

92. Tex.Civ.App., 391 S.W.2d 167.

93. The reservation was of a $1/16$th interest in form similar to the example above, and it was held that it reserved only a right to $1/16 \times 1/8$, or $1/128$th, of gross production.

94. Both the Hudgins and the Grissom case relied upon the early Texas case of Klein v. Humble Oil & Refining Co., 126 Tex. 450, 86 S.W.2d 1077, as a basis of the holding that the lease rights passed to the grantee. It would seem that the cases are distinguishable as to the wording of the reservation, as the clause in the Klein case stated that grantors "were not to *participate in any oil lease* or rental bonuses * * *" (emphasis supplied) which is a broader phrase than merely "rentals and bonuses" and might be construed as including the power to execute oil and gas leases.

95. Westbrook v. Ball, 222 Miss. 788, 77 So.2d 274; Martin v. Snuggs, Tex.Civ. App., 302 S.W.2d 676. This, of course, is with reference to the context of a grant with a reservation in the form of a mineral interest. The converse would also be true where A conveyed the mineral interest to B which provided that B would not be entitled to bonus or rentals. Also see: Houston v. Moore Investment Co., Tex. Civ.App., 559 S.W.2d 850.

96. 222 Miss. 788, 77 So.2d 274; Martin v. Snuggs, Tex.Civ.App., 302 S.W.2d 676.

97. Also see Martin v. Snuggs, Tex. Civ.App., 302 S.W.2d 676, which cited and followed the Mississippi case and further attempted to distinguish the Hudgins case. However, the court in effect reached the same result as in Hudgins by granting reformation which had the effect of placing in the grantee the exclusive right to lease the reserved interest. Cf. Shepard v. John Hancock Mutual Life Insurance Co., 189 Kan. 125, 368 P.2d 19, where it would seem that the Kansas court, in a suit to quiet title on the basis that a royalty interest violated the rule against perpetuities, in effect reformed a reservation of a royalty to a mineral interest to avoid the effect of the rule.

doubtful and following a policy of liberality in favor of the grantee. The opposite conclusion is compelled by a finding that reservation is certain in the first instance, i. e., of a fully participating mineral interest, and that only certain specific rights have been carved out. However, should the fact that only part of the economic benefits were severed from what is otherwise a reserved mineral interest make the grant or reservation ambiguous? If so, how resolve the ambiguity? Again we are confronted with the dilemma of whether the policy of the courts should be directed, in this instance, to resolving the precise intent of the parties (if any, in fact, existed) or formulating a rule of construction of practical application. It is no secret that in the great majority of instances involving construction of instruments as here presented the original parties are no longer locatable. The use of parol evidence to determine meaning in instruments found in a chain of title should be minimized to promote certainty of titles. Although the Hudgins court found it preferable that the right to lease follow the right to bonus, how may one treat them as inseparable? Does bonus follow the right to lease or the right to lease follow bonus?[98] If one be granted, does the other always follow? As all interests are definable and alienable, it would seem that the view of the courts exemplified by Westbrook v. Ball is a preferable, if not entirely accurate, reconstruction of intent. The preferable remedy, if one exists, is in reformation for mistake.

(J) Effect of Recitals to Other Instruments

A reference back to another instrument, if sufficiently certain, may have the result of modifying the interests contained in the instrument containing the reference.

Although an instrument from its terms may be fairly susceptible of a construction that it grants or reserves a mineral or royalty interest, a reference to a prior instrument may have the effect of characterizing the interest granted or reserved as being identical to the interest embodied in such prior instrument. For example, where O reserves "an undivided $3/4$ths of all the oil, gas and minerals in, on and under said land, being the same interest reserved in deed heretofore executed by A to B, to which reference is here made," and the former deed reserves a $3/16$ royalty interest, the question is squarely presented as to whether O intended to reserve a $3/4$ mineral interest or merely a $3/16$ royalty. Although controlling effect will normally not be given to the reference unless it is concluded that the instrument clearly requires this result, the presence of express language of reference, such as "to which reference is here made" or "to which refer-

---

98. See Houston v. Moore Investment Co., Tex.Civ.App., 559 S.W.2d 850, where grantor reserved an undivided one-half mineral interest, less the right to lease. The deed was held not ambiguous and that grantor also owned the bonus. Grantor owned all incidents of the mineral interest, minus only those expressly granted, i.e., the right to lease.

ence is here made for all purposes," will no doubt tend to influence a conclusion that such limiting effect was intended.⁹⁹

§ 2.8 Attributes of the Mineral Estate—Conveyances of Royalty and Mineral Interests for a Limited Term

Conveyances of fractional interests, royalty and mineral, are often made for limited periods of time. Although in the early days of oil and gas development such limited term interests were merely for an extended term of years, it has now become common to convey such interests for a fixed term of years that may be extended upon development and production.¹ An example of such term interest would be a grant of a $\frac{1}{16}$th royalty interest for "a term of ten years and as long thereafter that oil, gas, or other minerals are produced from the above described land." Upon production within the fixed or primary term, the royalty interest would continue past the end of the primary term until such time as the production ceased.

The use of such defeasible interests has proved very helpful in avoiding undue partitioning of the fully participating mineral interests. In many areas of the country mineral interests in tracts of land have become so spread out among owners that it becomes impossible to develop the property, as it is not possible to acquire leases from a sufficiently large percentage of the owners to make development profitable. Remedial legislation has been attempted in several states allowing the leasing of interests of "unknown owners" and using the courts as judicial trustees, but they, for the most part, have not proved particularly helpful.²

As most of the law that has developed in connection with term mineral and royalty grants has been in connection with the nature of acts necessary to propel the deed past the primary term, detailed discussion of the nature of the term grant is covered elsewhere.³

---

99. See Pich v. Lankford, 157 Tex. 335, 302 S.W.2d 645, although here the limiting effect was denied. Martin v. Knight, 290 Ala. 171, 275 So.2d 117 (where reference to prior deed controlled the interest passing to grantee in later conveyance. A good example of uncertain draftsmanship).

1. See Beatty v. Baxter, 208 Okl. 686, 258 P.2d 626; Archer County v. Webb, 161 Tex. 210, 338 S.W.2d 435.

2. For instance see Art. 2320b, Tex. Civ.Stat.

3. See Chapter 6, § 6.5(A), infra, Chapter 9, § 9.3, infra.

CHAPTER 3

CONVEYANCES, PARTITION, AND ADVERSE POSSESSION OF THE MINERAL ESTATE

Analysis

Sec.
3.1 Conveyances of the Mineral Estate—Description of Fractional Interests.
  (A) General.
  (B) Description of Quantum of Interest——Undivided Interests.
  (C) Description of Quantum of Interest——Percentage Interests and Mineral or Royalty Acre Interests.
3.2 Problems Commonly Encountered in Conveyances or Reservations of Fractional Interests in the Mineral Estate.
  (A) General—Use of Parol Evidence.
  (B) Reservations and Exceptions—Effect of False Recitals of Fact, and Effect of Those Made in Favor of Third Parties.
  (C) Reservations and Exceptions of Fractional Mineral or Royalty Interests from Conveyances of Undivided Mineral or Royalty Interests.
  (D) The Effect of an Exception or Reservation in an Instrument in Which Grantor has Breached His Covenant of Warranty by Overconveyance—After Acquired Title and the Doctrine of Duhig v. Peavy-Moore Lumber Co.
  (E) Estoppel by Deed as to a Reserved Interest Contained in a Deed Executed by One Without Title to One With Title.
3.3 Partition of the Mineral Estate.
  (A) Basis for Judicial Partition of Concurrently Owned Interests in the Minerals.
  (B) Elements Necessary for Partition of the Mineral Estate.
    (1) Necessity of a Possessory Interest.
    (2) The Concept of Estates of Equal Dignity or of Right to Possession.
    (3) Necessity of Ownership Throughout the Entire Tract to be Partitioned.
    (4) Method of Partition.
  (C) Equitable Partition.
3.4 Adverse Possessors—Effect of Surface Possession.
  (A) Non-user.
  (B) No Severance of Surface and Minerals.
  (C) Prior Severance of Surface and Minerals.
  (D) Tacking of Possession Between Successive Possessors.
  (E) Merger of Severed Estate.
3.5 Adverse Possession—Actual Possession of the Minerals.
  (A) Acts of Actual Possession.
  (B) Rights Acquired—Claiming under Color of Title.
  (C) Rights Acquired—Not Claiming under Color of Title.

§ 3.1 Conveyances of the Mineral Estate—Description of Fractional Interests

(A) General

In a prior chapter consideration has been given to the question of the nature of interests that may be created in the mineral estate. The present chapter primarily directs attention to problems of ownership and conveyance of fractional interests in the mineral estate.

It is beyond the scope of this volume to consider all variations in local law affecting conveyances of the mineral estate. Generally speaking, such conveyances must conform to the formalities and solemnities required by statutes of frauds and conveyances relating to deeds and contracts of sale of realty.[1] A deed of a mineral interest is required to be executed by persons or entities capable of owning or conveying property, the land and interests therein to be conveyed must be described with legal sufficiency, the instrument must be properly acknowledged or proved for record to entitle it to recordation, and, needless to say, it must be properly executed, delivered and accepted, all in accordance with local law of the situs of the property. As is the case with other conveyances, consideration is not a prerequisite for validity of the instrument, but is necessary to entitle the grantee to the protection of the recording statutes and the operation of the bona fide purchaser doctrine as it relates to prior equitable rights and interests.

(B) Description of Quantum of Interest—Undivided Interests

In most jurisdictions a conveyance or reservation creating concurrent ownership of the mineral estate, in absence of express words of survivorship, will be presumed to create a tenancy in common between the concurrent owners. In some jurisdictions concurrent ownership may be created in the form of a joint tenancy, or, if between husband and wife, a tenancy by the entireties.

Consider that O is the owner in fee simple of the mineral estate in Blackacre, a section of land containing 640 acres. O desires to convey to A $1/4$ of the mineral estate. O's attorney prepares a deed granting and conveying "an undivided one-fourth ($1/4$)" interest in the minerals together with specific rights of ingress and egress for the purposes of exploration, development and production. A conveyance of an "undivided" fractional interest in land creates a concurrent ownership of the mineral estate in the grantee with other owners of interests in the minerals. Today such concurrent ownership, in absence of specific intent being manifested in the instrument, will usually create a tenancy in common.[2]

---

1. See Chapter 1, § 1.3, supra.

2. In some jurisdictions a conveyance to husband and wife will create a tenancy by the entireties. Riddle v. Ellis, 139 Okl. 68, 281 P. 286. It is stated by Professor Powell that in not more than twenty-one jurisdictions is this form of owner-

The predominant characteristic of a tenancy in common is the unity of possession of each tenant in the land. Each tenant is separately vested with a non-exclusive possessory right in all of Blackacre, which interest will pass to his heirs, devisees, or successors by voluntary or involuntary conveyance. In the example above, O and A, as tenants in common in the minerals, each own a separate fractional share in all of the minerals underlying Blackacre; however, without partition, neither tenant has the exclusive right to possession to any particular or separate portion of the mineral estate.

It is not always desired to create a tenancy in common. In jurisdictions where it is feasible, parties may create a joint tenancy or a tenancy by the entireties.[3] A joint tenancy differs from a tenancy in common in that the surviving joint tenant has a right to the property, whereas upon the death of a tenant in common the property will pass to the heirs and devisees of the deceased, not to the surviving tenant in common. A tenant by the entireties is a joint tenancy where the tenants are husband and wife.

The rights of use and possession of the land by the joint tenant and the tenant in common may be treated as being equivalent, with differences in the methods of concurrent ownership being found in connection with termination of the tenancy or conveyance of interests. An illustration of a failure to appreciate the survivorship rights of the wife where property is owned as tenants by the entireties is illustrated in the Arkansas case of Tyler v. Boucher.[4] In this case $1/4$ of the minerals in 20 acres of land was conveyed to H and W as tenants by the entireties. Following a conveyance of one-half of their interest ($1/8$ of the minerals) to another, H attempted to convey the entire remaining $1/8$ mineral interest to A, without the joinder of his wife. H's conveyance, therefore, was effective only to convey H's interest ($1/16$ of the minerals) for a term equal to H's lifetime. In an attempt to adjust this situation, H and W later conveyed a $1/128$ royalty interest to A. The result was that if W survived H, the conveyance of H and W to A would not serve to convey W's survivorship interest in H's $1/16$ mineral interest, W owning the entire $1/8$ mineral interest subject only to a right in A to $1/128$ of gross production as a royalty. Since the deed of H could not bind the survivorship interest of W in H's $1/16$ interest, and as the later deed conveyed only a royalty interest, which conveyed neither W's survivorship right in H's interest nor any right to W's mineral interest other than royalty, these interests were retained in W if she survived H.

ship of substantial importance. See 4 Powell on Real Property, §§ 621–624.

Fast v. Fast, 209 Kan. 24, 496 P.2d 171 (unless limited, a conveyance of an undivided interest in described land, will also carry with it a corresponding undivided interest in the underlying mineral estate).

3. Hardy v. Greathouse, 406 Ill. 365, 94 N.E.2d 134; Tyler v. Boucher, 225 Ark. 806, 285 S.W.2d 524.

4. 225 Ark. 806, 285 S.W.2d 524.

This result may be contrasted to one in a jurisdiction where H and W own as tenants in common. Here W would have no survivorship rights in H's $1/16$ mineral interest, and although H could not convey W's interest in the minerals (except in those jurisdictions where he might have this power as community manager) his first deed would be effective as a fee simple conveyance of his own interest. As a result, A would be entitled to the $1/16$ mineral interest received from H, together with the $1/128$ royalty interest from W. W, on the other hand, would own only a $1/16$ mineral interest subject to A's royalty interest.

(C) Description of Quantum of Interest—Percentage Interests and Mineral or Royalty Acre Interests

The quantum of ownership of the mineral estate may be denoted by percentage interests, undivided interests, or of a particular number of acres of royalty or minerals.

A designation of a fractional interest as an undivided interest or percentage interest denotes a fixed fraction in the land described, regardless of the actual amount of land contained in the description.

The exact quantum of ownership indicated in a conveyance or reservation of a mineral or royalty acre interest is determined by forming a fraction whose numerator equals the number of mineral or royalty acres conveyed and whose denominator consists of the actual acreage contained in the land described.

By the better view the remedy for breach of warranty of title in a conveyance of a fractional number of mineral or royalty acres in certain described land, is in damages for the value of the lost mineral or royalty interest in that portion of the described land to which title has failed.

At least three methods have been used to denote the quantum of the mineral interest conveyed or reserved. Assume that O owns Blackacre, containing 20 acres of land, and desires to convey to A one-fourth of the minerals that he owns. He may do so by conveying a fractional interest in the minerals, a percentage interest [5] in the minerals, or a mineral acre interest.[6]

---

5. Pauley v. Faucett, 124 Cal.App.2d 406, 269 P.2d 89.

6. Examples of mineral acre interests: Carroll v. Funk, C.A.9th, 222 F.2d 508; Edwards v. Carter Oil Co., 226 Ark. 215, 288 S.W.2d 954; Superior Oil Co. v. Vanderhoof, D.C.Mont., 297 F.Supp. 1086 (effect of outstanding royalty); Smith v. Anisman, La.App., 85 So.2d 351; Wade v. Roberts, Okl., 346 P.2d 727; Woods v. Sims, 154 Tex. 59, 273 S.W.2d 617; Daniel v. Allen, Tex.Civ.App., 129 S.W.2d 392; Texas Osage Co-operative Royalty Pool v. Garcia, Tex.Civ.App., 176 S.W.2d 798; Pan-American Petroleum Corp. v. Texas Pacific Coal & Oil Co., Tex.Civ.App., 340 S.W.2d 548; of royalty acre interests: Dickens v. Tisdale, 204 Ark. 838, 164 S.W.2d 990; Tyler v. Boucher, 225 Ark. 806, 285 S.W.2d 524; Inslee v. Palmer, 153 Kan. 147, 109 P.2d 208; Halbert v. Green, Tex.Civ.App., 285 S.W.2d 767. The term has also been applied to the working interests in a lease, El Paso Natural Gas Co. v. Kelly, C.A.10th, 308 F.2d 820. See Tyler v. Boucher, concerning a 5 acre mineral interest in a 20 acre tract of land, where the royalty interest was variously described as (a) $1/128$ of gross production, (b) $1/16$ of royalty, and (c) a $1\!1/4$ acre royalty interest. They are all equivalent as (b) is equal to $1/16 \times 1/8$, or $1/128$ royalty interests, and (c) equals $1\!1/4 / 20 \times 1/8$, or $1/16 \times 1/8$, or $1/128$ royalty interest.

A conveyance of "an undivided one-fourth (1/4) interest in and to" the minerals will convey to A one-fourth of the minerals in the described land. The quantum of interest that A acquires is in no way dependent upon the actual acreage contained in the land. A's interest is calculated by applying the fraction contained in the conveyance against the total mineral estate in the land described. A conveyance by percentage or decimal equivalent is merely a conveyance of a fractional interest in a different form. The conveyance to A may have conveyed "an undivided 25%" of the minerals, or if converted to a decimal form "an undivided 0.25000000" of the minerals. In each instance A owns one-fourth of the minerals.

There has evolved, apparently as a holdover from the earlier days of more or less rough and ready conveyancing, a conveyance of a fractional interest defined in terms of acres of interest. For instance, in the example above, when O owns what he considers to be 20 acres of land he may have negotiated with A to convey to him "five acres of minerals," or a "five acre mineral" interest. This is merely another method of stating a fractional interest. A mineral acre is equivalent to all of the minerals in one acre of land. In constructing the fractional interest of A in the minerals, the acre interest conveyed in the deed is the numerator, and the denominator is the actual number of acres contained in the land described. If O's tract of land contains 20 acres, A's mineral interest is equal to $5/20$, or an undivided twenty five percent of or a one-fourth interest in the minerals in Blackacre. It should be observed that at this point neither O nor A may actually know the exact quantum of the minerals that each owns. If an accurate survey reflects that only 19.5 acres are contained in the described land, A's fractional interest is larger than he may have thought, i.e., $5/19.5$ equals 25.64% of the minerals. The converse is also true; if the tract is larger than thought, A's fractional interest will be decreased. The decrease in A's interest may be a result of natural causes such as accretion to land abutting a watercourse.[7]

When the "acre interest" mode of delineation of the quantum of interest is used for conveyance of royalty, a question is presented as to the definition of "royalty acre." In the above example, O conveys to A "a five acre royalty interest" in the minerals in Blackacre. A receives a non-cost bearing interest in gross production, but how much? Does A receive $5/20$ × gross production, viz., a royalty of 25% of production, or does A receive $5/20$ of royalty actually provided to the landowner under any present or future lease, or perhaps $5/20$ × the customary royalty provided to the landowner under oil and gas leases?

A royalty acre has been defined as "royalty accruing from production computed on an acre basis,"[8] and a fair inference from the few cases found would be that the phrase is equivalent to "$5/20$ths of roy-

---

7. Wade v. Roberts, Okl., 346 P.2d 727.

8. Inslee v. Palmer, 153 Kan. 147, 109 P.2d 208.

alty."[9] Where the oil and gas lease provides for a $1/8$ royalty, A would receive $5/20 \times 1/8$, or a $1/32$ royalty interest. However, such construction may or may not be followed by other courts. The use of royalty acres should be avoided at all costs.

Due to the inability to fix the fractional interest with certainty from the face of the instrument, the use of "acre interest" fractions should be discouraged. When encountered, one requires a staked survey of the property by a reputable surveyor, or, more preferably a correction instrument executed by all parties fixing the quantum of interest in a fractional form. Neither expedient, however, may prove particularly satisfactory. A staked survey of rural property may prove exorbitantly expensive as compared to the value of the interest conveyed. Where not all persons are *sui juris* or available, such an agreement may prove impossible to obtain. Even if available, the parties may not agree; however, in some cases a remedy of reformation has been availed of, resulting in a judgment of a fixed fractional share.[10] As the remedy of reformation is traditionally an equitable action, and as such being an *in personam* proceeding, absence from the jurisdiction may prevent the availability of the remedy. In some jurisdictions reformation of a deed is treated as a *quasi in rem* action, and parties may be constructively served with process.

Where a conveyance is made of a stated fractional interest, followed by a recital of mineral or royalty acres, e.g., "an undivided one-fourth interest in the minerals, it being my intent to convey 24 mineral acres", the redundant recital has usually been ignored.[11] However, in the Oklahoma case of Wade v. Roberts,[12] the recitation acted as a limitation upon the fractional interest granted. In that case a conveyance was made of "an undivided $5/32$ interest amounting to an undivided five (5) acre interest." It was later found that, due to accretion, a $5/32$ undivided interest would then amount to a 7.385 acre interest. The court held that the latter portion of the clause evidenced an intent that the fractional interest would not exceed a five acre interest. It is interesting to speculate what the court would have concluded if due to erosion the tract had decreased.

It is to be deplored that some draftsmen seem called upon to couple a recital of an acre interest to a statement of a definite fraction, producing an ambiguous instrument. Parol evidence would seem to

---

9. Dickens v. Tisdale, 204 Ark. 838, 164 S.W.2d 990.

10. See Texas Osage Co-operative Royalty Pool v. Garcia, Tex.Civ.App., 176 S.W.2d 798.

11. Texas Gulf Producing Co. v. Griffith, 218 Miss. 109, 65 So.2d 834; Ford v. Jones, 226 Miss. 716, 85 So.2d 215; Fantham v. Goodrich, 238 S.W.2d 572, reversed 150 Tex. 601, 244 S.W.2d 510; Woods v. Sims, 154 Tex. 59, 273 S.W.2d 617.

An alternative approach has been to construe the instrument against the party who prepares it: Williams v. Phillips Petroleum Co., D.C.Ala., 453 F.Supp. 967, rehearing denied C.A.5th, 614 F.2d 293; Johnston v. Hayes, Fla.App., 352 So.2d 951; Light v. Crowson Well Service, Inc., La., 313 So.2d 803.

12. Okl., 346 P.2d 727; also see Woods v. Sims, 154 Tex. 59, 273 S.W.2d 617.

§ 3.1   CONVEYANCES, PARTITION, POSSESSION   107

be clearly admissible to determine the actual intent of the parties. By application of the rule that in construction of an instrument it should be construed in favor of the grantee, it is arguable that the grantee should have an alternative right to choose the most advantageous construction. However, the courts have construed the instrument against the grantee, where the grantee prepared the instrument.[13]

The law is not settled whether a conveyance by mineral or royalty acres is void for indefiniteness under the statute of frauds; however, the preferable view is that it is not void.[14] The quantum conveyed or reserved may be made certain by ascertainment of the actual acreage described. However the question might have been decided as an original proposition, today public policy would seem to require support of such conveyances due to the large number of titles that would now be adversely affected by such a decision.

In addition to the constructional problem of definition of interest where a conveyance is made of mineral or royalty acres, there may be added the unresolved question of remedy for breach of warranty. Consider that O conveys one-fourth of the minerals in Blackacre, described as containing 100 acres of land. It is subsequently discovered that title to the west 10 acres of the land described is owned by T. Is it of consequence that A was conveyed "an undivided one-fourth interest in Blackacre," or "a twenty-five acre mineral interest in Blackacre"? It is clearly the law that in the event of conveyance of an undivided fractional interest, A owns one-fourth of the minerals in the remaining 90 acres and has a cause of action for damages for failure of title to one-fourth mineral interest in the west 10 acres.

Is the result similar where the conveyance was of mineral acres? Traditionally, A's damage is the value of the difference between what A would have had if the title had been as represented and as it actually existed, or for the value of a $2\frac{1}{2}$ acre mineral interest, viz, A would own a mineral interest of $^{25}/_{100}$ in 90 acres of land together with a cause of action for damages for loss of $2\frac{1}{2}$ mineral acres. However, one case [15] has indicated that O would be obligated to make up, out of the remaining acreage, a sufficient amount of the mineral estate so as to give to A an interest in 90 acres equivalent to that he would have received in the 100 acres. This, of course, is equal to giving A the identical right he would have had if the deed had described only

---

13. See cases at ftn. 12, supra.

14. Only three cases were found by the author: Knox v. Rutherford, Tex.Civ. App., 168 S.W.2d 313 (void); Pan-American Petroleum Corp. v. Texas Pacific Coal & Oil Co., Tex.Civ.App., 340 S.W.2d 548, refused n.r.e. (valid); Krebs v. Hodgson, Miss., 274 So.2d 122 (valid). However, the first case appears to bottom the decision on a consideration that the instrument did not describe the life, condition or terms of the mineral interest conveyed, rather than a defect in the manner of describing the fractional interest.

15. Daniel v. Allen, Tex.Civ.App., 129 S.W.2d 392, and see discussion in Hollyfield v. Rovenger, Tex.Civ.App., 262 S.W.2d 114. In the Alabama case of Williams v. Phillips Petroleum Co., D.C.Ala., 453 F.Supp. 967, the court refused to follow the Daniel case.

90 acres of land, i.e., $^{25}/_{90}$, or 27.77% of the minerals in the 90 acres of land.

The situations are different. In the latter case the parties are merely determining the amount of acreage actually contained in the description, which may or may not change A's supposed fractional interest in the land. Although A's fractional interest may thereby differ somewhat from what he supposed, A's total interest in the minerals does not change. Where a mineral deed conveys to A a 25 acre mineral interest in a tract supposed to contain 100 acres, but which surveys out to 90 acres, A's interest is increased from 25.00% to 27.77%. However, A's total mineral interest is unchanged, 27.77% of 90 acres equalling 25.00% of 100 acres.

Where a breach of warranty has occurred, the problem is not the ascertainment of the acreage contained in the deed description, but the fact that O did not own the land he purported to convey and to which he warranted title. For here the deed described 100 acres, but of the 100 acres described O owned only 90 acres. Traditionally the remedy for breach of warranty has been money damages for the value of the lost interest, usually stated in terms of consideration paid. No reason can be perceived for treating a conveyance by mineral or royalty acres differently from one by a stated fraction. To follow the approach of Daniel v. Allen[16] could lead to absurd results. In instances where the area lost is not large, a lessee may well be able to drill as many wells as he could have on the original acreage, with the same drainage area and total production, but with a substantial increase in the return from production to the acre interest grantee. Where the area lost is in excess of half of the described land, the grantee might receive all or a substantial portion of the production. Such a result can hardly be said to be within the manifested intent of the parties who have merely chosen, not wisely, an alternative method of stating a fractional interest in the mineral estate. At least one court has refused to reach this result, stating that the remedy is for breach of warranty, for value of the interest lost, not to make up the deficiency from other minerals owned by grantor in the tract.[17]

§ 3.2 Problems Commonly Encountered in Conveyances or Reservations of Fractional Interests in the Mineral Estate

Normally, an exception or reservation will be given effect wherever found in the body of an instrument, although some authority exists to the effect that an exception in or following the habendum clause will serve only to limit the warranty and not the conveyance.

---

16. Tex.Civ.App., 129 S.W.2d 392.

17. Williams v. Phillips Petroleum Co., D.C.Ala., 453 F.Supp. 967.

(A) General—Use of Parol Evidence

If the purpose of litigation is to determine title, any attack upon an instrument in the chain of title will be a collateral attack, and parol evidence will be excluded unless the instrument is ambiguous. If the purpose of litigation is a direct attack upon the instrument itself, parol evidence will be readily admitted to determine intent of the parties.

It is a basic rule of interpretative law that extrinsic evidence will not be considered in the interpretation of a written instrument unless the instrument is ambiguous. In the interpretation of instruments affecting oil and gas interests, courts will give effect to manifestations of intent without regard to common law restrictions as to form. The modern trend is to apply the "four corners rule," i.e., disregard the position of provisions in an instrument and determine intent from a reading of the whole instrument. For example, an intent to reserve an interest to the grantor will be given effect wherever found in the instrument, although some cases are still found that would apply the earlier rule that an exception or reservation in or following the warranty clause will serve to limit the warranty, but not the grant. Examples may be found, of course, where this approach has been carried to an extreme, with the result that a court has come to conclusions very probably not in the minds of any of the parties at the time of the transactions.

In analyzing and understanding the action of a court in permitting or excluding parol evidence consideration must be given to the framework in which the litigation was presented. A distinction must be made whether the cause of action was one to determine title to Blackacre, or to set aside, modify, or reform a particular instrument.

If the suit is one for title, the purpose of the litigation is to determine ownership of a certain described tract of land. Any attack upon an instrument in the chain of title is merely collateral to the purpose of the litigation. It is here that the above stated rule of parol evidence is applied, and parol evidence is normally excluded where the introduction of such evidence is for the purpose of making a collateral attack upon an unambiguous instrument.

Where the purpose of the litigation is not to determine title to a tract of land, but for the very purpose of setting aside, modifying or reforming a writing, such litigation constitutes a direct attack upon the instrument. In this type of litigation the question presented is whether the instrument, as prepared, actually represents and reflects the true intention of the parties. Parol evidence bearing upon the intent of the parties is freely admitted, for only by comparing intent as evidenced by parol evidence with the writing as prepared may the litigation be resolved.[1]

---

1. Edwards v. Carter Oil Co., 226 Ark. 215, 288 S.W.2d 954 (mutual mistake); Smalley v. Rogers, 232 Miss. 705, 100 So.2d 118 (reformation); Continental Oil Co. v. Doornbos, Tex.Civ.App., 386 S.W.2d 610, reversed Tex., 402 S.W.2d 879 (reformation); Wiseman v. Priboth,

Although courts usually follow the above distinction between direct and collateral attacks upon written instruments, instances may be found where relief in the form of reformation, modification, etc., has been given in suits for the purpose of determining title.[2]

(B) Reservations and Exceptions—Effect of False Recitals of Fact, and Effect of Those Made in Favor of Third Parties

A mineral interest which is excepted from or reserved in a deed, and which is supported by a false recital of fact, will be retained by the grantor and will not pass to the grantee. It is probably the majority view that a reservation or exception in favor of a third party will be ineffective to benefit the third party, and the interest will not pass to the grantee but will be retained by the grantor. In reaching this result, technical distinctions between a reservation and an exception will be ignored.

O conveys Blackacre to A by a deed containing a recital following the granting clause: " * * * subject to the one-half interest in mineral and oil rights as conveyed to William Henderson." However, no such conveyance of a mineral interest has ever been made. The question is presented as to the ownership of this ½ mineral interest. No contention may be made that the reservation would operate in favor of Henderson, as it contains no operative words to this effect. Since it is the intent of the recital that the interest not pass to the grantee, it is generally held that the ½ mineral interest will be retained by the grantor.[3]

An example of a case involving a reservation accompanied by a false recital of fact is that of Union Oil Co. of California v. Colglazier.[4] In this case A, who owned no interest in the minerals, executed a deed with a reservation of a one-half mineral interest. B, a subsequent grantor, who owned the minerals, later executed a deed with a reservation of " * * * (c) an undivided one half interest in the oil and gas * * * the same having been reserved to (A) * * * " The court held that the reservation was effective as it clearly appeared that the grantor intended to reserve the mineral rights. The false recital of fact, where such intent is shown, will not void the exception.

A different situation exists where the grantor attempts to make a reservation in favor of a third party, e.g., O conveys Blackacre to A and reserves an undivided one-half interest in the minerals to T. It is probably the prevailing view that the reservation in favor of T is

Tex.Civ.App., 310 S.W.2d 600 (mutual mistake—reformation).

2. See Gettel v. Hester, 165 Neb. 573, 86 N.W.2d 613, and Garrett v. Dils Co., 157 Tex. 92, 299 S.W.2d 904.

3. Brown v. Brown, Ky., 404 S.W.2d 286; Noffsinger v. Brown, Ky., 408 S.W.2d 436; Richardson v. Moore, 198 Miss. 741, 22 So.2d 494; Oldham v. Fortner, 221 Miss. 732, 74 So.2d 824; Wilson v. Gerard, 213 Miss. 177, 56 So.2d 471; West v. Arrington, Miss., 183 So.2d 824. But cf. Gibson v. Sellars, Ky., 252 S.W.2d 911.

4. Ala., 360 So.2d 965. However, see Melton v. Davis, Tex.Civ.App., 443 S.W.2d 605, refused n. r. e.

§ 3.2   CONVEYANCES, PARTITION, POSSESSION   111

void.[5] The most common example is where property is owned as the separate property of one spouse. Later both spouses execute a deed and reserve an interest in the minerals "to the grantors." The rationale in voiding the reservation to the spouse executing the deed but who owned no interest in the property, is that a reservation is of some interest owned by the grantor.[6] An exception to this rule is sometimes found where spouses reserved to themselves, and to the survivor, a life estate in the property. In some cases the reservation of a life estate to the non-owning spouse has been upheld.[7]

The denial of a reservation of an interest to the non-owning spouse (or other party) has been criticized on the ground that an intent to pass title should be given effect, even though not couched in formal granting language, and some supporting authority for this view point exists.[8]

Some courts, in reaching a result that the reservation be given effect, have found that the language of the reservation in the deed served to create a trust in favor of the parties named in the reservation.[9]

If T (or W, the spouse) does not benefit by the attempted reservation, will the interest now be owned by O or by A? A distinction could be made on the technical ground of whether the attempted creation of rights in T was by way of reservation or exception. An exception is technically considered as the withholding from the grantee of an interest already existing in the grantor. Upon failure of an exception the interest would thereupon remain in O, as no intent was manifested that it should, in any event, pass to A. On the other hand, a reservation is viewed as a new interest created in favor of the grantor after the property had passed to the grantee. Upon failure of an attempted reservation, it could be argued that the interest has passed to the grantee and remains there when the reservation fails. This distinction, if followed, could lead to differences in result, depending upon conceptualism in a jurisdiction as to the nature of ownership of the mineral estate. In an ownership-in-place jurisdiction a mineral interest is a corporeal interest, and in all probability the inter-

---

5. See: Ogle v. Barker, 224 Ind. 189, 68 N.E.2d 550; Leidig v. Hoopes, Okl., 288 P.2d 402; Sword v. Sword, Ky., 252 S.W.2d 869; Harris, Reservations in Favor of Strangers to the Title, 6 Okl.L. Rev. 127.

6. Leidig v. Hoopes, Okl., 288 P.2d 402; Ryan v. Fort Worth National Bank, Tex.Civ.App., 433 S.W.2d 2. In the Ryan case the wife of a partner joined her husband in execution of a partnership deed, containing a reservation to the grantors. It was invalid in favor of the wife.

7. Krug v. Reissig, Wyo., 488 P.2d 150. The case contains a good discussion of the different lines of authority.

8. Long-Bell Lumber Co. v. Granger, 222 La. 670, 63 So.2d 420, and see footnote 10, infra.

9. Burns v. Bastien, 174 Okl. 40, 50 P.2d 277, which contained the following reservation:

"Reserving an undivided three-fourths interest in and to all the royalties of oil and gas under and pertaining to said premises, which reservation of royalties shall belong to George Bastien, Charles Bastien, and E. E. Mead, share and share alike."

est attempted to be passed to T would be considered as an exception from O's deed. In a non-ownership state a right to the minerals is viewed as a profit à prendre, an incorporeal interest, and the interest might be considered a reservation rather than an exception.[10]

However, the majority of jurisdictions ignore the technical distinctions between an exception and a reservation and treat each as a limitation on the interest passing to the grantee[11], and the rights of the parties will be determined from intent as manifested by the entire instrument. It therefore appears to be the general view that, however framed, upon failure of the interest to pass to T, it will be owned by the grantor, O.[12]

(C) Reservations and Exceptions of Fractional Mineral or Royalty Interests from Conveyances of Undivided Mineral or Royalty Interests

In determining the quantum of a mineral or royalty reservation or exception contained in a conveyance of a fractional interest, where intent is not clear whether the reserved interest is proportional to the fractional interest conveyed or to the entire mineral estate, some authorities have

---

10. Restatement of the Law of Property, § 473 (1944), comment (a). It would seem consistent with modern conveyancing practices to allow creation of interests in third parties where such intent clearly appears regardless of absence of formal words of grant.

11. Brown v. Kirk, 127 Colo. 453, 257 P.2d 1045; Elrod v. Heirs, Devisees, etc., 156 Neb. 269, 55 N.W.2d 673; Edwards v. Brusha, 18 Okl. 234, 90 P. 727; Ewing v. Trawick, 208 Okl. 311, 256 P.2d 182; generally the term "subject to" is given the same significance as a reservation or exception, see Kelley v. Haas, Ky., 262 S.W.2d 687; Bulger v. McCourt, 179 Neb. 316, 138 N.W.2d 18; and Freeman v. Southland Paper Mills, Inc., Tex.Civ. App., 573 S.W.2d 822. However, classification as an exception or reservation may be decisive in determining whether the interest retained is personal to the grantor or will pass to his heirs and assigns. Since an excepted interest may be owned in fee by the grantor, or may be subject to conveyancing statutes which allow the interest to run to the heirs or assigns of the grantor, words of inheritance will not be necessary in the creation of the exception. Corporeal interests retained by the grantor are normally classified as being reservations, unless the conveyancing statutes of a particular jurisdiction are construed as applying to retained (not granted) interests, words of inheritance may be necessary to prevent the retained interest from being personal to the grantor. Silvis v. Peoples Natural Gas Co., 386 Pa. 453, 126 A.2d 706; Freeport Coal Co. v. Valley Point Mining Co., 141 W.Va. 397, 90 S.E.2d 296.

Early Oklahoma cases, now not followed, drew a distinction between the grant and the reservation of a mineral interest, where the rights of ingress and egress for development were not expressly included in the instrument. Where omitted from a grant of the mineral interest it was held that the conveyance was void. However, where omitted from a reservation, the rights would be implied. See Newbern v. Gould, 162 Okl. 82, 19 P.2d 157, and Morgan v. McGee, 117 Okl. 212, 245 P. 888.

12. Reservation void in favor of stranger to title and instrument: Sword v. Sword, Ky., 252 S.W.2d 869; White v. Hogge, Ky., 291 S.W.2d 22; Joiner v. Sullivan, Tex.Civ.App., 260 S.W.2d 439. Reservation void in favor of party to instrument, but stranger to title: Leidig v. Hoopes, Okl., 288 P.2d 402 (reservation to wife of grantor); Pruitt v. Burrow, Okl., 291 P.2d 349 (reservation in favor of husband of grantor). However, some courts have distinguished between the situation where the third party is a stranger to both the title and the deed, and where a party to the deed, but a stranger to the title, and have allowed the reservation in the latter instance. Long-Bell Lumber Co. v. Granger, 222 La. 670, 63 So.2d 420. Also see cases at footnote 3, supra.

treated the reservation or exception as being ambiguous and have examined surrounding circumstances to determine the intent of the parties.

In a majority of the cases, the reservation or exception has been viewed as not being ambiguous, and intent is determined by construction of the instrument. A distinction has been made whether a retained interest is reserved from the land "conveyed" or from the land "described." If the former, it has been treated as indicating an intent that the retained interest is proportional to the fractional interest conveyed; if the latter, proportional to the entire mineral estate.

Where grantor conveys an undivided interest in the minerals and retains an interest with a recital that the retained interest is "out of" grantor's interest, the recital will be construed as indicating the source of the retained interest and will not modify the amount of the interest retained.

Frequently, upon the sale of an undivided interest in the minerals the grantor will retain a small fractional mineral or royalty interest. Confusion as to the amount of the retained interest has been caused by use of imprecise language. This is illustrated in the early case of Hooks v. Neil.[13] O, the owner of an undivided one-half interest in the minerals underlying Blackacre, executed and delivered a deed to A which conveyed the undivided one-half interest and reserved " * * * a one thirty-second of all the oil in or under said land and premises herein described and conveyed." All parties agreed that the instrument was not ambiguous, and litigated the issue of whether the quantum of the reserved interest was referable to the entire mineral estate or merely to the interest conveyed. The court held that the reservation was referable only to the interest conveyed, i.e., equal to one sixty-fourth ($1/64$) of gross production, apparently upon the rather fallacious ground that the grantor could not make a reservation from an interest not owned by him.[14] The reasoning of the court is suspect, as the issue involved was the determination of the fraction of production in which A would share. In any event, the grantor had a sufficient interest in the mineral estate to allow the retention of either fraction of royalty, $1/32$ or $1/64$.

Hooks v. Neil was distinguished in the case of King v. First National Bank of Wichita Falls,[15] which also involved a grant of an undivided one-half interest in the minerals, but the reservation omitted the word "conveyed," i.e., " * * * reserving $1/8$ royalty in oil and gas that may be produced from the hereinabove described land." It was held that the reservation was $1/8$ of the entire mineral estate and not $1/8$ of the $1/2$ interest conveyed. The court distinguished the Hooks case on the basis that the reference there was to land "con-

---

13. Tex.Civ.App., 21 S.W.2d 532.

14. Also see Whitaker v. Neal, Tex. Civ.App., 187 S.W.2d 147; Dowda v. Hayman, Tex.Civ.App., 221 S.W.2d 1016; and cf. Krauss v. Fry, 209 La. 250, 24 So. 2d 464, where in a conveyance of a one-half mineral interest there was retained " * * * one-half ($1/2$) of all of the oil, gas and other mineral rights in, under and that may be produced from the above described land * * * ". The reservation was found ambiguous and parol evidence was allowed in construction of the instrument. In this case the reservation, on its face, is equal to the conveyance.

15. 144 Tex. 583, 192 S.W.2d 260, 163 A.L.R. 1128.

veyed," or to the interest granted, whereas here the reference was to the land "described." The use of the word "described" was construed as indicating an interest in the physical land itself and not merely in the interest therein conveyed by the grantor. This distinction between a reference to "land conveyed" and "land described" has been applied to the royalty reserved in oil and gas leases upon fractional interests in the mineral estate, as well as in deeds of mineral interests.[16]

Limiting phraseology such as is found in the Hooks case may inadvertently limit the scope of a grant of a mineral interest where the deed contains a reference back to instruments in the prior chain of title. Such references are primarily inserted in order to preserve continuity of title by harmonizing property descriptions which changed from time to time as parties in the antecedent title prepared deed descriptions from updated surveys. In order to insure the inclusion of all the property, properly supported by the antecedent chain of title, it is customary to include a metes and bounds description reflecting the most recent field notes, with references back to instruments in the prior chain of title for further descriptive purposes. Some care

---

16. Price v. Atlantic Refining Co., 79 N.Mex. 629, 447 P.2d 509; R. Lacy, Inc. v. Jarrett, Tex.Civ.App., 214 S.W.2d 692 (lease); Ferguson v. Morgan, 220 Miss. 266, 70 So.2d 866 (deed); McElmurray v. McElmurray, Tex.Civ.App., 270 S.W.2d 880 (deed); and cf. Fatherree v. McCormick, 199 Miss. 248, 24 So.2d 724. The late Professor Wilmer D. Masterson, Jr., in discussing the distinction suggested that the draftsman, if he desired that the reserved interest not be considered as being only proportional to the interest owned by the grantor, use the word "physical" preceding the word "land," viz., "O hereby reserves an undivided $1/16$ interest in all of the oil, gas and other minerals in, on, under, or that may be produced from the above described physical land * * *." Further clarifying recitals may also be desirable. See Masterson, Double Fraction Problems in Instruments Involving Mineral Interests, 11 S.W.L.J. 281; and cf. Barber, Duhig to Date: Problems in the Conveyancing of Fractional Mineral Interests, 13 S.W.L.J. 320, and Meyers and Williams, Oil and Gas Conveyancing: Grants and Reservations by Owners of Fractional Mineral Interests, 43 Va.L.Rev. 639.

In Middleton v. Broussard, Tex., 504 S.W.2d 839 the court expressly followed Hooks v. Neil (citing the text) in construing the following language:

" * * * and also a one-sixty-fourth ($1/64$) royalty right and interest in and to said *tracts* of land, * * * " (emphasis supplied)

and

"An undivided one-sixty-fourth ($1/64$) royalty interest in and to all of the oil, gas and other minerals in and under and that may be produced and saved from all of the above *described* land and premises, * * * " (emphasis supplied)

The court distinguished between a reference to the interest conveyed and to an interest in the entire land, and held:

"From the words in the Broussard deed, it appears that the grantors intended to convey the one-sixty-fourth royalty in all of the lands described. The deed does not limit the royalty to the lands "conveyed." It describes certain tracts and surveys out of which the Broussards granted a lesser undivided *surface* estate."

" * * * The Broussard deed does not purport to limit the royalty interest to what was conveyed. The grantors by their Paragraph Ninth in the deed state that the royalty grant is 'An undivided one-sixty-fourth ($1/64$) royalty interest in and to *all* of the oil, gas and other minerals in and under and that may be produced and saved from all of the above described land and premises * * *' (emphasis supplied) We conclude under the Hooks rule that the grantors conveyed the one-sixty-fourth royalty to all of the lands described."

should be given to the form of the reference. Where the reference is in the form of " * * * (metes and bounds description) and being the same land described in that certain deed executed by John Doe and wife, Jane Doe, as Grantors, to Richard Green, as Grantee, dated January 1, 1939, Recorded in Volume 375, Page 15, Deed Records, Dallas County, Texas, to which reference is made only for a further description of said land. * * *," only the specific description of the land in the former deed will be incorporated by the reference.[17] However, if the reference back recites "being the same land conveyed in deed executed by John Doe, etc.", the granting clause in the incorporating instrument will be limited to that quantum of estate actually conveyed in the reference instrument.[18] A like result will occur if a reference is made to a former instrument "for all purposes." [19]

An interesting illustration of the effect of such reference is presented in the case of Sharp v. Fowler.[20] O, the owner of Blackacre executed deed No. 1 to A, in which deed O reserved all of the minerals. O later executed deed No. 2 to A, conveying the minerals previously reserved in the former deed. In the instrument in question, A conveyed Blackacre to B, describing the land by metes and bounds, and following the description with a recitation that the land was "the same land described" in deed No. 1, to which it made reference. It was held that the effect of the reference to deed No. 1 was merely to point to the former deed for a further description of the land, and the reference back did not limit the grant in the deed to B to the same interest that had passed to A in deed No. 1, i.e., the surface of the land. This may be contrasted with the result in Winters v. Slover,[21] where A executed a deed of trust and mortgage to Bank with a recitation that the property described was "the same land conveyed by O to A (making reference to the former deed)." In the former deed O had conveyed only a $1/2$ interest in Blackacre to A, and it was held that the deed of trust was limited by the reference to a like conveyance.

Some courts have viewed a reference back to "land conveyed" as ambiguous and have allowed evidence of surrounding circumstances to be considered to determine the intent of the parties.[22] In one

17. Sharp v. Fowler, 151 Tex. 490, 252 S.W.2d 153; Crumpton v. Scott, Tex.Civ. App., 250 S.W.2d 953.

18. Winters v. Slover, 151 Tex. 485, 251 S.W.2d 726.

19. Harris v. Windsor, 156 Tex. 324, 294 S.W.2d 798.

In the case of Pfisterer v. Noble, Miss., 320 So.2d 383, grantor previously had conveyed all of the minerals, but had later repurchased a $1/8$ mineral interest. Grantor then conveyed the land by a deed containing the following clause:

"This conveyance and warranty herein are made subject to prior reservations and conveyances of all the oil, gas and other minerals in, on and under said lands."

The court held the language was not ambiguous and the quoted language served to except from the operation of the deed *all* of the mineral estate. The $1/8$ mineral interest remained in the grantor.

20. 151 Tex. 490, 252 S.W.2d 153.

21. 151 Tex. 485, 251 S.W.2d 726.

22. Kilfoyle v. Wright, D.C.Ala., 188 F.Supp. 899, affirmed in part and reversed in part, C.A.5th, 300 F.2d 626; Krauss v. Fry, 209 La. 250, 24 So.2d 464.

case [23] a reference back to a former deed, if allowed to modify the grant in the instrument containing the reference, would have had the effect of conveying a substantially larger tract than the one described. It was held that to give such effect to the reference was outside the obvious intent of the parties, and the reference was held to refer to the quality of the estate granted in the former deed and not to the extent of the land described.

The question of whether the amount of a fractional interest is proportional to the interest owned by a grantor or to the entire mineral estate also arises in conveyances of undivided interests which contain references to the fractional interest owned by the grantor at the time of the conveyance. O, owning an undivided one-half interest in the minerals, may convey to A "$1/4$ of the minerals out of the interest owned by the grantor" or "$1/4$ of the minerals out of my $1/2$ mineral interest." Did the grantor intend A to receive a full $1/4$ mineral interest which would be subtracted from O's interest, or only to receive an interest proportional to O's interest, i.e., $1/4$ of $1/2$, or a $1/8$ mineral interest? In the few cases found, the phrase "out of" has been construed as meaning "taken from" or "subtracted from," indicating the source of the interest rather than the quantum.[24]

For instance, in the case of Black v. Shell Oil Co.,[25] a deed was executed conveying an undivided one-half interest in the minerals. Following the granting clause and description of the land, the following language appears:

> "It being the intention of grantors herein to convey one-half of the minerals out of the interest owned by them in above-described tract of land."

It was held that "out of" referred to the source of the title out of which the $1/2$ mineral interest was to be taken and did not operate to reduce the amount of the mineral interest acquired by the grantees.

(D) The Effect of an Exception or Reservation in an Instrument in Which Grantor has Breached His Covenant of Warranty by Overconveyance—After Acquired Title and the Doctrine of Duhig v. Peavy-Moore Lumber Co.

Where a grantor conveys an interest in the minerals and in the same instrument reserves a mineral interest, and where there is a prior interest outstanding that is not excepted from the operation of the deed, so that effect may not be given to both the interest that grantor has purported to convey and the interest grantor has attempted to reserve, under the rule of Duhig v. Peavy-Moore Lumber Co., the grantee is not limited to a suit in damages for failure of title, but the attempted reservation will fail to the extent necessary to make the grantee whole. Where complete failure

---

23. Taylor v. Kerlin, Tex.Civ.App., 327 S.W.2d 793.

24. Minchen v. Hirsch, Tex.Civ.App., 295 S.W.2d 529; Black v. Shell Oil Co., Tex.Civ.App., 397 S.W.2d 877.

25. Tex.Civ.App., 397 S.W.2d 877, refused n.r.e., however, cf. Hartman v. Potter, Utah, 596 P.2d 653.

§ 3.2   CONVEYANCES, PARTITION, POSSESSION   117

of the reserved interest is insufficient to make the grantee whole, he will also have a cause of action in damages for failure of title.

Regardless of the Duhig rule, parties may contract for the payment of the economic benefits in a proportion different from ownership of the nominal title. It has been held such intent may be evidenced by a recital of payment of benefits from an existing lease.

The Duhig rule has been rejected as a device by which to reduce royalty in oil and gas leases on fractional interests, where the lease does not include a proportional reduction clause.

It is a familiar proposition of property law when a grantor, O, purports to convey Blackacre to A, at a time when O does not have title, that in the event O later acquires Blackacre, or an interest therein, O will be estopped by his deed to later claim that title to such interest is in O and not in A. Although it is generally stated that the doctrine of after acquired title is based upon the covenant of warranty,[26] the proper rationale is that of estoppel by deed, viz., that a grantor cannot later claim against his former solemn pronouncement that he has conveyed Blackacre to the grantee. This is evident in the fact that after acquired title will pass under deeds without warranty as well as under deeds with warranty. The after acquired title doctrine is, of course, applicable to interests in the mineral estate.[27]

In connection with conveyances of fractional interests in the mineral estate, a mutation of the after acquired title rule has occurred which has come to be referred to as the "Duhig Doctrine," from the case of Duhig v. Peavy-Moore Lumber Co.[28] This case was concerned with the effect of a conveyance by a Grantor, O, to Grantee, A, made by warranty deed of all of Blackacre, which deed contained a reservation to Grantor of a $1/2$ mineral interest. At the time of the conveyance a prior interest of an undivided $1/2$ mineral interest was outstanding in T, a third party. No mention was made in O's deed of T's prior interest. In a contest between O and A, O contended that the interest which he had reserved was in addition to T's interest and that, as a result, the minerals were owned $1/2$ by T and $1/2$ by O, A's only interest being in the surface of the land. As both O and A took subject to T's outstanding interest, obviously each may not own an undivided $1/2$ interest.

In determining upon whom the loss should fall, it would appear that the court had two possible solutions. The first was to give effect to the reservation by O, leaving A with no interest in the minerals, but with a cause of action for breach of warranty for failure of title as to an undivided $1/2$ interest. The remedy would be in damages

26. See Continental Oil Co. v. Tate, 211 La. 852, 30 So.2d 858; Brannon v. Varnado, 234 Miss. 466, 106 So.2d 386; Murphy v. Athans, Okl., 265 P.2d 461; Bryan v. Everett, Okl., 365 P.2d 146; McMahon v. Christmann, 157 Tex. 403, 303 S.W.2d 341, 304 S.W.2d 267; Body v. McDonald, 79 Wyo. 371, 334 P.2d 513.

27. See discussion in Hemingway, After-Acquired Title in Texas, Parts I and II, 20 S.W.L.J. p. 97 and p. 310.

28. 135 Tex. 503, 144 S.W.2d 878. Also see: Kadrmas v. Sauvageau, N.D., 188 N.W.2d 753; Murphy v. Athans, Okl., 265 P.2d 461; and, Bryan v. Everett, Okl., 365 P.2d 146.

for the value of the interest lost, usually measured by the consideration paid by A.[29] On the other hand the court might have voided the reserved interest of O on the ground of repugnancy, in that (disregarding the surface ownership) the reservation had the effect of nullifying the grant of the mineral interest to A.[30] The result would have been to place title to the remaining $1/2$ mineral interest in A, with no interest left in O.

The court did neither. Based somewhat upon the covenant of warranty basis of after acquired title, and partly upon estoppel by deed representations, the court held that where an interest is outstanding in the mineral estate so that full effect may not be given to both the granting clause and the reserved interest, the grantor may not claim any reserved interest until the grantee is made whole. Consequently, all of O's reserved interest was taken away from O and vested in A.

In applying the Duhig rule, the courts have not been consistent as to the underlying rationale. Drawing an analogy to cases involving passage of after acquired title, a dichotomy exists between cases bottomed upon the contractual scope of the warranty clause, i.e., that one may not claim an interest inconsistent with the warranty, and those which would see the rule as raising an estoppel against the grantor to deny what he has purported to convey, without regard to the presence or scope of a warranty. The latter would seem to be the proper basis for the rule, and the estoppel should not be regarded as being formed by the scope of the warranty.[31] Although not apparent in decisions applying or denying the Duhig rule, it is arguable that different results will occur depending upon whether the rule is viewed as being based upon the covenant of warranty or upon an estoppel by representation. A situation in point concerns the materiality of whether the Duhig rule will be applied in situations where the grantee has knowledge of the prior outstanding interest. Where estoppel is the rationale applied, it might be anticipated that knowledge by the grantee will prevent the estoppel from arising. On the other hand, if the rule is viewed as being based upon contract, knowledge of the grantee should be viewed as immaterial, as one may contract

---

29. See Taylor v. Wallace, 20 Colo. 211, 37 P. 963; Wilson v. Taylor Executors, 9 Ohio St. 595, 75 Am.Dec. 488; Hollingsworth v. Mexia, 14 Tex.Civ.App. 363, 37 S.W. 455.

30. See Lucas v. Thompson, 240 Miss. 767, 128 So.2d 874; Montgomery v. Ebony Hills Improvement Co., Tex.Civ.App., 229 S.W.2d 830.

31. Continental Oil Co. v. Tate, 211 La. 852, 30 So.2d 858; Brannon v. Varnado, 234 Miss. 466, 106 So.2d 386; Kadrmas v. Sauvageau, N.D., 188 N.W.2d 753; Murphy v. Athans, Okl., 265 P.2d 461; Bryan v. Everett, Okl., 365 P.2d 146; McMahon v. Christmann, 157 Tex. 403, 303 S.W.2d 341, 304 S.W.2d 267; Body v. McDonald, 79 Wyo. 371, 334 P.2d 513; American Republics Corp. v. Houston Oil Co. of Texas, C.A.5th, 173 F.2d 728, cert. denied, 338 U.S. 858, 70 S.Ct. 101, 94 L.Ed. 526; Coyne v. Butler, Tex.Civ.App., 396 S.W.2d 474. Cf. Language in Duhig v. Peavy-Moore Lumber Co., note 28 supra; Body v. McDonald, 79 Wyo. 371, 334 P.2d 513.

See discussion, Hemingway, After-Acquired Title in Texas, Part One and Two, 20 S.W.L.J. p. 97, p. 310.

§ 3.2   CONVEYANCES, PARTITION, POSSESSION   119

to bind himself to deliver an interest he does not own, or warrant a conveyance although he has no title. However, it appears that results will be the same in either event, and that knowledge of the grantee will be ignored.[32] This may be seen in the case of Body v. McDonald,[33] where it was argued that in the case in hand the grantee had knowledge of the prior outstanding interest, and therefore it differed from the Duhig case. The court denied the asserted distinction and admonished counsel that they had not properly distinguished between an estoppel in pais and an estoppel by deed, citing the early landmark case of Ayer v. Philadelphia & Face Brick Co.,[34] for such distinction. Here Justice Holmes conceived of estoppel by deed as emanating from the scope of the warranty clause and denied that knowledge of the grantee would effect the estoppel.[35] As the scope of the warranty clause was said to be determined by the contractual undertakings there expressed, knowledge of the grantee would have no effect upon the ability of the grantor to so bind himself, and, hence, no effect upon the estoppel thereby raised.

As a practical matter, the question of knowledge is probably ever-present, actually or constructively. When the prior interest is recorded, a subsequent grantee is charged with constructive notice by the recording acts. If the prior interest is not recorded, the grantee may be subject to the basic rule that a grantee is bound by the terms of instruments which form links in his chain of title, whether recorded or not. For example, A conveys to B by deed containing a reservation to A of an undivided ¼ mineral interest, which deed is unrecorded; B then conveys Blackacre to C; C conveys to D without mention of the reserved interest in A. If the interest in A is a legal interest, both C and D take subject to A's reserved interest, although without actual knowledge. This may be contrasted with the situation where A conveys an undivided ¼ mineral interest to X before he conveys to B. In this case if the deed to X is unrecorded it will be cut off by

---

32. Brown v. Kirk, 127 Colo. 453, 257 P.2d 1045; Body v. McDonald, 79 Wyo. 371, 334 P.2d 513.

33. 79 Wyo. 371, 334 P.2d 513.

34. 159 Mass. 84, 34 N.E. 177.

35. "The title may be said to inure by way of estoppel when explaining the reason why a discharge in bankruptcy does not affect this operation of the warranty; but if so, the existence of the estoppel does not rest on the prevention of fraud or on the fact of a representation actually believed to be true. It is a technical effect of a technical representation, the extent of which is determined by the scope of the words devoted to making it. * * * But the scope of the conventional assertion is determined by the scope of the warranty which contains it. Usually the warranty is of what is granted, and therefore the scope of it is determined by the scope of the description. But this is not necessarily so; and when the warranty says that the grantor is to be taken as assuring you that he owns and will defend you in the encumbered fee, it does not matter that by the same deed he avows the assertion not to be the fact. The warranty is intended to fix the extent of responsibility assumed, and by that the grantor makes himself answerable for the fact being true. In short, if a man by a deed says, I hereby estop myself to deny a fact, it does not matter that he recites as a preliminary that the fact is not true. The difference between a warranty and an ordinary statement in a deed is, that the operation and effect of the latter depends on the whole context of the deed, whereas the warranty is put in for the express purpose of estopping the grantor to the extent of its words."

subsequent purchasers without notice for value by virtue of the recording acts. In the later example the instrument does not form a link in either B or C's chain of title, and they are not claiming through the instrument to X.

Variations [36] in application of the Duhig rule may be illustrated as follows:

(1) O conveys to A all of Blackacre by a deed containing a reservation of a $3/8$ mineral interest. At the time, a $1/4$ mineral interest is outstanding in T. To determine the rights of O, it is necessary to determine what O has purported to convey to A, and this interest must then be compared with the interest owned by O at the time of the conveyance.

The interest which a grantor purports to convey is determined by the scope of the granting language less any reserved or excepted interests. For instance, in the above example, the granting clause is unrestricted, which would result in placing the entire mineral estate in A, but for the effect of the later reservation of a $3/8$ interest. The net effect of the deed is to purport to convey to A an undivided $5/8$ interest in the minerals (in these examples the ownership of the surface estate will be ignored). However, at the time that O conveyed, he owned only $3/4$ of the minerals. Obviously, it is impossible for A to receive $5/8$ of the minerals and at the same time for O to reserve $3/8$ of the minerals, as this gives no effect to the prior outstanding interest. To allow full effect to the reserved $3/8$ interest of O would reduce A's interest to $3/8$, rather than the $5/8$ that O purported to convey. Under the Duhig rationale, a sufficient portion of O's reserved mineral interest will be taken from O to make A whole, viz., $1/4$ of the minerals. The state of the title is that T owns a $1/4$ mineral interest, A owns $5/8$ of the minerals, and O has title to the remaining $1/8$.

An extension of this example occurs where A conveys to B, with a reservation of an undivided one-fourth mineral interest; B conveys to C; C conveys to D, etc., with each subsequent deed containing the

---

36. For cases involving the Duhig situation, see: American Republics Corp. v. Houston Oil Co., C. A. 5th, 173 F.2d 728, cert. denied 338 U.S. 858, 70 S.Ct. 101, 94 L.Ed. 526; Brown v. Kirk, 127 Colo. 453, 257 P.2d 1045; Dixon v. Abrams, 145 Colo. 86, 357 P.2d 917; Fatherree v. McCormick, 199 Miss. 248, 24 So.2d 724; Salmen Brick & Lumber Co. v. Williams, 210 Miss. 560, 50 So.2d 130; Garraway v. Bryant, 224 Miss. 459, 80 So.2d 59, 61 A.L.R.2d 1387; Merchants & Manufacturers Bank v. Dennis, 229 Miss. 447, 91 So.2d 254; Brannon v. Varnado, 234 Miss. 466, 106 So.2d 386; Lucas v. Thompson, 240 Miss. 767, 128 So.2d 874; Gettel v. Hester, 165 Neb. 573, 86 N.W.2d 613; Kadrmas v. Sauvageau, N. D., 188 N.W.2d 753; Murphy v. Athans, Okl., 265 P.2d 461; Birmingham v. McCoy, Okl., 358 P.2d 824; Bryan v. Everett, Okl., 365 P.2d 146; Klein v. Humble Oil & Refining Co., 126 Tex. 450, 86 S.W.2d 1077; Fantham v. Goodrich, 238 S.W.2d 572, reversed 150 Tex. 601, 244 S.W.2d 510; Benge v. Scharbauer, 152 Tex. 447, 259 S.W.2d 166; McMahon v. Christmann, 157 Tex. 403, 303 S.W.2d 341, 304 S.W.2d 267; Miles v. Martin, 159 Tex. 336, 321 S.W.2d 62; Howell v. Liles, Tex.Civ.App., 246 S.W.2d 260; McLain v. First National Bank of Fort Worth, Tex. Civ.App., 263 S.W.2d 324; Coyne v. Butler, Tex.Civ.App., 396 S.W.2d 474; Selman v. Bristow, Tex.Civ.App., 402 S.W.2d 520; Body v. McDonald, 79 Wyo. 371, 334 P.2d 513.

same reservation of a one-fourth interest. If A owned the entire fee prior to A's conveyance to B, the result is that A owns $1/4$ of the minerals and D (or the last grantee) owns the surface and $3/4$ of the minerals. Each reservation was merely protection as to A's $1/4$ interest and did not serve to reserve any additional interest in the subsequent grantor.

(2) The second example deals with the situation where the reserved interest of O is insufficient to make A whole. This result will occur in example (1) if the quantum of T's outstanding interest and O's reserved interest are reversed, i.e., a prior outstanding interest of a $3/8$ mineral interest and a reserved interest of $1/4$. Here O has purported to convey to A an undivided $3/4$ mineral interest at a time when he only owns $5/8$. Under Duhig, A will pick up all of O's reserved interest and in addition will have a cause of action in damages for breach of warranty for an additional $1/8$.[37]

(3) As noted above, A's remedy depends upon the interest that O has purported to convey. For instance, if in example (1) O had also excepted an additional $1/4$ mineral interest from the conveyance, the deed would have purported to have conveyed all of the minerals less the reserved $3/8$ interest and the excepted $1/4$ interest, or only a $3/8$ interest. The reservation of O would have been given full effect as, obviously, there would be no overconveyance. Overconveyance will also be prevented if the granting clause itself is reduced to give cognizance to the prior interest, viz., in example (1) if O had granted only an undivided $3/4$ mineral interest, with reservation to O of an additional $3/8$ interest.

Such limitation of the grant also may occur where the deed makes reference to a prior grant in the chain of title. Consider the situation where L conveys Blackacre to M, reserving an undivided $1/4$ mineral interest. Later in the chain of title O conveys Blackacre to A, reserving an undivided $3/8$ mineral interest. The deed contains the following recital after the metes and bounds description: " * * *, being the same property conveyed by L to M (specific reference to the deed) to which deed reference is here made for all purposes." It has been held that a reference back to a former deed for all purposes will limit the quantum of the conveyance in the deed containing the reference to the same quantum of estate passing in the former deed. In this case the granting clause in O's deed would be limited to an undivided $3/4$ interest in the mineral estate, and the net effect of A's deed would be to purport to convey to A a $3/8$ interest.[38] Again the reservation of O would be given full effect.

---

37. But see Brannon v. Varnado, 234 Miss. 466, 106 So.2d 386 (point as to cause of action not discussed); and McLain v. First National Bank of Fort Worth, Tex.Civ.App., 263 S.W.2d 324 (court reformed deed to avoid result). See Scarmardo v. Potter, Tex.Civ.App., 613 S.W.2d 756, which did not discuss the point specifically. It was also rejected in the Duhig case, see discussion in text following this footnote.

38. However, courts have refused to recognize the reference as a limitation.

The Duhig decision may be criticized on the ground that the court did not properly interpret a recital in the granting clause in the deed. Following the description was the recital: " * * * and being the same tract of land formerly owned by the Talbot-Duhig Lumber Company, and after the dissolution of said company, conveyed to W. J. Duhig by B. M. Talbot." The referred-to deed conveyed only an undivided $1/2$ mineral interest to B. M. Talbot. The court was of the opinion that the effect of the recital was to indicate the source of title and not in limitation of the granting clause. A contrary construction would have prevented the result in the Duhig case.

(4) The case of Benge v. Scharbauer,[39] provided a modification of the Duhig rule as to payments or benefits under an existing oil and gas lease. Restating the facts: At a time that an undivided $1/4$ mineral interest is outstanding in T, O conveys Blackacre to A by deed containing a reservation of an undivided $3/8$ mineral interest to the grantor. The deed contains a recital that the grantee shall have the right to lease; however, "said leases shall provide for the payment of three-eighths ($3/8$) of all the bonuses, rentals and royalties to the grantors." Applying the Duhig rule to the title of the parties: T owns $1/4$ of the minerals, and since O has purported to convey $5/8$ of the minerals to A at a time when he owned only a $3/4$ mineral interest, a $1/4$ mineral interest will be subtracted from O's reserved interest and given to A. A therefore owns $5/8$ of the mineral estate and O the remaining $1/8$. However, the parties may contract to divide the economic benefits in proportions different from the proportions in which they own the title, and in Benge it was held that by the recital they had so contracted. The results may be tabulated as follows:

	Title to Mineral Estate	Ownership of Economic Benefits
T	$1/4$	$1/4$
O	$1/8$	$3/8$
A	$5/8$	$3/8$

The Benge case may be criticized on the grounds that not only is it highly unrealistic to attempt to separate the economic benefits of the mineral estate from the nominal title, but also that the recital does not evidence an intention to contract for economic benefits in a proportion different from the ownership of the nominal title. As pointed out in the dissenting opinion, had the outstanding interest been $3/8$ rather than $1/4$, O would have received $3/8$ of the economic benefits when owning none of the title to the mineral estate, and although " * * * such an arrangement may be one within the power of a grantor to contract for, few sane people would so contract." [40]

The majority opinion is based upon the proposition that the parties had contracted for such a result. It would seem that the proposition is sound that the parties may do so; however, the pertinent inquiry is

---

39. 152 Tex. 447, 259 S.W.2d 166, at page 171.

40. Benge v. Scharbauer, 152 Tex. 447, 259 S.W.2d 166, at page 171.

§ 3.2   CONVEYANCES, PARTITION, POSSESSION   123

whether they have undertaken to do so. In the recital the same fraction, ³/₈, is used both in referring to title and to the payment to be made under the lease, and it is difficult to see how the parties have indicated an intent to deal with the economic benefits differently from the title.

As discussed in a later section,[41] in Texas the recital providing for the payment of specific benefits under an oil and gas lease which is outstanding at the time of the execution of a mineral deed, came into existence due to early case law which indicated that a conveyance of the mineral estate made "subject to" an outstanding oil and gas lease would serve only to pass the reversionary interest under the lease and none of the economic benefits.[42] Although the early cases are no longer considered authoritative,[43] a custom grew up whereby a mineral conveyance made at a time when a lease was outstanding would expressly include economic benefits payable under the lease in proportion to the mineral interest conveyed.

In the Benge case the difference in result is not due to a differing intent of the parties concerning the nominal title and the economic benefits. On the contrary, the use of the recital is to insure inclusion of benefits incident to the conveyed mineral estate. The difference in result as to title and benefits occurred solely by application of a rule of property, i.e., the Duhig doctrine. Although the Benge case is authoritative in Texas as to its facts, a much clearer indication of contractual intent than was present in the case would seem necessary to reach this result.

(5) O conveys Blackacre to A by deed containing a reservation of a $1/16$ royalty interest, at a time when there is an outstanding $1/2$ mineral interest in T. The deed purports to convey all of the minerals, subject to the royalty retained by the grantor. The question raised here is whether the Duhig rule will be applied to the reserved royalty interest of O. The issue has been squarely presented only in cases involving oil and gas leases where the lessor has reserved a full $1/8$ royalty interest while executing a lease on less than all of the minerals.[44] In several cases where the proportionate reduction clause was omitted from the lease, or expressly made inapplicable to a reserved royalty interest, attempts were made to reduce royalty on the basis of Duhig by taking a sufficient portion of the reserved royalty from the lessors until the royalty remaining was proportionate to the mineral interests leased.

41. See Chapter 9, §§ 9.1, 9.2, infra.

42. See Hager v. Stakes, 116 Tex. 453, 294 S.W. 835; and Caruthers v. Leonard, Tex.Com.App., 254 S.W. 779.

43. Harris v. Currie, 142 Tex. 93, 176 S.W.2d 302, and cf. Wright v. Carter Oil Co., 97 Okl. 46, 223 P. 835. Also see Atlantic Refining Co. v. Shell Oil Co., 217 La. 576, 46 So.2d 907 (express agreement).

44. Gibson v. Turner, 156 Tex. 289, 294 S.W.2d 781; McMahon v. Christmann, 157 Tex. 403, 303 S.W.2d 341, 304 S.W.2d 267; and see Hemingway, After-Acquired Title in Texas, Part II, 20 S.W. L.J. 310, at 324.

In these cases application of the Duhig rule has been denied on several grounds: (a) that the clause of warranty only applies to the interest granted and not to the interest reserved; (b) that a distinction must be made whether the interest retained is a reservation or an exception; (c) that automatic extinguishment of the royalty in the lease situation does not comport with the intent of the parties in the customary lease situation; and (d) that the doctrine will apply only to like interests.[45]

In lease cases the Texas court has clearly moved to a warranty basis to deny application of the Duhig rule, which seems unsupportable. Although a warranty covenant may not attach to a grantor's reserved interest, the reservation taken in connection with the granting clause defines the interest that grantor purports to convey and would support an estoppel without regard to the presence or absence of warranty. No judicial basis can be discovered for drawing a distinction upon the ground of whether the retained interest is in the form of an exception or reservation. A much sounder ground upon which to deny application of the Duhig rule to royalty reservations in conveyances of mineral interests would be that of impracticability, in that the grant and reservation are of unlike interests. In the above example, A owns only $1/2$ of the minerals, which interest would entitle him to a $1/16$ royalty (when the customary lease royalty is $1/8$), together with the right to lease, bonus and delay rentals incident to the interest. If Duhig were applied on the basis of comparable royalty lost, all of the reserved royalty would pass to A, and he would also have a cause of action for the other incidents of the mineral interest which he did not receive.

However, it cannot be predicted with accuracy what quantum of royalty will be provided for in a later lease. Also, any breach from overconveyance will involve incidents of title other than royalty, and it may not be said that the transferring of a portion of the grantor's reserved royalty interest would put the parties on a parity. In all probability, A should be limited to the traditional remedy of a suit for damages breach of warranty for loss of the mineral interest, and any interest he acquires will be burdened by the reserved royalty interest of O.

(6) A different situation from that discussed in (5), above, is where A conveys the fee and reserves a royalty interest, and where subsequent grantors also convey the fee and reserve a like royalty interest. For instance if A and all subsequent grantors were to reserve a $1/16$ royalty interest, the last grantee would hold title subject to A's $1/16$ royalty. All other reservations by subsequent grantors would serve merely to except from the conveyance the burden of A's royalty interest, and would not reserve additional royalties.

45. Id., supra, note 44.

§ 3.2 CONVEYANCES, PARTITION, POSSESSION 125

In this situation if the last grantee, e.g., D, were to execute an oil and gas lease with a $1/8$ royalty, both A and D would receive $1/16$ of production.

If A were to have conveyed a $1/16$ royalty interest to X and then executed a deed to the land with a reservation of a $1/16$th royalty interest, (and with D finally receiving this interest) royalty would be shared by X and D with each receiving $1/16$th of production.

Duhig has clearly been applied to royalty conveyances and reservations where only royalty interests have been involved.[46]

In this connection, the Duhig situation with regard to royalty should not be confused with the case where A, owning the fee, makes multiple conveyances to different grantees. For instance, A might execute deeds to each of three different grantees, e.g., B, C, and D, with each grantee receiving a $1/16$th royalty interest. A then executes an oil and gas lease to Rex Oil Co. Where all the deeds have been recorded, or the lessee otherwise has notice of them, lessee is subject to such royalty conveyances. The lessee will receive only a $13/16$ working interest, and will be bound to pay B, C, and D their royalty interests. A will receive nothing if the royalty reserved in the lease does not provide for more than a $3/16$ royalty.

The acceptance of the Duhig rule has not been overwhelming. Judicial restriction of the rule has occurred in Texas, its birthplace, and application to reservations of royalty in oil and gas leases has been flatly rejected.[47] Following the reasoning of the oil and gas lease cases, a serious doubt has been raised whether the doctrine will be applied in conveyances of the mineral estate with reservations of royalty interests. At least one judge has raised the question of whether Duhig relief should be granted in any event.[48]

In jurisdictions that apply the rule, draftsmen will be plagued with the problem of preparation of conveyances containing reservations or exceptions of fractional mineral interests when it is not possible or convenient to examine the underlying title for the purpose of discovering such prior outstanding interests. To avoid the Duhig result, as well as possible breach of warranty, it has been suggested that any such reservation or exception expressly be made "in addition to any prior recorded outstanding mineral or royalty interests." [49]

---

46. Selman v. Bristow, Tex.Civ.App., 402 S.W.2d 520, writ refused n. r. e., Tex., 406 S.W.2d 896; Haddad v. Boon, Tex.Civ.App., 557 S.W.2d 805, appeal after remand Tex.Civ.App., 609 S.W.2d 609, error granted; Jackson v. McKenney, Tex.Civ.App., 602 S.W.2d 124.

47. McMahon v. Christmann, 157 Tex. 403, 303 S.W.2d 341, 304 S.W.2d 267; and see Forrest v. Hanson, Tex., 424 S.W.2d 899, refusing to apply Duhig where other lands were involved.

48. See dissenting opinion in Salmen Brick & Lumber Co. v. Williams, 210 Miss 560, 50 So.2d 130. But see McClung v. Lawrence, Tex., 430 S.W.2d 179, applying Duhig to a reserved non-participating royalty interest.

49. See Masterson, Double Fraction Problems in Instruments Involving Mineral Interests, 11 S.W.L.J. 281; and cf. Barber, Duhig to Date: Problems in the Conveyancing of Fractional Mineral Interests, 13 S.W.L.J. 320. However, the

(E) Estoppel by Deed as to a Reserved Interest Contained in a Deed Executed by One Without Title to One With Title

Application of the principle of estoppel by deed may have the effect of placing title in a grantor who has no title, where a conveyance is made to one with title and the deed contains a reservation back to the grantor. This may be illustrated by the example where T acquires title to Blackacre by adverse possession and then leaves the land. Subsequently O, who has paper title, but who has unknowingly lost title by adverse possession, conveys Blackacre to T, or to T's successors in title, by deed containing a reservation of a fractional mineral or royalty interest. It has been suggested [50] that T, by acceptance of the deed from O, is estopped to deny the reservation by O. The result seems inequitable, in that T is faced with partial loss of title to one without title and for which loss T has paid the consideration! However, acceptance by a grantee of a deed is sufficient to bind him on an assumption of payment of outstanding indebtedness. Is an accepting grantee bound by all recitals in a conveyance which run in favor of the grantor? It may be significant that in one of the cases which apparently so held, the grantee actually had asserted the deed as evidence of a muniment of title.[51]

§ 3.3 Partition of the Mineral Estate

In most jurisdictions, the mineral co-tenant has an absolute right to partition. Equitable grounds are generally considered only in relation to the manner of partition, although in a few jurisdictions may be considered as defensive matters upon which to defeat partition.

Parties may either expressly or impliedly contract against partition. In some jurisdictions an implication against partition may arise from the existence of a joint operating agreement.

For a right of partition of the mineral estate to exist, it is usually stated that there must be joint ownership of a possessory interest throughout the land to be partitioned, and of estates of equal dignity or of right of possession.

Where partition is made of the mineral estate, although some jurisdictions prefer partition by sale, i.e., to sell the entire tract in controversy and partition the proceeds, the usual method is to partition in kind

---

question arises whether the attorney for a grantee can be persuaded to accept a deed with a blanket exception which would have the effect of destroying the grantor's warranty as to any outstanding interests.

50. Greene v. White, 137 Tex. 361, 153 S.W.2d 575, 136 A.L.R. 626; Adams v. Duncan, 147 Tex. 332, 215 S.W.2d 599; Klein v. First National Bank of Chicago, Tex.Civ.App., 266 S.W.2d 448; but cf. Dean v. Hidalgo County Water Improvement District No. 2, Tex.Civ.App., 320 S.W.2d 29, refused n.r.e.; and see Hemingway, After-Acquired Title in Texas, Part II, 20 S.W.L.J. 310, at 329.

51. Adams v. Duncan, note 50, supra. In this case the instrument was relied upon in prior litigation.

However, the doctrine was denied in Dean v. Hidalgo County Water Improvement District No. 2, note 50 supra, on the ground that the grantee of the deed received nothing from the transaction.

among the several parties and to partition by sale only where partition in kind would be inequitable.

(A) Basis for Judicial Partition of Concurrently Owned Interests in the Minerals

Traditionally, owners of concurrent possessory interests in land have enjoyed the right of judicial partition. Normally adjunct to the powers of the Court of Chancery, the right of partition as a creature of equity has been partially or totally displaced by statute throughout the United States.[1] The right to partition possessory concurrent interests in the mineral estate exists in all states having petroleum production, either as a matter of common law or by reason of statutory enactment. In a few jurisdictions statements may be found to the effect that equitable issues must be shown on the face of the petition to entitle the owner to partition.[2] In a majority of the states, however, equitable grounds do not have to be pleaded as part of the cause of action, as (1) the mineral co-tenant has an absolute right to partition, with equitable principles applied only to the manner of partition,[3] or (2) equitable grounds are considered defensive matters upon which to deny partition where it would be considered oppressive or fraudulent.[4]

A denial of partition will result, however, where it is shown that the parties either expressly or impliedly have contracted against partition, where such express or implied agreement is limited in duration to a reasonable time.[5] Parties may also validly contract for a specific method of partition, again if limited to a reasonable period of time.[6]

Agreements not to partition have been implied from joint operating agreements,[7] by the reservation of the right to lease in a convey-

1. For a compilation of the various types of concurrent ownership subject to partition and a listing of state statutes, see Volume 4, Powell on Real Property, § 609, note 4.

2. Overton v. Porterfield, 206 Ark. 784, 177 S.W.2d 735; Beardsley v. Kansas Natural Gas Co., 78 Kan. 571, 96 P. 859; Clark v. Mercer Oil Co., 139 Okl. 48, 281 P. 283. These cases involve the partition of the leasehold estate, and the courts in the latter two cases considered the interest to be one in personal property and not subject to the partition statutes relating to realty.

3. Bacon v. Wahrhaftig, 97 Cal.App. 2d 599, 218 P.2d 144; Rudman v. Baine, Fla.App., 133 So.2d 760; Watters v. People, 23 Misc.2d 402, 195 N.Y.S.2d 785, affirmed 12 A.D.2d 886, 210 N.Y.S.2d 39; Wight v. Ingram-Day Lumber Co., 195 Miss. 823, 17 So.2d 196; Moseley v. Hearrell, 141 Tex. 280, 171 S.W.2d 337; Chaffin v. Hall, Tex.Civ.App., 210 S.W.2d 191;

Medina Oil Development Co. v. Murphy, Tex.Civ.App., 233 S.W. 333.

4. Sadler v. Public National Bank & Trust Co. of New York, C. A. 10th, 172 F.2d 870; Seeligson v. Eilers, D.C.Kan., 131 F.Supp. 639, reversed C.A. 10th, 231 F. 14; Holland v. Shaffer, 162 Kan. 474, 178 P.2d 235, 173 A.L.R. 845; Gillet v. Powell, 174 Kan. 88, 254 P.2d 258; Strait v. Fuller, 184 Kan. 120, 334 P.2d 385; Tuggle v. Davis, 292 Ky. 27, 165 S.W.2d 844, 143 A.L.R. 1087; Henkel v. Henkel, 282 Mich. 473, 276 N.W. 522; Coker v. Vierson, 170 Okl. 528, 41 P.2d 95; Henson v. Bryant, Okl., 330 P.2d 591.

5. Saulsberry v. Saulsberry, 290 Ky. 132, 160 S.W.2d 654; Delta Drilling Co. v. Oil Finance Corp., 195 La. 407, 196 So. 914; Roberts v. Jones, 307 Mass. 504, 30 N.E.2d 392, 132 A.L.R. 663.

6. Robinson v. Speer, Fla.App., 185 So.2d 730.

7. Sadler v. Public National Bank & Trust Co. of New York, C. A. 10th, 172

ance of the minerals,[8] from an obligation to drill an offset well,[9] and from the fact that the mineral lands were subjected to a pooling or unitization agreement.[10]

The greatest area of litigation has occurred in connection with agreements for operations, management and exploration. Not every agreement concerning operations or management will result in an implication against partition, and the existence of only a mining partnership will not raise the implication.[11]

The implication of an agreement not to partition from the existence of an operating agreement seems to have originated in Texas. The case of Elrod v. Foster[12] denied a right of partition of the leasehold estate to one who had contracted to pay his proportional part of the expenses of drilling and developing. The effect of the partition would have been to work a cancellation of the drilling contract and to have relieved the promisor from his obligation for expenses of development. It was further thought that retention in the agreement of a preferential right to purchase indicated an intent to retain the co-tenancy relationship.

The case has been followed,[13] but sharply distinguished in later cases.[14] In Warner v. Winn[15] the court stated: "An agreement against partition will be implied when a granting of such relief would destroy the estate sought to be partitioned. * * * It seems reasonably clear that when parties contract for the drilling of wells, and such drilling is either made the consideration for the transfer of a mineral estate or is necessary to extend or perpetuate a lease, it must be inferred that the parties to the drilling agreement did not intend for the estate to be partitioned. * * * On the other hand, it can hardly be said that each and every covenant or provision relating to property held in common carries with it the implication that no parti-

F.2d 870; Thomas v. Witte, 214 Cal.2d 322, 29 Cal.Rptr. 412; Elrod v. Foster, Tex.Civ.App., 37 S.W.2d 339; Warner v. Winn, Tex.Civ.App., 191 S.W.2d 747; Sibley v. Hill, Tex.Civ.App., 331 S.W.2d 227; Long v. Hitzelberger, Tex.Civ.App., 602 S.W.2d 321, farm-out agreement.

In McInteer v. Gillespie, 31 Okl. 644, 122 P. 184, it was held that an implied agreement not to partition resulted from an agreement among co-tenants to develop and promote property for sale by lots. Although there was some evidence of an express agreement, the court stated that such implied agreement would be raised where the purpose for which property was acquired would be defeated by partition. Does this mean that if mineral property was otherwise subject to partition that if no production was present and the result of partition in kind would be to divide the land into areas smaller than the applicable spacing requirements that partition would be denied? Or would the court merely partition by sale?

8. Odstrcil v. McGlaun, Tex.Civ.App., 230 S.W.2d 353; Allison v. Smith, Tex. Civ.App., 278 S.W.2d 940.

9. Moss & Urschel v. Clark, Tex.Civ. App., 82 S.W.2d 1090.

10. Thomas v. Witte, 214 Cal.App.2d 322, 29 Cal.Rptr. 412.

11. Browne v. Loriaux, 189 Kan. 56, 366 P.2d 1016; Moseley v. Hearrell, 141 Tex. 280, 171 S.W.2d 337. No implied agreement against partition results merely from the severance of the minerals from the surface.

12. Tex.Civ.App., 37 S.W.2d 339.

13. Sibley v. Hill, Tex.Civ.App., 331 S.W.2d 227.

14. Goodloe & Meredith v. Harris, 127 Tex. 583, 94 S.W.2d 1141; Warner v. Winn, Tex.Civ.App., 191 S.W.2d 747.

15. Tex.Civ.App., 191 S.W.2d 747.

tion shall be had." Commenting upon the fact that all wells had been drilled when the action for partition was brought, and in answer to the contention that the agreement to operate and manage the property would raise an implied agreement against partition, the court further stated: "Warner contends that this paragraph placed upon Winn the duty to continue to manage and operate the leases and wells here involved. This is true, but the covenant is independent in the sense that Winn's failure to abide by the terms thereof would not divest him of title to the property which he had acquired by virtue of having fulfilled the drilling obligations contained in the contract. From such a covenant, the breach of which is compensable in damages, an agreement not to partition the property held by the parties will not be implied." Therefore, in Texas, where drilling is being performed for an interest, an agreement against partition will be implied for as long as development is to continue. However, following the completion of the drilling program an agreement to operate and manage the properties, without more, will not be sufficient to raise the implication.[16]

It appears to be the view in other jurisdictions that the existence of an operating agreement which does not contain an express statement against partition will not be sufficient to support an implication of a contract against partition.[17] However, in the two Oklahoma cases noted, special weight was given by the courts to the fact that other co-tenants had refused to pay their proportionate share of the expenses, or severe disputes had arisen, making peaceable joint operation of the properties impossible.

(B) Elements Necessary for Partition of the Mineral Estate

Although precise requirements differ between jurisdictions, it may be generally stated that the following elements are necessary to sustain a statutory action for partition of the mineral estate:

1. Joint ownership;
2. Possessory interest;
3. Estates of equal dignity or of right to possession;
4. Throughout the land to be partitioned.

This may be restated that the parties desiring judicial partition must be joint owners (usually tenants-in-common, although the stat-

---

16. In Sibley v. Hill, Tex.Civ.App., 331 S.W.2d 227, it was held that agreement against partition was implied from an express reference that the operating agreement would last throughout the life of production coupled with a preferential right to purchase.

Also in the case of Long v. Hitzelberger, Tex.Civ.App., 602 S.W.2d 321 an implied covenant against partition was found from the execution of a farmout agreement and the execution of an operating agreement relating thereto. It was held that where two wells were to be drilled, the purpose of the agreement was not satisfied and the implication against partition was still in effect where only one well had been drilled.

17. Delta Drilling Co. v. Oil Finance Corp., 195 La. 407, 196 So. 914 (based partially upon statute); Sweeney v. Bay State Oil & Gas Co., 192 Okl. 28, 133 P.2d 538; Komarek v. Perrine, Okl., 382 P.2d 748.

utes of a particular state should be examined to determine the concurrent interests that are subject to partition) of possessory estates or interests which are of equal dignity, or of equal right to possession, in the minerals throughout the tract of land to be partitioned.

(1) Necessity of a Possessory Interest

The effect of partition is to sever the right of possession and not of title. That is to say that the quantum of title of each co-owner in the tract of land is neither enlarged nor diminished, but is exclusively confined to a part of the total tract partitioned. Before partition, each co-tenant has the non-exclusive right to possession of the entire property; following partition, each owner has the exclusive right of possession to a portion of the entire tract. As partition acts on the right of possession of each owner, it is often stated that the owner of a non-possessory interest in land, such as an easement, has neither the right to compel nor to defeat partition. In cases involving mineral interests it is generally held that owners of non-possessory interests in the minerals, by themselves, have no right to partition. Such non-possessory interests would include ownership of landowner's royalty, overriding royalty, production payments,[18] etc., as well as leases in non-ownership [19] jurisdictions.

Although in most cases it will be apparent whether the interest involved is a possessory or non-possessory interest in the minerals, a question of who has the right of partition of the minerals will be presented where there has been a division of the economic benefits of the mineral estate.[20] For instance, consider the situation where O conveys all of Blackacre to A and reserves to himself and his successors an undivided one-half ($\frac{1}{2}$) interest in the minerals, less, however, the right to lease, bonus and delay rentals as to the reserved interest.[21] Or, where O so reserves a one-half ($\frac{1}{2}$) mineral interest, less the right to bonus and delay rentals.[22] A solution as to the first example may be found in those jurisdictions that would classify the re-

---

18. Delta Drilling Co. v. Oil Finance Corp., 195 La. 407, 196 So. 914 (based partially upon statute); Sweeney v. Bay State Oil & Gas Co., 192 Okl. 28, 133 P.2d 538; Komarek v. Perrine, Okl., 382 P.2d 748.

19. See: Hudgins v. Lincoln National Life Insurance Co., D.C.Tex., 144 F.Supp. 192; Chaffin v. Hall, Tex.Civ.App., 210 S.W.2d 191; Newcomb v. Blankenship, Tex.Civ.App., 256 S.W.2d 700; Hall v. Vernon, 47 W.Va. 295, 34 S.E. 764, reversed by Preston v. White, 57 W.Va. 278, 50 S.E. 236.

20. Pasteur v. Niswanger, 226 Ark. 486, 290 S.W.2d 852; Watford Oil & Gas Co. v. Shipman, 233 Ill. 9, 84 N.E. 53; Zeigler v. Brenneman, 237 Ill. 15, 86 N.E. 597, case also contains a good discussion of co-tenant rights; Beardsley v. Kansas Natural Gas Co., 78 Kan. 571, 96 P. 859; Strait v. Fuller, 184 Kan. 120, 334 P.2d 385; Gulf Refining Co. v. Hayne, 138 La. 555, 70 So. 509, based upon the Louisiana adoption of the civil law concept of *dominium*. This was later changed by statute, see Amerada Petroleum Corp. v. Murphy, 204 La. 721, 16 So.2d 244; Hall v. Douglas, 104 W.Va. 286, 140 S.E. 4.

21. See Skelly Oil Co. v. Cities Service Oil Co., 160 Kan. 226, 160 P.2d 246, and cases collected by note 79, Chapter 2, § 2.7(H), supra.

22. Hudgins v. Lincoln National Life Insurance Co., D.C.Tex., 144 F.Supp. 192, and cases collected by note 86, Chapter 2, § 2.7(I), supra.

served interest as a royalty interest. What of the jurisdictions that would classify the reserved interest as a "non-participating mineral interest"?

In both examples the question presented is whether the owner of some of the economic benefits (that do not include the right to lease) will have the right of self development.[23] As the right to lease may be defined as the right to grant the development rights to another, it would seem by the better view that the intent of the parties must be presumed to be that the one acquiring the right to lease the property would have an exclusive right of development. Hence, the right of partition would follow the right to possession and development, which in these situations would be in the owner of the right to lease.

(2) The Concept of Estates of Equal Dignity or of Right to Possession

The determination of whether both plaintiff and defendant have equal rights of possession and dignity has unique significance in judicial partition of interests in the mineral estate. The question has arisen where the entire fee is being partitioned in connection with attempts of a life tenant to partition his remainderman, and in similar situations. The life tenant has no right to partition his remainderman, as the life tenant and the remainderman do not have equal rights of possession, or own estates of equal dignity. This is, of course, because a remainderman has no right of possession until the life tenancy has come to an end. A similar question has been raised where A owns a life estate in an undivided one-half ($\frac{1}{2}$) interest in Blackacre, B owns the remainder interest as to the one-half ($\frac{1}{2}$) undivided interest, and C owns the remaining one-half ($\frac{1}{2}$) interest in fee. It has been held that A and B may not compel partition of C, not on the ground that A and B together do not have an estate of equal dignity or right of possession with C, but on the ground that B, the owner of a non-possessory interest, can neither compel nor defeat partition, the joinder of B adding nothing to A's interest. Traditionally, if A and C desired partition C would institute the action and join A and B as parties defendant. As C has a possessory interest and his estate is of equal dignity and of equal right of possession with the combined interests of A and B, partition would be granted.

Due to the fact that possessory and non-possessory interests may be created out of the landowner's mineral estate and out of the leasehold estate of a lessee, the question arises as to what constitutes estates of equal dignity, or right of possession, for purposes of judicial partition. Whether a non-possessory interest may be added to the possessory interests of a plaintiff to create an estate of equal dignity to defendant's interest has assumed considerably more importance

---

23. See discussion in Chapter 2, § 2.7(H), (I), supra.

than it did in connection with partition of land where the minerals were not involved.

The concept that estates of both the plaintiff and defendant be of equal right of possession or dignity is well put in an early Texas case. Suit for partition was brought by the lessee of an undivided one-half ($^1/_2$) mineral interest, joining as defendants the fee owner of the other one-half interest and plaintiff's own remainderman. In denying the right of partition, the court stated: "In our opinion, the lessee here cannot compel the lessor, the owner of the fee, and his cotenants, to partition. The estate of leasehold here differs from, and is of less dignity than, and is subservient to, the estate of freehold; the two estates are by no means common, or of a kind. The lease held by appellant in terms limits appellant to the right to go upon the leased premises for the 'sole and only purpose' of saving and removing oil and gas, and the uses incident to that purpose. It conveyed only a particular and very limited estate in land whereof the grantor held the general estate. It did not convey the exclusive dominion of any part of the premises so as to make the lessee a tenant in common, or joint tenant of the owner of the fee." In discussing the concept of equal dignity the court further said: "As we understand the rule to be in Texas, as well as in all the other states, perhaps, unless the plaintiff in a partition proceeding has an equal right to possession, he cannot compel partition. A joint owner of the fee, or of any interest in the fee, may compel partition of the land, and in this way have his portion of the fee or interest therein segregated from all the other portions, and given over to his exclusive use and enjoyment. This is true because the owners of that interest have the equal or joint right to possess, the estates of all are of equal dignity, and the interest of each owner is in kind, and capable of partition. The partition is of the possession, and not of the title." [24]

Cases dealing with partition of interests in the minerals may be categorized as follows (fractions are illustrative only):

	Plaintiff		Defendant
1.	mineral interest owner ($^1/_2$)	v.	mineral interest owner ($^1/_2$)
2.(a)	surface owner ($^3/_4$) + mineral interest owner ($^3/_4$)	v.	surface owner ($^1/_4$) + mineral interest owner ($^1/_4$)
(b)	fee owner ($^1/_4$)	v.	surface owner ($^1/_2$) + mineral interest owner ($^1/_2$)
(c)	surface owner ($^1/_2$) + mineral interest owner ($^1/_2$)	v.	fee owner ($^1/_4$)

24. Medina Oil Development Co. v. Murphy, Tex.Civ.App., 233 S.W. 333; also see Seeligson v. Eilers, D.C.Kan., 131 F.Supp. 639, reversed C.A.10th, 231 F.2d 14; Gulf Refining Co. v. Hayne, 138 La. 555, 70 So. 509.

§ 3.3   CONVEYANCES, PARTITION, POSSESSION

	Plaintiff		Defendant
3.	(a) mineral interest owner ($^3/_4$)	v.	mineral interest owner ($^1/_4$) (subject to lease)
	(b) mineral interest owner ($^3/_4$)	v.	mineral interest owner ($^1/_4$) (subject to common lease)
4.	mineral interest owner ($^1/_4$)	v.	lessee (also joining any carved out interests such as O.R.R.I. and production payments, $^3/_4$)
5.	lessee ($^3/_4$)	v.	lessee ($^1/_4$)
	(common lessor not party to the action)		
6.	lessee ($^3/_4$)	v.	lessee ($^1/_4$)
	(separate lessors not parties to the action)		
7.	lessor ($^3/_4$) + lessee ($^3/_4$)	v.	lessor ($^1/_4$) + lessee ($^1/_4$)

In all cases plaintiffs have a possessory interest in the mineral estate, except where the lessee's rights are considered to be in the nature of personalty and are not covered by a specific statute. It should be noted that the nature of interests of both plaintiff and defendant are the same except in numbers 2, 4 and 7, where the interests of either or both plaintiff and defendant must be added together to equal the interest on the other side, which is either a fee simple in the entire land or a fee simple in the mineral estate.

The above examples may be classified into four rather broad groupings. The first general classification includes partition of the mineral estate where no lease is outstanding and would include examples 1 and 2(a), (b), (c).

It appears that in all jurisdictions owners of undivided interests in the minerals have the right to partition against the other joint owners of the mineral estate. For example: A, the owner of an undivided one-half ($^1/_2$) interest in the minerals, may partition his interest and join as defendants B and C, who own an undivided one-eighth ($^1/_8$) and an undivided three eighths ($^3/_8$), respectively,[25] (example 1). By the better view, an owner of an undivided interest in the mineral estate should have the right of partition of the minerals apart from the surface, whether or not plaintiff or defendants also own the surface estate. However, this does not appear to be the rule in Kentucky when A, the owner of an undivided interest in the mineral estate, sues B, the owner of the rest of the minerals and the surface estate (example 2(b)). In this factual context partition has been denied on the ground

---

25. Holland v. Shaffer, 162 Kan. 474, 178 P.2d 235, 173 A.L.R. 845; Gillet v. Powell, 174 Kan. 88, 254 P.2d 258; Tuggle v. Davis, 292 Ky. 27, 165 S.W.2d 844, 143 A.L.R. 1087; Stern v. Great Southern Land Co., 148 Miss. 649, 114 So. 739; Phillips v. Phillips, 170 Neb. 733, 104 N.W.2d 52; Watters v. People, 23 Misc. 2d 402, 195 N.Y.S.2d 785, affirmed 12 A.D.2d 886, 210 N.Y.S.2d 39; Wolfe v. Stanford, 179 Okl. 27, 64 P.2d 335; Henson v. Bryant, Okl., 330 P.2d 591; Moseley v. Hearrell, 141 Tex. 280, 171 S.W.2d 337; Hardin v. Eubank, Tex.Civ.App., 245 S.W.2d 554; Preston v. White, 57 W.Va. 278, 50 S.E. 236, but cf. Robertson Consolidated Land Co. v. Paull, 63 W.Va. 249, 59 S.E. 1085.

that it is prejudicial to the owner of the surface estate.[26] Apparently partition is allowed when plaintiff, rather than defendant, is the owner of the surface and an interest in the minerals [27] (example 2(c)).

It also appears to be the general rule that the owner of an undivided interest in the minerals may join as party plaintiff the owner of the corresponding undivided interest in the surface and compel partition of the fee estate against the remaining owners of the mineral and surface estates (example 2(a)).

Some problems have arisen as to the manner of partition where the quantum of interests in the surface and mineral estates are not equal. In some cases the surface and mineral estates have been partitioned separately, in kind, in the same suit. In others the surface and mineral estates have been partitioned by sale, with an apportionment of the proceeds. In the Oklahoma case of Jones v. Hayton,[28] land for which partition was sought was owned by some 60 parties, with 54 owning an interest in the minerals and the surface, and 6 owning an interest in the minerals only. Partition by sale was decreed, and an appraisal was made which valued the surface at $11,600 and the minerals at $2,400. At the sale separate bids were made of $8,000 for the surface and $5,000 for the minerals. The bid accepted, however, was a combined bid of $13,000. In apportioning the proceeds, it was held that the $13,000 should be distributed to the surface and minerals in the ratio of the bids actually made at the sale, and not the ratio established by appraisal, which was treated as a mere estimate of value.[29]

The second general classification of cases also involves the partition of the mineral estate, but where there is an outstanding lease (examples 3(a) and (b)). There should be no objection to partition of the underlying mineral estate where it is subject to a common lease (example 3(b)).[30] Upon partition by sale or in kind no prejudice would result to the lessee, and, where partitioned in kind, the mineral owners would then share in future production only from wells drilled on their respective tracts of land. If production has been obtained upon the tract so that partition may prejudice one of the mineral owners, partition will generally be by sale rather than in kind.

A different situation exists where the lessors have each leased to a different lessee, for instance, where A executes a lease to Humble Oil Co. on an undivided one-half mineral interest, and his co-tenant, B,

---

26. Ball v. Clark, 150 Ky. 383, 150 S.W. 359; Harkins v. Hatfield, 221 Ky. 91, 297 S.W. 1109.

27. Terteling Brothers, Inc. v. Bennett, Ky., 287 S.W.2d 607.

28. Okl., 329 P.2d 1056. Also see: Ellis v. Cook, 205 Okl. 13, 234 P.2d 412; and, Starnes v. Miller, Okl., 505 P.2d 180.

29. Also see Union Trust Co. of New York v. Illinois Midland & Railway Co., 117 U.S. 434, 6 S.Ct. 809, 29 L.Ed. 963;
Vollum v. Beall, 83 A. 1095; Coker v. Vierson, 170 Okl. 528, 41 P.2d 95.

30. See Williams v. Skinner, 195 Okl. 321, 157 P.2d 181; Cox v. Lasley, 52 O.B. A.J. 2211 (1981); Consolidated Gas Supply Corp. v. Riley, __ W.Va. __, 247 S.E.2d 712; but cf. Fry v. Dewees, 151 Kan. 488, 99 P.2d 844; and Spikes v. Magnolia Petroleum Co., 158 Kan. 659, 149 P.2d 348, where partition was denied on the basis of outstanding lease.

leases his remaining interest to Texaco. May A and B partition the mineral estate without joinder of the lessees? If so, may partition be in kind? At least one case has permitted partition in kind of the underlying mineral estate, without partition of the leases.[31] It is difficult to perceive how the resulting production will be divided where the mineral estate is held in severalty and the leasehold estate by tenants in common. What is the status of that portion of Texaco's lease as to the lands set aside to A? On principle, it would seem to be the better rule that if partition is to be allowed the owners of the underlying mineral estate, where co-tenants lease to different lessees, it be by sale and not in kind.

In some non-ownership jurisdictions, where the interest of the lessee is classified as personalty, the right of partition may exist solely in the owner of the mineral estate, and upon partition in kind the lessee's right will follow its lessor's interest.[32]

Partition has also been allowed where the plaintiff has joined as defendants all parties whose total interest will equal a mineral interest (example 4). For example, A may join as party defendants: B, the owner of an undivided interest in the minerals and lessor to Rex Oil Co.; Rex Oil Co., the owner of the leasehold estate; and also the owners of any carved-out interests from the leasehold estate, such as owners of overriding royalty interests, production payments, etc. The fact that some of the carved out interests are non-possessory should not defeat partition.[33]

The third category of cases involves partition by the lessee, without the joinder of its lessor (examples 5 and 6). In those jurisdictions where the lessee's interest is considered to be a corporeal interest in realty, the lessee may maintain partition of the leasehold estate.[34] As in the case of a mineral owner partitioning the minerals subject to the lease, it appears that a distinction should be made between the situation where the leases are subject to a common lessor and where each lease has been executed by different lessors. In the former situation, partition may be allowed either in kind or by sale [35] (example 5).

In the latter situation (example 6), royalty will be held in co-tenancy, and the leasehold estate in severalty. While a lease of Texaco may be segregated to the West one-half of the tract, its lessor would

---

31. Amerada Petroleum Corp. v. Massad, Tex.Civ.App., 239 S.W.2d 730.

32. Zeigler v. Brenneman, 237 Ill. 15, 86 N.E. 597; Watford Oil & Gas Co. v. Shipman, 233 Ill. 9, 84 N.E. 53.

33. Collier v. Collier, 184 Okl. 38, 84 P.2d 603; Rolls v. Woods, Tex.Com.App., 291 S.W. 532.

34. Strait v. Fuller, 184 Kan. 120, 334 P.2d 385; Browne v. Loriaux, 189 Kan. 56, 366 P.2d 1016; Union Gas & Oil Co. v. Wiedemann Oil Co., 211 Ky. 361, 277 S.W. 323; Black v. Sylvania Producing Co., 105 Ohio St. 346, 137 N.E. 904; Clark v. Mercer Oil Co., 139 Okl. 48, 281 P. 283; Belgam Oil Co., Inc., v. Wirt Franklin Petroleum Corp., Tex.Civ.App., 209 S.W.2d 376, but cf. Pasteur v. Niswanger, 226 Ark. 486, 290 S.W.2d 852; Watford Oil & Gas Co. v. Shipman, 233 Ill. 9, 84 N.E. 53; Zeigler v. Brenneman, 237 Ill. 15, 86 N.E. 597; Beardsley v. Kansas Natural Gas Co., 78 Kan. 571, 96 P. 859.

35. Cases note 34, supra.

still own royalty in the East one-half. Although some courts in this factual situation have allowed partition of the leases in kind,[36] in principle it would seem that partition, if allowed, should be by sale.

The fourth and last category is that where plaintiffs, lessor and lessee, sue defendants, lessor and lessee, for partition (example 7). In cases not concerned with the mineral estate it has been stated that a non-possessory interest owner can neither compel nor defeat partition. The problem here concerns the issue of whether the addition of the lessor to the plaintiff's side of the docket adds anything. Cases dealing with partition of the mineral estate have added to the general law of partition, as partition by A and his lessee against B and his lessee has been allowed on the basis that adding the interests will result in interests of equal dignity or right to possession on both sides of the docket. This is well illustrated by the Texas case of Chaffin v. Hall,[37] where plaintiffs were the lessor and lessee of an undivided three-fourths interest in the minerals, and the defendants were the lessor and lessee of the remaining one-fourth. Defendant lessor maintained that as her interest was non-possessory she could not be partitioned. Partition was allowed in kind, with each lessee and its respective lessor being awarded a tract in severalty.[38]

(3) Necessity of Ownership Throughout the Entire Tract to be Partitioned

It is generally stated that in order to compel partition the moving party must own a possessory interest in the minerals throughout the entire tract being partitioned.[39] This does not mean, however, that if A owns an undivided interest in 80 acres out of a 100-acre tract that he cannot bring suit for partition describing only the 80-acre tract in which he owns an interest. In Gilbreath v. Douglas,[40] it was held that partition would be allowed as to the Southwest one-fourth of a section of land to a depth of 2512 feet, on the ground that this was the largest portion of land in which all the parties were co-tenants. It was argued by the defendants that the partition was only partial, as their co-tenancy was in the south one-half and unlimited in depth. In awarding partition the court not only limited it in depth but also in duration, to two years from July 8, 1963 and as long thereafter as there was production in paying quantities, the period of the determinable fee owned by plaintiffs.

---

36. See Sweeney v. Bay State Oil & Gas Co., 192 Okl. 28, 133 P.2d 528; Harper v. Ford, Okl., 317 P.2d 210.

37. Tex.Civ.App., 210 S.W.2d 191.

38. Also see Overton v. Porterfield, 206 Ark. 784, 177 S.W.2d 735; Newcomb v. Blankenship, Tex.Civ.App., 256 S.W.2d 700; Gilbreath v. Douglas, Tex.Civ.App., 388 S.W.2d 279.

39. Rudman v. Baine, Fla.App., 133 So.2d 760; Harper v. Ford, Okl., 317 P.2d 210; Luckel v. Barnsdall Oil Co., Tex.Civ.App., 74 S.W.2d 127; Gilbreath v. Douglas, Tex.Civ.App., 388 S.W.2d 279.

40. Tex.Civ.App., 388 S.W.2d 279 and also see Luckel v. Barnsdall Oil Co., Tex. Civ.App., 74 S.W.2d 127; Cf. Ellis v. Cook, 205 Okl. 13, 234 P.2d 412.

In the Oklahoma case of Harper v. Ford [41] the court allowed partition of two leaseholds that covered different depths, were for different terms, and contained other different provisions. Plaintiff was lessee of a lease that covered an undivided $3/4$ interest in the minerals in a ten acre tract, down to the bottom of the Cromwell sand, found at a depth of about 2600 feet below the surface of the ground. Defendant was the lessee of the other $1/4$ interest in the minerals in the same tract of land, but whose lease covered all depths. It was held that upon execution of the leases they became co-tenants, and either could obtain partition without the consent of the other. Partition was allowed as to depths covered by both leases, i.e., to the bottom of the Cromwell sand.

Cases covering all the minerals in part of the land should be distinguished from those cases where all of the mineral interests in the tract partitioned have not been subject of the partition action.[42] For instance, can A, owning an undivided $1/4$ interest in Blackacre, partition B, who owns an undivided $1/2$ interest in Blackacre? The result would be that the remaining undivided $1/4$ interest would still be owned in common. At least one state has allowed such partition, but only where consented to by all parties before the court.

It may be stated that partition may be maintained, if the other elements for partition exist, as to that portion of the land in which unity of possession of the mineral estate exists between the litigants. This is certainly true as to partition by sale, and probably as to partition in kind.

(4) Method of Partition

As in most jurisdictions judicial partition is a matter of right, equitable considerations are not usually taken into account in determining whether partition should be granted; however, such considerations are relevant to the method of partition applied. Partition may be by sale, where the property is sold and the proceeds distributed among the owners, or in kind, where each party's undivided interest in the whole is converted into an interest in severalty in a specified portion of the tract.

The jurisdictions are divided on whether partition should be by sale or in kind, where the land is undeveloped for petroleum products. A number of jurisdictions are of the opinion that where petroleum products are concerned the only equitable manner of partition is by sale.[43] It is felt that, as it is impossible to determine without develop-

---

41. Okl., 317 P.2d 210.

42. See: Ellis v. Cook, 205 Okl. 13, 234 P.2d 412; Starnes v. Miller, Okl., 505 P.2d 180.

43. Union Gas & Oil Co. v. Wiedemann Oil Co., 211 Ky. 361, 277 S.W. 323; Terteling Brothers, Inc. v. Bennett, Ky., 287 S.W.2d 607; Osborn v. Osborn, 267 Ky. 757, 103 S.W.2d 262; Thompson v. Mack, La.App., 195 So. 50; Fortney v. Tope, 262 Mich. 593, 247 N.W. 751; but cf. Henkel v. Henkel, 282 Mich. 473, 276 N.W. 522; Stern v. Great Southern Land Co., 148 Miss. 649, 114 So. 739; Hall v. Vernon, 47 W.Va. 295, 34 S.E. 764; Preston v. White, 57 W.Va. 278, 50 S.E. 236,

ment the amount and extent of oil or gas products underlying a tract of land, partition in kind could result in unwittingly awarding tracts of greatly unequal value to the various participants.

In probably the majority of petroleum-producing states, the view is that partition in kind is preferable unless it can be shown by the party opposing partition that partition in kind is inequitable.[44] If the land is undeveloped for petroleum products and is not in proximity to production, a presumption may be raised that petroleum products, if any, underlie the lands equally.[45]

Even in jurisdictions that would award partition in kind in the first instance, if production exists upon the land or in the vicinity, partition will be by sale unless it can be shown that petroleum products actually underlie the lands more or less equally.[46] In some jurisdictions partition will be by sale where parties owning both the surface and minerals are joined and their interests are not owned equally.[47] In such a situation it may be possible to have the estates in the minerals and the surface partitioned separately, partitioning the minerals by sale, and the surface in kind. If the disparity is too great, partition may be made by sale of each estate separately.[48]

Where partition is in kind, the land should be subdivided into tracts no smaller than the prevailing minimum spacing pattern allowed by the particular conservation agency of the jurisdiction as to

apparently reversing the preceding case and providing for partition in kind, but cf. Robertson Consolidated Land Co. v. Paull, 63 W.Va. 249, 59 S.E. 1085, which relies upon Hall v. Vernon and doesn't mention the Preston case.

44. Jenks v. Jenks, 292 Ala. 328, 294 So.2d 147; Beardsley v. Kansas Natural Gas Co., 78 Kan. 571, 96 P. 859; Wight v. Ingram-Day Lumber Co., 195 Miss. 823, 17 So.2d 196; Blake v. St. Catherine Gravel Co., 218 Miss. 713, 67 So.2d 712; but cf. Stern v. Great Southern Land Co., 148 Miss. 649, 114 So. 739; Jones v. Hayton, Okl., 329 P.2d 1056; Coker v. Vierson, 170 Okl. 528, 41 P.2d 95; Wolfe v. Stanford, 179 Okl. 27, 64 P.2d 335; Henson v. Bryant, Okl., 330 P.2d 591; Ellis v. Cook, 205 Okl. 13, 234 P.2d 412; Starnes v. Miller, Okl., 505 P.2d 180; Amerada Petroleum Co. v. Massad, Tex.Civ.App., 239 S.W.2d 730.

45. Henderson v. Chesley, 116 Tex. 355, 292 S.W. 156; Humble Oil & Refining Co. v. Lasseter, Tex.Civ.App., 95 S.W.2d 730; Amerada Petroleum Co. v. Massad, Tex.Civ.App., 239 S.W.2d 730.

46. Phillips v. Phillips, 170 Neb. 733, 104 N.W.2d 52; Williams v. Skinner, 195 Okl. 321, 157 P.2d 181; Henderson v. Chesley, 116 Tex. 355, 292 S.W. 156; Humble Oil & Refining Co. v. Lasseter, Tex.Civ.App., 95 S.W.2d 730. The Texas case of White v. Smyth, 147 Tex. 272, 214 S.W.2d 967, 5 A.L.R.2d 1348, presents an interesting situation involving asphalt, where one co-tenant attempted to partition in kind and have set off to himself an area which was rich in asphalt. The court refused partition in kind where it was estimated that some 1800 borings would have to be made to determine the extent and volume of the asphalt, which underlay the land in sporadic and unequal amounts. The court also ordered an accounting of the entire proceeds received from the sale of the asphalt rather than on the price of the extracted material, on the ground that the processing did not constitute a manufacturing process.

47. Coker v. Vierson, 170 Okl. 528, 41 P.2d 95; Wolfe v. Stanford, 179 Okl. 27, 64 P.2d 335; Jones v. Hayton, Okl., 329 P.2d 1056.

48. Coker v. Vierson, 170 Okl. 528, 41 P.2d 95; Jones v. Hayton, Okl., 329 P.2d 1056, here the land was owned by 60 parties with 54 owning interests in both the surface and in the minerals, with 6 owning only a mineral interest. Also see Ellis v. Cook, 205 Okl. 13, 234 P.2d 412.

production reasonably expected in the area.[49] Where large tracts of land are involved, the courts will usually "checkerboard" the allotted subdivided tracts, i.e., awarding to each litigant alternate tracts.[50]

(C) Equitable Partition

A and B are co-tenants in Blackacre, which contains 640 acres of land. A, being somewhat confused as to the nature of his interest, agrees to sell to C the east one-half of Blackacre, and does so by executing a deed to C. Obviously, the deed will convey A's interest in the tract described; however, as B has not joined in the deed, what are the rights of C against B?

Although some jurisdictions hold that A's deed creates no rights in C as to B's interest in the land,[51] a body of law exists which would find an equity created in C's favor, which may be enforced against B by partition, if to do so would not prejudice B's rights.[52] Where the value of the land remaining after A's conveyance would be equal to or greater than the value of B's undivided interest in the entire tract, a court of equity may decree a partition on the ground that C may be protected by such partition and B is not hurt. Although few cases have been found, it would appear that the co-tenant's grantee may not claim the specific segregated tract described in his deed as a matter of right by operation of a rule of property.[53] The basis of the rule has been well stated by a lower Texas court: [54]

"The deeds of a tenant in common to specific parcels of the land are not absolutely void. They are always good as against the grantor. Such deeds do not convey or destroy any of the title of the nonjoining co-tenants to their undivided interest to the lands described in the deeds. The nonjoining cotenants may avoid such deeds, *if and to the extent only they are injured by such deeds.* Though one cotenant has no power to divest the title of other cotenants by selling specific parts of the common property, yet un-

---

49. Wight v. Ingram-Day Lumber Co., 195 Miss. 823, 17 So.2d 196; Blake v. St. Catherine Gravel Co., 218 Miss. 713, 67 So.2d 712.

50. Phillips v. Phillips, 170 Neb. 733, 104 N.W.2d 52; Henderson v. Chesley, 116 Tex. 355, 292 S.W. 156; Humble Oil & Refining Co. v. Lasseter, Tex.Civ.App., 95 S.W.2d 730. Note Watters v. People, 23 Misc.2d 402, 195 N.Y.S.2d 785, affirmed 12 A.D.2d 886, 210 N.Y.S.2d 39, where a New York court subdivided a tract diagonally.

51. Ball v. Clark, 150 Ky. 383, 150 S.W. 359; and see Luckel v. Barnsdall Oil Co., Tex.Civ.App., 74 S.W.2d 127.

52. Pellow v. Arctic Mining Co., 164 Mich. 87, 128 N.W. 918; Thomas v. Southwestern Settlement & Development Co., 132 Tex. 413, 123 S.W.2d 290; 17 Tex.L.Rev. 509; Simpson-Fell Oil Co. v. Stanolind Oil & Gas Co., 136 Tex. 158, 125 S.W.2d 263; 136 Tex. 158, 146 S.W.2d 723; 17 Tex.L.Rev. 507; Merriweather v. Jackson, Tex.Civ.App., 38 S.W.2d 599; Larrison v. Walker, Tex.Civ.App., 149 S.W.2d 172.

53. Pellow v. Arctic Mining Co., 164 Mich. 87, 128 N.W. 918; Thomas v. Southwestern Settlement & Development Co., 132 Tex. 413, 123 S.W.2d 290; 17 Tex.L.Rev. 509; Simpson-Fell Oil Co. v. Stanolind Oil & Gas Co., 136 Tex. 158, 125 S.W.2d 263; 136 Tex. 158, 146 S.W.2d 723, 17 Tex.L.Rev. 507.

54. Larrison v. Walker, Tex.Civ.App., 149 S.W.2d 172.

der the well-settled doctrine of equitable partition the court in adjusting the equities of all the interested parties will protect such purchasers by setting aside to them the particular tracts purchased, if it can be done without injury to the other owners, where, as here, the acreage of the common property is of equal and uniform value; and will set aside to the nonjoining cotenants the equivalent of their interest in all the land out of the unsold tract if it is sufficient to satisfy same; and if the unsold tract is not sufficient to fully satisfy the interest of the nonjoining cotenants, then the remainder of their interest will be satisfied out of that sold, in the inverse order of the execution of such deeds."

The courts have differed in their views as to the time at which the grantee's rights attach to the specific tract and when values should be determined, i.e., at the time of the conveyance or at the time of the decree of partition.[55]

The doctrine of equitable partition may also be applied where, following the conveyance by one co-tenant of a specific tract out of the common property, the nonjoining co-tenant conveys all of the remaining portion of the common property to another. In this situation the conveyance of the first co-tenant has been treated as a continuing offer of partition that has been accepted by the latter conveyance. Some courts have upheld the partition on the ground of ratification.[56]

The doctrine of equitable partition has obvious value as a curative device where property is owned in common, and co-tenants deal with specific portions of the land without an express partition. The doctrine has been applied to conveyances or leases of mineral estates where tenants in common execute mineral or royalty deeds or mineral leases describing specific portions of lands held in common.[57] The doctrine, however, will not be applied to effect horizontal partition, i.e., to sever or separate the mineral from the surface estate.[58]

§ 3.4 Adverse Possessors—Effect of Surface Possession

Where no prior severance of the minerals from the surface has occurred, acquisitive possession of the surface of the land will also run to and mature title to the mineral estate. In ownership jurisdictions and most non-ownership jurisdictions mineral interests cannot be lost by non-

---

55. Pan American Production Co. v. Hollandsworth, Tex.Civ.App., 294 S.W.2d 205; Thomas v. Southwestern Settlement & Dev. Co., 132 Tex. 413, 123 S.W.2d 290, 17 Tex.L.Rev. 509 (determine value at time of trial); Germany v. Turner, 132 Tex. 491, 123 S.W.2d 874 (determine value at time of conveyance).

56. Simpson-Fell Oil Co. v. Stanolind Oil & Gas Co., 136 Tex. 158, 125 S.W.2d 263; 136 Tex. 158, 146 S.W.2d 723; 17 Tex.L.Rev. 507; Merriweather v. Jackson, Tex.Civ.App., 38 S.W.2d 599.

57. All cases cited in this Section involve mineral interests.

58. See Thomas v. Southwestern Settlement & Development Co., 132 Tex. 413, 123 S.W.2d 290; 17 Tex.L.Rev. 509; equitable partition was denied where one cotenant conveyed the surface and the other claimed the minerals on the ground that the conveyance of the surface was a continuing offer to partition the common property (simplified facts).

user, although in some non-ownership states they may be lost by abandonment.

Where a severance of the minerals has occurred, subsequent possession of the surface will not mature title to the minerals. Where acquisitive possession has begun, there must be an actual or constructive ouster of the possessor to interrupt possession.

In general, acquisitive possession begun as to both the surface and the minerals may be tacked between successive surface possessors, and, through the doctrine of inurement, title will be acquired to both surface and minerals. The result is the same although later possessors claim through instruments attempting to sever the minerals from the surface.

In the situation where the minerals are severed from the surface and later re-acquired by the grantor, the cases are unsettled whether the surface and minerals will be treated as having merged. If treated as merged, the minerals would be acquired by a later adverse possessor of the surface. If no merger is deemed to have occurred the later adverse possessor will acquire only the surface, and not the minerals.

(A) Non-user

In most jurisdictions title to the minerals or a right to the minerals may not be lost by non-user or abandonment. They may, however, be lost by adverse use and possession of the surface by a third party. This is true in all ownership jurisdictions and in most non-ownership states.

In Louisiana acquisitive prescription of mineral interests is not recognized, as discontinuous servitudes may be acquired only by conveyance.[1] However, as mentioned previously, mineral and royalty interests in Louisiana may be lost by non-user for ten years under the doctrine of liberative prescription.[2] Three other jurisdictions, Georgia,[3] Tennessee[4] and Virginia,[5] have enacted prescriptive statutes that provide results similar to Louisiana. However, in other non-ownership jurisdictions an interest in the minerals is not lost by non-user. There must be adverse use and possession of the servient lands sufficient to give rise to a cause of action.[6] In some jurisdictions, such as California, if an interest in the minerals is classified as incorporeal, it may be abandoned if an intent is found to do so.[7]

1. In general see Summers, The Law of Oil and Gas, §§ 138, 139. See: Savage v. Packard, 218 La. 637, 50 So.2d 298; and Nabors, The Louisiana Mineral Servitude and Royalty Doctrines: A Report to the Mineral Law Committee of the Louisiana State Law Institute, 25 Tul.L.R. 30.

2. Vincent v. Bullock, 192 La. 1, 187 So. 35; Wemple v. Nabors Oil & Gas Co., 154 La. 483, 97 So. 666.

3. Ga.Laws 1975, p. 725, Code Ann., § 85-407.1, and see: Nelson v. Bloodworth, 238 Ga. 264, 232 S.E.2d 547.

4. Tenn.Code Ann. § 64-704 (ten year period).

5. Va.Code 1950, §§ 55-154, 55-155, amended 1956 (35 year period).

6. Dabney-Johnston Oil Corp. v. Walden, 4 Cal.2d 637, 52 P.2d 237; Gerhard v. Stephens, 69 Cal.Rptr. 612, 442 P.2d 692; Jilek v. Chicago, Wilmington & Franklin Coal Co., 382 Ill. 241, 47 N.E.2d 96, 146 A.L.R. 871; Melton v. Sneed, 188 Okl. 388, 109 P.2d 509.

7. Gerhard v. Stephens, 69 Cal.Rptr. 612, 442 P.2d 692.

(B) No Severance of Surface and Minerals

Where no separation of the minerals from the rest of the land has occurred prior to the entry of the trespasser, adverse possession of the surface will mature title to all of the land, including the minerals.[8]

Where the surface possessor has begun his possession subsequent to a severance or separation of the minerals from the rest of the land by the true owner, the adverse possessor, upon maturing of his title, will acquire the surface estate only and not the minerals.[9] This is true whether or not the possessor has notice of the prior severance.[10]

The rationale of the courts has been based on notice to the owner of a claim against his estate. Where no conveyance has been made of the minerals at the time of the entry of the trespasser, surface occupancy will give sufficient notice to the owner. However, where the minerals have been conveyed away prior to the entry of the trespasser, acts peculiar to the use and possession of the surface would not apprise the mineral owner of an intent to appropriate the minerals, even if he were cognizant of them. Where the adverse possessor is using the land for chicken raising and farming he is doing no act inconsistent with possession of the mineral estate. In fact, the mineral owner would have no cause of action against him. In an Oklahoma case [11] where gas was taken from an off-tract well for use in connection with a minnow pond, brooder, and dwelling house, where no other operations were done in respect to on-tract wells, and where no reports were made to state administrative agencies, it was held that the acts were insufficient to put the owner of the minerals on notice of a claim by the surface possessors.

In Kentucky, when there has been prior severance, the denial of acquisition of the minerals by surface possession is upon a different basis. Under common law decisions and a state statute, the surface possessor is a trustee of the mineral estate for the benefit of the

---

8. Clanahan v. Morgan, 268 Ala. 71, 105 So.2d 429; Gerhard v. Stephens, 69 Cal.Rptr. 612, 442 P.2d 692; Ates v. Yellow Pine Land Co., Fla.App., 310 So.2d 772, citing and quoting the text; Dixon v. Henderson, Tex.Civ.App., 267 S.W.2d 869. For an interesting case involving adverse possession of minerals under accreted lands, and which of two claimants had constructive possession, see: Seigle v. Thomas, Okl., 627 P.2d 417.

9. United Fuel Gas Co. v. Dyer, C.A.4th, 185 F.2d 99; Pollard v. Simpson, 240 Ala. 401, 199 So. 560; Bodcaw Lumber Co. v. Goode, 160 Ark. 48, 254 S.W. 345, 29 A.L.R. 578; Brian v. Valley View Cattle Ranch, Inc., 35 Colo.App. 428, 535 P.2d 237; Jilek v. Chicago, Wilmington & Franklin Coal Co., 382 Ill. 241, 47 N.E.2d 96, 146 A.L.R. 871; Piney Oil & Gas Co. v. Scott, 258 Ky. 51, 79 S.W.2d 394; Ward v. Woods, Ky., 310 S.W.2d 63; Moffett v. International Paper Co., 243 Miss. 562, 139 So.2d 655; Lehfeldt v. Adams, 130 Mont. 395, 303 P.2d 934; Bilby v. Wire, N.D., 77 N.W.2d 882; Gill v. Fletcher, 74 Ohio St. 295, 78 N.E. 433; Sautbine v. Keller, Okl., 423 P.2d 447; Medusa Portland Cement Co. v. Lamantina, 353 Pa. 53, 44 A.2d 244; Broughton v. Humble Oil & Refining Co., Tex.Civ. App., 105 S.W.2d 480; Smith v. Pittston Co., 203 Va. 408, 124 S.E.2d 1; Kanawha & Hocking Coal & Coke Co. v. Carbon County, Utah, 535 P.2d 1139; Thornock v. Cook, Utah, 604 P.2d 934; McCoy v. Lowrie, 42 Wn.2d 24, 253 P.2d 415.

10. United Fuel Gas Co. v. Dyer, C.A.4th, 185 F.2d 99.

11. Hassell v. Texaco, Inc., Okl., 372 P.2d 233.

owners thereof.¹² This is apparently treated as a true trusteeship, and actual repudiation of the relationship must be made prior to the time acquisitive possession may commence.¹³ Theoretically, it would appear that continued possession of the surface after repudiation of the trusteeship would be sufficient to commence acquisitive possession. This has been indicated in at least one case,¹⁴ but is in contradiction to early cases dealing with hard minerals, where a new entry was required.

(C) Prior Severance of Surface and Minerals

Generally, any conveyance or judicial act that will create a separation of the surface and minerals will be sufficient to prevent acquisition of the minerals by subsequent surface possession.¹⁵ This is also true in most non-ownership states in which a conveyance or reservation of the minerals will create an incorporeal hereditament ¹⁶ in the land.

A question still remains whether the execution of an oil and gas lease will prevent a later adverse possessor from acquiring the mineral estate.

In those states that view the mineral estate as a corporeal interest in real property, the courts have held that the execution of an oil and gas lease will have the same effect as the prior severance of the mineral estate by deed.¹⁷ The same result should be reached in non-ownership jurisdictions that view the oil and gas lease as creating an incorporeal interest in real property, although few cases have been reported dealing with the question.¹⁸

Where an oil and gas lease is viewed as merely creating a contractual right,¹⁹ the execution of an oil and gas lease prior to entry will

---

12. Piney Oil & Gas Co. v. Scott, 258 Ky. 51, 79 S.W.2d 394; Curtis-Jordan Oil & Gas Co. v. Mullins, 269 Ky. 514, 106 S.W.2d 979; Inland Steel Co. v. Isaacs, Ky., 291 S.W.2d 522; Ward v. Woods, Ky., 310 S.W.2d 63.

13. Piney Oil & Gas Co. v. Scott, 258 Ky. 51, 79 S.W.2d 394; Inland Steel Co. v. Isaacs, Ky., 291 S.W.2d 522.

14. Ward v. Woods, Ky., 310 S.W.2d 63.

15. Brian v. Valley View Cattle Ranch, Inc., 35 Colo.App. 428, 535 P.2d 237; Moffett v. International Paper Co., 243 Miss. 562, 139 So.2d 655; Johnson v. Unknown Heirs, 140 Mont. 128, 368 P.2d 577; Ventro v. Clinchfield Coal Corp., 199 Va. 943, 103 S.E.2d 254; Sautbine v. Keller, Okl., 423 P.2d 447 (judicial decree); Rio Bravo Oil Co. v. McEntire, 128 Tex. 124, 95 S.W.2d 381 (contract of sale); Weems v. Hawkins, Tex.Civ.App., 278 S.W.2d 439 (lease); but cf. Crain v. Pure Oil Co., C.A.8th, 25 F.2d 824; Continental Oil Co. v. Chicago & North Western Railway Co., D.C.Wyo., 148 F.Supp. 411; Dixon v. American Liberty Oil Co., 226 La. 911, 77 So.2d 533.

16. Gerhard v. Stephens, 69 Cal.Rptr. 612, 442 P.2d 692; Jilek v. Chicago, Wilmington & Franklin Coal Co., 382 Ill. 241, 47 N.E.2d 96, 146 A.L.R. 871.

17. Weems v. Hawkins, Tex.Civ.App., 278 S.W.2d 439, cf. Continental Oil Co. v. Chicago & North Western Railway Co., D.C.Wyo., 148 F.Supp. 411.

18. See Fadem v. Kimball, Okl.App., 612 P.2d 287 in which the court states that the Oklahoma Supreme Court had not decided whether the execution of an oil and gas lease effected a severance, and the court found it unnecessary to decide the point in the case under consideration. The question there presented was one of ouster rather than severance.

19. Dixon v. American Liberty Oil Co., 226 La. 911, 77 So.2d 533.

not prevent the acquisition of the mineral rights by a later adverse possessor.[20]

It may occur that less than all of the minerals have been severed from the land at the time that limitation was begun. O conveys to A all of Blackacre, reserving an undivided one-half interest in the minerals. AP then enters and stays for the limitation period. The general view would seem to be that he would acquire only that portion of the mineral estate that had not been separated from the surface, i.e., a one-half mineral interest.[21]

A more serious problem in relation to a partial severance occurs where adverse possession is begun and completed during the time that an oil and gas lease is outstanding. O executes an oil and gas lease to Black Gold Oil Co. for a ten-year primary term, reserving to O a $1/8$ landowner's royalty. AP enters and completes adverse possession of the surface under a limitation statute with a lesser time period. It is assumed that Oil Co. has never been in physical possession of the mineral estate. What will AP pick up besides the surface rights?

Assuming that these acts occur in a jurisdiction in which the execution of an oil and gas lease effects a severance of the minerals from the rest of the land, the answer would seem to depend upon whether an oil and gas lease severs all $8/8$ of the mineral estate, or only $7/8$ of the minerals, leaving $1/8$ in the lessor. However, if the latter is the case, the AP would acquire the $1/8$ landowner's royalty even though it is a non-possessory interest. It has been held [22] that the owner of a possessory interest may lose his non-possessory interest by adverse possession where, by virtue of the possessory interest, he could have ejected the adverse possessor to protect the non-possessory interest. Where the only interest owned is a non-possessory interest, such as non-participating royalty interest owned by a third party, it will not be lost by adverse possession.

The same reasoning would seem to apply to the possibility of reverter if it is also considered as not being severed from the rest of the land by the oil and gas lease. If one followed the view that only $7/8$ of the mineral estate is severed by an oil and gas lease, a distinction would have to be made between a lease on oil, where title to royalty oil is retained by the lessor, and a lease on gas, where title to

---

20. Crain v. Pure Oil Co., C.A.8th, 25 F.2d 824; Dixon v. American Liberty Oil Co., 226 La. 911, 77 So.2d 533.

21. Buckner v. Wright, 218 Ark. 448, 236 S.W.2d 720; Fadem v. Kimball, Okl. App., 612 P.2d 287; Birdwell v. American Bonding Co., Tex.Civ.App., 337 S.W.2d 120; Dixon v. Henderson, Tex.Civ.App., 267 S.W.2d 869. However, in the case of Smith v. Nyreen, N.D., 81 N.W.2d 769, concerning possession of the surface and an *unsevered* undivided $1/9$ of the minerals it was held, *inter alia*, that adverse possession had run against all of the mineral estate under the concept that the possessor's interest was undivided and pervaded all of the minerals. But cf. Bilby v. Wire, N.D., 77 N.W.2d 882.

22. Elcan v. Childress, 40 Tex.Civ. App. 193, 89 S.W. 84, and see Strong v. Garrett, 148 Tex. 265, 224 S.W.2d 471.

§ 3.4   CONVEYANCES, PARTITION, POSSESSION

royalty gas passes to the lessee, and the only claim the lessor has is for a money payment.[23]

The view that an oil and gas lease severs only $7/8$ of the minerals is the older view [24] and does not seem to be borne out by the later cases. Under the more modern and probably prevailing view in ownership jurisdictions, an oil and gas lease should be considered as severing the entire mineral estate, including the landowner's royalty and possibility of reverter, so that adverse possession completed during the interim period would not acquire such rights.[25]

As can be seen from the above, where an instrument in the prior chain of title has conveyed or separated the mineral estate from the rest of the land, subsequent adverse possession of the land will not re-acquire the mineral estate. Where adverse possession is relied upon for title curative purposes, care must be taken to determine if a prior severance of the minerals has occurred. Consider the following: O is the owner of Blackacre in fee. He enters into a contract of sale with A. A in his title examination determines that there is a break in the chain of title, in that a gap exists from 1915 to 1918. A deed is found from X to Y in 1915, and a deed from L to M dated in 1918 (regular title exists from M to O). From a detailed investigation it can be determined that the property was in continuous use and possession of the record owners from 1918 to date, sufficient to satisfy the applicable statute of adverse possession. Can A's attorney assure A that he has title to both the surface and mineral estates? Technically, he cannot. It is possible that a conveyance was made from Y to L between 1915 and 1918 which reserved the minerals to Y, and which deed was never placed of record.[26] It is a general rule of law that one is bound by all instruments in the chain of title through which he claims. Hence, A would be bound by a severance contained in Y's deed, and subsequent adverse possession of the surface by record owners would not have matured title to the minerals. This situation must be distinguished from the one in which Y makes a conveyance of the minerals to S, through whom A does not claim (Y subsequently conveying all of the land to L, through whom A claims through a regular chain of title). If S does not timely record, under the operation of the recording statutes he is subject to being cut off by subsequent purchasers for value without notice of S's interest.

Although severance prior to surface possession may prevent acquisition of the minerals by such possession, where the possession

---

23. See Chapter 7.

24. For a discussion of the older view see Walker, The Nature of Property Interests Created by an Oil and Gas Lease in Texas, 7 Tex.L.Rev. 539, 579.

25. Warmack v. Henry H. Cross Co., 237 Ark. 869, 377 S.W.2d 47; Saunders v. Hornsby, Tex.Civ.App., 173 S.W.2d 795. In the latter case the view was expressed that possession and occupancy of the mineral estate was in the oil and gas lessee at all times. Also see Yttredahl v Federal Farm Mortgage Corp., N.D., 104 N.W.2d 705; and Wisness v. Paniman, N.D., 120 N.W.2d 594.

26. Steed v. Crossland, Tex.Civ.App., 252 S.W.2d 784; Mountain Missions School, Inc. v. White, 204 Va. 256, 130 S.E.2d 452.

has begun, a subsequent severance of the minerals by the true owner will not interrupt the adverse possessor's running of the statute as to either the surface or the minerals. For example: nine years after AP's entrance, O conveys all the minerals to L. AP completes the possession period (ten years) without being dispossessed. AP will mature title to the surface and the minerals. It is the general rule that once adverse possession has begun, it may only be interrupted by an ouster, actual or constructive.[27] An actual ouster would consist of physical removal of the AP from the premises, and a constructive ouster, the successful prosecution of an action in ejectment to a judgment. A conveyance or reservation of the minerals [28] or the execution of an oil and gas lease [29] does not constitute an ouster and, hence, will not interrupt possession.

(D) Tacking of Possession Between Successive Possessors

Where AP goes into possession of the surface and later conveys the surface to AP_2, who continues the possession, such possession will mature title to both the surface and minerals, under the doctrine of inurement.[30] This would appear to be the rule in most states; however, it is rejected in Tennessee.[31]

In order for tacking of sucessive periods of possession to exist between adverse possessors it is necessary that privity of estate exists between them. Such privity is satisfied by a transfer of possession from one possessor to another, and may be orally or by deed. It may be that AP transfers Blackacre to AP_2 by deed, reserving the minerals to the grantor. Upon completion of the possession period by AP_2, title to all of Blackacre will be acquired. The deed between AP and AP_2 is a nullity insofar as title is concerned, which is still in O; however, it does serve to establish privity between the possessors. Upon completion of the possession period, the parties will be estopped to claim against the terms of the instrument.[32] Therefore, in the above example AP will own the minerals, and AP_2 the surface.

27. Huddleston v. Peel, 238 Miss. 798, 119 So.2d 921; Rio Bravo Oil Co. v. Staley Oil Co., 138 Tex. 198, 158 S.W.2d 293.

28. Huddleston v. Peel, 238 Miss. 798, 119 So.2d 921; Cargill v. Buie, Tex.Civ. App., 343 S.W.2d 746.

29. Ates v. Yellow Pine Land Co., Fla. App., 310 So.2d 772, citing and quoting from the text; Fadem v. Kimball, Okl. App., 612 P.2d 287; Rio Bravo Oil Co. v. Staley Oil Co., 138 Tex. 198, 158 S.W.2d 293.

30. Lykes Brothers, Inc. v. McConnel, Fla.App., 115 So.2d 606; Pierson v. Case, 272 Ala. 527, 133 So.2d 239; Temples v. First National Bank of Laurel, 239 Miss. 446, 123 So.2d 852; Stern v. Franklin, Okl., 288 P.2d 412; Houston Oil Co. of Texas v. Moss, 155 Tex. 157, 284 S.W.2d 131.

31. Northcut v. Church, 135 Tenn. 541, 188 S.W. 220; some question may exist whether it is the rule followed in Oklahoma, see: Shellenberger v. Hicks, Okl., 370 P.2d 292.

32. Since the deed is a nullity and distribution of the minerals after completion of possession is based on estoppel, completion of the period may be by the possession of either the claimant of the surface or the minerals. Clanahan v. Morgan, 268 Ala. 71, 105 So.2d 429; Pierson v. Case, 272 Ala. 527, 133 So.2d 239; Lykes Brothers, Inc. v. McConnel, Fla. App., 115 So.2d 606; Temples v. First National Bank of Laurel, 239 Miss. 446,

It appears, however, that a different result may occur when the deed is executed between adverse possessors prior to entry. For example, O is the true owner of land. A, thinking that he has paper title to the land, executes a deed to B, which reserves the minerals to A. Upon entry and completion of possession by B, only title to the surface will have been acquired.[33] The deed to B had the effect of qualifying the claim of B to the interest set forth in the deed.

It could be argued that this also should be the result when the deed is exchanged after possession has been begun by AP. As the deed to AP_2 reserved the minerals, only the claim of AP as to the surface was continued, and AP_2's possession was so qualified. The cases, however, do not so hold. Apparently this is on the ground that possession was begun as to the entire fee and will continue as long as possession is continued. The deed between AP and AP_2 is a nullity and will not interrupt possession once begun.

(E) Merger of Severed Estate

A troublesome problem concerns the situation where O, the owner in fee of Blackacre, conveys all the minerals to B. Later, B conveys the minerals back to O. AP then enters and completes possession of the surface. Does AP pick up the minerals? This, of course, depends upon whether after the re-conveyance of the mineral estate O is considered the owner of the fee in Blackacre or the owner of two separate fee estates, one in the surface and the other in the minerals.

Merger generally will not occur between estates of equal dignity or where there exists no intent that the interests merge. There is some authority for the proposition that merger will not occur after the re-conveyance; thus, AP acquires only the surface, and not the minerals. This conclusion has been criticized; however, authority on the point is meager.[34] One consequence of the non-merger theory is that, once the minerals are severed from the surface, subsequent surface possession is insufficient to cure defects in the underlying mineral estate.

Although it may be the law that a previously severed mineral estate will not merge with the surface estate by re-conveyance to its owner, merger will occur, if no intent is found to the contrary, where O has reserved a lesser interest such as a reversionary interest in the minerals. O, the owner of Blackacre in fee, executes an oil and gas lease to Black Gold Oil Co. for a five-year primary term. At the end

---

123 So.2d 852. Also see: Adams v. Duncan, 147 Tex. 332, 215 S.W.2d 599.

33. Thomas v. Southwestern Settlement & Development Co., Tex.Civ.App., 131 S.W.2d 31; Birdwell v. American Bonding Co., Tex.Civ.App., 337 S.W.2d 120.

34. Ferguson v. Hilborn, Okl., 402 P.2d 914; Humphreys-Mexia Co. v. Gammon, 113 Tex. 247, 254 S.W. 296, 29 A.L.R. 607. But cf. Jones v. McFaddin, Tex.Civ.App., 382 S.W.2d 277; McElroy, Adverse Possession of Mineral Estates, 11 Baylor L.Rev. 253; comment 25 Tex.L. Rev. 157, 159; and Sledge v. Craven, Tex.Civ.App., 254 S.W.2d 888 (no merger).

of the five-year term no production is being obtained from the land, and the lease therefore terminates. AP later enters and does acts to the surface sufficient to mature title to the surface. Does he also acquire the minerals? The answer is yes. Upon execution of the oil and gas lease either a determinable fee or an interest in the nature of a profit à prendre is created in the lessee. In the first instance the lessor retains a possibility of reverter, and in the latter the fee subject to the profit. Upon the termination of the lease, merger will occur, and O will thereupon own the fee simple in an unsegregated estate. A later AP will acquire both the surface and the minerals.

§ 3.5 Adverse Possession—Actual Possession of the Minerals

Following a severance of the mineral estate, adverse possession thereof may be acquired by continuous operations and production of oil and gas for the statutory period.

Where such production occurs in relation to an oil and gas lease or other written instrument, the better view is that title, when matured, will relate to all the minerals and to the territorial extent evidenced in such instrument. Constructive possession will not affect tracts in a chain of title other than that upon which production occurs.

Where such production occurs not in relation to a written instrument, the nature and extent of title matured depends upon the claim evidenced by the possessor. As to the minerals so affected, such claim should presumptively be the same as that manifested under an oil and gas lease.

To this point, the problem considered has been the acquisition of the minerals by adverse possession of the surface. Adverse possession may also be directly made of the mineral estate. The following apocryphal story is illustrative of its importance: Black Gold Oil Co. acquired an oil and gas lease from O. O claimed that the lease was voidable and brought suit to set aside the lease and for conversion of the oil produced. The case was one that over a period of years traveled numerous times from trial court to supreme court. Ultimately the lease was set aside. Following this final judgment, Oil Co. filed suit for title to the oil, alleging that they had actually produced oil from the leased premises for a period of time in excess of the statutory period, and that title had been acquired by actual adverse possession of the mineral estate. Oil Co. also contended that as the basic suit of the lessor was only to set aside a voidable lease and not in ejectment as well, it did not serve to interrupt the possession of the lessee. Judgment was granted for the lessee. It was rumored that the lessor's attorney was to receive a contingent fee equal to one-third of the amount recovered. Production at the time the lease was set aside amounted to several million dollars. A painful lesson in pleading!

(A) Acts of Actual Possession

As illustrated above, acquisitive possession of the mineral estate may be made by the actual drilling into the reservoir and producing petroleum products for the requisite period under the statutes of a particular jurisdiction relating to adverse possession or prescription of land. The drilling and production must be continuous for the required period and accompanied by other acts required, such as paying taxes, etc.[1]

Not all acts relating to the minerals will be sufficient to mature title to the mineral estate. Execution of an oil and gas lease, without accompanying acts to reduce the minerals to possession, is insufficient,[2] as is mere surface mining for a period of three or four months.[3] In one case[4] the possessor took gas from an abandoned well to use in connection with a minnow pond, brooder, and dwelling house. It was held that such acts did not constitute possession of the severed mineral estate, as the gas was not produced from wells located on the tract involved, no operations were done in respect to other wells, no cleaning was done or equipment was installed, and no reports were submitted to state administration agencies. The court stated that no notice would be given to the owners of the mineral estate from casual observation or inspection of the land in question. It has also been held that removal of oil or gas from under a tract of land by means of wells located on adjacent or nearby tracts, even if included in the same production unit, is insufficient.[5]

To be adverse, the acts done in relation to the mineral estate must be sufficient to manifest a denial of a right or to assert an inconsistent claim to the mineral estate. Such acts must clearly not be acts consistent with surface usage of the land. It is questionable what acts, such as continuous operations, short of actual appropriation of petroleum products from the land would be sufficient to mature title. This would seem especially true in a non-ownership jurisdiction, where title vests in the minerals only upon actual removal and reduction to possession.

---

1. Day v. Pounders, 231 Miss. 63, 94 So.2d 620; Kilpatrick v. Gulf Production Co., Tex.Civ.App., 139 S.W.2d 653; Webb v. British American Oil Producing Co., Tex.Civ.App., 281 S.W.2d 726; Gossett v. Tidewater Associated Oil Co., Tex.Civ.App., 436 S.W.2d 416.

2. Francis v. Francis, 288 Ky 685, 157 S.W.2d 289; Viersen v. Boettcher, Okl., 387 P.2d 133.

3. Claybrooke v. Barnes, 180 Ark. 678, 22 S.W.2d 390, 67 A.L.R. 1436.

4. Hassell v. Texaco, Inc., Okl., 372 P.2d 233.

5. Brizzolara v. Powell, 214 Ark. 870, 218 S.W.2d 728, (off-tract well did not mature title to A's interest in 40-acre tract in unit, where A did not authorize unitization of his interest). The result was based upon lack of notice; Dixon v. American Liberty Oil Co., 226 La. 911, 77 So.2d 533; Dye v. Miller & Viele, Utah, 587 P.2d 139, (the court held producer could not have possession by "remote control" through lessee-operator to cut off tax title, where unit well was in the unit but not on the land involved, and statute required the land be "actually occupied or * * * in actual possession.") and cf. Sanford v. Alabama Power Co., 256 Ala. 280, 54 So.2d 562.

(B) Rights Acquired—Claiming under Color of Title

Actually, very few cases have arisen dealing with actual possession of the mineral estate; however, several rather serious questions need to be considered. Consider that O is the owner of Greenacre. X, believing himself to be the owner of the mineral estate, elects to develop the minerals himself. He thereupon drills two wells in the corner of Greenacre, which contains some 300 acres of land. After production for an applicable period, what has X acquired? Assume that the wells are completed in the Woodbine formation at a depth of 5000 feet and produce only oil. Will X acquire only the rights in oil produced from the Woodbine formation, or will he also acquire the rights to gas and all other minerals, as well? Would it make a difference if X was a lessee?

The question of the extent of constructive possession of a possessor who is actually mining petroleum products has not been authoritatively answered by judicial decision. A smattering of cases, including those dealing with hard minerals, have denied possession beyond the actual well being drilled.[6] The rationale was that the true owner cannot be constructively ousted underground merely by the reduction of minerals to actual possession in a small portion of the tract of land. Surface possession is distinguished, in that the possessor has the ability of immediate occupancy as to those portions described in a deed that he is not then actually occupying.[7]

It would appear that the most recent and the better reasoned of the cases present the rule that a possessor under color of title can maintain constructive possession of the mineral estate, where petroleum products are being withdrawn, to the limits of the instrument to which possession is referable.[8] The leading case is Diederich v. Ware,[9] where actual possession was from two producing wells situated upon 56 acres of land. It was held that the possessor acquired title to all the minerals in the entire tract described in the deed. The rationale of the court was that, as fugacious minerals were being withdrawn, the entire stratum was affected, and dominion was exercised to the oil under the entire tract of land.

This raises a question whether title should be matured only to the stratum affected by the withdrawal, or to all depths. A strict application of the rationale of the Ware case might lead to a restriction

---

6. Sanford v. Alabama Power Co., 256 Ala. 280, 54 So.2d 562; Laney v. Monsanto Chemical Co., 233 Ark. 645, 348 S.W.2d 826; Piney Oil & Gas Co. v. Scott, 258 Ky. 51, 79 S.W.2d 394.

7. See Piney Oil & Gas Co. v. Scott, 258 Ky. 51, 79 S.W.2d 394.

8. Kinder v. La Salle County Carbon Coal Co., 310 Ill. 126, 141 N.E. 537; Diederich v. Ware, Ky., 288 S.W.2d 643; Vance v. Guy, 223 N.C. 409, 27 S.E.2d 117; Mohoma Oil Co. v. Ambassador Oil Corp., Okl., 474 P.2d 950 (held that working interest in lease acquired by adverse possession by actual production, under color of title, was extinguished when production ceased); Kilpatrick v. Gulf Production Co., Tex.Civ.App., 139 S.W.2d 653.

9. Ky., 288 S.W.2d 643, rejecting the rationale of Piney Oil & Gas v. Scott.

that title is matured only to the particular stratum. However, some limitation statutes state that, upon completion of the particular acts necessary, "full title" is acquired to "the land". It is believed that under such statutes, although actual withdrawal has affected only one horizon, title is matured to all of the minerals described in the instrument to which possession is referable and to all depths.[10] In the absence of such statutory language, and where the possessor is in possession under an oil and gas lease or mineral deed, his possession should be referable to the lease or deed to determine the extent of the claim. Where the lease or deed describes all minerals in a tract of land, possession would include the petroleum products as to all depths throughout the tract of land described.

The claim of an adverse possessor in possession under an oil and gas lease will not be extended beyond the land described by the lease held by the possessor. Where Black Gold Oil Co. has pooled its lease with the lessee of the adjoining land, and where it is contractually provided in Black Gold's lease that production anywhere in the pool will be deemed to be production from all lands included in the pool, it has been held that if the unit well is on land covered by the adjoining lease it will not be considered production from the land against which the adverse possession of the minerals is claimed, even if actual drainage occurs from under the tract in question.[11]

(C) Rights Acquired—Not Claiming under Color of Title

Where the possessor is not claiming under color of title, the territorial extent of the claim will be referable to the statutes of a particular jurisdiction. In Texas, for instance, an adverse possessor may acquire up to 160 acres of land where he is not claiming under a deed or has not fenced the property. It has been suggested that the possessor be limited to the drainage area around the well bore or to an area equal to the minimum spacing allowed in the jurisdiction.

Where no lease is involved, the question becomes one of intent as to the nature of the rights claimed. Although it might be held that the self-developer should be limited in claim to the particular products produced, it would seem more reasonable that his claim would extend to the products usually included in the mineral estate under oil and gas leases normally used in the area.

---

10. Mohoma Oil Co. v. Ambassador Oil Corp., Okl., 474 P.2d 950; Maloy v. Smith, Okl., 341 P.2d 912; Kilpatrick v. Gulf Production Co., Tex.Civ.App., 139 S.W.2d 653.

11. Brizzolara v. Powell, 214 Ark. 870, 218 S.W.2d 728; Dye v. Miller & Viele, Utah, 587 P.2d 139.

CHAPTER 4

TRESPASS, SURFACE AND SUB-SURFACE, AND THIRD PARTY CLAIMS

Analysis

Sec.
4.1 The Geophysical Surface Trespasser.
  (A) The Right to Explore.
  (B) Surface Geophysical Exploration Where a Trespass is Involved.
  (C) Surface Geophysical Exploration with no Physical Entry.
  (D) Surface Geophysical Exploration That Causes Physical Damage.
4.2 The Geophysical Sub-Surface Trespasser.
  (A) Sub-Surface Trespass That Results in No Production.
  (B) Sub-Surface Trespass That Results in Production or Drainage.
    (1) Recovery and Remedy.
    (2) The Good-Faith Trespasser.
    (3) Directional Underground Trespass.
    (4) Discovery and Limitations.
  (C) Trespass Caused by Underground Intrusion of Injected Substances.
  (D) Conversion Caused by Negligent Sub-Surface Operations.
4.3 Slander of Title Affecting Oil and Gas Interests.

§ 4.1 The Geophysical Surface Trespasser

Where an oil and gas lease does not grant to the lessee the exclusive right to explore, such exclusive right will not be implied from the right to drill, mine and extract petroleum products. In this case a non-exclusive right to explore will co-exist in both the lessor and the lessee. However, where the mineral rights have been separated from the rest of the land, and where no lease is involved, the owner of the mineral rights will have the exclusive right to explore.

Where the geophysical trespasser has wrongfully entered land and conducted geophysical surveying operations, the landowner may recover for direct physical damage and for the value of the loss of exploration rights as to lands directly explored. Where the landowner is successful in establishing a causal connection between the loss of value of rights in the mineral estate and the communication of information gathered by the trespasser, it is probable that the landowner may recover for the value of such loss.

Where no physical entry has been made on the land, recovery by the landowner of the value of exploration rights has been denied. However, where damage has occurred from geophysical operations and a causal connection has been established, even though no physical entry has occurred, the majority of jurisdictions will impose liability without fault for such damage. An exception is Texas, which requires an additional finding of negligence. It is not settled whether the doctrine of *res ipsa loquitur* will be applied in Texas.

(A) The Right to Explore

Where O has conveyed the minerals to A, and Black Gold Oil Co. desires to enter and explore for possible petroleum production, to whom should it turn for permission? As O owns the surface rights and Black Gold must make an entry on the surface of the land for exploration purposes, will O's permission be sufficient? On the other hand, A owns the mineral estate that is being explored and the acts of exploration without A's consent may be unwarranted acts of interference with the minerals. Should Black Gold also acquire permission from A?

Where a separation of the mineral rights has occurred, it has been held that for purposes of mineral development and exploration the mineral rights are dominant.[1] In absence of contractual language to the contrary, the owner of the minerals has a right to use as much of the surface as is reasonably necessary for mineral exploration and development purposes.[2] Black Gold then would have to acquire permission only from the owner of the mineral estate. However, as a matter of practice, the exploring party will usually obtain a damage release from the owner of the surface. The consideration for the damage release will approximate the cost of the damage that may occur in the course of the exploration. It is desirable for the prospective mineral developer to keep the good will of the surface owner.

In some of the early cases the question of exploration rights arose after the property had been leased for oil and gas development. Conflicts arose as to whether the lessor or lessee, or both, had a right thereafter to explore. In one Texas case, where the oil and gas lease did not grant to the lessee an "exclusive" right to explore, as well as to drill, mine and remove the minerals, it was held that a non-exclusive right to explore co-existed in both the lessor and lessee.[3] It is not only in the early cases that the question has been presented. In a recent Wyoming case,[4] state and federal leases were executed which conveyed to the lessee an exclusive right to "drill for, mine, extract and remove" the minerals, but not an exclusive right to explore. As in the Puckett case, it was held that the lease did not by implication grant to the lessee the exclusive right to explore. The lessor was allowed to grant to third persons the right to shoot and explore. In the modern lease form the problem of a co-existing right in the lessor

---

1. Wall v. Shell Oil Co., 209 Cal.App. 2d 504, 25 Cal.Rptr. 908; Hurley v. Northern Pacific Railway Co., 153 Mont. 199, 455 P.2d 321; Warren Petroleum Corp. v. Monzingo, 157 Tex. 479, 304 S.W.2d 362, 65 A.L.R.2d 1352; Stradley v. Magnolia Petroleum Co., Tex.Civ.App., 155 S.W.2d 649.

2. Phillips Petroleum Co. v. Cowden, C.A.5th, 241 F.2d 586, 67 A.L.R.2d 433, affirming prior appeal 256 F.2d 408.

3. Shell Petroleum Corp. v. Puckett, Tex.Civ.App., 29 S.W.2d 809 but cf. Wilson v. Texas Co., Tex.Civ.App., 237 S.W.2d 649, where an exclusive right to explore was granted to the lessee and it was held no co-existing right to explore remained in the lessor during the life of the lease.

4. Ready v. Texaco, Inc., Wyo., 410 P.2d 983, 28 A.L.R.3d 1419.

has generally been avoided by granting the lessee "exclusive" rights of exploration.[5]

Usually, negotiation for exploration rights is not difficult. However, if one is representing the landowner, it is necessary that certain minimal provisions be included for her protection, the absence of which may cause hard feelings between the attorney and her client. Understandably, many of the rural landowners are more concerned with continued proper operations of their farm or ranch than with the possibility of future production of petroleum products. Where agreements for exploration allow men and equipment to roam lands at will and contain no provision for restoration, etc., the wronged landowner can become a most unwelcome sight to behold to the attorney who represented her. The following matters should be discussed and agreed upon for inclusion in the exploration contract:

A. Authority.
  1. Governmental units, if shooting on a road—does county or state have authority, etc?
  2. Who has authority for off-shore exploration?
  3. Surface owner v. mineral owner.
  4. Mineral owner v. oil and gas lessee.

B. Specific matters.
  1. Description of land to be explored, entrances to be used, and roadways over the lands, repair of fences, prevention of escape of livestock, etc.
  2. Term—commencement and termination of permit.
  3. Methods to be used and amount and types of equipment.
     a. gravimetric.
     b. seismic.
     c. magnetic.
     d. core samples.
     e. other.
  4. Personnel—number, housing and attendant services, if any, etc.
  5. Number and location of shot holes, size of explosives.
  6. Consideration for the permit—by the acre, by the shot, etc.
  7. Insurance and indemnity provisions—as to personal injury and damage to property, crops, and animals.
  8. Filling up holes and restoration of land and improvements.

---

5. Typical language in the lease: " * * * hereby grants, leases and lets exclusively unto Lessee for the purpose of investigating, exploring, prospecting, drilling and mining for and producing oil, gas and all other minerals, laying pipelines, building roads, tanks, power stations, telephone lines and other structures thereon * * * ".

§ 4.1   TRESPASS, SURFACE, SUB-SURFACE   155

9. Use of water and timber, etc.
10. Confidential nature of information, use without landowner's consent, disclosure of information to owner or others.
11. Hunting and firearms on the land, etc.
12. Assignability.

Where the landowner may contemplate use of the land for subdivision purposes, agreement should be made in the initial instrument restricting exploration to specific areas for exploration and development that will not unduly interfere with the use of the land for subdivision purposes.

As the exploration contract usually will include an option to obtain oil and gas leases on the lands described, provision should be made that the appropriate provisions for the landowner's protection in the exploration contract also be carried forward into any leases to be executed. This may be so stated in the contract. However, it is better practice to attach the form of lease, which will be executed in the event of the exercise of the option, as an exhibit to the contract. Appropriate provisions for the protection of the landowner may then be inserted directly in the form of the oil and gas lease to be used.

(B) Surface Geophysical Exploration Where a Trespass is Involved

This section excludes those operations that, although they take place on the surface of the land involved, have for their purpose the piercing of a petroleum reservoir. They are discussed in the following section. Here the discussion is directed primarily to situations where the operations are generally seismic in character or where similar operations are carried out on the surface or slightly beneath the surface for the purpose of discovering whether the sub-strata is favorable for the discovery of petroleum products.

Although such operations in the mind of the public are viewed as "searching for oil", technically, this is not the case. Instead, it is known that various configurations of sub-structures are favorable for the retention of petroleum products. Geophysical operations are usually directed at finding petroleum products indirectly, by the discovery of underground formations that are favorable for the accumulation of such products. The actual discovery of the products sought comes about only by actual drilling into the sub-structure. Surface geophysical exploration employs various tests, some of which may cause minor damage to the land, such as seismic tests that chart reflection waves from explosive charges.

In the course of the exploration and search for oil, either by mistake, inadvertence, or willfulness, geophysical tests have been run on lands without proper authorization. In such cases the geophysical explorer is a trespasser. There is no question that the landowner may recover from the trespasser for the actual damage done to his land, to restore it to the condition it was in prior to the trespass.[6] This apparently is true even if the cost of restoration is greater than the market value of the land itself.[7]

However, direct damage to the land itself as a result of a geophysical trespass in most instances will not comprise the greatest loss to the landowner. The landowner will also have lost the value of the exploration rights. If the result of the exploration demonstrates that the land is valueless for oil and gas production, he also may have lost the value of the right to execute oil and gas leases on the land or to sell other interests in the mineral estate.

It would appear to be settled that where a trespass is proved the landowner may recover for the loss of the exploration rights.[8] Recovery for the loss of such rights has been allowed under the theory of conversion,[9] implied contract,[10] and trespass.[11] In Texas, the landowner may waive the tort and sue in assumpsit for the reasonable rental value of the land for exploration purposes.[12] The leading case is probably that of Phillips Petroleum Co. v. Cowden.[13] In this case T, geophysical trespasser, entered P's land and located six shot holes thereon. P owned 2682 acres and claimed as damages the reasonable value of the rights to seismographic exploration for the entire acreage. The basis of P's claim was that the information acquired by T related to the entire tract of P's land. T, on the other hand, stated that it had occupied effectively only 81.1 acres and, furthermore, that the information acquired was of such poor quality it was useless.

The court allowed recovery for the reasonable value of the use and occupancy of the land. It was pointed out that the value of the use is independent from the value of the right to the trespasser. Also, the court limited recovery only to such land from which informa-

---

6. Angelloz v. Humble Oil & Refining Co., 196 La. 604, 199 So. 656; Picou v. Fohs Oil Co., 222 La. 1068, 64 So.2d 434; Harrell v. Vahlsing, Inc., Tex.Civ.App., 248 S.W.2d 762; Shell Petroleum Corp. v. Scully, C.A.5th, 71 F.2d 772.

7. Shell Petroleum Corp. v. Scully, C.A.5th, 71 F.2d 772.

8. Angelloz v. Humble Oil & Refining Co., 196 La. 604, 199 So. 656; Estes v. Browning, 11 Tex. 237; Gulf, Colorado & Santa Fe Railway Co. v. Dunman, 85 Tex. 176, 19 S.W. 1073; Harrell v. Vahlsing, Inc., Tex.Civ.App., 248 S.W.2d 762; Shell Petroleum Corp. v. Scully, C.A.5th, 71 F.2d 772; Phillips Petroleum Co. v. Cowden, C.A.5th, 241 F.2d 586, 67 A.L.R.2d 433, affirming prior appeal, 256 F.2d 408. But see Picou v. Fohs Oil Co., 222 La. 1068, 64 So.2d 434, where damages would be limited to actual physical damage where the entry is in good faith.

9. Angelloz v. Humble Oil & Refining Co., 196 La. 604, 199 So. 656; but cf. Shell Petroleum Corp. v. Moore, C.A.5th, 46 F.2d 959.

10. Harrell v. Vahlsing, Inc., Tex.Civ. App., 248 S.W.2d 762.

11. Picou v. Fohs Oil Co., 222 La. 1068, 64 So.2d 434; Shell Petroleum Corp. v. Moore, C.A.5th, 46 F.2d 959; Shell Petroleum Corp. v. Scully, C.A.5th, 71 F.2d 772.

12. Estes v. Browning, 11 Tex. 237; Phillips Petroleum Co. v. Cowden, C.A. 5th, 241 F.2d 586, 67 A.L.R.2d 433, affirming prior appeal 256 F.2d 408; cf. Shell Petroleum Corp. v. Moore, C.A.5th, 46 F.2d 959. In the event P waives the trespass may he recover for actual damage to the land? It would seem not, Harrell v. Vahlsing, Inc., Tex.Civ.App., 248 S.W.2d 762, but cf. Shell Petroleum Corp. v. Scully, C.A.5th, 71 F.2d 772.

13. C.A.5th, 241 F.2d 586, 67 A.L.R.2d 433, affirming prior appeal 256 F.2d 408.

tion was directly gathered, i.e., that "occupied" by the exploration. The value of the use and occupancy of the land was computed on the basis of the reasonable amount of P's land that would have been included in a voluntary contract between the parties. Interestingly, upon remand the jury found that the entire tract of P would have been included in the agreement.

In the proper case the landowner may recover for the loss of value of the leasing rights and the loss of value of other interests he might have sold in the mineral estate where (1) the geophysical trespasser has communicated the results of his findings to third parties and (2) they tend to demonstrate that the land is useless for oil and gas production purposes. In Angelloz v. Humble Oil & Refining Co.,[14] T entered and ran a seismographic survey on a part of P's land. P was allowed to recover an amount equal to bonus money for execution of oil and gas leases. It was shown that he had been offered bonus money to execute a lease prior to T's entry, but was unable to lease for any amount following the trespass. P was also able to establish a causal connection between the trespass and the loss of leasing ability by showing that T released information to third parties that the land in the area surveyed was dry.

In Thomas v. Texas Co.,[15] in a similar situation, P asked for the value of the loss of sale of a perpetual non-participating royalty interest as a result of the alleged activities of T in publishing a report showing that the area was dry. In this case the remedy was refused on the basis that P had offered no proof of the trespass or that the results actually had been communicated to third parties. The evidence further tended to show that T was engaged in surveying a very large area with a series of 153 tests. The shots on P's land were shots numbered 29 and 30, and any information available from them was inconclusive. The court also felt the loss of the sale was due to too high an asking price.[16] However, the court did not indicate that the petition did not state a cause of action.

These cases demonstrate the difficulty in establishing a causal connection between the trespass and the fall in value of the leasing rights or of other interests in the minerals. It might be argued that in any event P has not suffered a compensable loss, as the trespass merely demonstrated that he had no minerals in which to sell an interest, and that it is unconscionable to allow a recovery.[17] The better view is that P did suffer a compensable loss, i.e., the opportunity to lease or sell an interest in the mineral estate. There is no reason to prefer the trespasser who wrongfully removed the opportunity over

---

14. 196 La. 604, 199 So. 656.

15. Tex.Civ.App., 12 S.W.2d 597.

16. P had asked a consideration of $600 per acre for sale of the rights, whereas the highest sale price existing in the area was not in excess of $400 per acre.

17. This argument was put forward in Martel v. Hall Oil Co., 36 Wyo. 166, 253 P. 862, 52 A.L.R. 91, dealing with the trespasser who drills a dry hole, see § 4.2, infra.

the landowner. Where the causal connection is established, the landowner should be able to establish his loss by opinion evidence, as in other cases of trespass. A loss of specific bargain should not be required.[18]

(C) Surface Geophysical Exploration with no Physical Entry

Where the geophysical explorer has not made an entry upon the land in order to obtain the information, the landowner has generally been denied recovery for a taking of information concerning his mineral rights. For example, where shot holes have been placed on adjoining land, with receiving stations on opposite adjoining land, so that seismic waves pass through the property, recovery has been denied.[19] The same result would apparently follow where information was gathered by magnetometer in aircraft passing over the property. Although no tort has been recognized for invasion of privacy or for conversion of information as to the mineral estate, it would seem that where valuable sub-surface information has been obtained without actual entry upon the property, recovery should be allowed. This result could be reached viewing the acts as comprising a new tort, or by extending the traditional scope of trespass to cover any type of energy wave caused to pass through the property of another. In this situation the value of the exploration rights may be lost by the use of modern technology, and it is ridiculous that the law not compensate for such taking because of archaic and outmoded concepts.

(D) Surface Geophysical Exploration That Causes Physical Damage

Petroleum jurisprudence is replete with cases involving damage to water wells and other improvements caused by surface geophysical exploration.[20] A typical situation occurs where P is located some dis-

---

18. See Summers Oil and Gas, § 660, where he would analogize the situation to one of defamation of property and would require for recovery that the statement communicated be false and that loss of specific bargain be shown. Although such analogy may be made, it would seem the better view in oil and gas cases to recognize the extreme sensitivity of mineral interests to communications regarding their value, especially where the trespasser usually is the only one in a position to have any concrete knowledge about sub-surface conditions. This, of course, makes falsity extremely difficult and expensive to establish. No case was found requiring the statement to be false.

19. Kennedy v. General Geophysical Co., Tex.Civ.App., 213 S.W.2d 707, has been cited for this proposition. However, here liability was denied where shot holes were placed on one side of P's land but it was shown that no straight lines existed over P's land from the shot holes to the recording instruments. The court also stated the usual rule that vibrations are not sufficient to constitute a trespass.

20. For example see: Western Geophysical Co. of America v. Mason, 240 Ark. 767, 402 S.W.2d 657; Western Geophysical Co. v. Rowell, 126 Ga.App. 427, 190 S.E.2d 921; Pate v. Western Geophysical Co. of America, La.App., 91 So. 2d 431; Langlinais v. Geophysical Service, Inc., 237 La. 585, 111 So.2d 781; Hoyt v. Amerada Petroleum Corp., La. App., 69 So.2d 546; Gullatt v. Ashland Oil & Refining Co., La.App., 243 So.2d 820; Burgess v. Travelers Ins. Co., La. App., 254 So.2d 163; Phillips Petroleum Co. v. Smith, Miss., 184 So.2d 631; Teledyne Exploration Co. v. Dickerson,

§ 4.1   TRESPASS, SURFACE, SUB–SURFACE   159

tance from the geophysical operations. Following blasting during a seismographic survey, P finds his water well dry, or cracks are found in his house and other improvements, or his oil well sands up and becomes useless. Is the fact of the coincidental blasting and drying up of the well or other damage a sufficient showing for liability?

Although vibrations have been considered an insufficient invasion to constitute a trespass, recovery has been allowed for actual damage caused by underground vibrations.[21] To present a *prima facie* case, plaintiff must (1) establish a causal connection between the geophysical operations and the resultant damage and (2) also demonstrate that the operator did not comply with the standard of conduct required in such operations.

Generally, the coincidence of the operation and the damage is in itself insufficient to establish a causal connection.[22] Testimony that the charge was placed at a different level [23] or of the condition of the well before and after the detonation,[24] is in itself insufficient to support a causal connection. To establish a causal connection by circumstantial evidence, it is necessary to show, in reference to the conditions existing prior to the operations, that it is highly improbable that the injury would have occurred but for the operations being conducted. Where the well or improvement has been in satisfactory existence for a number of years prior to the damage,[25] or where the detonation occurred in relatively close proximity to and at the same depth as the well damaged,[26] it has been found that a causal connection existed. This is also true where direct eyewitness testimony is offered as to the effect of the geophysical operations on the improvement.[27]

In most jurisdictions, where a causal connection is established between the operations and the damage, the defendant will be held lia-

---

Miss., 253 So.2d 817; Shell Oil Co. v. Cavanaugh, Miss., 295 So.2d 1; Seismograph Service Corp. v. Buchanan, Okl., 316 P.2d 185; Ft. Worth & Denver City Railway Co. v. Beauchamp, 95 Tex. 496, 68 S.W. 502; Comanche Duke Oil Co. v. Texas Pacific Coal & Oil Co., Tex.Com.App., 298 S.W. 554; Humble Oil & Refining Co. v. Grucholski, Tex.Civ.App., 376 S.W.2d 950.

21. Note 20, supra.

22. Chevron Oil Co. v. Snellgrove, 253 Miss. 356, 175 So.2d 471; Phillips Petroleum Co. v. Smith, Miss., 184 So.2d 631. However, see Teledyne Exploration Co. v. Dickerson, Miss., 253 So.2d 817 (where landowner was in house at time seismic shots exploded on adjacent tracts of land and observed shaking of home and later cracks in walls). Also see Burgess v. Travelers Insurance Co., La.App., 254 So.2d 163 and Western Geophysical Co. v. Rowell, 126 Ga.App. 427, 190 S.E.2d 921 where damage was directly observed.

Lack of causal connection was found in Shell Oil Co. v. Cavanaugh, Miss., 295 So.2d 1.

23. Western Geophysical Co. of America v. Martin, 253 Miss. 14, 174 So.2d 706.

24. Continental Oil Co. v. Hinton, 253 Miss. 233, 175 So.2d 512.

25. Langlinais v. Geophysical Service Inc., 237 La. 585, 111 So.2d 781; Stanolind Oil & Gas Co. v. Lambert, Tex.Civ.App., 222 S.W.2d 125.

26. Western Geophysical Co. of America v. Mason, 240 Ark. 767, 402 S.W.2d 657.

27. Pate v. Western Geophysical Co. of America, La.App., 91 So.2d 431; Teledyne Exploration Co. v. Dickerson, Miss., 253 So.2d 817; Seismograph Service Corp. v. Buchanan, Okl., 316 P.2d 185; Superior Oil Co. v. King, Okl., 324 P.2d 847.

ble, on the ground of strict or absolute liability.[28] This is an extension of the doctrine of Rylands v. Fletcher and would impose liability without fault where the act resulted from inherently dangerous activities.

A distinction is made in Mississippi between the situations (1) where the actor is a trespasser or is operating on an adjoining tract of land and (2) where he is on the land lawfully. In the first situation (after a consideration and rejection of the distinction between the case where blasting has caused ejection of articles upon the surface of the land, calling for strict liability on the part of the actor, and the case where damage is caused by vibrations with no physical trespass, calling for a finding of negligence), the Mississippi courts placed themselves in the camp of absolute liability.[29] However, if the actor, such as a lessee, is lawfully on the land, negligence must be shown as a requisite for liability.[30]

An exception to applying strict liability is made in Texas, which emphatically rejected the Rylands doctrine in the case of Turner v. Big Lake Oil Company.[31] Whether the damage is caused by vibrations or by intrusion of salt water or other substances across property lines, Texas will require a showing of negligence or nuisance.[32] In Comanche Duke Oil Co. v. Texas Pac. Coal & Oil Co.,[33] such damage was caused by the negligent use of excessive amounts of nitro in a well on an adjoining tract of land. The court stated that where the use of one tract of land necessarily causes transmission of forces or motions into adjacent tracts, but where such use is reasonable, the resulting damages to adjoining properties are *damnum absque injuria*. The court indicated that liability would result where the use of the land was unlawful, or lawful and unreasonable.

The doctrine of *res ipsa loquitur* would seem to be applicable where the requisite elements are present, i.e., that operation of the activity be entirely within the control of the defendant, and that the damage would not have occurred in the absence of negligence. It has been applied in Louisiana.[34] At least one Texas case appears un-

---

28. Pate v. Western Geophysical Co. of America, La.App., 91 So.2d 431; Central Exploration Co. v. Gray, 219 Miss. 757, 70 So.2d 33; Gullatt v. Ashland Oil & Refining Co., La.App., 243 So.2d 820; Burgess v. Travelers Insurance Co., La. App., 254 So.2d 163; Continental Oil Co. v. Hinton, 253 Miss. 233, 175 So.2d 512; Teledyne Exploration Co. v. Dickerson, Miss., 253 So.2d 817; States Exploration Co. v. Reynolds, Okl., 344 P.2d 275.

29. Central Exploration Co. v. Gray, 219 Miss. 757, 70 So.2d 33; Continental Oil Co. v. Hinton, 253 Miss. 233, 175 So. 2d 512; but compare Western Geophysical Co. of America v. Martin, 253 Miss. 14, 174 So.2d 706; Teledyne Exploration Co. v. Dickerson, Miss., 253 So.2d 817.

30. Cities Service Oil Co. v. Corley, Miss., 197 So.2d 244.

31. 128 Tex. 155, 96 S.W.2d 221.

32. Comanche Duke Oil Co. v. Texas Pacific Coal & Oil Co., Tex.Com.App., 298 S.W. 554; Klostermann v. Houston Geophysical Co., Tex.Civ.App., 315 S.W.2d 664; Sinclair Oil & Gas Co. v. Gordon, Tex.Civ.App., 319 S.W.2d 170; Humble Oil & Refining Co. v. Grucholski, Tex. Civ.App., 376 S.W.2d 950; Roskey v. Gulf Oil Corp., Tex.Civ.App., 387 S.W.2d 915.

33. Tex.Com.App., 298 S.W. 554.

34. Langlinais v. Geophysical Service Inc., 237 La. 585, 111 So.2d 781; Hoyt v. Amerada Petroleum Corp., La.App., 69 So.2d 546.

settled whether the doctrine would be applied in the proper case.[35] It has been expressly rejected in some cases [36] on the ground that it was not shown that the damage would not have occurred but for negligence. The requirement of negligence may be removed contractually.[37]

§ 4.2 The Geophysical Sub-Surface Trespasser

Where one without right has wrongfully entered and drilled a dry hole, the landowner may recover the market value of the leasing or exploratory rights, on the theory of trespass. Where such act is accompanied by a claim of right, the landowner may have an alternative remedy for slander of title, requiring loss of a specific bargain and allowing a defense of good faith. At least one jurisdiction would reject liability in either instance.

Where one without right has wrongfully entered and drilled a producing well and is considered to have entered in willful or negligent disregard of the owner's rights, he is considered to have entered in bad faith and must account to the owner for all products that have been produced and converted, without credit for any costs of development or production. However, where he is considered to have entered under an honest and reasonable belief in his claim, in most jurisdictions, he will be allowed, in accounting to the owner, to offset against the value of the products converted the reasonable costs of drilling, completing and producing. In no event will the credit for costs exceed the extent to which a benefit has been conferred upon the owner. Some early cases, from areas having a history of hard mineral mining, allowed the owner to recover upon the basis of the royalty to which he normally would have been entitled, rather than upon the value of gross production less costs.

Actual or constructive notice of another's right should not constitute bad faith *per se*; however, it appears to be the view of the majority of the courts that an entry following the commencement of litigation is in bad faith. This view seems erroneous.

A body of law has been emerging that tends to treat authorized secondary recovery operations that result in a sub-surface intrusion into surrounding producing areas as creating a non-actionable trespass, or in some cases no tort is recognized.

Where, due to negligent operations, products are drained from adjoining producing wells or reservoirs such drainage will constitute a conversion of the products drained.

(A) *Sub-Surface Trespass That Results in No Production*

It should be pointed out that in this Section, 4.2, the term "sub-surface trespass" is directed at acts which, although occurring on the

---

35. Klostermann v. Houston Geophysical Co., Tex.Civ.App., 315 S.W.2d 664.

36. Stanolind Oil & Gas Co. v. Lambert, Tex.Civ.App., 222 S.W.2d 125; Roskey v. Gulf Oil Corp., Tex.Civ.App., 387 S.W.2d 915.

37. Humble Oil & Refining Co. v. Grucholski, Tex.Civ.App., 376 S.W.2d 950.

surface of land overlying the mineral rights in question, nevertheless have for their purpose the piercing of possible petroleum reservoirs.

The problem approached in this section is exemplified by the case of Humble Oil & Refining Co. v. Kishi.[1] In this case the land was owned in undivided interests by Kishi and Lang. Kishi was the owner of the surface and an undivided $3/4$ of the minerals, and Lang owned the remaining $1/4$ undivided interest in the minerals. Kishi executed an oil and gas lease dated December 23, 1919. However, the lease was not signed by Lang until January 29, 1920, at which time it was delivered. The lease provided for a three-year primary term.

On January 23, 1923, Humble entered and began the drilling of a well under an express claim of right that the lease was still in effect as to all interests. Kishi protested the entry, to which Lang had consented. The well came in a dry hole. The market value of the right to lease then fell from $1000 an acre to zero. Kishi brought suit for the fall in market value caused by the drilling of the dry hole, alleging that Humble had drilled the well under an unwarranted claim of right.

Humble claimed that it had drilled the well in good faith, relying upon the fact that the lease did not expire until three years from the time that Lang executed and delivered the lease. In this Humble was in error, as the body of the lease itself stated that the primary term would commence upon the date of the lease, or December 23, 1919. It therefore would expire three years later, on December 23, 1922, which was prior to Humble's entry. As Kishi had not ratified the lease, it had expired as to his interest at the time of the entry of Humble.

The trial court awarded only nominal damages of $1.00. Upon appeal, it was held that Kishi was entitled to a proportional part ($3/4$) of the market value of the leasing rights of $1000 per acre, or $750 per acre. Upon re-hearing, the former opinion was superseded and the case was remanded. The court would not indulge in the presumption that the $3/4$ interest was leasable at $3/4$ of total market value.

In both opinions of the Commission of Appeals, the court emphasized that the entry of Humble was not wrongful in itself, but that it asserted a wrongful claim: "Though it did so in good faith (entered), without any intention to injure Kishi, it asserted a right it did not have. * * * The entry made upon this land was unlawful, not because the company had no right to make entry, but because the entry made was in denial of Kishi's right. The character of the entry made was unlawful, and was the sole cause of the injury complained of. The company had no right to deprive Kishi of the value of his property by making the unwarranted claim that the lease theretofore executed by him gave it the right of entry, * * *."

---

1. Humble Oil & Refining Co. v. Kishi, Tex.Com.App., 276 S.W. 190; Humble Oil & Refining Co. v. Kishi, Tex. Com.App., 291 S.W. 538; Humble Oil & Refining Co. v. Kishi, Tex.Civ.App., 299 S.W. 687.

The case raises two basic questions. First, was the court correct in its measure of damages in the case, and second, on a broader consideration, what should be the measure of damages where the act of the trespasser has "changed a pleasant uncertainty to an unpleasant certainty"?

The first question seems to be answered in the negative. The petition was framed as a slander of title suit, i.e., disparagement of title by reason of an unwarranted claim. The court seems to have said as much; however, the measure of damages was that allowed for trespass, i.e., the loss of market value of the leasing rights caused by the act.

An act of trespass is compensated by measuring loss of market value caused by the act. Damages may be established by expert testimony as to such inherent loss. In a slander of title action a loss of a specific bargain is required. None was shown in this case. Good faith is also a defense in a slander action. The alleged good faith of Humble was answered by the court's statement that it asserted a right it did not have.[2] Here the court essentially gave a trespass measure of damages in a slander of title action.

It appears from the case that if a loss of a specific sale had been required no damages would have been recoverable. On the other hand, if the case were viewed as a trespass case the court would have had to remove the hurdle that a claimant of an undivided interest in Texas, as in most jurisdictions, is not a trespasser but enters under a claim of right. On basic considerations as to the form of action and the nature of the recovery allowed the case seems incorrect. However, it may now be stated that in Texas where one enters, authorized by an owner of an undivided interest in the minerals, but wrongfully asserts a right to other undivided interests, he is a trespasser as to such interests.

The Kishi case is a classic case where the court was trying to compensate for the loss of speculative value but could not find an historic "cubbyhole" in which the case would fit.

The Kishi case has been severely criticized on the ground that Kishi was compensated in a situation in which he could have conferred no correlative benefit. Martel v. Hall Oil Co.,[3] expressly rejected Kishi in the following language: "It may be, though there is no showing to that effect, that plaintiffs might have sold their rights for a considerable sum of money. They would then have been the gainers, and the purchaser would have been the loser. They would, upon their own theory, have pocketed a lot of money, but for what? What would they have given in return? Nothing. They would have

---

2. It is doubtful that good faith and reasonable reliance could have been shown here. Today the invalidity of the lease seems plain on its face; it may have been otherwise in 1919.

3. 36 Wyo. 166, 253 P. 862, 52 A.L.R. 91.

sold something of no value whatever. They would, upon their own theory, have received something for nothing in return." In the Martel case no showing was made as to the value of the mineral leasing rights, but it seems clear the court would have denied a recovery in any event.

At least one other case has reached the same result as Kishi.[4] It would also seem that the court in Martel is incorrect in its philosophy that the seller would receive something for nothing. What Kishi could have sold was the right to explore his property. In such a situation there is never a guarantee that petroleum products will be found. Where one has entered and wrongfully exercised a right that it did not have, the landowner should be compensated for the exercise of the right. Whether or not oil is discovered is immaterial.

(B) Sub-Surface Trespass That Results in Production or Drainage

(1) Recovery and Remedy

Consider the following situation: Black Gold Oil Co. acquires a lease on Blackacre from A, relying upon a title opinion from counsel that A has title to the minerals. After Black Gold drills a well and produces for a time, it is discovered that O, not A, actually is the owner of the mineral estate. There is no doubt that Black Gold has converted the oil of O; however, does Black Gold have any rights in this situation? An example is found in the early Kentucky case of Swiss Oil Corp. v. Hupp,[5] where the lessee acquired a "top lease" of properties based on an attorney's opinion that a prior lease had expired. This result was reinforced by litigation in the trial court holding that the second lease was good. The lessee thereafter drilled six wells, again relying upon an attorney's opinion. The trial court was later reversed, and it was held that the first lease was still in force. In the interim period defendant lessee had produced 67,527 barrels of oil valued at $142,849.28. In accounting for the proceeds the defendant contended that as it had acted in good faith, it should be allowed credit for the costs of drilling the well and production. The court stated the rule to be that " * * * wrongdoers find the way of the transgressor hard under the law. They are held to a strict accountability for their malappropriation of another's property. Complete restitution without credit for expenses incurred or deduction of costs of production is required. But those who invade the property of another inadvertently or under a bona fide belief or claim of right and extract minerals are allowed credit for proper expenditures in obtaining or producing them. While not allowed any profit, they are not to be penalized."

4. Matheson v. Placid Oil Co., 212 La. 807, 33 So.2d 527, and see Humble Oil & Refining Co. v. Luckel, Tex.Civ.App., 154 S.W.2d 155; and, Brixey v. Union Oil Co. of California, D.C.Ark., 283 F.Supp. 353.

5. 253 Ky. 552, 69 S.W.2d 1037.

§ 4.2   TRESPASS, SURFACE, SUB–SURFACE   165

Where the trespasser producing petroleum products is considered to have been in good faith, it is generally held that, in accounting for the products converted, he may offset against the value of the products withdrawn the reasonable costs of (1) drilling, (2) completing the well, and (3) operating and producing the products.[6] Such credit is limited in amount to the extent that the operations have enhanced the property of the owner.[7] The right of the good-faith trespasser is one of reimbursement out of production.[8] Where there has been insufficient production, the trespasser will not recover his costs.[9]

Little difficulty is incurred by the trespasser who has remained in possession until recoupment of his costs, but what of the sub-surface trespasser who is ousted prior to payout? It does not appear that the owner has an obligation to allow the trespasser to stay in possession until he has recouped his costs or to continue reimbursement after the trespasser is ousted.[10] However, under general equity practice the trespasser may be allowed the value of his costs, to the extent that they enhance the property, by way of an equitable lien against the property until satisfied.[11]

In some jurisdictions, betterment statutes have been enacted allowing a good-faith trespasser to recover the value of his improvements to the extent that they have benefitted the owner. Although such statutes usually do not expressly include subsurface trespassers, they have sometimes been included by judicial interpretation.[12] In Texas some question remains whether equity practice is cumulative with the statutory remedy, or whether the statute is exclusive. The better view would seem to be that the remedies are cumulative.[13]

Where the improvements of the trespasser have not added to or enhanced the value of the owner's property, the only credit allowed

---

6. Lambach v. Town of Mason, 386 Ill. 41, 53 N.E.2d 601; Barnes v. Winona Oil Co., 83 Okl. 253, 200 P. 985, 23 A.L.R. 189; Edwards v. Lachman, Okl., 534 P.2d 670; Bender v. Brooks, 103 Tex. 329, 127 S.W. 168; American Trading and Production Corp. v. Phillips Petroleum Co., Tex Civ.App., 449 S.W.2d 794, refused n. r. e.; Williamson v. Jones, 43 W.Va. 562, 27 S.E. 411. At least two Illinois cases in the federal system have rejected the distinction between a good faith and a bad faith trespasser: Shell Oil Co. v. Manley Oil Corp., D.C.Ill., 50 F.Supp. 21; Superior Oil Co. v. Harsh, D.C.Ill., 50 F.Supp. 358. But cf. Shell Oil Co. v. Dye, C.A. 7th, 135 F.2d 365; Lambach v. Town of Mason, 386 Ill. 41, 53 N.E.2d 601. From the last case it would seem Illinois now recognizes a distinction.

7. Greer v. Stanolind Oil & Gas Co., C.A.10th, 200 F.2d 920; Edwards v. Lachman, Okl., 534 P.2d 670; Carter Oil Co. v. McCasland, C.A.10th, 207 F.2d 728.

8. Lawrence Oil Corp. v. Metcalfe, 266 Ky. 819, 100 S.W.2d 217.

9. Miller v. Tidal Oil Co., 161 Okl. 155, 17 P.2d 967, 87 A.L.R. 811.

10. But see Lawrence Oil Corp. v. Metcalfe, 266 Ky. 819, 100 S.W.2d 217.

11. Pomeroy v. Pearce, Tex.Com. App., 2 S.W.2d 431.

12. Belcher v. Elliott, C.A.6th, 312 F.2d 245; 12 O.S. 1481 (Okl.); Article 7393, Vernon's Ann.Tex.Civ.St.; Also see Ky. K.R.S. 381.460; Utah U.C.A.1953, § 57–6–1.

13. Pomeroy v. Pearce, Tex.Com. App., 2 S.W.2d 431, Wood v. Cahill, 21 Tex.Civ.App. 38, 50 S.W. 1071; but cf. Schwethelm v. Collozo, Tex.Civ.App., 159 S.W.2d 161.

will be for lifting and production costs.[14] In Carter Oil Company v. McCasland,[15] the trespasser entered under an ambiguous instrument. Here Carter executed a partial assignment of oil and gas leases insofar as they covered producing horizons above a depth of 4,000 feet. The assignor-trespasser interpreted the assignment as assigning the leases only to that portion of a producing horizon that existed above the 4,000-foot depth. Assignee, and the court, interpreted the assignment as assigning all of a producing horizon (both that portion below as well as that above 4,000 feet) when any part of it extended above 4,000 feet. Assignor drilled into horizons below 4,000 feet that also extended and were produced by assignee above this depth. It was held that he was a good-faith trespasser but had not enhanced the property of the assignee, who had upstructure wells which would eventually drain all of the products found below 4,000 feet. No credit was allowed for the costs of drilling, completing, or equipping the well.

Although credit will be denied for non-beneficial costs, costs beyond those encountered in the typical case will be allowed if they are found to be reasonable costs of development. Credit has been allowed for the cost of drilling an unprofitable directional branch well, which was later plugged back, on the ground that it was a reasonable cost of exploration.[16] In a similar case, credit was allowed where a well was drilled to a depth of 7,327 feet and plugged back to 3,949 feet.[17] Analogies have been made between the costs for which credit is given to the good-faith trespasser and those allowed, in an accounting between co-tenants, where one co-tenant is drilling an undivided interest in the minerals. Generally, each co-tenant may drill as a matter of right. However, they may not convert another co-tenant's oil. Accounting is made on the basis that the producing co-tenant may retain all proceeds of production until he has recouped his costs of drilling, completing, and producing. In Burnham v. Hardy Oil Co.,[18] for instance, in addition to the ordinary costs of development and production allowed the co-tenant, he was allowed to recoup the costs of pipe-line construction and a pumping station. It is questionable whether a recoupable cost for a co-tenant drilling as a matter of right should necessarily be a recoupable cost for one who has entered wrongfully, although in good faith. Although strong analogies may be made between these two situations, they are not basically the same. At present no authoritative decision exists in this area.

14. Carter Oil Co. v. McCasland, C.A.10th, 207 F.2d 728; Edwards v. Lachman, Okl., 534 P.2d 670; American Trading and Production Corp. v. Phillips Petroleum Co., Tex.Civ.App., 449 S.W.2d 794 refused n.r.e. (illegal well); Greer v. Stanolind Oil & Gas Co., C.A.10th, 200 F.2d 920; Greer v. Stanolind Oil & Gas Co., C.A.10th, 200 F.2d 920; Pan American Petroleum Corp. v. Candelaria, C.A. 10th, 403 F.2d 351.

15. C.A.10th, 207 F.2d 728.

16. Champlin Refining Co. v. Aladdin Petroleum Co., 205 Okl. 524, 238 P.2d 827.

17. Martel v. Hunt, 195 La. 701, 197 So. 402.

18. Tex.Civ.App., 147 S.W. 330, affirmed 108 Tex. 555, 195 S.W. 1139.

Some early cases from jurisdictions having a history of hard mineral mining awarded to the landowner, not the amount of gross production that was converted minus expenses, but the amount of royalty that the owner would have received had the land been under lease.[19] The rule was changed in Kentucky, in the case of Swiss Oil Corp. v. Hupp,[20] as to oil and gas cases where the dispute was between the lessee and the trespasser. However, the court indicated that the royalty rule would be retained where the dispute was between the trespasser and the landowner. It now appears that in the latter case the landowner will have an election whether to recover on a royalty or gross proceeds basis.[21] The Kentucky rule as to hard minerals has also been modified to allow recovery of gross proceeds less expenses.

Where the trespasser has entered in bad faith and removed petroleum products from the land, he will be liable for the full value of the products converted, without deduction of costs of any kind.[22] If gas is wrongfully withdrawn and commingled with other gas owned by the trespasser, he will be liable for the value of all the gas produced and sold from both wells.[23]

A classic case of fraudulent removal of oil by directional drilling was presented in Alphonzo E. Bell Corp. v. Bell View Oil Syndicate.[24] In this case defendant directionally drilled upstructure and bottomed the well on adjoining land. Every effort had been made to conceal the illegal drilling. When discovered, defendant used considerable ingenuity in its defense of the case. It was argued that as California was a non-ownership jurisdiction and title to oil or gas was not acquired until produced, each lessee had the right to bottom its wells as it saw fit in the reservoir in order to withdraw its proportionate part of the oil. It was further argued that each lessee was entitled to a pro-rata portion of the oil in the reservoir without regard to where a well was positioned. The court denied all arguments, holding that

19. Alaska Placer Co. v. Lee, Alaska, 553 P.2d 54; Stark v. Pennsylvania Coal Co., 241 Pa. 597, 88 A. 770; Young v. Ethyl Corp., C.A.8th, 581 F.2d 715, cert. denied 439 U.S. 1089, 99 S.Ct. 871, 59 L.Ed.2d 56, appeal after remand 635 F.2d 681 (removal of salt brine. The court refused to allow damages on enhanced value); Swiss Oil Corp. v. Hupp, 253 Ky. 552, 69 S.W.2d 1037; and see Summers, Oil and Gas, § 24, p. 62.

20. 253 Ky. 552, 69 S.W.2d 1037. This is the rule in other jurisdictions, see Bender v. Brooks, 103 Tex. 329, 127 S.W. 168.

21. Stephens v. Preston's Heirs, 300 Ky. 843, 190 S.W.2d 468.

22. Pacific Western Oil Co. v. Bern Oil Co., 13 Cal.2d 60, 87 P.2d 1045; Alphonzo E. Bell Corp. v. Bell View Oil Syndicate, 24 Cal.App.2d 587, 76 P.2d 167; Gribben v. Carpenter, 323 Pa. 243, 185 A. 712; Mayhew v. Callard, C.A.7th, 312 F.2d 295. However State severance taxes are recoupable by the bad-faith trespasser. Also see Steeple Oil & Gas Corp. v. Amend, Tex.Civ.App., 392 S.W.2d 744, reversed, Tex., 394 S.W.2d 789, where a lessee tried to recoup costs of drilling and completion by applying a rule similar to that of a good-faith trespasser, where it had drilled a well after the lease had lapsed due to failure to pay shut-in royalties. Denied in intermediate Court of Appeals and reversed on a procedural ground.

23. Gribben v. Carpenter, 323 Pa. 243, 185 A. 712.

24. 24 Cal.App.2d 587, 76 P.2d 167.

bottoming a well on another's land was a trespass, and that defendant was entitled only to that portion of the oil that it could withdraw from wells bottomed on its own lands. D was found to be a willful trespasser and was denied recoupment of costs. The court was doubtless impressed by the efforts at concealment in this case.

Where the producer of petroleum products has been classified as a bad-faith trespasser, a purchaser of such products with notice will be jointly liable for the conversion.[25] No right exists in such assignee to credits for improvements.

In accounting to the owner for products that were converted, it is the amount of the oil or gas that was wrongfully produced that must be accounted for, not that which is ultimately lost from recovery by the owner. In one case,[26] where the well of the owner was located upstructure from the well of the trespasser, it was argued that only oil that would have been ultimately lost from recovery by the owner should be accounted for. In other words, the accounting should be reduced by the amount that the trespasser would have produced by a well that had been properly bottomed. The contention was denied and accounting was made for the value of all oil wrongfully removed from the property.

It appears to be the general rule that where products are converted by a trespasser, value will be determined as being the market value of the products at the time of the conversion.[27] Where the market has fallen since the time of the conversion, the trespasser may not replace the oil converted rather than account for it on the basis of the value at the time of the conversion.[28] In some cases the trespasser has had to account for such products under the rule that a converter is liable for the highest intermediate value between the time of conversion and time of trial.[29]

Interest is generally allowed on the net amount of oil accounted for by the trespasser.[30] However, where the reasonable expenses of a good-faith trespasser exceed the amount of gross production, no recovery is made by the landowner, and no interest is payable.[31]

Where interest is payable, the courts have differed as to the time from which it is first computed. Not only do some courts have discretion as to the time interest will become payable, disagreement has

---

25. Probst v. Bearman, 76 Okl. 71, 183 P. 886.

26. Alphonzo E. Bell Corp. v. Bell View Oil Syndicate, 24 Cal.App.2d 587, 76 P.2d 167.

27. Barnes v. Winona Oil Co., 83 Okl. 253, 200 P. 985, 23 A.L.R. 189; Texas Co. v. State, 154 Tex. 494, 281 S.W.2d 83.

28. Swiss Oil Corp. v. Hupp, 253 Ky. 552, 69 S.W.2d 1037.

29. Probst v. Bearman, 76 Okl. 71, 183 P. 886.

30. Swiss Oil Corp. v. Hupp, 253 Ky. 552, 69 S.W.2d 1037; Miller v. Tidal Oil Co., 161 Okl. 155, 17 P.2d 967, 87 A.L.R. 811; Champlin Refining Co. v. Aladdin Petroleum Co., 205 Okl. 524, 238 P.2d 827; Texas Co. v. State, 154 Tex. 494, 281 S.W.2d 83; Shell Oil Co. v. Manley Oil Corp., D.C.Ill., 50 F.Supp. 21.

31. Miller v. Tidal Oil Co., 161 Okl. 155, 17 P.2d 967, 87 A.L.R. 811.

occurred as to the time at which the sum owed by a geophysical trespasser becomes a liquidated amount. At least three viewpoints have been expressed: (a) Interest is payable from the time of the conversion on the net amount for which the trespasser must account, although a later accounting is necessary to fix the principal amount;[32] (b) Interest is payable only from the time that the principal amount is fixed by judgment;[33] and (c) Interest is payable from the time that the proceeds from production exceed the operating costs.[34]

The first would seem to be the preferable viewpoint. No reason can be perceived upon which to allow the trespasser to have use of converted money of the owner interest free from the time of the sale of the products to the time of a later trial at which the accounting is made. Under this view, interest would be payable from the time the products should have been sold, if a market existed for the products at the time of the conversion, although the products were not sold until a later time. As very few cases exist dealing with the problem, it cannot be said that any particular rule predominates.

(2) The Good-Faith Trespasser

From the above discussion it may be seen that the good-faith geophysical trespasser is in a more advantageous position than one who is considered as being willful or in bad faith. The question follows, what is good faith? Many cases have attempted to answer the question.[35] As stated in the Kentucky case of Swiss Oil Co. v. Hupp:[36] "The test to be applied is that of intent, but being a state of mind, it can seldom be proved by direct evidence. The conditions and behavior are usually such that the court can determine whether the trespass was perpetrated with a spirit of wrongdoing, with a knowledge it was wrong, or whether it was done under a bona fide mistake, where the circumstances were calculated to induce or justify the reasonably prudent man, acting with a proper sense of the rights of others, to go in and continue along the way. And in judging the trespasser's acts, regard must be had for conditions as they then appeared rather than as disclosed in the light cast backwards by the

---

32. Texas Co. v. State, 154 Tex. 494, 281 S.W.2d 83 (from the time the products removed have been sold); Shell Oil Co. v. Manley Oil Corp., D.C.Ill., 50 F.Supp. 21 (from the date sold).

33. Swiss Oil Corp. v. Hupp, 253 Ky. 552, 69 S.W.2d 1037.

34. Champlin Refining Co. v. Aladdin Petroleum Co., 205 Okl. 524, 238 P.2d 827.

35. Lambach v. Town of Mason, 386 Ill. 41, 53 N.E.2d 601; Belcher v. Elliott, C.A.6th, 312 F.2d 245; Swiss Oil Corp. v. Hupp., 253 Ky. 552, 69 S.W.2d 1037; Lebow v. Cameron, Ky., 394 S.W.2d 773; Martel v. Hunt, 195 La. 701, 197 So. 402; Barnes v. Winona Oil Co., 83 Okl. 253, 200 P. 985, 23 A.L.R. 189; Sapulpa Petroleum Co. v. McCray, 136 Okl. 269, 277 P. 589; Miller v. Tidal Oil Co., 161 Okl. 155, 17 P.2d 967, 87 A.L.R. 811; Ballard v. Stanolind Oil & Gas Co., C.C.A.5th, 80 F.2d 588; Bender v. Brooks, 103 Tex. 329, 127 S.W. 168; Gulf Production Co v Spear, 125 Tex. 530, 84 S.W.2d 452; Steeple Oil & Gas Corp. v. Amend, Tex.Civ.App., 392 S.W.2d 744, reversed Tex., 394 S.W.2d 789; Hall Oil Co. v. Barquin, 33 Wyo. 92, 237 P. 255; Mayhew v. Callard, C.A.7th, 312 F.2d 295; Superior Oil Co. v. Harsh, D.C.Ill., 50 F.Supp. 358.

36. 253 Ky. 552, 69 S.W.2d 1037.

future." Or, as was stated in Miller v. Tidal Oil Co.,[37] whether the "taking is without culpable negligence or willful disregard of the rights of others and in the honest and reasonable belief that it was rightful." There must be some reasonable doubt of the other party's exclusive or dominant right,[38] and the action of the trespasser classified as "innocent", "unintentional",[39] or with a "honest belief."[40]

For a person to be in good faith not only must he have so believed, the basis for such belief must have been adequate to support such a belief. A person may not keep himself ignorant and then claim to be in good faith; the reliance must be reasonable. In several cases reliance has been deemed to have been reasonable where the trespasser has relied upon advice of counsel,[41] such as in the interpretation of ambiguous instruments.[42] However, where counsel have no adequate basis for advice upon which the trespasser relied, it would seem that reliance is not reasonable. In Humble Refining Co. v. Kishi,[43] the question of good faith was not considered by the court; however, had the action been viewed as one concerning slander of title, the good faith of Humble would have been in question. It is doubtful whether Humble's reliance upon house counsel or outside counsel that the lease was still in effect would have been sufficient to support a claim of good faith.

It is sometimes stated that the trespasser must also have been claiming under color of title.[44] However, it would seem that this is

37. 161 Okl. 155, 17 P.2d 967, 87 A.L.R. 811; also see Sapulpa Petroleum Co. v. McCray, 136 Okl. 269, 277 P. 589, "An honest intention to abstain from taking any unconscientious advantage of another, even through forms or technicalities of the law, together with an absence of all information or belief of facts which would render the transaction unconscientious."; and Gulf Production Co. v. Spear, 125 Tex. 530, 84 S.W.2d 452, "Good faith under one state of facts would not be good faith under a slightly different state of facts. In general, it may be said that to act in good faith in developing a tract of land for oil and gas one must have both an honest and reasonable belief in the superiority of his title."

38. Lebow v. Cameron, Ky., 394 S.W.2d 773.

39. Bender v. Brooks, 103 Tex. 329, 127 S.W. 168.

40. Alaska Placer Co. v. Lee, Alaska, 553 P.2d 54; Bender v. Brooks, 103 Tex. 329, 127 S.W. 168; Sapulpa Petroleum Co. v. McCray, 136 Okl. 269, 277 P. 589.

The burden of proof as to the existence of good faith is normally on the trespasser. However, in some jurisdictions it appears that the owner has the burden of establishing lack of good faith: Sapulpa Petroleum Corp. v. McCray, 136 Okl. 269, 277 P. 589; Barnes v. Winona Oil Co., 83 Okl. 253, 200 P. 985; Dilworth v. Fortier, Okl., 405 P.2d 38.

41. Alaska Placer Co. v. Lee, Alaska, 553 P.2d 54; Whittaker v. Otto, 248 Cal. App.2d 666, 56 Cal.Rptr. 836; Swiss Oil Corp. v. Hupp., 253 Ky. 552, 69 S.W.2d 1037; Lebow v. Cameron, Ky., 394 S.W. 2d 773; Martel v. Hunt, 195 La. 701, 197 So. 402.

42. Lambach v. Town of Mason, 386 Ill. 41, 53 N.E.2d 601 (ambiguous dedication); Belcher v. Elliott, C.A.6th, 312 F.2d 245 (ambiguous instrument).

43. Tex.Com.App., 276 S.W. 190; or rehearing Com.App., 291 S.W. 538, and see § 4.1, infra.

44. Whittaker v. Otto, 248 Cal.App.2d 666, 56 Cal.Rptr. 836; Barnes v. Winona Oil Co., 83 Okl. 253, 200 P. 985, 23 A.L.R. 189; Sapulpa Petroleum Co. v. McCray, 136 Okl. 269, 277 P. 589 (had minerals). See: Sick v. Bendix United Geophysical Corp., La.App., 341 So.2d 1308 discussing LSA–R.S. 9:2721 and LSA–C.C. art. 2266, protecting from trespass those who deal with the record owner, in good faith and rely upon the title to immovable property. The statutes do not protect those

§ 4.2   TRESPASS, SURFACE, SUB–SURFACE   171

not always a necessary element for belief to be reasonable. A reasonable risk of title may be taken.[45] In at least one case, good faith was found where the reliance had been upon a title derived through adverse possession.[46] However, the trespasser will not be in good faith when pursuing a wholly speculative claim [47] or is acting with actual disregard for the rights of others.[48]

To what extent may the trespasser be in good faith after he has actual or constructive knowledge of a claimed right of another? This is a vital question. Does the mere fact that an instrument disclosing another's claim has been filed of record make a subsequent entry by a trespasser one in bad faith? Would it make a difference if the trespasser had seen the instrument prior to entry, or had been told by the claimant? Should entry after a title suit has been filed against the trespasser constitute bad faith? The case law is meager and not conclusive. In all the above situations, the person making the entry has notice of the other's claim, although some are stronger assertions of the claim than others.

In the early United States Supreme Court case of Guffey v. Smith,[49] a distinction was drawn between notice given constructively and actually. The court was of the opinion that constructive notice was insufficient to constitute the later entry as one in bad faith. The court said: "They paid a substantial sum for it, were let into possession by the lessor, and were not conscious that they were invading the rights of others. True, the prior lease had been properly recorded, but as they consulted an abstractor before consummating the transaction with Willett, and were advised that the title was clear, the constructive notice resulting from the recording of the prior lease was not inconsistent with an honest, though mistaken, belief on their part that they had acquired a perfect right to take and dispose of the oil."

The cases are inconsistent as to the effect of actual notice. In Guffey v. Smith, the court continued: "But the expenses incurred after August 1, 1907, are upon a different footing. On that date Solley and his associates were actually and fully informed of the prior lease and of the complainants' purpose to insist upon the rights conferred

who deal with neither the true owner nor the record owner.

45. Belcher v. Elliott, C.A.6th, 312 F.2d 245; Lebow v. Cameron, Ky., 394 S.W.2d 773.

46. Bender v. Brooks, 103 Tex. 329, 127 S.W. 168.

47. Dethloff v. Ziegler Coal Co., 82 Ill.2d 393, 45 Ill.Dec. 175, 412 N.E.2d 526; Ballard v. Stanolind Oil & Gas Co., C.A. 5th, 80 F.2d 588.

48. Hall Oil Co. v. Barquin, 33 Wyo. 92, 237 P. 255. Also see Steeple Oil & Gas Corp. v. Amend, Tex.Civ.App., 392 S.W.2d 744, reversed Tex., 394 S.W.2d 789, where attempt of lessee to apply good faith doctrine, where lease lapsed due to late payment of shut-in royalty, was denied on ground lessee was sole cause of loss of lease.

See: Edwards v. Lachman, Okl., 534 P.2d 670, where lessee was in good faith until he had directional survey made that showed that the well was bottomed across the property line. It was held that production afterwards was in bad faith as a matter of law.

49. 237 U.S. 101, 35 S.Ct. 526, 59 L.Ed. 856.

by it, and to obtain redress for the invasion of those rights, so what was done thereafter cannot be regarded as anything less than a willful taking and appropriation of the oil which was subject to complainants' superior right." Although other cases have agreed with the court in the Guffey case,[50] it appears that the majority of opinion is to the effect that actual notice will be treated as only one of the elements to be considered along with the other surrounding circumstances in determining good or bad faith.[51]

A different result exists where litigation is pending at the time of entry, and the cases are nearly unanimous in holding that a later entry is made in bad faith;[52] this is true even where the trial court has upheld the trespasser.[53] A sharp distinction has been made between cases where litigation was pending prior to entry and where the entry was peaceable and suit was later filed.[54]

It is arguable whether notice of any kind, including the filing of suit should, *per se*, make a later entry one in bad faith. Not only should the matter of notice be examined, but the quality of reliance in an honest belief must also be examined and weighed. It certainly is not demonstrable that the litigant or claimant usually prevails. To treat notice as the sole determinant of good or bad faith places the trespasser with an honest and reasonable belief in the superiority of his title in an untenable position. This is especially true when dealing with oil and gas products, where delay may occasion the loss of valuable products by drainage.

Questions have also arisen where the trespasser entered peaceably and later received notice, or suit was later filed. Is he now in bad faith for subsequent operations? Apparently, where the trespasser

---

50. Guffey v. Smith, 237 U.S. 101, 35 S.Ct. 526, 59 L.Ed. 856; Shell Oil Co. v. Dye, C.C.A.7th, 135 F.2d 365.

51. Mayhew v. Callard, C.A.7th, 312 F.2d 295; Jenkins v. Pure Oil Co., Tex.Civ.App., 53 S.W.2d 497.

52. Probst v. Bearman, 76 Okl. 71, 183 P. 886; Texas Co. v. Pettit, 107 Okl. 243, 220 P. 956; Houston Production Co. v. Mecom Oil Co., Tex.Com.App., 62 S.W.2d 75. But see Lebow v. Cameron, Ky., 394 S.W.2d 773; Joyce, Administrator v. Zachary, Administrator, Ky.App., 434 S.W.2d 659; Jenkins v. Pure Oil Co., Tex.Civ.App., 53 S.W.2d 497, where T's title lay in parol T held not to be in bad faith; Whelan v. Killingsworth, Tex.Civ.App., 537 S.W.2d 785.

53. Texas Co. v. Pettit, 107 Okl. 243, 220 P. 956, also see Shell Oil Co. v. Manley Oil Corp., D.C.Ill., 50 F.Supp. 21.

Compare the following two cases:

In Alaska Placer Co. v. Lee, Alaska, 553 P.2d 54, an entry was held to be in good faith where it was made upon advice of counsel, and after appeal of a judgment sustaining lease, but which was later reversed and forfeiture sustained. In this case the court found that the trespasser had an honest and reasonable belief that the taking was lawful.

However, in Whelan v. Killingsworth, Tex.Civ.App., 537 S.W.2d 785, where plaintiff, assignor of leases, brought suit to rescind assignment and prevailed in trial court, and during pendency of appeal entered under writ of possession and drilled two producing wells, was held to be in bad faith, entering *pendente lite*, the court classifying entry made pending final outcome of suit as the same as entry made after suit filed and before judgment.

54. Joyce v. Zachary, Ky., 434 S.W.2d 659; Barnes v. Winona Oil Co., 83 Okl. 253, 200 P. 985, 23 A.L.R. 189; and see Houston Production Co. v. Mecom Oil Co., Tex.Com.App., 62 S.W.2d 75.

§ 4.2   TRESPASS, SURFACE, SUB–SURFACE   173

is in good faith at the time that suit is filed, he will not lose his status as a good-faith trespasser until such time as a final judgment has been entered.[55] In the case of Gulf Refining Co. of Louisiana v. United States,[56] the court stated: "The moral quality of their possession was not affected by the institution of the government's suit, or the resistance which they interposed before judgment to the government contentions * * * An appeal is not a new suit in an appellate court but a continuation of the suit in the court below * * * and the suit is pending until the appeal is disposed of."

(3) Directional Underground Trespass

In the last several years cases have been appearing in greater quantity concerning the drilling and production out of slanted wells bottomed on adjacent tracts of land. Probably the most noted of the cases is that of Alphonzo E. Bell Corp. v. Bell View Oil Syndicate.[57] The act of deliberately slanting the well to take advantage of up-structure production was concealed from the California regulatory agency, and an attempt was made to justify the well on the ground that as it was drilled in a non-ownership state it could be bottomed anywhere in the formation. The case states the generally applied rule [58] that the underground trespass of a slanted well is subject to injunction, and damages may be recovered for the products converted. As the intrusion constitutes a continuing trespass it is subject to injunction without a showing of a specific amount of damage.[59]

Injunctive relief is also available to the owner of a mineral estate where a petroleum operator, with permission of the owner of the overlying surface, is using a portion of such surface as a well site for the directional drilling of a well through a part of the underlying mineral estate into an adjacent tract.[60]

In the East Texas field many wells were found to have been directionally drilled and were protected from discovery by the use of dummy wells that produced from pipelines connected to other wells and the filing of false reports with the commission. It was in connection

---

55. Gulf Refining Co. of Louisiana v. United States, 269 U.S. 125, 46 S.Ct. 52, 70 L.Ed. 195; Sapulpa Petroleum Co. v. McCray, 136 Okl. 269, 277 P. 589.

56. 269 U.S. 125, 46 S.Ct. 52, 70 L.Ed. 195.

57. 24 Cal.App.2d 587, 76 P.2d 167, also see note 24, supra. In this case it is noted the court would allow the royalty owner a cause of action for trespass. Would this be true if royalty is payable in money rather than in kind?

58. Pacific Western Oil Co. v. Bern Oil Co., 13 Cal.2d 60, 87 P.2d 1045; Union Oil Co. of California v. Domengeaux, 30 Cal.App.2d 266, 86 P.2d 127; Hancock Oil Co. v. Meeker-Garner Oil Co., 118 Cal. App.2d 379, 257 P.2d 988; Hastings Oil Co. v. Texas Co., 149 Tex. 416, 234 S.W.2d 389.

59. Hancock Oil Co. v. Meeker-Garner Oil Co., 118 Cal.App.2d 379, 257 P.2d 988; Hastings Oil Co. v. Texas Co., 149 Tex. 416, 234 S.W.2d 389.

60. Hancock Oil Co. of California v. Meeker-Garner Oil Co., 118 Cal.App.2d 379, 257 P.2d 988; Chevron Oil Co. v. Howell, Tex.Civ.App., 407 S.W.2d 525. Where the lease covers state lands, such as a river bed, a right of condemnation may exist for the purpose of acquisition of drilling sites on abutting lands. Coastal States Gas Producing Co. v. Pate, Tex., 309 S.W.2d 828.

with these wells that an administrative discovery rule was enacted.[61] Liability for conversion of oil from the deviated wells has been extended to those actually having control of the operations. In Harrington v. Texaco, Inc.,[62] the operator of a group of leases was held to be jointly and severally liable with the leasehold owners on the basis of the control of the operator over the leases. Liability was for the full amount of the oil converted, without regard to the amount of the oil he had actually received. Such liability has also been extended to a bank that was the holder of a mortgage on leasehold interests together with a production payment payable from runs from a deviated well. The bank's liability was based upon its apparent control over operations conferred in the security instruments.[63]

Where the deviated well has produced from the same pool as it would have if it had not been deviated, and if allowables have not been exceeded, in Texas [64] at least, the lessee may receive permission to redrill and straighten the wells.

(4) Discovery and Limitations

Limitation against a cause of action for sub-surface trespass will begin to run at the time that the landowner knows or through the use of reasonable care should have known about the trespass.[65] At least one state has a short time limitation statute against underground trespass.[66]

Where the landowner suspects that the adjoining lessee is draining his subsurface, he may bring discovery proceedings ancillary to litigation for conversion, both in state and federal courts.[67] Some jurisdictions have provisions for administrative discovery, which is initi-

---

61. Hastings Oil Co. v. Texas Co., 149 Tex. 416, 234 S.W.2d 389 (Section V, Texas statewide Rule No. 54).

62. C.A.5th, 339 F.2d 814.

63. Pan American Petroleum Co. v. Long, C.A.5th, 340 F.2d 211. However, in Schlumberger Well Surveying Corp. v. Nortex Oil & Gas Corp., Tex., 435 S.W.2d 854, a conspiracy to defraud by sale of deviated wells was denied as to a well-surveying company whose logs reflected a total length of 1500 to 1700 feet longer than the producing depth of the field. Actual knowledge of the conspiracy and intent to participate by the well-surveying company was required to be shown for liability to exist. The court would not raise such facts by inference.

64. Harrington v. Railroad Commission, Tex., 375 S.W.2d 892.

Also see Lachman v. Sperry-Sun Well Surveying Co., C.A.10th, 457 F.2d 850, where directional survey found well bottomed on adjoining tract of land and contract with surveying company contained a clause binding the company to non-disclosure of the results of the survey. Company's employee informed owner of adjacent land, who sued owner of well and recovered. Owner of well was denied recovery against surveying company for breach of non-disclosure clause which, although generally enforceable, could not be enforced against an illegal act, i.e., the illegal bottoming of the well.

65. Pacific Western Oil Co. v. Bern Oil Co., 13 Cal.2d 60, 87 P.2d 1045; Alphonzo E. Bell Corp. v. Bell View Oil Syndicate, 24 Cal.App.2d 587, 76 P.2d 167.

66. § 349¾, West's Ann.Cal.Code Civ. Proc., and see Stafford v. Union Oil Co. of California, 173 Cal.App.2d 307, 343 P.2d 380.

67. Williams v. Continental Oil Co., C.A.10th, 215 F.2d 4 (Rule 34, Federal Rules of Civil Procedure); Hastings Oil Co. v. Texas Co., 149 Tex. 416, 234 S.W.2d 389 (Section V, Texas statewide Rule No. 54).

ated by the state regulatory body upon notice from a landowner.[68] Such statutes may or may not provide for notice and hearing to the suspected wrongdoer.

(C) Trespass Caused by Underground Intrusion of Injected Substances

Recently a body of law has been developing with regard to the injection of substances into reservoirs, with authority from state regulatory agencies, which intrude into adjacent mineral areas. This is an outgrowth of increasing use of secondary recovery operations involving the injection of substances, such as salt water, for pressuring purposes. Such injection is usually performed under the authority of state conservation regulatory bodies. Where such injection results in the flooding of producing wells or merely intruding into adjoining sub-space, is the intrusion actionable?

Where such injection is done voluntarily without authorization, and results in damage to adjacent wells, the injector will be liable in damages for destruction of the wells.[69] However, where injection was into an existing salt water formation that extended under the adjoining lands and was of such great extent that the injected materials were quite small compared to the size of the reservoir into which they were injected, and where no communication existed with producing horizons, no actionable tort was committed.[70] The injector was neither liable in damages (there were none) nor subject to injunctive relief. In some early cases in non-ownership jurisdictions no tort was recognized, due to application of a principle that, when injected, the substances traveled across ownership lines and title was then lost. This doctrine was applied in the early landmark case of Hammonds v. Central Kentucky Natural Gas Co.,[71] in which the injector was sued for trespass after injection of gas for storage purposes into an underground reservoir. It has since been remarked that the plaintiff should have drilled a well and withdrawn and sold the products. This was attempted in a recent Texas case,[72] where the courts rejected the approach of the Hammonds case and stated that after gas was produced title was acquired, and when it was later injected for storage purposes title had not been abandoned. Therefore the withdrawal was a conversion. It might be asked whether the injector in this case had committed an enjoinable trespass.

However, where the injection is part of an approved water flood program and results in the flooding out of surrounding wells it has been indicated that the public policy of prevention of waste will su-

---

68. See L & G Oil Co. v. Railroad Commission, Tex., 368 S.W.2d 187.

69. West Edmond Hunton Lime Unit v. Lillard, Okl., 265 P.2d 730.

70. West Edmond Salt Water Disposal Association v. Rosecrans', 204 Okl. 9, 226 P.2d 965.

71. 255 Ky. 685, 75 S.W.2d 204.

72. Lone Star Gas Co. v. Murchison, Tex.Civ.App., 353 S.W.2d 870, 94 A.L.R.2d 529. Also see Emeny v. United States, Ct.Cl., 412 F.2d 1319 (ownership of underground reservoir for storage purposes).

persede the right of the adjoining property owner to enjoin the program. In the Texas case of Railroad Commission v. Manziel,[73] it was held that such authorized injection did not constitute a trespass. However, it would seem more desirable to classify the intrusion into the adjoining sub-surface as a trespass that was not actionable due to overriding public policy.

Where wells on surrounding lands are lost due to authorized water flood programs, is such loss one that should in effect be compensated for? Should compensation be allowed in the guise of damages payable by the intruder? This appears to have been the rationale of the case of Tidewater Oil Co. v. Jackson,[74] which awarded compensatory damages and reads somewhat like a condemnation case. The fundamental problem presented is that property values have been lost by private action authorized by a state conservation regulatory body for the public purpose of preventing waste in the production of petroleum products. Viewed as analogous to an indirect exercise of power by the regulatory body, if treated merely as the exercise of the police power, no compensation would be recognized. However, as a water flood program may destroy legally acquired and existing economic values indirectly for a public purpose but which will directly serve to increase production and income to private producers, it would seem to be sufficiently different from the traditional exercise of police power as to require the payment of compensation. If the water flood program results in increased production from other wells of the adjoining owners, such increase should be offset against the alleged loss.

(D) Conversion Caused by Negligent Sub-Surface Operations

A producer may be guilty of conversion where, although a well is bottomed on his land, drainage of products from adjacent lands occurs as a result of negligent or wrongful operations. This is well illustrated in the Texas case of Elliff v. Texon Drilling Co.,[75] where a gas well, the Driscoll-Sevier No. 2, blew out due to use of drilling mud of insufficient weight. The well cratered and burned and the fire was communicated to the Elliff No. 1, on adjoining lands, which also cratered and burned. Products were lost from the Elliff well both through its well bore and underground to and through the Driscoll-Sevier well. Defendants were ingenious (as were the attorneys

---

73. Tex., 361 S.W.2d 560, 93 A.L.R.2d 432.

Also see: Baumgartner v. Gulf Oil Corp., 184 Neb. 384, 168 N.W.2d 510, cert. denied 397 U.S. 913, 90 S.Ct. 914, 25 L.Ed.2d 93, where court stated that orthodox rules of trespass are not appropriately applied to subsurface intrusions under authorized secondary recovery unit; and, Mowrer v. Ashland Oil & Refining Co., C.A.7th, 518 F.2d 659, allowing recovery on an amalgamation of nuisance and strict liability theories.

74. C.A.10th, 320 F.2d 157, cert. denied 375 U.S. 942, 84 S.Ct. 347, 11 L.Ed. 2d 273.

75. 146 Tex. 575, 210 S.W.2d 558, 4 A.L.R.2d 191.

in the Bell View Oil Syndicate, cited above),[76] and argued that liability should in part be denied on the ground that the law of capture would convert the title of the plaintiff's gas, which was subject to underground drainage to defendant's land, to defendants as soon as it crossed the ownership line. Defendants also cited cases from Louisiana to support a non-ownership theory. The court held (1) that as to the latter argument, Texas was an ownership jurisdiction and the Louisiana cases had no application, and (2) that the rule of capture only operated in instances where drainage was due to legitimate operations.

The rule of capture is a corollary to the ownership view of mineral rights. Where A has bottomed a well on his own land, and it in turn drains products from under B's land, technically A will be guilty of converting B's oil in the event that it can be identified. The rule of capture states that A owns all oil removed from wells properly drilled on his land. In effect, title changes from B to A as it passes to A's properly drilled well. It is interesting to note that in both the Elliff and Bell cases the defense attorneys applied considerable legal imagination in attempting to apply fundamental principles as to the nature of the petroleum products while beneath the ground. In each instance it was argued that the proper measure of damages was not the amount of products that had been drained from the land of plaintiffs, but rather the amount of products that plaintiffs would have otherwise produced. Of course, where a gas field is involved, as in the Elliff case, although the amount of products drained was substantial, the effect on the recoverable reserves under the Elliff land was negligible. The effect of the defendant's arguments would have been to prorate the loss of products over all of the landowners whose reserves were affected by the withdrawal.

§ 4.3 Slander of Title Affecting Oil and Gas Interests

When dealing with oil and gas interests, which are subject to severe economic fluctuations, a serious question arises as to the extent that one may claim title in himself without liability. It generally has been held that malice must be shown for the owner to recover damages. Where one has acted without just or reasonable cause and where there has been a loss of a specific bargain, damages may be recovered. Where actual ill will has been the motivating factor, punitive damages may be recovered.

Action based upon good faith will generally be a defense.

It is generally the law that in the absence of statute or contractual provision, there exists no duty to release an expired oil and gas lease of record. Texas is one jurisdiction where such a common law duty apparently exists. Several jurisdictions have statutes imposing damages for failure to release an expired oil and gas lease. Where such a statutory duty exists, the cause of action is based upon breach of contract, and it is not necessary to establish either malice or the loss of a specific bargain.

---

76. Note Martel v. Hall Oil Co., 36 Wyo. 166, 253 P. 862, 52 A.L.R. 91, supra.

O is the owner of Blackacre. He leases the property to Black Gold Oil Company for a period of five years and as long thereafter as oil, gas or other petroleum products are sold. At the end of the five year primary term Black Gold Oil Company is engaged in drilling a well with a rig capable of drilling only to a depth of 2000 feet, although oil is not expected at a lesser depth than 8000 feet. At the time that Black Gold Oil Company reaches a depth of 1500 feet, O is approached by Pure Petroleum Company, which would pay a bonus of $5,000 for a lease on the land. O asks for a release from Black Gold Oil Company, which refuses to release. Black Gold says that it is in the process of moving a larger rig onto the land, but never does so, due to transportation problems. Six months later, Black Gold executes and delivers a release to O. In the interim, a dry hole was drilled on an adjoining tract of land, and O is unable to lease to anyone. Does O have a cause of action against Black Gold Oil Company?[1]

The problem has arisen in other contexts: X files an instrument of record evidencing a claim in himself in the mineral estate;[2] X is in possession of Blackacre under color of title and refuses to remove therefrom despite a demand from what later turns out to be the true owner;[3] X refuses to release an oil and gas lease during the primary term, although the last delay rental payment was skipped for a reason deemed adequate to X;[4] X brings suit claiming the minerals in Blackacre, which suit he later loses.[5] During each of these acts, the true owner loses the opportunity to lease the land, or the market value falls due to the apparent cloud cast upon the title to the land by such acts.

In cases dealing with oil and gas interests more so than in the case of other interests not subject to rapid economic fluctuations, a serious question has arisen as to what extent one who ultimately loses may assert a claim against the mineral estate and not be liable in damages.

Traditionally, an action for slander of title will contain the following elements: (1) The uttering and publishing of the slanderous words,[6] (2) which were false,[7] (3) which publishing was malicious,[8] (4) that plaintiff possessed an estate or interest in the property slan-

---

1. Hunt Oil Co. v. Berry, 227 Miss. 234, 86 So.2d 7.

2. Frankfort Oil Co. v. Snakard, C.A. Okl., 279 F.2d 436; Reaugh v. McCollum Exploration Co., 139 Tex. 485, 163 S.W.2d 620; Winn v. Warner, Tex.Civ.App., 199 S.W.2d 560.

3. Hunt Oil Co. v. Berry, 227 Miss. 234, 86 So.2d 7; Humble Oil & Refining Co. v. Luckel, Tex.Civ.App., 171 S.W.2d 902.

4. Berryman v. Sinclair Prairie Oil Co., C.C.A.10th, 164 F.2d 734.

5. Sellars v. Grant, C.A.5th, 196 F.2d 677.

6. Berryman v. Sinclair Prairie Oil Co., C.C.A.10th, 164 F.2d 734; Solberg v. Sunburst Oil & Gas. Co., 76 Mont. 254, 246 P. 168; Witherspoon v. Green, Tex. Civ.App., 274 S.W. 170; Wheelock v. Batte, Tex.Civ.App., 225 S.W.2d 591;

7, 8. See notes 7 and 8 on page 179.

§ 4.3   TRESPASS, SURFACE, SUB–SURFACE   179

dered,[9] and (5) that plaintiff sustained special damages.[10] Of special interest in oil and gas cases are the elements dealing with the definition of malice and the necessity of showing a special loss.

A disparaging statement about particular property has a tendency to depreciate its market value through its effect upon the opinions of other people. If an owner were able to recover upon mere allegations and proof that the statements have decreased the market value of the land, the courts would be flooded with litigation. The restraining doctrine is a requirement that more must be shown, viz. malice. The term includes both "actual" and "implied" malice. Actual or express malice includes a desire to injure,[11] bad or evil motive, ill will [12] or wrongful motive.[13] It has generally been held that actual or express malice must be shown in order for a recovery to include exemplary or punitive damages.[14] Actual malice has been found where one has asserted a right known to be false,[15] or where such claim is not based upon a reasonable belief,[16] or where actual intent to injure existed.[17] In Winn v. Warner,[18] it was found that where defendant had filed an affidavit claiming an interest in the property, which prevented the execution of an oil and gas lease by plaintiff, he was motivated as much by a feeling of actual ill will toward the plaintiff as he was by a desire to protect his interest in the property.

Implied malice, which is necessary for a recovery of actual damages,[19] indicates an act that was done without a just cause or ex-

Barquin v. Hall Oil Co., 28 Wyo. 164, 202 P. 1107.

7. Humble Oil & Refining Co. v. Luckel, Tex.Civ.App., 171 S.W.2d 902.

8. Berryman v. Sinclair Prairie Oil Co., C.A.10th, 164 F.2d 734; Sinclair Refining Co. v. Jones Super Service Station, 188 Ark. 1075, 70 S.W.2d 562; Draper v. J. B. & R. E. Walker, Inc., 115 Utah 368, 204 P.2d 826; Frankfort Oil Co. v. Snakard, C.A.10th, 279 F.2d 436; Jarrett v. Ross, 139 Tex. 560, 164 S.W.2d 550; Barquin v. Hall Oil Co., 28 Wyo. 164, 202 P. 1107; "An action for slander of title lies only against one who falsely and maliciously denies or impugns * * * title to property, or where one unnecessarily intermedles with the affairs of another with which he is wholly unconcerned." Solberg v. Sunburst Oil & Gas. Co., 76 Mont. 254, 246 P. 168.

9. Reaugh v. McCollum Exploration Co., 139 Tex. 485, 163 S.W.2d 620.

10. Berryman v. Sinclair Prairie Oil Co., C.A.10th, 164 F.2d 734; Hunt Oil Co. v. Berry, 227 Miss. 234, 86 So.2d 7; Solberg v. Sunburst Oil & Gas. Co., 76 Mont. 254, 246 P. 168; Shell Oil Co. v. Howth, 138 Tex. 357, 159 S.W.2d 483; Humble Oil & Refining Co. v. Luckel, Tex.Civ.App., 171 S.W.2d 902; Wheelock v. Batte, Tex.Civ.App., 225 S.W.2d 591; Barquin v. Hall Oil Co., 28 Wyo. 164, 202 P. 1107.

11. Glieberman v. Fine, 248 Mich. 8, 226 N.W. 669.

12. Winn v. Warner, Tex.Civ.App., 199 S.W.2d 560; Wheelock v. Batte, Tex.Civ.App., 225 S.W.2d 591.

13. Frankfort Oil Co. v. Snakard, C.A.10th, 279 F.2d 436.

14. Winn v. Warner, Tex.Civ.App., 199 S.W.2d 560; Wheelock v. Batte, Tex.Civ.App., 225 S.W.2d 591; Kidd v. Hoggett, Tex.Civ.App., 331 S.W.2d 515.

15. Sinclair Refining Co. v. Jones Super Service Station, 188 Ark. 1075, 70 S.W.2d 562; Kidd v. Hoggett, Tex.Civ.App., 331 S.W.2d 515.

16. Glieberman v. Fine, 248 Mich. 8, 226 N.W. 669.

17. Winn v. Warner, Tex.Civ.App., 199 S.W.2d 560.

18. Tex.Civ.App., 199 S.W.2d 560.

19. Winn v. Warner, Tex.Civ.App., 199 S.W.2d 560; Wheelock v. Batte, Tex.Civ.App., 225 S.W.2d 591; Kidd v. Hoggett, Tex.Civ.App., 331 S.W.2d 515.

cuse,[20] one not done in good faith.[21] Malice may be implied from the assertion of a fact known to be false.[22]

As in the case of the geophysical trespasser, the good faith of one accused of the slandering of the title of another is an ameliorating circumstance. A corollary of the definition of malice is that actions done under a reasonable belief, or in good faith, are not malicious in a suit of slander of title.[23] For instance, in the case of Berryman v. Sinclair Prairie Oil Co.,[24] plaintiff was unable to prove that the claim of the lessee (that the lease was held in effect by drilling over a delay rental payment date) was made in bad faith, where lessee would not release until the well had come in dry and lessor had lost an opportunity to lease. The mere failure to release the lease under the circumstances, with resultant loss to lessor, was insufficient to establish liability for damages. Good faith has been found: (1) Where suit was filed, but lost, where reasonable doubt existed as to the rights of the parties on a close question, and the suit was filed on advice of counsel; [25] (2) a refusal to release a lien due to an honest although mistaken belief that the lien was valid; [26] (3) where a claim was asserted upon the advice of counsel where the material facts were fully and correctly revealed to the attorney from whom the advice was obtained; [27] (4) where a claim to property was made under the color of title and the advice of an attorney, or upon reasonable belief that the party had title to the property acquired.[28] The test for good faith seems similar to that employed in determining good faith for a geophysical trespasser.[29]

It seems clearly to be the law in oil and gas cases that in addition to the other elements of slander of title, it is necessary that the injured party show more than merely general damages. He must show that he has been specifically injured by the loss of a particular bargain.[30] It will not be sufficient to show that there was a ready mar-

20. Glieberman v. Fine, 248 Mich. 8, 226 N.W. 669.

21. Winn v. Warner, Tex.Civ.App., 199 S.W.2d 560.

22. Sinclair Refining Co. v. Jones Super Service Station, 188 Ark. 1075, 70 S.W.2d 562; Kidd v. Hoggett, Tex.Civ. App., 331 S.W.2d 515.

23. Berryman v. Sinclair Prairie Oil Co., C.A.10th, 164 F.2d 734; Sinclair Refining Co. v. Jones Super Service Station, 188 Ark. 1075, 70 S.W.2d 562; Noble v. Johnson, 180 Okl. 169, 68 P.2d 838; Mollohan v. Patton, 110 Kan. 663, 202 P. 616, on rehearing, 205 P. 643; Sellars v. Grant, C.A.5th, 196 F.2d 677; Humble Oil & Refining Co. v. Luckel, Tex.Civ.App., 171 S.W.2d 902; Winn v. Warner, Tex. Civ.App., 199 S.W.2d 560; Wheelock v. Batte, Tex.Civ.App., 225 S.W.2d 591.

24. C.A.10th, 164 F.2d 734.

25. Sellars v. Grant, C.A.5th, 196 F.2d 677.

26. Mollohan v. Patton, 110 Kan. 663, 202 P. 616, on rehearing 110 Kan. 663, 205 P. 643.

27. Noble v. Johnson, 180 Okl. 169, 68 P.2d 838.

28. Sinclair Refining Co. v. Jones Super Service Station, 188 Ark. 1075, 70 S.W.2d 562; Humble Oil & Refining Co. v. Luckel, Tex.Civ.App., 171 S.W.2d 902.

29. See § 4.2(B)(2), supra; Noble v. Johnson, 180 Okl. 169, 68 P.2d 838; Berryman v. Sinclair Prairie Oil Co., C.C.A. 10th, 164 F.2d 734.

30. Berryman v. Sinclair Prairie Oil Co., C.A.10th, 164 F.2d 734; Hunt Oil Co. v. Berry, 227 Miss. 234, 86 So.2d 7; Solberg v. Sunburst Oil & Gas Co., 76 Mont. 254, 246 P. 168; Dixon v. McCann, 87 Okl. 109, 206 P. 597; Shell Oil Co. v.

ket for property similar to plaintiffs; it must be shown that a particular offer to buy or lease was made and lost due to the cloud cast upon plaintiff's title. As discussed in an earlier section, if the case of Humble Oil & Refining Co. v. Kishi [31] had been treated as a case of slander of title, it would not have been sufficient to show that surrounding property could be leased for a certain figure during the drilling of the well and that upon the drilling of the dry hole that the ability to so lease was lost.

However, where a statutory duty is violated, the injured party may recover for the decrease in market value or may be given statutory damages.[32] In the case of Mollohan v. Patton [33] defendant refused to release an expired oil and gas lease. This violated a Kansas statute requiring the release of expired leases, with statutory damages of $100 being provided for such failure, in addition to such other damages as might be shown by the injured party. During this period two dry holes were drilled on adjoining properties. The plaintiff was allowed to testify as to the damages occasioned by the failure to release. He stated that he had sold oil and gas leases for a three year period and that, in his opinion, the property in question could have been leased for $500, had the land been freed of defendant's lease.

Assuming that plaintiff can show that he had lost a specific bargain during the period that his title was clouded, of what significance is the fact that the property has market value at the time of trial with the cloud removed? In the Texas case of Reaugh v. McCollum Exploration Co.,[34] two of four joint owners of the minerals executed an oil and gas lease with the understanding that it would not be effective or binding until all joint owners had signed. Lessee, however, filed the lease of record with only the two signatures and would not release it upon request of the lessors. During the period that the lease was

Howth, 138 Tex. 357, 159 S.W.2d 483; Humble Oil & Refining Co. v. Luckel, Tex.Civ.App., 171 S.W.2d 902; Wheelock v. Batte, Tex.Civ.App., 225 S.W.2d 591; Barquin v. Hall Oil Co., 28 Wyo. 164, 202 P. 1107. It is generally stated that recovery may be had for loss of profits where such loss is a natural and probable consequence of the act and where the amount is shown with sufficient certainty, but that anticipated profits cannot be recovered as they would be too uncertain. Humble Oil & Refining Co. v. Luckel, Tex.Civ.App., 171 S.W.2d 902. However in the case of Winn v. Warner, Tex.Civ. App., 199 S.W.2d 560, it was held that in the case of willful slander, the wrongdoer was liable for all results that should have been contemplated, foreseen or might have been anticipated, i.e. in this case the amount of future production that was lost.

31. Tex.Com.App., 276 S.W. 190, set aside in rehearing 291 S.W. 538, see Section 4.2, supra. Also see Hunt Oil Co. v. Berry, 227 Miss. 234, 86 So.2d 7, where plaintiff was allowed the loss of bonus where a prospective lessee discovered a former instrument on record clouding plaintiff's title, but was denied recovery for the fall in market value of the leasing rights where a well drilling on nearby land during this period came in dry.

32. §§ 53–312 and 53–313, Ark.Stats. (double damages); Mollohan v. Patton, 110 Kan. 663, 202 P. 616, on rehearing, 110 Kan. 663, 205 P. 643; Erne v. Broiles, 173 Kan. 882, 252 P.2d 612; Kan. St.Ann., §§ 55–201 and 55–202 ($100 statutory damages).

33. 110 Kan. 663, 202 P. 616, in rehearing 110 Kan. 663, 205 P. 643. It is somewhat questionable whether the testimony would have been admitted over timely objection.

34. 139 Tex. 485, 163 S.W.2d 620.

wrongfully of record, lessors lost a possible lease of the property. It was alleged that they had lost an opportunity to lease for $250 per acre, and they also sued for exemplary damages in the sum of $5,000. The suit combined an action to remove the cloud cast by defendant's lease and an action for damages. It was held that the proper measure of damages was the amount for which they could and would have sold the lease, had the sale not been frustrated, less the amount for which they could have sold a lease on the land at the time of the trial with the cloud removed. It was indicated by defendants that at the time of the trial the land could have been leased for $400 to $600 per acre with the cloud removed! Would the plaintiffs have been in a better position if they had only brought suit for damages for slander of title, and not to remove the cloud? Would they then have merely received the value of the lost bargain without deduction? If required to deduct the amount for which the land could have been leased at the time of trial with the cloud, the deduction would have been only for a nominal amount.[35]

Where damages are received for slander of title, interest is payable on the value of the lost bargain from the time of the loss of sale to the time of trial.[36]

Several cases have appeared that seem to have confused slander of title with other types of actions. Discussion has already been made of the Kishi case.[37] Another case of interest is that of American Surety Co. of New York v. Marsh.[38] In this case defendant oil company claimed that its lease was still in effect and would not release the lease. Following suit in trial court, which defendant lost, it filed a supersedeas bond whereby the surety company would be liable for all damages during the period to final judgment. During this period of time plaintiff lost an opportunity to lease for $60,000, as he could not deliver immediate possession. Although the judgment was later affirmed in plaintiff's favor, a dry hole had been drilled on nearby property in the interim period. Leasing rights on the subject property were then worth no more than $2,000. The court expressly followed the rationale set forth in the Kishi case and stated that as defendant had asserted a claim that it did not have, the fact that it may have been in good faith would not be a defense. It would seem that the case is more nearly the classic case of slander of title than was the Kishi case, and that the good faith of the defendant should have been considered. However, from a reading of the opinion, one gets the strong feeling that the defendant was not in good faith in asserting its lease, which may have subjectively influenced the court.

Recurring problems in the oil and gas field are whether a lessee has a duty to release an expired lease and whether the failure or re-

---

35. Humble Oil & Refining Co. v. McLean, Tex.Civ.App., 268 S.W. 179.

36. Reaugh v. McCollum Exploration Co., 139 Tex. 485, 163 S.W.2d 620.

37. Note 31, supra.

38. 146 Okl. 261, 293 P. 1041.

§ 4.3 TRESPASS, SURFACE, SUB–SURFACE 183

fusal to so release, which causes a specific loss to the landowner, constitutes a slander on his title for which damages are recoverable. It appears to be the view at common law that a mortgagee was under no obligation to release a lien when the debt that it secured had been satisfied.[39] This also appears to be the majority viewpoint concerning the release of an expired oil and gas lease where no contractual [40] or statutory duty [41] to release exists.

In the Wyoming case of Barquin v. Hall Oil Co.,[42] which concerned the release of an expired oil and gas lease, the court drew a distinction between the situation where all elements of slander of title existed and the mere failure to release an expired oil and gas lease. The court refused to extend the slander of title action from the situation where the instrument was void from the outset when recorded to the case where the instrument was valid when recorded but the rights thereunder later terminated. The court was bothered by the fact that as originally published the instrument was valid, but became cancelled by reason of subsequent events. No way was seen by which the instrument became republished after it was void. Other courts have relied upon the earlier mortgage cases and have applied the same rule: That no duty to release an expired oil and gas lease exists.[43]

It would seem to be the rule in Texas, however, that a common law duty does exist to release an oil and gas lease after it has terminated,[44] and there is some indication that this may be the rule as to mortgages.[45] In the case of Wheelock v. Batte,[46] it was stated that in order for the failure to release an oil and gas lease to be actionable, such act must be malicious, and that good faith on the part of one asserting the lease would be a defense to the action. In this case good faith was shown by the lessee, the circumstances being such that the lessor, anxiously trying to declare the lease terminated, had misled the lessee, which in turn had resulted in the lessee terminating his operations on the lease.

39. Draper v. Walker, 115 Utah 368, 204 P.2d 826.

40. Solberg v. Sunburst Oil & Gas. Co., 76 Mont. 254, 246 P. 168.

41. Mollohan v. Patton, 110 Kan. 663, 202 P. 616, in rehearing 110 Kan. 663, 205 P. 643.

See Oklahoma statute 41 O.S. 40 requiring lessee to file release for record in county where land lies within 60 days after termination of lease. However, lessor is not precluded from bringing suit for slander of title within the 60 day period. Crosbie v. Absher, 174 Okl. 593, 51 P.2d 970.

42. 28 Wyo. 164, 202 P. 1107.

43. Hasquet v. Big West Oil Co., C.C.A.9th, 29 F.2d 78; Draper v. Walker, 118 Utah 368, 204 P.2d 826; Wheelock v. Batte, Tex.Civ.App., 225 S.W.2d 591. In Witherspoon v. Green, Tex.Civ.App., 274 S.W. 170, the lease was still within the primary term. Should a distinction be drawn between this situation and one where the lease is outside the primary term and expires through cessation of production?

44. Witherspoon v. Green, Tex.Civ. App., 274 S.W. 170; Simmons v. Ledger Co., Tex.Civ.App., 79 S.W.2d 336; cf. Wheelock v. Batte, Tex.Civ.App., 225 S.W.2d 591.

45. Knox v. Farmers State Bank, Tex. Civ.App., 7 S.W.2d 918; Simmons v. Ledger Co., Tex.Civ.App., 79 S.W.2d 336.

46. Tex.Civ.App., 225 S.W.2d 591.

In the later Texas case of Kidd v. Hoggett,[47] the lessee attempted to hold the lease by making a shut-in royalty payment, but the well was not a commercial producer. It was stated that a duty existed in Texas at common law to release a terminated lease of record. The court did not seem to be concerned with the requirement of additional publication of an expired lease, but followed earlier case law that the failure to clear the record of an instrument clouding the title is a publication.[48] The court clarified the definition of malice, asserting that malice sufficient for actual damages would be deliberate conduct without a reasonable cause.[49] Under the Kidd ruling, damages apparently would be limited to loss of a specific sale.

Where the lessee is guilty of the failure to release an oil and gas lease and the duty is contractual, the cause of action is based upon breach of contract. It is not necessary to show malice. It has been held that recovery may be had for the general loss of market value, and loss of specific bargain need not be shown.[50] This is also true where statutes have been passed requiring release of liens and of oil and gas leases.[51] A number of states have legislation requiring such release.[52]

---

47. Tex.Civ.App., 331 S.W.2d 515.

48. Witherspoon v. Green, Tex.Civ. App., 274 S.W. 170; Knox v. Farmers State Bank, Tex.Civ.App., 7 S.W.2d 918; Solberg v. Sunburst Oil & Gas. Co., 76 Mont. 254, 246 P. 168.

49. "How malice is defined, however, is another matter. Malice as a basis for recovery of actual damages, as distinguished from punitive damages should mean that the act or refusal was deliberate conduct without reasonable cause. * * * Malice as a basis for recovery of punitive damages should mean actual malice, that is, ill will, bad or evil motive, or such gross indifference to or reckless disregard of the rights of others as will amount to a willful or wanton act."

50. Solberg v. Sunburst Oil & Gas. Co., 76 Mont. 254, 246 P. 168.

51. Mollohan v. Patton, 110 Kan. 663, 202 P. 616, in rehearing 110 Kan. 663, 205 P. 643; Erne v. Broiles, 173 Kan. 882, 252 P.2d 612; Dixon v. McCann, 87 Okl. 109, 206 P. 597; 41 O.S. 40 (Okl.); §§ 53–312 and 53–313, Ark.Stats.

52. See Hasquet v. Big West Oil Co., C.C.A. 9th, 29 F.2d 78; Draper v. Walker, 118 Utah 368, 204 P.2d 826; Barquin v. Hall Oil Co., 28 Wyo. 164, 202 P. 1107 and Summers, Oil & Gas Law, § 472.

CHAPTER 5

THE OIL AND GAS LEASE—LEASES FROM OWNERS OF CONCURRENT, SUCCESSIVE, OR RESTRICTED INTERESTS

Analysis

Sec.
5.1 Co-tenants.
    (A) Right of a Co-tenant to Develop and Produce.
    (B) Accounting to a Non-joined Co-tenant by a Producing Co-tenant.
    (C) Co-tenant Leasing.
    (D) Ratification by a Non-joined Co-tenant.
5.2 Life Tenant and Remainderman.
    (A) Leases From a Life Tenant or a Remainderman.
    (B) Joint Leases by Life Tenant and Remainderman.
    (C) Leases Preceding the Life Estate—The Open Mine Doctrine.
    (D) Application of the Uniform Trust Act and the Uniform Principal and Income Act.
5.3 The Determinable Fee Estate, Estates Subject to a Power of Termination, and Fee Estates Subject to Executory Interests.
5.4 Lands Subject to Servitudes and Restrictions.
5.5 Landlord and Tenant.
5.6 Lands Subject to Security Interests.
5.7 Leases From Persons Acting in a Representative Capacity.
    (A) Attorneys-in-Fact.
    (B) Trustees.
    (C) Administrators, Executors, and Guardians.
    (D) Business Entities.
    (E) Governmental Entities.
    (F) Unascertainable or Unknown Owners.

§ 5.1 Co-tenants

In the majority of jurisdictions each co-tenant, or his lessee, has a non-exclusive right to enter the common premises, to explore, and to produce petroleum products. In a minority of jurisdictions a co-tenant does not have the right to produce oil and gas products without the consent of his fellow co-tenants; such production is considered waste and may be enjoined.

Where the right of a co-tenant exists to produce petroleum products, he may not convert the interests of other owners and must account to them for their respective shares. Accounting is upon the basis of the proportionate interest of the non-joined owner, less the reasonable costs of development, production and marketing attributable to each such interest. The right of the producing co-tenant to payment for such costs is one of recoupment from production, and he may retain production attributable to other non-joined owners until such time that costs are satisfied.

In the absence of a contractual agreement or unusual circumstances, where each co-owner has leased his interest to a different lessee, each lease is independent of the other, and the acts of a lessee under one lease will not inure to the advantage of the other lessee. In such a situation, when production is acquired, the producing co-tenant will account to the lessee of the non-joined interest, who will distribute such share in accordance with the latter's lease contract.

A non-joined co-tenant may ratify an existing lease executed by other co-owners where such lease purports to cover the interest of the ratifying co-owner. The ratifying co-owner will be entitled to his proportionate share of the economic benefits paid under the lease.

(A) Right of a Co-tenant to Develop and Produce

The basic question involved, concerning the right of one co-tenant to develop the minerals underlying the commonly owned land, is whether a co-tenant has the right to remove petroleum products without the agreement of his co-owners. Petroleum products, unlike solid minerals, are capable of movement to places of lower pressure. If production on adjacent tracts of land is draining the oil or gas from under the commonly owned tract, unless production is obtained on the commonly owned tract, the whole of the petroleum products may be lost. In virtually all jurisdictions one co-tenant has the right to drill for and to remove petroleum products if they are in imminent danger of being lost.[1] This is not universally true, however, where the existence of the mineral estate is not being threatened. In several jurisdictions, notably Illinois, Louisiana, and West Virginia, production of petroleum products by one co-tenant may be enjoined by another co-tenant.[2]

However, the majority of jurisdictions view production of the mineral estate by a co-tenant not as waste but as enjoyment of the estate.[3] Under the majority view, each co-tenant has the non-exclusive

---

1. New Domain Oil & Gas Co. v. McKinney, 188 Ky. 183, 221 S.W. 245; Texas & Pacific Coal & Oil Co. v. Kirtley, Tex.Civ.App., 288 S.W. 619; Law v. Heck Oil Co., 106 W.Va. 296, 145 S.E. 601; Prairie Oil & Gas Co. v. Allen, C.C.A. 8th, 2 F.2d 566, 40 A.L.R. 1389. For a discussion of the rights of co-tenants in the mineral estate generally see: Williams, The Effect of Concurrent Interests on Oil and Gas Transactions, 34 Tex.L.Rev. 519; Summers, Oil and Gas, § 222, Power of a Cotenant to Lease for Oil and Gas.

2. Zeigler v. Brenneman, 237 Ill. 15, 86 N.E. 597, Gulf Refining Co. of Louisiana v. Carroll, 145 La. 299, 82 So. 277, but cf. Scott v. Hunt Oil Co., La.App., 152 So.2d 599; South Penn Oil Co. v. Haught, 71 W.Va. 720, 78 S.E. 759; Law v. Heck Oil Co., 106 W.Va. 296, 145 S.E. 601. See Thaxton v. Beard, 157 W.Va. 381, 201 S.E.2d 298, where co-tenant did not object to entry by fellow co-tenant. The result in these states is an outgrowth of the rule at common law since 1285 (Statute of Westminister II, 13 Edw. 1, C. 22) that a co-tenant is subject to waste in development of the joint property without consent of the other co-owners. For a discussion of statutes in these jurisdictions attempting to ameliorate this situation, see Summers, Oil and Gas Law, § 222, pp. 59–64.

3. Slade v. Rudman Resources, Inc., 237 Ga. 848, 230 S.E.2d 284 (a case of first impression in which Georgia adopted the majority rule); Krug v. Krug v. Cities Service Petroleum Co., 5 Kan.App. 2d 426, 618 P.2d 323.

Moody v. Wagner, 167 Okl. 99, 23 P.2d 633; Prairie Oil & Gas Co. v. Allen, C.C.A. 8th, 2 F.2d 566, 40 A.L.R. 1389; and see note 1, supra.

right to enter, explore, and produce his share of the petroleum products.[4] He cannot exclude his fellow co-tenants from doing likewise.[5] Each co-tenant has the right to execute a lease upon his interest.[6] Thereupon the lessee becomes a co-tenant [7] with the other undivided interest owners in the minerals and will enjoy the same right to develop and produce that existed in his lessor.[8] However, where the lessee claims the entire right in the land to the exclusion of other co-owners, he is a trespasser as to the other interests.[9]

Each lessee of an undivided interest has a right to deal exclusively with his interest. This includes the right to an exclusive location where not in conflict with the existing locations of other co-tenants,[10] and the right to place his interest in a unit and to share in production from other lands in the unit.[11] However no duty exists to drill for other co-tenants or to represent them before regulatory bodies.[12] The right of the lessee of the owner of an undivided interest in the minerals is to the use and possession of the property, and he is not merely relegated to the right of partition where a dispute arises with other co-owners.[13]

(B) Accounting to a Non-joined Co-tenant by a Producing Co-tenant

Where a co-tenant, or a lessee from a co-tenant, has the right to go on the joint property, drill, and produce petroleum products, he

4. Burnham v. Hardy Oil Co., Tex.Civ. App., 147 S.W. 330, and see note 3, supra.

5. Slade v. Rudman Resources, Inc., 237 Ga. 848, 230 S.E.2d 284; Krug v. Krug v. Cities Service Petroleum Co., 5 Kan.App.2d 426, 618 P.2d 323; Moody v. Wagner, 167 Okl. 99, 23 P.2d 633; Earp v. Mid-Continent Petroleum Corp., 167 Okl. 86, 27 P.2d 855, 91 A.L.R. 188; Prairie Oil & Gas Co. v. Allen, C.C.A. 8th, 2 F.2d 566, 40 A.L.R. 1389.

6. Sun Oil Co. v. Oswell, 258 Ala. 326, 62 So.2d 783; Little v. Mountain View Dairies, 35 Cal.2d 232, 217 P.2d 416, Petroleum Exploration Corp. v. Hensley, Ky., 284 S.W.2d 828; Amundson v. Gordon, 134 Mont. 142, 328 P.2d 630; Schank v. North American Royalties, Inc., N.D., 201 N.W.2d 419; Moody v Wagner, 167 Okl. 99, 23 P.2d 633; Earp v. Mid Continent Petroleum Corp., 167 Okl. 86, 27 P.2d 855, 91 A.L.R. 188; McIntosh v. Ropp, 233 Pa. 497, 82 A. 949; Hughes v. Cantwell, Tex.Civ.App., 540 S.W.2d 742; Prairie Oil & Gas Co. v. Allen, C.C.A. 8th, 2 F.2d 566, 40 A.L.R. 1389. However, the lease must be of the undivided interest, not all of a segregated or carved-out part of the joint lands. Medina Oil Development Co. v. Murphy, Tex.Civ.App., 233 S.W. 333.

7. New Domain Oil & Gas Co. v. McKinney, 188 Ky. 183, 221 S.W. 245; Earp v. Mid-Continent Petroleum Corp., 167 Okl. 86, 27 P.2d 885, 91 A.L.R. 188.

8. Earp v. Mid-Continent Petroleum Corp., 167 Okl. 86, 27 P.2d 855, 91 A.L.R. 188; Hughes v. Cantwell, Tex.Civ.App., 540 S.W.2d 742; but cf. Gulf Refining Co. of Louisiana v. Carroll, 145 La. 299, 82 So. 277. In such jurisdictions the lease is treated as being valid between the co-tenant and his lessee, but entry and development may not be made thereunder upon objection of other co-owners.

9. Riddle v. Ellis, 139 Okl. 68, 281 P. 286; Foster v. Weaver, 118 Pa. 42, 12 A. 313; Humble Oil & Refining Co. v. Kishi, Tex.Com.App., 276 S.W. 190, rehearing 291 S.W. 538.

10. Gibson & Jennings v. Amos Drilling Co., 196 Okl. 143, 162 P.2d 1002.

11. Superior Oil Co. v. Roberts, Tex., 398 S.W.2d 276; Whelan v. Placid Oil Co., Tex.Civ.App., 274 S.W.2d 125.

12. Zimmerman v. Texaco, Inc., Tex. Civ.App., 409 S.W.2d 607, writ refused Tex., 413 S.W.2d 387.

13. Garcia v. Sun Oil Co., Tex.Civ. App., 300 S.W.2d 724.

may not convert that portion of the oil or gas belonging to his fellow co-owners. As each barrel of oil or cubic foot of gas that is produced is owned by all of the tenants in common, the producing co-tenant therefore must account to all for their respective shares of the products produced. However, if the producing co-tenant has a right to production from wells not located upon the jointly owned lands, as where the lease interest is unitized and production is from other lands in the unit, and where no contractual relationship exists with the non-joined co-tenants, the latter have no right to share.[14]

Each non-joining co-tenant has the right to receive his proportionate share of the products produced, but must bear the reasonable costs of development, production, and marketing.[15] The producing co-tenant, however, has a right of recoupment, and he may retain all of the production until he has recouped his costs. Where production is insufficient to cover the costs of development and production, the non-joined co-tenant is under no personal liability for his share of the excessive costs.[16]

This may be illustrated by the following examples: (1) A and B are co-tenants in Blackacre, which contains 100 acres of land. A decides to develop the land for oil and gas purposes, and at the cost of $100,000 drills a well and is successful in producing oil and gas. A, however, must account to B for B's share of the production. Although it might be argued that A should return to B one-half of each barrel of oil, starting from the first production, it is generally held that A may retain B's share until he has recovered the reasonable costs of drilling the well, at which time A will pay to B one-half of production minus one-half of future production expenses.

---

14. Superior Oil Co. v. Roberts, Tex., 398 S.W.2d 276.

15. McMillan v. Powell, 235 Ark. 932, 362 S.W.2d 721; Slade v. Rudman Resources, Inc., 237 Ga. 848, 230 S.E.2d 284; Krug v. Krug v. Cities Service Petroleum Co., 5 Kan.App.2d 426, 618 P.2d 323; New Domain Oil & Gas Co. v. McKinney, 188 Ky. 183, 221 S.W. 245; Gillispie v. Blanton, 214 Ky. 49, 282 S.W. 1061; Moody v. Wagner, 167 Okl. 99, 23 P.2d 633; Earp v. Mid-Continent Petroleum Corp., 167 Okl. 86, 27 P.2d 855, 91 A.L.R. 188; Burnham v. Hardy Oil Co., Tex.Civ. App., 147 S.W. 330; Texas & Pacific Coal & Oil Co. v. Kirtley, Tex.Civ.App., 288 S.W. 619; Prairie Oil & Gas Co. v. Allen, C.C.A. 8th, 2 F.2d 566, 40 A.L.R. 1389; Thaxton v. Beard, 157 W.Va. 381, 201 S.E.2d 298. Also cf. Rosse v. Northern Pump Co., Tex.Civ.App., 353 S.W.2d 287, citing Texas & Pacific Coal & Oil Co. v. Kirtley, Tex.Civ.App., 288 S.W. 619, which would apparently classify the co-tenant producing without express permission of his fellow co-owners as a bad faith trespasser, with no right of recoupment of expenses. This is not the prevailing view in Texas, but is a remnant of the good faith-bad faith trespasser analogy that was applied in earliest cases dealing with co-tenant production. This would have been a natural outgrowth from jurisdictions where each co-tenant lacked the right to develop without consent of other joint owners. See: Zeigler v. Brenneman, 237 Ill. 15, 86 N.E. 597; Gulf Refining Co. of Louisiana v. Carroll, 145 La. 299, 82 So. 277; South Penn Oil Co. v. Haught, 71 W.Va. 720, 78 S.E. 759; Law v. Heck Oil Co., 106 W.Va. 296, 145 S.E. 601.

16. Krug v. Krug v. Cities Service Petroleum Co., 5 Kan.App.2d 426, 618 P.2d 323; Moody v. Wagner, 167 Okl. 99, 23 P.2d 633; Earp v. Mid-Continent Petroleum Corp., 167 Okl. 86, 27 P.2d 855, 91 A.L.R. 188; Prairie Oil & Gas Co. v. Allen, C.C.A. 8th, 2 F.2d 566, 40 A.L.R. 1389.

This example is illustrated by the Texas case of Bullard v. Broadwell,[17] where landowner A executed a deed to B of an undivided one-third interest in the minerals. A reserved the right to lease. A, the owner of the undivided two-thirds mineral interest, drilled a producing well. The deed to B did not contain a clause providing for a royalty to B in the event of self-development by A. In the litigation that followed, A contended that B was only entitled to $1/3$ of the usual $1/8$ royalty, or a royalty of $1/24$ of production. B on the other hand contended that he was entitled to $1/3$ of gross production, minus the reasonable costs of drilling, completing, and producing. B also sued A for conversion of his portion of the minerals.

In this case of first impression in Texas, the court held for B, and stated that as a non-joined co-tenant B was entitled to his proportionate part of gross production, minus reasonable costs. The court did consider and reject the view that in cases of self-development by a co-tenant the non-joined co-tenant was entitled to a proportionate part of the usual royalty.

The court also denied the count in conversion on the ground that the non-joined co-tenant was not entitled to any of the proceeds of production until the producing co-tenant had recouped the reasonable cost of development and production.

(2) Similar to the first example is the one in which A does not desire to develop the property himself. Instead, he executes an oil and gas lease to Black Gold Oil Company in return for a royalty of $1/8$ of production. Since A owns and has leased only an undivided one-half mineral interest, Black Gold will be obligated to pay to A only one-half of the stated royalty, i.e., a $1/16$. B owns the other one-half interest, which is unleased. In this contractual context, Black Gold will bear all the costs of development and production, and A will bear none in the development of the "A-Black Gold" one-half interest. Black Gold's interest is therefore termed the "cost-bearing interest," and A's interest is termed the "non-cost-bearing interest." Upon execution of the lease, A and Black Gold became co-tenants in A's undivided one-half interest and as to B. When the producing well is completed, Black Gold, in accordance with the contractual provisions of the lease with A, must account to A for $1/16$ of each barrel of oil (or m.c.f. of gas, as the case may be) whether or not Black Gold will ever recover its costs of development and production. However, Black Gold may retain B's one-half interest in production until such time as Black Gold has recovered its development and production costs. Hence, A will immediately begin to receive royalty payments from the first production, whereas B will not receive payments until Black Gold has recouped its costs, if, in fact, this ever occurs.

It should be noted that the payments to B are not in the nature of royalty, as B does not have a contractual arrangement with Black

---

17. Tex.Civ.App., 588 S.W.2d 398, refused n. r. e.

Gold, but are the return to B of B's interest in the minerals as a non-joined co-tenant, i.e., one-half of gross production less one-half of the costs of development and production.[18]

It is speculative as to which interest may be the more valuable, A's or B's. If the well never pays out, or if unusual costs of well workover and maintenance are encountered, B's interest may well prove the less valuable.

In jurisdictions that have a tradition of hard mineral mining, as in cases concerning the good-faith trespassers, the right of the co-tenant to share has sometimes been limited to a royalty interest. It is not believed this view is followed in any jurisdiction at the present time. However, an aftermath of the royalty view is still found in Kentucky. Kentucky apparently will apply the royalty rule to production that has occurred up to the time the non-joined co-tenant brings suit, at which time it will convert to a return of gross proceeds minus expenses of future production.[19] In one Kentucky case,[20] the royalty rule was applied where a lease provided for the payment of $150 royalty per well per year on gas wells. Gas from the well on jointly owned property was not metered. Rather than speculate as to the amount of gas produced from the well, the non-joined owner was relegated to his proportionate share of the stated lease royalty. West Virginia also applied the royalty rule in the case of South Penn Oil Co. v. Haught,[21] where gross proceeds were $16,000 and costs and expenses exceeded $40,000. The non-joined owner was awarded a $1/32$ royalty on his $1/4$ mineral interest. This case seems to be clearly wrong, and goes beyond the rationale behind the recoupment theory. When the venture is a failure, and the producer has taken all the risk, although he has no right to convert another's oil, there would seem to be no basis upon which to make a royalty payment to the non-consenting owner who has done nothing.

The right of the producing co-tenant to recoup costs is limited (1) only to reasonable costs incurred in connection with the lease in which the co-tenancy exists and (2) to the amount of production from the lease.[22]

Litigation has occurred regarding the nature of costs and expenses that constitute reasonable costs of development, production, and marketing, where overhead costs, interest upon capital advanced, dry holes incident to a drilling program and other non-direct costs relative to the production in which the non-joined owners may share, have been incurred. The general rule of thumb that has been applied is that expenses, both direct and indirect, reasonably incident to the

---

18. See note 17, supra.

19. New Domain Oil & Gas Co. v. McKinney, 188 Ky. 183, 221 S.W. 245; Gillispie v. Blanton, 214 Ky. 49, 282 S.W. 1061.

20. Petroleum Exploration Corp. v. Hensley, Ky., 284 S.W.2d 828.

21. 71 W.Va. 720, 78 S.E. 759.

22. McMillan v. Powell, 235 Ark. 932, 362 S.W.2d 721; Superior Oil Co. v. Roberts, Tex., 398 S.W.2d 276; Rosse v. Northern Pump Co., Tex.Civ.App., 353 S.W.2d 287; Prairie Oil & Gas Co. v. Allen, C.C.A. 8th, 2 F.2d 566, 40 A.L.R. 1389.

drilling, production, and marketing functions, are recoupable. Understandably, the courts have not been consistent as to which particular costs are considered to be reasonable.

Examples of costs and expenses that have been deemed to be reasonable and recoupable are the following: Increased costs of materials that represent a warehousing charge to enable the lessee to keep sufficient materials on hand to prevent shortages;[23] the cost of a pumping plant and pipe necessary to market the products produced;[24] customary overhead expenses;[25] processing charge for gas in order to make it marketable;[26] and the costs of drilling of marginal wells or dry holes pursuant to a comprehensive drilling and development plan, where the non-joined owners would share in benefits from the entire program.[27] On the other hand, it has also been held that the cost of dry holes is not to be borne by the non-joining owner,[28] and a recent case [29] has denied the right of the producing co-tenant to charge for the reasonable use of capital advanced for development of the lands.

The rationale of cost sharing by the non-consenting co-owner is to prevent unjust enrichment, i.e., one who enjoys the fruits of another's labors should also share in the costs of the enterprise. Upon this basis it may be seen that the non-joined co-owner is not on the same basis in respect to cost sharing as is a co-venturer. Only those costs that would prevent unjust enrichment should be recoupable, not the producing co-owner's general costs of doing business. It would seem the better view to limit cost recoupment to the direct costs of drilling, production and marketing.

(C) Co-tenant Leasing

Although the law seems clear that the producing co-tenant must account to the non-joining co-tenant for his proportionate share of production less the reasonable costs and expenses of development and production, problems of accounting and recoupment become complicated where more than one co-tenant leases for development of his interest in the minerals. In Earp v. Mid-Continent Petroleum Corporation,[30] under simplified facts, A and B were co-tenants in the minerals. A owned an undivided $2/33$ of the minerals, and B owned the remaining $31/33$ interest in the minerals. Each executed a separate lease to a different lessee. A leased to Wagner, and B to Mid-Continent

---

23. Moody v. Wagner, 167 Okl. 99, 23 P.2d 633.

24. Burnham v. Hardy Oil Co., Tex. Civ.App., 147 S.W. 330.

25. New Domain Oil & Gas Co. v. McKinney, 188 Ky. 183, 221 S.W. 245; Moody v. Wagner, 167 Okl. 99, 23 P.2d 633.

26. Moody v. Wagner, 167 Okl. 99, 23 P.2d 633.

27. Connette v. Wright, 154 La. 1081, 98 So. 674 (had received share of production under decision orders); Moody v. Wagner, 167 Okl. 99, 23 P.2d 633.

28. Burnham v. Hardy Oil Co., Tex. Civ.App., 147 S.W. 330.

29. Cox v. Davison, Tex., 397 S.W.2d 200.

30. 167 Okl. 86, 27 P.2d 855, 91 A.L.R. 188, also see Moody v. Wagner, 167 Okl. 99, 23 P.2d 633 growing out of the same factual situation.

Petroleum Corporation. The lease executed to Wagner provided it would be for a term of "five years and as long thereafter as oil and gas, or either of them, should be produced from said land *by the lessee.*" (emphasis supplied). Wagner paid the first year delay rental, but thereafter neither paid delay rentals nor drilled.

During the second year of the leases, Mid-Continent drilled a producing well on the land. During the primary term of the lease Mid-Continent paid to its own lessor, B, a royalty of $1/8 \times 31/33$ and paid a royalty of $1/8 \times 2/33$ to A. A claimed that he was entitled to the full $2/33$ of production as the Wagner lease had expired at the end of the second year of the primary term by reason of the failure of Wagner to either drill or pay delay rentals. Wagner, on the other hand, asserted that his lease was continued in effect by the activities of Mid-Continent. No contractual agreement existed between Wagner and Mid-Continent.

The court found that an ambiguity existed between the habendum clause in Wagner's lease, requiring production to be "by the lessee," and the delay rental clause. The latter provided that the necessity for payment of delay rentals would continue only: "If no well be commenced * * * by the last day of each year of the primary term." It did not require such well to be commenced "by the lessee." [31]

Applying the familiar contract principle that parties to a contract may construe an ambiguous provision by their acts, the court found that, due to the execution of a division order by A recognizing Wagner's interest and accepting payment, the parties had construed the drilling of the well by Mid-Continent as satisfying the delay rental clause in Wagner's lease, and that the acts of Mid-Continent had kept Wagner's lease alive during the primary term. However, it was expressly pointed out that as there was no agreement making the well of Mid-Continent also Wagner's well, the production of Mid-Continent would not serve to propel Wagner's lease beyond its primary term.

During both the primary term of the Wagner lease and afterwards, Mid-Continent must account to the A-Wagner interest on the basis of a non-joined co-tenant interest. During the period that the Wagner lease was in existence, $2/33$ of gross production less expenses (after recoupment of the costs of drilling, production, and marketing) must be paid to the non-joined co-tenants, A-Wagner. It is indicated in the Earp case that while the Wagner lease was in effect, the share from the producing co-tenant was to be distributed by Wagner ac-

---

31. See Mattison v. Trotti, C.A.5th, 262 F.2d 339, where the phrase "by the lessee" was not included in the habendum clause and it was argued that, as in the Earp case as to delay rentals, any production would keep a co-tenant's lease alive. This construction was rejected, and it was held that the operations as to each lease were independent. Present day leases generally do not include the phrase "by the lessee" in either the habendum or delay rental clause.

Hughes v. Cantwell, Tex.Civ.App., 540 S.W.2d 742 (a case of first impression in the Texas courts which adopts the view of the Earp case; "by the lessee" not included in the clause).

cording to the terms of the A-Wagner lease. That is to say, Wagner was to disburse to A a royalty interest as provided for in their lease. After the lease of Wagner terminated, A received the entire $2/33$ of gross production minus expenses of production.

The conclusion that the share of the non-joined co-tenant should be distributed according to the terms of a valid lease between such co-tenant and his lessee may lead to a peculiar result. Assume the following:

A executes his lease to Rex Oil Company, and B executes a corresponding lease to Humble. Humble drills a successful producing well. As mentioned above, B will share immediately to the extent of his royalty interest (i.e., $1/16$) from the first barrel of oil, Humble will be entitled (1) to $7/16$ of production out of B's interest (the remaining interest in B's one-half after deduction of B's $1/16$ royalty) and (2) to retain the remaining one-half interest of A-Rex until recoupment of costs. This means that no payment will be made to A-Rex until payout. Rex Oil Co., however, under its lease is contractually obligated to absorb the costs incident to the undivided one-half interest of A-Rex, and therefore Rex Oil Co. must pay to A the value of $1/16$ of production commencing from the production of the first barrel of oil by Humble.

Rex Oil Co. would recoup the prior royalty payments made to A from the $8/16$ A-Rex interest which would be paid by Humble at the time of payout of the cost of the well. However, if the well never paid out, Rex would have had to pay royalty on A's undivided one-half interest without receiving a cent from production. This is obviously an unsatisfactory state of affairs for Rex Oil Company, and would be highly unusual under present day practices.

The normal procedure would be to execute a joint operating agreement, whereby all of the leasehold interests would be operated by one party, with all lessees sharing in the cost of the wells according to the proportion of their interests.[32] Any well thereby becomes the well of each of the co-tenants and will serve to extend each lease beyond the primary term. Payment is also straightforward, with each of the lessors receiving his share of the royalty out of the first barrel of production. Also, each lessee will be paid its share in the proceeds of production and will be liable for its share of the expenses. However, here there would be no period of time, unless the parties used some type of carried interest arrangement, that one of the lessees would hold all production until recoupment. Furthermore, the liability of each of the lessees under the joint operating agreement is contractual and is not limited in amount merely to the share of each in production.

32. Schank v. North American Royalties, Inc., N.D., 201 N.W.2d 419; Hughes v. Cantwell, Tex.Civ.App., 540 S.W.2d 742; Willson v. Superior Oil Co., Tex.Civ. App., 274 S.W.2d 947, refused n.r.e.

In the absence of estoppel factors or complicating contractual language, it is the law generally (1) that each co-tenant may execute a valid lease upon his own interest, (2) that each lease is independent, and (3) that the payments, operations or acts of lessees of other co-tenants will have no effect upon the continued validity of any other particular co-tenant's lease.[33]

A few practical remarks may be made in connection with the acquisition of leases from co-owners of jointly owned lands. From the landowner's standpoint, it is probably a material consideration that no one of the co-owners be bound upon the lease unless all are bound. This of course can be done by a statement in the lease instrument that it will not be binding upon any party lessor until it has been properly executed and acknowledged by all of the parties. The lessee has a corollary consideration that he be able to acquire all signatures of lessors within a reasonable time. To speed the execution of a lease among joint owners, multiple copies of the instrument may be prepared and used, with one copy mailed to each co-owner. This is a much faster and surer method than circulating one copy of the lease, and has the additional advantage of revealing the holdup in the chain of execution if one develops. Caution should be taken that each copy contain the statement that although the instrument is being executed in multiple copies, that each copy of the multiple copies constitutes one and the same instrument.

Where the lessee desires to examine the title before acquiring title to the lease, multiple execution of the lease may prove difficult, as people tend to get out of pocket during periods of delay. The easiest method is to have a completely executed lease deposited in a bank, together with a time draft which must be paid by the lessee before acquiring the lease. The time of the draft should correspond with a reasonable examination period for the lease. Where a proper escrow deposit has been made, the intervening death of a party lessor should not prevent title passing to the lessee upon the payment of the draft and delivery of the lease to the lessee. An alternative procedure is to have a power of attorney executed empowering a joint owner who will be available to execute the lease. This, of course, will not suffice to acquire the interest of one who has died in the interim period.

(D) Ratification by a Non-joined Co-tenant

Where it is not possible to acquire the signatures of all co-tenants on the lease instrument, it may be possible to acquire a ratification of the lease at a later date, in form sufficient to satisfy the statute of

---

33. Schank v. North American Royalties, Inc., N.D., 201 N.W.2d 419; Hughes v. Cantwell, Tex.Civ.App., 540 S.W.2d 742 (in both cases co-tenant's lessee did not pay delay rentals during primary term of lease, due to drilling activities of lessee from another co-tenant and the leases terminated as there was no joint operating agreement or other contractual relationship between the lessees of the various co-tenants). Also see: Willson v. Superior Oil Co., Tex.Civ.App., 274 S.W.2d 947, refused n.r.e.

frauds and conveyances in a particular jurisdiction.[34] Ratification may be desired from two divergent standpoints. The lessee may want a ratification by the remaining co-tenants [35] of an existing lease which covers only a portion of the interests. On the other hand, a non-joining co-tenant may later desire to ratify and come within the terms of an existing lease. May he do so? Where the existing lease has purported to lease all of the interests in the land, by describing the land without limitation to the undivided interests leased, the non-joined co-tenant may ratify the lease.[36] This apparently may be done either by delivery of a unilateral instrument to the lessee,[37] or by a suit brought to ratify.[38]

Where the non-joined co-tenant later ratifies a lease executed by his fellow co-tenant, he will be treated as a co-lessor and will be paid a royalty proportionate to his mineral interest, i.e., a $1/16$ royalty for a one-half mineral interest, which royalty will commence with the first production.[39] Several cases have indicated that where ratification has occurred, the ratifying co-tenant is to be considered a lessor from the beginning and is entitled to his proportionate share of all economic benefits paid to leasing co-tenants up to the time of ratification, including bonus.[40]

In some jurisdictions ratification may inadvertently result. In Texas a non-joining co-tenant may ratify a prior lease by execution of an instrument affecting the land when it is made "subject to the lease." [41] Under these cases, where A, the owner of one-half of the minerals in Blackacre, executes a mortgage on his one-half interest "subject to the oil and gas lease previously made by B," ratification of the prior lease would result, whether or not intended. As such

34. Ratification differs from an estoppel. An estoppel involves facts and conduct which in equity become a bar to a right. A ratification on the other hand involves a grant or conveyance. In certain situations such as in the Earp case an estoppel based on acts and conduct may be sufficient to continue a lease in effect. However, in some situations, such as a lease from a married couple upon their marital homestead in Texas, not only must a conveyance be involved but the instrument must contain a joint acknowledgment for validity, and no estoppel would be recognized.
Thaxton v. Beard, 157 W.Va. 381, 201 S.E.2d 298.

35. Ratification in favor of the lessee may be accomplished by execution of a division order by the non-joining co-tenant where the division order contains words of grant or confirmation. In some jurisdictions, such as Texas, where the homestead is involved it may be necessary to have a joint acknowledgement of husband and wife. See Texas & Pacific Coal & Oil Co. v. Kirtley, Tex.Civ.App., 288 S.W. 619.

36. Brooks v. Mull, 147 Kan. 740, 78 P.2d 879; Texas & Pacific Coal & Oil Co. v. Kirtley, Tex.Civ.App., 288 S.W. 619; Van Deventer v. Gulf Production Co., Tex.Civ.App., 41 S.W.2d 1029; Shield v. Shield, Tex.Civ.App., 286 S.W.2d 252.

37. Brooks v. Mull, 147 Kan. 740, 78 P.2d 879.

38. Shield v. Shield, Tex.Civ.App., 286 S.W.2d 252.

39. Thaxton v. Beard, 157 W.Va. 381, 201 S.E.2d 298. For a discussion of the proportionate reduction clause see Chapter 7, § 7.8, infra.

40. Brooks v. Mull, 147 Kan. 740, 78 P.2d 879; Shield v. Shield, Tex.Civ.App., 286 S.W.2d 252.

41. Van Deventer v. Gulf Production Co., Tex.Com.App., 41 S.W.2d 1029 (option agreement and later deed); Humble Oil & Refining Co. v. Clark, 126 Tex. 262, 87 S.W.2d 471 (mineral deed).

recitations are usually made to protect the mortgagor or others from liability on the warranty clause, the ensuing ratification is a wholly unintended result. Such cases are clearly wrong.

Where fellow co-tenants are not easily found, obtaining the joinder or ratification may prove vexing. In jurisdictions where fractional undivided interests in the mineral estate may last perpetually, a very real problem may be presented to the lessee as to whether he will be able to accumulate a sufficiently large interest in the minerals to make development economically feasible. In an attempt to alleviate the situation where owners of fractional interest cannot be found, statutes have been enacted providing for a statutory trustee for the leasing of these interests. Execution of leases is supervised by judicial process, with payments for the benefit of the absent owners to be made to the statutory trustee, or into the registry of the court.[42]

§ 5.2 Life Tenant and Remainderman

Neither a life tenant nor a remainderman, without the joinder of the other, may develop or remove petroleum products from the land in which the successive estates or interests exist. The life tenant may not commit waste, and the remainderman has no right of possession until the death of the life tenant. An exception is where the instrument creating the life estate expressly authorizes the life tenant to lease and develop without the joinder of the remainderman.

However, the life tenant and the remainderman may execute joint leases for the development of the property. Where production ensues, it appears to be the general rule that royalties and bonus are to be treated as corpus of the estate to be conserved for the remainderman and invested, the life tenant to enjoy the interest therefrom. In some jurisdictions partition will be made by purchase of an annuity to return the estimated income of the fund for the life expectancy of the life tenant. Withdrawal of the fund for investment may be made by the life tenant secured by a refunding surety bond to be performable at the death of the life tenant. Delay rentals (and bonus in Oklahoma and some other jurisdictions) are treated as ground rent, or income from the land, and are payable to the life tenant.

Where a mine has been opened for oil and gas production prior to the creation of the life estate, be it legal or conventional, the open mine doctrine will apply and all economic benefits will thereafter be payable to the life tenant. Although the existence of a producing well is sufficient in all jurisdictions to open the mine, it has been held in some jurisdictions that an oil and gas lease that is in existence but without production at the time of creation of the life estate is sufficient for the open mine doctrine to apply. In these cases the courts find a devotion or dedication of the lands to mining purposes prior to the creation of the life estate sufficient for application of the open mine doctrine.

42. Scott v. Sampson, Tex.Civ.App., 333 S.W.2d 220 (Vernon's Ann.Tex.Civ. Stat., Art. 2320b).

It is believed that the extent to which a mine is considered open for oil and gas purposes will be determined by reference to the lease in effect at the time the life estate is created. Under such lease further wells may be drilled to such depths and for such products as are authorized under the lease, whether or not so producing at the time of the creation of the life estate.

Where the life estate is held in trust and where no provisions are made for the apportionment of economic benefits under a lease the provisions of the Uniform Trust Act will apply (if adopted in that particular jurisdiction). Where the life estate is not held in trust, little uniformity exists as to the application of the Uniform Principal and Income Act.

(A) Leases From a Life Tenant or a Remainderman

The preceding section dealt with the development of lands for oil and gas purposes where ownership of the land was held in concurrent estates or interests. As was seen, each owner of a concurrent interest has a co-equal right to possession, use, and development of the land for production of oil and gas. This is not the case, however, where successive estates or interests are involved, for no owner of a successive estate or interest in land has, in himself, the full right of development. Where a life estate has been created, neither the life tenant nor the remainderman may develop the land for oil and gas without the agreement of the other.[1] The remainderman does not have a right of possession until the death of the life tenant, and the life tenant, who has a possessory estate in the land, may use it only for purposes consistent with ownership of a possessory interest of limited duration. That is to say, the corpus of the estate must be conserved for the benefit of the remainderman. This has been well stated in the early case of Koen v. Bartlett:[2]

> " * * * the owners of the inheritance have no more right to approach by a tunnel, and break and enter his superficial close, than they have to break and enter his close on the surface. Their estate of inheritance is vested in right of interest, but not in right of enjoyment. Their estate is expectant on the determination of the life estate. It is the duty of the life tenant to spare and preserve the corpus of the inheritance, and of the owners of the fee in expectancy to wait, for they have no present right of use and enjoyment, and cannot exercise any right by anticipation; and their respective duties point out their respective rights."

---

1. Burden v. Gypsy Oil Co., 141 Kan. 147, 40 P.2d 463; Meredith v. Meredith, 193 Ky. 192, 235 S.W. 757, and 204 Ky. 608, 264 S.W. 1109; Rowe v. Bird, Ky., 304 S.W.2d 775, 56 Mich.L.Rev. 654; Eide v. Tveter, D.C.N.D., 143 F.Supp. 665; Orndoff v. Consumer's Fuel Co., 308 Pa. 165, 162 A. 431, 31 Mich.L.Rev. 998. In general see Summers Oil and Gas Law, §§ 223, 224, 225, 613; Williams, The Effect of Various Conditions of Ownership on Oil and Gas Transactions, 5 Utah L.Rev. 1; Woodward, The Open Mine Doctrine in Oil and Gas Cases, 35 Tex.L. Rev. 538; Statutes applying to apportion income and principal see footnote 20–24 Walker, pp. 345–346; Open Mine Doctrine in Mississippi. Miss.L.J. 35:436 May 1964.

2. 41 W.Va. 559, 23 S.E. 664.

Production of petroleum products by a life tenant causes a diminution of the mineral estate, is classified as waste, and may be enjoined by the remainderman.[3]

The life estate involved may be a conventional life estate created by deed, trust, or will,[4] or a legal life estate in the nature of a probate homestead,[5] a dower right,[6] a right of curtesy,[7] or one created by the statutes of descent and distribution.[8]

What the life tenant or remainderman may not do by himself, he may not do through a nominee or a lessee. It has been stated by the courts that neither the life tenant nor the remainderman has the right,[9] nor can grant,[10] a lease covering only his interest, and that such a lease is void[11] and of no effect.

Although such a leasehold interest may not be developed in absence of consent of the other owner, it is not correct to say that such leases are void in a strict sense. The interests of both a life tenant and a remainderman are alienable, and the lessee merely stands in the shoes of his respective lessor. It has been held that a lease from a life tenant is not intrinsically bad because it may contemplate waste.[12] Even though the lessee from a life tenant may be enjoined

---

3. Heyser v. Frankfort Oil Co., C.A.10th, 316 F.2d 441, cert. denied 375 U.S. 824, 84 S.Ct. 64, 11 L.Ed.2d 56; Swayne v. Lone Acre Oil Co., 98 Tex. 597, 86 S.W. 740; Koen v. Bartlett, 41 W.Va. 559, 23 S.E. 664. It was originally held in English common law cases that the legal life tenant was impeachable for waste, while the conventional life tenant was not. Although the law was changed prior to adoption of the common law in the United States, an attempt was made in early oil and gas cases to apply such distinction. See Davis v. Atlantic Oil Producing Co., C.A.5th, 87 F.2d 75, 16 Tex.L.Rev. 420; Swayne v. Lone Acre Oil Co., 98 Tex. 597, 86 S.W. 740; and comment therein in Davis v. Bond, 138 Tex. 206, 158 S.W.2d 297.

4. Meredith v. Meredith, 193 Ky. 192, 235 S.W. 757, and 204 Ky. 608, 264 S.W. 1109; Davis v. Bond, 138 Tex. 206, 158 S.W.2d 297; Mitchell v. Mitchell, Tex.Civ. App., 298 S.W.2d 236, reversed on other grounds 157 Tex. 346, 303 S.W.2d 352; Clyde v. Hamilton, Tex., 414 S.W.2d 434.

5. Warren v. Martin, 168 Ark. 682, 272 S.W. 367; Lawley v. Richardson, 101 Okl. 40, 223 P. 156, 43 A.L.R. 802; Heyser v. Frankfort Oil Co., C.A.10th, 316 F.2d 441, cert. denied 375 U.S. 824, 84 S.Ct. 64, 11 L.Ed.2d 56; Swayne v. Lone Acre Oil Co., 98 Tex. 597, 86 S.W. 740; Petrus v. Cage Brothers, Tex.Civ.App., 128 S.W.2d 537; White v. Blackman, Tex. Civ.App., 168 S.W.2d 531; Thompson v. Thompson, 149 Tex. 632, 236 S.W.2d 779, noted in 30 Tex.L.Rev. 134; Youngman v. Shular, 155 Tex. 437, 288 S.W.2d 495, noted in 10 Sw.L.J. 449; 34 Tex.L.Rev. 328; 3 U.C.L.A.L.Rev. 601. But see Brandenburg v. Petroleum Exploration, 218 Ky. 557, 291 S.W. 757, probate homestead held not to have the attributes of a life estate.

6. Yost v. Ratliff, Ky., 246 S.W.2d 447; Seager v. McCabe, 92 Mich. 186, 52 N.W. 299; Aldridge v. Houston Oil Co., 116 Okl. 281, 244 P. 782.

7. Orndoff v. Consumer's Fuel Co., 308 Pa. 165, 162 A. 431, 31 Mich.L.Rev. 998.

8. Cook v. Cook, Tex.Civ.App., 331 S.W.2d 77; Bergendahl v. Blanco Oil Co., Tex.Civ.App., 440 S.W.2d 81; Davis v. Atlantic Oil Producing Co., C.A.5th, 87 F.2d 75, 16 Tex.L.Rev. 420.

9. Burden v. Gypsy Oil Co., 141 Kan. 147, 40 P.2d 463; Meredith v. Meredith, 193 Ky. 192, 235 S.W. 757, and 204 Ky. 608, 264 S.W. 1109; Rowe v. Bird, Ky., 304 S.W.2d 775, 56 Mich.L.Rev. 654.

10. Orndoff v. Consumer's Fuel Co., 308 Pa. 165, 162 A. 431, 31 Mich.L.Rev. 998.

11. Eide v. Tveter, D.C.N.D., 143 F.Supp. 665.

12. Hardie v. Chew Fish Yuen, 258 Cal.App.2d 301, 65 Cal.Rptr. 594; Orndoff v. Consumer's Fuel Co., 308 Pa. 165, 162 A. 431, 31 Mich.L.Rev. 998. But

by the remainderman from conducting geophysical operations, the lessee has the right to acquire the interest or consent [13] of the remainderman. Likewise, the lessee of the remainderman has the right to enjoin waste by the life tenant or his assignees, and also to develop the land upon the death of the life tenant, if this occurs prior to the expiration of the primary term of the lease.[14]

An exception to the rule that a life tenant may not grant a developable leasehold interest in the oil and gas without the joinder of the remainderman exists where (1) a conventional life estate has been created and the instrument creating the life estate expressly authorizes the life tenant to lease and develop the minerals without the joinder of the remainderman,[15] or (2) where such right exists due to a statutory enactment.[16] There is some authority for the proposition that a life tenant may develop without the joinder of the remainderman where it is reasonably necessary to prevent destruction of the mineral estate through drainage.[17] Where authority exists for the development of the minerals solely by the life tenant or his nominee, all economic benefits will be payable to the life tenant.[18]

(B) Joint Leases by Life Tenant and Remainderman

Where the ownership of the mineral estate is divided between a life tenant and a remainderman, although neither may open a mine or drill for oil and gas separately, they may do so jointly.[19] Normally this is done through the joint execution of an oil and gas lease; however, the same result will occur where one party executes the lease and the other adopts or ratifies the executed lease by an instrument in writing containing words of grant.[20] It has been held that where the life tenant and the remainderman each execute a lease to the same lessee, both identical in term and provisions, there is a merger of the two leases in the hands of the lessee.[21]

---

cf. Eide v. Tveter, D.C.N.D., 143 F.Supp. 665.

13. Burden v. Gypsy Oil Co., 141 Kan. 147, 40 P.2d 463. But cf. Eide v. Tveter, D.C.N.D., 143 F.Supp. 665; What is the effect of the remainderman ratifying a lease void as to the life tenant?

14. Welborn v. Tidewater Associated Oil Co., C.A.10th, 217 F.2d 509.

15. Bruner's Will, 363 Pa. 552, 70 A.2d 222; Amarillo Oil Co. v. McBride, Tex.Civ.App., 67 S.W.2d 1098; Guest v. Bizzell, Tex.Civ.App., 271 S.W.2d 472.

16. Ark.Stats. §§ 52–215 to 52–223 and see Love v. McDonald, 201 Ark. 882, 148 S.W.2d 170; life estate resulting from conversion of an estate tail, see Waller v. Rhyne, 232 Ark. 501, 338 S.W.2d 670.

17. See Love v. McDonald, 201 Ark. 882, 148 S.W.2d 170.

18. Amarillo Oil Co. v. McBride, Tex. Civ.App., 67 S.W.2d 1098; Guest v. Bizzell, Tex.Civ.App., 271 S.W.2d 472.

19. Haskell v. Wood, 256 Cal.App.2d 799, 64 Cal.Rptr. 459; Meredith v. Meredith, 193 Ky. 192, 235 S.W. 757, and 204 Ky. 608, 264 S.W. 1109; Barnes v. Keys, 36 Okl. 6, 127 P. 261.

20. Burden v. Gypsy Oil Co., 141 Kan. 147, 40 P.2d 463. The instrument must comply with the formalities of conveyance for a particular jurisdiction.

21. Union Gas & Oil Co. v. Wiedemann Oil Co., 211 Ky. 361, 277 S.W. 323; Weekley v. Weekley, 126 W.Va. 90, 27 S.E.2d 591, 150 A.L.R. 689.

An interesting situation occurred in the case of Rowe v. Bird,[22] where both the life tenant and the remainderman executed separate leases to different groups of lessees. Although a substantial amount of the leasehold estate under both leases came into the hands of the one group, it was held that no merger resulted, as the leases were neither coincident in time nor of identical terms. Here the commencement of the term of the second lease was some two years later than that of the first lease. However, merger will apparently result where a fractional interest under both leases comes into the same ownership if the leases are otherwise substantially identical.[23] In this situation the producing owner of the portion of the merged lease would account to the other owners of interests in the mineral estate on the basis of a co-tenancy in the non-joined life estate-remainder interest.[24]

Upon the execution of a joint lease, a problem remains as to the manner in which the proceeds from production are to be apportioned between the life tenant and the remainderman. Traditionally, in absence of an agreement, the life tenant may enjoy only the income from land in which he has a life estate, whereas the remainderman may enjoy only the corpus of the estate. If economic benefits derived from the land are classified as income, they are apportionable to the life tenant; however, even if classified as the return of corpus, they are not presently apportionable to the remainderman, as he has no right to the estate until the death of the life tenant. The sums will be retained by the court and invested, and the interest paid to the life tenant until his death, at which time the entire fund will be paid over to the remainderman, or his heirs or distributees. The economic benefits derived from the production of oil and gas must therefore be classified either as the return of income or of corpus.

As the production of petroleum products constitutes a wasting asset industry, any production of the mineral estate is also a partial consumption of it. If a benefit is classified as an interest in production, in all probability it will be treated as a return of part of the corpus of the mineral estate.

Royalty payments obviously are a return of the corpus of the estate and are to be conserved for the benefit of the remainderman.[25] Such classification should be extended to royalty substitutes. Bonus payments, paid as consideration for title to the minerals, are normally considered as payments of advance royalties and should be treated as

---

22. Ky., 304 S.W.2d 775, 56 Mich.L. Rev. 654.

23. See Weekley v. Weekley, 126 W.Va. 90, 27 S.E.2d 591, 150 A.L.R. 689, treated as a joint lease where an undivided ¼ interest was acquired in both leases by the same party.

24. Swayne v. Lone Acre Oil Co., 98 Tex. 597, 86 S.W. 740.

25. Haskell v. Wood, 256 Cal.App.2d 799, 64 Cal.Rptr. 459; Burden v. Gypsy Oil Co., 141 Kan. 147, 40 P.2d 463; Meredith v. Meredith, 193 Ky. 192, 235 S.W. 757, and 204 Ky. 608, 264 S.W. 1109; Barnes v. Keys, 36 Okl. 6, 127 P. 261; Davis v. Bond, 138 Tex. 206, 158 S.W.2d 297; Clyde v. Hamilton, Tex., 414 S.W.2d 434.

a return of corpus.[26] This is also true as to shut-in royalties paid in lieu of gas production.[27] Delay rentals, on the other hand, have been considered ground rents or income from the land, and are payable to the life tenant.[28]

It therefore appears to be the general rule that where a joint lease is executed by the life tenant and remainderman, in absence of an agreement to the contrary, royalties and bonus will be retained for the benefit of the remainderman and invested, and interest thereon paid to the life tenant until death,[29] but delay rentals will be payable directly to the life tenant.

As is the case generally, in respect to economic benefits from lands subject to life estates, the parties may desire to free the funds from the necessity of being tied up for the duration of the life of the life tenant. Where the life tenant is a relatively young person compared to the remainderman, it is highly possible that the remainderman will not outlive the life tenant and therefore never enjoy the estate. On the other hand, the life tenant may desire to be able to presently enjoy the life income from the estate. Where all the parties are *sui juris* and agree as to a method of division, the funds will be partitioned according to the terms of such an agreement.[30]

Where the parties cannot agree as to a method of partitioning the proceeds, in several jurisdictions a judicial partition will be made on the basis of life expectancy of the life tenant.[31] However, in one state [32] it was held that neither the life tenant nor the remainderman may obtain a judicial partition, as it would not do justice between the parties. It was stated that if the life tenant did not live according to the expectancy tables and lived longer than expected, he would have received less than his due, and if the life tenant lived a shorter period the remainderman would have been shorted.

Where agreement cannot be had between the parties, and partition is not judicially possible, the funds may be withdrawn by the life tenant upon the furnishing of a refunding surety bond,[33] which guar-

---

26. Mills v. Mills, 275 Ky. 431, 121 S.W.2d 962; Clyde v. Hamilton, Tex., 414 S.W.2d 434. However, in Oklahoma bonus is classified as rentals and would be payable to the life tenant. Aldridge v. Houston Oil Co., 11 Okl. 281, 244 P. 782; Dixon v. Mapes, 181 Okl. 376, 73 P.2d 1131; Franklin v. Margay Oil Corp., 194 Okl. 519, 153 P.2d 486.

27. Mills v. Mills, 275 Ky. 431, 121 S.W.2d 962.

28. Aldridge v. Houston Oil Co., 116 Okl. 281, 244 P. 782; Weekley v. Weekley, 126 W.Va. 90, 27 S.E.2d 591, 150 A.L.R. 689.

29. But see Yost v. Ratliff, Ky., 246 S.W.2d 447, where due to the circumstances involved, royalty, not only interest thereon, was payable to the life tenant. Also see note 26, supra, as to Oklahoma cases classifying bonus as rentals and payable to the life tenant.

30. Meredith v. Meredith, 193 Ky. 192, 235 S.W. 757, 204 Ky. 608, 264 S.W. 1109.

31. Burden v. Gypsy Oil Co., 141 Kan. 147, 40 P.2d 463; Barnes v. Keys, 36 Okl. 6, 127 P. 261.

32. Graser v. Graser, 147 Tex. 404, 215 S.W.2d 867.

33. Ramirez v. Flag Oil Corp. of Delaware, Tex.Civ.App., 266 S.W.2d 270. In absence of such withdrawal apparently neither party has the right to invest the funds.

antees that the funds will be returned to the registry of the court upon the death of the life tenant. This allows the life tenant to invest the funds free of court control during his lifetime.

(C) *Leases Preceding the Life Estate—The Open Mine Doctrine*

The open mine doctrine has been held to apply to production of petroleum products.[34] Briefly stated, where a mine has been opened prior to the creation of a life estate, the life tenant is entitled to the entire production from the mine,[35] not just the interest income from production. The doctrine is well stated, in the West Virginia case of Koen v. Bartlett,[36] decided in 1895:

> " * * * that if these mines of oil and gas had been open when Kerns, * * * came in as tenant for life of the immediate freehold, then he would have a right to work them during the continuance of his estate, and take the issues and profits thence produced; for these two are derivative parts of one estate; each, in quantity of ownership and order of enjoyment, is measured and determined by time; and, though both are vested in right, the life tenant has the hither segment,—the immediate freehold,—and therefore, the sole right to hold, use, and enjoy. And if the mine is 'open' when he comes in, then we conclude that the one who had the right to say has, by his actions, which speak louder than words, manifested his intention that it may be worked. Hence the life tenant may lawfully mine, sever, and convert the mineral from land into personalty; and this is something in which the owner of the expectant estate of inheritance has no right * * * The rule is well settled that a tenant for life, when not precluded by restraining words, may not only work open mines, but may work them to exhaustion; and it is settled law that the rents of an open mine are income and go to the tenant for life * * * A mine lawfully leased to be opened is an 'open mine,' within the reason

---

34. Mills v. Mills, 275 Ky. 431, 121 S.W.2d 962 (bonus and rentals); Mills v. Taylor, Ky., 268 S.W.2d 412 (royalties, bonus, and rentals); Aldridge v. Houston Oil Co., 116 Okl. 281, 244 P. 782 (rentals and bonus); Clyde v. Hamilton, Tex., 414 S.W.2d 434 (royalties and bonus); Moore v. Vines, Tex., 474 S.W.2d 437; Weekley v. Weekley, 126 W.Va. 90, 27 S.E.2d 591, 150 A.L.R. 689 (bonus).

35. Haskell v. Wood, 256 Cal.App.2d 799, 64 Cal.Rptr. 459; Andrews v. Andrews, 31 Ind.App. 189, 67 N.E. 461; Mills v. Taylor, Ky., 268 S.W.2d 412; Bruner's Will, 363 Pa. 552, 70 A.2d 222; Aldridge v. Houston Oil Co., 116 Okl. 281, 244 P. 782; In re Shailer's Estate, Okl., 266 P.2d 613; Heyser v. Frankfort Oil Co., C.A.10th, 316 F.2d 441, cert. denied 375 U.S. 824, 84 S.Ct. 64, 11 L.Ed.2d 56; Petrus v. Cage Brothers, Tex.Civ. App., 128 S.W.2d 537; White v. Blackman, Tex.Civ.App., 168 S.W.2d 531; Youngman v. Shular, 155 Tex. 437, 288 S.W.2d 495, noted in 10 Sw.L.J. 449; Moore v. Vines, Tex., 474 S.W.2d 437; Bergendahl v. Blanco Oil Co., Tex.Civ. App., 440 S.W.2d 81; 34 Tex.L.Rev. 328; 3 U.C.L.A.L.Rev. 601; Clyde v. Hamilton, Tex., 414 S.W.2d 434; Koen v. Bartlett, 41 W.Va. 559, 23 S.E. 664.

Where a conventional life estate is involved, if the instrument creating the life estate gives the life tenant authority to open mines and produce, it is viewed that the instrument opens the mine, and the open mine doctrine will apply to production thereafter. Bruner's Will, 363 Pa. 552, 70 A.2d 222.

36. 41 W.Va. 559, 23 S.E. 664.

of the rule as laid down in these cases; and when lawfully opened and worked as in this case, during the time that the freehold estate of the life tenant continues, the profits issuing therefrom, thus lawfully severed and produced, belong of right to him; for the term 'profit,' in law, comprehends the produce of the soil, whether it arise above or below the surface, including product of mines, as well as the herbage growing on the surface."

As applied in hard mineral mining, the open mine doctrine applied only to the mine that was open at the time the life estate was created, and did not apply to mines subsequently opened. The opening of new pits or galleries was not considered the opening of a new mine.[37]

The application of the open mine doctrine to petroleum production raises many questions: As to oil and gas production, what is a mine? Does the open mine doctrine apply only to wells producing at the time that the life estate was created? Does the producing horizon in which production exists constitute the "open mine" so that other wells may be drilled into such formations? If the producing wells are productive of gas only, or of oil only, does the "open mine" consist only of the products produced from the lands covered by the oil and gas lease? Or will an "open mine" be determined by reference to the lease under which the producing wells have been drilled, so that the lessee may thereafter fully develop the existing lease as an "open mine"? Two questions are involved: First, when is a mine deemed to be open, and, second, what is the extent of the opened mine?

It appears to be the rule in all jurisdictions that a mine is opened when it is in actual production at the time that the life estate is created.[38] It has been held, and there appears to be authority in early case law, that a mine is opened by the execution of a lease on the land for mining purposes.[39]

In the Texas case of Youngman v. Shular,[40] H and W executed an oil and gas lease upon their homestead. Prior to the time that production was obtained, H died, creating in the surviving W a probate homestead, which in Texas has all the attributes of a legal life estate. After the death of H, The Texas Company drilled five wells on the lease and was paying one-half of the $1/8$ royalty to W. (The other one-half was paid to an assignee of H and W, which interest was assigned prior to the death of H). Three daughters brought suit for the royal-

---

37. Haskell v. Wood, 256 Cal.App.2d 799, 64 Cal.Rptr. 459.

38. Mills v. Taylor, Ky., 268 S.W.2d 412; Lawley v. Richardson, 101 Okl. 40, 223 P. 156, 43 A.L.R. 802; White v. Blackman, Tex.Civ.App., 168 S.W.2d 531; Clyde v. Hamilton, Tex., 414 S.W. 434. However, the open mine doctrine may be negated either expressly or by implication, where a conventional life estate is involved. See Koen v. Bartlett, 41 W.Va. 559, 23 S.E. 664.

39. Youngman v. Shular, 155 Tex. 437, 288 S.W.2d 495, noted in 10 Sw.L.J. 449; 34 Tex.L.Rev. 328; 3 U.C.L.A.L. Rev. 601; Moore v. Vines, Tex., 474 S.W.2d 437; Koen v. Bartlett, 41 W.Va. 559, 23 S.E. 664.

40. 155 Tex. 437, 288 S.W.2d 495, noted in 10 Sw.L.J. 449; 34 Tex.L.Rev. 328; 3 U.C.L.A.L.Rev. 601.

ty interest of W on the ground that they were entitled to the corpus of the production from the wells as remaindermen, and that W was only entitled to interest on the royalty fund. The court found that the lease had opened the mine, and that all royalties were payable to the widow. In passing, the court commented upon the fact that no distinction would be made between a legal life estate created by law and a conventional life estate created by voluntary instrument.

In the process of holding an executed lease will open a mine the case also removed all doubt that in Texas, and apparently in other jurisdictions, that where there is production at the time of the creation of the life estate, the lessee has the right to drill additional wells to which the open mine doctrine will apply and from which all economic benefits will be paid to the life tenant.[41]

In an aftermath to the Youngman case, a lower Texas appellate court in the case of Mitchell v. Mitchell [42] found itself presented with implications suggested in the Youngman case by Judge Garwood regarding the application of the open mine doctrine to oil and gas leases executed by the life tenant after termination of the oil and gas lease that was in existence at the time of the creation of the life estate. The court was faced with three different situations. In the first of these situations the chronological order of events was as follows: Lease No. 1 was executed; the life estate was created; lease No. 1 terminated due to no production; and lease No. 2 was executed. It was held that the open mine doctrine applied to lease No. 2, and that bonus and royalties were payable to the life tenant, on the ground that the land had been devoted or dedicated to petroleum development and production at the time that the life estate was created. The court held that the situation was similar to cases where it was held that the mine did not close where work was discontinued for a time and then the mine was reworked, and that the reworking constituted a continuation of the former open mine. Supporting cases usually distinguish the concept of abandonment from that of a temporary cessation.

In the second situation lease No. 1 was executed and production was obtained under the lease, but ceased, which caused the first lease to terminate. The life estate was then created. Lease No. 2 was executed, and production was obtained. Again the court held that the open mine doctrine applied to Lease No. 2, upon reasoning similar to that in the first situation: That lease No. 2 was merely a continuation of the purposes of the lessors in lease No. 1.

However, in the third situation the court denied the application of the open mine doctrine. Here the facts were identical to situation number two, with the exception that no production was obtained un-

---

41. Andrews v. Andrews, 31 Ind.App. 189, 67 N.E. 461; Lawley v. Richardson, 101 Okl. 40, 223 P. 156, 43 A.L.R. 802; Mitchell v. Mitchell, 298 S.W.2d 236, reversed on other grounds 157 Tex. 346, 303 S.W.2d 352; Clyde v. Hamilton, Tex., 414 S.W.2d 434.

42. 298 S.W.2d 236, reversed on other grounds 157 Tex. 346, 303 S.W.2d 352.

der the first lease prior to its termination. The cases may be diagrammed as follows:

(1) Lease No. 1—Life Est.—no production & termination—Lease No. 2—Production=OMD applies

(2) Lease No. 1—production, cessation & termination—Life Est.—Lease No. 2—production=OMD applies

(3) Lease No. 1—no production & termination—Life Est.—Lease No. 2=OMD does not apply.

It is hard to distinguish between the three situations. If both the drilling of a well and the execution of a lease will constitute the opening of a mine, what is the difference in the termination of lease No. 1 where a well has been drilled and where one has not been drilled? The rationale supportive of the result in (1) and (2) is distinguishable from the case of a hard mineral mine which is open, work is then temporarily stopped, and then again continued. In (1) and (2) production or operations were discontinued to the point that a new lease arrangement had to be entered into in order to work the mine. Also some case law exists to the effect that the execution of a lease by the life tenant after the expiration of the lease existing at the time that the life estate was created would not serve to extend and continue the original lease.[43]

The speculations concerning the implications of the Youngman case were set to rest in Texas in the Texas Supreme Court case of Moore v. Vines.[44] In the Vines case, an oil and gas lease was executed by the life tenant and by the remainderman, after the termination of a prior oil and gas lease which was in existence at the time the life estate was created. The open mine doctrine applied to the prior lease. The question involved in the case was whether the open mine doctrine applied to the second lease, which would entitle the life tenant to all payments under the second lease.

It was held that the open mine doctrine applied to the prior lease which was in existence at the time that the life tenancy was created, but that the open mine doctrine ceased to be applied at the time of the termination of such lease. The implication that the open mine doctrine may apply to leases executed by the life tenant after the termination of a lease in existence at the time the life estate is created, as the result of some kind of dedication for such purpose due to execution of the first lease, was denied. The court stated:

"The better view, in our opinion, is that the open mine doctrine is not applicable beyond the lease in existence at the time of the

---

43. See Daniels v. Charles, 172 Ky. 238, 189 S.W. 192 and see Warren v. Martin, 168 Ark. 682, 272 S.W. 367; Heyser v. Frankfort Oil Co., C.A.10th, 316 F.2d 441, cert. denied 375 U.S. 824, 84 S.Ct. 64, 11 L.Ed.2d 56, to the effect that execution of a later lease will constitute abandonment of the probate homestead in the minerals. Cf. Thompson v. Thompson, 149 Tex. 632, 236 S.W.2d 779, noted in 30 Tex.L.Rev. 134.

44. Tex., 474 S.W.2d 437.

vesting of the life estate * * *. The rights of [the life tenant] in such respect rested on this lease and expired upon its termination. The lease executed after the vesting of the life estate was not the equivalent of an open mine at such prior time. [The] life tenant was not authorized by the will * * * to lease the land for mineral development nor was he given enjoyment of the proceeds from any such lease. Under these circumstances we are unable to attribute an intent * * * that the land should continue to be leased for mineral development for the benefit of [the life tenant] with a resulting diminishment in the value of the interest of the remaindermen."

A similar result to that in the Vines case is also found in the Oklahoma case of Nutter v. Stockton.[45] Here an oil and gas lease was followed by the creation in a will of a conventional life estate. After the expiration of the first lease, the life tenant executed a second lease, which the remainderman refused to ratify. The court held that where the first lease expired and no intent was shown in the will that the life tenant have the authority to execute additional leases, the open mine doctrine would not apply. As in the Vines case the court rejected the construction that the execution of the first lease prior to the creation of the life estate evidenced an intent to devote the land to continuing oil and gas exploration.

In regard to the second question, concerning the extent of the open mine, although cases are few, the extent to which the mine was opened would seem to be referable to the terms of the lease. Where the lease covers all the land in question and authorizes both oil and gas wells, where production exists from oil wells, and gas production is later found at lower depths, the open mine doctrine should also cover the production of the gas wells, or any other production allowable under the lease. As the rationale supporting the drilling of additional wells after the creation of the life estate is that the drilling is not being done by the life tenant but by the authority of the original lessor,[46] the extent of the dedication of the land for mining purposes should be described and limited by the intent of the lessor in the wording of the lease.

The open mine doctrine will apply either to conventional or legal life estates. The former are created by deed, trust, or will, and the latter by the operation of law. A common circumstance that gives rise to the creation of a legal life estate occurs many times when one

---

45. Okl., 626 P.2d 881. Also see Heyser v. Frankfort Oil Co., C.A.10th, 316 F.2d 441, cert. denied 375 U.S. 824, 84 S.Ct. 64, 11 L.Ed.2d 56. In the Heyser case the life estate was created by the probate homestead in W after the death of H, who also left children. W executed a second lease after the expiration of the first lease. The court held that the open mine doctrine did not apply to the second lease. However, the execution of the second lease by W also had the effect of abandoning the homestead rights of W. This resulted in W being a co-tenant with the children, terminating the life tenant-remainderman relationship.

46. Andrews v. Andrews, 31 Ind.App. 89, 67 N.E. 461.

§ 5.2   OWNERS OF INTERESTS   207

spouse dies leaving a surviving spouse. A right of dower,[47] curtesy,[48] or a forced share[49] may carry the characteristics of a legal life estate, as will the probate homestead in Texas and Oklahoma.[50] In Kentucky[51] the probate homestead merely gives a right of occupancy and not a life estate.

Where the lease is executed or is producing, as the case may be, prior to the creation of the particular legal life estate, the open mine doctrine will apply to such interests. However, one significant difference does exist between the legal life estate and the conventional life estate in regard to the application of the open mine doctrine. In jurisdictions such as Texas and Oklahoma, where H and W own lands and execute oil and gas leases prior to H's death, H is powerless to prevent the application of the open mine doctrine to lands covered by the probate homestead even though he may have prepared an estate plan expressly providing for the apportionment of proceeds of production between takers under his will.[52] This was one of the reasons that Judge Garwood opposed the application of the open mine doctrine to the probate homestead in the case of Youngman v. Schular.[53] Where an interest in the nature of the probate homestead is not involved, the grantor of a conventional life estate may expressly provide for the apportionment of proceeds in a manner different from that provided by law applying to leases by the life tenant and remainderman, or under the open mine doctrine.

(D) Application of the Uniform Trust Act and the Uniform Principal and Income Act

Where the life estate is contained in a trust, and where no provision is made for the apportionment of proceeds of production and other economic benefits payable under an oil and gas lease, it is expressly provided in the Uniform Principal and Income Act of 1962[54] that the remainderman will receive $27\frac{1}{2}\%$ of the gross proceeds (not to

---

47. Seager v. McCabe, 92 Mich. 186, 52 N.W. 299; but cf. Yost v. Ratliff, Ky., 246 S.W.2d 447.

48. Orndoff v. Consumer's Fuel Co., 308 Pa. 165, 162 A. 431, 31 Mich.L.Rev. 998 (joint lease with remainderman).

49. Cook v. Cook, Tex.Civ.App., 331 S.W.2d 77; Bergendahl v. Blanco Oil Co., Tex.Civ.App., 440 S.W.2d 81; Davis v. Atlantic Oil Producing Co., C.A.5th, 87 F.2d 75, 16 Tex.L.Rev. 420.

50. Aldridge v. Houston Oil Co., 116 Okl. 281, 244 P. 782; Swayne v. Lone Acre Oil Co., 98 Tex. 597, 86 S.W. 740; Petrus v. Cage Brothers, Tex.Civ.App., 128 S.W.2d 537; White v. Blackman, Tex. Civ.App., 168 S.W.2d 531; Youngman v. Shular, 155 Tex. 437, 288 S.W.2d 495, noted in 10 Sw.L.J. 449; 34 Tex.L.Rev. 328; 3 U.C.L.A.L.Rev. 601.

51. Brandenburg v. Petroleum Exploration, 218 Ky. 557, 291 S.W. 757.

52. Mitchell v. Mitchell, 298 S.W.2d 236, reversed on other grounds 157 Tex. 346, 303 S.W.2d 352; Cook v. Cook, Tex. Civ.App., 331 S.W.2d 77; Clyde v. Hamilton, Tex., 414 S.W.2d 434.

53. 155 Tex. 437, 288 S.W.2d 495, noted in 10 Sw.L.J. 449; 34 Tex.L.Rev. 328; 3 U.C.L.A.L.Rev. 601.

54. § 9. [Disposition of Natural Resources]

(a) If any part of the principal consists of a right to receive royalties, overriding or limited royalties, working interests, production payments, net profit interests, or other interests in minerals or other natural resources in, on or under land, the receipts from taking the natural re-

exceed 50% of the net proceeds, after deducting the expense and carrying the charge on such property) attributable to the royalty and bonuses, while the life tenant will receive the remaining $72\frac{1}{2}\%$ of production and the income (rentals).

Where the life estate is not contained in a trust, some application has been made of the Uniform Principal and Income Acts, prepared in 1931 and revised in 1962. Section 9 of the 1931 Act[55] provides that where no provision has been made, the life tenant is entitled to income from the corpus of the production but that the corpus will be preserved for the remainderman. This is a restatement of the common law rule. The 1931 Act applies to interests whether or not they are held in trust, and would therefore also apply to the ordinary legal or conventional life estate. Of the states that have adopted the 1931 Act, seven of them have adopted a different basis for apportionment of the proceeds of production of natural resources from that stated in the Act, which provisions apparently would apply to the proceeds of production from an oil and gas lease. It is not known whether these provisions would displace the rules applicable where the open mine

---

sources from the land shall be allocated as follows:

(1) If received as rent on a lease or extension payments on a lease, the receipts are income.

(2) If received from a production payment, the receipts are income to the extent of any factor for interest or its equivalent provided in the governing instrument. There shall be allocated to principal the fraction of the balance of the receipts which the unrecovered cost of the production payment bears to the balance owed on the production payment, exclusive of any factor for interest or its equivalent. The receipts not allocated to principal are income.

(3) If received as a royalty, overriding or limited royalty, or bonus, or from a working, net profit, or any other interest in minerals or other natural resources, receipts not provided for in the preceding paragraphs of this section shall be apportioned on a yearly basis in accordance with this paragraph whether or not any natural resource was being taken from the land at the time the trust was established. Twenty-seven and one-half per cent of the gross receipts (but not to exceed 50% of the net receipts remaining after payment of all expenses, direct and indirect, computed without allowance for depletion) shall be added to principal as an allowance for depletion. The balance of the gross receipts, after payment therefrom of all expenses, direct and indirect, is income.

(b) If a trustee, on the effective date of this Act, held an item of depletable property of a type specified in this section he shall allocate receipts from the property in the manner used before the effective date of this Act, but as to all depletable property acquired after the effective date of this Act by an existing or new trust, the method of allocation provided herein shall be used.

(c) This section does not apply to timber, water, soil, sod, dirt, turf, or mosses.

55. § 9. Disposition of Natural Resources

Where any part of the principal consists of property in lands from which may be taken timber, minerals, oils, gas or other natural resources and the trustee or tenant is authorized by law or by the terms of the transaction by which the principal was established to sell, lease or otherwise develop such natural resources, and no provision is made for the disposition of the net proceeds thereof after the payment of expenses and carrying charges on such property, such proceeds, if received as rent on a lease, shall be deemed income, but if received as consideration, whether as royalties or otherwise, for the permanent severance of such natural resources from the lands, shall be deemed principal to be invested to produce income. Nothing in this section shall be construed to abrogate or extend any right which may otherwise have accrued by law to a tenant to develop or work such natural resources for his own benefit.

doctrine would apply.[56] The 1962 Act, on the other hand, applies only to interests in trust and will not be applicable where the life estate is not so contained.

Where the states have changed Section 9 the apportionment method adopted varies greatly. In Texas,[57] for instance, royalty and bonus are apportioned according to the old percentage depletion formula of the Internal Revenue Code, (principal is $27\frac{1}{2}\%$ of the gross proceeds, not to exceed 50% of the net, and the income consists of the balance of the proceeds). The figures are fixed by the state statute.

In Oklahoma,[58] on the other hand, bonus is treated as income, and royalty is apportioned by the following formula: "Such percentage thereof *as is permitted to be deducted for depletion* under the *then* existing laws of the United States for federal income tax purposes shall be treated as principal * * *" (emphasis added) and the balance treated as income. This tying of the principal allocation to the federal income tax depletion provisions raises many problems. In the first instance, depletion of an economic interest in production must be the greater of percentage or cost depletion. The statutory provision would seem to require this calculation before allocation could be made.

Additional problems would seem to be caused by the provisions of the Tax Reduction Act of 1975. This act repealed percentage depletion for all but the independent producers and royalty owners and a few others, as defined in the act. It provides for a decreasing percentage from $27\frac{1}{2}\%$ to 15% in 1984. This decreasing percentage would also seem to apply to the determination of principal under the Oklahoma act. Production over the average daily production permitted by the act and production after a transfer of a proven property loses all right to percentage depletion. If royalty production in trust consisted in part of such production the question remains unanswered whether it would be deemed to be income. Acts such as that of Oklahoma, which are tied to the federal income tax provisions, would seem to be in need of revision.

56. States changing Section 9 of the 1931 Principal and Income Act are: Alabama, Code of Ala. Tit. 58, § 83; Colorado, C.R.S. '63, 57–4–9; Illinois, S.H.A. ch. 30, § 168; New Mexico, 1953 Comp. § 33–5–26; Oklahoma, 60 Okl.St.Ann. § 175.33; Pennsylvania, 20 P.S. § 3470.9; Texas, Art. 7425b, Section 33; Vermont, 14 V.S.A. § 3309; Wisconsin, W.S.A. 701.20.

In Commercial National Bank in Nacogdoches v. Hayter, Tex.Civ.App., 473 S.W.2d 561 (it was held that apportionment under the Texas Trust Act was mandatory in a testamentary trust where royalties were not directed to be paid to income beneficiaries and the term "income" was not defined).

57. Tex.Rev.Civ.Stat. art. 7425b, § 33.

58. 60 Okl.St.Ann. § 175.33.

§ 5.3 The Determinable Fee Estate, Estates Subject to a Power of Termination, and Fee Estates Subject to Executory Interests

The owner of a determinable or conditional fee, or one subject to an executory interest, unless expressly prohibited by the instrument creating the interest, has full interest in the minerals and may execute oil and gas leases and enjoy the full economic benefits from production during the duration of the fee interest.

The owner of the future interest will not have a cause of action for damages or for injunctive relief due to such production, even if there exists a reasonable possibility that the future interest will soon become possessory. It is probable that where the lease does not cover the future interest and the possessory estate comes to an end, the lease will terminate, and the lessee will have the status of a good-faith trespasser.

Unlike the owner of a life estate, the owner of the fee has full power to lease the subject land for oil and gas purposes. This is true whether or not the fee is subject to being cut short by the owner of the possibility of reverter, power of termination, or executory interest.[1]

Where the grant is limited in respect to the use of the land, unless expressly prohibited, the land may be used for secondary purposes, such as leasing and production for oil and gas, where such secondary use does not diminish the use of the land for the primary purpose stated in the limitation.[2]

The leading case is that of Skipper v. Davis,[3] where land was sold to a church "to be used for church purposes only and that in case the same is abandoned as such, that the title shall be revested * * *" in the grantors. Some time after the small rural church was estab-

---

1. Regular Predestinarian Baptist Church of Pleasant Grove v. Parker, 373 Ill. 607, 27 N.E.2d 522, 137 A.L.R. 635; Williams v. McKenzie, 203 Ky. 376, 262 S.W. 598; Sun Oil Co. v. Stout, La.App., 46 So.2d 151; Frensley v. White, 208 Okl. 209, 254 P.2d 982; Davis v. Skipper, 125 Tex. 364, 83 S.W.2d 318. In general see Browder, Defeasible Fee Estates in Oklahoma—An Addendum, 6 Okl.L.Rev. 482; Mosburg, Oil and Gas, and the Defeasible Fee, 12 Okl.L.Rev. 233; Williams, The Effect of Various Conditions of Ownership on Oil and Gas Transactions, 5 Utah L.Rev. 1; American Law of Property, Sections 4.104 and 4.105; and Restatement of the Law of Property Sections 49, 193, 194.

2. United States v. Illinois Central Railroad Co., C.A.7th, 187 F.2d 374 (for railroad); Regular Predestinarian Baptist Church of Pleasant Grove v. Parker, 373 Ill. 607, 27 N.E.2d 522, 137 A.L.R. 635 (church); Dees v. Cheuvronts, 240 Ill. 486, 88 N.E. 1011 (school); Williams v. McKenzie, 203 Ky. 376, 262 S.W. 598 (school district); City of Grand Rapids v. Central Land Co., 294 Mich. 103, 292 N.W. 579 (park, highway, street and boulevard purposes); Priddy v. School District No. 78, Cotton County, 92 Okl. 254, 219 P. 141, 39 A.L.R. 1334 (school); Frensley v. White, 208 Okl. 209, 254 P.2d 982 (church); Davis v. Skipper, 125 Tex. 364, 83 S.W.2d 318 (church). Cf. City of Grand Rapids v. Central Land Co., 294 Mich. 103, 292 N.W. 579; Sun Oil Co. v. Stout, La.App., 46 So.2d 151, which draws a distinction between donations for religious and community service purposes, which are treated as conveyances, and donations for other uses, which are held to create servitudes only and no interest in the minerals; United States v. Union Pacific Railroad Co., 353 U.S. 112, 77 S.Ct. 685, 1 L.Ed.2d 693, belatedly holding that Section 2 of the Right of Way Act of July 1, 1862, grants only a surface estate in the lands, distinguishing earlier cases which held that a limited base fee was created.

3. 125 Tex. 364, 83 S.W.2d 318.

§ 5.3 OWNERS OF INTERESTS 211

lished, the land was leased, and oil was found on the land. The membership of the church was then closed, and at about the same time the grantors apparently had second thoughts about the wisdom of conveying the land. Suit was brought on the reverter clause on the grounds: (1) That the leasing of the land for petroleum production and the resulting production constituted a breach of the limitation, (2) that production of oil and gas constituted waste to the holders of the possibility of reverter, and (3) that the limitation clause was a restrictive covenant that created an equitable right in gross in favor of the grantors.

The lower appellate court granted an injunction but was reversed by the Texas Supreme Court. The Court stated: "As plaintiffs have only a possibility of reverter, are they in a position to maintain an action for injunction to prevent the drilling of the oil well and the production of oil from the land? * * * So long as there is no abandonment of the land for church purposes, the trustees of the church have therein what has been termed a 'base, qualified or determinable fee.' Such an estate is a fee because by possibility it may endure forever; but 'as it depends upon the concurrence of collateral circumstances which qualify and debase the purity of the donation, it is therefore a qualified or base fee.' It follows, therefore, that the grantee under such a deed as is involved here may use the land to the extent of producing the oil and gas therefrom, and, conversely, the holder of a mere possibility of reverter has no such estate as authorizes him to maintain an injunction to prevent such use of the land." The court also found that the clause did not constitute a restrictive covenant.

As stated above, normally the owner of a limited fee is not subject to the doctrine of waste nor must he account to his reversioner for any portion of the economic benefits from the lease. However, where it appears reasonably certain that the future interest will vest, and that the owner of the limited fee is engaging in unconscionable or wanton conduct that will diminish the value of the estate for the holder of the future interest, the owner of the limited fee may be subject to an injunction to prevent waste.[4] The burden will be upon the hold-

---

4. Restatement of Property:
§ 49. Privilege to Use the Affected Land.
  The privilege of the owner of a possessory estate in fee simple defeasible to use the land is identical with that of an owner of a possessory estate in fee simple absolute, except that the privilege is limited by a duty not to commit waste.
Comment:
  a. Normal slightness of restriction on use. The duty not to commit waste is a duty, the extent of which is correlative to the degree of protection to which the owner of the future interest is entitled as against uses made by, or conduct of, the owner of the possessory estate. The future interest after an estate in fee simple defeasible must be either a possibility of reverter, a power of termination or an executory interest. Any one of these future interests normally is so tenuous that any substantial restriction upon the uses or conduct of the owner of such an estate would be unreasonable (see §§ 193, 194).
§ 193. Future Interest in Fee Simple Following a Present Estate in Fee Simple Defeasible or in Fee Simple Conditional—Injunctive Relief.

er of the future interest to establish these facts. It is the position of the American Law Institute that production of oil and gas is not an activity that would be classified as wanton or unconscionable conduct, and that conduct not wrongful when done will not be rendered wrongful by the estate's coming to an end.[5] If this view is followed, production of petroleum products by the owner of a limited fee will not be classified as waste or subject to injunctive relief.

When a future interest in fee simple is preceded only by a present estate in fee simple defeasible (defined § 16) or in fee simple conditional (defined § 17), then the owner of such future interest can obtain the appropriate prohibitive injunction against threatened conduct of the owner of the present estate when

(a) a reasonable probability exists that such future interest will become a present interest; and

(b) the conduct of the owner of such present estate threatens to destroy, or substantially to diminish the market value of that which the owner of the future interest would otherwise acquire upon his interest becoming a present interest; and

(c) such conduct is either wanton or unconscionable; and

(d) the owner of such present estate has no present absolute power to destroy this future interest and thereby to acquire for himself the economic advantages of ownership thereof.

h. Conduct which is within Clauses (b) and (c).

The traditional illustrations of conduct within Clauses (b) and (c) are the cutting of ornamental timber, or of unripe timber, and the destruction of the mansion house. In this connection "ornamental timber" includes all those trees and shrubs which the last owner of the estate in fee simple absolute manifested an intention to have left standing. Any conduct which a reasonable man, in the management and utilization of land owned by him in fee simple absolute, normally would make is not such conduct as comes within Clauses (b) and (c). Thus the owner of an estate in fee simple defeasible or in fee simple conditional normally is not restricted in cutting timber for sale, in opening mines, in drilling for oil, or in removing or altering buildings.

Also see:

§ 194. Future Interest in Fee Simple Following a Present Estate in Fee Simple Defeasible or in Fee Simple Conditional—No Recovery of Damages.

When a future interest in fee simple is preceded only by a present estate in fee simple defeasible (defined § 16) or in fee simple conditional (defined § 17), then the owner of such future interest

(a) while his interest continues to be future, cannot recover damages from the owner of such present estate for conduct of such present owner decreasing the value of the future interest; and

(b) after his interest becomes a present interest, cannot recover damages from the owner of such formerly present estate, or from his personal representative, for any conduct of such former owner while in possession other than conduct which would have been sufficient to base the granting of a prohibitive injunction under the rule stated in § 193.

Reprinted with permission of American Law Institute.

5. Comment to Section 194:

a. Rationale. The fee simple character of the present estate normally includes an uncertainty as to whether the present estate will ever end. This fact precludes for the duration of this uncertainty any recovery of damages by the person to whom the future interest has been limited. Thus the rule stated in Clause (a) excludes both the individual recovery of damages of the type allowed under the rules stated in §§ 187 and 191 and also the representative recovery of damages of the type allowed under the rules stated in §§ 189(1)(c) and 192(a). The rule stated in Clause (b) is a further application of the inference of fact that the creation of a present estate in fee simple defeasible or in fee simple conditional manifests the intent of the creator thereof to confer large liberty of action upon the recipient thereof. Conduct not wrongful when done is not rendered wrongful by the doer's estate coming to an end. Reprinted with permission of American Law Institute.

Although the owner of the limited fee estate may lease and produce petroleum products during the life of the limited fee estate, what is the status of a lease that does not include the future interest when the estate terminates, and the future interest becomes possessory? Consider the situation where O conveys Blackacre to A, for so long as the University football team does not win the Conference football championship. A then leases the land to Texaco, Inc., for oil and gas exploration and production. Texaco drills a producing oil well, and three years later University wins the football crown. What is the status of the Texaco lease? Since the future interest was not covered by the lease, presumably, upon occurrence of the event, the lease is lost, and Texaco would be in the situation of the good-faith trespasser.[6]

As a practical matter, the owner of a future interest should be joined in the execution of the lease. It may be possible to obtain such interest by the payment of only a small cash payment; however, where a larger payment or an additional payment out of production is demanded the amount of consideration will have to be weighed against the possibility that the future interest will become possessory.

§ 5.4 Lands Subject to Servitudes and Restrictions

Where lands to be leased are subject to servitudes or restrictions, care must be used to determine that a lease covers all rights to possession or occupancy in the land.

A fruitful area for litigation is where leases are taken upon rights-of-way, strips adjoining roadways, etc. In these situations the language of the granting clause in the particular instrument must be carefully studied in order to determine the nature of the rights created. Where sufficiently broad, a conveyance of a right-of-way may constitute a full fee conveyance. Where only an easement has been created, however, the owner of such interest does not have the right to lease; this right remains in the owner of the mineral estate.[1]

Although the owner of an easement right does not have the right to execute oil and gas leases, he may enjoin third parties, including lessees of the minerals, from interfering with the enjoyment of the easement. The lessee of mineral rights under lands subject to such rights may find himself forced to drill directionally in order to remove the petroleum products.

When acquiring deeds for a roadway, it has become customary for government agencies to use a deed form that will enable them to use

---

6. See Andrews v. Brown, Tex.Civ.App., 283 S.W. 288, affirmed Com.App. 10 S.W.2d 707, where the court refused to discuss this situation.

1. See: Texas Co. v. Newton Naval Stores Co., 223 Miss. 468, 78 So.2d 751, 49 A.L.R.2d 1182; Aubert v. St. Louis-San Francisco Railway Co., 207 Okl. 537, 251 P.2d 190; Haines v. McLean, 154 Tex. 272, 276 S.W.2d 777.

gravel, caliche, sand, etc., for road building purposes. However, in many instances, the granting clause used may be broad enough to embrace the entire mineral estate. The careful draftsman of an instrument conveying a right-of-way or other surface rights will expressly reserve the mineral estate, other than that which will be necessary for the purposes of the grant, together with the right to drill directionally to remove the minerals.

Another situation is where the land to be leased is a strip of land adjoining other land of the grantor. A common illustration is that concerning ownership of the strip of land underlying a roadway adjoining property to be leased. When O conveys Blackacre to A by a boundary description without mention of the roadways abutting Blackacre, who has the right to lease the strip—O, who originally owned the land at the time the road right-of-way was executed, or A?

The ownership of such strips is covered in any elementary text of real property, and local law will have to be referred to to determine the rules of construction that are to be followed. Normally, however, unless an express intent to exclude such strip can be found in the instrument, it will be presumed that the strip of land followed the conveyance to A. In the majority of jurisdictions, the mere fact that it is not included within the boundary description, or that the description of the property commenced in the common boundary line of the street and the property rather than in the center line of the street does not indicate such an intent to exclude the strip.[2] However, this is not true where the same grantor owns land on both sides of the right-of-way or street.[3] Many other examples of strip ownership may be encountered; however, they are too extensive to be covered in this treatise.

§ 5.5 Landlord and Tenant

Where the minerals are severed either by deed or by oil and gas lease prior to the execution of a non-mineral lease for years, the tenant for years will be subject to the rights of the owners of the mineral estate to use so much of the land as is reasonably necessary for the development and production of oil and gas.

Where no mineral severance has occurred, and the owner of the land executes a non-mineral lease "for agricultural purposes," or other use incident to the surface, it appears to be the trend that such lease will be treated as separating the surface from the mineral estate, so that the non-mineral lease will be subject to the use of the surface for development of the minerals. There is some authority for the proposition that in such

2. Joens v. Baumbach, 193 Cal. 567, 226 P. 400; In re Parkway in the City of New York, 209 N.Y. 344, 103 N.E. 508; New Orleans & Northeastern Railroad Co. v. Morrison, 203 Miss. 791, 35 So.2d 68; Rio Bravo Oil Co. v. Weed, 121 Tex. 427, 50 S.W.2d 1080, 85 A.L.R. 391; MacCorkle v. City of Charleston, 105 W.Va. 395, 142 S.E. 841, 58 A.L.R. 231. Contra: Salter v. Jonas, 39 N.J.L. 469, and see Hamlin v. Attorney General, 195 Mass. 309, 81 N.E. 275.

3. Couch v. Texas & Pacific Railway Co., 99 Tex. 464, 90 S.W. 860, and see In re Robbins, 34 Minn. 99, 24 N.W. 356.

instances the later oil and gas lease would constitute a breach of the covenant of quiet enjoyment of the prior lease.

Where no mineral severance has occurred, and a non-mineral lease is executed for years without restriction on use, the better view is that the execution of a later oil and gas lease would not be effective, as the possessory right to all of the land for the term of years is in the prior tenant. The production of petroleum products by a tenant for years under an unrestricted lease will constitute waste and may be enjoined.

O, the owner of Blackacre in fee, executes a lease to farmer Jones "for agricultural purposes only." Subsequently, Black Gold Oil Company sends their "lease hound" into the area and asks him to secure a block of oil and gas leases. Lease hound secures a lease from O and assigns it to Black Gold Oil Company. When it attempts to enter the property Black Gold is confronted by farmer Jones and is told that farmer Jones has the primary right to the land under his prior agricultural lease. Black Gold is charged with notice of the prior rights from the possession of farmer Jones. Whose right is superior?

Very little authority is found defining the rights of parties where a prior non-mineral lease is involved. Partly, if not altogether, this is due to the fact that the later oil and gas lessee will normally be able to secure a "Tenant's Consent Agreement" by a payment to the prior tenant covering estimated damages for use of the surface in the petroleum operations. The agreement subordinates the right of the prior tenant to the later oil and gas lease.

In some situations a severance of the mineral rights or estate may have occurred prior to the execution of the non-mineral lease.[1] Here the non-mineral lessee will have acquired his interests subject to the right of the owners of the severed minerals to enter and develop the land for oil and gas.[2]

Where a prior severance of the minerals has not occurred by way of deed or by statutory enactment, the rights of the subsequent oil and gas lessee will depend upon the nature of the rights created under the prior lease.

In the illustration above, may the lessee for "agricultural purposes only" obtain injunctive relief against the entry of the later oil and gas lessee, or if entry has occurred, damages for injury to the use of the surface for farming purposes? Does such action by the oil and gas lessee constitute a breach of the covenant of quiet enjoy-

---

1. Herein defined as a lease not primarily for mining purposes.

2. Where a later non-mining lease is expressly made subject to the rights of developers of the mineral estate, the latter will be liable only for negligent conduct. Where merely later in time and therefore subject to the rights of prior outstanding mineral interests of which the later non-mineral lessee has or is charged with notice, the developer of the minerals has a right to use only that portion of the surface as is reasonably necessary for such operations. Kemmerer v. Midland Oil & Drilling Co., C.A.8th, 229 F. 872; Anderson-Prichard Oil Corp. v. McBride, 188 Okl. 384, 109 P.2d 221; Mid-Continent Petroleum Corp. v. Rhodes, 205 Okl. 651, 240 P.2d 95; Pace v. State ex rel. Rice, 191 Miss. 780, 4 So. 2d 270; Placid Oil Co. v. Lee, Tex.Civ. App., 243 S.W.2d 860.

ment? Although development and production of petroleum products will constitute a substantial interference with the use of the premises by the agricultural lessee, the trend of the law apparently is to answer the question in the negative.[3]

The rationale for a negative answer has been a view by the courts that a lease for years for a purpose relating to surface occupancy creates a separation or severance of the minerals from the surface. An analogy has been drawn to the situation where O, the owner of the fee, executes a deed conveying the surface only, leaving the minerals in the grantor. When this view is followed, the surface lessee takes his rights subject to the burden of an easement in favor of the dominant mineral estate, allowing the use of so much of the surface as is reasonably necessary for development and production of oil and gas. This doctrine is aptly stated by the court in Stanolind Oil & Gas Co. v. Wimberly:[4] "Since appellee's lease was for 'grazing purposes only,' and not a conveyance of the minerals, it operated as a severance of the mineral estate owned by Mrs. Allison from the leasehold surface estate acquired by appellee under his grazing lease. Appurtenant to such mineral estate, which appellant subsequently acquired, as well as to the mineral estate theretofore acquired by it though not specifically granted, was the right of ingress and egress, and the right to use so much of the surface of the land as might be reasonably necessary to enforce and enjoy the mineral estate so acquired."

This result may be questioned on the ground of whether the grantor at the time of making the non-mineral lease intended to subject the leasehold to the burden of an easement in favor of the minerals, especially in situations where no oil or gas development has occurred in the area. This situation is distinguishable from one where a severance in fee has been made of the mineral estate and if no easement for development existed the value of the mineral estate would be lost. In the case of an estate for years, upon termination of the possessory estate, an event certain to occur, the mineral estate may be developed by the then fee owner, if desired. The social utility of land for agri-

---

3. Anderson-Prichard Oil Corp. v. McBride, 188 Okl. 384, 109 P.2d 221; Stanolind Oil & Gas Co. v. Wimberly, Tex.Civ. App., 181 S.W.2d 942; Hagar v. Martin, Tex.Civ.App., 277 S.W.2d 195. In Hagar v. Martin, O executed a gravel lease to A. O then executed to B a lease for "dairy farming." While the dairy lease was in effect the first gravel lease terminated and O executed a second gravel lease to C. It was held that the right to the minerals stayed in O in the interim period, and the dairy tenant was subject to the rights of C under the second gravel lease. Although the court stated that the first gravel lease severed the minerals, which stayed in O and passed to C, the same result would occur if it had viewed the dairy lease as creating the severance. But see: Republic Natural Gas Co. v. Melson, Okl., 274 P.2d 543, where the court stated: "That contention, however, does not take into consideration the fact that plaintiff had leased the premises for 'agricultural purposes,' and had gone into possession several weeks prior to the execution and delivery of defendant's mineral lease and several months prior to the drilling operations. Therefore, the oil and gas lease was subject to plaintiff's rights under the agricultural lease and defendant was liable for all damage done to plaintiff's crops." Under the Melson view would the dairy lease, B, in Hagar v. Martin have been superior to C, the later gravel lease?

4. Tex.Civ.App., 181 S.W.2d 942.

cultural uses is at least as great as it is for extraction of petroleum products.

Although in many cases a lease for years "for agricultural purposes," "for grazing purposes," "for dairy farming," or other use incident to the surface will create a separation of the surface and mineral estate, what of the lease for years of land which contains no restrictions on use, or reservations or exceptions?

In two cases where the question was posed, unfortunately, the ultimate decision was that a mineral severance had occurred either prior to the non-mineral lease in question, or that the non-mineral lease covered only the surface. Gulf Refining Co. of Louisiana v. Terry [5] was concerned with a lease that covered "the above described land" and contained no restrictions on use. It was executed by the county in 1846. An oil and gas lease was executed in 1929. It was held that the county could not lease for oil and gas during the term of the 99-year lease, as the term "land" included the minerals. However, the Gulf case was later expressly overruled in the case of Pace v. State ex rel. Rice [6] where it was stated that where the sovereign was concerned, the lease would be construed against the grantee, that the usual purposes for which lands are leased were agricultural purposes, and that the minerals would not pass unless clearly stated.

A similar result occurred in Kemmerer v. Midland Drilling Co.,[7] again concerning leases where a sovereign right was indirectly concerned. The lands concerned were Indian lands, and it was held that in enacting a prior federal statute authorizing the leasing for oil and gas in what was formerly Indian territory, Congress had in effect severed the minerals from the rest of the land. Following this enactment O leased the land without restriction to A, who went into possession of the surface. O then leased to B for oil and gas purposes. Due to the prior federal enactment, it was held that the prior lease to A was subject to the mineral rights theretofore severed. However, in a strong dissenting opinion, Justice Sanborn stated:

> "The main question in the case is: May the owner of a tract of land who has leased it for years without any reservation, restriction, or exceptions to a lessee who has taken possession thereof under a lease, vest in a second lessee by a subsequent lease of the right to take oil or gas from the land, or by any other subsequent grant or lease, the right to deprive the first lessee of his right to the exclusive possession of every part of the surface of and of the land itself during the term of his prior lease? The majority answer this question in the affirmative. It seems to me that it should be answered in the negative.

* * *

5. 163 Miss. 869, 142 So. 457.
6. 191 Miss. 780, 4 So.2d 270.
7. C.A.8th, 229 F. 872.

"This lease contains no restrictions to agricultural, mining, or any other purpose; no exceptions, no reservations. It was a lease not of the surface only, nor of any stratum only, but of the lands and premises described in it.

* * *

"While one is the owner of a tract of land, he may separate it into different strata, and grant the right to one stratum to one party, and the right to another stratum to another party; but when he has parted with all his right and title to all of his tract he can no longer subdivide it, or grant any right in it."

Where no prior severance has occurred, by the terms of the lease the possessory right to the entire fee would be in the tenant. It would therefore seem that a later lease for oil and gas purposes would not pass any possessory right in the land. For the oil and gas lease to become effective, the lessee would also have to acquire a like lease or ratification from the tenant for years. However, where the prior lease is without restriction and is a periodic tenancy, and after the execution of a later oil and gas lease, upon the expiration of the first period the petroleum lease will become prior.[8]

Where the non-mineral lease for years is limited or restricted, the tenant for years may not execute effective oil and gas leases on the lands. The lessor, owner of the reversion, is in the same position as either a reversioner subject to an estate for life or a vested remainderman following a life estate. The doctrine of waste will apply, and the tenant for years may not commit waste by removing petroleum products from under the land.[9] As in the case of the life tenant, a lease for development of the premises would have to be obtained from the tenant for years and from the lessor.

§ 5.6 Lands Subject to Security Interests

Where land is subject to an outstanding mortgage, the ability of the mortgagor to execute an effective oil and gas lease, will depend upon whether the particular jurisdiction follows a title or lien theory of mortgages.

In a title-theory-of-mortgages jurisdiction, production of petroleum products by the mortgagor will constitute an injury to the security of the mortgagee. In a lien- or hybrid-theory jurisdiction, injury to the security of the mortgagor will not occur until his security is impaired. This is usually stated to be when the value of the property becomes less than the balance of the debt. Where the mortgage is superior to a later oil and gas lease, a subordination agreement normally will be acquired by the lessee from the mortgagee.

If a subordination agreement is not obtained, a foreclosure of the prior mortgage will destroy the later lease. However, if the lessee did not

---

8. Robinson Drilling Co. v. Moses, Tex.Civ.App., 256 S.W.2d 650. However, the periodic tenant in possession must have either actual or constructive notice of the later-in-time oil and gas lease.

9. See § 5.2, supra.

assume to pay the prior debt, a right of marshalling may be available upon foreclosure.

Consider the situation where O, the landowner, has purchased land for which part of the purchase money has been borrowed from a lending institution. For security of the lending institution, O executed a mortgage describing all of Blackacre. O then desires to execute an oil and gas lease to Black Gold Oil Co. What will be the relative positions of the mortgagee and the lessee? The same situation may occur where the security instrument is executed incident to a loan for improvements. If O is the owner of the entire fee, surface and mineral, at the time of the execution of the mortgage and the lease, the lease of Black Gold Oil Co. will be subject to the mortgage.

The rights of Black Gold Oil Co. will vary according to the jurisdiction in which the land is situated. Some states follow the common law theory of mortgages, under which title and the right to possession to the property passes to the mortgagee.[1]

Other states follow the lien theory of mortgages.[2] In the latter jurisdictions the mortgagor retains title and possession to the property, subject to security rights of the mortgagee. These rights are non-possessory in character, being in the nature of a right to sell the subject property upon default. Assuming that the mortgagee buys in at a foreclosure sale, in a lien state its right thereupon becomes possessory. An intermediate or hybrid theory is followed in some jurisdictions, where the right of the mortgagee becomes possessory upon default.[3]

Although no cases were found, in those states which recognize the mortgage as passing title and possession to the mortgagee, it would appear that the mortgagor would be unable to execute a lease that would be effective to vest either title to or the right to possession of the minerals.[4] In such states an oil and gas lease should be executed or ratified by both the mortgagee and the mortgagor. In those jurisdictions the right of the mortgagor to do acts on the land is in the nature of a license, and is usually limited to acts that are proper in the course of good husbandry. This view would deny the right of the mortgagor, or his lessee, to develop the land for oil and gas. Where title to or possession of the land, including the minerals, is in the mortgagee, removal of oil or gas from the land is an injury to the mortgagee's interest, enjoinable in equity and compensible in damages for the products removed. It has been held that where the mortgagor has opened a mine prior to the execution of the mortgage,

---

1. Osborne, Mortgages, §§ 13, 14, 15. In general see: Ledbetter, Mortgages of Land Affecting Subsequent Mineral Interests, 32 Tex.L.Rev. 740; Vagts, Impact of the Uniform Commercial Code on the Oil and Gas Mortgage, 43 Tex.L.Rev. 825.

2. Osborne, Mortgages, § 15.
3. Osborne, Mortgages, § 14.
4. Osborne, Mortgages, § 125.

under the open mine doctrine, he has the right to continue production.[5]

In states following a lien or hybrid concept, the owner of the land subject to the mortgage has a right to execute an oil and gas lease that will invest the lessee with the right to possession, limited only by provisions of the mortgage or safeguards erected by judicial decision.[6] Unless the mortgage instrument defines removal of such products as waste, the limitation on the right of the mortgagor or his lessee to remove petroleum products is that point at which the security of the mortgagee is impaired.[7] In the Texas case of Carroll v. Edmondson,[8] it was held that security is not impaired until the value of the property is reduced below the balance due on the debt. The case has been criticized on the ground that the true test for impairment of security is not when the value of the property becomes less than the balance owing, but when the ratio of the value of the property to the balance due is diminished.

For instance, it is customary for lending institutions not to lend 100% on the dollar, but to require that a cushion of value exist in the collateral property to support the loan. A bank might lend $6,000 on property worth $10,000. Assume that the collateral property is damaged or the value lessened so that when $3,000 is owing upon the debt, the remaining property worth is only $4,000. On the original loan the ratio of property value to loan outstanding is 5 to 3, but in the latter instance it is reduced to 4 to 3. Under the Carroll case the security is not impaired; however, it is arguable that where the loan balance/property value ratio is lessened, security is impaired.

In most instances, removal of petroleum products in lien- and hybrid-theory states would seem not to affect the security ratio of most loans. Usually the loan appraisal will be directed at values for surface usage and will not include the value of the minerals. Unless the operations for development are sufficiently injurious to the surface to affect the security ratio, removal of petroleum products will leave the ratio unaffected.

In both title and lien states the mortgagee would be overjoyed if petroleum products could be found on non-residential property, for this will constitute an additional source of income to the mortgagor. In title states the payment of the economic benefits under the lease would seem to be payable directly to the mortgagee. In absence of an effective assignment, they are not so payable in lien- or hybrid-theory states, at least until the mortgagee acquires the right of possession. However, the oil and gas lessee is at least as anxious to have his lease out from under the prior mortgage. Therefore, in the

---

5. Federal Land Bank of New Orleans v. Mulhern, 180 La. 627, 157 So. 370, 95 A.L.R. 948, 9 Tul.L.Rev. 283.

6. Osborne, Mortgages, §§ 126, 127.

7. Of course, removal of such products may be made an event of default under an express clause of the mortgage, see Federal Land Bank of New Orleans v. Mulhern, 180 La. 627, 157 So. 370, 95 A.L.R. 948, 9 Tul.L.Rev. 283.

8. Tex.Com.App., 41 S.W.2d 64.

usual situation in which an oil and gas lease is executed after the mortgage is executed, the lending institution will execute a subordination agreement,[9] subordinating the mortgage to the oil and gas lease, its equipment, and the products produced thereunder.[10] In return, the mortgagor executes an assignment of the economic benefits from the lease to the mortgagee.

Where the oil and gas lease is acquired subsequent to the mortgage, and the lessee does not assume payment of any part of the prior indebtedness, and where the bonus for the lease is not reduced by reason of the outstanding security instrument, the lease is "subject to" the lien of the prior mortgage, but the lessee is not personally liable for payment. Where the debtor defaults and the mortgage is foreclosed, normally all of the property will be sold, and the later oil and gas lease, unless a subordination was obtained, will be wiped out.[11]

However, in equity, where O executes a mortgage and then sells off parcels of land and the purchasers do not assume payment of any part of the debt, the mortgagor's retained land at the time of each sale is looked at as the primary fund for collateral security of the debt. In the event of default, if the rights of the mortgagee will not be injured, the purchaser from O has the right that O's property as the primary fund be sold first to see if it will satisfy the balance outstanding.

Where several persons have so purchased, each in turn may assert the right that the land which remained in O's ownership at the time each bought be sold first. Hence, upon sale, O's retained land, if any, is sold first, followed, until satisfaction of the debt, by a sale of each tract of land purchased from O, with the land sold the latest in time being sold first. The doctrine is called marshalling, and, where asserted, the lands will be sold in the inverse order of their alienation. The right to marshall must be asserted during the judicial foreclosure. In states that allow out-of-court foreclosure by a trustee, the right to marshall may be asserted by enjoining the trustee's sale and forcing a judicial foreclosure.

The doctrine of marshalling has been applied to severed mineral estates, where the severance occurred either by deed or oil and gas

---

9. See Frede v. Lauderdale, Tex.Civ. App., 322 S.W.2d 379, where an argument was unsuccessfully made that the subordination agreement actually was a release of the minerals from the mortgage.

10. See Continental Securities Corp. v. Wetherbee, 187 La. 773, 175 So. 571, where it was held that an exception clause in the mortgage which read: "This act of mortgage does not, in any way, affect or apply to the oil and/or gas which has been or may be produced * * * shall have the right to sell said oil and/or gas * * * free from any lien, privilege, or incumbrance resulting from this mortgage * * *," freed the production from the well from the mortgage, but that all physical equipment used in connection with the well, including pipe, rigs, etc., were caught by the mortgage.

11. Skelly Oil Co. v. Johnson, 209 Ark. 1107, 194 S.W.2d 425; State ex rel. Commissioners of Land Office v. Reynolds, 201 Okl. 400, 206 P.2d 184; Noble v. Kahn, 206 Okl. 13, 240 P.2d 757, 35 A.L.R.2d 119.

lease. In such cases it has been required that the surface be sold prior to the sale of the minerals.¹² Where the mortgagee can show that hardship will occur due to the fact that the land will thereby be offered piecemeal, the right to marshall will be denied. It also may be waived by the parties by not claiming the right during the judicial foreclosure,¹³ by stipulation during trial, or by express clauses in the mortgage.

Maurer v. Arab Petroleum Corporation,¹⁴ concerned a mineral deed that contained the following clause: "Grantor further agrees that Grantee, its heirs, executors, administrators and assigns shall have the right at anytime to redeem for Grantor or its heirs, executors, administrators and assigns by payment, any deed of trust, taxes, judgments or other liens on the above described land, in the event of default of payment of Grantors, and be subrogated to the rights of the holder or holders thereof." In holding that the clause constituted a waiver of the right to marshall by the grantee, the court stated that the clause constituted a recognition that the prior vendor's lien was to remain a common charge upon the whole premises. The case seems wrong. The clause is general in its nature and protective as to any number of encumbrances that might become prior to the mineral interest of the grantee. It doesn't presently purport to recognize any lien as a charge upon the mineral interest. The case may have an extensive application if followed, as most oil and gas leases contain similar provisions. It is thought that the preferable view is that the inclusion of such a clause is not a waiver of the right to marshall.

One acquiring an oil and gas lease must determine that former security instruments are either barred of record or by an applicable statute of limitations. Where land is acquired subject to an existing lien, care must be taken to see that no extensions of the indebtedness have been made by the persons primarily liable for the debt, as such extensions may be binding during the extension period as to all property subject to the lien, whether or not the owner of such property has joined in the extension.¹⁵ Special care must be taken of federal tax liens which may be extended beyond the six-year limitation period without the extension being recorded. In these cases a release will be required.¹⁶

Unexpected results may occur where the priority of the senior and junior chains of title may become reversed by operation of the doctrine of after-acquired title. O gives a mortgage to Bank, and than executes to B a mineral deed, which is recorded, as was the mort-

12. Miller v. Cisco, 279 Ky. 440, 130 S.W.2d 783; Dowling v. Springer, 186 Okl. 656, 100 P.2d 278; Continental Oil Co. of Texas v. Graham, Tex.Civ.App., 8 S.W.2d 719; 7 Tex.L.Rev. 323.

13. First National Bank in Wellington v. McClellan, Tex.Civ.App., 117 S.W.2d 807.

14. 134 Tex. 256, 135 S.W.2d 87, 131 A.L.R. 1, 18 Tex.L.Rev. 460.

15. Texas Land and Mortgage Co. v. Cohen, 138 Tex. 464, 159 S.W.2d 859; Countiss v. Baldwin, Tex.Civ.App., 151 S.W.2d 235.

16. The Federal Tax Lien Act of 1966, Public Law 89–719, 80 Stat. 1125.

gage. Bank forecloses and buys in the property and later re-sells it to O. O then executes an oil and gas lease to Rex Oil Company. The lease is a nullity. Upon re-acquiring the title to Blackacre, title to the minerals passed *eo instante* to B. Although B's title was junior to that of the bank, when Bank sold to O and the minerals passed to B by estoppel by deed, B's mineral deed became senior. Since it was recorded, Rex Oil Company, a subsequent purchaser, is charged with constructive notice of the deed. Likewise, if O had executed an oil and gas lease to B, who did not go into possession or record, upon re-acquisition of title by after-acquired title following the foreclosure, the oil and gas lease to Rex Oil Company would have cut off the unrecorded lease to B. After passage of the after-acquired title, B would have been in the senior chain of title, but was unrecorded as to Rex, a subsequent purchaser for value.[17]

§ 5.7 Leases from Persons Acting in a Representative Capacity

It has been held that a power of attorney authorizing an agent to "sell and convey" land does not include the power to execute oil and gas leases. However, in the case of a trust where the trustee is empowered to "sell, convey, and manage" the trust estate, it is generally held that the trustee has the power to execute leases for oil and gas. Where the trustee does not have an express power to sell any part of the lands in trust, any power to lease for oil and gas will have to be implied from the facts and circumstances surrounding the use of the land at the time the trust was executed in relation to the purposes of the trust.

The courts are divided as to whether an oil and gas lease executed by a trustee, under common law, may last beyond the termination of a trust. Statutory authority authorizing oil and gas leases by trustees provides for a life beyond termination of the trust.

Proceeds payable to trusts providing for beneficiaries of successive interests are apportionable between the successive beneficiaries of the trust as though the interests were not in trust. However, apportionment may differ where expressly so stated by the trustor, or by applicable state statute.

By the better view, where the trust is located in one state and the oil or gas production in another, the views of the state of the situs of production should control, both as to the characterization of the nature of the economic benefits from the lease and as to the allocation rule applied.

In the absence of legislation or of an express or implied power in a will to execute an oil and gas lease, administrators and executors of decedents' estates and guardians of minors and incompetents have no power to execute such leases. However, most jurisdictions with substantial oil and gas production have enacted statutes permitting the execution of oil and gas leases and the dealing with oil and gas interests by dependent administrators, executors, and guardians.

---

17. See Scott v. Cohen, C.C.A.5th, 115 F.2d 704; Caswell v. Llano Oil Co., 120 Tex. 139, 36 S.W.2d 208; Cherry v. Farmers Royalty Holding Co., 138 Tex. 579, 160 S.W.2d 908.

Where no express authority exists in a will, it is thought to be the general rule that a power to sell land will not include the power to execute oil and gas leases, although there exist a few cases to the contrary. Where independent administration of a decedent's estate exists, it is doubtful whether such executors have power to execute oil and gas leases, where no express power is set forth in the will (and where recourse cannot be made to legislation relating to dependent personal representatives).

In community property jurisdictions a spouse may have authority as community survivor, where the other spouse is either dead or incompetent, to execute oil and gas leases.

Where future interests run to unascertainable persons, leases may be obtained that bind such interests either through a judicial action applying the doctrine of virtual representation, or by legislation allowing leasing of such interests by means of statutory trusteeships under judicial control.

In many instances it will be necessary to obtain leases from persons acting in a representative capacity. This may include any of the following:

(1) Attorneys-in-fact, acting under a power of attorney.

(2) Trustees.

(3) Guardians of minors and incompetents.

(4) Administrators, executors, and independent executors of decedents' estates.

(5) Community survivors, qualified and unqualified.

(6) Partnerships, corporations, and other business entities.

(7) Political subdivisions, including cities, towns, and school districts.

(8) Sovereign entities, federal, state, and local.

(9) Unascertainable owners of future interests.

Obviously, in such situations, leases must be obtained from persons with authority to bind the entity owning the mineral estate. In any particular jurisdiction, recourse must be made to local law in order to determine the particular steps to be taken in acquiring the lease.

In general, where a lease is obtained from one in a representative capacity, it is necessary to determine that the grant of supporting authority is sufficiently broad to encompass the acts contemplated as to the mineral estate. In this regard it is necessary to determine whether the authority relates to the execution of oil and gas leases, allows the execution of mineral conveyances, authorizes the reception of delay rentals or shut-in royalties, or the execution of pooling and unitization agreements.

Not only must such authorization exist, it must be in effect at the time of the act or acts envisioned. Therefore, not only must this determination be made in an initial instance, it should also be made each

§ 5.7   OWNERS OF INTERESTS   225

time that it is necessary to deal with one in a representative capacity. An instance is that of periodic payments under an oil and gas lease. The guardianship of a minor or incompetent will cease with the majority of the minor or the restoration of the mentally incompetent. The authority of the administrator or executor will cease upon closing of the estate or (where an order of distribution is not required) upon the payment of all the debts of the estate. Keeping these general comments in mind, we will now turn to a brief consideration of the problems involved in each of the above enumerated categories.

(A) Attorneys-in-Fact

A dearth of authority exists relating to the ability of one acting under a power of attorney to execute an oil and gas lease for his principal. Normally, however, the authority of the agent is strictly construed and will only extend by implication to such matters which are necessary for carrying the authority into effect. In the Texas case of Bean v. Bean,[1] it was held that where authority existed to "grant, sell, and convey" certain land, the agent had only a "naked power of sale of land, and such power does not include the right to lease it." The court predicated its interpretation of the scope of the power on the common everyday parlance of the average owner who would not understand that a right to sell land also carries with it the right to sell minerals apart from it.

Although a general rule cannot be formulated from the existing state of authorities, a careful draftsman will include specific powers to deal with the minerals apart from the surface where such are desired by the parties. The power of attorney dealing with the minerals will also be subject to other rules of law regarding delegation of powers, including the rule that unless the power delegated is coupled with an interest in the land, the authority will terminate upon the death of the principal.

(B) Trustees

Whether or not a trustee has the power to execute an oil and gas lease upon lands which are the *res* of a trust, will depend upon the terms of the trust, or in the absence of authority so provided, upon legislation that may exist in a particular jurisdiction. Authority to lease may be found from the terms of the trust where expressly set

---

1. Tex.Civ.App., 79 S.W.2d 652. Also see: Bolton v. Rouss, 144 La. 134, 80 So. 226. The Bean case was later distinguished in the Texas case of Avis v. First National Bank of Wichita Falls, 141 Tex. 489, 174 S.W.2d 255, which dealt with the power of a trustee to lease. In this case the court found an implied power to lease for oil and gas purposes from the clause that granted the trustee the "full, ample, complete and absolute power to manage, control, sell and dispose of said trust property, rent, make leases thereon, and in every way handle same. * * * " Would a similar power in a power of attorney authorize the execution of oil and gas leases? Customarily the power of a trustee is construed more broadly than is that of the agent. In general see American Law of Property, §§ 12.55 and 12.80.

forth in the instrument, or by necessary implication from the purposes of the trust. Where expressly set forth, no particular problem is presented other than that the prescribed procedure is followed by the trustee.

Where authority is not expressly set forth, the power to lease may be implied from the express powers set forth in the trust when related to the general purpose of the trust. It is generally held that where the trustee is invested with full power to sell and dispose of the estate, this power will also include the right to execute oil and gas leases.[2] Several cases justify the result on the rationale that the power to sell the fee also includes the power to carve out lesser interests such as an oil and gas lease,[3] whereas other jurisdictions reason that as oil and gas are part of the realty, a strict construction of the trust verbiage would include petroleum leases.[4] The Texas case of Avis v. First National Bank of Wichita Falls,[5] found a power to lease for oil and gas in a trust instrument that granted to the trustee "full, ample, complete and absolute power to manage, control, sell, and dispose of said trust property." The court stressed that this was more than a naked power to sell, and that the scope of a trustee's duties are normally broader than an agent's, thereby distinguishing the case of Bean v. Bean,[6] which concerned a power of attorney.

In the Kansas case of Heffelfinger v. Scott,[7] a power to lease for oil and gas was found from the general purposes of the trust where the trustees were directed to sell land and reinvest in securities. There it was found that it would be economically unsound to sell all of the farm land at the same time, as it would cause a depressed market. As there was considerable oil and gas activity in the vicinity at the time, and a trustee is charged with making the land productive, the court held that the trustees did have an implied power to execute oil and gas leases. A supporting rationale was that the land was in danger of being drained, and that if the trustees did not then lease they would be unable to do so in the future.

Where the express power contained in the trust gives the trustee the power to "lease and manage" or some variation thereof which does not include an express power to sell the trust property, the

2. Layman v. Hodnett, 205 Ark. 367, 168 S.W.2d 819; Heyl v. Northern Trust Co., 312 Ill.App. 207, 38 N.E.2d 374; Heffelfinger v. Scott, 142 Kan. 395, 47 P.2d 66; Ilari v. Ewing, 314 Ky. 182, 234 S.W.2d 293; Franklin v. Margay Oil Corp., 194 Okl. 519, 153 P.2d 486; but cf. In re Bruner's Will, 363 Pa. 552, 70 A.2d 222, 18 A.L.R.2d 92, where such implication of power to lease for oil and gas was denied. In general see: Goodpasture, Apportionment of Receipts from Mineral Interests under the Oklahoma Trust Act, 20 Okl.L.Rev. 29; Hoffman, The Oil and Gas Lease as a Trust Asset, 7 U.C.L.A.L. Rev. 358; Power of a Trustee to Execute Oil and Gas Leases, 33 Ind.L.Rev. 227; Brown, The Oil and Gas Lease as a Private Trust Res, 9 Okl.L.Rev. 10; Blake, The Trustee's Power to Lease for Oil and Gas, 22 So.Calif.L.Rev. 115.

3. Ilari v. Ewing, 314 Ky. 182, 234 S.W.2d 293; Franklin v. Margay Oil Corp., 194 Okl. 519, 153 P.2d 486.

4. Layman v. Hodnett, 205 Ark. 367, 168 S.W.2d 819; Heffelfinger v. Scott, 142 Kan. 395, 47 P.2d 66.

5. 141 Tex. 489, 174 S.W.2d 255.

6. Tex.Civ.App., 79 S.W.2d 652.

7. 142 Kan. 395, 47 P.2d 66.

courts sometimes have found an implied power to lease for oil and gas purposes from an examination of the purposes of the trust in connection with the circumstances surrounding the use of the property at the time of the execution of the trust instrument.[8] In Lanyon Zinc Co. v. Freeman, a Kansas case,[9] farming land was placed in trust, and the trustee was given the power "to lease and maintain the same in repair and good condition with a view to obtain the best income therefrom without permitting the same to deteriorate in value or quality." The trustee executed an oil and gas lease. It was held that the lease was not within the power of the trustee, interpreting the language of the trust in light of the facts and circumstances surrounding the trust at the time it was made. It was found that the owner was the resident of another state, the land was devoted to farming at that time, and that no oil and gas activity was occurring in the vicinity.

However, in a later somewhat similar case the Kansas court [10] came to an opposite conclusion. Here oil and gas leases were in existence at the time that the trust took effect. The trust empowered the trustee "to follow, as nearly as possible and practicable, the general policy I have pursued in the management of my estate." It was found that to carry out the intent of the trustor, the trustee had the implied power to renew the oil and gas leases when they expired. Likewise, the California court [11] found an implied power to lease lands which were in danger of being drained, where the trust stated that its purpose was to secure the largest return possible on the investment.

In jurisdictions having considerable activity in the petroleum industry, legislation has been passed authorizing the execution of oil and gas leases by trustees.[12] The Uniform Trustees' Powers Act, Section 3(c)(11) does contain authority relating to the execution of oil and gas leases by trustees.[13] Where no statute exists, and no express or implied authority is found in the terms of the trust, a trustee has no power to execute oil and gas leases.

8. Ohio Oil Co. v. Daughetee, 240 Ill. 361, 88 N.E. 818; Lanyon Zinc Co. v. Freeman, 68 Kan. 691, 75 P. 995.

9. 68 Kan. 691, 75 P. 995.

10. First National Bank in Wichita v. Magnolia Petroleum Co., 144 Kan. 645, 62 P.2d 891.

11. Adams v. Cook, 15 Cal.2d 352, 101 P.2d 484. The language is very similar to that in Lanyon Zinc Co. v. Freeman, supra note 8.

12. Florida Stats.Ann. § 691.63(3); Michigan Comp.Laws Ann. § 27.3178 (465); Montana Rev.Code, 1947, §§ 86–315, 86–317; Nebraska R.R.S.1943, §§ 57–210 through 57–212, amended 1953, c. 190; 60 Okl.Stat.Ann. §§ 71–73, 175.24(C), 175.24(H); Vernon's Ann.Tex. Civ.Stat. art. 7425b–25; Virginia Code, 1950, § 8–675, as amended; Washington R.C.Ann. § 30.99.070; Wyoming Stat. § 4–25.

13. "To enter into a lease or arrangement for exploration and removal of minerals or other natural resources or enter into a pooling or unitization agreement." In effect in Florida, F.S.A. §§ 737.401–737.406; Idaho, I.C. §§ 68–104 to 68–113; Kansas, K.S.A. §§ 58–1201 to 58–1211; Kentucky, KRS 386.800 to 386.840; Maine, 18–A M.R.S.A. §§ 7–401 to 7–407; Mississippi, Code 1972, §§ 91–9–101 to 91–9–119; Montana, MCA 72–21–101 to 72–21–206; New Hampshire, RSA 564–A:1 to 564–A:11; Oregon, ORS 128.003 to 128.051; Utah, U.C.A. 1953, 75–7–401 to 75–7–408; Wyoming, W.S. 1977, §§ 4–8–101 to 4–8–111.

Where authority permits the leasing of trust property for oil and gas, some question exists as to the term for which such lease may extend. It is the normal rule that where a trust is for a fixed term, a lease may not extend beyond the term, and where it is not for a fixed term, a lease may only have a duration of the probable duration of the trust.[14] Where no statute was involved,[15] some decisions have allowed the oil and gas lease to extend beyond the termination of the trust, but there are cases to the contrary.[16] Most legislation expressly provides that leases executed by trustees pursuant to such acts may have a duration beyond the termination of the trust.

Where production occurs in relation to oil and gas properties upon which leases have been executed by a trustee, and where successive estates are involved, such as life tenant and remainderman, the same general principles will apply to such interests as where they are not held in trust. Where no authority is vested in the trustee to execute oil and gas leases, but where leases or production have occurred prior to the creation of the interest in trust, the open mine doctrine will apply, and all of the economic benefits from the leases will be payable to or held, under the terms of the trust, for the life tenant.[17]

Where no lease has been executed prior to the creation of the interest in trust, neither the trustee nor the life tenant has the right to execute oil and gas leases upon the remainder interest, and to the extent that production occurs from land in which such interest occurs, the remainderman will be treated as a non-joined co-tenant and will be entitled to his proportionate share of gross production less expenses.[18]

Where authority exists for the execution of oil and gas leases after creation of the interests in trust, allocation must be made between the successive estates of the economic benefits from the lease. Again, where the trust is not subject to the Uniform Principal and Income Act or other state enactments, such allocation will be made in the same manner as if the interests were not in trust.[19] However, if

---

14. Scott, The Law of Trusts, § 189.2; and see Williams v. Nylund, C.A.10th, 268 F.2d 91.

15. Adams v. Cook, 15 Cal.2d 352, 101 P.2d 484.

16. Wingert v. T. W. Phillips Gas & Oil Co., 398 Pa. 100, 157 A.2d 92.

17. In re Bruner's Will, 363 Pa. 552, 70 A.2d 222, 18 A.L.R.2d 92.

18. Martin v. Humble Oil and Refining Co., D.C.Miss., 199 F.Supp. 648, affirmed C.A.5th, 298 F.2d 163.

19. Under the normal rule, royalty and usually bonus are treated as corpus and are invested to maintain the estate, with the life tenant being entitled to the income therefrom. Central Standard Life Insurance Co. v. Gardner, 17 Ill.2d 220, 161 N.E.2d 278; Millikin Trust Co. v. Jarvis, 34 Ill.App.2d 180, 180 N.E.2d 759; Franklin v. Margay Oil Corp., 194 Okl. 519, 153 P.2d 486; Avis v. First National Bank of Wichita Falls, 141 Tex. 489, 174 S.W.2d 255. In California, at common law the apportionment made was $27\frac{1}{2}\%$ to corpus and $72\frac{1}{2}\%$ to income. In the Matter of the Estate of Sloan v. St. Aubyn, 222 Cal.App.2d 283, 35 Cal.Rptr. 167; whereas in Illinois, apportionment was determined by capitalizing the royalty income at 5% to determine the fund that yields such income. Heyl v. Northern Trust Co., 312 Ill.App. 207, 38 N.E.2d 374. Also see text and footnotes at § 5.2, supra.

the trustor manifests an intent that either the life tenant or the remainderman will take all of the benefits of production from the lease, no apportionment will be made.

In the Mississippi case of First National Bank of Laurel v. Commercial National Bank & Trust Co.,[20] where the trustor stated that "the entire income" should be paid to the life tenant, it was held that the term would include all of the royalty. The result was based upon the court's interpreting the intent of the trustor as to the meaning of "entire income" in the layman sense, as including all payments from the lease.

The National Conference of Commissioners on Uniform State Laws has promulgated two versions of the Uniform Principal and Income Act. The first act was written in 1931, and Section 9 provides for allocation of income from natural resources. However, it merely states the general rule that payments representing return of corpus of an estate will be held for the remainderman and invested, with the income to be paid to the income beneficiaries. At last count 13 states have adopted the 1931 Act; however, several of the states have changed the apportionment rule to treat some part of the payments received as presently payable to the income beneficiaries.[21]

In 1962 the Commissioners drafted a revised version of the Act. Section 9 of the revised Act provides for apportionment on the basis

---

20. 247 Miss. 667, 157 So.2d 502.

Also see: Commercial National Bank in Nacogdoches v. Hayter, Tex.Civ.App., 473 S.W.2d 561 (where it was held that apportionment under the Texas Trust Act was mandatory in a testamentary trust where royalties were not directed to be paid to income beneficiaries and the term "income" was not defined).

21.

Table of Jurisdictions Wherein 1931 Act Has Been Adopted

Jurisdiction	Laws	Effective Date	Statutory Citation
Alabama	1939, p. 902	9-19-1939	Code of Ala.1975, §§ 19-3-270 to 19-3-282.
Arizona	1951, c. 138	3-29-1951	A.R.S. §§ 14-7401 to 14-7416.
Colorado	1955, c. 151	4-7-1955	C.R.S. '73, 15-1-401 to 15-1-417.
Connecticut	1939, No. 254a		C.G.S.A. §§ 45-110 to 45-119.
Kentucky	1956, c. 176	2-27-1956	KRS 386.190 to 386.340.
Montana	1959, c. 277	3-17-1959	MCA 72-25-101 to 72-25-302.
Oklahoma	1941, p. 250	5-31-1941	60 Okl.St.Ann. §§ 175.3, 175.26 to 175.36.
Pennsylvania	1972, No. 164	7-1-1972	20 Pa.C.S.A. §§ 8101 to 8112.
Tennessee	1955, c. 81	3-1-1955	T.C.A. §§ 35-701 to 35-715.
Texas	1943, c. 148, p. 232	4-19-1943	Vernon's Ann.Civ.St. arts. 7425b-4, 7425b-26 to 7425b-36.
Vermont	1957, No. 171	6-1-1957	14 V.S.A. §§ 3301 to 3313.
Virginia	1936, c. 432	3-30-1936	Code 1950, §§ 55-253 to 55-268.
West Virginia	1953, c. 95	90 days after 3-13-1953	Code 36-6-1 to 36-6-17.

Also see text at § 5.2, supra.

of the depletion allowance used for federal income tax purposes, and is set out below.[22] It appears that 23 states have adopted the act.[23]

22. § 9. [Disposition of Natural Resources].—(a) If any part of the principal consists of a right to receive royalties, overriding or limited royalties, working interests, production payments, net profit interests, or other interests in minerals or other natural resources in, on or under land, the receipts from taking the natural resources from the land shall be allocated as follows:

(1) If received as rent on a lease or extension payments on a lease, the receipts are income.

(2) If received from a production payment, the receipts are income to the extent of any factor for interest or its equivalent provided in the governing instrument. There shall be allocated to principal the fraction of the balance of the receipts which the unrecovered cost of the production payment bears to the balance owed on the production payment, exclusive of any factor for interest or its equivalent. The receipts not allocated to principal are income.

(3) If received as a royalty, overriding or limited royalty or bonus, or from a working, net profit, or any other interest in minerals or other natural resources, receipts not provided for in the preceding paragraphs of this section shall be apportioned on a yearly basis in accordance with this paragraph whether or not any natural resource was being taken from the land at the time the trust was established. Twenty-seven and one-half per cent of the gross receipts (but not to exceed 50% of the net receipts remaining after payment of all expenses, direct and indirect, computed without allowance for depletion) shall be added to principal as an allowance for depletion. The balance of the gross receipts after payment therefrom of all expenses, direct and indirect, is income.

(b) If a trustee, on the effective date of this Act, held an item of depletable property of a type specified in this section he shall allocate receipts from the property in the manner used before the effective date of this Act, but as to all depletable property acquired after the effective date of this Act by an existing or new trust, the method of allocation provided herein shall be used.

(c) This section does not apply to timber, water, soil, sod, dirt, turf or mosses.

23.

Table of Jurisdictions Wherein 1962 Act Has Been Adopted

Jurisdiction	Laws	Effective Date	Statutory Citation
Arkansas	1971, No. 318	3-17-1971	Ark.Stats. §§ 58–601 to 58–616.
California	Stats.1967, c. 1508	7-1-1968	West's Ann.Civ.Code, §§ 730 to 730.17.
Florida	1974, c. 74—106	7-1-1975	West's F.S.A. §§ 738.01 to 738.15.
Hawaii	1973, c. 200	5-29-1973	HRS §§ 557–1 to 557–16.
Idaho	1963, c. 187		I.C. §§ 68–1001 to 68–1016.
Illinois	1981, P.A. 82-390	1-1-1982	S.H.A. ch. 30, §§ 501 to 517.
Indiana	1969, c. 69	3-7-1969	IC 30-4-5-1 to 30-4-5-11.
Kansas	1965, c. 344	6-30-1965	K.S.A. 58-901 to 58-917.
Maryland	1965, c. 877	6-1-1965	Code, Estates and Trusts, §§ 14-201 to 14-214.
Michigan	1965, No. 340	1-1-1966	M.C.L.A. §§ 555.51 to 555.68.
Minnesota	1969, c. 1006	1-1-1970	M.S.A. §§ 501.48 to 501.63.
Mississippi	1966, c. 371	1-1-1967	Code 1972, §§ 91-17-1 to 91-17-31.
Nevada	1969, p. 708	7-1-1969	N.R.S. 164.140 to 164.370.
New Mexico	1969, c. 239	4-3-1969	NMSA 1978, §§ 46-3-1 to 46-3-15.
New York	1966, c. 952	9-1-1967	McKinney's EPTL 11-2.1.
North Carolina	1973, c. 729	1-1-1974	G.S. §§ 37-16 to 37-40.
North Dakota	1969, c. 541		NDCC 59-04.1-01 to 59-04.1-17.
Oregon	1975, c. 717	9-13-1975	ORS 129.005 to 129.125.
South Carolina	1963, c. 269	6-3-1963	Code 1976, §§ 21-35-10 to 21-35-210.
Utah	1979, c. 89	1-1-1980	U.C.A.1953, 22-3-1 to 22-3-15.
Washington	1971, c. 74	1-1-1972	West's RCWA 11.104.010 to 11.104.940.
Wisconsin	1957, c. 300	7-9-1957	W.S.A. 701.20.
Wyoming	1963, c. 189	2-26-1963	W.S.1977, §§ 2-3-601 to 2-3-614.

A conflict appears in the treatment given to the characterization of payments made to the trust where the trust is located in one state and the producing property in another. Few cases have been found. In the case of Millikin Trust Company v. Jarvis,[24] the Illinois court treated bonus and royalty as constituting personal property and applied the law of the forum in apportionment of the proceeds. Other jurisdictions,[25] deeming payments from an oil and gas lease to be in the nature of realty, have applied the law of the situs of the property. It is submitted that the proper view is (a) to characterize the economic benefits from production by the law of situs of the property (where no designation of a particular state law is made in the trust instrument for construction of the trust for allocation purposes), and (b) to also apply the allocation rules of the law of the situs of the property.[26]

(C) Administrators, Executors, and Guardians

This section will deal generally with the authority of fiduciaries of estates of decedents and persons under disability to execute oil and gas leases. However, no attempt will be made to examine the specific laws and statutes of each jurisdiction.

In relation to the estates of decedents, where it is desired to acquire oil and gas leases while the estate is in administration, it may be necessary to deal with administrators of decedents dying intestate, executors under court supervision, or those able to administer independently of court supervision in the case of decedents dying testate. In community property states, where the decedent dies intestate, a community survivor may have the inherent power to execute an oil and gas lease.

It generally may be stated that neither an administrator of an intestate's estate nor a guardian of an estate of a minor or an incompetent has power to execute an oil and gas lease unless the statutes of the particular jurisdiction so provide. This is also true as to the executor of a testate estate, where the will does not include a power to lease. However, a court may authorize execution of an oil and gas lease on a minor ward's estate to conserve the estate from waste by drainage from wells on adjoining tracts of land.[27]

Due to the increase in oil and gas activity over the last several decades, many jurisdictions have enacted statutes empowering the probate court to authorize execution of oil and gas leases by such personal representatives.[28]

24. 34 Ill.App.2d 180, 180 N.E.2d 759.

25. In re Estate of McClure, 21 Misc. 2d 470, 192 N.Y.S.2d 290.

26. See § 277 and 279, Restatement of the Law of Trusts, Second, Proposed Official Draft, Part III, dated April 22, 1969.

27. Newell v. McMillan, 139 Kan. 94, 30 P.2d 126.

28. Alabama: Code, Tit. 21, § 48; Arkansas: Ark.Stats. § 57-640; California: West's Ann.Prob.Code, § 1538; Colorado: C.R.S. '63, § 153-10-21; Florida: F.S.A. § 745.02; Idaho: I.C. § 15-905; Illinois: S.H.A. ch. 3, § 222a (1965

A problem incurred in connection with some of the earlier statutes was that, although they empowered the execution of such leases, no provisions were included that would allow the extension of the primary term of the oil and gas lease beyond the period of administration, unless production was obtained.[29] Later legislation not only provides for the extension of such leases beyond the period of administration or the duration of minority or incompetence, but also provides that such representatives may execute all such instruments that relate to the oil and gas development generally. These include division orders, pooling and unitization agreements, etc.[30]

Where the decedent dies testate and the will expressly empowers the executor to execute oil and gas leases, obviously no problem exists. However, what if the will merely gives the executor the power to sell the estate? Although several cases have come to the conclusion that the power to sell land also includes the power to execute oil and gas leases,[31] it is doubtful that this may be stated as a general rule.[32] The office of executor, normally, is quite limited in scope compared to that of a trustee. The function of the executor is to pay debts and distribute the property. As a matter of fact, under most of the statutes, the real property vests immediately, upon death, in the heirs and devisees, subject to the power of the administrator or executor to sell the property during administration of the estate. This, of course, is the rule at common law as to land. The executor does have the power to sell property of the estate to pay debts, but this power cannot be equated to the power to tie up a part of the estate beyond the period of distribution, which the execution of an oil and gas lease normally would do.

Where dependent administration by an executor is involved, in cases of doubt, recourse may be had to the probate court for leasing under applicable statutory authority. However, several jurisdictions, such as Washington and Texas, allow for and make extensive use of the independent executor, who, after qualifying, essentially operates free from court supervision. In such jurisdictions it may not be possible to have recourse to such legislation. In Texas it has been held

---

Amend.); Indiana: Burns' Ann.St. § 31–401; Kansas: K.S.A. § 59–1807; Kentucky: KRS 387.150; Louisiana: LSA–R.S. 9:711; Michigan: M.C.L.A. § 709.5; Mississippi: Code 1942, § 415; Nebraska: R.R.S.1943, § 57–210; New Mexico: 1953 Comp. § 32–1–20; Nevada: N.R.S. 149.060; North Dakota: NDCC 38–10–04; Ohio: R.C. § 2111.26; Oklahoma: 58 Okl.St.Ann. §§ 808, 924; South Dakota: SDC 30–18–8, 30–29–10; Texas: V.A.T.S.Probate Code, § 367; Virginia: Code 1950, § 8–675; West Virginia: Code, 37–1–2; Wyoming: W.S.1957, § 4–23. Also see Davis, Ancillary Administration of Oil and Gas Leases in Kansas: A Legal Conundrum, 5 Kan.L.Rev. 452.

29. See: Tex.Rev.Civ.Stat., 1925, arts. 3554–3557, and cf. present legislation: V.A.T.S. Probate Code, § 367(C)(7).

30. For instance see the provision of the Texas Probate Code, §§ 369, 370, 371, 372.

31. Layman v. Hodnett, 205 Ark. 367, 168 S.W.2d 819; Oliver v. Culpepper, 209 Ark. 326, 190 S.W.2d 457.

32. Lanyon Zinc Co. v. Freeman, 68 Kan. 691, 75 P. 995; Irons v. Fort Worth Sand & Gravel Co., Tex.Civ.App., 260 S.W.2d 629; Smith v. Womack, Tex.Civ. App., 231 S.W. 840.

that although an independent executor is within the general probate code definition of the term "personal representative," he does not come within the class of personal representatives that may lease for oil and gas pursuant to statutory authority.[33]

It is considered doubtful, in Texas, whether the independent executor has the power to execute oil and gas leases where no authority is contained in the will. It is also questioned whether authority to execute oil and gas leases will be implied from an express power to sell, where extensive powers of management and control are not present.[34] It has been held in Texas that the independent executor has powers to settle an estate which are as broad as those of an executor operating under court supervision.[35] As to the question of whether or not execution of an oil and gas lease constitutes an act in settlement of an estate, it has been argued that the powers of the independent executor should be considered to be at least as extensive as those now applying to dependent executors under the present statutes.[36]

Where an independent executor is empowered to execute oil and gas leases, the problem still exists whether the lease can extend beyond the period of administration. When debts no longer exist, the power of the independent executor is terminated. The situation has generally been avoided through the expedient of requiring all parties in interest, viz., the independent executor and the heirs or devisees, to join in the execution of the lease. If the independent executor is also a devisee, he should execute the lease in both his representative and individual capacities.[37]

If no authority exists in an executor or administrator to execute oil and gas leases, leases taken from the heirs or devisees during the period of administration are subject to being displaced by sales of the land by the administrator or executor for the payment of the debts of the estate. Unless an arrangement may be made to withdraw such land from administration by the use of a substitute fund, such as a bond, leases taken during such period are of doubtful effect.

---

33. Marshall v. Hobert's Estate, Tex. Civ.App., 315 S.W.2d 604.

34. Smith v. Womack, Tex.Civ.App., 231 S.W. 840; Irons v. Fort Worth Sand & Gravel Co., Tex.Civ.App., 260 S.W.2d 629; but cf. Oliver v. Culpepper, 209 Ark. 326, 190 S.W. 457, and see, Woodward, Independent Administrations Under the New Texas Probate Code, 34 Tex.L.Rev. 687.

35. Roy v. Whitaker, 92 Tex. 346, 48 S.W. 892, modified 49 S.W. 367.

36. Woodward, Independent Administrations Under the New Texas Probate Code, 34 Tex.L.Rev. 687.

37. Prior to the amendment of the Texas Probate Code it was the practice of Texas attorneys to take leases with such dual execution although all debts of the estate may have been paid, as there existed no statutory method of closing the independent administration. This has been remedied with addition of provisions providing for the closing of the estate by the filing of an affidavit by the independent executor. V.A.T.S. Probate Code, § 151. However, such filing is permissive and not mandatory, and when no such affidavit has been filed the problem of whether the independent executor may act in a representative capacity will still exist.

In community property jurisdictions, upon the dissolution of the marital partnership by death of a spouse, the surviving spouse generally has the power to administer the estate of the decedent that is similar to the powers of a surviving partner to wind up partnership business. Where debts exist, the community survivor has the power to execute oil and gas leases and convey mineral interests in the land.[38] If the decedent died testate, this power may be lost when an executor is appointed for the estate.[39] In some community property jurisdictions, the power of the spouse as community survivor exists where the other spouse has become insane.[40]

Leases of minors or incompetents, executed prior to majority or after adjudication of insanity, are voidable upon the reaching of majority, or upon restoration of the incompetent.[41] Prior to enactment of statutes allowing the leases of a guardian to extend beyond the period of majority, where such leases existed and no production was obtained prior to this period, if the minor at age 21 did not ratify the lease it would terminate. However, if the lease was executed or ratified by a minor in a jurisdiction where the disabilities of minority were removed prior to reaching majority the resulting lease would extend beyond the period of majority.

In the situation of a minor, or of an incompetent after adjudication of incompetency, the oil and gas lease must be acquired from the guardian of the respective estate.

---

38. Griffin v. Stanolind Oil and Gas Co., 133 Tex. 45, 125 S.W.2d 545; Union Producing Co. v. Sanborn, D.C.Tex., 194 F.Supp. 121.

39. Tracy v. Lion Oil Co., Tex.Civ. App., 312 S.W.2d 562. In community property states, property may be divided into the separate property of each spouse, general community property, and special community property. Management and control of the various types of property may exist in either the husband, or the wife, and upon the death of one spouse, in the surviving spouse as community survivor, or in the executor or administrator of the decedent. Recourse must be made to local law to determine who has the power to lease. See: Huie, Changes Made by the Texas Probate Code in the Administration of Community Property, 34 Tex.L.Rev. 700; and Hudspeth, The Matrimonial Property Act of 1967—Six Areas of Change, 31 Tex. Bar J. 477.

40. Texas: V.A.T.S. Probate Code, §§ 157, 160, 161, 167.

41. Where an attack is to be made upon such an instrument, it is necessary to determine whether the instrument is void or merely voidable. In the first instance suit may be for title, but in the latter it must be for rescission of the instrument. In most jurisdictions these are different actions, and different limitation statutes apply. In at least one jurisdiction the tolling provisions in the limitation statutes applying to suits for title and to suits for rescission are different. A further admonition may be made in the event a suit for rescission is brought—that it be coupled with a count for title, in order to interrupt any adverse possession period that may have commenced by the lessee's producing from the property. Where possession is not interrupted, in the conceivable instance that recovery of title by rescission is not accomplished prior to the defendant's maturing title by limitation, plaintiff would find himself with a very hollow victory.

(D) Business Entities

Oil and gas leases obtained from corporations, partnerships, and unincorporated associations, churches, etc., primarily involve the conformity of such leases to local law. In the case of the corporation, if the execution of an oil and gas lease is not within the purposes of the corporation, either expressly or impliedly, a specific supporting resolution of the board of directors should be obtained and placed of record with the lease. Such resolution should be ratified by the stockholders.

Where partnership lands are concerned, if the particular jurisdiction has passed the Uniform Partnership Act, or has legislation of a similar nature, the lease, executed by the managing partner, may be taken in the partnership name. However, where no such legislation is in force, it will be necessary to obtain the signatures of all of the partners.

It is necessary to determine the exact legal structure of churches in order to determine the body that holds title to the property involved and those having authority to execute oil and gas leases. In the case of some denominations it will be necessary to see that the particular method of conveying property as described in their by-laws, discipline, etc., be carried out. Where it is necessary to have a congregation vote to authorize the lease, it is suggested that the attorney representing the lessee be present to determine that the meetings are regular and properly documented.

In most jurisdictions an unincorporated association is not considered to be a legal entity and cannot hold or convey property in the association name. Conveyances must be taken from all members, or from a duly constituted board of trustees, if one exists, that holds the property for the association.

(E) Governmental Entities

Little may be said in a general nature of leases obtained from governmental entities, federal, state, or local, due to the diversity in the provisions of the supporting legislation. Again, it is necessary to determine the proper procedure and whether legislation is sufficiently broad to support the resulting lease. Although many oil and gas leases are obtained on federal lands, such consideration is omitted from this treatise, as it is felt that it would unduly lengthen the work, and that it is adequately discussed elsewhere.

Although most states that have important oil and gas production have enacted statutes regulating the execution of oil and gas leases on state lands, none of the states has as extensive an ownership of the minerals in state lands as does Texas, which retained all of her public domain upon entrance into statehood. Due to certain relinquishment acts, no question is presented in Texas as to the ownership of the minerals underlying lands that were patented prior to September 1, 1895. The minerals as to such grants are vested in the owners of the lands. However, since that date, patents of lands in Texas may have reserved the minerals to the State.

Until 1911, if the lands patented were classified as mineral lands, which served to reserve the minerals to the State, such classification appeared upon the face of the patent. After such date the classification may or may not appear upon the face of the patent, which necessitates that one leasing such lands correspond with the Texas State Land Office to obtain a statement of facts. Such statement sets forth the history of the land and its severance from the sovereignty of the soil, together with the classification of the land as patented.

No relinquishment act served to vest the minerals in the owners of the surface so reserved as to lands patented after September 1, 1895. From 1895 until 1919 a deteriorating relationship existed between the landowners of lands in which the State owned the minerals and the State of Texas. This was caused by the fact that leases were made by the State in which the landowner did not participate and whose lands were injured by the lessees. Rumors of armed conflict existed. Upon this background, in 1919, the so-called Relinquishment Act of 1919 [42] was passed. The act actually did not relinquish any of the minerals back to the landowners; however, it did constitute the landowner the agent of the State of Texas for oil and gas leasing purposes. The act provided for minimum rentals and royalties, and further provided that the landowner would share in the resulting economic benefits equally with the State.

As to all lands patented in the State of Texas between September 1, 1895, and August 21, 1931,[43] that were classified as mineral, the landowner has no right to sell the minerals, which are owned by the State of Texas. The only conveyance of the minerals that such land-

---

42. Tex.Rev.Civ.Stat., 1925, Arts. 5367–5382; and see Greene v. Robison, 117 Tex. 516, 8 S.W.2d 655; State v. Standard, Tex., 414 S.W.2d 148; Standard v. Sadler, Tex., 383 S.W.2d 391; Hawkins, El Sal Del Rey, dealing with Texas relinquishment acts prior to Sept. 1, 1895.

43. As to the cut-off date of the Texas Relinquishment Act, the author received a letter dated March 3, 1975, from Mr. Virgil C. Morelle, Attorney for the General Land Office, containing, in part, the following information:

Dear Professor Hemingway:

We have in our library your excellent Hornbook "The Law of Oil and Gas." At page 211, last paragraph, there is the following statement concerning the Texas Relinquishment Act:

"As to all lands patented in the State of Texas between September 1, 1895, and *August 21, 1931*, which were classified as mineral, the landowner has no right to sell the minerals under the land, * * *." (Emphasis added)

Several other writers have also indicated that the Relinquishment Act has no application to any public school land sold after August 21, 1931.

We note, however, that the Sales Act of 1931 (Ch. 271, Gen.Laws, Acts of the 42nd. Legis., Reg.Sess.1931, P. 452, Art. 5421c, V.T.C.S.), as construed in Caples v. Cole, 102 S.W.2d 173, Tex.Sup.1937, apparently became effective immediately after its passage, which was May 29, 1931, rather than 90 days after adjournment. If so, it would appear that the cut-off date of the Relinquishment Act is May 29, 1931 rather than August 21, 1931.

owner may make is of royalty limited in duration to the life of any lease in existence at the time of the conveyance.[44] Where lands were severed from the sovereignty of the soil subsequent to August 21, 1931,[45] the patentee acquired title to the surface and all the minerals, with the State of Texas reserving a $\frac{1}{16}$th non-participating royalty interest.

(F) Unascertainable or Unknown Owners

As mentioned in § 5.1, frustrating problems may be presented to persons trying to obtain oil and gas leases from co-tenants who cannot be found after diligent search. The same holds true where future interests are created in favor of non-ascertainable persons. For instance, Grandpa dies leaving Blackacre to son John, for life, with remainder to John's children. At the time the lease is to be obtained, John is 73 years of age and has no children. In fact, he is a bachelor. Can Black Gold rely upon a lease obtained from John? The same question may be asked if the remainder were to John's heirs. In the latter case, jurisdictions which still follow the Rule in Shelley's case would convert the contingent remainder in John's heirs to a vested remainder in John. As no estate intervenes between the life estate and vested remainder of John, they would merge into the fee. However, many jurisdictions that formerly followed the Rule have changed it by statute so that the remainder may be created. In these cases the only limitation upon the remainder would be the rule against perpetuities, which might void the remainder. Where void, the attorney may still be presented with the problem of locating the owners of the reversion in the land.

Where rules of law or construction, such as the Rule in Shelley's case and the Doctrine of Worthier Title,[46] are not available, it may still be possible to join such unascertainable owners through a judicial action by use of the doctrine of Virtual Representation. The doctrine of Virtual Representation is a quasi-class action where living ascertainable persons having a natural relationship with the class to be joined, and not having an adverse interest to the class, may be viewed as representing the unascertained group.[47] In many jurisdictions, statutes have been passed allowing for the leasing of future interests

---

44. Lewis v. Oates, 145 Tex. 77, 195 S.W.2d 123.

45. See note 43, supra.

46. Simes, Handbook of the Law of Future Interests, Chapter 5 (Shelley's rule), Chapter 6 (Doctrine of Worthier Title).

47. Simes, Handbook of the Law of Future Interests, Chapter 10, § 49.

In Amarex, Inc. v. Sell, Okl., 566 P.2d 456 where the state statute provides for the appointment of a trustee for the leasing of interests of contingent remaindermen, it was held that although such appointment was necessary as to unascertained contingent remaindermen, it was not the exclusive method of leasing and that ascertained contingent remaindermen who had reached their majority were bound by their execution of the lease.

running to unascertainable persons.[48] Generally these statutes set up some pattern of statutory trusteeship subject to judicial control.

48. Illinois: S.H.A. ch. 104, § 27; Kentucky: KRS 353.300–353.380; Nebraska: R.R.S.1943, §§ 57–222 to 57–224; N.D.: Laws 1951, c. 187, §§ 1–2, amended Laws 1955, c. 216, § 1; Oklahoma: 60 Okl.St.Ann. §§ 71–73; Texas: Vernon's Ann.Civ.Stat., article 2320c; West Virginia: Code, 36–2–1.

CHAPTER 6

THE OIL AND GAS LEASE—DURATION

Analysis

Sec.
6.1 The Nature of an Oil and Gas Lease.
6.2 Classification of Oil and Gas Leases by Duration.
6.3 Keeping the Lease Alive During the Primary Term—The Delay Rental.
 (A) The Delay Rental—Payment Date.
 (B) The Delay Rental—Tender.
 (C) The Delay Rental—Notice of Assignment by the Mineral Owner.
 (D) The Delay Rental—Effect of Operations During the Primary Term.
 (E) The Delay Rental—Effect of Improper Payment.
 (F) The Delay Rental—Estoppel, Waiver, and Ratification of an Improper Payment by the Mineral Owner.
6.4 Propelling the Lease Past the Primary Term and Keeping It Alive During the Secondary Term by Production of Oil or Gas—Definition of "Production."
 (A) Production—Quantum of Production, i.e., Paying Quantities.
 (B) Production—Sporadic Production and Temporary Cessation of Production.
6.5 Propelling the Lease Past the Primary Term and Keeping It Alive During the Secondary Term—Contractual Substitutes for Production—The Nature of Shut-In Royalties.
 (A) Shut-In Royalties—Time of Payment.
6.6 Propelling the Lease Past the Primary Term by Operations—Completing the Well Drilling at the End of the Primary Term.
6.7 Propelling the Lease Past the Primary Term by Operations—Commencement of Drilling Operations.
6.8 Keeping the Lease Alive by Operations During the Secondary Term—The Dry Hole Clause.
6.9 Keeping the Lease Alive by Operations During the Secondary Term—The Continuous Operations Clause.

§ 6.1 The Nature of an Oil and Gas Lease

When construing an instrument that is in the form of a deed but which contains many of the provisions commonly found in an oil and gas lease, the courts will try to determine the motivating intent behind the instrument. Where a substantial consideration for the transaction will not be realized without production, there is a strong tendency to construe the instrument as a lease, as the parties were primarily looking to the expectation of production for a financial return. This conclusion is fortified by the presence of covenants calling for exploration and development and for termination. Where such factors do not exist the prevailing view is that the instrument is a deed.

Regardless of the theory of ownership of the mineral estate adopted, the great majority of the producing jurisdictions treat the interest created by an oil and gas lease as a nonpossessory interest in real property, i.e., an incorporeal hereditament, a profit à prendre. A few jurisdictions, such as Texas, treat the oil and gas lease as creating a corporeal interest in real property, a determinable fee. Although early cases were concerned with the form of the granting clause as to whether a license or a lease was created, today virtually all jurisdictions determine the interest created without regard to the wording of the clause.

The earliest oil and gas leases were strongly influenced by the experience of the draftsmen with hard mineral leases or long-term leases between landlord and tenant. At times it became extremely difficult to determine whether a certain instrument was a mineral deed or an oil and gas lease. Most of the litigation arose years after the instrument was executed, when suit was brought to terminate the apparent interest on the basis that the instrument constituted a lease which had terminated due to non-development.[1] Other consequences of classification as a deed or a lease concern whether obligations to develop that normally are implied in a lease but not in a deed will be implied under the instrument,[2] the tax consequences of the transaction,[3] the validity of the instrument,[4] and its conformity with local law relating to forms of conveyancing and recording.[5]

In making a determination whether an instrument is a deed or lease, the courts try to determine the intent of the parties from the face of the instrument in relation to the facts and circumstances existing at the time of its execution. Factors considered include the nature and extent of the following:

---

1. Adams v. Elkhorn Coal Corp., 199 Ky. 612, 251 S.W. 654; Duncan v. Mason, 239 Ky. 570, 39 S.W.2d 1006; Bardhill v. Sellers, Ky., 298 S.W.2d 5; Dougherty v. Greene, 218 Miss. 250, 67 So.2d 297; Crain v. Pure Oil Co., C.A.8th, 25 F.2d 824.

2. Bardhill v. Sellers, Ky., 298 S.W.2d 5; Dougherty v. Greene, 218 Miss. 250, 67 So.2d 297; Crain v. Pure Oil Co., C.A. 8th, 25 F.2d 824 (lease); Davis v. Mann, C.A.10th, 234 F.2d 553; Kentucky Natural Gas Corp. v. Carter, 303 Ky. 559, 198 S.W.2d 311; Danciger Oil & Refining Co. of Texas v. Powell, 137 Tex. 484, 154 S.W.2d 632; Texas Co. v. State of Texas, 154 Tex. 494, 281 S.W.2d 83 (deeds). However, covenants to develop sometimes will be implied in deeds. See Freeport Sulphur Co. v. American Sulphur Royalty Co., 117 Tex. 439, 6 S.W.2d 1039.

3. See West v. Commissioner of Internal Revenue, C.A.5th, 150 F.2d 723, cert. denied 326 U.S. 795, 66 S.Ct. 488, 90 L.Ed. 484. If a sale, the transaction would be subject to tax on the basis of a long term capital gain; if a lease, treated as ordinary income subject to depletion.

4. Texas Co. v. State of Texas, 154 Tex. 494, 281 S.W.2d 83, (instrument construed as a deed and held to be invalid as a conveyance of minerals under the Texas Relinquishment Act). See § 5.7.

5. See Kan.Stat.Ann. § 79–420 which requires a deed, but not a lease, severing the mineral estate to be recorded for tax purposes. Some jurisdictions may require deeds and oil and gas leases to be recorded in separate records, which may affect constructive notice of the instrument. However, if both are considered as a part of the deed records it would seem in the absence of particular language in a statute precluding notice, that recording in the wrong record would still impart constructive notice.

§ 6.1   THE OIL AND GAS LEASE—DURATION   241

(a) Amount of monetary consideration for the instrument.[6]

(b) Form of granting clause.[7]

(c) Reservation of payments out of production.[8]

(d) Express duty to develop.[9]

(e) Term of grant.[10]

(f) Presence of easements for development and use of equipment.[11]

(g) Presence of an obligation to drill a well.[12]

(h) Right to remove fixtures.[13]

(i) Provision for termination.[14]

Both an absolute grant of the minerals and an oil and gas lease contemplate and place in the hands of the grantee the right to explore for and develop the mineral estate. Hence, in each case an intent to obtain petroleum production may be said to exist in the minds of the parties. However, the touchstone is found in the nature of the motivation for the particular conveyance, viz., is the primary expectation of benefit and reward from the transaction that of prompt, if not immediate, exploration of the premises for oil and gas production, or, is

---

6. Adams v. Elkhorn Coal Corp., 199 Ky. 612, 251 S.W. 654; Duncan v. Mason, 239 Ky. 570, 39 S.W.2d 1006; Kentucky Natural Gas Corp. v. Carter, 303 Ky. 559, 198 S.W.2d 311; Texas Co. v. State of Texas, 154 Tex. 494, 281 S.W.2d 83; Feather v. Baird, 85 W.Va. 267, 102 S.E. 294.

7. Kentucky Natural Gas Corp. v. Carter, 303 Ky. 559, 198 S.W.2d 311; Feather v. Baird, 85 W.Va. 267, 102 S.E. 294.

8. Adams v. Elkhorn Coal Corp., 199 Ky. 612, 251 S.W. 654; Duncan v. Mason, 239 Ky. 570, 39 S.W.2d 1006; Davis v. Mann, C.A.10th, 234 F.2d 553; Kentucky Natural Gas Corp. v. Carter, 303 Ky. 559, 198 S.W.2d 311; Texas Co. v. State of Texas, 154 Tex. 494, 281 S.W.2d 83; Feather v. Baird, 85 W.Va. 267, 102 S.E. 294 (deeds); Dougherty v. Greene, 218 Miss. 250, 67 So.2d 297; Eggleston v. Sinclair Oil & Gas Co., 132 Okl. 81, 269 P. 306; Crain v. Pure Oil Co., C.A.8th, 25 F.2d 824; West v. Commissioner of Internal Revenue, C.A.5th, 150 F.2d 723, cert. denied 326 U.S. 795, 66 S.Ct. 488, 90 L.Ed. 484 (leases).

9. Adams v. Elkhorn Coal Corp., 199 Ky. 612, 251 S.W. 654; Davis v. Mann, C.A.10th, 234 F.2d 553; Kentucky Natural Gas Corp. v. Carter, 303 Ky. 559, 198 S.W.2d 311 (deeds); Eggleston v. Sinclair Oil & Gas Co., 132 Okl. 81, 269 P. 306; Crain v. Pure Oil Co., C.A.8th, 25 F.2d 824; West v. Commissioner of Internal Revenue, C.A.5th, 150 F.2d 723, cert. denied 326 U.S. 795, 66 S.Ct. 488, 90 L.Ed. 484 (leases).

10. Adams v. Elkhorn Coal Corp., 199 Ky. 612, 251 S.W. 654; Duncan v. Mason, 239 Ky. 570, 39 S.W.2d 1006.

11. Adams v. Elkhorn Coal Corp., 199 Ky. 612, 251 S.W. 654; Bardhill v. Sellers, Ky., 298 S.W.2d 5; Clark v. Wilson, Ky.Ct.App., 316 S.W.2d 693; Eggleston v. Sinclair Oil & Gas Co., 132 Okl. 81, 269 P. 306.

12. Bardhill v. Sellers, Ky., 298 S.W.2d 5.

13. Eggleston v. Sinclair Oil & Gas Co., 132 Okl. 81, 269 P. 306; Crain v. Pure Oil Co., C.A.8th, 25 F.2d 824.

14. Adams v. Elkhorn Coal Corp., 199 Ky. 612, 251 S.W. 654; Duncan v. Mason, 239 Ky. 570, 39 S.W.2d 1006 (deeds); Bardhill v. Sellers, Ky., 298 S.W.2d 5; Dougherty v. Greene, 218 Miss. 250, 67 So.2d 297; Crain v. Pure Oil Co., C.A.8th, 25 F.2d 824 (leases).

it found in the monetary payments for the property, with the possibility of production constituting a secondary consideration?[15]

The courts have attempted to look through form to the substance of the transaction. The fact that an instrument is titled either a "Mineral Deed" or an "Oil and Gas Lease" will have little effect upon the construction of the instrument.[16] The mere fact that the instrument provides for a payment out of production will not convert what is otherwise a mineral deed into an oil and gas lease.[17] However, if it is found that the only substantial return for the execution of the instrument will come from production or not at all, there exists a strong tendency to construe the instrument as an oil and gas lease.[18] This is especially true where other clauses normally associated with oil and gas leases are also present.

In the case of Crain v. Pure Oil Co.,[19] the instruments there construed were each entitled "Oil and Gas Deed," recited a consideration of $1.00, contained a provision for payments out of production, but contained no express covenant for exploration or for termination. In construing the instruments as constituting oil and gas leases, the court stated:

"It is provided that, if found, the mining, extracting and producing must commence within one year from date of discovery, but no effort need ever be made to discover the same if this is in fact a deed, so that the Sanchos would receive $1.00 for the mineral interest and no other benefit, and grantees could hold the mineral rights indefinitely and never make any effort to discover oil or gas. Such construction is unreasonable, unjust, inequitable, and unconscionable. Reasonable men would not enter into any such contract, and certainly it was not the intention of the parties that grantees could indefinitely tie up the mineral rights in this land, and that any benefit to the Sanchos should be at the option of the grantee."

The same result has occurred where the consideration for the grant was not the reservation of a payment out of production, but was payment in stock of the company acquiring the instrument, which stock would have no value but for production from the land.[20]

However, where the instrument has many of the provisions commonly found in an oil and gas lease, but provides for a substantial

---

15. Davis v. Mann, C.A.10th, 234 F.2d 553 (primary use for agriculture).

16. Davis v. Mann, C.A.10th, 234 F.2d 553 ("Warranty Deed"); Eggleston v. Sinclair Oil & Gas Co., 132 Okl. 81, 269 P. 306 ("Oil & Gas Mining Lease"); Crain v. Pure Oil Co., C.A.8th, 25 F.2d 824 ("Oil and Gas Deed").

17. See Davis v. Mann, C.A.10th, 234 F.2d 553.

18. Dougherty v. Greene, 218 Miss. 250, 67 So.2d 297; Eggleston v. Sinclair Oil & Gas Co., 132 Okl. 81, 269 P. 306; Crain v. Pure Oil Co., C.A.8th, 25 F.2d 824; West v. Commissioner of Internal Revenue, C.A.5th, 150 F.2d 723, cert. denied 326 U.S. 795, 66 S.Ct. 488, 90 L.Ed. 484.

19. C.A.8th, 25 F.2d 824.

20. Bardhill v. Sellers, Ky.Ct.App., 298 S.W.2d 5; Clark v. Wilson, Ky., 316 S.W.2d 693.

§ 6.1 THE OIL AND GAS LEASE—DURATION

cash consideration, or deferred cash payments, the courts have looked at the transaction as an absolute grant of the mineral estate.[21] In the case of Danciger Oil and Refining Co. of Texas v. Powell,[22] the instrument provided for a $50,000 cash payment, with a further payment of $50,000 out of $1/8$ of production. However, the deferred installment payments were due and payable in the future in any event, whether or not production was sufficient. No provisions were found requiring the grantee to explore or develop the premises. The court construed the instrument as a deed, rather than a lease.

Although in construing an instrument as a deed or a lease the courts have given primary consideration to the nature of the consideration provided for in the instrument, such construction is also aided by the absence or presence of express provisions calling for the development of the premises or termination in the event of the lack of such development. Where an instrument has provided for payments out of production but has expressly negated any duty to develop for the minerals, it has been held to be a deed.[23] On the other hand, where express development obligations exist an opposite result has occurred.[24] In several instances where the instrument contained provisions common to both oil and gas leases and mineral deeds, the courts have been guided by clauses which have expressly stated the intention of the parties as to the nature of the instrument.[25]

As in the cases dealing with the nature of ownership of the mineral estate,[26] various concepts have been utilized in defining the nature of the interest of the lessee created under an oil and gas lease. Although jurisdictions that view the interest in the mineral estate prior to production as non-possessory are precluded from treating the interest of the lessee as a possessory interest, ownership jurisdictions

---

21. Adams v. Elkhorn Coal Corp., 199 Ky. 612, 251 S.W. 654; Duncan v. Mason, 239 Ky. 570, 39 S.W.2d 1006; Kentucky Natural Gas Corp. v. Carter, 303 Ky. 559, 198 S.W.2d 311; Danciger Oil & Refining Co. of Texas v. Powell, 137 Tex. 484, 154 S.W.2d 632; Texas Co. v. State of Texas, 154 Tex. 494, 281 S.W.2d 83; Feather v. Baird, 85 W.Va. 267, 102 S.E. 294.

22. 137 Tex. 484, 154 S.W.2d 632.

23. Adams v. Elkhorn Coal Corp., 199 Ky. 612, 251 S.W. 654; Danciger Oil & Refining Co. of Texas v. Powell, 137 Tex. 484, 154 S.W.2d 632; Texas Co. v. State of Texas, 154 Tex. 494, 281 S.W.2d 83.

24. Bardhill v. Sellers, Ky., 298 S.W.2d 5; Eggleston v. Sinclair Oil & Gas Co., 132 Okl. 81, 269 P. 306; West v. Commissioner of Internal Revenue, C.A. 5th, 150 F.2d 723, cert. denied 326 U.S. 795, 66 S.Ct. 488, 90 L.Ed. 484. The conclusion is reinforced where an express provision is found for termination upon non-development. See Dougherty v. Greene, 218 Miss. 250, 67 So.2d 297, where termination was provided for in the event of non-payment of minimum royalties.

25. Texas Co. v. State of Texas, 154 Tex. 494, 281 S.W.2d 83 (Where it was stated that the instrument was to be "construed as a conveyance in fee of all oil, gas and other minerals" held to be a deed). Danciger Oil & Refining Co. of Texas v. Powell, 137 Tex. 484, 154 S.W.2d 632 (Where instrument was subject "only to the limitations and covenants hereinafter set forth" held, in construing instrument as a deed, to exclude the implication of covenants additional to those set forth in the instrument, such as a covenant to explore or develop).

26. See: § 1.3. Nature of Ownership of the Mineral Estate, supra, and generally, Summers, Oil and Gas Law, Volume 1A, Legal Interest Created by Oil and Gas Leases.

are not limited to the view that only a corporeal possessory interest in the minerals is created. As a matter of fact, several jurisdictions that follow the ownership theory of the mineral estate find the interest of the lessee to be a nonpossessory incorporeal interest.[27] One such jurisdiction finds the interest of the lessee to be personalty.[28]

Such dichotomy of viewpoint can be traced to the earliest case to consider the nature of the lessee's interest under an oil and gas lease. This is the case of Funk v. Halderman,[29] decided in Pennsylvania in 1866. Here the granting clause of the lease provided that the lessee have the "free and uninterrupted use, privilege, and liberty to go on any part of" certain described lands. The court applied the English distinction between a lease and a license, and held that the instrument created a license, as it conferred only an "exclusive right" to go on the land. However, the court further defined the interest as constituting a license coupled with an interest in the minerals so that it was not revocable at the will of the grantor.

Later Pennsylvania decisions have distinguished the factual situation in the Funk case and have held where the granting clause purports to grant, demise and lease the land for oil and gas production, rather than an exclusive privilege to take oil and gas, that a corporeal possessory estate is created in the minerals in the lessee.[30] It appears now that Alabama and Ohio [31] are the only jurisdictions which are influenced by the form of the granting clause in defining the nature of the lessee's interest.

It is interesting to note that only three of a possible thirteen ownership jurisdictions find that the interest of the lessee in an oil and gas lease is a corporeal possessory interest.[32] By far the majority of

27. Arkansas; Kansas; Montana; Ohio; Pennsylvania; Tennessee; West Virginia.

28. Kansas.

29. 53 Pa. 229.

30. Kelly v. Keys, 213 Pa. 295, 62 A. 911 (license-nonpossessory interest); Barnsdall v. Bradford Gas Co., 225 Pa. 338, 74 A. 207 (lease-possessory interest).

31. Alabama: Moorer v. Bethlehem Baptist Church, 272 Ala. 259, 130 P.2d 367; Ohio: no authoritative decision is found defining the exact nature of the oil and gas lease in Ohio. However, it appears that the lease-license distinction will be applied. Woodland Oil Co. v. Crawford, 55 Ohio St. 161, 44 N.E. 1093; Jones v. Wood, 9 Ohio Cir.Ct.R. 560. It appears that Ohio is tending toward the ownership theory of the mineral estate, Kelly v. Ohio Oil Co., 57 Ohio St. 317, 49 N.E. 399; but cf. Back v. Ohio Fuel Gas Co., 160 Ohio St. 81, 113 N.E.2d 865.

32. Texas is the mainstay of the view that an oil and gas lease creates a corporeal possessory interest in real property, i.e., a determinable fee in the minerals. Stephens County v. Mid-Kansas Oil & Gas Co., 113 Tex. 160, 254 S.W. 290; Sheffield v. Hogg, 124 Tex. 290, 77 S.W.2d 1021. However, between 1915 and 1923 the form of the granting clause was instrumental as to the interest created. Texas Co. v. Daugherty, 107 Tex. 234, 176 S.W. 717. Also see Walker, Nature of the Property Interests Created by an Oil and Gas Lease in Texas, 11 Tex.L. Rev. 399. Mississippi follows the Texas view, and the form of the granting clause does not affect the result, Stokely v. State, 149 Miss. 435, 115 So. 563; Lloyd's Estate v. Mullen Tractor & Equipment Co., 192 Miss. 62, 4 So.2d 282; Sistrunk v. Graham, 215 Miss. 552, 61 So.2d 335; and see Hall, The Application of the Determinable Fee Theory in Construing the Mississippi Mineral Lease, 19 Miss.L.J. 291; New Mexico is apparently committed to the Texas view, Bolack v. Hedges, 56 N.M. 92, 240 P.2d 844; Heath v. Gray, 58 N.M. 665, 274 P.2d 620.

§ 6.1   THE OIL AND GAS LEASE—DURATION

the oil and gas producing jurisdictions classify the interest of the lessee as a nonpossessory interest in land, an incorporeal hereditament, i.e., a profit à prendre.[33] Two jurisdictions classify the lessee's interest as one in personal property,[34] and another two jurisdictions would so classify the lessee's interest prior to the time that discovery is made.[35]

---

33. Arkansas: Pasteur v. Niswanger, 226 Ark. 486, 290 S.W.2d 852; Henry v. Gulf Refining Co., 176 Ark. 133, 2 S.W.2d 687; California: Callahan v. Martin, 3 Cal.2d 110, 43 P.2d 788; Gerhard v. Stephens, 69 Cal.Rptr. 612, 442 P.2d 692; and see Hightower, The Oil and Gas Lease in California, 3 U.C.L.A.L.Rev. 424; Illinois: Poe v. Ulrey, 233 Ill. 56, 84 N.E. 46; Central Standard Life Insurance Co. v. Gardner, 17 Ill.2d 220, 161 N.E.2d 278; Indiana: Heller v. Dailey, 28 Ind.App. 555, 63 N.E. 490; Kansas: although Kansas is an ownership state as to the mineral estate it appears that an oil and gas lease in Kansas creates an interest in personalty, Potucek v. Blair, 176 Kan. 263, 270 P.2d 240; Rowan v. Harburney Oil Co., C.A.10th, 91 F.2d 122; however, cf. Rowan v. Harburney Oil Co., C.A.10th, 91 F.2d 122; and Dickey v. Coffeyville Vitrified Brick & Tile Co., 69 Kan. 106, 76 P. 398; Palmer Oil & Gas Co. v. Parish, 61 Kan. 311, 59 P. 640; Robinson v. Smalley, 102 Kan. 842, 171 P. 1151; Burden v. Gypsy Oil Co., 141 Kan. 147, 40 P.2d 463. It is treated as an interest in realty for purposes of the homestead statute, and the statute of frauds; also see Poole, The Nature of the Lessee's Interest Under an Oil and Gas Lease in Kansas, 5 Kan.Bar.J. 306; Scott, Creation of Oil and Gas Royalty and Mineral Interests, J.B.A.Kan. 234; Kentucky: Central Kentucky Natural Gas Co. v. Smallwood, Ky., 252 S.W.2d 866; Piney Oil & Gas Co. v. Allen, 235 Ky. 767, 32 S.W.2d 325; Swiss Oil Co. v. Hupp, 253 Ky. 552, 69 S.W.2d 1037; Louisiana: Serio v. Chadwick, La.App., 66 So.2d 9; Dixon v. American Liberty Oil Co., 226 La. 911, 77 So.2d 533; Reagan v. Murphy, 235 La. 529, 105 So.2d 210; and see Daggett, Mineral Rights, 20 La.L.Rev. 237; Nature of a Mineral Lease in Louisiana, 25 Tul.L.Rev. 497; Maryland: Kiser v. Eberly, 200 Md. 242, 88 A.2d 570, (however, the case does not classify the real property interest found); Montana: Voyta v. Clonts, 134 Mont. 156, 328 P.2d 655; Herigstad v. Hardrock Oil Co., 101 Mont. 22, 52 P.2d 171; Williard v. Federal Surety Co., 91 Mont. 465, 8 P.2d 633; Broderick v. Stevenson, Consolidated Oil Co., 88 Mont. 34, 290 P. 244; and see Shepherd, Oil and Gas Leasehold and Other Estates, 14 Montana L.Rev. 1; Sullivan, Survey of Oil and Gas Law in Montana as it relates to the Oil and Gas Lease, 16 Montana L.Rev. 1; North Dakota: it is probable that a non-possessory interest in real property is created, Petroleum Exchange Inc. v. Poynter, N.D., 64 N.W.2d 718; Alfson v. Anderson, N.D., 78 N.W.2d 693; Ulrich v. Amerada Petroleum Corp. N.D., 66 N.W.2d 397; Oklahoma: Kelly v. Harris, 62 Okl. 236, 162 P. 219; Rich v. Doneghey, 71 Okl. 204, 177 P. 86; Kolachny v. Galbreath, 26 Okl. 772, 110 P. 902; Wyoming: Boatman v. Andre, 44 Wyo. 352, 12 P.2d 370; and see Everett, Wyoming Decisions Relative to the Law of Oil and Gas and Comments with Respect to Form "88" Leases, 6 Wyo.L.J. 223. The nature of the lessee's interest is not clear in Arizona; Colorado, see March, The Interest of Landowner and Lessee in Oil and Gas in Colorado, 25 Rocky Mt.L.Rev. 117; Michigan; Nebraska, see Merrill, The Oil and Gas Lease-Major Problems, 41 Neb.L.Rev. 488; and Utah.

34. New York: New York Laws, 1883, Chap. 372, for all purposes except taxation; Wagner v. Mallory, 169 N.Y. 501, 62 N.E. 584; Washington: Walla Walla Oil Gas & Pipe Line Co. v. Vallentine, 103 Wash. 359, 174 P. 980; and see Burnside, Nature of Interests Created by Oil Leases in Illinois, 24 Wash.U.L.Q. 91; also see Kansas, note Wagner v. Mallory, 169 N.Y. 501, 62 N.E. 584, supra.

35. West Virginia: (cases differ; however, it appears that prior to discovery the interest of the lessee is an "inchoate and contingent" interest), Shearer v. United Carbon Co., 143 W.Va. 482, 103 S.E.2d 883; Core v. New York Petroleum Co., 52 W.Va. 276, 43 S.E. 128; Eastern Oil Co. v. Coulehan, 65 W.Va. 531, 64 S.E. 836, but cf. Charter v. Maxwell, 132 W.Va. 282, 52 S.E.2d 753; Tennessee cites and apparently follows the West Virginia view, Morris v. Messer, 156 Tenn. 54, 299 S.W 782.

For the most part, it is somewhat misleading to label the lessee's interest as either a possessory or non-possessory interest in land. The nature of the lessee's interest in any particular jurisdiction will depend upon its treatment by the courts in connection with the statute of frauds; tax liability; dower and curtesy; actions concerning real property such as ejectment; venue and jurisdiction of courts; joinder of parties; conveyancing statutes; homestead rights; creation and foreclosure of vendor's, materialmen's and laborer's liens; real estate brokers' commissions and license; corporate franchise taxes on tangible property owned by the corporation, etc. Although these problems no longer pose pressing problems in most producing jurisdictions, having been settled by judicial decision or statute, in most of the states that consider the interest of the lessee to be basically a non-possessory interest, decisions concerning the precise nature of the interest in particular instances are far from consistent.[36]

§ 6.2 Classification of Oil and Gas Leases by Duration

Although early draftsmen were strongly influenced by leases used for hard mineral mining, a more flexible structure was evolved for use by the oil and gas lessee.

The "drill or pay" lease allowed the lessor to hold the lessee liable for payment of delay rentals during the entire primary term, or to terminate the lease in the event of non-compliance by the lessee.

The "unless" lease, however, became the most commonly used lease in the industry, as it allows the lessee freedom of action in either paying the delay rentals or of drilling, with the only result of non-compliance being the loss of the lease.

As mentioned previously, draftsmen of early oil and gas leases were influenced by instruments pertaining to hard mineral mining. Essentially, however, a different factor was present, although not immediately recognized: The nature of petroleum products as migratory substances. Where hard minerals were concerned, no problem was presented by the failure to remove such minerals for a long period of time, other than loss of immediate income from production. This, of course, is not the case where petroleum products, due to tardy development, are being drained by production from adjacent lands. For this reason the fee conveyance or long-term lease were soon abandoned in order to gain flexibility in the event of a failure of the lessee to develop.[1]

---

36. See Summers, Oil and Gas Law, ch. 7, Legal Interest Created by Oil and Gas Leases.

1. Gulf Oil Corp. v. Southland Royalty Co., Tex., 496 S.W.2d 547 (an example of a lease with a 50-year fixed term that caused extensive litigation as the field was still highly productive at the end of the 50 years!).

In general see Summers, Oil and Gas Law, Volume 2, Chapter 11. Many early leases were conveyances for periods of 15 to 99 years. Upon appreciation of the migratory nature of oil and gas, they were followed by leases covering small acreage containing short terms of several months in which the lessee must drill or forfeit. When deeper wells were necessary the lessee needed a longer term

§ 6.2   THE OIL AND GAS LEASE—DURATION   247

The first form of lease to gain widespread popularity was the so-called "or" lease form.[2] Under this form of lease, land was leased for a fixed period of time, which initial period could be extended by production. During each year of the initial period the lessee covenanted to either drill a well or pay a sum of money to the lessor to delay operations. Such sum is called a delay rental. It was held that the lessee had no right to terminate the lease, and the lessor could not force the lessee to drill a well, but could bring suit for the rentals.[3] Since the lessee had no right to terminate, he either had to drill a well or was absolutely obligated to pay rentals during the entire term of the lease.

Later, a forfeiture clause was added by which the lessor could elect to terminate the lease upon failure of the lessee to drill. The lessee attempted to claim benefit of the clause where he had failed to drill, but it was held that the forfeiture clause was for the benefit of the lessor and not the lessee.[4] Therefore, under this form of "or" lease the lessee was again obligated to either drill or pay, but the lessor could elect to sue for the rentals during the term of the lease, or could terminate the lease for failure of the lessee to do either.

In an attempt to alleviate this situation a surrender clause was added to the lease, whereby the lessee could elect to surrender the lease and avoid further liability for rentals where he desired not to develop the land. However, some courts looked at the oil and gas lease as an executory contract. As it was customary for the lessee to pay only a very nominal consideration, with the lessor looking to development for return, courts looked at the lease containing a surrender clause as placing no obligation upon the lessee and held the lease to be invalid.[5] Although later cases have upheld such leases without the necessity of payment of a substantial additional consideration for the surrender clause,[6] it was this state of affairs that led the oil and

within which he could block up larger acreage and acquire greater amounts of capital; hence leases with a fixed term of five or ten years were developed. See Shannon v. Long, 180 Ala. 128, 60 So. 273; Karns v. Tanner, 66 Pa. 297; Guffey Petroleum Co. v. Oliver, Tex.Civ.App., 79 S.W. 884.

2. O'Hara v. Coltrin, ___ Colo.App. ___, 637 P.2d 398; Carroll v. Eaton, 168 Mont. 150, 541 P.2d 64; Norman Jessen & Associates, Inc. v. Amoco Production Co., N.D., 305 N.W.2d 648; Cohn v. Clark, 48 Okl. 500, 150 P. 467; Girolami v. Peoples Natural Gas Co., 365 Pa. 455, 76 A.2d 375; McElroy, Unless vs. Or: An Appraisal, 6 Baylor L.Rev. 415.

3. Butler v. Nepple, 54 Cal.2d 589, 6 Cal.Rptr. 767, 354 P.2d 239; Sugg v. Williams, 191 Ky. 188, 229 S.W. 72; Jackson v. Twin State Oil Co., 95 Okl. 96, 218 P. 324.

4. Galey v. Kellerman, 123 Pa. 491, 16 A. 474; and see, Poe v. Ulrey, 233 Ill. 56, 84 N.E. 46; Cohn v. Clark, 48 Okl. 500, 150 P. 467; Hickernell v. Gregory, Tex. Civ.App., 224 S.W. 691.

5. Eclipse Oil Co. v. South Penn Oil Co., 47 W.Va. 84, 34 S.E. 923; Federal Oil Co. v. Western Oil Co., 7th Cir., 112 F. 373, affirmed 121 F. 674. See Summers, Oil and Gas Law, Vol. 2, §§ 223–243 for a discussion of the variations in these early lease forms and the error of the early courts in holding that such leases were tenancies at will.

Also see footnote 2, supra.

6. Brown v. Wilson, 58 Okl. 392, 160 P. 94 (It was this case that led attorneys in Tulsa, Oklahoma, to develop the "unless" form lease); Rich v. Doneghey, 71 Okl. 204, 177 P. 86; Corsicana Petroleum Co. v. Owens, 110 Tex. 568, 222 S.W. 154.

gas industry to look for an alternative form of oil and gas lease. This was found in the "unless" type lease.

The "unless" lease form is commonly referred to as the "Producer's 88 Lease." This title resulted from the act of a Tulsa, Oklahoma printer who numbered his printed forms, and in printing an "unless" lease form designated it as number "88." Since landowners became willing to accept the 88 lease form, its use was encouraged by other printers who also called their "unless" form leases "Producer's 88" leases. An examination of lease forms in current use will reveal that they are still designated as "Producer's 88 Form Lease," or "Producer's 88 Lease, Revised," which may or may not set forth the last date of revision.[7]

With the increasing awareness of the landowner as to the subtleties of oil and gas law, no longer will printed forms with such a designation be naively accepted and executed by a landowner. However, many oil companies still print up such forms (or have them printed up) which contain provisions thought beneficial, for this is both cheaper and does not generate the suspicion that a typed lease still may do upon occasion.

The form of the "unless" lease resembles the form of the "or" lease in many respects. Each contains a fixed term. The fixed term is referred to as the primary term of the lease. The primary term may be for any term of years that is agreeable to the parties. In recent years the primary term of the oil and gas lease in common use appears to have become shortened from the former customary term of ten years to five or three years. In areas of high activity, leases are routinely found with short terms of three months to a year. Many contain an obligation well clause. Such short terms are favorable to the landowner, as they force the lessee to promptly begin to develop the property or lose the lease.

The primary term of the "unless" lease is followed by a secondary term, which is indefinite in duration and is dependent upon production for continued existence. A similar secondary term is also provided for in the "or" lease form.

It is in the structure of the primary term that the "unless" and the "or" form leases may be distinguished. As seen above, the lessee using the "or" form lease is under an absolute obligation to drill or pay at the end of each year of the primary term. Upon failure to do either, the lessor has a right to terminate. This right of termination is in the nature of a forfeiture due to non-compliance with a condition

---

7. The designation is generally that of an "unless" form lease. As most printed forms of the Producer's 88 lease are promulgated by various oil and gas companies, the terms necessarily will differ according to the understanding of a particular company as to desirable provisions in the lease. For this reason the designation of a lease as a Producer's 88 is not legally descriptive of the estate or interest that it creates in the lessee. See Fagg v. Texas Co., Tex.Com.App., 57 S.W.2d 87, and Walker, Defects and Ambiguities in Oil and Gas Leases, 28 Tex.L. Rev. 895; Veasey, The Law of Oil and Gas, 18 Mich.L.Rev. 652.

subsequent. Such forfeiture is not automatic upon non-compliance, but must be judicially asserted by the lessor, and may be prevented by good cause shown by the lessee.

On the other hand, the modern "unless" form lease expressly provides that the primary term shall terminate upon any anniversary date of the lease during its primary term, *unless* the lessee either pays the delay rental then due or commences the operations for the drilling of a well prior to each such date. Any year during the primary term when the lessee does not either commence operations or pay the delay rental he will lose his lease; however, there is no obligation upon him to do either act. As will be seen in later sections of this work, in most jurisdictions the termination of the "unless" lease for non-compliance is treated as a common law limitation upon the estate or interest of the lessee. The lease terminates automatically upon non-compliance.

The "unless" form of oil and gas lease is in almost exclusive use in this country, as it has achieved the desired flexibility for the lessee without the resulting liability of the "or" lease form. However, some thought has been given in the oil industry to going back to a modified "or" form lease to escape some of the limitation features of the "unless" lease.

§ 6.3 Keeping the Lease Alive During the Primary Term—The Delay Rental

The delay rental provision allows the lessee to pay an annual rental in lieu of development for each year of the primary term. Under the customary "unless" lease a failure of the lessee to either commence a well or pay the delay rental on or prior to the anniversary date for each year of the lease within the primary term will result in termination of the lease. Such provision is properly construed as a common law limitation on the estate of the lessee.

Rex Oil Company executes an "unless" type oil and gas lease upon Blackacre with a ten-year primary term. As will be seen in later sections,[1] Rex must have production in paying quantities or some contractual substitute such as shut-in royalty payments or development operations at the end of the primary term in order for the lease to be propelled into the secondary term. The failure of the lessee to be so producing or operating at the end of the primary term will result in the termination of the lease, either by its own terms or under a decree of cancellation, depending upon the jurisdiction the lessee is operating in. However, what must Rex Oil Company do to keep the lease alive during the ten-year primary term?

It was held in cases involving the earliest forms of oil and gas leases that the lease would be terminated if the lessee did not commence development and exploration within a reasonable time from

---

1. See §§ 6.10 and 6.11, infra.

the execution of the lease.[2] The same result would occur where, during the primary term, the lessee had achieved production which then ceased and the lessee did nothing more on the land during the primary term. The rationale for termination of the lease was usually phrased in terms that the lease had been lost through abandonment.[3]

When the leasehold interest is viewed as an interest in personalty, a finding of abandonment may result where the lessee has ceased operations with an intent to abandon.[4] However, the normal rule is that title to interests in realty may not be abandoned. Where O owns Lot 6, Block 14, of the Glad Acres Subdivision, he may not lose title by leaving the lot with an intention to abandon. Title will remain in O unless lost due to adverse possession of the property by a third party, or by sale for nonpayment of taxes or similar charges.

However, even in ownership jurisdictions abandonment has been used as a supporting rationale for termination of a lease where the lessee has ceased operations. In Texas Company v. Davis,[5] the Texas Supreme Court found that the lease had terminated where nothing had been done from 1904 to 1919, which was still within the primary term. The rationale was abandonment. The court stated that the lessee had abandoned the purpose of the lease. Title was lost when the lessee had permanently stopped and abandoned exploration and development of the leased premises.

Under the early forms of leases, in order to prevent abandonment of the lease due to non-development, the lessee must have been more or less continually engaged in some type of development, exploration, or production activities. However, any production during the primary term will be sufficient to prevent termination, even though not in paying quantities[6] or sufficient to maintain the lease in the secondary term. This is a correct result as the habendum clause does not apply during the primary term. The primary term of the lease is a period for development and exploration. As long as the lessee is actively engaged in exploration and development during this period, nothing more should be required. However, after the end of the primary term the lease must be a profitable proposition to both the lessor and the lessee, or it will terminate. One must be careful when speaking

---

2. Cameron v. Lebow, Ky., 338 S.W.2d 399; Texas Co. v. Davis, 113 Tex. 321, 254 S.W. 304. As to this Section in general, see Summers, Oil and Gas, Chapter 11; Bond, Delay Rental Instructions, 14 Okla.L.Rev. 475; Conger, Problems Presented in Connection With Paying Delay Rentals on Oil and Gas Leases, 2 La.B.J. 193; Holder, Payment of Delay Rentals, 5 La.B.J. 183; Merrill, Abandonment of Oil and Gas Leases, 11 Cornell L.Q. 499; Moses, Relationship Between the Lessor and the Depository Bank in Mineral Leases, 18 Tex.L.Rev. 262; Williams, Delay Rental and Related Clauses of Oil and Gas Leases, 38 Minn.L.Rev. 97; and see 26 W.Va.L.Q. 149.

3. Hill v. Larcon Co., D.C.Ark., 131 F.Supp. 469; Texas Co. v. Davis, 113 Tex. 321, 254 S.W. 304.

4. See Gerhard v. Stephens, 68 Cal.2d 864, 69 Cal.Rptr. 612, 442 P.2d 692.

5. 113 Tex. 321, 254 S.W. 304.

6. Baker v. Huffman, 176 Kan. 554, 271 P.2d 276; Long v. Magnolia Petroleum Co., 166 Neb. 410, 89 N.W.2d 245; Murphy v. Garfield Oil Co., 98 Okl. 273, 225 P. 676.

§ 6.3   THE OIL AND GAS LEASE—DURATION   251

of "production" to determine in what regard the term is being used. The term "production" may have several connotations depending upon the context in which it is being applied.[7]

In the above illustration, concerning early lease forms, the lessee had to do something, either drill or pay during the entire primary term of the lease to prevent termination. It was to prevent this burden that the delay rental payment was devised and the "unless" lease came into prominence. Under the customary "unless" lease [8] it is provided that the lease will terminate at the end of the first year of the primary term "unless" the lessee does either of two things: (1) commence the operations for the drilling of a well,[9] or (2) pay a rental payment to the lessor for the express purpose of delaying development. It is the majority view that payment of delay rental postpones the obligation for initial exploration and development for the entire period for which it is paid.[10] Therefore, if the lessee pays the delay rental on or before the anniversary date for each year of the primary term the lease will be maintained in full force and effect to the last day of the primary term without the need for development. However, if no development has occurred or is occurring at the end of the primary term the lease will terminate.

Under the "unless" lease form no obligation rests upon the lessee to pay the delay rental,[11] but non-payment will result in termination of the lease. The "unless" clause in the lease is properly construed as creating a common law limitation on the estate and not a right of forfeiture in the lessor.[12]

---

7. "Production" may use the following definitions:

(a) In connection with the habendum clause, the lessee normally need make a profit only over operating expenses, see § 6.11, infra.

(b) During the primary term any production is sufficient.

(c) However, for the lessee to be obligated to drill additional wells after the initial well, it must be shown that anticipated production from the additional wells will pay not only the operating costs, but will also be sufficient to return the cost of drilling and completing the additional well, and pay a profit. See Chapter 8, § 8.3(A), infra.

8. A customary provision is as follows:

If operations for drilling are not commenced on said land or on acreage pooled therewith as above provided on or before one year from this date, the lease shall then terminate as to both parties, unless on or before such anniversary date Lessee shall pay or tender to Lessor or to the credit of Lessor in _____ Bank at _____, Texas, (which bank and its successors are Lessor's agent and shall continue as the depository for all rentals payable hereunder regardless of changes in ownership of said land or the rentals) the sum of _____ Dollars ($_____), (herein called rentals), which shall cover the privilege of deferring commencement of drilling operations for a period of twelve (12) months. In like manner and upon like payments or tenders annually, the commencement of drilling operations may be further deferred for successive periods of twelve (12) months each during the primary term.

9. Earlier leases provided that the well had to be "completed" rather than commenced prior to any particular payment date.

10. Humphreys v. Fletcher, 27 N.M. 639, 204 P. 70; but cf. Cameron v. Lebow, Ky., 338 S.W.2d 399.

11. Brunson v. Carter Oil Co., D.C. Okl., 259 F. 656; Stady v. Texas Co., 150 Kan. 420, 94 P.2d 322; Johnson v. Smallenberger, 237 La. 11, 110 So.2d 119.

12. Mattison v. Trotti, C.A.5th, 262 F.2d 339; Kugel v. Young, 132 Colo. 529, 291 P.2d 695. O'Hara v. Coltrin, __

In order to avoid the loss of a lease through improper payment of delay rentals lessees have executed "paid-up" leases. These are leases under which the delay rentals are paid in advance for the entire primary term of the lease. Unless care is used, this practice can result in creating some additional problems for the lessee.

A special form of paid-up lease should be used. Where the usual "unless" lease is used, containing a delay rental clause, and the rentals are merely paid in advance, no notice is given by the lease that delay rentals have been paid. Rent is not apportionable as to time, but accrues on the date due. Unless otherwise stated in the lease, delay rentals are due and payable on the due date shown in the lease. Where no notice is given by the lease of paid-up rentals, liability would exist for such payments to later purchasers of the reversion of the mineral estate from the lessor. "On or before" payment provisions relate to the time payment may be made, not to the determination of the proper payee. Therefore, a paid-up lease should show on its face that all delay rentals have been paid in advance, and that no subsequent owner of the reversion is entitled to delay rentals. Also, the delay rental clause should be stricken from the lease form, along with other provisions relating to the payment of delay rentals.

The purpose of payment of delay rentals is to postpone the necessity of drilling an exploratory well during the period of time for which delay rentals have been paid. The paid-up lease form should contain express language that relieves the lessee from drilling an exploratory well during the entire primary term of the lease.

The Internal Revenue Service has taken the position that where payments have been made for the extension of a lease for a period of more than one year, the payments are in the nature of a bonus and not rentals.[13] Although delay rental payments may be deducted by the lessee as a business expense, bonus must be capitalized and depleted. Bonus payments would be ordinary income to the lessor, subject to cost depletion. Under recent revenue rulings of the I.R.S.[14] cash bonus is not subject to percentage depletion by the lessor. Cost depletion is available to the lessor if a basis can be shown in the mineral estate and the lessor can calculate future production. Where the surface and the minerals are purchased together, lessor may not be able to show a basis for the mineral estate where a value for the minerals was not designated or allocated at the time of purchase.[15]

Colo.App. ___, 637 P.2d 398; Trigg v. United States, Department of Interior, C.A.10th, 630 F.2d 1370.

13. Rev.Rul. 80–49.

14. Rev.Rul. 81–44, also see Rev.Rul. 81–266, where it is still the position of the IRS that the lessee provide for bonus exclusion in computation of percentage depletion.

15. Plow Realty Co. of Texas, 4 T.C. 600; Rev.Rul. 69–539.

(A) The Delay Rental—Payment Date

Delay rentals are due and payable on or before the anniversary date shown in the body of the lease, not on or before the anniversary date of the date of execution, acknowledgment or delivery. Ambiguity may occur in the payment date through amendment of the lease by a subsequent instrument. The better view is that payment of delay rentals is not excused during a period of challenge by the lessor of the lessee's title.

Under the form of "unless" lease now commonly in use the delay rental must be paid on or before the anniversary date of the lease for each successive year during the primary term that the lessee desires to so keep the lease alive.[16] Since failure to so pay is a terminal provision of the lease there should be no ambiguity as to the date upon which each delay rental is to become due. However, at times controversy has arisen as to the date of the lease for delay rental payment purposes. In the case of Hughes v. Franklin,[17] the first line in the body of the lease contained the date of October 8. The lessors were tenants in common, and the lease was circulated until the last party lessor had executed it on November 26, the date of delivery. A delay rental payment made on the anniversary date of delivery was held to be late, as the date in the body of the lease controlled over the date of execution, acknowledgment or delivery. This appears to be the general rule.[18] Where the payment date falls upon a Sunday or holiday, it apparently will be paid timely if payment is made upon the next ensuing business date.[19]

Strangely, one form of the unless lease, apparently in an effort to clarify the problem of conflicting dates, has worded the "unless" clause so that it reads: "If drilling operations are not commenced on the leased premises on or before one (1) year from the *effective* date hereof, this lease will then terminate unless * * *." It would seem that by introducing the word "effective" the draftsman is creating the very problem to be avoided. The word "effective" is not otherwise defined in the instrument, and it is arguable that this would be the date of delivery. In the case of tenants in common, delivery may occur upon a different date as to each lessor, for, unless otherwise restricted, the instrument will become effective as to each upon execution and delivery. This, of course, would lead to an extremely difficult situation for the lessee. The dates of delivery would not be set forth in the lease, would lie in parol, and would occasion separate payments for each party lessor.

---

16. Apparently some conflict in the decisions occurred under early lease forms calling for a "completion" of the well. See Summers, Oil & Gas, § 341.

17. 201 Miss. 215, 29 So.2d 79.

18. Hughes v. Franklin, 201 Miss. 215, 29 So.2d 79; Greer v. Stanolind Oil & Gas Co., C.A.10th, 200 F.2d 920.

19. See Durell v. Miles, 53 N.M. 264, 206 P.2d 547; Semans v. Adams, Tex.Civ. App., 228 S.W. 353. Cf. McLaughlin v. Brock, Tex.Civ.App., 225 S.W. 575, where payment made following holiday which fell on last day, held not timely and lease terminated. See Summers, § 346.

An ambiguity in delay rental payment date may also result from an amendment of the oil and gas lease. Assume that one of the parties signs the lease on January 1, at a time when some question has arisen as to his capacity. At a later time, July 7, when no question remains as to his capacity he executes another lease identical in form except for the date and the statement that the second lease was executed "in lieu and correction of" the first lease. Lessee then waits to the anniversary date of the second lease, July 7, to pay the delay rental; is it paid timely? It was held in the case of Humble Oil & Refining Company v. Mullican,[20] that the delay rental was improperly paid. The basis of the decision was that it was not the intent of the parties that the second lease completely replace the first but that it was executed merely to remove any doubts concerning the capacity of the lessor.

Whether or not one agrees with the result, the case raises a question as to the manner in which amendments of the original lease should be handled in regard to the date delay rentals are to be paid. Where the second instrument is not to entirely replace the first, one method is to execute a lease identical in form and backdated to bear the same lease date as the original lease. Obviously the second lease will have no legal effect until signed and delivered; however, all of the operative dates will be identical with the original lease, including the primary term.

The parties to the lease have the power in advance of the payment date to extend the period for payment of the delay rental. However, it has been held where the lessor has top leased prior to an extension agreement, the second lessee who had not joined in the agreement was not bound by it. A failure of the lessee to pay on the original anniversary date terminated the lease.[21]

The courts are divided on the question of whether it is necessary for the lessee to continue to pay or tender delay rental payments where the lessee's title is being questioned by the lessor.[22] As the delay rental clause is generally viewed as constituting a common law limitation on the lease which will automatically terminate upon non-payment it would seem that, unless acts of the lessor might result in an estoppel or waiver of the payments, the conservative lessee is compelled to take the view that termination by non-payment is not affected by the acts of the lessor questioning the lease.

---

20. 144 Tex. 609, 192 S.W.2d 770.

21. Willan v. Farrar, 176 Neb. 1, 124 N.W.2d 699. Also see, Brown, Effect of Top Leases: Obstruction of Title and Related Considerations, 30 Bay.L.R. 213 (1978).

22. Valentine Oil Co. v. Powers, 157 Neb. 71, 59 N.W.2d 150 (holding that payment is not excused); Mitchell v. Simms, Tex.Com.App., 63 S.W.2d 371. Cases holding that further payment is excused during period of challenge to lessee's title: Gheen v. Diamond Shamrock Corp., Tex.Civ.App., 529 S.W.2d 289 (that objection to tender made by check instead of in cash must be made at time of tender by lessee), also see UCC § 2–511(2), (3); Kugel v. Young, 132 Colo. 529, 291 P.2d 695, noted 3 U.C.L.A.L.Rev. 609; Leonard v. Busch-Everett Co., 139 La. 1099, 72 So. 749; Twyford v. Whitchurch, C.A. 10th, 132 F.2d 819.

(B) The Delay Rental—Tender

Where a depository bank has been designated by the lessors under the customary form of the "unless" lease, receipt by the bank on or before the due date will constitute a proper tender, whether or not the money is actually credited to the lessor's account or clears the payee bank prior to the due date.

Where the lease provides for "mailing" to the lessor or depository bank, a timely deposit in the mails of the rental check, properly addressed and stamped, will constitute a good tender, although the payment never reaches the addressee, or is late.

For a tender of delay rentals to be good it must be made by the lessee, or his employee or agent on his behalf, and not by an unauthorized third party.

A depository bank only has limited authority to receive rental payments and to credit them to the account of the lessor. It cannot defeat a proper tender made by the lessee by directing the manner in which it will accept payments, nor bind the lessor by the acceptance or crediting of late or improper payments to the lessor's account.

Under the customary "unless" lease where all parties executing the lease are named in the premises and are defined as "Lessor", the lessee may make delay rental payments to such parties jointly. Where the lease may not be so construed the lessee must pay each party lessor his proportionate share, separately.

Virtually all "unless" lease forms call for the lessee to "pay or tender" the delay rentals to the lessor. Where the payment is made to the lessor individually no particular problems exist, except that the payment must actually be presented to the lessor on or prior to the rental payment date. Unless payment by check is provided, the lessor may demand payment in money. However, most lessors designate a depository bank to which payments are to be made for the lessor's account, in which payments by check are impliedly authorized.

The usual procedure is that clerks in the lessee's office prepare and mail delay rental checks to the designated depository bank several weeks early to allow for normal delay in the mails. Accompanying the delay rental check is a receipt form called a "Delay Rental Receipt." The receipt lists the name of the lease, the property covered thereby, the amount of the delay rental, the names of the lessors to be paid, and the period of time that is covered by the payment. The depository bank upon receiving the check and receipt will stamp one copy of the receipt showing the date and time that the check was received by the bank for credit to the account of the lessor. This copy is returned to the lessee for his records.

A complete file on the lease should contain the executed lease, cancelled bonus check, and all delay rental receipts from the depository bank. Where assignment of the lease, or a part of it, is to be made, this material, or copies thereof should be examined, together with records of operations and production upon the subject lease, for a determination that the lease has been continually held in effect. If the record of delay rentals, operations, shut-in royalties, etc., does not show a sufficiently complete picture of the continued validity of the lease, appropriate requirements will have to be made.

Where payment is made to a depository bank a question has arisen whether mere receipt by the bank is sufficient if credit to the account of the lessor or clearing of the check to the payee bank is not accomplished prior to the rental payment date. It appears to be the general view that a good tender is merely the receipt by the bank, on or before the rental due date, of a check for which funds exist, payable to the proper parties lessor. Credit to the account of the lessor or clearing of the check to the payee bank is not required.[23] The courts treat the depository bank as the agent of the lessor for the receipt of the rental check, therefore receipt by the agent is treated as receipt by the principal.[24] This is generally true although an express appointment is not made in the lease instrument.[25] The same result has occurred although the lease required that payment be "paid or credited" to the lessor,[26] rather than "paid or tendered."

An illustration of such tender is found in the case of Gulf Production Company v. Perry,[27] where the lessee had timely sent the checks to the depository bank. However, the bank would not credit the rental to the account of the lessors as they had no account at the bank. It was held that this was a good tender as it was in compliance with the contractual provisions of the lease. The failure of the bank to credit the account of the lessor was not chargeable to the lessee, as the bank was the agent of the lessor.

For a tender to be good it is necessary that sufficient funds be on deposit, or that special arrangements have been made in advance, so that the check will in fact be honored by the payee bank. In Nelson Bunker Hunt Trust Estate v. Jarmon,[28] the lessee tendered the check to the depository bank, and it was returned twice. Before again tendering the check the lessee made a loan of $500 and had it credited to his account. The check was again submitted, but it was returned marked "insufficient funds." The lessee had never kept a running balance of his account and was not aware until a month later that the check was in fact not good. It was held that the check was never good and the lease therefore terminated. The case can be contrasted with another Texas case, that of Hamilton v. Baker.[29] The check of

---

23. Gulf Refining Co. v. Bagby, 200 La. 258, 7 So.2d 903; Kronmiller v. Hafner, 75 S.D. 439, 67 N.W.2d 353; Gulf Production Co. v. Perry, Tex.Civ.App., 51 S.W.2d 1107; but cf. Chapple v. Kansas Vitrified Brick Co., 70 Kan. 723, 79 P. 666; Harter v. Edwards, 108 Kan. 346, 195 P. 607.

24. Kronmiller v. Hafner, 75 S.D. 439, 67 N.W.2d 353.

25. Note 24, supra.

26. Burbidge v. Noe, N.D., 69 N.W.2d 286.

27. Tex.Civ.App., 51 S.W.2d 1107. This case also contains a copy of a typical delay rental receipt.

28. Tex.Civ.App., 345 S.W.2d 579.

29. 147 Tex. 240, 214 S.W.2d 460, noted in 27 Tex.L.Rev. 561.

§ 6.3   THE OIL AND GAS LEASE—DURATION   257

the lessee was presented to the bank and was refused; however, the lease did not terminate. Here the lessee had talked to a vice-president of the bank and had arranged that the bank would honor the check, even if insufficient funds were shown to be in the account. A proper notation was made upon the lessee's ledger sheet. However, a clerk changed the sheet without copying the notation. The check was in fact good when it was presented and constituted a good tender.

A good tender may also be made where the lessor accepts a substitute consideration. In Gulf Production Co. v. Continental Oil Co.,[30] the lessor accepted syndicate certificates in lieu of cash. The agreement of the lessor to accept a substitute for cash continued the lease in effect.

The more recent lease forms usually provide that the delay rental be "mailed or delivered" to lessor or to said bank on or before such date of payment. Assume that Rex Oil Company has delay rentals due and payable on or before the 1st of April of each year of the primary term. On March 21 it mails a check in the proper amount, in a properly addressed and stamped envelope which either reaches the depository bank or lessor two days late due to the delay in the mails, or never reaches them. Has lessee made a sufficient tender so as to maintain the lease in effect? Where the lease has expressly allowed mailing of the delay rentals a sufficient compliance with the provisions of the lease has been met and the tender is good.[31] Where the delay rental is properly and timely mailed, the postal service is deemed to be the agent of the lessor, and proper deposit in the mail constitutes a proper tender although thereafter lost and never delivered.[32]

On the other hand, where the lease clause calls for the delay rental to be "paid or delivered" either to the lessor or the depository bank, such payment must actually be received on or before the due date. Also, if lost in the mails the tender is not good.

Accordingly, where the lease provides for mailing of delay rentals, if the rental is improperly mailed, the tender is not good. An interesting case in this regard is that of Skelly Oil Company v. Kidd.[33] In this case the lessee and lessor changed the depository bank. The lessee prepared the change of depository. The name of the town was mistakenly written as "Eustage, Texas", instead of "Eustace, Texas." The lessor executed the instrument without noticing the mistake. The lessee mailed the delay rental addressed to the bank at Eustage, Texas; however, the post office, rather than returning the letter, sent it to a bank with the same name in Carthage, Texas,

30. 139 Tex. 183, 164 S.W.2d 488, noted in 21 Tex.L.Rev. 326.

31. Baker v. Potter, 223 La. 274, 65 So.2d 598; Corley v. Olympic Petroleum Corp., Tex.Civ.App., 403 S.W.2d 537; Skelly Oil Co. v. Kidd, Tex.Civ.App., 417 S.W.2d 186; cf. Ballard v. Miller, 87 N.M. 86, 529 P.2d 752 (1975).

32. Corley v. Olympic Petroleum Corp., Tex.Civ.App., 403 S.W.2d 537.

33. Tex.Civ.App., 417 S.W.2d 186.

which credited the amount to the account of the lessors. It was held that the lease did not terminate, as the lessee had actually complied with the terms of the lease as amended.

One case has held that where a lease provides for mailing, the lessee may also use a substitute method of equal reliability. In Baker v. Potter,[34] instead of mailing the rental payment, the lessee wired the money to the depository bank by Western Union, on the last day of the primary term. The money was received two hours later, 10:30 a. m., and the bank was notified. However, the money was not delivered to the bank until the following day due to internal procedures of Western Union. The court stated that a designation of the mails did not exclude use of another agent of equal reliability, and, as mailing the last day of the primary term would suffice, depositing in Western Union was equally efficacious. It is doubtful whether the case may be relied upon as a general precedent, as the lessee did not strictly conform to the provisions of the lease, and many jurisdictions construe the lease strictly against the lessee. Where the substitute method is chosen by the lessee, such agency would be deemed to be the agent of the lessee, rather than the lessor, and timely receipt by the depositing bank would seem required.

Where a depository bank has been designated by the lessors in the lease, as mentioned above, it is generally held that the bank is the agent of the lessors in receiving delay rental checks.[35] This is true whether or not the lease contains an express appointment of the bank as agent.[36] However, the agency of the bank is limited to the purposes set forth in the lease.[37] Normally this means that the sole authority of the bank is to receive properly tendered delay rental checks and to deposit them to the account of the lessors.

The bank has no authority to refuse a properly tendered rental due to internal procedures of the bank and so defeat the tender of the lessee, nor to direct the manner in which the payment should be made.[38] As the bank has no authority to defeat a properly tendered rental by the lessee, it also has limited authority to bind the lessor. The bank has no authority to bind the lessor by acceptance of improper or untimely tendered delay rentals.

However, in one case,[39] where the depository bank was changed and the rental check was sent to the second bank, but somehow was forwarded to the original depository bank, it was held that the lease did not terminate. The court stated as one basis for its holding that

---

34. 223 La. 274, 65 So.2d 598.

35. Wagner v. Mounger, 253 Miss. 83, 175 So.2d 145; Carroll v. Roger Lacy, Inc., Tex.Civ.App., 402 S.W.2d 307.

36. Kronmiller v. Hafner, 75 S.D. 439, 67 N.W.2d 353.

37. Kouns v. Southwood, 203 Ark. 469, 158 S.W.2d 37; Wagner v. Mounger, 253 Miss. 83, 175 So.2d 145.

38. Brazell v. Soucek, 130 Okl. 204, 266 P. 442; also see Kugel v. Young, 132 Colo. 529, 291 P.2d 695, noted 3 U.C. L.A.L.Rev. 609.

39. Carroll v. Roger Lacy, Inc., Tex. Civ.App., 402 S.W.2d 307.

§ 6.3   THE OIL AND GAS LEASE—DURATION

the second bank was the agent of the lessor who was bound by the action of such bank in missending the rental payment. The case may be criticized upon the ground that such act was outside the limited authority set forth in the lease to accept and credit rental payments.

It should be pointed out that the usual "unless" lease states that: "*Lessee* shall pay or tender to lessor * * *". The lessee is bound by the terms of the lease. If the payment is not made by the lessee or his agent acting upon his behalf the payment is improper, and the lease will terminate.[40]

The usual "unless" lease provides that the lessee may make a joint payment where the lease is executed by two or more lessors. This is a result of (1) the premises of the lease defining the landowners executing the lease, whether one or more, as "Lessor," and (2) the delay rental clause stating that the lessee may "pay or tender to Lessor or to the depository hereinafter designated, for deposit to Lessor's credit * * *" the amount of delay rentals. As defined, "Lessor" will include all parties who are named in the premises.

Where one or more parties execute the lease the lessee will send to the depository bank a delay rental check that will include the total amount and the names of the lessors to whose accounts the sum should be credited. However, under the lease the lessee is not charged with making a specific allocation.[41] The bank may, in some cases, have to require a delay rental division order wherein all lessors will designate the proportion of the delay rentals to which they are entitled. Needless to say, this relieves the lessee of a troublesome burden, for an erroneous allocation of delay rentals by the lessee may cause a portion of the lease to terminate.

Where the lease may not be so construed or does not authorize joint payment, the lessee must pay each mineral owner his proportionate share.[42] However, in these circumstances, if the instrument is ambiguous a joint payment may be proper.[43]

Under the normal lease, where the original lessor has assigned a portion of the minerals underlying the lease the lessee will have the duty of allocation and mailing of separate checks, as most leases do not provide for a joint payment in this instance.

---

40. Wagner v. Mounger, 253 Miss. 83, 175 So.2d 145.

See Brannon v. Gulf States Energy Corp., Tex., 562 S.W.2d 219 (where check in amount of lease rental was paid by third party claiming it was bonus for new lease; however, it was held that as accompanying letter referred to payment as "lease rentals" acceptance by lessor revived first lease which had terminated due to non-payment of rentals).

41. Gulf Production Co. v. Perry, Tex. Civ.App., 51 S.W.2d 1107; York v. McBee, Tex.Civ.App., 308 S.W.2d 951.

In Trad v. General Crude Oil Co., Tex. Civ.App., 468 S.W.2d 612 (where delay rental was properly and timely deposited by lessee, improper allocation by bank to credit of lessor as attorney in fact for others held not to terminate the lease as bank in making such allocation was agent of lessors).

42. Superior Oil Co. v. Jackson, 207 Okl. 437, 250 P.2d 23.

43. Superior Oil Co. v. Jackson, 207 Okl. 437, 250 P.2d 23; Perkins v. Magnolia Petroleum Co., Tex.Civ.App., 148 S.W.2d 266.

To illustrate the above, in the first instance if A and B execute a joint lease to Rex Oil Company, Rex, unless restricted by the lease, will normally be able to pay A and B by a joint check in the total amount of the delay rentals. However, where A has executed a lease to Rex Oil Company, and later A assigns a one-half interest in the minerals, subject to the lease, to B, Rex will have to pay A and B by separate checks.

Where a joint payment is made, however, it must be made to the correct parties. In the case of Rushing v. Griffin,[44] the lessors were two married men. The check that was forwarded to the depository, however, included the name of the wife of one of the lessors. It was held that the check was properly rejected by the lessors and the lease terminated.

Where an allocation is made, the lessee must be certain not to short one of the parties entitled to delay rentals. For instance, assume that the delay rentals on Blackacre total $100. A assigns a one-third interest in the minerals to B and also a one-third interest in the minerals to C. How should Rex Oil Company pay the rentals? One-third of $100 would come out to two payments of $33.33 and one payment of $33.34. Actually, two of the payments are short, as three x $33.33 is only $99.99. Two of the three parties have not received the correct payment of the delay rental and could claim that the lease was terminated as to their interests. It is cheap insurance for the lessee to make sure that each party is paid the extra penny. This may also be said in other instances where landowners are claiming a larger amount of delay rental than the lessee feels is correct. The lessee can always make the overpayment and litigate the amount actually due, and the lease will stay in effect as to such interests. However, if the lessee tenders the lesser amount, and in following litigation it is found that the larger amount was correct, the lease is lost. A rule of thumb: When in doubt, overpay. The rule is a consequence of the interpretation that in most jurisdictions the "unless" clause is treated as a common law limitation and not merely a covenant.

(C) The Delay Rental—Notice of Assignment by the Mineral Owner

Where the lessor has sold his interest in the minerals and no clause is contained in the lease requiring notice of the change of ownership to the lessee, the lessee, at its peril, must determine the actual ownership of the delay rentals, and the lease will terminate as to such interest if paid to the wrong person.

Lease clauses requiring notice and the furnishing of copies of instruments reflecting changes in ownership in the mineral estate are valid, and the lessee is only required to pay those who have furnished it proper copies of such instruments. Connecting instruments in the chain of title may

---

44. 240 La. 31, 121 So.2d 229.

§ 6.3 THE OIL AND GAS LEASE—DURATION

be required. Apparently, where such a clause is present, the lessee may not rely upon recorded instruments in lieu of those furnished under the clause.

O executes to Black Gold Oil Company an oil and gas lease that contains no particular provisions regarding the payment of the delay rentals in the event of assignment of the underlying mineral estate by O. Prior to a rental payment date, O executes a deed of the land, including the minerals, to A. Black Gold is given no notice of the sale, and upon the next delay rental payment date pays the rentals to O. The lease will terminate. As seen in an earlier section the owner of the mineral estate on the rental payment date is entitled to the delay rentals.[45] This is so even though the lessee has no actual notice of the transfer. Therefore, unless some provision of the lease requires the lessor's assignee or grantee to notify the lessee of the transfer of mineral interests, the lessee will have to search the records for recorded instruments reflecting transfers that affect the underlying mineral estate of all leases that it has. This obviously has been an onerous burden, and one around which protective contractual provisions have been drafted.

It is customary now to find a provision in the assignment clause of the oil and gas lease which requires a transferee to furnish a copy of the instrument reflecting such transfer a certain number of days, 30 or 45, prior to the next ensuing rental payment date.[46] It is generally held that such provisions are valid and that both the lessor, his grantees and assigns, and the lessee are bound by the clause.[47] Where such clause is present in a lease and the lessor has sold all or part of the minerals to another party and no notice has been given to the lessee, the lessee is protected if it tenders the delay rentals to the last person from whom it has received notice.[48] In the above example, if Black Gold's lease contained such a clause and A did not give proper timely notice to Black Gold, a payment of the delay rentals to O would be proper, and the lease would not lapse. The clause relieves the lessee of the burden of record search, and the lessee is not bound

---

45. See § 6.5, infra. But cf. Crowder v. James, 110 Okl. 214, 236 P. 891; Reserve Gas Co. v. Carbon Black Manufacturing Co., 72 W.Va. 757, 79 S.E. 1002, to the effect if no clause is contained in the lease, lessee may pay the original lessor, and recording of transfer is not notice to lessee. The latter point would seem correct, as the lessee in paying delay rentals is not in the position of a subsequent purchaser as to title.

46. "The rights of either party hereunder may be assigned in whole or in part, and the provisions hereof shall extend to their heirs, successors and assigns; but no change or division in ownership of the land, rentals or royalties, however accomplished, shall operate to enlarge the obligations or diminish the rights of Lessee; and no change or division in such ownership shall be binding on Lessee until thirty (30) days after Lessee shall have been furnished by registered U.S. mail at Lessee's principal place of business with a certified copy of recorded instrument or instruments evidencing same."

47. Garelick v. Southwest Gas Producing Co., Inc., La., 129 So.2d 520; Jackson v. United Producers' Pipe Line Co., Tex.Civ.App., 33 S.W.2d 540; Cassity v. Smith, Tex.Civ.App., 193 S.W.2d 991.

48. Jackson v. United Producers' Pipe Line Co., Tex.Civ.App., 33 S.W.2d 540; Cassity v. Smith, Tex.Civ.App., 193 S.W.2d 991.

by constructive notice of the recorded instruments showing change of title to the mineral estate.[49]

Even where notice is furnished, the lessee may be entitled to require further information before being required to pay rentals to the party shown as grantee in the instrument. Assume, again in the above example, that after the sale by O to A, that A in turn sold the property to B. B gave notice timely to Black Gold Oil Company. Apparently, Black Gold may require that all links in the chain of title be furnished showing the connection of B to O.[50]

It also appears that the clause works in reverse, that is to say, that if the lease contains a notice clause and the lessee attempts to rely upon the record the lessee will be charged if the record is incorrect and the lessee has paid on such basis. In the case of Atlantic Refining Co. v. Shell Oil Co.,[51] the lease contained a notice of assignment clause. O, the owner of the mineral estate subject to the lease, executed a deed to A of an undivided one-half interest in the minerals. As executed, the deed had deletions whereby the grantee would receive no part of the delay rentals. However, as recorded, the deed showed no deletions. Relying upon the recorded deed, lessee paid one-half of the delay rentals to A. It was held that the lease terminated, as the lessee was not entitled to rely upon the record. Strangely, here there was no need to furnish a copy of the deed to the lessee, as the deed did not make a change in the parties to whom the delay rentals were payable.

Some problems have occurred concerning the inter-relationship of the time that the lessee actually mails out delay rentals and the furnishing of notice of assignment under early lease notice clauses. These clauses did not provide that notice had to be received a certain number of days prior to the next rental payment date. Consequently, what was the position of the lessee where he had already mailed out rental payments by the time that he received notice of change of ownership still prior to the payment date? This was the situation in the case of Gulf Refining Co. v. Shatford.[52] Here the assignee of the minerals did not notify the lessee for six months after the transfer. Upon receiving notice, the lessee requested certified copies or photostats. These were received by the lessee ten days prior to the rental payment date; however, the lessee had mailed rental checks the day before. Where the lessee had the right to pay "on or before" the rental payment date, the court held that the payments were properly sent out where it was not an unreasonable time in advance of a payment date. A lessee will not desire to wait until the last minute to pay rental payments. As virtually all payments are mailed, a lessee will desire to have a sufficient cushion of time so that a correct pay-

---

49. Garelick v. Southwest Gas Producing Co., Inc., La., 129 So.2d 520.

50. Pearce v. Southern Natural Gas Co., 220 La. 1094, 58 So.2d 396.

51. 217 La. 576, 46 So.2d 907.

52. C.A.5th, 159 F.2d 231. Without a clause in the lease, if mailed too far in advance, the lessee may be obligated to pay twice.

§ 6.3   THE OIL AND GAS LEASE—DURATION   263

ment may be made if the first attempt is lost in the mails or incorrectly sent. To avoid the problem presented in the Shatford case, as discussed above, many notice of assignment clauses now contain a provision that the notice of change of ownership must be received 30 to 45 days prior to the rental payment.

(D) The Delay Rental—Effect of Operations During the Primary Term

The dry hole clause was made operative during the primary term of the lease to allow the lessee to return to the payment of delay rentals where it had drilled a dry hole or had production that ceased. In absence of such clause the lessee is not authorized to return to payment of delay rentals, and a lease may be in danger of loss by abandonment. The wording of some dry hole clauses may cause a shift in the date of payment of delay rentals. A better approach is to tie return to delay rentals to the next anniversary date of the lease after the expiration of a stated number of days.

Under the "unless" form lease it is provided that the lease will terminate on any anniversary date of the lease during the primary term "unless" the lessee either pays or tenders the delay rentals or commences the operations for the drilling of a well. The prior discussion relates to the payment of delay rentals as a method of keeping the lease alive during the primary term. The alternate procedure is to commence the operations for the drilling of a well.[53] Under the early "unless" lease drilling a well could pose a problem for the lessee. Pure Oil Company acquires an "unless" lease upon Blackacre. The lease contains a ten-year primary term. Pure pays delay rentals for the first two years of the lease. However, during the third year of the primary term of the lease Pure begins the drilling of a well. The well comes in dry prior to the next rental payment date. How can Pure keep the lease alive? If Pure does nothing the lease may be subject to loss due to abandonment. Therefore Pure tenders the delay rental due for the fourth year of the primary term. However, the lessor may reject the payment on the ground that the delay rental clause does not provide for the return to delay rentals after operations are commenced upon the lease. The lessor is supported in his reasoning by the wording of the "unless" clause which reads: "If drilling operations are not commenced on the leased premises on or before * * *." Since drilling operations have been commenced

---

53. See Logan v. The California Co., 231 Miss. 836, 97 So.2d 924, where court rejected argument of lessor that drilling was not an alternative method to keep the lease alive and insisted delay rentals be paid during periods of operations also. See § 6.7, infra, for a discussion of what constitutes "commencement" of drilling operations. The cases are divided whether drilling in violation of state conservation rules will satisfy the "unless" clause. Goble v. Goff, 327 Mich. 549, 42 N.W.2d 845 (No); Novak v. Bruner, Tex. Civ.App., 320 S.W.2d 439 (Yes, rules do not affect property rights).

the clause is no longer applicable. Therefore, if the lessee did not continue operations upon the lease it may be lost.[54]

The dry hole clause was worded to apply during the primary term in order to avoid the above result.[55] As commonly worded, the clause provides that if the lessee drills a dry hole during the primary term, or has production that ceases, the lease will not terminate if the lessee resumes the payment of delay rentals.[56] Therefore, the dry hole clause, as commonly used, allows the lessee in the position of Pure Oil Company above to return to delay rentals. Some of the early forms allowed the lessee to return to delay rentals in the event that a dry hole was drilled but omitted to include cessation of production as an event allowing return to delay rentals. In such cases after cessation of production if the lessee did not continue operations upon the lease, it terminated.[57]

A question that has not been satisfactorily answered by the courts is the consequence of not returning to the payment of delay rentals for the next rental payment period after he has drilled a dry hole or had production that has ceased.[58] Where the clause is worded so as to require the lessee to either continue operations or return to payment of delay rentals, no problem exists, as the lease will terminate if neither act is done. However, some of the leases have clauses that merely authorize the return to delay rentals to avoid termination of the lease. It would seem that the better view, in keeping with the

---

54. Hill v. Larcon Co., D.C.Ark., 131 F.Supp. 469; but cf. Baker v. Huffman, 176 Kan. 554, 271 P.2d 276.

55. Vaughn v. Hearrell, Ky., 347 S.W.2d 542; Auzenne v. Lawrence Oil Co., La., 179 So.2d 533; Logan v. The California Co., 231 Miss. 836, 97 So.2d 924; Moyer v. Walker, C.A.10th, 276 F.2d 681; Colby v. Sun Oil Co., Tex.Civ.App., 288 S.W.2d 221; Mattison v. Trotti, C.A.5th, 262 F.2d 339. However, where separate leases are held from co-tenants, drilling by one lessee does not relieve the other lessee from paying delay rentals, Mattison v. Trotti, C.A.5th, 262 F.2d 339, and see §§ 6.6–6.9, infra.

A typical dry hole clause:

"If prior to discovery and production of oil, gas or other mineral on said land or on acreage pooled therewith Lessee should drill a dry hole or holes thereon, or if after discovery and production of oil, gas or other mineral, the production thereof should cease from any cause, this lease shall not terminate if Lessee commences operations for drilling or reworking within sixty (60) days thereafter or if it be within the primary term, commences or resumes the payment or tender of rentals or commences operations for drilling or reworking on or before the rental paying date next ensuing after the expiration of sixty days from date of completion of dry hole or cessation of production. If at any time subsequent to sixty (60) days prior to the beginning of the last year of the primary term and prior to the discovery of oil, gas or other mineral on said land, or on acreage pooled therewith, Lessee should drill a dry hole thereon, no rental payment or operations are necessary in order to keep the lease in force during the remainder of the primary term."

56. Where an "unless" form lease is given a primary term of one year or less, it would seem to allow indefinite propelling of lease term by payment of annual delay rentals. Such conflict in provisions results from careless draftsmanship, and the general result is that the clause in conflict with the habendum clause must yield. See Vaughn v. Hearrell, Ky., 347 S.W.2d 542, overruling insofar as possible Simpson v. Buckner's Administrator; and Lloyd's Estate v. Mullin Tractor & Equipment Co., 192 Miss. 62, 4 So.2d 282.

57. See Hill v. Larcon Co., D.C.Ark., 131 F.Supp. 469; Auzenne v. Lawrence Oil Co., La., 179 So.2d 533.

58. See Moyer v. Walker, C.A.10th, 276 F.2d 681.

intent of the parties and whether the clause is worded positively or negatively, is that if operations are not again commenced upon the lease, failure to pay the next ensuing delay rental will result in termination of the lease.

Where the lease contains a dry hole clause that is effective during the primary term of the lease, conflicts have arisen as to the date for the payment of the next delay rental where a dry hole has been drilled or production has ceased. In the case of Superior Oil Co. v. Stanolind Oil & Gas Company,[59] a lease was executed upon March 3, 1944. A well was drilled that was completed as a dry hole on February 3, 1945. The dry hole clause provided as follows:

> "Should the first well drilled on the above described land be a dry hole, then and in that event, if a second well is not commenced on said land *within twelve months thereafter*, this lease shall terminate as to both parties, unless the lessee on or before the expiration of said twelve months shall resume the payment of rentals *in the same amount and in the same manner as hereinbefore* provided." (emphasis supplied)

As can be seen from the above clause it is not clear, after the drilling of a dry hole, whether the next payment date is twelve months from the drilling of the dry hole, or on the next anniversary date of the lease.

In this case no payment was made until early 1946, when a delay rental check was sent to the depository bank with the notation that it was "in payment of delay rentals for the period of February 3, 1946, to February 3, 1947." Similar payments were made through the year 1948. The lessee then sold the lease. The assignee, assuming that the dry hole clause provided that delay rentals would be due on or before the anniversary date of the lease, tendered the next delay rental payment upon February 5, 1949, which date was between the anniversary date of the drilling of the dry hole, February 3, and the anniversary date of the lease, March 3. It was held that the lease terminated due to a late payment by the assignee. The court stated that the dry hole clause was ambiguous, but that it had been construed by a course of action of the parties in relation to payment and the delay rental receipts. The payment date as so construed was February 3, the anniversary date of the completion of the dry hole.

Differences in the wording of the dry hole clause may vary the result. In Harrel v. The Atlantic Refining Co.,[60] the clause provided that:

> "Should the first well drilled on the above described land be a dry hole, then, and in that event, if a second well is not commenced on said land *within twelve months from the expiration of the last rental period for which rental has been paid*, this lease shall terminate as to both parties, unless the lessee on or before the expi-

---

59. 150 Tex. 317, 240 S.W.2d 281.   60. D.C.Okl., 123 F.Supp. 70.

ration of said twelve months shall resume the payment of rentals in the same amount and in the same manner as hereinbefore provided."

The anniversary date of the lease was June 15. The June, 1952, rental was timely paid. In August, 1952, lessee drilled a dry hole and no delay rental was tendered on June 15, 1953. The court held that due to the wording of the dry hole clause, no rental payment was due until *after* the expiration of 12 months from the end of a year for which rentals had been paid. The last rental period was June, 1952, and the expiration of this rental period was June, 1953. The Court held that the clause added an additional 12 months to resume rental payments after June, 1953.

Much of the confusion that exists in some of the cases is due to the fact that the lease in its relationship between the delay rental clause and the dry hole clause is either ambiguous or tends to set up a date that can vary from the anniversary date of the lease. As the payment of delay rentals is generally considered to involve a common law limitation upon the lease, the lessee that accepts a lease that is less than crystal clear in this regard is courting disaster. In no event should there be any possibility of the change in date for the payment of delay rentals.

The better approach is to obligate the lessee to resume the payment of delay rentals (or commence operations) on or before the rental payment date next ensuing after the completion of a dry hole or after production ceases. However, if Rex Oil Company completes a dry hole on the day before rental payments are due he may find his lease terminating before he can properly tender a payment to the lessee. For this reason the more recent lease forms have inserted a time period prior to the anniversary date of the lease, during which period if a well were completed as dry or production ceased, the lessee would be excused from tendering payment for the next year.

For instance, Black Gold has a lease that states that if it drills a dry hole during the primary term or has production that ceases, the lease will not terminate if the lessee commences operations for the drilling of a well or resumes the payment of delay rentals upon the delay rental payment date next ensuing after the expiration of three months from the completion of the dry hole or cessation of production. The anniversary date of the lease is January 1, and is for a five-year primary term ending December 31, 1983. Black Gold completes a dry hole on November 15, 1979. As this is within three months of the January 1, 1980, anniversary date of the lease, Black Gold is excused from the payment of delay rentals until January 1, 1981.[61] Also, if the dry hole were to be completed on November 15, 1982, he need not pay a delay rental for the year 1983, and the lease will be held until the end of the primary term. An alternative ap-

---

61. Colby v. Sun Oil Co., Tex.Civ. App., 288 S.W.2d 221.

proach to the three-month time period is to divide the delay rentals into 12ths and merely authorize the lessee to pick up the next monthly payment after the expiration of 15 days. One case [62] would have the lessee pay the proportionate part of the delay rental for the period until the next anniversary date of the lease and then resume paying on the regular payment date.[63]

(E) The Delay Rental—Effect of Improper Payment

Where an improper payment of delay rentals has been made, it is the general view that the payment will not be excused where it is due solely to the mistake of the lessee, its employees, or its agents. On the other hand, virtually all jurisdictions except Texas will excuse an improper payment where it is caused by an independent third party over which the lessee has no control. Apparently all jurisdictions will excuse an improper delay rental payment made by the lessee where it has been furnished and relied on an ambiguous instrument, or a confusing situation has been caused by the owners of the mineral estate.

Heretofore, insofar as the payment of delay rentals has been concerned, the discussion has been directed to what constitutes a good tender of delay rental payments. In this section the discussion is directed to the consequences of late or improper payment of rentals. When, if at all, will an improper payment of delay rentals be excused, without the interposition of a waiver or estoppel on the part of the lessor?

Whether or not a jurisdiction will relieve from an improper payment of delay rentals will depend, to a certain extent, upon the view of that jurisdiction as to the nature of the terminal provisions of the "unless" clause. A majority of jurisdictions appear to view the "unless" clause as creating a limitation upon the estate of the lessee, which will terminate automatically by its own terms in the event the lessee does not strictly comply with its provisions.[64] On the other hand, a number of jurisdictions view the termination as a forfeiture in equity,[65] and several jurisdictions appear to vary in their treatment

---

62. Fawvor v. United States Oil of Louisiana, Inc., La., 162 So.2d 602.

63. It is also suggested that, where practical, delay rentals and shut-in royalties be identical in amount. Not only will this avoid animosity by the land owner, if the delay rentals are somewhat larger than shut-in royalties where a shut-in gas well is drilled, but will also prevent termination of the lease in the event the lessee mistakenly pays one instead of the other. In this regard see Davis v. Laster, 242 La. 735, 138 So.2d 558, 96 A.L.R.2d 332.

64. Kugel v. Young, 132 Colo. 529, 291 P.2d 695, noted 3 U.C.L.A.L.Rev. 609 (Colorado); O'Hara v. Coltrin, ___ Colo. App. ___, 637 P.2d 398; Morton v. Sutcliffe, 175 Kan. 699, 266 P.2d 734 (Kansas); Johnson v. Smallenberger, 237 La. 11, 110 So.2d 119 (Louisiana); Richard v. Tarpon Oil Co., La.App., 269 So.2d 261, writ denied La., 271 So.2d 262, states the view that in Louisiana a lease will ipso facto terminate due to an intentional failure by lessee to properly pay delay rentals, but will be treated as a forfeiture with equitable considerations applicable where the lessee attempts to pay and comply with the lease, but does so improperly. Valentine Oil Co. v. Powers, 157 Neb. 71, 59 N.W.2d 150 (Nebraska); Woodside v. Lee, N.D., 81 N.W.2d 745 (North Dakota); Appling v. Morrison, Tex.Civ.App., 227 S.W. 708 (Texas).

65. Cordell v. Enis, 162 Ark. 41, 257 S.W. 375 (Arkansas); Ledford v. Atkins,

of the effect of the clause.[66] A jurisdiction that treats termination of the lease due to noncompliance with the delay rental clause as a forfeiture may apply equitable principles to prevent loss of the lease in situations in which the courts feel that it would be inequitable not to do so. On the other hand, a jurisdiction that views the termination as a limitation would technically be precluded from using equity principles to prevent loss of the lease.

At the outset it may be stated that a tender of delay rentals is not proper unless it is paid both timely and in the correct amount. Most of the cases dealing with improper payment deal with late payment of the rentals. The cases fall into the following categories:

(a) Where the lessee attempts to make payment, but the payment is improper solely through a mistake of the lessee, whether or not he is acting in good faith.[67]

(b) Where the lessee attempts to make payment, but the payment is late due to the acts of an independent third party beyond the control of the lessee.[68]

(c) Where the lessee attempts to make a payment, but it is improper due to confusion or ambiguity caused by the lessor.[69]

Very few cases are found where the improper payment is excused where it is solely due to the mistake of the lessee or his employees, although dicta is found in several cases espousing this view.[70] Where

---

Ky., 413 S.W.2d 68 (Kentucky). See Ballard v. Miller, 87 N.M. 86, 529 P.2d 752.

66. Morton v. Sutcliffe, 175 Kan. 699, 266 P.2d 734; cf. Young v. Moncrief, 117 Kan. 698, 232 P. 871 (Kansas); Phillips Petroleum Co. v. Curtis, C.A.10th, 182 F.2d 122; cf. Oldfield v. Gypsy Oil Co., 123 Okl. 293, 253 P. 298 (Oklahoma).

67. Excused: Cordell v. Enis, 162 Ark. 41, 257 S.W. 375; Ledford v. Atkins, Ky., 413 S.W.2d 68 (illness). Not excused: Vaughan v. Doss, 219 Ark. 963, 245 S.W.2d 826 (mailed to wrong bank); Johnson v. Smallenberger, 237 La. 11, 110 So.2d 119 (non-payment); Rushing v. Griffin, 240 La. 31, 121 So.2d 229 (named erroneous person in joint check); Hughes v. Franklin, 201 Miss. 215, 29 So.2d 79 (sent on anniversary date of execution rather than date of lease); Valentine Oil Co. v. Powers, 157 Neb. 71, 59 N.W.2d 150; Ellison v. Skelly Oil Co., 206 Okl. 496, 244 P.2d 832 (mailed to wrong bank); Phillips Petroleum Co. v. Curtis, C.A. 10th, 182 F.2d 122 (error of employee); Young v. Jones, Tex.Civ.App., 222 S.W. 691 (wrong amount: $73.29 instead of $76.25); Ford v. Barton, Tex.Civ.App., 224 S.W. 268 (illness); Empire Gas & Fuel Co. v. Saunders, C.A.5th, 22 F.2d 733 (mistake of lessee in construing instrument); Good Hope Refineries, Inc. v. Benavides, C.A.1st, 602 F.2d 998, cert. denied 444 U.S. 992, 100 S.Ct. 523, 62 L.Ed.2d 421 (bankruptcy of lessee); Trigg v. United States, Department of Interior, C.A.10th, 630 F.2d 1370 (bankruptcy of lessee).

68. Excused: Young v. Moncrief, 117 Kan. 698, 232 P. 871 (mailed correctly—never received); Gloyd v. Midwest Refining Co., C.A.10th, 62 F.2d 483 (mailed correctly—lost in mail); Ballard v. Miller, 87 N.M. 86, 529 P.2d 752 (lost in mail, lease not terminated); Oldfield v. Gypsy Oil Co., 123 Okl. 293, 253 P. 298 (properly addressed—delivered to wrong bank); Brazell v. Soucek, 130 Okl. 204, 266 P. 442 (bank clerk did not deposit timely); Twyford v. Whitchurch, C.A.10th, 132 F.2d 819 (change in bank through receivership—no notice to lessee).

69. Kouns v. Southwood, 203 Ark. 469, 158 S.W.2d 37; Schwartzenberger v. Hunt Trust Estate, N.D., 244 N.W.2d 711 (mistake by lessee in ascertaining acreage, lease terminated). Humble Oil & Refining Co. v. Harrison, 147 Tex. 216, 205 S.W.2d 355, noted in 26 Tex.L.Rev. 826; Ploeger v. Humble Oil & Refining Co., Tex.Civ.App., 416 S.W.2d 553.

70. Young v. Moncrief, 117 Kan. 698, 232 P. 871; Kays v. Little, 103 Kan. 641,

the acts of the lessee in paying are not in good faith, no jurisdiction will excuse the late payment. However, some authority has been found excusing an improper payment where the lessee is acting in good faith. An Arkansas [71] case held the lease was not forfeited where the lessee paid the delay rental late because the payment date was overlooked. Here the court emphasized that the lessee and lessor were good friends, had seen each other nearly every day, and the lessee had paid a large bonus of $4,000. The court stated that equity abhors a forfeiture and will seize upon slight circumstances to avoid the result. However, the case also may be rested upon grounds of waiver, as the lessor kept the check a week before declaring a forfeiture, which was deemed to be an unreasonable length of time. It is probable that the court would have terminated the lease had the lessor promptly rejected the payment.

A Kentucky [72] court also excused a late payment occasioned solely by the circumstances of the lessee. Here, when the payment became due the lessee, which was a partnership, did not make the payment timely, as the managing partner was in a comatose condition and seriously ill. The payment was 13 days late. The court held that it would not terminate a lease where the lessee had made a substantial investment and the delay rental is late due to extraordinary circumstances. It should be noted both Arkansas and Kentucky view the clause as merely occasioning a forfeiture in equity.

The majority view is that where the mistake is solely caused by the lessee or his employees, the improper payment of delay rentals will not be excused. Where the check is mailed late, [73] or addressed to the wrong depository bank,[74] or is made out in the wrong amount,[75] (in one case $73.39 instead of $76.25) the courts will not give relief, and the lease will terminate.

In the case of Empire Gas & Fuel Co. v. Saunders,[76] a lease was executed upon four quarter sections of land. The lessor later sent a copy of a deed whereby an undivided $1/2$ interest in two quarter sections, or a total of an undivided $1/4$ interest in the minerals under lease, was conveyed. However, by inadvertance the lessee construed the conveyance as passing all of the minerals under the two quarter sections and accordingly sent a check for $1/2$ of the delay rentals to the assignee. It was held that the mistake was solely that of the

---

175 P. 149, 1 A.L.R. 675; Oldfield v. Gypsy Oil Co., 123 Okl. 293, 253 P. 298; Richard v. Tarpon Oil Co., La.App., 269 So.2d 261, writ refused La., 271 So.2d 262; Ballard v. Miller, 87 N.M. 86, 529 P.2d 752, on ground lessee manifested an intent to keep lease in effect.

71. Cordell v. Enis, 162 Ark. 41, 257 S.W. 375.

72. Ledford v. Atkins, Ky., 413 S.W.2d 68; but cf. Ford v. Barton, Tex.Civ.App., 224 S.W. 268 (illness not excused).

73. Hughes v. Franklin, 201 Miss. 215, 29 So.2d 79; Phillips Petroleum Co. v. Curtis, C.A.10th, 182 F.2d 122.

74. Vaughan v. Doss, 219 Ark. 963, 245 S.W.2d 826; Ellison v. Skelly Oil Co., 206 Okl. 496, 244 P.2d 832.

75. Schwartzenberger v. Hunt Trust Estate, N.D., 244 N.W.2d 711. Young v. Jones, Tex.Civ.App., 222 S.W. 691.

76. C.A.5th, 22 F.2d 733.

lessee and that the lease terminated insofar as it covered the interest of the assignor. The burden of paying a correct delay rental payment was placed upon the lessee, and lessor was under no duty to notify of the incorrect payment.

In an interesting Oklahoma case, Phillips Petroleum Co. v. Curtis,[77] the delay rental was late due to a mistake of an employee of the lessee. In Oklahoma, as discussed below, the cases of Oldfield v. Gypsy Oil Co.,[78] Brazell v. Soucek,[79] and Gloyd v. Midwest Refining Co.,[80] which allowed relief for improper payment caused by a third party over which the lessee had no control, had been interpreted as also giving relief where the mistake was caused solely by the lessee. However, in the Phillips [81] case these three cases were distinguished. The Oklahoma court stated that the "unless" clause constituted a limitation upon the estate of the lessee, not a forfeiture, and that:

"In no case, so far as we have been able to discover, has the Supreme Court of Oklahoma held that the lessee was entitled to equitable relief from the termination of an 'unless' lease by reason of failure to pay the delay rental within the time specified in the lease, where the failure, although unintentional, was caused by a mistake of an employee or agent of the lessee in the performance of his duties, acting under the direction, supervision and control of the lessee."

In the second category are found a number of jurisdictions that would give relief where the lessee has, in good faith, timely attempted to pay delay rentals, but which were not timely received due to acts of third parties over which lessee has no control. The landmark case is that of Oldfield v. Gypsy Oil Co.[82] In this case the delay rental check was timely mailed in a properly addressed and stamped envelope, but it was delivered by the post office to the wrong bank. The lessee didn't discover this until after the due date. The court viewed the effect of the "unless" clause as allowing an abandonment of the lease by non-payment of delay rentals, rather than a limitation. This allowed the court to look behind the acts of the lessee to his intent to abandon. It was held the lease did not terminate. The rationale of the result was that where the lessee shows itself "ready, desirous, prompt and eager to comply" and acts within ample and reasonable time, late payment due to mistake of a third party will be excused.

The Oldfield case has been extensively followed in Oklahoma where third-party acts resulted in late or non-receipt of delay rentals. It was later followed in New Mexico in the case of Gloyd v. Midwest Refining Co.,[83] where the delay rental was lost in the mail. The court

77. C.A.10th, 182 F.2d 122.
78. 123 Okl. 293, 253 P. 298.
79. 130 Okl. 204, 266 P. 442.
80. C.A.10th, 62 F.2d 483.

81. Also see Ellison v. Skelly Oil Co., 206 Okl. 496, 244 P.2d 832.
82. 123 Okl. 293, 253 P. 298.
83. C.A.10th, 62 F.2d 483. Ballard v. Miller, 87 N.M. 86, 529 P.2d 752 (follows

stated that the lease would terminate only upon an intentional failure of the lessee to pay, and broadly enunciated a rule that if the failure to pay was not intentional, but due to accident or mistake, equity will relieve the error. These cases are broad enough to support a conclusion that where the mistake is caused solely by the lessee, but is in good faith, the mistake will be excused. However, as mentioned above, the Oklahoma case of Phillips Petroleum Co. v. Curtis,[84] has attempted to narrow the application of the Oldfield rule to that of delay caused by an independent agency. Although the Curtis case is a federal case the basic rationale has been reiterated and supported in the Oklahoma Supreme Court case of Ellison v. Skelly Oil Co.[85]

At least one jurisdiction, Texas, apparently will not allow relief where the improper payment is caused by a third party independent agency. In the case of Appling v. Morrison,[86] rentals were timely mailed but arrived late due to a delay in the mails. It was held that the lease terminated. The court emphasized that a limitation upon the estate of the lessee was involved and that equitable principles would not be applied to save the lease. This strict view would still seem to be the adjudicated view in Texas.

The only manner in which the lessee in Texas may find relief from an erroneous payment is in the third category of cases, where the lessor has furnished the lessee with an ambiguous instrument or confusing situation, which the lessee must interpret at his peril. The landmark case applying relief where the instrument furnished the lessee was ambiguous is Humble Oil & Refining Company v. Harrison.[87] Here the total amount paid by the lessee was correct, but the allocation to the various owners of the mineral estate was erroneous.

A, who owned an undivided ¾ interest in the minerals, executed a lease covering his interest to Humble. A later executed a mineral deed to B wherein he conveyed an undivided ½ interest in the described land. The deed contained the following clauses: "In the above described tract of land the Grantors own three-fourths (¾) of the minerals and are hereby conveying two-thirds (⅔) of their said three-fourths (¾) of the minerals, or an undivided one-half of the said minerals." However, this was later followed by a clause that stated: It is understood and agreed that one-half (½) of the money rentals,

---

the Gloyd case that lease not terminated where rental lost in the mail and never delivered, on ground the acts of the lessee manifested an intent not to terminate the lease by timely use of a customary method of payment).

84. C.A.10th, 182 F.2d 122.

85. 206 Okl. 496, 244 P.2d 832.

86. Tex.Civ.App., 227 S.W. 708. However, in Texas where the lease has provided for payment by mailing it has been held tender is good upon timely deposit in the mail in a properly addressed and stamped envelope, the postal service being deemed the agent of the lessor. See Corley v. Olympic Petroleum Corp., Tex.Civ.App., 403 S.W.2d 537, and text at footnotes 31, 32, supra. Cf. Ballard v. Miller, 87 N.M. 86, 529 P.2d 752, which does not mention the agency rationale.

87. 146 Tex. 216, 205 S.W.2d 355, noted in 26 Tex.L.Rev. 826. Also see Schwartzenberger v. Hunt Trust Estate, N.D., 244 N.W.2d 711 (mistake in acreage by lessee, lease terminated).

which may be paid * * * is to be paid to the Grantee * * *." Humble construed the clauses as passing to the grantee one-half of the rentals payable under A's lease, $\frac{1}{2} \times \frac{3}{4}$ or $\frac{3}{8}$ of the total rentals payable as to all of the minerals. It was found by the Court that Humble had misconstrued the clauses and that what was passed to the grantee was a right, not to one-half of the rentals payable under A's lease, but to one-half of all the rentals payable as to the entire mineral estate. Humble was excused from the wrongful payment on the ground that the assignee of the lessor had furnished an ambiguous instrument. The imposition of the proper construction of an ambiguous instrument upon the lessee at his peril would be to impose an additional burden upon the lessee. This is in conflict with the assignment clause which normally provides that either party may assign his interest under the lease, but that no such assignment may impose an additional burden upon the lessee. The case has been followed in Texas in connection with an ambiguous judgment.[88]

A somewhat similar result occurred in Arkansas,[89] where the assignee of the lessor conveyed an undivided $\frac{1}{8}$ interest in the minerals to B. The land was subject to a lease. However, the parties felt that the acknowledgment was defective and the instrument was re-acknowledged and re-filed for record. As re-recorded, the instrument did not contain the prior recording certificate, which the clerk had omitted. Atlantic Refining Co. examined title and paid B for both interests, or a total of an undivided $\frac{1}{4}$ interest. It was held that the lease did not terminate (1) as the lessee was not negligent and (2) the confusing situation was caused by the lessors and assigns. The Court found that it would be inequitable to forfeit the lease in this situation.

(F) The Delay Rental—Estoppel, Waiver, and Ratification of an Improper Payment by the Mineral Owner

It is questionable whether a notice of default clause will prevent the termination of a lease for improper payment of delay rentals that would not otherwise be excused. However, in virtually all jurisdictions acceptance and retention for an unreasonable length of time of delay rentals that have been improperly paid will cause the lease to be maintained in effect. The courts are not precise in the application of the doctrines of estoppel, waiver, or ratification in reaching this result.

In an attempt to prevent termination of the lease for improper payment of delay rentals, clauses have been inserted providing that upon an incorrect but good-faith attempt to pay delay rentals, the lease will not terminate until expiration of a stated number of days following receipt of written notice from the lessor to the lessee of the improper payment. Of the few cases on the books, two [90] have held

---

88. Ploeger v. Humble Oil & Refining Co., Tex.Civ.App., 416 S.W.2d 553.

89. Kouns v. Southwood, 203 Ark. 469, 158 S.W.2d 37.

90. Lewis v. Grininger, 198 Okl. 419, 179 P.2d 463; Clovis v. Carson Oil Co., D.C.Mich., 11 F.Supp. 797.

§ 6.3 THE OIL AND GAS LEASE—DURATION

that the clauses were void, as they conflicted with and were repugnant to the delay rental clause. It has been argued that notice clauses may be effective in regard to the breach of covenants but where the provision involved is a limitation on the estate the lease terminates before the clause can take effect. In two cases the clauses have been given effect.[91] One of these cases is the case of Woolley v. Standard Oil Company of Texas,[92] where the lease contained the following clause:

> "If lessee shall, in good faith and with reasonable diligence, attempt to pay any rental, but shall fail to pay or incorrectly pay some portion thereof, this lease shall not terminate unless lessee, within thirty (30) days after written notice of its error or failure, shall fail to rectify the same."

Here the lessee attempted to correctly pay delay rentals. The correct amount was furnished to the bank; however, incorrect instructions were issued by the lessee for allocation among the parties entitled thereto. The bank made out the checks and sent them out. Although estoppel was relied upon as one ground on which the lease did not terminate, the court expressly found as an alternative ground that the notice clause was valid. As the clause was valid, the question presented was not whether the lessee was negligent, but whether he acted in good faith. It was found that the lessee did act in good faith even though the error rested exclusively with the lessee.

Although a notice clause may be thought to be in conflict with the wording of the "unless" clause, a better approach to instrument interpretation and construction is to view the instrument as a whole and to give effect to the intention of the parties as found thereon. The position of the notice clause is analogous to that of the well completion clause and the habendum clause, where the former clause is now held to modify the latter and allow the lessee to finish the well drilling at the end of the primary term. It is certainly arguable that the notice clause modifies the "unless" clause. It is illogical to reason that if the provision constitutes a limitation upon the estate it may not be modified by further provisions if this is the intent of the parties. Certainly there is nothing sacred about the automatic termination effect of the "unless" clause.

In the foregoing sections the discussion has been directed to what constitutes a good tender of delay rentals and when an improper payment of delay rentals may be excused. An additional element may present itself where the lessee has made an improper attempt to pay a delay rental, which would normally not be excused, but where the conduct of the lessor is such that the lease should not be treated as being terminated. Cases in this area come within the rationale of

---

91. Woolley v. Standard Oil Co. of Texas, C.A.5th, 230 F.2d 97; Dietrich v. Davis, La.App., 246 So.2d 710 (notice clause effective).

92. C.A.5th, 230 F.2d 97.

estoppel, waiver, and ratification. Prior to a discussion of the specific situations it might be wise to generally define the terms. Although the result may be the same, i.e., the lease does not terminate, the three rationales are essentially different:

(1) An estoppel will arise where one person by his conduct misleads another to the other's detriment. The essential basis of estoppel is that of a false or misleading representation by conduct. One then is denied to change his position where it will cause harm to the other.

(2) A waiver, on the other hand, has no element of misrepresentation. A waiver is an intentional release or relinquishment of a known right. It is essentially an election to dispense with or forego a right.

(3) A ratification, in connection with an oil and gas lease, is in effect a re-grant of the property. Although an estoppel or waiver may lie in parol, a ratification of an oil and gas lease must satisfy both the statutes of frauds and conveyances of particular jurisdictions.

The courts have not been precise in their treatment of binding the mineral owner where it is deemed that through his conduct the lease should not terminate although the payment of the delay rental was improper.

Although there would seem to be no duty upon the lessor to speak [93] when he receives an improper delay rental payment, so as to raise an estoppel by silence, virtually all jurisdictions have held that acceptance of an improper delay rental payment and retention of it for any length of time will not result in termination of the lease.[94] The courts seem to speak in terms of estoppel of the lessor to then attack the wrongful payment after unreasonable retention of the money; however, it would seem that waiver of wrongful payment would be a more precise rationale. Although the owner of the mineral estate may not legally be charged with misrepresentation by retention of the rental where no duty to speak exists, this is not to say such conduct should not be interpreted as a waiver of the right to

---

93. Johnson v. Smallenberger, 237 La. 11, 110 So.2d 119; but cf. Calhoun v. Gulf Refining Co., 235 La. 494, 104 So.2d 547; Hove v. Atchison, C.A.8th, 238 F.2d 819. The Calhoun case involved an unusual situation where the lessor contended the lease terminated as payments were not paid according to the terms of the lease, where he received rental payments in excess of those called for in the lease. However, see Richard v. Tarpon Oil Co., La.App., 269 So.2d 261, writ denied La., 271 So.2d 262, (where lessee deposited delay rental check to lessor as curator rather than individually, lessor was estopped to claim termination of the lease where lessor knew of mistake in time to inform lessee, but did not do so).

94. Kugel v. Young, 132 Colo. 529, 291 P.2d 695, noted 3 U.C.L.A.L.Rev. 609; Walter v. Ashland Oil & Refining Co., 300 Ky. 43, 187 S.W.2d 425; Hutchinson v. Schneeberger, Ky., 374 S.W.2d 483; Davis v. Laster, 242 La. 735, 138 So.2d 558, 96 A.L.R.2d 332; Nadeau v. Texas Co., 104 Mont. 558, 69 P.2d 586; Norman Jessen & Associates v. Amoco Production Co., N.D., 305 N.W.2d 648. Humphreys v. Fletcher, 27 N.M. 639, 204 P. 70; Woolley v. Standard Oil Co. of Texas, C.A.5th, 230 F.2d 97. See note 93, supra.

declare the lease terminated. And, as mentioned earlier, where a depository bank is being used, the bank has no authority to estop the lessor or waive an improper payment.

In jurisdictions such as Texas where the delay rental payment has been improperly made the lease immediately terminates of its own accord. It would seem improper to state that a new grant has thereafter been made due to estoppel or waiver. However, both doctrines have been applied in Texas.[95] In Texas the lessor not only has to retain the rental payment but in one case it seems implied that he also has to use the proceeds.[96] Although the cases talk in terms of estoppel it again would seem that waiver is the proper terminology.

Ratification radically differs from both estoppel and waiver and normally would not result merely from the retention of improperly paid rental payments. Obviously the owners of the mineral estate may ratify an expired or terminated lease by use of a separate instrument including words of grant that in effect re-grant the lands on the same terms and conditions as the former lease. The lease may be incorporated by reference in the ratifying instrument. However, in some jurisdictions a ratification may inadvertently occur. Assume that O executes an oil and gas lease to Pure Oil Company. During the primary term the lessee does not pay the delay rentals and the lease expires. However, after the lease has expired, O sells to B the land that was subject to the lease. In the body of the lease following the description, in order to avoid a question of breach of warranty, the draftsman states that the land is "subject to" the lease to Pure Oil Company and refers to it by recording reference. In Texas the courts have held that the execution of a "subject to" deed has the effect of ratifying the expired lease.[97] These cases are erroneous. The only intent of the parties is to avoid the breach of warranty of a lease that is still within the primary term and that has not been released of record. Without further language there is no basis to find that the parties intended to ratify the lapsed lease.

Not only is the underlying rationale different for estoppel, waiver and ratification, they also differ in effect. Where the lease has terminated, it may not be revived by estoppel or waiver where homestead rights of the parties are involved. Normally, specific acts of execu-

---

95. Mitchell v. Simms, Tex.Com.App., 63 S.W.2d 371; McCoy v. Texon Royalty Co., Tex.Civ.App., 124 S.W.2d 877; Woolley v. Standard Oil Co. of Texas, C.A.5th, 230 F.2d 97. In Brannon v. Gulf States Energy Corp., Tex., 562 S.W.2d 219 (acceptance of late delay rental payment revived lease "as though it had never terminated").

96. Mitchell v. Simms, Tex.Com.App., 63 S.W.2d 371; McCoy v. Texon Royalty Co., Tex.Civ.App., 124 S.W.2d 877; but cf. Woolley v. Standard Oil Co. of Texas, C.A.5th, 230 F.2d 97. Where the lessee has $500 in his bank account and delay rentals of $300 are thereafter deposited, and where the lessor then withdraws $400 to pay bills, has he "used" the delay rental money? If money is considered to be withdrawn on a "first in-first out" basis the answer would be no. But cf. Uniform Commercial Code § 4–303(2).

97. Grissom v. Anderson, 125 Tex. 26, 79 S.W.2d 619; Humble Oil & Refining Co. v. Clark, 126 Tex. 262, 87 S.W.2d 471.

tion are prescribed by statute to convey the homestead,[98] which will preclude revival of the lease by anything less than a written instrument containing words of grant and executed and acknowledged as prescribed.

Revival of a terminated lease by estoppel or waiver on the one hand and ratification on the other may be affected both by the recording acts and the notice of assignment clause in the oil and gas lease. Consider the following facts, which are essentially the same as found in the Texas case of Mitchell v. Sims:[99] A owns Blackacre and leases the land to Rex Oil Company. The lease contains a notice of assignment clause. After the execution of the lease A sells an undivided one-half interest in the minerals to B. B records, but does not send a copy of the deed to Rex Oil Company. Rex Oil Company misses the rental payment date, but sends a late check that A withdraws and uses in such a manner that it would be found that A has either waived the late payment or is estopped to terminate the lease. As Rex did not know of B, no payment was sent to B. What is the result?

Although A may estop himself there is no relationship between A and B that would impute the waiver or estoppel from A to B. Therefore, only A's one-half interest is affected by the waiver or estoppel and is still under the lease. The lease has expired as to B's interest. Where the lease had terminated at the time the late payment was made, the notice of assignment provision does not operate to protect Rex Oil Company. As the lease went out, so did the protection of the notice of assignment clause. Had the payment been timely made, Rex's payment to A would have been proper and would have held the entire lease, including the interest of B.

Changing the facts slightly, the same conveyances have been made but the deed to B has not been recorded. Rex misses the delay rental payment; however, instead of merely paying the rental payment late and hoping that A would somehow bind himself by acceptance, Rex has A execute an instrument in writing with words of grant, ratifying the lease as it covers the entire land. Rex files the instrument of record. Rex, instead of acquiring a revival of the lease by estoppel, has acquired it by grant and now occupies the position of a bona fide purchaser for value of the lease interest. As the deed to B was not recorded, it would be cut off by the recording acts. Here Rex acquires a good lease on the entire mineral interest. Had the deed to B been recorded, Rex again would have acquired only half a loaf.

98. Mitchell v. Simms, Tex.Com.App., 63 S.W.2d 371.

99. Tex.Com.App., 63 S.W.2d 371.

§ 6.4 Propelling the Lease Past the Primary Term and Keeping It Alive During the Secondary Term by Production of Oil or Gas—Definition of "Production"

The customary habendum clause calls for "production" to propel the oil and gas lease past the primary term. The jurisdictions are divided in their interpretation of the term. In a substantial number of jurisdictions production does not include marketing of the products. In these jurisdictions discovery of petroleum products will be sufficient, although in most of these jurisdictions discovery must be of products capable of being produced in paying quantities. Where so discovered, the lessee will have a reasonable time to secure production. Utmost good faith and diligence is required.

In the other jurisdictions, actual production of petroleum products is required. Where discovery of petroleum products has occurred sufficient to produce in paying quantities, but no products are being actually produced and marketed, the lease will terminate at the end of the primary term unless it is being held under other provisions of the lease.

In the preceding section we have seen how a lease may be kept alive during the primary term by the payment of delay rentals or operations. Assuming that the lease has been so kept alive, it is then necessary to satisfy the habendum clause of the lease in order to propel the lease past the end of the primary term and into the secondary term. The habendum clause customarily used in the unless form lease provides that the lease will extend into the secondary term "as long as oil and gas is produced therefrom." Some variations may be found, namely in the use of the term "production." Sometimes it is called "paying production", or "production in paying quantities," or where oil and gas is "found" or "found and produced." Generally the courts in a particular jurisdiction will treat the terms as synonyms, although in a few distinction is made between the terms "produced" and "found," as will be seen later.

A dichotomy is found in the construction of the term "produced." One line of construction would construe the term as requiring marketing and sale of the products to satisfy the habendum clause,[1] whereas the other line of construction would not require marketing.[2]

---

1. Lamczyk v. Allen, 8 Ill.2d 547, 134 N.E.2d 753; Elliott v. Crystal Springs Oil Co., 106 Kan. 248, 187 P. 692; Baldwin v. Blue Stem Oil Co., 106 Kan. 878, 189 P. 920; Reese Enterprises v. Lawson, 220 Kan. 300, 553 P.2d 885; Home Royalty Association Inc. v. Stone, C.A.10th, 199 F.2d 650; Smith v. Sun Oil Co., 172 La. 655, 135 So. 15; Kinne v. Swanson Consolidated Oil Co., 293 Mich. 509, 292 N.W. 472; Town of Tome Land Grant, Inc. v. Ringle Development Co., 56 N.M. 101, 240 P.2d 850; Greer v. Salmon, 82 N.M. 245, 479 P.2d 294; Feland v. Placid Oil Co., N.D., 171 N.W.2d 829; Hanna v. Shorts, 163 Ohio St. 44, 125 N.E.2d 338; Waddle v. Lucky Strike Oil Co., Tenn., 551 S.W.2d 323; Stanolind Oil & Gas Co. v. Barnhill, Tex.Civ.App., 107 S.W.2d 746; Cox v. Miller, Tex.Civ.App., 184 S.W.2d 323; Morrison v. Swaim, Tex.Civ.App., 220 S.W.2d 493; Holchak v. Clark, Tex. Civ.App., 284 S.W.2d 399; and cf. Fox v. Thoreson, Tex., 398 S.W.2d 88; Monsanto Co. v. Tyrrell, Tex.Civ.App., 537 S.W.2d 135; Bell v. Mitchell Energy Corp., Tex. Civ.App., 553 S.W.2d 626.

2. Barrett v. Dorr, 140 Ind.App. 295, 212 N.E.2d 29; Pennagrade Oil & Gas Co. v. Martin, 211 Ky. 137, 277 S.W. 302; Fey v. A.A. Oil Corp., 129 Mont. 300, 285 P.2d 578; Christian v. A.A. Oil Corp., 161 Mont. 420, 506 P.2d 1369; Gypsy Oil Co.

One of the first cases to hold that discovery prior to the end of the primary term of the lease was sufficient to propel the lease into the secondary term is the West Virginia case of Eastern Oil Co. v. Coulehan.[3] In this case the lessee had discovered gas in an upper stratum prior to the end of the primary term of the lease. However, instead of completing the well the lessee chose to drill to a greater depth. The lessor prevented the lessee from drilling for about 12 hours. Upon continuing drilling, gas was found in greater quantities in a lower sand, some 12 hours after the expiration of the primary term of the lease. Hence, at the end of the primary term no actual production of gas had occurred. The court held that discovery prior to the end of the primary term vested the lessee with an estate in the minerals and that he had a reasonable time after discovery to find a market for the gas and make a marketing connection.

The Coulehan case was later construed in South Penn Oil Co. v. Snodgrass,[4] where it was stated that the discovery necessary to vest the minerals in the lessee need not be in paying quantities.[5] It is not clear whether or not West Virginia requires discovery in paying quantities, as a later West Virginia case stated that the lessee must show that the reasonable result of the discovery will be paying production.[6]

That discovery must be in paying quantities is the view of the Oklahoma courts[7] and would seem consistent with the view that production sufficient to eventually hold the lease in virtually all jurisdictions

v. Marsh, 121 Okl. 135, 248 P. 329, 48 A.L.R. 876; McVicker v. Horn, Robinson and Nathan, Okl., 322 P.2d 410, noted 11 Okl.L.Rev. 464; 13 S.W.L.J. 134; Townsend v. Creekmore-Rooney Co., Okl., 332 P.2d 35; Hunter v. Clarkson, Okl., 428 P.2d 210; Flag Oil Corp. of Delaware v. King Resources Co., Okl., 494 P.2d 322; Gard v. Kaiser, Okl., 582 P.2d 1311; McEvoy v. First National Bank and Trust Co. of Enid, Okl., 624 P.2d 559; Bristol v. Colorado Oil & Gas Corp., C.A.10th, 225 F.2d 894, noted 58 W.Va.L.Rev. 309; Cox v. Gulf Oil Corp., C.A.10th, 301 F.2d 122; Summerville v. Apollo Gas Co., 207 Pa. 344, 56 A. 876; Benedum-Trees Oil Co. v. Davis, C.A.6th, 107 F.2d 981; Eastern Oil Co. v. Coulehan, 65 W.Va. 531, 64 S.E. 836; South Penn Oil Co. v. Snodgrass, 71 W.Va. 438, 76 S.E. 961; Ohio Fuel Oil Co. v. Greenleaf, 84 W.Va. 67, 99 S.E. 274; and see Pryor Mountain Oil & Gas Co. v. Cross, 31 Wyo. 9, 222 P. 570. On the habendum clause generally see Summers, Oil and Gas Law, Chapter 10, §§ 292–298; Hall, Application of the Determinable Fee Theory in Construing the Mississippi Mineral Lease, 19 Miss.L.J. 291; Moses, Habendum Clause in Oil and Gas Leases, 7 S.T.L.J. 12; Habendum Clause as a Special Limitation on Oil and Gas Leases in Texas, 11 S.W.L.J. 340; Production in Paying Quantities in an Oil and Gas Lease, 25 Tul.L.Rev. 506.

3. 65 W.Va. 531, 64 S.E. 836.

4. 71 W.Va. 438, 76 S.E. 961.

5. As will be seen, paying quantities usually denotes some element of profit to the lessee over expenses of production.

6. Ohio Fuel Oil Co. v. Greenleaf, 84 W.Va. 67, 99 S.E. 274.

7. Gypsy Oil Co. v. Marsh, 121 Okl. 135, 248 P. 329, 48 A.L.R. 876; McVicker v. Horn, Robinson and Nathan, Okl., 322 P.2d 410, noted 11 Okl.L.Rev. 464; 13 S.W.L.J. 134.

Kansas follows the rule that actual production is necessary to continue the lease in effect past the end of the primary term. However, where the lease contains a clause allowing the lessee to finish the well being drilled at the end of the primary term the Kansas decisions have adopted the "Oklahoma" rule allowing the lessee a reasonable time to secure a market. See Tate v. Stanolind Oil & Gas Co., 172 Kan. 351, 240 P.2d 465 and Sword v. Rains, C.A.10th, 575 F.2d 810. See discussion § 6.5(A), infra, footnote 10.

§ 6.4   THE OIL AND GAS LEASE—DURATION

requires production in paying quantities. It would be the better view that "production" in these states may be defined as being a well which is completed and capable of producing oil or gas in paying quantities. This, also, is the Oklahoma view.[8]

In Oklahoma and other states that view discovery as sufficient to satisfy the habendum clause, the lessee will have a reasonable time within which to market the products. The rationale is that upon discovery the lessee is vested with an interest in the minerals under the lease. Physical non-production of oil and gas will not terminate the lease as long as the lessee is acting as a reasonably prudent lessee under the circumstances. In Stewart v. Amerada Hess Corp.,[9] a case dealing with cessation of production in paying quantities, the Oklahoma Supreme Court stated:

> "The 'thereafter' clause is hence not ever to be regarded as akin in effect to the common-law conditional limitation or determinable fee estate. The occurrence of the limiting event or condition does not automatically effect an end to the right. Rather, the clause is to be regarded as fixing the life of a lease instead of providing a means of terminating it in advance of the time at which it would otherwise expire. In short, the lease continues in existence so long as interruption of production in paying quantities does not extend for a period longer than reasonable or justifiable in light of all the circumstances involved. But under *no* circumstances will cessation of production in paying quantities *ipso facto* deprive the lessee of his extended-term estate."

If non-production is not due to exhaustion of products, the courts will consider equitable considerations to determine whether the conduct of the lessee justifies the continuation of the lease.

In such jurisdictions, once a lessee has found or discovered petroleum products (in absence of complete cessation of production, which may amount to an abandonment of the lease by the lessee, or in absence of exhaustion of the producing formations), the lease will not terminate by its own terms. A suit must be brought by the lessor for cancellation of the lease. In this situation, however, a court will usually give relief against cancellation where absence of production is caused by unusual circumstances or by those essentially beyond the control of the lessee, where it was not at fault in failing to anticipate the result.

As to a well being drilled at the end of the primary term, and in which oil or gas is discovered, but not marketed until after the end of the primary term, such considerations will be weighed to determine

---

8. Western States Oil & Land Co. v. Helms, 143 Okl. 206, 288 P. 964; Kolachny v. Galbreath, 26 Okl. 772, 110 P. 902; Frank Oil Co. v. Belleview Gas and Oil Co., 29 Okl. 719, 119 P. 902; Parks v. Sinai Oil and Gas Co., 83 Okl. 295, 201 P. 517; State v. Carter Oil Co. of West Virginia, Okl., 336 P.2d 1086.

9. Okl., 604 P.2d 854, citing Hunter v. Clarkson, Okl., 428 P.2d 210.

whether the lease should continue in effect until marketing is accomplished.

The conduct of the lessee required is that of good faith in using reasonable diligence in finding a market. However, such conduct is not unlimited, but will only exist for a reasonable time. Diligence and reasonable time are related terms in the promulgation of a rule of conduct based on equitable considerations. Although the terms are not synonymous, reasonable time is related to the diligence of the lessee in finding a market.[10]

The problem of securing actual production from the lease prior to the end of the primary term is much greater where gas rather than oil is found. Oil may immediately be produced and stored above ground, and a readily available market usually exists. Transportation to market may be done by truck if pipeline facilities are not available. This is not true in the case of gas. If the gas well is a discovery well it is usual that pipeline facilities will not be found nearby. Gas may not be produced and effectively stored above the ground due to the great quantities of gas used. If no pipeline facilities are available, unless the lessee has the available capital a gathering line will not be constructed until a sufficient number of wells have been developed in the field to economically justify the building of such a line. Therefore, unless the lease is being held in effect by virtue of other provisions,[11] a considerable time gap may exist between the discovery of the gas and actual production.

In the case of Bristol v. Colorado Oil and Gas Corporation,[12] a gas well was shut in following the primary term for some 7⅔ years prior to the securing of a market. The court held that the lease had not terminated, and stated that the lessee had used extraordinary diligence in securing a market. Factors considered were that the well was located in wildcat territory over twenty miles from a pipeline. More than 14 wells were drilled on the block, and extensive negotiations were carried on with all purchasing companies that might be interested. No drainage existed. Large amounts were spent; the original well cost $120,000 and each of the others in excess of $50,000 each. The price of gas had significantly increased during this period.

In contrast to the above jurisdictions, is the view that the wells must be physically producing at the end of the primary term, i.e., that

---

10. McVicker v. Horn, Robinson and Nathan, Okl., 322 P.2d 410, noted 11 Okl. L.Rev. 464; 13 S.W.L.J. 134; Bristol v. Colorado Oil & Gas Corp., C.A.10th, 225 F.2d 894, noted 58 W.Va.L.R. 309. However, see Jath Oil Co. v. Durbin Branch, Okl., 490 P.2d 1086, an Oklahoma case holding lease automatically terminated where production cessation held not temporary. Also the presence of a shut-in royalty clause effective during the primary term will not modify the reasonable time in which gas must be marketed in Oklahoma, see Flag Oil Corp. of Delaware v. King Resources Co., Okl., 494 P.2d 322.

11. See § 6.5, infra, relating to shut in royalties, and § 6.6, infra relating to operations at the end of the primary term.

12. C.A.10th, 225 F.2d 894, noted 58 W.Va.L.R. 309.

§ 6.4   THE OIL AND GAS LEASE—DURATION   281

discovery alone is insufficient to hold the lease and propel it into the secondary term.

This latter line of authority is well illustrated by the cases of Stanolind Oil & Gas Co. v. Barnhill [13] and Cox v. Miller.[14] In both cases gas was found in quantities sufficient for paying production; however, no market was available. In the Stanolind case a sour gas well was involved that was capable of producing 7,000,000 cubic feet of gas per day. Production, however, was insufficient to support a carbon black plant, and gas, therefore, could not be produced. In the Miller case the well was capable of the production of 1,000,000 cubic feet of gas per day, but no pipeline was available to transport the gas to market. In both cases, as no physical production was present at the end of the primary term it was held that the leases had terminated.

Jurisdictions such as Texas follow the view that absence of production terminates an oil and gas lease by its own terms, due to the determinable limitation contained in the habendum clause.[15] This is a common law limitation on the estate, and equitable principles are not applicable to relieve the lessee in hardship situations. In Baldwin v. Blue Stem Oil Co.,[16] a lease was executed for a primary term of three years, which ended January 17, 1919. The lessee waited until December 7, 1918 to commence a well, which was not finished by the end of the primary term. It was argued on behalf of the lessee that completion was delayed due to the fact that the weather was inclement, producing large amounts of rain, mud, blizzard conditions, and sickness among the crew. In addition, government regulations prevented acquisition of casing, coal, and other supplies necessary to complete the well before the end of the primary term. It was held that the lease terminated at the end of the primary term due to no production, and

13. Tex.Civ.App., 107 S.W.2d 746.

14. Tex.Civ.App., 184 S.W.2d 323.

15. See Elliott v. Crystal Springs Oil Co., 106 Kan. 248, 187 P. 692; Hanna v. Shorts, 163 Ohio St. 44, 125 N.E.2d 338; Morrison v. Swaim, Tex.Civ.App., 220 S.W.2d 493; Holchak v. Clark, Tex.Civ. App., 284 S.W.2d 399; but cf. Fox v. Thoreson, Tex., 398 S.W.2d 88. In Elliott v. Crystal Springs the court emphasized the fact that drilling and operations had ceased for over seven months and no prospects existed to secure a market at an early date. The court leaves open the question whether a judgment forfeiting the lease would have been entered if early prospects of securing a market existed where the lessee had spent large sums developing the lease. In jurisdictions that view the lease as an estate subject to cancellation in equity, notice under a notice clause giving lessee a specified time period to acquire production is a valid condition precedent to an action of forfeiture, see Christian v. A.A. Oil Corp., 161 Mont. 420, 506 P.2d 1369. However, in jurisdictions viewing lack of actual production in paying quantities as a special limitation on the estate, a notice clause is generally viewed as ineffective, see Waddle v. Lucky Strike Oil Co., Inc., Tenn., 551 S.W.2d 323; Preston v. Lambert, Tex.Civ.App., 489 S.W.2d 955; Waggoner & Zeller Oil Co. v. Deike, Tex.Civ.App., 508 S.W.2d 163; Lynch v. Southern Coast Drilling Co., Inc., Tex. Civ.App., 442 S.W.2d 804.

16. 106 Kan. 848, 189 P. 920; and Home Royalty Association Inc. v. Stone, C.A.10th, 199 F.2d 650. But cf. Elliott v. Crystal Springs Oil Co., 106 Kan. 248, 187 P. 692, where the Kansas court entertaining a suit to cancel left open the question of application of equitable considerations.

(A) Production—Quantum of Production, i.e., Paying Quantities

Paying production, or production in paying quantities, is usually defined as that quantum of production that would return a profit to the lessee, however small, over lifting or production costs, even though the cost of drilling and equipping the well might never be repaid.

Where production has become marginal or sporadic, in order to determine whether production should be deemed to be in paying quantities a majority of jurisdictions apply a subjective approach and will look to a number of factors and relevant circumstances to determine whether or not a prudent lessee would continue to operate the lease for profit and not for speculation. Some jurisdictions apply an objective approach and will determine paying quantities upon a mathematical computation.

In determining paying production there will be included all income attributable to the working interest of the lease, with deductions for landowner's royalty, severance taxes, license and permit fees, labor, electricity, transportation expense, replacement and repair of producing equipment, and direct costs of supervision. Views differ on inclusion of costs of depreciation of producing equipment, administrative overhead, and on the time period to be considered during which income and costs are compared to determine if production is in paying quantities.

In those jurisdictions that require actual production prior to the end of the primary term, a question arose early in the history of the petroleum industry as to the quantum of production that was necessary to continue the lease into the secondary term. The habendum clause contained in the customary lease merely stated that the lease would continue for " * * * so long as oil and gas, or either of them, is produced * * *." Normally, qualifying words were not present. Should any amount of production, however small, serve to satisfy this provision?

It has been indicated that any production capable of division and payment to the royalty owners is sufficient.[17] However, by far the majority view is that some element of profit to the lessee would be required, and as so defined the term "production" was equated to "paying production" or "production in paying quantities." [18] The definition and elements of such production is set forth below.

---

17. See Enfield v. Woods, 198 Ky. 328, 248 S.W. 842.

Hisle v. Keltner, Ky.App., 495 S.W.2d 773 (production only need be capable of division).

18. West v. Russell, 12 Cal.App.3d 638, 90 Cal.Rptr. 772; Reese Enterprises, Inc. v. Lawson, 220 Kan. 300, 553 P.2d 885; Noel Estate, Inc. v. Murray, 223 La. 387, 65 So.2d 886; Berthelote v. Loy Oil Co., 95 Mont. 434, 28 P.2d 187; Treasure County v. Berggren, 154 Mont. 1, 459 P.2d 271; Hanna v. Shorts, 163 Ohio St. 44, 125 N.E.2d 338; Stewart v. Amerada Hess Corp., Okl., 604 P.2d 854; Mason v. Ladd Petroleum Co., Okl., 630 P.2d 1283; Waddle v. Lucky Strike Oil Co., Inc., Tenn., 551 S.W.2d 323; Garcia v. King, 139 Tex. 578, 164 S.W.2d 509; Clifton v. Koontz, 160 Tex. 82, 325 S.W.2d 684, noted 14 S.W.L.J. 539; Gas Ridge, Inc. v. Suburban Agricultural Properties, Inc., C.A.5th, 150 F.2d 363, rehearing denied

§ 6.4   THE OIL AND GAS LEASE—DURATION   283

Before proceeding to a discussion of the nature of production in paying quantities it might be well to mention that such production will normally keep the lease alive not only as to the tract of land upon which the well is situated, but as to all land described in the lease, whether or not it is contiguous.[19]

Also, although the modern lease calls for the production of "oil and gas, or either of them," if the habendum clause requires production of "oil *and* gas" the phrase has been construed to mean that production of either of the products will satisfy the clause.[20] But where gas has been produced from another well and then reinjected into the ground, it has been held that production of such stored gas at a later time does not constitute such production as will keep the lease in effect.[21] Production of gas solely under the free gas clause for domestic use of the lessor also will not be sufficient.[22] To satisfy the habendum clause, production must be by the lessee, and production by another without the lessee's consent will not suffice to keep the lease alive.[23]

"Paying quantities" has been characterized to denote such production to the lessee. In other words, production must include an element of profit to the lessee. The nature and rationale of such profitability has been well stated in the Texas case of Garcia v. King:[24]

"It should be noted that we are here dealing with a situation in which under normal conditions all of the producing wells on the lease in question at the time of the termination of the primary period were not producing enough oil or gas to pay a profit over and above the cost of operating the wells. In order to understand and properly interpret the language used by the parties we must consider the objects and purposes intended to be accomplished by

150 F.2d 1020, cert. denied 326 U.S. 796, 66 S.Ct. 487, 90 L.Ed. 485.

19. See Ricketts v. Welch, Okl., 488 P.2d 361; Turner v. McBroom, Okl., 565 P.2d 44; Mathews v. Sun Oil Co., Tex., 425 S.W.2d 330; Orive v. Sun Oil Co., Tex.Civ.App., 346 S.W.2d 383; and § 9.10(A), infra.

20. Rostocil v. The United Oil and Gas Royalty Association, 177 Kan. 15, 274 P.2d 761.

21. Smallwood v. Central Kentucky Natural Gas Co., Ky., 308 S.W.2d 439; also see West v. Continental Oil Co., C.A. 5th, 194 F.2d 869 where production from abandoned well held sufficient to excuse payment of delay rentals during the primary term.

22. Metz v. Doss, 114 Ill.App.2d 195, 252 N.E.2d 410, delivery of gas under free gas clause for household use plus expenditure of large sums for development of gas storage reservoir, not sufficient; Goodwin v. Wright, ___ W.Va. ___, 255 S.E.2d 924, only production was of gas under free gas clause for domestic use, not sufficient.

23. Buckles v. Wil-Mc Oil Corp., Okl., 585 P.2d 1360, production by assignee of farm-out; Continental Oil Co. v. Osage Oil & Refining Co., C.A.10th, 69 F.2d 19 and see Earp v. Mid-Continent Petroleum Corp., 167 Okl. 86, 27 P.2d 855; Simmons v. Wilson, Tex.Civ.App., 216 S.W.2d 847.

24. 139 Tex. 578, 164 S.W.2d 509, the court cites and follows Gypsy Oil Co. v. Marsh, 121 Okl. 135, 248 P. 329, 48 A.L.R. 876 and Parks v. Sinai Oil & Gas Co., 83 Okl. 295, 201 P. 517.

Also see: West v. Russell, 12 Cal.App. 3d 638, 90 Cal.Rptr. 772; Reese Enterprises v. Lawson, 220 Kan. 300, 553 P.2d 885; Mason v. Ladd Petroleum Co., Okl., 630 P.2d 1283; Stewart v. Amerada Hess Corp., Okl., 604 P.2d 854. The statement of the rule is virtually identical in the various jurisdictions.

them in entering into the contract. The object of the contract was to secure development of the property for the mutual benefit of the parties. It was contemplated that this would be done during the primary period of the contract. So far as the lessees were concerned, the object in providing for a continuation of the lease for an indefinite time after the expiration of the primary period was to allow the lessees to reap the full fruits of the investments made by them in developing the property. Obviously, if the lease could no longer be operated at a profit, there were no fruits for them to reap. The lessors should not be required to suffer a continuation of the lease after the expiration of the primary period merely for speculation purposes on the part of the lessees. Since the lease was no longer yielding a profit to the lessees at the termination of the primary period, the object sought to be accomplished by the continuation thereof had ceased, and the lease had terminated."

In defining the term "paying quantities" the court said: "It has been generally held that paying quantities when used in this connection, means paying quantities to the lessee. If a well pays a profit, even small, over operating expenses, it produces in paying quantities, though it may never repay its costs and the enterprise as a whole may prove unprofitable."

As may be seen, the definition of paying quantities is whether the well produces a profit to the lessee over lifting or production costs.[25] Lifting or production costs are the costs of producing the well and do not include costs of drilling, completing, or equipping the well. Whether or not the well may ultimately pay out its costs of drilling and completing is not considered.[26]

---

25. West v. Russell, 12 Cal.App.3d 638, 90 Cal.Rptr. 772 (1970); Reese Enterprises v. Lawson, 220 Kan. 300, 553 P.2d 885 (1976). In the latter case the court defines costs as all current costs of operation and production, including all direct costs such as labor, trucking, transportation expense, replacement and repair of equipment, taxes, licenses and permit fees, operator's time on the lease, maintenance and repair of roads, entrances, and gates, and expenses incurred in complying with state laws requiring plugging of abandoned wells and prevention of pollution; Berthelote v. Loy Oil Co., 95 Mont. 434, 28 P.2d 187; Treasure County v. Berggren, 154 Mont. 1, 459 P.2d 271; Mason v. Ladd Petroleum Co., Okl., 630 P.2d 1283; Gypsy Oil Co. v. Marsh, 121 Okl. 135, 248 P. 329, 48 A.L.R. 876; Kerr v. Hillenberg, Okl., 373 P.2d 66; Garcia v. King, 139 Tex. 578, 164 S.W.2d 509; Clifton v. Koontz, 160 Tex. 82, 325 S.W.2d 684, 79 A.L.R.2d 774, noted 14 S.W.L.J. 539. See Briggs v. Waggoner, Okl., 375 P.2d 896 where habendum clause called for "commercial and paying quantities to the lessor," held, lessee only had to make a profit and expenses.

26. Noel Estate, Inc. v. T. W. Murray, 223 La. 387, 65 So.2d 886; Berthelote v. Loy Oil Co., 95 Mont. 434, 28 P.2d 187; Treasure County v. Berggren, 154 Mont. 1, 459 P.2d 271; Gypsy Oil Co. v. Marsh, 121 Okl. 135, 248 P. 329, 48 A.L.R. 876; Kerr v. Hillenberg, Okl., 373 P.2d 66; Garcia v. King, 139 Tex. 578, 164 S.W.2d 509. However, it should be noted that the definition of "production" for purposes of satisfying the habendum clause differs from the definition of "production" as related to other matters. Production during the primary term sufficient to excuse payment of delay rentals generally does not include an element of profit to the lessee, whereas production sufficient to impose duties to offset or develop additional wells includes recov-

§ 6.4   THE OIL AND GAS LEASE—DURATION   285

In most jurisdictions the profit to the mineral owner in the form of the amount of royalty payable to the lessor is not considered. However, this is not the rule in Louisiana, where paying production must return a sufficient consideration to the lessor.[27]

The simple test set forth above is satisfactory as long as production stays at levels which continue to pay a profit to the lessee over production costs. However, this generally is not the nature of petroleum production throughout the life of a well. Eventually production will fall off and become sporadic. Many wells are never better than marginal at best. For many years oil men have been burdened with the problem of whether a marginal well would continue the lease in effect under the habendum clause. The tests set forth above do not, except in the most general terms, deal with the problems of cyclical production or the period over which the well should be tested to determine whether production is profitable.

The problem is not as difficult in those jurisdictions that view termination of a lease as subject to a suit for cancellation in equity as it is in those jurisdictions that view the lease as subject to a determinable limitation. In the former jurisdictions a subjective test developed, and equity could give relief in situations where production had decreased or had become sporadic but where a reasonably prudent operator would continue to operate.

In the Oklahoma case of Henry v. Clay,[28] lessee was producing from one oil well at the end of the primary term of the lease. After the end of the primary term, for a nine-month period expenses were $949.12 and income $902.97, or a loss of $46.15. In holding that the lease did not lapse, the court stated:

> "We further hold that the standard by which the judgment and good faith of the lessee is measured is whether the lease is producing, or by the exercise of reasonable skill and diligence could be made to produce, sufficient oil and gas to justify a reasonable and prudent operator in continuing the operation thereof."

In the landmark case of Clifton v. Koontz,[29] Texas adopted a subjective approach very similar to that quoted above from Henry v. Clay in determining if production in paying quantities is present in marginal well situations. The case is an extension of Garcia v. King and may allow a marginal well to continue a lease in effect in situations even where it is produced at a loss. The case is therefore high-

ery of costs of drilling and completion in addition to a profit over lifting costs. See § 8.3(A), infra.

27. See Noel Estate, Inc. v. T. W. Murray, 223 La. 387, 65 So.2d 886. An early Oklahoma case briefly discussed whether production could be considered as being in paying quantities where the return to the lessor did not equal the delay rentals; however, this does not appear to be an element considered in later opinions, Gypsy Oil Co. v. Marsh, 121 Okl. 135, 248 P. 329, 48 A.L.R. 876; Mason v. Ladd Petroleum Co., Okl., 630 P.2d 1283. See Briggs v. Waggoner, Okl., 375 P.2d 896.

28. Okl., 274 P.2d 545.

29. 160 Tex. 82, 325 S.W.2d 684, noted 14 S.W.L.J. 539.

ly significant in jurisdictions that treat the lease as automatically terminating under the Garcia v. King rule.

The question presented in Clifton v. Koontz was whether a lease had terminated due to cessation of production. It was alleged that for a 16-month period production had ceased to be in paying quantities, as from June 1955 through September 1956 there was an overall loss of $216.16. In September 1956, reworking was commenced that resulted in the well being put back on production. Output was increased some 1800%. For the nine-month period prior to June 1955 the lease had been profitable. It was held that the lease did not terminate. The court stated that under the lease a 60-day period was provided after production ceased during which reworking could be commenced without lapse of the lease. Since no production would have been necessary to maintain the lease for this 60-day period it was not considered by the court in the total period. Considering the amended period from June 1955 to July 1956, a profit was made of $111.25. The court also stated that the loss in production during the last three months (July through September) was due to operations in preparation for reworking the well. However, the court did not bottom its holding upon the fact that during the amended period a small profit had been made, but stated:

"The generally accepted definition of 'production in paying quantities' is stated in the Garcia case, to be as follows: 'If a well pays a profit, even small, over operating expenses, it produces in paying quantities, though it may never repay its costs, and the enterprise as a whole may prove unprofitable.'

"In the case of a marginal well, such as we have here, the standard by which paying quantities is determined is whether or not under all the relevant circumstances a reasonably prudent operator would, for the purpose of making a profit and not merely for speculation, continue to operate a well in the manner in which the well in question was operated.

"In determining paying quantities, in accordance with the above standard, the trial court necessarily must take into consideration all matters which would influence a reasonable and prudent operator. Some of the factors are: The depletion of the reservoir and the price for which the lessee is able to sell his produce, the relative profitableness of other wells in the area, the operating and marketing costs of the lease, his net profit, the lease provisions, a reasonable period of time under the circumstances, and whether or not the lessee is holding the lease merely for speculative purposes.

"The term 'paying quantities' involves not only the amount of production, but also the ability to market the product at a profit. Whether there is a reasonable basis for the expectation of profitable returns from the well is the test."

§ 6.4   THE OIL AND GAS LEASE—DURATION   287

The court relegated the Garcia v. King test of profit over the lifting expenses to merely one of the elements a reasonably prudent operator would consider in determining whether such operator would continue to operate the lease for the purpose of making a profit and not for speculation. The court goes on to say that there can be no arbitrary period [30] for determining the question of whether or not a lease has terminated, for many reasons may exist to cause a slowing up in production. Seasonal variation in production due to proration rules of the state conservation commission is one of the factors pointed out.

The approaches applied by the Oklahoma and the Texas courts as to the acts of the lessee are very similar. Under either approach, whether a lease will terminate due to cessation of production in paying quantities will depend upon the surrounding facts and circumstances, including the reason for the marginal production, the relative profitability in the past, and prospects for future production. Prior to the Clifton case the latter would form no part of the conclusion under the Garcia v. King rule.[31]

In at least one jurisdiction, Kansas, the court, in Reese Enterprises v. Lawson,[32] has stated that determination of whether a well is producing in paying quantities will be determined by a mathematical computation. Kansas applies an objective test, and good faith of the operator is not a factor.

In determining whether a well is producing in paying quantities both income and cost of lifting or production of the well are to be considered.

The cases have been consistent that all income attributable to the working interest, or lessee's interest, under the lease is to be considered.[33] To determine the income for purposes of determining paying

---

30. See Transport Oil Co. v. Exeter Oil Co., Ltd., 84 Cal.App.2d 616, 191 P.2d 129; Reese Enterprises, Inc. v. Lawton, 220 Kan. 300, 553 P.2d 885; Texaco Inc. v. Fox, 228 Kan. 589, 618 P.2d 844; Ballanfonte v. Kimbell, Tex.Civ.App., 373 S.W.2d 119. But cf. Renner v. Huntington-Hawthorne Oil and Gas Co., 39 Cal.2d 93, 244 P.2d 895; Transport Oil Co. v. Exeter Oil Co., Ltd., 84 Cal.App.2d 616, 191 P.2d 129, where the parties attempted to further define "paying quantities" in the lease.

31. See Fick v. Wilson, Tex.Civ.App., 349 S.W.2d 622, which held lapse in production of 110 days did not terminate the lease, citing Clifton v. Koontz. In discussing the fact that for nine months prior to the 110 day period the lease produced at a profit, the court stated: "For appellants to prevail, it would have to be held as a matter of law that production for the 9 month period preceding May 13, had no probative value relevant to the issue of production in paying quantities. * * * Clifton v. Koontz forbids such a conclusion; and, to the contrary, supports the view such evidence is relevant and material."

32. 220 Kan. 300, 553 P.2d 885 (the court states good faith of the lessee is not a factor).

33. Clifton v. Koontz, 160 Tex. 82, 325 S.W.2d 684; Reese Enterprises, Inc. v. Lawton, 220 Kan. 300, 553 P.2d 885; Mason v. Ladd Petroleum Co., Okl., 630 P.2d 1283. In Bell v. Mitchell Energy Corp., Tex.Civ.App., 553 S.W.2d 626, holding that a marginal well had not ceased production in paying quantities under the Clifton test, the court allowed the jury to take into account increased gas price approval by the Federal Power Commission granted retroactively, which the assignee of the lease did not take into account

production, all income attributable to any non-cost bearing interest that has been created out of the working interest will be added back.[34] If lessee, Rex Oil Company, had assigned the lease to Black Gold Oil Company and reserved to itself an overriding royalty interest equal to $1/16$ of $7/8$ of total production, the income payable to Rex would be included in the income of the working interest of Black Gold to determine the total income from the lease.

The courts have not been consistent as to what costs should be subtracted in determining production in paying quantities. Only costs of removing the petroleum products from the ground, and not costs of drilling, completing and equipping a well should be considered.

Lifting and production costs that have been required to be deducted include:[35] labor costs of pumpers and others operating equipment on the lease, day-to-day power and supplies; severance taxes;[36] license and permit fees; replacement and repair of producing equipment,[37] maintenance and repair of roads, entrances, and gates; and electricity and telephone costs. The jurisdictions vary, however, in treatment of costs of depreciation.[38] Cases are beginning to appear considering administrative overhead and camp expense. Kansas, in the case of Reese Enterprises v. Lawson, discussed above, has included costs of plugging abandoned wells where required by state law. However, this latter expense would not seem to be an expense relating to the cost of production.

One of the first cases dealing with the problem of depreciation on equipment is that of Bales v. Delhi-Taylor[39] Oil Corporation. In the Bales case, income and expenses from the well in question during the applicable period were as follows:

when he elected to abandon the lease and reassigned it.

A similiar decision is found in Oklahoma in the case of a Barby v. Singer, Okl., 648 P.2d 14, holding that a lessee did not lose a marginal lease where it refused to plug and abandon a stripper well pending congressional action which resulted in a retroactive price increase. It also held that the retroactive price increase could be considered in determining whether the lease should be cancelled or kept in effect. In Texas the question would be whether the lease had terminated due to failure to produce in paying quantities. In Oklahoma under the vesting concept, the question is whether the lease should be cancelled due to the failure of the lessee to act as would a reasonably prudent operator in the circumstances. See discussion, footnote 9, supra.

34. Transport Oil Co. v. Exeter Oil Co., Ltd., 84 Cal.App.2d 616, 191 P.2d 129; Clifton v. Koontz, 160 Tex. 82, 325 S.W.2d 684, 79 A.L.R.2d 774, noted 14 S.W.L.J. 539.

35. See footnote 34, supra.

36. Persky v. First State Bank of Vernon, Tex.Civ.App., 117 S.W.2d 861.

37. Clifton v. Koontz, 160 Tex. 82, 325 S.W.2d 684, 79 A.L.R.2d 774, noted 14 S.W.L.J. 539; Skelly Oil Co. v. Archer, 163 Tex. 336, 356 S.W.2d 774; Sullivan and Garnett v. James, Tex.Civ.App., 308 S.W.2d 891.

38. Texaco v. Fox, 228 Kan. 589, 618 P.2d 844, cf. Stewart v. Amerada Hess Corp., Okl., 604 P.2d 854, and Bales v. Delhi-Taylor Oil Corp., Tex.Civ.App., 362 S.W.2d 388.

39. Tex.Civ.App., 362 S.W.2d 388, following Skelly Oil Co. v. Archer, 163 Tex. 336, 356 S.W.2d 774.

§ 6.4   THE OIL AND GAS LEASE—DURATION   289

Month	Income	Lease Expense	Plant Expense	Net
Sept., 1958	$512.00	$141.00	$18.00	$353.00
Oct.	436.00	118.00	13.00	305.00
Nov.	312.00	101.00	9.00	202.00
Dec.	270.00	93.00	13.00	164.00
Jan., 1959	109.00	128.00	4.00	−21.00
Feb.	116.00	111.00	5.00	
Mar.	34.00	76.00	1.00	−43.00

It was argued, however, that a depreciation expense of $365.00 per month should have been included. This would result in a net loss for each month after August 1958. The equipment subject to depreciation was that of salvageable equipment, and the figure was book depreciation. The court came to the conclusion that depreciation would be proper, but that it should be based upon actual depreciation and apply only to producing equipment. It was held that the lease did not terminate, as a reasonably prudent operator would have so operated for a profit, and that the landowner had not sustained his burden of proof as to the character of equipment and the depreciation figures applied thereto.

Oklahoma cases have been consistent with the Texas cases in holding that actual depreciation of producing equipment must be deducted. In Stewart v. Amerada Hess Corp.,[40] a case of first impression in Oklahoma, the court distinguished depreciation of producing or lifting equipment from that of original investment equipment. The court stated:

> "The cost of drilling a producing well—i.e. the expense incurred before oil is actually lifted from the ground—is not an item to be considered in computing production in 'paying quantities.' The lifting of oil which marks the commencement of production stage is coincidental with the completion of a well. At that stage, critical here, only those expenses which are directly related to lifting operations can be included in determining if Amerada's lease remained in force beyond its primary term.
>
> * * *
>
> "Other out-of-state authority reasons that since the original investment in a well may not be considered in computing oil lifting expenses, neither should producing equipment depreciation. * * * Depreciation of equipment used in lifting operations is regarded as production expense in some states. The rationale for this rule is that while depreciation of the original investment in

---

40. Okl., 604 P.2d 854; also see Transport Oil Co. v. Exeter Oil Co., Ltd., 84 Cal.App.2d 616, 191 P.2d 129; Clifton v. Koontz, 160 Tex. 82, 325 S.W.2d 684, 79 A.L.R.2d 774, noted 14 S.W.L.J. 539; Skelly Oil Co. v. Archer, 163 Tex. 336, 356 S.W.2d 774; Sullivan and Garnett v. James, Tex.Civ.App., 308 S.W.2d 891; Bales v. Delhi-Taylor Oil Corp., Tex.Civ. App., 362 S.W.2d 388; but cf. Whitaker v. Texaco, Inc., C.A.10th, 283 F.2d 169.

the drilling of a well may not be *stricto sensu* an out-of-pocket lifting expense, production-related equipment does have value that is being reduced through its continued operation. We adopt this reasoning as sound and hold that depreciation should be mandatorily included as an item of lifting expense in determining whether there is production in 'paying quantities.' "

The Stewart case was expressly rejected in Kansas in the case of Texaco, Inc. v. Fox,[41] wherein the court refused to include depreciation of equipment as an expense to be considered. Although the opinion apparently rejects all equipment depreciation, it appears from the opinion that only depreciation on original investment was involved.

Administrative overhead and camp expense is generally stated as an expense to be included. However, few cases have dealt with the allocation of such expenses to a lease. It would seem obvious that expenses of administration that are immediately connected with production from the lease would be considered. This would include expenses of a supervisor in visiting the lease for such purposes. But what of office overhead of a lessee's district offices, or central headquarters?

In Mason v. Ladd Petroleum Corp.,[42] the Oklahoma court limited inclusion of such expenses to those that were directly related to the producing operation of a lease. It was further stated that the treatment of such expenses in a joint operating agreement would not be determinative of the treatment of such costs in determining production in paying quantities. In an interesting part of the opinion the court stated:

"But while a district office may be convenient and even necessary as a pragmatic approach to making a corporate giant functional in the corporate administration of its lease operations, we deem the expense of such an office to be too indirectly and too remotely related to defendant's lifting or producing operations in connection with the Sherman No. 1 well to be included in determining whether the well operates at a profit. The district office expense relates to and is made necessary by reason of corporate convenience or necessity, and not by reason of anything necessary or convenient for the lifting operations of the well. Here we distinguish between what may be corporate convenience and necessity on the one hand, and the convenience and necessity of those functions which relate directly to the production or 'lifting expenses' intimate to the actual production of a well on the other hand. To do otherwise is to lose sight of the real issue, that is, whether a well yields production income in excess of the cost of the production. The owner and operator of an oil and gas leasehold estate may for whatever reason be multi-tiered, and may for whatever reason, accounting or otherwise, be capable of attributing a portion or percentage of its over-all operational expense to an individ-

---

41. 228 Kan. 589, 618 P.2d 844. 42. Okl., 630 P.2d 1283.

ual well, an attempted application of such expenses to lifting expenses of a well to determine the issue before us will but lead to the absurdity of determining a well to be a non-producer in the hands of a corporate giant, yet a producer in the hands of a single leasehold owner-operator who is unfettered by such attendant complexities."

Where more than one well is operated, a question arises as to the method of allocation of expenses among leases. In Sullivan and Garnett v. James,[43] lessee operated some 5 wells situated on various leases. As to one lease the method of allocation of expenses was critical in determining whether it was producing in paying quantities. The expenses involved were expenses of operation and administration, which were the same for all wells. If allocated equally on a per well basis, expenses of the lease involved would exceed the income. However, if allocated proportionally to production from each lease, apparently the income from the subject lease would have exceeded expenses. The court held that indirect expenses should be allocated on a per lease basis, and that the lease in question had terminated.

(B) Production—Sporadic Production and Temporary Cessation of Production

In a number of the producing states the courts treat termination of a lease as involving a cancellation or forfeiture in equity. In these states where production has ceased or is no longer deemed to be in paying quantities, cancellation of the lease will not be decreed where, in view of relevant circumstances, such decree would be unreasonable.

In Texas and several other jurisdictions termination of a lease under the habendum clause is treated as a determinable limitation on the lessee's estate. A cessation of production results in automatic termination except in those cases where the cessation is deemed "temporary." In such jurisdictions cessation of production will be deemed "temporary" where stoppage is due to mechanical or production breakdowns.

Where stoppage of production is treated as temporary, the lessee, unless limited by the terms of the lease, will have a reasonable time to remedy the stoppage and again begin production. A line of cases would limit the time in which production will be deemed to be temporary by application of time limits contained in lease clauses under which operations can cease without termination of the lease.

When a lease has terminated due to cessation of production, later acceptance of royalty payments, without more, will not estop the mineral owner nor constitute a waiver of the termination.

---

43. Tex.Civ.App., 308 S.W.2d 891. The case is conceptually unsatisfactory, as the court affirms on the basis that both theories were submitted to the jury. Also Clifton v. Koontz was not cited nor its effect considered by the court whether nevertheless a reasonably prudent operator would have continued to so operate the lease. Where wells from more than one lease are operated as one administrative unit, should all wells be considered as producing in paying quantities where income exceeds expenses on any reasonable basis of allocation?

Upon wrongful interference of the mineral owner with the lessee, the lessee may cease operations and will be awarded additional equal or reasonable time to the term of the lease, after cessation of the litigation.

In the foregoing section the question was whether or not production existed in paying quantities. Although some overlap occurs between this section and the preceding one, here the assumption is made, unless otherwise stated, that for a lesser or greater period of time, as the case may be, actual production has ceased.

Where production has ceased, according to a strict reading of the habendum clause, the lease should thereupon terminate according to its own terms. However, as mentioned above, in a number of jurisdictions termination of a lease involves a cancellation or forfeiture of the lease in equity. In these jurisdictions discovery of oil or gas vests the lessee with a right to remove the minerals, and cessation of production will not form a basis for termination where (1) the lessee has not capped or otherwise intentionally abandoned the lease, or (2), where the lessee, in good faith, is using reasonable diligence to put the lease back in production during a continuing period of possibility of profitable production.[44]

The forerunner of these decisions appears to be the case of Lamb v. Vansyckle,[45] where, after the end of the primary term, production ceased for some 56 days. The court held that it would not adopt the rule of automatic limitation on the lessee's estate and also would not decree a forfeiture where in view of all circumstances such decree would be unreasonable. The court therefore rejected both the Texas view of strict limitation upon the estate, and the Louisiana view [46] that the lessor in order to prove termination had the burden of proof of showing either an intentional abandonment or that the well was no longer capable of paying production. Although intentional abandonment would be a cause for forfeiture, cessation of ability to produce in paying quantities need not be.

An illustrative case is that of Hoff v. Girdler Corp.,[47] which involved the production of helium. A lease was executed with a primary term of five years and so long thereafter as minerals were produced. The lease was executed in March 1929; helium was discovered and produced until August 1, 1930. The United States

---

44. Saulsberry v. Siegel, 221 Ark. 152, 252 S.W.2d 834; Barrett v. Dorr, 140 Ind. App. 295, 212 N.E.2d 29; Gillespie v. Ohio Oil Co., 260 Ill. 169, 102 N.E. 1043; Gillespie v. Wagoner, 28 Ill.2d 217, 190 N.E.2d 765; Lamb v. Vansyckle, 205 Ky. 597, 266 S.W. 253; Stimson v. Tarrant, C.A.9th, 132 F.2d 363, but cf. Berthelote v. Loy Oil Co., 95 Mont. 434, 28 P.2d 187; Stewart v. Amerada Hess Corp., Okl., 604 P.2d 854; Cotner v. Warren, Okl., 330 P.2d 217, noted 13 S.W.L.J. 382; Kerr v. Hillenberg, Okl., 373 P.2d 66; Hunter v. Clarkson, Okl., 428 P.2d 210; Jath Oil Co. v. Durbin Branch, Okl., 490 P.2d 1086. See discussion § 6.4(A) at footnote 9, supra.

45. 205 Ky. 597, 266 S.W. 253; expressly cited and followed: Barrett v. Dorr, 140 Ind.App. 295, 212 N.E.2d 29; Gillespie v. Wagoner, 28 Ill.2d 217, 190 N.E.2d 765; Cotner v. Warren, Okl., 330 P.2d 217, noted 13 S.W.L.J. 382; Hunter v. Clarkson, Okl., 428 P.2d 210.

46. Tyson v. Surf Oil Co., 195 La. 248, 196 So. 336.

47. 104 Colo. 56, 88 P.2d 100.

was the sole purchaser, but terminated the contract of purchase in the spring of 1930 due to development of government-owned helium production facilities. The lessee attempted to develop foreign markets, but the government prevented the export of helium. Lessee had expended nearly $500,000 on the development of the well, which was capable of production in paying quantities, but for which no market existed. The lessee thereafter kept the facilities in good repair and was attempting to expand a domestic market. In a suit for cancellation of the lease on the basis of abandonment it was held that the lease was not subject to cancellation on the ground that no abandonment had occurred. The lessee had shown no intent to abandon. On the contrary, the lessee had used every effort to maintain the well and facilities, in which lessee had a very substantial investment, and had attempted to develop a market. A not unreasonable time had elapsed, and the lessor was not being injured, as no drainage was occurring. As the present lessee could not obtain a market under the existing circumstances, it was felt unreasonable to terminate the lease and occasion a great financial loss to the lessee.

Factors that the courts have looked to in determining whether a lease would be subject to cancellation where production has ceased, have included the following:

(1) Ability of lease or well to produce in commercial quantities; [48]

(2) no available market [49] or other reasons for cessation of production; [50]

---

48. Saulsberry v. Siegel, 221 Ark. 152, 252 S.W.2d 834; Hoff v. Girdler Corp., 104 Colo. 56, 88 P.2d 100; Elliott v. Crystal Springs Oil Co., 106 Kan. 248, 187 P. 692; Tyson v. Surf Oil Co., 195 La. 248, 196 So. 336; Greer v. Salmon, 82 N.M. 245, 479 P.2d 294 where no production for four years due to leak between well and meter, no royalty paid, and well at all times capable of production in paying quantities, held not temporary cessation and lease expired; Stimson v. Tarrant, C.A.9th, 132 F.2d 363; but cf. Gillespie v. Ohio Oil Co., 260 Ill. 169, 102 N.E. 1043.

49. Hoff v. Girdler Corp., 104 Colo. 56, 88 P.2d 100; Stimson v. Tarrant, C.A.9th, 132 F.2d 363.

50. Saulsberry v. Siegel, 221 Ark. 152, 252 S.W.2d 834 (derrick burned down and production ceased for four years); Wilson v. Talbert, 259 Ark. 535, 535 S.W.2d 807 (no effort to replace ruptured tank for four months and another available nearby and not used); Elliott v. Crystal Springs Oil Co., 106 Kan. 248, 187 P. 692 (couldn't buck pressure of high pressure gathering line); Barrett v. Dorr, 140 Ind. App. 295, 212 N.E.2d 29 (mismanagement); Feland v. Placid Oil Co., N.D., 171 N.W.2d 829 (salt water pit filled); Gard v. Kaiser, Okl., 582 P.2d 1311 (low gas pressure); State v. Amoco Production Co., Okl., 645 P.2d 468 (collapsed casing); Cotner v. Warren, Okl., 330 P.2d 217, noted 13 S.W.L.J. 382 (internal business problems; however, in Gillespie v. Wagoner, 28 Ill.2d 217, 190 N.E.2d 765 it was held cessation of production due to financial trouble was not a sufficient reason); Kerr v. Hillenberg, Okl., 373 P.2d 66 (change to secondary production methods); Cole v. Philadelphia Co., 345 Pa. 315, 26 A.2d 920 (drilling to lower sand); Hunter v. Clarkson, Okl., 428 P.2d 210 (sporadic production); Reynolds v. McNeill, 218 Ark. 453, 236 S.W.2d 723, noted 30 Tex.L.R. 527 (shut down for repairs caused by breakdown of producing equipment); Amoco Production Co. v. Braslau, Tex., 561 S.W.2d 805 (collapsed casing); Casey v. Western Oil and Gas, Inc., Tex. Civ.App., 611 S.W.2d 676, refused n.r.e. (negotiation for a higher price, and equipment stolen from lease).

(3) reasonable diligence [51] and good faith [52] shown by the lessee in attempting to secure a market; [53]

(4) period of time of cessation; [54]

(5) large financial investment by the lessee; [55]

(6) lessor not being injured; [56]

(7) no intent shown from the circumstances that lessee is abandoning the lease, etc.[57]

In a suit for cancellation of the lease the court will balance the above factors to determine whether a forfeiture should be adjudicated.

The problem of cessation of production from the lease also arises and affects term mineral and royalty grants. It is customary in many term deeds to grant the interest for a fixed term with a habendum clause identical or similar to that found in an oil and gas lease. For instance, O may grant to A a $^1/_{16}$ royalty interest in the land for a term of five years and as long thereafter as oil or gas is produced therefrom. The grantee, or his assigns, does not have a possessory interest in the minerals and the duration of the grant is dependent upon production from the land at the end of the term of the grant in the deed. Production as defined in the term deed is usually defined in the same manner as that in the oil and gas lease, and calls for production in paying quantities to continue the deed past the fixed term.[58]

Assume that there is an oil and gas lease upon the land and from which oil is being produced after the end of the term of the deed.

---

51. Barrett v. Dorr, 140 Ind.App. 295, 212 N.E.2d 29; Gillespie v. Wagoner, 28 Ill.2d 217, 190 N.E.2d 765; Stimson v. Tarrant, C.A.9th, 132 F.2d 363.

52. Kerr v. Hillenberg, Okl., 373 P.2d 66.

53. Such actions can only extend the lease for a reasonable time: Saulsberry v. Siegel, 221 Ark. 142, 252 S.W.2d 834; Hoff v. Girdler Corp., 104 Colo. 56, 88 P.2d 100; Lamb v. Vansyckle, 205 Ky. 597, 266 S.W. 253; Hunter v. Clarkson, Okl., 428 P.2d 210.

54. Kelwood Farms, Inc. v. Ritchie, 1 Kan.App.2d 472, 571 P.2d 338.

55. Saulsberry v. Siegel, 221 Ark. 152, 252 S.W.2d 834; Hoff v. Girdler Corp., 104 Colo. 56, 88 P.2d 100; Elliott v. Crystal Springs Oil Co., 106 Kan. 248, 187 P. 692.

56. Hoff v. Girdler Corp., 104 Colo. 56, 88 P.2d 100 (lessor not hurt), cf. Elliott v. Crystal Springs Oil Co., 106 Kan. 248, 187 P. 692.

57. Intent to abandon shown from capping of wells, Locke v. Palmore, 308 Ky. 637, 215 S.W.2d 544; Tyson v. Surf Oil Co., 195 La. 248, 196 So. 336. Also see Kelwood Farms, Inc. v. Ritchie, 1 Kan.App.2d 472, 571 P.2d 338.

58. Kelwood Farms, Inc. v. Ritchie, 1 Kan.App.2d 472, 571 P.2d 338; Texaco, Inc. v. Fox, 228 Kan. 589, 618 P.2d 844 (1980); Stuart v. Pundt, Tex.Civ.App., 338 S.W.2d 167, error refused; Amoco Production Co. v. Braslau, Tex., 561 S.W.2d 805. In Oklahoma the situation is not clear, with opposing viewpoints being expressed in a federal case, Panhandle Eastern Pipe Line Co. v. Isaacson, C.A.10th, 255 F.2d 669, which would treat production under a lease and a term deed as the same, and an Oklahoma Court of Appeals case, whose publication was not directed by the Oklahoma Supreme Court, and therefore is not considered as precedent, McEvoy v. First National Bank and Trust Co. of Enid, Okl. App., 624 P.2d 559, which held that production under term deed requires actual production and not just discovery.

However, some time thereafter the well on the lease is shut down for any of the reasons set forth above, and further assume that a court in the same jurisdiction would find that the lease had not been abandoned nor would they decree a forfeiture. Does the term deed terminate? It appears to be the law in those jurisdictions that would not find a forfeiture, that the term deed does not terminate as long as equity would not decree a forfeiture of the lease.[59] An abandonment of the lease, however, would also terminate the term deed.[60]

In these jurisdictions it might be argued that the term deed should be construed more strictly than the oil and gas lease, as many of the factors that the courts take into account in balancing equities do not exist in the case of the non-possessory term interest. Here the grantee has not expended large sums of money in development of the lease, and being a non-possessory interest holder his acts cannot affect whether the lease will be held in effect. Few cases are found discussing the position of the term deed grantee vis-a-vis the lessee. However, in the Oklahoma case of Beatty v. Baxter,[61] the court was of the opposite opinion, that more liberality should be shown the term deed owner than the lessee, for the reason that he is at the mercy of the acts of the lessee.

Where production has ceased, Texas and several other jurisdictions follow the view that the habendum clause imposes a determinable limitation upon the interest of the lessee. Surrounding circumstances should have no influence upon the termination of the estate where production in paying quantities has ceased, even for an instant.[62] Although this appears to be the result where no production in paying quantities has been achieved during the primary term, or where production has totally ceased, the result of strict termination has been modified in Texas (1) by the case of Clifton v. Koontz,[63] where a marginally producing lease is concerned and expenses exceed income, and (2) in those situations where production has ceased in situations where the Texas courts would treat the cessation of production only as "temporary."[64] Be this as it may, however, Texas,

---

59. Beatty v. Baxter, 208 Okl. 686, 258 P.2d 626; Postier v. Postier, Okl., 296 P.2d 138. The statement may be subject to criticism for being overly broad; however, although not expressly discussed, it would seem that the underlying rationale in the Beatty case would be to extend the duration of the term deed to all matters where cessation of production would not result in termination of the lease, and not just from temporary cessation due to mechanical breakdowns. Compare with temporary cessation cases in jurisdictions following the Texas view. Amoco Production Co. v. Braslau, Tex., 561 S.W.2d 805.

60. Owens v. Day, 207 Okl. 341, 249 P.2d 710.

61. 208 Okl. 686, 258 P.2d 626.

62. Renner v. Huntington-Hawthorne Oil and Gas Co., 39 Cal.2d 93, 244 P.2d 895; Kahn v. Arkansas River Gas Co., 122 Kan. 786, 253 P. 563; Francis v. Pritchett, Tex.Civ.App., 278 S.W.2d 288. The same view is accorded term royalty or mineral interests at the end of or after the fixed term: Sellers v. Breidenbach, Tex.Civ.App., 300 S.W.2d 178; Midwest Oil Corp. v. Lude, Tex.Civ.App., 376 S.W.2d 18.

63. 160 Tex. 82, 325 S.W.2d 684, noted 12 Okl.L.Rev. 179, 14 S.W.L.J. 539.

64. Wilson v. Holm, 164 Kan. 229, 188 P.2d 899; Watson v. Rochmill, 137 Tex. 565, 155 S.W.2d 783; Midwest Oil Corp.

and those following its view, starts with the basic premise that, after the expiration of the primary term, lack of production in paying quantities automatically terminates the oil and gas lease, without the necessity for notice or adjudication.[65] The lessee must strictly comply with the terms of the habendum clause or he will speedily lose the lease, save for the few areas in which the courts give relief.

Two cases are illustrative of the Texas view. The first is the Kansas case of Kahn v. Arkansas River Gas Co.,[66] which involved a lease with a one-year primary term. A large gas well was drilled and produced for a while; however, production was stopped when the well pressure became too low to buck the line pressure of the gathering line. The lessee needed to drill more wells to develop the lease for a new market. Lessee had spent some $29,000 in development of the well, which was capable of production of 1,500,000 cubic feet of gas per day. Lessee had also entered into a contract with nearby towns but needed a pipeline to deliver the gas. The court held that as the lease was not otherwise being held, it expired of its own terms when production ceased.

The second case is the Texas case of Gulf Oil Corporation v. Reid,[67] whereby a gas well capable of producing gas in commercial quantities was brought in after the end of the primary term. The shut-in royalty was not paid for about a month after the primary term, and the Supreme Court of Texas held that the lease had terminated due to failure to produce. Although the case demonstrates the Texas approach, that there must be no time gap between the end of the primary term, operations, and production or substitute production, it was decided after Clifton v. Koontz, and is hard to square with the decision that a reasonably prudent operator would have operated the lease for profit and not for speculation. However, some later cases have seemingly distinguished the Koontz case as applying only to marginal well production, and not to the situation where production has totally ceased,[68] or where, as in the Reid case, has never begun.

As mentioned above, the Texas courts have held that the lease does not terminate in those instances where the cessation was deemed to be "temporary." Such situations may be distinguished from those described immediately above, where production was treated as having totally ceased.

An early case dealing with the question of whether a lease would terminate due to stoppages in production necessary to repair or re-

v. Winsauer, 159 Tex. 560, 323 S.W.2d 944; Amoco Production Co. v. Braslau, Tex., 561 S.W.2d 805.

65. But see Francis v. Pritchett, Tex. Civ.App., 278 S.W.2d 288, where gas well was shut in after primary term without payment of shut in royalties, court cancelled lease except for 20 acres around well. Result seems to be incorrect view of the nature of the habendum clause in Texas.

66. 122 Kan. 786, 253 P. 563.

67. 161 Tex. 51, 337 S.W.2d 267.

68. Hall v. McWilliams, Tex.Civ.App., 404 S.W.2d 606.

work the well was the Texas case of Watson v. Rochmill.[69] In this case tubing stopped up, and production ceased for a period of two years and seven months. During this time a watchman was on the property, taxes were paid, the well was swabbed out and worked on, and over $8,000 was spent on repairs. Two years after the well was shut down, the landowner brought suit to declare that the lease was terminated. The lessee also alleged that oil could have been produced but was not, due to low gravity, as there was no market to justify such production. It was held that the lease had terminated. The court stated that "upon cessation of production after termination of the primary term, the lease automatically terminated. The strictness of the above rule has been modified where there is only a temporary cessation of production due to sudden stoppage of the well or some mechanical breakdown of the equipment used in connection therewith, or the like. Under such circumstances there are authorities which hold that the lessee is entitled to a reasonable time in which to remedy the defect and resume production." It was found in the Rochmill case that the stoppage was not temporary in nature and was not brought about by mechanical breakdowns or other condition in connection with the well or associated equipment.

The conclusion that temporary cessations due to mechanical or production breakdowns will not terminate the lease is not consistent with the rationale that an oil and gas lease creates a determinable fee in the lessee, and appears to be an equitable encroachment to cover situations which must normally occur in the course of operations.[70] For such purposes temporary stoppages of production do not constitute a cessation of production within the scope of the habendum clause. Obviously the stoppage in production herein tolerated without constituting a cessation of production would seem to comprise a much narrower area in scope than the equitable considerations considered in jurisdictions that treat the cancellation of an oil and gas lease as a forfeiture in equity.[71] However, later Texas cases have somewhat broadened the area of matters to be considered. In Midwest Oil Corporation v. Winsauer,[72] the Texas court found although a stoppage of 174 days had occurred, due in part to obstructions in pipe and litigation, that a term royalty interest, in the secondary term,

---

69. 137 Tex. 565, 155 S.W.2d 783, 137 A.L.R. 1032.

70. Wilson v. Holm, 164 Kan. 229, 188 P.2d 899; Frost v. Gulf Oil Corp., 238 Miss. 775, 119 So.2d 759, 100 A.L.R.2d 876; Watson v. Rochmill, 137 Tex. 565, 155 S.W.2d 783, 137 A.L.R. 1032; Midwest Oil Corp. v. Winsauer, 159 Tex. 560, 323 S.W.2d 944; Stuart v. Pundt, Tex. Civ.App., 338 S.W.2d 167; Campbell v. Seaman, Tex.Civ.App., 427 S.W.2d 705; Amoco Production Co. v. Braslau, Tex., 561 S.W.2d 805 (following Stuart v. Pundt, where it was held that cessation was temporary where a casing collapsed and a new well was drilled to the same sand. In Amoco the Texas Supreme Court held cessation was temporary where a casing collapsed and well then completed in a *new* sand. However, the court emphasized that this sand had been encountered during the original drilling and the case did not concern cessation of production during a period of further, additional, or deeper exploration).

71. Footnotes 48–57, supra.

72. 159 Tex. 560, 323 S.W.2d 944; Amoco Production Co. v. Braslau, Tex., 561 S.W.2d 805.

would not terminate, as the stoppage was merely temporary. The court emphasized that the well's ability to produce and the lessee's good faith are also factors to be taken into account. Strangely, the Texas Supreme Court cited Beatty v. Baxter [73] and other cases from jurisdictions having fundamentally an equitable philosophy toward the termination of a lease that is past the primary term.

The later case of Amoco Production Co. v. Braslau [74] represents an extreme extension of the Texas cases, or, perhaps signals a change in underlying rationale in Texas cases dealing with production and temporary cessation of production. In this case the question was whether a term royalty interest had terminated. There was production from a lease on the land, during the fixed term of the royalty deed. While drilling the well on the lease, four separate sands had been identified by the lessee. Completions were made in two of the sands. After production ceased due to depletion from the two sands, efforts were made to recomplete in the other two sands. The well was lost due to collapse of casing in the well bore. Lessee then commenced and drilled well number two. It was completed 103 days after production had ceased and some 20 days after the expiration of the fixed term of the royalty deed. The court held that the stoppage was temporary and that the term royalty deed did not terminate under its habendum clause. The court stressed that it did not have before it the extension or preservation of a term royalty during a period of further or deeper exploration. The court relied on the earlier case of Stuart v. Pundt,[75] also involving a term interest, where the lessee drilled a new well into the same producing sand and the court held that cessation was only temporary and the term interest did not terminate.

If the case is to be supported solely on the basis of the temporary cessation of production concept, why did the deed not terminate automatically upon cessation of production due to depletion of products in the reservoir? This is usually not defined as temporary cessation, but as permanent cessation.[76] No problem would seem to have been encountered with the lease, as it would be maintained under the provisions of the continuous operations clause. However, such provisions usually do not appear in a term deed.

The court seems to rely upon some type of "discovery" theory, in that it stresses that "indications of production" were found in the other sands. This is not sufficient under the Texas cases to constitute production in paying quantities under the habendum clause.

It is interesting to compare the Oklahoma case of State v. Amoco Production Co.,[77] which dealt with a situation where production ceased due to a collapsed casing and the lessee drilled to the same

---

73. 208 Okl. 686, 258 P.2d 626.
74. Tex., 561 S.W.2d 805.
75. Tex.Civ.App., 338 S.W.2d 167, error refused.
76. Sunray DX Oil Co. v. Texaco, Inc., Tex., 417 S.W.2d 424, refused n.r.e.
77. Okl., 645 P.2d 468.

formation in a second well. The Oklahoma Supreme Court held that the cessation was temporary and that the lessee had used due diligence in restoring production. The court relied upon both Texas cases of Braslau and Pundt. Since Oklahoma applies the vesting theory as to producing sands in which oil or gas is discovered in paying quantities, it would seem that the court did not have to rely upon the Texas cases. A lease in Oklahoma will not terminate as to a producing sand that has not become depleted when the lessee is acting with prudence and due diligence. A contrast between the Oklahoma cases and the Braslau case is found in that Oklahoma will not recognize a "discovery" unless the well has been cased, completed, and tested, and is capable of production in paying quantities.[78] In Oklahoma "an indication of production," as encountered in the Braslau case, would not have been sufficient, and if other provisions were not present in a lease, or in a term deed, it would seem the interest would have terminated due to permanent cessation of production.[79]

Texas is not the only jurisdiction that, while basically viewing termination under the habendum clause as a determinable limitation, has cited cases from jurisdictions such as Oklahoma in support of a conclusion that temporary stoppages do not terminate a lease. The Mississippi case of Frost v. Gulf Oil Corporation,[80] cited both the Winsauer [81] and Cotner [82] cases. This raises a question as to what extent jurisdictions such as Texas and Mississippi have modified their view as to the nature of the habendum clause, and are moving to the view of other jurisdictions that a lease will not be terminated when in view of all the circumstances it would not be reasonable.

As can be seen from the above discussion, a lease will not be treated as having terminated due to stoppages in production from breakdowns or for reworking operations. This view has also been applied to term deeds. The factual area in which this will result will depend upon the view of the particular jurisdiction as to the nature of the oil and gas lease. However, such stoppage will only be tolerated for a reasonable period of time in relation to the facts and circumstances.

A line of cases has developed holding that the parties have contracted for a period of time during which such stoppage can be treated as temporary. In development of the lease the so-called naked habendum clause, i.e., without contractual modification, can be prolonged only by production, which is defined as including temporary stoppages as discussed above. Apparently for protection where re-

78. Hoyt v. Continental Oil Co., Okl., 606 P.2d 560; but cf. Frost v. Gulf Oil Corp., 238 Miss. 775, 119 So.2d 759, can, within reasonable time, complete and produce from other discovered reservoir.

79. See cases in Oklahoma cited in footnote 67, § 6.4(B), supra, as to the situation whether discovery is sufficient to constitute production under a term deed.

80. 238 Miss. 775, 119 So.2d 759, 100 A.L.R.2d 876.

81. 159 Tex. 560, 323 S.W.2d 944.

82. Okl., 330 P.2d 217, noted 13 S.W. L.J. 382.

working and other non-productive operations became necessary on producing wells, a clause was drafted to provide the express right to so rework or operate and that during such period of time the lease would not lapse. The clause is generally drafted to provide a time period, usually of 60 days.

Starting with the case of Woodson Oil Co. v. Pruett,[83] a line of authority [84] has construed the clause to the effect that the time stated in the reworking clause is a contractual limit on temporary stoppages. In this case no drilling or reworking was done on the well for a period of 190 days, and the court cancelled the lease on the ground that the stoppage had continued for more than the 60 days allowed by the drilling or reworking clause.

It was argued in a later Texas case,[85] that in light of Clifton v. Koontz that the clause should not be regarded as an exclusive statement of when stoppage is to be deemed temporary, but that the court should look to see if a reasonably prudent operator would nevertheless have so operated the lease for purpose of profit and not just for speculation. The court rejected the application of the Koontz case on the ground that it applied only to marginal production, not to the situation where production had ceased.

The 60-day drilling or reworking clause has been applied to limit the time within which work may be started to remedy the cause of a temporary cessation of production in two recent cases by the Supreme Courts of Texas and Oklahoma.

In the Texas case of Samano v. Sun Oil Co.[86] production from a well ceased due to mechanical difficulties. The lease contained the following habendum clause:

"[T]his lease shall remain in force for a term of ten years from this date, called primary term, and as long thereafter as oil, gas or other mineral is produced from said land, or as long thereafter as Lessee shall conduct drilling or reworking operations thereon with

---

83. Tex.Civ.App., 281 S.W.2d 159.
"If at the expiration of the primary term, Lessee is conducting operations for drilling a new well or re-working an old well, or if after the expiration of the primary term, production on this lease shall cease, this lease nevertheless shall continue as long as said operations continue or additional operations are had, which additional operations shall be deemed to be had where not more than Sixty (60) days elapse between abandonment of operations on one well and commencement of operations on another well, and if production is discovered this lease shall continue as long as additional operations are had."

84. Hoyt v. Continental Oil Co., Okl., 606 P.2d 560; Samano v. Sun Oil Co., Tex., 621 S.W.2d 580; Hall v. McWilliams, Tex.Civ.App., 404 S.W.2d 606; Haby v. Stanolind Oil and Gas Co., C.A.5th, 228 F.2d 298.

85. Hall v. McWilliams, Tex.Civ.App., 404 S.W.2d 606.

86. Tex., 621 S.W.2d 580. In the case of Shelton v. Taylor, Tex.Civ.App., 615 S.W.2d 912, the court held that the clause did not limit the temporary cessation doctrine, on the basis that the sixty-day drilling or reworking clause was not contained in the habendum clause, as it was in Samano. Shelton was following the lower court opinion in Samano, which was later reversed by the Supreme Court. It is apparent that Samano will be applied where the sixty-day clause is a separate clause in the lease.

no cessation of more than sixty consecutive days until production results, * * *"

Sun did nothing to restore production for a period of seventy-three days. Here there was a total cessation of production. The court held that the sixty day clause limited the "reasonable time" that the lessee would ordinarily have to restore production after a temporary cessation. The court rejected Gulf's argument that the clause did not apply after the end of the primary term, and held that when production stopped the express wording of the clause applied. Gulf therefore had sixty days within which to begin drilling or reworking operations. As it did not do so, the lease terminated.

A similar result occurred in the Oklahoma case of Hoyt v. Continental Oil Co.[87] In this case production in paying quantities ceased, although production did not cease entirely. The court construed cessation of production in paying quantities after the end of the primary term as cessation of production under the sixty day clause requiring drilling or reworking within such time period. The lessee was negotiating for a new gas purchase contract at a higher price for sale of gas from a formation from which the well was not producing. The well was later recompleted in the new formation. The court held that the lease had terminated. In applying the sixty day clause as a limitation of the reasonable operator rule in cases of temporary cessation of production, the court stated:

"On this point the record clearly demonstrates production in paying quantities was not obtained for an uninterrupted period far in excess of the 60-day provision in the lease executed by the parties. Where the parties have bargained for and agreed on a time period for a temporary cessation clause that provision will control over the common law doctrine of temporary cessation allowing a 'reasonable time' for resumption of drilling operation. * * * As the New Mexico Court noted on this subject in Greer v. Salmon,[88] supra, quoting from Haxlett 'Effect of Temporary Cessation Of Production on Leases and Term Royalties', Southwestern Legal Foundation, Tenth Annual Institute on Oil and Gas Law and Taxation, 201 at 248:

'The courts have been unanimous in construing this clause as meaning that cessation of production for longer than the stipulated period cannot be considered "temporary". In effect, the provision is construed as giving the lessee a fixed period of time within which to resume production or commence additional drilling or reworking operations in order to avoid termination of the lease; the period of grace having been fixed by agreement of the parties, it cannot be extended by the courts, no matter what the circumstances or cause of the cessation.'"

87. Okl., 606 P.2d 560.

88. 82 N.M. 245, 479 P.2d 294.

The apparent blanket application of the clause by the courts gives some cause for concern, and raises questions that have not yet been answered. It is questionable whether the parties to the lease have intended that the sixty day clause replace the common law doctrine relating to temporary cessation of production. The scope of the wording of the clause is much more narrow than the causes that may lead to temporary cessation of production. This may come about by many factors that cannot be remedied by either drilling or reworking of the well. These can include negotiation for a higher sales price of gas, vandalism or theft of equipment from the lease, washout of roads, rupture of storage tanks, loss of market, government regulations, and financial difficulties, to name a few. It would seem that the application of the clause should be limited to matters that may be remedied by drilling or reworking operations. This approach was taken by the Arkansas court in the case of Wilson v. Talbert,[89] where the court would apply the sixty day drilling or reworking clause only to matters of depletion or threatened depletion that could be averted only by extensive measures such as drilling a new well or reworking or deepening or plugging back of an old well. The clause would not be applied to temporary cessations of production by causes beyond the control of the lessee.

It appears to be the majority view that once the lease has terminated due to non-production, a later resumption of production by the lessee and acceptance of royalty payments by the landowners, without more, will not serve to waive the termination, ratify the lease, or estop the landowner.[90] The rationale is that upon termination the lessee is a trespasser, and any production that is paid to the landowner is merely his own property.[91] Therefore, no basis for estoppel exists, and no intent to ratify or waive is shown. In most jurisdictions the only manner in which the lease may be revived is by a new grant in writing signed by the landowners and containing words of grant.[92]

Depending upon the jurisdiction, where petroleum products have not been discovered or are not being produced in paying quantities at or prior to the end of the primary term of the lease, it will expire according to its own terms. However, where the landowner has wrongfully repudiated the lease or brought about unsuccessful litigation in an attempt to terminate the lease, the courts have given relief to the lessee.[93] Where it appears to the overanxious lessor that the

---

89. 259 Ark. 535, 535 S.W.2d 807.

90. Renner v. Huntington-Hawthorne Oil and Gas Co., 39 Cal.2d 93, 244 P.2d 895; Watson v. Rochmill, 137 Tex. 565, 155 S.W.2d 783, 137 A.L.R. 1032; Hastings v. Pichinson, Tex.Civ.App., 370 S.W.2d 1; Gas Ridge, Inc. v. Suburban Agricultural Properties, Inc., C.A.5th, 150 F.2d 363, rehearing denied 150 F.2d 1020, cert. denied 326 U.S. 796, 66 S.Ct. 487, 90 L.Ed. 485; Haby v. Stanolind Oil & Gas Co., C.A.5th, 228 F.2d 298.

91. See Gas Ridge, Inc. v. Suburban Agricultural Properties, Inc., C.A.5th, 150 F.2d 363, rehearing denied 150 F.2d 1020, cert. denied 326 U.S. 796, 66 S.Ct. 487, 90 L.Ed. 485.

92. Hastings v. Pichinson, Tex.Civ. App., 370 S.W.2d 1.

93. Greer v. Carter Oil Co., 373 Ill. 168, 25 N.E.2d 805; Violette v. Gaertner, 261 Mich. 6, 245 N.W. 554; Fey v. A. A. Oil Corp., 129 Mont. 300, 285 P.2d 578; Stahl v. Van Vleck, 53 Ohio St. 136, 41

lessee will not be able to fulfill the terms of the lease, he many times has acted in such a way that the lessee has found himself faced with the dilemma that if he continues operations he may put himself in the position of a bad-faith trespasser or if he drills a dry hole he may be liable for the destruction of the market value of the leasehold.

The interference by the lessor has taken many forms such as physical ejectment from the land,[94] written rejection of the lease,[95] the bringing of suit for cancellation of lease or injunction against operations,[96] or the execution of top leases to take effect immediately.[97]

Any of these actions constitutes a cloud on the title of the lessee, and it has been held that they constitute a continuing legal excuse for the lessee to suspend operations until the particular matters are settled.[98] Where it is found that the landowner has acted wrongfully, the courts have either increased the lease term by an amount of time identical to that lost due to the actions of the landowner,[99] or have given the lessee a reasonable additional period as indicated by the circumstances in the case.[1]

In one case, however, a remedy was denied, where the lessee had waited until six days prior to the end of the primary term of the lease to commence a well, which under the terms of the lease had to be producing by the end of the primary term. The landowner ejected

N.E. 35; Gisinger v. Hart, 115 Ohio App. 115, 184 N.E.2d 240; Simons v. McDaniel, 154 Okl. 168, 7 P.2d 419; Continental Oil Co. v. Osage Oil & Ref. Co., C.A.10th, 69 F.2d 19; Miller v. Hodges, Tex.Com. App., 260 S.W. 168; Kothmann v. Boley, 156 Tex. 56, 308 S.W.2d 1; Midwest Oil Corp. v. Winsauer, 159 Tex. 560, 323 S.W.2d 944; Silverman v. Emerson, Tex. Civ.App., 257 S.W. 612; Heard v. Pratt, Tex.Civ.App., 257 S.W. 660; Shell Oil Co. v. Goodroe, Tex.Civ.App., 197 S.W.2d 395; but cf. Atlantic Richfield Co. v. Hilton, Tex.Civ.App., 437 S.W.2d 347 (letter held not a repudiation).

However see Burger v. Wood, Okl. App., 575 P.2d 977, which held no termination where interference was by surface owner and not by lessor-mineral owner. It is hard to view the acts of a third party as obstructing the rights of the lessee so as to cause an extension of the lease term. The rights of the reversionary mineral interest owner should not be affected by the acts of a third party.

94. Fey v. A. A. Oil Corp., 129 Mont. 300, 285 P.2d 578.

95. Violette v. Gaertner, 261 Mich. 6, 245 N.W. 554; Fey v. A. A. Oil Corp., 129 Mont. 300, 285 P.2d 578; Kothmann v. Boley, 156 Tex. 56, 308 S.W.2d 1; Shell Oil Co. v. Goodroe, Tex.Civ.App., 197 S.W.2d 395; Midwest Oil Corp. v. Winsauer, 159 Tex. 560, 323 S.W.2d 944.

96. Greer v. Carter Oil Co., 373 Ill. 168, 25 N.E.2d 805; Stahl v. Van Vleck, 53 Ohio St. 136, 41 N.E. 35; Miller v. Hodges, Tex.Com.App., 260 S.W. 168.

97. Simons v. McDaniel, 154 Okl. 168, 7 P.2d 419; Shell Oil Co. v. Goodroe, Tex. Civ.App., 197 S.W.2d 395.

A top lease may suffer from two infirmities. If it is to take effect upon the expiration of the existing lease it will violate the Rule Against Perpetuities and also constitute an obstruction of the present lease. Both may be avoided by executing a present lease of the reversionary mineral interest. By having the lease subject to the present lease, it does not constitute an obstruction and does not constitute an executory interest.

98. Fey v. A. A. Oil Corp., 129 Mont. 300, 285 P.2d 578.

99. Violette v. Gaertner, 261 Mich. 6, 245 N.W. 554; Stahl v. Van Vleck, 53 Ohio St. 136, 41 N.E. 35; Continental Oil Co. v. Osage Oil & Refining Co., C.A. 10th, 69 F.2d 19; Silverman v. Emerson, Tex.Civ.App., 257 S.W. 612; Heard v. Pratt, Tex.Civ.App., 257 S.W. 660.

1. Greer v. Carter Oil Co., 373 Ill. 168, 25 N.E.2d 805; Miller v. Hodges, Tex. Com.App., 260 S.W. 168; Kothmann v. Boley, 156 Tex. 56, 308 S.W.2d 1.

the lessee from the land. A remedy for the lessee was denied on the ground that in no event could he have acquired production prior to the end of the primary term.[2]

§ 6.5 Propelling the Lease Past the Primary Term and Keeping It Alive During the Secondary Term—Contractual Substitutes for Production—The Nature of Shut-In Royalties

The shut-in gas clause provides for a substitute or contractual method of production that will maintain the lease in force and effect when a gas well is drilled and for which no market exists. However, for a well to be maintained by the payment of shut-in royalties it must be capable of producing gas in paying quantities.

Where liquid components are produced in paying quantities from a gas well, it has been held that shut-in royalties cannot be paid under a lease that provides for such payments on wells that produce "gas only." However, the lessee under this view will lose his lease if he is unable to re-inject the gas, for he will be unable either to pay shut-in royalties or to produce liquid components.

The shut-in gas clause primarily evolved to provide a method to keep an oil and gas lease alive at the end of the primary term, or in the secondary term, when a gas well had been drilled upon the premises and could not be produced due to lack of a market or market connection. This was especially important in those jurisdictions, like Texas, that strictly view the habendum clause of the oil and gas lease as imposing a determinable fee upon the lessee.

As has been seen, in those jurisdictions unless oil or gas is being actually produced in paying quantities at or after the end of the primary term, the lease will automatically terminate. As gas cannot be stored above the ground, unless there is a nearby market and pipeline connection available after the end of the primary term, the lease will terminate.

The problem is not so acute in jurisdictions, such as Oklahoma, that find that discovery of petroleum in paying quantities will keep the lease alive past the end of the primary term where, within a reasonable time, the lessee is using reasonable diligence to secure a marketing outlet for the well. In either jurisdiction a shut-in gas clause can be convenient, as many times the field must be developed to the point that sufficient producing wells are available to economically justify a pipeline connection. This may take a period of years. Therefore the shut-in gas clause is commonly provided for in the modern oil and gas lease.

The effect of the shut-in gas clause is to modify the habendum clause and provide for a substitute or contractual method of production in lieu of actual production of gas. The older forms provided for

---

2. Gisinger v. Hart, 115 Ohio App. 115, 184 N.E.2d 240. Here no clause existed in the lease allowing the lessee to finish the well drilling at the end of the primary term.

a minimal payment where a gas well was drilled and shut in. However, where a gas well was drilled during the primary term and the amount of the shut-in royalty was substantially less than delay rentals, landowners became unhappy. This in turn led to litigation by landowners where the delay rentals were very large. To alleviate this problem it is now customary, where possible, to provide that the shut-in royalties will be in the same amount as the delay rentals. Several variations of the shut-in royalty clause are set forth below.[1]

---

1. (a):

"* * * and (c) if at any time while there is a gas well or wells on the above land (and for the purposes of this clause (c) the term 'gas well' shall include wells capable of producing natural gas, condensate, distillate or any gaseous substance and wells classified as gas wells by any governmental authority) such well or wells are shut in, and if this lease is not continued in force by some other provision hereof, then it shall nevertheless continue in force for a period of ninety days after such well or wells are shut in, and during such ninety-day period lessee or any assignee hereunder may pay or tender an advance annual royalty equal to the amount of delay rentals provided for in this lease for the acreage then held under this lease by the party making such payment or tender, and if such payment or tender is made, this lease shall continue in force and it shall be considered that gas is being produced from the leased premises in paying quantities within the meaning of paragraph 2 hereof for one (1) year from the date such well or wells are shut in, and in like manner subsequent advance annual royalty payments may be made or tendered and this lease shall continue in force and it will be considered that gas is being produced from the leased premises in paying quantities within the meaning of said paragraph 2 during any annual period for which such royalty is so paid or tendered; such advance royalty may be paid or tendered in the same manner as provided herein for the payment or tender of delay rentals; royalty accruing to the owners thereof on any production from the leased premises during any annual period for which advance royalty is paid may be credited against such advance payment."

(b) Suggested model. Shut-in royalty clause by Professor William J. Flittie, 6 Summers, p. 20:

"§ 1132. Optional Shut-in Royalty Clause—Mandatory Payment Clause

"If at any time before or after expiration of the primary term there is not paying production attributable to this lease or other existing facts as would excuse payment of delay rentals or hold the lease beyond its primary term as the case may be, but there is a well or wells capable of producing natural gas, condensate, distillate, or classified as gas wells by governmental authority, or which though not so classified cannot be produced without wasting gas to an extent forbidden by governmental authority or contrary to good operating practices, and such wells are shut in before or after production therefrom without surrendering this lease or portion thereof where the wells are located, lessee shall be absolutely obligated to pay, within one year from the next rental anniversary date if within the set primary term, and before the end of the current annual period measured by the end of the primary term if after the end of the set primary term or if a shut-in continues into such period, and successively by such annual intervals thereafter until production is commenced or resumed, an amount equal to what delay rentals, if payable, would compute on acreage then held, and it will be considered the absolute binding obligation to make such payment, giving rise to an enforceable debt obligation if not paid, is in law constructive production equivalent to actual production in paying quantities. Payment shall be to owners of royalty as these may differ from owners of minerals, but otherwise in the same manner as payment of delay rentals hereunder. If lessee shall surrender this lease or any portion thereof during such annual intervals lessee nevertheless shall be obligated to make the current payment on the basis of acreage held at commencement of the interval, it being conclusively intended hereby that the lease was in law a producing lease with this royalty payment obligation incurred being constructive production. It is intended this shut-in provision may be used successively and to

Since the payment of shut-in royalties is a substitute for the payment of actual royalty, and when so paid is considered as constituting production within the meaning of the habendum clause, wells upon which shut-in royalties are paid must also be the equivalent of a producing well. That is to say, in order to maintain a lease in force by the payment of shut-in royalties the well must be capable of production in paying quantities at the time that it is shut in.[2] Where the well is not so capable of producing, the payment of shut-in royalties is futile.

Early forms of the shut-in royalty clause have caused serious construction problems relating to their application to wells that produce other than dry gas. Some gas wells also produce liquid products. Where no market exists for either the gas or the wet products, may such wells be shut in and shut-in royalties paid thereon so as to maintain the lease in effect? Clauses found in the earlier lease forms which permitted shut-in royalties to be paid on wells that were producing "gas only" have led to litigation concerning the shutting in of wet gas wells.

The first case of note dealing with this problem was the case of Vernon v. Union Oil Company of California.[3] An oil and gas lease was executed containing a five-year primary term that expired on December 5, 1956. A gas well was completed and shut in upon July 23, 1956, and was not put on actual production until March 5, 1957. Shut-in royalties were paid timely. However, lessors claimed that the lease had terminated as the clause only applied to wells capable of producing "gas only."

cover intervals greater than an annual interval if shut-ins continue so long, but the implied covenants are not suspended hereby. The maximum payment in an annual interval except as royalty on actual production causes it to be exceeded shall be the amount computed according to this provision once for each annual period. Lessee shall be entitled to credit royalties paid on actual production during an annual period against annual shut-in payments, and if not taken at the time a shut-in payment is made may take and adjust for this credit in succeeding annual periods or recoup from royalty on actual production at any time."

On the shut-in royalty generally, see Summers, Oil and Gas Law, Chapter 10, § 299; Clarke, Shut-in Gas Well Clause in Oklahoma Oil and Gas Leases, 32 Okla.B.A.J. 1795; Kolb, Problems Arising in the Payment of Shut-in Gas Well Royalty in Texas, 2 S.T.L.J. 62; Malone, The Evolution of Shut-In Royalty Law, 11 Baylor L.Rev. 19; Masterson, The Shut-In Royalty Clause in an Oil and Gas Lease, 12 S.W.L.J. 459; Moses, Recent Problems in Connection with Shut-in Gas Royalty Provisions in Oil and Gas Leases, 10 Loyola L.Rev. 1; Moses, Shut-in Gas Well Problems, 33 Miss.L.J. 267; Shut-in Gas Well Payment—Royalty or Rental, 24 La.L.Rev. 384; Constructional and Drafting Problems in Shut-in Royalty Clauses, 3 U.C.L.A.L.Rev. 564.

2. Kidd v. Hoggett, Tex.Civ.App., 331 S.W.2d 515; Duke v. Sun Oil Co., C.A.5th, 320 F.2d 853, rehearing denied 323 F.2d 518.

Christian v. A. A. Oil Corp., 161 Mont. 420, 506 P.2d 1369; Greer v. Salmon, 82 N.M. 245, 479 P.2d 294. Hoyt v. Continental Oil Co., Okl., 606 P.2d 560.

3. C.A.5th, 270 F.2d 441, noted 38 Tex.L.Rev. 807. The clause involved contained the following language:

"* * * where gas from a well producing gas only is not sold or used, Lessee may pay as royalty $50.00 per well per year, and upon such payment it will be considered that gas is being produced within the meaning of Paragraph 2 (the habendum clause) hereof. * * *"

The lessor contended that "gas" means the state in which it is marketed under normal conditions. The lessee, on the other hand, said that "gas" included everything in the reservoir that was produced at the mouth of the well. This constituent element theory would include as "gas" all liquids that were later separated out. The parties also differed as to the significance of the word "only." The lessor argued that it would include wells from which dry gas was the sole product produced, and the lessee contended that it merely excluded wells that would be classified as "oil" wells.

The court looked at the purpose of the lease and the differences in storage and production of oil and gas. It was concluded that reservoir conditions were important only as they affected the state of the final product, and the test of whether "gas" was being produced should be applied at the marketing point. Upon this analysis, liquid components produced from a well primarily producing gas were not considered part of the "gas" produced.

The question of whether shut-in royalty may be made on a well capable of producing liquid components as well as gas, however, was said to turn upon the purpose of the shut-in clause. As it was a substitute for gas production it would be necessary to hold a gas lease by payment of shut-in royalty when a gas well was shut in and it was not possible to achieve production in paying quantities of either the gas or the liquid components. Therefore, the court held that it was proper to hold the lease by payment of shut-in royalties where it was not reasonable to operate the lease for the production of liquid components alone.

The approach of the court in the Vernon case was followed in the later case of Duke v. Sun Oil Co.,[4] which also concerned payment of shut-in royalties on a well capable of producing condensate, where the clause applied to "gas only" wells. The court stated the test to be whether a reasonably prudent or diligent operator acting in good faith would have undertaken to complete the well as a well for the production of liquid components rather than a gas well. The question was held to be one for the jury.

It is rather unfortunate that the courts did not attempt to resolve the problem of what constituted "gas only" production by reference to the products produced and the reservoir conditions. A parallel problem exists in connection with the payment of royalty for actual production where a clause provides for a royalty upon "gas." Here the courts have attempted to determine the question on the basis of the constituent element theory—that everything coming out of the mouth of a gas well in gaseous form will be considered "gas" for the purposes of royalty payment. These cases were cited in the Vernon case, but were not followed.

4. C.A.5th, 320 F.2d 853, rehearing denied 323 F.2d 518.

The Vernon and Duke cases do not help the lessee where condensate is produced from a gas well in paying quantities, but where the gas cannot be reinjected into the ground. In these circumstances the lessee could neither produce nor pay shut-in royalties, and in jurisdictions such as Texas the lease would terminate.

Later lease forms provide that shut-in royalties may be paid where liquid components are being produced from a gas well.

In one case the question presented was whether a shut-in royalty could be paid on a well that was not shut in, but from which the only production was for domestic uses under the "free gas" clause of the lease. It was held [5] that this did not constitute production under the habendum clause of the lease, and it was kept alive by the payments of shut-in royalties.

(A) Shut-In Royalties—Time of Payment

Where constructive production, such as the payment of shut-in royalties, is being used to maintain a lease in effect, payments must be made prior to or on the dates that actual production must exist to maintain a lease in effect.

To be entirely safe a lessee should pay succeeding shut-in royalty payments on or before the date of the capping of the well. Where a well is shut-in during the last year of the primary term and the first shut-in royalty payment is made between the date of capping of the well and the anniversary date of the lease, some confusion exists in the cases as to the proper date for successive payments. A trend in the cases seems to be that the lessee will be bound by the period shown in the shut-in royalty receipt and payments later than the period reflected in the receipt will not be timely.

Where no provision is contained in the lease limiting the time during which a lease may be maintained by constructive production, it would seem that the lessee may only so hold the lease for a period of time that a prudent lessee would hold it to acquire a market.

Unless special provisions are contained therein, a term mineral or royalty deed will not be maintained by the payment of shut-in royalties under an existing lease.

In jurisdictions that require actual production prior to the end of the primary term there must be no time gap between the end of the primary term and beginning of actual production [6] or, if after the primary term, no time gap in actual production. Likewise where the lessee is relying upon constructive production to maintain the lease in

---

5. Mitchell Energy Corp. v. Blakley, Tex.Civ.App., 560 S.W.2d 740, refused n.r.e.

6. Doty v. Key Oil, Inc., 83 Ill.App.3d 287, 38 Ill. Dec. 922, 404 N.E.2d 346; Lamczyk v. Allen, 8 Ill.2d 547, 134 N.E.2d 753; Freeman v. Magnolia Petroleum Co., 141 Tex. 274, 171 S.W.2d 339; Union Oil Co. of California v. Ogden, Tex.Civ.App., 278 S.W.2d 246. In the Ogden case the court intimated that if facilities for gas purchase were located nearby and imminent the lessee would have a reasonable time after the primary term to make a market connection. This would seem to be contra to the Texas rationale, see Gulf Oil Corp. v. Reid, 161 Tex. 51, 337 S.W.2d 267.

effect there must also be no time gap between the end of the primary term and constructive production, or if after the primary term, between the tacking of actual and constructive production.

As constructive production is a substitute for actual production, for constructive production to maintain a lease it must be effective at the same times that actual production must occur to maintain the lease. Where a lease is being maintained by constructive production a time gap may occur (1) by failure to pay shut-in royalties before the end of the primary term, (2) where a gas well is completed after the end of the primary term by failure to pay shut-in royalties prior to capping the well, (3) where the lease is being held at the end of the primary term by gas production, which well is later shut in, by failure to pay shut-in royalties prior to the shutting in of the well, or (4) where the lease is being held by constructive production at the end of the primary term, by not commencing actual production prior to the end of the period for which shut-in royalties have been paid.

In Texas it has been held that a shut-in royalty must be paid prior to the end of the primary term in order to propel the lease into the secondary term by means of such constructive production. In the landmark case of Freeman v. Magnolia Petroleum Co.,[7] a gas well was completed and shut in on December 22, 1939. The end of the primary term was April 7, 1940. The lessee did not pay the shut-in royalty prior to the end of the primary term, but claimed under the clause that it could pay any time within one year after the capping of the well. The court held against the lessee on the ground that the fee determined at the end of the primary term where neither actual or constructive production had thereupon been commenced.[8]

Where the shut-in royalty is not paid so as to prevent a time gap between the capping of the gas well and the payment of the royalty, interaction of other clauses in the lease may serve to maintain the lease in effect during the period.

In the Kansas case of Tate v. Stanolind Oil and Gas Co.,[9] the court came to the conclusion that a reasonable time existed to find a market for gas for a well shut in during the primary term, but upon which no shut-in royalty had been paid, although Kansas requires production to propel the lease into the secondary term. The court based the result upon the intent of the parties as evidenced from other parts of the lease. It was reasoned that as the lease contained a well completion clause, viz., allowing the lessee to finish the well drilling at the end of the primary term, it thereby reflected an intent that

---

7. 141 Tex. 274, 171 S.W.2d 339. Also see Doty v. Key Oil, Inc., 83 Ill.App.3d 287, 38 Ill.Dec. 922, 404 N.E.2d 346.

8. However, Robinson v. Continental Oil Co., D.C.Kan., 255 F.Supp. 61 held shut-in royalties were timely paid within a year after the capping of the well, but an alternative ground of decision apparently was the fact that lessor top-leased shortly after the well was shut-in, which resulted in a lease contest that would afford an excuse for delay in payment. Also see Shell Oil Co. v. Goodroe, Tex.Civ. App., 197 S.W.2d 395, as to effect of top leasing by lessor.

9. 172 Kan. 351, 240 P.2d 465.

the parties contemplated a reasonable period after the expiration of the primary term within which the lessee could secure production. The conclusion of the court seems unsupportable. However, as modern leases commonly contain a similar clause, the effect of the decision is to give Kansas the equivalent of the Oklahoma rule that discovery alone is sufficient to propel a lease past the primary term.

In Oklahoma, as mentioned above, production in paying quantities is equated to discovery of products that are capable of production in paying quantities. The lessee then has a reasonable time to secure actual production. It is the rule in Oklahoma that the reasonable time period to secure actual production is not limited by the presence of the usual shut-in royalty clause unless the clause expressly so states.[10] Therefore, neither nonpayment of shut-in royalty after the end of the primary term, nor the failure to secure actual production prior to the end of the shut-in royalty period will terminate the lease if the lessee is acting as a reasonably prudent lessee under the circumstances in securing actual production. Where the clause is so conditioned the lease would terminate.

The shut-in royalty clause in Oklahoma, during the period of the clause, does act to remove doubt that the lessee is acting as a reasonably prudent lessee in securing a market and also provides a minimum payment for the lessor.

Although the general rule is that the shut-in royalty must be paid so as to leave no time gap between the capping of the well and the payment of the shut-in royalty, where such gap occurs but does not extend beyond the period allowed for continuous operations the lease may not terminate.

As is discussed in another section, to prevent the lapse of a lease due to the drilling of a dry hole after the end of the primary term or where production ceases after the end of the primary term, express clauses (the continuous operations and dry hole clauses) have been commonly included in the lease, providing that the lease will not lapse where operations are conducted on the lease which result in production and where no gap in operations occurs for more than a stated number of days, usually sixty.

The situation that has arisen relating to the interaction of the payment of shut-in royalties and the continuous operations clause occurs where a well is drilling at the end of the primary term and is completed and shut in as a gas well after the end of the primary term. Assume that the shut-in royalty is paid 45 days after the capping of the well; does the 60-day period in the continuous operations clause have the effect of extending the term of the lease for sixty days after the well was capped? If so, the shut-in royalty was timely paid, although not paid at or prior to the capping of the well. Under the properly

---

10. Flag Oil Corp. of Delaware v. King Resources Co., Okl., 494 P.2d 322; Gard v. Kaiser, Okl., 582 P.2d 1311.

drawn continuous operations clause the answer is that such payment of the shut-in royalty is timely.

That this result depends upon the particular wording of the continuous operations clause in the lease must be emphasized. Wording of lease provisions varies widely, and this can be clearly illustrated by the following two cases dealing with this problem. The first case is that of Gulf Oil Corporation v. Reid.[11] Here the primary term ended December 9, 1948. The gas well was capped on January 18, 1949, but the shut-in royalty was not paid until February 19, 1949. Under all authorities if the royalty payment had been made on or before the date of capping of the gas well it would have been timely. However, here a time gap of about a month intervened. The Texas Supreme Court held that the lease terminated, and that lack of a market was not an excuse. It was held that the sixty-day continuous operations clause did not apply.

The clause contained in the lease provided that the lease would not lapse "so long as not more than sixty (60) days are allowed to elapse between the completion or *abandonment* of one well and the commencement of operations on another until production is obtained." The court reasoned that where the well had been shut in it had not been abandoned and therefore the continuous operations clause did not apply to extend the lease for 60 days beyond the time the well was capped. The lease had therefore terminated prior to the payment of the shut-in royalty.

However, in the later case of Skelly Oil Co. v. Harris,[12] the court found that where actual production of gas began 41 days after the capping of a gas well, and for which no shut-in royalty was paid, the lease did not terminate. It was here held that the lease would automatically be extended for a period of 60 days following the cessation of operations on the lease. The clause here provided: "* * * the lease shall remain in force so long as operations are prosecuted with *no cessation* of more than sixty (60) consecutive days." Since the capping of the well constituted cessation of operations, the 60-day period of the continuous operations clause was held to have extended the lease for such period for all purposes. The court stated:

> "The 60-day clause thus allows the lessee that period after completion of a well capable of producing within which to begin either *actual* or *constructive* production" (emphasis supplied).

Therefore, under such a clause if Rex Oil Co. completes a shut-in gas well 30 days prior to the end of the primary term, the 60-day

---

11. 161 Tex. 51, 337 S.W.2d 267.

12. 163 Tex. 92, 352 S.W.2d 950, noted 17 S.W.L.J. 272; followed in Duke v. Sun Oil Co., C.A.5th, 320 F.2d 853, rehearing denied 323 F.2d 518; and see Shell Oil Co. v. Goodroe, Tex.Civ.App., 197 S.W.2d 395.

In Skelly v. Harris the well was drilled within a unit but not on the lease lands involved. It was held that operations on unit lands were the same as if a leasehold well had been drilled.

extension would add 30 days after the end of the primary term within which to pay the shut-in royalty.

To avoid the time-gap problem more recent lease forms provide that shut-in royalties may be paid within a 90-day period following the capping of the well.

Where the gas well is shut in prior to the last year of the primary term, a question arises whether shut-in payments must be made during each year of the primary term in order to keep the lease alive. Where the question of abandonment of the lease is not involved it would seem that unless the shut-in clause of the lease requires that a payment be made to continue the lease in effect during each year of the primary term, that it is not necessary to do so, but that the total payment may be made prior to the last day of the primary term.[13]

The problem has largely been solved by the use of a shut-in clause that ties into the delay rental clause as to the amount and time of payments. Here it is provided that where a completed well is shut in shut-in royalties will be commenced in the same amounts and times as the payment of delay rentals. Therefore, the payment would be made on the next applicable delay rental payment date.[14] The use of this clause avoids bad feeling on the part of the landowner where the delay rental payments were considerably greater in amount than the shut-in royalty payments.

Several rather severe problems have occurred in connection with the timely payment of shut-in royalties. The first problem area occurs where a gas well is capped during the last year of the primary term and the shut-in royalty payment is made between the date of capping the well and the end of the primary or an extended term. For instance, Rex Oil Company shuts in a gas well on July 1, pays the shut-in royalty on August 1, and the primary term ends on September 1. When is the next payment due? Unless affected by contractual considerations or provisions in the lease or on the shut-in rental receipt, the lessee would be safe in paying any time within one year from the date of capping of the well, and should, under commonly used oil and gas lease forms, be safe in paying within one year from the date of the first shut-in royalty payment.

This question was raised in the case of Duke v. Sun Oil Co.,[15] where a gas well was completed after the end of the primary term and the shut-in royalty was paid prior to the end of the 60-day extended term under the continuous operations clause. Query: When is the second payment due? The court appears in the first instance to tie the second payment date into the anniversary date of capping of the gas well; however, on rehearing, the court states: "[W]e conclude that we ought not at this stage to hold as a matter of law that the

---

13. See Sohio Petroleum Co. v. V. S. & P. R. R., 222 La. 383, 62 So.2d 615.

14. See Phillips Petroleum Co. v. Harnly, Tex.Civ.App., 348 S.W.2d 856.

15. C.A.5th, 320 F.2d 853, rehearing denied 323 F.2d 518.

§ 6.5   THE OIL AND GAS LEASE—DURATION   313

anniversary date for payments of shut-in royalty was established by the actual date of the shut-in of the well, or alternatively, by the date Lessors received the initial check." The case was remanded for further development of the underlying facts regarding payment of the royalties.

Although normally the date of capping of the well or date of payment of the shut-in royalty will determine the anniversary date of further royalty payments, it is customary for the lessee to send a "Shut-in Royalty Receipt" to the depository bank of the lessor, one copy of which is stamped by the bank and returned to the lessee to indicate that the payment was timely received. The receipt sets forth a description of the lease, the land involved, the parties being paid, and the period for which the payment is being made. It has been held that the period of payment shown on the receipt is controlling as to the period of time covered by the payment.[16] Where this differs from the date of capping of the well or of the date of the first payment, it may have the effect of changing the date that future payments are due, if the well is not put on production prior to that time.

In Steeple Oil & Gas Corp. v. Amend,[17] the primary term of the lease ended October 9, 1957. A gas well was brought in and capped on August 1, 1957. The shut-in royalty payment was made on September 24, 1957 and recited that it was paid for the period from August 9, 1957 to August 9, 1958. The second payment was made September 22, 1958, within a year from the first payment, but not within a year from the date recited upon the receipt. The court held that the parties were bound by the period shown on the receipt. The court did not discuss the proper date for payment where no receipt was involved.

A similar situation occurred in the case of Shell Oil Co. v. Goodroe,[18] where, due to falling pressure which made it impossible to buck the line pressure in the gathering line, a gas well was shut in. This was done on July 25, 1944. The shut-in royalty was not paid until October 16, 1944, which was held to be a timely payment within the 90-day period of the continuous operations clause in the lease. The shut-in royalty receipt stated that the royalty was paid for the period from "July 25, 1944 to July 25, 1945," tying it back to the actual date of the capping of the well. It was held that a tender, refused by the lessor, on July 12, 1945 was good, and that the period indicated in the receipt would constitute the period during which the royalty payment was in effect. The effect of these cases seems to be that if, in relation to the facts in the Goodroe case, the second payment had been made after July 25 and prior to October 16, the payment would have been late.

16. Shell Oil Co. v. Goodroe, Tex.Civ.App., 197 S.W.2d 395; Steeple Oil & Gas Corp. v. Amend, Tex.Civ.App., 337 S.W.2d 809; Phillips Petroleum Co. v. Harnly, Tex.Civ.App., 348 S.W.2d 856.

17. Tex.Civ.App., 337 S.W.2d 809.
18. Tex.Civ.App., 197 S.W.2d 395.

The above discussion deals with the situation where a well has been capped and the first shut-in royalty payment is properly made sometime after the capping of the well, and raises a question as to the time for the second payment. What, however, is the effect of intermittent production during the year that the payment has been made? Assume that Rex Oil Company completes a gas well after the primary term, on July 1. It is shut in on that date and a shut-in royalty is paid. Gas is produced from December until February, at which time the well is again capped due to a breakdown in equipment. Does a shut-in payment have to be made in February? If not, when is the next shut-in payment due? There is no doubt that a payment could be made in February upon capping of the well, which would serve to keep the lease alive for a year from that time. Where the well is valuable and is greatly in excess in value of the amount of the shut-in royalty, the prudent thing to do would be to pay an additional shut-in payment.

However, most lease forms provide that upon the proper payment of the shut-in royalty it will be considered that constructive production will hold the lease under the habendum clause for a year from the effective date of the payment. Therefore, it would seem that the lessee could with safety wait until the anniversary date of the original capping of the well, in this illustration July 1, (the expiration date shown on the shut-in royalty receipt) to make the payment.

No cases were found expressly dealing with this problem, although by analogy the case of Phillips Petroleum Company v. Harnly [19] may have some application. In this case the primary term ended on November 9, 1956. A gas well was completed during the last year of the primary term in March 1956. Production from this well occurred during the last year of the primary term, from March 1956 until July 1956. The well was capped on July 30, 1956, prior to the end of the primary term. Shut-in royalties were tendered on the last day of the primary term, November 9, 1956, but were refused by the lessor. The court held that the shut-in royalties were properly tendered.

The lease in this case provided that shut-in royalties would be payable "in the amount and time of the delay rentals." The anniversary date of payment of delay rentals was November 9. The court held that the date of payment was proper and also served to apply for the period from November 9 to November 9, the anniversary date of the lease, rather than from the anniversary date of capping of the well, July 30 to July 30. Here again the court found that the contractual language of the parties controlled as to the period of the payment of the royalty. It therefore may be concluded that, in absence of other factors, a shut-in royalty payment made on the anniversary date as indicated by the shut-in royalty receipt will be proper and timely, as will one made on the anniversary date of the capping of the well, if

19. Tex.Civ.App., 348 S.W.2d 856.

§ 6.5   THE OIL AND GAS LEASE—DURATION   315

the date of capping of the well does not fall later than the period indicated in the shut-in royalty receipt.

As in the case of delay rentals, a check is an unconditional payment, unless specified otherwise in the lease.[20] The manner of apportionment of shut-in royalties among royalty owners, payment to the depository bank, and notice as to change of ownership and address are the same as in the case of payment of delay rentals, and are discussed elsewhere.[21]

Where the lessee has shut in a gas well and is holding it by means of payments of shut-in royalties there is authority to the effect that he may not indefinitely so hold the lease without actual production, although the shut-in clause is not limited in time. The time has been stated to be that during which a diligent lessee would hold it for the purpose of securing a market.[22] As such, the test seems identical with that used in Oklahoma as to the period of time a lessee can hold a lease upon which petroleum products have been found in commercial quantities but which are not being actually produced at the end of the primary term due to lack of a market.

More frequently leases are being found where a limit has been inserted beyond which time the lessee cannot hold the lease without actual production.[23] Selling gas to an adjoining lease, also owned by the lessee in question, for the purposes of operation of a heater-treater has been held to be insufficient production to hold the lease after the time limit that the lease may be held by payment of shut-in royalties.[24]

Heretofore the discussion has concerned the continuation of the oil and gas lease in effect under the habendum clause by means of constructive production by payment of shut-in royalties. Will the payment of shut-in royalties by the lessee, which the lessor has agreed to be production under the habendum clause of the lease, also constitute production in the case of the term mineral and royalty deeds? The answer is, "No."[25] It has been held that the definition of production in the oil and gas lease as comprising payment of shut-in royalties, is not binding as a definition of contractual production for all purposes from the same land. Even if the owner of the term mineral deed ratifies the lease, or joins in the original lease with the lessor, it has been the view of the courts that constructive production

20. Phillips Petroleum Co. v. Harnly, Tex.Civ.App., 348 S.W.2d 856; Duke v. Sun Oil Co., C.A.5th, 320 F.2d 853, rehearing denied 323 F.2d 518.

21. See § 6.4, supra.

22. Lelong v. Richardson, La., 126 So.2d 819.

23. Hastings v. Pichinson, Tex.Civ.App., 370 S.W.2d 1 (3 years); Patton v. Rogers, Tex.Civ.App., 417 S.W.2d 470.

24. Patton v. Rogers, Tex.Civ.App., 417 S.W.2d 470.

25. Archer County v. Webb, 161 Tex. 210, 338 S.W.2d 435, noted 39 Tex.L.R. 365; Holland v. Vela De Pena, Tex.Civ.App., 343 S.W.2d 750; Investors Royalty Co. v. Childrens Hospital Medical Center, Tex.Civ.App., 364 S.W.2d 779; Midwest Oil Corp. v. Mengers, Tex.Civ.App., 372 S.W.2d 247; Ramage v. Potter, Tex.Civ.App., 373 S.W.2d 399; Midwest Oil Corp. v. Lude, Tex.Civ.App., 376 S.W.2d 18; Union Producing Co. v. Scott, D.C.Tex., 173 F.Supp. 361, affirmed C.A.5th, 267 F.2d 469.

by the lessee under the lease will not serve to keep term mineral and royalty grants alive in absence of similar provisions for the payment of shut-in royalties in the term grants.[26]

For instance, O grants to B a five-year term mineral interest in ¼ of the minerals in Blackacre. On the same day O executes to Rex Oil Company an oil and gas lease with a three-year primary term and containing a shut-in royalty clause. Rex drills a gas well that is shut in at the end of the primary term of the lease and keeps the lease alive by payments of shut-in royalty. At the end of the five-year term of the mineral deed, the term grant of B will terminate unless Rex has begun actual production.

It is suggested that the customary term mineral or royalty grant incorporate a clause to the effect that if an oil and gas lease is in effect on the land at the end of the term, but that actual production is not occurring, that the term grant will not terminate, but will remain in effect for so long as such lease remains in effect on the land. This, of course, will indirectly incorporate for the benefit of the owner of the term grant all provisions contained in the oil and gas lease which enable the lessee to keep the lease alive without production. This will include the payment of delay rentals if the lease is still within its primary term.

§ 6.6 Propelling the Lease Past the Primary Term by Operations—Completing the Well Drilling at the End of the Primary Term

There exists a split of authority whether under the modern "unless" lease a lessee may complete a well after the end of the primary term that he has commenced prior to the end of the term. One view, known as the Oklahoma view, would find a conflict between the habendum clause and the drilling portion of the delay rental clause and in giving effect to both clauses would find an intent to permit the Lessee to finish the well.

In what may be the majority view, it is considered that the habendum clause is dominant and controls, and the lessee will not be permitted to complete the well. The lease will terminate due to lack of production in paying quantities. It is the better reasoned view.

A "well completion clause," which expressly provides for the completion of a well drilling at the end of the primary term, is customarily included in the modern lease. However, it has been interpreted as only applying to the well drilling at the end of the primary term.

In previous sections it was assumed that at the end of the primary term (1) actual production was in effect, (2) oil or gas had been dis-

---

26. Archer County v. Webb, 161 Tex. 210, 338 S.W.2d 435, noted 39 Tex.L.R. 365; Midwest Oil Corp. v. Lude, Tex.Civ.App., 376 S.W.2d 18; Union Producing Co. v. Scott, D.C.Tex., 173 F.Supp. 361, affirmed C.A.5th, 267 F.2d 469, rejecting, as applicable to shut-in royalties, cases which held that where the owner of the reversion and the term mineral grant executed or ratified an oil and gas lease containing pooling provisions that constructive production from an off-tract unit well would serve to keep the lease alive, would also serve to keep the term grant alive. See § 7.13(B), infra.

covered but not produced, or (3) a gas well had been drilled, capped, and shut-in royalties had been paid, and that one of these circumstances had propelled the lease into the secondary term. All of these methods of propelling the lease past the primary term relate either to methods of finding or production of petroleum products. It is axiomatic that under the modern lease where oil or gas has neither been discovered nor is being produced at the end of the primary term the lease will terminate. However, if the lessee is in the act of drilling a well at the end of the primary term, may he complete it?[1]

Under the modern "unless" lease form the lessee may keep the lease alive until the end of the primary term by the timely payment of delay rentals.[2] Such payment serves to delay development to the last day of the period for which the delay rental has been paid. Where such payments are made during each year of the primary term, the lessee may delay beginning development of the lease until the last day of the primary term.

Since by payment of delay rentals the lessee has the right to begin the well on the last day of the primary term, does he thereby also have a reasonable time after the end of the primary term to complete it? The courts have been in conflict in answering the question almost since the beginning of oil and gas production.

One line of authority takes the position that a conflict exists between the habendum clause, which requires a *completed* well (or at least discovery) prior to the end of the primary term, and the "unless" clause, which requires payment of rentals only if a well has not been *commenced* prior to the next rental payment date. The "unless" clause then customarily continues that such right to pay and postpone development will continue for like periods with like payments. This "unless" clause usually does not specifically refer to the habendum clause nor limit the time for such payments to the primary term of the lease.[3] The other line of authority finds no conflict be-

---

1. Generally see Summers, Oil and Gas, §§ 300.1, 303, 349; Walker, The Nature of Property Interests Created by an Oil and Gas Lease in Texas, 8 Tex.L.R. 483; Fuller, Extension of an Oil and Gas Lease by a Well Commencement, 17 Okla.L.Rev. 57; Berman, Dry Hole Drilling Operations and 30 Day–60 Day Drilling Operation Clauses, 38 Tex.L.Rev. 270, and Extending the Texas Oil and Gas Lease by the Habendum, Dry Hole, and Shut-in Royalty Clauses, 14 S.W.L.J. 365.

2. See § 6.3, supra.

3. Tate v. Stanolind Oil and Gas Co., 172 Kan. 351, 240 P.2d 465; Lester v. Mid-South Oil Co., Ky., 296 F. 661; Simpson v. Buckner's Administrator, 247 Ky. 564, 57 S.W.2d 464; Simons v. McDaniel, 154 Okl. 168, 7 P.2d 419, noted 10 Tex.L. Rev. 518; Champlin Refining Co. v. Magnolia Petroleum Co., 178 Okl. 203, 62 P.2d 249; Hicks v. Mid-Kansas Oil & Gas Co., 182 Okl. 61, 76 P.2d 269; Champlin v. Sinclair Oil and Gas Co., Okl., 344 P.2d 268; Moncrief v. Pasotex Petroleum Co., C.A.10th, 280 F.2d 235, cert. denied 364 U.S. 912, 81 S.Ct. 277, 5 L.Ed.2d 227; Texas Co. v. Curry, Tex.Civ.App., 229 S.W. 643; DeFlores v. Smith, Tex.Civ. App., 236 S.W. 505; cf. State ex rel. Commissioners of Land Office v. Carter Oil Co., Okl., 336 P.2d 1086, noted 13 Okl.L. Rev. 82; Humphrys v. Skelly Oil Co., C.A.5th, 83 F.2d 989. Although two early Texas cases appear to apply this rationale, in view of the dominant position the Texas courts place on the habendum clause, these cases cannot be said to reflect the present view of the Texas courts.

tween the habendum and "unless" clauses, or, if a conflict is found, the habendum clause is held to be the dominant and controlling statement of intent.[4]

The landmark case in holding that the lessee has a right to finish the well drilling at the end of the primary term, due to the conflict between the "unless" clause and the habendum clause is that of Lester v. Mid-South Oil Co.[5] The case concerned an "unless" lease form with a five-year primary term and the right to delay the commencement of a well by annual payments of delay rentals. The primary term ended April 9. A well was started on April 8 and was completed 14 days after the end of the primary term. It was held that the lease did not terminate, but that the right to commence a well under the "unless" clause modified the termination aspect of the habendum clause. In this manner the court attempted to give effect to both clauses. This conclusion has come to be known as the "Oklahoma" rule and was adopted in the case of Simons v. McDaniel.[6]

Although the jurisdictions that apply the Oklahoma rule usually refer to the conflict in the clauses as creating an ambiguity, parol evidence apparently is not admissible for explanation of the intent of the parties.[7] It is interesting to note that the basis of the Oklahoma rule is the apparent conflict between the two clauses; however, a recent Oklahoma case[8] has reached the same conclusion where the lease did not contain a delay rental clause. The case would seem insupportable under the Simons case.

The opposite view, that the lessee does not have a right to finish the well drilling at the end of the primary term, is espoused in the early Michigan case of Fagan & Co. v. Burns.[9] The case was decided after Lester v. Mid-South Oil Co. In the Fagan case the lessee began operations two days before the end of the primary term, and it was held that the lease terminated. The lease involved a form that had been prepared for a five-year primary term, with the usual "unless" delay rental clause. However, the term had been shortened to one year. Normally, a lease with a one-year primary term would not include a delay rental provision. The court held that the drilling com-

---

4. Valer Oil Co. v. Souza, 6 Cal.Rptr. 301, 182 Cal.App.2d 790; Perkins v. Saunders, 109 Kan. 372, 198 P. 954; Browning v. Cavanaugh, Ky., 300 S.W.2d 580; Vaughn v. Hearrell, Ky., 347 S.W.2d 542; Fagan & Co. v. Burns, 247 Mich. 674, 226 N.W. 653, 67 A.L.R. 522.

5. Ky., 296 F. 661.

6. 154 Okl. 168, 7 P.2d 419, noted 10 Tex.L.Rev. 518. This case contains a lengthy dissent and together with the majority opinion collects and comments on the then existing authority on the question.

7. Hicks v. Mid-Kansas Oil & Gas Co., 182 Okl. 61, 76 P.2d 269.

8. Moncrief v. Pasotex Petroleum Co., C.A.10th, 280 F.2d 235, cert. denied 364 U.S. 912, 81 S.Ct. 277, 5 L.Ed.2d 227. See comment of Dean Kuntz in 12 Oil & Gas Reporter 1087. Where a lease is classified in Oklahoma as a "completion" lease, requiring the completion of a well rather than merely its commencement prior to the end of the applicable rental period to excuse payment, no conflict occurs and the Simons case does not apply. See State ex rel. Commissioners of Land Office v. Carter Oil Co., Okl., 336 P.2d 1086, noted 13 Okl.L.Rev. 82.

9. 247 Mich. 674, 226 N.W. 653, 67 A.L.R. 522.

mencement provisions in the "unless" clause did not have the effect of modifying the habendum clause because of the following: (a) The "unless" clause did not purport to modify the habendum clause; (b) the "unless" clause could not change a condition subsequent, when breached, to an extension of the lease; and (c) the object of the "unless" clause was to abrogate the implied duty of the lessee that would otherwise exist to develop within the fixed term. The court stated, [T]he fixed term is not extended by mere indirect, ambiguous and negative language in the development (delay rental) clause; but it may and must, if at all, be extended by direct and affirmative provisions therefor."

The better reasoned view would seem to be that the drilling provisions of the "unless" clause have no application after the end of the primary term. As the provisions for payment of delay rentals are for the purpose of delay of development during the primary term, drilling by the lessee that will discontinue the need for rental payments should be likewise limited. The apparent majority view would support the conclusion that unless the habendum clause was expressly and appropriately modified in the lease, the lessee may not finish the well drilling at the end of the primary term.[10]

To relieve the uncertainty in those jurisdictions that do not follow the Oklahoma view, a clause has been inserted into the lease expressly allowing the lessee to complete the well drilling at the end of the primary term. For want of a better name it may be called "the well completion clause," referring to the operation of the clause as allowing completion of the well drilling at the end of the primary term. Such a clause, properly drawn, modifies the habendum clause and is effective. A typical clause reads as follows:

> "If at the expiration of the primary term oil, gas or other mineral is not being produced on said land but lessee is then engaged in drilling or reworking operations thereon, this lease shall remain in force so long *as operations* are prosecuted with no cessation of more than thirty (30) consecutive days, and if they result in the production of oil, gas or other mineral so long thereafter as oil, gas or other mineral is produced from said land * * *."[11] (Emphasis supplied).

---

10. It would appear Kentucky has repudiated Simpson v. Buckner's Administrator, 247 Ky. 564, 57 S.W.2d 464 and would support this statement: Browning v. Cavanaugh, Ky., 300 S.W.2d 580; Vaughn v. Hearrell, Ky., 347 S.W.2d 542. This would also seem to be the Kansas view, Perkins v. Saunders, 109 Kan. 372, 198 P. 954, but cf. Tate v. Stanolind Oil and Gas Co., 172 Kan. 351, 240 P.2d 465.

11. This clause was involved in the case of Rogers v. Osborn, 152 Tex. 540, 261 S.W.2d 311, noted 6 Bay.L.Rev. 106; 32 Tex.L.Rev. 240. Some forms of the clause are drafted in terms of the lessee "commencing operations to drill a well" prior to the end of the primary term. Some writers refer to the clause as the "well commencement clause." However, it is the author's predisposition that well completion clause is more descriptive of the operation of the clause, i.e., not to commence a well, but to complete one.

It may generally be stated that the well completion clause has been interpreted as applying only to the well drilling at the end of the primary term.[12] This interpretation has also been applied where the habendum clause stated that the lease would have a duration as "long as oil and gas is produced or said premises are developed or operated."[13]

Where the only clause applying to the factual situation and modifying the habendum clause is the well completion clause, cases attempting to apply it to other than the well drilling at the end of the primary term fall into two classes. In the first group are the cases where operations for the drilling of well #2 are carried on while the well that was drilling at the end of the primary term is still drilling. In the case of Skelly Oil Co. v. Wickham,[14] the well drilling at the end of the primary term was completed as a dry hole, and well #2, which was begun prior to the completion of the first well, came in as a producer. The pertinent clause read as follows:

> "If the lessee shall commence to drill a well within the term of this lease *or any extension thereof*, the lessee shall have the right to drill such well to completion with reasonable diligence and dispatch, and if oil or gas, or either of them, be found in paying quantities, this lease shall continue and be in force with like effect as if such well had been completed within the term of years herein first mentioned." (Emphasis supplied)

It was held that the lease had terminated as the operative language in the clause referred only to the well drilling at the end of the primary term. The extension of the lease to allow completing the well drilling at the end of the primary term was not such an extension during which other wells could be commenced and was not an extension of the lease for all purposes.

The second category of cases concerns the typical well completion clause quoted above. Here the factual situation may be similar to that in the Skelly Oil Co. case, or the lessee may complete as a dry

---

12. See Rogers v. Osborn, 152 Tex. 540, 261 S.W.2d 311, noted 6 Bay.L.Rev. 106; 32 Tex.L.Rev. 240. LeBar v. Haynie, Wyo., 552 P.2d 1107. In this case lessee commenced operations for drilling a well prior to the end of the primary term, which operations were stopped on July 13, after the end of the primary term. The rig was moved off, with no drilling operations until August 27 which deepened the well and which was then completed as a producer. The court held that the well drilling at the end of the primary term was "completed" as a producer from the deeper depth. Landowner unsuccessfully contended well was "completed" as a dry hole at the lesser depth and recompletion to deeper horizon was a new well not applicable under the well completion clause. The case raises the interesting question of when a well is "completed." Also see Barrett v. Ferrell, Tex.Civ.App., 550 S.W.2d 138, and § 8.13, note 3, infra.

13. Gasaway v. Pendergrass, Ky., 350 S.W.2d 460; Statex Petroleum v. Petroleum, Inc., C.A.10th, 308 F.2d 815, 96 A.L.R.2d 315; Skelly Oil Co. v. Wickham, C.A.10th, 202 F.2d 442. Cf. Pardue v. Mark, Tex.Civ.App., 279 S.W.2d 594; Morrison v. Swaim, Tex.Civ.App., 220 S.W.2d 493. In the latter case the lease was continued on the ground that due to a procedural error operations were not found to have ceased.

14. C.A.10th, 202 F.2d 442.

§ 6.7   THE OIL AND GAS LEASE—DURATION   321

hole the first well, which was drilling at the end of the primary term, and then begin well No. 2 within 30 days thereafter. It has been held that operations referred to in the clause only have reference to the well drilling at the end of the primary term.[15] Again, although well No. 2 may be completed as a producer, the lease will terminate.

§ 6.7 Propelling the Lease Past the Primary Term by Operations—Commencement of Drilling Operations

In order to determine whether the activities of a lessee prior to the end of the primary term are sufficient to constitute the commencement of operations to drill a well, the courts will look to the financial and technological ability of the lessee and his subjective intent or good faith to diligently complete the well. When satisfied as to the above, a minimum of activities of the lessee on the drill site are sufficient to constitute the commencement of operations to drill a well, although spudding of the well has not occurred prior to the end of the primary term.

Although contractual variations may be found,[1] the vast majority of well completion clauses have a condition that the lessee must have commenced operations for the drilling of a well prior to the end of the primary term. Such operative language has been generally interpreted to mean that operations for the drilling of a well, and not the actual spudding in or drilling of the hole, must have commenced prior to the end of the primary term.

Where the wording of the clause requires the lessee to start operations for the drilling of a well before the end of the primary term, obviously the actual "spudding in" of a well prior to the end of the primary term satisfies the clause.[2] Where operations only are envisioned prior to the end of the primary term, the parties have agreed that something less than spudding in will suffice. What acts of the lessee will be satisfactory? Generally the lease does not specify in this regard. Where the lessee has waited to the last day of the primary term to enter the land and has staked the location and placed

---

15. Rogers v. Osborn, 152 Tex. 540, 261 S.W.2d 311, noted 6 Bay.L.Rev. 106; 32 Tex.L.Rev. 240; cf. Pardue v. Mark, Tex.Civ.App., 279 S.W.2d 594. Lease forms drafted after the Rogers case have been modified in many cases so that the well completion clause will apply to the well drilling at the end of the primary term or to any subsequent wells.

1. Lewis v. Nance, 20 Cal.App.2d 71, 66 P.2d 708, noted in 12 So.Calif.L.Rev. 96, where clause required lessee to start "the drilling of a well for oil * * *", held to require actual drilling of the hole and not just preliminary operations; and see State ex rel. Commissioners of Land Office v. Carter Oil Co., Okl., 336 P.2d 1086, noted 13 Okl.L.Rev. 82. It should be noted that the language in the delay rental clause calling for the commencement of a well before the next ensuing anniversary date of the primary term to suspend the necessity of paying the next delay rental, is similar to language in the well completion clause. Generally speaking, the test of whether a lessee has "commenced" the operations to drill a well is the same for either of the clauses.

2. See Wehran v. Helis, La., 152 So.2d 220. Here the lease provided operations would be considered as having commenced if materials were placed on the site prior to the end of the primary term. On the next to the last day the drilling barge and derrick became stuck in the canal. However, the well was spudded in the next day. Huhn v. Marshall Exploration, Inc., La.App., 337 So.2d 561 ("operations for drilling").

timbers on the site, will this be sufficient to satisfy the clause? Will it make a difference whether or not the lessor (1) obtains an injunction to prevent the lessee from going on the land in connection with a suit to declare that the lease has terminated, or (2) waits to sue for cancellation of the lease until after the lessee has drilled and completed a producing well?

The cases are replete with examples of activities of the lessee immediately prior to the last day of the primary term. Lessees have entered at the end of the primary term and have placed materials on the site,[3] drilled water wells,[4] dug slush pits,[5] secured permits to drill,[6] built roads for equipment,[7] entered into drilling contracts,[8] staked locations,[9] moved equipment on the location,[10] and have leveled the site,[11] as well as various combinations of these activities.

However, the attitude of the courts has been that more than the factual situation of the well site must be looked at to determine whether the acts of the lessee are sufficient to constitute operations for the drilling of a well. A two-fold test [12] is applied, with the courts looking first at the objective manifestation of the lessee's intent as reflected by the activities at the well site. The courts then look to the subjective intent of the lessee, viz., were the acts done with good faith in an attempt to commence a well? In the situation where the lessor has not attempted to interrupt the lessee and he has actually diligently completed the well after the primary term it is usually

---

3. Guleke v. Humble Oil & Refining Co., Tex.Civ.App., 126 S.W.2d 38. Sufficient: Breaux v. Apache Oil Corp., La. App., 240 So.2d 589 (began building road and turn-around at well); Allen v. Continental Oil Co., La.App., 255 So.2d 842, writ denied, 260 La. 701, 257 So.2d 156 (staked location, acquired well permit, built access road, dug slush pits, laid gas and water lines, spudder rig hole to 35 feet and pipe set); Huhn v. Marshall Exploration, Inc., La.App., 337 So.2d 561 (drilled through plug of abandoned well); LeBar v. Haynie, Wyo., 552 P.2d 1107 (used water rig to drill).

4. Note 3, supra.

5. Walton v. Zatkoff, 372 Mich. 491, 127 N.W.2d 365; Jones v. Moore, Okl., 338 P.2d 872; Guleke v. Humble Oil & Refining Co., Tex.Civ.App., 126 S.W.2d 38.

6. Haddock v. McClendon, 223 Ark. 396, 266 S.W.2d 74; Vickers v. Peaker, 227 Ark. 587, 300 S.W.2d 29.

7. Haddock v. McClendon, 223 Ark. 396, 266 S.W.2d 74.

8. Vickers v. Peaker, 227 Ark. 587, 300 S.W.2d 29.

9. Vickers v. Peaker, 227 Ark. 587, 300 S.W.2d 29; Iberian Oil Corp. v. Texas Crude Oil Co., La., 212 F.Supp. 941; Jones v. Moore, Okl., 338 P.2d 872; Guleke v. Humble Oil & Refining Co., Tex.Civ.App., 126 S.W.2d 38; Petersen v. Robinson Oil & Gas Co., Tex.Civ.App., 356 S.W.2d 217.

10. Vickers v. Peaker, 227 Ark. 587, 300 S.W.2d 29; Petersen v. Robinson Oil & Gas Co., Tex.Civ.App., 356 S.W.2d 217.

11. Walton v. Zatkoff, 372 Mich. 491, 127 N.W.2d 365; also see Moore Oil, Inc. v. Snakard, D.C.Okl., 150 F.Supp. 250; Whelan v. R. Lacy, Inc., Tex.Civ.App. 251 S.W.2d 175.

12. Haddock v. McClendon, 223 Ark. 396, 266 S.W.2d 74; Vickers v. Peaker, 227 Ark. 587, 300 S.W.2d 29; Illinois Mid-Continent Co. v. Tennis, 122 Ind.App. 17, 102 N.E.2d 390; Breaux v. Apache Oil Corp., La.App., 240 So.2d 589; Allen v. Continental Oil Co., La.App., 255 So.2d 842, writ denied 260 La. 701, 257 So.2d 156. Walton v. Zatkoff, 372 Mich. 491, 127 N.W.2d 365; Jones v. Moore, Okl., 338 P.2d 872; Stolz, Wagner & Brown v. Duncan, D.C.Okl., 417 F.Supp. 552; Petersen v. Robinson Oil & Gas Co., Tex. Civ.App., 356 S.W.2d 217; Geier Jackson, Inc. v. James, D.C.Tex., 160 F.Supp. 524.

found that the lessee was in good faith as to the activities performed prior to the end of the primary term.[13] However, where the lessor has interrupted the lessee and when little has been done on the lease site prior to the end of the primary term, it is much more difficult to establish good faith on the part of the lessee.[14]

Necessarily, proof of good faith or the lack of it must be found from the circumstances. Where a substantial sum has been expended by the lessee prior to interruption by the lessor it has been found that he was in good faith.[15] The ability of the lessee, both financial and technological, to carry on the drilling to completion will have a bearing upon the finding of the courts as to the good faith of the lessee, or the lack of it. In the case of Geier-Jackson, Inc. v. James,[16] the lessee's activities included building a road, knocking down trees and grading ground, laying water lines, and drilling for a water well. The lessee had drilling rigs capable of drilling to 12,000 feet. However, it was held that these activities and capability were insufficient, as there was evidence that the president of the corporation, which also owned a lease on adjoining land upon which a producing well was located, did not have a present intent to diligently drill the lease. In Fremont Lumber Co. v. Starrell Petroleum Co.,[17] the lessee had a present intent to perform, but it was held that the activities of the lessee at the end of the primary term were insufficient where it was shown that the only asset of the company was the lease. It owned no machinery or equipment, had no employees or geologists, and had no borrowing power.

It may be concluded that where the lessee has the ability to drill the well to completion and no showing can be made of a lack of present intent to diligently carry on drilling activities until completion, very little in the way of physical activities must be performed on the site to support a conclusion that the lessee has commenced operations for the drilling of a well prior to the end of the primary term of the lease. A minimum of physical activities would seem to include the staking of the well site plus some acts to the land itself such as leveling the site and digging slush pits.[18]

---

13. Breaux v. Apache Oil Corp., La. App., 240 So.2d 589 (good faith plus due diligence required); Allen v. Continental Oil Co., La.App., 255 So.2d 842, writ denied 260 La. 701, 257 So.2d 156 (substantial preparation prior to end of primary term plus diligence resulting in actual production); Peterson v. Robinson Oil & Gas Co., Tex.Civ.App., 356 S.W.2d 217.

14. Haddock v. McClendon, 223 Ark. 396, 266 S.W.2d 74.

15. Haddock v. McClendon, 223 Ark. 396, 266 S.W.2d 74.

16. Tex., 160 F.Supp. 524; also see Illinois Mid-Continent Co. v. Tennis, 122 Ind.App. 17, 102 N.E.2d 390.

17. 364 Or. 773, 364 P.2d 773 However, where the equipment initially used by the lessee is inadequate to drill to the anticipated depth, or roads are inadequate to handle required heavy machinery, a showing by the lessee that other adequate equipment is available, or adequate facilities will be provided, coupled with a reasonable showing why not used or provided at the out-set will suffice. See Haddock v. McClendon, 223 Ark. 396, 266 S.W.2d 74; Guleke v. Humble Oil & Refining Co., Tex.Civ.App., 126 S.W.2d 38.

18. In Vickers v. Peaker, 227 Ark. 587, 300 S.W.2d 29, staked location and moved equipment on site; Walton v. Zatkoff,

§ 6.8 Keeping the Lease Alive by Operations During the Secondary Term—The Dry Hole Clause

During the secondary term the dry hole clause allows the lessee a stated number of days after the completion of a well as a dry hole to commence additional drilling activities. If they result in a producing well the lease will be maintained in effect. The lessee may tack between the well completion clause and the dry hole clause. However, if a well is completed as a "wet" hole, i.e., some production but insufficient to produce a profit, one case indicates that the well is not considered a dry hole. The view has been criticized.

Assume that Rex Oil Co., lessee, has a lease that provides for a five-year primary term. The lease also contains a well completion clause. Rex has kept the lease alive during the primary term by the payment of delay rentals. Several weeks prior to the end of the primary term Rex begins operations for the drilling of a well that is completed as a dry hole after the end of the primary term. Unless other provisions are present in the lease, it will terminate, as no production exists at the end of the extended term of the lease.

To relieve from such termination of the lease, where the lessee desires to drill again in such circumstances, a clause known as the dry hole clause is commonly included in the modern oil and gas lease. Although, as usually drawn, the clause also applies to dry holes drilled during the primary term [1] (to allow the lessee to again commence the payment of delay rentals), we here will only examine its operation after the end of the primary term.

As it applies to a dry hole drilled after the end of the primary term, a common provision reads as follows:

> "If prior to discovery of oil or gas on said land Lessee should drill a dry hole or holes thereon, * * * this lease shall not terminate if lessee commences additional drilling or reworking operations within sixty (60) days thereafter * * *".[2]

Where the clause expressly modifies the habendum clause,[3] it has the effect of keeping the lease in effect for sixty days after a dry hole

---

372 Mich. 491, 127 N.W.2d 365, leveled site and dug slush pits; Jones v. Moore, Okl., 338 P.2d 872, staked location and dug slush pits; Petersen v. Robinson Oil & Gas Co., Tex.Civ.App., 356 S.W.2d 217, staked location and leveled site; Terry v. Texas Co., Tex.Civ.App., 228 S.W. 1019, placed timbers on ground and moved machinery on site; Guleke v. Humble Oil & Refining Co., Tex.Civ.App., 126 S.W.2d 38, made location, placed materials on site, drilled a water well. Cf. Forney v. Ward, 25 Tex.Civ.App. 443, 62 S.W. 108, hauling timbers on site insufficient, expressly not followed in Terry v. Texas Co., supra.

Apparently re-entering an abandoned well will constitute a compliance with the well completion clause, Kothmann v. Boley, 158 Tex. 56, 308 S.W.2d 1; Phillips v. Suntex Oil & Gas Co., Tex.Civ.App., 419 S.W.2d 422; however, the drilling of an input well for secondary production will not, Petroleum Engineers Producing Corp. v. White, Okl., 350 P.2d 601.

1. Freeland v. Edwards, 11 Ill.2d 395, 142 N.E.2d 701; Vaughn v. Hearrell, Ky., 347 S.W.2d 542; and see § 6.3(D).

2. Clause is taken from Rogers v. Osborn, 152 Tex. 540, 261 S.W.2d 311, noted 6 Bay.L.Rev. 106; 32 Tex.L.Rev. 240.

3. See Freeland v. Edwards, 11 Ill.2d 395, 142 N.E.2d 701; Browning v. Cavanaugh, Ky., 300 S.W.2d 580: Vaughn v. Hearrell, Ky., 347 S.W.2d 542; although

§ 6.8 THE OIL AND GAS LEASE—DURATION

has been drilled. During this time, the lessee may drill an additional well, which, if it is completed as a producer, will keep the lease in effect. Likewise, if well #2 is completed as a dry hole, the clause will serve to keep the lease in effect for sixty days thereafter, during which time the lessee may, if he desires, drill an additional well.

It should be noted, however, that the clause as commonly written, has at least one trap for the unwary. Assume that Rex Oil Co. drills a well during the primary term of the lease. The well produces for a few years and then production falls off till it ceases to produce, also during the primary term. During the last year of the primary term the lessee begins the drilling of a well, which is completed as a dry hole after the end of the primary term. Does the dry hole clause now apply, as written above, to give the lessee sixty days to begin another well? The answer is, "No",[4] where the clause is worded: "If *prior to discovery* of oil or gas * * *," as discovery has already occurred, and the dry hole clause no longer applies.

Cases have arisen dealing with the interaction or tacking between the well completion clause and the dry hole clause. Consider two variations of the same problem:

(a) Rex Oil Company is operating under a lease that contains a well completion clause providing that if the lessee is conducting operations for the drilling of a well at the end of the primary term the lease will not lapse if such operations are prosecuted with no cessation of more than thirty (30) consecutive days, and if they result in paying production the lease will be kept alive by such production. The lease has no dry hole clause. Lessee finishes the well drilling at the end of the primary term as a dry hole, and then commences a second well within 30 days which is completed as a producer. Does well #2 keep the lease alive?

(b) Here the facts are the same, except (1) the lease also contains a dry hole clause and (2) the first well is completed with a small amount of oil run from the well, far below that necessary to constitute production in paying quantities. Will well #2 keep the lease alive?

The first illustration raises the question of whether the well completion clause will apply to wells other than the one which is actually drilling at the end of the primary term, i.e., to subsequent wells. The second illustration poses the question of what constitutes a dry hole. Both questions were dealt with in the case of Rogers v. Osborn.[5]

---

no case was found from Oklahoma or jurisdictions following the Oklahoma rule as to modification of the habendum clause by the delay rental clause, it is believed a dry hole type clause would have the effect of modifying the habendum clause although not expressly so stating.

4. Continental Oil Co. v. Boston-Texas Land Trust, C.A.5th, 221 F.2d 124. It would seem discovery must be of petroleum products in paying quantities to have this result.

5. Rogers v. Osborn, 152 Tex. 540, 261 S.W.2d 311, noted 6 Bay.L.Rev. 106; 32 Tex.L.Rev. 240.

The lease contained both a well completion clause [6] and a continuous operations clause.[7] The first well was completed after the end of the primary term. About all the production that resulted was a periodic flowing of "oily mud." It was found in answer to one of lessee's special issues that the well was not a dry hole. The Texas Supreme Court stated that, therefore, the dry hole clause had no application. The court also held that the lessee could not tack well No. 2 to well No. 1 under the well completion clause. The result was based on the wording of the clause that referred only to "operations." As other clauses in the lease which allowed the tacking of wells spoke of "*additional* drilling or reworking operations," it was reasoned the omission of the word "additional" in the well completion clause demonstrated an intent the clause only refer to operations in connection with the well drilling at the end of the primary term. Hence, under the approach of this case, the answer to both of the above problems would be that the second well in neither case kept the leases in effect.

In both illustrations the well completion clause, as worded, would apply only to the well drilling at the end of the primary term. In the second illustration the lessee could not tack to the dry hole clause, as it was found that a wet but economically poor well was not a "dry hole." The conclusion of the court that an unprofitable well is not a dry hole has rightly been strongly criticized.

That Rogers v. Osborn may be strictly construed in Texas is indicated in a later case in that jurisdiction. In Pardue v. Mark,[8] the lease provided for a five-year primary term and would be continued in effect thereafter by production or ", * * * as long as operations are being carried on." The well drilling at the end of the primary term was dry, and the lessee skidded the rig to a new location and completed the well as a producer. It was held that the lease was continued in effect and that Rogers v. Osborn did not apply.

---

6. "If at the expiration of the primary term oil, gas or other mineral is not being produced on said land but lessee is then engaged in drilling or re-working operations thereon, this lease shall remain in force so long as operations are prosecuted with no cessation of more than thirty (30) consecutive days, and if they result in the production of oil, gas or other mineral so long thereafter as oil, gas or other mineral is produced from said land * * *."

7. "* * * if after discovery of oil or gas the production thereof should cease from any cause, this lease shall not terminate if lessee commences additional drilling or re-working operations within sixty (60) days thereafter * * *."

It should be noted that in the well completion clause the 30-day period refers to the maximum length of time that can elapse and operations will be considered continuous. In the continuous operations clause as above set forth, it would seem that the 60-day period refers not to a time gap as to operations being conducted on a well but to the time within which additional operations must commence. Therefore it would seem under these clauses if Black Gold's well ceases to produce, and drilling operations start on well No. 2 within 45 days, that no arbitrary time limit will apply to operations on well No. 2, after which operations will not be considered continuous. However, this view has been rejected in cases of first impression in both Oklahoma and Texas. See discussion in § 6.4, supra.

8. Pardue v. Mark, Tex.Civ.App., 279 S.W.2d 594, and see cases collected in Summers, Oil and Gas Law, § 300, note 92.

§ 6.9 Keeping the Lease Alive by Operations During the Secondary Term—The Continuous Operations Clause

During the secondary term, the continuous operations clause allows the lessee to return to drilling activities where an existing producing well ceases to produce. In the proper circumstances the well completion clause, the dry hole clause, and the continuous operations clause are cumulative and may be tacked.

Definitional problems as to what constitutes a "dry hole" have created difficulties in tacking between the clauses where a previous well is not a duster, but does not produce in paying quantities.

Where the continuous operations clause provides that the lease will not lapse if operations are prosecuted with no interruption of more than 60 consecutive days, upon cessation of operations the lease will not lapse until the additional expiration of 60 days. It appears to be the increasing view of the courts that such extension will be for all purposes.

We have seen how special clauses have been developed to aid the lessee in developing the lease, by modification of the habendum clause, in allowing him to complete the well drilling at the end of the primary term, and by providing for additional time to drill an additional well where a well so drilling comes in dry. However, protection is not complete. Assume that at the end of the primary term Rex Oil Co. has a well producing in paying quantities, or is drilling a well at the end of the primary term that is completed as a paying producer. Assume further that either of these wells, some time after the end of the primary term, ceases to produce in paying quantities. In those jurisdictions that do not follow a "vesting" concept [1] the lease will terminate, in absence of a saving clause that modifies the habendum clause. Obviously the well completion clause will not apply as no well is now drilling, and the dry hole clause will not apply as the lessee drilled a producer, not a dry hole. Therefore, additional phraseology has been added to the dry hole clause. This phraseology

---

1. In those jurisdictions that view discovery of production in paying quantities as "vesting" the lessee with an interest in the lease, the lease may not automatically terminate upon cessation of actual production. The lessee may be able to begin drilling to different formations without the necessity of a continuous operations clause. The result would be dependent upon whether a jurisdiction views the "vesting" as applying to all formations under a lease or just the formations in which production has been discovered.

In Oklahoma the lessee is viewed as being vested with an interest only in the producing formation in which products have been discovered in paying quantities. The lease will not terminate unless the lessee has abandoned the lease or production has ceased due to depletion of the products in the formation. Apparently, during the time that production is continuing from one reservoir, the lessee may drill to other formations and continue production either from the presently producing formation or from the other formation. After depletion of production from the present formation the lessee may then continue production from the other formation.

However, if production from the present formation has stopped due to depletion of the products, the lease then will terminate (if no other production then exists), and the lessee may not then drill to deeper or other formations without a continuous operations clause. See Parks v. Sinai Oil and Gas Co., 83 Okl. 295, 201 P. 517; Roach v. Junction Oil and Gas Co., 72 Okl. 213, 179 P. 934; Western States Oil & Land Co. v. Helms, 143 Okl. 206, 288 P. 964; and, Anthis v. Sullivan Oil & Gas Co., Okl., 203 P. 187.

is sometimes referred to as the continuous drilling or continuous operations clause. A typical provision is that found in Rogers v. Osborn:

> "* * * if after discovery of oil or gas the production thereof should cease from any cause, this lease shall not terminate if lessee commences additional drilling or reworking operations within sixty (60) days thereafter * * *."

Few problems have been presented in regard to what constitutes sufficient operations to keep the lease in effect, if they are commenced within the particular time limit stated in the clause. Analogies have been drawn to cases dealing with commencement of drilling operations in the delay rental and well completion clauses.[2] An example of such activities is given in the footnotes.[3] The burden is on the lessor [4] to show that such activities were not carried on continuously without cessation for the required number of days.

The effect of the clause is to keep the lease in effect for the stated number of days after production has ceased, and if operations are started within such time and result in a producing well they will maintain the lease in effect. Here if Rex Oil Co. has a producing well after the end of the primary term which ceases to produce, and within the required number of days stated in the continuous operations clause begins the drilling of a new well or reworking the old well, which results in production in either case, the lease will be maintained in effect.

---

2. Texas Co. v. Leach, 219 La. 613, 53 So.2d 786; Lone Star Producing Co. v. Walker, Miss., 257 So.2d 496 (example of facts where operations considered not continuous).

Where questions have arisen as to what constitutes "reworking" activities, in two cases they have been construed as requiring more than the ability of the formation to feed products into the well bore, and include any operations that are necessary to obtain production. House v. Tidewater, La.App., 219 So.2d 616, writ refused 253 La. 1081, 221 So.2d 516; Bell v. Mitchell Energy Corp., Tex.Civ.App., 553 S.W.2d 626. As to what constitutes a completed well see Barrett v. Ferrell, Tex.Civ.App., 550 S.W.2d 138, writ refused n.r.e., drilling to a depth that would reasonably preclude the probability of finding oil or gas at a further depth—here dealing with well completed as a dry hole.

3. Texas Co. v. Leach, 219 La. 613, 53 So.2d 786 held re-working started within 60 days after shut-down:

9/7/47—shut down.
9/10/47—relegged derrick.
9/11/47—pulled tubing.
9/16/47—strengthened and reworked bridge for heavy equipment.
9/25/47—doped tubing and rods.
10/1/47—repaired gas line for power.
11/14/47—racked and doped tubing.
11/21/47—repaired road and bridges.
11/26/47—prepared for cable tubing.
11/27/47—crews started actual reworking of wells.

Also see Morrison v. Swaim, Tex.Civ.App., 220 S.W.2d 493.

4. Texas Co. v. Leach, 219 La. 613, 53 So.2d 786; Morrison v. Swaim, Tex.Civ.App., 220 S.W.2d 493; Chandler v. Drummet, Tex.Civ.App., 557 S.W.2d 313 (lease terminated, as operations not begun within 60 days after dry hole, on rationale that clause places time limitation on implied obligation to develop within a reasonable time).

§ 6.9   THE OIL AND GAS LEASE—DURATION

The well completion clause, the dry hole clause, and the continuous operations clause, in the modern lease form, are cumulative in effect.[5] For instance, assume that Black Gold Oil Company is drilling a well at the end of the primary term of the lease, which well is completed after the end of the primary term as a dry hole. Within twenty days lessee begins the drilling of well #2, which is completed as a producer. Well #2 produces for three years and production then ceases. Within forty-five days, lessee begins operations for the drilling of well #3, which also comes in as a dry hole. Lessee again begins drilling operations on well #4, thirty days after the dry hole, and this well is completed as a producer in paying quantities. The lease is maintained in effect if the beginning of operations in each case is within the period required by the various clauses.

The lessee is able to complete well #1 after the end of the primary term either under the well completion clause, or without one in a jurisdiction following the Oklahoma rule. The dry hole clause allows the commencement of additional drilling activities where the well drilling at the end of the primary term came in dry. When well #2 ceases to produce, the lessee is able to maintain the lease in effect under the continuous operations clause, and is able to tack well #4 when the third well was completed as a dry hole.

The operative words in cumulative usage of the various clauses has caused litigation. In order for the continuous operations clause to apply, it is normally provided that production must cease. No cases have been found discussing the problem of when production ceases under the continuous operations clause except to apply the same test of cessation of production that is usual to apply in a particular jurisdiction as to cessation of production under the habendum clause.

However, for the dry hole clause to apply, it is usually provided that the lessee must have drilled a "dry hole." This, in turn, raises the question of what is a dry hole. The question was squarely presented in the case of Rogers v. Osborn.[6] In this case the lessee was drilling a well at the end of the primary term, which well was completed after the end of the primary term. The well was not a commercial producer, and would periodically only produce oily mud. The lessee began another well within the time limits of both the well completion clause and the continuous operations clause.

As discussed previously, the court held that the well completion clause would only apply to the well drilling at the end of the primary term. In the trial court the lessee submitted a special issue which

---

5. Union Sulphur Co. v. Texas Gulf Sulphur Co., Tex.Civ.App., 42 S.W.2d 182; Rogers v. Osborn, 152 Tex. 540, 261 S.W.2d 311, noted 6 Bay.L.Rev. 106; 32 Tex.L.Rev. 240; Stanolind Oil & Gas Co. v. Newman Brothers Drilling Co., 157 Tex. 489, 305 S.W.2d 169, noted 56 Mich. L.Rev. 823; Phillips v. Suntex Oil & Gas Co., Tex.Civ.App., 419 S.W.2d 422; St. Louis Royalty Co. v. Continental Oil Co., C.A.5th, 193 F.2d 778.

6. 152 Tex. 540, 261 S.W.2d 311, noted 6 Bay.L.Rev. 106; 32 Tex.L.Rev. 250.

was answered by the jury to the effect that the well was not a dry hole. Without discussion, the Supreme Court of Texas held that the lessee was bound by the finding. As the well was not a dry hole, the lessee could not come within the provisions of the continuous operations clause, and the lease terminated. The case has come to be known as the "wet hole" case. It has been argued by various writers, and would seem justly subject to criticism, that for purposes of maintaining the lease in effect any well incapable of producing in paying quantities should be treated as a dry hole.

The later Texas case of Stanolind Oil & Gas Co. v. Newman Bros. Drilling Co.,[7] where the first well drilled was dry, demonstrates the interaction of the well completion and continuous operations clause, and involves the same lease form as used in Rogers v. Osborn.

A case similar in result to that of Rogers v. Osborn, but relating to operations in a unit is that of Sunac Petroleum Corporation v. Parkes.[8] In this case the subject lease was in a unit for production of *gas*. At the end of the primary term of the lease a well was drilling in the unit, but not on the subject lease. It was completed after the end of the primary term of the subject lease as a well capable of producing oil, but not gas. Within 13 days thereafter a well was started on the subject lease and was subsequently completed as a producing well. It was argued that, under the normal rule, where a lease is submitted to a unit operations any well on the unit would satisfy the habendum clause of every lease in the unit, including the modifying clauses dealing with wells drilling at the end of the primary term, dry holes, or production that ceases.

There is no doubt that the unit well drilling at the end of the primary term of the subject lease satisfied the well completion clause of the subject lease and propelled it past the primary term. The lease then was in effect up until the unit well was completed as an oil well. The court drew a strong analogy to the Osborn case and concluded that the prior unit well was not a dry hole. As it could not satisfy the unit, which was for gas only, it could not be considered a producer upon which production had ceased. A dissenting justice argued that any well insufficient to propel a lease past the primary term should be classified as a dry hole.

The case is also similar to the Osborn case in that the second well was started within the 30-day time limit imposed in the well completion clause. Again, the court followed the Osborn case and held that the well completion clause applies only to the well drilling at the end of the primary term.

In both the Rogers and Sunac case the court was more concerned with the construction of the wording of the clause than with the purpose of the clause. "Dry hole" within the intention of the parties

---

7. 157 Tex. 489, 305 S.W.2d 169, noted 56 Mich.L.Rev. 823.

8. Tex., 416 S.W.2d 798.

would seem to indicate a well that does not carry out the purpose of the lease, i.e., that the well produce at a profit. This approach has apparently been applied by the courts in Oklahoma in the case of Hoyt v. Continental Oil Company,[9] where cessation of production was defined as being cessation of production in paying quantities and not total cessation of production. This is an enlightened approach and should be followed by other jurisdictions.

Due to the problem raised in the Osborn case, many lease forms have been amended to provide that the periods stated in each clause are now the same, sixty days, and the well completion clause has been amended so that it will apply not only to the well drilling at the end of the primary term, but also to subsequent wells begun within sixty days. The effect is to allow a second well to satisfy the well completion clause whether or not the first well is actually dry, as it is not necessary to tack to the continuous operations clause. A typical form of the clauses as amended is [10]

> "6. If prior to discovery of oil, gas or other mineral on said land * * * Lessee should drill a dry hole or holes thereon, or if after discovery of oil, gas or other mineral, the production thereof should cease from any cause, this lease shall not terminate if lessee commences additional drilling or reworking operations within 60 days thereafter * * * If at the expiration of the primary term, oil, gas or other mineral is not being produced on said land,

---

[9]. Okl., 606 P.2d 560.

[10]. Another form:

6. If prior to discovery and production of oil, gas or other mineral on said land or on acreage pooled therewith, Lessee should drill a dry hole or holes thereon, or if after discovery and production of oil, gas or other mineral, the production thereof should cease from any cause, this lease shall not terminate if Lessee commences operations for drilling or reworking within sixty (60) days thereafter or if it be within the primary term, commences or resumes the payment or tender of rentals or commences operations for drilling or reworking on or before the rental paying date next ensuing after the expiration of sixty days from date of completion of dry hole or cessation of production. If at any time subsequent to sixty (60) days prior to the beginning of the last year of the primary term and prior to the discovery of oil, gas or other mineral on said land, or on acreage pooled therewith, Lessee should drill a dry hole thereon, no rental payment or operations are necessary in order to keep the lease in force during the remainder of the primary term. If at the expiration of the primary term, oil, gas or other mineral is not being produced on said land, or on acreage pooled therewith, but Lessee is then engaged in drilling or reworking operations thereon or shall have completed a dry hole thereon within sixty (60) days prior to the end of the primary term, the lease shall remain in force so long as operations on said well or for drilling reworking of any additional well are prosecuted with no cessation of more than sixty (60) consecutive days, and if they result in the production of oil, gas or other mineral, so long thereafter as oil, gas or other mineral is produced from said land or acreage pooled therewith. Any pooled unit designated by Lessee in accordance with the terms hereof, may be dissolved by Lessee by instrument filed for record in the appropriate records of the county in which the leased premises are situated at any time after the completion of a dry hole or the cessation of production on said unit. In the event a well or wells producing oil or gas in paying quantities should be brought in on adjacent land and within three hundred thirty (330) feet of and draining the leased premises, or acreage pooled therewith, Lessee agrees to drill such offset wells as a reasonably prudent operator would drill under the same or similar circumstances.

or on acreage pooled therewith, but lessee is then engaged in drilling or reworking operations thereon or shall have completed a dry hole thereon within sixty (60) days prior to the end of the primary term, the lease shall remain in force so long as *operations on this or on any subsequent well* are prosecuted with no cessation of more than sixty (60) consecutive days, and if they result in the production of oil, gas or other mineral, so long thereafter as oil, gas or other mineral is produced from said land or acreage pooled therewith."

An additional question has arisen in connection with both the well completion and continuous operations clauses. As sometimes written, both clauses may contain phraseology that operations must be prosecuted with "no cessation of more than 60 consecutive days." Of what effect upon the term of the lease is the stated number of days? Rex Oil Co., after the primary term of the lease, has a well that ceases to produce. Within 15 days he begins the drilling of a second well and prosecutes operations for 45 days. He then discontinues operations. When does the lease terminate? If the continuous operations clause contains wording that operations must be commenced within 60 days from the time of cessation of operations and continued with no cessation of more than 60 consecutive days, it would seem that the lease will not terminate immediately upon the cessation of operations, as the lessee has till the last of the 60-day period to again commence operations. Where such wording is present, that the lease will not terminate until the end of the stated period, viz., 60 days after cessation of operations, the term of the lease is automatically extended for the stated period following the drilling of a dry hole, cessation of production, or discontinuation of operations.

However, for what purpose is the extension of the term? Is it merely for the commencement of drilling operations on the lease or is it for all purposes? That is to say, if substitute methods of keeping the lease alive become operative during this stated period, other than drilling or reworking operations, will they keep the lease alive?

It increasingly appears to be the view of the courts that, unless contractual language of the lease is restrictive, the extension of the lease is treated as being for all purposes. The landmark case is that of Skelly v. Harris.[11] The facts were that a unit well was drilling at the end of the primary term. The well was not located upon lands covered by the subject lease. The unit well was completed as a gas well after the end of the primary term and was capped. Some 41 days later production commenced. It was held that the lease was held in effect. The court stated:

> "When the language of the 60-day clause is given its ordinary and commonly accepted meaning, it contemplates and permits either a temporary interruption or a final discontinuance of the operations

---

11. 163 Tex. 92, 352 S.W.2d 950; noted 17 S.W.L.J. 272.

in progress at the end of the primary term. If such operations result in production at a time when there has been cessation of more than sixty consecutive days, the lease remains in force so long thereafter as production continues. The 60-day clause thus allows the lessee that period after completion of a well capable of producing within which to begin *either actual or constructive production."* (Emphasis supplied).

There seems to be no doubt as to the court's language that any method available to satisfy the habendum clause during the extension period will maintain the lease in effect. If the lessee had paid a shut-in royalty within the 60-day period the lease would likewise have been kept in effect.

The Skelly case may be distinguished from the case of Gulf Oil Corp. v. Reid,[12] where under similar facts it was held that payment of the shut-in royalty was not timely. Payment was made after the capping of the well, but before the stated time limit in the continuous operations clause. However, the clause involved in the Reid case did not predicate the running of the 60-day extension period from the time that operations ceased, but from the "completion or *abandonment* of one well and the commencement of operations on another." Where the first well was a capped gas well the court held that it had not been abandoned and hence the lessee could not come within the quoted clause. This being so, the lease term came to an end when the well was capped.

It is interesting to note that one case [13] has analogized the period that the lease is held in effect by the payment of shut-in royalties to be the contractual equivalent of actual production, to the extent that the extension period of the continuous operations clause will apply at the expiration of the period that the shut-in royalty is payable. Thus, under this approach, if Rex Oil Company were keeping the lease in effect by payment of shut-in royalties, at the end of the payment period, under a Harris v. Skelly type clause, the lease would not terminate for an additional 60-day period. This 60-day extension would be for all purposes.

This is upon the rationale that by treating shut-in royalty payments as equivalent to actual production, the expiration of the period for which the payment is made is the same as cessation of actual production. Hence, under this approach, cessation of constructive production is equal in operative effect to cessation of actual production. This result is the logical extension of the statement in most oil

---

12. 161 Tex. 51, 337 S.W.2d 267. A question was raised whether operations for laying a pipeline to the gathering line would have kept the lease alive during the interim period, but was not answered by the court on final appeal. It would seem that such operations, if being conducted on the lease, would have been sufficiently connected with the well to have the effect of maintaining the lease in effect.

13. Citizens National Bank of Emporia, Kansas v. Socony Mobil Oil Co., Tex. Civ.App., 372 S.W.2d 718.

and gas leases that while payment of shut-in royalties is being made it will be considered that "gas is being produced from this lease in paying quantities."

CHAPTER 7

THE OIL AND GAS LEASE—ROYALTY AND OTHER PARTICULAR LEASE CLAUSES

Analysis

Sec.
7.1 Products Covered by the Royalty Clauses—Introduction.
7.2 Royalty on Gas Produced From an Oil Well—Casinghead Gas and Gasoline.
  (A) Where No Clause Provision.
  (B) Express Clause Provision.
7.3 Royalty on Liquid Components Produced From a Gas Well—Condensate and Distillate.
7.4 Compensation for Royalty Based Upon "Market Value," "Market Price," and "Proceeds."
  (A) General.
  (B) Market Price.
  (C) Market Value.
  (D) Proceeds.
  (E) Market Price or Value Royalty Clauses and the Long-Term Gas Sales Contract Problem.
  (F) Expenses of Transportation and Preparation for Market.
  (G) "FERC–Out" and "Market–Out" Clauses.
7.5 Division and Transfer Orders.
  (A) Nature of the Division Order.
  (B) Effect of the Division Order.
  (C) Modification or Termination of Division Orders.
7.6 Minimum Royalty Clause.
7.7 Description and Mother-Hubbard Clause.
7.8 The Proportionate Reduction and Warranty Clauses.
7.9 The Surrender Clause.
7.10 Lessee's Right to Remove Fixtures From the Lease.
7.11 The Force Majeure Clause.
7.12 The Free Gas Clause.
7.13 Pooling and the Pooling Clause.
  (A) Formation of Units.
  (B) Basis and Authority of the Lessee to Pool.
  (C) Designation of Pooling.
  (D) The Effect of Production and Operations Within the Unit Upon Acreage Within and Outside of the Unit.
  (E) Allocation of Production.
7.14 The Entirety and Assignment Clauses.
7.15 Lessor's Special Inspection Clause.

§ 7.1 Products Covered by the Royalty Clauses—Introduction

Early lease clauses merely provided for royalty payments upon production of oil and gas. Gas was a waste product, and flat-rate royalty clauses were preferred. Difficulties were encountered as to the coverage of the lease and the payment of royalties upon casinghead gas (gas produced from an oil well) and upon condensate (liquids produced from casinghead gas and from a gas well). The modern lease form customarily provides royalty payments equal to a fraction of production on oil and gas and all products integral with production of oil and gas.

The modern oil and gas lease conveys the right to explore for minerals other than oil and gas. However, it is to petroleum production that both the lessee and the lessor look for compensation and return from the venture. Therefore, in this chapter the discussion will be directed to compensation to the lessor from oil and gas production, and from production of products that are integral with the production of oil and gas.[1]

In the earliest leases primary emphasis was upon the production of oil; gas was considered to be a waste product and was vented into the air. The then-customary provisions were that the lessor was entitled to a fractional portion, usually $1/8$,[2] of the oil, in kind,[3] to be delivered to his tanks, or the value of such fractional part of the oil so run to be paid to his credit. On gas produced the older provisions were for the payment of a flat rate per well per year to be paid for gas wells where gas was sold or used off the premises.[4] In a few in-

---

1. In general see: Arata, "Timely Payments of Royalties", Loyola L.Rev. 163; Brown, Gas Royalty Provisions and the Rights of Lessors and Lessees with Respect to Sale of Gas, 30 N.D.L.Rev. 5; Ethridge, Oil and Gas Division Orders, 19 Miss.L.J. 127; Hardwicke, Evolution of Casinghead Gas Law, 8 Tex.L.Rev. 1; Hardwicke, Problems Arising Out of Royalty Clauses in Oil and Gas Leases in Texas, 29 Tex.L.Rev. 790; Mosburg, Analysis of Producer Gas Sale Contracts, 17 Okla.L.Rev. 249; Moses, "In lieu" Royalty Agreements in the Oil Industry, 3 Houston L.Rev. 84; Sneed, Value of Lessor's Share of Production Where Gas Only is Produced, 25 Tex.L.Rev. 641; and, Summers, Oil and Gas, §§ 587–597.2.

2. In some jurisdictions, such as California, the customary royalty provided is $1/6$. The quantum of royalty will in the last analysis depend upon the respective bargaining power of the lessor and lessee. This in turn will in large part depend upon the amount and quality of the lands being leased, or subject to lease.

3. A typical clause: "the equal one-eighth of all oil produced and saved upon said premises, to be delivered in any pipe line to which (any) well or wells may be connected, to the credit of the party of the first part." Where the clause provides for payment of oil in kind but specifies no place of delivery, it has been held that the lessor may require delivery into tank cars where inconvenience to the lessee would not be increased thereby. See: Tremont Lumber Co. v. Louisiana Oil Refinery Co., 187 La. 454, 175 So. 25; Atwood v. Humble Oil & Refining Co., C.A.5th, 338 F.2d 502.

4. A typical early clause: "If gas is found, second party agrees to pay first party $200.00 for the product each year, payable quarterly, for the product of each well, while the same is being used off the premises." Flat rate gas royalties today are largely obsolete. When such clauses were used differences existed as to the obligation to pay when a gas well was completed but no gas was produced or used off the premises. The more common clause fixed an obligation to pay royalty only if gas was marketed or used. See Ohio Oil Co. v. Lane, 59 Ohio St. 307, 52 N.E. 791; Iams v. Carnegie Natural Gas Co., 194 Pa. 72, 45 A. 54; and see Summers, Oil and Gas, § 588.

§ 7.1   ROYALTY AND OTHER CLAUSES   337

stances there were provisions for the gas to be paid in kind, although such provisions were not often seen due to the impracticability of the connection of a pipeline to the well.[5]

Following the flaring of gas as a waste product, the next development was that liquid components in gas became valuable whether produced (1) from the gas produced from an oil well (called casinghead gas) or (2) from wells that produced gas, but no oil. The casinghead gas, which is produced along with oil from the casinghead of an oil well, was run through separators at the wells, and a substance called drip gasoline or casinghead gasoline was removed. The gas then was either vented to the air, or was piped to a central treating plant and run through absorption towers. This removed the remaining wet elements by absorption into the oil through which the gas was run. After absorption the remaining or "residue" gas was vented to the air.

Not all gas wells produce "dry" gas; some produce "wet" gas, which is rich in liquid components. These components, first called distillate, but today more commonly called condensate, were removed by processes similar to those used in the treatment of the casinghead gas.

Controversies arose as to whether the liquid elements were "oil" or "gas," and even whether they were, in fact, covered by the lease. Where determined to be covered by the lease there was disagreement on how royalty should be paid.

As lease royalty clauses developed, specific provisions were inserted in the leases to spell out the coverage and royalty obligations of the lessee for oil, gas, casinghead gas, liquids produced from casinghead gas, and condensate. Also, as gas became more valuable the form of the gas royalty payment was changed from a flat rate royalty to a share in a fractional amount of the gas produced.[6] As men-

---

5. Molter v. Lewis, 156 Kan. 544, 134 P.2d 404; Reed v. Hackworth, Ky.App., 287 S.W.2d 912; Tremont Lumber Co. v. Louisiana Oil Refinery Co., 187 La. 454, 175 So. 25; Martin v. Amis, Tex.Com. App., 288 S.W. 431 (providing for delivery in kind); Clear Creek Oil & Gas Co. v. Bushmiaer, 165 Ark. 303, 264 S.W. 830; Parnell, Inc. v. Giller, Trustee, 237 Ark. 267, 372 S.W.2d 627; Matzen v. Hugoton Production Co., 182 Kan. 456, 321 P.2d 576; Gilmore v. Superior Oil Co., 192 Kan. 388, 388 P.2d 602; Ashland Oil & Refining Co. v. Staats, Inc., D.C. Kan., 271 F.Supp. 571; Warfield Natural Gas Co. v. Allen, 261 Ky. 840, 88 S.W.2d 989; La Fitte Co. v. United Fuel Gas Co., C.A.6th, 284 F.2d 845 (providing for payment in money).

With the possibility of gas shortages and the higher prices for gas, an "in kind" provision is now appearing in more leases. This is especially true in leases on state lands.

6. Following is an example for a comprehensive royalty clause:

"The royalties to be paid by Lessee are:

(a) On oil, one-eighth (1/8th) of that produced and saved from said land, same to be delivered at the wells or to the credit of Lessors in the pipe line to which the wells may be connected; Lessors' interest in either case shall bear its proportion of any expense for treating oil to make it marketable as crude."

(b) On gas, including casinghead gas and all gaseous substances produced from said land and sold or used off the premises except in the manufacture of gasoline or other products therefrom in accordance with the provisions of Sub-

tioned above, the royalty clause generally does not provide for delivery of gas in kind, but for payment of the price or value of a share of the gas that is sold or used off the premises. It should be noted that under the normal oil royalty clause, where delivery in kind is provided, title to the royalty oil does not pass to the lessee, but is retained by the lessor; on the other hand, however, where payment is to be made of the value of a portion of the gas, title to the gas passes to the lessee when the lease is executed.

Today state conservation regulations prevent the venting of gas to the air. It is necessary either to sell the gas or re-inject it into the

division 3(d) below, the market value at the mouth of the well of one-eighth (1/8th) of the gas sold or used.

(c) On distillate, condensate, and other products separated or extracted by use of oil and gas separators of conventional type or other equipment at least as efficient, from gas, including casinghead gas or other gaseous substance produced from said land, the market value at the separator of one-eighth (1/8th) of the distillate, condensate and other products so separated and extracted, it being understood and agreed that said gas, before being sold or used will be run through such separators or other equipment unless (1) the same is processed in an absorption or extraction plant, or (2) the liquid hydrocarbon content of said gas is so small as to make the installation and operation of separators or other comparable equipment unprofitable, or (3) the pressure of said gas is such that running the same through separators or other comparable equipment will so reduce the pressure that Lessee will be unable to sell and deliver the separated gas against existing gathering system or pipeline pressures.

(d) In the event that any gas, including casinghead gas, from said land shall be processed in an absorption or extraction plant owned or operated in whole or in part by Lessee or any assignee of Lessee, or any affiliated, parent or subsidiary company or either of them (it being understood and agreed that nothing herein contained shall require Lessee or any assignee to so process such gas), then in lieu of the royalties hereinabove provided on gas and the products extracted therefrom, Lessors shall be paid as royalties on such gas and the products therefrom the following:

(1) On distillate, condensate, and other products which are condensed and extracted from the gas by running such gas through an adequate conventional type oil and gas separator on the leased premises, one-eighth (1/8th) of the market value at the well of the products which are so recovered and sold or used.

(2) On products extracted from the gas in the absorption or extraction plant, but excluding products which are recovered by means described in the preceding subparagraph (1), one-eighth (1/8th) of the market value of the products so extracted and recovered, the market value to be determined immediately upon extraction and prior to further refining of such products.

(3) On residue gas (that remaining after having been processed for the liquid hydrocarbons herein contained) sold, or used, the market value at the plant of one-eighth (1/8th) of such residue gas sold or used less compression, dehydration and treating costs, if any.

The recovery of products covered by this lease shall be calculated by the making of periodical tests in accordance with modern and sound engineering practice prevailing in the industry at the time of the test. Lessors, or any of them, their agents and representatives, shall, at their own risk, have the right to witness any testing or gauging of oil, gas condensate or distillate on the leased premises and of witnessing any drilling or other operations relating to the development of said land or the production of oil, gas condensate or distillate therefrom.

(e) On all other minerals mined and marketed, one-eighth (1/8th), either in kind or value at the well or mine, at Lessee's election, except that on sulphur the royalty shall be three dollars ($3.00) per long ton on all sulphur produced and saved.

ground. Residue gas is either dehydrated and sold to gas pipeline companies or other purchasers, or is re-injected into the ground. Such re-injected residue gas may later be sold, and a royalty is then payable upon such sales or use. However, if one owns a term royalty interest that was in effect at the time of original production but not at the later time when the re-injected gas was produced, it has been held that the term royalty owner will not share in the royalty payments made at the time of the sale.[7]

A case that dramatizes the difference between the old flat rate royalty clause on gas and the more modern clause is Southland Royalty Company v. Pan American Petroleum Corporation.[8] The royalty clauses in the case provided as follows:

"(a) to deliver to the credit of lessor, free of cost, in the pipeline to which they may connect their wells, the equal one-eighth part of all oil produced and saved from the leased premises and *⅛ of the net proceeds of potash and other minerals at the mine.* (Emphasis supplied).

"(b) to pay the lessor One Hundred Dollars, each year in advance for the gas from each well where gas only is found while the same is being used off the premises * * *."

Lessee had drilled three gas wells and was producing and selling more than one million dollars worth of gas each year. Royalty payments were made under clause (b), the flat rate clause. Lessors brought suit for royalty based upon clause (a), which provided for ⅛ of the proceeds. In an opinion that seems justifiable only upon the basis of the inequity of paying three hundred dollars each year for a million dollars worth of gas, the Texas Supreme Court found for the lessors.

The rationale was that clause (b) only referred to gas being "used off the premises" (which it interpreted to mean being used off the premises by the lessee) and not to gas being sold.[9] It was also held that gas was included in the definition of "other minerals" contained in clause (a), which clause also referred to products being sold. From this reasoning the court stated, "The first royalty clause, as amended, imposes a clear legal obligation to pay royalty of ⅛ of the net proceeds on gas sold, including gas sold for use by others off the premises, and which in its second and third royalty clauses does not impose a clear legal obligation to pay flat-rate royalties on gas sold for use by others off the premises but are ambiguous in that respect."

7. Bezzi v. Hocker, C.A.10th, 370 F.2d 533.

8. Tex., 378 S.W.2d 50.

9. Tyson v. Surf Oil Co., 195 La. 248, 196 So. 336.

As to other cases interpreting the phrase "used off the premises" see cases and discussion at footnote 7, § 7.2(B), infra.

The court was not bothered by the phrase "at the mine" used in clause (a), as it interpreted an oil and gas lease as a mine. The court also stated that "potash and other minerals" was not limited to hard minerals of a like character, under the doctrine of *ejusdem generis.* In what seems to be an erroneous statement [10] the court further stated that the doctrine had never been recognized in Texas.

It seems clear that the court, in the guise of the constructional process, applied equity principles to relieve what it felt was unjust enrichment of the lessees caused by a lease executed in 1925. However, it also seems obvious that the parties had no subjective intent to include gas in clause (a) by use of the term "other minerals." In the granting clause of the lease, as well as in royalty clause (a), the word "Potash" was added. At the time the lease was drawn up, 1925, gas was of little value, but oil and potash had a wide market. The lessors, somewhat ineptly perhaps, merely provided for a share of the value of the minerals that at that time had a market value. The case is a good example of problems that may arise where old lease forms have been kept in effect for a long period of time. Without the amendment to clause (a), the court would have had no alternative but to find for the lessees.

Non-payment of royalty in all jurisdictions except Louisiana will merely give rise to a suit for accounting by the lessee.[11] In Louisiana, prior to the enactment of the Louisiana Mineral Code,[12] non-payment of royalty could cause the cancellation of an oil and gas lease.[13]

However, for delay in payment to have constituted grounds for forfeiture of the lease prior to the Code, such delay must have been unreasonable.[14] Louisiana courts did not declare a forfeiture in all cases where a royalty payment delay had occurred. Such delay may have been excused on the ground that it was reasonable. As one Louisiana court stated:[15]

> "In this case there were grounds for honest doubt as to the rights of the parties. This court has not, and will not, penalize a litigant lessee by dissolving a lease held technically in default when there is a bona fide defense. The plaintiff's request for cancellation should, therefore, be denied."

---

10. See text and footnotes Chapter 1, § 1.1, supra.

11. See Cannon v. Cassidy, Okl., 542 P.2d 514, for majority view that lease is not subject to termination for delay in payment of royalties.

12. LSA-R.S. 31:137–31:143, effective January 1, 1975.

13. Melancon v. The Texas Co., 230 La. 593, 89 So.2d 135, 4 U.C.L.A.L.Rev. 485; Bollinger v. The Texas Co., 232 La. 637, 95 So.2d 132; Pierce v. Atlantic Refining Co., La.App., 140 So.2d 19. But cf. Hebert v. Sun Oil Co., La.App., 223 So.2d 897, writ refused La., 227 So.2d 147.

14. Bailey v. Meadows, La.App., 130 So.2d 501; and see cases cited in footnote 13 in main text.

15. Rudnick v. Union Producing Co., 209 La. 943, 25 So.2d 906.

§ 7.1 ROYALTY AND OTHER CLAUSES

Areas in which a good-faith dispute led to a delay in royalty payments for which the court would not declare a forfeiture:

(a) Deduction of costs.[16]

(b) Construction of lease terms.[17]

(c) Title problems.[18]

(d) Time delay not unreasonable.[19]

Cancellation of an oil and gas lease in Louisiana for non-payment of royalties has been mitigated by the provisions of the Louisiana Mineral Code.[20] Cancellation will be avoided by payment by the lessee of royalties upon notice by the lessor of non-payment.[21] This ap-

---

16. Greene v. The Carter Oil Co., La. App., 152 So.2d 611, writ refused La., 153 So.2d 414; Boutte v. Chevron Oil Co., D.C.La., 316 F.Supp. 524.

17. Greene v. The Carter Oil Co., supra, note 16.

18. Bonsall v. Humble Oil & Refining Co., D.C.La., 201 F.Supp. 516, affirmed C.A.5th, 300 F.2d 150; Broadhead v. Pan American Petroleum Corp., La.App., 166 So.2d 329, writ refused La., 167 So.2d 679; Bouterie v. Kleinpeter, 258 La. 605, 247 So.2d 548; Canik v. Texas International Petroleum Corp., La.App., 308 So.2d 453; Fawvor v. United States Oil of Louisiana, Inc., La.App., 162 So.2d 602; Nunez v. Superior Oil Co., D.C.La., 406 F.Supp. 261; Touchet v. Humble Oil & Refining Co., D.C.La., 191 F.Supp. 291; Wilson v. Sun Oil Co., La.App., 265 So.2d 344, affirmed La., 290 So.2d 844.

19. Alvord v. Sun Oil Co., La.App., 271 So.2d 561, writ denied La., 273 So.2d 299 (1 year); Hibbert v. Mudd, La.App., 272 So.2d 697, reversed La., 294 So.2d 518 (19 months). Also see case in footnote 18, supra.

20. LSA-R.S. 31:137–31:143:

Art. 173. If a mineral lessor seeks relief for the failure of his lessee to make timely or proper payment of royalties, he must give his lessee written notice of such failure as a prerequisite to a judicial demand for damages or dissolution of the lease.

Art. 138. The lessee shall have thirty days after receipt of the required notice within which to pay the royalties due or to respond by stating in writing a reasonable cause for nonpayment. The payment or nonpayment of the royalties or stating or failing to state a reasonable cause for nonpayment within this period has the following effect on the remedies of dissolution and damages.

Art. 139. If the lessee pays the royalties due in response to the required notice, the remedy of dissolution shall be unavailable unless it be found that the original failure to pay was fraudulent. The court may award as damages double the amount of royalties due, interest on that sum from the date due, and a reasonable attorney's fee, provided the original failure to pay royalties was either fraudulent or willful and without reasonable grounds. In all other cases, such as mere oversight or neglect, damages shall be limited to interest on the royalties computed from the date due, and a reasonable attorney's fee if such interest is not paid within thirty days of written demand therefor.

Art. 140. If the lessee fails to pay royalties due or fails to inform the lessor of a reasonable cause for failure to pay in response to the required notice, the court may award as damages double the amount of royalties due, interest on that sum from the date due, and a reasonable attorney's fee regardless of the cause for the original failure to pay royalties. The court may also dissolve the lease in its discretion.

Art. 141. In a case where notice of failure to pay royalties is required, dissolution should be granted only if the conduct of the lessee, either in failing to pay originally or in failing to pay in response to the required notice, is such that the remedy of damages is inadequate to do justice.

Art. 142. A mineral lease may be dissolved partially or in its entirety. A decree of partial dissolution may be made applicable to a specified portion of land, to a particular stratum or strata, or to a particular mineral or minerals.

Art. 143. A mineral lessee cannot be evicted by summary process.

21. LSA-R.S. 31:137–139.

pears to be true even in those instances where the non-payment was intentional or not due to reasonable cause.

Upon non-payment and notice by the lessor, lessee may also respond by stating a reasonable cause for non-payment.[22] In this regard, the cases prior to the enactment of the Code would seem applicable.

Where the lessee does not respond satisfactorily to notice of non-payment by the lessor, cancellation will be available,[23] but only in cases where the remedy of damages is inadequate to do justice. The alternative remedy, and the one which will normally be imposed, is that of damages double the amount of royalties due, interest on that sum from the date due, and a reasonable attorney's fee.[24]

In some states, and Louisiana after passage of the Mineral Code, interest may be allowable for unreasonable delay in rental payment.[25]

§ 7.2 Royalty on Gas Produced from an Oil Well—Casinghead Gas and Gasoline

Where no mention is made in the lease royalty clauses of casinghead gas or gasoline, the courts have prevented unjust enrichment of the lessee who attempted to pay for such production under a flat rate gas clause by either classifying the products as coming within the oil royalty clause, under which a fractional portion of production is returned to the lessor, or, in Oklahoma, holding that they are not covered by the lease, in which case the lessor is entitled to the value of the products less the reasonable costs of production.

Some leases have provided that the lessee may acquire gas produced from an oil well by the payment of a flat rate per year. The better reasoned cases hold that title to the gas with all its constituent elements passes to the lessee and that additional royalty is not payable upon the gasoline extracted therefrom. A few cases have reached an opposite result, apparently in an effort to relieve unjust enrichment.

The inequity of the flat rate clause for gas produced from an oil well has been alleviated in the more modern lease form that provides for payment of the value of a fractional interest in production of casinghead gas and gasoline extracted therefrom.

(A) *Where No Clause Provision*

Although the early leases provided for royalty payments on oil and gas, it was found that some anomalies existed in definition. In this section the discussion is directed to royalties payable upon gas that is produced from the casinghead of an oil well[1] and upon liquid substances extractable therefrom.

---

22. LSA-R.S. 31:138.
23. LSA-R.S. 31:140–143.
24. LSA-R.S. 31:139, 140.
25. Lippert v. Angle, 211 Kan. 695, 508 P.2d 920, LSA-R.S. 140.

1. The appendix to the opinion in Reynolds v. McMan Oil & Gas Co., Tex. Com.App., 11 S.W.2d 778, rehearing denied 14 S.W.2d 819, contains a discussion of the early production methods of cas-

Production of oil was found to be enhanced by the release of gas in the production of oil. The gas was vented to the air. It was later inghead gas and its processing, excerpts of which are set forth:

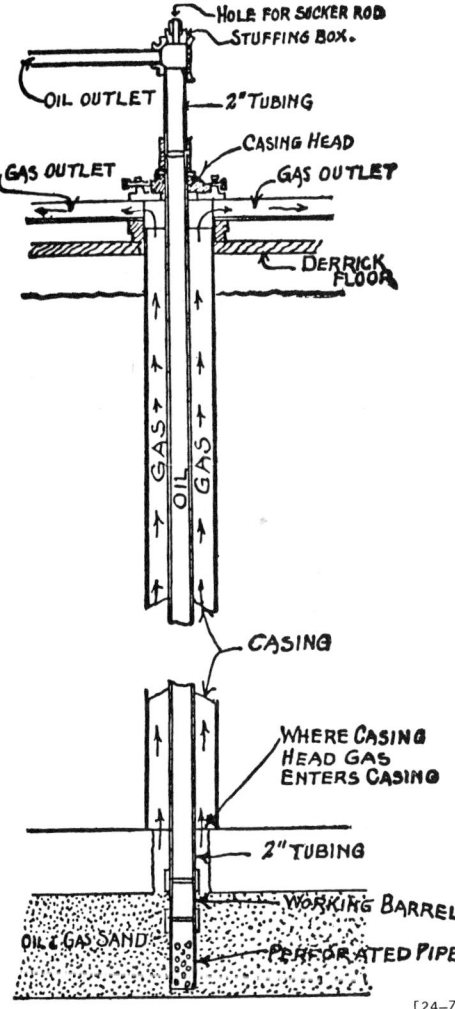

The above print will be helpful to understand the discussion of the method of producing casinghead gas. The Bulletins and Technical Papers quoted from, are prepared and published by the Bureau of Mines, Department of the Interior, Washington, D.C.

"A casinghead is the cast iron fitting that screws on the top of the casing of an oil well, through which the casinghead gas flows.

"There are various sizes and designs of casingheads. Their size varies according to the casing, generally from $2\tfrac{3}{4}$ in. up to 10 in., and the opening in the top from one to four inches. The side openings vary from one to three inches, two inch being the most commonly used. The top is generally placed on top of a gasket and held in place by set screws through the casinghead. In the early days when the gas was not needed for local heating or flambeau torches, the side openings were left open and the casinghead gas flowed into the atmosphere." Wescott, Handbook of Casinghead Gas (3d Ed.) pp. 6 to 8.

Bulletin 95, p. 137, and Morrison, Oil and Gas Rights, p. 960, thus define casinghead gas:

"Natural gas rich in oil vapors. So named as it is usually collected, or separated from the oil, at the casinghead. Frequently called combination gas or wet gas."

"The gas is essentially a mixture of natural gas and the vapors of the lighter components of petroleum. The proportion of vapor has been obviously increased by the loss of methane from the natural storage reservoir in the earth. Wescott, p. 10.

"When the well is worked for petroleum, the coincident reduction of pressure on the petroleum permits the release of dissolved natural gas and vapors of petroleum in the form of the gaseous substance known as casinghead gas." Id. p. 11.

"When dry natural gas is passed over or through oil carrying gasoline, the latter will slowly vaporize or change into a gas when under the right temperature and pressure conditions until the gas becomes saturated with gasoline vapors. The lighter gasoline vapors would vaporize first.

"This process is commonly spoken of as 'the natural gas picking up the gasoline.'" Id. p. 12.

"Casinghead gas is the name given to the gas which flows from oil wells, and, as a rule, comes from the same 'sand' or formation, as the oil, and should not be confused with dry or natural gas which comes from a sand other than the oil sand and is usually under high pressure. Its name is derived from the fact that it is taken from the well through the casinghead. It consists of a mixture of the lighter members of the methane series, namely,

found that such gas was impregnated with liquid petroleum substances that could be removed from the gas by means of separators at the well or by absorption plant processing. The product removed is natural gasoline, sometimes called casinghead gasoline. For convenience in discussion, gas produced from an oil well, before processing, will be called "casinghead gas", the liquid components will be termed "gasoline", and the gas after processing, "residue gas."

The earliest cases dealing with the problem of casinghead gas and gasoline were those that involved no clause which specifically provided for royalty upon such products. Generally, the oil clauses provided for a royalty of a fractional part of production, usually $1/8$, and a payment of a flat rate per well per year on gas. Several questions were presented: Was the casinghead gas produced from the oil well to be paid for under the flat rate gas royalty clause? Was gasoline that was extracted from casinghead gas to be paid for under the oil royalty clause, or was it covered at all?

The first case to litigate the question of payment for casinghead gas royalties was Locke v. Russell,[2] decided in 1915. The lessee produced oil and casinghead gas from which he extracted gasoline. He accounted for the products by paying for the oil and the gasoline upon the basis of $1/8$ of the production. The lessor sued for flat rate gas royalty on the basis that the casinghead gas produced from the oil well came within the scope of the gas clause. The court held that casinghead gas production did not constitute the well a gas well for payment of the flat rate gas royalty, and in pasing stated:

> "Because as properly defined, gasoline is a colorless inflammable fluid, the first and highest distillant of crude petroleum; represents the lightest portions of crude oil; and is extracted from it by distillation, very much as whiskey is distilled and in much the same sort of apparatus. Being the most volatile component of petroleum, it readily separates from it, and, in the process of distillation, is the oil drawn off at the lowest temperature."

methane, ethane, propane, butane, pentane, etc., but heavier hydrocarbons than predominate in natural gas." Id. p. 35.

"Casinghead gas represents gas that occurs in contact with oil and hence has an excellent chance to mingle with and carry out of the well some of the lighter vapors—the gasoline of the oil.

"When the pressures are not too high, considerable quantities of vapors from the lighter constituents of the oil are carried by the gases, just as water vapor is carried in the atmosphere. The carrying power of all gases is the same, provided no chemical reactions take place, and air can carry just as much gasoline vapor as can natural gas." Bulletin 148, p. 12.

"The air in passing through the oil sand picks up and carries with it some of the lighter constituents of the oil, that is—gasoline." Bulletin 120, p. 59.

"A promising field for the absorption process lies in the treatment of gas from oil wells producing from a sand into which air has been forced under pressure to increase the oil production. This gas, as it flows from the wells, can be treated by the absorption process and the gasoline it contains extracted." Bulletin 120, p. 66.

2. 75 W.Va. 602, 84 S.E. 948, and see Summers, Oil and Gas, § 592.

§ 7.2　ROYALTY AND OTHER CLAUSES　345

The view that casinghead gas and gasoline constitute part of the oil is the law of Texas and, apparently, the view of Louisiana, at least as to the gasoline.

In Wemple v. Producers Oil Co.,[3] the lease provided for ⅛ royalty on oil and a flat rate of $200 per year for each well from which gas was produced and used off the premises. Gasoline was extracted from the casinghead gas, and it was held that royalty was properly payable under the oil clause of the lease. The court, however, also indicated that if any residue gas was used off the premises, royalty would be payable under the flat rate gas clause, contra to the Locke case. The court stressed that at the time the lease was drawn up, in 1914, the parties had no knowledge that gasoline extracted from the casinghead gas might be the most valuable product produced from the lease. Therefore, there was no intent that extracted gasoline would be paid for under the flat rate gas clause. Although the case has been interpreted as classifying casinghead gasoline as oil, the result is also squarely bottomed upon the prevention of unjust enrichment.

The Texas case of Livingston Oil Corporation v. Waggoner,[4] based upon the authority of both the Locke and Wemple cases, concludes that casinghead gas, which was sold to a processing plant at 10 cents per mcf, was includable in the oil royalty clause. Although the lessee contended that the payment upon the oil production also included payment for the casinghead gas produced and therefore no liability existed for an additional payment, the court held that royalty was payable separately upon the sale of the casinghead gas.

The Oklahoma courts have taken a different position, that casinghead gas is neither oil nor gas under the royalty clauses of an oil and gas lease. Therefore, where not expressly mentioned in the royalty clauses, it is not covered by the lease. The case of Hammett Oil Co. v. Gypsy Oil Co.,[5] is illustrative of this view. Here oil was found and produced. In 1913 the lessee entered into a contract for the manufacture of gasoline from casinghead gas. The lessors contended that casinghead gas and gasoline were not covered by the lease and still belonged to the lessors. The court sustained the lessors. The court alluded to the fact that at the time the transactions took place, 1913, the parties did not understand that casinghead gas from an oil well was either oil or gas. The lessors could recover for the value of the casinghead gas or gasoline minus the reasonable expenses of production. This apparently is the present view of the Oklahoma courts.[6]

3. 145 La. 1031, 83 So. 232.

4. Tex.Civ.App., 273 S.W. 903; for an example of a casinghead gas sales contract see Saulsbury Oil Co. v. Phillips Petroleum Co., C.A.5th, 142 F.2d 27, cert. denied 323 U.S. 727, 65 S.Ct. 62, 89 L.Ed. 584.

5. 95 Okl. 235, 218 P. 501, 34 A.L.R. 275. The theory of recovery is that the lessee is a good-faith converter.

6. Ludey v. Pure Oil Co., 157 Okl. 1, 11 P.2d 102. Broswood Oil Co. v. Sand Springs Home, 178 Okl. 550, 62 P.2d 1004.

It can be seen that in cases involving leases that did not mention casinghead gas or gasoline, but did contain flat rate gas clauses under which the lessees based payment, the courts prevented unjust enrichment by using two basic approaches. The courts either classified the products as being within the oil clause or as not being covered by the lease.

(B) Express Clause Provision

The second category of cases involves a lease royalty clause, in addition to clauses relating to oil and gas, that provides for a flat rate payment for "gas produced from an oil well," or "casinghead gas sold or used off the premises," or some variation thereof. The pertinent question involved is whether payment under such clause also passes title to the lessee to the "wet" elements in the casinghead gas without the need for further payment. Very few cases are found in this area. It would seem to be the majority construction that payment for the gas also included payment for all constituent elements thereof as it came out of the well.

In the Oklahoma case of Mussellem v. Magnolia Petroleum Co.,[7] the lease contained an additional lease clause that provided for a payment of $50 per year for "gas produced from an oil well and used off the premises." The lessee paid the designated sum for casinghead gas and then removed gasoline on the leased premises. The lessor, trying to come within the purview of the Oklahoma cases holding that casinghead gas not provided for in the lease was not covered thereby, argued that where the lessee processed the gas on the leased premises, it was not "used off the premises." The court re-

---

7. 107 Okl. 183, 231 P. 526. Cf. Southland Royalty Co. v. Pan American Petroleum Corp., Tex., 378 S.W.2d 50.

Barby v. Cabot Corp., C.A.10th, 465 F.2d 11: (no additional royalty due on processed value of liquids where clause provided for "market value *at the wellhead* or if used off the premises market value *at the well*.") (emphasis supplied) The court held royalty payable upon the best price for the whole gas stream sold at the wellhead, which included the unprocessed value of the liquids in the gas.

Consistent with construction of the Mussellem case is Lackey v. Ohio Oil Co., C.A.10th, 138 F.2d 449, which interpreted the phrase "used off the premises" as meaning appropriated to a purpose foreign to utilization for development of the lease, whether by lessee or another. Contrary to the interpretation of the Texas court in the Southland case (see discussion in main text at note 8, § 7.1, supra) this would include sales of gas.

The clause "used off the premises," came into use when no market for natural gas existed. It allowed the payment of royalty when gas was not used for development of the lease. In light of this historical development, the view of the Texas court in the Southland case seems expedient rather than definitive in its construction that the clause does not include gas sold. Also see: Kingery v. Continental Oil Co., D.C.Tex., 434 F.Supp. 349 (sale 3½ miles away was a sale "off the premises").

Interestingly, in Butler v. Exxon Corp., Tex.Civ.App., 559 S.W.2d 410, royalty on gas "sold at the wells" included deliveries made over the lease line. Also see Skaggs v. Heard, D.C.Tex., 172 F.Supp. 813.

The definitive statement of the Texas court as to the meaning of "off the premises" is found in the case of Exxon Corp. v. Middleton, Tex., 613 S.W.2d 240, on remand Tex.Civ.App., 619 S.W.2d 477. "Premises" was defined as the land described in the lease. "Sold off the premises" is gas sold outside the leased land. See discussion in § 7.4, infra.

jected the argument on the ground that any use of the gas not in the development of the lease was a use "off the premises." Basically, the lessee should not have to pay royalty upon petroleum products used in the operation and development of the lease; therefore, any use foreign to the development of the premises was a use "off the premises."

As to payment for liquid components in the gas, in an opinion that discusses the nature of the components in the reservoir, the court came to the conclusion that, upon compliance with the clause, title to the casinghead gas, which by definition contains "wet" elements, passed to the lessee, and no further royalty obligation existed as to the gasoline produced.

In Texas a similar rationale is found in the case of Magnolia Petroleum Co. v. Connellee.[8] In this case the wording of the clause was that the lessee pay $25 per year for "casinghead gas sold or used off the premises." Again, the lessee manufactured large quantities of gasoline from casinghead gas and in turn paid the lessor $25 under the above clause. In holding that no additional royalty was payable for the gasoline extracted, the court stated that it was the common understanding of the parties that the lessee, upon such payment, would acquire title to all casinghead gas as it came from the well and that it included all constituent elements and wet elements. The constituent element theory has also had application to wet elements produced from gas wells and would seem to be the better constructional view.

However, some authority exists to the contrary. In the case of Gilbreath v. States Oil Corporation,[9] an additional royalty clause was inserted in the lease that stated that the lessee would pay $25 per year for "gas produced from an oil well." Following the Louisiana case of Wemple v. Producers Oil Company,[10] that the parties' lack of knowledge precluded an intent that the above clause would apply to other than gas used for fuel and heat, the court held, in effect, that casinghead gas and gasoline extracted therefrom was not covered by the clause. Being part of the oil, royalty was payable under the oil royalty clause of $1/8$ of production. It should be noted that, although the same argument was made in the Musselem case, cited above, the court held that such lack of understanding was immaterial and that it would not change the contract of the parties.

A similar rationale to the Gilbreath case is found in the Texas case of Reynolds v. McMan Oil Company.[11] Here the clause was not materially different from the one in Magnolia v. Connellee, which had been decided earlier. The clause provided that lessee would pay $100 per year for "gas produced from any oil or gas well and used off the

---

8. Tex.Com.App., 11 S.W.2d 158.

9. C.A.5th, 4 F.2d 232.

10. 145 La. 1031, 83 So. 232; and see note 3 supra.

11. Tex.Com.App., 11 S.W.2d 778, rehearing denied 14 S.W.2d 819.

premises." The lessee again manufactured large quantities of gasoline from casinghead gas. However, the court held that the lessee was obligated to pay an additional royalty on the gasoline extracted under the oil royalty clause. In reaching the decision that the quoted clause did not cover the gasoline extracted, the court inquired as to the understanding and knowledge of the parties concerning the use of casinghead gas at the time the lease was executed. It was found that it was not within the intention of the parties that the clause would fix title to gas produced from an oil well for purposes other than for light and fuel.

The court attempted to distinguish the Reynolds case from the Connellee case on the basis of differences in the wording of the clauses; however, it would seem that little difference exists. The court also rather lamely tried to find that the lessee's use of the gas was not "off the premises" and, therefore, the clause was inapplicable. Some writers have stated that there is a square conflict in the Texas decisions between the Connellee and Reynolds cases; however, the court in both opinions states that casinghead gas is part of the oil. They differ on the applicability of the quoted clauses, which seem nearly identical in purport. The Connellee case applies the clause, and Reynolds does not. The non-applicability in Reynolds seems not to be predicated upon a different conceptual basis as to the nature of casinghead gas and gasoline, but upon the intent of the parties, as shown from the surrounding circumstances, as to applicability of the clause. Reynolds does not reach the question of whether, if the clause were applicable, gasoline extracted thereunder would be considered a constituent element of the casinghead gas.

Where the lease clause provides for a royalty upon casinghead gas and casinghead gasoline based upon the value of a fractional part of that sold or used off the premises, the conflict of the older cases [12] caused by the lessee acquiring gasoline of great value by the payment of flat rate gas royalties, does not occur. The consideration here involved is the rate at which the royalty should be paid, and is discussed in a later section.

§ 7.3 Royalty on Liquid Components Produced From a Gas Well—Condensate and Distillate

Royalty on condensate or distillate, liquids that are extracted from gas wells, are payable under the gas royalty clause of the lease. By the majority view royalty payments for gas will include the condensate, and no further royalty liability will exist upon the extraction of condensate from the gas either by the lessee or third-party processors.

Under the normal lease royalty clause on gas, royalty is paid on the basis of a fractional portion of the value [1] of the gas produced.

---

12. Katschor v. Eason Oil Co., 178 Okl. 634, 63 P.2d 977.

1. Actually the phraseology by which "value" is defined in the clause differs widely from form to form. Variations are found, such as "market value," "market price," "proceeds," "price received," etc. See § 7.4, infra.

§ 7.3 ROYALTY AND OTHER CLAUSES 349

As discussed in the preceding section, early gas royalty clauses provided for a flat rate payment for gas produced. However, some gas wells also produce large quantities of fluids that may be extracted from the gas, either at the well or by more sophisticated processes. Such liquid is called condensate or distillate. Actually, in chemical composition it is identical with gasoline extracted from casinghead gas. In this section the discussion is directed to the payment of royalties upon liquids or condensate from gas wells. At times it may be difficult to determine whether a well should be classified as either a gas or oil well, and the classification of the state conservation agency for proration purposes may not be binding in this regard.

In the foregoing section, it was concluded that where no clause was present in the lease, casinghead gas and gasoline were classified as oil, and royalty was payable under the oil royalty clause, in the majority of jurisdictions. This has not generally been true as to condensate from gas wells. The majority of the decisions have concluded, upon one basis or the other, that the liquid components of gas production, where no clause is present in the lease directing payment of royalties upon such products, are part of the gas and payable, if at all, under the gas royalty clause.

Being classifiable as gas, the further question remains whether the payment of either a flat royalty [2] or fractional portion [3] of gas production will also serve to satisfy a royalty obligation upon the condensate extracted therefrom, either by the lessee, or by a processor to whom the lessee sells the gas and from whom he receives payment both for the gas and the condensate removed.

The landmark cases, which have been followed in other jurisdictions, are the Texas cases of Humble Oil & Refining Company v. Poe [4] and Lone Star Gas Co. v. Stine.[5] These cases applied the approach of the earlier case of Magnolia Petroleum Co. v. Connellee,[6] which dealt with casinghead gas and gasoline extracted therefrom. It was held that upon the payment for gas under the gas royalty clause, the lessee acquired title to the gas as it came from the well, together with and including all the constituent elements thereof. As such constituent elements included the condensate, a further payment of royalty on the extracted condensate was not necessary. These cases have been applied whether or not the extraction was done by the lessee [7] or by a third party processor.[8] It also has been held that

---

2. Coyle v. Louisiana Gas & Fuel Co., 175 La. 990, 144 So. 737; Humble Oil & Refining Co. v. Poe, Tex.Com.App., 29 S.W.2d 1019; Lone Star Gas Co. v. Harris, Tex.Civ.App., 45 S.W.2d 664, rehearing denied 45 S.W.2d 998.

3. Wall v. United Gas Public Service Co., 178 La. 908, 152 So. 561; O'Neal v. Union Producing Co., D.C.La., 57 F.Supp. 440; McCoy v. United States Gas Public Service Co., D.C.La., 57 F.Supp. 444; Maddox v. The Texas Co., D.C.Tex., 150 F.Supp. 175.

4. Tex.Com.App., 29 S.W.2d 1019.

5. Tex.Com.App., 41 S.W.2d 48, 82 A.L.R. 1299.

6. Tex.Com.App., 11 S.W.2d 158.

7. Wall v. United Gas Public Service Co., 178 La. 908, 152 So. 561; O'Neal v. Union Producing Co., D.C.La., 57 F.Supp. 440; McCoy v. United States Gas Public

---

8. See note 8 on page 350.

condensate royalty will not be payable under a clause in the lease that provides for payment for gas produced from an oil well.[9] The same result has been reached where the royalty clause expressly included the royalty payment upon condensate as being included within the gas royalty clause.[10]

One case that reached a contrary result is the case of Coyle v. Louisiana Gas & Fuel Company.[11] This lease contained a clause providing for $1/8$ royalty upon oil, gas produced from "gas only" wells, and gas from oil wells. The lessor contended that he was entitled to additional royalty upon the condensate produced from gas that was sold to a third party processor. The lessee was paid both for the gas and the condensate removed. The court held that the lessor was entitled to share in the proceeds from the extracted condensate. The rationale of the case is much like that used in the early cases that classified casinghead gas as oil to prevent unjust enrichment of the lessee. In the Coyle case the court stressed that the parties, at the time of the execution of the lease, had no knowledge or appreciation of the value of condensate that could later be extracted from the gas. The court held that if the condensate was not regarded as being covered by the lease the lessee was not entitled to it, and if covered by the lease the lessee was obligated to pay the lessor $1/8$ of the value of the condensate less the proportionate costs of processing. It would seem that the rationale of the case is not followed in Louisiana in the later cases.[12]

It is obvious that in dealing with casinghead gas and gasoline, distillate, and condensate, the careful draftsman will expressly include

Service Co., D.C.La., 57 F.Supp. 444; Humble Oil & Refining Co. v. Poe, Tex. Com.App., 29 S.W.2d 1019; Lone Star Gas Co. v. Stine, Tex.Com.App., 41 S.W.2d 48, 82 A.L.R. 1299.

8. Freeland v. Sun Oil Co., C.A.5th, 277 F.2d 154, cert. denied D.C., 364 U.S. 826, 81 S.Ct. 64, 5 L.Ed.2d 55; Lone Star Gas Co. v. Harris, Tex.Civ.App., 45 S.W.2d 664, rehearing denied 45 S.W.2d 998; Maddox v. The Texas Co., D.C.Tex., 150 F.Supp. 175. However, in both the Freeland and Maddox cases dicta was contained to the effect that if condensate could be removed by drips it would be deemed to be "oil".

9. O'Neal v. Union Producing Co., D.C.La., 57 F.Supp. 440; McCoy v. United States Gas Public Service Co., D.C. La., 57 F.Supp. 444; Lone Star Gas Co. v. Harris, Tex.Civ.App., 45 S.W.2d 664, rehearing denied 45 S.W.2d 998.

10. Roy v. Arkansas-Louisiana Gas Co., 200 La. 233, 7 So.2d 895, where the royalty clause on gas reads as follows:

"To pay lessor at the rate of Two Hundred ($200.00) Dollars per year * * * for each well producing gas (whether casinghead gas or otherwise) while such gas is not being utilized or sold off the premises * * * but during the time such gas shall be utilized or sold off the premises * * * shall be paid one-half of one cent ($1/2$ of 1¢) per thousand cubic feet of such gas production, including gasoline, whether recovered by drips, absorption, plant or otherwise * * *."

11. 175 La. 990, 144 So. 737; other cases containing express clauses are Freeland v. Sun Oil Co., C.A.5th, 277 F.2d 154, cert. denied 364 U.S. 826, 81 S.Ct. 64, 5 L.Ed.2d 55, and Read v. Britain, Tex., 422 S.W.2d 902.

12. Wall v. United Gas Public Service Co., 178 La. 908, 152 So. 561; Roy v. Arkansas-Louisiana Gas Co., 200 La. 233, 7 So.2d 895; O'Neal v. Union Producing Co., D.C.La., 57 F.Supp. 440; McCoy v. United States Gas Public Service Co., D.C.La., 57 F.Supp. 444. The Roy case contains an excellent discussion of the nature of condensate production and of the products extracted.

provisions spelling out the royalty liability of the lessee in the various situations.[13]

§ 7.4 Compensation for Royalty Based Upon "Market Value," "Market Price," and "Proceeds"

Where gas royalty is computed upon "market price at the well," proof of comparable sales in the field will establish such price, and opinion evidence is irrelevant. Where no market exists in the field, in absence of unlawful combination or suppression of price, royalty will be computed upon receipts from the marketing outlet for the products less the costs and expenses of marketing and transportation. Where the royalty obligation is predicated upon "market value at the well" the courts have reached virtually the same results as where based upon market price.

Royalty payable upon the "proceeds" of the sale of gas will be computed on the basis of aggregate gross receipts from all products less the costs of marketing and transportation. The presence of actual sales in the field is immaterial.

Although the courts seem agreed that the lessee should not have the exclusive burden of expense of transportation to a distant market, the cases are in conflict as to the division between lessee and lessor of the costs of ordinary market preparation, such as compression and dehydration.

In the situation where gas production has been sold by the lessee under a long-term contract of sale and the gas royalty clause provides for the payment based upon "market value" of the gas, the majority of jurisdictions impose a royalty liability based upon the sale price of current sales in the area. This is true even though current sales are for a higher price than that provided for in the contract of sale and the lessee is unable to acquire a price increase for the sale of gas.

The jurisdictions differ as to what constitutes comparable sales. Although some will look at all sales in the area, a majority of jurisdictions will not treat sales between regulated and nonregulated markets as comparable.

At least one jurisdiction, Oklahoma, has held that the price received for sales of gas under an arm's-length long-term gas sales contract is "market value" for such gas sales.

(A) General

As mentioned in previous sections, royalty clauses on gas, and sometimes on casinghead gas, usually provide for the payment of a money sum to the royalty owner, rather than payment by delivery of the products in kind. Substantial differences in language are found defining the basis upon which payment should be made. Variations include: "sales made by the lessee," "rate received by lessee,"[1] "mar-

---

13. See clause note 6, § 7.1, supra.

1. Skaggs v. Heard, D.C.Tex., 172 F.Supp. 813; Cotiga Development Co. v. United Fuel Gas Co., 147 W.Va. 484, 128 S.E.2d 626.

ket price,"[2] "market price at the well,"[3] "market value,"[4] "market value at the well,"[5] "proceeds from the sale,"[6] "proceeds at the well,"[7] "net proceeds at the well,"[8] "gross income received."[9] Although superficially similar, the variations in wording produce dissimilar results.

Before proceeding to a detailed examination of the case law on the subject, some general observations may be made. Clauses that define the royalty in terms of a "market *price* at the well" or the "*price* received by the lessee" denote a royalty return based upon actual sales in the vicinity of the well. However, where the terminology is "market *value*," a distinction is made between actual sales in the vicinity and market value that can be established by opinion evidence.[10] Although market value may turn out to be close to actual sales in the vicinity, theoretically such sales are merely one factor to be included in the determination. Finally, the concept of "proceeds" looks to the receipts from the sales of the petroleum products, wherever made. Although all definitions may be subject to adjustment, due to the circumstances existing, it may be seen that the basic concepts are not identical.

(B) Market Price

The first cases to be examined are those dealing with clauses that look to a market price at the well. Where there are comparable sales of similar products in the field, such sales will determine the rate upon which royalty is computed.[11] Price can only be proved by actual

---

2. Wall v. United Gas Public Service Co., 178 La. 908, 152 So. 561.

3. Clear Creek Oil & Gas Co. v. Bushmiaer, 165 Ark. 303, 264 S.W. 830; Sartor v. United Carbon Co., 183 La. 287, 163 So. 103; Tyson v. Surf Oil Co., 195 La. 248, 196 So. 336; Shamrock Oil & Gas Corp. v. Coffee, C.A.5th, 140 F.2d 409; Texas Oil & Gas Corp. v. Vela, Tex., 429 S.W.2d 866; Phillips Petroleum Co. v. Bynum, C.A.5th, 155 F.2d 196, cert. denied 329 U.S. 714, 67 S.Ct. 44, 91 L.Ed. 620.

4. Armstrong v. Skelly Oil Co., C.A.5th, 55 F.2d 1066 (second case).

5. Parnell, Inc. v. Giller, Trustee, 237 Ark. 267, 372 S.W.2d 627; Freeland v. Sun Oil Co., C.A.5th, 277 F.2d 154, cert. denied 364 U.S. 826, 81 S.Ct. 64, 5 L.Ed. 2d 55; Katschor v. Eason Oil Co., 178 Okl. 634, 63 P.2d 977; LeCuno Oil Co. v. Smith, Tex.Civ.App., 306 S.W.2d 190; Phillips Petroleum Co. v. Ochsner, C.A. 5th, 146 F.2d 138.

6. Molter v. Lewis, 156 Kan. 544, 134 P.2d 404; Matzen v. Hugoton Production Co., 182 Kan. 456, 321 P.2d 576, 73 A.L.R.2d 1045; Warfield Natural Gas Co. v. Allen, 261 Ky. 840, 88 S.W.2d 989; Ladd v. Upham, Tex.Civ.App., 58 S.W.2d 1037, affirmed 128 Tex. 14, 95 S.W.2d 365.

7. Gilmore v. Superior Oil Co., 192 Kan. 388, 388 P.2d 602; Schupbach v. Continental Oil Co., 193 Kan. 401, 394 P.2d 1; Ashland Oil & Refining Co. v. Staats, Inc., D.C.Kan., 271 F.Supp. 571.

8. Natural Gas Distributing Corp. v. Williams, Tex.Civ.App., 355 S.W.2d 194; Phillips Petroleum Co. v. Johnson, C.A. 5th, 155 F.2d 185.

9. La Fitte Co. v. United Fuel Gas Co., C.A.6th, 284 F.2d 845.

10. The stated distinction between "market price" and "market value" is probably more theoretical than real, and many courts seemingly make no distinction. However, see Swain v. Santa Fe Pacific Railroad Co., 24 Ariz.App. 349, 538 P.2d 1150.

11. Swain v. Santa Fe Railway Co., 24 Ariz.App. 349, 538 P.2d 1150 (actual transactions in area). Wall v. United Gas Public Service Co., 178 La. 908, 152 So. 561; Sartor v. United Carbon Co., 183 La.

transactions, if such exist. It is not based upon market value, fair market value, or reasonable worth.[12] Price relates to actual sales; value or worth relates to opinion. Where comparable sales exist in the field, market price will not be based on a reconstructed sales price at the well by virtue of the gross-receipts-less-expenses method.[13] Nor will it necessarily be determined by the contract price for which the gas or other products are sold, if such contract price does not reflect the current market price.[14] Non-comparable sales will not serve as a basis for royalty payments,[15] nor will a field price that is artificially set.

It has been held, however, that where no market price exists in the field, in absence of unlawful combination or suppression of market price such sales may constitute the market price upon which royalty is payable.[16] In effect, this is a re-creation of a market price at the well. The cases have held that where no market can be shown at

287, 163 So. 103; Texas Oil & Gas Corp. v. Vela, Tex., 429 S.W.2d 866; Shamrock Oil & Gas Corp. v. Coffee, C.A.5th, 140 F.2d 409. But cf. Cotiga Development Co. v. United Fuel Gas Co., 147 W.Va. 484, 128 S.E.2d 626, which provided for royalty computed upon the rate received by lessee. It was held lessee was in error basing royalty upon the general area rate or field price rather than upon amounts actually received.

12. Shamrock Oil & Gas Corp. v. Coffee, C.A.5th, 140 F.2d 409. (Where actual sales exist opinion evidence is irrelevant.)

13. Wall v. United Gas Public Service Co., 178 La. 908, 152 So. 561; Johnson v. Jernigan, Okl., 475 P.2d 396.

14. Texas Oil & Gas Corp. v. Vela, Tex., 429 S.W.2d 866; Foster v. Atlantic Refining Co., C.A.5th, 329 F.2d 485. In each case the court held the lessee was obliged to pay gas royalty on the basis of current market price in the field, rather than upon amounts received under long-term contracts of sale. The market price had greatly appreciated from the time the contracts were executed.

In both the Vela and the Foster cases the courts emphasized that financial hardship of the lessee caused by such lease interpretaton was not a factor to be taken into account by the court. The basic question involves the situation of the lessee selling gas under long-term sales contracts. Many of these contracts are for periods of time of twenty years. Where the gas is under the jurisdiction of the Federal Power Commission prospects of substantial price increases are slim. The lessee is caught in an economic trap. It is a fact that gas companies have spent tremendous sums in developing gas fields to create markets, which has caused a large increase in the value of gas. At the time of the entering into the contracts in the Vela and Foster cases, gas had relatively little value.

Under the contracts and the effect of the above opinions the lessors will benefit from a situation that has come about by the action of the gas producers, but in which they will not share. It is no realistic answer to say that the lessee is bound by the letter of the contract.

Since the first edition of the Hornbook, increased litigation has occurred in the area of royalty payment liability under the market price or value clause where long term gas sales contracts exist. See expanded discussion § 7.4(E), infra.

15. Phillips Petroleum Co. v. Bynum, C.A.5th, 155 F.2d 196, cert. denied 329 U.S. 714, 67 S.Ct. 44, 91 L.Ed. 620; cf. Sartor v. United Carbon Co., 183 La. 287, 163 So. 103.

Also see discussion of comparable sales between regulated and nonregulated markets in § 7.4(E), infra.

16. Clear Creek Oil & Gas Co. v. Bushmiaer, 165 Ark. 303, 264 S.W. 830; Wall v. United Gas Public Service Co., 178 La. 908, 152 So. 561; Phillips Petroleum Co. v. Bynum, C.A.5th, 155 F.2d 196, cert. denied 329 U.S. 714, 67 S.Ct. 44, 91 L.Ed. 620. Some confusion seems to exist as to the area in which lack of market price must be shown. In Sartor v. United Carbon Co., 183 La. 287, 163 So. 103, it was held the showing need not be made to the entire parish, and in Phillips Petroleum Co. v. Bynum, to the county, but not to the entire field.

the well royalty will be based on the price received at a distant point, less the costs and expenses of transportation. Such costs of transportation will be shared by the lessor, as no duty exists upon the lessee to construct facilities to transport products to a distant market.[17] Although the cases are not altogether clear, it would seem that it would be improper to use the receipts-less-expenses method to determine market price in the field, where comparable sales of such products are made in the field.

An alternative to the receipts-less-expenses approach, where no market price is shown to exist in the field, would be to allow evidence of fair or reasonable market value in the field to be used as a basis for royalty computation.[18]

(C) Market Value

In contrast to the clauses that provide for market price are those that provide for royalty computation based upon market value. Market value is determined at the well. As mentioned above, value is distinguishable from price. The price of a product may or may not reflect the intrinsic value of it. It also may be that a product may have different values for differing uses, but only one market. Generally, value is established by opinion evidence concerned with comparable sales and intrinsic uses of the product or like products. However, it appears that where actual sales of gas or petroleum products exist in the field, the cases treat market value the same as market price, and generally indicate that an actual market in the field will be practically conclusive evidence of value.[19]

In Phillips Petroleum Co. v. Ochsner,[20] the lessee was taking gas from plaintiff's wells and trading it with the pipeline company for equal volumes of gas in another party of the county. The gas that the lessee acquired in trade was used for processing for removal of condensate in his plant, and the gas of the plaintiff's well was actually sold for heat and light purposes by the pipeline. Plaintiff sued to have royalties based upon the market value of gas for heat and light.

---

17. Vedder Petroleum Corp. v. Lambert Lands Co., 50 Cal.App.2d 102, 122 P.2d 600; Matzen v. Hugoton Production Co., 182 Kan. 456, 321 P.2d 576, 73 A.L.R.2d 1045; Reed v. Hackworth, Ky., 287 S.W.2d 912; Wall v. United Gas Public Service Co., 178 La. 908, 152 So. 561; Johnson v. Jernigan, Okl., 475 P.2d 396; Freeland v. Sun Oil Co., C.A.5th, 277 F.2d 154, cert. denied 364 U.S. 826, 81 S.Ct. 64, 5 L.Ed.2d 55; LeCuno Oil Co. v. Smith, Tex.Civ.App., 306 S.W.2d 190.

18. Texas Oil & Gas Corp. v. Vela, Tex., 429 S.W.2d 866; Brown, Gas Royalty Provision and the Rights of Lessors and Lessees with Respect to Sale of Gas, 30 N.D.L.Rev. 5.

19. Phillips Petroleum Co. v. Ochsner, C.A.5th, 146 F.2d 138; cf. Shamrock Oil & Gas Corp. v. Coffee, C.A.5th, 140 F.2d 409; Phillips Petroleum Co. v. Bynum, C.A.5th, 155 F.2d 196, cert. denied 329 U.S. 714, 67 S.Ct. 44, 91 L.Ed. 620.

Lippert v. Angle, 211 Kan. 695, 508 P.2d 920 (proof of market value); Lightcap v. Mobil Oil Corp., 221 Kan. 448, 562 P.2d 1 (market value equated to "proceeds" where no free market exists and amounts received set by FPC regulation. Excellent review of cases dealing with market value, market price, and proceeds).

20. C.A.5th, 146 F.2d 138.

§ 7.4   ROYALTY AND OTHER CLAUSES   355

The court held that there was a market at the mouth of the well for gas sales for extraction of condensate, but not for heat and light purposes. Although opinion evidence could have established a market value for heat and light purposes, the court held that the value was controlled by the market that in fact existed. The only market that existed at the mouth of the well was for gasoline extraction purposes.

Where no market exists at the mouth of the well, the market value cases also re-create a value thereby computing receipts less expenses of processing and transportation.[21] It would seem, then, that although the computation of royalty based upon market price or market value at the well theoretically differ, as a practical matter the courts have reached almost identical results in either instance.

(D) Proceeds

The third group of cases comprises those that attempt to set forth a royalty formula based on "proceeds." Phraseology may differ as to whether the proceeds are to be those "from the sale" of the petroleum products or "at the well." Some clauses talk of "net" proceeds. However, it appears that the differences in terminology are not emphasized and that the royalty computation will generally be made on the basis of the aggregate sales price ultimately received from the separate sales of the constituent products less the cost of marketing, transportation, and treatment.[22] As usually applied, actual sales in the field or other evidence of market value in the field is irrelevant.

---

21. Parnell, Inc. v. Giller, Trustee, 237 Ark. 267, 372 S.W.2d 627; LeCuno Oil Co. v. Smith, Tex.Civ.App., 306 S.W.2d 190. Cf. Freeland v. Sun Oil Co., C.A. 5th, 277 F.2d 154, cert. denied 364 U.S. 826, 81 S.Ct. 64, 5 L.Ed.2d 55; Katschor v. Eason Oil Co., 178 Okl. 634, 63 P.2d 977; Armstrong v. Skelly Oil Co., C.A. 5th, 55 F.2d 1066 (second case). In Freeland v. Sun Oil Co, C.A.5th, 277 F.2d 154, cert. denied 364 U.S. 826, 81 S.Ct. 64, 5 L.Ed.2d 55, the court stated:

"It stands for the proposition that in determining market value costs which are essential to make a commodity worth anything or worth more must be borne proportionately by those who benefit. To put it another way: in the analytical process of reconstructing a market value where none otherwise exists with sufficient definiteness, all increase in the ultimate sales value attributable to the expense incurred in transporting and processing the commodity must be deducted. The royalty owner shares only in what is left over, whether stated in terms of cash or an end product.

"In this sense he bears his proportionate part of that cost, but not because the obligation (or expense) of production rests on him. Rather, it is because that is the way in which Louisiana law arrives at the value of the gas at the moment it seeks to escape from the wellhead."

22. Molter v. Lewis, 156 Kan. 544, 134 P.2d 404; Matzen v. Hugoton Production Co., 182 Kan. 456, 321 P.2d 576, 73 A.L.R.2d 1045; Ashland Oil & Refining Co. v. Staats, Inc., D.C.Kan., 271 F.Supp. 571; Natural Gas Distributing Corp. v. Williams, Tex.Civ.App., 355 S.W.2d 194; Phillips Petroleum Co. v. Johnson, C.A. 5th, 155 F.2d 185; Holbein v. Austral Oil Co., C.A.5th, 609 F.2d 206. However, compare Warfield Natural Gas Co. v. Allen, 261 Ky. 840, 88 S.W.2d 989; Reed v. Hackworth, Ky.App., 287 S.W.2d 912; La Fitte Co. v. United Fuel Gas Co., C.A.6th, 284 F.2d 845, which hold if the lease is silent as to the place and price of sales, that such sales are at the mouth of the well; hence, lessee could pay on the basis of field rate or price. The cases seem clearly erroneous.

Also see West v. Alpar Resources, Inc., N.D., 298 N.W.2d 484; Ladd v. Upham, Tex.Civ.App., 58 S.W.2d 1037, affirmed Com.App., 128 Tex. 14, 95 S.W.2d 365,

(E) Market Price or Value Royalty Clauses and the Long-Term Gas Sales Contract Problem

As mentioned above, the courts have encountered increased litigation in the situation where gas is being sold by the lessee under a long-term contract of sale and royalty is to be paid under the lease on the basis of market price or market value. Since the case of Phillips Petroleum Co v. The State of Wisconsin [23] (sometimes called Phillips I), in June 1954, the price of gas sold in interstate commerce for resale has been regulated. Regulation was by the Federal Power Commission (FPC) until October 1, 1977, when it was superseded by the Federal Energy Regulatory Commission (FERC). From the 1950's the price being paid for gas in the intrastate market rose steadily, and by the 1970's greatly exceeded the price in the interstate market.

No problem existed in connection with the payment of royalty on gas sales under a lease that provided for royalty payment based upon the proceeds or amount received. In this case the amounts received by the lessee were the basis for royalty payments.

The situation was far different where the lease provided for royalty payments based upon market price or value. As discussed above, market price or value is determined from actual sales in the field or area. Where current sales for gas in the field or area exceeded the maximum price provided for in long-term gas sales contracts, was the lessor entitled to royalty payments based on the current price, or only on amounts received by the lessee under the gas sales contracts? The problem was not confined to interstate versus intrastate prices, but also extended to intrastate sales under long-term sales contracts versus intrastate current gas sales.

The landmark case is that of Texas Oil & Gas Corp. v. Vela,[24] a Texas decision in 1968, which involved only intrastate sales. In this

---

and concurring opinion in Matzen v. Hugoton Production Co., 182 Kan. 456, 321 P.2d 576, 73 A.L.R.2d 1045, to the effect that "proceeds" means gross receipts without deduction of expenses.

In Phillips Petroleum Co. v. Johnson, C.A.5th, 155 F.2d 185, the royalty clause used two different bases for computation: (a) "net proceeds" from gas sales and (b) if "used," but not sold, "fair market value." It was held that neither commingling of gas with other gas or separating out condensate by drip separators was a "use".

Professor Sneed, in "Value of Lessor's Share of Production where Gas Only is Produced," 25 Tex.L.Rev. 641, discussed the conclusion in Saulsbury Oil Co. v. Phillips Petroleum Co., C.A.5th, 142 F.2d 27, cert. denied 323 U.S. 727, 65 S.Ct. 62, 89 L.Ed. 584, that operating expenses, direct general expenses, retirements, ad valorem taxes, other direct taxes, Federal income taxes, capital stock taxes, social security taxes, unemployment taxes, indirect overhead adjusted to a current basis and depreciation were items to be proportionately deducted from the lessors' share and stated that it created an accounting problem which is staggering. Also see Huie, Walker and Woodward, Cases in Oil and Gas, pp. 603–606 and 612–613.

Also see:

Waechter v. Amoco Production Co., 217 Kan. 489, 537 P.2d 228 (complex case stating, in effect, that proceeds are determined by price set by final government order); Lightcap v. Mobil Oil Corp., 221 Kan. 448, 562 P.2d 1, footnote 19 supra. Johnson v. Jernigan, Okl., 475 P.2d 396 (allowing lessee deduction of pipeline transportation charges).

23. 347 U.S. 672, 74 S.Ct. 794, 98 L.Ed. 1035, rehearing denied 348 U.S. 851, 75 S.Ct. 17, 18, 99 L.Ed. 670.

24. Tex., 429 S.W.2d 866.

§ 7.4   ROYALTY AND OTHER CLAUSES   357

case the lease provided for gas royalty of " * * * one-eighth of the market price at the wells of the amount so sold or used." Gas was being sold by the lessee under a gas sales contract that provided for 2.3 cents per Mcf, whereas current prices being paid for gas in the field ranged from 13 cents to 17 cents per Mcf.

The court held for the lessor, and found that the royalty obligation was to be based upon the current price for gas in the field and not the price being received under the gas sales contract. The court specifically stated that the sales of gas occurred upon each delivery under the contract and not at the time the contract was executed. Proof of market price or value was to be made from comparison with comparable sales of gas, which were defined as sales comparable in time, quality, and availability to marketing outlets. The case has been greatly criticized on the ground that under an irrevocable long-term gas sales contract, the contract is the market.

At least one jurisdiction has avoided the Pandora's box opened by the Vela case. Oklahoma, in the case of Tara Petroleum Corp. v. Hughey,[25] held that under a market price royalty clause, where the contract has been entered into at arm's length, the contract price is the market.

In jurisdictions following the Vela approach several problems have emerged. One problem is whether the market price or value clause or the proceeds or amount realized clause applies, where they are both present in the same royalty provision. These clauses were involved in the Texas case of Exxon v. Middleton.[26] In this case the lease contained the following royalty clause provisions:

[1] " * * * on gas * * * *sold or used off the premises* * * * the *market value* at the well of one-eighth of the gas so sold or used."

and

Where the FPC has decreed higher royalty payments in the Vela situation, due to higher price in the field over the dedication price, such increase may be included as a component of producer's cost in application for a higher ceiling gas price to be paid, i.e., flow-through of incremental royalty costs to customer. Pennzoil Producing Co. v. FPC, C.A.5th, 553 F.2d 485. In Mobil Oil Corp. v. FPC, 463 F.2d 256, cert. denied 406 U.S. 976, 92 S.Ct. 2409, 2410, 2413, 32 L.Ed.2d 676, rehearing denied 402 U.S. 902, 903, 93 S.Ct. 100, 103, 34 L.Ed.2d 165, 166, the court held that the FPC did not have jurisdiction over royalty payments made on gas sales and that they were not subject to FPC rate regulation.

25. Okl., 630 P.2d 1269. Also see Pierce v. Texas Pacific Oil Co., Inc., C.A. 10th, 547 F.2d 519, a forerunner of the Tara case. The Pierce case dealt with the split-stream sales situation. Here, two or more lessees each sell their production to different purchasers. In Oklahoma the royalty payable to each lessor is based on the average price of all sales. This gives the lessor whose lessee is selling the higher-priced gas a lower royalty than where based solely on the sales of its lessee. See Shell Oil Co. v. Corporation Commission, Okl., 389 P.2d 951, which has become known as the "Blanchard case." Also see Hemus & Co. v. Hawkins, D.C.Tex., 452 F.Supp. 861, for another split-stream case.

26. Tex., 613 S.W.2d 240, on remand 619 S.W.2d 477.

[2] " * * * that on gas *sold at the wells* the royalties shall be one-eighth of the *amount realized* from such sale. * * *" (emphasis supplied).

The question presented is when is gas "sold or used off the premises," and when is it "sold at the wells"?

In a somewhat earlier case in Texas, that of Butler v. Exxon Corp.,[27] the court, in construing identical royalty clauses, had held that delivery and sale of gas at a point some 100 feet off the lease was a sale of gas "at the well." The court apparently defined a sale as being "at the well" when gas was sold in the vicinity of the field of production, rather than at a more remote location.

This rather indefinite construction of "at the well" was overruled in the Middleton case.[28] In the Middleton case the product was sold at a processing plant located off the lease. The court held that this was "a sale off the premises" to which the market value royalty provisions applied. Justice Campbell defined "at the wells" and "off the premises" as follows:

> "We conclude 'off the premises' modifies both 'sold' and 'used.' The 'premises' is the land described in the lease agreement. Therefore, sold 'off the premises' means gas which is sold outside the leased premises. Thus, 'sold at the wells' means sold at the wells within the lease, and not sold at the wells within the fields."

The extent to which the method of royalty payment provided for in the lease may be modified by execution of a division order is discussed below.[29]

A much more difficult question is that of valuation or determination of price under the market price or value clause. The courts generally state that comparable sales may be used as evidence from which market value or price may be determined. Sales are comparable when they are substantially similar as to conditions of sale, adjusted by volume, location, and quality factors.[30]

It appears that at least three jurisdictions would consider intrastate sales in determining market value where gas is dedicated to and is being sold into the interstate market.[31] In one jurisdiction it may

---

27. Tex.Civ.App., 559 S.W.2d 410, refused n.r.e., appeal after remand 585 S.W.2d 881, set aside Tex., 619 S.W.2d 399.

28. See footnote 26, supra. Middleton also held that where a lease was in a unit and the unit well was not on the lease, the resulting production was not "at the wells" of that lease. It was stated that pooling did not extend the boundary lines of the leased premises to the unit boundary lines.

29. § 7.5, infra.

30. Lippert v. Angle, 211 Kan. 695, 508 P.2d 920, sales under substantially similiar conditions; Montana Power Co. v. Kravik, 189 Mont. 87, 586 P.2d 298, appeal after remand __ Mont. __, 616 P.2d 321, sales adjusted by volume, location, and quality factors; Texas Oil & Gas Corp. v. Vela, Tex., 429 S.W.2d 866, comparable in time, quality, and availability to marketing outlets.

31. Lightcap v. Mobil Oil Corp., 221 Kan. 448, 562 P.2d 1, cert. denied 434 U.S. 876, 98 S.Ct. 228, 54 L.Ed.2d 156; Shell Oil Co. v. Williams Inc., La.App., 411 So.2d 634; Montana Power Co. v. Kravik, 189 Mont. 87, 586 P.2d 298, appeal after remand __ Mont. __, 616 P.2d 321.

be that only intrastate sales will be considered.[32] However, the trend of the cases seems to be that, at least prior to the enactment of the Natural Gas Policy Act of 1978,[33] sales into a regulated market and sales into a nonregulated market will not be treated as comparable.

The dichotomy between regulated and nonregulated sales has emerged from a series of cases in the federal courts [34] and has been followed in two Texas cases.[35]

In the decision of the Federal District Court in Brent v. Natural Gas Pipeline Co. of America,[36] the court dealt with sales of gas irrevocably dedicated and sold in interstate commerce. Again, royalty owners were complaining about a deficiency in royalty payments under a market value royalty clause. Lessors tried to introduce intrastate sales as evidence of market value. The court held that only interstate sales were relevant and comparable. The court based its result in part on the case of California v. Southland Royalty Co.,[37] and stated that although the case was not directly in point that " * * * the reasoning of that opinion convinces this court the FPC jurisdiction over interstate gas may alter the private rights of parties not subject to that jurisdiction, to the extent that such jurisdiction may limit the scope of sales which can be considered in determining 'market value' of interstate gas." The court further held:

> "In conclusion the court finds that there are two distinct markets for gas in the geographical area where defendant's wells are located, the interstate market and intrastate market. The gas in this case has been irrevocably dedicated to the former. Therefore, only gas sales in the relevant geographical area, made by producers of the same vintage as the gas in question, are comparable to determine the 'market value' of the gas involved in this case."

The case was affirmed in the case of Kingery v. Continental Oil Co.,[38] wherein the court stated:

> " * * * instead we held only that the market value of interstate gas is to be determined by comparison with the sales of com-

---

32. Montana Power Co. v. Kravik, 189 Mont. 87, 586 P.2d 298, appeal after remand ___ Mont. ___, 616 P.2d 321.

33. 15 U.S.C. §§ 3301–3432(b) (Supp. II 1978) (NGPA).

34. Kingery v. Continental Oil Co., D.C.Tex., 434 F.Supp. 349, allowing consideration of intrastate gas sales, but which was reversed on this point by Kingery v. Continental Oil Co., C.A.5th, 626 F.2d 1261, holding that intrastate sales are not comparable. The later Kingery case also affirmed Brent v. Natural Gas Pipeline Co. of America, D.C. Tex., 457 F.Supp. 155; and see, Hemus & Co. v. Hawkins, D.C.Tex., 452 F.Supp. 861.

35. Exxon Corp. v. Middleton, Tex., 613 S.W.2d 240, on remand 619 S.W.2d 477; First National Bank in Weatherford v. Exxon Corp., Tex.Civ.App., 597 S.W.2d 783, writ granted, affirmed Tex., 622 S.W.2d 80.

36. D.C.Tex., 457 F.Supp. 155, affirmed Kingery v. Continental Oil Co., C.A.5th, 626 F.2d 1261.

37. 436 U.S. 519, 98 S.Ct. 1955, 56 L.Ed.2d 505, rehearing denied 439 U.S. 885, 99 S.Ct. 230, 231, 58 L.Ed.2d 200.

38. C.A.5th, 626 F.2d 1261.

parable gas on the interstate market. This is so because this gas could not be sold on the intrastate market and thus its value on that market was zero. (citation omitted) Since sellers and buyers of gas in interstate commerce cannot lawfully contract for a price above that allowed by federal regulation, prices above that figure are simply not comparable. This is as far as we need to go to decide cases before us and that is as far as we do go."

As can be seen from the above quotation, the Kingery court did not mention the factor of "vintage" of the gas being sold.

In the Texas case of Exxon v. Middleton,[39] dealing with sales in the intrastate market, the court also followed the approach of Brent and Kingery. The court found that it was improper to consider interstate sales where the gas contract was for sales within the state. The case illustrates the evidentiary problems involved in determining current prices for gas sales. In this case sales in a seven county area were considered. However, the testimony of an expert that considered only the three highest sales in the area was stated to be improper. At least one court has indicated that an average of all sales in the field would not necessarily be binding as to determination of the current price.[40] Another case deemed improper the average of prices testified to by several experts, where the resulting average was not a price testified to by any one witness.[41]

In Middleton, Justice Campbell expanded the discussion of what sales may be deemed comparable.

"Sales comparable in time occur under contracts executed contemporaneously with the sale of the gas in question. Sales comparable in quality are those of similar physical properties such as sweet, sour, or casinghead gas. Quality also involves the legal characteristics of the gas; that is, whether it is sold in a regulated or unregulated market, or in one particular category of a regulated market. Sales comparable in quantity are those of similar volumes to the gas in question. To be comparable, the sales must be made from an area with marketing outlets similar to the gas in question. Gas from fields with outlets to interstate markets only, for instance, would not be comparable to gas from a field without outlets only to the intrastate market."

Since the Natural Gas Policy Act of 1978 [42] has extended the regulation structure to intrastate sales of gas as well as to interstate sales, it may be that the importance of the above cases is diminished. However, it seems probable that comparable sales may still be separated along lines of interstate and intrastate sales.

---

39. See footnote 26 supra.

40. Texas Oil & Gas Corp. v. Vela, Tex., 429 S.W.2d 866.

41. Exxon Corp. v. Jefferson Land Co., Tex.Civ.App., 573 S.W.2d 529, writ refused n.r.e., Tex., 618 S.W.2d 529.

42. See footnote 33, supra.

§ 7.4 ROYALTY AND OTHER CLAUSES

(F) Expenses of Transportation and Preparation for Market

Where the clause designates proceeds to be determined "at the well," the lessee will bear line losses between the well and the ultimate sales point.[43] Also, it may be that the lessor will only be entitled to royalty on the products as they pass through the well mouth, and not upon the enhanced value caused by processing into separate products of higher economic value after leaving the well and before arriving at the point of sale.

As indicated above, the lessee is not exclusively chargeable with the costs of transportation of the products to a distant market. This appears to be true whether or not the formula for computation relates to the mouth of the well or at the ultimate point of sale.[44] As stated in Matzen v. Hugoton Production Co.:[45]

> "It was as much Hugoton's duty to find a market on the leased premises without cost to the plaintiffs as it was to find and produce the gas; but that duty did not extend to providing a gathering system to transport and process the gas off the leases at a large capital cost with attending financial hazards in order to obtain a market at which the gas might be sold."

However, what of the costs of preparation of the products for market that did not involve large capital expenditures, such as the cost of dehydration, compression, and otherwise preparing the product for market? The costs of compression usually fall within the duty of the lessee to market the products and will be borne by the lessee and not shared by the lessor.[46] On the other hand, some courts would charge the lessor with his proportionate share of the costs of dehydration and other preparation for market.[47] Where the royalty clause applies the compensation formula "at the well," some courts have approached the question by charging the lessee with all non-extraordinary costs of market preparation.[48] However, an analysis

---

43. Scott v. Steinberger, 113 Kan. 67, 213 P. 646; Ashland Oil & Refining Co. v. Staats, Inc., D.C.Kan., 271 F.Supp. 571.

Johnson v. Jernigan, Okl., 475 P.2d 396 (allowing deduction).

44. Matzen v. Hugoton Production Co., 182 Kan. 456, 321 P.2d 576, 73 A.L.R.2d 1045; Ashland Oil & Refining Co. v. Staats, Inc., D.C.Kan., 271 F.Supp. 571; Reed v. Hackworth, Ky., 287 S.W.2d 912; Johnson v. Jernigan, Okl., 475 P.2d 396.

45. 182 Kan. 456, 321 P.2d 576, 73 A.L.R.2d 1045.

46. Gilmore v. Superior Oil Co., 192 Kan. 388, 388 P.2d 602; Schupbach v. Continental Oil Co., 193 Kan. 401, 394 P.2d 1; Ashland Oil & Refining Co. v. Staats, Inc., D.C.Kan., 271 F.Supp. 571; Skaggs v. Heard, D.C.Tex., 172 F.Supp. 813; But see: Harding v. Cameron, D.C. Okl., 220 F.Supp. 466, which states the Oklahoma rule that compression costs are proportionately charged against the lessor.

47. Vedder Petroleum Corp., Ltd. v. Lambert Lands Co., 50 Cal.App.2d 102, 122 P.2d 600; West v. Alpar Resources, Inc., N.D., 298 N.W.2d 484. Johnson v. Jernigan, Okl., 475 P.2d 396; Freeland v. Sun Oil Co., C.A.5th, 277 F.2d 154, cert. denied 364 U.S. 826, 81 S.Ct. 64, 5 L.Ed. 2d 55; Holbein v. Austral Oil Co., C.A. 5th, 609 F.2d 206.

48. Gilmore v. Superior Oil Co., 192 Kan. 388, 388 P.2d 602; Schupbach v. Continental Oil Co., 193 Kan. 401, 394 P.2d 1; Ashland Oil & Refining Co. v. Staats, Inc., D.C.Kan., 271 F.Supp. 571.

362   THE OIL AND GAS LEASE   Ch. 7

on the basis of the nature of the cost or the place of sale is unsatisfactory.

The better approach would seem to be whether such costs are conceived to be within the implied obligation of the lessee to market the products from the lease. Those cases would charge all such costs to the lessee that they find are within such an implied obligation.[49] On the other hand, the contrary result is justified upon the counter-argument that where the lessee has, by such acts or treatment, given or enhanced the value of the product the lessor should not share in the enhanced value without sharing part of the costs.[50] It cannot be said that any particular view prevails, with the exception that Kansas[51] appears to find the costs chargeable against the lessee only, whereas the opposite view appears to be espoused in Louisiana.[52]

(G) "FERC-Out" and "Market-Out" Clauses

Deregulation of some natural gas, and the resulting fluctuating market, has led to the wide-spread use of price-reduction clauses in gas purchase contracts. "FERC-out" clauses allow the purchaser to reduce the price it pays to the seller, to compensate for any reduction in price that the purchaser can charge when that reduction is caused by FERC regulations. "Market-out" clauses allow the purchaser to reduce the price it pays whenever it determines that the market into which it sells will not bear the currently-demanded price. The "market-out" clause may be tied to a price determined by the price of an alternate fuel, e.g., "85% of the monthly average cost of Number 2/diesel, as used in the * * * area," or may be subject solely to the buyer's opinion. The seller is given the options of accepting the reduced price or cancelling the contract, although it must usually agree that if it cancels the contract it will not sell to a different purchaser at or below the proposed lower price.

§ 7.5 Division and Transfer Orders

Under the general view, a division order is a revocable authorization to the purchaser of production for payment upon a stated basis to the owners of production. It is revocable at the will of either party, but both are bound until the division order is terminated. By the better view, an owner of production who has executed a division order is not so contractually

---

49. Ashland Oil & Refining Co. v. Staats, Inc., D.C.Kan., 271 F.Supp. 571; West v. Alpar Resources, Inc., N.D., 298 N.W.2d 484; Johnson v. Jernigan, Okl., 475 P.2d 396; and Sneed, Value of the Lessee's Share of Production where Gas Only is Produced, 25 Tex.L.Rev. 641.

50. Wall v. United Gas Public Service Co., 178 La. 908, 152 So. 561; Freeland v. Sun Oil Co., C.A.5th, 277 F.2d 154, cert. denied 364 U.S. 826, 81 S.Ct. 64, 5 L.Ed. 2d 55.

51. Gilmore v. Superior Oil Co., 192 Kan. 388, 388 P.2d 602; Schupbach v. Continental Oil Co., 193 Kan. 401, 394 P.2d 1; Ashland Oil & Refining Co. v. Staats, Inc., D.C.Kan., 271 F.Supp. 571.

52. Wall v. United Gas Public Service Co., 178 La. 908, 152 So. 561; Sartor v. United Carbon Co., 183 La. 287, 163 So. 103.

bound or estopped by the division order that he cannot recover for underpayment from owners of production who have been overpaid. He may not recover from the purchaser of production.

(A) Nature of the Division Order

When production is obtained, the lessee or the purchaser of production must account to the owners of the royalty interests as provided for under the royalty clauses of the lease. Where a rightful owner is not properly paid, the lessee or purchaser of production will be subject to a suit for accounting for unpaid royalty plus interest. In some instances it may be subject to a suit for conversion.

In order to protect itself, the lessee or purchaser of production normally will require that all persons entitled to a share in production execute a "division order" or "declaration of interest."[1] Such instrument declares the portion of production to which each is entitled, and also may contain additional provisions relating to computation of price, warranty by the sellers, notice of change of ownership, etc.[2]

1. Generally see Summers, Oil and Gas, § 590.

2. Summers lists the matters covered as follows (Vol. 3A, § 590):

(a) Warranty by the sellers that they are the legal owners of the proportion of the oil produced set opposite their respective names in the order.

(b) Legal description of the property, including the numbers of the wells from which the oil purchased is produced.

(c) Authorization of the purchaser to take the oil, giving credit to each seller for the proportion of the amount opposite his name.

(d) Termination of the order on written notice by sellers and sometimes by either party.

(e) Oil taken to become the property of the purchaser.

(f) Price to be paid for the oil taken, date and method of payment.

(g) Authority of purchaser to deduct taxes payable by purchaser.

(h) Successors, personal representatives and assigns of sellers bound by the order.

(i) Seller bound by the order, although other owners have not signed.

(j) Seller required to furnish abstract of title or other evidence of title at any time on demand by purchaser.

(k) Failure to furnish abstract, or any dispute concerning seller's title to the land or the oil, authorizes purchaser to withhold payment, without interest,* until title is determined, unless the seller furnishes a satisfactory indemnity bond.

(*l*) Seller required to give purchaser notice of any suit affecting the title to the land or the oil and to indemnify the purchaser against all costs incurred in defending such suit.

(m) Purchaser not bound by any transfer or incumbrance of seller's interest until after written notice thereof, signed by the seller or transferee, and the receipt of the instrument of transfer.

(n) Warranty by producer that the oil has been produced in conformity with all applicable laws and administrative rules.

* The cases seem divided as to interest on suspended runs: Shutts v. Phillips Petroleum Co., 222 Kan. 527, 567 P.2d 1292; Helmley v. Ashland Oil Co., 1 Kan.App.2d 532, 571 P.2d 345; Sterling v. Marathon Oil Co., 223 Kan. 686, 576 P.2d 635; Wolfe v. Texas Co., C.A. 10th, 83 F.2d 425; Wolfe v. Prairie Oil & Gas Co., C.A.10th, 83 F.2d 434; Wolfe v. Shell Petroleum Corp., C.A. 10th, 83 F.2d 438; Gulf Pipe Line Co. v. Warren, Tex.Civ.App., 45 S.W.2d 719; Gulf Pipe Line Co. v. Nearen, 135 Tex. 50, 138 S.W.2d 1065; Lasater v. ConVest Energy Corp., Tex.Civ.App., 615 S.W.2d 340, refused n.r.e. Phillips Petroleum Co. v. Williams, C.A.5th, 158 F.2d 723. Interest has been allowed on suspended royalties during the pendency of FERC action on rates: Mad-

In order to determine the proper ownership of the products being purchased, as well as the extent and scope of the production,[3] the purchaser of production will prepare, usually through house counsel, a division order title opinion. This is done from an examination of abstracts and other materials relating to the title of the mineral estate from which production is being purchased. Where title defects are found, the purchasing company will withhold payment until the defects have been corrected to the satisfaction of the purchaser's attorneys. The requiring of additional curative title matters by the purchaser of production may in some cases cause embarrassment to the lessee's attorney who has passed title to the lease. For this reason the attorney for the lessee should assure himself that he is using standards for title examination that are comparable to those of the attorney of the purchaser of production. The attorney for the lessee may have the feeling that someone is always looking over his shoulder, for, normally, another will examine title behind him.

From the division order title opinion, the division order is drawn up. Where transfers of interest have occurred and notice has been furnished to the purchaser of production, house counsel will examine such instruments and prepare a memorandum for the preparation of transfer orders, to substitute the new interest for the old under the division order.

The nature of the division order prepared will depend to some extent upon the nature of the production from the lease. This will affect the question of title to the products and the complexity of the computation of royalty valuation.[4] As was noted in prior sections, the oil royalty clause usually provides for the delivery of royalty oil in kind to the lessor or royalty owner, or to his credit if sold by the lessee. In this instance, title to the royalty oil is reserved in the lessor[5] and does not pass to the lessee. Where the oil is sold by the lessee, the lessee becomes the agent[6] of the royalty owner, and must account for the money received in sale of the lessor's oil. In the case of oil production, the purchaser therefore buys oil both from the lessor and from the lessee. It will prepare a division order to be signed

---

dox v. Gulf Oil Corp., 222 Kan. 733, 567 P.2d 1326, cert. denied 434 U.S. 1065, 98 S.Ct. 1242, 55 L.Ed.2d 767; Gray v. Amoco Production Co., 223 Kan. 441, 573 P.2d 1080; Shutts v. Phillips Petroleum Co., 222 Kan. 527, 567 P.2d 1292, cert. denied 434 U.S. 1068, 98 S.Ct. 1246, 55 L.Ed.2d 769, rehearing denied 435 U.S. 961, 98 S.Ct. 1594, 55 L.Ed.2d 811; Phillips Petroleum Co. v. Stahl Petroleum Co., Tex., 569 S.W.2d 480.

3. Division Orders may be limited to segregated portions of the lease, areas, depths, or formations covered. They may also be limited to specific production from pooled production.

4. In the case of production of liquids from gas the division order may contain numerous technical provisions relating to the matter of product measurement and valuation. For problems involved see Danciger Oil & Refineries v. Hamill Drilling Co., 141 Tex. 153, 171 S.W.2d 321.

5. Shreveport-El Dorado Pipe Line Co. v. Bennett, 172 Ark. 804, 290 S.W. 929; Wolfe v. Texas Co., C.A.10th, 83 F.2d 425; Tidewater Associated Oil Co. v. Clemens, Tex.Civ.App., 123 S.W.2d 780.

6. Shreveport-El Dorado Pipe Line Co. v. Bennett, 172 Ark. 804, 290 S.W. 929; Wolfe v. Texas Co., C.A.10th, 83 F.2d 425.

by all owners of an interest in production, whether such interests are derivative from the lessor or carved out of the lessee's interest.

However, a slightly different arrangement is sometimes found in the case of gas production or casinghead gas production. Under the customary gas royalty clause the lessee is required to account to the lessor or royalty owner for the value of the gas produced. Title to the gas passes to the lessee upon execution of the lease. The relationship between the lessee and the lessor is not one of principal and agent, but of debtor and creditor.[7] Since the title to the gas is in the lessee, in those cases where the lessee is financially responsible, or has posted a bond, the purchasing company will pay all proceeds to the lessee, who in turn will circulate a division order to the owners of the other interests in production. If the lessee owns the entire working interest, only the landowner's royalty interest, or derivative interests, will be shown in the gas division order.

No cases have been found that emphasize the difference in relationship between the lessor and lessee under the oil and gas royalty clauses. However, where no division order has been signed and the royalty owner retains title to the royalty oil, the lessee may be guilty of conversion if he sells the royalty oil after notice from the royalty owner that he will not accept the posted price and desires to take delivery in kind.[8] Where no demand is made upon the lessee, and the lessor has failed to furnish tanks for delivery of royalty oil, the lessee has implied authority to market the royalty oil and pay the current posted price.[9]

(B) Effect of the Division Order

The function of a division order is to provide a direction or authorization to the purchasing company to pay the proceeds of production to the owners of production. Where all owners have executed the division order, the purchaser is protected in so paying, even though such division of interest set forth is incorrect.[10] When an assignment of an interest occurs, the parties are requested to execute a transfer order, which evidences the sale of the interest on the one hand, and, on the other, the substitution of the new owner under the provisions of the division order.[11]

---

7. Tidewater Associated Oil Co. v. Clemens, Tex.Civ.App., 123 S.W.2d 780.

8. Southern Oil Corp. v. Waggoner, C.A.5th, 276 F. 487.

9. Wolfe v. Texas Co., C.A.10th, 83 F.2d 425; Wolfe v. Prairie Oil & Gas Co., C.A.10th, 83 F.2d 434; Wolfe v. Shell Petroleum Corp., C.A.10th, 83 F.2d 438. The court indicated that acceptance of benefits by the lessor constituted a ratification of the acts of the lessee, as an agent acting without authority.

10. Chicago Corp. v. Wall, 156 Tex. 217, 293 S.W.2d 844; Exxon Corp. v. Middleton, Tex., 613 S.W.2d 240, on remand Tex.Civ.App., 619 S.W.2d 477.

11. Where an assignment of an interest subject to producing lease occurs, the parties should make the transfer of lease benefits occur at a time co-incident with the transfer of interest under the transfer order. Usually this is as of 7:00 o'clock A.M. on the first day of the month. Where the assignment is effective at another time an appropriate allo-

Although division orders customarily cover all of the land under a lease, they may cover only particular producing sands or parts of a lease. It has been held that a payment made in accordance with a division order covering part of a lease did not relieve the purchaser of production from liability for failure to pay the correct royalty on production from the part of the lease not covered by the division order. In Shreveport-El Dorado Pipe Line Co. v. Bennett,[12] the purchaser of production prepared division orders covering the south 40 acres of the leased land. However, production was also from the north 20 acres. Lessor had executed a division order on the south 40 acres, but it did not cover the north 20 acres, in which he had a different interest. Lessor received royalty payments as to the north 20 acres in accordance with interests shown in the division order on the south 40 acres. It was held that he was not estopped, either by the execution of the division order or by receipt of royalty, from asserting his correct interest against the purchaser of production.

The opposite result has also occurred. Where the purchaser of production was of the opinion that a tract was not covered by the division order, but after litigation it was found to be included,[13] the purchaser of production was required to pay on the basis of the division order as to all tracts and interests actually covered thereby.

The division order customarily will contain a notice clause, viz., that change in payment will not be made until notice to the purchaser of production. The clause is valid as to those signing the division order, but is not effective when an interest is established in the leased tract by a third party.[14]

Where the parties have signed division orders, questions have arisen whether the owners are bound by the provisions of division orders that differ from the royalty provisions of the lease.

(A) Where the production being purchased consists of gas or liquids recovered from gas, a complex situation exists as to the manner of measuring and valuing the products. The oil and gas lease normally does not provide a detailed procedure for such determinations. However, division orders covering gas and condensate many times do have detailed provisions relating to such matters. In actual fact, the provisions of the division order may provide a substantially different method of valuation than that set forth in the lease.

(B) When dry gas is being sold to pipeline companies under long-term contracts of sale, the royalty payment under the division order

cation should be made by the seller to the buyer.

12. 172 Ark. 804, 290 S.W. 929.

13. Magnolia Petroleum Co. v. King, Tex.Civ.App., 271 S.W. 201. The tract described was "Lot 2 containing 15 acres". Lot 2 was found upon accurate survey to contain an additional .56-acre strip. Although payment had been made upon a different ownership basis as to the .56-acre strip, it was held the lease and division order covered "Lot 2". Therefore, payment was required to be made as to the .56-acre strip as was made to the 15-acre tract.

14. Tidewater Associated Oil Co. v. Hammer, Tex.Civ.App., 163 S.W.2d 232.

§ 7.5 ROYALTY AND OTHER CLAUSES

may be tied into and related to the price paid under the contract. Where interstate gas sales are involved, reserves are dedicated under the contract and are under the jurisdiction of FERC. Contract prices for current gas sale contracts may be much higher than prices under older contracts.[15]

Division orders are generally viewed as being in the nature of revocable authorizations to pay, binding the sellers of the products to the purchasing company until revoked. This view has generally been followed in connection with division orders that change the method of royalty payment from the lease. In Phillips Petroleum Co. v. Williams,[16] the court, holding that a division order does not constitute a novation of the lease, stated:

> " * * * division and transfer orders, with their definite declaration that the market value of the gas at the mouth of the well is to be the measure of lessor's rights and lessee's obligations, and their clear and full provisions for precisely arriving at the value, * * * until withdrawn or modified, * * * constitute the precise and definite basis for payments, and payments made in accordance with them are final and binding. * * * Binding as they are, however, in respect of payments made and accepted under them, these division or transfer orders did not rewrite or supplant the lease contract. They are binding only for the time and to the extent that they have been or are being acted on and made the basis of settlements and payments, and from the time that notice is given that settlements will not be made on the basis provided in them, they cease to be binding. As to persons who did not sign division or transfer orders, payments made to and accepted by, or settlements made with them, on the basis provided for in these orders, will be equally binding. If, however, the evidence shows not that the payments were received upon the basis provided in these agreements, but that they were received merely as payments tendered by the company and accepted by the recipients on the faith and in the belief that they were being paid the amount due them, the mere acceptance of these payments would not constitute an accord and satisfaction or a binding settlement."

The Williams case was followed in Exxon Corp. v. Middleton,[17] where it was held that payments made and accepted under the divi-

---

15. See discussion at § 7.4(E), supra.

16. C.A.5th, 158 F.2d 723, and see Hafeman v. Gem Oil Co., 163 Neb. 438, 80 N.W.2d 139; Stanolind Oil & Gas Co. v. Terrell, Tex.Civ.App., 183 S.W.2d 743.

17. Tex., 613 S.W.2d 240, on remand Tex.Civ.App., 619 S.W.2d 477, citing the text; and see Chicago Corp. v. Wall, 156 Tex. 217, 293 S.W.2d 844; and Huber Corp. v. Denman, C.A.5th, 367 F.2d 104. Maddox v. Gulf Oil Corp., 222 Kan. 733, 567 P.2d 1326, cert. denied 434 U.S. 1065, 98 S.Ct. 1242, 55 L.Ed.2d 767. In the Texas cases of Butler v. Exxon Corp., Tex.Civ.App., 559 S.W.2d 410, refused n.r.e., appeal after remand 585 S.W.2d 881, set aside Tex., 619 S.W.2d 399, and Amoco Production Co. v. First Baptist Church of Pyote, Tex.Civ.App., 579 S.W.2d 280, refused n.r.e. 611 S.W.2d 610. Justice Osborn took the position that the execution of a division order would not change the rights of the lessor under the lease. In the latter case he cited Professor Merrill: " * * * the purposes for which the [division] order is ex-

sion orders that provided for payment based on "amounts realized" were effective until the division orders were revoked. The effect of the division order was to change the method of payment of royalty from "market value" under the lease clause to "amount realized" under the division order. At least one case has reached the conclusion that the division order is not supported by consideration, and if no estoppel exists, the lessor may recover for royalty payments based on the lease clause.[18] The Middleton case would reach the same result whether the division order ran to the lessee or to a third party purchaser.

It has been generally stated by various writers that the execution of a division order may operate to ratify an invalid lease from which production was being purchased. It is true that a co-tenant may ratify acts of another co-tenant who is dealing with the entire jointly owned property. The question, however, is whether the execution of division order, without more, will constitute such a ratification. An act of ratification should reflect an intent of the party to ratify the acts of another. It would normally seem that the subjective intent of parties executing division orders is not to recognize another's interest in the tract.

Although cases do contain the above general statement, the majority of cases holding that ratification has occurred involve division orders that contain express words of ratification.[19] One case has held that where no such express statement is found, the execution of a division order is merely one of the circumstances to be taken into account in finding a showing of intent to so ratify.[20] Where execution

ecuted and the type of economic duress which prescribes it repel the implication that it is intended to affect the obligations of the operator to the royalty owner. The better reasoned decisions are in accordance with this view, and hence the mere execution of a division order, or the acceptance of payments in accordance therewith from the purchaser, ought not to preclude the royalty owner from asserting a breach of implied obligation against the operator."

This viewpoint of Justice Osborn was overruled by the Middleton decision; however, Justice Osborn has persisted in the view. See the dissents in The First National Bank in Weatherford v. Exxon Corp., Tex.Civ.App., 597 S.W.2d 783, affirmed 622 S.W.2d 80, for which writ has been granted by the Texas Supreme Court; and, Lasater v. ConVest Energy Corp., Tex.Civ.App., 615 S.W.2d 340, refused n.r.e.

18. In Simpson v. United Gas Pipe Line Co., 196 Miss. 356, 17 So.2d 200, the court took the position that the division order was a contract which bound the parties for sufficient consideration to the terms of the gas purchase contract over the entire 15-year lease.

19. Kaufman v. Arnaudville Co., La. App., 186 So.2d 337; Gonsoulin v. Shell Oil Co., D.C.La., 321 F.Supp. 900, affirmed C.A.5th, 445 F.2d 861 (ratification of wrongful unit allocation); Corey v. Sunburst Oil and Gas Co., 72 Mont. 383, 233 P. 909; National Forge Co. v. Carlson, 452 Pa. 516, 307 A.2d 202 (ratification of wrongful drilling location); Texas and Pacific Coal and Oil Co. v. Kirtley, Tex.Civ.App., 288 S.W. 619; American Refining Co. v. Tidal Western Oil Corp., Tex.Civ.App., 264 S.W. 335, error refused 114 Tex. 583, 278 S.W. 1114. But cf. Eagle Oil Co. v. Sinclair Prairie Oil Co., D.C. Okl., 24 F.Supp. 612; and Johnson v. Texas Gulf Coast Corp., Tex.Civ.App., 359 S.W.2d 91 (no authority cited to sustain ratification holding); Yelderman v. McCarthy, Tex.Civ.App., 474 S.W.2d 781 (ratification of invalid exercise of pooling power—express statement on check).

20. Barr v. Wall, Tex.Civ.App., 265 S.W.2d 208.

§ 7.5   ROYALTY AND OTHER CLAUSES   369

of the division order is followed by long acquiescence in the acts of the lessee, ratification may be found.[21]

(C) Modification or Termination of Division Orders

It is the general view that division orders are terminable at the will of either party, seller or purchaser.[22] This is not to say that a division order, if so drawn, would not be a binding contract for a definite period,[23] but that, as customarily prepared, they are not so viewed. The purchaser is bound to pay according to the terms of the division order until terminated, and the seller is also so bound to the purchaser.[24] It is also the general view that a division order does not constitute a conveyance or transfer of title.[25]

Although the purchaser of production is protected if all parties execute a division order even though some of the interests are incorrectly stated, may one of the owners of production, who is receiving a lesser interest than entitled to, be estopped to assert his correct interest against an overpaid interest owner after the execution of a division order stating that he is the owner of the incorrect interest? The better view is that such party may assert his interest as against the overpaid owner.[26] The contract of the owner of an interest in production is with the purchaser of production,[27] not with other owners and sellers.[28] Although not bound contractually or estopped [29] by execu-

21. Duval v. W. T. Carter & Brothers, Tex.Civ.App., 207 S.W.2d 962. Where one co-tenant is dealing with the common property the other co-tenant may share by acceptance of benefits and acquiescence or by other acts deemed to be a ratification. It is doubtful whether execution of a division order alone is sufficient.

22. Welch v. Pauline Oil & Gas Co., 133 Okl. 122, 271 P. 651; Malarnee v. Pauline Oil & Gas Co., 133 Okl. 192, 271 P. 937; Snider v. Snider, 208 Okl. 231, 255 P.2d 273; Chicago Corp. v. Wall, 156 Tex. 217, 293 S.W.2d 844; Phillips Petroleum Co. v. Williams, C.A.5th, 158 F.2d 723.

23. Simpson v. United Gas Pipe Line Co., 196 Miss. 356, 17 So.2d 200; Headley v. Hoopengarner, 60 W.Va. 626, 55 S.E. 744.

24. Purchaser bound: Texas Co. v. Pettit, 107 Okl. 243, 220 P. 956; cf. Budde v. Navarro Oil Co., Tex.Civ.App., 145 S.W.2d 321. Seller bound: Hershey v. Hershey, 3 Ill.App.2d 307, 122 N.E.2d 69; Wagner v. Sunray Mid-Continent Oil Co., 182 Kan. 81, 318 P.2d 1039; Simpson v. United Gas Pipeline Co., 196 Miss. 356, 17 So.2d 200; Dale v. Case, 217 Miss. 298, 64 So.2d 344, 37 A.L.R.2d 811; Chicago Corp. v. Wall, 156 Tex. 217, 293 S.W.2d 844; Phillips Petroleum Co. v. Williams, C.A.5th, 158 F.2d 723.

25. Hershey v. Hershey, 3 Ill.App.2d 307, 122 N.E.2d 69; Brown Land & Royalty Co. v. Green, C.A.5th, 198 F.2d 74, cert. denied 344 U.S. 913, 73 S.Ct. 335, 97 L.Ed. 704; Snider v. Snider, 208 Okl. 231, 255 P.2d 273; Thompson v. Thompson, 149 Tex. 632, 236 S.W.2d 779; Padgett v. Padgett, Tex.Civ.App., 309 S.W.2d 262. Also see Hamman v. Cooperative Refinery Association, Mo.App., 372 S.W.2d 474, where the court held execution of a division order was necessary to the validity of an assignment. On principle the case seems incorrect.

26. Hershey v. Hershey, 3 Ill.App.2d 307, 122 N.E.2d 69.

27. Wagner v. Sunray Mid-Continent Oil Co., 182 Kan. 81, 318 P.2d 1039; Simpson v. United Gas Pipeline Co., 196 Miss. 356, 17 So.2d 200; Chicago Corp. v. Wall, 156 Tex. 217, 293 S.W.2d 844.

28. Hershey v. Hershey, 3 Ill.App.2d 307, 122 N.E.2d 69.

29. Hershey v. Hershey, 3 Ill.App.2d 307, 122 N.E.2d 69; Wagner v. Sunray Mid-Continent Oil Co., 182 Kan. 81, 318 P.2d 1039; Brown Land & Royalty Co. v. Green, C.A.5th, 198 F.2d 74, cert. denied 344 U.S. 913, 73 S.Ct. 335, 97 L.Ed. 704; Simpson v. United Gas Pipeline Co., 196

tion of the division order as to other sellers under the general view, some jurisdictions have reached a contrary result.[30]

§ 7.6 Minimum Royalty Clause

The minimum royalty clause is used in instances where the landowner desires that cash payments for royalty be maintained at a minimum level, where actual production could result in a lesser royalty, and where the landowner has sufficient bargaining power to cause the insertion of the clause. A sample clause is set forth in the footnotes.[1] Cash payments in lieu of actual royalty, such as minimum

---

Miss. 356, 17 So.2d 200; Dale v. Case, 217 Miss. 298, 64 So.2d 344, 37 A.L.R.2d 811; Hafeman v. Gem Oil Co., 164 Neb. 438, 80 N.W.2d 139; Chicago Corp. v. Wall, 156 Tex. 217, 293 S.W.2d 844.

30. Simpson v. United Gas Pipeline Co., 196 Miss. 356, 17 So.2d 200; Texas Co. v. Pettit, 107 Okl. 243, 220 P. 956; Childers v. Neely, 47 W.Va. 70, 34 S.E. 828; Headley v. Hoopengarner, 60 W.Va. 626, 55 S.E. 744.

1. After the end of each lease year, Lessees shall compute the value of all of the royalties stipulated in Section 3 hereof which have accrued on all production (if any), during such lease year from all portions of the above described land remaining subject to this lease. In determining such value, production, severance and regulatory taxes paid on such production shall not be included. The resulting figures shall be called "accrued royalty". The minimum amounts payable under this lease for each lease year shall be, in any event, not less than $_____ (per lease year), if during the primary term, and not less than $_____ (per lease year), if after the expiration of the primary term of this lease, which amount shall be called "minimum royalty". If for any such lease year the accrued royalty plus any delay rentals (where the lease is still in the primary term) or shut-in gas well royalties that have been paid for such lease year is as much as or exceeds the minimum royalty, then the terms of this paragraph shall not apply. If, however, for any such lease year the accrued royalty, together with any amounts paid as delay rentals or shut-in gas well royalties is less than the minimum royalty, then Lessees shall within sixty (60) days following the close of such lease year, pay or tender to the persons entitled to receive the royalties hereunder, or to their credit in the depository bank named herein, the difference between the minimum royalty and an amount equal to the accrued royalty plus any delay rentals and shut-in gas well royalties paid for such year. If such payment is not made within such 60-day period, any of the Lessors may declare this lease terminated after giving ten (10) days' notice by registered mail to Lessees of the existence of such default, provided that Lessees have not paid to Lessors such payment within the 10-day notice period. The 10 days shall commence to run with the mailing of the registered notice. Any such payments or tenders may be made in the manner and at the place, and subject to all of the terms and provisions stipulated in Section 6 hereof for the payment of delay rentals. Should this lease be partially assigned as to one or more segregated portions or tracts, prior to the commencement of a lease year, then the minimum payment required of each such segregated portion or tract remaining subject to the lease at the commencement of any particular lease year shall be calculated separately on the basis above set out, and failure to make payment of the minimum payment due on one segregated portion or tract (segregated at the commencement of the lease year) shall give rise under the provisions of this paragraph to a right of termination only as to such tract or tracts and will not affect this lease as to those segregated portions or tracts for which such payments are duly made or tendered. Credits for accrued royalties during the lease year in the case of such segregated tracts shall be computed so that the segregated tract from which there has been production during the lease year will receive a credit for the full amount of accrued royalty from such tract unless the amount of such accrued royalty from one segregated tract exceeds the minimum payment owing on such tract for the particular lease year, in which event the excess of such accrued royalty shall be credited on an acreage basis to the remaining tracts which were subject to the lease at the be-

royalty payments and shut-in royalty payments, are viewed as royalty and not as rentals.[2]

§ 7.7 Description and Mother-Hubbard Clause

The Mother-Hubbard, or cover-all, clause will generally serve to pick up small strips of land or irregularly shaped excess acreage that lies outside of the tract of land particularly described in an oil and gas lease or deed. Where the land that would be subject to the operation of the clause is substantial in size it has been held that the clause is ambiguous as compared to the presumed intent of the parties, and the court will look to parol evidence to determine the scope of the clause. By the better view, only objective evidence of intent should be considered.

It is unsettled whether the clause will serve to give constructive notice to subsequent purchasers of the excess acreage.

With one exception, description problems pertaining to the land included in mineral and royalty deeds and oil and gas leases do not differ greatly from description problems in non-mineral conveyances. The exception is the use of the "Mother-Hubbard," or "cover-all," clause in conveyances of mineral interests. Such clauses have become almost universal in oil and gas leases and have been found with greater frequency in mineral and royalty deeds. The Mother-Hubbard clause is placed after the particular description of the land affected and may read as follows:

> "This lease also covers and includes all land owned or claimed by lessor adjacent or contiguous to the land particularly described above, whether the same be in said survey or surveys or in adjacent surveys, although not included within the boundaries of the land particularly described above. For the purpose of calculating the rental payments hereinafter provided for, said land is estimated to comprise 100.00 acres whether it actually comprises more or less."[1]

ginning of the lease year. The terms of this paragraph shall apply both during and after the primary term of this lease, although, as stated above, the minimum royalty during the primary term shall be $_____ per year during the primary term and after the primary term shall be $_____. The term "lease year" shall mean an annual period beginning on an anniversary of the date of this lease. The provisions of this paragraph with reference to minimum royalty shall in no way affect the provisions of this lease relating to shut-in gas well royalties or the duty of the Lessees to fully develop the leased premises. The provisions of this section are not intended to and do not provide for a continuance of the lease by making the minimum royalty payments where there is no production in paying quantities but shall be applicable only if and when the lease is being continued in force by production in paying quantities of oil, gas, or other mineral, or by payment of delay rentals (during the primary term) or shut-in gas well royalties or by drilling or reworking operations as elsewhere provided in this lease.

2. Morriss v. First National Bank of Mission, Tex.Civ.App., 249 S.W.2d 269. Also see Andretta v. West, Tex., 415 S.W.2d 638; Pan American Petroleum Corp. v. Robinson, Tex.Civ.App., 405 S.W.2d 698. In Hixon v. Parker, 317 Ark. 210, 307 S.W.2d 210, the Arkansas Court dealt with the effect of the Force Majeure clause on minimum royalty payments.

1. Gardner v. Amerada Petroleum Corp., D.C.Tex., 91 F.Supp. 134, from which case the clause is adopted.

The use of the Mother-Hubbard clause was caused by a somewhat common situation. Lessee, Pure Oil Company, desires to lease Blackacre from O. O executes a lease containing the same land description that was used in the deed to him. However, it is later discovered that the fence lines of O on the west side of the tract lie outside of the land as described in the deed, and the extra land has been picked up by adverse possession. Therefore, the land actually owned by O is in excess of that described in both the deed and the lease. The Mother-Hubbard clause was inserted in the lease to pick up such strips or excess acreage.

Two problems are presented as to the operation of the Mother-Hubbard clause: First, how does the clause operate to pick up excess acreage, and, second, what is the effect of such clause upon subsequent purchasers of land that may be included in the clause, but which is not particularly described in the deed or lease? Some authority exists as to the first problem, but little or none exists as to the second.

Although not particularly discussed in the cases that deal with the operation of the Mother-Hubbard clause, considerable variation in wording exists. Probably the major difference is that some of the clauses are worded so as to include the additional land, if any, within the description clause of the instrument,[2] and may actually use additional words of grant.[3] As to this type clause it may be concluded that words of grant apply to the Mother-Hubbard language.

The former type of clause does not expressly purport to include excess acreage within the granting language of the instrument, but merely states that it is the intention of the grantor or lessor to include such land.[4] No discernable difference can be seen in the cases due to the difference in wording. However, where it is found that substantially large tracts may be subject to the operation of the clause, the inclusion of granting language may have some bearing as to the intent of the parties to include large tracts within the scope of the instrument.

The wording of the clause also varies as to the territorial scope of the clause. Some clauses include only "contiguous" lands,[5] others "adjacent or contiguous" lands,[6] and still others "adjoining"[7] lands. Clauses are found that limit such land to that located in the "same

---

2. United Gas Public Service Co. v. Mitchell, 188 La. 651, 177 So. 697; Cummings v. Midstates Oil Corp., 193 Miss. 675, 9 So.2d 648; Gardner v. Amerada Petroleum Corp., D.C.Tex., 91 F.Supp. 134.

3. Dennis v. Pace Petroleum Co., Tex. Civ.App., 230 S.W.2d 585.

4. Sun Oil Co. v. Burns, 125 Tex. 549, 84 S.W.2d 442; Gulf Production Co. v. Spear, 125 Tex. 530, 84 S.W.2d 452; Sun Oil Co. v. Bennett, 125 Tex. 540, 84 S.W.2d 447; Mann v. Rio Bravo Oil Co., Tex.Civ.App., 107 S.W.2d 653.

5. United Gas Public Service Co. v. Mitchell, 188 La. 651, 177 So. 697.

6. Cummings v. Midstates Oil Corp., 193 Miss. 675, 9 So.2d 648; Gardner v. Amerada Petroleum Corp., D.C.Tex., 91 F.Supp. 134.

7. Sun Oil Co. v. Burns, 125 Tex. 549, 84 S.W.2d 442; Sun Oil Co. v. Bennett, 125 Tex. 540, 84 S.W.2d 447.

survey,"[8] whereas others would include such lands in "adjoining"[9] or "adjacent"[10] surveys.

In the Texas case of Gardner v. Amerada Petroleum Corp.,[11] the court defined the terms "adjacent," "adjoining," and "contiguous." Here the question involved was whether a lot in a subdivision on one side of a street was picked up by the Mother-Hubbard clause contained in a lease of acreage on the opposite side of the street. The clause purported to cover lands of lessor "adjacent or contiguous" to the particularly described acreage. "Adjacent" was defined as tracts of land that are separated by an intervening object, but which are "near to, or in the neighborhood of" the particular described land; "adjoining" as being tracts of lands that touch in some part; and "contiguous" as tracts of land that have all or most of one side in contact. It was held that the subdivision lot was both adjacent and contiguous to the particularly described acreage. It was adjacent as it was nearby, although perhaps not touching. However, it was also viewed as being contiguous under the general view that the owners of land bounded by a street own to the middle of the street. Therefore, the acreage and the subdivision tracts had sides in contact under the street.

If the term "adjacent" is given the same definition as to surveys, it may be that under a literal interpretation the clause would pick up land of the lessor two surveys away. However, some limitation of the term "survey" is found in the cases. In Texas Osage Co-operative Royalty Pool v. Thomas,[12] the court interpreted the term "survey" as not designating the base survey by which land is severed from the sovereignty of the soil, but only the particularly described tract of land, which was incorrectly described in the instrument in question.

In the majority of cases, where small strips of land are involved, the clause has operated to pick up the strip on the basis that the grant covered the strip.[13] Although no description of the strip is included in the clause, it apparently operates on the basis that a grantor may make an effective grant of all the land that he owns in a described area. In one case,[14] however, it appears that the court viewed the clause as merely vesting the grantee with a contract right

---

8. Gulf Production Co. v. Spear, 125 Tex. 530, 84 S.W.2d 452; Mann v. Rio Bravo Oil Co., Tex.Civ.App., 107 S.W.2d 653.

9. Sun Oil Co. v. Burns, 125 Tex. 549, 84 S.W.2d 442; Sun Oil Co. v. Bennett, 125 Tex. 540, 84 S.W.2d 447; Smith v. Allison, 157 Tex. 220, 301 S.W.2d 608.

10. Cummings v. Midstates Oil Corp., 193 Miss. 675, 9 So.2d 648; Gardner v. Amerada Petroleum Corp., D.C.Tex., 91 F.Supp. 134.

11. D.C.Tex., 91 F.Supp. 134.

12. Tex.Civ.App., 270 S.W.2d 450; Gulf Production Co. v. Spear, 125 Tex. 530, 84 S.W.2d 452.

13. Sun Oil Co. v. Burns, 125 Tex. 549, 84 S.W.2d 442; Gulf Production Co. v. Spear, 125 Tex. 530, 84 S.W.2d 452; Sun Oil Co. v. Bennett, 125 Tex. 540, 84 S.W.2d 447; Mann v. Rio Bravo Oil Co., Tex.Civ.App., 107 S.W.2d 653; Alexander v. Byrd, Tex.Civ.App., 114 S.W.2d 915; Dennis v. Pace Petroleum Co., Tex.Civ. App., 230 S.W.2d 585.

14. United Gas Public Service Co. v. Mitchell, 188 La. 651, 177 So. 697.

to have the instrument reformed to include a particular description of any additional lands, when discovered.

Difficulty has arisen when the Mother-Hubbard clause is applied to the actual facts of land ownership of the grantor and it is found that it would include within its terms, not just small strips of land, but substantially large tracts. In the case of Smith v. Allison,[15] the specifically described lands in a deed consisted of two quarter sections, in which the grantor was conveying an undivided one-half interest. The two quarter sections were opposite each other, one being the southeast one-fourth (SE ¼) and the other the northwest one-fourth (NW ¼). The grantor also owned an undivided ¼ mineral interest in the northeast one-fourth (NE ¼) of the same section, which lay between the two tracts specifically described, and additionally owned minerals in the entire two sections that adjoined the subject lands, on the north and on the east. The Mother-Hubbard clause read as follows:

> "The parties, however, intend this deed to include, and same is hereby made to cover and include, not only the above described land, but also any and all other land and interest in land owned or claimed by Grantor in said survey or surveys in which the above described land is situated or adjoining the above described land. * * *"

In a suit for title it was claimed that the clause had the effect of including an undivided ¼ of the minerals in the northeast quarter section owned by the grantor. No claim was made to the minerals in either of the other full sections of land in which the grantor owned minerals.

The case sets forth three opinions: majority, concurring, and dissenting. The majority and the dissenting justices found the clause ambiguous. The majority found a patent ambiguity between the granting clause of the deed, which evidenced an intent to convey only an undivided one-half mineral interest, and the Mother-Hubbard clause, which showed an intent to convey the full fee in the disputed quarter section and the two full sections of land. The court allowed parol evidence as to the intent of the parties. The grantor, over objection, was allowed to testify as to her subjective intent in the conveyance. It was found that there was no intent to include the disputed quarter section.

The dissenting opinion, on the other hand, found a latent ambiguity that resulted when the description in the deed and the Mother-Hubbard clause were applied to the land owned by the grantor. As the traditional purpose of the Mother-Hubbard clause is to pick up small excess acreage, the presence of substantially large tracts that could be included within the wording of the clause was deemed ambiguous.

---

15. 157 Tex. 220, 301 S.W.2d 608; also see Gulf Producing Co. v. Spear, 125 Tex. 530, 84 S.W.2d 452, which would consider the clause in connection with surrounding circumstances.

§ 7.7   ROYALTY AND OTHER CLAUSES

However, the dissenting justice would allow only objective, not subjective, parol evidence to explain the ambiguity. The dissent reasoned that as no such evidence was introduced to explain the scope of the clause and as the disputed quarter section literally came within its terms, it should have passed under the terms of the deed. The concurring opinion would, as a matter of law, restrict the operation of the clause to picking up small strips and excess acreage.

The dissenting opinion would seem to present the traditionally accepted view of the operation of the clause, the creation of the ambiguity, and the better treatment of parol evidence. The Allison case result against the operation of the clause to pick up substantial acreage has been stated in other opinions [16] and follows the judicial view that the clause is disfavored by the law.[17]

Where the Mother-Hubbard clause is inserted in an oil and gas lease, the careful lessee should make certain that any excess acreage that may be caught by the clause will not change the delay rental obligation. In many cases the total monetary payment for delay rentals is computed upon a sum-per-acre basis. If the acreage would vary, the total sum to be paid may also vary, resulting, perhaps, in an underpayment. To prevent this result, it is customary to insert a provision that for the purposes of payment of delay rentals the lease is deemed to contain a stated number of acres, whether it actually covers a greater or lesser amount.

It should also be pointed out that it is not customary for Mother-Hubbard clauses to be inserted in either mineral or royalty deeds. The need for such coverage, however, in a deed conveyance is at least as great as it is in the case of a lease. When the deed is executed after the execution of the oil and gas lease, the grantee should be assured of economic benefits from all lands from which the lessee may produce. This is especially true in the case of the term deed, where its continued existence may depend upon such production.

An unsolved and practically untreated question arises in connection with the rights of third-party purchasers of the strip or other excess land presumably covered by an earlier Mother-Hubbard clause. Assume A owns 100 acres of land, but actually has 109 acres under fence. The 9-acre excess is in the form of a strip on the west side of the subject tract. A executes an oil and gas lease with a Mother-Hubbard clause sufficient to pick up the excess acreage, but which describes only the 100 acre tract by metes and bounds. The lease is recorded. Later, A has the land surveyed and finds the additional 9 acres. A sells the 9 acres to B, who has no actual notice of the oil and gas lease and its Mother-Hubbard clause. Is B a bona fide purchaser for value without notice of the 9-acre tract of land un-

---

16. The Texas Co. v. Newton Naval Stores Co., Inc., 223 Miss. 468, 78 So.2d 751, 49 A.L.R.2d 1182; Continental Oil Co. v. Walker, 238 Miss. 21, 117 So.2d 333; Texas Osage Co-operative Royalty Pool v. Thomas, Tex.Civ.App., 270 S.W.2d 450.

17. Continental Oil Co. v. Walker, 238 Miss. 21, 117 So.2d 333.

der the recording acts so as to cut off the rights of the lessee under the clause?

Three cases have been found that bear on the question. In two Texas cases it appears that B would be charged with notice of the lease and the operation of the clause. In Gulf Producing Co. v. Spear,[18] the court was dealing with two leases. The one prior in time contained a Mother-Hubbard clause. As to its effect on the later lessee, the court stated that it, "gave notice of the intention of the parties to include in it all land owned or claimed by the lessor in the Hollingworth survey. This statement of the lessor's intention and the incomplete and incorrect description of the last line of the tract described by metes and bounds were enough to put subsequent purchasers upon inquiry as to the land intended to be leased." The particular description in the prior lease was defective and in examining the supporting authority [19] for the above statement it would appear that the court's statement should be limited to the facts of the case and not be extended to the case where no defect in the description is found. In the other Texas case,[20] it was merely stated that where the subsequent purchaser knew of the prior lease, he failed to meet the burden that he was an innocent purchaser of the lot in question. Actually, neither case can be cited as authority that recordation of a lease with a Mother-Hubbard clause is notice to a subsequent purchaser of the excess, but not specifically described lands.

In the third case, from Louisiana, United Gas Public Service Co. v. Mitchell,[21] the court reached an opposite result, that the third-party purchaser was not bound by the Mother-Hubbard clause. Here the court viewed the clause as not automatically including the excess lands within the scope of the granting instrument. It was stated that the lessee merely had a contract right to have such lands included when they were discovered. The acquisition of these lands by a subsequent purchaser cut off the right.

Another area of difficulty, and one as to which there appears to be little or no case authority, is whether a deed with a Mother-Hubbard clause that conveys less than all the interest of the grantor will operate to pick up the remaining interest? For instance, the grantor owns all of the minerals and conveys an undivided one-half of the minerals in a deed that contains the clause. Does the clause operate to convey the other one-half to the grantee? A second similar situation is where the deed containing a Mother-Hubbard clause conveys Blackacre, and then excepts or reserves an area from the grant. Where grantor reserves a three-acre tract from the general conveyance, does the clause operate to pass it to the grantee?

18. 125 Tex. 530, 84 S.W.2d 452.

19. Carter v. Hawkins, 62 Tex. 393.

20. Gardner v. Amerada Petroleum Corp., D.C.Tex., 91 F.Supp. 134.

21. 188 La. 651, 177 So. 697.

§ 7.8   ROYALTY AND OTHER CLAUSES   377

In both cases it can be strongly argued that the Mother-Hubbard clause should not have the effect to pass such interests to the grantee. Such conclusion can result from giving effect to an expressed intent not to pass the excepted or reserved interest or by treating the instrument as ambiguous and allowing parol evidence as to the intent of the parties.[22]

§ 7.8   The Proportionate Reduction and Warranty Clauses

When an oil and gas lease is treated as a sale in gross, rather than by the acre, the lessee will be unable to reduce rentals and royalties in the event that the mineral interest effectively leased is less than supposed. When full interest leases are obtained upon partial interests, it is customary for a lessee to rely upon the proportionate reduction or lesser-interest clause to reduce rentals and royalties to the proportion of the interest leased. However, one case has indicated that if a partial-interest lease is obtained, the lessee will not be entitled to reduce rentals under the clause.

The proportionate reduction, or lesser-interest clause, is inserted in an oil and gas lease for the lessee's protection in case it is later found that the lease covers a smaller interest in the minerals than the lessee believed it was leasing.[1] Such lesser interest may be due to failure of title as to the lessor's interest or where the lessee believed that the quantum of the lessor's interest was greater than that actually owned. In such situations the lessee will desire to pay economic benefits in proportion to the interest that is owned by the lessor and is effectively leased.

Assume that Rex Oil Company leases Blackacre, containing 320 acres, from O. It is thought that O owns the full fee interest in the minerals, and a lease is prepared purporting to so lease. The lease provides for payment of $1/8$ royalties and delay rentals of $320.00, based upon a calculation of $1.00 per acre leased. However, it is later found that O owns only an undivided $3/4$ interest in the mineral estate, and that his lease covers only such interest. A owns the other $1/4$ interest, and Rex obtains a lease upon such undivided interest, providing for royalties of $1/4 \times 1/8$, or $1/32$, and delay rentals in the amount of $80.00. If there is no specific clause contained in O's lease, can

---

22. In Lewis v. East Texas Finance Co., Tex.Civ.App., 123 S.W.2d 803, reversed 136 Tex. 149, 146 S.W.2d 977 the lease granted a described tract of land "not including the road." It was held that the Mother-Hubbard clause should not operate where express intent to withhold an interest was shown, and that, in any event, the presence of the Mother-Hubbard clause made the instrument ambiguous and parol evidence was properly admitted in the trial court.

Upon appeal to the Texas Supreme Court, the case was reversed on the ground that only an easement was excepted. The court held that the instrument was not ambiguous and that parol evidence should have been excluded. The court did not discuss the effect of the presence of the Mother Hubbard clause. Lewis v. East Texas Finance, 136 Tex. 149, 146 S.W.2d 977.

1. In general see Summers, Oil and Gas, §§ 342, 609.2; Jones, Problems Presented by Joint Ownership of Oil, Gas and Other Minerals, 32 Tex.L.Rev. 697.

Rex Oil Company reduce the payments to $3/4$ of the amounts shown in the lease?

As the question is stated, the lease constitutes a sale in gross, and not by the acre. If it were the latter, in the event of failure of title, the consideration and economic benefits under the lease would be reducible to the quantum of the estate actually leased.[2] However, where a sale is in gross, the rule is that the consideration may not be so reduced. These cases have been applied to oil and gas leases, where it has been held that in absence of a proportionate reduction clause, rentals and royalties may not be reduced.[3] The proportionate reduction clause that has been inserted in leases customarily reads as follows:

> "Without impairment of Lessee's rights under the warranty in event of failure of title, it is agreed that if Lessor owns an interest in the oil, gas or other minerals on, in or under said land less than the entire fee simple estate (whether or not this lease purports to cover the whole or a fractional interest) then the royalties and rentals to be paid Lessor shall be reduced in the proportion that his interest bears to the whole undivided fee and in accordance with the nature of the estate of which Lessor is seized."

The general effect of the clause is to allow the lessee to reduce royalty and rental payments to correspond to the interest effectively covered by the lease.[4] In the above example, Rex Oil Company would reduce the payments to O to $3/4 \times 1/8$, or $3/32$, royalty, and $3/4 \times \$320.00$, or \$240.00, delay rentals. The total royalty and rental obligation payable to O and A would be $1/8$ royalty and \$320.00 delay rentals. Without the proportionate reduction clause, the total royalty and rental obligation would be $5/32$ royalty and \$400.00 rentals. The increased royalty obligation would reduce the lessee's interest in production from $7/8$ to $27/32$.

Assume further, in connection with the above illustration, that Rex Oil Company is aware that O owns $3/4$ of the minerals and A $1/4$ of the minerals. Rex desires to lease both interests and not to have more than the normal royalty and rental obligation. Therefore, Rex prepares two oil and gas leases. O's lease covers all of Blackacre

---

2. Wells v. Shadoin, 202 Ky. 456, 260 S.W. 12; Dilworth v. Fortier, Okl., 405 P.2d 38; Coker v. Benjamin, Tex.Civ.App., 83 S.W.2d 373.

3. Piney Oil & Gas Co. v. Allen, 235 Ky. 767, 32 S.W.2d 325; Foster v. Hopkins, Tex.Civ.App., 68 S.W.2d 380. Where a lease is executed purportedly covering an undivided interest, and a full royalty is reserved, the courts have generally rejected the view that the reference in the royalty clause that payment is of production "under this lease" or "from the premises" would serve to limit the payment to the proportion of royalty corresponding to the undivided mineral interest lease. Pollock v. McAlester Fuel Co., 215 Ark. 842, 223 S.W.2d 813; Probst v. Ingram, Okl., 373 P.2d 58; Williams v. Sohio Petroleum Co., 18 Ill.App. 2d 194, 151 N.E.2d 645; and see Chapter 3, §§ 3.0–3.2. Also see King v. First National Bank, 144 Tex. 583, 192 S.W.2d 260; Hooks v. Neill, Tex.Civ.App., 21 S.W.2d 532.

4. See Hove v. Atchison, D.C.N.D., 138 F.Supp. 486; Williams v. Sohio Petroleum Co., 18 Ill.App.2d 194, 151 N.E.2d 645.

and provides for 1/8 royalty and $320 delay rentals. The lease contains a proportionate reduction clause. An identical lease is prepared for A. Under these leases Rex reasons that no matter what the undivided interests of O and A, they are effectively covered in the two leases, and whatever quantum of title that O and A may respectively own, lessee may reduce both royalty and rental payments proportionally. In this the lessee is correct.[5] However, O's attorney advises O not to sign, as the lease has overstated O's interest, and would subject O to liability on his warranty of title. In this the attorney is also correct. Although the proportionate reduction clause serves to reduce Rex's royalty and rental obligation, it does not serve to reduce what O purports to convey or diminish O's obligation on the warranty to the interest actually owned.[6] O thereupon refuses to sign unless the warranty clause is struck from the lease. Rex argues that traditionally the warranty clause is included to help pick up after acquired title and it not asserted as a breach of warranty,[7] and refuses to strike the clause.

To counter the impasse, O's attorney suggests that, in the alternative, they prepare an oil and gas lease merely purporting to convey the undivided interest that O owns; therefore, there would be no breach of warranty. The lessee argues that if O owns more than a $3/4$ undivided interest it would not be picked up under the lease. It also argues that the case of Texas Company v. Parks[8] has made it uncertain as to its right to reduce rentals and royalties under a partial-interest lease.

In the Parks case, the granting clause of the lease was expressly limited to an undivided one-half (1/2) interest in the described land, which contained 320 acres, delay rentals were stated to be $160.00, and royalty 1/8. Lessee tendered delay rentals of $80.00 under the proportionate reduction clause, which was apparently similar to the one set forth above although it did not contain the language within the parentheses. Lessor sued for termination of the lease on the ground that the delay rentals were not reducible. The court held for the lessor. Two rationales are set forth for this result. The first had

---

5. Williams v. Sohio Petroleum Co., 18 Ill.App.2d 194, 151 N.E.2d 645.

6. Berwick Mud Co. v. Stansbury, La. App., 205 So.2d 147; Klein v. Humble Oil & Refining Co., 126 Tex. 450, 86 S.W.2d 1077, noted 14 Tex.L.Rev. 563; Griffin v. Stanolind Oil & Gas Co., 133 Tex. 45, 125 S.W.2d 545; Reeves v. Republic Production Co., Tex.Civ.App., 177 S.W.2d 1011. Although the proportionate reduction clause protects the lessee by allowing him to reduce payments to the interest owned by lessor, it does not have a corresponding benefit for the lessor. It will not reduce, to the interest owned, the interest lessor purports to convey. Lessor remains liable on his warranty. In Griffin v. Stanolind Oil & Gas Co., 133 Tex. 45, 125 S.W.2d 545, the court stated:

"This clause is but a covenant respecting the contingency of failure of title in whole or in part. Its legal effect is no greater than a similar covenant for the reduction of unpaid purchase money which is sometimes inserted in a deed which purports a grant of fee simple title to an entire tract of land."

7. This has been traditionally true, but would be little protection in the event lessee decided to assert a breach of warranty.

8. Tex.Civ.App., 247 S.W.2d 179, noted 4 Bay.L.Rev. 541.

to do with the mechanical wording of the lease clauses. In the lease form, the grant of an undivided $\frac{1}{2}$ interest in the land was defined as "said land." The court stated that delay rentals could not be reduced, as lessor owned the entire fee simple estate in "said land," viz., as defined in the lease, an undivided one-half interest. Second, as the lessor had conveyed the entire interest he had purported to convey, the lessee had no right to reduce the delay rentals: "The property referred to as the land is the same as that actually owned and conveyed by the lessors."

On rehearing, it was strongly argued that the holding in respect to the rentals would endanger the right of the lessee to reduce royalties. The court stated: "Neither do we agree with appellant's argument that the effect of our opinion 'is to place in jeopardy the right of the lessee to reduce royalty under every producing oil and gas lease in this State in which an undivided or fractional interest was described, rather than the entire fee simple interest, in the granting clause.' Looking to the description of the land leased, we believe the lessee, or his assigns, would have no difficulty in determining the amount of royalty interest which appellees should receive if and as oil is produced from said land. We need not state here that a formula used or the reason given for determining amount of rental due under a lease should necessarily be the same formula used to ascertain proportionate royalty interests in the oil if and as oil is produced."

This statement might be small solace to the lessee who next attempted to reduce royalties only to be told the proportionate reduction clause did not apply. No basis can be perceived for the court's discrimination between the treatment on rentals and royalties. Factually, however, it may be noted that royalty in the lease had not been reduced, but that it appears that delay rentals were. At the rate of $1 per acre, $320 delay rentals would be payable. The amount stated in the lease appears to be reduced one-half to $160. Was the lessee attempting to proportionately reduce an already reduced amount?

If one may rely upon the court's statement that royalties may be reduced but rentals not, one method of preparing a partial-interest lease would be to state the royalty in the full amount, delay rentals in the reduced amount, and strike the word "rentals" from the proportionate reduction clause. Another method of using a partial-interest lease would be to reduce both the amount of the rentals and royalties and strike the entire proportionate reduction clause from the lease.

In summary then, methods that may be used where a lease of a partial mineral interest, i.e., an undivided mineral interest, is attempted:

> (1) Use a full-interest lease with a proportionate reduction clause, and, if possible, strike the warranty clause or modify it to warrant only the interest that the lessor believes he is leasing. This is probably the better method, as it protects the lessor from

breach of warranty and allows the lessee to take leases from all undivided interest owners and reduce all economic benefits (except bonus)[9] to the interests actually leased.

(2) Use a partial-interest lease, with the granting clause conveying only the undivided interest lessor is purporting to convey. Reduce all payments in the lease to the interest owned, leave in the warranty clause, but strike the proportionate reduction clause. This will give maximum protection to the lessor, but not protect the lessee in the event of failure of title.

(3) Use a partial-interest lease, reduce the amount of the rentals but not the royalties, leave in the warranty and proportionate reduction clauses, and strike the word "rentals" from the latter clause. Not much can be said for this method, except that it may be workable in Texas if the court follows the dicta in the Parks case as to royalties. The same virtues and drawbacks exist as in (2), with the additional consideration that the court may decide against interpreting the reduction clause as applying where the lessor owned the specific interest he intended to lease.

(4) Use a partial-interest lease with all amounts stated in full. Do not define "said land" in the granting clause, and include the parenthetical phrase in the clause set forth. It is problematical if this removes all doubt of the application of the Parks case.

Several cases have arisen where the amounts stated in the body of the lease were subject to reduction by the proportionate reduction clause; however, the parties had provided for additional royalties by means of a rider attached to the lease. Where no modifying language appears on the rider, such payments are also subject to reduction.[10] Where specifically limited, the clause will not apply.

In McMahon v. Christmann,[11] the rider stated that the additional payment to the lessor would be "without reduction" and was held not to be subject to the clause. However, in another case,[12] where the prefatory phrase stated, "Notwithstanding anything to the contrary contained in the foregoing lease, it is understood and agreed * * *," it was held that the major purpose of the clause was to change the amount of shut-in royalties. The court stated that there was nothing contrary between the gas clause in the rider and as stated in the lease, which statements were identical. Therefore, the royalty amounts were reducible. The court also seemed to find the quot-

---

9. Normally, bonus would be paid in cash prior to execution of the lease and would not be affected by the proportionate reduction clause. However, in Probst v. Ingram, Okl., 373 P.2d 58, lessor reserved a production payment, which the court classified as deferred bonus. The bonus payment was held not to be reducible, as the proportionate reduction clause only applied to "rentals and royalties".

10. McMahon v. Christmann, 157 Tex. 403, 303 S.W.2d 341, noted in 5 U.C. L.A.L.Rev. 558; Newport Oil Co. v. Lamb, Tex.Civ.App., 352 S.W.2d 861; Finder v. Nyegaard, Tex.Civ.App., 367 S.W.2d 217.

11. 157 Tex. 403, 303 S.W.2d 341, noted in 5 U.C.L.A.L.Rev. 558.

12. Finder v. Nyegaard, Tex.Civ.App., 367 S.W.2d 217.

ed statement meaningless. The same results are found applicable to provisions for additional royalty payments typed in the lease, if not specifically stated to be free of the clause.[13]

If the lease actually conveys a lesser interest than supposed and contains a proportionate reduction clause, the lessee may reduce rentals and royalties in proportion to the interest effectively leased. However, will estoppel by deed operate to prevent the operation of the clause? It is a general rule of construction that a grantee is estopped from denying the terms of an instrument through which he claims. Where Rex Oil Company accepts a lease with the reservation of a $1/8$ royalty to the lessor and containing a proportionate reduction clause, will estoppel by deed prevent the lessee from reducing the rentals and royalties under the clause? The answer appears to be that the lessee is not so estopped, and that the clause prevents the estoppel.[14]

As mentioned in an earlier chapter,[15] in some jurisdictions, estoppel by deed has operated to diminish reserved interests in a deed where there has been an overconveyance. This was generally stated in the Texas case of Duhig v. Peavy-Moore Lumber Co.[16] In several of the following cases, an attempt was made to apply the Duhig result to reduce royalties in an oil and gas lease where no proportionate reduction clause was present. In the first case, Gibson v. Turner,[17] it was argued that the Duhig doctrine should operate to reduce royalty in proportion to the $9/40$ interest leased. The court refused to apply the Duhig doctrine on the ground that no title was outstanding, as the lessee had acquired it. However, in the later case of McMahon v.

---

13. Pollock v. McAlester Fuel Co., 215 Ark. 842, 223 S.W.2d 813; McMahon v. Christmann, 157 Tex. 403, 303 S.W.2d 341, noted in 5 U.C.L.A.L.Rev. 558; Probst v. Ingram, Okl., 373 P.2d 58. Such perpetual payments out of production, in addition to the normal landowners royalty, are sometimes referred to as "overriding royalties." Another and more common use of the term "overriding royalty" refers to perpetual payments out of production that are carved out of the lessee's interest (working interest), and are payable to persons other than the landowner.

14. Arkansas Louisiana Gas Co. v. Evans, 232 Ark. 495, 338 S.W.2d 666, 87 A.L.R.2d 595; Reeves v. Republic Production Co., Tex.Civ.App., 177 S.W.2d 1011. In the latter case the court stated:

" * * * the fact that the lessee in this case may happen to own the title to the minerals in the land leased to it by the lessor, and that lessor's title fails because of such ownership by the lessee, is a very unusual circumstance. But there is nothing in this unusual circumstance to deprive the lessee of the benefit of the provision in the lease for its protection against the failure of title to property which lessor assumed to lease. There is nothing in such circumstances to support the conclusion that the lessee thereby intended to convey to the lessor oil rights which the lessee owns and holds title to independently of the lessor. The lease does not by its terms purport to do so. And, so far from such a circumstance making it inequitable for the lessee to claim the benefit of the saving clause, it rather presents an additional weighty reason why the lessee should not be required to pay the lessor royalties on production from land which the lessor does not own the title to."

15. See Chapter 3, § 3.2(D)(5), supra.

16. 135 Tex. 503, 144 S.W.2d 878.

17. Gibson v. Turner, 156 Tex. 289, 294 S.W.2d 781; and see Hemingway, After-Acquired Title in Texas, 20 S.W.L.J. 310, 321–326.

Christmann,[18] title was outstanding. Here the court flatly stated that Duhig would have no application to oil and gas leases.

It should be noted, and contrasted with the Gibson case, that although there the court found no outstanding title, such factor would not prevent the operation of the proportionate reduction clause. In Reeves v. Republic Production Co.,[19] the lessee had a part of the title purported to be covered by a lease from O. Nevertheless, lessee could reduce the payments to O under the proportionate reduction clause in the lease.

§ 7.9 The Surrender Clause

The surrender clause affords the lessee with a unilateral means to be released from non-accrued obligations as to portions of the lease so surrendered. A question exists whether partial releases of particular producing formations may be made under the customary clause.

Virtually all modern oil and gas lease forms contain a form of clause allowing the lessee to surrender the lease, or parts thereof.[1] A commonly found clause reads as follows:

"5. * * * Lessee may at any time or times execute and deliver to Lessor or to the depository above named or place of record a release or releases covering any portion or portions of the above described premises and thereby surrender this lease as to such portion or portions and be relieved of all obligations as to the acreage surrendered, and thereafter the rentals payable hereunder shall be reduced in the proportion that the acreage covered hereby is reduced by said release or releases."[2]

The effect of the surrender clause is to provide the lessee with a unilateral method of securing a release from the obligations of the lease.[3] Under most surrender clauses a partial surrender of the lease may be made. Relief may be desired in any of the following situations:

(a) Rex, upon exploration of the land covered by the lease, desires to develop only a small portion of the lease. He wishes to release the remainder of the lease and be relieved from the obligation of paying delay rentals upon the portion not to be developed.

(b) Rex, during or after the primary term, desires only to develop a small portion of the lease and does not wish to be obligated to drill offset wells on lands which he does not deem suitable for development.

18. 157 Tex. 403, 303 S.W.2d 341, noted in 5 U.C.L.A.L.Rev. 558.

19. Tex.Civ.App., 177 S.W.2d 1011.

1. See Chapter 6, §§ 6.1, 6.2, supra, discussing the surrender clause, the "drill or pay" lease, and development of the "unless" lease. Also see Summers, Oil & Gas Law, §§ 235, 241, 242, 336, 522–525.

2. Shell Oil Co. v. Stansbury, Tex.Civ. App., 401 S.W.2d 623.

3. Osborn v. Finklestein, 189 Ind. 90, 126 N.E. 11; Coastal Club v. Shell Oil Co., D.C.La., 51 F.Supp. 819; s. c. D.C. La., 56 F.Supp. 641.

(c) Same as (b), above, where Rex has discovered oil in paying quantities, but does not desire to further develop other portions of the lease, and desires to be relieved of the implied obligation to further develop as to the other lands.

By exercise of the surrender clause all three objectives may be accomplished. Rex may execute a release and will be relieved of obligations as to the land released, viz., to pay delay rentals, drill offsets, or develop such released lands.[4] However, the release of such obligations operates only as to future obligations and normally will not serve to discharge such obligations that have already accrued.[5]

As can be seen, the right of the lessee of an "unless" lease to secure a partial release is important and is usually provided for in the lease. However, may the lessee make partial releases as to particular producing formations? In the Texas case of Shell Oil Co. v. Stansbury,[6] it was held that the clause, which is quoted above, did not authorize partial releases as to particular producing formations. This result was based upon the wording of the clause, which referred to "the acreage" surrendered. Acreage was construed as allowing only vertical and not horizontal release. The court seemed bothered by the problem of payment of delay rentals where only a particular formation was released from the lease, as delay rentals were calculated to be reduced in proportion that the "acreage" was reduced. Some lease forms expressly provide for the release of particular producing formations.

It has also been held that surrender of a portion of the land covered by the lease will not serve to proportionately reduce royalties. A California case, Beverly Hills Oil Co. v. Beverly Hills Unified School District,[7] involved a lease with a 50% royalty, a surrender clause similar to that quoted above, and no provision for delay rentals. The lessee released the northerly $3/5$ of the lease and argued that the royalty obligation was reduced to 20%. As rentals were not present in the lease, the lessee contended that the term "rentals" was interchangeable with the word "royalties" and denoted the same. The court held for the lessor. It was stated that although in California royalties, technically, were deemed to be rent, the terms had substantially different meanings within the context of the lease. Further, it would be unreasonable to reduce royalties upon release of a portion of the lease, as no particular relationship existed between the surrendered acreage and production of the retained wells, whereas a direct relationship exists between the quantum of delay rentals paya-

---

4. Beverly Hills Oil Co. v. Beverly Hills Unified School District, 264 Cal. App.2d 603, 70 Cal.Rptr. 640; Superior Oil Co. v. Dabney, 147 Tex. 51, 211 S.W.2d 563; Shell Oil Co. v. Stansbury, Tex.Civ.App., 401 S.W.2d 623; Pan American Petroleum Corp. v. Robinson, Tex.Civ.App., 405 S.W.2d 698. See Stockton v. Weeks, 51 Cal.App.2d 447, 125 P.2d 110 (reduction of installment bonus).

5. Edmonds v. Mounsey, 15 Ind.App. 399, 44 N.E. 196.

6. Tex.Civ.App., 401 S.W.2d 623.

7. 264 Cal.App.2d 603, 70 Cal.Rptr. 640.

§ 7.10   ROYALTY AND OTHER CLAUSES   385

ble and the acreage under the lease. The same distinction would exist between rentals and shut-in royalties. As shut-in royalties are not usually classifiable as rentals, they would not be reducible under the commonly used surrender clauses.

Wording of the clauses differs as to the formalities necessary for release of a lease, or part thereof. Limitations may be placed upon the time of release,[8] notice to the lessor,[9] recording of the surrender, the necessity for payment of money or accrued rentals,[10] configuration of the tracts that may be surrendered,[11] multiple exercise of the clause, etc. Where such limitations are set forth, the lessee must comply in order to have an effective surrender of the lease.[12]

§ 7.10 Lessee's Right to Remove Fixtures From the Lease

Where no provision exists in the lease, the lessee may remove his fixtures, i.e., equipment, machinery, derrick, pumps, casing, etc., during the term of the lease or within a reasonable time after the termination thereof. Many lease clauses state that such fixtures may be removed "at any time"; however, this has been consistently construed as meaning "within a reasonable time."

An oil and gas lessee, where no provision is present in the lease, may remove his fixtures, i.e., machinery, equipment, derrick, pumps, casing, etc., within the term of the lease or within a reasonable time after the termination of the lease.[1] Where it is found that an unreasonable time has elapsed, title to the fixtures not removed will pass to the lessor on the ground of abandonment.

Although such right exists without a provision in the lease, it has become customary to insert a provision relating to removal of fixtures. A common provision is as follows:

"Lessee shall have the right at any time to remove all machinery and fixtures placed on said premises, including the right to draw and remove casing."

The courts have held that such clause does not give the lessee an unlimited time to remove fixtures, but "at any time" shall mean "within a reasonable time."[2] Therefore, it would seem that the right

---

8. Ward v. Tripple State Natural Gas & Oil Co., 131 Ky. 711, 115 S.W. 819; and see State ex rel. Dickgraber v. Sheridan, 126 Mont. 447, 254 P.2d 390; Brown v. Wilson, 58 Okl. 392, 160 P. 94.

9. Eastern Oil Co. v. Beatty, 71 Okl. 275, 177 P. 104.

10. Title Insurance & Trust Co. v. Amalgamated Oil Co., 63 Cal.App. 29, 218 P. 71; Burress v. Diem, 23 Okl. 776, 101 P. 1116; Jackson v. Pure Oil Operating Co., Tex.Civ.App., 217 S.W. 959.

11. Alfson v. Anderson, N.D., 78 N.W.2d 693.

12. Benson v. Nyman, 136 Kan. 455, 16 P.2d 963.

1. Delk v. Craig, 235 Ark. 200, 357 S.W.2d 522. The rationale is that such equipment constitutes trade fixtures. In general see Summers, Oil and Gas Law, § 526.

2. Hill v. Larcon Co., D.C.Ark., 131 F.Supp. 469; Pratt v. Gerstner, 188 Kan. 148, 360 P.2d 1101; Davis v. Howard, Ky., 276 S.W.2d 460; Cox v. Miller, Tex. Civ.App., 184 S.W.2d 323; Vermillion v. Fidel, Tex.Civ.App., 256 S.W.2d 969. But see Sunray DX Oil Co. v. Texaco, Inc., Tex.Civ.App., 417 S.W.2d 424.

of the lessee to remove fixtures is the same under the above clause as it is where there is no clause.

What constitutes a reasonable time will depend upon the facts and circumstances in each instance.[3] In Texas the question is one for the jury.[4] It has been stated that determinations of a reasonable time will be affected by the damage to the lessor caused by the non-removal of the fixtures. In Pratt v. Gerstner,[5] it was held that landowner's claim of damage due to interference with the raising of pine trees due to the stacking of materials on the land could not be sustained where the area occupied by such materials was small.

The right to remove fixtures may be lost when it would be inequitable to allow such removal. In Woodson Oil Co. v. Pruett,[6] the lessee lost the lease, although it still had a producing well thereon. The court denied the right of the lessee to remove the casing because it would have had the effect of destroying the well. The well was thereafter produced by the lessor. The court allowed rental to be paid to the lessee until the well ceased to produce. An alternative remedy would have been to enter judgment in favor of lessee for the value of the casing.

A somewhat contrary result was reached in the case of Blankenship v. United Fuel Gas Co.,[7] where gas for domestic usage was being produced from a well. The well was not producing in paying quantities. The lessee desired to shut in the well and remove the casing to prevent salt water flooding to other wells. It was held that the lessee had a contract right to remove his equipment and that he was not acting maliciously in seeking to remove the equipment.

Where the lease has terminated, but before lessee has removed his fixtures, use of such equipment by other parties will constitute a conversion. In Texas Co. v. Sorrell,[8] the original lessee obtained permission to abandon a well. The lease was abandoned, and lessee claimed a right to remove the casing from the well. However, before this could be done, lessor again leased to lessee No. 2, who re-worked

---

3. Delk v. Craig, 235 Ark. 200, 357 S.W.2d 522 (4 months not unreasonable); Pratt v. Gerstner, 188 Kan. 148, 360 P.2d 1101 (29 months after cessation of production and 22 months after termination of the lease was unreasonable); Texas Co. v. Sorrell, D.C.Mont., 116 F.Supp. 137 (6½ months not unreasonable); Cox v. Miller, Tex.Civ.App., 184 S.W.2d 323 (September, 1939, to April, 1943, not unreasonable where lessee made continuous efforts to market with apparent knowledge and acquiescence of lessor).

4. Cox v. Miller, Tex.Civ.App., 184 S.W.2d 323; Vermillion v. Fidel, Tex.Civ. App., 256 S.W.2d 969.

5. 188 Kan. 148, 360 P.2d 1101.

6. Tex.Civ.App., 298 S.W.2d 856. Also see Powers v. Bridgeport Oil Co., 238 Ill. 397, 87 N.E. 381; Eubank v. Twin Mountain Oil Corp., Tex.Civ.App., 406 S.W.2d 789; Patton v. Rogers, Tex.Civ. App., 417 S.W.2d 470.

7. Ky., 307 S.W.2d 928.

8. D.C.Mont., 116 F.Supp. 137. Also see Lund v. Starz, 355 Mich. 497, 94 N.W.2d 912; Proper v. Butcher, Ohio App., 175 N.E.2d 528. Lessee also may have the right, where lessor wrongfully interferes with removal, to bring an action to recover the property or enjoin lessor's interference. Hill v. Larcon Company, D.C.Ark., 131 F.Supp. 469; Baker v. Vanderpool, 296 Ky. 663, 178 S.W.2d 189.

the well and increased its productivity. It was held that the second lessee was guilty of a conversion of the casing.

In a few cases the question has arisen whether the lessee has lost the right to remove the fixtures where he has released the lease.[9] The general result has been that the right to remove fixtures was not lost. However, the concurring opinion in Pratt v. Gerstner,[10] would reach the opposite result on the ground that the right to remove fixtures only exists by virtue of the clause in the lease, and when the lease was released the right to remove was lost with it. The underlying assumption would seem contra to the weight of authority.

Contractual restrictions may be inserted into the clause. If so contained, they are binding upon the lessee. The clause in Wade v. Lillard[11] had a 60-day restriction upon the time within which the fixtures could be removed. It was indicated that the lessee was bound by the time limit. A clause may contain a prohibition against removal,[12] which is also binding.

§ 7.11 The Force Majeure Clause

The force majeure clause is inserted in an oil and gas lease to excuse the lessee from non-performance of lease obligations when the non-performance is caused by circumstances beyond the reasonable control of the lessee.

It is a familiar principle of contract law that where an obligation is undertaken that is unconditional and absolute, inability to perform is not an excuse where the act promised is not inherently impossible of performance.[1] In construction contracts and allied areas it has become obligatory to place contractual language excusing performance due to circumstances of extreme and unreasonable difficulty beyond the reasonable control of the party charged with performance. Such clauses are commonly referred to as force majeure clauses.

Similar situations occur in connection with the drilling and development of oil and gas leases. For instance, where a lessee is operating after the end of the primary term to complete a well that he has begun prior to the end of the primary term, will he be excused for non-performance due to weather conditions, etc., which last longer than the period stated in the well completion clause? In Baldwin v. Blue Stem Oil Co.,[2] the lessee waited until the end of the last year of a three-year primary term of the lease to commence the drilling operations on a well. The well was not completed prior to the end of the term, and no other lease provision applied to save the lease. The

---

9. Pratt v. Gerstner, 188 Kan. 148, 360 P.2d 1101; Texas Co. v. Sorrell, D.C. Mont., 116 F.Supp. 137.

10. 188 Kan. 148, 360 P.2d 1101.

11. 201 Okl. 520, 207 P.2d 771.

12. Johnson v. Hinkel, 29 Cal.App. 78, 154 P. 487.

1. Baldwin v. Blue Stem Oil Co., 106 Kan. 848, 189 P. 920; Graham-Loftus Oil Corp. v. Mountain View Development Corp., 37 Cal.App.2d 315, 99 P.2d 357; Ellwood v. Nutex Oil Co., Tex.Civ.App., 148 S.W.2d 862.

2. 106 Kan. 848, 189 P. 920.

lease did not have a force majeure clause. The lessee contended that his non-performance should be excused, as he was prevented from timely performance by rains, blizzards, sickness of the drilling crew and shortages of fuel and casing due to federal rules and regulations in force during World War I. The court held that impossibility so caused did not excuse performance, and the lease terminated.

A similar situation occurred in the case of Haby v. Stanolind Oil & Gas Co.,[3] which has become known as the "Sprayberry decision." Oil production occurred in the Sprayberry field with the production of casinghead gas. Some of the producers had facilities to re-cycle the gas back into the reservoir, whereas others did not. The Texas Railroad Commission found that production of gas that was flared and not returned to the reservoir was waste and ordered the wasteful producers to shut down to prevent waste. The Commission also ordered the non-wasteful producers to shut down to protect the correlative right of the wasteful producers to produce. Although this latter order was later held to be invalid, during a period of some years the field was shut in. The well in question was drilled under a lease that did not have a force majeure clause. The well was shut in under the order later held invalid. It was held that the lease was terminated, although cessation of production was caused by government regulation.

Other cases involving circumstances beyond the lessees' control include strikes and boycotts,[4] undue price rises,[5] rain and floods,[6] non-availability of a market,[7] scarcity of materials,[8] zoning ordinances,[9] and governmental orders and regulations.[10]

It has become common to include force majeure clauses in oil and gas leases. Such lease clauses vary from the simple [11] to those that

---

3. C.A.5th, 228 F.2d 298, noted 35 Tex.L.Rev. 149. Although the parties apparently contracted with reference to governmental orders, the court felt such subjective intent was controlled by specific provisions of the lease, such as the continuous operations clause, which provided the lease would terminate where production ceased "from any cause" unless operations or production was obtained within a specified time.

4. Hixon v. Parker, 228 Ark. 317, 307 S.W.2d 210.

5. Butler v. Nepple, 54 Cal.2d 589, 6 Cal.Rptr. 767, 354 P.2d 239.

6. Illinois Mid-Continent Co. v. Tennis, 122 Ind.App. 17, 102 N.E.2d 390; Baldwin v. Blue Stem Oil Co., 106 Kan. 848, 189 P. 920; Logan v. Blaxton, La. App., 71 So.2d 675.

7. Lamczyk v. Allen, 8 Ill.2d 547, 134 N.E.2d 753.

8. Prairie Oil Co. v. Carleton, 91 Cal. App.2d 555, 205 P.2d 81.

9. Baldwin v. Kubetz, 148 Cal.App.2d 937, 307 P.2d 1005.

10. Haby v. Stanolind Oil & Gas Co., C.A.5th, 228 F.2d 298, noted 35 Tex.L. Rev. 149; Baldwin v. Blue Stem Oil Co., 106 Kan. 848, 189 P. 920; Gillham v. Jenkins, 206 Okl. 440, 244 P.2d 291; Hunter Co. v. Vaughn, 217 La. 459, 46 So.2d 735.

11. Illinois Mid-Continent Co. v. Tennis, 122 Ind.App. 17, 102 N.E.2d 390: "In the event lessee is prevented from complying with the drilling obligations imposed by this lease, by reason of floods, or impassable roads, then lessee shall have such additional time to comply with such drilling obligations as it was prevented from meeting such requirements by reason of floods or the impassable condition of roads." Prairie Oil Co. v. Carleton, 91 Cal.App.2d 555, 205 P.2d 81: "Paragraph 10 provides that: 'The drilling and operating requirements of this lease shall be suspended while, but only as long as Lessee is prevented from complying therewith, in whole or in part, by

are so complex and all-encompassing as to practically relieve the lessee from all duties.[12] Such proliferation of the clause has no doubt been due to the fact that early forms, copied from building construction agreements, at times were not broad enough to adequately protect the lessee. In Haby v. Stanolind Oil & Gas Co.,[13] discussed above, the cause of the cessation of production was due to government regulation. It is doubtful, if the lease had contained a force majeure clause, whether at that time it would have included a provision concerning government regulations. It is essential that the draftsman use a clause of sufficient breadth but not so broad as to become meaningless.

Where a force majeure clause is present in the lease, if the lessee can satisfy the burden of proof that the conditions which occurred were those contemplated by the clause, default due to such conditions will be excused for so long as the condition persists. Cases are found involving orders of a conservation commission of the state[14] and the shortage of materials.[15]

On the other hand, where the lessee is unable to discharge the burden of establishing such facts, the default will not be excused.[16] In the case of Lamczyk v. Allen,[17] the lessee attempted to rely upon

---

strikes, lockouts, war or inability (other than financial) of Lessee to obtain material or supplies, as well as delays in transportation, accidents and other matters of any kind or nature whatsoever beyond the control of Lessee, or when the price of oil falls below forty (40) cents per barrel at the well.'" See Summers, Oil & Gas Law, Form, §§ 1137, 1357.

12. Logan v. Blaxton, La.App., 71 So. 2d 675, see clause footnote 19, infra.

13. Note 3, supra.

14. Hunter Co. v. Vaughn, 217 La. 459, 46 So.2d 735.

15. Prairie Oil Co. v. Carleton, 91 Cal. App.2d 555, 205 P.2d 81; Caddell v. Threshold Development Co., Tex.Civ. App., 609 S.W.2d 871, (lessor's "lockout" of lessee); Gilbert v. Smedley, Tex.Civ. App., 612 S.W.2d 270, refused n.r.e., (bankruptcy as "cause beyond control" of lessee's assignees of lease within the force majeure clause).

16. Illinois Mid-Continent Co. v. Tennis, 122 Ind.App. 17, 102 N.E.2d 390 (shut down for 259 days due to rains); Lamczyk v. Allen, 8 Ill.2d 547, 134 N.E. 2d 753; Baldwin v. Kubetz, 148 Cal.App. 2d 937, 307 P.2d 1005; Butler v. Nepple, 54 Cal.2d 589, 6 Cal.Rptr. 767, 354 P.2d 239; Logan v. Blaxton, La.App., 71 So.2d 675.

17. 8 Ill.2d 547, 134 N.E.2d 753. The lease contained the following clause:

Paragraph 16 provided: "If, after production has been obtained, operations under this lease are delayed, interrupted or prevented by acts of God, fire, riots, wars, strikes, inability to obtain equipment due to governmental order or action, or by failure of carriers to transport equipment, or by regulation by State or Federal action, this lease shall not terminate or be forfeited and no right of damages shall exist against lessee by reason thereof, provided operations are commenced or resumed within a reasonable time after removal of such cause or causes. If at any time within three months prior to the expiration of the primary term of this lease, production has not been obtained and the commencement or continuance of operations for the drilling of a well on said lands is delayed or prevented by any of the causes, mentioned in this paragraph, the said primary term and all other terms of this lease may be extended for successive periods of time while such cause or causes exist, by continuing the payment or tender of delay rentals in the manner and amount and for the periods of time as provided in Paragraphs 7 and 8 of this lease for deferment of the commencement of drilling operations during the said primary term."

the force majeure clause to relieve him from termination of the lease where a gas well was shut in and shut-in royalties were not paid. The lessee claimed that the lease should be held in effect under the clause due to non-availability of a market. The court stated that the clause: "* * * contemplates a condition where there has been production of gas together with its delivery and sale but that, due to certain conditions after production, suspension of operations is caused by no reasonable market being available, and provides for resumption within a reasonable time after removal of the cause." Since production had never been obtained, it was held that the clause did not apply. In Butler v. Nepple,[18] the lessee argued that the force majeure clause should apply due to sharply increased prices for casing and materials. The court found that there existed no factual evidence upon which to base a finding that the price increase was extreme and unreasonable and stated, "Even in the case of a force majeure provision in a contract, mere increase in expense does not excuse the performance unless there exists extreme and unreasonable difficulty, expense, injury or loss involved." In another case the lessee tried to excuse a deliberate shut-down from November 1951 to May 19, 1952, due to seasonable rains. The court was unimpressed.[19]

Paragraph 17 provided: "It is further agreed that during any period of over-production the lessee may curtail production and prorate runs from said lands on a basis equal to any curtailment or proration in effect on adjoining lands, or in compliance with any proration order issued by any governmental authority. Operations hereunder may be suspended or discontinued during such time as the price of oil produced from said lands shall be less than 75 cents per barrel at the well, or for such time as there shall be no reasonable market for the oil and/or gas that may be produced from said lands, and this lease shall not terminate or be forfeited and no right of damages shall exist by reason of such suspension or discontinuance, provided operations are resumed within a reasonable time after removal of such cause."

18. 54 Cal.2d 589, 6 Cal.Rptr. 767, 354 P.2d 239.

19. Logan v. Blaxton, La.App., 71 So. 2d 675. The court stated: "Should the defendant be relieved of his obligation to produce and market the oil during and for the reason of the seasonal rains each year, and covering a like period of time as contended here, that is, from November to May, inclusive, and then, by the terms of the lease, be allowed six months to begin operations again, such delay would extend into the next rainy season, and the effect would be that he could hold the lease perpetually without any activity on his part. We could not so construe the terms of this lease."

The cause involved was so broad as to almost be meaningless:

"(a) The term 'Force Majeure' as used herein shall mean and include: * * * lack of labor or means of transportation of labor or material; *Acts of God*; insurrection; *flood*; strike.

"(b) If by reason of Force Majeure as herein defined, lessee is prevented from or delayed in drilling, completing or producing any well or wells for oil, gas or other mineral on the leased premises, then while so prevented or during the period of such delay lessee shall be relieved from all obligations, whether express or implied, imposed on lessee under this lease, to drill, complete or produce such well or wells on the leased premises, and lessee shall not be liable in damages and this lease shall not be subject to cancellation for failure of lessee to drill, complete or produce such well or wells during the time lessee is relieved from all obligations to do so. Provided, this provision shall not relieve lessee from the necessity of paying rentals during the primary term in order to continue this lease in force under the specifications of paragraphs 4 and 6 above.

Where the clause applies, the lessee has a reasonable time under the facts and circumstances to resume operations under the lease.[20]

§ 7.12 The Free Gas Clause

Many oil and gas leases contain a clause for the use of free gas by the lessor for domestic purposes in the heating and lighting of dwelling houses on the leased property. A typical clause is found in United Fuel Gas Co. v. McCoy,[1] which provides:

> "Lessor may lay a line to any gas well on said land and take gas produced from said well for his own use for heat and light in two dwelling houses on said land."

The clause may limit the amount of free gas to be allotted to the lessor or the surface possessor,[2] assignment,[3] place responsibility on the lessor to make the connection on the well,[4] or state that it is a personal covenant which does not run with the land.[5] The provision for the use of free gas by the lessor, or possessor of the surface, may sometimes be inserted in the royalty clause.[6]

"(c) If upon or at any time after the expiration of the primary term hereof, while this lease is in force, lessee cannot maintain same in effect because prevented by Force Majeure from fulfilling the particular requirement (operations on or continued production from the leased premises as the case may be) necessary so to do as specified in paragraph 2 hereof, then while so prevented and for six months thereafter this lease shall nevertheless continue in effect; and if within such six months lessee either commences operations on or resumes production from the leased premises, as the case may be, this lease shall continue in effect thereafter as though Force Majeure had not intervened. During any period this lease is continued in force after its primary term by Force Majeure as herein provided, lessee shall pay to the owners of the royalty hereunder, or to the credit of such owners in the depositary bank above named, as royalty, an amount equal to $1 per acre per year for each acre retained hereunder. Such payments shall be made annually, and shall become due on each anniversary hereof while such Force Majeure continued, except the first payment shall be made within a reasonable time after occurrence of Force Majeure and shall be proportionate in amount to the unexpired portion of the then current year, if for less than a year. Nothing herein shall impair the right of lessee to release this lease as to all or any portion of the lands covered hereby and to be relieved of all obligations thereafter accruing as to the acreage released.

"(d) The specification of causes of Force Majeure herein enumerated shall not exclude other causes from consideration in determining whether lessee has used reasonable diligence wherever required in fulfilling any obligations or conditions of this lease, express or implied, and any delay of not more than six months after termination of Force Majeure shall be deemed justified."

20. Wilson v. Talbert, 259 Ark. 535, 535 S.W.2d 807; Caddell v. Threshold Development Co., Tex.Civ.App., 609 S.W.2d 871; Gilbert v. Smedley, Tex.Civ.App., 612 S.W.2d 270, refused n.r.e.

1. Ky., 307 S.W.2d 176.

2. Note 1 supra.

3. Salisbury v. Columbian Fuel Corp., Ky., 387 S.W.2d 864; United Fuel Gas Co. v. McCoy, Ky., 307 S.W.2d 176; Ludolph v. Tuel & Thoenen Inc., 6 Ohio Misc. 117, 214 N.E.2d 696, 35 O.O.2d 239.

4. Sinclair Oil & Gas Co. v. Huffman, Okl., 376 P.2d 599.

5. Lyons v. Gambill, 242 Ky. 696, 47 S.W.2d 532; Howell v. Kentucky-West Virginia Gas Co., Ky., 275 S.W.2d 429.

6. Sinclair Oil & Gas Co. v. Huffman, Okl., 376 P.2d 599.

The lessor or the possessor of the surface estate only has a privilege or right to use gas as it is expressed in the lease.[7] The majority of the controversies arising out of the clause deal with the meaning of "domestic purposes." Where the clause places no limitation upon the amount or extent of use, the lessor is not entitled to an unlimited amount of gas, but will be limited to such use as is customary and reasonable for domestic purposes.[8] However, an excessive use of gas by the lessor does not generally give the lessee the right to terminate the connection.[9] Where the lessor is not entitled by the terms of the lease to the free use of gas, but the lessee furnishes it as an accommodation, the lessee will not be estopped from terminating the supply.[10]

The term "dwelling house," which is used in many free gas clauses, has been interpreted to extend beyond the ordinary meaning of the phrase and includes the residence, garage, work house and separate sleeping quarters.[11] It extends to the cluster of buildings in the curtilage.[12]

Free use of gas for irrigation purposes has not been included within the clause on the ground that it is the custom and practice of the area where the leasehold is situated.[13] A specific provision relating to gas for irrigation purposes must be included. Oklahoma, through the passage of legislation,[14] sought to require the lessee, who is producing gas for sale or for off-premises use, to make gas available to the lessor for the operation of irrigation wells on the land at a reasonable price. However, the Oklahoma Supreme Court, in Phillips Petroleum Co. v. Corporation Commission of Oklahoma,[15] held that this statute was unconstitutional. The basis for the decision was that the statute was not a valid regulation under the police power of the State but would, if enforced, constitute a taking of producer's property without due process of law.

Usually, provisions for the benefit of the lessor are referable to and run with the mineral ownership of the land. But this is not the case in the use of the free gas clause. This clause is usually for the

---

7. Ludolph v. Tuel & Thoenen Inc., 6 Ohio Misc. 117, 214 N.E.2d 696, 35 O.O.2d 239.

8. Ludolph v. Tuel & Thoenen Inc., 6 Ohio Misc. 117, 214 N.E.2d 696, 35 O.O.2d 239; Summers, Oil & Gas Law, § 587.

9. Scurry Area Canyon Reef Operators Corp. v. Popnoe, Tex.Civ.App., 283 S.W.2d 819.

10. Cranston v. Miller, 208 Ark. 156, 185 S.W.2d 920; Ludolph v. Tuel & Thoenen Inc., 60 Ohio Misc. 117, 214 N.E.2d 696, 35 O.O.2d 239.

11. Smith v. State, 80 Fla. 315, 85 So. 911; Horst v. Handke, 190 Iowa 658, 180 N.W. 762; United Carbon Co. v. Conn, Ky., 351 S.W.2d 189.

12. United Carbon Co. v. Conn, Ky., 351 S.W.2d 189.

13. Phillips Petroleum Co. v. Buster, C.A.10th, 241 F.2d 178.

14. 52 Okl.St.Ann. §§ 250–256.

15. Okl., 312 P.2d 916.

benefit of the surface owner,[16] and runs for the benefit of the surface owner and the mineral estate owner.[17]

However, the benefit of the free gas clause may be personal or run with the land according to the intention of the parties.[18] "For the use of the grantor's immediate family"[19] or "for the use of any of the children of the grantor living on the farm or land herein described"[20] are phrases in the clause which indicate that this is a personal covenant and does not run with the land. But if the language of the clause makes it applicable to the possessor of the surface estate or "for the life of the well"[21] the clause runs with the land and successive possessors of the surface are entitled to the benefit of the clause.

Where there has been a subdivision of the property a problem may arise as to whether the owners of the property on which there is not a producing well are entitled to the benefits of the clause. The answer would seem to be that they would not be so entitled. In Warfield Natural Gas Co. v. Moore,[22] the court held that in the case where the dwelling house entitled to free gas under the lease had been destroyed and another erected in its place, the lessor would be entitled to the use of free gas if the new house had been built to replace the one destroyed. However, if the one subsequently built on the property was not to replace the original, such subsequent dwelling would not be entitled to the benefit of the clause, as it was not the intention of the parties to the lease that such subsequent dwelling would be covered by the clause.

The result in the above case may be contrasted with that in the Kansas case of Jackson v. Farmer,[23] which has the effect of putting the lessee in the public utility business. In the Jackson case four

---

16. United Fuel Gas Co. v. McCoy, Ky., 307 S.W.2d 176; Warfield Natural Gas Co. v. Small, 282 Ky. 347, 138 S.W.2d 488.

17. Jackson v. Farmer, 225 Kan. 732, 594 P.2d 177.

18. Patrick v. Allen, Ky., 350 S.W.2d 481; Warfield Natural Gas Co. v. Small, 282 Ky. 347, 138 S.W.2d 488.

19. Lyon v. Gambill, 242 Ky. 696, 47 S.W.2d 532.

20. Howell v. Kentucky-West Virginia Gas Co., Ky., 275 S.W.2d 429.

21. Patrick v. Allen, Ky., 350 S.W.2d 481.

Slife v. Kundtz Properties, Inc., 40 Ohio App.2d 179, 318 N.E.2d 557, 69 O.O.2d 178 (case remanded, as stating cause of action, to determine if successors entitled to benefit of clause although original house razed and land subdivided and later house built. " * * * for the purpose of heating the residence now upon the premises * * * so long as the wells produce gas." (emphasis added) The later part of the clause interpreted as indicating gas use not limited to original house).

22. 281 Ky. 689, 136 S.W.2d 1086.

23. 225 Kan. 732, 594 P.2d 177. The court further stated that the principal dwelling did not have to be on the land at the time the lease was executed. As a matter of fact, it was built later. The effect of the unitization in this case was to treat all the unit land as one lease for application of the free gas clauses that were present in the individual leases. This may be contrasted with the reasoning of the court in Exxon v. Middleton, footnote 23 § 7.4, supra, that sales of gas from the unit well would not be treated as sales "at the well" for leases in the unit and upon which the unit well was not located. The rationale there was that unitization for purposes of the royalty clause did not constitute the unit as one lease.

leases, each on a quarter section, were unitized into one unit. The only unit well was located on the southwest one-fourth of the section. The lease on the northwest one-fourth of the section contained a free gas clause. The court held that the principal dwelling owner on the northwest one-fourth of the section had a right to take gas from the unit well to satisfy the clause. The court further stated that each principal dwelling on each of the leases forming the unit had a similar right! The rationale for this result was that after unitization it was all treated as one lease.

Where the lease provides that the gas to be used by the lessor is to be appropriated from production of the wells on the leased premises, or contains language indicating an intention that the duty to furnish gas is contingent upon production from the lease, the lessee is under no independent duty to furnish free gas until production is attained. However, if the lease does not so qualify, then the lessee may be under a separate and independent duty to furnish gas.[24] Where the use of a compressor was required to increase the flow into the lessor's line, it was held, in Bassell v. West Virginia Central Gas Co.,[25] that the lessee may furnish gas from other sources. The lessee is not relieved of its duty to furnish free gas when the amount of production is reduced.[26]

On the other hand, the lessee is free to operate its affairs in a lawful and businesslike manner, and the lessor may not interfere with such operation. Where the lease provides for the free use of gas by the lessor, he may not interfere with the installation of a meter on the lessor's line to determine the amount being used.[27] The lessee is not required to operate its well so that the lessor may be furnished with gas. It may plug the wells if it is desirable and remove all machinery and equipment on the premises, if provided for in the lease.[28] It would be advantageous to the lessee to include in the free gas clause words to the effect that lessor will provide the line to the well for the taking of the free gas and that such is done at the lessor's risk. Such a provision places the burden on the lessor for the construction of the line, and when the well ceases production the privilege ceases.[29]

Lessor may use both legal and equitable remedies if the lessee, or his successors, refuses to furnish the gas as is required by the lease or threatens to terminate the supply.[30] The lessor may obtain a temporary injunction to maintain the status quo until the point may be settled. In the event of breach of the covenant by the lessee, the

---

24. Summers, Oil & Gas Law, § 587.
25. 86 W.Va. 198, 103 S.E. 116, 12 A.L.R. 1398.
26. Pittsburgh & West Virginia Gas Co. v. Nicholson, 87 W.Va. 540, 105 S.E. 784, 12 A.L.R. 1392.
27. United Carbon Co. v. Ramsey, Ky., 350 S.W.2d 454.
28. Ludolph v. Tuel & Thoenen Inc., 60 Ohio Misc. 117, 214 N.E.2d 696, 35 O.O.2d 239.
29. Note 28, supra.
30. Note 28, supra.

lessor or the person who is entitled to the free gas may bring an action for damages,[31] specific performance,[32] or to enjoin the lessee from interfering with the lessor's use of the gas.[33] The measure of the amount of damages is the value of the gas which should have been provided [34] or the difference in the value of the property with and without the free gas.[35]

§ 7.13 Pooling and the Pooling Clause

Pooling may be defined as the combination of leases or parts of leases for the development and production of oil, gas, and associated products. Some primary reasons for pooling are more effective and efficient development, conservation of oil and gas, the elimination of unnecessary wells, the combination of enough land to enable the lessee to drill a well with a full proration allowance, the sharing of risks, holding acreage for future production, directional drilling, and to use secondary and enhanced methods of production for additional recovery of products.

Terminology is not precise. The terms "pooling" and "unitization" many times are incorrectly used interchangeably. "Pooling" usually refers to the combination of enough land to form a single-well drilling unit with a full allowable. "Unitization," on the other hand, normally refers to field-wide or partial field-wide operation. Field-wide or partial field-wide unitization is used for operations for the purpose of causing products to migrate across lease lines. These operations include water flooding to create a pressure barrier to move products, pressure maintenance operations such as gas cycling, which removes liquid products and reinjects gas back into the formation to help maintain primary production pressure, and enhanced recovery procedures such as CO_2 injection and injection of other miscible displacement fluids. The latter is a form of tertiary recovery. Secondary recovery uses a displacement substance that does not modify the properties of the substance being displaced. An example is the use of a water drive in an oil field. Tertiary recovery differs, as the displacement fluid or process modifies the properties of the product being displaced.

Another method of sharing the risk and the products where lands of large size are being developed is known as the area of interest unit or the working interest owner unit. These have been used in areas of west Texas. The sharing is done by the lessees under an operating agreement. They are not approved by the Texas Railroad Commission. It is hard to say whether the agreement creates a unitization in

---

31. Summers, Oil & Gas Law, § 587.

32. Indiana Natural Gas & Oil Co. v. Hinton, 159 Ind. 398, 64 N.E. 224; Sheridan Oil Co. v. Cunningham, 186 Okl. 618, 99 P.2d 497.

33. Kimble v. Wetzel Natural Gas Co., 134 W.Va. 761, 61 S.E.2d 728.

34. Scurry Area Canyon Reef Operators Corp. v. Popnoe, Tex.Civ.App., 283 S.W.2d 819; Harbert v. Hope Natural Gas Co., 76 W.Va. 207, 84 S.E. 770.

35. Indiana Natural Gas & Oil Co. v. Hinton, 159 Ind. 398, 64 N.E. 224.

the sense of a full unit agreement. The agreement does not purport to affect the royalty interest in the lands covered. However, the royalty may be pooled in the spacing units at the time of drilling, the pooling is provided for in the individual leases.

Pooling is normally done under the provisions of the oil and gas lease and pools both the royalty and working interest in the lands covered. Field-wide and partial field-wide unitization is usually accomplished through separate agreements by the working interest owners and by the royalty owners.

Pooling or unitization may also be distinguished on the basis of whether it is done by voluntary agreement or by force pooling or unitization under a statute. Force pooling statutes differ greatly, and not all jurisdictions that have force pooling statutes also have force unitization statutes.

It must be emphasized that the individual instruments allowing pooling or unitizing be read carefully. This is especially true of pooling under a lease pooling clause. The clauses differ greatly in coverage and provisions.

Pooling as herein discussed is limited in scope to the voluntary formation of oil or gas drilling units of sufficient size so that the lessee will comply with spacing requirements for such production. Excellent materials are available for those interested in the more complex aspects of pooling and unitization and should be consulted by those actively interested in the area.[1]

(A) Formation of Units

The formation of units for pooled production can result, in some jurisdictions, from the execution of a joint or community lease by the several owners of segregated tracts of land, or from lessees' acting pursuant to the authority vested in them by lease clauses allowing pooling.

A community lease may result where owners of contiguous tracts of land execute a single lease describing such lands. For example A, B, and C are the owners of tracts 1, 2, and 3. Rex Oil Company obtains a lease describing all the land, by perimeter description. The lease is executed by A, B and C. In some jurisdictions it is held that a community lease results as a matter of law.[2] That is to say that the lessee may develop the entire land as one tract without regard to inside offsets, royalty will be paid to the lessors on an apportionment

---

1. See Summers, Oil and Gas Law, §§ 950–978; Hoffman, Voluntary Pooling and Unitization; Myers, The Law of Pooling and Unitization, Voluntary-Compulsory.

2. Higgins v. California Petroleum & Asphalt Co., 109 Cal. 304, 41 P. 1087; Parker v. Parker, Tex.Civ.App., 144 S.W.2d 303; Howell v. Union Producing Co., C.A.5th, 392 F.2d 95; Lynch v. Davis, 79 W.Va. 437, 92 S.E. 427. In these jurisdictions lack of intent to pool or knowledge of the consequences of execution of a joint lease is immaterial. Also see Chapter 9, § 9.4, infra.

§ 7.13   ROYALTY AND OTHER CLAUSES   397

basis, and production on any part of the lands will keep the lease alive as to all lands.

In other jurisdictions such joint execution may raise a rebuttable presumption of pooling,[3] while in others the courts will try to determine the intent of the parties from the instrument and surrounding circumstances without regard to a presumption.[4]

In those jurisdictions that find a pooling of the lands described in the common lease, this result is not varied where the lands described are not contiguous[5] or where execution of the lease is done by counterpart copies.[6] In the latter event all copies should describe the entire lands and include the name of all parties "lessor" in the granting clause.

In view of the development and judicial interpretation of the express pooling clause, the use of the community lease as a deliberate means of effectuating pooling has been virtually abandoned. Where it is desired to pool lands for oil and gas development it is the current practice to include a pooling clause in the lease or to obtain an amendment to the lease providing for pooling.[7] A basic pooling clause may read as follows:[8]

> "Lessee, at its option, is hereby given the right and power to pool or combine the acreage covered by this lease or any portion

---

3. Peerless Oil & Gas Co. v. Tipken, 190 Okl. 396, 124 P.2d 418; cf. Nabors v. Producers Oil Co., 140 La. 985, 74 So. 527.

4. Brown v. Sugar Creek Syndicate, 195 La. 865, 197 So. 583; Leonard v. Barnes, 75 N.M. 331, 404 P.2d 292.

5. Shell Petroleum Corp. v. Calcasieu Real Estate & Oil Co., 185 La. 751, 170 So. 785.

6. Irick v. Hubbell & Webb, Okl., 280 P.2d 733. A partial rationale for the community lease result is that in the premises of the customary oil and gas lease, following the blank for insertion of names, all parties are collectively defined as "Lessor". Royalty from production from the lease is also payable to "lessor", raising a conclusive or rebuttable presumption of apportionment, depending upon the jurisdiction.

7. The amendment clause would be essentially identical to that found in the oil and gas lease, but should be executed to conform to the statutes of frauds and conveyances in a particular jurisdiction. This is especially important in jurisdictions, such as Texas, that follow the cross-conveyance theory and have special conveyancing rules as to the marital homestead.

8. This clause was involved in litigation in the case of Tiller v. Fields, Tex. Civ.App., 301 S.W.2d 185. Another more detailed clause:

> "Lessee, at its option, is hereby given the right and power to pool or combine the acreage covered by this lease, or any portion thereof as to oil and gas, or either of them, with other land, lease or leases in the immediate vicinity thereof to the extent hereinafter stipulated, when in Lessee's judgment it is necessary or advisable to do so in order properly to explore or to develop and operate said leased premises in compliance with the spacing rules of the Railroad Commission of Texas, or other lawful authority, or when to do so would, in the judgment of Lessee, promote the conservation of oil and gas in and under and that may be produced from said premises. Units pooled for oil hereunder shall not substantially exceed 40 acres each in area, and units pooled for gas hereunder shall not substantially exceed in area 640 acres each plus a tolerance of 10% thereof, provided that should governmental authority having jurisdiction prescribe or permit the creation of units larger than those specified, units thereafter created may conform substantially in size with those prescribed by governmental regulations. Lessee under the provisions hereof may pool or combine acreage covered by this lease, or any portion

thereof with other land, lease or leases in the immediate vicinity thereof, when in Lessee's judgment it is necessary or advisable to do so in order properly to develop and operate said premises in compliance with the spacing rules of the Railroad Commission of Texas or other lawful authority, or when to do so would, in the judgment of Lessee, promote the conservation of the oil and gas in and under and that may be produced from said premises. Lessee shall execute in writing an instrument identifying and describing the pooled acreage. The entire acreage so pooled into a tract or unit shall be treated, for all purposes except the payments of royalties on production from the pooled unit, as if it were included in this lease. If production is found on the pooled acreage, it shall be treated as if production is had from this lease, whether the well or wells be located on the premises covered by this lease or not.

thereof as above provided as to oil in any one or more strata and as to gas in any one or more strata. The units formed by pooling as to any stratum or strata need not conform in size or area with the unit or units into which the lease is pooled or combined as to any other stratum or strata, and oil units need not conform as to area with gas units. The pooling in one or more instances shall not exhaust the rights of the Lessee hereunder to pool this lease or portions thereof into other units. Lessee shall file for record in the appropriate records of the county in which the leased premises are situated an instrument describing and designating the pooled acreage as a pooled unit. Lessee may at its election exercise its pooling option after commencing operations for or completing an oil or gas well on the leased premises, and the pooled unit may include, but it is not required to include, land or leases upon which a well capable of producing oil or gas in paying quantities has theretofore been completed or upon which operations for the drilling of a well for oil or gas have theretofore been commenced. Operations for drilling on or production of oil or gas from any part of the pooled unit which includes all or a portion of the land covered by this lease regardless of whether such operations for drilling were commenced or such production was secured before or after the execution of this instrument or the instrument designating the pooled unit, shall be considered as operations for drilling on or production of oil or gas from land covered by this lease whether or not the well or wells be located on the premises covered by this lease, and the entire acreage constituting such unit or units, as to oil and gas, or either of them, as herein provided, shall be treated for all purposes, except the payment of royalties on production from the pooled unit, as if the same were included in this lease. For the purpose of computing the royalties to which owners of royalties and payments out of production and each of them, shall be entitled on production of oil and gas, or either of them, from the pooled unit, there shall be allocated to the land covered by this lease and included in said unit a pro rata portion of the oil and gas, or either of them, produced from the pooled unit after deducting that used for operations on the pooled unit. Such allocation shall be on an acreage basis—that is to say, there shall be allocated to the acreage covered by this lease and included in the pooled unit that pro rata portion of the oil and gas, or either of them, produced from the pooled unit which the number of surface acres covered by this lease and included in the pooled unit bears to the total number of surface acres included in the pooled unit. Royalties hereunder shall be computed on the portion of such production, whether it be oil and gas, or either of them, so allocated to the land covered by this lease and included in the unit just as though such production were from such land. The production from an oil well will be considered production from the lease or oil pooled unit from which it is producing and not as production from a gas pooled unit; and production from a gas well will be considered as production from the lease or gas pooled unit from which it is producing and not from an oil pooled unit."

§ 7.13   ROYALTY AND OTHER CLAUSES   399

In lieu of the royalties elsewhere herein specified, Lessor shall receive on production from a unit so pooled only such portion of the royalty stipulated herein as the amount of his acreage placed in the unit or his royalty interest therein on an acreage basis bears to the total acreage so pooled in the particular unit involved."

The express pooling clause will generally cover and include the following areas:

(1) Basis and authority of the lessee to pool or combine acreage.

(2) The method of designation of the pooled acreage.

(3) The effect of production within the unit upon acreage within and outside of the unit.

(4) Allocation of production.

(B) Basis and Authority of the Lessee to Pool

It is fundamental that where an express pooling clause is relied upon as the basis for formation of drilling units, that the basis and authority of the lessee to pool must be in reference to the authority as contained in the clause. Although such clauses are liberally interpreted to achieve the result intended by the parties,[9] an exercise of the power not in compliance with the clause is void.[10]

Where the lease clause expressly provides for pooling and the lessee has complied with the provisions of the lease, a question still remains whether the pooling authority has been exercised in good faith. In the Texas case of Elliott v. Davis[11] the court stated that the

---

9. Tiller v. Fields, note 8, supra. Also see Banks v. Mecom, Tex.Civ.App., 410 S.W.2d 300.

10. Leach v. Brown, Tex.Civ.App., 353 S.W.2d 920; Texaco, Inc. v. Lettermann, Tex.Civ.App., 343 S.W.2d 726.

Questions of interpretation of the wording of the pooling clause sometimes prove troublesome. In many forms the lessee is authorized to pool the lease with "lands or leases in the vicinity" of the lease. Obviously, this phrase has no precise meaning, and some lessees seem to have taken a very liberal view of the geographic scope of the phrase.

Some clauses allow the pooling of "contiguous" tracts of land, as contrasted to "adjacent" tracts. At least one case has construed "contiguous" as requiring that the tracts touch at least at one point, and that "adjacent" means that the tracts are nearby, but not actually touching. See discussion at § 7.7. If the tracts do not actually touch, pooling under clauses permitting pooling only if contiguous tracts would seem invalid, if the above distinction is applied.

Doubt arises as to the authority of the lessee to pool in situations where the lease authority varies from the unit size allowed by governmental authority. Is a unit invalid where the lease allows gas units to 640 acres and one is formed by the lessee, where the authorized unit for proration purposes by the state authority is only 320 acres? Is the lessee in good faith where the lease allows a unit not to exceed 160 acres "or as permitted by governmental authority?" If the rules of the state commission allow pooling for units larger than 160 acres, but the drainage area of the well does not exceed 160 acres, is a larger unit valid? See Jones v. Killingsworth, Tex., 403 S.W.2d 325.

In Yelderman v. McCarthy, Tex.Civ. App., 474 S.W.2d 781, pooling was held invalid where the lessee formed a 320-acre gas unit and only 40-acre unit authority was provided for in the lease.

11. Tex.Civ.App., 553 S.W.2d 223. Also see, Texas Mineral Interest Pooling Act: Effect Upon the Executive Right

lessee's exercise of the pooling authority must be fair and in good faith in regard to the circumstances, the reasonable development of the property, and the interests of both the lessor and the lessee. The court stated that the lessee was not in a fiduciary relationship with the lessor.

Pooling to bring in worthless land or land condemned by prior drilling has been held to have been an exercise in bad faith.[12] Where not expressly permitted by the lease clause, pooling after drilling has been held to have been a bad-faith exercise.[13] Such pooling, of course, dilutes the interest of the owners in the drill site. However, the courts have reached an opposite result in this situation where the circumstances justified such pooling.[14]

It is a common practice of lessees to pool in order to preserve lease acreage. For example, assume Rex Oil Company has acquired four separate leases, one on each quarter of a particular section. Each lease contains a pooling clause. Rex forms a 40-acre square unit which is primarily located on acreage covered by the lease on the SE ¼, but which includes small acreage from the other leases:

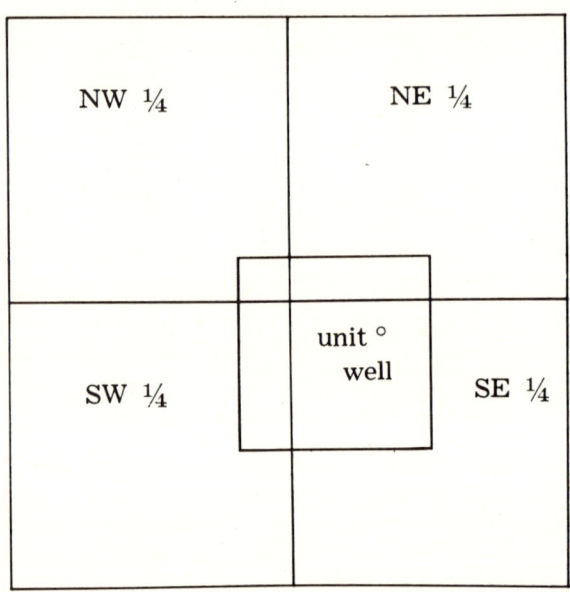

[32-Z]

Holder's Authority to Pool, 17 S.T.L.J. 435 (1976).

Also see Pritchett v. Forest Oil Corp., Tex.Civ.App., 535 S.W.2d 708 (no fiduciary relationship).

12. Southwest Gas Producing Co. v. Seale, Miss., 191 So.2d 115; Imes v. Globe Oil & Refining Co., 184 Okl. 79, 84 P.2d 1106.

13. Mallett v. Union Oil & Gas Corp., 232 La. 157, 94 So.2d 16.

14. Boone v. Kerr-McGee Oil Industries, C.A.10th, 217 F.2d 63; Gillham v. Jenkins, 206 Okl. 440, 244 P.2d 291; Expando Production Co. v. Marshall, Tex. Civ.App., 407 S.W.2d 254; cf. Mallett v. Union Oil & Gas Corp. of La., 232 La. 157, 94 So.2d 16; Southwest Gas Producing Co. v. Seale, Miss., 191 So.2d 115; Imes v. Globe Oil & Refining Co., 184 Okl. 79, 84 P.2d 1106.

As discussed below, under the express terms of the leases, production from the unit well will keep all four leases alive past their primary terms. However, in this situation, three of the lessors will receive a very small portion of production. Where the intent of such pooling is not to comply with spacing requirements, but is to preserve the lease acreage of the other leases, is such pooling a good-faith exercise of the pooling power?

An interesting Texas case involving this type of situation is that of Amoco Production Co. v. Underwood,[15] which was decided after and which cited the case of Davis v. Elliott, above. In this case lessors brought suit to cancel a unit designation. The unit contained 688 acres out of eight leases, which contained a total of 2,252 acres. The unit included 45 acres which were down structure and upon which a reasonably prudent operator would not drill. The unit excluded 90 acres of productive acreage. Leases were within 2 days of the end of the primary term at the time of the pooling.

It was held that the pooling was not in good faith. The court stated that the question of good faith is a matter of fact. The court stressed the fact that the lessee at the time of pooling had no intention of further developing the remaining acreage outside of the unit.

The result of the case may be supported on the ground that the lessee had included non-productive acreage in the unit. However, the court also stressed as a factor in the decision that the lessee had no intent to develop the remaining acreage. Implicit in the holding would seem to be the possible approval of such pooling where the lessee could show the intent and capability to develop the remaining acreage within a reasonable time. It does not appear that the court is stating that any pooling is invalid when done when sufficient acreage exists in the lease for a location without pooling, as this would be narrower than the authority contained in the lease clause.[16]

When the lessee has once validly exercised the pooling power during the life of the lease, may he thereafter again exercise the power? Many pooling forms now expressly provide for successive exercise. Even without such a provision, where such later exercise follows the termination of the first unit, it has been held that the lessee may successively exercise the power.[17] In the following situation it would

---

15. Tex.Civ.App., 558 S.W.2d 509.

16. "Lessee, at its option, is hereby given the right and power to pool or combine the land covered by this lease, or any portion thereof, as to oil and gas, or either of them, with any other land, lease or leases when in Lessee's judgment it is necessary or advisable to do so *in order to properly develop* and operate said premises, such pooling to be into a well unit or units not exceeding forty (40) acres, plus an acreage tolerance of ten percent (10%) of forty (40) acres, for oil, and not exceeding six hundred and forty (640) acres, plus an acreage tolerance of ten percent (10%) of six hundred and forty (640) acres, for gas, except that larger units may be created to conform to any spacing or well unit pattern that may be prescribed by governmental authorities * * *" (emphasis supplied).

17. Texaco, Inc. v. Lettermann, Tex. Civ.App., 343 S.W.2d 726.

seem that no problem would exist as to the successive exercise of the pooling power:

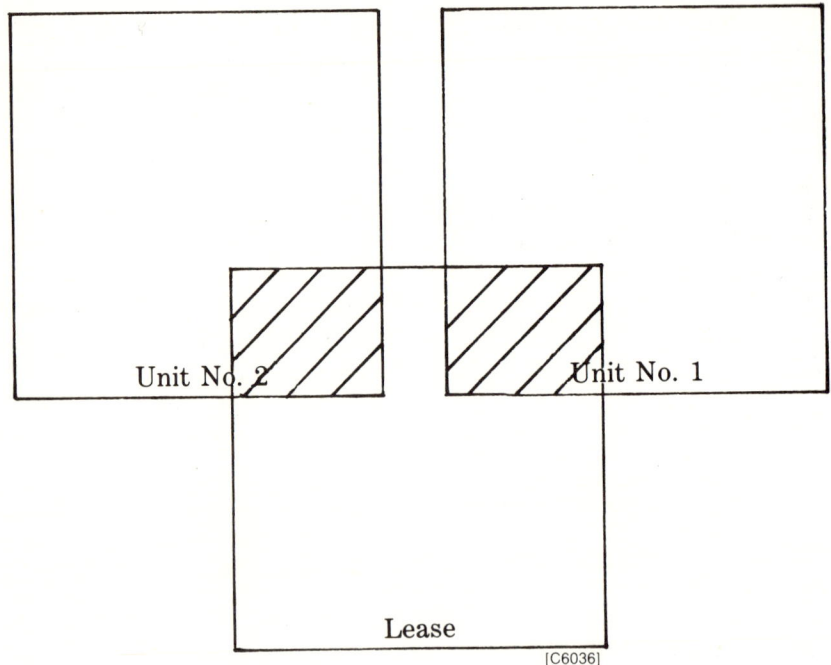

Here the formation of Unit No. 2 does not affect the rights of the owners of interests in Unit No. 1. This would also be true if the lease were pooled to all depths for gas and then later pooled to all depths for oil. On the other hand, if the effect of such exercise is to alter or to modify an existing unit, the later exercise, unless authorized by the lease, is void.[18] To validate such pooling all owners of interests in the first unit would have to ratify the second unit.

The rationale prohibiting the modification of an existing unit is that such alteration would change the interest of the present owners and, therefore, would not constitute a good-faith exercise of the authority. In one case, however, an opposite result was reached.[19]

Even where not specifically authorized in the lease, it appears that, unless specifically prohibited, the lessee may limit pooling to particular products, particular formations or intervals, or portions of the lease.[20] Unless the lease otherwise states, if leases are pooled for one product and the well produces another product, such production will only perpetuate the lease from which it is being produced and not other leases in the unit.[21] One Texas case[22] applied the doctrine of

18. Grimes v. La Gloria Corp., Tex. Civ.App., 251 S.W.2d 755.

19. Expando Production Co. v. Marshall, Tex.Civ.App., 407 S.W.2d 254.

20. Kenoyer v. Magnolia Petroleum Co., 173 Kan. 183, 245 P.2d 176; Trawick v. Castleberry, Okl., 275 P.2d 292.

21. Sunac Petroleum Corp. v. Parkes, Tex., 416 S.W.2d 798.

22. 152 Tex. 540, 261 S.W.2d 311, and see discussion at § 6.8, supra.

Rogers v. Osborn to an oil well drilled on a gas unit. The unit well was drilled in the unit on other lands. Within a few days after the oil well was brought in, lessee began drilling on its lease. The court held that the latter lease had terminated since the drilling was done after the end of the primary term and that the gas unit well did not constitute either a dry hole, as it was producing, or production that ceased, as the production did not apply to other lands in the unit. Therefore the new well could not be tacked onto the unit well to keep the latter lease alive.

Several cases have dealt with the problem of whether production from a gas unit well is unitized as to liquids from a wet gas well.[23] It has been held that if the products come out of the mouth of the well in gaseous form, or are in gaseous form in the reservoir, they are pooled.

Pooling as to less than all of the interest owners would seem valid, although at least one case has reached an opposite result.[24]

A related problem is where the lessee has the power to pool as to a substantial amount of the minerals, but only the right to lease the remainder. In one jurisdiction it has been held that the right to lease does not include the right to pool. In the case of Brown v. Smith,[25] the lessee acquired a community lease; however, as to a certain 20 acres, one of the lessors did not own the minerals, but merely held the right to lease. It was held the 20-acre tract was not pooled. The owner of the 20-acre tract would not share in production except from her 20 acres. Therefore, the lessee would have to use separate measuring tanks both for unit wells on the 20 acres and off the 20 acres. The court also indicated the lessee would be obligated to drill inside offsetting wells. It would, therefore, be mandatory in such situations to acquire either a power to pool or a ratification of the pooling from all non-participating royalty owners whose lands are included in the unit.

---

23. Blocker v. Christie, Mitchell & Mitchell Co., Tex.Civ.App., 340 S.W.2d 320, error refused; Skelly Oil Co. v. Savage, 202 Kan. 239, 447 P.2d 395, citing the Blocker case. Also see Martin v. Kostner, 231 Kan. 315, 644 P.2d 430, which held that gas being produced from a gas unit which contained substantial liquids was pooled. The lease clause prohibited pooling of "casinghead gas." It was factually found that the gas being produced was "associated gas" in a combination well, and that the gas was not casinghead gas.

24. Kenoyer v. Magnolia Petroleum Co., note 19, supra. But cf. Union Oil Co. v. Touchet, 229 La. 316, 86 So.2d 50. However, see Guaranty National Bank and Trust of Corpus Christi v. May, Tex.Civ.App. 395 S.W.2d 80, holding joinder of all royalty owners necessary to create pooling of royalty interest. Also see Pan American Petroleum Corp. v. Vines, Tex.Civ.App., 459 S.W.2d 911, holding all royalty owners were indispensable parties to construe the meaning of a unit division order.

25. 141 Tex. 425, 174 S.W.2d 43. See Minchen v. Fields, 162 Tex. 73, 345 S.W.2d 282. But see Le Blanc v. Haynesville Mercantile Co., 230 La. 299, 88 So.2d 377, following the rule that the holder of the power to lease has the power to pool the interest to which the power relates.

In the situation where the holder of the power to lease has authorized pooling and the lease has been pooled by the lessee, such pooling may be ratified by the royalty interest owner either by an instrument expressly ratifying the pooling [26] or, in some instances, by the acceptance of royalty checks for the amount of the pooled royalty.[27]

Does the execution of a joint lease by the owner of a term mineral interest and the owner of the reversionary interest in the tract pool the reversionary interest? In a slightly different format, does the execution of a lease containing pooling powers, by the owner of the reversionary interest, and the execution of a lease by the owner of the term mineral interest, containing pooling powers, result in a pooling of the reversionary interest by later exercise of the pooling powers? Where the unit well is drilled on lands in which the term mineral interest is located production will keep the term mineral interest alive past the primary term of such interest. But, will such production maintain the term interest in the following situation? O owns all the minerals in a section of land and sells A a one-half mineral interest with a term of 5 years and as long as oil and gas is produced, in the SE ¼ of the section. O and A sign a joint lease, or O signs a separate lease with pooling power as to the entire section and A signs a lease with pooling power as to her interest in the SE ¼. The unit well is drilled on the NW ¼ of the section:

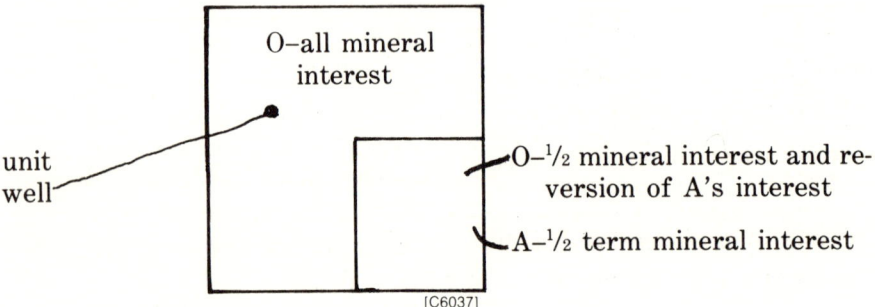

In Southland Royalty Co. v. Humble Oil & Refining Co.,[28] under simplified facts, O, the owner of Blackacre, conveyed to A an undivided one-half mineral interest in the north one-half of the land. The mineral deed was for 20 years and as long as production was obtained from "said land." O and A jointly leased to Rex Oil Company, and production was obtained from the south one-half of the land. It was held that the well held the term interest of A past the end of the 20-year term, on the basis that a community lease had resulted, and that O's reversion was modified by the joint lease.

---

26. Montgomery v. Rittersbacher, Tex., 424 S.W.2d 210, dealing with the ratification by the royalty owner of pooling under the entirety clause of a lease. This case is also an example of double pooling. Also see Ruiz v. Martin, Tex. Civ.App., 559 S.W.2d 839, refused n. r. e.

27. Yelderman v. McCarthy, Tex.Civ. App., 474 S.W.2d 781, but cf. Westbrook v. Atlantic Richfield Co., Tex., 502 S.W.2d 551, requiring words of ratification or revival.

28. 151 Tex. 324, 249 S.W.2d 914.

§ 7.13   ROYALTY AND OTHER CLAUSES   405

This case was further extended in the case of Spradley v. Finley,[29] where, under essentially the same fact situation, O and A executed separate leases with pooling clauses. In holding the term interests were extended, the court stated that the term "said land" in the term deed had been contractually construed in the pooling clauses to mean all lands included in the unit.

There are few cases relating to this problem. However, Kansas now appears to have adopted the view of the Southland Royalty case in Texas. In the Kansas case of Classen v. Federal Land Bank of Wichita,[30] the Kansas court has apparently reversed its view that off land unit production would not keep the term interest alive.[31] Although no case as such has been decided in Oklahoma, an early Federal case[32] seemed to reach a similar result as that in Southland Royalty. However, a recent Oklahoma Court of Appeals case,[33] which was not directed to be published by the Oklahoma Supreme Court, and therefore not considered as precedent in Oklahoma, reached the result that only actual physical production from the lands in which a term interest was located was sufficient to maintain such interest. As Dean Kuntz commented, "It is probable, then, that the impact of this case is to neutralize the effect of the federal case, with the result that what appeared to be an answer to the question can no longer be accepted."[34]

(C) Designation of Pooling

It is commonly provided in the lease that the lands will be considered pooled upon the execution and filing of record of a "Declaration of Pooling". Such designation merely identifies the leases and the lands involved and states the exercise of the authority as to a certain described area and depth. Pooling therefore is relatively simple.[35] The harder question is: How does one unpool?

---

29. 157 Tex. 260, 302 S.W.2d 409. The court again held the reversionary interest of the grantor was included, although the draftsman had stated the lease was "less" the acreage covered by the term grant. However, the courts have apparently backed away from allowing the lease definition of "production from said land" to modify and define the phrase in term deeds for other purposes. In Scott v. Union Production Co., C.A. 5th, 267 F.2d 469, where the term deed expired at a time when a lease on the reversion was being held by payment of delay rentals, the court refused to impute the contractual result from the lease, i.e., that "upon payment it will be considered gas is being produced from said land," as sustaining production to the term mineral grant.

30. 228 Kan. 426, 617 P.2d 1255.

31. Smith v. Home Royalty Association, Inc., 209 Kan. 609, 498 P.2d 98; Friesen v. Federal Land Bank of Wichita, 277 Kan. 522, 608 P.2d 915.

32. Panhandle Eastern Pipe Line Co. v. Isaacson, C.A.10th, 255 F.2d 669.

33. McEvoy v. First National Bank and Trust Co. of Enid, Oklahoma, Okl. App., 624 P.2d 559.

34. 69 Oil and Gas Reporter at page 496.

35. However, the procedure set forth in the lease clause must be followed or the unit may be invalid. In at least two cases it has been held that where the clause states that the designation be filed for record in the county where the land is located, the unit is not effectively formed until the designation is filed. Yelderman v. McCarthy, Tex.Civ.App., 474 S.W.2d 781, refused n. r. e. and Sauder v. Fry,

To answer this question it is necessary to consider the effect of pooling. Although most jurisdictions apparently consider pooling as merely contractually effecting an apportionment of production,[36] some jurisdictions view pooling as actually constituting a cross conveyance of title, at least for some purposes.[37] Texas, the foremost proponent of the cross-conveyance view, finds such result for purposes of joinder of parties,[38] but not to the extent that such cross conveyance can serve to cut off a prior equity by a bona fide purchaser.[39] Where the cross-conveyance view is followed, a unilateral release of an interest by one party will not serve to unpool his tract.[40] In such jurisdictions a partition involving joinder of all parties or a voluntary instrument effecting a re-conveyance would seem necessary.[41] Although customary and effective in fieldwide unitization agreements, termination or unpooling provisions are seldom seen in pooling clauses of leases.[42] It is also widely felt that appropriate provisions in the pooling agreement would prevent a cross conveyance in jurisdictions such as Texas.[43]

(D) The Effect of Production and Operations Within the Unit Upon Acreage Within and Outside of the Unit

According to the express provisions of the usual pooling clause, production or operations anywhere upon unit lands is deemed to be production or operations from all lands in the unit. The result of this provision is twofold: first, as the habendum clause of an oil and gas lease is indivisible,[44] unit production or operations will serve to hold

---

Tex.Civ.App., 613 S.W.2d 63. In the last case the unit well was begun on lands of another lease in the unit before the end of the primary term of a lease contributing lands to the unit. The designation of pooling was apparently executed at about the same time that the well was begun. The unit well was finished after the end of the primary term of the contributing lease and the designation was not filed until after the end of the primary term of such lease. It was held that the lease had terminated as the unit was not effective until the unit or pooling declaration was filed.

36. Kenoyer v. Magnolia Petroleum Co., 173 Kan. 183, 245 P.2d 176; Merrill Engineering Co. v. Capital National Bank, 192 Miss. 378, 5 So.2d 666; Sinclair Crude Oil Co. v. Oklahoma Tax Commission, Okl., 326 P.2d 1051; Lynch v. Davis, 79 W.Va. 437, 92 S.E. 427.

37. Tanner v. Title Insurance & Trust Co., 20 Cal.2d 814, 129 P.2d 383; Tanner v. Olds, 29 Cal.2d 110, 173 P.2d 6, 167 A.L.R. 1219; Veal v. Thomason, 138 Tex. 341, 159 S.W.2d 472; Belt v. Texas Co., Tex.Civ.App., 175 S.W.2d 622; Renwar Oil Corp. v. E. L. Lancaster, 154 Tex. 311, 276 S.W.2d 774. Also see Ragsdale v. Superior Oil Co., 40 Ill.2d 68, 237 N.E.2d 492.

38. Veal v. Thomason, 138 Tex. 341, 159 S.W.2d 472. See Douglas v. Butcher, Tex.Civ.App., 272 S.W.2d 553, allowing a class action in partition suit involving 3200 royalty owners, and Leach v. Brown, Tex.Civ.App., 251 S.W.2d 553. See Masterson, The Nature of Unitized Title, 10 S.W.L.J. 157.

39. Sohio Petroleum Co. v. Jurek, Tex.Civ.App., 248 S.W.2d 294, and see Fussell v. Rinque, Tex.Civ.App., 269 S.W.2d 442.

40. See Tanner cases, supra, note 37.

41. Garza v. DeMontalvo, 147 Tex. 525, 217 S.W.2d 988; Struss v. Stoddard, Tex.Civ.App., 258 S.W.2d 413. But cf. Howell v. Union Producing Co., C.A.5th, 392 F.2d 95.

42. See Grimes v. La Gloria Corp., Tex.Civ.App., 251 S.W.2d 755.

43. See § 956, Summers, Oil and Gas Law; Hoffman, Voluntary Pooling and Unitization, p. 167.

44. See Chapter 9, § 9.10(A), infra.

§ 7.13   ROYALTY AND OTHER CLAUSES   407

all lands of all of the leases in effect, whether such lands are inside or outside of the unit.[45] The remedy for non-development is not cancellation of the lease, but enforcement of the implied obligation to reasonably develop.

The second result of the combined effect of the habendum and pooling clauses of the lease is that such unit production during the primary term will alleviate the payment of delay rentals as to all lands included in each of the leases.

To prevent these results, the lessor may include a specific provision that lands outside the unit will not be held by production within the unit. These clauses have become known as "Pugh" clauses, and they usually segregate the lands under lease outside the unit from lands included in the unit for purposes of payment of delay rentals or perpetuation by unit production, or both.[46]

The Pugh clause, as all clauses in the lease, must be read carefully, as some provide that production from the unit well will not perpetuate lease lands outside the unit after the primary term of the leases, but do relieve the payment of delay rentals during the primary term.

Two cases have dealt with the question of whether a Pugh clause operates to effect a horizontal severance of the lease. Assume that the lease contains a Pugh clause as set forth below.[47] Lessee assigns the lease as to depths below 5000 feet. Lessee unitizes or pools the lease to all depths above 5000 feet and drills a producing well on the unit. Does the unit production hold the lease as to any part below 5000 feet? A Kansas case,[48] in federal court, held that the Pugh clause effected a horizontal severance and that the part of the lease not in the unit, including lower depths, terminated. However, a later Oklahoma case,[49] involving the same lease form, held that the clause did not effect a horizontal severance and that the lease was held as to lower depths. The court emphasized the presence of wording such as "Tract or tracts," "Premises," "lands," and "leasehold estates," and

---

45. Somers v. Harris Trust & Savings Bank, 1 Kan.App.2d 397, 566 P.2d 775 (a case of first impression adopting the doctrine of Scott v. Pure Oil Co); Scott v. Pure Oil Co., C.A.5th, 194 F.2d 393; but cf. Union Oil Co. v. Touchet, 229 La. 316, 86 So.2d 50; Alexander v. Holt, La.App., 116 So.2d 532. In several states if pooling is compulsory, acreage outside the unit will not be held: Texas Gulf Producing Co. v. Griffith, 218 Miss. 109, 65 So.2d 447, and see Whitaker v. Texaco, Inc., C.A.10th, 283 F.2d 169.

46. See Fremaux v. Buie, La.App., 212 So.2d 148; Humble Oil & Refining Co. v. Hutchins, 217 Miss. 636, 64 So.2d 733; Bennett v. Sinclair Oil & Gas Co., C.A.5th, 405 F.2d 1005.

47. "(b) During the primary term hereof and until production has been obtained, from this or the consolidated leasehold, the lessee shall be privileged to pay the annual delay rentals stipulated herein on any part of this leasehold included in a consolidation of estates or not so included, and thereby continue this lease in full force and effect as to the part or portions thereof upon which rentals are so paid, but this lease, insofar as it covers any tract or tracts not included in a consolidation of estates held in force by production as herein provided, shall terminate at the expiration of the primary term hereof, unless oil, gas, or other minerals is or can be produced from a well or wells thereon."

48. Rogers v. Westhoma Oil Co., C.A.10th, 291 F.2d 726.

49. Rist v. Westhoma Oil Co., Okl., 385 P.2d 791 (1963).

that the wording of the clause said nothing of "depths, levels or strata." The decisions of the Oklahoma court seems consistent with the clause in those cases.

Although it would seem possible to draft a Pugh clause that would effect a horizontal severance, unless specifically covered, a problem would remain as to the proper payment of delay rentals. Delay rental clauses provide for payment based on surface acreage and would have to be modified. How would delay rentals be paid in the above example if the lease were not assigned as to lower depths, but the lessee formed a unit of 160 acres out of larger lease acreage, but pooled only down to 5000 feet?

Pooling may have other unintended results. It may have the effect of pooling the free gas clause in the lease.[50]

(E) Allocation of Production

Where all interests in the minerals are included in the unit, the lease clause normally provides production will be allocated in the proportion which each lease contributes acreage to the unit as compared to the total acreage in the unit. Where three leases are pooled and contribute respectively A—15 acres, B—12 acres and C—13 acres to a 40-acre drilling unit, production attributable to royalty and working interests will be allocated in the ratios of $^{15}/_{40}$, $^{12}/_{40}$, and $^{13}/_{40}$:[51]

---

50. See Jackson v. Farmer, 225 Kan. 732, 594 P.2d 177 and discussion of the free gas clause in § 7.12, supra.

51. Where only part of the mineral interests are included in the unit, computations must be adjusted accordingly. A leases all of a 30-acre tract, B all of a 10-acre tract and C an undivided one-half interest in a 20 acre tract. The leases of A, B, and C contain pooling provisions. D owns the other one-half interest and does not lease. Lessee pools the leases of A, B, and C. Although surface acreage equals 60 acres, only 50 acres are committed to the unit. If a well is drilled on A's or B's tract, sharing will be as follows:

$A-^{30}/_{50} \times ^{1}/_{8} = ^{3}/_{40}$ R.I.
$B-^{10}/_{50} \times ^{1}/_{8} = ^{1}/_{40}$ R.I.
$C-^{10}/_{50} \times ^{1}/_{8} = ^{1}/_{40}$ R.I.
D–Nothing
Lessee–$^{7}/_{8} = ^{35}/_{40}$ W.I.

Former Rule 40(B), now Rule 051.02.02.040, of the Texas Railroad Commission provides that if a tract to be pooled has an outstanding interest for which pooling authority does not exist, the tract may be assigned to a unit where authority exists in the remaining undivided interest, provided that total gross acreage in the tract is included for allocation purposes, and the Certificate filed with the Commission shows that a certain undivided interest is outstanding in the tract.

In this situation the following allocation of production has been made:

$A-^{30}/_{60} \times ^{1}/_{8} = ^{1}/_{16}$ R.I.
$B-^{10}/_{60} \times ^{1}/_{8} = ^{1}/_{48}$ R.I.
$C-^{10}/_{60} \times ^{1}/_{8} = ^{1}/_{48}$ R.I.
D–Nothing
Lessee:
$^{60}/_{60} \times ^{7}/_{8} = ^{7}/_{8}$ W.I.
$^{10}/_{60} \times ^{7}/_{8} = ^{1}/_{48}$ W.I. If D ratifies the unit this amount will be paid to D out of lessee's share.

If the well is on C's tract, D shares as a non-joined co-tenant. The other one-half of production is allocated in the unit:

$A-^{30}/_{50} \times ^{1}/_{16} = ^{13}/_{80}$ R.I.
$B-^{10}/_{50} \times ^{1}/_{16} = ^{1}/_{80}$ R.I.
$C-^{10}/_{50} \times ^{1}/_{16} = ^{1}/_{80}$ R.I.
D–one-half of gross production minus one-half of costs.
Lessee–$^{7}/_{8} \times ^{1}/_{2} = ^{35}/_{80}$ W.I.

§ 7.15   ROYALTY AND OTHER CLAUSES   409

$$A-{}^{15}/_{40} \times {}^{1}/_{8} = {}^{15}/_{320} \text{ R.I.}$$
$$B-{}^{12}/_{40} \times {}^{1}/_{8} = {}^{12}/_{320} \text{ R.I.}$$
$$C-{}^{13}/_{40} \times {}^{1}/_{8} = {}^{13}/_{320} \text{ R.I.}$$
$$\text{Lessee-} \qquad {}^{7}/_{8} \text{ W.I.}$$

The first column is the acreage allocation to each tract, the second column the royalty payable under the lease, and the final figure is the royalty allocation to each tract.[52]

§ 7.14   The Entirety and Assignment Clauses

The entirety and assignment clauses are discussed in Chapter 9, infra.

§ 7.15   Lessor's Special Inspection Clause

The following clause actually appeared as a type written rider in an oil and gas lease, otherwise usual in form which was recorded on January 17, 1957, in Jefferson Davis Parish, Louisiana:

> "If a well should be located on the surface of the land herein leased, then in lieu of Lessor being furnished an electrical log, Lessor shall have the right to be lowered head first down the casing equipped with a two cell battery flashlight to a depth of 7,000 feet, or some lesser depth if heaving shales be encountered.
>
> "Lessee agrees that Lessor will be lowered at a rate of speed not to exceed that rate which any prudent operator would lower his Lessor into a well bore. It is further understood that if lowering line should part, immediate fishing operations shall be commenced, and in no event shall Lessor be cemented, plugged and abandoned."

The author would like to thank Ms. Linda M. Harris, an attorney with Tenneco Oil Exploration and Production, for the clause. The author encountered the clause in an actual lease and had intended to include it in the first edition, but was unable to do so as it had been lost.

In the situation where the well is on D's land, how would allocation be made of the remaining one-half of production under Rule 40, set forth above?

52. Where more than one person owns an interest in any particular tract that is committed to the unit, computation is much facilitated by first computing the royalty and working interest to be allocated to each tract in the unit. The percentage of ownership in each tract can then be applied against such allocation figure. Where complex ownership situations are encountered this is much easier than attempting to compute each individual unit share directly.

CHAPTER 8

COVENANTS OF THE LESSEE TO PROTECT, DEVELOP, AND ADMINISTER THE LEASE

Analysis

Sec.
8.1 The Basis and Nature of Covenants Implied in Oil and Gas Leases.
8.2 Implied Covenants to Develop the Lease—To Drill an Initial Well.
8.3 ____ After Production Is Acquired.
  (A) Profitability to the Lessee.
  (B) Reasonable Diligence of the Lessee.
  (C) Exploration and Development of Other Areas and Formations Where Profitabiity Cannot Be Shown.
8.4 ____ Effect of Express Provisions in the Lease.
8.5 Implied Covenant of Protection—Duty to Protect Against Drainage.
8.6 The Effect of an Express Offset Clause on the Implied Covenant to Protect Against Drainage.
8.7 Implied Covenant of Protection—Not to Depreciate the Lessor's Interest.
8.8 The Implied Covenant to Protect Against Drainage as Affected by Operations to Stimulate Production and Statutory Enactments.
8.9 Implied Covenants—Other Miscellaneous Covenants.
  (A) The Covenant to Use Reasonable Care in Operations.
  (B) The Covenant to Produce.
  (C) The Covenant to Market.
  (D) The Covenant to Seek Favorable Administrative Action.
8.10 Remedies for Breach of Implied Covenants—Damages.
8.11 ____ Cancellation of Lease.
8.12 Breach of Implied Covenants—Effect of Release.
8.13 Breach of an Express Clause to Drill.

§ 8.1 The Basis and Nature of Covenants Implied in Oil and Gas Leases

Covenants are implied when an oil and gas lease does not express the lessee's obligations relating to development, protection, and management of the lease. It would appear to be the view of the courts that such covenants are implied in fact rather than in law.

In this section consideration is directed at covenants of the lessee that are implied within the context of the leasing transaction.[1] Upon

---

1. On implied covenants generally, see: Summers, Oil and Gas Law, §§ 395–400, 431–472; Brown, Implied Covenant for Additional Development, 13 S.W. L.J. 149; Brown, Proposed New Covenant of Further Exploration: Reply to Comment, 37 Tex.L.Rev. 303; Kuntz, Prudent Operator and Further Development, 9 Okla.L.Rev. 255; Limes, Geological Proof of Drainage, 11 Inst.Min.L. 33; Logan, Nonproducer Speculation in Oil and Gas: Sublease and Assignment, 4 Kan.L.Rev. 396; Meyers, Compulsory Joinder of Parties in Implied Covenant

the execution of an oil and gas lease, the lessee has the entire possession of the leased premises for the purposes of development and management of the property for the production of oil and gas. The primary interest and consideration of the lessor is in the royalty payments to be returned from production. As has been seen, an oil and gas lease is a conveyance with numerous contractual provisions. However, traditionally, matters relating to the development of the lease and protection of the lessor's interest have not been expressly included in the lease. Covenants have been implied to cover the matter of development and protection. In recent years, implied covenants have been somewhat expanded to cover matters concerning the management of the lease. The major implied covenants may be summarized as follows:

(A) Implied covenants to develop the lease.

   (1) To drill an initial well.

   (2) To reasonably develop the lease after production has been acquired.

(B) Implied covenants of protection.

   (1) To protect against drainage.

   (2) Not to depreciate the lessor's interest.

(C) Implied covenants relating to management and administration of the lease.

   (1) To produce and market.

   (2) To operate with reasonable care.

   (3) To use successful modern methods of production and development.

   (4) To seek favorable administration action.

Litigation, 16 Stan.L.Rev. 43; Merrill, Prudent Operator and Further Development—Oklahoma Rule, 5 Okla.L.Rev. 453; Merrill, Implied Covenant of Further Exploration in Oklahoma, 13 Okla.L.Rev. 249; Meyers, Implied Covenant of Further Exploration, 34 Tex.L.Rev. 553; Meyers, Covenant of Further Exploration: A Comment, 37 Tex.L.Rev. 179; Meyers, Two Drilling Covenants Implied in Oil and Gas Leases, 38 Minn.L.Rev. 127; Meyers and Williams, Implied Covenants in Oil and Gas Leases: Drainage Caused by the Lessee, 40 Tex.L.Rev. 923; Meyers and Williams, The Implied Duty to Explore Further: Recent Texas Developments, 41 Tex.L.Rev. 789; Smith, The Implied Duty to Explore Further. Recent Texas Developments—A Disagreement, 42 Tex.L.Rev. 199; Walker, The Nature of Property Interests Created by an Oil and Gas Lease in Texas, 11 Tex.L.Rev. 399; Implied Covenants in Oil Leases—Drainage, 61 Dick.L.Rev. 91; Reasonable Development of Multiple Reservoir Fields in Louisiana, 9 Loyola L.Rev. 194; Implied Covenant to Protect Leased Premises from Drainage where Lessee is Responsible for Drainage, 35 Miss.L.J. 280; Conn, Trends in the Application of the Implied Covenant of Further Development, 12 Okla.L.Rev. 470; Implied Covenants of Exploration in Oil and Gas Leases, 37 Tul.L.Rev. 90.

The exact basis for implication of such covenants is disputed. The majority of the cases state that such covenants are implied to carry out the intentions of the parties.

"At the outset it should be noted that when parties reduce their agreements to writing, the written instrument is presumed to embody their entire contract, and the court should not read into the instrument additional provisions unless this be necessary in order to effectuate the intention of the parties as disclosed by the contract as a whole. An implied covenant must rest entirely on the presumed intention of the parties as gathered from the terms as actually expressed in the written instrument itself, and it must appear that it was so clearly within the contemplation of the parties that they deemed it unnecessary to express it, and therefore omitted to do so, or it must appear that it is necessary to infer such a covenant in order to effectuate the full purpose of the contract as a whole as gathered from the written instrument. It is not enough to say that an implied covenant is necessary in order to make the contract fair, or that without such a covenant it would be improvident or unwise, or that the contract would operate unjustly. It must arise from the presumed intention of the parties as gathered from the instrument as a whole." [2]

Professor Merrill is the leading proponent of the proposition that such covenants are implied to insure a course of fair dealing between the parties where the control is vested exclusively in the hands of one of the parties, the lessee.

"It is undoubtedly one of the presuppositions of the taking of the lease by the lessee that he shall be able to determine the policy to be followed in respect to development and operation. The magnitude of the investment required, the hazardous nature of the enterprise, the need for stability in titles and property values, all de-

---

2. Danciger Oil & Refining Co. of Tex. v. Powell, 137 Tex. 484, 154 S.W.2d 632, 137 A.L.R. 408. In Adkins v. Adams, C.A.7th, 152 F.2d 489, arising in Illinois, the court stated, "The courts cannot make contracts for parties, and can declare implied covenants to exist only when there is a satisfactory basis in the express contracts of the parties which makes it necessary to imply certain duties and obligations in order to effect the purposes of the parties in the contracts made. Before a covenant will be implied in the express terms of a contract, it must appear therefrom that it was so clearly in the contemplation of the parties as that they deemed it unnecessary to express it, and therefore omitted to do so, or that it is necessary to imply such covenant in order to give effect to and effectuate the purpose of the contract as a whole." In the early landmark case of Brewster v. Lanyon Zinc Co., C.A.8th, 140 F. 801, the court stated, "It is conceded, as indeed it must be, that the lease contains no express stipulation as to what, if anything, should be done in the way of searching for and producing oil or gas after the first five years; but it does not follow from this that it is silent on the subject, or that the matter is left absolutely to the will of the lessee. Whatever is implied in a contract is as effectual as what is expressed. Implication is but another name for intention, and if it arises from the language of the contract when considered in its entirety, and is not gathered from the mere expectations of one or both of the parties, it is controlling."

However, the lessee is not a fiduciary as to the lessor. Craig v. Champlin Petroleum Co., C.A.10th, 435 F.2d 933.

mand that he be not required to comply with any and all demands for development or protection which the lessor may see fit to make. Is not the real basis of the doctrine of implied covenants in oil and gas leases to be found in a theory of enforcing that conduct which, under the circumstances, fair dealing between lessor and lessee fairly demands that the latter pursue?"[3]

There is much to be said for the implied-in-law approach championed by Professor Merrill. Although courts state that they are effectuating the intent of the parties, seldom is an actual inquiry to intent reported. To a great extent, the decisional process in finding or denying the existence of an implied covenant is one of constructing a standard of conduct in the circumstances, not expressly covered by the lease, where fairness will not condone the lessee as the sole arbiter.

Controversy also exists as to whether the covenants are implied in law or in fact. If the former, they do not constitute part of the contract itself. If the latter, they are considered as being part of the contract and are subject to the same laws affecting limitations,[4] venue,[5] etc., as the written lease. It appears that the majority view is that implied covenants are implied in fact[6] and not in law.

§ 8.2 Implied Covenants to Develop the Lease—To Drill an Initial Well

Where the lease is silent, there exists an implied covenant to drill an exploratory well within a reasonable time. However, with the possible exceptions of Indiana and Kentucky, it has consistently been held that an express provision to delay drilling by the payment of delay rentals negates such implied covenant.

Under an oil and gas lease the financial return to the lessor is dependent primarily upon production. When the lease contains no express provision for the drilling of an exploratory well, nor provisions to the contrary, a covenant is implied that the lessee drill an exploratory well within a reasonable time.[1] Such covenant was originally implied in the lease forms in early use. It is generally not implied in

---

3. Merrill, Covenants Implied in Oil and Gas Leases, 2nd Ed. §§ 222, 223.

4. Indian Territory Illuminating Oil Co. v. Rosamond, 190 Okl. 46, 120 P.2d 349, 138 A.L.R. 246 (expressly rejecting Prof. Merrill's implied in law theory); Texas Pacific Coal & Oil Co. v. Stuard, Tex.Civ.App., 7 S.W.2d 878.

5. Petroleum Producers Co. v. Steffens, 139 Tex. 257, 162 S.W.2d 698.

6. Gillet v. Elmhurst Investment Co., 111 Kan. 755, 207 P. 843; Warfield Natural Gas Co. v. Allen, 248 Ky. 646, 59 S.W.2d 534, 91 A.L.R. 890. Indian Territory Illuminating Oil Co. v. Rosamond, 190 Okl. 46, 120 P.2d 349, 138 A.L.R. 246.

Texas Pacific Coal & Oil Co. v. Stuard, Tex.Civ.App., 7 S.W.2d 878. Petroleum Producers Co. v. Steffens, 139 Tex. 257, 162 S.W.2d 698. Professor Merrill is a vigorous advocate of the implied in law approach; See Merrill, Covenants Implied in Oil and Gas Leases, §§ 7 and 220, and the cases collected therein.

1. Mansfield Gas Co. v. Alexander, 97 Ark. 167, 133 S.W. 837; Carlisle v. Lady, 109 Cal.App. 567, 293 P. 686; Cole v. Butler, 103 Kan. 419, 173 P. 978; Harris v. Ohio Oil Co., 57 Ohio St. 118, 48 N.E. 502; New State Oil & Gas Co. v. Dunn, 75 Okl. 141, 182 P. 514; Magnolia Petroleum Co. v. Page, Tex.Civ.App., 141 S.W.2d 691.

connection with lease forms presently being employed by the oil and gas industry. Under the modern "unless" lease, the parties expressly contract for delay in drilling, by payment of delay rentals, which removes the implied obligation to drill an initial or exploratory well.[2] Under such form of lease, payment of delay rentals releases the lessee from the duty to drill an exploratory well during the primary term. At the end of the primary term, however, the lease will terminate if the lessee is not engaged in drilling at that time or does not have production in paying quantities.

In Indiana and Kentucky a covenant is implied that the lessee will have an obligation to develop after demand, although the lease is being held by delay rentals.[3] This view has been rejected in most other jurisdictions.[4]

§ 8.3 Implied Covenants to Develop the Lease—After Production Is Acquired

All jurisdictions impose a prudent operator rule to determine whether lease development satisfies the implied covenant of further development. This rule requires that operations be mutually profitable to both lessor and lessee and be diligently prosecuted in relation to the circumstances in each case. Within such relationship the lessee has an implied duty, after production is acquired, to develop the lease to its fullest extent.

By the prevailing view, in Oklahoma, Texas, and several other jurisdictions, it is not a breach of the prudent operator standard when the lessee holds portions of a lease for long periods of time without development, where profitability of further development cannot be shown.

The proposed implied covenant of further exploration, that the lessee has an obligation to drill to other portions of the lease or to other formations where profitability cannot be shown, has not been accepted by the courts.

As discussed in the preceding section, under the modern lease form, no implied obligation exists upon the lessee to drill an exploratory well during the primary term. However, once production has been acquired by the lessee, an implied covenant may exist that the lessee engage in further development of the lease. Such implied cov-

---

2. Warm Springs Development Co. v. McAulay, 94 Nev. 194, 576 P.2d 1120; Southwestern Oil Co. v. Kersey, 80 Okl. 135, 195 P. 120; Coats v. Brown, Tex.Civ.App., 301 S.W.2d 932; Morris v. Messer, 156 Tenn. 54, 299 S.W. 782; Carper v. United Fuel Gas Co., 78 W.Va. 433, 89 S.E. 12.

3. See Consumers' Gas Trust Co. v. Littler, 162 Ind. 320, 70 N.E. 363; Monarch Oil, Gas & Coal Co. v. Richardson, 124 Ky. 602, 99 S.W. 668; Cameron v. Lebow, Ky., 338 S.W.2d 399; McMahan v. Boggess, Ky., 302 S.W.2d 592; and Summers, Oil & Gas Law, § 397.

4. The Indiana and Kentucky view has been rejected in (Arkansas) Grooms v. Minton, 158 Ark. 448, 250 S.W. 543; (Illinois) Poe v. Ulrey, 233 Ill. 56, 84 N.E. 46; (Kansas) Rolander v. Sanderson, 141 Kan. 809, 43 P.2d 1061; (Mississippi) Lloyd's Estate v. Mullen Tractor & Equipment Co., 192 Miss. 62, 4 So.2d 282; (Ohio) Kachelmacher v. Laird, 92 Ohio St. 324, 110 N.E. 933; (Oklahoma) Eastern Oil Co. v. Beatty, 71 Okl. 275, 177 P. 104; (Texas) Hitson v. Gilman, Tex.Civ.App., 220 S.W. 140; Link v. State's Oil Corp., Tex.Civ.App., 229 S.W. 693; (Tenn.) Morris v. Messer, 156 Tenn. 54, 299 S.W. 782.

enant may exist either during [1] or after the end of the primary term, after production has been acquired. It is the purpose of this section to discuss the basis and extent of such implied covenant.

It is not every situation of production that will give rise to the implied covenant to further develop. Nor will the judgment of the lessee be the sole determining factor as to the further duty of the lessee.[2] The standard is whether a reasonably prudent lessee in the same or similar circumstances would further develop.[3] The rule has been stated as follows:

"A lessee must conduct its operations to promote the mutual advantage and profit of both lessor and lessee, and to act as would a reasonable and prudent operator under similar circumstances and conditions. In seeking the answer to the crucial issue as to whether or not the lessee has developed the lease according to the standards of a reasonable, prudent operator, we have considered all of the facts. Specifically, we have considered: (a) geological data, (b) the number and location of wells drilled both on the leased premises and adjoining lands, (c) the productive capacity of producing wells, (d) the cost of drilling operations, (e) the time interval between the completion of the last well and the demand for additional operations, and (f) the acreage involved in the disputed lease." [4]

1. Berry v. Wondra, 173 Kan. 273, 246 P.2d 282; McMahan v. Boggess, Ky., 302 S.W.2d 592; Texas Pacific Coal & Oil Co. v. Stuard, Tex.Civ.App., 7 S.W.2d 878; Coats v. Brown, Tex.Civ.App., 301 S.W. 2d 932; cf. Link v. State's Oil Corp., Tex. Civ.App., 229 S.W. 693.

2. Daughetee v. Ohio Oil Co., 263 Ill. 518, 105 N.E. 308; Brewster v. Lanyon Zinc Co., C.A.8th, 140 F. 801; Fontenot v. Austral Oil Exploration Co., D.C.La., 168 F.Supp. 36, modified and affirmed C.A. 5th, 266 F.2d 956; Spiller v. Massey & Moore, Okl., 406 P.2d 467; Kleppner v. Lemon, 176 Pa. 502, 35 A. 109. See dissent Clifton v. Koontz, 160 Tex. 82, 325 S.W.2d 684, 79 A.L.R.2d 774.

3. Reynolds v. Smith, 231 Ark. 566, 331 S.W.2d 112; Zappia v. Garner, 259 Ark. 794, 536 S.W.2d 714; Elliott v. Pure Oil Co., 10 Ill.2d 146, 139 N.E.2d 295; Temple v. Continental Oil Co., 182 Kan. 213, 320 P.2d 1039, rehearing denied 183 Kan. 471, 328 P.2d 358; Renner v. Monsanto Chemical Co., 187 Kan. 158, 354 P.2d 326; Rush v. King Oil Co., 220 Kan. 616, 556 P.2d 431; Sanders v. Birmingham, 214 Kan. 769, 522 P.2d 959; Brewster v. Lanyon Zinc Co., C.A.8th, 140 F. 801; Nunley v. Shell Oil Co., La.App., 76 So.2d 111, noted 15 La.L.Rev. 853; Dupree v. Relco Exploration Co., Inc., La. App., 354 So.2d 1083; Fontenot v. Austral Oil Exploration Co., D.C.La., 168 F.Supp. 36, modified and affirmed, C.A. 5th, 266 F.2d 956; Superior Oil Co. v. Devon Corp., C.A.8th, 604 F.2d 1063 (case of first impression); Skelly Oil Co. v. Boles, 193 Okl. 308, 142 P.2d 969; Barnes v. Mack Oil Co., Okl., 376 P.2d 279; Spiller v. Massey & Moore, Okl., 406 P.2d 467; Carter v. United States Smelting, Refining and Mining Co., Okl., 485 P.2d 748; West v. Sun Oil Co., Okl., 490 P.2d 1073; Dixon v. Anadarko Production Co., Okl., 505 P.2d 1394; Amoco Production Co. v. Alexander, Tex., 622 S.W.2d 563; Wes Tex Land Co. v. Simmons, Tex.Civ.App., 566 S.W.2d 719; Carter Oil Co. v. Mitchell, C.A.10th, 100 F.2d 945, noted in 17 Tex.L.Rev. 509; Trust Co. of Chicago v. Samedan Oil Corp., C.A.10th, 192 F.2d 282; Blythe v. Sohio Petroleum Co., C.A.10th, 271 F.2d 861; Kleppner v. Lemon, 176 Pa. 502, 35 A. 109; cf. Sand Springs Home v. Clemens, Okl., 276 P.2d 262.

4. Fontenot v. Austral Oil Exploration Co., D.C.La., 168 F.Supp. 36, modified and affirmed C.A.5th, 266 F.2d 956. In Oklahoma the duty is broader than merely a duty to drill, see Barnes v. Mack Oil Co., Okl., 376 P.2d 279.

Several other definitions are set forth below.⁵ The rule, as usually set forth, stresses two factors, (1) that such operations be mutually profitable to both the lessor and the lessee, and (2) that the lease be developed with reasonable diligence.

(A) Profitability to the Lessee

As the prudent operator rule is stated above, the lessee is not required to further develop unless it will be profitable to both the lessor and the lessee. As the lessor owns a non-cost-bearing interest, any development that results in production will be profitable to the lessor. This, however, is not true as to the lessee. As it has the cost-bearing interest, in the usual situation it has no duty to further develop unless production can be acquired in paying quantities. The definition of paying quantities as used herein differs from the definition of paying quantities necessary to keep a lease in effect past the end of the primary term. As used in the latter sense, such production must merely pay the costs of operations, whether or not the well will ultimately pay out. As used to imply drilling duties upon the lessee, it must be shown that such production would, in all probability, pay a reasonable profit as well as the costs of drilling and development of the well.⁶ The burden is on the lessor to show that the lessee would be able to drill further wells at a profit.

---

5. "Prudent Operator Test: As the term suggests, it imposes upon the lessee the implied duty to do whatever in the circumstances would be reasonably expected of a prudent operator of a particular lease, having a rightful regard for the interest of both the lessor and the lessee. * * * [T]he implied covenants of the lease impose no obligation upon the lessee to develop the lease beyond the point where it would be profitable to him, even if some benefit to the lessor would result therefrom. And, that the one seeking cancellation has the burden of proving that the drilling of additional wells would probably result in profitable production." Trust Co. of Chicago v. Samedan Oil Corp., C.A.10th, 192 F.2d 282.

"Under such circumstances, the lessee's obligation as to the development is measured by the rule of reasonable diligence or what an ordinarily prudent and diligent operator would do and he is not required to continue in the performance of these duties or to engage in the performance of such implied duties unless there is a reasonable expectation of profit, not only to the lessor, but also to the lessee." Clifton v. Koontz, 160 Tex. 82, 325 S.W.2d 684, 79 A.L.R.2d 774.

"It is necessary that the lessor show the quality of oil and gas being produced from the premises as indicated by prior exploration and development; the local market and demand therefor; the character of the natural reservoir—whether such as to permit the drainage of a large area by each well—and the usages of the business. Among economic factors to be considered are the cost of drilling, equipment and operation of wells; cost of transportation, cost of storage, the prevailing price; general market conditions as influenced by supply and demand or by regulation of production through governmental agencies." Sanders v. Birmingham, 214 Kan. 769, 522 P.2d 959.

6. Poindexter v. Lion Oil Refining Co., 205 Ark. 978, 167 S.W.2d 492; Daughetee v. Ohio Oil Co., 263 Ill. 518, 105 N.E. 308; Elliott v. Pure Oil Co., 10 Ill.2d 146, 139 N.E.2d 295; Baker v. Collins, 29 Ill.2d 410, 194 N.E.2d 353; Harris v. Morris Plan Co., 144 Kan. 501, 61 P.2d 901; Temple v. Continental Oil Co., 182 Kan. 213, 320 P.2d 1039, rehearing denied 183 Kan. 471, 328 P.2d 358; Brewster v. Lanyon Zinc Co., C.A.8th, 140 F. 801; Sohio Petroleum Co. v. Miller, 237 La. 1013, 112 So.2d 695; Fontenot v. Austral Oil Exploration Co., D.C.La., 168 F.Supp. 36, modified and affirmed C.A.5th, 266 F.2d 956; Skelly Oil Co. v. Boles, 193 Okl. 308, 142 P.2d 969; Trawick v. Castleberry, Okl., 275 P.2d

In the case of Harris v. Morris Plan Co.,[7] the lessee drilled one well on 200 acres of land in 1927. The well was abandoned in 1934 and the lessee contended that it was not then profitable to drill, as the price of oil was too low. Evidence, however, showed that there were 25 producing wells to the north and some 30 producing wells about the same distance to the southeast. Other persons were willing to enter and drill the leased premises. It was held that the lessee had breached the implied covenant to develop. On the other hand, in the case of Baker v. Collins,[8] the lessee had one producing well upon 210 acres of land. It was shown that the lessee had expended large sums to produce. Lessee had drilled three other wells on the lease that were either dry or had stopped producing. The one remaining well produced only one-half barrel per day. It was held that the covenant to further develop was not breached.

Although the element of profitability to the lessee is customarily required to be shown by the lessor as a condition precedent to the implication of a covenant to further develop, it also may be related to the diligence of the lessee in developing the lease. In the following sections, discussion will be directed to situations (a) where the lessee has allowed a considerable period of time to pass without development and (b) where the known profitable formations have been fully developed and other areas of the same formation or other formations exist without development.

(B) *Reasonable Diligence of the Lessee*

Even in those situations where profitability of further development has been shown, the lessee will not have breached an implied covenant of further development where it is shown that the lessee is proceeding with due diligence. Whether the lessee has diligently developed will be determined in connection with the facts and circumstances of the particular situation.[9]

292; Spiller v. Massey & Moore, Okl., 406 P.2d 467; Trust Co. of Chicago v. Samedan Oil Corp., C.A.10th, 192 F.2d 282; Kleppner v. Lemon, 176 Pa. 502, 35 A. 109; Texas Pacific Coal & Oil Co. v. Barker, 117 Tex. 418, 6 S.W.2d 1031, 60 A.L.R. 936, noted 7 Tex.L.Rev. 438; Fort Worth National Bank v. McLean, Tex. Civ.App., 245 S.W.2d 309; Clifton v. Koontz, 160 Tex. 82, 325 S.W.2d 684, 79 A.L.R.2d 774; Felmont Oil Corp. v. Pan American Petroleum Corp., Tex.Civ.App., 334 S.W.2d 449; Pan American Petroleum Corp. v. Hardy, Tex.Civ.App., 370 S.W.2d 904. Also see cases footnote 3, supra.

7. 144 Kan. 501, 61 P.2d 901.

8. 29 Ill.2d 410, 194 N.E.2d 353.

Two other cases where the lessee acted as a reasonably prudent lessee and the courts found that the implied covenant of reasonable development had not been breached are: Frazier v. Justiss Mears Oil Co., Inc., La.App., 391 So.2d 485, writ refused La., 395 So.2d 340; and West v. Sun Oil Co., Okl., 490 P.2d 1073. In each case the lessee had made substantial investment in exploration of the area and in drilling other wells to determine the advisability of further drilling on the leases or of drilling to deeper formations.

9. Baker v. Collins, 29 Ill.2d 410, 194 N.E.2d 353; Middleton v. California Co., 237 La. 1039, 112 So.2d 704; Dupree v. Relco Exploration Co., Inc., La.App., 354 So.2d 1083; West v. Sun Oil Co., Okl., 490 P.2d 1073 (good discussion of facts excusing further development); Skelly Oil Co. v. Boles, 193 Okl. 308, 142 P.2d 969; Crocker v. Humble Oil & Refining

In Oklahoma the passage of an unreasonable length of time during which no development has occurred, will operate to shift the burden of proof as to profitability of development. Where less than a reasonable time has elapsed, the burden is on the lessor to show profitability; following such lapse of time the burden is on the lessee to show that further drilling would be unprofitable.[10] In other jurisdictions, such as Texas, it appears that the burden of showing profitability remains upon the lessor.[11]

In recent years a question has arisen whether the lessee has breached his covenant to further develop where the lessor is unable to show that further development would be profitable to the lessee. The forerunner is found in the case of Sauder v. Mid-Continent Petroleum Corp.[12]

The Sauder case arose in Kansas. It involved a lease upon two adjoining tracts of land, one of 320 acres and the other of 40 acres. The lease was executed in 1916. Two wells were drilled on the 40-acre tract as offsets in 1920–21. No other development occurred. The lessor requested further development of the 320-acre tract and in 1930 brought suit for cancellation. The defense of the lessee was that the sands pinched out and that production from the 320-acre tract of land was highly unlikely. Although the lessor did not prove that the lessee could drill at a profit on the 320-acre tract, the court ruled that the lease as to that tract would be cancelled unless development was begun within a reasonable time.

The court was concerned that the lessee had held a half-section of land for 17 years without the drilling of an exploratory well, had refused to further develop such tract, and had also refused to release it. The court stated that the lessee could not hold the major portion of the leased premises indefinitely by production from a small part of

---

Co., Okl., 419 P.2d 265; Carter Oil Co. v. Mitchell, C.A.10th, 100 F.2d 945, noted in 17 Tex.L.Rev. 509. Cf. Sohio Petroleum Co. v. Miller, 237 La. 1013, 112 So.2d 695, decided the same day as the Middleton case, with opposite results.

10. West v. Sun Oil Co., Okl., 490 P.2d 1073; Dixon v. Anadarko Production Co., Okl., 505 P.2d 1394 (although a drainage case, the question might be asked whether the court is broadening the area in which the burden of proof will shift to the lessee to all cases in which the lessee has superior knowledge of the facts); Mitchell v. Amerada Hess Corp., Okl., 638 P.2d 441; Magnolia Petroleum Co. v. Rockhold, 192 Okl. 628, 138 P.2d 809; Magnolia Petroleum Co. v. Wilson, C.A.10th, 215 F.2d 317. Cf. Trawick v. Castleberry, Okl., 275 P.2d 292, no breach of duty, where, although burden shifted to lessee as there had been no development for an unreasonable time, lessee demonstrated present well would never pay out.

11. Clifton v. Koontz, 160 Tex. 82, 325 S.W.2d 684, 79 A.L.R.2d 774. Also see: Sanders v. Birmingham, 214 Kan. 769, 522 P.2d 959; Frazier v. Justiss Mears Oil Co., Inc., La.App., 391 So.2d 485, writ refused La., 395 So.2d 340; Superior Oil Co. v. Devon Corp., C.A.8th, 604 F.2d 1063.

12. 292 U.S. 272, 54 S.Ct. 671, 78 L.Ed. 1255, 93 A.L.R. 454, noted 40 W.Va.L.Q. 175. Also see Harris v. Morris Plan Co., 144 Kan. 501, 61 P.2d 901.

Cf. Sanders v. Birmingham, 214 Kan. 769, 522 P.2d 959 (that a 17-year delay was not sufficient in itself to show breach of covenant of reasonable development, without showing of profitability. No discussion of holding for speculative purpose).

Ch. 8 PROTECT, DEVELOP, ADMINISTER LEASE 419

the land. The action of the lessee not only withheld royalty from the lessor but prevented him from making other arrangements for development. Holding the lease for an extremely long period of time for speculative purposes was a breach of the prudent operator rule.

Following the Sauder case, Arkansas,[13] Kentucky,[14] Maryland,[15] Ohio,[16] and Oklahoma[17] have reached similar results. It is probable that it will not be followed in Texas.[18] Oklahoma is the foremost proponent of the view that the lessee has breached the implied covenant of further development where it is found the lessee is holding the lease for speculative purposes. This generally occurs where (1) the lessee has held the lease for a very long period of time without development, although (2) it cannot be shown that other wells could be profitably drilled. For a time the Oklahoma courts were unclear whether cancellation in such a case resulted from abandonment of the lease by the lessee, or from breach of the implied covenant to develop. This was authoritatively decided in the case of Doss Oil Royalty Co. v. Texas Co.[19] Suit was brought for cancellation of the undeveloped portions of two leases. No wells had been drilled for 14 years, and the leases had not been fully developed. The court condemned an attempt to indefinitely freeze undeveloped portions of leases for speculative purposes. The court restricted the loss of a lease from abandonment to situations where the lessee had physically relinquished the premises and adopted the Sauder view that a breach of the implied covenant of further development was involved. The case was remanded for a determination whether such delay could be justified by the lessee.

13. Nolan v. Thomas, Ark., 309 S.W.2d 727, noted 12 Ark.L.Rev. 213.

14. Cameron v. Lebow, Ky., 338 S.W.2d 399 (17 years, but relief denied on the ground that the lessor had not made a demand.).

15. Humble Oil & Refining Co. v. Romero, C.A.5th, 194 F.2d 383.

16. Lake v. Ohio Fuel Gas Co., 2 Ohio App.2d 227, 207 N.E.2d 659 (22 years).

17. Doss Oil Royalty Co. v. Texas Co., 192 Okl. 359, 137 P.2d 934 (14 years); Magnolia Petroleum Co. v. Rockhold, 192 Okl. 628, 138 P.2d 809; Skelly Oil Co. v. Boles, 193 Okl. 308, 142 P.2d 969; McKenna v. Nichlos, 193 Okl. 526, 145 P.2d 957; Sand Springs Home v. Clemens, Okl., 276 P.2d 262 (12 years); Coal Oil & Gas Co. v. Styron, Okl., 303 P.2d 965; Wolfson Oil Co. v. Gill, Okl., 309 P.2d 282 (35 years); Crocker v. Humble Oil & Refining Co., Okl., 419 P.2d 265 (36 years); Mitchell v. Amerada Hess Corp., Okl., 638 P.2d 441; Trust Co. of Chicago v. Samedan Oil Corp., C.A.10th, 192 F.2d 282; Magnolia Petroleum Co. v. Wilson, C.A.10th, 215 F.2d 317.

18. Sauder was followed in Willingham v. Bryson, Tex.Civ.App., 294 S.W.2d 421, noted 35 Tex.L.Rev. 617; 34 Dicta 348, 11 S.W.L.J. 390; 5 U.C.L.A.L.Rev. 567, which was overruled in Clifton v. Koontz, 160 Tex. 82, 325 S.W.2d 684, 79 A.L.R.2d 774. The tenor of the Clifton case is very strongly for the element of profitability; however, the case expressly excepted from the opinion situations where a long time had elapsed or large acreage was involved. Also see Amerada Petroleum Co. v. Doering, C.A.5th, 93 F.2d 540; Sinclair Oil & Gas Co. v. Masterson, C.A.5th, 271 F.2d 310, noted in 60 Col.L.Rev. 741 and 14 S.W.L.J. 407 and Felmont Oil Corp. v. Pan American Petroleum Corp., Tex.Civ.App., 334 S.W.2d 449.

19. 192 Okl. 359, 137 P.2d 934. Also see Magnolia Petroleum Co. v. Rockhold, 192 Okl. 628, 138 P.2d 809; Skelly Oil Co. v. Boles, 193 Okl. 308, 142 P.2d 969; McKenna v. Nichlos, 193 Okl. 526, 145 P.2d 957.

Another example of the Oklahoma rule is found in Sand Springs Home v. Clemens,[20] where only one small producing well and one dry hole were drilled on a 120-acre of land during a period of 12 years. The court decreed partial cancellation on the ground that the lessee could not hold the entire lease indefinitely for speculative purposes and stated: "If such be the case, no injury could result to defendant by a cancellation of the lease as to the undeveloped portion of the lands embraced therein. Equity and justice to the plaintiff require that it be done."

The Oklahoma courts view such cancellation as an exercise of their equity powers. This view of the Oklahoma courts is well stated in Trust Co. of Chicago v. Samedan Oil Corp.,[21] where the court, in discussing the development of Oklahoma law, stated,

"With Doss Royalty Co. v. Texas Co., the Oklahoma Court discarded abandonment for mere lapse of time as a distinct ground for cancellation of a lease, and very properly, we think, incorporated lapse of time as a part of the concept of the implied covenant to exercise due diligence. * * * 'In other words, after the passage of a reasonable length of time, the duty to drill additional wells becomes progressively greater, and the standard of the prudent operator becomes progressively of less importance in determining whether such duty exists' * * * Predominant in all these cases is a conscientious effort to arrive at a just and equitable adjustment of the conflict of the parties to the lease, having in mind the rights and duties imposed by their contract, express or implied. The rule of the Doss case is one of essentially equitable cognizance to effectuate justice."

As indicated in the Doss case where the lessee can justify such lapse of time without development, the lease will not be subject to cancellation. Generally such delay is excused where it can be shown that the lessee was engaged in geological studies concerning the further exploration of the lease in other or deeper sands. Accordingly, under these cases, the implied covenant of the lessee to further develop includes not only a duty to drill, but also to make preparation for the development of other possibly producing sands. Such studies and preparations, coupled with an intent to drill related to such programs, will be sufficient justification for delay.[22] This is illustrated in the

---

20. Okl., 276 P.2d 262.
21. C.A.10th, 192 F.2d 282.
22. Reynolds v. Smith, 231 Ark. 566, 331 S.W.2d 112; Middleton v. California Co., 237 La. 1039, 112 So.2d 704; Skelly Oil Co. v. Boles, 193 Okl. 308, 142 P.2d 969; Barnes v. Mack Oil Co., Okl., 376 P.2d 279; Carter Oil Co. v. Mitchell, C.A. 10th, 100 F.2d 945, noted in 17 Tex.L. Rev. 509; Blythe v. Sohio Petroleum Co., C.A.10th, 271 F.2d 861; Sun Oil Co. v. Frantz, C.A.10th, 291 F.2d 52. Cf. Olson v. Signal Drilling and Exploration Inc., 151 Mont. 122, 439 P.2d 763. Here, plaintiff attempted to show there had been a breach of the implied covenant to develop by the lessee on the ground that in a proposed, but not executed, unit agreement the production percentage to be allocated to the undrilled tract was evidence that drilling by the lessee was justified. It is interesting to note that in rejecting such figures as evidence of damage, that such figures, if applied to portions of the lease from which plaintiff acquired production, would show actual production in excess

case of Reynolds v. Smith,[23] where seven wells, of which three were producers, had been drilled to a depth of 3000 to 3500 feet. It was shown that no lack of reasonable development had occurred as to the 3,000' depth, and that, as to greater depths, the wells would cost from $40,000 to $70,000, which could be justified only by drilling in blocks of 500 acres. The nearest deep well was some nine miles distant, and the depth was wildcat under this lease. It was held that the lessee had acted as a reasonably prudent operator, who would not drill deeper with only 120 acres under lease.

(C) Exploration and Development of Other Areas and Formations Where Profitability Cannot Be Shown

From an analysis of the above cases and the Texas case of Willingham v. Bryson,[24] Professor Meyers logically suggested that a new implied covenant may have been in the process of emerging.[25] He suggested that the covenant be named the implied covenant of further exploration. The term exploration was used to differentiate the factual situation to which it applied from that of development. In other words, the implied covenant of development or further development would only attach when it could be shown that the lessee would be able to drill at a profit to himself. However, independent of this covenant, there also existed an additional covenant that the lessee drill exploratory wells upon portions of the lease even where it could not be shown that they could be drilled at a profit. This could include other parts of the same formation, such as the Sauder case, as well as other formations. If the lessee retained the lease for an unreasonable length of time without such exploration, such unexplored portions of the lease would be subject to cancellation.

Although usually referred to as part of the implied covenant of further development, it would appear that the courts of Arkansas,

---

of percentage allocated, hence, plaintiff was not damaged. A fine example of a sword cutting two ways.

In Renner v. Monsanto Chemical Co., 187 Kan. 158, 354 P.2d 326, lessee unsuccessfully defended on ground state proration formula showed additional wells would constitute waste.

Also see Wolfson Oil Co. v. Gill, Okl., 309 P.2d 282, contemplation of secondary recovery operations, which had not proven feasible in other areas in the same sand, was not sufficient justification.

23. 231 Ark. 566, 331 S.W.2d 112, also see Barnes v. Mack Oil Co., Okl., 376 P.2d 275; Carter Oil Co. v. Mitchell, C.A. 10th, 100 F.2d 945, noted in 17 Tex.L. Rev. 509; Blythe v. Sohio Petroleum Co., C.A.10th, 271 F.2d 861.

24. Willingham v. Bryson, Tex.Civ. App., 294 S.W.2d 421, noted 35 Tex.L. Rev. 617; 34 Dicta 348, 11 S.W.L.J. 380; 5 U.C.L.A.L.Rev. 567.

25. One of the more interesting exchanges in law review literature occurred between Professor Meyers and Mr. Earl A. Brown; Meyers, Implied Covenant of Further Exploration, 34 Tex.L.Rev. 553; Brown, Implied Covenant for Additional Development, 13 S.W.L.J. 149; Meyers, Covenant of Further Exploration: A Comment, 37 Tex.L.Rev. 179; Brown, Proposed New Covenant of Further Exploration: Reply to Comment, 37 Tex.L. Rev. 303. It is also interesting to note that in the case book, Oil and Gas, by Williams, Maxwell and Meyers, in the section concerning implied development and exploration covenants, the Masterson case is inserted virtually in full, but the Clifton case is omitted, without comment.

Kansas, Kentucky, Maryland, and Ohio may have adopted a covenant very similar to that proposed by Professor Meyers.[26] Uncertainty exists as to the existence of a covenant to drill in Texas where profitability cannot be shown. Such covenant was indicated in the Texas case of Willingham v. Bryson,[27] which followed the Sauder case and dealt with drilling to deeper sands. However, the case was emphatically overruled in the later case of Clifton v. Koontz.[28]

In the Clifton case plaintiffs asked for a partial cancellation of the lease on the ground "* * * 3. That the implied covenant second above stated [to further explore] required and obligated said working interest owners to drill a second or additional well on said land as a test well looking to the production [of] oil, gas or other minerals therefrom prior to this date;". The court found that the lessors had not discharged their burden.

> "The petitioners did not discharge the burden which rested upon them to prove, as required, that the lessees failed to measure up to the standard of the prudent operator. While it is true that each separate stratum or horizon would be entitled to separate development yet it is equally true that the burden rests upon the lessor to prove that the producing stratum required additional wells, or that strata different from that from which production is being obtained, in reasonable probability exist, and that by the drilling of additional wells there would be a reasonable expectation of profit to the lessee."

As to a new covenant to explore, the court disposed of its application in Texas with the following language:

> "We hold that there is no implied covenant to explore as distinguished from the implied covenant to conduct additional development after production in paying quantities has been obtained * * *. This theory is untenable and is diametrically opposed to our established 'prudent operator' rule where expectation of profit is an essential element. * * * We decline to follow the theory advanced that there is an implied covenant to explore as distinguished from the implied covenant to develop."

However, the court modified its language with the limitation:

> "* * *, it should be noted that we do not have a factual situation where the lease covers several thousand acres and an effort is being made to hold such vast acreage by showing production from a comparatively small area. Neither are we confronted with a situation where an unreasonably long length of time has elapsed since the last development of the leased premises. Therefore, we do not pass upon these questions."

---

26. See notes 13 through 16 supra.

27. Tex.Civ.App., 294 S.W.2d 421, noted 35 Tex.L.Rev. 617; 34 Dicta 348, 11 S.W.L.J. 380; 5 U.C.L.A.L.Rev. 567.

28. 160 Tex. 82, 325 S.W.2d 684, 79 A.L.R.2d 774.

Ch. 8   PROTECT, DEVELOP, ADMINISTER LEASE

It appears certain from the opinion that the court has held that no obligation rests upon the lessee in Texas to explore other formations unless it may be shown by the lessor that the possibility of profit exists. In view of the modifying language, it is uncertain what the view will be in a factual situation such as the Sauder case if the lessor has requested further development of the same formation, is unable to show profitability and the lessee has not developed for a very long period of time, or expressly refuses to develop further.

Two subsequent cases in Texas dealt with the situation where large acreage was being held. The case of Sinclair Oil & Gas Co. v. Masterson [29] involved some 91,000 acres of land. The decision of the Court of Appeals of the Fifth Circuit was handed down after the decision of the Texas Supreme Court in Clifton v. Koontz. The Circuit Court of Appeals found that the facts in the Masterson case came within the exception stated by the Texas Supreme Court and expressly found an implied covenant of exploration. However, following the Masterson case, the El Paso Court of Civil Appeals, in Felmont Oil Corp. v. Pan American Petroleum Corp.,[30] also involving large acreage, expressly repudiated the implied covenant of exploration and the Masterson decision. Writ of error was refused, "no reversible error," by the Texas Supreme Court.

Although this constituted an affirmation of the lower court opinion, under the Texas procedural system an "n. r. e." affirmation does

---

29. C.A.5th, 271 F.2d 310, noted in 60 Col.L.Rev. 741 and 14 S.W.L.J. 407.

30. Tex.Civ.App., 334 S.W.2d 449. The court stated the following elements as to a cause of action for failure to develop:

"(1) That the lessees failed to measure up to the standards of the prudent operator;

(2) That producing strata or horizons, which they contend should have been further explored or drilled, required additional wells;

(3) That strata or horizons other than those from which production is being obtained (on which further exploration or drilling is sought), exists in reasonable probability;

(4) That by the drilling of additional wells, there would be a reasonable expectation of profit, not only to the lessor, but also to the lessee."

The court rejected Masterson and followed Koontz: "In the Koontz case (supra), the Supreme Court specially pointed out that it did not have before it a factual situation where the lease covers several thousand acres, and an effort is being made to hold such vast acreage by showing production from a comparatively small area, nor did it have a situation where an unreasonably long time had elapsed since the last development of the leased premises. In its opinion, the court did not pass upon these questions. Such questions are, however, inescapably before us in the case now under consideration.

"Out of the 10,240 acres covered by Lease 'A,' lessee-appellees own 5,685 acres; and, out of the 21,120 acres covered by Lease 'B', lessee-appellees own 13,325 acres."

" * * * Obviously, all and every part of each so vast a lease cannot be fully explored and completely developed in a single operation. After production, the lessee is required to reasonably develop the remainder of the lease held by him, and if he fails to do so, he may suffer the loss of all or part of his leasehold estate."

"We hold here, as was held by the Supreme Court in the Koontz case, supra, that there is no implied covenant to explore, as distinguished from the implied covenant to conduct, additional development after production in paying quantities has been obtained."

Also see Amerada Petroleum Co. v. Doering, C.C.A.5th, 93 F.2d 540.

not raise the opinion to the stature of a Supreme Court Opinion. It merely is an agreement with the result in the case and not necessarily an approval of the reasoning. For this reason, "n. r. e." opinions are less than satisfactory indicators in Texas for precedent evaluation. As the Masterson case is not binding upon the state courts, under the Erie doctrine, it may only be concluded that no authoritative precedent exists in Texas as to the modifying situations indicated in the Clifton opinion.

Any question that may have existed whether Oklahoma would impose an implied covenant of further exploration, has been answered in the case of Mitchell v. Amerada Hess Corp.[31] In the two earlier cases of Blyth v. Sohio Petroleum Co.[32] and Carter Oil Co. v. Mitchell,[33] the question posed was whether the lessee had breached an implied obligation to drill deep tests. In both cases the court refused cancellation although a long period of time had elapsed without development. In each case the basis for non-cancellation was that the lessee had spent considerable time and effort in investigating such deep tests, and such drilling would require substantial investments. In both cases the shallower sands had been fully developed. However, neither case was dismissed for failure to state a cause of action, but on the basis that the lessee was satisfying the standard of a reasonably prudent operator.

In Mitchell v. Amerada Hess Corp.[34] lessors were attempting to cancel leases so they could re-lease for high bonuses and other economic benefits generally prevailing in the area. The leases had been held by production for some 23 years. However, lessors maintained that other productive formations existed that had not been explored by the lessees. It was part of the cause of action that lessees had breached an implied covenant to explore, i.e., drill wells to other formations although it could not be shown that such wells would recover the costs of drilling and producing.

The court stated the issue: "Would a prudent operator, having due consideration for the interest of both the lessee and lessor, considering all factors, including what is known about the market, the geology and adjoining activity, drill the proposed well?" The court rejected the proposition that the lessee would have an obligation to drill other wells without consideration of a profit to the lessee. "It is simply not realistic to ignore profit as a consideration of the standard of a prudent operator simply because the lessor demands a wildcat be

---

31. Okl., 638 P.2d 441.

32. C.A.10th, 271 F.2d 861; also see Reynolds v. Smith, 231 Ark. 566, 331 S.W.2d 112; Magnolia Petroleum Co. v. Rockhold, 192 Okl. 628, 138 P.2d 809; Barnes v. Mack Oil Co., Okl., 376 P.2d 279; Sinclair Oil & Gas Co. v. Bishop, Okl., 441 P.2d 436.

33. C.C.A.10th, 100 F.2d 945, noted in 17 Tex.L.Rev. 509.

34. Okl., 638 P.2d 441. In Louisiana it appears that a lessee has a positive duty to develop all formations and all depths, as a reasonably prudent operator. See Dupree v. Relco Exploration Co., Inc., La.App., 354 So.2d 1083; Vetter v. Morrow, La.App., 361 So.2d 898; Waseco Chemical & Supply Co. v. Bayou State Oil Corp., La.App., 371 So.2d 305, writ denied La., 374 So.2d 656.

drilled on a productive lease rather than an additional well to a productive formation."

The court re-emphasized the prudent operator doctrine and rejected the implied covenant to further explore:

"We thus hold there is no implied covenant to further explore after paying production is obtained, as distinguished from the implied covenant to further develop. In addition to the speculative burden the offered covenant would place on lessees, the covenant as tendered is substantially served by the covenant for further development as it is interpreted in this jurisdiction while limiting the duty to drill additional wells to those instances where a prudent operator would expect a probability of potential profit from the well contemplated. * * * where the lessor has established an unreasonable or unconscionable length of time in developing an oil and gas lease, the lessee shoulders the burden of proof to excuse his delay, facilitating cancellation of leases owned by dilatory or speculative lessees."

It appears to be the trend that the lessee will not have an obligation to drill further wells where profitability cannot be shown. This appears to be true not only in cases dealing with the implied covenant for reasonable development but also with the implied covenant to drill protection wells.

Where a duty exists to develop other formations, a duty exists to develop each such reservoir separately. In the Texas case of Pan American Petroleum Corp. v. Hardy,[35] the lessee concealed the fact that known reservoir "A" overlay reservoir "B". Upon discovery that reservoir "B" could be developed at a profit to the lessee, suit was brought. The court rejected lessee's argument that it could offset production from the "A" reservoir against production they should have developed in the "B" reservoir. As the reservoirs were in fact separate, they should be developed separately.

§ 8.4 Implied Covenants to Develop the Lease—Effect of Express Provisions in the Lease

The parties to a lease, by express language, may eliminate any implied duty of the lessee to develop. Where the express clause is inconsistent with an implied covenant to develop, the express clause will control. If the express clause shows an intent to fully state the duty of the lessee to develop the lease, no covenant to further develop will be implied.

A statement in an oil and gas lease that the lessee shall have no duty to develop the lease is valid and will eliminate any implied duty of development.[1] In some instances the clause is limited in extent [2]

---

35. Tex.Civ.App., 370 S.W.2d 904.

1. Linn v. Wehrle, 35 Ohio App. 107, 172 N.E. 288 (" * * * there shall be no implied covenant to drill or protect mines"); Adkins v. Adams, C.C.A.7th, 152 F.2d 489 (" * * * at such times

2. See note 2 on page 426.

or as to the products covered.³ At times the negation of an implied duty to develop is found in the nature of the discretion given to the lessee. In Ralph v. Magnolia Petroleum Co.,⁴ where the lease contained a provision that drilling and mining for oil, gas and other minerals would be wholly at the option of the grantee, it was held that no implied obligation to develop existed. On the other hand, in Cowden v. Broderick & Calvert,⁵ the lease contained the phrase, "Lessor agrees that all other development shall be at the discretion of the lessee." It was held that "discretion" did not mean the uncontrolled will of the lessee, and such discretion was subject to an equitable standard of what is just and proper under the circumstances. Therefore, the exercise of discretion by the lessee was subject to court review. An intent to negate an implied duty to develop has been found,⁶ in the deletion of express provisions relating to development that had been contained in the lease.

A more difficult situation arises where the language in the lease does not totally negate a duty to drill, but merely sets forth an express development program. The question involved is whether it is the intent of the parties that the express provisions totally supplant an implied covenant of further development, or merely relate to a portion of the duty to develop. Although the problem cannot be said to be rare, it is somewhat unusual, as in most cases the parties to the lease are unable to formulate a satisfactory express program of lease development at the time of the execution of the lease. Where the lessee is developing in a semi-proven area, such express provisions are sometimes found.

Gulf Production Co. v. Kishi⁷ concerned the problem of whether an express clause negated a further implied covenant to develop. The lease acreage, the requirements of the clause,⁸ and the wells drilled and produced were as follows:

and in such manner as the lessee may elect.")

2. Simms Oil Co. v. Flewellen, 138 Tex. 63, 156 S.W.2d 521, exempted lessee for 20 years:

"It is further agreed that in no event shall the lessee and his assigns be required to exercise his option to develop said premises in less time than twenty years unless a producing oil or gas well is brought in on an adjoining or adjacent tract of land and that in that event the said lessee shall commence drilling of an offset well within six months after such well on the adjoining tract has been brought in or else shall forfeit this lease as a penalty for such non-development."

3. In Wilkins v. Nelson, 161 La. 437, 108 So. 875, the lease imposed an express duty to drill an oil well when one was drilled within a half mile of the lease. The lessee drilled a gas well and never drilled for oil. It was held no implied duty existed to drill for oil, as no oil well was ever drilled within the specified distance.

4. Tex.Civ.App., 95 S.W.2d 222. Also see Skinner v. Ajax Portland Cement Co., 109 Kan. 72, 197 P. 875 ("It is entirely optional with the lessee as to when, during the term of this lease, it shall be obliged to drill either for oil or gas.")

5. 131 Tex. 434, 114 S.W.2d 1166, 117 A.L.R. 61.

6. Smith v. Tullos, 195 La. 400, 196 So. 912.

7. 129 Tex. 487, 103 S.W.2d 965.

8. (a) Clause as to Lease No. 1:

"If oil shall be found on said premises in paying quantities, then unless lessee shall within 60 days from such finding of oil in paying quantities, be-

Ch. 8   PROTECT, DEVELOP, ADMINISTER LEASE   427

	Acreage	Clause Required	Actually Drilled
Lease #1	150 acres	12 wells	15 wells (12 producing)
Lease #2	20 acres	4 wells	6 wells (all producing)
	170 acres	16 wells	21 wells (18 producing).

Lessors brought suit for damages for the royalty that would have been produced had the lessees reasonably developed the premises.

It was alleged that reasonable development called for 15 wells to be drilled per year on Lease No. 1 and 5 wells per year on Lease No. 2. The court held that the express covenant excluded an implied covenant for further development to drill in excess of the number of wells called for by the express clauses. The rationale of the decision is that implied covenants arise only out of necessity in absence of an express stipulation with respect to development of the leased premises. Where the parties have expressed themselves on the matter of development there is no room for an additional implied covenant, even if the express covenant would be inadequate for reasonable development. However, if the express clause reflects, but does not fully state the lessee's duty as to development, the extent to which a reasonably prudent operator would thereafter drill will form the basis for an implied covenant of additional development.[9] The result in the case is consistent with other authority holding that where the express clause is totally inconsistent with an implied covenant to develop, the latter does not arise.[10]

---

gin the drilling of another well and unless lessee shall thereafter continue to drill other wells (beginning each additional well within 60 days from the completion of the last prior well), until a total of 12 wells shall have been drilled on said premises, this lease shall on such failure at any time cease to be effective except as to, and the lessee shall on such failure lose its rights hereunder, except as to an area equal to five (5) acres, for each producing well, which total area may be selected by lessee, both as to location and shape, and as to which this lease and lessee's rights hereunder, shall remain effective so long as production or explorations are continued by lessee on such retained area in accordance with the other terms of this lease; lessee having expressly the right to drill as many additional wells as it pleases on such retained area. It is expressly stated that such alternative right to drill 12 wells or to forfeit the lease with the exception of the retained area at any time during the drilling of such 12 wells is at lessee's election."

(b) Clause as to Lease No. 2:

"Should oil in paying quantities be found on the leased premises, then additional wells shall be drilled thereon until as many as four producing wells are drilled and such additional wells shall be drilled within not more than 90 days interval between the completion or abandonment of one and commencement of work on another and a failure to drill such additional wells shall terminate this lease as to all land except 5 acres in a square around each producing well, with the well in the center."

9. See Sinclair Oil & Gas Co. v. Masterson, C.A.5th, 271 F.2d 310, noted in 60 Col.L.Rev. 741 and 14 S.W.L.J. 407, where the court took the view the express clause did not exclude an implied covenant to further development, but merely accelerated that portion of development covered by the clause.

10. Central States Production Corp. v. Jordan, 184 Okl. 262, 86 P.2d 790; Texas Pacific Coal & Oil Co. v. Barker, 117 Tex. 418, 6 S.W.2d 1031, 60 A.L.R. 936, noted 7 Tex.L.Rev. 438.

When the clause merely requires an exploratory well to be drilled, the implied covenant to further develop will not be eliminated.[11] Where the extent of the express clause may be construed to apply to only a portion of the development of the lease, the implied covenant will arise to the extent a reasonably prudent operator would further develop the lease.[12]

In some instances, through inept draftsmanship, an express clause has the result of leaving the lessee in the same position that he would have been in without the clause or in an inferior position. An example where the clause left the implied covenant of further development in effect is found in Endicott v. DeBarbieri.[13] Here the clause stated, "It is further agreed that in the event the first test well on the above described lands shall be completed as a commercial producer of oil and gas, or either of them, then additional wells shall be drilled each six months in accordance with the spacing regulations promulgated by the Conservation Division of the Corporation Commission of the State of Kansas until the lease is fully developed." No spacing regulations were promulgated by the state as to the field in question. The lessee contended that the reasonable operator rule would require only one well on the lease. However, the court said that the lessee would have to drill one well each six months until one well had been drilled for every ten acres. To be relieved of the obligation to drill to this density the lessee would have to have such regulations promulgated.

On the other hand, in the case of Texas Pacific Coal & Oil Co. v. Barker,[14] under the clause involved,[15] the court stated that the lessee had a duty to continue drilling until it could show that a test on the merged property proved that further development would be unprofitable. As the case arose in Texas, it would appear that the effect of

---

11. Brewster v. Lanyon Zinc Co., C.C.A.8th, 140 F. 801. But cf. Hughes v. Busseyville Oil & Gas Co., 180 Ky. 545, 203 S.W. 515, (no duty to further develop after drilling of the first well).

12. Alford v. Dennis, 102 Kan. 403, 170 P. 1005 (language construed to apply only to wells to be drilled to a stated date, after which implied covenant attached); Rhoads Drilling Co. v. Allred, 123 Tex. 229, 70 S.W.2d 576 (express agreement construed as merely supplemental to implied obligation and not in lieu thereof).

13. 189 Kan. 301, 369 P.2d 241.

14. 117 Tex. 418, 6 S.W.2d 1031, 60 A.L.R. 936, noted 7 Tex.L.Rev. 438.

15. "As a further consideration for the execution of this merger agreement, the Texas Pacific Coal & Oil Company hereby agrees that within 30 days from the date of the delivery of the merger agreement * * * that it will begin actual drilling of a well for oil and gas on some portion of said merged premises and will prosecute said drilling with reasonable diligence until oil or gas is obtained in paying quantities or until such depth has been reached as should obtain oil or gas in the Ranger field, taking into consideration the depth of other producing wells in said section of the county. * * *, and it further agrees that it will dedicate at least one string of tools to the development of said merged tracts, and will keep the same operating until the said tract of land is developed, or until sufficient proofs have been made on said tract of land as to convince the said lessee that other portions of it are dry and unworthy of further tests."

the clause was to shift the burden of whether or not a well could be drilled at a profit to the lessee.

The cases dealing with the effect of spacing orders of conservation commissions and orders of other governmental agencies have been conflicting. Decisions have ranged from eliminating the implied covenant to the extent that it conflicts with such orders,[16] allowing payment of compensatory royalties where the wells could not be drilled,[17] to not precluding the implied covenant to the extent it would be "reasonable under the circumstances."[18] Unless the lessee is being unjustly enriched by the operation of the order, it would seem that the better view is that the implied covenant would be superseded by the order, to the extent of the conflict.

§ 8.5 Implied Covenant of Protection—Duty to Protect Against Drainage

In the absence of a lease provision, a covenant will be implied that the lessee shall prevent drainage from the lease by the drilling of offsetting wells, where such wells would be drilled by a reasonably prudent operator, i.e., would return profit to the lessee over the costs of drilling, completing, equipping, and producing. The duty of offset will exist as to each producing formation. The common law duty may be varied or affected by:

(a) **express provisions of the lease, and statutory enactments;**

(b) **ownership of a leasehold interest in the draining tract by the lessee; or,**

(c) **secondary recovery operations or alterations to stimulate production.**

O executes an oil and gas lease to Pure Oil Company. While the lease is being held by production from the center of the lease, it is found that the adjoining land has been leased and that several wells have been drilled thereon. Lessor assumes that as a result of this activity petroleum products are being drained from under his land to the adjoining land. The lease is silent regarding any duty of the lessee to prevent drainage. What is the lessee's obligation, if any, in this regard?

In prior sections the discussion was directed to the implied covenant of the lessee to reasonably develop the leased premises for the mutual benefit of the lessor and lessee. As the major consideration to the lessor for an oil and gas lease is the return from the products produced, in the absence of a negating clause, the lessee has an obligation to develop the premises for the greatest return, where such development will also return a profit to the lessee. Likewise, the

---

16. U. V. Industries, Inc., v. Danielson, ___ Mont. ___, 602 P.2d 571.

17. Cook v. El Paso Natural Gas Co., C.A.10th, 560 F.2d 978, a drainage case with a common lessee that appears to be based upon unjust enrichment of the lessee.

18. Rush v. King Oil Co., 220 Kan. 616, 556 P.2d 431.

lessee may not sit back and allow the products to be drained from under the land, as the lessor may not protect himself, having no possessory interest in the minerals. The question is not so much whether a covenant to prevent drainage will be implied, but rather what is the scope of the liability of the lessee to prevent drainage? Is the lessee obliged to prevent all drainage?

As in the case of the implied covenant to develop, the standard applied is that of the reasonably prudent operator.[1] The lessee is not an insurer against drainage.[2] He is charged with the obligation that he use the same efforts that a reasonably prudent operator would. The rule is well stated in the case of Gerson v. Anderson-Prichard Production Corp.:[3]

> "But the lessee does not bear an implied obligation to drill an offset well to prevent drainage unless, taking into consideration all existing facts and circumstances, it would probably produce oil in sufficient quantity to repay the whole sum required to be expended, including the cost of drilling, equipping, and operating the well and also pay a reasonable profit on the entire outlay. No obligation rests upon the lessee to carry the operations beyond the point where they are profitable to him, even if some benefit to the lessor would result from them."

This appears to be the rule in all jurisdictions. Therefore, the lessee is not obligated to prevent all drainage. Only when drainage is substantial and the drilling of an offset well in all probability would produce a profit for the lessee, does the implied obligation attach. The obligation to drill protection wells exists separately as to each

---

1. Rush v. King Oil Co., 220 Kan. 616, 556 P.2d 431; Shell Oil Co. v. James, Miss., 257 So.2d 488; America Southwest Corp. v. Allen, Miss., 336 So.2d 1297; West v. Sun Oil Co., Okl., 490 P.2d 1073 (1971); Elliott v. Pure Oil Co., 10 Ill.2d 146, 139 N.E.2d 295; Renner v. Monsanto Chemical Co., 187 Kan. 158, 354 P.2d 326; North American Petroleum Co. v. Knight, Okl., 321 P.2d 964, noted in 11 Okl.L.Rev. 340; Sunray Mid-Continental Oil Co. v. McDaniel, Okl., 361 P.2d 683, noted 15 Okl.L.Rev. 76; Spiller v. Massey & Moore, Okl., 406 P.2d 467; Texas Pacific Coal & Oil Co. v. Barker, 117 Tex. 418, 6 S.W.2d 1031, 60 A.L.R. 936, noted 7 Tex.L.Rev. 438; Hutchins v. Humble Oil & Refining Co., Tex.Civ.App., 161 S.W.2d 571; Chapman v. Sohio Petroleum Co., Tex.Civ.App., 297 S.W.2d 885; Vega Petroleum Corp. v. Hovey, Tex.Civ. App., 604 S.W.2d 388; Shell Petroleum Corp. v. Shore, C.A.10th, 72 F.2d 193, noted in 13 Tex.L.Rev. 140; Gerson v. Anderson-Prichard Production Corp., C.C.A.10th, 149 F.2d 444; Tide Water Associated Oil Co. v. Stott, C.C.A.5th, 159 F.2d 174, cert. denied 331 U.S. 817, 67 S.Ct. 1306, 91 L.Ed. 1835. The rule is also stated in Spiller v. Massey & Moore, Okl., 406 P.2d 467.

"There is no implied obligation on the part of an oil and gas lessee to drill an offset well to a well on adjoining premises, * * * save and except where the drilling of such well would probably, taking all of the existing facts and circumstances into consideration, produce sufficient oil to repay the cost of drilling, equipping, and operating such well, and also to produce a reasonable profit on the entire outlay, and neither the lessee or lessor is the arbiter of whether an offset well should be drilled * * * but both are bound by what a reasonable prudent operator would do under similar circumstances, and under no circumstances will a lessee be required to drill an offset or an additional well when the same would probably not result profitably to him."

2. Tide Water Associated Oil Co. v. Stott, C.C.A.5th, 159 F.2d 174, cert. denied 331 U.S. 817, 67 S.Ct. 1306, 91 L.Ed. 1835.

3. C.C.A.10th, 149 F.2d 444.

producing formation. The burden is on the lessor to show that the offset well may be drilled at a profit.[4]

The common law duty to protect the lease from drainage by drilling of offsetting wells may be varied by:

(a) An express clause in the lease, and statutory enactments;

(b) the fact that the lessee also owns a lease on the draining tract of land;

(c) secondary recovery or other operations to stimulate production.

§ 8.6 The Effect of an Express Offset Clause on the Implied Covenant to Protect Against Drainage

An express clause relating to the obligation of the lessee to drill offset or protection wells will control and displace an implied covenant to otherwise protect from drainage.

Where the oil and gas lease contains an express clause relating to the duty of the lessee to drill offsetting wells, such clause will control, and no further obligation to protect against drainage will be implied.[1] The usual clause incorporates the prudent operator standard of profitability plus a limitation as to the maximum distance without which a well drilled on other land will not be required to be offset. The effect of the clause is to exempt wells outside of this distance from imposing an obligation of protection on the lessee though they may in fact be draining the leased premises.

Old clauses, that are still found in oil and gas leases, which usually state the maximum offset distance as 150 to 200 feet, were designated prior to imposition of spacing regulations or at a time that very small spacing distances existed. These clauses may well serve to exempt the lessee from ever having an obligation to offset, as no wells under modern spacing regulations may be drilled within such distances. However, one case has held that such clauses are ineffective and do not displace the implied covenant to drill a protection well.[2] The better drawn clause should include two offset distances, one for oil wells and the other for gas wells, at least sufficient for anticipated spacing.

4. Breaux v. Magnolia Petroleum Co., La.App., 121 So.2d 280.

America Southwest Corp. v. Allen, Miss., 336 So.2d 1297; Cone v. Amoco Production Co., 87 N.M. 294, 532 P.2d 590 (no substantial drainage). See Bolton v. Coats, Tex., 533 S.W.2d 914 (Held classification as gas reservoir does not relieve from liability (1) for past drainage of oil and distillate; or (2) under implied covenant against future drainage of oil and distillate from same reservoir).

1. Hartman Ranch Co. v. Associated Oil Co., 10 Cal.2d 232, 73 P.2d 1163; Davis v. Mose, 112 Okl. 38, 239 P. 447; Burt v. Deorsam, Tex.Civ.App., 227 S.W. 354; Wolter v. Houston Oil Co. of Texas, Tex. Civ.App., 74 S.W.2d 706; Magnolia Petroleum Co. v. Page, Tex.Civ.App., 141 S.W. 2d 691; Coats v. Brown, Tex.Civ App., 301 S.W.2d 932.

2. Williams v. Humble Oil and Refining Co., C.A.5th, 432 F.2d 165, rehearing denied 435 F.2d 772, cert. denied 402 U.S. 934, 91 S.Ct. 1526, 28 L.Ed.2d 868 (short offset distance did not displace implied covenant to drill protection well).

Attempts have been made to draft the clause so it will be effective if the spacing regulations change, which they may very well do, from the time of the execution of the lease to the time of draining production on other lands. In Shell Oil Co. v. Stansbury,[3] the clause was drafted to impose a duty to offset when a well was located "* * * on adjoining land and *within offset distance as fixed by the spacing rules of any governmental regulatory body* having jurisdiction for the field in which said well is located and draining the leased premises." The court interpreted the distance requirements set in Texas as spacing requirements but not as fixing offset distances. It was held that the clause did not apply and that the common law prudent operator rule, without a distance limitation, controlled. The court stated:

> "Appellant contends that the provision that no well shall be drilled nearer than 330 feet to any property line, lease line or subdivision line was an offset distance. We do not consider it so to be. It is a spacing rule but not an offset distance for the purpose of determining the obligation of the lessee to drill an offset well.
> * * * A lessor and lessee may contract so that lessee is never under obligation to drill an offset well. To so contract, however, the language must be very clear. In this lease there is no contract that lessee shall not be under obligation to drill an offset well. The offset clause under consideration recognized that under the Statewide Field Rules no maximum offset distance had been fixed but that in the future governmental authority could have a rule fixing a maximum offset distance. There being no offset distance fixed by any governmental authority, Shell was obligated to drill such offset wells as a reasonably prudent operator would drill under the same or similar circumstances on the Stansbury land to protect it from drainage."

Some express offset clauses make the judgment of the lessee conclusive.[4] Such clauses have been generally upheld as being within the scope of the power to contract and not against public policy. In Wolter v. Houston Oil Co. of Texas,[5] the clause protected against drainage through wells on "adjoining lands." A gas well was drilled some 396.5 feet away and was apparently draining the lessor's land. It was held that no obligation to protect existed, as there was an intervening 80-acre tract between the lessor's land and the land on which the gas well had been drilled. The court held that the land on which the gas well was situated was not "adjoining."

However, it is not every express clause that will displace the implied covenant to protect against drainage. In numerous cases the parties have inserted express clauses relating to reasonable develop-

---

3. Tex.Civ.App., 401 S.W.2d 623, refused n. r. e. 410 S.W.2d 187.

4. Magnolia Petroleum Co. v. Page, Tex.Civ.App., 141 S.W.2d 691 ("The judgment of the lessee when not fraudulently exercised in carrying out the purposes of this lease shall be conclusive."); Coats v. Brown, Tex.Civ.App., 301 S.W.2d 932.

5. Tex.Civ.App., 74 S.W.2d 706.

ment of the lease. Such clauses are normally construed as relating only to the implied covenant to develop and do not affect or displace the implied covenant to offset.[6] To remove the implied obligation to offset, the express clause must relate to protection wells as well as to exploration and development of the lease.

Some authority exists to support the proposition that where an obligation to drill a protection well exists, either under an implied or express covenant, such obligation will be subordinate to the power of the state conservation agency to combine land and form drilling units.[7] In Hood v. Southern Production Co.,[8] the lessee was not liable for non-performance where the land that it otherwise would have been under an obligation to protect was placed in a mandatory gas unit and the lessee was prohibited by the orders of the state agency from drilling upon the leased premises.

In a similar case, Cook v. El Paso Natural Gas Co.,[9] it was held that the lessor was entitled to payment of a compensatory royalty for such drainage, where the lessee had leases on the two adjoining tracts of land.

The effect of the express offset clause where the lessee also owns the lease on the land on which the draining well is located is discussed in the following section.

§ 8.7 Implied Covenant of Protection—Not to Depreciate the Lessor's Interest

Some jurisdictions appear to recognize an implied covenant that is to be distinguished from the obligation to protect the lessor's interest from substantial drainage to other lands. The lessee is obligated not to deplete the lessor's interest by lessee's affirmative acts, i.e., to conserve the mineral resources of the lessor and to refrain from depletory acts.

Within this concept the lessee may be liable for drainage where the lessee is also the owner of the draining lease. In some jurisdictions such liability may exist even though the lessor cannot prove that a well drilled on his drained tract would be profitable. However, the majority of cases would impose an element of profitability to the lessee under application of the reasonably prudent operator rule.

By the better view, liability of the lessee under such implied covenant would not be limited by express offset clause provisions.

O executes a lease that contains no express offset clause to Black Gold Oil Company. Black Gold also has a lease upon the adjoining

---

6. Hartman Ranch Co. v. Associated Oil Co., 10 Cal.2d 232, 73 P.2d 1163; Stanolind Oil & Gas Co. v. Christian, Tex. Civ.App., 83 S.W.2d 408. But cf. Williams v. Humble Oil & Refining Co., D.C. La., 290 F.Supp. 408, (short offset distance did not displace implied covenant), C.A.5th, 432 F.2d 165.

7. Hood v. Southern Production Co., 206 La. 642, 19 So.2d 336; Rush v. King Oil Co., 220 Kan. 616, 556 P.2d 431 (1976); U. V. Industries, Inc. v. Daniel son, ___ Mont. ___, 602 P.2d 571 (1979); Cook v. El Paso Natural Gas Co., C.A. 10th, 560 F.2d 978; also see discussions at footnotes 4, § 8.5, supra, and 9, infra.

8. 206 La. 642, 19 So.2d 336.

9. C.A.10th, 560 F.2d 978.

property from its lessor, "A". Black Gold drills a well that produces oil in paying quantities on the lease from A. O requests Black Gold to drill on his lease, which Black Gold refuses to do. O believes that Black Gold is draining his property by means of the well on A's tract of land and brings suit for damages for failure of Black Gold to drill a protection well. During the course of the trial O is able to establish that in all probability drainage to A's tract exists. However, O is unable to prove that Black Gold can drill the offsetting well at a profit. Can O recover?

In a preceding section it was found that the general rule is that an implied obligation rests upon the lessee to drill a protection well only where the lessor can show that it may be drilled at a profit. Is the lessee in the same position where he is also the lessee of the draining well? Some cases hold that the lessee is not in the same position, and that where the lessee is also the owner of the draining well, recovery may be had even when the lessor is unable to show the well would be profitable to the lessee.[1]

The basis for liability in most of these cases has been distinguished from the ordinary implied covenant to prevent drainage to the lessor's tract. Instead, the courts talk in terms of an additional implied covenant. In Bush Oil Co. v. Beverly-Lincoln Land Co.,[2] the lessee was draining the subject lease by producing from adjoining land. The court found that at least one-fourth of the production from the adjoining well came from drainage from the subject tract of land. In affirming liability for drainage the court stated that it was not within the contemplation of the parties at the time of the execution of the lease that the lessee by his adjacent lease could drain the lessor and, " * * * there is an implied obligation on the part of an oil and gas lessee to refrain from taking any affirmative course of action which will result in draining a substantial quantity of the oil and gas from the lessor's property and producing the same through the lessee's well on adjacent premises belonging to a different lessor." The

---

1. Bush Oil Co. v. Beverly-Lincoln Land Co., 69 Cal.App.2d 246, 158 P.2d 754; Geary v. Adams Oil & Gas Co., D.C. Ill., 31 F.Supp. 830; Millette v. Phillips Petroleum Co., 209 Miss. 687, 48 So.2d 344; Phillips Petroleum Co. v. Millette, 221 Miss. 1, 72 So.2d 176, noted in 30 N.Y.U.L.Rev. 730. Also see Hartman Ranch Co. v. Associated Oil Co., 10 Cal. 2d 232, 73 P.2d 1163; Hughes v. Busseyville Oil & Gas Co., 180 Ky. 545, 203 S.W. 515; Gerson v. Anderson-Prichard Production Corp., C.C.A.10, 149 F.2d 444; Cone v. Amoco Production Co., 87 N.M. 294, 532 P.2d 590 (New Mexico court discusses the contrasting views, but takes no position as to substantial drainage show); Cook v. El Paso Natural Gas Co., C.A.10th, 560 F.2d 978 (only need proof of drainage). But cf. Pierce v. Goldking Properties, Inc., La.App., 396 So.2d 528, writ denied 400 So.2d 904; Haken v. Harper Oil Co., Okl.App., 600 P.2d 1227; Shell Oil Co. v. Stansbury, Tex.Civ.App., 401 S.W.2d 623, refused n.r.e. 410 S.W.2d 187; Monsanto Chemical Co. v. Andreae, 245 Miss. 11, 147 So.2d 116; Shell Oil Co. v. James, Miss., 257 So.2d 488; Kleppner v. Lemon, 176 Pa. 502, 35 A. 109; Hutchins v. Humble Oil and Refining Co., Tex. Civ.App., 161 S.W.2d 571; Tide Water Associated Oil Co. v. Stott, C.C.A.5th, 159 F.2d 174, cert. denied 331 U.S. 817, 67 S.Ct. 1306, 91 L.Ed. 1835, which are either unclear or would apparently require proof of profitability.

2. 69 Cal.App.2d 246, 158 P.2d 754.

court expressly held that in this situation the lessor did not have to show that a reasonably prudent operator would drill the offset well.[3]

In both Mississippi and Texas the courts recognize that the lessee may not disparage his lessor's lease, and, although earlier cases were unclear, it now appears from later decisions that it is necessary for the lessor to show that the protection well could be drilled at a profit. In Mississippi the decision in Millette v. Phillips Petroleum Co.,[4] followed by the appeal upon remand, Phillips Petroleum Co. v. Millette,[5] seems to apply the rule that profitability need not be shown. In a situation where the lessee was draining the subject lease by adjacent production the Court in the first decision had the following to say:

> "So there is presented for decision the question whether the implied duty of a mineral lessee to conserve the interests of its lessor extends to protection against, or a duty to compensate for, its own act of drainage. * * * Although oil is a fugacious product and ordinarily belongs to the producer who captures it upon his own lands, yet when such producer is under an obligation to do nothing to destroy or deplete the lands of his lessor, he may not with impunity impair the value of his lessor's property. This responsibility is separable from a duty to drill offset wells, and an express covenant which absolves the lessee from this method of development does not relieve the lessee of liability for substantial drainage by him."

Upon remand the trial court found that the cost of drilling the well would not be recovered and found for the lessor. This was affirmed upon appeal.

However, following the Millette duo, the Mississippi Supreme Court handed down the opinion in Monsanto Chemical Co. v. Andreae.[6] The court refused to follow the Millette cases in a similar

3. In Geary v. Adams Oil & Gas Co., D.C.Ill., 31 F.Supp. 830, where damages were assessed in a similar situation, the court made the following observation:

"If the defendant had no interest in the adjoining leases on the north and south, it would seem that its defense, based on the foregoing facts, might be sound. But here the mind is haunted by the fact that the defendant is the beneficiary of the oil drained from plaintiff's land by the wells on the north and south which belong to the defendant. It has not only been saved the cost of drilling, equipping and operating a protecting well but it gets the oil anyway without plaintiffs being paid for it."

4. 209 Miss. 687, 48 So.2d 344.

5. 221 Miss. 1, 72 So.2d 176, noted in 30 N.Y.U.L.Rev. 730. Although the court in the first case appears to talk in terms of unjust enrichment of the lessee, the court in the second seems at least in part to base recovery on the contract to pay royalty contained in the lease.

"Royalty is to be paid for oil produced and saved from said land. It does not limit their royalty to one-eighth of the oil produced and saved from said land through wells drilled on said land, but obligates appellant to pay them the royalty on the oil produced and saved from said land regardless of how it may be produced or where it may be drawn to the surface."

6. 245 Miss. 11, 147 So.2d 116. In distinguishing the Millette cases, the court states: "It is true that in Millette the Court said that neither the rule of capture nor the prudent operator rule was applicable to that case under the facts there. That was, however, a very different case from the case we have here. As stated by Judge Hall, the appellant's position in that case was entitled to scant consideration in a court of equity because

situation, limiting the Millette holding to situations where the lessee was guilty of bad faith in refusing to either drill or release the lease, and substantial drainage occurs. It appears that the prudent operator test will be applied in other than such limited situations. It does not appear that the Monsanto case overrules the Millette cases, but rather severely limits their application. Subsequent cases appear to require profitability under the reasonably prudent operator rule.[7]

A similarly uncertain situation occurred in Texas. In the case of Shell Oil Co. v. Stansbury,[8] the fact situation was similar to that of the Millette cases. Liability was found for drainage in a decision in a Texas Court of Civil Appeals. A writ of error was refused by the Texas Supreme Court with the notation, "no reversible error." As has been mentioned elsewhere, such notation merely indicates that the lower opinion is affirmed, but that the Supreme Court does not necessarily concur in the reasoning. Such cases are of doubtful value as precedents. However, in this instance, the Supreme Court took a rather unusual step in writing a short opinion accompanying the refusal of the writ. In the opinion it indicated that the well in Stansbury could be drilled at a profit and that a reasonably prudent operator would have so drilled. The court then makes the statement:

> "We disapprove any language in the opinion of Hutchins v. Humble Oil & Refining Co., 161 S.W.2d 571 (Tex.Civ.App.1942, writ ref. w. o. m.) which conflicts with the principle that a lessee is under a duty to protect his lessor against depletion of the lessor's minerals by the affirmative act of the lessee upon adjacent land."

In the Hutchins case,[9] which also involved the drainage by a lessee from a well he owned on adjacent land, the court held that the lessor could not recover on a dual basis: (a) he could not show that the offset well could be drilled at a profit; and (b) the express offset clause distance was controlling, and the draining well was beyond the offset clause maximum distance. It is difficult to determine what the court was disapproving. As discussed below, it has been held in some cases that where the lessee is draining his own lessor, the offset

---

Phillips had refused to drill a well on appellee's land, contending that no oil could be produced from it, and had also refused to cancel the lease so that the lessor might undertake to find some other operator to drill, and after refusing this, had further declined to accept a substantial consideration for cancellation of the lease. Phillips refused to do anything and refused to let anybody else do anything to ascertain whether there was any oil on Millette's land. We do not have such a case here." It also appears that the court in the Monsanto case is of the opinion the protection well involved in the Millette cases could be drilled at a profit.

7. Shell Oil Co. v. James, Miss., 257 So.2d 488 (apparently recognizing the reasonably prudent operator rule in all cases except in limited cases where Millette may apply), also see Monsanto Chemical Co. v. Sykes, 245 Miss. 207, 147 So.2d 290.

8. Tex.Civ.App., 401 S.W.2d 623, refused n. r. e. 410 S.W.2d 187. Smith, The Implied Duty to Explore Further: Recent Texas Developments—A Disagreement, 42 Tex.L.Rev. 199.

9. Here the lessee owned the adjacent land in fee. Also see Kleppner v. Lemon, 176 Pa. 502, 35 A. 109 and Tide Water Associated Oil Co. v. Stott, C.C.A.5th, 159 F.2d 174, cert. denied 331 U.S. 817, 67 S.Ct. 1306, 91 L.Ed. 1835.

clause has no effect. The court in the Stansbury case may have been either disapproving the fact that the offset clause controlled or the holding that the lessor had to prove that the well could be drilled at a profit. As the court in the Stansbury case found that a well could be drilled at a profit and that the express offset clause was ineffective, either consideration of the court's statement is dicta, strong as it may be. It may only be concluded that further opinions will be necessary to clarify this language.

The holding in the Stansbury case appears to have been clarified by the Texas Supreme Court in the case of Amoco Production Co. v. Alexander.[10] The court, in a common lessee drainage case, stated that the express offset distance in the lease will not limit the lessee's obligation to protect from drainage when the lessee is the one causing the drainage. It then stated, "In drainage cases, Texas courts place upon the lessor the burden to prove that substantial drainage has occurred and that an offset well would produce oil or gas in *paying quantities.*" (emphasis supplied). As to the obligation to drill the protection well the lessee would not have a greater duty than a reasonably prudent operator.

In Louisiana the implied covenant against drainage may be satisfied by including the land in the unit with the draining well, if a reasonably prudent operator would do so.[11] As the duty to unitize due to drainage will exist whether or not the draining well is on the land of a common lessee, no greater duty exists in the common lessee situation than if the lessee on the draining land is a third party.

Oklahoma will apply the reasonably prudent operator rule in the common lessee situation. However, in this situation the burden of proof as to what a reasonably prudent operator would do will shift to the lessee, due to its superior knowledge of the facts.[12]

Three cases have dealt with the effect of an express clause upon the obligation of a lessee not to drain his lessor. In one of the three cases the court held that the express clause distance controlled and that no liability attached, although drainage was by the lessee of his own lessor.[13] In the other two cases the lessee was liable in damages. In the first Millette[14] case an express offset clause contained a 150-foot distance within which the lessee had a duty to drill protection wells. The well in that case was 570 feet from the lease line, and, therefore, beyond the maximum distance as stated in the clause. The court found that no duty to offset existed due to the clause, then, as

---

10. Tex., 622 S.W.2d 563, noted in 12 St. Mary's L.J. 600 (1980).

11. Pierce v. Goldking Properties, Inc., La.App., 396 So.2d 528, writ denied, La., 400 So.2d 904.

12. Haken v. Harper Oil Co., Okl. App., 600 P.2d 1227. Some statements of the court in this case raise the question whether the burden of proof will be shifted to the lessee in all cases where the lessee has superior knowledge of the facts.

13. Hutchins v. Humble Oil and Refining Co., Tex.Civ.App., 161 S.W.2d 571.

14. Millette v. Phillips Petroleum Co., 209 Miss. 687, 48 So.2d 344. Cf. Williams v. Humble Oil & Refining Co., D.C.La., 290 F.Supp. 408, (short distance clause did not displace implied covenant).

discussed above, found liability on the basis of different implied covenant. In the Texas Stansbury [15] case an express clause was also involved, but, as construed by the court, the clause was ineffective. In the situations where liability is recognized upon a basis different from the ordinary obligation to drill protection wells, it would seem that the view of the court in the Millette case is sound, and that an express offset clause would not preclude liability of the lessee.

§ 8.8 The Implied Covenant to Protect Against Drainage as Affected by Operations to Stimulate Production and Statutory Enactments

By the better view, no breach of the implied covenant to protect against drainage exists where an output well is changed to an input well to stimulate production, although such change is technically a breach of the duty to offset. But where the result of such change is to increase drainage away from the subject lease, liability may occur.

Some diversity in case law exists where a technical breach of the duty to protect from drainage occurs through secondary recovery operations. For instance, where the lessee has a well that is an offset well that is tending to prevent drainage from the subject lease, and changes the well to an input well for pressuring purposes that increase the total recoverable product from the land, should the lessee be liable for the product which is drained away in consequence of changing the well?

Three cases have been found that bear upon an answer. In the first case, Mitchell v. Union Drilling & Petroleum Co.,[1] the lessee merely plugged the well, which allowed drainage to other lands. Accordingly, it was held it had violated the implied covenant to protect from drainage. And, in Ramsey v. Carter Oil Co.,[2] the court found that the lessee by changing an offset well to an input well had breached the covenant to protect from drainage even though the drainage to other lands was replaced by other products. Although the evidence tended to show that re-pressuring would increase total production by some 34,000 to 110,000 barrels, the court ignored such increased production. It looked merely to the local situation surrounding the changed well, stated that the lessee's purpose in the lease is not to impoverish the lessor, and, as such act will drive lessor's oil from the land, it was a trespass upon the lessor's right. The view of the court in this relatively early case is extraordinary for its shortsightedness.

---

15. Shell Oil Co. v. Stansbury, Tex. Civ.App., 401 S.W.2d 623, refused n. r. e. 410 S.W.2d 187. The holding in the Stansbury case was clarified in the later case of Amoco Production Co. v. Alexander, Tex., 622 S.W.2d 563, and see discussion at footnote 10, supra.

1. 1 Cal.2d 56, 32 P.2d 1069.
2. C.A.Ill., 74 F.Supp. 481, affirmed 172 F.2d 622, cert. denied 337 U.S. 958, 69 S.Ct. 1535, 93 L.Ed. 1757.

In the later case of Carter Oil Co. v. Dees,[3] in a nearly identical situation, an Illinois court found no liability. The rationale was that the lease purpose should be determined from the lease as a whole as it affects the interest of both the lessor and lessee. This later case seems clearly correct, and is in line with more current views.

The Texas case of Amoco Production Co. v. Alexander [4] involved field wide drainage away from the lessor's lease and the common lessee situation. In this case lessee was the owner of 80% of the leases in the field. Lessors were down-structure in the field, and oil was drained away from their lands. Their leases provided for a $1/6$th royalty whereas lessee's up-structure leases provided for a $1/8$th royalty. The field was under active water drive for production. Lessors alleged that lessee had "plugged back" wells in the lower part of the structure, which resulted in oil from lessors' land being produced from lessee's up-structure wells. The court held that the implied covenant to prevent drainage operated as to field wide drainage as well as to local drainage. Oil was as much lost to lessors by either. The court further stated that lessee's responsibilities to its other lessors in the field would not control where they were not parties to the suit. The reasonably prudent operator standard would not be reduced merely because lessee had other lessors in the same field.

Some jurisdictions have statutes that require offsetting wells be drilled in certain circumstances, upon notice by the lessor.[5] Failure to so drill may result in termination of the lease.

§ 8.9 Implied Covenants—Other Miscellaneous Covenants

In addition to the implied obligations discussed in the preceding sections, from time to time the courts have discussed other covenants that will be implied when the lease is silent on the subject:

   (a) To use reasonable care in operations, including use of proven modern methods of development and operations.

   (b) To produce.

   (c) To market.

   (d) To seek favorable administrative action in aid of the other obligations of the lessee.

(A) The Covenant to Use Reasonable Care in Operations

That the lessee should use reasonable care in development and operations seems self-evident. The covenant involves the standard of care to be applied to the lessee's acts and the nature of the methods employed.

---

3. 340 Ill.App. 449, 92 N.E.2d 519, noted 1951 U.Ill.L.F. 336.

4. Tex., 622 S.W.2d 563, citing § 8.1 of the Hornbook.

5. Acts of Arkansas, 1939, Act 348, § 1, Ark.Stats. § 53–508; Laws of Iowa, 1939, p. 88, Ch. 63, § 2, I.C.A. § 84.2; Kentucky Rev.Stat. 353.040; Virginia Laws 1948, c. 223, Code 1950, § 47–105. Also see Summers, Oil and Gas Law, § 399.

Some of the early cases held that the judgment of the lessee was not reviewable as to the manner and method in which the lease was developed and produced.[1] Today, however, it seems unquestionable that the reasonably prudent operator test will be applied to such acts of the lessee [2] in developing and producing the lease.

This view is well set forth in the landmark case of Empire Oil & Refining Co. v. Hoyt.[3] Here a well was flooded out during acidization, due to the failure to place an inert blanket of calcium chloride in the well bore to prevent erosion from the producing sands into water-bearing sands below. The lessee asserted that it was not negligent because the operations were customary practice in the field. In denying this contention the court stated that custom in the field is not conclusive because custom may be negligent. The standard of care was characterized as follows:

" * * * where oil has been found in quantities, the question of further development and its method is not subject to determination of either of the parties alone, as the object and purpose of the operation is to obtain a benefit for both the lessor and the lessee. Neither, in the absence of some stipulation to that effect, is made arbiter of the extent of care with which the operation shall proceed and each is bound by standards of what is reasonable, or putting it another way, the care to be exercised is what would be reasonably expected of operators of ordinary prudence having regard to the interest of both lessee and lessor and, although the lessee acts in good faith, if, in so doing, he commits some act which a reasonably prudent person would not do under the same or similar circumstances, he is liable for the resulting damages. * * * It is manifest that it was implied that the lessee would exercise reasonable diligence to avoid the destruction of the oil pool by water encroachment."

Within this context, liability has been found on the part of the lessee in situations where it failed to complete the well properly,[4] failed to operate the well with due prudence,[5] and failed to use proven methods of operation and development.[6] In connection with the

---

1. See Warfield Natural Gas Co. v. Allen, 248 Ky. 646, 59 S.W.2d 534, 91 A.L.R. 890.

2. Indiana Oil, Gas & Development Co. v. McCrory, 42 Okl. 136, 140 P. 610; Rhoads Drilling Co. v. Allred, 123 Tex. 229, 70 S.W.2d 576; Empire Oil & Refining Co. v. Hoyt, C.C.A.6th, 112 F.2d 356, comment 19 Tex.L.Rev. 80, and noted in 47 W.Va.L.Q. 65; Newell v. Phillips Petroleum Co., C.C.A.10th, 144 F.2d 338.

3. C.C.A.6th, 112 F.2d 356, comment 19 Tex.L.Rev. 80, and noted in 47 W.Va. L.Q. 65.

4. Warner v. Shell Petroleum Corp., 132 Kan. 837, 297 P. 682 (failed to set casing down to the oil sand, allowing soft shale to break up and clog the well); also see Warfield Natural Gas Co. v. Allen, 248 Ky. 646, 59 S.W.2d 534, 91 A.L.R. 890 (failed to case off fresh water, allowing the well to flood out).

5. Indiana Oil, Gas & Development Co. v. McCrory, 42 Okl. 136, 140 P. 610 (negligence, carelessness and want of diligence); Newell v. Phillips Petroleum Co., C.C.A.10th, 144 F.2d 338 (here no liability, as lessor failed to show that unrestricted production would have ultimately produced more oil).

6. Williams v. Humble Oil & Refining Co., C.A.5th, 432 F.2d 165 (failure to ful-

methods of completion used by the lessee is the further question of whether the lessee should be compelled to test and complete in multiple formations. In addition to the reasonably prudent operator test, the Oklahoma case of Sinclair Oil & Gas Company v. Bishop,[7] sets forth the view that the lessee is not under a duty to make multiple tests and completions unless it can be shown that such operations would not endanger the presently producing formation and that such completion would probably be profitable.

In several cases the lessee has been held to have breached the covenant relating to reasonable operation where it did not use proven modern methods of development and operation. In Rhoads Drilling Co. v. Allred,[8] it was held that where lessee failed to install a pump on an oil well from which the flow had substantially declined the lessee did not act as a reasonably prudent operator. A similar result is found in Wadkins v. Wilson Oil Corporation,[9] for failure to acidize, which was then recognized as a customary and progressive practice in the field. Following the rationale of these cases it would seem that they could be extended to such matters as secondary recovery operations, deeper recovery, etc., where it may be shown that such operations would be profitable to the lessee, and proven methods of operation were available.

(B) The Covenant to Produce

In accordance with the rationale discussed earlier, that the lease must be operated for the mutual benefit of both the lessor and the lessee, where a well is capable of being produced in paying quantities, the lessee has an implied obligation to produce the well so long as such production remains profitable.[10] In one case [11] it was held that the lessee did not have the obligation to produce the well up to the maximum allowable where the rate of production would recover to the lessor an amount equal to or in excess of the ratio of lessor's acreage to the acreage in the entire field multiplied by total production from the entire field. It would seem that in most situations a failure to produce up to the allowable would recover less than the

ly inform lessor of opportunity to unitize); Shaw v. Henry, 216 Kan. 96, 531 P.2d 128 (failure of lessee to drill salt water disposal well required by State Board of Health); Waseco Chemical & Supply Co. v. Bayou State Oil Corp., La. App., 371 So.2d 305, writ denied, La., 374 So.2d 656 (failure to institute secondary recovery procedures); Wadkins v. Wilson Oil Corp., 199 La. 656, 6 So.2d 720; Rhoads Drilling Co. v. Allred, 123 Tex. 229, 70 S.W.2d 576. Also see, Prudent Operator Standard: Does it Include a Duty to Use Enhanced Recovery? 40 La. L.R. 974 (1980).

7. Sinclair Oil & Gas Co. v. Bishop, Okl., 441 P.2d 436. The court indicates that if exercised in good faith lessee's judgment will prevail as to the manner in which a well is completed.

8. 123 Tex. 229, 70 S.W.2d 576.

9. 199 La. 656, 6 So.2d 720.

10. Louisiana Gas Lands v. Burrow, 197 La. 275, 1 So.2d 518; Okmulgee Supply Corp. v. Anthis, 189 Okl. 139, 114 P.2d 451.

11. Louisiana Gas Lands v. Burrow, 197 La. 275, 1 So.2d 518, but cf. Biskamp v. General Crude Oil Co., Tex.Civ.App., 452 S.W.2d 515.

total recoverable oil or gas under the lease. Unless justified by the surrounding circumstances, such failure to so produce would seem contrary to the view that the lessee reasonably operate for the benefit of the lessor. However, the lessee does not violate the covenant to produce where such production would violate a state rule or regulation relating to wasteful production.[12]

Where a well is producing in paying quantities, a lessee may not shut down the well without an opportunity for the lessor to have a determination that the well has in fact ceased producing in paying quantities.[13] Destruction of a producing well is compensable in damages for the royalties that the lessor would have received if the well had not been destroyed.[14] Where a lump sum payment is recovered, it must be reduced to present worth.[15]

(C) The Covenant to Market

As in the case of the covenant to produce, the lessee is also under an implied obligation to market with due diligence the products produced. Obviously, without marketing the lessor will not realize any benefit from the lease. The question arises as to what constitutes due diligence. Where the lease contains an express clause requiring that the lessee "market the production * * *, to the end that the Lessor and the Lessee may derive the speediest return practicable for the * * * gas recoverable thereunder * * *" it would seem that the lessee would be under an obligation to sell at the first reasonable opportunity.[16] Without such wording it has been held that the lessee may withhold products from the market for a reasonable time in order to receive the best price.

In Gazin v. Pan-American Petroleum Corporation,[17] a gas well was shut in from 1956 until 1960 in order to obtain a better contract as to price and period than was available at the time the well was shut in. It was held that the lessee had not breached the covenant to market

---

12. Sinclair Oil & Gas Co. v. Bishop, Okl., 441 P.2d 436.

13. Warner v. Shell Petroleum Corp., 132 Kan. 837, 297 P. 682; Okmulgee Supply Corp. v. Anthis, 189 Okl. 139, 114 P.2d 451; Gallaspy v. Warner, Okl., 324 P.2d 848. Shut down of a producing well may also have a collateral effect, Mitchell v. Union Drilling & Petroleum Co., 1 Cal. 2d 56, 32 P.2d 1069; Carter Oil Co. v. Dees, 340 Ill.App. 449, 92 N.E.2d 519, noted 1951 U.Ill.L.F. 336 and Ramsey v. Carter Oil Co., D.C.Ill., 74 F.Supp. 481, affirmed 172 F.2d 622, cert. denied 337 U.S. 958, 69 S.Ct. 1535, 93 L.Ed. 1757 (possible breach of covenant to offset, by permitting drainage to other tracts).

Casing may not be removed from a producing well although the lease provides for removal "at any time", Okmulgee Supply Corp. v. Anthis, 189 Okl. 139, 114 P.2d 451.

14. Warner v. Shell Petroleum Corp., 193 Kan. 837, 297 P. 682; Okmulgee Supply Corp. v. Anthis, 189 Okl. 139, 114 P.2d 451; Gallaspy v. Warner, Okl., 324 P.2d 848.

15. Gallaspy v. Warner, Okl., 324 P.2d 848.

16. Craig v. Champlin Petroleum Co., C.A.10th, 435 F.2d 933 (no breach of covenant where no available purchaser, here 6–9 miles away. Lessee not a fiduciary as to lessor).

Cotiga Development Co. v. United Fuel Gas Co., 147 W.Va. 484, 128 S.E.2d 626. Also see Summers, Oil & Gas Law, § 400.

17. Okl., 367 P.2d 1010.

as the lessee had used due diligence to obtain a satisfactory market within this period. In this case the court held that by acceptance of delay rentals for 2½ years that lessors had waived their right to demand marketing during such period. However, it would appear from a reading of the case that the same result would have occurred without the waiver.

Although the lessee has an obligation to market the products from the wells, it has been repeatedly held that he does not have to stand the expense of a long and costly gathering system to transport the products to the nearest market.[18] As in the case of other implied covenants, an express covenant on the same subject matter will displace the implied covenant.[19]

The lessee also has an obligation to obtain the best price reasonably possible. Under a gas royalty clause providing for payment of part of the "market price or market value," this would be the best current market price reasonably available. What is the obligation of the lessee under a "proceeds" gas royalty clause?

In the Texas case of Amoco Production Co. v. First Baptist Church of Pyote,[20] lessee was selling gas as part of production from a four-way split-stream gas well. One lessee sold into interstate commerce under jurisdiction of the then Federal Power Commission. Two lessees sold intrastate with contracts that contained annual price redetermination clauses. Amoco sold its gas to Pioneer Natural Gas Corporation. Amoco also had other gas under prior contract with Pioneer. Under the new contract, Pioneer agreed to raise the price it would pay for all gas, old and new, to the rate provided for in the new split gas sales contract. This contract also had a price redetermination clause. Under the gas contracts of the other lessees from the same gas well, sales were made for 0.625 cents per Mcf, which increased over a four-year period to $1.95 per Mcf. Under the Pioneer gas sales contract, gas was sold initially for 0.17 cents per Mcf and increased over the same four-year period to a high of only 0.72 cents per Mcf. Lessor sued for underpaid royalty. The court held that the lessee was not a fiduciary as to the lessor, but did have the obligation to act fairly and in good faith as to the lessor's interests. It was further held that the lessee had breached its obligation to reasonably market. Part of the consideration to lessee for the gas sales contract was a higher price for gas under existing production with Pioneer. Although this was of benefit to lessee's other lessors, it was not of benefit to lessor in this suit.

---

18. Ashland Oil & Refining Co. v. Staats, Inc., D.C.Kan., 271 F.Supp. 571, and § 7.4(E), supra, Chapter 7.

19. Brimmer v. Union Oil Co. of California, C.C.A.10th, 81 F.2d 437, 105 A.L.R. 454, cert. denied 298 U.S. 668, 56 S.Ct. 833, 80 L.Ed. 1391.

20. Tex.Civ.App., 579 S.W.2d 280, writ refused n. r. e. Tex., 611 S.W.2d 610, citing §§ 7.4(c) and 8.9(c) of the Hornbook.

The court points out that the lessee had an obligation to obtain the best price possible by exercise of reasonable effort. In refusing writ of error, the Texas Supreme Court made the further statement that although the lessee had a duty to seek a fair market for the gas, such obligation would not convert a "proceeds" gas royalty clause to a "market price" gas royalty clause with Vela-type accounting problems.

Apparently, the court would find the same obligation to seek a fair market for gas sales at the time the original gas sales contract is executed, whether the gas royalty clause is a "proceeds" or "market price" clause. However, in Texas at least, if the market price of the gas then increased, under a "proceeds" type gas royalty clause, the lessee would not be liable for future royalty payments based upon the increased gas sales prices.

(D) The Covenant to Seek Favorable Administrative Action

Although only mentioned recently by the courts, it appears that in certain circumstances the lessee has an implied obligation to seek favorable administrative action in aid of the discharge of the obligations under the lease, express or implied.

In Baldwin v. Kubetz,[21] where the failure to properly operate resulted in a failure to obtain a zoning variance, the court expressly noted the existence of an implied covenant to seek administrative action to carry out the purposes of the lease. It was also mentioned in Sinclair Oil & Gas Co. v. Bishop,[22] where the lessee could not operate wells to produce oil, as such production would result in waste due to the flaring of gas. As wasteful flaring wells on other tracts were draining the subject lease, the court said that it was the duty of the lessee to go to the Corporation Commission in an attempt to stop the flaring of gas by the wasteful wells. Where proper development, protection, or production of the lease may be accomplished by appropriate administrative action, these cases would recognize an implied obligation to seek such action.

In Amoco Production Co. v. Alexander, discussed earlier,[23] it was held that the lessee had breached its duty as a reasonably prudent operator in failing to apply for exceptions to the Texas spacing rules to allow the drilling of protection wells on the updip corner of plaintiff's lease that was being drained by fieldwide drainage. The court stated, "The duty to seek favorable administrative action may be classified under the implied covenants to protect the lease, or to manage

---

21. 148 Cal.App.2d 937, 307 P.2d 1005.

22. Okl., 441 P.2d 436. But cf. Sunray DX Oil Co. v. Crews, Okl., 448 P.2d 840.

See Forman v. Mac Kellar Drilling Co., Okl., 430 O.B.A.J. 457; also see Williams v. Humble Oil & Refining Co., C.A.5th 432 F.2d 165, note 6, supra.

23. See discussion at § 8.7, fn. 10, and § 8.8 fn. 4, supra.

and administer the lease. Regardless of the category, the standard of care in testing Amoco's performance is that of a reasonably prudent operator under similar facts and circumstances."

This covenant is consistent with the basic view that where the lessee has all of the operating rights the lessee is also operating for the benefit of the lessor. Other examples where such covenant might be applied are: resisting the granting of an exception to the spacing regulations for a well on adjoining property; instituting action by the state commission,[24] where it is appropriate, to survey wells on adjoining property to determine if they are directionally drilled onto the subject land; attempting to have the subject lease included within a producing unit under forced pooling statutes,[25] where the tract is being drained and lessee is unable to acquire a drilling permit.

§ 8.10 Remedies for Breach of Implied Covenants—Damages

Breach of implied covenants that result in undue loss of production may be compensated by the royalty that the lessor would have received had the wells been properly operated or drilled. In some jurisdictions the payment of delay rentals will serve to postpone or waive the obligation of a lessee to drill a protection well. By the better view, the covenant to protect the lease from drainage should not be affected by such payments.

Where the lessee has breached an implied covenant to develop,[1] to drill protection wells,[2] to market,[3] or to produce a well capable of production in paying quantities,[4] recovery may be had in damages for the breach of such covenant. In most jurisdictions, generally speaking, such damages are measured by royalties that the lessor would have received if the lessee had properly produced.

Where the lessee has breached the implied covenant of development the majority rule is that the lessor may recover in damages for the amount of royalty he would have received had a reasonably prudent operator developed the lease.[5] Where it is shown that such

---

24. Amoco Production Co. v. Ware, 269 Ark. 313, 602 S.W.2d 620 (holding no duty to appeal an order of the state commission).

25. Pierce v. Goldking Properties, Inc., La.App., 396 So.2d 528, writ denied La., 400 So.2d 904 (Duty to unitize as a reasonably prudent operator).

1. Brewster v. Lanyon Zinc Co., 8th Cir., 140 F. 801; Midland Gas Corp. v. Reffitt, 286 Ky. 11, 149 S.W.2d 537; Howerton v. Kansas Natural Gas Co., 82 Kan. 367, 108 P. 813; Waggoner Estate v. Sigler Oil Co., 118 Tex. 509, 19 S.W.2d 27.

2. Geary v. Adams Oil & Gas Co., D.C. Ill., 31 F.Supp. 830; America Southwest Corp. v. Allen, Miss., 336 So.2d 1297 (1976); Harris v. Ohio Oil Co., 57 Ohio St. 118, 48 N.E. 502; Wes-Tex Land Co. v. Simmons, Tex.Civ.App., 566 S.W.2d 719.

3. Cotiga Development Co. v. United Fuel Gas Co., 147 W.Va. 484, 128 S.E.2d 626.

4. Warner v. Shell Petroleum Corp., 132 Kan. 837, 297 P. 682; Okmulgee Supply Corp. v. Anthis, 189 Okl. 139, 114 P.2d 451; Gallaspy v. Warner, Okl., 324 P.2d 848.

5. Brewster v. Lanyon Zinc Co., C.C.A.8th, 140 F. 801; Daughetee v. Ohio Oil Co., 263 Ill. 518, 105 N.E. 308; Midland Gas Corp. v. Reffitt, 286 Ky. 11, 149 S.W.2d 537; Texas Pacific Coal & Oil Co. v. Barker, 117 Tex. 418, 6 S.W.2d 1031, 60 A.L.R. 936, noted 7 Tex.L.Rev. 438; Waggoner Estate v. Sigler Oil Co., 118 Tex. 509, 19 S.W.2d 27.

wells would have been gas wells and the lease contained a flat rate gas clause, the recovery will be based upon the flat rate, and not upon the actual production from the well.[6] Products lost from recovery due to breach of the covenant to develop may also be recovered. In General Crude Oil Co. v. Harris,[7] the lease was situated in the East Texas Field. This field was subject to a water drive that moved oil from the west to the east. An element of damages allowed was the oil lost from recovery due to the general field movement.

The royalty rule has been criticized in the case of recovery of damages for breach of the covenant of reasonable development. It has been argued that where no drainage occurs the oil is still in place beneath the ground. Where the lessee later develops the field and pays royalty upon such production the lessor will obtain a double recovery. It was suggested in the Texas case of Texas Pacific Coal & Oil Co. v. Barker,[8] that to prevent such double recovery the lessee credit against royalty payments from future production the amounts so decreed. This suggestion was later followed in the West Virginia case of Cotiga Development Co. v. United Fuel Gas Co.,[9] which involved breach of an express covenant relating to marketing.

In the early case of Grass v. Big Creek Development Co.,[10] the suggestion was made that an appropriate recovery in damages would be the interest upon the royalty that the lessor would have received. The interest rule seems to have been rejected in virtually all jurisdictions.[11]

Where the covenant breached has been to prevent drainage, the courts consistently seem to have allowed damages based upon royalty that the lessor would have received had the proper offset wells been drilled.[12] However, the courts are not clear whether the royalty is to

6. Howerton v. Kansas Natural Gas Co., 82 Kan. 367, 108 P. 813.

7. Tex.Civ.App., 101 S.W.2d 1098.

8. 117 Tex. 418, 6 S.W.2d 1031, 60 A.L.R. 936, noted 7 Tex.L.Rev. 438.

9. 147 W.Va. 484, 128 S.E.2d 626.

10. 75 W.Va. 719, 84 S.E. 750. Also see Lyon v. Miller, 24 Pa. 392.

11. Macon v. Trowbridge, 38 Colo. 330, 87 P. 1147; Daughetee v. Ohio Oil Co., 263 Ill. 518, 105 N.E. 308; Stoddard v. Illinois Improvement & Ballast Co., 275 Ill. 199, 113 N.E. 913; Gilmore v. Ontario Iron Co., 86 N.Y. 455; Powell v. Burroughs, 54 Pa. 329; Texas Pacific Coal & Oil Co. v. Barker, 117 Tex. 418, 6 S.W.2d 1031, 60 A.L.R. 936, noted 7 Tex. L.Rev. 438. Also see criticism of rule in Summers, Oil & Gas Law, § 435, pp. 47–50.

12. Brewster v. Lanyon Zinc Co., C.C.A.8th, 140 F. 801; Geary v. Adams Oil & Gas Co., D.C.Ill., 31 F.Supp. 830; Mitchell v. Union Drilling & Petroleum Co., 1 Cal.2d 56, 32 P.2d 1069; Phillips Petroleum Co. v. Millette, 221 Miss. 1, 72 So.2d 176, noted in 30 N.Y.U.L.Rev. 730; North American Petroleum Co. v. Knight, Okl., 321 P.2d 964, noted in 11 Okl.L.Rev. 340; Christie, Mitchell & Mitchell Co. v. Howell, Tex.Civ.App., 359 S.W.2d 658. See Carson v. Ozark Natural Gas Co., 191 Ark. 167, 83 S.W.2d 833, where gas drainage was in question. As lease contained a flat rate gas clause it was held the lessee could pay the flat rate in lieu of drilling an offset well.

American Southwest Corp. v. Allen, Miss., 336 So.2d 1297 (court allowed future continuing damages, as lump sum payment thought unfair due to changing future conditions, where lessee refused to drill offset well and circumstances affecting reasonable prudent operation in 1969, time of breach, different than those existing at time of trial some years later).

be paid upon the production that would have occurred had the protection wells been drilled, or on the amount of products that were drained from the lease due to failure to properly protect. Obviously, these may not be equivalent measures. As the lessee is liable only for loss of substantial and not all drainage (not being an insurer against drainage, having only to use such measures as a reasonably prudent operator would use), it would seem that the proper measure would be the royalty the lessor would have received from production had the protection well or wells been properly drilled.

Where the lessee has breached an implied covenant, and the lessor sues for damages the major problem confronting the lessor is not the measure of damages, but the proof of damages. In order to recover, the lessor has the burden to prove such damages with reasonable certainty,[13] by substantial evidence.[14] Where the implied covenant of further development is breached, not only must the lessor show the number of wells that a reasonably prudent operator would have drilled, but also the amount of production that would have occurred if they had been drilled. Proof is similar in the case of non-drilling of protection wells. Since direct evidence is not available, such proof must be made by use of experts,[15] and such geological data[16] as the lessor is able to accumulate. In this regard the oil corporation with a geological department has a great advantage over the lessor.

Where the breach of covenant occurs during the primary term, payment of delay rentals may affect the right of the lessor to recover. Obviously, where no development has occurred payment of delay rentals will serve to allow the lessee to postpone drilling of an initial well for each year of the primary term for which delay rentals have been paid. But what is the effect of payment of delay rentals where it is later found that the lease was being drained by production from adjoining lands? It appears to be the majority rule that payment of a delay rental by the lessee will excuse, in whole or in part, the lessee from drilling an offset well during the period for which the rental is paid.[17]

---

13. See Cone v. Amoco Production Co., 87 N.M. 294, 532 P.2d 590; Carter v. United States Smelting, Refining & Mining Co., Okl., 485 P.2d 748.

Texas Pacific Coal & Oil Co. v. Barker, 117 Tex. 418, 6 S.W.2d 1031, 60 A.L.R. 936, noted 7 Tex.L.Rev. 438.

14. Temple v. Continental Oil Co., 182 Kan. 213, 320 P.2d 1039, rehearing denied 183 Kan. 471, 328 P.2d 358.

15. Howerton v. Kansas Natural Gas Co., 82 Kan. 367, 108 P. 813. Temple v. Continental Oil Co., 182 Kan. 213, 320 P.2d 1039, rehearing denied 183 Kan. 471, 328 P.2d 358; Vonfeldt v. Hanes, 196 Kan. 719, 414 P.2d 7; Midland Gas Corp. v. Reffitt, 286 Ky. 11, 149 S.W.2d 537. These cases contain good examples of the type and nature of evidence used.

16. Temple v. Continental Oil Co., 182 Kan. 213, 320 P.2d 1039, rehearing denied 183 Kan. 471, 328 P.2d 358; Midland Gas Corp. v. Reffitt, 286 Ky. 11, 149 S.W.2d 537.

17. Sun Oil Co. v. Oswell, 258 Ala. 326, 62 So.2d 783; Blair v. Clear Creek Oil & Gas Co., 148 Ark. 301, 230 S.W. 286, 19 A.L.R. 430; Clear Creek Oil & Gas Co. v. Brunk, 160 Ark. 574, 255 S.W. 7; Poindexter v. Lion Oil Refining Co., 205 Ark. 978, 167 S.W.2d 492; Hood v. Southern Production Co., 206 La. 642, 19 So.2d 336; Lindow v. Southern Carbon Co., D.C.La., 5 F.Supp. 818; Lake v. Ohio

Rex pays O the delay rental for the year 1968 in January, and in July, 1968 it is found that drainage exists that a reasonably prudent operator would offset. When does the duty to drill arise? The leading case holding that the payment of the rental serves to relieve the lessee from thereafter drilling an offset well during the entire period for which the rental is paid is Carper v. United Fuel Gas Co.[18] The rationale is that drainage could only be prevented by the drilling of an offset well. Since the lessor has agreed to accept money rental to delay drilling, he is not entitled to both the drilling of an offset well and to the payment of rentals. In these jurisdictions lessor must demand drilling and communicate a refusal to accept further delay rentals during the period for which the last rental was paid. Lessee's obligation to drill a protection well commences at the beginning of the next period. Where delay rentals have been accepted for a year of the primary term, in these jurisdictions, no obligation to drill a protection well would arise during such year.

Some courts [19] take a modified view that no liability will attach during the period for which the delay rental is paid until such time as the lessor makes demand upon the lessee for protection and notifies the lessee that no further delay rentals will be accepted. In these jurisdictions the lessee would be obligated to drill the offset well from the time of the demand and could not wait until the end of the period for which the delay rentals had been paid. Hence, if demand were made July 1, 1968, under the Carper case, no liability would ensue until January 1, 1969. However, under the modified view, liability would ensue upon demand, July 1, 1968.

In both groups of jurisdictions acceptance of delay rentals after knowledge of the breach of the implied covenant to prevent drainage will serve as a waiver of the prior default.[20] However, some courts have held that where the obligation to drill an offset well is express, acceptance of delay rentals will not serve as a waiver.[21]

Both Texas [22] and Mississippi [23] have emphatically rejected the payment of delay rentals as either postponing the time until which the lessee would be obliged to drill a protection well or waiving a breach of the covenant that occurred prior to the acceptance of a later delay rental payment. The reasoning of the courts, and the better

Fuel Gas Co., 2 Ohio App.2d 227, 207 N.E.2d 659; Carper v. United Fuel Gas Co., 78 W.Va. 433, 89 S.E. 12.

18. 78 W.Va. 433, 89 S.E. 12; also see Lindow v. Southern Carbon Co., D.C.La., 5 F.Supp. 818.

19. Blair v. Clear Creek Oil & Gas Co., 148 Ark. 301, 230 S.W. 286, 19 A.L.R. 430; Clear Creek Oil & Gas Co. v. Brunk, 160 Ark. 574, 255 S.W. 7; Poindexter v. Lion Oil Refining Co., 205 Ark. 978, 167 S.W.2d 492.

20. Sun Oil Co. v. Oswell, 258 Ala. 326, 62 So.2d 783; Clear Creek Oil & Gas Co. v. Brunk, 160 Ark. 574, 255 S.W. 7; Lake v. Ohio Fuel Gas Co., 2 Ohio App.2d 227, 207 N.E.2d 659.

21. Hood v. Southern Production Co., 206 La. 642, 19 So.2d 336.

22. Texas Co. v. Ramsower, Tex. Comm.App., 7 S.W.2d 872, rehearing denied 10 S.W.2d 537, noted 7 Tex.L.Rev. 661.

23. Millette v. Phillips Petroleum Co., 209 Miss. 687, 48 So.2d 344.

view, is that delay rentals are merely for delay in development of the lease and are not a substitute for protection. Liability, therefore, in these jurisdictions will attach at the time that a reasonably prudent operator would have drilled the protection well. Payment of delay rentals has no effect upon such liability.

In all jurisdictions, when the offset well is drilled, such operations will serve to relieve the lessee of further delay rental obligation if the well is a producer.

§ 8.11 Remedies for Breach of Implied Covenants—Cancellation of Lease

In a few jurisdictions damages are the only remedy for the breach of implied covenants. In probably a majority of the jurisdictions, courts will exert equity powers to decree a cancellation where it has been shown that damages are inadequate. Other jurisdictions will decree cancellation without first showing the remedy at law is inadequate. Where cancellation is decreed it has become customary to cast it in the form of an alternative decree, i.e., that lessee remedy the breach within a stated period of time or the lease will be cancelled in whole or in part.

As mentioned in the preceding section, an action for damages is usually available as a remedy where the lessee has breached implied covenants. Damages are, at best, a poor remedy from the lessor's point of view due to the difficult burden of proof that he must meet. From the lessee's standpoint, damages are unsatisfactory where the effect is to award double damages. In most jurisdictions an additional remedy is available in the nature of full or partial cancellation of the lease.[1]

However, some variation exists among jurisdictions as to cancellation as a remedy. In a few jurisdictions it is held that damages are the only remedy available for breach of implied covenants, and cancellation will not be decreed.[2] The rationale is that the basis of the cause of action is a breach of a covenant and not a condition.

On the other hand, in probably a majority of the jurisdictions, cancellation may be pursued where it is first shown that the remedy in

---

1. Sauder v. Mid-Continent Petroleum Corp., 292 U.S. 272, 54 S.Ct. 671, 78 L.Ed. 1255, 93 A.L.R. 454, noted 40 W.Va.L.Q. 175; Poindexter v. Lion Oil Refining Co., 205 Ark. 978, 167 S.W.2d 492; Nolan v. Thomas, 228 Ark. 572, 309 S.W.2d 727, noted 12 Ark.L.Rev. 213; Alford v. Dennis, 102 Kan. 403, 170 P. 1005; Harris v. Morris Plan Co., 144 Kan. 501, 61 P.2d 901; Stamper v. Jones, Shelburne & Farmer, Inc., 188 Kan. 626, 364 P.2d 972; Brewster v. Lanyon Zinc Co., C.C.A. 8th, 140 F. 801; Kleppner v. Lemon, 176 Pa. 502, 35 A. 109; Waggoner Estate v. Sigler Oil Co., 118 Tex. 509, 19 S.W.2d 27; Rendleman v. Barlett, Tex.Civ.App., 21 S.W.2d 58; Hull v. Magnolia Petroleum Co., C.C.A. 5th, 119 F.2d 123. These cases involve both the implied covenant to offset and the implied covenant to develop.

2. Geary v. Adams Oil & Gas Co., D.C.Ill., 31 F.Supp. 830; Harris v. Ohio Oil Co., 57 Ohio St. 118, 48 N.E. 502; McCutcheon v. Enon Oil & Gas Co., 102 W.Va. 345, 135 S.E. 238. Cf. El Rio Oils, Canada, Ltd. v. Chase, 95 Cal.App.2d 402, 212 P.2d 927.

damages is inadequate.[3] The foremost proponent of the view is Texas. In Waggoner Estate v. Sigler Oil Co.,[4] the court, after recognizing that damages are the appropriate remedy for breach of implied covenants, made the following observation:

> "And, despite our refusal to treat as a limitation or as a condition subsequent the implied covenant for reasonable development of premises leased for the mining of oil and gas, after they have been discovered, should there be a breach of such covenant for which an action for damages, for any reason, furnishes no adequate remedy, our courts, in the exercise of equitable jurisdiction, will compel the lessee to fully perform his obligation, which constitutes a fundamental consideration for, and object of, the lease, or submit to cancellation of the lease."

As can be seen from the court's statement, the basis for cancellation in the jurisdictions that follow the above view is that equity will give relief where the remedy at law is inadequate.

In the third group of jurisdictions, cancellation will be decreed as a remedy for breach of an implied covenant without the necessity of first pursuing a remedy in damages.[5] The apparent basis of this remedy is that for a continuing breach of implied covenants the court will imply a condition for which forfeiture may be had. In some instances both damages and cancellation may be an appropriate remedy.[6]

Where the remedy pursued is that of damages, notice, other than filing of suit, is normally not required.[7] However, notice and demand is usually required prior to bringing suit for cancellation, in order to put the lessee in default.[8] This rule appears to be particularly strongly applied in Kentucky and Louisiana. Where, however, it ap-

---

3. Howerton v. Kansas Natural Gas Co., 82 Kan. 367, 108 P. 813; Alford v. Dennis, 102 Kan. 403, 170 P. 1005; Brewster v. Lanyon Zinc Co., C.A. 8th, 140 F. 801; Waggoner Estate v. Sigler Oil Co., 118 Tex. 509, 19 S.W.2d 27; Rendleman v. Barlett, Tex.Civ.App, 21 S.W.2d 58; General Crude Oil Co. v. Harris, Tex.Civ. App., 101 S.W.2d 1098; Wes-Tex Land Co. v. Simmons, Tex.Civ.App. 566 S.W.2d 719; Amerada Petroleum Co. v. Doering, C.C.A.5th, 93 F.2d 540, 114 A.L.R. 1385.

4. 118 Tex. 509, 19 S.W.2d 27.

5. Nolan v. Thomas, 228 Ark. 572, 309 S.W.2d 727, noted 12 Ark.L.Rev. 213; Poindexter v. Lion Oil Refining Co., 205 Ark. 978, 167 S.W.2d 492; Sapp v. Massey, Ky., 358 S.W.2d 490; Lafitte Co. v. United Fuel Gas Co., Ky., 177 F.Supp. 52; Carter v. Arkansas-Louisiana Gas Co., 213 La. 1028, 36 So.2d 26; Libby v. DeBaca, 51 N.Mex. 95, 179 P.2d 263; Doss Oil Royalty Co. v. Texas Co., 192 Okl. 359, 137 P.2d 934.

6. See Webb v. Graf, 289 Ky. 644, 159 S.W.2d 433.

7. See General Crude Oil Co. v. Harris, Tex.Civ.App., 101 S.W.2d 1098, and Ky.Rev.Stat. § 353.040 requiring demand in suits for damages as well as for cancellation where breach relates to duty to drill an offset well.

8. Cameron v. Lebow, Ky., 338 S.W.2d 399; Sapp v. Massey, Ky., 358 S.W.2d 490; Lafitte Co. v. United Fuel Gas Co., D.C.Ky., 177 F.Supp. 52; Lindow v. Southern Carbon Co., D.C.La., 5 F.Supp. 818; Fey v. A. A. Oil Corp., 129 Mont. 300, 285 P.2d 578; Doss Oil Royalty Co. v. Texas Co., 192 Okl. 359, 137 P.2d 934; Brown v. Shafer, Okl., 325 P.2d 743.

Ch. 8   PROTECT, DEVELOP, ADMINISTER LEASE

pears that the lessee would not have performed in the event of notice, notice will not be required.[9]

Where cancellation is decreed, it has become customary, unless it is apparent that the lessee will not further perform, to cast the judgment in the form of an alternative decree.[10] One of the first cases to employ the alternative decree is that of Sauder v. Mid-Continent Petroleum Corporation.[11] Here the lessee attempted to hold 320 acres under lease for 17 years by production from two small wells located on an adjacent 40-acre tract of land, also under the same lease. Holding that the lessee had breached the implied covenant of reasonable development, the court decreed that the lease as to the 320-acre tract would be cancelled unless the lessee began development within a reasonable time. This type of decree has become popular in all jurisdictions that will cancel a lease for breach of implied covenants. Although partial vertical cancellation has been decreed as to partial acreage under the lease, some cases have also applied to a particular producing formation, or depth.[12] Horizontal partial cancellation has been expressly rejected in Louisiana.[13]

§ 8.12 Breach of Implied Covenants—Effect of Release

O executes an oil and gas lease to Pure Oil Company. The lease contains a release clause, allowing the lessee to release the lease at any time. The usual release clause states that upon release all obligations of the lessee will be extinguished. However, release under the clause usually does not serve to release the lessee from accrued obligations such as to offset, develop, pay rentals, or drill an obligation well. Where obligations have not yet accrued at the time of release, the effect of the clause will be to release the lessee from further liability.[1]

Where the lease contains express drilling obligations and other express covenants which the lessor desires to be carried out in any event, the release clause should be modified to that extent. In this

---

9. Harris v. Morris Plan Co., 144 Kan. 501, 61 P.2d 901; Sapp v. Massey, Ky., 358 S.W.2d 490.

10. Sauder v. Mid-Continent Petroleum Corp., 292 U.S. 272, 54 S.Ct. 671, 78 L.Ed. 1255, 93 A.L.R. 454, noted 40 W.Va.L.Q. 175; Poindexter v. Lion Oil Refining Co., 205 Ark. 978, 167 S.W.2d 492; Alford v. Dennis, 102 Kan. 403, 170 P. 1005; Stamper v. Jones, Shelburne & Farmer, Inc., 188 Kan. 626, 364 P.2d 972; Waggoner Estate v. Sigler Oil Co., 118 Tex. 509, 19 S.W.2d 27; Rendleman v. Barlett, Tex.Civ.App., 21 S.W.2d 58.

11. 292 U.S. 272, 54 S.Ct. 671, 78 L.Ed. 1255, 93 A.L.R. 454, noted 40 W.Va.L.Q. 175.

12. Jones v. Interstate Oil Corp., 115 Cal.App. 302, 1 P.2d 1051; McKenna v. Nichlos, 193 Okl. 526, 145 P.2d 957; Barnes v. Mack Oil Co., Okl., 376 P.2d 279; and, see Sinclair Oil & Gas Co. v. Masterson, C.A.5th, 271 F.2d 310, noted in 60 Col.L.Rev. 741 and 14 S.W.L.J. 407.

13. Coyle v. North American Oil Consolidated, 201 La. 99, 9 So.2d 473.

1. Sunray-Mid-Continent Oil Co. v. McDaniel, Okl., 361 P.2d 683; Superior Oil Co. v. Dabney, 147 Tex. 51, 211 S.W.2d 563. See also Chapter 7, § 7.9, supra.

regard, express provision should be made in the case of deferred bonus payments under the lease.

§ 8.13 Breach of an Express Clause to Drill

By far the majority view is that damages for the failure to drill a well under an express drilling obligation is the cost of the drilling of the well. In Texas, damages are based upon the royalty that would have been received had the well been drilled, with liquidated damage clauses being commonly employed.

In previous sections, discussion has been directed at implied covenants and remedies for breach of such covenants. Frequently an express provision is found in an oil and gas lease requiring the lessee to drill a well to a certain depth or condition. Such provisions are also found in farm-out agreements and other instruments. Where an unqualified obligation exists to drill, what is the remedy of the obligee for a breach of the covenant?[1]

It is the majority rule that the proper measure of damages for the failure to drill a well in such circumstances is the cost of the drilling of the well.[2] Such cost of drilling, however, does not include equipment for the testing and completing of the well, just the expense of drilling proper.[3] Where a well has been partially drilled and then abandoned, the cost of drilling will only include the cost of drilling the abandoned well, if this can successfully be done.[4]

Although the cost of drilling rule is by far the majority rule, it has been criticized on the ground that such damages are not what the lessor bargained for. The loss of bargain of the lessor, rather, is the production that would have occurred had the well been drilled, together with the increase in market value of the mineral estate during the drilling period. On this basis, Texas[5] has refused to follow the

---

1. In general, see Maxwell, Damages for Breach of Express and Implied Drilling Covenants, 5 Rocky Mt. Law Inst. 435; Moses, Measure of Damages for the Breach of a Drilling Obligation Under a Mineral Lease in Louisiana, 14 Tul.L.Rev. 89–9; Scott, The Measure of Damages for Breach of a Covenant to Drill a Test Well for Oil and Gas, 9 Kan.L.Rev. 281; Measure of Damages for Breach of an Express Covenant to Drill a Test Well, 8 Wyo.L.J. 142–51.

2. Landauer v. Huey, 143 Colo. 76, 352 P.2d 302; Gartner v. Missimer, 178 Kan. 566, 290 P.2d 827, noted 3 U.C. L.A.L.Rev. 586, 13 Wash. & Lee L.Rev. 207; In the Matter of Stannard's Estate v. Reynolds, 179 Kan. 394, 295 P.2d 610; Fisher v. Tomlinson Oil Co., Inc., 215 Kan. 616, 527 P.2d 999; Jones v. Whittington, La.App., 171 So.2d 764; Ardizonne v. Archer, 72 Okl. 70, 178 P. 263; Smith v. Kious, 194 Okl. 17, 147 P.2d 442 and see Waldrip v. Hamon, D.C. Okl., 136 F.Supp. 412.

3. See Smith v. Kious, 194 Okl. 17, 147 P.2d 442.

See Barrett v. Ferrell, Tex.Civ.App., 550 S.W.2d 138 (where contract called for drilling and completing well, it was held an obligation to "complete" the well does not mean to complete as a producer with installation of producing equipment unless expressly called for by the contract or by necessary implication. Here dry hole drilled and obligation to complete satisfied by drilling to required depth).

4. Gartner v. Missimer, 178 Kan. 566, 290 P.2d 827, noted 3 U.C.L.A.L.Rev. 586; 13 Wash. & Lee L.Rev. 207.

5. Guardian Trust Co. v. Brothers, Tex.Civ.App., 59 S.W.2d 343; Fain-McGaha Corp. v. Owens, 132 Tex. 109, 121 S.W.2d 982; Hardwick v. Jackson, Tex. Civ.App., 315 S.W.2d 440, cf. Texas Pac.

cost-of-drilling rule. Under the view of Guardian Trust Co. v. Brothers,[6] where the lessee (or another) has failed to comply with an express obligation to drill, it is incumbent upon the lessor to prove the royalty lost from such failure. Although it may be that such rule is more consistent with the bargain, it is practically impossible of proof in those situations where obligation wells would be of the most benefit. Where the land involved is located in wildcat or semi-proven territory, in all probability it will be impossible to prove the amount of any production that would be forthcoming if the well had been drilled. In such situations the loss-of-royalty rule is practically a guarantee against liability on the part of the driller.

In Texas, as well as in other jurisdictions, the obligee may also show loss of market value due to the failure to drill the well, but proof must include a showing whether the obligee would have "ridden the well down" or would have sold off interest in the mineral estate during the drilling period.[7] Although the cases are not clear, it seems intimated that proof short of reflecting actual negotiations for such sales will be inadequate.

In order to insure a damage recovery in Texas, the practice has been to include a liquidated damage clause in the event of default. Where damages may not be proved, obviously it cannot be shown that the clause would constitute a penalty. Where such clause includes a sum approximating the cost of drilling of the well the remedy is the same as the majority rule. In one case an alternative to the liquidated damage clause was the use of a deferred bonus to be paid if the well were not drilled.[8]

Whether or not the particular jurisdiction follows the cost-of-drilling or the lost-royalty rule, the draftsman should assure himself, if it is his desire, that the provision for the obligation will be worded as a condition rather than as a covenant. Where the latter occurs, it may not be possible, upon default, to obtain cancellation of the underlying instrument of which the clause was a part. The clause should be worded so as to express a right to terminate upon default, either in the form of a condition subsequent or a determinable limitation.

Coal & Oil Co. v. Stuard, Tex.Civ.App., S.W.2d 878, an earlier view.

6. Tex.Civ.App., 59 S.W.2d 343.

7. Sanzenbacher v. Howard-Clay Oil Co., C.C.A. 8th, 283 F. 13; Durbin Bond & Co., Inc. v. Gillis, C.A.5th, 242 F.2d 176.

8. Harrell v. Bakhaus, Tex.Civ.App., 315 S.W.2d 685.

CHAPTER 9

TRANSFERS BY THE LESSOR AND BY THE LESSEE

Analysis

Sec.
9.1 Post-Lease Conveyances by the Lessor That Are Expressly "Subject to" an Outstanding Lease—Effect Upon the Quantum of Interests Conveyed.
9.2 _____ Effect as to the Land Covered by the Conveyance.
9.3 _____ Effect Upon the Lease to Which the Reference Is Made and Upon the Duration of the Deed in Which the Recitation Is Contained.
9.4 Post-Lease Conveyances of the Lessor—Apportionment or Non-apportionment of Rentals and Royalties.
9.5 The Entirety Clause.
9.6 Transfers by the Lessee.
9.7 Contracts to Assign Oil and Gas Leases.
9.8 Assignment of Oil and Gas Leases.
9.9 Creation of Non-Cost-Bearing Interests From the Lessee's Interest.
 (A) Definition of Fraction.
 (B) Costs to Be Borne.
 (C) Extent of Production From Which Paid and Minerals Covered.
 (D) Graduated, Sliding Scale, or Conversion Provisions.
 (E) Implied Covenants.
 (F) Effective Date.
 (G) Mortgage Upon Oil and Gas Interests.
9.10 Divisibility of Covenants.
 (A) Habendum Clause and Modifying Clauses.
 (B) Delay Rentals.
 (C) Divisibility of Implied Covenants.
9.11 Relationship of Lessor, Lessee, and Owners of Non-Cost-Bearing Interests.
 (A) Creation of a Fiduciary Relationship.
 (B) Assignment of Leases as Affecting Liability Upon Express and Implied Covenants.

In this chapter, attention is directed to conveyances and assignments made by the lessor and lessee. Obviously, a lessee may make conveyances and assignments only after the execution of a lease; however, it is possible for the landowner to convey interests in the minerals both before and after the execution of a lease. Conveyances by the landowner prior to the execution of an oil and gas lease have been covered in prior sections of the book,[1] and herein only conveyances after the execution of a lease will be discussed.

---

1. See Chapter 2; and Chapter 3, §§ 3.1–3.2(E), supra. In general, see Summers, Transfers of Oil and Gas Rents and Royalties, 10 Tex.L.Rev. 1; Gam-

Where an oil and gas lease has been executed, the lessor will no longer have a possessory right to explore and develop the minerals, but will have the right to royalty, the right to bonus payable out of future production, the right to delay rentals, the right to shut-in royalties, and other economic benefits payable under the lease. In addition, he will also have the reversionary rights in the mineral estate. The lessor may convey all or part of such interests, in severalty or in undivided interests, as has been discussed elsewhere.[2] In this chapter, discussion wil be directed to a conveyance by a lessor, or by his successors, that:

(1) Is made expressly "subject to" the outstanding lease as it affects the quantum of the interests conveyed;

(2) conveys only a part of the land covered by the lease; and

(3) is made expressly "subject to" the outstanding lease and revives or ratifies such lease.

§ 9.1 Post–Lease Conveyances by the Lessor That Are Expressly "Subject to" an Outstanding Lease—Effect Upon the Quantum of Interests Conveyed

Although a few early cases are to the contrary, it appears to be the established view that a conveyance of the minerals that is expressly made "subject to" an outstanding lease conveys rentals, royalties, and other economic benefits relating to the outstanding lease and also conveys a reversionary interest in the minerals.

Due to decisions in early cases, a mineral deed form came into common usage that, in addition to the customary mineral granting clause, (1) expressly granted specific interests under an existing lease and (2) restated the permanent ownership of the mineral reversionary interest. Such deeds commonly have been construed as containing two different grants, one grant of the benefits under the outstanding lease and the other of the permanent mineral interest. Where conflicting provisions exist between the granting clause and the restated reversionary mineral interest, the cases are not uniform. One view would allow the granting clause to control; the other would look to the entire instrument in an attempt to determine intent. The use of a clause to restate ownership of the reversionary mineral interest is unnecessary.

A great deal of unnecessary confusion has been created in situations where, following the execution of an oil and gas lease, the lessor has conveyed an interest in the minerals. This confusion is partly due to early decisions concerning the interests that will pass to the grantee, where a deed is executed expressly "subject to" an outstanding oil and gas lease. This confusion has been compounded in in-

---

mage, Mineral Deed to Fractional Undivided Interest Subject to Existing Lease, 17 Tex.L.Rev. 346; Lee, Ambiguity and the "Subject to" Clause in Texas Mineral Conveyancing, 5 S.T.L.J. 313; Masterson, Double Fraction Problems in Instruments Involving Mineral Interests, 11 Sw.L.J. 281; Meyers & Williams, Oil and Gas Conveyancing: Grants and Reservations by Owners of Fractional Mineral Interests, 43 Va.L.Rev. 639. See Summers, Oil & Gas Law, §§ 600, 601, 606.

2. See Chapter 2, supra.

stances where a draftsman has prepared the deed without a thorough understanding of the interests owned by the lessor and of those interests that are to be passed to the grantee.

Assume the following situation: O leases Blackacre to Pure Oil Company, using an ordinary "unless" form lease with a primary term of ten years. The lease is recorded. No mention of the outstanding lease is made in the deed.[1] Upon execution of the lease, the landowner owns:

(a) The right to benefits payable under the present outstanding lease, i.e., rentals, royalties, production payments, bonus payable out of future production, shut-in royalties, etc.; and,

(b) the reversionary interest in the minerals, including the right to execute future leases and the right to economic benefits payable thereunder.

Later, O executes a deed describing all of Blackacre. Unless expressly limited, in virtually all jurisdictions the economic benefits as well as the reversionary interest in the minerals will pass to the grantee.[2] However, the grantor will have breached his warranty by not excepting the outstanding lease from the conveyance. Following normal conveyancing technique, the draftsman will include a statement that the conveyance is "subject to" the outstanding oil and gas lease, identifying the lease by reference to its recordation.

In most jurisdictions the "subject to" phrase is treated as a saving clause against a breach of warranty.[3] However, in an early Texas case, Caruthers v. Leonard,[4] it was held that the effect of the phrase was only to pass the reversionary interest in the minerals to the grantee, with the grantor retaining the economic benefits under the present lease. The case indicated that in order to pass such economic benefits there must be a separate assignment of such benefits in the conveyance. The case has since been overruled.[5] It appears to be

---

1. As the lease is recorded, the later conveyance is burdened by the outstanding oil and gas lease. If not recorded, the lease would be cut off by a bona fide purchaser for value.

2. Wright v. Carter Oil Co., 97 Okl. 46, 223 P. 835; Hager v. Stakes, 116 Tex. 453, 294 S.W. 835; Theo Oil Co. v. Thomas, Tex.Civ.App., 108 S.W.2d 555; Harris v. Currie, 142 Tex. 93, 176 S.W.2d 302; Alfrey v. Ellington, Tex.Civ.App., 285 S.W.2d 383. But cf. California where community lease: Tanner v. Title Insurance & Trust Co., 20 Cal.2d 814, 129 P.2d 383. Unpaid but accrued rental and royalties are owned by the transferor; unaccrued benefits under the lease pass to the transferee. See Duvall v. Stone, 54 N.M. 27, 213 P.2d 212.

3. French v. Querbes, 200 La. 654, 8 So.2d 631; Wright v. Carter Oil Co., 97 Okl. 46, 223 P. 835; Kokernot v. Caldwell, Tex.Civ.App., 231 S.W.2d 528; Bass v. Harper, Tex.Civ.App., 437 S.W.2d 648, reversed Tex., 441 S.W.2d 825.

4. Tex.Com.App., 254 S.W. 779. It was held that rentals under the present lease did not pass to the grantee. The rationale was that rentals were for delay in drilling on the surface of the land and therefore not appurtenant to the mineral interest. Hence, a grant of the reversionary interest in the minerals did not carry with it the rentals. Also see Tipps v. Bodine, Tex.Civ.App., 101 S.W.2d 1076.

The prevailing view is to the contrary. See note 3, supra.

5. Hager v. Stakes, 116 Tex. 453, 294 S.W. 835; Harris v. Currie, 142 Tex. 93, 176 S.W.2d 302.

the present view in Texas that all economic benefits from the lease will now pass under a deed expressly "subject to" an outstanding lease. However, the effects of the Caruthers case are still felt. The main effect of the Caruthers decision was the creation of a printed deed form containing three main divisions of the granting clause. The use of this printed form has become widespread and has been the subject of extensive litigation.

The clauses are as follows:[6]

(1) The granting clause, which is identical to the granting clause in other mineral conveyances.

(2) The "subject to" clause, which generally reads: "Said land being now under an oil and gas lease executed in favor of _____, it is understood and agreed that this sale is made subject to the terms of said lease, but covers and includes _____ of all of the oil royalty, and gas rental or royalty due and to be paid under the terms of said lease. It is understood and agreed that _____ of the money rentals which may be paid to extend the term within which a well may be begun under the terms of said lease is to be paid to the said Grantee * * *."

(3) The "future lease" clause. The draftsman of this form found it necessary to restate the ownership of the mineral estate in the event that the present lease terminated and that future leases were executed. It is extremely unfortunate that this was done, for, after the expiration of the outstanding lease, the ownership of the mineral estate would normally be determined under clause (1). This restatement of ownership as contained in the future lease clause could hardly have been more inept. " * * * in event that the above described lease for any reason becomes cancelled or forfeited, then and in that event an undivided _____ of the lease interest and all future rentals on said land for oil, gas and other mineral privileges shall be owned by said Grantee, he owning _____ of _____ of all oil, gas and other minerals in and under said lands, together with interest in all future rents." Not only is the entire clause redundant of clause (1), it contains two statements concerning the ownership of rentals and also uses the term "lease interest" which was not at that time judicially defined. A more effective trap for the unwary can hardly be imagined.

Again assume that O has executed an oil and gas lease to Pure Oil Company, reserving a landowner's royalty of $\frac{1}{8}$. A desires to buy one-eighth of O's interest. As O owns all the minerals, A should purchase a $\frac{1}{8}$ mineral interest in Blackacre. O and A go to a stationery

---

6. The quoted materials are from Garrett v. Dils Co., 157 Tex. 92, 299 S.W.2d 904, noted 12 S.W.L.J. 394. Also see Stanley v. Slone, 216 Ky. 114, 287 S.W. 360; Armstrong v. Bell, 199 Miss. 29, 24 So.2d 10; Tipps v. Bodine, Tex.Civ.App., 101 S.W.2d 1076; Schubert v. Miller, Tex. Civ.App., 119 S.W.2d 139; Richardson v. Hart, 143 Tex. 392, 185 S.W.2d 563; Gibson v. Watson, Tex.Civ.App., 315 S.W.2d 48; Delta Drilling Co. v. Simmons, 161 Tex. 122, 338 S.W.2d 143; Etter v. Texaco, Inc., Tex.Civ.App., 371 S.W.2d 702.

store and purchase the above mineral deed form. In filling out the form, O and A do not distinguish between a mineral interest and a royalty interest. A fills out the form and asks O what he owns. As O is getting $1/8$ of production as a royalty, he answers that he owns $1/8$. A then fills in clause (1) with the figure $1/64$, or $1/8$ of what A mistakenly believes O owns. If the parties stopped here, A would own a $1/64$ mineral interest, entitling her to $1/64$ *of* benefits under the lease, including $1/64$ of $1/8$ ($1/512$) royalty interest under the normal $1/8$ lease.

Clause (2), the "subject to" clause, reads as a percent of royalty. As A assumes that she is to have $1/8$ of O's interests, she places the fraction $1/8$ in the clause, so that she will receive $1/8$ of royalty. This would entitle her to a $1/64$ royalty under the present lease. Therefore, after merely filling in the blanks in the first two paragraphs, the parties have stated two different interests in royalty, one eight times larger than the other.

Had the parties stopped at this point, although expressed intent is somewhat uncertain, the construction of the conveyance and the result is fairly predictable. In the case of Hoffman v. Magnolia Petroleum Co.,[7] the Supreme Court of Texas announced the so-called "two-grant doctrine." Briefly, this means that the grantor may grant two separate estates. The first is the permanent mineral interest of the grantee, and the second is the right to rentals and royalties under an outstanding lease. When the outstanding lease terminates, the mineral interests of the parties will be determined by the first clause.

This doctrine is well set forth in Richardson v. Hart.[8] "It is clear, we think, that the instrument conveyed two separate and distinct estates in the land. The first was a permanent interest in the minerals in place which was to subsist during and beyond the life of the existing lease. The other was the royalty to be due and payable under the lease. The first estate is determined in the first and fourth paragraphs of the deed which precisely define and prescribe the interest conveyed as being $1/16$ of $1/8$, or $1/128$ of all the oil, gas or other minerals in and under or produced from the land. This estate is fixed as a permanent grant irrespective of the existence, duration or termination of this or any future lease, and, in the absence of an agreement to the contrary, would determine the proportionate share of the grantee or his assigns in the royalties in the oil or other minerals produced from the land. Without any stipulation as to royalties the interest thus conveyed would carry with it by operation of law, the right to $1/128$ of the royalties paid under any lease. However, the parties did not leave the matter of the payment of royalties under the

---

7. Tex.Com.App., 273 S.W. 828.

8. 143 Tex. 392, 185 S.W.2d 563. Also see Little v. Mountain View Dairies, 35 Cal.2d 232, 217 P.2d 416; Paddock v. Vasquez, 122 Cal.App.2d 396, 265 P.2d 121, noted 32 Tex.L.Rev. 766; Smith v. Grubb, 402 Ill. 451, 84 N.E.2d 421; Hinkle v. Gauntt, 201 Okl. 432, 206 P.2d 1001; Woods v. Sims, 154 Tex. 59, 273 S.W.2d 617; Gibson v. Watson, Tex.Civ. App., 315 S.W.2d 48.

Ch. 9   TRANSFERS BY LESSOR AND LESSEE   459

existing lease to be determined by operation of law. In the third paragraph of the deed they made a covenant in regard thereto which passed to the grantee the second estate above mentioned. The fact that it fixes the share in the present royalties the same as would have obtained by operation of law does not lessen its force and effect as a conveyance. As is often the case, such payment of royalty might have been larger or smaller than a pro rata share."

Again, in Woods v. Sims,[9] the court stated, "In the absence of a stipulation with respect to the royalty payable under the lease, the conveyance of an interest in the minerals in place carries with it by operation of law the right to a corresponding interest in the royalty. It does not follow, however, that the interest in the royalty must be the same as the mineral interest conveyed where the instrument provides otherwise. Mineral deeds such as those involved in this case convey separate and distinct estates in the land, including (1) a permanent interest in the minerals in place which subsists during and beyond the life of the existing lease, and (2) an interest in the royalty to be due and payable under the lease." Therefore, had A and O stopped with the "subject to" clause, A would be entitled to a $1/64$ royalty payable under the present lease and a $1/64$ permanent mineral interest, entitling her to a $1/512$ royalty under future leases.

Severe constructional problems have not arisen where only the granting clause and the "subject to" clause have been used. However, where the parties have also used the future lease clause, i.e., clause (3), to restate mineral ownership upon termination of a present lease, many suits have arisen involving construction of the language used, the results of which have not been uniform or predictable.

In resolving the construction of these instruments the courts have usually followed the modern view of construction that the intention of the parties will be found from the "four corners"[10] of the instrument. Therefore, the courts will attempt to give effect to each word and phrase used. Normally, parol evidence is excluded,[11] and it is rare to find a court declaring the language ambiguous, however incomprehensible the instrument may be.[12]

The four corners rule becomes difficult to apply where internal inconsistencies occur between the granting clause and the future lease clause. It is with the quantum of the permanent mineral interest that the courts have had the most difficulty.

9. 154 Tex. 59, 273 S.W.2d 617.

10. Barnard v. Jamison, 78 Cal.App. 2d 136, 177 P.2d 341; Dale v. Case, 217 Miss. 298, 64 So.2d 344, 37 A.L.R.2d 811; Krutzfeld v. Stevenson, 86 Mont. 463, 284 P. 553; Tipps v. Bodine, Tex.Civ.App., 101 S.W.2d 1076; Kokernot v. Caldwell, Tex.Civ.App., 231 S.W.2d 528; Gibson v. Watson, Tex.Civ.App., 315 S.W.2d 48; Bass v. Harper, Tex.Civ.App., 437 S.W.2d 648, reversed Tex., 441 S.W.2d 825.

11. Armstrong v. Bell, 199 Miss. 29, 24 So.2d 10, but cf. Smith v. Grubb, 402 Ill. 451, 84 N.E.2d 421.

12. Tipps v. Bodine, Tex.Civ.App., 101 S.W.2d 1076; Garrett v. Dils Co., 157 Tex. 92, 299 S.W.2d 904, noted 12 S.W. L.J. 394; Delta Drilling Co. v. Simmons, 161 Tex. 122, 338 S.W.2d 143; Etter v. Texaco, Inc., Tex.Civ.App., 371 S.W.2d 702.

Two distinct approaches are applied. In both approaches it is stated that the permanent mineral interest is to be found by construing the granting clause and future lease clause in relation to each other.[13] Where effect cannot reasonably be given to both clauses,[14] one line of authority would reject inconsistencies in the future lease clause and allow the granting clause to control.

The other view rejects any repugnancy between the two clauses and attempts to find intent from a consideration of all clauses in the deed in relationship to each other.[15]

Illustrative of the latter view is the case of Garrett v. Dils,[16] from which the above mineral deed form was quoted. In the Dils case the clauses stated the following fractional interests as passing to the grantee:

(a) Granting clause: $1/64$ mineral interest.

(b) "Subject to" clause: $1/8$ of the royalty and rental.

(c) Future lease clause: $1/8$ of the lease interest and all future rentals, " * * * he owning one-eighth of one-eighth of all oil, gas and other minerals in and under said lands, together with one-eighth interest in all future rents."[17]

The outstanding lease expired. At issue was the ownership of the incidents in the mineral estate as to future leases.

---

13. Richardson v. Hart, 143 Tex. 392, 185 S.W.2d 563; Woods v. Sims, 154 Tex. 59, 273 S.W.2d 617.

14. Paddock v. Vasquez, 122 Cal.App.2d 396, 265 P.2d 121, noted 32 Tex.L.Rev. 766; Krutzfeld v. Stevenson, 86 Mont. 463, 284 P. 553 (expressly rejecting prior Montana decisions to the contrary); Schubert v. Miller, Tex.Civ.App., 119 S.W.2d 139; Richardson v. Hart, 143 Tex. 392, 185 S.W.2d 563; Woods v. Sims, 154 Tex. 59, 273 S.W.2d 617; Gibson v. Watson, Tex.Civ.App., 315 S.W.2d 48; Etter v. Texaco, Inc., Tex.Civ.App., 371 S.W.2d 702.

In Woods v. Sims, 154 Tex. 59, 273 S.W.2d 617, the clauses involved were:

(a) *granting clause:* an undivided $25/200$ths mineral interest in 200 acres described by metes and bounds, with the statement, "it being the intention of the grantor to convey and the grantee to purchase an undivided 25 acre mineral interest."

(b) *"subject to" clause:* $25/200$ths of benefits under the lease.

(c) *reversionary interest clause:* an undivided $25/200$ths mineral interest.

The land actually contained 226.88 acres. Construing clauses (a) and (c) together the court held the permanent grantee was entitled to:

(1) $25/200$ths $\times$ $1/8$ royalty under present leases.

(2) $25/226.88$ $\times$ $1/8$ royalty under future leases.

15. Stanley v. Slone, 216 Ky. 114, 287 S.W. 360; Armstrong v. Bell, 199 Miss. 29, 24 So.2d 10; Dale v. Case, 217 Miss. 298, 64 So.2d 344, 37 A.L.R.2d 811; Tipps v. Bodine, Tex.Civ.App., 101 S.W.2d 1076.

16. 157 Tex. 92, 299 S.W.2d 904, noted 12 S.W.L.J. 394.

17. Under this form the same fractions should be used throughout the form. To convey a $1/8$ mineral interest as in the above example, "$1/8$" should have been inserted in all the blanks, and the future lease and reversionary interest clause modified as follows:

(1) granting clause: $1/8$ mineral interest.

(2) "subject to" clause: $1/8$ of royalty and rentals under the present lease.

(3) future lease and reversionary interest: $1/8$ of the lease interest and future rentals, * * * he owning $1/8$ of all oil, gas and other minerals in and under said lands, together with $1/8$ interest in all future rents.

Ch. 9   TRANSFERS BY LESSOR AND LESSEE   461

Had the deed not contained a future lease clause, it is clear that the grantee would have owned a $1/64$ permanent mineral interest. The court, as is customary in these cases, held that the deed was not ambiguous and proceeded to apply the four corners rule of construction. However, in so doing, the court departed from the two-grant doctrine and stated, "Had other language in the deed not disclosed what the parties understood 'one sixty-fourth' to mean, it would be our duty to give those words their usual meaning and construe the deed as a mineral deed to an undivided one sixty-fourth of the minerals in place. But there follows the granting clause language which clearly defines what the parties understood one sixty-fourth of the minerals to mean." The court then refered to the "subject to" clause. "Construing all of these provisions together it is made certain that what the parties intended to convey, had there been production under the then existing lease, was a royalty of one sixty-fourth or one-eighth of the one-eighth royalty retained in the lease." The court, rather than treating each clause as a separate grant, found that the statement of royalty to be received under the present lease clause had defined the mineral estate in the granting clause, i.e., a $1/8$ mineral interest!

The court then stated that no intent existed in the future lease clause to convey a lesser interest under future leases. The court continued with reasoning that the author finds difficult to accept: "As pointed out above, there was granted one sixty-fourth of the minerals which the parties construed to mean one-eighth of the one-eighth royalty under the then existing lease. The provision for ownership of the minerals under future leases is that the grantee shall own 'one-eighth of one-eighth' of the minerals. Had that fraction been expressed as one sixty-fourth, it should be given the same meaning as in the granting clause which the parties understood and agreed to be a one sixty-fourth royalty or one-eighth of the one-eighth royalty. Instead of employing the fraction one sixty-fourth in defining the ownership under a subsequent lease, the provision is for one-eighth of one-eighth. Clearly, that does not denote a less interest than a one sixty-fourth, but on the contrary it emphasizes the fact that the intention was to convey one-eighth of the royalty under future leases the same as under the original lease. The court takes judicial knowledge of the fact that the usual royalty provided in mineral leases is one-eighth. The parties doubtless assumed that the royalty under future leases would be one-eighth, as it was under the lease in existence when the deed was executed."

The case is subject to criticism on at least two grounds. First, the future interest clause is so indefinite that it should not control over the clear statement of the mineral estate granted under the granting clause. Second, it is obvious that the parties have attempted to convey a $1/8$ mineral interest and have misstated the fractional interests. However, the case involved a suit in trespass to try title, and the instrument was found not to be ambiguous. It appears obvious that

Hemingway Law of Oil & Gas 2nd Ed. HB—17

the Texas court has given equitable relief of reformation by construction in a suit for title.

Where no present lease exists, neither the "subject to" clause nor the future interest clause should be given effect in construing the grant of a permanent interest in the minerals. In Gibson v. Watson,[18] which involved a deed form similar to that used in the Dils case, but which stated in the "subject to" clause that it was "not leased," the court would not consider the "subject to" or the future lease clause for constructional purposes.

Since rentals, royalties, and other economic benefits may be conveyed separately from the reversionary interest in the minerals,[19] the future lease clause may also have the effect of distributing such benefits under future leases in proportions different from the ownership of the reversionary mineral interest.

The Texas courts have held that the term "lease interest" as used in these clauses denotes the right to lease.[20] In Etter v. Texaco,[21] the granting clause conveyed a $1/32$ mineral interest, which would include $1/32$ of the royalty, rentals and the right to lease. This was followed by the future lease clause that stated, "* * * and in the event that the said above described lease for any reason becomes cancelled or forfeited, then and in that event, *the lease interests and all future rentals* on said land, for oil, gas and mineral privileges shall be owned by [the grantor]." By construing these clauses together it was found that the grantee received a $1/32$ of royalty under future leases, but the right to lease and rentals had been reserved by the grantor. This approach has been followed by other cases in Texas.[22]

In conclusion, where such a mineral deed form has been employed and the fractions are not consistent, it will be necessary to have a judicial determination and construction of the instrument. Since, by the general view, a conveyance of the minerals subject to an outstanding lease will carry with it proportional benefits under the existing lease and in the reversionary interest in the minerals, it is unnecessary to provide a separate conveyance of benefits under the existing lease. However, where the draftsman would feel more comfortable with a separate assignment of such benefits, care should be taken that the fractions stated are consistent with those in the granting clause. If it is desired to grant a different fractional interest under the existing lease than is proportional to the granting clause, this should be expressly stated in the "subject to" clause. Under no cir-

---

18. Tex.Civ.App., 315 S.W.2d 48.

19. Elkhorn Coal Corp. v. Slone, 210 Ky. 761, 276 S.W. 826; French v. Querbes, 200 La. 654, 8 So.2d 631; Wright v. Carter Oil Co., 97 Okl. 46, 223 P. 835; and see note 2, supra.

20. Garrett v. Dils Co., 157 Tex. 92, 299 S.W.2d 904, noted 12 S.W.L.J. 394.

21. Tex.Civ.App., 371 S.W.2d 702.

22. Tipps v. Bodine, Tex.Civ.App., 101 S.W.2d 1076; Richardson v. Hart, 143 Tex. 392, 185 S.W.2d 563; Garrett v. Dils Co., 157 Tex. 92, 299 S.W.2d 904, noted 12 S.W.L.J. 394; Delta Drilling Co. v. Simmons, 161 Tex. 122, 338 S.W.2d 143; Etter v. Texaco, Inc., Tex.Civ.App., 371 S.W.2d 702.

cumstances is it necessary or desirable to use a clause to redefine mineral ownership as to future leases or in the mineral reversion.

§ 9.2 Post-Lease Conveyances by the Lessor That Are Expressly "Subject to" an Outstanding Lease—Effect as to the Land Covered by the Conveyance

If an interest in the minerals is conveyed by a deed made expressly subject to an outstanding lease, where the land described is only a part of the land covered by the outstanding lease, the normal recital in the "subject to" clause may have the effect of assigning lease benefits relating to the entire land covered by the lease and not only that part of the land described in the deed. In these instances the so-called "insofar as" clause should be included.

Where the lessor desires to convey an interest in the minerals after the execution of an oil and gas lease, he may convey such interest in all or part of the land covered by the lease. Where the conveyance relates to all of the land covered by the lease, no particular problem exists as to the land from which the grantee will receive economic benefits under the present lease.

O executes a lease upon Blackacre, which covers 640 acres of land. Later O conveys to A an undivided one-half interest in the entire 640 acres. In the "subject to" clause the draftsman would state that the land is subject to the outstanding lease but that the interest conveyed covers and includes one-half of the rentals and royalties payable under the terms of said lease. Since A would then own an undivided interest in all of the land covered by the lease, no problem is encountered in determining A's interest. A would receive the stated interest in rentals and in royalties from wells drilled anywhere on the lease. However, where the interest conveyed is in only a portion of the land subject to the lease, the use of the "subject to" clause without modification may lead to unexpected results.

Referring to the above illustration, assume that the conveyance is made, but that the undivided one-half of the minerals are conveyed only in the southwest one-fourth (SW$\frac{1}{4}$) of the land. In the deed the draftsman includes the same recitation as to the present lease, "* * * but covers and includes one-half of the rentals and royalties payable under the *terms of said lease.*" Rentals and royalties payable under the "terms of said lease" relate to the entire 640 acres. Query: Does the grantee, by reason of the recitation, have a right to one-half of the rentals and royalties from the entire lease?

Again, assume that royalties in the lease are $\frac{1}{8}$ and the rentals are $1.00 per acre. If it is held that the grantee is entitled to the economic benefits from the present lease relating only to the SW$\frac{1}{4}$, A would be entitled to $\frac{1}{2} \times \$160.00$, or $80.00 rentals, and $\frac{1}{16}$ royalty only from wells drilled on the SW$\frac{1}{4}$. If the recitation is controlling, A would be entitled to one-half of all rentals, or $320.00, and a $\frac{1}{16}$ royalty from wells drilled anywhere on the lease.

In the Texas case of Hoffman v. Magnolia Petroleum Co.,[1] from which the above illustration is taken, the court held that the two-grant doctrine applied. In other words, separate grants were made (1) of the permanent interest in the minerals, and (2) of the interest under the present lease. Therefore, the clauses would not be construed together to determine the extent of the interest of the grantee. It was held that the effect of the recitation was to convey to the grantee one-half of the rentals and royalties under the entire lease, not just as to the $SW^1/_4$. It is submitted that although the two-grant theory may be applied to the quantum of the interest conveyed, it should be rejected as to the land covered by the conveyance. It apparently has been rejected in Louisiana,[2] and a later Texas case[3] has rejected its application.

To avoid the result of Hoffman v. Magnolia, where the effect is that the conveyance will include benefits from lands covered by the lease but which are not described in the deed, the draftsman should include the so-called "insofar as" clause. This is merely an additional phrase following the "subject to" clause, e.g., "* * * covers and includes one-half of the rentals and royalties payable under said lease, *insofar as said lease covers the above described land.*" This effectively restricts the assignment of benefits under the existing lease to the portion of the land conveyed. It may be used in all conveyances of interests conveyed subject to an outstanding lease. It is effective where an interest in partial tracts is conveyed, but merely redundant where an interest in the entire tract is conveyed.

§ 9.3 Post-Lease Conveyances by the Lessor That Are Expressly "Subject to" an Outstanding Lease—Effect Upon the Lease to Which the Reference Is Made and Upon the Duration of the Deed in Which the Recitation Is Contained

Where the conveyance is made expressly subject to an outstanding lease, in the case of a royalty conveyance the danger is always present that unless care is used by the draftsman the royalty interest may be interpreted as having a duration measured by the life of the mentioned lease.[1] The result is that if the royalty is tied to an existing lease, upon the termination of the named lease the royalty interest will terminate also. In one case where the recitation was to "the royalty interest in a lease to Producers,"[2] it was held that the royalty was limited to the life of the lease then in effect.

---

1. Tex.Com.App., 273 S.W. 828, noted 30 Tex.L.Rev. 395.

2. See French v. Querbes, 200 La. 654, 8 So.2d 631.

3. Robinson v. Humble Oil & Refining Co., Tex.Civ.App., 301 S.W.2d 938.

1. Duvall v. Stone, 54 N.M. 27, 213 P.2d 212; Commerce Trust Co. v. Lyon, Tex.Civ.App., 284 S.W.2d 920; Kaiser v. Love, 163 Tex. 558, 358 S.W.2d 586 and see Summers, Oil & Gas Law, § 602.

2. Commerce Trust Co. v. Lyon, Tex. Civ.App., 284 S.W.2d 920.

Ch. 9 TRANSFERS BY LESSOR AND LESSEE 465

An opposite result is found in the case of Kaiser v. Love.[3] The case involved a deed with a reservation of "all the oil and gas rights in the above tract of land hereby conveyed in the full terms as set forth in a particular oil and gas lease." The rationale of the case was that a reservation of the "oil and gas rights in the above tract of land" was sufficiently definite without reference to the lease. The phrase was also construed as including the possibility of reverter in the minerals and was therefore broader than royalty payable under a particular lease. The result was that a mineral, and not a royalty, interest was reserved.

It has been argued that the "subject to" clause in a term mineral deed has the positive effect of incorporating the lease into the deed. In Kokernot v. Caldwell,[4] a term mineral deed was executed after the execution of an oil and gas lease. The deed was expressly made subject to the outstanding lease, and it was then provided that the deed was to stay in effect for a term of 20 years. In the "subject to" clause it was recited that the deed covered and included $1/2$ of the royalties payable under said lease, and it was argued that the only way in which it could include $1/2$ of royalty under the lease was to extend the deed during the life of the lease. This contention has been uniformly rejected by the courts. The phrase is to subordinate and not to create rights.

In Bass v. Harper,[5] a conveyance was made of a $1/2$ mineral interest. The conveyance was made "subject to the mineral reservation contained in [prior deed]." It was stipulated that the prior deed reserved a $6/14$ of royalty. The question presented in the case was who would bear the burden of the outstanding royalty interest, the grantor or grantee in the deed. It was the grantor's contention that as a $1/2$ mineral interest was entitled to $7/14$ of royalty, and as the grant was subject to the burden of the outstanding interest, the grantee was entitled to only $7/14$ minus $6/14$, or $1/14$, of royalty. The grantee countered with the view that the "subject to" clause was merely a protection on the warranty, and not a reservation by implication. The court held for the grantor. The rationale was that the grant, and not the warranty, was made subject to the outstanding interest.

The same problem exists where assignments of interests in the leasehold estate are made by the lessee when there are prior outstanding interests. In either case the draftsman should be careful to spell out who will bear the burden of the prior outstanding interest. If the burden is to be borne proportionately, the later conveyance should so state.

---

3. 163 Tex. 558, 358 S.W.2d 586.

4. Tex.Civ.App., 231 S.W.2d 528. No provision was contained in the deed for extension of the term by production past the fixed 20-year period. Also see Fleming v. Ashcroft, 141 Tex. 41, 175 S.W.2d 401.

5. Tex.Civ.App., 437 S.W.2d 648, reversed Tex., 441 S.W.2d 825.

The effect of executing deeds subject to lapsed oil and gas leases, and effectually reviving such leases, is covered elsewhere.[6]

§ 9.4 Post-Lease Conveyances of the Lessor—Apportionment or Non-apportionment of Rentals and Royalties

In virtually all jurisdictions, where land subject to an oil and gas lease is subdivided, unless an agreement exists to the contrary, royalties will be paid upon production from the lease on a non-apportionment basis, viz., they will be paid only to the owners of the land from which the production is obtained.

Delay rentals, on the other hand, are analogous to common law rent, are viewed as issuing from all of the land under lease, and will be shared on an apportioned basis, viz., all owners of land under lease will share in the proportion that the tract of land in which they own an interest bears to the total land under lease.

O owns Blackacre, containing 640 acres of land. O leases the entire tract of land to Shell Oil Company. O reserves a $1/8$ landowner's royalty, and the lease provides for delay rentals of $1.00 per acre. While the lease is in effect, O conveys the south 320 acres of Blackacre to A, including all of the minerals and rights under the outstanding lease, insofar as they pertain to the south 320 acres of land. After holding the lease for two years by the payment of delay rentals, Shell drills three wells, all on the south 320 acres. To whom should Shell have paid the rentals, and who is entitled to the royalties?

Delay rentals are equivalent to common law rents, are deemed to have issued from all of the land, and are payable to all who have an interest in the land at the time the rent is due. Therefore, rents and delay rentals are payable on an apportionment basis, viz., to each owner in the proportion that the land owned bears to the total tract upon which rentals are paid. In the above illustration, O and A would each be entitled to $320 delay rentals.

The question early arose whether royalties from production should be paid upon an apportionment basis, like delay rentals, or on a non-apportionment basis, viz., only to the owner of the tract from which petroleum products are produced. The earliest case is that of Wettengel v. Gormley.[1] In this case O, the landowner, leased 600 acres of land, which consisted of three separate farms. Upon his death, while the lease was still in effect, the farms passed, one apiece, to his three children. All the wells were drilled upon one of the farms. The court held that all would share in the royalties from the production in proportion to the acreage of the particular farm owned.

---

6. See §§ 5.1(D), and 6.3(F).

1. 160 Pa. 559, 28 A. 934. In general, see Summers, Oil & Gas Law, §§ 600, 601, 606; Huie, Apportionment of Oil and Gas Royalties, 78 Harv.L.Rev. 1112, Masterson, Division Order Problems Created by Apportionment of Royalty, 10 Okla.L. Rev. 289; Mosburg, Effect of Lessor's Assignment of Part of Leased Premises Upon Right to Receive Oil and Gas Royalties, 11 Okla.L.Rev. 149.

The rationale was threefold: (a) That oil and gas was a fugacious substance moving beneath the surface of the ground, and ownership of it was not like the ownership of realty; (b) that an oil and gas lease was similar to a lease for general tillage, the rents for which are apportionable among all the owners of the land; and (c) that oil was producible equally from all of the tract, therefore the wells were also producing the oil of the other children, in which production they should share. Upon the second appeal [2] the court affirmed the apportionment rule, with a somewhat different rationale. Royalties were treated as personal property, but were analogized to rentals. As rents they were deemed to issue from each and every part of the land, not being payable by the acre or by the farm, but upon total production within the 600 acres.

The Gormely case has been rejected in virtually every producing jurisdiction [3], with the exception of California.[4] Therefore, under the overwhelming weight of authority, where a conveyance of part of the land has been made by the lessor, or his successor, subsequent to the execution of a lease (unless agreement has otherwise been made in the lease [5] or by separate instrument between all the parties), royalties will be paid only to the owners of the land on which the wells have been drilled. The rationale of these cases, even in the non-ownership jurisdictions, is that when oil or gas is beneath a tract of land it is part of the real estate and that a deed of such land conveys every right of the grantor in the land, including the oil and gas, or the

---

2. Wettengel v. Gormley, 184 Pa. 354, 39 A. 57.

3. Osborn v. Arkansas Territorial Oil & Gas Co., 103 Ark. 175, 146 S.W. 122; Moshiek v. Lininger, 130 Colo. 266, 274 P.2d 965; Central Pipe Line Co. v. Hutson, 401 Ill. 447, 82 N.E.2d 624, noted 62 Harv.L.Rev. 1242; Fairbanks v. Warrum, 56 Ind.App. 337, 104 N.E. 983; Carlock v. Krug, 151 Kan. 407, 99 P.2d 858; Hurst v. Paken Oil Co., 287 Ky. 257, 152 S.W.2d 981; Merrill Engineering Co. v. Capital National Bank of Jackson, 192 Miss. 378, 5 So.2d 666; Raley v. Moore, 60 N.M. 200, 289 P.2d 957; Northwestern Ohio Natural Gas Co. v. Ullery, 68 Ohio St. 259, 67 N.E. 494; Kimbley v. Luckey, 72 Okl. 217, 179 P. 928; Galt v. Metscher, 103 Okl. 271, 229 P. 522; Japhet v. McRae, Tex.Com.App., 276 S.W. 669, noted 4 Tex.L.Rev. 339; Garza v. DeMontalvo, 147 Tex. 525, 217 S.W.2d 988; McElvain v. The Texas Co., Tex.Civ.App., 273 S.W.2d 676; McKinnon v. Lane, Tex.Civ.App., 285 S.W.2d 269; Coates v. DeGarcia, Tex.Civ.App., 286 S.W.2d 691; Pittsburg & West Virginia Gas Co. v. Ankrom, 83 W.Va. 81, 97 S.E. 593; Shut-in royalties are probably included in the definition of "royalty," see Robinson v. Milam, 125 W.Va. 218, 24 S.E.2d 236.

In Minchen v. Fields, 162 Tex. 73, 345 S.W.2d 282, it was held that an additional payment to lessor out of future production, of $60,195.00 out of $1/32$ of $7/8$, constituted a deferred bonus payment. As bonus was payable for consideration for the whole lease, the payment was held to be apportionable among all owners of mineral interests subject to the lease, whether or not wells were located on their lands.

4. Standard Oil Co. of California v. John P. Mills Organization, 3 Cal.2d 128, 43 P.2d 797; Higgins v. California Petroleum and Asphalt Co., 109 Cal. 304, 41 P. 1087; (unaccrued royalty is an incorporeal hereditament and is classified as rent); cf. McIntire's Administrator v. Bond, 227 Ky. 607, 13 S.W.2d 772, 64 A.L.R. 630, (adopting the apportionment view, but overruled in Hurst v. Paken Oil Co., 287 Ky. 257, 152 S.W.2d 981).

5. See § 9.5, infra, for a discussion of the entirety clause. A proportionate reduction clause does not operate as an entirety clause. See Carlock v. Krug, 151 Kan. 407, 99 P.2d 858.

rights thereto.[6] The Gormley case has been criticized on the ground that an oil and gas lease is unlike a lease for general tillage and that the court was incorrect in its assumption that each acre would produce equally, as a ground or basis for unjust enrichment.[7]

Examples of the apportionment and non-apportionment views may be illustrated in connection with the case of Japhet v. McRae.[8] In this case the landowner, O, owned 15 acres of land, and executed an oil and gas lease to Oil Company. O subsequently sold the north 5 acres to A, who in turn sold to B an undivided 3-acre interest in the north 5 acres. Subsequently, O sold the south 10 acres to A, who in turn sold to C. A gas well was drilled on the south 10 acres. In applying the non-apportionment view, C would receive a full $1/8$ royalty from production. Likewise, if a well had been drilled on the north 5 acres, A would receive $1/8$ royalty $\times$ his undivided interest in the tract ($2/5 \times 1/8$), or $2/40$ royalty. B would receive $1/8 \times$ his undivided interest ($3/5 \times 1/8$), or $3/40$ royalty.

If the apportionment view is followed, each owner of an interest in land under lease will receive a proportion of production from all wells on the lease, whether or not they are located on his tract of land. In computation, first the royalty from each well would be apportioned or allocated to each tract in proportion to the entire acreage under lease. In this example, the north 5 acres would have an allocation of $5/15 \times 1/8$, or $1/24$ of production. Of this interest, A would receive $2/5 \times 1/24$, or $2/120$ R.I., and B $3/5 \times 1/24$, or $3/120$ R.I. C would receive the royalty allocated to the south 10 acres, or $2/3 \times 1/8$, which equals $2/24$, or $10/120$ R.I.

Several other situations may result in apportionment of royalties:

(1) Execution of a joint lease by owners of tracts of land in severalty;

(2) Conveyances "subject to" an existing lease that come within the rule of Hoffman v. Magnolia; and

(3) Where lease contains an entirety clause.

In the factual situation herein discussed, it is important to note the sequence of facts. Here the tract is first leased as an entirety from one ownership, and then subdivided by the lessors, or by their succes-

---

6. Osborn v. Arkansas Territorial Oil & Gas Co., 103 Ark. 175, 146 S.W. 122; Moshiek v. Lininger, 130 Colo. 266, 274 P.2d 965; Central Pipe Line Co. v. Hutson, 401 Ill. 447, 82 N.E.2d 624, noted 62 Harv.L.Rev. 1242; Fairbanks v. Warrum, 56 Ind.App. 337, 104 N.E. 983; Northwestern Ohio Natural Gas Co. v. Ullery, 68 Ohio St. 259, 67 N.E. 494; Kimbley v. Luckey, 72 Okl. 217, 179 P. 928; Pittsburg & West Virginia Gas Co. v. Ankrom, 83 W.Va. 81, 97 S.E. 593. Northwestern Ohio Natural Gas Co. v. Ullery, 68 Ohio St. 259, 67 N.E. 494 has an excellent review of the development of case law in this area, as does Carlock v. Krug, 151 Kan. 407, 99 P.2d 858.

7. Japhet v. McRae, Tex.Com.App., 276 S.W. 669, noted 4 Tex.L.Rev. 339.

8. Tex.Com.App., 276 S.W. 669, noted 4 Tex.L.Rev. 339. Also see Gault v. Metscher, 103 Okl. 271, 229 P. 522 (where south half of land sold after lease, lessee tried to put well on dividing line, but placed it 4 feet north of the line. Under non-apportionment view, owner of north tract entitled to all royalty).

sors. This must be distinguished from the situation where the owners of several tracts join in a joint lease. In the latter situation the result is an apportionment of royalties from the view that such execution of a joint lease results in pooling of the tracts by implication of law. In Texas [9] this result occurs as a matter of law, and parol evidence is not admissible to show a contrary intent. In other jurisdictions [10] such execution raises a presumption of a pooled lease.

As an example of implied pooling, assume the same example as set forth above; however, conveyances to A, B, and C were executed prior to the execution of an oil and gas lease. A, B, and C then execute the same lease. In this case apportionment would be applied as indicated above, where A receives a $2/120$ R.I., B a $3/120$ R.I., and C a $2/24$ or $10/120$ R.I.

Where a client presents a situation in which owners of land are desiring to execute a joint lease, it is essential that the practitioner be careful to determine whether the owners are owners of undivided interests or interests in severalty. In the latter instance they may not desire to create a pooled lease.

The second situation that results in a kind of apportionment is found where jurisdictions follow the view of Hoffman v. Magnolia.[11] Here, O owned a tract of land that he leased. He then conveyed to A an undivided one-half mineral interest in the SW $1/4$. However in the "subject to" clause of the deed, O recited that it was subject to a present lease and covered and conveyed $1/2$ of the royalties and rentals payable *"under said lease."* The court held that the grant of rentals and royalties under the present lease extended to all payments as to all lands under the lease, and not only insofar as the lease covered the SW $1/4$. This situation may be used to illustrate the differences between non-apportionment, apportionment, and application of the Hoffman rule:

(a) *Non-Apportionment.* Assume the phrase "under said lease" was not included, and the jurisdiction applied the non-apportionment rule. O would get the full $1/8$ royalty from all wells on lands covered by the lease except those on the SW $1/4$. As to wells on the SW $1/4$, O would get $1/2$ of the royalty, as would A, each receiving a $1/16$ royalty.

(b) *Apportionment.* Same facts as (a); however, the jurisdiction follows the apportionment view. O and A will receive their interests in production from all wells, wherever situated on the lease. In allocating royalty between the SW $1/4$ and the rest of the

9. Parker v. Parker, Tex.Civ.App., 144 S.W.2d 303, and see § 7.13(A), supra.

10. See Higgins v. California Petroleum and Asphalt Co., 109 Cal. 304, 41 P. 1087; Peerless Oil and Gas Co. v. Tipken, 190 Okl. 396, 124 P.2d 418. But cf. French v. Querbes, 200 La. 654, 8 So.2d 631.

However, parties to a joint lease may provide for payment of royalties on a non-apportionment basis by proper provisions, Phillips Petroleum Co. v. McIlroy, D.C.Tex., 178 F.Supp. 107.

11. See § 9.2, supra, at note 1.

leased land, the allocation to SW $\frac{1}{4}$ would be $^{160}/_{640} \times \frac{1}{8}$, or a $\frac{1}{32}$ royalty. The remainder of the leased land would receive $^{480}/_{640} \times \frac{1}{8}$ ($\frac{3}{32}$ royalty). As to the SW $\frac{1}{4}$, both O and A would receive their interest ($\frac{1}{2}$) $\times$ the royalty allocated to the tract, i.e., each would receive $\frac{1}{2} \times \frac{1}{32}$ ($\frac{1}{64}$ royalty).

As to the remainder of the leased land, O is the sole owner, and would receive the entire allocation of royalty to these tracts, a $\frac{3}{32}$, or $\frac{6}{64}$, royalty. Therefore, out of total production A would receive a $\frac{1}{64}$ royalty, and O, combining his interest in both tracts, would receive $\frac{7}{64}$ royalty from any well drilled on the lease. (Incidentally, this is the same computation that would be made if the conveyance had been made to A prior to the lease, and O and A had executed a joint lease that pooled the tracts).

(c) *Application of Hoffman v. Magnolia.* Assume the same facts as in (a), above, but the phrase *"under said lease"* is included. This also has the effect of apportioning production, but not on the same basis as in (b). Again it does not matter where the well is located on the leased tract. O and A will receive the same share in any well. Here, however, the interests are not determined by the mineral interests each owns, but by the recitation in the "subject to" clause contained in the deed to A. If the Hoffman view is followed, A will receive $\frac{1}{2}$ of royalty from any well. Therefore, from any well on the lease both O and A will receive a $\frac{1}{16}$ royalty. The differences may be summarized in chart form:

	Location of Wells	
	SW $\frac{1}{4}$	Rest of Leased Land
(a) Non-apportionment		
O	$\frac{1}{16}$ R.I.	$\frac{1}{8}$ R.I.
A	$\frac{1}{16}$ R.I.	None
(b) Apportionment		
O	$\frac{7}{64}$ R.I.	$\frac{7}{64}$ R.I.
A	$\frac{1}{64}$ R.I.	$\frac{1}{64}$ R.I.
Apportionment—Hoffman v. Magnolia		
O	$\frac{1}{16}$ R.I.	$\frac{1}{16}$ R.I.
A	$\frac{1}{16}$ R.I.	$\frac{1}{16}$ R.I.

In situations where the subdivision of the land is made after the execution of an oil and gas lease, it does not matter whether the subdivision is voluntary or involuntary, and the non-apportionment rule has been applied where the subdivision was the result of voluntary conveyance,[12] voluntary partition,[13] descent of property by inheritance

---

12. Northwestern Ohio Natural Gas Co. v. Ullery, 68 Ohio St. 259, 67 N.E. 494; Galt v. Metscher, 103 Okl. 271, 229 P. 522; Grelling v. Allen, Tex.Civ.App., 218 S.W.2d 896; McElvain v. The Texas Co., Tex.Civ.App., 273 S.W.2d 676.

13. McIntire's Administrator v. Bond, 227 Ky. 607, 13 S.W.2d 772, 64 A.L.R. 630.

or will,[14] judicial partition,[15] and sales by a trustee in bankruptcy.[16] In the majority of jurisdictions the owner of the tract from which production issues will be entitled to the royalties or to other payments out of production.

In some instances the interrelation of the non-apportionment rule and application of well spacing regulations has given rise to inequities.[17] In Ryan Consolidated Petroleum Corporation v. Pickens,[18] two lessees had leases on adjoining tracts. Due to the application of Texas Rule 37,[19] which relates to well spacing, only one well could be drilled on the two adjoining tracts. Although each lessee had to include the description of both tracts in applications for a permit to drill a well as an exception to Rule 37, when the well was authorized for one lessee, it was held that he was the only one entitled to production from the well. The other lessee, due to application of Rule 37, could not obtain a well permit on his land nor, under the non-apportionment view, share in the production from the other. This case was instrumental in leading to the passage of the Texas forced pooling stat-

14. Wettengel v. Gormley, 160 Pa. 559, 28 A. 934.

15. Coates v. DeGarcia, Tex.Civ.App., 286 S.W.2d 691.

16. Pittsburg & West Virginia Gas Co. v. Ankrom, 83 W.Va. 81, 97 S.E. 593.

17. See Ryan Consol. Petroleum Corp. v. Pickens, 155 Tex. 221, 285 S.W.2d 201, cert. denied 351 U.S. 933, 76 S.Ct. 790, 100 L.Ed. 1462; Nale v. Carroll, 155 Tex. 555, 289 S.W.2d 743; Mueller v. Sutherland, Tex.Civ.App., 179 S.W.2d 801; Republic Natural Gas Co. v. Baker, C.A. 10th, 197 F.2d 647.

18. 155 Tex. 221, 285 S.W.2d 201, cert. denied 351 U.S. 933, 76 S.Ct. 790, 100 L.Ed. 1462.

19. Rule 37 sets the minimum spacing distances for well drilling in the state. It is held that the Rule comes into effect as to land in any particular part of the state when (a) production occurs within reasonable proximity of the tract of land, or (b) the land is subdivided for the purpose of oil and gas exploration. Nash v. Shell Petroleum Corp., Tex.Civ.App., 120 S.W.2d 522; Railroad Commission v. Delhi-Taylor Oil Corp., Tex.Civ.App., 302 S.W.2d 273. Any tract of land that is smaller than the spacing distance when the Rule comes into effect may be entitled to a well to prevent drainage, unless it is being effectively drained from other lands by the lessee. Gulf Land Co. v. Atlantic Refining Co., 134 Tex. 59, 131 S.W.2d 73; Railroad Commission v. Humble Oil & Refining Co., Tex.Civ.App., 193 S.W.2d 824; Railroad Commission v. Williams, 163 Tex. 370, 356 S.W.2d 131; Coloma Oil & Gas Corp. v. Railroad Commission, 163 Tex. 483, 358 S.W.2d 566.

Where the tract is subdivided subsequent to the time that Rule 37 attaches in the area, and such subdivided tracts are smaller than the spacing regulations, the subdivision is called a "voluntary subdivision." This is somewhat of a misnomer, as it will be so called whether the subdivision is voluntary or involuntary. After the Order of May 29, 1934, the only exception upon which a well could be obtained upon such a tract is to prevent waste. See Gulf Land Co. v. Atlantic Refining Co., supra. This has been defined as meaning the existence of peculiar geophysical characteristics so that the well on this tract would be the only one that could remove the products. No exception, as to this type of small tract, is allowed to prevent drainage. Under the rule of the "Centurary case" (Railroad Commission v. Magnolia Petroleum Co., 130 Tex. 484, 109 S.W.2d 967), where an application is made upon a tract that is classified as a voluntary subdivision, the Railroad Commission of Texas will reconstruct the tract as it existed at the time Rule 37 attached in the area. If this reconstructed tract has no well, as a total tract it is entitled to a well, unless being effectively drained by the applicant from other lands. This is what happened in the Pickens case, and the tract as reconstructed was entitled to one well. Each applicant had to include a description of the reconstructed tract in the application. The Pickens case held that such description did not result in equitable pooling of the tracts.

utes.[20] In some jurisdictions,[21] where land must be included in a proration unit, all lands included in the unit will share on an apportioned basis.

§ 9.5 The Entirety Clause

Where conveyances of segregated portions of land have been made after execution of the lease, an entirety clause allows the lessee to treat a lease as a unit for the purpose of paying royalties. The effect of the clause is to pool royalties. It is the majority view that subsequent conveyances, without the consent of the lessee, can not place segregated tracts on a non-apportionment basis.

It is the better view that a "now or hereafter" entirety clause will not have the result of pooling royalty upon segregated tracts of differing ownership at the time of execution of the lease.

Nearly all jurisdictions will divide royalty upon a non-apportionment basis where conveyances of mineral or royalty interests are made in segregated parts of the lands covered by the lease. Payment of royalty on a non-apportionment basis may prove difficult to the lessee where several separate tracts are involved and the quantum of royalty ownership varies between the tracts. In this situation the lessee is unable to treat the lease as a unit, in the regard that separate measuring equipment will be necessary for each tract of land with differing ownership.[1] It was for the convenience and benefit of the lessee that an additional clause was added to the assignment clause of the lease. This clause has been named the entirety

---

20. Mineral Interest Pooling Act, Natural Resources Code § 102.001 et seq.

Although the Texas Mineral Interest Pooling Act was enacted to avoid the result in Ryan v. Pickens, the Act as originally written was interpreted as not being subject to implementation by a royalty owner, see Railroad Commission of Texas v. Coleman, Tex., 460 S.W.2d 404. This case, together with Northwest Oil Co. v. Railway Commission, Tex.Civ. App., 462 S.W.2d 371 (which held that the owner of a working interest could not implement the Act unless it could prove it had drilled or proposed to drill a well), led to an amendment of Art. 6008c, Vernon's Ann.Civ.St., which has changed these results, Superior Oil Co. v. Railway Commission, Tex.Civ.App. 519 S.W.2d 479.

The Texas Act contains a "muscle-in" clause, whereby small tracts can be combined into units with adjacent larger tracts. However, lessee may not form tracts so as to leave over isolated unassigned small tracts to muscle in on adjacent tracts, Broussard v. Texaco, Inc., Tex., 479 S.W.2d 270.

21. Griffith v. Gulf Refining Co., 215 Miss. 15, 60 So.2d 518, noted 24 Miss.L.J. 258.

Leonard Crude Oil Co. v. Walton, 39 Mich.App. 293, 197 N.W.2d 503.

1. Under the customary assignment clause found in oil and gas leases each party has the right to assign, where the effect of such assignment will not increase the burdens of the lessee. Therefore, conveyances of lands subject to the lease may or may not affect the manner in which royalty is paid. However, such conveyances will not impose the additional burden upon the lessee of drilling inside offsets, i.e., drilling offset wells across division lines inside the boundaries of the original lease, where the division lines are created by such subsequent conveyances.

Ch. 9   TRANSFERS BY LESSOR AND LESSEE   473

clause.[2] The effect of the clause is to allow the lessee to pay royalties on an apportionment basis.

By way of illustration are simplified facts from the Oklahoma case of Eason v. Rosamund.[3] A was the owner of adjoining 40-acre tracts of land and executed a lease on both tracts to Black-Gold Oil Company. The lease contained an entirety clause. Subsequently, deeds were executed by A to B and C that conveyed to each a 5-acre mineral interest in the west 40 acres. Under each deed without regard to the entirety clause in the lease, the grantee was to receive $5/40$ of $1/8$ of royalty, or a total payment of $1/64$ royalty, as to wells drilled on the west 40 acres.

If no entirety clause were contained in the lease, A then would receive the full $1/8$ royalty from production from the east 40 acres, and would receive $1/8$ minus the interests of B and C, or a total of $3/32$ royalty from production from the west 40 acres. B and C would each receive $1/64$ royalty from production from the west 40 acres.

The effect of an entirety clause in the lease is to put the production on a pooled basis, so that each will share in production from any well on the lease in the proportion that the area of the tract in which they own interest bears to the entire acreage under lease. And, most important from the standpoint of the lessee is the fact that the interest of all parties in production will be the same as to all wells:

Tract (1), West 40 Acres:

	Interest in Tract [4]		Tract share of Production from Lease [5]		Royalty Under Lease		Interest in Production Under Lease
A	$3/4$ (30 acre int.)	x	$40/80$	x	$1/8$	=	$6/128$ R.I.
B	$1/8$ (5 acre int.)	x	$40/80$	x	$1/8$	=	$1/128$ R.I.
C	$1/8$ (5 acre int.)	x	$40/80$	x	$1/8$	=	$1/128$ R.I.

Tract (2), East 40 Acres:

A	All ($40/40$)	x	$40/80$	x	$1/8$	=	$8/128$ R.I.
B	None						
C	None						

Total Royalty Payable Under Lease $16/128$ or $1/8$ R.I.

---

2. A typical clause, from Gypsy Oil Co. v. Schonwald, 107 Okl. 253, 231 P. 864:

"If the leased premises are hereafter owned in severalty or in separate tracts, the premises, nevertheless, shall be developed and operated as an entirety, and royalties shall be paid to each separate owner in the proportion that the acreage owned by him bears to the entire leased acreage."

In general, see Summers Oil and Gas Law, § 612; Hardwicke & Hardwicke, Apportionment of Royalty to Separate Tracts: The Entirety Clause and the Community Lease, 32 Tex.L.Rev. 660;

Masterson, Division Order Problems Created by Apportionment of Royalty, 10 Okl.L.Rev. 289; Effect of Entirety Clauses on Grantees Taking Under Deeds Subject to Lease, 34 Neb.L.Rev. 697.

3. 173 Okl. 10, 46 P.2d 471.

4. Although in most cases this interest would be stated in undivided interests, in the Eason case 5 ac. mineral interests were conveyed, which are converted to undivided interests by placing the acre interest as the numerator and the number of acres in the tract as

5. See note 5 on page 474.

The total payment to a royalty owner as to any well upon the lease is determined by adding together his or her interests in all tracts under the lease. A, therefore, as to any well, is entitled to a total of $^{14}/_{128}$ R.I., and B and C, each, a $^1/_{128}$ R.I.

The entirety clause, as commonly worded, relates to conveyances of minerals and royalty which are made after execution of the lease. Such clauses generally are held to be valid, and have the effect of spreading royalty to all owners of tracts under the lease.[6]

Some conflict has occurred in the decisions whether the lessor, or his successors, may thereafter convey an interest in the land subject to a lease with an entirety clause, where the effect of such conveyance is to place the tract conveyed upon a nonapportionment basis.[7] The problem is caused by the conflict between, (1) the entirety clause in a lease, which would allow an owner in a tract without production to share in production from another tract, and (2) a deed executed after the lease that conveys a stated royalty or mineral interest in only a segregated tract of land under the lease. The situation is amply illustrated in the facts of the Texas case of Cockrell v. Texas Gulf Sulphur Co.,[8] which involved sulphur production rather than oil and gas.

Under simplified facts, O owned 729.7 acres of land and executed an oil and gas lease upon the tract. The lease, which contained an entirety clause,[9] provided for sulphur payments of 50 cents per long

---

the denominator, i.e., $^5/_{40} = ^1/_8$ mineral interest. See Chapter 3, § 3.1(C), supra.

5. The share of each tract in production is proportional to the entire acreage under lease. In the example each tract contained 40 acres, with 80 total acres under lease. Where several tracts are involved and are of irregular size, computation is easier if a percentage of production is computed for each tract, with the individual ownership interest then applied against such allocated percentage.

6. Harley v. Magnolia Petroleum Co., 378 Ill. 19, 37 N.E.2d 760, 137 A.L.R. 900; Hoffman v. Sohio Petroleum Co., 179 Kan. 84, 292 P.2d 1107; Ruthven & Co. v. Pan American Petroleum Corp., 206 Kan. 639, 482 P.2d 28; Rauner v. Jones, 159 Neb. 385, 67 N.W.2d 347; Krone v. Lacy, 168 Neb. 792, 97 N.W.2d 528; Schrader v. Gypsy Oil Co., 38 N.M. 124, 28 P.2d 885; Smith v. Amerada Petroleum Corp., N.D., 136 N.W.2d 483; Gypsy Oil Co. v. Schonwald, 107 Okl. 253, 231 P. 864; Cockrell v. Texas Gulf Sulphur Co., 157 Tex. 10, 299 S.W.2d 672, noted 35 Tex.L. Rev. 872; but cf. Shell Petroleum Corp. v. Calcasieu Real Estate & Oil Co., 185 La. 751, 170 So. 785; Shell Petroleum Corp. v. Carter, 187 La. 382, 175 So. 1.

Query: Is a grantor who conveys a $^1/_4$ mineral interest in a tract subject to an oil and gas lease, subject to a suit for breach of warranty by the grantee, where due to the entirety clause in the lease grantee is entitled to a $^1/_{64}$ royalty payment rather than a $^1/_{32}$ which he expected under the deed?

Ruthven & Co. v. Pan American Petroleum Corp., 206 Kan. 639, 482 P.2d 28 (proportionate reduction clause does not apply to well located on part of lease which is 100% leased although other tracts under lease only partially leased).

7. Cannot place on non-apportionment basis: Rauner v. Jones, 159 Neb. 385, 67 N.W.2d 347; Hafeman v. Gem Oil Co., 163 Neb. 438, 80 N.W.2d 139.

8. 157 Tex. 10, 299 S.W.2d 672, noted 35 Tex.L.Rev. 872.

9. "It is further agreed that all the conditions and terms herein shall extend to the heirs, executors, legal representatives, successors in interest and assigns of the parties hereto; but no change of ownership of the land, or part thereof, shall impose any additional obligations or burden on the Lessee, and to that end Lessors hereby covenant for themselves, their heirs, assigns and successors in interest, that in case of any change of ownership of said land, or part thereof, whether by conveyance, will, inheritance,

ton. O sold other interests in the land until at the time of execution of the deed in question she owned only an undivided $\frac{1}{8}$ mineral interest in the west 400.0 acres and an undivided $\frac{1}{2}$ mineral interest in the east 329.7 acres. O then sold the 729.7 acres by warranty deed to A. The deed was expressly subject to the lease [10] and provided for the following reservations and exceptions of sulphur, with the royalty in each tract proportionately reduced to O's mineral ownership:

"5. $6\frac{1}{2}$ cents per ton of 2240 pounds on all sulphur produced and marketed from the west 400 acres of said above described premises.

"6. 25 cents per ton of 2240 pounds on all sulphur produced and marketed from the east 329.7 acres of said above described premises."

Sulphur was produced from the west 400.0 acres but not from the east 329.7 acres. O conveyed her interest to B, and B was paid on the basis of $6\frac{1}{2}$ cents from production from the west 400.0 acres. B claimed, however, that payment should be based upon the entirety clause in the lease and that under such clause B was entitled to a total of 14.72180347 cents per ton. The calculation was based upon the interest that O owned at the time of the conveyance to A:

West 400 acres:

$^{400}/_{729.7}$ x $\frac{1}{8}$ (O's int.) x 50 cents (lse. royalty) = 3.42606551 cents

East 329.7 acres:

$^{329.7}/_{729.7}$ x $\frac{1}{2}$ x 50 cents   =   11.29573796

O's total royalty under entirety clause   14.72180347

The lessee claimed that as the deed did not contain a clause providing for payment of royalty upon an apportionment basis, the proper royalty payment was 6.5 cents per ton. B, on the other hand, contended, and was sustained by the Court, that as the only right to royalty that O owned at the time of the deed was royalty payable upon an apportioned basis, she could not convert this royalty to a

partition or otherwise, all rentals and royalties accruing hereunder shall be paid to the new owners in proportion to their ownership of the whole of the land hereby leased so that no owner of a segregated part of said land shall be entitled to the whole royalties accruing from developments on said segregated tract, but only to such part of such royalty as the acreage in his tract is to the whole acreage embraced in this lease; this covenant shall be taken and construed as a covenant running with the land and binding on all successors in interest to Lessors herein."

10. "Following the habendum clause, and at the beginning of the warranty clause, we find the following: " * * * and subject to the aforesaid oil, gas and mineral leases and mineral and/or royalty conveyances, grantor does hereby bind herself, her heirs, etc."

"It was further provided: 'it is expressly understood and agreed that the reservations and exceptions hereinabove enumerated shall be perpetual and shall apply whether such oil, gas, casinghead gas and/or gasoline, sulphur and/or other mineral or minerals is produced under the existing or any future lease or leases by the lessee or lessees therein or by the grantees herein, its successors and assigns, or otherwise'."

non-apportionment basis by reserving a specific royalty as to each tract of land.

Some cases have held that although the lessor and the lessee are bound by the entirety clause in the lease, purchasers from the lessor are not.[11] Several rationales have been advanced to support this conclusion: that the deed modified the lease, nullifying the entirety clause;[12] that the deed is to be construed without reference to the lease;[13] or that the purchasers are bound by the deed and not the lease.[14] In reference to the above illustration these courts would hold that the lessee was correct in paying B 6.5 cents royalty from production. However, in these cases the lessee was not a party to the suit or was not claiming that such a change in royalty payment would result in increased burdens or decreased rights to him. It appears that if the lessee could show that paying royalty upon non-apportionment basis would cause him substantial detriment, the entirety clause would have been enforced.[15]

The weight of authority [16] is that the lessor, or his succesors, cannot deal with the land so as to place royalty payments on a non-apportionment basis. In Cockrell v. Texas Gulf Sulphur Co.[17] the above illustration), the court held that the parties, without the joinder of the lessee, could not place the royalty payments upon a non-apportionment basis. It was held that where the subsequent deed was expressly "subject to" the lease, the lease modified the deed.[18] Other courts have held that the entirety clause is a covenant running with the land,[19] which restricts the power of parties subsequent to alienate the mineral estate free of the entirety clause.[20]

---

11. Alsip's Administrator v. Onstott, Ky., 283 S.W.2d 711; Shell Petroleum Corp. v. Carter, 187 La. 382, 175 So. 1; Coyne v. Simrall Corp., C.C.A.6th 140 F.2d 574, cert. denied 323 U.S. 723, 65 S.Ct. 56, 89 L.Ed. 581; Iskian v. Consolidated Gas Utilities Corp., 207 Okl. 615, 251 P.2d 1073 (lessors and grantees to pay all additional costs of lessee, and only for the life of the lease), but see note 16, infra.

12. Alsip's Administrator v. Onstott, Ky., 283 S.W.2d 711.

13. Iskian v. Consolidated Gas Utilities Corp., 207 Okl. 615, 251 P.2d 1073 (lessors and grantees to pay all additional costs of lessee, and only to last for the life of the lease), but see note 16, infra.

14. Shell Petroleum Corp. v. Carter, 187 La. 382, 175 So. 1.

15. Shell Petroleum Corp. v. Carter, 187 La. 382, 175 So. 1; Iskian v. Consolidated Gas Utilities Corp., 207 Okl. 615, 251 P.2d 1073.

16. Turner v. Brookshear, C.A.10th, 271 F.2d 761; Rauner v. Jones, 159 Neb. 385, 67 N.W.2d 347; Hafeman v. Gem Oil Co., 163 Neb. 438, 80 N.W.2d 139, noted 5 U.S.C.A.L.Rev. 555; Krone v. Lacy, 168 Neb. 792, 97 N.W.2d 528; Schrader v. Gypsy Oil Co., 38 N.M. 124, 28 P.2d 885; Gypsy Oil Co. v. Schonwald, 107 Okl. 253, 231 P. 864; Eason v. Rosamond, 173 Okl. 10, 46 P.2d 471, but cf. Iskian v. Consolidated Gas Utilities Corp., notes 11 and 13, supra; Cockrell v. Texas Gulf Sulphur Co., 157 Tex. 10, 299 S.W.2d 672, noted 35 Tex.L.Rev. 872.

17. 157 Tex. 10, 299 S.W.2d 672, noted 35 Tex.L.Rev. 872.

18. Schrader v. Gypsy Oil Co., 38 N.M. 124, 28 P.2d 885; Cockrell v. Texas Gulf Sulphur Co., 157 Tex. 10, 299 S.W.2d 672, noted 35 Tex.L.Rev. 872.

19. Hafeman v. Gem Oil Co., 163 Neb. 438, 80 N.W.2d 139, noted 5 U.C.L.A.L. Rev. 555; Krone v. Lacy, 168 Neb. 792, 97 N.W.2d 528.

20. Rauner v. Jones, 159 Neb. 385, 67 N.W.2d 347; Gypsy Oil Co. v. Schonwald, 107 Okl. 253, 231 P. 864; Eason v. Rosamond, 173 Okl. 10, 46 P.2d 471; Turner v.

The previous discussion has been directed to the situation where conveyances of segregated tracts were made subsequent to the time that the lease was executed. However, as to time of application, entirety clauses found in leases are of two types. The customary "hereafter" [21] clause is applied to conveyances made after the lease is executed. However, "the now or hereafter" [22] clauses speak to the situation where ownership of the land is in separate tracts at the time the lease is executed.

Several cases have dealt with the question of the effect of the "now or hereafter" entirety clause where leases were executed upon several tracts of land with differing ownership. In the case of Jul-Brookshear, C.A.10th, 271 F.2d 761. In Gypsy v. Schonwald the court stated:

"In the instant case the lessor-owner of the entire 100 acres executed the lease on it as entirety. That he had the right to place therein any provision which he deemed either to his advantage or to the advantage of a subsequent purchaser of a fractional interest in the land or the mineral estate therein seems clear as an incident to his ownership. He had the right to limit his sale thereof or manner of the use thereof as to its entirety or any acreage within the whole, or any estate arising from any part thereof. What he did in fact was in the nature of a covenant which burdened his remainder to the extent that one purchasing subsequent to said lease contract, and subject to it, acquired an interest in the royalty on the whole acreage, prorated as the fraction thereof purchased bore to the entire tract * * *. The clause here in question was, as to subsequent agreements of sale, tantamount to a severance of the owner's estate in the oil and gas mineral from the estate in the land itself, and the covenanting that owners of a fraction of the whole estate in either should share in the oil and gas as per the pro rata clause thereof. If the purchaser succeeds by contract to the west 80 or a fraction thereof as to fee or mineral right, he takes same burdened with that agreement in the lease, and as the contract affects the mineral rights, it goes to all underneath the acreage covered by the lease. * * * If said clause is a valid clause, Clark in executing the lease placed a restriction upon his power to alienate any part of his estate in the land covered by the lease, with a right on the part of the subsequent grantee of such fractional interest to participate in the royalty, except in accordance with the said lease provision itself. The lessee, the plaintiff in error in this court, has been complying with the terms of its lease, and the question really at issue is: Can it be required to accommodate itself to the wishes of a subsequent purchaser of a fraction of the real estate or mineral interest therein, so as to allow him to secure a part of the royalty from a fractional portion of the land, under a conveyance made by the lessor, subsequent to the recordation of the lease, and against the acquisitions which the lessor had contracted with the lessee in the lease itself? We take it that if said clause is a valid contractual provision, after the premises have been found to be productive of oil and gas, and the primary purpose of the lease, to wit, the development, has been fully carried out by the lessee it cannot be compelled to do other than pay the royalty, as per the terms of the lease and whatever contract was made between the lessor and a subsequent purchaser could not be made effective to alter the duty of the lessee as to the royalty interest other than is set forth in its lease contract."

21. See note 2, supra.

22. "If the leased premises are now or shall hereafter be owned in severalty or in separate tracts, the premises, nevertheless, shall be developed and operated as one lease, and all royalties accruing hereunder shall be treated as an entirety and shall be divided among and paid to such separate owners in the proportion that the acreage owned by each such separate owner bears to the entire leased acreage." Taken from Thomas Gilcrease Foundation v. Stanolind Oil & Gas Co., 153 Tex. 197, 266 S.W.2d 850, noted 6 Bay.L.Rev. 232.

Ruthven & Co. v. Pan American Petroleum Corp., 206 Kan. 639, 482 P.2d 28.

Tex Drilling Co., Inc. v. Pure Oil Co.,[23] O executed a lease covering three tracts of land. Tract (1) contained 80 acres, Tract (2) contained 160 acres, as did Tract (3). However, O owned varying interests in the three tracts:

Tract (1) 80 acres, $3/4$ undivided interest = 60 acre mineral int.
Tract (2) 160 acres, all of the tract = 160 acre mineral int.
Tract (3) 160 acres, $1/4$ undivided interest = 40 acre mineral int.
Total interest under lease = $\overline{260}$ acre mineral int.

Oil production occurred upon Tract (3). A and B, who also owned interests in Tract (3), contended that O was entitled to only $1/4$ of $1/8$, or $1/32$, royalty in production from this tract. O, on the other hand, asserted that as the lease contained a "now or hereafter" type of entirety clause,[24] he was entitled to royalty from the well on Tract (3) equal to the sum of the interests he owned in the tracts under lease, in proportion to the entire lease, viz. $260/400 \times 1/8$, or $13/160$. Percentage-wise, A and B assert O is entitled to 3.125% of gross production as a royalty, and O asserts he is entitled to 8.125%.

The first case to deal with this type situation was the case of Thomas Gilcrease Foundation v. Stanolind Oil & Gas Co.[25] It was held that the entirety clause would apply to the different tracts owned at the time of the execution of the lease, supporting O in the above illustration. The court emphasized the portion of the clause that referred to ownership "in severalty or in separate tracts." The court stated: "But, however the term 'in severalty' may be applied in this connection we think that in purview of the 'entirety clause' under the facts here before us the ownership of petitioner is in 'separate tracts' and the words 'are now' must be given the effect of making

---

23. D.C.Colo., 201 F.Supp. 874.

24. Identical with that in note 22, supra.

25. 153 Tex. 197, 266 S.W.2d 850, noted 6 Bay.L.Rev. 323.

Strange results may occur where a lease contains a "now and hereafter" entirety clause, and the court follows the Gilcrease case. Assume that A owns two adjoining tracts of land with 80 acres each. In the west tract A owns $1/4$ of the minerals, and in the east tract A owns $3/4$ of the minerals. Under the Gilcrease case, from a well drilled under either tract, A will receive a total of $1/4 \times 1/8 \times 1/2$ from the west tract plus $3/4 \times 1/8 \times 1/2$ from the east tract. Added together this would be $1/64$ plus $3/64 = 4/64$, or $1/16$ royalty from any well.

Further assume that B owns $1/4$ of the minerals in the east tract and C owns $3/4$ of the minerals in the west tract. They also execute separate leases on their interests to the same lessee as does A.

Oil Company drills wells on both tracts, with well #1 on the west tract, and well #2 on the east tract. Total royalty payments on both tracts would be as follows:

Tract 1 (west tract)
A $1/16$ (on an entirety basis)
B   0 (does not own an interest in tract)
C $3/32$ ($3/4 \times 1/8$, on a non-apportionment basis)
     $\overline{5/32}$ total royalty

Tract 2 (east tract)
A $1/16$ (on an entirety basis)
B $1/32$ ($1/4 \times 1/8$, on a non-apportionment basis)
C $\underline{0}$ (does not own an interest in tract)
     $3/32$ total royalty

the clause applicable at the time of the execution of the lease. We have been cited no authority to the effect that ownership in different undivided interests, in segregated portions of the leased premises does not qualify as an ownership 'in separate tracts.'"

However, the opposite result has been reached in the cases of Jul-Tex Drilling Company, Inc. v. Pure Oil Co. and Ruthven & Co. v. Pan American Petroleum Corp.,[26] which rejected the Gilcrease decision.[27] In Jul-Tex the court felt that application of the entirety clause to this set of facts was essentially unfair. It also emphasized the meaning of the phrase "leased premises," stating: "The application of the entirety clause to lands embraced by the lease and subdivided at the time or subsequently, is understandable. The lessee can treat the lands as a unit and can pay royalties on a proportionate basis and thus the result is more equitable. However, there is no apparent justification for applying the clause where, as here, there are separate leases applicable to the subdivided area. Here the lease in suit, although it describes 400 acres, is effective only as to the acreage owned by the Nelsons, (O), for this reason the 'leased premises' here are not 'owned in severalty.' The leased premises include only the acreage demised in the Nelson lease, and no other. The premises demised in the Johnson and Burnham leases are not the same as the premises leased by the Nelsons, and the Nelsons are not entitled to a royalty calculated by relating their acreage to that outside their lease merely because it is part of the quarter section in which Johnson and Burnham have an interest."

The view of the Jul-Tex and Ruthven cases seems the better view, that "leased premises" relates to the interest in the minerals contained in the lease. The denominator should relate to the interest leased, not to the surface acreage covered by the lease.

Reformation has been attempted in instances where mineral deeds have been executed subsequent to an oil and gas lease containing an entirety clause and the parties to the deed did not realize the effect of the clause. In most cases reformation has been denied.[28] However, even if allowed, the further question remains whether the deed could be asserted against the lessee so as to place royalty sharing upon a

---

26. Jul-Tex Drilling Co., Inc. v. Pure Oil Co., D.C.Colo., 201 F.Supp 874, and Ruthven & Co. v. Pan American Corp., 206 Kan. 639, 482 P.2d 28.

27. See Smith v. Amerada Petroleum Corp., N.D., 136 N.W.2d 483; Stroud v. D-X Sunray Oil Co., Okl., 376 P.2d 1015, see Comment 1 Houston L.Rev. 48. In the latter case the lease contained only a "hereafter" type entirety clause, and it was held the clause had no application to the situation where tracts were owned in severalty at the time of execution of the lease. The Gilcrease case was distinguished.

28. Segelke v. Kilmer, 145 Colo. 538, 360 P.2d 423; Harley v. Magnolia Petroleum Co., 378 Ill. 19, 37 N.E.2d 760, 137 A.L.R. 900; Hafeman v. Gem Oil Co., 163 Neb. 438, 80 N.W.2d 139, noted 5 U.S. C.A.L.Rev. 555; Turner v. Brookshear, C.A.10th, 271 F.2d 761. Contra: Coyne v. Simral Corp., C.C.A.6th, 140 F.2d 574, cert. denied 323 U.S. 723, 65 S.Ct. 56, 89 L.Ed. 581.

non-apportionment basis.[29] Under the general view above discussed the answer would be in the negative.

§ 9.6 Transfers by the Lessee

In the preceding sections discussion has been directed to the post-lease transfers of the lessor. In the following sections attention will be given to some of the common transfers of the lessee. A lessee may assign the entire leasehold estate to another. He also may make an assignment of part of the lease either as to an individed interest in the lease, to certain depths only, or to particular producing formations. Any of these assignments may be to all or to a segregated part of the land covered by the lease.

The lessee may, in any of the above assignments, reserve a non-cost-bearing interest out of production, termed an "overriding royalty" interest. Such non-cost-bearing interests may be used for financing operations upon the lease, as in the case of a production payment, which is an overriding royalty interest limited in amount to a certain sum, and which may be given for materials or services. In some cases large scale financing may be acquired by execution of a mortgage on the leasehold interests of a lessee, including his reserves.

In other instances the lessee may finance operations upon the lease by means of sharing agreements, such as farmout, bottom hole, and dry hole letters. Or financing may be provided by other undivided interest owners in the lease by use of carried interest or net profit agreements, mining partnerships, or, more recently, by oil and gas syndication. Such agreements and assignments will be discussed in the following sections.

§ 9.7 Contracts to Assign Oil and Gas Leases

In virtually all jurisdictions contracts to execute leases and assignments of leases, as well as non-cost-bearing interests out of the working interest, come within the Statute of Frauds and must be in writing. Such instruments may be avoided on the ground of uncertainty where the leasehold estate is not described in full.

In nearly all jurisdictions contracts to execute oil and gas leases or to assign oil and gas leases are required to be in writing to satisfy the Statute of Frauds.[1] This generally appears to be true even where one jurisdiction would treat an oil and gas lease as personalty.[2] Not

---

29. See Segelke v. Kilmer, 145 Colo. 538, 360 P.2d 423; Turner v. Brookshear, C.A.10th, 271 F.2d 761.

1. Borden v. Case, 270 Ala. 293, 118 So.2d 751, 81 A.L.R. 982; Petroleum Exchange v. Poynter, N.D., 64 N.W.2d 718; Fagg v. Texas Co., Tex.Com.App., 57 S.W.2d 87; Tennant v. Dunn, 130 Tex. 285, 110 S.W.2d 53; Taber v. Pettus Oil & Refining Co., 139 Tex. 395, 162 S.W.2d 959, 141 A.L.R. 808; Cherry v. Salinas, Tex.Civ.App., 355 S.W.2d 833; Paine v. Moore, Tex.Civ.App., 464 S.W.2d 477.

2. See Robinson v. Smalley, 102 Kan. 842, 171 P. 1155; McKenna v. Wallis, D.C.La., 200 F.Supp. 468, affirmed C.A.5th, 366 F.2d 210.

only are oil and gas leases [3] and their assignments [4] within the Statute of Frauds, so are other interests that may be carved out of the working interest of the lessee, such as production payments,[5] overriding royalty interests,[6] carried interests,[7] etc.

The primary defect concerning the contract to execute or assign leases is found in the description of the leasehold interest to be created or assigned. In Fagg v. Texas Company,[8] which involved a suit for specific performance to execute an oil and gas lease, the contract stated, "It is further agreed and understood by both parties hereto that an 88 form lease, properly describing the surplus tract of land. * * * [was to be placed in escrow.]" The court held that the description of the lease to be executed was insufficient, stating, "The character, extent, and duration of the rights to oil and gas in place, which the proposed lessee was to acquire, constituted an essential part of the subject-matter of the agreement, and called for means of identification. The particular character of the rights which were to be acquired by the proposed lessee, or the extent or duration of such rights, is not in any wise disclosed or made ascertainable. The provision relative to 'an 88 form lease' can shed no light on those matters, for the reason that the character of printed matter contained in any designated class of oil and gas lease forms depends on what matter various designers of such forms may deem appropriate—and may vary accordingly. As we see it, the reference to 'an 88 form lease' is as incapable of definite application as if the term 'oil and gas lease form' had been used instead." This has been followed in other cases.[9]

To avoid the lease description problem in the situation of a contract to execute an oil and gas lease, a full unexecuted copy of the lease [10] to be executed should be annexed to the contract as an exhibit

3. Borden v. Case, 270 Ala. 293, 118 So.2d 751, 81 A.L.R. 982; Fagg v. Texas Co., Tex.Com.App., 57 S.W.2d 87; Cherry v. Salinas, Tex.Civ.App., 355 S.W.2d 833.

4. Petroleum Exchange Inc. v. Poynter, N.D., 64 N.W.2d 718; Taber v. Pettus Oil & Refining Co., 139 Tex. 395, 162 S.W.2d 959, 141 A.L.R. 808.

5. Tennant v. Dunn, 130 Tex. 285, 110 S.W.2d 53.

6. Robichaux v. Pool, La.App., 209 So. 2d 77; Gruss v. Cummins, Tex.Civ.App., 329 S.W.2d 496.

7. LaRue v. Wiggins, Tex.Civ.App., 277 S.W.2d 808.

8. Tex.Com.App., 57 S.W.2d 87.

9. In Taber v. Pettus Oil & Refining Co., 139 Tex. 395, 162 S.W.2d 959, 141 A.L.R. 808, a contract to assign leases was held void for uncertainty where the contract provided "It is also understood and agreed that the assignments are to be regular Texas Standard Form No. 86, properly executed," and that it was to cover "one-hundred and sixty acres of oil and gas leases," where neither the terms of the lease nor of the assignment could be ascertained at the time the memo was executed without resorting to parol evidence. Also, in Cantrell v. Garrard, Tex. Com.App., 240 S.W.533 a contract to sell "an oil and gas lease * * * what is known as a commercial lease, providing for one-eighth royalty to landowner" was held to violate the statute.

Weaver v. Farr, Tex.Civ.App., 314 S.W.2d 440 held the description insufficient to describe either the land or the lease, where they were described as, "125 acre Crank Lease, 80 acre Dorsey Lease", etc. Reference to the leases in escrow was insufficient to cure the defect.

10. It has been held that mutuality of contract is not destroyed by the fact that the lease to be assigned contains a sur-

thereto, but with all the blanks filled in, and referred to by reference in the contract. In the case of a contract to assign a lease, a complete copy of the assignment should be annexed as an exhibit in which reference should be made to the lease as recorded, including the full recording data.

A short check list of matters to be included in a contract to assign an oil and gas lease is as follows:

(a) Description of leases to be assigned and the interests purchased. The specific interest to be purchased should be specified, including a designation of how the burden of any prior outstanding interest should be borne. This is partially discussed above.

(b) Description of personal property to be purchased. Again the better approach is to annex as an exhibit copies of the bill of sale, or other title documents that will be used in closing the transaction. This not only assures that such equipment will be properly described, but forces the parties to acquire all necessary information prior to drawing up the contract. This is important, but is not practiced by all attorneys. The contract should be the evidence of a complete transaction, and not merely the basis for further negotiations.

(c) Description of the consideration. Although the contract should set forth the formula to be used, again reference may be made to the form of assignment attached to the contract, which will contain a description of any retained overriding royalty interests or production payments.

(d) Title and producing information. In this section, the attorney for the purchaser, in addition to acquiring complete supplemental abstracts down to date, should be certain to make provision for obtaining the files of the seller relating to the payment of delay rentals, production history, logs, core analysis, workover reports, etc., so that it may be determined that the lease has been kept in full force and effect from the time of execution. It should also be provided that all delay rental receipts, original title opinions, title curative files, lease operating files, abstracts and supplemental abstracts, should become the property of the purchaser upon closing.

(e) Where it is necessary that a relatively long period of time elapse from the execution of the contract to the closing of the transaction, the contract should spell out the obligations of the parties relative to keeping the lease alive during this period, such as payment of delay rentals, continuing production, etc.

(f) Where a producing lease is involved, provision should be made regarding the turning over of operations upon the closing of

---

render clause. Although the lessee can terminate his obligations under the lease, the clause has no effect upon the obligations of the parties to the contract, Alfson v. Anderson, N.D., 78 N.W.2d 693.

the transaction. As it is customary to pay accrued runs upon the 1st day of a month at 7:00 o'clock a. m., prorations will have to made to adjust this date to the date of closing.

Other matters are similar to the usual contract of sale in connection to remedies upon default, time for abstract examination and curing of title objections, pro-rata adjustments of taxes, and the escrow of an executed assignment and other instruments to a depository bank.

§ 9.8 Assignment of Oil and Gas Leases

Under the customary assignment clause found in oil and gas leases, the interest of the lessee is freely assignable. The lessee's interest in the lease may be wholly or partially assigned. A partial assignment may relate to the transfer of an undivided interest, specific depths or formations, particular products, limited parts of the lands covered by the lease, or a combination thereof.

Oil and gas leases may be transferred and assigned either in whole or in part. The oil and gas lease customarily provides that the interest of either the lessor or lessee may be assigned so long as it does not increase the burdens of the lessee.[1]

The lessee may make the following assignments:

(a) Complete assignment of the lease without reservations of any interest therein;

(b) Complete assignment of the lease with reservation of a non-cost-bearing interest such as an overriding royalty interest;

(c) Partial assignment of the lease by assignment of undivided interests;

(d) Partial assignment of the lease as to depths;

(e) Partial assignment of the lease as to products covered; or

(f) Partial assignment of the lease as to portions of the leased land.

---

1. In general, see Summers, Oil & Gas Law, §§ 541, 546, 553, 553.1, 554, 555 and 556. A common assignment provision:

"The rights of either party hereunder may be assigned in whole or in part, and the provisions hereof shall extend to their heirs, successors and assigns; but no change or division in ownership of the land, rentals or royalties, however accomplished, shall operate to enlarge the obligations or diminish the rights of Lessee; and no change or division in such ownership shall be binding on Lessee until thirty (30) days after Lessee shall have been furnished by registered U. S. mail at Lessee's principal place of business with a certified copy of recorded instrument or instruments evidencing same. In the event of assigment hereof in whole or in part, liability for breach of any obligation hereunder shall rest exclusively upon the owner of this lease or of a portion thereof who commits such breach. * * * In event of assignment of this lease as to a segregated portion of said land, the rentals payable hereunder shall be apportionable as between the several leasehold owners ratably according to the surface area of each, and default in rental payment by one shall not affect the rights of other leasehold owners hereunder."

Where the assignment is partial, it may combine one or more of elements (c) through (f), as well as the reservation of a non-cost-bearing interest.

As mentioned above, the lessee may transfer all of his interests in the lease to another, with (or without) the reservation of a non-cost-bearing interest in production. This would be the situation where Texaco, Inc. assigned all the lease to Sunoco, with a reservation of a $1/16$ of $7/8$ overriding royalty.

The lessee also may transfer undivided interests in the lease, so that the assignee and the assignor become co-tenants in the lease, e.g., Sunoco may assign half of its interest in the lease to Humble Oil and Refining Company. In this case both Sunoco and Humble would bear one-half of the costs of the development of the lease. However, a problem exists, according to the form of the assignment, as to the quantum of production each will receive, depending upon the manner in which the burden of the outstanding override of Texaco is borne.[2]

The following possibilities exist:

(1) The assignor will bear the full burden of the outstanding overriding interest, in which case Sunoco would bear one-half of the costs but receive only $49/128$ of production ($1/2$ of production attributable to the working interest *less* the $1/16$ of $7/8$ overriding royalty interest). Humble would receive $7/16$ of gross production.

(2) The converse of the above, where the assignee would bear the full burden of the outstanding overriding interest.

(3) Both assignor and assignee proportionately share the burden of the outstanding overriding royalty interest.

The above situations will be created according to the modifying language used in the assignment. Where the assignor merely assigns the interest in the lease, e.g., "an undivided one-half interest in the following described oil and gas lease," without mention of any outstanding interests, the assignor will bear the burden of such interests. This is illustrated in (1) above. However, on the other hand, if the language is modified, e.g., "an undivided one-half interest in the following described oil and gas lease, subject, however, to any outstanding overriding royalty interests or production payments," the burden of all such interests will be borne by and subtracted from the interest of the assignee.

Normally, such a broad exception of outstanding interests will not be acceptable to the parties. In the usual case the parties are cognizant of the interests outstanding, and the assignment will expressly apportion the burden of such interest upon the appropriate party. Where the assignment is of an undivided interest in the lease, the customary agreement is that all such burdens will be borne in propor-

---

2. Bass v. Harper, Tex.Civ.App., 437 S.W.2d 648, reversed Tex., 441 S.W.2d 825.

tion to the undivided interest assigned. Where this is the intent, the granting clause in the assignment should be worded appropriately, e.g., "an undivided one-half interest in and to the following described oil and gas lease, being proportionately subject, however, to the burden of the following described outstanding interests: * * *."

It should also be noted that where all interests in the lease are proportionately subject to the burden of outstanding non-cost-bearing interests, computation of each interest is greatly simplified. For example, assume that two overriding royalties are outstanding: (a) $3/32$ of $8/8$ in A; (b) $1/32$ of $8/8$ in B. For simplicity of computation all fractions are of $8/8$, rather than of $7/8$ of $8/8$ of production. In actuality most overriding royalty interests carved out of the working interest are expressed as a fraction of $7/8$ of total production. The reason that most non-cost-bearing interests are expressed as a fraction of $7/8$, is probably that the interest of the lessee, i.e., "the working interest," is *usually* $7/8$ of gross production. When the lessee agrees to convey $1/16$ of his interest to X for materials and supplies, the intention is probably to convey $1/16$ of what he receives from production under the lease, or of $7/8$. However, the only difference between $1/16$ of $7/8$ and $1/16$ of $8/8$ is that the latter is a marginally larger fraction. Normally, both are reduced to decimals for computational purposes.

It cannot be stressed too strongly that where interests are carved out of the lessee's interest, the term "working interest" should not be substituted for the exact fraction of production. Where an overriding royalty interest of $1/16$ of $7/8$ is created, a better statement of the fraction is $1/16$ of $7/8$ of $8/8$ of production. In no event should it be worded as $1/16$ of $7/8$ of the lessee's working interest, as such phrase is patently ambiguous, i.e., $1/16$ of $7/8$ of $7/8$?

Returning to the above illustration, Black-Gold Oil Company is the owner of the oil and gas lease, subject to the two stated overriding royalty interests, and a $1/8$ landowner's royalty. Black-Gold in turn conveys and assigns to Humble Oil and Refining Co. an undivided $1/4$ interest in the lease, and to Pure Oil Company an undivided $3/8$ interest in the lease. All interests are made *proportionately* subject to the burden of the outstanding interests (excluding landowner's royalty). Since all interests are proportionately subject to the outstanding interests, they may all be subtracted "off the top" of the lessee's interest in production under the lease. The total of the two interests outstanding is $4/32$ of $8/8$. Therefore, the lessee's interest after subtraction of such interests is $7/8$ less $4/32$, or $28/32 - 4/32 = 24/32$. In this the owners of the lessee's interest under the lease will share as follows:

		Share of production	Share of cost
Humble	$1/4$ x $24/32$ =	$6/32$	$1/4$
Pure	$3/8$ x $24/32$ =	$9/32$	$3/8$
Black-Gold	$3/8$ x $24/32$ =	$9/32$	$3/8$
		$24/32$	100%

As can be seen, this is a much easier method of calculation than calculating each interest individually, i. e., Humble: $1/4$ of $7/8 - 1/4$ ($3/32$ of $8/8 + 1/32$ of $8/8$) etc. This is especially true where numerous interests are outstanding and decimal equivalents of such interests must be used.

As mentioned above, assignments of oil and gas leases may be partial assignments in matters other than undivided interests in the lease. Such assignments may be partial or limited as to the formations or depths covered by the assignments,[3] to particular products,[4] or to only part of the lands covered by the lease.

Where the assignment is limited as to depth, care must be exercised as to the manner in which the depth limitation is set forth. Although it is customary to find depths limited to particular named producing formations, such as "to the bottom of the Woodbine sand," the designation by relation to a named formation would seem subject to uncertainty at best, and may lead to litigation concerning what sand the producer is completed in. However, if a particular depth limitation is to be expressed in feet below the surface of the ground, engineering studies should be made to insure that all of the intended formation is included in the designation. If this is not possible, designation by formation name may still be preferable, although it may lead to litigation, as stated above.

In one case [5] the assignment was of certain leases "insofar as said leases cover producing horizons above a depth of 4000 feet." It was held that the assignee owned all of a formation where any part of it extended above 4000 feet, and that the assignor had no right to produce from such formation below 4000 feet. The court also stated that although the assignor was a trespasser in good faith, he was not entitled to recoupment of costs. The wells of assignor conferred no benefit upon the assignee, as the assignee could completely produce the oil from these formations from higher wells. The case has been criticized. The assignment should have assigned the leases "down to a depth of 4000 feet below the ground, said depth being measured from the derrick floor."

Although a warranty clause is not usually found in lease assignments, many times being expressly negated, the purchaser of producing leases should consider the use of a comprehensive warranty. A sample clause is set forth below.[6]

---

3. Hanlin v. Westhoma Oil Co., C.A.10th, 291 F.2d 726; Ascher v. Mid-States Oil Corp., 222 La. 812, 64 So.2d 182; Joyce v. Wyant, D.C.Mich., 105 F.Supp. 979, affirmed 202 F.2d 863; Palmer Oil Corp. v. Phillips Petroleum Co., 204 Okl. 543, 231 P.2d 997; Carter Oil Co. v. McCasland, C.A.10th, 190 F.2d 887.

4. See: Arrington v. El Paso Natural Gas Co., D.C.Okl., 233 F.Supp. 522; Cain v. Neumann, Tex.Civ.App., 316 S.W.2d 915.

5. Carter Oil Co. v. McCasland, C.A.10th, 190 F.2d 887.

6. TO HAVE AND TO HOLD the above described property, interests and rights unto the said Assignee, together with all and singular, the rights and appurtenances thereto in anywise belonging, forever; and Assignors do hereby bind themselves, their heirs, administra-

§ 9.9 Creation of Non-Cost-Bearing Interests From the Lessee's Interest

Two general types of non-cost-bearing interests may be carved out of the lessee's interest. The first is an overriding royalty interest, a continuing interest in production throughout the life of the lease. The other is the production payment, which is limited in amount and which may be payable from production of particular products.

In many instances non-cost-bearing interests are carved from the interest of the lessee. They are non-cost bearing as they do not bear any part of cost or expense of development or operation. Such interests may be designated as overriding royalty interests, or may be limited in amount to a certain sum. In the latter case they are usually designated as production payments, although earlier usage was to refer to the particular product out of which the sum was payable, e.g., oil payment.

The production payment is merely a limited overriding royalty, and in those jurisdictions where royalty is treated as an interest in realty, such designation usually applies to the non-cost-bearing interests carved out of the lessee's interest.[1] Overriding royalty interests are used many times to compensate for the acquisition of a lease. A acquires a lease upon Blackacre for Pure Oil Company. Upon assignment of the lease to Pure, an overriding royalty interest is reserved in A. Pure, upon a later complete or partial assignment of the lease,

---

tors, executors, successors and assigns, to the extent hereinafter indicated, to warrant and forever defend all and singular, the said property interests and rights unto the said Assignee, his heirs and assigns, against every person whomsoever claiming or to claim the same or any part thereof, and, without limitation on the foregoing, Assignors, and each of them, warrant (1) that they are the lawful owners of the above described three oil, gas and mineral leases, and each of them, and all rights, titles, interests and estates thereunder, (2) that the net leasehold estate herein conveyed (after deduction of all the outstanding interests) consists of not less than three-fourths ($^3/_4$ths) of eight-eighths ($^8/_8$ths) of all of the oil, gas and other minerals, in, to, under and that may be produced from the said leases and each of them, land described in said oil, gas and mineral leases, have been paid, (3) that all rentals and royalties payable under the leases have been paid in full, (4) that each of said leases is in full force and effect and is a valid and subsisting oil, gas and mineral lease against the hereinabove described land, (5) that Assignors and each of them, have good right and authority to sell and convey the same, and (6) that said leases and mineral leasehold estates and each of them, herein described, are free from any overriding royalties or production payments, liens, encumbrances or claims of any type or character.

1. See Davis v. Lewis, 187 Okl. 91, 100 P.2d 994; Tennant v. Dunn, 130 Tex. 285, 110 S.W.2d 53; Walker, Oil Payments, 20 Tex.L.Rev. 259. Overriding royalty interests are varied. A common variation is that of a convertible override. The owner of the override generally has an option to convert it to a stated percentage of the working interest after working interest owners have recovered costs and expenses of developing and drilling a well. This is also called a "back-in." For an example see Energy Oils, Inc. v. Montana Power Co., C.A.9th, 626 F.2d 731.

Another variation of the overriding royalty interest is a "net profits" interest. Here the amount of the production payable to the owner of the interest is based upon the net profits formula contained in the instrument. Commonly, only the term "net profits" is used, which raises questions of what expenses may be deducted to determine net profits.

or of an interest in the lease, may desire to retain a continuing interest in production as partial compensation for the assignment.

The limited overriding royalty interest, or production payment, is customarily used as a device for repayment of a loan or for payment for goods and services rendered. In some instances it is also used as a device for limited additional compensation for an assignment of a lease. Normally, the production payment differs from security for a debt, as no personal obligation exists to pay the stated sum where the wells do not have sufficient production to pay out,[2] and no lien is created upon the property as security for the stated sum.[3] However, in some cases the instruments have been drawn so as to create an absolute liability in addition to the production payment.[4]

Following is a list of matters to be considered in the drafting of an overriding royalty or production payment, some of which are discussed below:

(1) Define the fraction from which it is payable;

(2) Define the minerals from which it is payable;

(3) State costs, if any, to be borne by the interest;

(4) Attachment of the interest to renewal leases;

(5) Effect of the proportionate reduction clause on the interest;

(6) Effect of the implied covenants of the lessee;

(7) Limitations upon depth or formations, etc.;

(8) Graduated, sliding scale, or conversion provisions;

(9) Effect of the pooling of the lease;

(10) Warranty, quitclaim etc.;

(11) Effective date of instrument.

(A) Definition of Fraction

As in the case of all interests carved out of the lessee's interest, care must be used in defining the fraction or quantum of interest. Pure Oil Co. assigns to A an overriding royalty of $1/16$. Consider the following statements of interest:

(a) $1/16$ out of the lessee's $7/8$ interest;

(b) $1/16$ out of $7/8$;

(c) $1/16$ out of $7/8$ working interest;

(d) $1/16$ out of $7/8$ leasehold.

In each instance the statement of the interest is ambiguous. In all four cases the interest is susceptible of two constructions: (1) that

---

2. Prince Brothers Drilling Co. v. Fuhrman Petroleum Corp., Tex.Civ.App., 150 S.W.2d 314.

3. But see National Bank of Tulsa v. Warren, 177 Kan. 281, 279 P.2d 262; Davis v. Lewis, 187 Okl. 91, 100 P.2d 994.

4. Danciger Oil & Refining Co. of Texas v. Powell, 137 Tex. 484, 154 S.W.2d 632, 137 A.L.R. 408.

the interest is a full $1/16$ interest (or $8/128$) and is merely payable out of the lessee's interest; or (2) that the quantum of the interest is of the lessee's interest under the lease, and not of full production, i.e., $1/16 \times 7/8 = 7/128$. In both (c) and (d), an additional interpretation may be made that the interest is equal to $1/16 \times 7/8 \times 7/8 = 49/1008$. This is due to the fact that the terms "working interest" and "leasehold estate" have a common meaning as the right to $7/8$ of production. Since the fraction $7/8$ and the particular phrase both appear in the clause it might be assumed by some that both be given effect. Therefore, it is necessary that the draftsman define the fraction precisely. If it is the intent that a full $1/16$ interest be created the clause should read, "'$1/16$ of $8/8$ of production," or, "'$1/16$ of gross production." If the lesser interest, the phrase may read, "'$1/16$ of $7/8$ of $8/8$ of production," or, "'$1/16$ of $7/8$ of gross production."

An additional problem will occur where the lease from which the non-cost-bearing interest is created does not cover the full interest in the minerals. In the above illustration assume that the lease of Pure Oil Company covers only a one-half interest in the minerals. Two constructional problems occur. The first is whether the proportionate reduction clause in the lease applies to reduce the overriding royalty or production payment in proportion to the interest under lease. However, by the lease terms the proportionate reduction clause applies only to interests created under the lease.

The second problem is just the converse of the first. Where the non-cost-bearing interest is created under the $1/2$ interest lease of Pure above, will it be automatically reduced in amount, due to the drafting of the assignment? It is the normal practice to tie the non-cost-bearing interest to the lease from which it is created. In the above illustration Pure drafts the following clause:

"* * * an overriding royalty of $1/16$ of $7/8$ of $8/8$ of all of the oil, gas and other minerals *produced and saved under and by virtue of said lease.*"

Query: As the lease covers only half of the minerals, does the non-cost-bearing interest refer only to the half mineral interest under the lease? Under some authority it would seem that the answer is yes, and that the overriding royalty interest created is only a $1/32$.[5]

To protect against either undesired result a clause should be inserted into the instrument providing that the non-cost-bearing interest will or will not be reduced, regardless of the interest under lease. Also a further provision may be inserted to deal with the effect of failure of title to the lease interest:

"Although it is believed that the net mineral interest in the said lease owned by the Assignor amounts to not less than a 0.875000 working interest, if by reason of failure of title in whole

---

5. Cf. Fry v. Farm Bureau Oil Co., 3 Ill.2d 94, 119 N.E.2d 749; Whitten v. Daws, 226 Miss. 96, 83 So.2d 744, and Oldland v. Gray, C.A.10th, 179 F.2d 408, and see Whitson Co. v. Bluff Creek Oil Co., 156 Tex. 139, 293 S.W.2d 488.

or in part, or for any other reason, the net mineral leasehold interest actually acquired by Assignor in said lease should be less than the interests hereinabove set forth, then the overriding royalty interest herein assigned to Assignee shall not be reduced in amount as hereinabove set forth."

Where it is desired that the overriding royalty be reduced the phrase may be changed to read, "then the overriding royalty interest herein assigned to Assignee shall bear its proportionate part of such loss and shall be reduced proportionately." Where a partial interest lease is assigned and it is desired that the interest not be reduced due to title loss, recitations in the above clause should be changed appropriately.

(B) Costs to Be Borne

Overriding royalty interests and production payments have been defined as non-cost-bearing interests, in that they normally do not bear any part of costs of development and production.[6] However, they usually bear the burden of production and severance taxes unless expressly negated. Where there is a possibility of gas production, the owner of the cost-bearing interest may wish to consider whether such non-cost-bearing interests should bear their proportionate part of costs incident to marketing, such as costs of dehydration, compression, and transportation to the market. Where the amount of such non-cost-bearing interest outstanding is relatively large, the bearing of the entire burden of such costs may be distinctly disadvantageous to the lessee.

(C) Extent of Production From Which Paid and Minerals Covered

As in the case of royalty payments under the lease, the careful draftsman will define both the minerals that are subject to the override or production payment and the production from which they are payable, e.g., "saved, marketed, or used off the premises," and the same problems of construction will apply.[7]

(D) Graduated, Sliding Scale, or Conversion Provisions

Where the wells to which the non-cost-bearing interest relate enjoy good production with minimal costs for re-working and repairs, outstanding non-cost-bearing interest may be borne by the owners of the working interest with a minimum of economic burden. However, most wells, after a time, become more costly to operate. At this time outstanding non-cost-bearing interests may make the wells unprofitable to operate. To avoid this result, draftsmen have created sliding

---

6. In the creation of the interests it is usually stated they are "free of all costs and expense." Cf. Cities Service Oil v. McCrory, Tex.Civ.App., 191 S.W.2d 791; and Stanolind Oil & Gas Co. v. Terrell, Tex.Civ.App., 183 S.W.2d 743.

7. See Chapter 7, supra.

scale overriding interests. That is to say that when production falls below a certain point the non-cost-bearing interest will convert to a smaller fraction, e.g., an overriding interest of $^1/_{16}$ of $^7/_8$ of gross production will be reduced to a $^1/_{32}$ of $^7/_8$ of gross production. Many problems have been encountered in drafting such provisions: (a) definition of the event upon which the non-cost-bearing interest will be reduced;[8] (b) whether the interest will again be increased when costs are reduced;[9] (c) whether reduction of such interests will be upon the basis of each well, or upon the basis of all wells on the lease;[10] (d) the average period over which such production should be measured;[11] (e) minerals covered;[12] etc. It appears to be the present trend that sliding scale or graduated overriding royalty interests are being replaced by interests that convert to cost-bearing working interests when costs rise to a certain point.

(E) *Implied Covenants*

Although uncertainty of opinion exists,[13] under current case law covenants for protection of non-cost-bearing interests are probably implied. For this reason, the assignee of the non-cost-bearing interest, if desired, should attempt to include a clause in the assignment that the implied covenants of the lessee will also run to the owner, successors and assigns, of the overriding royalty or production payment. Likewise, where no such covenants are intended, they should be expressly negated in the assignment.

(F) *Effective Date*

In order to comply with the bookkeeping systems of most oil companies, the change of ownership should be made effective as of the beginning of runs on the 1st day of the next succeeding month at

---

8. Agey v. Barnard, Tex.Civ.App., 123 S.W.2d 484; Johnston v. Cole, Tex.Civ. App., 135 S.W.2d 524; Ferguson v. Housh, Tex.Civ.App., 227 S.W.2d 590.

9. Midas Oil Co. v. Whitaker, Tex.Civ. App., 123 S.W.2d 495; Exum v. Laub, C.C.A.5th, 87 F.2d 73.

10. Butler v. Jenkins Oil Corp., 128 Tex. 356, 97 S.W.2d 466; Midas Oil Co. v. Whitaker, Tex.Civ.App., 123 S.W.2d 495; Exum v. Laub, C.C.A.5th, 87 F.2d 73.

11. McLachlan v. Stroube, Tex.Civ. App., 324 S.W.2d 279; Exum v. Laub, C.C.A.5th, 87 F.2d 73; Kingwood Oil Co. v. Loehr, C.A.5th, 200 F.2d 551.

12. Butler v. Jenkins Oil Corp., 128 Tex. 356, 97 S.W.2d 466.

Wahlenmaier v. American Quasar, Tex. Civ.App., 517 S.W.2d 390 (royalty to be $^1/_8$ when production exceeded 350 barrels, $^1/_{16}$ when under. On gas produced, held "barrels" not ambiguous and applied only to oil production. Could not include gas production on basis of barrels of equivalent liquified gas).

13. Although some decisions find no implication of implied covenants to non-cost-bearing interest owners upon assignment of a lease, McNeil v. Peaker, 253 Ark. 747, 488 S.W.2d 706; Henderson Co. v. Murphy, 189 Ark. 87, 70 S.W.2d 1036; Kile v. Amerada Petroleum Corp., 118 Okl. 176, 247 P. 681; the trend of authority seems increasingly to recognize such implied covenants: Cook v. El Paso Natural Gas Co., C.A.10th, 560 F.2d 978; Phillips Petroleum Co. v. Taylor, C.C.A.5th, 116 F.2d 994; Cole Petroleum Co. v. United States Gas & Oil Co., 121 Tex. 59, 41 S.W.2d 414, 86 A.L.R. 719; Bolton v. Coats, Tex., 533 S.W.2d 914; Wes-Tex Land Co. v. Simmons, Tex.Civ.App., 566 S.W.2d 719.

seven o'clock a.m. Where change of ownership is made as to a producing interest upon an interim date, an appropriate accounting must be made by the parties.

(G) Mortgage Upon Oil and Gas Interests

In many instances the lessee, in order to raise capital with which to develop oil and gas properties, obtains a loan secured by lien upon producing leases.[14] The bank or financing institution will make an independent appraisal of the reserves of the producing leases, and the amount of the loan will be based upon this estimate. Although such transactions may be of varying complexity, some comment may be made as to inclusion of provisions in a simple mortgage of such properties. Such provisions would include the following:

(1) An adequate description of the oil and gas leases and the working interest owned by the mortgagor, as well as an adequate description of all personal property and fixtures included on the lease. The mortgage should contain an after-acquired property clause and a future indebtedness clause.

(2) Full covenants of the mortgagor as to all matters necessary to keep the leases in full force and effect.

(3) Full warranty as to the interests conveyed under each lease; that each lease is in full force and effect; and that no liens have attached to the leases.

(4) A requirement that the mortgagor furnish monthly reports of runs and production for the property, as well as reports of monthly expenses for operating and development costs.

(5) Covenants that the mortgagor will continuously operate the leases in accordance with the best usage and custom in the field, insofar as a reasonably prudent operator would do so.

(6) Mortgage should be filed both as a mortgage on realty and as a fixture filing under the Uniform Commercial Code.

(7) Although many mortgages contain a general clause relating to assignments of rights of the mortgagor to the mortgagee, such clauses in lien-theory jurisdictions are not effective until after default or foreclosure. Therefore, such clauses are unsatisfactory as a means of assuring that a present assignment of runs will be applied to the secured indebtedness. It is therefore necessary to include an express assignment of runs. An illustrative example of such provision follows:

---

14. Also see Chapter 5, § 5.6, dealing with oil and gas leases on lands subject to security interests.

ASSIGNMENT OF PRODUCTION

"As further security for the payment of the indebtedness secured hereby, Grantor has TRANSFERRED, ASSIGNED and CONVEYED, and does hereby TRANSFER, ASSIGN and CONVEY unto said Bank, hereinafter sometimes called 'Bank', its successors and assigns, all oil, gas, casinghead gas, distillate and other minerals, and the proceeds therefrom, produced and to be produced, from the interests of Grantor in the leases, properties and interests above described, from and after the first (1st) day of _____, at seven (7:00) o'clock a. m., and Grantor hereby authorizes and empowers the said Bank, and its successors and assigns, to demand, collect and receive said oil, gas, casinghead gas, distillate and other minerals, and the proceeds therefrom, produced and to be produced from the interests of Grantor in said properties, and to execute any release, receipt, division order, transfer order and relinquishment or other instrument that may be required or necessary to collect and receive such production or the proceeds therefrom; and Grantor hereby authorizes and directs all pipeline companies, gathering companies and others purchasing production from said properties above described or having in their possession any production from said properties, or the proceeds therefrom, to pay and deliver to Bank, its successors and assigns, all such production or proceeds therefrom accruing; and Grantor agrees that all division orders, transfer orders, receipts and other instruments which the said Bank or its successors or assigns may from time to time execute and deliver for the purposes of collection or receipting for such production or the proceeds therefrom may be relied upon in all respects and that the same shall be binding upon Grantor and Grantor's heirs, legal representatives, successors and assigns. Grantor agrees to execute and deliver all necessary, convenient and appropriate instruments, including transfer and division orders, which may be required in connection with the receipt of such production or the proceeds therefrom by said Bank or its successors or assigns and to indemnify and keep and hold harmless said Bank and its successors and assigns from all parties whomsoever having or claiming an adverse interest in said leases, properties and interests and the production and proceeds therefrom and in this respect agrees to pay all expenses, costs, charges and reasonable attorney's fees which may be incurred by the said Bank or by its successors or assigns, as to any of said matters.

"The proceeds actually received by the Bank or by any of its successors or assigns from the production from Grantor's interests in said properties may be held by said Bank or by its successors or assigns and applied first to the payment of all accrued interest on the above note and any other indebtedness secured hereby and then to the payment of the principal of such note and other indebtedness owing by Grantor to said Bank or to its successors or assigns in such production or the proceeds therefrom upon the indebtedness secured hereby, the payment of such proceeds to the said Bank or its successors or assigns by such pipeline company, gathering company or other person receiving, handling or purchasing such production shall operate as a full and final discharge of all liability of such pipeline company, gathering company or other person in the premises."

§ 9.10 Divisibility of Covenants

A covenant is said to be indivisible where the compliance with the covenant as to one segregated tract under a lease is also compliance as to all tracts under the lease.

A covenant is said to be divisible where, in such situation, compliance or failure to comply affects only the particular segregated tract, without effect upon the other tracts subject to the lease.

The habendum clause and modifying clauses are treated as indivisible in most jurisdictions, Louisiana being an exception. The delay rental clause is normally made divisible under the provisions of the modern lease. Opinion differs whether implied covenants of the lessee are divisible or indivisible.

As is discussed elsewhere,[1] the lessee is obligated upon certain covenants which run to the lessor, and perhaps to other owners of non-possessory interests in the minerals. These covenants may be expressed in the lease, such as the duty to drill, to discover or produce in paying quantities at the end of the primary term of the lease, and to pay delay rentals, or may be implied, such as the obligation to further develop when paying production is encountered, protect against unreasonable drainage, etc. Where only one tract of land is subject to or covered by the lease, each covenant relates to the entire tract; however, where the lease covers more than one tract of land, a problem arises whether satisfaction of any particular covenant as to a particular tract will also satisfy the lease as to all tracts under the lease. Although such separation of tracts can come about by partial assignment of the lease, it may also be due to the fact that the lease as originally drawn covers more than one tract of land.

By way of illustration: Lessor owns tracts (1) and (2) and executes one lease upon both tracts of land. Although they are in the same vicinity they are separated somewhat by other lands. The lessee drills a producing well upon tract (1) but does not drill any wells upon tract (2). At the end of the primary term is the lease kept in effect upon both tracts of land, or only upon tract (1)? The same question may be asked if the tracts were adjoining, or where only one tract was described in the lease and lessee later executed an assignment upon the west $\frac{1}{2}$ to another lessee who drilled the producing well. In each of these cases, does the extension of the primary term pertain

---

1. See § 9.9 supra, and Chapter 8.

only to the tract upon which the well was drilled, or does it satisfy the habendum clause as to all lands covered by the lease?

If the well satisfies only the covenant as to the tract upon which it is drilled, the covenant is said to be divisible, or divided as to each separate tract under the lease. That is to say, that satisfaction of the covenant, or the consequences of failure to satisfy the covenant, pertains to each tract separately. In effect it is the same as if there were a separate lease on each separate tract. In the above illustration, if the covenant is treated as divisible the lease would be kept alive only as to the tract upon which the well was drilled and would lapse as to all other land described in the lease. If treated as indivisible the well would keep the lease alive after the primary term as to all of the lands described.

It appears to be the general rule that the habendum clause, and modifying clauses of the habendum clause such as the well completion, continuous drilling, shut-in royalty, and dry hole clauses, are treated as being indivisible,[2] although Louisiana reaches a contrary result.[3] Under the terms of the customary lease, the delay rental clause is divisible, due to the provisions of the express clause allowing assignments, which states that delay rentals must be paid separately as to each tract after assignment. Diversity of opinion exists as to whether implied covenants are indivisible or divisible.

(A) Habendum Clause and Modifying Clauses

As stated above, it is the general view that the habendum clause, fixing the term of the lease, is indivisible. If a well is drilled any place upon the lease, it will satisfy the habendum clause as to all land covered by the lease. O leases 640 acres of land to Rex Oil Company, and Rex assigns the lease as to a certain 150 acres to Pure Oil Company. When Pure later drills a well producing in paying quantities, the entire 640 acres will be held by the well.

Where large acreage is involved, the lessor often will insert a clause that severs a specified amount of the acreage from the rest of the lease and which will be kept alive by operations. In the above example, if 4000 acres had been leased, the lessor could have provided that only 300 acres could be maintained by each producing well.

---

2. Cowman v. Phillips Petroleum Co., 142 Kan. 762, 51 P.2d 988; Gypsy Oil Co. v. Cover, 78 Okl. 158, 189 P. 540; Sinclair Prairie Oil Co. v. Campbell, C.C.A.5th, 164 F.2d 907; Berry v. Tide Water Association Oil Co., C.A.5th, 188 F.2d 820; Harris v. Michael, 70 W.Va. 356, 73 S.E. 934. Cf. Nafco Oil & Gas, Inc. v. Tartan Resources Corp., Tex.Civ.App., 522 S.W.2d 703 (habendum clause expressly made divisible).

3. Roberson v. Pioneer Gas. Co., 173 La. 313, 137 So. 46, 82 A.L.R. 1264; Noel Estate, Inc. v. Murray, 223 La. 387, 65 So.2d 886; Eota Realty Co. v. Carter Oil Co., 225 La. 790, 74 So.2d 30.

It is uncertain whether the Louisiana Mineral Code, La.R.S. 31:130, would change this result. The express provision so states, but the comment explains that the purpose is to preserve established law.

Any acts that will satisfy the habendum clause under the lease terms will also serve to perpetuate the entire lease. In the above example where Pure drilled the 150-acre tract, the drilling could have resulted in a shut-in gas well. The payment of shut-in gas well rentals is a contractual substitute for production.[4] This being so, such payment will not only satisfy the habendum clause as to the 150-acre tract, but also as to the balance of acreage under the lease. The same result would be reached if Pure had pooled the 150 acres with the like acreage from any other lease into a 300-acre gas unit, and a producing gas well were drilled upon the other 150-acre tract. Contractually, under the pooling clause, production any place on a unit is treated as production from all lands covered by the unit. Therefore, unit production is also production from Pure's 150 acres. As this satisfies the habendum clause as to the 150 acres, it will do so for the entire 640 acres and keep the whole Rex lease alive.

The principle is the same whether the habendum clause is satisfied by production, substitutes for production, or other modifying clauses in the lease. Assume in the above example that at the end of the primary term[5] Pure had a well drilling on its 150-acre tract and completed it after the end of the primary term, under the well completion clause of the lease. Since this clause modifies and satisfies the habendum clause as to the 150 acres, it does so for all the land under the lease.

It has been indicated that such result will occur where the operations are done on other unit lands in a unit. Alluding again to the 300-acre gas unit above, assume that the operator is drilling a well on unit lands, but not Pure's 150 acres, at the end of the primary term of Pure's lease. The well comes in dry, but within the continuous operation time stated in Pure's lease, operator begins another unit well on other unit lands that results in a shut-in gas well capable of producing in paying quantities. Shut-in royalties are timely paid. It is submitted that such operations are imputed to Pure's portion of the lease by virtue of the pooling clause. Since they satisfy the habendum clause of Pure's lease, the entire 640 acres have been held (in absence of a contractual or statutory "Pugh" clause).[6]

Where one is obtaining a partial assignment of an oil and gas lease and the base lease is past the primary term, it will be necessary to determine that sufficient production timely occurred to perpetuate the lease and has done so continually up to the time of the assignment. If no clause is present in the base lease limiting the indivisibility of the habendum clause, assignee may safely rely upon such production as also maintaining the lease as to the assigned portions, unless a different view obtains in the particular jurisdiction.

4. Berry v. Tide Water Association Oil Co., C.A.5th, 188 F.2d 820.

5. See Chapter 6, supra.

6. See Sunac Petroleum Corp. v. Parkes, Tex., 416 S.W.2d 798; Skelly Oil Co. v. Harris, 163 Tex. 92, 352 S.W.2d 950. Also see § 7.13(D), supra, for a discussion of the "Pugh" clause.

(B) Delay Rentals

Under most of the express clauses dealing with assignment of the lease, it is provided that upon assignment of the lease as to a segregated portion of the land, the payment of rentals will be apportioned according to the ownership of surface area of the lands covered by the lease, and failure of one owner to pay will not affect the rights of the other owners.[7] The clause therefore makes the payment of delay rentals divisible as to the separate ownership of tracts of land under lease.

By way of illustration: A leases 640 acres of land to Texaco, Inc. Texaco thereafter assigns the lease as to the south one-half of the land to Black-Gold Oil Company. Delay rentals are $640 per year. Texaco, Inc. timely pays $320 to A, and Black-Gold does not. The result under the clause is that the lease goes out as to the Black-Gold tract, but remains in effect as to the Texaco, Inc. tract. This result may be contrasted with the conveyance of an undivided one-half interest in the 640 acres by Texaco, Inc. to Black-Gold. In this event the clause does not cover the assignment, and the duty to pay delay rentals is treated as being indivisible. Hence, if Texaco, Inc. pays its portion of the delay rentals, but Black-Gold does not, the entire lease will terminate.

The clause may relate to ownership of undivided interests in one of the segregated tracts. Under the above illustration, where Black-Gold acquires assignment of the lease as to the south one-half of the land, it may in turn assign undivided interests in the lease as to such tract to an investment group, e.g., C, D, and E. Although payment of delay rentals is treated separately as to both the north and south tracts, all delay rentals must be paid as to each segregated tract. As to the south one-half, it is not sufficient that Black-Gold or any particular member of the investment group pay merely its particular portion of the delay rentals. The total $320 must be paid. For this reason, where the leasehold estate, or a portion of it, is held in undivided interests by several persons, either as operators or non-operators, it is customary that one member of the group, usually the operator, have the responsibility to pay the entire delay rental obligation on the tract, subject to reimbursement from the other owners.[8]

---

7. "In event of assignment of this lease as to a segregated portion of said land, the rentals payable hereunder shall be apportionable as between the several leasehold owners ratably according to the surface area of each, and default in rental payment by one shall not affect the rights of other leasehold owners hereunder. If six or more parties become entitled to royalty hereunder, Lessee may withhold payment thereof unless and until furnished with a recordable instrument executed by all such parties designating an agent to receive payment for all." See: Armstrong v. McGough, 157 Ark. 173, 247 S.W. 790, 29 A.L.R. 236; Hitson v. Gilman, Tex.Civ.App., 220 S.W. 140.

8. Hyaldahl v. Alphin, 176 Ark. 1176, 290 S.W. 44; Broyles v. Gilman, Tex.Civ. App., 222 S.W. 685. However, it is customary that such agreement be in writing and provide for contribution from the other parties. It is probable that under such agreement an equitable lien would

The assignment clause pertaining to the divisibility of delay rental payments is inadequate in the event of partial assignments of the lease where such assignments result in horizontal rather than vertical severances of the leasehold estate. For instance, what is the delay rental obligation of Black-Gold where it assigns the lease as to all depths from 5000 feet below the ground, downward? Or where it is assigned a particular producing formation? The lease clause simply does not apply. Where no production exists upon the lease, or is not contemplated prior to the next rental payment date, it would appear that the entire rental must be paid, and the proportions bearable by each party would be subject to agreement.

(C) Divisibility of Implied Covenants

Diversity of opinion exists whether, upon assignment of the lease as to segregated portions, implied covenants are to be treated as divisible or indivisible.[9] For simplification, the discussion is addressed to the implied covenant to protect against drainage and the implied covenant to further develop. It would appear that from the nature of the covenant to protect against drainage, pragmatically, such covenant would be divisible. Although the covenant itself is applicable to the entire leasehold, the duty to drill an offset well on a segregated tract does not arise unless that particular tract is threatened with drainage.[10] Where other segregated tracts within the same leasehold are not threatened with drainage, there is no duty to drill an offset well to protect them.

The duty to reasonably develop, however, originally exists as to the entire lease acreage. The leading case cited for the proposition that implied covenants are divisible is Cosden Oil Co. v. Scarborough.[11] In this case some 10,254 acres of land were leased, and the lease as to some 400 acres was assigned to defendant. Some production having been found on the lease, lessor took the position that each assignee must independently develop his own holdings. The lease contained an extended clause relating to assignment, which did not expressly cover implied covenants. The court reversed a lower court decision decreeing partial cancellation, on the ground that the facts arise against the leasehold interests of the parties for whose benefit the payments were made. Also see Merrill, The Partial Assignee—Done in Oil, 20 Tex.L. Rev. 298.

9. See Summers, Oil & Gas Law, §§ 513, 516; Brown, Assignments of Interests in Oil & Gas Leases, Farmout Agreements, Bottom-Hole Letters, Reservations of Overrides and Oil Payments, Southwestern Legal Foundation Fifth Annual Institute in Oil and Gas Law and Taxation; Williams and Meyers, Oil and Gas Law, § 409; Lesar, Divisibility of Covenants in Oil and Gas Leases, 25 Ky. L.J. 142. As to implied covenants generally, see Chapter 8, supra.

10. See Lindow v. Southern Carbon Co., D.C.La., 5 F.Supp. 818. No obligation to maintain inside offsets against internal drainage should result from assignment of segregated portions of the lease. No such obligation existed as to the lease as a whole and such result is contrary to the usual lease provision that partial assignment of the lease will not increase the lessee's burdens thereunder.

11. C.C.A.5th, 55 F.2d 634.

did not support a finding that the implied obligation to develop had been breached. However, the court stated that the covenant to reasonably develop was divisible and related to each assigned tract separately.

The rationale for this holding, seemingly, is found in the intention of the parties, as reflected in the assignment clause, that assigned acreage be treated separately. However, the court stated its holding categorically: "There is ample authority for the view we take that the lease is indivisible as to the fixing of the term; divisible as to the implied covenant to develop. It accords with reason and common sense. In taking it, however, we take it not partially but fully. That is, we find that as assignee, after production of oil has terminated the obligation to pay rentals and had fixed in the original lessee and his assigns a determinable fee, stands as to the tract that he owns in the same position with reference to due diligence as his assignor stands to the tract retained, obligated to the same extent and no more, to do further development." Although other cases have followed this view,[12] substantial authority exists to the contrary, that the implied covenant to further develop is indivisible.[13]

Where the viewpoint is taken that the implied covenant to further develop is indivisible, it will be necessary for the lessor, as part of his burden of proof, to show that the lease as a whole has not been reasonably developed. Where the covenant is treated as divisible, the lessor would have to maintain such burden of proof only as to the tract assigned. But, where each tract is treated, in effect, as subject to an independent lease, should the duty to further develop exist where no production is from the separate tract? Where the covenant is viewed as indivisible, nearby production on other portions of the lease would be available for such proof.

In view of the indecisiveness of the authorities, something may be said for treating the implied covenant of further development as being divisible. Where different lessees own the lease to certain portions of the land, why should they not be burdened with separate obligations as to the tracts in which they own the leasehold interest? On the other hand, no clear authority exists for such a conclusion. Later Texas decisions diminish the authority of Cosden.[14] Although the customary assignment clause clearly divides the obligation to pay de-

---

12. Standard Oil Co. of Louisiana v. Giller, 183 Ark. 776, 38 S.W.2d 766; Alphin v. Gulf Refining Co., D.C.Ark., 39 F.Supp. 570; American Wholesale Corp. v. F. & S. Oil & Gas Co., 242 Ky. 356, 46 S.W.2d 498; Dixon v. Anadarko Production Co., Okl., 505 P.2d 1394; Cox v. Sinclair Gulf Oil Co., Tex.Civ.App., 265 S.W. 196; Sinclair Oil & Gas Co. v. Bryan, Tex.App., 291 S.W. 692; Atwood v. Humble Oil & Refining Co., C.A.5th, 338 F.2d 502, cert. denied 381 U.S. 926, 85 S.Ct. 1562, 14 L.Ed. 684.

13. Hughes v. Cordell, 174 Ark. 757, 296 S.W. 735; Greenwood v. Texas-Interstate Pipeline Co., 143 Kan. 686, 56 P.2d 431; Worrell v. Parsons, 133 Okl. 61, 271 P. 155; Galt v. Metscher, 103 Okl. 271, 229 P. 522; Duke v. Stewart, Tex.Civ. App., 230 S.W. 485; Dacamara v. Binney, Tex.Civ.App., 146 S.W.2d 440.

14. See Dacamara v. Binney, Tex.Civ. App., 146 S.W.2d 440.

lay rentals, it does not do so as to other obligations, either express or implied. The court in the Cosden case sees no reason why some of the lessee's obligations should not be divisible while others are nondivisible; however, the question may also be asked, "Unless so stated in the lease why should they not be treated consistently?" Does not the application of a divisibility approach change the obligation of the lessee, where the original obligation applied to the lease as a whole? Furthermore, the assignment clause usually expresses a general intent that assignment of the lease should not increase the burdens of the lessee. It would seem the preferable view that unless otherwise expressly stated in the lease, all covenants of the lessee, express or implied, be treated as indivisible. Since courts increasingly are applying partial cancellation of the lease as a remedy for failure to reasonably develop, it may be, from a practical view, that little difference in result will occur, regardless of whether treated as divisible or indivisible.[15]

§ 9.11 Relationship of Lessor, Lessee, and Owners of Non-Cost-Bearing Interests

The creation of a non-cost-bearing interest carved from the working interest will not in itself create a fiduciary relationship between the owner of the working interest and the owner of the said interest. Such relationship may be otherwise created by the acts of the parties or by contractual provisions in the assignment.

In a few jurisdictions reservation of a non-cost-bearing interest in an assignment of an interest in the lease will create a sub-lease rather than an assignment, with the result that covenants will not run to the sublessee. In a majority of jurisdictions the distinction appears to be ignored by the courts.

(A) Creation of a Fiduciary Relationship

O, the owner of Blackacre, executes an oil and gas lease to Big-Rich Oil Company. Big-Rich assigns the lease to Black-Gold Oil Company, reserving an overriding royalty interest of $1/16$ of $7/8$ of gross production. The lease contains a five-year primary term; at the end of the five-year term Black-Gold has done nothing on the lease, and it expires. Big-Rich thereby sues Black-Gold for damages, to be measured by the royalty it would have received if wells had been drilled upon the tract covered by the lease. The basis of the suit is that Big-Rich has a non-possessory interest in the land and therefore cannot enter and develop, and, as it trusted Black-Gold, a fiduciary relationship was created which Black-Gold has violated.

It appears to be well established that no fiduciary relationship, *per se*, exists between the owner of the working interest in an oil and

---

15. It would seem to have some bearing, however, on lessor's burden as to the extent of evidence necessary.

gas lease and the owners of non-possessory interests in the minerals.¹ At least, no greater duty exists than that which exists to the owner of the landowner's royalty. Where the owner of the leasehold estate allows the lease to terminate under its own terms, without other fault on its part, the non-possessory interests based upon such interest will also terminate.[2]

This rule is a boon to the title examiner. Many times oil and gas titles can become extremely confused, with the underlying lease being a supporting basis for a complex title structure. If it can be determined that the base lease is outside the primary term and has terminated by its own terms, not only is the lease eliminated from consideration, so are all portions of the title based thereon.

However, this is not to say that a fiduciary relationship can never exist between the owner of the leasehold estate and owners of non-possessory interests carved therefrom. A fiduciary relationship may be created because of other circumstances in the relationship of the parties, or from provisions in the assignment.

The most common situation where assertion of a fiduciary relationship is made is where the lessee causes or allows the base oil and gas lease to expire, after he has top leased the same land, so as to extinguish non-cost-bearing interests dependent upon the base lease. For instance, O executes an oil and gas lease to Pure Oil Company; Pure assigns the lease to Big-Rich Oil Company, with the reservation of an overriding royalty of a $1/16$ of $7/8$ of gross production. In the last year of the primary term of the lease Big-Rich Oil Company obtains a new lease from O that will begin upon the termination of the old lease, and that will in effect, cut out the override of Pure Oil Company. Big-Rich could also do this by leasing and then not paying the next delay rental due. Will the override of Pure Oil Company be imposed upon the new lease of Big-Rich? The answer appears to be no, unless, as mentioned above, a fiduciary relationship can otherwise be found in the relationship of Pure and Big-Rich, or some provision is found in the assignment.

An example of a fiduciary relationship being created due to the circumstances of the parties is found in the case of MacDonald v. Follett.[3] Leases were obtained in 1934 in which MacDonald and Fol-

1. See Summers, Oil and Gas, § 554. Henry v. Gulf Refining Co., 179 Ark. 138, 15 S.W.2d 979; Chase v. Trimble, 69 Cal. App.2d 44, 158 P.2d 247; Robinson v. Eagle-Picher Lead Co., 132 Kan. 860, 297 P. 697, 75 A.L.R. 840; Hawkins v. Klein, 124 Okl. 161, 255 P. 570; MacDonald v. Follett, 142 Tex. 616, 180 S.W.2d 334.

Tyra v. Woodson, Tex., 495 S.W.2d 211; Rankin v. Naftalis, Tex., 557 S.W.2d 940; Echols v. Yeates Development Co., Tex. Civ.App., 565 S.W.2d 277.

2. La Laguna Ranch Co. v. Dodge, 18 Cal.2d 132, 114 P.2d 351, 135 A.L.R. 546; Cameron Meadows Land Co. v. Bullard, La.App., 348 So.2d 193; Brannan v. Sohio Petroleum Co., D.C.Okl., 161 F.Supp. 155, affirmed C.A.10th, 260 F.2d 621; Rogers National Bank of Jefferson v. Pewitt, Tex.Civ.App., 231 S.W.2d 487; Gordon v. Empire Gas & Fuel Co., C.C.A.5th, 63 F.2d 487.

3. 142 Tex. 616, 180 S.W.2d 334. Also see Brannan v. Sohio Petroleum Co., C.A.10th, 248 F.2d 316, on second trial D.C.Okl., 161 F.Supp. 155, affirmed C.A. 10th, 260 F.2d 621.

lett equally shared in a $1/32$ overriding royalty interest. In 1937, at a time when the leases were to expire, MacDonald agreed with Follett to enter into negotiations so that renewal leases would be obtained and that overrides would be obtained in the renewal leases for their mutual benefit. Without the knowledge of Follett, MacDonald negotiated for renewal leases for the benefit of the lessee and obtained a like $1/32$ override for himself. No part of the override was assigned to Follett. Follett contended that a fiduciary relationship existed between the parties, and that equity should impress a constructive trust upon the renewal leases and override for one-half of the $1/32$ for the benefit of Follett. The court so held. However, the court stated, "Whether or not joint owners of overriding royalty interests sustain relations of trust and confidence toward each other depends upon the facts and surrounding circumstances. They do not sustain that relationship by virtue alone of their being joint owners." The court found the relationship from the promise of MacDonald to deal with the leases for the mutual benefit of both parties. Other circumstances that have led the courts to find a fiduciary relationship are the existence of a mining partnership or the prevention of unjust enrichment.[4]

A provision in the assignment will have the effect of creating a cause of action where a lease is terminated and non-cost-bearing interests are cut out. In Probst v. Hughes,[5] in the assignment in which an overriding royalty was reserved, it was expressly stated that the interest would "apply to all modifications, renewals and extensions" by the assignee or its assigns. The lease was allowed to expire, and a second lease was secured without the override. It was contended that the clause was not effective, as a new lease was neither an extension or renewal of the first lease. The court held that the clause created a fiduciary relationship and that the person in a position of trust was under a duty to seek renewal of the original lease if he desired to develop the property. The court imposed the override upon the second lease by way of constructive trust. The court distinguished assignments where no clause was included, and stated that the reservation of an overriding royalty interest did not of itself raise a fiduciary relationship.

See Echols v. Yeates Development Co., Tex.Civ.App., 565 S.W.2d 277.

4. Simmons v. Wilson, Tex.Civ.App., 216 S.W.2d 847; Brannan v. Sohio Petroleum Co., supra, note 3.
Tyra v. Woodson, Tex., 495 S.W.2d 211 (must be fiduciary relationship apart from the joint venture agreement); Foley v. Phillips, 211 Kan. 735, 508 P.2d 975 (venturer can acquire for own account property outside of, i.e., not the natural outgrowth, of the scope of the venture); Rankin v. Naftalis, Tex., 557 S.W.2d 940 (no fiduciary relationship as to lease acquired as: (1) no actual fraud involved, (2) did not reacquire original property, (3) original contract did not embrace a general business for continued acquisition of mineral interests, and (4) lease was not acquired upon basis of information received in drilling venture activities).

5. 143 Okl. 11, 286 P. 875, 69 A.L.R. 929.

A similar case is Hivick v. Urschel,[6] where a clause was included in the assignment of a production payment that provided that a 30-day notice would be given to the owner of the production payment before release of the lease. In this case a breach of the clause was held to be a tort, and resulted in the court's imposing the production payment by way of a constructive trust upon the new lease. The Hivick case may be contrasted with the Probst case, where the constructive trust was based upon a breach of contract. It may be asked in the Hivick case what would be the remedy if the lease had simply been improperly released, without obtaining a new lease?

(B) Assignment of Leases as Affecting Liability Upon Express and Implied Covenants

Assume the situation where the leasehold estate is owned by Big-Rich Oil Company and is assigned to Texaco, Inc. with the reservation of an overriding royalty of a $1/16$ of $7/8$ of gross production. To what extent may O, the lessor, enforce express and implied covenants against Texaco, Inc. or against Big-Rich Oil Company?

Two general areas of discussion are indicated. The first is the extent to which an assignor, Big-Rich Oil Company, will remain liable for breaches of express and implied covenants in an oil and gas lease after assignment. The second area, as to liability of Texaco, Inc., concerns the effect of the reservation of an overriding royalty interest, or other non-cost bearing interest, upon the assignment of an interest in an oil and gas lease, that is to say, whether such a reservation will create a sub-lease.

As to the first issue, it may be stated that as to express covenants, the lessee will remain liable upon the lease after assignment, as the lessee had privity of contract with the lessor.[7] Scant authority is found as to continued liability upon implied covenants after assignment, although one case indicates continued liability.[8] At common law the assignor was obligated after assignment as to covenants based upon privity of contract but not upon privity of estate. If this view is followed, in those jurisdictions that view implied covenants as covenants implied in fact,[9] they would form part of the express provi

---

6. 171 Okl. 17, 40 P.2d 1077; also see Rees v. Briscoe, Okl., 315 P.2d 758.

However, care must be used in drafting notice clauses. In the following cases no liability resulted due to clause wording: Phillips v. Inexco Oil Co., Inc., Tex.Civ.App., 540 S.W.2d 546 (no right of reassignment where notice clause and right of reassignment applied when lessee desired to abandon and drop lease; instead lessee drilled producing well); Walton v. Atlantic Refining Co., Wyo., 501 P.2d 802; also see: Guinand v. Atlantic Richfield Co., C.A.10th, 485 F.2d 414 (clause provided for right of reassignment upon 30-day notice if lessee desired to terminate lease, and no right of reassignment where lease terminated through carelessness or inadvertence).

7. Whale v. Rice, 173 Okl. 530, 49 P.2d 737; Curry v. Texas Co., Tex.Civ. App., 8 S.W.2d 206.

As to Louisiana see the new Louisiana Mineral Code, La.R.S. 31:126–132, which changes results in some instances as to cases arising after the code was enacted.

8. Gillet v. Elmhurst Investment Co., 111 Kan. 755, 207 P. 843.

9. See Chapter 8, § 8.1, supra.

sions of the lease, and the lessee would remain liable as to such implied covenants after assignment. Where implied covenants are treated as implied in law, seemingly no liability would exist after assignment. However, little authority exists, and the writers are not agreed as to the probable result.[10]

The converse situation deals with the liability of the assignee of the lease. At common law, where the entire estate was transferred for the entire term, it was held that an assignment resulted and that privity of estate existed between the owner of the reversion in the land and the transferee. Where less than the entire estate was transferred, or for less than the entire term, a sub-lease resulted, and neither privity of contract nor of estate existed between the owner of the reversion in the land and the transferee. Although some jurisdictions hold that a transfer of an oil and gas lease with the reservation of an overriding royalty or other non-cost-bearing interest, creates a sub-lease,[11] in many cases either no clear holding has been made, or the concept has been ignored.[12]

The consequences that may result from classifying the transactions as a sub-lease rather than an assignment are:

(1) That the assignee is bound [13] upon covenants that run with the land, and the sub-lessee is not,[14] there being no privity of contract or estate between the sub-lessee and the lessor.

(2) The lessor has only a derivative method of enforcing covenants, by proceeding against the assignor. For this reason some assignors include a clause of express assumption by the assignee of all of the express and implied obligations of the lessee. Where such assumption exists some courts have applied a third-party beneficiary theory similar to that applied where a later purchaser expressly assumes the burden of an outstanding mortgage, providing a direct action by the lessor against the sub-lessee.

---

10. Merrill, Covenants Implied in Oil and Gas Leases; Walker, The Nature of the Property Interests Created by an Oil and Gas Lease, 11 Tex.L.Rev. 399; Warren, Transfer of the Oil and Gas Lessee's Interest, 34 Tex.L.Rev. 386.

11. Garner v. Knudsen, 129 Cal.App. 2d 747, 277 P.2d 890; Smith v. Sun Oil Co., 165 La. 907, 116 So. 379; Sunburst Oil & Refining Co. v. Callender, 84 Mont. 178, 274 P. 834; Shearer v. United Carbon Co., 143 W.Va. 482, 103 S.E.2d 883; Haynes v. Eagle-Picher Co., C.A.10th, 295 F.2d 761, cert. denied, 369 U.S. 828, 82 S.Ct. 846, 7 L.Ed.2d 794. Also see Hamblen v. Placid Oil Co., Tex.Civ.App., 279 S.W.2d 127, reversed on other grounds 155 Tex. 494, 289 S.W.2d 553; Moore v. Campbell, D.C.Tex., 267 F.Supp. 126.

Pepper v. The Pyramid Oil & Gas Corp., La.App., 287 So.2d 620, also see note 7, supra.

12. Texas Co. v. Mattocks, 211 Ark. 972, 204 S.W.2d 176; Connell v. Kanwa Oil, 161 Kan. 649, 170 P.2d 631; Davis v. Lewis, 187 Okl. 91, 100 P.2d 994.

13. See Phillips Petroleum Co. v. Taylor, C.C.A.5th, 115 F.2d 726; Gillet v. Elmhurst Investment Co., 111 Kan. 755, 207 P. 843.

14. See Hartman Ranch Co. v. Associated Oil Co., 10 Cal.2d 232, 73 P.2d 1163.

Pepper v. The Pyramid Oil & Gas Corp., La.App., 287 So.2d 620 (sublease, no liability by sublessee for non-payment of delay rentals as no privity of contract or estate. Result would be changed under new Louisiana Mineral Code, see note 36, supra).

(3) The sub-lessee cannot execute a release of the lease so as to terminate the lessor-assignor relationship.[15]

It appears that most of the cases dealing with liability of assignees where a reservation of a non-cost-bearing interest appears in the chain of title have not applied the assignment—sublease distinction. It is the view of the author that such distinction is improperly applied in the oil and gas field.[16]

15. Saling v. Flesch, 85 Mont. 106, 277 P. 612.

16. Also see Merrill, The Partial Assignee—Done in Oil, 20 Tex.L.Rev. 298.

*

TABLE OF CASES

References are to Pages

Abney v. Lewis, 49
Acker v. Guinn, 5, 12, 13, 15, 16, 18, 19, 20
Adams v. Cook, 227, 228
Adams v. Duncan, 126, 147
Adams v. Elkhorn Coal Corp., 240, 241, 243
Adams v. Grigsby, 11
Adams v. Riddle, 25
Adams County v. Smith, 8, 10
Adkins v. Adams, 412, 425
Agajanian v. Cuccio, 54
Agey v. Barnard, 491
Ahne v. Reinhart and Donovan Co., 7
Alaska Placer Co. v. Lee, 167, 170, 172
Aldridge v. Houston Oil Co., 198, 201, 202, 207
Aleut Corp. v. Arctic Slope Regional Corp., 13
Alexander v. Byrd, 373
Alexander v. Holt, 407
Alexander v. King, 60
Alford v. Dennis, 428, 449, 450, 451
Alfrey v. Ellington, 456
Alfson v. Anderson, 245, 385, 482
Allen v. Continental Oil Co., 322, 323
Allen v. Farmers' Union Co-op. Royalty Co., 4, 5, 12, 14, 16, 17
Allison v. Smith, 35, 37, 38, 42, 47, 128
Alphin v. Gulf Ref. Co., 499
Alsip's Adm'r v. Onstott, 476
Alvord v. Sun Oil Co., 341
Amarex, Inc. v. Sell, 237
Amarillo Oil Co. v. McBride, 199
Ambarann Corp. v. Old Ben Coal Corp., 2, 4
Ambassador Oil Corp. v. Robertson, 9, 11
Amerada Petroleum Co. v. Doering, 419, 423, 450
Amerada Petroleum Corp. v. Massad, 135, 138
Amerada Petroleum Corp. v. Murphy, 130
America Southwest Corp. v. Allen, 430, 431, 445, 446

American Petroleum Corp. v. Robinson, 384
American Ref. Co. v. Tidal Western Oil Corp., 368
American Republics Corp. v. Houston Oil Co. of Texas, 118, 120
American Sur. Co. of New York v. Marsh, 182
American Trading and Production Corp. v. Phillips Petroleum Co., 165, 166
American Wholesale Corp. v. F. & S. Oil & Gas Co., 499
Amoco Production Co. v. Alexander, 415, 437, 438, 439, 444
Amoco Production Co. v. Braslau, 293, 294, 295, 296, 297, 298, 299
Amoco Production Co. v. First Baptist Church of Pyote, 367, 443
Amoco Production Co. v. Guild Trust, 2, 4
Amoco Production Co., State v., 293, 298
Amoco Production Co. v. Underwood, 401
Amoco Production Co. v. Ware, 445
Amundson v. Gordon, 69, 84, 88, 187
Anderson & Kerr Drilling Co. v. Bruhlmeyer, 2, 3, 4, 5, 14
Anderson-Prichard Oil Corp. v. McBride, 215, 216
Andretta v. West, 43, 44, 371
Andrews v. Andrews, 202, 204, 206
Andrews v. Brown, 213
Angelloz v. Humble Oil & Ref. Co., 156, 157
Anthis v. Sullivan Oil & Gas Co., 327
Appling v. Morrison, 267, 271
Archer County v. Webb, 42, 100, 315, 316
Ardizonne v. Archer, 452
Arkansas Louisiana Gas Co. v. Evans, 382
Armstrong v. Bell, 457, 459, 460
Armstrong v. Lake Champlain Granite Co., 7, 8, 10, 17
Armstrong v. McCraken, 76, 94, 96
Armstrong v. McGough, 497
Armstrong v. Skelly Oil Co., 352, 355
Arnold v. Ashbel Smith Land Co., 71, 81, 82, 89

TABLE OF CASES
References are to Pages

Arrington v. El Paso Natural Gas Co., 486
Arrington v. United Royalty Co., 53, 54
Ascher v. Mid-States Oil Corp., 486
Ashland Oil, Inc. v. Phillips Petroleum Co., 9
Ashland Oil & Ref. Co. v. Staats, Inc., 337, 352, 355, 361, 362, 443
Associated Oil Co., People v., 30
Ates v. Yellow Pine Land Co., 142, 146
Atlantic Oil Co. v. County of Los Angeles, 54
Atlantic Ref. Co. v. Shell Oil Co., 123, 262
Atlantic Richfield Co. v. Hilton, 303
Atwood v. Humble Oil & Ref. Co., 336, 499
Atwood v. Rodman, 2, 8, 10, 11
Aubert v. St. Louis-San Francisco Ry. Co., 213
Auzenne v. Lawrence Oil Co., 264
Avery v. Moore, 2
Avis v. First Nat'l Bank of Wichita Falls, 225, 226, 228
Ayer v. Philadelphia & Face Brick Co., 119

Back v. Ohio Fuel Gas Co., 26, 28, 30, 244
Bacon v. Wahrhaftig, 127
Bailey v. Meadows, 340
Baker v. Collins, 416, 417
Baker v. Huffman, 250, 264
Baker v. Potter, 257, 258
Baker v. Vanderpool, 386
Baldwin v. Blue Stem Oil Co., 277, 281, 387, 388
Baldwin v. Kubetz, 388, 389, 444
Bales v. Delhi-Taylor Oil Corp., 288, 289
Ball v. Clark, 134, 139
Ballanfonte v. Kimbell, 287
Ballard v. Miller, 257, 268, 269, 270, 271
Ballard v. Stanolind Oil & Gas Co., 169, 171
Banks v. Mecom, 399
Bannard v. New York State Natural Gas Corp., 3
Barby v. Cabot Corp., 346
Barby v. Singer, 288
Bardhill v. Sellers, 240, 241, 242, 243
Barker v. Campbell-Ratcliff Land Co., 2, 3
Barker v. Levy, 78, 79
Barnard v. Jamison, 459
Barnard v. Monongahela Natural Gas Co., 24, 25
Barnes v. Keys, 199, 200, 201

Barnes v. Mack Oil Co., 415, 420, 421, 424, 451
Barnes v. Winona Oil Co., 165, 168, 169, 170, 172
Barnett v. Morris, 69
Barnsdall v. Bradford Gas Co., 244
Barquin v. Hall Oil Co., 179, 181, 183, 184
Barr v. Wall, 368
Barrett v. Dorr, 277, 292, 293, 294
Barrett v. Ferrell, 320, 328, 452
Barton v. Wichita River Oil Co., 3, 6
Bass v. Harper, 456, 459, 465, 484
Bassell v. West Virginia Central Gas Co., 394
Baumgartner v. Gulf Oil Corp., 176
Bean v. Bean, 225, 226
Bearden v. Knight, 50
Beardsley v. Kansas Natural Gas Co., 127, 130, 135, 138
Beatty v. Baxter, 100, 295, 298
Belcher v. Elliott, 165, 169, 170, 171
Belgam Oil Co. v. Wirt Franklin Petroleum Corp., 135
Bell v. Mitchell Energy Corp., 277, 287, 328
Bell, People ex rel. Carrell v., 16
Bell Corp., Alphonzo E. v. Bell View Oil Syndicate, 167, 168, 173, 174, 177
Bellport v. Harrison, 55, 56, 57, 71
Belt v. Texas Co., 406
Bender v. Brooks, 165, 167, 169, 170, 171
Benedum-Trees Oil Co. v. Davis, 278
Benge v. Scharbauer, 120, 122, 123
Bennett v. Scofield, 50
Bennett v. Sinclair Oil & Gas Co., 407
Benson v. Nyman, 385
Bergendahl v. Blanco Oil Co., 198, 202, 207
Berry v. Tide Water Ass'n Oil Co., 495, 496
Berry v. Wondra, 415
Berryman v. Sinclair Prairie Oil Co., 178, 179, 180
Berthelote v. Loy Oil Co., 282, 284, 292
Berwick Mud Co. v. Stansbury, 379
Besing v. Ohio Val. Coal Co. of Kentucky, 6, 8, 12, 14, 15, 16, 17, 19
Beury v. Shelton, 10, 13
Beverly Hills Oil Co. v. Beverly Hills Unified Sch. Dist., 384
Bezzi v. Hocker, 339
Bilby v. Wire, 142, 144
Bincent v. Bullock, 141
Birdwell v. American Bonding Co., 144, 147
Birmingham v. McCoy, 120

TABLE OF CASES
References are to Pages

Biskamp v. General Crude Oil Co., 441
Black v. Shell Oil Co., 116
Black v. Sylvania Producing Co., 135
Blair v. Clear Creek Oil & Gas Co., 447, 448
Blake v. St. Catherine Gravel Co., 138, 139
Blankenship v. United Fuel Gas Co., 386
Blocker v. Christie, Mitchell & Mitchell Co., 403
Blythe v. Hines, 9, 12, 13, 19
Blythe v. Sohio Petroleum Co., 415, 420, 421, 424
Board of Regents, State ex rel. Fatzer v., 48, 49, 62
Boatman v. Andre, 245
Bodcaw Lumber Co. v. Goode, 25, 27, 142
Body v. McDonald, 117, 118, 119, 120
Boggess v. Milam, 26
Bolack v. Hedges, 244
Bollinger v. Texas Co., 340
Bolton v. Coats, 431, 491
Bolton v. Rouss, 225
Bonsall v. Humble Oil & Ref. Co., 341
Bonzo v. Nowlin, 35, 38
Boone v. Kerr-McGee Oil Indus., 400
Borden v. Case, 480, 481
Bouterie v. Kleinpeter, 341
Boutte v. Chevron Oil Co., 341
Boyd v. United States, 7
Brady v. Smith, 10
Brandenburg v. Petroleum Exploration, 198, 207
Brannan v. Sohio Petroleum Co., 501, 502
Brannon v. Gulf States Energy Corp., 259, 275
Brannon v. Varnado, 117, 118, 120, 121
Brazell v. Soucek, 258, 268, 270
Breaux v. Apache Oil Corp., 322, 323
Breaux v. Magnolia Petroleum Co., 431
Brent v. Natural Gas Pipeline Co. of America, 359
Brewster v. Lanyon Zinc Co., 412, 415, 416, 428, 445, 446, 449, 450
Brian v. Valley View Cattle Ranch, Inc., 142, 143
Briggs v. Waggoner, 284, 285
Brimmer v. Union Oil Co. of California, 443
Bristol v. Colorado Oil & Gas Corp., 278, 280
Brixey v. Union Oil Co. of California, 164
Brizzolara v. Powell, 3, 149, 151
Broadhead v. Pan American Petroleum Corp., 341

Broderick v. Stevenson, Consolidated Oil Co., 245
Brooks v. Mull, 195
Broome's Estate, In re, 57
Broswood Oil Co. v. Sand Springs Home, 345
Broughton v. Humble Oil & Ref. Co., 142
Broussard v. Texaco, Inc., 472
Brown v. Brown, 110
Brown v. Kirk, 112, 119, 120
Brown v. Shafer, 450
Brown v. Smith, 47, 403
Brown v. Spilman, 24
Brown v. Sugar Creek Syndicate, 397
Brown v. Wilson, 247, 385
Brown Land & Royalty Co. v. Green, 369
Browne v. Loriaux, 128, 135
Browning v. Cavanaugh, 318, 319, 324
Broyles v. Gilman, 497
Bruner's Will, In re, 199, 202, 226, 228
Brunson v. Carter Oil Co., 251
Bryan v. Everett, 117, 118, 120
Buckles v. Wil-Mc Oil Corp., 283
Buckner v. Wright, 144
Budde v. Navarro Oil Co., 369
Bulger v. McCourt, 3, 4, 5, 112
Bullard v. Broadwell, 189
Bundy v. Myers, 3
Bundy v. United States Trust Co. of New York, 39
Bunker Hunt Trust Estate, Nelson v. Jarmon, 256
Burbidge v. Noe, 256
Burden v. Gypsy Oil Co., 29, 197, 198, 199, 200, 201, 245
Burdette v. Bruen, 2, 4, 5
Burger v. Wood, 303
Burgess v. Travelers Ins. Co., 158, 159, 160
Burke v. Southern Pac. Ry. Co., 2, 3
Burnet v. Harmel, 50
Burnham v. Hardy Oil Co., 166, 187, 188, 191
Burns v. Audes, 96
Burns v. Bastien, 70, 72, 73, 111
Burress v. Diem, 385
Burt v. Deorsam, 431
Bush Oil Co. v. Beverly-Lincoln Land Co., 434
Butler v. Exxon Corp., 346, 358, 367
Butler v. Jenkins Oil Corp., 491
Butler v. Nepple, 247, 388, 389, 390

Caddell v. Threshold Development Co., 389, 391
Cain v. Neumann, 9, 11, 486

TABLE OF CASES
References are to Pages

Calhoun v. Gulf Ref. Co., 274
California v. Southland Royalty Co., 359
Callahan v. Martin, 26, 29, 53, 54, 55, 56, 57, 71, 245
Camden Safe Deposit & Trust Co. v. Scott, 39
Cameron v. Lebow, 250, 251, 414, 419, 450
Cameron Meadows Land Co. v. Bullard, 501
Campbell v. Seaman, 297
Campbell v. Tennessee Coal, Iron & R.R. Co., 2, 13
Canik v. Texas Int'l Petroleum Corp., 341
Cannon v. Cassidy, 340
Canter v. Lindsey, 91
Cantrell v. Garrard, 481
Caples v. Cole, 236
Cargill v. Buie, 146
Carlisle v. Lady, 413
Carlisle v. United Producing Co., 61
Carlock v. Krug, 467, 468
Carothers v. Mills, 7
Carper v. United Fuel Gas Co., 414, 448
Carrell, People ex rel. v. Bell, 16
Carroll v. Bowen, 48, 72, 73, 75
Carroll v. Eaton, 247
Carroll v. Edmondson, 220
Carroll v. Funk, 104
Carroll v. Roger Lacy, Inc., 258
Carson v. Missouri Pac. R.R. Co., 8
Carson v. Ozark Natural Gas Co., 446
Carter v. Arkansas-Louisiana Gas Co., 450
Carter v. Hawkins, 376
Carter v. United States Smelting, Ref. and Mining Co., 415, 447
Carter Oil Co. v. Dees, 439, 442
Carter Oil Co. v. McCasland, 165, 166, 486
Carter Oil Co. v. Mitchell, 415, 418, 420, 421, 424
Carter Oil Co., State ex rel. Comm'rs of Land Office v., 317, 318, 321
Carter Oil Co. of West Virginia, State v., 279
Caruthers v. Leonard, 48, 49, 50, 123, 456, 457
Casey v. Western Oil and Gas, Inc., 293
Cassity v. Smith, 261
Casteel v. Crigler, 76, 77, 78, 79
Caswell v. Llano Oil Co., 28, 223
Cates v. Greene, 49
Central Exploration Co. v. Gray, 160
Central Kentucky Natural Gas Co. v. Smallwood, 245

Central Pipe Line Co. v. Hutson, 467, 468
Central Standard Life Ins. Co. v. Gardner, 228, 245
Central States Production Corp. v. Jordan, 427
Certain-Teed Products Corp. v. Comly, 8, 10
Chaffin v. Hall, 127, 130, 136
Champlin v. Sinclair Oil and Gas Co., 317
Champlin Ref. Co. v. Aladdin Petroleum Co., 166, 168, 169
Champlin Ref. Co. v. Magnolia Petroleum Co., 317
Chandler v. Drummet, 328
Chapman v. Sohio Petroleum Co., 430
Chapple v. Kansas Vitrified Brick Co., 256
Charter v. Maxwell, 245
Chase v. Trimble, 501
Cherry v. Farmers Royalty Holding Co., 223
Cherry v. Salinas, 480, 481
Chevron Oil Co. v. Howell, 173
Chevron Oil Co. v. Snellgrove, 159
Chicago Corp. v. Wall, 365, 367, 369, 370
Childers v. Neely, 370
Christian v. A. A. Oil Corp., 277, 281, 306
Christie, Mitchell & Mitchell Co. v. Howell, 446
Christman v. Emineth, 8, 11, 12, 13, 15, 19, 21
Cities Serv. Oil Co. v. Corley, 160
Cities Serv. Oil Co. v. McCrory, 490
Cities Serv. Oil Co. v. Sohio Petroleum Co., 58
Citizens Nat'l Bank of Emporia, Kansas v. Socony Mobil Oil Co., 333
Clanahan v. Morgan, 142, 146
Clark v. Mercer Oil Co., 127, 135
Clark v. Wilson, 241, 242
Classen v. Federal Land Bank of Wichita, 405
Claybrooke v. Barnes, 149
Clear Creek Oil & Gas Co. v. Brunk, 447, 448
Clear Creek Oil & Gas Co. v. Bushmiaer, 337, 352, 353
Clifton v. Koontz, 282, 284, 285, 286, 287, 288, 289, 291, 295, 296, 300, 415, 416, 417, 418, 419, 422, 423
Clovis v. Carson Oil Co., 272
Clyde v. Hamilton, 198, 200, 201, 202, 203, 204, 207
Coal Oil & Gas Co. v. Styron, 419
Coastal Club v. Shell Oil Co., 383

TABLE OF CASES

Coastal States Gas Producing Co. v. Pate, 173
Coates v. DeGarcia, 467, 471
Coats v. Brown, 414, 415, 431, 432
Cockrell v. Texas Gulf Sulfur Co., 474, 476
Cohn v. Clark, 247
Coker v. Benjamin, 378
Coker v. Hudspeth, 68
Coker v. Vierson, 127, 134, 138
Colby v. Sun Oil Co., 264, 266
Cole v. Berry, 10
Cole v. Butler, 413
Cole v. McDonald, 8, 10
Cole Petroleum Co. v. United States Gas & Oil Co., 491
Cole v. Philadelphia Co., 293
Collier v. Collier, 135
Coloma Oil & Gas Corp. v. Railroad Comm'n, 471
Colonial Royalties Co. v. Keener, 73, 74
Comanche Duke Oil Co. v. Texas Pac. Coal & Oil Co., 159, 160
Commerce Trust Co. v. Lyon, 464
Commercial Nat'l Bank in Nacogdoches v. Hayter, 209, 229
Commissioner v. _____ (see opposing party)
Commissioners of Land Office, State ex rel. v. Carter Oil Co., 317, 318, 321
Commissioners of Land Office, State ex rel. v. Reynolds, 221
Cone v. Amoco Production Co., 431, 434, 447
Connell v. Kanwa Oil, 504
Connette v. Wright, 191
Consolidated Gas Supply Corp. v. Riley, 134
Consumers' Gas Trust Co. v. Littler, 414
Continental Group, Inc. v. Allison, 12, 19, 21
Continental Oil Co. v. Boston-Texas Land Trust, 325
Continental Oil Co. v. Chicago & North Western Ry. Co., 143
Continental Oil Co. v. Doornbos, 109
Continental Oil Co. v. Hinton, 159, 160
Continental Oil Co. v. Osage Oil & Ref. Co., 283, 303
Continental Oil Co. v. Tate, 117, 118
Continental Oil Co. v. Walker, 375
Continental Oil Co. of Texas v. Graham, 222
Continental Securities Corp. v. Wetherbee, 221
Continental Supply Co. v. Texas Co., 55

Cook v. Cook, 198, 207
Cook v. El Paso Natural Gas Co., 429, 433, 434, 491
Cook v. McClellan, 73, 74
Corbett v. LaBere, 71
Corbin v. Moser, 71, 91
Cordell v. Enis, 267, 268, 269
Core v. New York Petroleum Co., 245
Corey v. Sunburst Oil and Gas Co., 368
Corlett v. Cox, 72, 78, 87
Corley v. Olympic Petroleum Corp., 257, 271
Cormier v. Ferguson, 71, 95
Corsicana Petroleum Co. v. Owens, 247
Cosden Oil Co. v. Scarborough, 498, 500
Cotiga Development Co. v. United Fuel Gas Co., 351, 353, 442, 445, 446
Cotner v. Warren, 292, 293
Couch v. Texas & Pac. Ry. Co., 214
Countiss v. Baldwin, 222
Cowden v. Broderick & Calvert, 426
Cowman v. Phillips Petroleum Co., 495
Cox v. Davison, 191
Cox v. Gulf Oil Corp., 278
Cox v. Lasley, 134
Cox v. Miller, 277, 281, 385, 386
Cox v. Sinclair Gulf Oil Co., 499
Coyle v. Louisiana Gas & Fuel Co., 349, 350
Coyle v. North American Oil Consol., 451
Coyne v. Butler, 118, 120
Coyne v. Simrall Corp., 476, 479
Craig v. Champlin Petroleum Co., 412, 442
Crain v. Pure Oil Co., 143, 144, 240, 241, 242
Cranston v. Miller, 392
Crocker v. Humble Oil & Ref. Co., 417, 419
Cronkhite v. Falkenstein, 4, 5, 7, 8, 10, 12, 14, 16, 17
Crosbie v. Absher, 183
Crowder v. James, 59, 261
Crumpton v. Scott, 115
Cumberland Mineral Co. v. United States, 9, 11, 12, 13, 14, 19
Cummings v. Midstates Oil Corp., 372, 373
Currie v. Harris, 49
Curry v. Texas Co., 503
Curtis-Jordan Oil & Gas Co. v. Mullins, 143

Dabney-Johnston Oil Corp. v. Walden, 29, 53, 54, 59, 71, 141
Dacamara v. Binney, 499

TABLE OF CASES
References are to Pages

Dale v. Case, 369, 370, 459, 460
Dallapi v. Campbell, 35, 36, 39, 40
Danciger Oil & Refineries v. Hamill Drilling Co., 364
Danciger Oil & Ref. Co. of Texas v. Powell, 240, 243, 412, 488
Daniel v. Allen, 104, 107, 108
Daniels v. Charles, 205
Daughetee v. Ohio Oil Co., 415, 416, 445, 446
Davis v. Atlantic Oil Producing Co., 198, 207
Davis v. Bond, 198, 200
Davis v. Elliott, 401
Davis v. Hardman, 48, 71, 72, 78, 86
Davis v. Howard, 385
Davis v. Hurst, 71
Davis v. Laster, 267, 274
Davis v. Lewis, 487, 488, 504
Davis v. Mann, 240, 241, 242
Davis v. Mose, 431
Davis v. Plunkett, 6
Davis v. Skipper, 210
Dawson v. Meike, 5, 7, 9, 12, 16, 17
Day v. Pounders, 149
Dean v. Hidalgo County Water Improvement Dist. No. 2, 126
DeBusk v. Cosden Petroleum Corp., 37, 39
Deer Lake Co. v. Michigan Land & Iron Co., Ltd., 9
Dees v. Cheuvronts, 210
DeFlores v. Smith, 317
Delk v. Craig, 385, 386
Delta Drilling Co. v. Oil Fin. Corp., 127, 129, 130
Delta Drilling Co. v. Simmons, 64, 457, 459, 462
Dennis v. Pace Petroleum Co., 372, 373
Deseret Livestock Co. v. State, 11
Dethloff v. Ziegler Coal Co., 171
Detlor v. Holland, 2, 3, 6, 7
Dickens v. Tisdale, 104, 106
Dickey v. Coffeyville Vitrified Brick & Tile Co., 245
Dickgraber, State ex rel. v. Sheridan, 385
Diederich v. Ware, 150
Dietrich v. Davis, 273
Dilworth v. Fortier, 170, 378
Dingess v. Huntington Development & Gas Co., 2, 3, 6
Dixon v. Abrams, 120
Dixon v. American Liberty Oil Co., 143, 144, 149, 245
Dixon v. Anadarko Production Co., 415, 418, 499

Dixon v. Henderson, 142, 144
Dixon v. McCann, 180, 184
Dixon v. Mapes, 201
Doochin v. Rackley, 8, 12, 13
Doss Oil Royalty Co. v. Texas Co., 419, 420, 450
Doster v. Friedensville Zinc Co., 2, 10, 17
Doty v. Key Oil, Inc., 308, 309
Dougan, United States v., 50
Dougherty v. Greene, 240, 241, 242, 243
Douglas v. Butcher, 406
Dowda v. Hayman, 113
Dowling v. Springer, 222
Drake v. O'Brien, 37
Draper v. J. B. & R. E. Walker, Inc., 179
Draper v. Walker, 183, 184
DuBois v. Jacobs, 19
Duhig v. Peavy-Moore Lumber Co., 117, 118, 119, 121, 382
Duke v. Stewart, 499
Duke v. Sun Oil Co., 306, 307, 308, 311, 312, 315
Duncan v. Mason, 240, 241, 243
Dunham v. Kirkpatrick, 2, 3, 7
Dunn v. Southwest Ardmore Tulip Creek Sand Unit, 11
Dupree v. Relco Exploration Co., 415, 417, 424
Duquesne Natural Gas Co. v. Fefolt, 53
Durbin Bond & Co. v. Gillis, 453
Durell v. Miles, 253
Duval v. Stone, 71, 456, 464
Duval v. W. T. Carter & Bros., 369
Dye v. Miller & Viele, 149, 151

Eagle Oil Co. v. Sinclair Prairie Oil Co., 368
Earp v. Mid-Continent Petroleum Corp., 187, 188, 191, 192, 283
Easley v. Melten, 17
Eason v. Rosamund, 473, 476
Eastern Oil Co. v. Beatty, 385, 414
Eastern Oil Co. v. Coulehan, 245, 278
Echols v. Yeates Development Co., 501, 502
Eclipse Oil Co. v. South Penn Oil Co., 247
Edmonds v. Mounsey, 384
Edwards v. Brusha, 112
Edwards v. Carter Oil Co., 104, 109
Edwards v. Lachman, 165, 166, 171
Eggleston v. Sinclair Oil & Gas Co., 241, 242, 243
Eide v. Tveter, 197, 198, 199
El Paso Natural Gas Co. v. Kelly, 104
El Rio Oils, Canada, Ltd. v. Chase, 449
Elcan v. Childress, 144

TABLE OF CASES

Elkhorn City Land Co. v. Elkhorn City, 2, 9, 11, 12
Elkhorn Coal Corp. v. Slone, 462
Elliff v. Texon Drilling Co., 30, 176, 177
Elliott v. Berry, 76
Elliott v. Crystal Springs Oil Co., 277, 281, 293, 294
Elliott v. Davis, 399
Elliott v. Pure Oil Co., 415, 416, 430
Ellis v. Cook, 134, 136, 137, 138
Ellison v. Skelly Oil Co., 268, 269, 270, 271
Ellwood v. Nutex Oil Co., 387
Elrod v. Foster, 128
Elrod v. Hiers, Devisees, etc., 112
Emeny v. United States, 175
Empire Gas & Fuel Co. v. Saunders, 268, 269
Empire Oil & Ref. Co. v. Hoyt, 440
Endicott v. DeBarbieri, 428
Energy Oils, Inc. v. Montana Power Co., 487
Enfield v. Woods, 282
Eota Realty Co. v. Carter Oil Co., 495
Erne v. Broiles, 181, 184
Estate of (see name of party)
Estes v. Browning, 156
Etter v. Texaco, Inc., 457, 459, 460, 462
Eubank v. Twin Mountain Oil Corp., 386
Evans, State v., 9, 10, 11, 14
Ewing v. Trawick, 112
Expando Production Co. v. Marshall, 400, 402
Extraction Resources, Inc. v. Freeman, 68, 84
Exum v. Laub, 491
Exxon Corp. v. First Nat'l Bank of Midland, 57
Exxon Corp. v. Jefferson Land Co., 360
Exxon Corp. v. Middleton, 346, 357, 358, 359, 360, 365, 367, 393

Fadem v. Kimball, 143, 144, 146
Fagan & Co. v. Burns, 318
Fagg v. Texas Co., 248, 480, 481
Fain-McGaha Corp. v. Owens, 452
Fairbanks v. Warrum, 467, 468
Fantham v. Goodrich, 106, 120
Farmers Canal Co. v. Potthast, 91
Farrell v. Sayre, 12
Fast v. Fast, 103
Fatherree v. McCormick, 114, 120
Fatzer, State ex rel. v. Board of Regents, 48, 49, 62
Fawvor v. United States Oil of Louisiana, Inc., 267, 341

Feather v. Baird, 241, 243
Federal Gas, Oil & Coal Co. v. Moore, 3, 4, 5, 6
Federal Land Bank of Houston v. United States, 45, 47
Federal Land Bank of New Orleans v. Mulhern, 220
Federal Land Bank of Wichita, Kansas v. Nicholson, 35, 39, 74
Federal Oil Co. v. Western Oil Co., 247
Feland v. Placid Oil Co., 277, 293
Felmont Oil Corp. v. Pan American Petroleum Corp., 417, 419, 423
Ferguson v. Hilborn, 147
Ferguson v. Housh, 491
Ferguson v. Morgan, 114
Fey v. A.A. Oil Corp., 277, 302, 303, 450
Fick v. Wilson, 287
Finder v. Nyegaard, 381
First Nat'l Bank in Weatherford v. Exxon Corp., 359, 368
First Nat'l Bank in Wellington v. McClellan, 222
First Nat'l Bank in Wichita v. Magnolia Petroleum Co., 227
First Nat'l Bank of Laurel v. Commercial Nat'l Bank & Trust Co., 229
Fisher v. Keweenaw Land Ass'n, 2, 12
Fisher v. Tomlinson Oil Co., 452
Flag Oil Corp. of Delaware v. King Resources Co., 278, 280, 310
Fleming v. Ashcroft, 465
Fleming Foundation v. Texaco, Inc. 5, 9, 11, 16, 28
Foley v. Phillips, 502
Fontenot v. Austral Oil Exploration Co., 415, 416
Ford v. Barton, 268, 269
Ford v. Jones, 106
Forman v. Mac Kellar Drilling Co., 444
Forney v. Ward, 324
Forrest v. Hanson, 125
Ft. Worth & Denver City Ry. Co. v. Beauchamp, 159
Fort Worth Nat'l Bank v. McLean, 417
Fortney v. Tope, 137
Foster v. Atlantic Ref. Co., 353
Foster v. Hopkins, 378
Foster v. Weaver, 187
Fox v. Thoreson, 277, 281
Francis v. Francis, 149
Francis v. Pritchett, 295, 296
Frank Oil Co. v. Belleview Gas and Oil Co., 279
Frankfort Oil Co. v. Snakard, 178, 179

TABLE OF CASES
References are to Pages

Franklin v. Margay Oil Corp., 201, 226, 228
Frazier v. Justiss Mears Oil Co., 417, 418
Frede v. Lauderdale, 221
Freeland v. Edwards, 324
Freeland v. Sun Oil Co., 350, 352, 354, 355, 361, 362
Freeman v. Magnolia Petroleum Co., 308, 309
Freeman v. Southland Paper Mills, Inc., 112
Freeport Coal Co. v. Valley Point Mining Co., 112
Freeport Sulphur Co. v. American Sulpher Royalty Co., 240
Fremaux v. Buie, 407
Fremont Lumber Co. v. Starrell Petroleum Co., 323
French v. Querbes, 456, 462, 464, 469
Frensley v. White, 210
Friesen v. Federal Land Bank of Wichita, 405
Froelich v. United Royalty Co., 25
Frost v. Gulf Oil Corp., 297, 299
Frost-Johnson Lumber Co. v. Nabors Oil & Gas Co., 26, 29
Fry v. Dewees, 134
Fry v. Farm Bureau Oil Co., 489
Fry v. Hurst, 27
Fry v. Smith, 76, 77
Funk v. Halderman, 244
Fussell v. Ringue, 406

Galey v. Kellerman, 247
Gallaspy v. Warner, 442, 445
Gallin v. Combs, 68, 87
Galt v. Metscher, 467, 470, 499
Garcia v. King, 282, 283, 284, 285, 286, 287
Garcia v. Sun Oil Co., 187
Gard v. Kaiser, 278, 293, 310
Gardner v. Amerada Petroleum Corp., 371, 372, 373, 376
Gardner v. Jones, 73, 76, 94, 96
Gardner v. Pan American Petroleum Corp., 79, 80
Garelick v. Southwest Gas Producing Co., 261, 262
Garner v. Knudsen, 504
Garraway v. Bryant, 120
Garrett v. Dils Co., 64, 89, 110, 457, 459, 460, 462
Gartner v. Missimer, 452
Garza v. DeMontalvo, 406, 467
Gas Products Co. v. Rankin, 26

Gas Ridge, Inc. v. Suburban Agric. Properties, Inc., 282, 302
Gasaway v. Pendergrass, 320
Gault v. Metscher, 468
Gazin v. Pan-American Petroleum Corp., 442
Geary v. Adams Oil & Gas Co., 434, 435, 445, 446, 449
Geller v. Smith, 50, 51, 61, 62
General Crude Oil Co. v. Harris, 446, 450
Geothermal Kinetics, Inc. v. Union Oil Co. of California, 9, 10, 12
Gerhard v. Stephens, 26, 29, 53, 54, 55, 141, 142, 143, 245, 250
Gerkins v. Kentucky Salt Co., 30
Germany v. Turner, 140
Gerson v. Anderson-Prichard Production Corp., 430, 434
Gettel v. Hester, 110, 120
Getty Oil Co. v. Royal, 70
Gheen v. Diamond Shamrock Corp., 254
Gibson v. Sellars, 3, 4, 110
Gibson v. Turner, 123, 382, 383
Gibson v. Tyson, 2, 7, 8, 9, 10
Gibson v. Watson, 457, 458, 459, 460
Gibson & Jennings v. Amos Drilling Co., 187
Gilbert v. Smedley, 389, 391
Gilbreath v. Douglas, 136
Gilbreath v. States Oil Corp., 347
Gilcrease Foundation, Thomas v. Stanolind Oil & Gas Co., 477, 478, 479
Gill v. Fletcher, 142
Gillespie v. Wagoner, 294
Gillespie v. Ohio Oil Co., 292, 293
Gillespie v. Wagoner, 292, 293
Gillet v. Elmhurst Inv. Co., 413, 503, 504
Gillet v. Powell, 127, 133
Gillham v. Jenkins, 400
Gillham v. Jenkins, 388
Gillispie v. Blanton, 188, 190
Gilmore v. Ontario Iron Co., 446
Gilmore v. Superior Oil Co., 337, 352, 361, 362
Girolami v. Peoples Natural Gas Co., 247
Gisinger v. Hart, 303, 304
Glass v. Skelly Oil Co., 57
Glieberman v. Fine, 179, 180
Gloyd v. Midwest Ref. Co., 268, 270
Goble v. Goff, 263
Gonsoulin v. Shell Oil Co., 368
Good Hope Refineries, Inc. v. Benavides, 268
Goodloe v. City of Richmond, 11
Goodloe & Meredith v. Harris, 128
Goodwin v. Wright, 283

TABLE OF CASES
References are to Pages

Gordon v. Empire Gas & Fuel Co., 501
Gossett v. Tidewater Associated Oil Co., 149
Grand Rapids, City of v. Central Land Co., 210
Graham-Loftus Oil Corp. v. Mountain View Development Corp., 387
Graser v. Graser, 201
Grass v. Big Creek Development Co., 446
Gray v. Amoco Production Co., 364
Gray-Mellon Oil Co. v. Fairchild, 26, 28
Greene v. Carter Oil Co., 341
Greene v. Robison, 57, 236
Greene v. White, 126
Greenshields v. Warren Petroleum Corp., 29, 55
Greenwood v. Texas-Interstate Pipeline Co., 499
Greer v. Carter Oil Co., 51, 302, 303
Greer v. Salmon, 277, 293, 306
Greer v. Stanolind Oil & Gas Co., 165, 166, 253
Grelling v. Allen, 470
Greyhound Leasing & Financial Corp. v. Joiner City Unit, 11
Gribben v. Carpenter, 167
Griffin v. Stanolind Oil and Gas Co., 234, 379
Griffith v. Gulf Ref. Co., 472
Griffith v. Taylor, 52, 61, 62, 64, 65
Grimes v. La Gloria Corp., 402, 406
Grissom v. Anderson, 275
Grissom v. Guetersloh, 96, 97, 98
Grooms v. Minton, 414
Gruss v. Cummins, 481
Guaranty Nat'l Bank and Trust of Corpus Christi v. May, 403
Guardian Trust Co. v. Brothers, 452, 453
Guest v. Bizzell, 199
Guffey v. Smith, 171, 172
Guffey Petroleum Co. v. Oliver, 247
Guinand v. Atlantic Richfield Co., 503
Guinn v. Acker, 8
Guleke v. Humble Oil & Ref. Co., 322, 323, 324
Gulf, Colorado & Santa Fe Ry. Co. v. Dunman, 156
Gulf Land Co. v. Atlantic Ref. Co., 471
Gulf Oil Corp. v. Reid, 296, 308, 311, 333
Gulf Oil Corp. v. Southland Royalty Co., 246
Gulf Pipe Line Co. v. Nearen, 363
Gulf Pipe Line Co. v. Pawnee Tulsa Petroleum Co., 70
Gulf Pipe Line Co. v. Warren, 363
Gulf Producing Co. v. Spear, 374, 376
Gulf Production Co. v. Continental Oil Co., 70, 257
Gulf Production Co. v. Kishi, 426
Gulf Production Co. v. Perry, 256, 259
Gulf Production Co. v. Spear, 169, 170, 372, 373
Gulf Ref. Co. v. Bagby, 256
Gulf Ref. Co. v. Goode, 71
Gulf Ref. Co. v. Hayne, 130, 132
Gulf Ref. Co. v. Stanford, 56, 87
Gulf Ref. Co. v. Shatford, 262, 263
Gulf Ref. Co. of Louisiana v. Carroll, 186, 187, 188
Gulf Ref. Co. of Louisiana v. Terry, 217
Gulf Ref. Co. of Louisiana v. United States, 173
Gullatt v. Ashland Oil & Ref. Co., 158, 160
Gypsy Oil Co. v. Cover, 495
Gypsy Oil Co. v. Marsh, 277, 278, 283, 284, 285
Gypsy Oil Co. v. Schonwald, 473, 474, 476, 477

Haby v. Stanolind Oil and Gas Co., 300, 302, 388, 389
Haddad v. Boon, 125
Haddock v. McClendon, 322, 323
Hafeman v. Gem Oil Co., 367, 370, 374, 476, 479
Hagar v. Martin, 216
Hager v. Stakes, 55, 123, 456
Hague v. Wheeler, 24
Hail v. Reed, 24
Haines v. McLean, 213
Haken v. Harper Oil Co., 434, 437
Halbert v. Green, 104
Halbert v. Hendrix, 29, 30
Hall v. Douglas, 130
Hall v. McWilliams, 296, 300
Hall v. Vernon, 130, 137, 138
Hall Oil Co. v. Barquin, 169, 171
Hamblen v. Placid Oil Co., 504
Hamilton v. Baker, 256
Hamilton v. Foster, 26
Hamlin v. Attorney Gen., 214
Hamman v. Cooperative Refinery Ass'n, 369
Hammett Oil Co. v. Gypsy Oil Co., 345
Hammonds v. Central Kentucky Natural Gas Co., 25, 28, 175
Hancock Oil Co. v. Meeker-Garner Oil Co., 173
Hanlin v. Westhoma Oil Co., 486
Hanna v. Shorts, 277, 281, 282

Hans v. Great Bend Brick & Tile Co., 8, 10
Hanson v. Ware, 42, 53, 56
Harbert v. Hope Natural Gas Co., 395
Hardcastle v. McCluskey, 54, 56, 58
Hardie v. Chew Fish Yuen, 198
Hardin v. Eubank, 133
Harding v. Cameron, 361
Hardwick v. Jackson, 452
Hardy v. Greathouse, 53, 55, 103
Harkins v. Hatfield, 134
Harley v. Magnolia Petroleum Co., 474, 479
Harper v. Ford, 136, 137
Harrel v. Atlantic Ref. Co., 265
Harrell v. Bakhaus, 453
Harrell v. Vahlsing, Inc., 156
Harrington v. Railroad Comm'n, 174
Harrington v. Texaco, Inc., 174
Harris v. Currie, 49, 123, 456
Harris v. Michael, 495
Harris v. Morris Plan Co., 416, 417, 418, 449, 451
Harris v. Ohio Oil Co., 413, 445, 449
Harris v. Skelly, 333
Harris v. Windsor, 115
Harriss v. Ritter, 89, 91
Harter v. Edwards, 256
Hartman v. Potter, 116
Hartman Ranch Co. v. Associated Oil Co., 431, 433, 434, 504
Haskell v. Wood, 199, 200, 202, 203
Hasquet v. Big West Oil Co., 183, 184
Hassell v. Texaco, Inc., 142, 149
Hastings v. Pichinson, 302, 315
Hastings Oil Co. v. Texas Co., 173, 174
Hathorn v. Natural Carbonic Gas Co., 11
Hawkins v. Klein, 501
Haynes v. Board of Comm'rs, 5
Haynes v. Eagle-Picher Co., 504
Hays v. Phoenix Mut. Life Ins. Co., 73, 85
Hays Estate, Inc., Stephen v. Togliatti, 11
Headley v. Hoopengarner, 369, 370
Heard v. Pratt, 303
Heath v. Gray, 244
Hebert v. Sun Oil Co., 340
Heffelfinger v. Scott, 226
Heinatz v. Allen, 7, 9, 11, 14
Heller v. Dailey, 29, 30, 245
Helmley v. Ashland Oil Co., 363
Helms v. Guthrie, 91
Hemus & Co. v. Hawkins, 357, 359
Henderson v. Chesley, 138, 139
Henderson Co. v. Murphy, 491
Hendler v. Lehigh Val. R.R. Co., 9, 10, 11
Henkel v. Henkel, 127, 137
Henry v. Clay, 285
Henry v. Gulf Ref. Co., 245, 501
Henson v. Bryant, 127, 133, 138
Herigstad v. Hardrock Oil Co., 245
Hern v. Skelly Oil Co., 96
Hershey v. Hershey, 369
Heyl v. Northern Trust Co., 226, 228
Heyser v. Frankfort Oil Co., 198, 202, 205, 206
Hibbert v. Mudd, 341
Hickernell v. Gregory, 247
Hickey v. Dirks, 85
Hicks v. Mid-Kansas Oil & Gas Co., 317, 318
Higgins v. California Petroleum & Asphalt Co., 396, 467, 469
Higgins Oil & Fuel Co. v. Guaranty Oil Co., 25
Highland v. Commonwealth of Pennsylvania, 2, 3, 4
Hightower v. Marktzky, 36, 37, 94
Hill v. Larcon Co., 250, 264, 385, 386
Hinkle v. Gauntt, 68, 69, 458
Hisle v. Keltner, 282
Hitson v. Gilman, 414, 497
Hivick v. Urschel, 503
Hixon v. Parker, 371, 388
Hoff v. Girdler Corp., 292, 293, 294
Hoffman v. Magnolia Petroleum Co., 458, 464, 469, 470
Hoffman v. Sohio Petroleum Co., 474
Holbein v. Austral Oil Co., 355, 361
Holchak v. Clark, 45, 277, 281
Holifield v. Perkins, 49
Holland v. Dolese Co., 9, 11, 13, 15, 19
Holland v. Shaffer, 127, 133
Holland v. Vela De Pena, 315
Hollingsworth v. Mexia, 118
Hollister Co. v. Cal–L Exploration Corp., 35, 41, 42, 43, 44
Hollyfield v. Rovenger, 107
Home Royalty Ass'n Inc. v. Stone, 277, 281
Homestake Exploration Corp. v. Schoregge, 25
Hood v. Southern Production Co., 433, 447, 448
Hooks v. Neil, 113, 114, 378
Horn v. Skelly Oil Co., 68
Horst v. Handke, 392
House v. Tidewater, 328
Houston v. Moore Inv. Co., 47, 96, 98, 99
Houston Farms Development Co. v. United States, 50

TABLE OF CASES
References are to Pages

Houston Oil Co. of Texas v. Moss, 146
Houston Production Co. v. Mecom Oil Co., 172
Hove v. Atchison, 274, 378
Howard v. Dillard, 35, 36, 37, 38, 94, 95
Howell v. Kentucky-West Virginia Gas Co., 391, 393
Howell v. Liles, 120
Howell v. Union Producing Co., 396, 406
Howerton v. Kansas Natural Gas Co., 445, 446, 447, 450
Hoyt v. Amerada Petroleum Corp., 158, 160
Hoyt v. Continental Oil Co., 299, 300, 301, 306, 331
Huber Corp. v. Denman, 367
Huddleston v. Peel, 146
Hudgins v. Lincoln Nat'l Life Ins. Co., 42, 45, 47, 96, 97, 98, 130
Hudson & Collins v. McGuire, 4
Hughes v. Busseyville Oil & Gas Co., 428, 434
Hughes v. Cantwell, 187, 192, 193, 194
Hughes v. Cordell, 499
Hughes v. Franklin, 253, 268, 269
Huhn v. Marshall Exploration, Inc., 321, 322
Huie Hodge Lumber Co. v. Railroad Lands Co., 2, 3, 4, 6
Hull v. Magnolia Petroleum Co., 449
Humble Oil & Ref. Co. v. Clark, 195, 275
Humble Oil & Ref. Co. v. Grucholski, 159, 160, 161
Humble Oil & Ref. Co. v. Guillory, 56
Humble Oil & Ref. Co. v. Harrison, 268, 271
Humble Oil & Ref. Co. v. Hutchins, 407
Humble Oil & Ref. Co. v. Kishi, 162, 163, 170, 181, 182, 187
Humble Oil & Ref. Co. v. Lasseter, 138, 139
Humble Oil & Ref. Co. v. Luckel, 164, 178, 179, 180, 181
Humble Oil & Ref. Co. v. McLean, 182
Humble Oil & Ref. Co. v. Mullican, 254
Humble Oil & Ref. Co. v. Poe, 349, 350
Humble Oil & Ref. Co. v. Romero, 419
Humble Oil & Ref. Co. v. West, 28
Humphreys v. Fletcher, 251, 274
Humphreys-Mexia Co. v. Gammon, 27, 147
Humphrys v. Skelly Oil Co., 317
Hunt Oil Co. v. Berry, 178, 179, 180, 181
Hunter v. Clarkson, 278, 279, 292, 293, 294
Hunter Co. v. Vaughn, 388, 389

Hurley v. North Pac. Ry. Co., 70, 153
Hurst v. Paken Oil Co., 467
Hutchins v. Humble Oil and Ref. Co., 430, 434, 436, 437
Hutchinson v. Schneeberger, 274
Hyaldahl v. Alphin, 497

Iams v. Carnegie Natural Gas Co., 336
Iberian Oil Corp. v. Texas Crude Oil Co., 322
Ilari v. Ewing, 226
Illinois Central R.R. Co., United States v., 210
Illinois Mid-Continent Co. v. Tennis, 322, 323, 388, 389
Imes v. Globe Oil & Ref. Co., 400
In re (see name of party)
Indian Territory Illuminating Oil Co. v. Rosamond, 413
Indiana Natural Gas & Oil Co. v. Hinton, 395
Indiana Oil, Gas & Development Co. v. McCrory, 440
Inland Steel Co. v. Isaacs, 143
Inslee v. Palmer, 104, 105
Investors Royalty Co. v. Childrens Hosp. Medical Center, 315
Irick v. Hubbell & Webb, 397
Irons v. Fort Worth Sand & Gravel Co., 232, 233
Iskian v. Consolidated Gas Utilities Corp., 59, 476

Jackson v. Farmer, 393, 408
Jackson v. McKenney, 125
Jackson v. Pure Oil Operating Co., 385
Jackson v. Twin State Oil Co., 247
Jackson v. United Producers' Pipe Line Co., 261
Jackson, Inc., Geier v. James, 322
Japhet v. McRae, 467, 468
Jarrett v. Ross, 179
Jath Oil Co. v. Durbin Branch, 280, 292
Jefferson Lake Sulphur Co. v. Lambert, 50
Jenkins v. Pure Oil Co., 172
Jenks v. Jenks, 138
Jessen & Associates, Inc., Norman v. Amoco Production Co., 247, 274
Jilek v. Chicago, Wilmington & Franklin Coal Co., 141, 142, 143
Joens v. Baumbach, 214
Johnson v. Hinkel, 387
Johnson v. Jernigan, 353, 354, 356, 361, 362
Johnson v. Smallenberger, 251, 267, 268, 274

TABLE OF CASES

Johnson v. Texas Gulf Coast Corp., 368
Johnson v. Unknown Heirs, 143
Johnston v. Cole, 491
Johnston v. Hayes, 106
Joiner v. Sullivan, 112
Jolly v. Wilson, 69, 73, 94, 95, 96
Jones v. Forest Oil Co., 25
Jones v. Hayton, 134, 138
Jones v. Interstate Oil Corp., 451
Jones v. Killingsworth, 399
Jones v. McFaddin, 147
Jones v. Moore, 322, 324
Jones v. Rock Island Improvement Co., 13
Jones v. Whittington, 452
Jones v. Wood, 244
Joyce v. Wyant, 486
Joyce v. Zachary, 172
Jul-Tex Drilling Co. v. Pure Oil Co., 477, 479

Kachelmacher v. Laird, 414
Kadrmas v. Sauvageau, 117, 118, 120
Kahn v. Arkansas River Gas Co., 295, 296
Kaiser v. Love, 59, 464, 465
Kalberer v. Grassham, 9, 11
Kale v. Ohio Fuel Gas Co., 419
Kanawha & Hocking Coal & Coke Co. v. Carbon County, 142
Kansas City Southern Ry. Co. v. Reinman, 17
Kansas Natural Gas Co. v. Board of Comm'rs of Neosho County, 29
Karns v. Tanner, 247
Katschor v. Eason Oil Co., 348, 352, 355
Kaufman v. Arnaudville Co., 368
Kays v. Little, 268
Keaton v. Murphy, 59
Kelley v. Haas, 112
Kelly v. Harris, 245
Kelly v. Keys, 244
Kelly v. Ohio Oil Co., 26, 244
Kelwood Farms, Inc. v. Ritchie, 294
Kemmerer v. Midland Oil & Drilling Co., 215, 217
Kennedy v. General Geophysical Co., 158
Kenoyer v. Magnolia Petroleum Co., 402, 403, 406
Kentucky Bank & Trust Co. v. Ashland Oil & Transp. Co., 53
Kentucky Diamond Mining & Developing Co. v. Kentucky Transvaal Diamond Co., 8, 10
Kentucky Natural Gas Corp. v. Carter, 240, 241, 243

Kentucky-West Virginia Gas Co. v. Browning, 2, 4, 6
Kerr v. Hillenberg, 284, 292, 293, 294
Keville v. Hollister Co., 35, 37, 39, 40, 41
Kidd v. Hoggett, 179, 180, 184, 306
Kile v. Amerada Petroleum Corp., 491
Kilfoyle v. Wright, 35, 85, 115
Kilpatrick v. Gulf Production Co., 149, 150, 151
Kimble v. Wetzel Natural Gas Co., 395
Kimbley v. Luckey, 467, 468
Kimsey v. Fore, 42, 44, 45
Kinder v. LaSalle County Carbon Coal Co., 8, 10, 150
King v. First Nat'l Bank of Wichita Falls, 113, 378
Kingery v. Continental Oil Co., 346, 359
Kingwood Oil Co. v. Loehr, 491
Kinne v. Swanson Consol. Oil Co., 277
Kirby Lumber Corp. v. Claypool, 27
Kiser v. Eberly, 25, 28, 245
Klein v. First Nat'l Bank of Chicago, 126
Klein v. Humble Oil & Ref. Co., 69, 94, 95, 98, 120, 379
Kleppner v. Lemon, 415, 417, 434, 436, 449
Klostermann v. Houston Geophysical Co., 160, 161
Knox v. Farmers State Bank, 183, 184
Knox v. Rutherford, 107
Koen v. Bartlett, 197, 198, 202, 203
Kokernot v. Caldwell, 456, 459, 465
Kolachny v. Galbreath, 245, 279
Komarek v. Perrine, 129, 130
Kothmann v. Boley, 303, 324
Kouns v. Southwood, 258, 268, 272
Kraker v. Unknown Heirs, 77
Krauss v. Fry, 113, 115
Krebs v. Hodgson, 107
Krone v. Lacy, 474, 476
Kronmiller v. Hafner, 256, 258
Krug v. Cities Serv. Petroleum Co., 186, 187, 188
Krug v. Reissig, 111
Krutzfeld v. Stevenson, 459, 460
Kugel v. Young, 251, 254, 258, 267, 274

L & G Oil Co. v. Railroad Comm'n, 175
La Fitte Co. v. United Fuel Gas Co., 337, 352, 355, 450
La Laguna Ranch Co. v. Dodge, 501
Lachman v. Sperry-Sun Well Surveying Co., 174
Lackey v. Corley, 80
Lackey v. Ohio Oil Co., 346
Lacy, Inc., R. v. Jarrett, 114

TABLE OF CASES

Ladd v. Upham, 352, 355
Lake v. Ohio Fuel Gas Co., 447, 448
Lamb v. Vansyckle, 292, 294
Lambach v. Town of Mason, 165, 169, 170
Lambert v. Pritchett, 6
Lamczyk v. Allen, 277, 308, 388, 389
Landauer v. Huey, 452
Lane v. Elkins, 64
Laney v. Monsanto Chem. Co., 150
Langlinais v. Geophysical Serv., Inc., 148, 159, 160
Lanyon Zinc Co. v. Freeman, 227, 232
Larrison v. Walker, 139
LaRue v. Wiggins, 481
Lasater v. ConVest Energy Corp., 363, 368
Lathrop v. Eyestone, 53, 54, 55, 56, 57, 58, 71, 83, 89, 93
Law v. Heck Oil Co., 186, 188
Lawley v. Richardson, 198, 203, 204
Lawrence Oil Corp. v. Metcalfe, 165
Lawsen v. Earp, 76, 94, 96
Layman v. Hodnett, 226, 232
Le Blanc v. Haynesville Mercantile Co., 47, 403
Leach v. Brown, 399, 406
LeBar v. Haynie, 320, 322
Lebow v. Cameron, 169, 170, 171, 172
LeCuno Oil Co. v. Smith, 352, 354, 355
Ledford v. Atkins, 267, 268, 269
Lehfeldt v. Adams, 142
Leidig v. Hoopes, 111, 112
Lelong v. Richardson, 315
Leonard v. Barnes, 397
Leonard v. Busch-Everett Co., 254
Leonard Crude Oil Co. v. Walton, 472
Lester v. Mid-South Oil Co., 317, 318
Lewis v. East Texas Fin., 377
Lewis v. Grininger, 272
Lewis v. Nance, 321
Lewis v. Oates, 57, 237
Leydig v. Commissioner, 54, 55, 56
Libby v. DeBaca, 450
Light v. Crowson Well Serv., Inc., 106
Lightcap v. Mobil Oil Corp., 354, 356, 358
Lindow v. Southern Carbon Co., 447, 448, 450, 498
Link v. State's Oil Corp., 414, 415
Linn v. Wehrle, 425
Lippert v. Angle, 342, 354, 358
Little v. Mountain View Dairies, 68, 69, 79, 187, 458
Lively v. Federal Land Bank of Louisville, 71
Livingston Oil Corp. v. Waggoner, 345

Lloyd's Estate v. Mullen Tractor & Equipment Co., 244, 264, 414
Locke v. Palmore, 294
Locke v. Russell, 344, 345
Lockey v. Corley, 80, 83
Logan v. Blaxton, 388, 389, 390
Logan v. California Co., 263, 264
Logue v. Marsh, 53, 55
Lone Star Gas Co. v. Harris, 349, 350
Lone Star Gas Co. v. Murchison, 25, 28, 53, 175
Lone Star Gas Co. v. Stine, 349, 350
Lone Star Producing Co. v. Walker, 328
Long v. Hitzelberger, 128, 129
Long v. Magnolia Petroleum Co., 250
Long-Bell Lumber Co. v. Granger, 111, 112
Longino v. Machen, 59, 70
Louisville Gas Co. v. Kentucky Heating Co., 26, 30
Louisiana Gas Lands v. Burrow, 441
Love v. McDonald, 199
Lucas v. Thompson, 118, 120
Luckel v. Barnsdall Oil Co., 136, 139
Ludey v. Pure Oil Co., 345
Ludolph v. Tuel & Thoenen Inc., 391, 392, 394
Lund v. Starz, 386
Luse v. Boatman, 3, 6
Lykes Bros., Inc. v. McConnel, 146
Lynch v. Davis, 396, 406
Lynch v. Southern Coast Drilling Co., 281
Lyon v. Gambill, 391, 393
Lyon v. Miller, 446

MacCorkle v. City of Charleston, 214
MacDonald v. Follett, 501
MacMaster v. Onstad, 2, 9, 11
McBride v. Hutson, 54
McClung v. Lawrence, 125
McClure, In re Estate of, 231
McCombs v. Stephenson, 9, 10, 11
McCoy v. Lowrie, 142
McCoy v. Texon Royalty Co., 275
McCoy v. United States Gas Public Serv. Co., 349, 350
McCutcheon v. Enon Oil & Gas Co., 449
McElmurray v. McElmurray, 114
McElvain v. Texas Co., 467, 470
McEvoy v. First Nat'l Bank and Trust Co. of Enid, 278, 294, 405
McGarraugh v. McGanaugh, 50
McInteer v. Gillespie, 128
McIntire's Adm'r v. Bond, 467, 470
McIntosh v. Ropp, 187
McIntosh v. Vail, 57

TABLE OF CASES
References are to Pages

McKenna v. Nichlos, 419, 451
McKenna v. Wallis, 480
McKinney's Heirs v. Central Kentucky Natural Gas Co., 2, 3, 6
McKinnon v. Lane, 467
McLachlan v. Stroube, 491
McLain v. First Nat'l Bank of Fort Worth, 120, 121
McLaughlin v. Brock, 253
McMahan v. Boggess, 414, 415
McMahon v. Christmann, 62, 117, 118, 120, 123, 125, 381, 382
McMillan v. Powell, 188, 190
McMullin v. Magnuson, 8, 10
McNabb v. South Eastern Gas Co. of West Virginia, 59
McNeese v. Renner, 78, 79
McNeil v. Peaker, 491
McVicker v. Horn, Robinson and Nathan, 278, 280
McWilliams v. Standard Oil Co., 59
Mack Oil Co. v. Laurence, 11, 15
Macon v. Trowbridge, 446
Maddox v. Gulf Oil Corp., 363, 367
Maddox v. Texas Co., 349, 350
Magnolia Petroleum Co. v. Connellee, 347, 348, 349
Magnolia Petroleum Co. v. King, 366
Magnolia Petroleum Co. v. Page, 413, 431, 432
Magnolia Petroleum Co. v. Rockhold, 418, 419, 424
Magnolia Petroleum Co., State v., 48
Magnolia Petroleum Co. v. Wilson, 418, 419
Malarnee v. Pauline Oil & Gas Co., 369
Mallett v. Union Oil & Gas Corp. of La., 400
Maloy v. Smith, 151
Manley v. Boling, 68
Mann v. Rio Bravo Oil Co., 372, 373
Mansfield Gas Co. v. Alexander, 413
Manufacturers Gas & Oil Co. v. Indiana Natural Gas & Oil Co., 24, 25, 26
Marias River Syndicate v. Big West Oil Co., 79, 82, 85, 86
Marshall v. Hobert's Estate, 233
Martel v. Hall Oil Co., 157, 163, 177
Martel v. Hunt, 166, 169, 170
Martin v. Amis, 337
Martin v. Humble Oil and Ref. Co., 228
Martin v. Knight, 100
Martin v. Kostner, 403
Martin v. Snuggs, 69, 96, 98
Marvel v. Merritt, 6

Mason v. Ladd Petroleum Co., 282, 283, 284, 285, 287, 290
Masterson v. Gulf Oil Corp., 61, 423, 424
Matheson v. Placid Oil Co., 164
Mathews v. Sun Oil Co., 283
Matter of (see name of party)
Mattison v. Trotti, 192, 251, 264
Matzen v. Hugoton Production Co., 337, 352, 354, 355, 356, 361
Maurer v. Arab Petroleum Corp., 222
Mayhew v. Callard, 167, 169, 172
Maynard v. McHenry, 3, 4
Maynard v. Ratliff, 52
Medina Oil Development Co. v. Murphy, 127, 132, 187
Medusa Portland Cement Co. v. Lamantina, 142
Meeks v. Harmon, 73, 75, 86
Melancon v. Cheramie, 89, 93
Melancon v. Texas Co., 53, 340
Melton v. Davis, 110
Melton v. Sneed, 70, 73, 141
Merchants & Mfrs. Bank v. Dennis, 120
Meredith v. Meredith, 197, 198, 199, 200, 201
Merrill Engineering Co. v. Capitol Nat'l Bank, 53, 54, 406, 467
Merriweather v. Jackson, 139, 140
Metz v. Doss, 283
Meyers v. Central Nat'l Bank of Okmulgee, 74
Midas Oil Co. v. Whitaker, 491
Mid-Continent Petroleum Corp. v. Rhodes, 215
Middleton v. Broussard, 114
Middleton v. California Co., 417, 420
Midland Gas Corp. v. Reffitt, 445, 447
Mid-Northern Oil Co. v. Walker, 3
Midwest Oil Corp. v. Lude, 295, 315, 316
Midwest Oil Corp. v. Mengers, 315
Midwest Oil Corp. v. Winsauer, 45, 295, 297, 303
Miles v. Martin, 120
Miller v. Cisco, 222
Miller v. Hodges, 303
Miller v. Ridgley, 26, 29
Miller v. Sooy, 55, 56, 58
Miller v. Speed, 69, 78, 79
Miller v. Tidal Oil Co., 165, 168, 169, 170
Millette v. Phillips Petroleum Co., 434, 435, 436, 437, 438, 448
Millikin Trust Co. v. Jarvis, 228, 231
Milling v. Collector of Revenue, 60
Mills v. Mills, 201, 202
Mills v. Taylor, 202, 203
Minchen v. Fields, 51, 52, 403, 467

TABLE OF CASES
References are to Pages

Minchen v. Hirsch, 116
Mining Corp. of Arkansas v. International Paper Co., 2, 6, 8, 11, 15
Mississippi River Fuel Corp. v. Fontenot, 30
Missouri Pac. R.R. Co. v. Strohacker, 2, 3, 6, 7
Mitchell v. Amerada Hess Corp., 418, 419, 424
Mitchell v. Espinosa, 27, 30
Mitchell v. Hannah, 78
Mitchell v. Mitchell, 198, 204, 207
Mitchell v. Simms, 254, 275, 276
Mitchell v. Union Drilling & Petroleum Co., 438, 442, 446
Mitchell Energy Corp. v. Blakley, 308
Mobil Oil Corp. v. FPC, 357
Moffett v. International Paper Co., 142, 143
Mohoma Oil Co. v. Ambassador Oil Corp., 150, 151
Mollohan v. Patton, 180, 181, 183, 184
Molter v. Lewis, 337, 352, 355
Monarch Oil, Gas & Coal Co. v. Richardson, 414
Moncrief v. Pasotex Petroleum Co., 317, 318
Monon Coal Co. v. Riggs, 2, 3, 7
Monsanto Chem. Co. v. Andreae, 434, 435, 436
Monsanto Chem. Co. v. Sykes, 436
Monsanto Co. v. Tyrrell, 277
Montana Power Co. v. Kravik, 358, 359
Montgomery v. Ebony Hills Improvement Co., 118
Montgomery v. Rittersbacher, 404
Moody v. Wagner, 186, 187, 188, 191
Moore v. Campbell, 504
Moore v. Vines, 202, 203, 205, 206
Moore Oil, Inc. v. Snakard, 322
Moorer v. Bethlehem Baptist Church, 30, 244
Morgan v. Farr, 59, 64
Morgan v. McGee, 70, 112
Morris v. Messer, 245, 414
Morrison v. Socolofsky, 8, 11, 12, 14, 15, 19
Morrison v. Swaim, 277, 281, 320, 328
Morriss v. First Nat'l Bank of Mission, 47, 51, 60, 61, 62, 371
Morten v. Sutcliffe, 267, 268
Moseley v. Hearrell, 127, 128, 133
Moser v. United States Steel Corp., 9, 13, 19, 21, 23
Moshiek v. Lininger, 467, 468
Moss & Urschel v. Clark, 128

Mounger v. Pittman, 78, 79, 89, 97
Mountain Forest Fur Farms of America, Inc. v. Cockrell, 35, 39
Mountain Missions Sch., Inc. v. White, 145
Mowrer v. Ashland Oil & Ref. Co., 176
Moyer v. Walker, 264
Mueller v. Sutherland, 471
Murbarger v. Franklin, 28
Murphy v. Athans, 73, 117, 118, 120
Murphy v. Dilworth, 64, 68, 69
Murphy v. Earp, 94, 96
Murphy v. Garfield Oil Co., 250
Murphy Oil Co. v. Burnet, 51
Murray v. Allard, 3, 7, 26
Mussellem v. Magnolia Petroleum Co., 346, 347

Nabors v. Producers Oil Co., 397
Nadeau v. Texas Co., 274
Nafco Oil & Gas, Inc. v. Tartan Resources Corp., 495
Nale v. Carroll, 471
Nance v. Donk Bros. Coal & Coke Co., 5
Nash v. Shell Petroleum Corp., 471
National Bank of Tulsa v. Warren, 488
National Forge Co. v. Carlson, 368
Natural Gas Distributing Corp. v. Williams, 352, 355
National Supply Co. v. McLeod, 30
Navajo Tribe of Indians v. United States, 9
Nelson v. Bloodworth, 141
Nephi Plaster & Mfg. Co. v. Juab County, 10
New Domain Oil & Gas Co. v. McKinney, 186, 187, 188, 190, 191
New Mexico & Arizona Land Co. v. Elkins, 9, 11
New Orleans & Northeastern R.R. Co. v. Morrison, 214
New State Oil & Gas Co. v. Dunn, 413
New York State Natural Gas Corp. v. Swan-Finch Gas Development Corp., 2
Newbern v. Gould, 70, 112
Newcomb v. Blankenship, 130, 136
Newell v. McMillan, 231
Newell v. Phillips Petroleum Co., 440
Newell, Inc. v. Randall, 9, 11, 12, 13
Newport Oil Co. v. Lamb, 381
Noble v. Johnson, 180
Noble v. Kahn, 221
Noble, United States v., 54, 55
Noel Estate, Inc. v. Murray, 282, 284, 285, 495

TABLE OF CASES
References are to Pages

Noffsinger v. Brown, 110
Nolan v. Thomas, 419, 449, 450
Norris v. Vaughan, 60
North American Petroleum Co. v. Knight, 430, 446
Northcut v. Church, 146
Northern Natural Gas Co. v. Grounds, 9
Northern Pac. Ry. Co. v. Soderberg, 2, 10, 11, 14
Northwest Oil Co. v. Railway Comm'n, 472
Northwestern Ohio Natural Gas Co. v. Ullery, 467, 468, 470
Novak v. Bruner, 263
Noxon v. Union Oil Co. of California, 51
Nunez v. Superior Oil Co., 341
Nunley v. Shell Oil Co., 415
Nutter v. Stockton, 206

Odstrcil v. McGlaun, 35, 37, 38, 39, 128
Ogle v. Barker, 111
O'Hara v. Coltrin, 247, 251, 267
Ohio Fuel Oil Co. v. Greenleaf, 278
Ohio Oil Co. v. Daughetee, 227
Ohio Oil Co. v. Indiana, 24, 26
Ohio Oil Co. v. Lane, 336
Ohio Oil Co., State v., 25
Okmulgee Supply Corp. v. Anthis, 441, 442, 445
Oldfield v. Gypsy Oil Co., 268, 269, 270
Oldham v. Fortner, 110
Oldland v. Gray, 489
Oliver v. Culpepper, 232, 233
Olson v. Dillerud, 8, 11, 12, 13, 15
Olson v. Signal Drilling and Exploration Inc., 420
O'Neal v. Union Producing Co., 349, 350
1,253.14 Acres of Land, United States v., 6, 8, 9, 10, 11, 12, 19
Orive v. Sun Oil Co., 283
Orndoff v. Consumer's Fuel Co., 197, 198, 207
Osborn v. Arkansas Territorial Oil & Gas Co., 467, 468
Osborn v. Finklestein, 383
Osborn v. Osborn, 137
Overton v. Porterfield, 127, 136
Owens v. Day, 295

Pace v. State ex rel. Rice, 215
Pacific Western Oil Co. v. Bern Oil Co., 167, 173, 174
Paddock v. Vasquez, 458, 460
Padgett v. Padgett, 369
Paine v. Moore, 480
Palmer v. Crews, 71
Palmer v. Lide, 91

Palmer Oil & Gas Co. v. Parish, 245
Palmer Oil Corp. v. Phillips Petroleum Co., 486
Pan American Petroleum Co. v. Long, 174
Pan American Petroleum Corp. v. Cain, 35, 36, 37, 38, 39
Pan American Petroleum Corp. v. Candelaria, 166
Pan American Petroleum Corp. v. Hardy, 417, 425
Pan American Petroleum Corp. v. Robinson, 371
Pan-American Petroleum Corp. v. Texas Pac. Coal & Oil Co., 104, 107
Pan American Petroleum Corp. v. Vines, 403
Pan American Production Co. v. Hollandsworth, 140
Panhandle Co-op. Royalty Co. v. Cunningham, 4, 5, 8, 12, 13, 14, 16, 19
Panhandle Eastern Pipe Line Co. v. Isaacson, 294, 405
Pardue v. Mark, 320, 321, 326
Pariani v. State, 9, 10, 12
Parker v. Parker, 396, 469
Parks v. Sinai Oil and Gas Co., 279, 283, 327
Parkway in the City of New York, In re, 214
Parmelee v. Nueces Royalty Co., 51
Parnell, Inc. v. Giller, Trustee, 337, 352, 355
Pasteur v. Niswanger, 130, 135, 245
Pate v. Western Geophysical Co. of America, 158, 159, 160
Patrick v. Allen, 393
Patterson v. Texas Co., 62
Patton v. Rogers, 315, 386
Pauley v. Faucett, 104
Paxton v. Benedum-Trees Oil Co., 72, 86
Payne v. Campbell, 71, 81, 89
Peabody Coal Co. v. Erwin, 12, 19
Pearce v. Southern Natural Gas Co., 262
Pease v. Dolezal, 76, 85
Peerless Oil & Gas Co. v. Tipken, 397, 469
Pellow v. Arctic Mining Co., 139
Pennagrade Oil & Gas Co. v. Martin, 277
Pennzoil Producing Co. v. FPC, 357
People v. _____ (see opposing party)
People's Gas Co. v. Tyner, 25
Pepper v. Pyramid Oil & Gas Corp., 504
Perkins v. Magnolia Petroleum Co., 259
Perkins v. Saunders, 318, 319

TABLE OF CASES
References are to Pages

Persky v. First State Bank of Vernon, 288
Petersen v. Robinson Oil & Gas Co., 322, 323, 324
Petroleum Engineers Producing Corp. v. White, 324
Petroleum Exchange Inc. v. Poynter, 245, 480, 481
Petroleum Exploration Corp. v. Hensley, 187, 190
Petroleum Producers Co. v. Steffens, 413
Petrus v. Cage Bros., 198, 202, 207
Pfister v. Brown, 7, 9, 12, 15
Pfisterer v. Noble, 115
Phillips v. Inexco Oil Co., 503
Phillips v. Phillips, 133, 138, 139
Phillips v. Springfield Crude Oil Co., 30
Phillips v. Suntex Oil & Gas Co., 324, 329
Phillips Petroleum Co. v. Buster, 392
Phillips Petroleum Co. v. Bynum, 352, 353, 354
Phillips Petroleum Co. v. Corporation Comm'n of Oklahoma, 392
Phillips Petroleum Co. v. Cowden, 153, 156
Phillips Petroleum Co. v. Curtis, 268, 269, 270, 271
Phillips Petroleum Co. v. Harnly, 312, 313, 315
Phillips Petroleum Co. v. Johnson, 352, 355, 356
Phillips Petroleum Co. v. McIlroy, 469
Phillips Petroleum Co. v. Millette, 25, 434, 435, 446
Phillips Petroleum Co. v. Ochsner, 352, 354
Phillips Petroleum Co. v. Richard, 68, 82, 94, 95
Phillips Petroleum Co. v. Smith, 158, 159
Phillips Petroleum Co. v. Stahl Petroleum Co., 364
Phillips Petroleum Co. v. State of Wisconsin, 356
Phillips Petroleum Co. v. Taylor, 491, 504
Phillips Petroleum Co. v. Texaco, Inc., 9
Phillips Petroleum Co. v. Williams, 363, 367, 369
Picard v. Richards, 56, 69, 71
Pich v. Lankford, 100
Picou v. Fohs Oil Co., 156
Pierce v. Atlantic Ref. Co., 340
Pierce v. Goldking Properties, Inc., 434, 437, 445
Pierce v. Texas Pac. Oil Co., 357
Pierson v. Case, 146
Piney Oil & Gas Co. v. Allen, 245, 378

Piney Oil & Gas Co. v. Scott, 142, 143, 150
Pittsburg & West Virginia Gas Co. v. Ankrom, 467, 468, 471
Pittsburgh & West Virginia Gas Co. v. Nicholson, 394
Placid Oil Co. v. Lee, 215
Ploeger v. Humble Oil & Ref. Co., 268, 272
Plow Realty Co. of Texas, 252
Poe v. Ulrey, 30, 245, 247, 414
Poindexter v. Lion Oil Ref. Co., 416, 447, 448, 449, 450, 451
Pollard v. Simpson, 142
Pollock v. McAlester Fuel Co., 378, 382
Pomeroy v. Pearce, 165
Portwood v. Buckalew, 42, 44, 45, 47
Postier v. Postier, 295
Potucek v. Blair, 245
Powell v. Burroughs, 446
Powers v. Bridgeport Oil Co., 386
Praetorian Diamond Oil Ass'n v. Garvey, 17
Prairie Oil & Gas Co. v. Allen, 186, 187, 188, 190
Prairie Oil Co. v. Carleton, 388, 389
Pratt v. Gerstner, 385, 386, 387
Preston v. Lambert, 281
Preston v. White, 130, 133, 137, 138
Price v. Atlantic Ref. Co., 114
Priddy v. School Dist. No. 78, Cotton County, 210
Prince Bros. Drilling Co. v. Fuhrman Petroleum Corp., 488
Pritchett v. Forest Oil Corp., 400
Probst v. Bearman, 168, 172
Probst v. Hughes, 502, 503
Probst v. Ingram, 51, 61, 62, 378, 381, 382
Proctor v. Graham, 27
Producers Pipe & Supply Co. v. James, 60, 61
Proper v. Butcher, 386
Pruitt v. Burrow, 112
Pryor Mountain Oil & Gas Co. v. Cross, 278
Psencik v. Wessels, 10, 14
Puget Mill Co. v. Duecy, 2, 11
Pure Oil Co. v. Kindall, 26, 27, 53, 55

Quintana Petroleum Co., State v., 53, 54, 55

Radke v. Union Pac. R.R. Co., 29, 30
Ragsdale v. Superior Oil Co., 406
Railroad Comm'n v. Delhi-Taylor Oil Corp., 471

TABLE OF CASES
References are to Pages

Railroad Comm'n v. Humble Oil & Ref. Co., 471
Railroad Comm'n v. Magnolia Petroleum Co., 471
Railroad Comm'n v. Manziel, 176
Railroad Comm'n v. Williams, 471
Railroad Comm'n of Texas v. Coleman, 472
Raley v. Moore, 467
Ralph v. Magnolia Petroleum Co., 426
Ramage v. Potter, 315
Ramirez v. Flag Oil Corp. of Delaware, 201
Ramsey v. Carter Oil Co., 438, 442
Randolph's Estate, In re, 54, 56, 58
Rankin v. Naftalis, 501, 502
Rathbun v. State, 25, 27, 28
Rauner v. Jones, 474, 476
Rawling v. Fisher, 36, 38
Read v. Britain, 350
Ready v. Texaco, Inc., 153
Reagan v. Murphy, 245
Reaugh v. McCollum Exploration Co., 178, 179, 181, 182
Reed v. Hackworth, 337, 354, 355, 361
Reed v. Wylie, 8, 12, 13, 15, 16, 19, 20, 22
Rees v. Briscoe, 503
Reese Enterprises v. Lawson, 277, 282, 283, 284, 287
Reeves v. Republic Production Co., 379, 382, 383
Regular Predestinarian Baptist Church of Pleasant Grove v. Parker, 210
Reiss v. Rummel, 9, 12, 19
Rendleman v. Barlett, 449, 450, 451
Renner v. Huntington-Hawthorne Oil and Gas Co., 287, 295, 302
Renner v. Monsanto Chem. Co., 415, 421, 430
Renwar Oil Corp. v. E.L. Lancaster, 406
Republic Natural Gas Co. v. Baker, 471
Republic Natural Gas Co. v. Melson, 216
Reserve Gas Co. v. Carbon Black Mfg. Co., 261
Resler v. Rogers, 13
Reynolds v. McMan Oil & Gas Co., 342, 347, 348
Reynolds v. McNeill, 293
Reynolds v. Smith, 415, 420, 421, 424
Reynolds, State ex rel. Comm'rs of Land Office v., 221
Rhoads Drilling Co. v. Allred, 428, 440, 441
Rich v. Doneghey, 26, 29, 245, 247
Richard v. Tarpon Oil Co., 267, 269, 274
Richardson v. Hart, 457, 458, 460, 462
Richardson v. Moore, 110
Rickelton v. Universal Constructors, Inc., 8, 9, 11, 12, 14
Ricketts v. Welch, 283
Riddle v. Ellis, 102, 187
Riddlesperger v. Creslenn Ranch Co., 13, 19, 23
Riedt v. Rock Island Improvement Co., 12, 13
Riffel v. Dieter, 86
Right of Way Oil Co. v. Gladys City Oil, Gas & Mfg. Co., 3, 4, 5
Rio Bravo Oil Co. v. McEntire, 143
Rio Bravo Oil Co. v. Staley Oil Co., 146
Rio Bravo Oil Co. v. Weed, 214
Rist v. Westhoma Oil Co., 407
River Rouge Minerals, Inc. v. Energy Resources of Minnesota, 8, 12, 16, 18, 19
Rives v. Gulf Ref. Co., 28
Roach v. Junction Oil and Gas Co., 327
Robbins, In re, 214
Roberson v. Pioneer Gas Co., 495
Roberts v. Jones, 127
Robertson Consol. Land Co. v. Paull, 133, 138
Robichaux v. Pool, 481
Robinson v. Continental Oil Co., 309
Robinson v. Eagle-Picher Lead Co., 501
Robinson v. Humble Oil & Ref. Co., 464
Robinson v. Milam, 467
Robinson v. Robbins Petroleum Corp., 11
Robinson v. Smalley, 245, 480
Robinson v. Speer, 127
Robinson Drilling Co. v. Moses, 218
Rock House Fork Land Co. v. Raleigh Brick & Tile Co., 10, 13, 17
Rogers v. Morgan, 87, 89, 94, 95
Rogers v. Osborn, 319, 320, 321, 324, 325, 326, 329, 330, 331, 403
Rogers v. Westhoma Oil Co., 407
Rogers Nat'l Bank of Jefferson v. Pewitt, 501
Rolander v. Sanderson, 414
Rolls v. Woods, 135
Roskey v. Gulf Oil Corp., 160, 161
Rosse v. Northern Pump Co., 188, 190
Rostocil v. United Oil and Gas Royalty Ass'n, 283
Rousselot v. Spanier, 58
Rowan v. Harburney Oil Co., 245
Rowe v. Bird, 197, 198, 200
Roy v. Arkansas-Louisiana Gas Co., 350
Roy v. Whitaker, 233
Rudman v. Baine, 127, 136
Rudnick v. Union Producing Co., 340

TABLE OF CASES
References are to Pages

Ruiz v. Martin, 404
Rupel v. Ohio Oil Co., 30
Rush v. King Oil Co., 415, 429, 430
Rushing v. Griffin, 260, 268
Ruthven & Co. v. Pan American Petroleum Corp., 474, 477, 479
Ryan v. Fort Worth Nat'l Bank, 111
Ryan v. Pickens, 472
Ryan Consol. Petroleum Corp. v. Pickens, 471
Rylands v. Fletcher, 160

Sachs v. Board of Trustees, 26
Sadler v. Public Nat'l Bank & Trust Co. of New York, 127
St. Louis Royalty Co. v. Continental Oil Co., 329
Saling v. Flesch, 505
Salisbury v. Columbian Fuel Corp., 391
Salmen Brick & Lumber Co. v. Williams, 120, 125
Salter v. Jonas, 214
Salzeider v. Brunsdale, 11
Samano v. Sun Oil Co., 300
Sand Springs Home v. Clemens, 415, 419, 420
Sanders v. Bell, 73, 77, 78, 79
Sanders v. Birmingham, 415, 416, 418
Sanford v. Alabama Power Co., 149, 150
Sanzenbacher v. Howard-Clay Oil Co., 453
Sapp v. Massey, 450, 451
Sapulpa Petroleum Co. v. McCray, 169, 170, 173
Sartor v. United Carbon Co., 352, 353, 362
Sauder v. Fry, 405
Sauder v. Mid-Continent Petroleum Corp., 418, 419, 421, 423, 449, 451
Saulsberry v. Saulsberry, 127
Saulsberry v. Siegel, 292, 293, 294
Saulsbury Oil Co. v. Phillips Petroleum Co., 345, 356
Saunders v. Hornsby, 145
Sautbine v. Keller, 142, 143
Savage v. Packard, 141
Scarmardo v. Potter, 121
Schank v. North American Royalties, Inc., 187, 194
Schlittler v. Smith, 42, 47, 56, 62, 71, 86
Schlumberger Well Surveying Corp. v. Nortex Oil & Gas Corp., 174
Schrader v. Gypsy Oil Co., 474, 476
Schubert v. Miller, 457, 460
Schupbach v. Continental Oil Co., 352, 361, 362

Schwartzenberger v. Hunt Trust Estate, 268, 269, 271
Schwethelm v. Collozo, 165
Scott v. Cohen, 223
Scott v. Hunt Oil Co., 186
Scott v. Laws, 26
Scott v. Pure Oil Co., 407
Scott v. Sampson, 196
Scott v. Steinberger, 361
Scott v. Union Production Co., 405
Scurry Area Canyon Reef Operators Corp. v. Popnoe, 392, 395
Seager v. McCabe, 198, 207
Seeligson v. Eilers, 127, 132
Segelke v. Kilmer, 479, 480
Seigle v. Thomas, 142
Seismorgraph Serv. Corp. v. Buchanan, 159
Sellars v. Grant, 178, 180
Sellars v. Ohio Val. Trust Co., 6
Sellers v. Breidenbach, 295
Selman v. Bristow, 120, 125
Semans v. Adams, 253
Serio v. Chadwick, 245
Shailer's Estate, In re, 202
Shamrock Oil & Gas Corp. v. Coffee, 352, 353, 354
Shank v. North American Royalties, Inc., 193
Shannon v. Long, 247
Sharp v. Fowler, 115
Shaw v. Henry, 441
Shaw v. Watson, 29
Shearer v. United Carbon Co., 245, 504
Sheffield v. Gibbs Bros. and Co., 13, 19, 23
Sheffield v. Hogg, 49, 53, 55, 244
Shell Oil Co. v. Cavanaugh, 159
Shell Oil Co. v. Corporation Comm'n, 357
Shell Oil Co. v. Dye, 165, 172
Shell Oil Co. v. Goodroe, 303, 309, 311, 313
Shell Oil Co. v. Howth, 179, 180
Shell Oil Co. v. James, 430, 434, 436
Shell Oil Co. v. Manley Oil Corp., 165, 168, 169, 172
Shell Oil Co. v. Stansbury, 383, 384, 432, 434, 436, 437, 438
Shell Oil Co. v. Williams Inc., 358
Shell Petroleum Corp. v. Calcasieu Real Estate & Oil Co., 397, 474
Shell Petroleum Corp. v. Carter, 474, 476
Shell Petroleum Corp. v. Moore, 156
Shell Petroleum Corp. v. Puckett, 153
Shell Petroleum Corp. v. Scully, 156
Shell Petroleum Corp. v. Shore, 430

Hemingway Law of Oil & Gas 2nd Ed. HB—19

TABLE OF CASES
References are to Pages

Shellenberger v. Hicks, 146
Shelton v. Taylor, 300
Shepard v. John Hancock Mut. Life Ins. Co., 55, 56, 58, 71, 96, 98
Sheppard v. Stanolind Oil & Gas Co., 62, 63
Sheridan, State ex rel. Dickgraber v., 385
Sheridan Oil Co. v. Cunningham, 395
Shield v. Shield, 195
Shreveport-El Dorado Pipe Line Co. v. Bennett, 364, 366
Shutts v. Phillips Petroleum Co., 363, 364
Sibley v. Hill, 128, 129
Sick v. Bendix United Geophysical Corp., 170
Silver v. Bush, 2
Silverman v. Emerson, 303
Silvis v. Peoples Natural Gas Co., 27, 112
Simmons v. Ledger Co., 183
Simmons v. Wilson, 283, 502
Simms Oil Co. v. Flewellen, 426
Simons v. McDaniel, 303, 317, 318
Simpson v. Buckner's Adm'r, 264, 317, 319
Simpson v. Burris, 73
Simpson v. United Gas Pipe Line Co., 368, 369, 370
Simpson-Fell Oil Co. v. Stanolind Oil & Gas Co., 139, 140
Simson v. Langholf, 25, 68, 72, 78, 79, 87
Sinclair Crude Oil Co. v. Oklahoma Tax Comm'n, 406
Sinclair Oil & Gas Co. v. Bishop, 424, 441, 442, 444
Sinclair Oil & Gas Co. v. Bryan, 499
Sinclair Oil & Gas Co. v. Gordon, 160
Sinclair Oil & Gas Co. v. Huffman, 391
Sinclair Oil & Gas Co. v. Masterson, 419, 423, 427, 451
Sinclair Prairie Oil Co. v. Campbell, 495
Sinclair Ref. Co. v. Jones Super Serv. Station, 179, 180
Singer v. Tatum, 9, 11, 14, 17
Sistrunk v. Graham, 244
Skaggs v. Heard, 346, 351, 361
Skelly v. Harris, 311, 332, 333
Skelly Oil Co. v. Archer, 288, 289
Skelly Oil Co. v. Boles, 415, 416, 417, 419, 420
Skelly Oil Co. v. Butner, 35, 36, 37, 38
Skelly Oil Co. v. Cities Serv. Oil Co., 94, 95, 130
Skelly Oil Co. v. Harris, 311, 496
Skelly Oil Co. v. Johnson, 221
Skelly Oil Co. v. Kidd, 257
Skelly Oil Co. v. Savage, 403

Skelly Oil Co. v. Wickham, 320
Skinner v. Ajax Portland Cement Co., 426
Skipper v. Davis, 210
Slade v. Rudman Resources, Inc., 186, 187, 188
Sledge v. Craven, 147
Slife v. Kundtz Properties, Inc., 393
Sloan, In the Matter of the Estate of v. St. Aubyn, 228
Sloan v. Peabody Coal Co., 4, 5, 8, 12, 16
Smalley v. Rogers, 109
Smallwood v. Central Kentucky Natural Gas Co., 283
Smith v. Allison, 373, 374
Smith v. Amerada Petroleum Corp., 474, 479
Smith v. Anisman, 69, 104
Smith v. County of Musselshell, 68, 69, 80, 82
Smith v. Grubb, 458, 459
Smith v. Home Royalty Ass'n, Inc., 405
Smith v. Kious, 452
Smith v. Nyreen, 144
Smith v. Pittston Co., 142
Smith v. State, 392
Smith v. Sun Oil Co., 277, 504
Smith v. Tullos, 426
Smith v. Womack, 232, 233
Snider v. Snider, 369
Sohio Petroleum Co. v. Jurek, 406
Sohio Petroleum Co. v. Miller, 416, 418
Sohio Petroleum Co. v. V. S. & P. R.R., 312
Solberg v. Sunburst Oil & Gas Co., 178, 179, 180, 183, 184
Somers v. Harris Trust & Sav. Bank, 407
South Penn Oil Co. v. Haught, 186, 188, 190
South Penn Oil Co. v. Snodgrass, 278
Southern Oil Corp. v. Waggoner, 365
Southland Royalty Co. v. Humble Oil & Ref. Co., 404, 405
Southland Royalty Co. v. Pan American Petroleum Corp., 5, 16, 339, 346
Southport Petroleum Co. of Delaware v. Fithian, 30
Southwest Gas Producing Co. v. Seale, 400
Southwestern Oil Co. v. Kersey, 414
Spikes v. Magnolia Petroleum Co., 134
Spiller v. Massey & Moore, 415, 417, 430
Spradley v. Finley, 405
Stady v. Texas Co., 251
Stafford v. Union Oil Co. of California, 174
Stahl v. Van Vleck, 302, 303

TABLE OF CASES

Stamper v. Jones, Shelburne & Farmer, Inc., 449, 451
Standard v. Sadler, 236
Standard, State v., 236
Standard Oil Co. of California v. John P. Mills Organization, 467
Standard Oil Co. of Louisiana v. Futral, 95
Standard Oil Co. of Louisiana v. Giller, 499
Stanley v. Slone, 457, 460
Stannard's Estate, In the Matter of v. Reynolds, 452
Stanolind Oil & Gas Co. v. Barnhill, 277, 281
Stanolind Oil & Gas Co. v. Christian, 433
Stanolind Oil & Gas Co. v. Lambert, 159, 161
Stanolind Oil & Gas Co. v. Newman Bros. Drilling Co., 329, 330
Stanolind Oil & Gas Co. v. Terrell, 367, 490
Stanolind Oil & Gas Co. v. Wimberly, 216
Stark v. Pennsylvania Coal Co., 167
Starling v. Preston, 69
Starnes v. Miller, 134, 137, 138
State Highway Comm'n, State ex rel. v. Trujillo, 11, 13
State Land Bd. v. State Dept. of Fish and Game, 2, 5, 16, 17
State Nat'l Bank of Corpus Christi v. Morgan, 51, 61, 62, 63
States Exploration Co. v. Reynolds, 160
Statex Petroleum v. Petroleum, Inc., 320
Steed v. Crossland, 145
Steeple Oil & Gas Corp. v. Amend, 167, 169, 171, 313
Stegall v. Bugh, 2, 6, 7
Stephens v. Preston's Heirs, 167
Stephens County v. Mid-Kansas Oil & Gas Co., 3, 26, 27, 28, 244
Sterling v. Marathon Oil Co., 363
Stern v. Franklin, 146
Stern v. Great Southern Land Co., 133, 137, 138
Stewart v. Amerada Hess Corp., 279, 282, 283, 288, 289, 290, 292
Stimson v. Tarrant, 292, 293, 294
Stocker & Sitler, Inc. v. Metzger, 2, 4
Stockton v. Weeks, 384
Stoddard v. Illinois Improvement & Ballast Co., 446
Stokes v. Tutvet, 30, 68, 69, 71, 79, 83, 86, 87, 88
Stokley v. State, 244
Stolz, Wagner & Brown v. Duncan, 322

Stone v. Texoma Production Co., 36, 38, 39
Stoughten's Appeal, 30
Stradley v. Magnolia Petroleum Co., 153
Strait v. Fuller, 127, 130, 135
Stratmann v. Stratmann, 55
Strong v. Garrett, 144
Strong v. Strong, 51
Stroud v. D-X Sunray Oil Co., 479
Struss v. Stoddard, 406
Stuart v. Pundt, 294, 297, 298
Sugg v. Williams, 247
Sullivan and Garnett v. James, 288, 289, 291
Sult v. A. Hochstetter Oil Co., 2, 10
Summerville v. Apollo Gas Co., 278
Sun Oil Co. v. Bennett, 372, 373
Sun Oil Co. v. Burns, 372, 373
Sun Oil Co. v. Frantz, 420
Sun Oil Co. v. Oswell, 25, 27, 187, 447, 448
Sun Oil Co. v. Stout, 210
Sun Oil Co. v. Whitaker, 11
Sunac Petroleum Corp. v. Parkes, 330, 402, 496
Sunburst Oil & Ref. Co. v. Callender, 504
Sunray DX Oil Co. v. Crews, 444
Sunray DX Oil Co. v. Texaco, Inc., 298, 385
Sunray Mid-Continental Oil Co. v. McDaniel, 430, 451
Superior Oil Co. v. Dabney, 384, 451
Superior Oil Co. v. Devon Corp., 415, 418
Superior Oil Co. v. Harsh, 165, 169
Superior Oil Co. v. Jackson, 259
Superior Oil Co. v. King, 159
Superior Oil Co. v. Railway Comm'n, 472
Superior Oil Co. v. Roberts, 187, 188, 190
Superior Oil Co. v. Stanolind Oil & Gas Co., 35, 37, 265
Superior Oil Co. v. Vanderhoof, 104
Swain v. Santa Fe Pac. R.R. Co., 352
Swayne v. Lone Acre Oil Co., 198, 200, 207
Swearingen v. Oldham, 69, 77, 94, 95
Sweeney v. Bay State Oil & Gas Co., 129, 130, 136
Swiss Oil Corp. v. Hupp, 164, 167, 168, 169, 170, 245
Sword v. Rains, 278
Sword v. Sword, 111, 112
Sykes v. Austin, 74
Sykes v. Dillingham, 51, 52, 61, 62, 64

Taber v. Pettus Oil & Ref. Co., 480, 481
Tanner v. Olds, 406

TABLE OF CASES
References are to Pages

Tanner v. Title Ins. & Trust Co., 406, 456
Tara Petroleum Corp. v. Hughey, 357
Tate v. Stanolind Oil & Gas Co., 278, 309, 317, 319
Taylor v. Kerlin, 116
Taylor v. Wallace, 118
Teas v. Twentieth Century-Fox Film Corp., 42, 47, 48
Teledyne Exploration Co. v. Dickerson, 158, 159, 160
Temple v. Continental Oil Co., 415, 416, 447
Temples v. First Nat'l Bank of Laurel, 146
Tennant v. Dunn, 480, 481, 487
Terry v. Texas Co., 324
Terteling Bros., Inc. v. Bennett, 134, 137
Texaco Inc. v. Fox, 287, 288, 290, 294
Texaco, Inc. v. Lettermann, 399, 401
Texas & Pac. Coal & Oil Co. v. Kirtley, 186, 188, 195, 368
Texas Co. v. Bowen, 71, 81
Texas Co. v. Curry, 317
Texas Co. v. Daugherty, 26, 244
Texas Co. v. Davis, 250
Texas Co. v. Fontenot, 51, 61, 62
Texas Co. v. Leach, 328
Texas Co. v. Mattocks, 504
Texas Co. v. Newton Naval Stores Co., 213, 375
Texas Co. v. Parks, 48, 49, 50, 379
Texas Co. v. Pettit, 172, 369, 370
Texas Co. v. Ramsower, 448
Texas Co. v. Sorrell, 386, 387
Texas Co. v. State, 168, 169, 240, 241, 243
Texas Gulf Producing Co. v. Griffith, 106, 407
Texas Land & Mortg. Co. v. Cohen, 222
Texas Oil & Gas Corp. v. Vela, 352, 353, 354, 356, 358, 360
Texas Osage Co-op. Royalty Pool v. Garcia, 104, 106
Texas Osage Co-op. Royalty Pool v. Thomas, 373, 375
Texas Pac. Coal & Oil Co. v. Barker, 417, 427, 428, 430, 445, 446, 447
Texas Pac. Coal & Oil Co. v. Stuard, 413, 415, 452
Thaxton v. Beard, 186, 188, 195
Theo Oil Co. v. Thomas, 49, 456
Thomas v. Southwestern Settlement & Development Co., 139, 140, 147
Thomas v. Texas Co., 157
Thomas v. Witte, 128
Thompson v. Mack, 137
Thompson v. Thompson, 198, 205, 369

Thornock v. Cook, 142
Tide Water Associated Oil Co. v. Stott, 430, 434, 436
Tidewater Associated Oil Co. v. Clemens, 364, 365
Tidewater Associated Oil Co. v. Hammer, 366
Tidewater Oil Co. v. Jackson, 176
Tiller v. Fields, 397, 399
Tipps v. Bodine, 456, 457, 459, 460, 462
Title Ins. & Trust Co. v. Amalgamated Oil Co., 385
Tome Land Grant, Inc., Town of v. Ringle Development Co., 277
Toothman v. Courtney, 72, 86
Touchet v. Humble Oil & Ref. Co., 341
Town of (see name of town)
Townsend v. Creekmore-Rooney Co., 278
Townsend v. Cable, 27
Townsend v. State, 24, 25
Tracy v. Lion Oil Co., 234
Trad v. General Crude Oil Co., 259
Transcontinental Oil Co. v. Emmerson, 26, 29, 30
Transport Oil Co. v. Exeter Oil Co., Ltd., 287, 288, 289
Trawick v. Castleberry, 402, 416, 418
Treasure County v. Berggren, 282, 284
Tremont Lumber Co. v. Louisiana Oil Refinery Co., 336, 337
Triger v. Carter Oil Co., 30
Trigg v. United States, Dept. of Interior, 252, 268
Trimble v. Kentucky River Coal Corp., 30
Trujillo, State ex rel. State Highway Comm'n v., 11, 13
Trust Co. of Chicago v. Samedan Oil Corp., 415, 416, 417, 419, 420
Tuggle v. Davis, 127, 133
Turner v. Big Lake Oil Co., 160
Turner v. Brookshear, 476, 479, 480
Turner v. McBroom, 283
Twentieth Century-Fox Film Corp. v. Teas, 52, 61, 62, 65
Twyford v. Whitchurch, 254, 268
Tyler v. Boucher, 103, 104
Tyra v. Woodson, 501, 502
Tyson v. Surf Oil Co., 292, 293, 294, 339, 352

U.V. Indus., Inc. v. Danielson, 429, 433
Ulrich v. Amerada Petroleum Corp., 245
Union Gas & Oil Co. v. Wiedemann Oil Co., 135, 137, 199
Union Oil Co. v. Touchet, 403, 407

TABLE OF CASES

Union Oil Co. of California v. Colglazier, 110
Union Oil Co. of California v. Domengeaux, 173
Union Oil Co. of California v. Ogden, 58, 308
Union Oil Co. of California, United States v., 9, 10
Union Pac. R.R. Co., United States v., 210
Union Producing Co. v. Sanborn, 234
Union Producing Co. v. Scott, 42, 46, 47, 315, 316
Union Sulphur Co. v. Texas Gulf Sulphur Co., 329
Union Trust Co. of New York v. Illinois Midland & Ry. Co., 134
United Carbon Co. v. Conn, 392
United Carbon Co. v. Ramsey, 394
United Fuel Gas Co. v. Dyer, 142
United Fuel Gas Co. v. McCoy, 391, 393
United Gas Public Serv. Co. v. Mitchell, 372, 373, 376
United States v. _____ (see opposing party)
Updike v. Smith, 29

Valentine Oil Co. v. Powers, 254, 267, 268
Valer Oil Co. v. Souza, 318
Van Deventer v. Gulf Production Co., 195
Vance v. Guy, 150
Vang v. Mount, 6, 8, 9, 11, 12, 13, 14, 15, 19
Vaughan v. Doss, 268, 269
Vaughn v. Hearrell, 264, 318, 319, 324
Veal v. Thomason, 406
Vedder Petroleum Corp. v. Lambert Lands Co., 354, 361
Vega Petroleum Corp. v. Hovey, 430
Ventro v. Clinchfield Coal Corp., 143
Vermillion v. Fidel, 385, 386
Vernon v. Union Oil Co. of California, 306, 307, 308
Vetter v. Morrow, 424
Vickers v. Peaker, 322, 323
Viersen v. Boettcher, 149
Violette v. Gaertner, 302, 303
Vogel v. Cobb, 9, 11
Vollum v. Beall, 134
Vonfeldt v. Hanes, 447
Voyta v. Clonts, 69, 88, 245

Waddle v. Lucky Strike Oil Co., 277, 281, 282
Wade v. Lillard, 387
Wade v. Roberts, 104, 105, 106
Wadkins v. Wilson Oil Corp., 441
Waechter v. Amoco Production Co., 356
Waggoner & Zeller Oil Co. v. Deike, 281
Waggoner Estate v. Sigler Oil Co., 445, 449, 450, 451
Wagner v. Mallory, 245
Wagner v. Mounger, 258, 259
Wagner v. Sunray Mid-Continent Oil Co., 369
Wahlenmaier v. American Quasar, 491
Waldrip v. Hamon, 452
Wall v. Shell Oil Co., 2, 4, 153
Wall v. United Gas Public Serv. Co., 349, 350, 352, 353, 354, 362
Walla Walla Oil Gas & Pipe Line Co. v. Vallentine, 245
Waller v. Rhyne, 199
Walter v. Ashland Oil & Ref. Co., 274
Walton v. Atlantic Ref. Co., 503
Walton v. Zatkoff, 322, 323
Ward v. Tripple State Natural Gas & Oil Co., 385
Ward v. Woods, 142, 143
Warfield Natural Gas Co. v. Allen, 337, 352, 355, 413, 440
Warfield Natural Gas Co. v. Moore, 393
Warfield Natural Gas Co. v. Small, 393
Warm Springs Development Co. v. McAulay, 414
Warmack v. Henry H. Cross Co., 145
Warner v. Shell Petroleum Corp., 440, 442, 445
Warner v. Winn, 128
Warren v. Amerada Petroleum Corp., 42, 46, 47
Warren v. Clinchfield Coal Corp., 2, 3, 4
Warren v. Martin, 198, 205
Warren Petroleum Corp. v. Monzingo, 153
Waseco Chem. & Supply Co. v. Bayou State Oil Corp., 424, 441
Watford Oil & Gas Co. v. Shipman, 30, 130, 135
Watkins v. Certain-Teed Products Corp., 5, 28
Watkins v. Slaughter, 71, 81, 94
Watson v. Rochmill, 295, 297, 302
Watters v. People, 127, 133, 139
Waugh v. Thompson Land & Coal Co., 17
Weaver v. Farr, 481
Weaver v. Richards, 2
Webb v. British American Oil Producing Co., 149
Webb v. Graf, 450
Weekley v. Weekley, 199, 200, 201, 202
Weems v. Hawkins, 143
Wemple v. Nabors Oil & Gas Co., 141

TABLE OF CASES
References are to Pages

Wehran v. Helis, 321
Welborn v. Tidewater Associated Oil Co., 199
Welch v. Pauline Oil & Gas Co., 369
Wells v. Shadoin, 378
Wemple v. Producers Oil Co., 345, 347
Wes-Tex Land Co. v. Simmons, 415, 445, 450, 491
West v. Aetna Life Ins. Co., 4, 5, 8, 12, 16, 17
West v. Alpar Resources, Inc., 355, 361, 362
West v. Arrington, 110
West v. Commissioner of Internal Revenue, 240, 241, 242, 243
West v. Continental Oil Co., 283
West v. Russell, 282, 283, 284
West v. Sun Oil Co., 415, 417, 418, 430
West Edmond Hunton Lime Unit v. Lillard, 175
West Edmond Salt Water Disposal Ass'n v. Rosecrans, 175
West Virginia Dept. of Highways v. Farmer, 19
Westbrook v. Atlantic Richfield Co., 404
Westbrook v. Ball, 96, 98, 99
Western Development Co. v. Nell, 2, 3, 4, 5, 6
Western Geophysical Co. v. Rowell, 158, 159
Western Geophysical Co. of America v. Mason, 158, 159
Western Geophysical Co. of America v. Martin, 159, 160
Western Nuclear, Inc. v. Andrus, 8, 9, 11, 12, 13, 14, 16, 17
Western States Oil & Land Co. v. Helms, 279, 327
Westmoreland & Cambria Natural Gas Co. v. De Witt, 25, 26
Wettengel v. Gormley, 466, 467, 468, 471
Weyerhaeuser Co. v. Burlington Northern, Inc., 6, 8, 9, 11, 12, 14
Whale v. Rice, 503
Wheelock v. Batte, 178, 179, 180, 181, 183
Whelan v. Killingsworth, 172
Whelan v. Placid Oil Co., 187
Whelan v. R. Lacy, Inc., 322
Whitaker v. Neal, 113
Whitaker v. Texaco, Inc., 289, 407
White v. Blackman, 198, 202, 203, 207
White v. Hogge, 112
White v. McVey, 53, 54
White v. Miller, 8, 10
White v. New York State Natural Gas Corp., 25

White v. Smyth, 138
Whitson Co. v. Bluff Creek Oil Co., 489
Whittaker v. Otto, 170
Whitten v. Daws, 489
Wight v. Ingram-Day Lumber Co., 127, 138, 139
Wilkins v. Nelson, 426
Willan v. Farrar, 254
Williams v. Continental Oil Co., 174
Williams v. Humble Oil & Ref. Co., 431, 433, 437, 440, 444
Williams v. McKenzie, 210
Williams v. Nylund, 228
Williams v. Phillips Petroleum Co., 106, 107, 108
Williams v. Skinner, 134, 138
Williams v. Sohio Petroleum Co., 367, 378, 379
Williams v. South Pennsylvania Oil Co., 6
Williams' v. Union Bank & Trust Co., 53
Williams' Adm'r v. Union Bank & Trust Co., 54
Williamson v. Jones, 165
Williard v. Federal Sur. Co., 245
Williford v. Spies, 13, 19
Willingham v. Bryson, 419, 421, 422
Willson v. Superior Oil Co., 193, 194
Wilson v. A. Cook Sons Co., 3
Wilson, Commissioner v., 48, 49, 50
Wilson v. Gerard, 110
Wilson v. Hecht, 73, 77, 78, 79
Wilson v. Holm, 295, 297
Wilson v. Olsen, 74, 86
Wilson v. Sun Oil Co., 341
Wilson v. Talbert, 293, 302, 391
Wilson v. Taylor Ex'rs, 118
Wilson v. Texas Co., 153
Wingert v. T.W. Phillips Gas & Oil Co., 228
Winn v. Warner, 178, 179, 180, 181
Wintermann v. McDonald, 42, 46
Winters v. Slover, 115
Wiseman v. Priboth, 109
Wisness v. Paniman, 145
Witherspoon v. Green, 178, 183, 184
Wolf v. Blackwell Oil & Gas Co., 5
Wolfe v. Prairie Oil & Gas Co., 363, 365
Wolfe v. Shell Petroleum Corp., 363, 365
Wolfe v. Stanford, 133, 138
Wolfe v. Texas Co., 363, 364, 365
Wolfson Oil Co. v. Gill, 419, 421
Wolter v. Houston Oil Co. of Texas, 431, 432
Wood v. Cahill, 165
Woodland Oil Co. v. Crawford, 244
Woods v. Sims, 104, 106, 458, 459, 460

TABLE OF CASES
References are to Pages

Woodside v. Lee, 267
Woodson Oil Co. v. Pruett, 300, 386
Woolley v. Standard Oil Co. of Texas, 273, 274, 275
Worrell v. Parsons, 499
Wright v. Brush, 52, 62
Wright v. Carter Oil Co., 49, 123, 456, 462
Wulf v. Shultz, 8, 12, 14, 16, 17, 19
Wynn v. Sklar & Phillips Oil Co., 84

Yelderman v. McCarthy, 368, 399, 404, 405
Yost v. Ratliff, 198, 201, 207

Young v. Ethyl Corp., 167
Young v. Jones, 268, 269
York v. McBee, 259
Young v. Moncrief, 268
Youngman v. Shular, 198, 202, 203, 204, 207
Yttredahl v. Federal Farm Mortg. Corp., 145

Zappia v. Garner, 415
Zeigler v. Brenneman, 130, 135, 186, 188
Zimmerman v. Texaco, Inc., 187

INDEX

References are to Pages

ABSOLUTE OWNERSHIP THEORY
See Ownership Theories.

ADMINISTRATORS
See Oil and Gas Leases.

ADVERSE POSSESSION
See, also, Prescription.
Actual possession of mineral estate,
Acts sufficient, 148.
Extent of constructive possession, 149, 150.
Strata and products acquired, 151.
Merger, 147.
No severance, 142.
Non-user, Louisiana, 141.
Prior severance,
General, 143.
Oil and gas lease, 144.
Partial, 144.
Tacking of possession, 146.

AFTER-ACQUIRED TITLE
Mortgages and deeds of trust, 222.

AGRICULTURAL LEASES
See, also, Surface Lease.
Oil and gas leases, 215, 216.

APPORTIONMENT AND NONAPPORTIONMENT
See, also, Royalty and Royalty Interests, 53.
Entirety clause, 472.
Changed to non-apportionment, 474–476.
Lessor conveyances "subject to" lease, 468.

ASSIGNMENT CLAUSE
Divisibility of covenants, 498, 499.

ASSIGNMENTS
See, also, Delay Rentals; Divisibility of Covenants; Transfer by Lessee.
Burden of outstanding interests, 484, 485.
Contracts to assign leases, 480.
Checklist, 482.
"88 form lease," 481.
Statute of frauds, 481.
Effective date, 491.
Fiduciary relationship, 500–503.

ASSIGNMENTS—Cont'd
Full and partial lease assignments, 483–486.
Implied covenants, subleases and assignments, 504, 505.
In connection with mortgage, 492.
Non-cost bearing interest, 483–493.
Checklist for mortgages, 492–494.
Cost burden, 490.
Definition of fraction, 489.
Fiduciary relationship, 500.
Graduated sliding scale or conversion interest, 490.
Implied covenants, 491.
Overriding royalty, 487, 488.
Production payments, 488.
Proportionate reduction clause, 489.
Overriding royalty interest, impressed upon new leases, 501, 502.
Partial assignments as to depth, 486.
As to products, 486.
Particular formations, 486, 487.
Renewal and extension clause, 502.
Subleases and assignments, 503, 504.
Subordination agreements, 221.
Warranty, 486.

BONUS
See, also, Bonus—Royalty Distinction.
Cash, 51.
Community property, 51.
Conflict of laws, 231.
Incorporeal interest, 51.
Life tenant and remainderman, 200, 201.
Nature, 50.
Out of production, 51.
Taxation, 51.
Term, interest, 51.

BONUS—ROYALTY DISTINCTION
Bonus, royalty, 63.
Construction problems, 63–65.
"Normal" royalty, 62, 63.
Parol evidence, 64.
Problems stated, 61.
Variable participating royalty, 65.

CARRIED INTERESTS
See Assignments.

CASINGHEAD GAS
See Royalty Clause.

533

INDEX

References are to Pages

CESSATION OF PRODUCTION
See Production in Paying Quantities; Shut-In Royalties.

COMMENCEMENT OF OPERATIONS
See Delay Rentals; Habendum Clause.

COMMUNITY LEASE
See Pooling and Unitization.

COMMUNITY PROPERTY
Bonus, 51.
Delay rentals, 50.
Royalty, 60.

COMPULSORY UNITIZATION
See Pooling and Unitization.

CONCURRENT INTERESTS
Joint tenancy, 103.
Tenants by the entireties, 103.
Tenants in common, 102, 103.

CONDENSATE
See Natural Gasoline; Royalty Clause.

CONFISCATION
See Drainage; Rule 37.

CONTINUOUS OPERATIONS CLAUSE
See, also, Divisibility of Covenants; Dry Hole Clause.
Automatic lease extension, 331–334.
Cessation of production, 325–327.
Definition of dry hole, 325, 329.
Modification of habendum clause, 324.
Shut in royalties, 310.
Tacking operations, 324.
Tacking various clauses, 328.

CONVERSION OF MINERALS
Division orders and transfer orders, 365.

CORPORATIONS
See Oil and Gas Leases.

CORPOREAL AND INCORPOREAL INTERESTS
Mineral interests and lease interests, 23–31.

CO-TENANTS
See Tenants in Common.

COVER-ALL CLAUSE
See Mother Hubbard Clause.

DECEDENTS' ESTATES
See Oil and Gas Leases.

DEEDS OF TRUST
See Mortgages and Deeds of Trust.

DEFEASIBLE TERM INTERESTS
See Term Interests.

DELAY RENTALS
See, also, Divisibility of Covenants; Lessor, Conveyances By; Well Completion Clause.
Apportionment, see Lessor, Conveyances By.
Appurtenant to the mineral estate, 49.
Assignment, 260.
  Chain of title, 261.
  No notice to lessee, 261.
  Notice to lessee, 261.
  Prior payment by lessee, 262.
Breach of implied covenant, 447.
Common law rents, 49.
Community property, 50.
Conveyances, "subject to" lease, 456.
Covenant to drill an initial well, 413.
Divisibility of covenants, 497.
Early leases, 250.
  Abandonment, 250.
Improper payment, 267.
  Acts of third party, 270.
  Ambiguous instrument, 271.
  Estoppel, 272–276.
  Homestead, 276.
  Limitation v. Forfeiture, 267.
  Notice of breach clause, 273.
  Ratification, 274, 275.
  Sole mistake of lessee, 270.
  Subject to deed, 275.
  Waiver, 273, 274, 276.
Incorporeal interest, 49.
Lessee's title threatened, 228.
Lessor, conveyances by, 463.
Life tenant and remainderman, 201.
Minimum royalty, 370.
Nature, 48.
Operations during primary term, 263.
  Dry hole, 264.
  Return to delay rentals, 264.
Paid up lease, 252.
Payment, allocation among lessors, 260.
Payment date, 253.
  Ambiguity, 253.
  Failure to pay, 253.
  Lease amendment, 254.
Pooling, Pugh clause, 406–408.
Primary term production, 250.
Reduction of delay rentals, 377–386.
Rule against perpetuities, 49.
Shut in royalty payments, 282.
Surrender clause, 383.
Taxation, 50.
Tender, 255.
  Credit by bank, 256.
  Delay in mail, 257.
  Delay rental receipt, 255.
  Depository bank, 255.
  Early payment by lessee, 262.
  Effective operations, 263.
  Joint lessors next payment, 259.
  Mailed, 257.
  Payment by third party, 259.

INDEX
References are to Pages

DELAY RENTALS—Cont'd
Payment to non-lessor, 258, 259, 260.
Receipt by bank, 255, 256.
Return to delay rentals, 264.
Substitute method, 258.
Top lease, 254.
Well at end of term, 317–319.

DESCRIPTION OF PROPERTY
See Mortgages and Deeds of Trust; Mineral Deeds; Oil and Gas Leases.

DEVELOPMENT COVENANTS
See, also, Implied Covenants.
Express clause, 425.
    Effect on implied covenants, 426.

DIRECTIONAL DRILLING
See Subsurface Trespass.

DISTILLATE
See, Condensate; Natural Gasoline; Royalty Clause.

DIVISIBILITY OF COVENANTS
Continuous operations clause, 495, 496.
Delay rentals, 497, 498.
Habendum clause and modifying clauses, 495, 496.
Implied covenants, 498, 499.
Partial assignment of leases, 498.
Pooling clause, 496.
Royalties, 494.
Well completion clause, 496.

DIVISION AND TRANSFER ORDERS
Conversion of products, 365.
Different from lease, 366–369.
Division order title opinion, 364.
Gas production, 366–369.
    Current market price, 366.
    Federal Power Commission, 367.
Gas royalty, 365.
Nature of, 363.
Notice of change, 365.
Oil royalty, 364.
Preparation, 364.
Protection by division order, 364–370.
Ratification of lease, 368.
Revocable, 367–369.
Title examination, 364.

DRAINAGE
See, also, Implied Covenants.
Express clause, 431.
    Lessee's judgment conclusive, 432.
Implied covenant against, 430.

DRILLING OBLIGATIONS
See, also, Implied Covenants.
Breach of express covenant, 452.
    Cost of drilling well, 452.
    Loss of market value, 452.
    Lost royalty rule, 453.

DRILLING OBLIGATIONS—Cont'd
Force majeure clause, 387.
Liquidated damage clause, 453.

DRILLING UNITS
See Pooling & Unitization.

DRIP GASOLINE
See Condensate; Natural Gasoline.

DRY HOLE CLAUSE
See, also, Continuous Operations Clause; Delay Rentals, Operations during primary term; Divisibility of Covenants; Shut-In Royalties; Sixty Day Clause; Well Completion Clause.
Definition of dry hole, 329.
Tacking various clauses, 329.

EASEMENTS
Oil and gas leases, 213.

ENTIRETY CLAUSE
See Oil and Gas Leases.

ESTOPPEL
Mineral reservations and exceptions, Duhig Doctrine, 116.

ESTOPPEL BY DEED
See, also, Mineral Reservations and Exceptions; Oil and Gas Leases.
Mineral reservations, 126.

EXCEPTIONS AND RESERVATIONS
See, also, Mineral Reservations and Exceptions.
Common law distinctions, 27.

EXECUTIVE RIGHT
See Power to Lease.

EXECUTORS AND ADMINISTRATORS
See Oil and Gas Leases.

FIXTURES
Removal of, 385.
    Producing well, 386.
    Time to remove, 385.

FORCE MAJEURE CLAUSE
See Oil and Gas Leases.

FORCED POOLING AND UNITIZATION
See Pooling and Unitization.

FREE GAS CLAUSE
See Oil and Gas Leases.

FUTURE INTERESTS
Determinable fee, 210.
Doctrine of worthier title, 237.

INDEX
References are to Pages

FUTURE INTERESTS—Cont'd
Estate subject to executory interests, 210.
Oil and gas leases, unascertainable owners, 237.
Rule in Shelley's case, 237.
Unascertainable owners, 237.
Waste, 211.

GAS DIVISION ORDER
See Division and Transfer Orders.

GAS ROYALTY
See Royalty Clause.

GEOPHYSICAL EXPLORATION
See Subsurface Trespass.

GEOPHYSICAL OPERATIONS
See Subsurface Trespass.

GOOD FAITH IMPROVEMENTS
See Subsurface Trespass.

GUARDIANS
See Oil and Gas Leases.

HABENDUM CLAUSE
See, also, Divisibility of Covenants; Oil and Gas Leases; Production in Paying Quantities; Shut-In Royalties.
Commencement of operations, 321.
    Ability of lessee, 322–323.
    Activities of lessee, 321.
    Good faith, 323.
    Spudding in, 321.
Conflict with well completion clause, 318.
Continuous operations clause, 310–312.
Dry hole, definition, 325, 326.
Effect of co-tenant production, 190, 192.
Indivisibility, 495.
Substitute production, shut-in royalties, 304.

IMPLIED COVENANTS
See, also, Divisibility of Covenants; Drilling Obligations, Breach of express covenant.
Administrative action, 444.
Against drainage, 429.
    Effect of express clause, 431.
    Field wide drainage, 439.
    Lessee's judgment conclusive, 432.
    Profitability to lessee, 430.
    Reasonably prudent operator rule, 430, 431.
Alternative decree, 451.
Basis, 411–413.
Breach of covenant, effect on delay rentals, 447.
Cancellation of lease, 449.
    Adequate remedy of law, 449.
    Notice, 450.

IMPLIED COVENANTS—Cont'd
    Partial cancellation, 451.
Covenant to market, 442.
Covenant to produce, 441.
Damages, 445.
    Notice, 450.
    Proof, 447.
Depreciation of lessor's interest,
    Also adjoining lessee, 433.
    Offset clause, 439.
    Profitability to lessee, 433–438.
    Prudent operator rule, 439.
Development,
    During and after primary term, 414.
    Express clause, 425.
    No profit to lessee, 418.
    Profit to lessee, 416.
    Reasonable diligence of lessee, 417.
    Reasonably prudent lessee test, 415.
    Spacing and other governmental orders, 429.
    To drill an initial well, 413.
Divisibility of covenants, 494.
Effect of pooling and secondary recovery operations, 438.
Express clause, effect on implied covenants, 425.
Field wide drainage, 439.
Further development,
    Large acreage, 421.
    Long time period, 421.
    No profitability shown, 421.
    Oklahoma view, 424.
    Other formations and depths, 421.
Further exploration, 421.
Implied authority to market, 364.
Implied in fact, 413, 504, 505.
Implied in law, 413, 504.
Nature of and scope, 410.
Reasonable care and operations, 439.
    Use of proven methods, 441.
Release of lease, 451.
Remedy, cancellation, 449.
Royalty interest rule, 445.
Spacing and other governmental orders, 429.
Subleases and assignments, 503–505.

INCORPOREAL INTERESTS
Bonus, 51.
Delay rentals, 49.
Oil and gas leases, deed or lease, 244.
Reservations, 27.
Royalty, 52.

IRRIGATION
See Oil and Gas Leases, Free gas clause.

LEASE, MINERAL
See Oil and Gas Leases.

LESSEES, ASSIGNMENTS BY
See Assignments.

INDEX
References are to Pages

LESSOR, CONVEYANCES BY
See, also, Oil and Gas Leases, Entirety clause.
Apportionment, 466.
　Two grant doctrine, 469.
Future leases, 458–462.
Land included in conveyance, 463.
Lease interest, 462.
Mineral-royalty distinction, 458.
Non-apportionment, 469.
Reversionary interest under lease, 455, 456.
"Subject to" lease, 455, 462.
　Apportionment, delay rentals and royalties, 466.
　Effect on well spacing, 471.
　Warranty, 465.
Two grant doctrine, 458, 464, 469.

LIFE TENANT AND REMAINDERMAN
Apportionment,
　Partition, 201.
　Uniform Principal and Income Act, 207.
Uniform Trust Act, 207.
Execution of leases, 199.
　Injunctive relief, 198.
Joint lease, 199.
　Proceeds apportionment, 200.
Lease from life tenant, 197.
Lease from remainderman, 197.
Open mine doctrine, 202.
　Conventional life estate, 203, 206.
　Definition of mine, 203.
　Legal life estate, 203, 206.
　Probate homestead, 203, 207.
　Texas Relinquishment Act, 57.

LIMITATION TITLE TO MINERALS
See Adverse Possession.

MARKET, DUTY TO
See Implied Covenants.

MARSHALLING OF ASSETS
Oil and gas leases, 221.
　Waiver, 222.

MINERAL ACRES
Mineral acre interest, 105–108.
　Breach of warranty, 107.
　Effect of accretion, 106.
　Indefiniteness, 107.
　Redundant recitals, 106, 107.
　Royalty acre interest 105, 106.

MINERAL DEEDS
See, also, Lessor, Conveyances By; Oil and Gas Leases, Deed or lease.
Conveyance of a fractional interest, 108.
　Fur corner rule, 109.
　Parol evidence, 109.
Deed-lease distinction, 240, 241.

MINERAL DEEDS—Cont'd
Description, effect of accretion, 106.
Description of fractional undivided interest, 102.
Direct and collateral attack, 109.
Mineral acre interest, 106.
Mother Hubbard clause, 375.
Percentage, 105.

MINERAL ESTATE
See, also, Tenants in Common.
Bonus, 50.
Bonus—royalty distinction, 61.
Delay rentals, 48.
Easements, 213.
Joint tenancy, 103.
Mineral acre interest, 104, 105.
Nature of, 33, 34.
Other minerals, 307.
Percentage interest, 105.
Power to lease, 34.
　Alienability, 36.
　Revocability of the power, 38.
　Rule against perpetuities, 39–41.
　Standard of exercise, 42.
　　Notice of default, 44.
Right to explore, 153.
　Oil and gas lessee, mineral or surface owner, 153.
Rights of way, 213.
Royalty, 52.

MINERAL INTEREST
See, also, Mineral Reservations and Exceptions; Trespass.
Conveyance of fractional interest, 108.
　Four corner rule, 109.
　Parol evidence, 109.
Fractional interest, 102.
Landlord and tenant, 214.
Marshalling, 221.
Mineral acres,
　Breach of warranty, 107.
　Effect of accretion, 106.
　Indefiniteness, 107.
　Redundant recitals, 106, 107.
Right to explore, 153.
　Check list, 154.
　Contractual language, 153.
　Damage release, 153.
　Exclusive, 153.
　Non-exclusive, 153.
　Surface v. Mineral owner, 153.
Tenants in common, 102, 103.
Term interest, 100.

MINERAL RESERVATIONS AND EXCEPTIONS
Breach of warranty, 117–119.
　Knowledge of grantee, 119.
Duhig doctrine, 116–125.
False recitals of fact, 110.
In favor of third parties, 110.

MINERAL RESERVATIONS AND EXCEPTIONS—Cont'd
Out of grantor's interest, 116.
Quantum of reserved interest, 112.
Reference to other instruments, 113–116.
Reservation,
  From conveyed property, 113, 114.
  From described property, 112, 113.

MINERAL–ROYALTY DISTINCTION
Bonus, 64.
Construction problems, 65, 66.
Conveyances by lessor, 457–459.
Effect of the quantum of interest,
  Mineral conveyances, 90, 92.
  Royalty conveyances, 90.
Landowner's interest and landowner's rights, 87.
Mineral interest, less various rights, 93, 96.
  Oklahoma view, 95.
Minerals, mineral estate, mineral rights, 50, 68, 71.
Oil and gas, produced and saved, 78.
Oil and gas in, and under, 68.
Oklahoma view, 72–80.
Parol evidence, 71, 72.
Profits, 86.
Recitals to other instruments, 99.
"Royalty,"
  Coupled with other language, 81.
  Express rights of ingress and egress, 85.
  Oklahoma view, 72.
  Plus oil and gas, in, and under the land, 81–83.
  Royalty interest, royalty rights, 70, 81, 85.
  Uncertain meaning, 72.

MINERALS
Application of ejusdem generis rule, 5, 12, 16–18.
Definitions, 10.
Early history, 1.
Fissionable materials, 8.
Geothermic matter, 9.
Including oil and gas, 1.
Inorganic substances, 8.
Intent test, 18.
Land as a mineral, 10, 13.
Local knowledge, 11.
Meaning, 15.
Meaning, date of, 16, 21.
Methods of extraction, 12, 20.
"Mineral" as ambiguous, 12, 14.
Pennsylvania rule, 3.
Restoration, effect on, 21.
Statutory definition, 13.
"Strohacker Doctrine," 7.
Surface, definition, 21, 22.
Surface interference, 20, 21.
Texas rule, 20.

MINERALS—Cont'd
Unambiguous, limiting language, 6.
Use of parol evidence, 4, 6.
Value, 10, 14.
Water, 8.

MINIMUM ROYALTY CLAUSE
See Royalty Clause.

MORTGAGES AND DEEDS OF TRUST
  See, also, Assignments; Oil and Gas Leases.
After acquired title, 222.
Assignments, checklist, 492–494.
Execution of leases, 219.
Extension of lien, 222.
Marshalling, waiver, 222.
Oil and gas leases, marshalling, 221.
Production,
  Impairment of security, 220.
  Waste, 219.
Subordination agreement, 220.

MOTHER HUBBARD CLAUSE
See Oil and Gas Leases, Mother Hubbard clause.

NATURAL GASOLINE
See Condensate; Oil and Gas Leases.

NET–PROFITS INTEREST
See Assignments.

NON–OWNERSHIP THEORY
See Ownership Theories.

OFFSET COVENANTS
See Implied Covenants.

OIL AND GAS LEASES
  See, also, Continuous Operations Clause; Division and Transfer Orders; Fixtures, Removal of; Habendum Clause, Commencement of operations; Implied Covenants; Minimum Royalty Clause; Royalty Clause; Shut-In Royalties.
Administrators and executors, 223, 231.
  Duration of lease, 232, 233.
  Independent executors, 233.
Agents and attorneys in fact, 225.
Agricultural leases, 215.
Breach of warranty, Duhig doctrine, 117, 118.
Community survivors, 234.
Continuous operations clause, see, also, Divisibility of Covenants.
Corporations, 235.
Co-tenant leasing, 191.
Cover all clause, see also, Mother Hubbard clause.
Deed or lease, 240.
  Consideration, 241, 242.
  Development obligations, 242.

INDEX

References are to Pages

OIL AND GAS LEASES—Cont'd
  Granting clause, 244.
    Incorporeal interest, 244, 245.
    License, 244.
  Deed-lease distinction, 240.
  Delay rentals, see Delay Rentals.
  Description, 371.
    Adjacent and contiguous and adjoining lands, 372.
    Recording acts, 376.
    Same survey, 373.
    Vacancies and strips, 372.
  Determinable fee, 210.
  Easements, 213.
  Effect of co-tenant production, 191.
  Ejusdem generis, 340.
  Entirety clause, 472.
    Changed to non-apportionment, 474–475.
    "Hereafter" clause, 477–480.
    "Now or hereafter" clause, 477–480.
  Estate subject to executory interests, 210.
  Force majeure clause, 387.
  Free gas clause, 391.
    Domestic purposes, 392.
    Duties and supply, 393, 394.
    Irrigation use, 392.
    Pooling, 393, 394.
  Future interest, waste, 211.
  Governmental entities, Relinquishment Acts, 235.
  Guardian, 231.
  Habendum clause,
    See, also, Divisibility of Covenants; Shut-In Royalties.
    Conflict with well completion clause, 318.
    Continuous operations clause, 327.
    Discovery, 278–279.
    Effect of co-tenant production, 191.
    Indivisibility, 495.
    Joint operating agreement, 193.
    Production in paying quantities, 277, 282.
    Substitute production, 304.
  Interference by lessor, 303.
  Land subject to mortgages, 218.
    After acquired title, 222.
    Execution of lease, 219.
    Impairment of security, 220.
    Possessory interest, 219.
    Subordination agreements, 221.
  Landlord and tenant, 214.
  Long term leases, 246.
  Minor, 234.
    Guardian's lease, 234.
    Ratification, 234.
  Mother Hubbard clause, 371.
    Contiguous adjacent and adjoining lands, 372.
    Large tracts, 374.
    Notice to later purchasers, 376.

OIL AND GAS LEASES—Cont'd
    Recording acts, 376.
    Reserved interests, 376.
    Same survey, 373.
    Strips and excess acreage, 372.
    Words of grant, 372.
  "Or" leases, 247, 248.
  Partnerships, 235.
    Uniform partnership act, 235.
  Political subdivisions, 235.
  Pooling clause,
    Allocation of production, 408.
    Area of interest units, 395.
    Authority to pool, 399.
      Good faith exercise, 401.
    Community leases, 396.
    Designation, 405.
    Effect of production, 406.
    Formation of units, 396.
    Modification, 401.
    Non-participating royalty, 403.
    Partial pooling, 400–403.
    Pooling by reversionary mineral owner, 404.
    Pugh clause, 407–408.
    Successive exercise, 401.
    Tertiary production, 395.
    Working interest owner units, 395.
  Possessory-nonpossessory interest, 244–246.
  Producers 88 Lease, 248.
  Production, see Production in Paying Quantities.
  Proportionate reduction clause, 377.
    See, also, Assignments.
    Breach of warranty, 379.
    Estoppel by deed, 382.
    Failure of title, 377.
    Full interest lease, 380.
    No outstanding title, 382.
    Partial interest lease, 381.
    Reduction of royalties and rentals, 378–379.
  Release clause, sublease and assignments, 504, 505.
  Restricted lands, 213.
  Royalty clause, 336.
  Sovereign, 235.
  Surface leases, 214.
    Waste, 218.
  Surrender clause, 383.
    Effect on lessees obligations, 384.
    Horizontal surrender, 384.
  Tenant's consent agreement, 214.
  Tenants in common,
    Accounting, 187.
      Royalty rule, 190.
    Non-available parties, 196.
    Ratification, 195.
    Recoupable cost and expenses, 190.
    Right to lease, 186.
    Right to produce, 186.
    Statutory trustee, 196.

OIL AND GAS LEASES—Cont'd
Top lease, 254.
Trust, conflict of laws, 231.
Trustees, 225.
    Uniform Principal and Income Act, 229.
    Uniform Trust Act, 227.
    Uniform Trustee's Powers Act, 227.
Unascertainable owners, 237.
Unincorporated associations, 235.
"Unless" leases, 248, 251.
Warranty clause, 377.
    Partial interest lease, 381.
    Reduction of rentals and royalties, 382.
Waste, 218.
Well completion clause, 317.
    See, also, Divisibility of Covenants.

OIL DIVISION ORDER
See Division and Transfer Orders.

OIL PAYMENTS
See Assignments.

OIL ROYALTY
See Royalty and Royalty Interests.

OVERRIDING ROYALTIES
See Assignments.

OWNERSHIP THEORIES
Absolute ownership, 25, 26.
    Severance of mineral estate, 27.
Ad hoc development, 30.
Early cases, 24.
Nature of mineral ownership, 23.
Non-ownership, 24, 29.
Non-ownership theory,
    Chattel real, 29.
    License, 29.
    Profit á prendre, 29.
    Real right, 29.
    Servitude, 29.
    Severance of mineral estate, 27, 28.

PARTIAL ASSIGNMENT
See Assignments.

PARTITION
By sale, 137.
Contract against,
    Operating agreement, 127, 128.
    Pooling agreement, 128.
    Reservation of right to lease, 127.
Equality of right to possession, 130.
    Non-possessory interest, 130.
Equitable basis, 127, 139.
    Co-tenants, 139.
    Horizontal severance, 140.
Equity considerations, 137, 138.
Fully developed territory, 138.

PARTITION—Cont'd
In kind, 138.
Judicial partition, 127.
Leasehold interest, 134.
Life tenant and remainderman, 201.
Matter of right, 127.
Non-possessory interest, 130.
Ownership in tract, 136.
Partially developed territory, 138.
Possessory interest, 130.
Statutory basis, 127.
Wildcat territory, 138.

PARTNERSHIPS
Oil and gas leases, 235.

PAYING QUANTITIES
See Habendum Clause; Production in Paying Quantities.

POOLING AND UNITIZATION
See, Oil and Gas Leases, Pooling clause.

POWER TO LEASE
    See, also, Oil and Gas Leases,
Alienability, 36.
Nature of the power, 35.
Revocability of the power, 38.
Rule against perpetuities, 39.
Standard of exercise, 42.
    Advantageous terms, 46.
    Bonus-royalty provisions, 47.
    Drainage, 46.
    Term interest, 45.

PRESCRIPTION
Louisiana, 116.
Tennessee, 116.
Virginia, 117.

PRIOR SURFACE LEASE
See Oil and Gas Leases.

PRODUCERS 88 LEASE
See Oil and Gas Leases.

PRODUCTION IN PAYING QUANTITIES
Cessation,
    Continuous operations clause, 327.
    Estoppel, 302.
    Interference of lessor, 303.
    Ratification, 302.
    Waiver, 302.
Deductible expenses, 288.
Definition of paying production, 277.
Definition of production, 277.
Depreciation of producing equipment, 289–291.
Discovery, 278.
Dry hole, definition, 329.
During primary term, 250.
Indivisibility of habendum clause, 283, 495.
Marginal wells, 285.

INDEX

PRODUCTION IN PAYING QUANTITIES—Cont'd
Oklahoma view, 279.
Production by other than lessee, 283.
Profitability,
    Over lifting cost, 283.
    Royalty return, 285.
Reasonable diligence, 278, 279.
Reasonably prudent lessee, 285, 286.
Sporadic production, 291.
Substitute production, see shut in royalties.
Temporary cessation, 293–297.
    Drilling to deeper sand, 298.
    Effect of 60 day clause, 298–302.
    Equitable considerations, 294.
    Mechanical breakdown, 295–298.
    Term, mineral and royalty, 294.
Texas view, 283.
West Virginia view, 278.
Within reasonable time, 278–280.

PROPORTIONATE REDUCTION CLAUSE
See Oil and Gas Leases, Proportionate reduction clause.

PUGH CLAUSE
See Oil and Gas Leases, Pooling clause.

QUALIFIED OWNERSHIP THEORY
See Ownership Theories.

RATIFICATION
See, also, Oil and Gas Leases.
Conveyance "subject to" lease, 195.
Co-tenant leases, 194.
Subject to deed, 275.

RECORDING
Oil and gas leases, Mother Hubbard clause, 375.

RELINQUISHMENT ACT
Texas Relinquishment Act 1919, p. 57.

RESERVATIONS AND EXCEPTIONS
See Mineral Reservations and Exceptions.

REVERSIONARY INTEREST
Leasing, unknown owners, 237.
Oil and gas leases, 194.

ROYALTY AND ROYALTY INTERESTS
See, also, Assignments; Bonus-Royalty Distinction; Divisibility of Covenants; Division and Transfer Orders; Lessor, Conveyances by; Mineral-Royalty Distinction; Shut-In Royalties.
Apportionment, see Lessor, Conveyances By.
Authority to pool, 399.

ROYALTY AND ROYALTY INTERESTS—Cont'd
Community property, 60.
Conflict of laws, 231.
Conveyances, 56.
    "Subject to" lease, 457, 464.
Duration, 56, 59, 60.
    Kansas, 71.
Gas royalty, 55, 336–362.
Incorporeal interest, 53, 54.
Life tenant and remainderman, 200.
Minimum royalty, 60.
Nature of,
    After lease, 53.
    Prior to lease, 53.
Non-participating royalty, 39, 96.
Oil royalty, 50.
Percentage interest, 105.
Personalty, 53, 54.
Quantum of reserved interest, 112.
Realty, 53.
Reduction of royalty, 378–382.
Royalty acre interest, 104.
Royalty acres,
    Breach of warranty, 107.
    Effect of accretion, 106.
    Indefiniteness, 107.
    Redundant recitals, 106.
    Reformation, 106.
Rule against perpetuities, 58.
Shut-in royalty, 60, 304.
Taxation, 60.
Term interest, 100.
Variable participating royalty, 65.

ROYALTY CLAUSE
See, also, Division and Transfer Orders.
Automatic lease extension, shut-in royalties, 333.
Casinghead gas, 342.
    No clause, 342, 347.
Condensate, 348.
    Constituent element theory, 349.
Constituent element theory, 348, 349.
Cost of preparation, 361.
Cost of transportation, 361.
Dehydration costs, 361.
Ejusdem generis, 340.
"FERC-out" and "market-out" clauses, 362.
Gas,
    Flat rate royalty, 336.
    FPC, FERC regulation, 356.
    Liquid components, 337.
Gas only, 350.
Long term gas sales contracts, 356.
Market price, 351, 352.
    Long term gas sales contracts, 356.
Market value, 351, 354.
    At the well, 358.

ROYALTY CLAUSE—Cont'd
Long term gas sales contracts, 356.
Minimum royalty, 370.
Net proceeds, 355.
Non-payment of royalties, 340.
"Of royalty", 91.
Payment in kind, 336, 338.
Proceeds, 355.
Shut-in royalty, continuous operations clause, 333.
Term interest, production of reinjected gas, 339.
Used off premises, 339, 346, 347, 358.

ROYALTY DEED
See, also, Lessor, Conveyances By.
Direct and collateral attack, 109.
Mother Hubbard clause, 371.
Percentage interest, 105.
Royalty acre interest, 106.

ROYALTY–MINERAL DISTINCTION
See Mineral-Royalty Distinction.

RULE AGAINST PERPETUITIES
Delay rentals, 49.
Power to lease, 39.
Royalty, 56, 58.

RULE OF CAPTURE
Subsurface damage, 176.

SECONDARY RECOVERY
See Subsurface Trespass, Injected substances.

SHUT–IN ROYALTIES
Condensate production, 307.
Distillate production, 307, 308.
Effect of continuous operations clause, 310.
Effect of sporadic production, 312.
"Gas only" clause, 306.
Nature, 60.
Receipt, 312–315.
Return to delay rentals, 314.
Tender,
    After dry hole, 310.
    After primary term ends, 310.
    Before primary term ends, 309.
    Date of payment, 312–314.
    Effect of shut-in royalty receipt, 312, 314.
    Time of payment, 308.
Term mineral and royalty grants, 315.

SIXTY DAY CLAUSE
See Continuous Operations Clause; Dry Hole Clause.

SLANDER OF TITLE
Acts constituting, 177.
Elements, 178.

SLANDER OF TITLE—Cont'd
Actual malice, 179.
Good faith, 180.
Implied malice, 179.
Measure of damages,
    Confusion with trespass, 182.
    Interest, 182.
    Release of lease, 183.
    Removal of cloud, 182.
    Statute, 181, 183.
Release of lease, 183.

"SUBJECT TO" LEASE
See, also, Lessor, Conveyances By.
Effect on Duhig doctrine, 121.

SUBLEASES
See, also, Assignments.
Effect upon express and applied covenants, 504, 505.

SUBSURFACE DAMAGE
Measure of damages, 176.
Negligent operations, 175, 176.
Rule of capture, 177.

SUBSURFACE TRESPASS
See, also, Subsurface Damage.
Accounting,
    Bad faith trespasser, 165, 166.
    Gross production minus expenses, 165.
    Royalty rule, 167.
Bad faith trespasser,
    Measure of damages, 168.
    Purchaser with notice, 168.
Betterment statutes, 165.
Damages,
    Bad faith trespasser, 168.
    Interest, 169.
Directional drilling,
    Discovery, 174.
    Limitation, 174.
    Remedy, 173.
Dry hole, 162.
Good faith trespasser,
    Accounting, 169.
    Actual notice, 171.
    Color of title, 170.
    Constructive notice, 172.
    Enhancement, 165.
    Good faith, 169.
    Pending litigation, 172.
    Reimbursement, 165.
        Non-beneficial costs, 166.
Injected substances, 175.
Measure of damage,
    Conversion, 164.
    Credit costs of drilling, 165.
    Production, 164.
    Slander of title, 163, 177.

INDEX

References are to Pages

SURFACE LEASE
Oil and gas leases, 215, 217.
Tenants consent agreement, 215.

SURFACE OWNER
Severance of mineral estate, 27.

SURRENDER CLAUSE
See Oil and Gas Leases.

TAXATION
Bonus, 51.
Delay rentals, 50.
Royalty, 60.

TENANCY BY THE ENTIRETIES
Mineral interest, 103.

TENANTS IN COMMON
See, also, Oil and Gas Leases.
Execution of instruments, 193.
Escrow, 194.
Mineral interest, 102.

TERM INTERESTS
Bonus, 51.
Conveyance "subject to" lease, 464.
Effect of pooling by reversionary mineral owner, 404, 405.
Exercise of power to lease, 45.
Production of reinjected gas, 339.
Royalty and mineral interests, 100.
Shut in royalties, 315.
Temporary cessation of production, 295.

TERM ROYALTY DEED
See Term Interests.

THIRTY DAY CLAUSE
See Dry Hole Clause; Well Completion Clause, 316.

TRANSFER BY LESSEE
See Assignments.

TRANSFER ORDERS
See Division and Transfer Orders.

TRESPASS
See, also, Subsurface Trespass.

TRESPASS—Cont'd
Geophysical operations, 153, 154.
Loss of exploration rights, 156.
Negligence, 160.
Physical damage, 159.
Res ipsa loquitur, 160.
Strict liability, 160.
Surface damages, 156, 198.
Value of leasing rights, 156, 157.
Use, 156.
Vibration damage, 158, 159.
No physical entry, 158.

TRUSTEES
See, also, Oil and Gas Leases.
Oil and gas leases, 226.

UNDERGROUND TRESPASS
See Subsurface Trespass.

UNIFORM PRINCIPAL AND INCOME ACT
Oil and Gas Leases, 207–209, 229.

UNITIZATION
See Pooling and Unitization.

"UNLESS" LEASE
Well drilling at end of term, 316–321.

WARRANTY OF TITLE
See Oil and Gas Leases.

WASTE
Oil and gas leases,
Future interests, 218.
Landlord and tenant, 214.

WELL COMPLETION CLAUSE
See, also, Divisibility of Covenants; Dry Hole Clause.
Dry hole clause, conflict with, 318.
Habendum clause,
Conflict with, 318.
Modification of, 319.
Tacking various clauses, 329.
Where no clause, 317–319.

†

THE LAW OF
OIL AND GAS

1986 Cumulative Pocket Part

by

Richard W. Hemingway

Eugene O. Kuntz Professor of
Oil, Gas and Natural Resources Law
University of Oklahoma

Insert this pocket part in back of volume

ST. PAUL, MINN.
WEST PUBLISHING CO.
1986

COPYRIGHT © 1986 By WEST PUBLISHING CO.
50 West Kellogg Boulevard
P.O. Box 64526
St. Paul, Minnesota 55164-0526
All rights reserved
Printed in the United States of America
ISBN 0-314-21321-X

Hemingway, Oil & Gas, 2nd Ed. HB
1986 P.P.

Preface

No attempt has been made to update the tax materials appearing in the text and appendix. This is due to the current confusion in Washington as to changes to be made in the tax statutes, and the fact that many discussed changes will substantially affect oil and gas interests. It is strongly recommended that consultation be had with tax practitioners experienced in the oil and gas field. It appears that the unsettled tax climate in the oil, gas, and natural resources field will continue for some time.

I especially wish to thank my research assistant, Ms. Kathlyn A. Rhodes, for her invaluable assistance in preparation of this supplement, as well as for all her help during the past two years.

RICHARD W. HEMINGWAY

Summary of Contents
(Including New or Retitled Sections)

Chapter	Page
1. Mineral Estate: Definition	1
2. Creation of Interests in the Oil and Gas Mineral Estate by the Landowner	5
§ 2.9 Dormant Mineral Acts	7
3. Conveyances, Partition, and Adverse Possession of the Mineral Estate	9
4. Trespass, Surface and Sub-Surface, and Third Party Claims	12
5. The Oil and Gas Lease—Leases From Owners of Concurrent, Successive, or Restricted Interests	13
6. The Oil and Gas Lease—Duration	14
7. The Oil and Gas Lease—Royalty and Other Particular Lease Clauses	18
8. Covenants of the Lessee to Protect, Develop, and Administer the Lease	22
9. Transfers by the Lessor and by the Lessee	24
Table of Cases	27

THE LAW OF
OIL AND GAS

CHAPTER 1

MINERAL ESTATE: DEFINITION

§ 1.1 "Minerals" as Including Oil, Gas and Petroleum Products

2. Richardson v. Citizens Gas & Coke Utility, 422 N.E.2d 704 (Ind.App. 1981), "coal and other minerals" and "coal, clay, mineral and mineral substance" held ambiguous, and as no oil and gas discovered in the county at the time, did not include oil and gas.

6. Richardson v. Citizens Gas & Coke Utility, 422 N.E.2d 704 (Ind.App. 1981), "coal and other minerals" and "coal, clay, mineral and mineral substance" held ambiguous, and as no oil and gas discovered in the county at the time, did not include oil and gas.

44. Not discovered in the county at time of execution of instrument. Richardson v. Citizens Gas & Coke Utility, 422 N.E.2d 704 (Ind.App.1981).

§ 1.2 "Minerals" and "Oil, Gas and Other Minerals" as Including Substances Other Than Petroleum Products

Add to text, p. 23:

The approach of the Texas courts in the Acker, Reed I & II cases was abandoned in the case of Moser v. United States Steel Co., 676 S.W.2d 99 (Tex.1984). In this case which involved uranium which could be removed by a non-destructive solvent method, the court reexamined the statements of Professor Kuntz in The Law Relating to Oil and Gas in Wyoming, 3 Wyo.L.J. 107 (1949). In particular, the court emphasized the following statement by Professor Kuntz:

"The rights of the surface owner to subjacent support and his right to the use of the top-soil in its place would have to be respected, and at the same time, the owner of the mineral fee should have a right of extraction. Since the right of extraction could only be exercised by destruction of the surface owner's enjoyment, it could only be accomplished with compensation for the damages to the surface estate. ... Specific mention of the substance, however, together with the usual provisions for extraction, would demonstrate a specific intention to make the surface right subject to the rights of access for purposes of extraction and would not make the mineral owner accountable for necessary damage following therefrom."

The court drew a distinction between the situation where the substance is specifically mentioned in the instrument and where it comes within the inclusive term of "other minerals." In the former the mineral is removable without compensation to the surface owner, limited by the reasonable use or accommodation doctrine. Where not specifically mentioned, whether or not a substance is a mineral will be determined by whether the substance is a mineral within the normal and natural meaning of the word, even though the presence or value is not known at the time of severance. The surface destruction test will not be applied to determine whether the substance is or is not part of the surface estate. Where deemed to be a mineral, but not specifically mentioned in the instrument, it is owned by the mineral estate owner who has a right to remove it, but must also compensate the surface owner for injury or destruction of the surface estate.

The court then stated that the rules announced in Moser are to be applied only prospectively from June 8, 1983. Some questions raised by the Moser opinion as to the prospective application of the case were answered in the case of Friedman v. Texaco.[65.5] The effective date of the Acker case was February 10, 1971. What about substances involved in severances prior to the 1971 date? Also what about substances severed prior to 1983 and merged after 1983 with the surface?

The court in Friedman held that where a severance has occurred prior to 1973, and the nature of the substance was not judicially determined prior to this date, that Acker-Reed will apply. Where severed prior to 1983 and then merged with the surface after 1983, Moser will apply. Since a great deal of the minerals in Texas were severed from the surface prior to 1983, the unfortunate Acker-Reed doctrine will continue to be applied.

2. Gelfius v. Chapman, 118 Ill. App.3d 290, 73 Ill.Dec. 798, 454 N.E.2d 1047 (1983) (coal); United States Steel Corp. v. Hoge, 503 Pa. 140, 468 A.2d 1380 (1983) (coal); Gladys City Co. v. Amoco Production Co., 528 F.Supp. 624 (Tex.1981) (salt); Moser v. United States Steel, 676 S.W.2d 99 (Tex.1984) (uranium); Friedman v. Texaco, 691 S.W.2d 586 (Tex.1985) (uranium); Storm Assoc., Inc. v. Texaco, Inc., 645 S.W.2d 579 (Tex.Civ.App.1982), affirmed 691 S.W.2d 586 (1985) (uranium); Martin v. Schneider, 622 S.W.2d 620 (Tex. Civ.App.1981) (uranium).

3. Spurlock v. Santa Fe Railroad Co., 143 Ariz. 469, 694 P.2d 299 (App. 1984), certiorari denied — U.S. —, 106 S.Ct. 3513, 87 L.Ed.2d 642 (1985) (helium).

9. TDC Engineering, Inc. v. Dunlap, 686 S.W.2d 346 (Tex.Civ.App.1985), lessee has the right to inject salt water produced from the lease into non-producing (surface) formations under dominant use doctrine. This does not include right to inject as to lands of lessor not covered by the lease or to lands covered by another lease.

10. Moser v. United States Steel, 676 S.W.2d 99 (Tex.1984) (uranium); Spurlock v. Santa Fe Railroad Co., 143 Ariz. 469, 694 P.2d 299 (App.1984), certiorari denied — U.S. —, 105 S.Ct. 3513, 87 L.Ed.2d 642 (1985) (helium).

11. Spurlock v. Santa Fe Railroad Co., 143 Ariz. 469, 694 P.2d 299 (App. 1984), certiorari denied — U.S. —, 105 S.Ct. 3513, 87 L.Ed.2d 642 (1985) (helium), where substance is known at time of severance lessee can reasonably destroy surface to mine; however, if unknown at time of severance lessee owns but cannot substantially interfere

§ 1.3 MINERAL ESTATE: DEFINITION 3

with surface owner's estate; Gladys City Co. v. Amoco Production Co., 528 F.Supp. 624 (Tex.1981) (salt), held that to constitute a "valuable" mineral, value must have been known at time lease was executed. Court distinguished a "valuable" mineral from an "other mineral."

13. Gelfius v. Chapman, 118 Ill. App.3d 290, 73 Ill.Dec. 798, 454 N.E.2d 1047 (1983), "oil, gas and other mineral" did not include coal.

14. Spurlock v. Santa Fe Railroad Co., 143 Ariz. 469, 694 P.2d 299 (App. 1984), certiorari denied ___ U.S. ___, 105 S.Ct. 3513, 87 L.Ed.2d 642 (1985) (helium) where mineral is unknown at the time of the severance, mineral is owned by owner of mineral estate but cannot be removed by methods that substantially interfere with the surface owner's estate; United States Steel Corp. v. Hoge, 503 Pa. 140, 468 A.2d 1380 (1983) (coalbed gas) held that the right to drill and operate for oil and gas included the right to the coalbed gas, which could be removed by methods which do not inflict substantial damage on the coal; Martin v. Schneider, 622 S.W.2d 620 (Tex.Civ.App.1981), court held that in determining whether uranium was included in the reservation of a "royalty in other minerals," where uranium was found at a depth of 20 feet and at an average depth of 55–66 feet, the surface destruction test would not be applied as the rights of a royalty owner do not include the right to produce. However, reservation in deed of "all mineral rights" was held to include lignite rights, although removal would cause surface damage by strip mining in Continental Group v. Allison, 404 So.2d 428 (La.1981), certiorari denied 456 U.S. 906, 102 S.Ct. 1753, 72 L.Ed.2d 163 (1982).

59. In an interesting non-application of Reed II, Martin v. Schneider, 622 S.W.2d 620 (Tex.Civ.App.1981), held that in determining whether uranium was included in the reservation of a "royalty in other minerals," where uranium was found at a depth of 20 feet and at an average depth of 55–66 feet, the surface destruction test would not be applied as the rights of a royalty owner do not include the right to produce.

65.5 691 S.W.2d 586 (Tex.1985); Storm Assoc., Inc. v. Texaco, Inc., 645 S.W.2d 579 (Tex.Civ.App.1982), affirmed 691 S.W.2d 586 (1985). Could the Acker-Reed rule be avoided by conveyance of the mineral estate to the owner of the surface estate, followed by a re-conveyance of the minerals, where this might be possible under the circumstances?

In Spurlock v. Santa Fe Railroad Co., 143 Ariz. 469, 694 P.2d 299 (App.1984), certiorari denied ___ S.Ct. ___, 105 S.Ct. 3513, 87 L.Ed.2d 642 (1985), the court held that where the substance was specifically named, or known to exist at the time of the severance, the mineral owner had full right to remove the substance, subject to the reasonable use doctrine, as in Moser. However, where the substance was not known at the time of the severance (and obviously not specifically named in the instrument) the mineral substance would be owned by the mineral estate owner, but it could not be removed if it would cause substantial damage or injury to the surface owner's estate.

§ 1.3 Nature of Ownership of the Mineral Estate

19. In Bagby v. Bredthauer, 627 S.W.2d 190 (Tex.Civ.App.1981), where grantor reserved a term royalty interest, the court held that it did not violate the rule against perpetuities by treating the reservation as creating a new interest in the grantor and leaving the possibility of reverter in the grantee. This in effect changed the grantee's interest from an executory interest to a reversion. As the latter is a vested interest the rule was not violated. The case is one of several cases dealing with reserved term interests as not violating the rule. A similar case was that of Earle v. International Paper Co., 429 So.2d 989 (Ala.1983) which also held a reserved term mineral interest did not violate the rule against perpetuities, using a strained application of common law rules as to future interests, in that the grantor owned a fee simple determinable and the grantee a reversion. Rather than twist the common law rules relating to future interests, a better approach would be to treat such interests as *sui generis* and fashion a rule of construction related to the realities of such transactions.

Cali v. De Mattei, 121 Ill.App.3d 623, 77 Ill.Dec. 262, 460 N.E.2d 121 (1984), after stating the technical common law distinction, ignored the technical distinction and held that the intent was to reserve an interest to the grantors where the term "excepting" was used.

22. Where the mineral and surface have been severed, they are normally treated separately. However, two cases have held that where surface ownership has been affected by accretion and erosion the severed mineral estate is likewise affected. Jackson v. Burlington Northern, Inc., ___ Mont. ___, 667 P.2d 406 (1983), citing and following Nilson v. Tenneco Oil Co., 614 P.2d 36 (Okl. 1980).

23. In Stucki v. Parker, 108 Idaho 929, 703 P.2d 693 (1985), it was held that a conveyance of "all the surface rights in and to * * *. The Grantor herein, however, reserves unto itself all phosphate and phosphate rock etc. * *," conveyed the surface less phosphate only, and was not a conveyance of the surface and minerals to grantee. Also see Reidt v. Rock Island, 521 P.2d 79 (Okl.1974) as to the meaning of "surface" cited in Stucki.

47. T-Vestco Litt-Vada v. Lu-Cal One Oil Co., 651 S.W.2d 284 (Tex.Civ. App.1983) n.r.e. (net proceeds interest was similar to a net profits or overriding royalty interest, and being a nonpossessory interest, the owner could not bring an action in trespass to try title, an ejectment action).

CHAPTER 2

CREATION OF INTERESTS IN THE OIL AND GAS MINERAL ESTATE BY THE LANDOWNER

Table of New or Retitled Sections

Sec.
2.9 Dormant Mineral Acts.

---

§ 2.2 Attributes of the Mineral Estate—The Power to Lease

(D) Standard of Exercise of the Power

38. Manges v. Guerra, 673 S.W.2d 180 (Tex.1984).

47. However, see Manges v. Guerra, 673 S.W.2d 180 (Tex.1984) wherein the court characterized the power as creating a fiduciary relationship; Comanche Land & Cattle Co., Inc. v. Adams, 688 S.W.2d 914 (Tex.Civ.App.1985) (utmost good faith).

48. Manges v. Guerra, 673 S.W.2d 180 (Tex.1984); Comanche Land & Cattle Co., Inc. v. Adams, 688 S.W.2d 914 (Tex.Civ.App.1985).

51. See Wells v. Berry, 434 So.2d 982 (Fla.App.1983) where suit brought by owner of term royalty interest to force holder of right to lease before the end of the term of the deed, was held to state a cause of action. The case contains a good discussion of authorities and cases as to when such an implied covenant may exist. The court summerized the case with the following statement: "In the final analysis, whether to imply a covenant in a particular instrument not otherwise specific on the subject depends upon a determination of the intent of the parties as gleaned from the circumstances surrounding the transaction. By itself, the mere absence of language expressly imposing the duty will not preclude an implication in the proper case."

In Manges v. Guerra, 673 S.W.2d 180 (Tex.1984) it was held that the holder of the right to lease had abused the power by leasing to himself after mortgaging the mineral interests subject to the power and thereby effectively removing the interests from competitive leasing. The lease was cancelled. Actual and punitive damages were awarded. The court reversed an order removing the defendant as holder of the power, on the basis that plaintiffs had elected damages as a remedy. Removal does not seem foreclosed as a remedy by the opinion. The court discussed the nature of the duty of the holder of the power to lease, as follows:

"The duty of utmost good faith owed by an executive has been settled since Schlitter v. Smith * * * That standard has been repeated (citations omitted) * * *." The fiduciary duty arises from the relationship of the parties and not from the contract. * * While a contract or deed may create the relationship, the duty of the executive arises from the relationship and not from express or implied terms of the contract or deed. That duty requires the holder of the executive right, Manges in this case, to acquire for the non-executive every benefit that he exacts for himself. R. Hemingway, The Law of Oil and Gas, Sec. 2.2(D) (2d ed.1983).

"In our opinion Manges' conduct amounted to a breach of his fiduciary duty as found by the jury in making the lease to himself, in agreeing upon a $5 nominal bonus for 25,911.62 acres of land, and in dealing with the entire mineral interest so that he received benefits that the non-executives did not receive. His taking one hundred percent of seven-eighths of the three producing wells, his taking one-half of the working interest, free and clear of costs, by his farm-out to Schero, was also the receipt of special benefits that the non-executives did not receive. Upon the basis of his receipt of special benefits, we must cancel the lease * * *."

59. Manges v. Guerra, 673 S.W.2d 180 (Tex.1984); Comanche Land & Cattle Co., Inc. v. Adams, 688 S.W.2d 914 (Tex.Civ.App.1985).

§ 2.5 Attributes of the Mineral Estate—The Right to Royalty

(A) Nature of Royalty Interests Prior to Lease

4. Denney v. Teel, 688 P.2d 803 (Okl. 1984), royalty from future leases is an interest in realty and its nature is governed by the law of the situs; Estate of Sellers v. Home State Bank, 7 Kan. App.2d 48, 637 P.2d 483 (1982), unaccrued royalty is an interest in real estate.

(B) Nature of Royalty Interests After Lease

12. Barby v. Cabot Corp., 598 F.Supp. 407 (D.C.Okl.1983) Lessor could not receive royalty in kind on condensate from a gas well on 5 leases which only provided for cash royalty on gas, and as to the remaining lease, could have royalty in kind but lessor would have to provide own facilities.

(C) Separation of Royalty Interests from the Mineral Estate—Nature and Duration of Such Interests

29. J.M. Huber Corp. v. Square Enterprises, Inc., 645 S.W.2d 410 (Tenn. App.1982), held that a nonparticipating royalty does not violate the Rule against Perpetuities. The case contains a good discussion of cases in this area.

§ 2.7 Attributes of the Mineral Estate—Interests Created When Fractional Interests Are Conveyed or Reserved

(G) The Effect of the Quantum of the Interest Conveyed or Reserved on the Mineral-Royalty Distinction, and Problems Occurring as to the Quantum of Production to Which a Mineral or Royalty Owner May be Entitled

(1) Royalty Consequences

74. Tiller v. Tiller, 685 S.W.2d 456 (Tex.Civ.App.1985) where instrument provided for "$1/9$ of the $1/8$ royalty" held that it was a $1/72$ royalty interest, and that would not be entitled to $1/9$ of the $1/5$ royalty provided for in later leases; it was not an "of royalty" interest.

(H) Effect of a Conveyance or Reservation of a Mineral Interest, Less the Right to Bonus, Delay Rentals and the Power to Lease

75. Dow Chemical Co. v. Warmack, 281 Ark. 77, 661 S.W.2d 376 (1983). In 1962 a royalty deed printed form was used to convey "all the oil, gas and other minerals" with a reservation of the right to lease, bonus and delay rentals, together with a typewritten clause that stated the parties intended to convey "10 royalty acres, non-participating." In question was bromine. The court held that the deed conveyed a non-participating royalty interest only as to the oil and gas. The deed conveyed a full mineral interest in the bromine and all other minerals. The rationale was that the reservation of the right to lease, bonus and delay rentals only applied to oil and gas.

HNG Fossil Fuels Co. v. Roach, 99 N.M. 216, 656 P.2d 879 (1982) held that the term "non-participating" removed the right to bonuses, delay rentals, the right to lease, and the right of ingress to explore for oil and gas from the conveyance; however, parol evidence was used to determine if the non-participating interest was a royalty interest or a non-participating mineral interest.

(I) Effect of a Conveyance or Reservation of a Mineral Interest, Less the Right to Bonus and Delay Rentals

89. Accord: Anderson v. Mayberry, 661 P.2d 535 (Okl.App.1983).

92. Accord: Anderson v. Mayberry, 661 P.2d 535 (Okl.App.1983).

95. Accord: Diamond Shamrock Corp. v. Cone, 673 S.W.2d 310 (Tex.Civ. App.1984).

98. In Andrus v. Kahao, 414 So.2d 1199 (La.1981) it was held that it was a rule of property in Louisiana that the bonus and rentals belong to the holder of the right to lease where no mention is made.

§ 2.8 Attributes of the Mineral Estate—Conveyances of Royalty and Mineral Interests for a Limited Term

1. See § 6.4(B), note 58, infra.

3. For a discussion of cases dealing with the rule against perpetuities and reserved term interests, see § 1.3 and discussion note 19.

§ 2.9 Dormant Mineral Acts

Several states have passed dormant mineral acts. These acts will terminate severed mineral interests where for a stated length of time interest in the mineral estate has not been demonstrated by the mineral owner. Such interest may be by way of actual production, paying of taxes, filing an instrument of record with a statement of claim within a statutory grace period, etc. The leading case holding such statutes constitutional is Texaco v. Short, 454 U.S. 516, 102 S.Ct. 781, 701 L.Ed.2d 738 (1982) upholding the Indiana Act as constitutional in a 5–4 decision. The Court was mostly concerned with the retroactive nature of the Act. Other cases dealing with the Indiana Act are Kirby v. Ashland Oil Cnc., 463 N.E.2d 1127 (Ind.App.1984) discussing acts that will prevent lapse and citing the Michigan Act; and, McCoy v. Richards, 581 F.Supp. 143 (D.C.Ind.1983), order affirmed 771 F.2d 1108 (7th Cir.1985). Also see Riddleberger v. Chesapeake Western Ry.,

327 S.E.2d 663 (Va.1985), declaring part of Virginia statute unconstitutional.

CHAPTER 3

CONVEYANCES, PARTITION, AND ADVERSE POSSESSION OF THE MINERAL ESTATE

§ 3.1 Conveyances of the Mineral Estate—Description of Fractional Interests

(C) Description of Quantum of Interest—Percentage Interests and Mineral or Royalty Acre Interests

8. Thibodeaux v. American Land & Exploration, Inc., 450 So.2d 990 (La. App.1984), writ denied 458 So.2d 118 (1984) again demonstrates unanticipated problems that may arise from the use of "acre" interests. The conveyance stated that the interest in no event should be less than 11.8 royalty acres. However, a later lease was made with a royalty of $1/5$. The court refused rescission. The use of royalty acres is stated in the words of one of the witnesses: "Supple testified that the term 'royalty acres' is a commonly used industry term. He also stated that production distribution is based on the ownership of royalty acres which are derived by converting ordinary acreage into royalty acreage on the basis of the standard one-eighth ($1/8$) royalty, which was the fraction ordinarily reserved by owners leasing their land for oil production. Thibodeaux, however, reserved a one-fifth royalty interest in the production under his lease with Stone Oil, thus, creating more royalty acreage on the land than would have existed under a one-eighth reservation. Harrison and Supple both calculated that the 20.5 acres owned by Thibodeaux and his children contained 47.1 royalty acres. In his deed to American Land Thidobeaux transferred one-half of his one-half interest, or one-fourth of the total (or 11.8) royalty acres."

§ 3.2 Problems Commonly Encountered in Conveyances or Reservations of Fractional Interests in the Mineral Estate

Read at bottom of p. 108:

.5 Goin v. Eater, 107 Ill.App.3d 887, 63 Ill.Dec. 496, 438 N.E.2d 234 (1982) held that an exception of "all coal, oil, gas and other minerals formerly reserved" only excepted from the grant minerals that grantor did not own, and that all of grantor's minerals were conveyed. Mueller v. Stangeland, 340 N.W.2d 450 (N.D.1983) held that the following language typed into the warranty clause: "all minerals ... not now owned by the vendor as disclosed by the records in the Office of the Register of Deeds ...," only modified the warranty and did not show an intent to reserve minerals from the grant, to grantor.

In Oklahoma an intent to reserve an interest must be shown by "apt language," Echolustee Oil Co. v. Johnson, 153 Okl. 92, 3 P.2d 227 (1931); Jarrett v. Moore, 159 Okl. 93, 14 P.2d 390 (1932). Both cases involved language in or at the end of the warranty clause in the form of "except an _____ interest." Where the wording in the form of "reserve to grantor" is used it has been held that the intent to reserve an interest is manifested. Westcott v. Bozarth, 202 Okl. 149, 211 P.2d 258 (1949); Erwin v. Poole, 446 P.2d 601 (Okl.1968); Barber v. Flynn, 628 P.2d 1151 (Okl. 1981).

(B) Reservations or Exceptions—Effect of False Recitals of Fact, and Effect of Those Made in Favor of Third Parties

5. Little v. Linder, 651 S.W.2d 895 (Tex.Civ.App.1983), reservation to "grantors ... heirs and assigns," did not serve to reserve interest to grantor wife who was a stranger to the title.

(D) The Effect of an Exception or Reservation in an Instrument in Which Grantor has Breached His Covenant of Warranty by Overconveyance—After Acquired Title and the Doctrine of Duhig v. Peavy-Moore Lumber Co.

28. Morgan v. Roberts, 434 So.2d 738 (Ala.1983); Peterson v. Simpson, 286 Ark. 177, 690 S.W.2d 720 (1985); Sibert v. Kubas, 357 N.W.2d 495 (N.D. 1984), changing the North Dakota Rule.

31. Blanton v. Bruce, 688 S.W.2d 908 (Tex.Civ.App.1985), applying Duhig to deed without warranty, citing the Text; cf. Peterson v. Simpson, 286 Ark. 177, 690 S.W.2d 720 (1985), adopts Duhig as to warranty deeds but rejects as to quick claim deeds, citing Hill v. Gilliam, 284 Ark. 383, 682 S.W.2d 737 (1985).

32. Sibert v. Kubas, 357 N.W.2d 495 (N.D.1984), constructive notice does not preclude Duhig.

§ 3.3 Partition of the Mineral Estate

(A) Basis for Judicial Partition of Concurrently Owned Interests in the Minerals

2. Oklahoma has enacted 12 O.S. § 1501 (1984) which provides that where the mineral estate is being partitioned that the petition shall specify and plaintiff shall establish by the preponderance of the evidence that (a) one or more co-owners are frustrating the development objectives of plaintiff for the mineral estate, and (2) that an order of the Oklahoma Corporation Commission to pool and develop would not effectuate a realization of the development objectives.

(B) Elements Necessary for Partition of the Mineral Estate

(2) The Concept of Estates of Equal Dignity or of Right to Possession

26. But see Dixieland Distilling Co. v. Keil, 664 S.W.2d 527 (Ky.App.1984) allowing partition of full severed mineral estate without joinder of surface owners, and commenting that defense of surface ownership exists where surface is unsevered from ownership of a part of the minerals.

27. See note 26, supra.

38. Witt v. Sheffer, 6 Kan.App.2d 868, 636 P.2d 195 (1981) held under the Kansas statute K.S.A. 60–1003 that all of the mineral estate may be partitioned, including personalty (oil and gas leases in Kansas), and that defendant in partition action that owned $100/320$ of the mineral estate could partition entire tract including 10 acres on which well was situated. Plaintiff wanted to partition all except the 10 acre tract.

In Cox v. Lasley, 639 P.2d 1219 (Okl. 1981) co-tenant of mineral estate and also owner of interest in leasehold had right to partition where other co-tenant did not plead or show hardship, fraud or oppression. Here plaintiff tried to partition and divest the Department of the Interior of jurisdiction over Indian

§ 3.5 CONVEYANCES, PARTITION, POSSESSION

lands under the lease, so that salt water could be injected on adjoining lands.

§ 3.5 Adverse Possession—Actual Possession of the Minerals

(A) Acts of Actual Possession

5. Accord, Hunt Oil Co. v. Moore, 656 S.W.2d 634 (Tex.Civ.App.1983), where it was held that unit production did not constitute actual adverse possession where the wells were located on other tracts of land.

(B) Rights Acquired—Claiming Under Color of Title

6. Only rights to coal mined could be acquired, no constructive possession of other minerals not loosened or actually mined. Thomason v. Mullinax, 403 So.2d 883 (Ala.1981). Also see Hurst v. Rice, 278 Ark. 94, 643 S.W.2d 563 (1982), where it was held that production of gas was not adverse to coal. Holding is limited to facts of case and court declines to generally hold whether or not adverse possession of one mineral can be adverse to others, where claim is made to all minerals.

9. See note 6, supra.

(C) Rights Acquired—Not Claiming Under Color of Title

Read following end of first paragraph in subsection (C):

11.5 See note 6, supra.

CHAPTER 4
TRESPASS, SURFACE AND SUB–SURFACE, AND THIRD PARTY CLAIMS

§ 4.1 The Geophysical Surface Trespasser

(A) The Right to Explore

3. Accord, Mustang Producing Co. v. Texaco, 754 F.2d 892 (10th Cir.1985), holding that the lessee's right to explore is not exclusive unless expressly made so in the lease.

(B) Surface Geophysical Exploration Where a Trespass is Involved

8. No right to damages was shown as to value of exploration rights and option to purchase a lease where only evidence of value was the mere willingness of trespasser to buy. Gulf Coast Real Estate Auction Co. v. Chevron Industries, Inc., 665 F.2d 574 (5th Cir. 1982).

(C) Surface Geophysical Exploration with No Physical Entry

19. In Ratliff v. Beard, 416 So.2d 307 (La.App.1982), writ denied 422 So.2d 154 (1982) it was held, *inter alia*, that aerial photography and viewing did not constitute a trespass or result in recoverable damages.

§ 4.2 The Geophysical Sub-Surface Trespasser

1. Winn v. Nilsen, 670 P.2d 588 (Okl.1983), lease term excludes first day and includes all of last day, i.e., lease dated 2/16/77 for a five year primary term, expires at midnight 2/16/82.

§ 4.3 Slander of Title Affecting Oil and Gas Interests

14. Zehner v. Post Oak Oil Co., 640 P.2d 991 (Okl.App.1981), (not released for publication by Oklahoma Supreme Court) where actual malace is shown, punitive damages are for the jury.

CHAPTER 5

THE OIL AND GAS LEASE—LEASES FROM OWNERS OF CONCURRENT, SUCCESSIVE, OR RESTRICTED INTERESTS

§ 5.1 Co-tenants

(A) Right of a Co-tenant to Develop and Explore

9. In Nelson v. Christianson, 343 N.W.2d 375 (N.D.1984) it was held that one co-tenant holding and entering under a deed of the whole tract from another co-tenant would constitute an ouster of other co-tenants. The court indicated that one co-tenant leasing from a third party of the entire tract for oil and gas, recording of affidavit of sole ownership and recording of contract of sale to entire tract would not constitute a hostile ouster. Acquisition of title by one co-tenant is presumed to be on behalf of all co-tenants, and constructive notice does not run to the other co-tenants. In this case there was no proof of acts of actual possession.

§ 5.2 Life Tenant and Remainderman

(A) Leases From a Life Tenant or a Remainderman

12. Hathorn v. Amoco Production Co., 472 So.2d 403 (Miss.1985), citing text.

13. See note 12, supra.

14. See note 12, supra.

§ 5.5 Landlord and Tenant

2. Oil and gas lease does not create relationship of landlord and tenant, and lessee can deny lessor's title. Cross v. Lowrey, 404 So.2d 645 (Ala.1981).

CHAPTER 6

THE OIL AND GAS LEASE—DURATION

§ 6.1 The Nature of an Oil and Gas Lease

34. An oil and gas lease in Kansas is not foreclosed by mortgage foreclosure unless provided for by statute, as an oil and gas lease is personalty in Kansas. Utica National Bank & Trust Co. v. Marney, 661 P.2d 1246 (Kan.1983).

§ 6.2 Classification of Oil and Gas Leases by Duration

5. Sidwell Oil and Gas Co., Inc. v. Lloyd, 230 Kan. 77, 630 P.2d 1107 (1981), is an example of mistaken creation of a no term lease, created by stating as the first delay rental payment date, the date that the three year primary term ended. Also see Federal Oil Co. v. Western Oil Co., cited in this note in main volume. Another common mistake that can create a no term lease, is where a lease is executed providing for a one year primary term. The parties do not strike the delay rental clause and provide for delay rentals with the first rental payment due on last day of the primary term.

§ 6.3 Keeping the Lease Alive During the Primary Term—The Delay Rental

(A) The Delay Rental—Payment Date

21. Where lessors wrongfully refused to accept last delay rental and repudiated the lease, lessee was relieved from any obligation to operate, pending judicial controversy over validity of lease. Tar Heel Energy Corporation v. Menking, 621 S.W.2d 450 (Tex.Civ.App. 1981), citing Kothman v. Boley, 158 Tex. 56, 308 S.W.2d 1 (1957).

(C) The Delay Rental—Notice of Assignment by the Mineral Owner

47. Both seller and buyer have equal responsibility to notify lessee of change of ownership. Brubaker v. Branine, 237 Kan. 488, 701 P.2d 929 (1985).

(E) The Delay Rental—Effect of Improper Payment

67. But cf. Latham v. Continental Oil Co., 558 F.Supp. 731 (D.C.Okl.1980) involved lease that originally covered 170 acres, recited as 160 acres. Lessee paid $17,000 for renewal lease which described 170 acres and provided for $170 delay rentals. Lessee paid $160 delay rentals as paid under original lease and lessors waited 6 weeks, until after payment date, to advise lessee that lease had terminated. Held: that the lease did not terminate and lessors had duty to advise lessee. Court seems to be applying general equity rules, but cites and relies upon cases where wrongful payment was prevented by acts of independent third parties.

§ 6.4 THE OIL AND GAS LEASE—DURATION

(F) The Delay Rental—Estoppel, Waiver, and Ratification of an Improper Payment by the Mineral Owner

91. In Kincaid v. Gulf Oil Corporation, 675 S.W.2d 250 (Tex.Civ.App.1984) writ ref., n.r.e., lease clause provided if a good faith effort was made to pay delay rental that the lease would not terminate but provision would be turned into an unconditional obligation, correctable after 30 days notice. It was held that the clause was valid and prevented lease from terminating where delay rental in correct amount was paid on last day but to wrong party.

Also see: Miami Oil Producers, Inc. v. Larson, ___ Mont. ___, 661 P.2d 1260 (1983), where notice clause required lessor, before bringing action "for any cause," to give notice to lessee. However, court held that clause did not apply to automatic termination of lease for non-production after primary term, or, to action on statute for release.

92. See note 91, supra.

93. But see Hove v. Atchison, 238 F.2d 819 (8th Cir.1956) where lessor found out lease covered additional acres and failed to notify lessee.

§ 6.4 Propelling the Lease Past the Primary Term and Keeping It Alive During the Secondary Term by Production of Oil or Gas—Definition of "Production"

(A) Production—Quantum of Production, i.e., Paying Quantities

18. See Pray v. Premium Petroleum Co., 662 P.2d 255 (Kan.1983) and Wrestler v. Colt, 233 Kan. 351, 644 P.2d 1342 (1983) "paying quantities" included by implication in oil and gas lease, where not expressly stated.

33. In Barby v. Singer, 648 P.2d 14 (Okl.1982) it was held that in determining whether production was in paying quantities, it was proper to consider the effect of a retroactive price increase under the Natural Gas Policy Act.

35. Pray v. Premier Petroleum Co., 233 Kan. 351, 662 P.2d 255 (1983), held that the cost of building a pipeline to the nearest market was not taken into account in determining whether production was in paying quantities, the costs were treated the same as costs of drilling and equipping a well.

(B) Production—Sporadic Production and Temporary Cessation of Production

48. In Pieszchalski v. Oslager, 128 Ill.App.3d 437, 83 Ill.Dec. 663, 470 N.E.2d 1083 (1984) the court distinguishes Gillespie v. Ohio Oil Co., cited in main text, which held that continuous minimal production was sufficient to keep lease alive after primary term, and lease terminated where minimal production was not continuous.

50. In Michigan Wisconsin Pipeline Co. v. Michigan National Bank, 118 Mich.App. 74, 324 N.W.2d 541 (1982) it was held that a lease did not terminate when awaiting the award, after the filing by the purchaser of the gas from the field of condemnation proceedings to condemn gas field for underground storage facilities, lessee ceased production except to maintain compressor and supply free gas to lessors, and that lessee had acted as a reasonable prudent operator.

Where production ceased during the determination of future use of tertiary recovery, where such recovery depended upon prospective but unassumed prospects and possibilities, such cessation was permanent and not temporary production, as production could not be resumed within a reasonable time. Wrestler v. Colt, 7 Kan.App.2d 553, 644 P.2d 1342 (1982).

51. Wagner v. Smith, 8 Ohio App.3d 90, 456 N.E.2d 523 (1982) held that where production ceased due to hole in casing allowing water to flood well in 1978, with attempted repairs in 1979, but no substantial efforts until 1981 after suit was filed, the actions of the

lessee were not conducted with due diligence and the lease terminated.

58. In Fransen v. Eckhardt, ___ P.2d ___ (Okl.1985) the Oklahoma Supreme Court apparently resolved the conflict between the two cases and held that actual production and receipt of benefits was necessary to constitute production to keep a term interest alive beyond the primary term of the deed. The court rejects the concept of "discovery" without marketing, which applies to oil and gas leases in Oklahoma, as to term interests. Although the court cites the text as supporting the result in the case, this is incorrect.

In Browning v. Griggsby, 657 S.W.2d 821 (Tex.Civ.App.1983), the court held that a term interest was indefeasibly vested when production existed on the date in the following clause, " * * * shall expire on October 25, 1958, unless at that time the above named minerals are being produced from the premises in paying quantities. The court would not imply a "thereafter" clause.

59. See Fransen v. Eckhart, note 58, supra.

§ 6.5 Propelling the Lease Past the Primary Term and Keeping It Alive During the Secondary Term—Contractual Substitutes for Production—The Nature of Shut-In Royalties

(A) Shut-In Royalties—Time of Payment

10. However, Oklahoma treats term interests differently than oil and gas leases, see Fransen v. Eckhardt, note 58, supra.

16. In Mayers v. Sanchez-O'Brien Minerals, 670 S.W.2d 704 (Tex.Civ.App. 1984) shut in payment period determined by date on shut in royalty receipt. Case is interesting case showing interrelationship between the various clauses in the lease, as the court held that the lease was also maintained by actual production obtained timely under the 60 day continuous operations clause.

§ 6.7 Propelling the Lease Past the Primary Term by Operations—Commencement of Drilling Operations

2. Murphy v. Amoco Production Company, 590 F.Supp. 455 (D.C.N.D. 1984), example of activities of preparation for drilling short of spudding in that were sufficient. Cf. Sheffield v. Exxon Corporation, 424 So.2d 1297 (Ala. 1982) where activities of negotiation of sales contract, internal corporate authority to drill, which did not include physical acts on the land, were not sufficient.

Several cases may be compared where the lessee did not have a deep rig available at the end of the primary term: Son-Lin Farms, Inc. v. Dyco Petroleum Co., 589 F.Supp. 1 (D.C.Okl. 1982) where it was held that lessee acted as a reasonably prudent operator, where within ten days of the end of the primary term lessee began drilling about 1–2 feet per day for two months and then moved a deep rig on the land and drilled to completion as a producer. In holding that the lease did not terminate the court stated that the intent of the lessee at the date of termination of the primary term was controlling, that the delay was caused by the inability of lessee to find a suitable rig, and that the lessee had proceeded under the circumstances as a reasonably prudent operator would have proceeded.

Herl v. Legleiter, 9 Kan.App.2d 15, 668 P.2d 200 (1983), where the court held that the lease terminated, where lessee built an access road, staked the location, constructed pits, and delivered mud, casing, etc. to the lease, but did not own a rig and had made no contract to obtain one. The court expressly did not decide whether the well must be spudded in prior to the end of the primary term; the difference, if any, between clauses providing for "commence to drill a well," "commence operations to drill a well," and "commence drilling operations;" or, the result if a lessee commenced drilling operations in good faith, with rig committed, and then could not carry through promptly be-

§ 6.7 THE OIL AND GAS LEASE—DURATION

cause of weather or other circumstances beyond his control.

Wilds v. Universal Resources Corporation, 662 P.2d 303 (Okl.1983) where Lessee was drilling with a rathole drilling rig at the end of the primary term. A business decision was made to use an available rotary rig at another location first. Directions were given to only drill a few feet per day. After 21 days the well had been drilled to a depth of 67 feet. The case was remanded to determine whether the lessee was in good faith and had acted with due diligence. It is interesting that the court does not discuss whether or not the lessee is in good faith due to a business decision to first use an available rig at another location.

The cases raise the question as to the good faith and intent of the lessee operating at the end of the primary term. Is a reasonably prudent operator more or less reasonably prudent where it does not foresee the necessity for securing a rig near the end of the primary term, or, makes a decision to use an available rig elsewhere for the overall benefit of its business?

14. See note 12, supra.

17. See note 12, supra.

CHAPTER 7

THE OIL AND GAS LEASE—ROYALTY AND OTHER PARTICULAR LEASE CLAUSES

§ 7.2 Royalty on Gas Produced From an Oil Well—Casinghead Gas and Gasoline

(A) Where No Clause Provision

2. For a modern case dealing with the basic nature of casinghead gas, see Martin v. Kostner, 231 Kan. 315, 644 P.2d 430 (1982), which dealt with the nature of casinghead gas in connection with the pooling of "gas rights." The court followed Lone Star Gas v. Stine, see text at footnote 5, Sec. 7.3, infra, and held that casinghead gas could only include gas coming out of solution, and that all other gas over this amount was gas well gas. In the case the well produced 34 million cubic feet of gas, and the court held that not more than 6 million cubic feet could have come out of the oil. The question of what constitutes casinghead gas has become the center of litigation concerning gas production in west Texas. The litigation has become known as the "white oil" cases. The ownership of approximately 27 billion dollars of reserves is at stake.

A counter argument to the concept of the Kostner case is that casinghead gas should be determined under the original reservoir conditions. Although some case law exists as to the nature of an oil well, gas well, and casinghead gas, virtually all of the litigation concerns actions of state regulation and conservation commissions in classifying wells for production and the prevention of waste. Slight case law exists dealing conceptually with the nature of oil and gas wells and or casinghead gas from the standpoint of ownership of the products, apart from lease definitions.

§ 7.3 Royalty on Liquid Components Produced From a Gas Well—Condensate and Distillate

5. See footnote 2., § 7.2(A), supra.

§ 7.4 Compensation for Royalty Based Upon "Market Value," "Market Price," and "Proceeds"

(E) Market Price or Value Royalty Clauses and the Long-Term Gas Sales Contract Problem

25. In Hillard v. Stephens, 276 Ark. 545, 637 S.W.2d 581 (1982), the Arkansas court adopted the approach of the Oklahoma court in Tara, that the market price was the price provided for in the long term contract, following and citing Henry v. Ballard & Cordell Corp., 401 So.2d 600 (La.App.1981) affirmed 418 So.2d 1334 (1982). However, cf. Diamond Shamrock Corp. v. Harris, 284 Ark. 270, 681 S.W.2d 317 (1984) where the court determined that market value was the current market price, rather than the price in the long term gas contract, where the contract was entered into 6 years before the lease was executed and the lessee had no notice or knowledge of the prior gas contract.

Although the Ballard case, above, seems to indicate that Louisiana would follow the contract price rule, the case was distinguished on its facts in the later Louisiana case of Shell Oil Co. v. Williams, 428 So.2d 798 (La.1983) which adopts the Vela rule. The court held "that market value must be determined by comparable sales in quality which also involve the legal characteristics of the gas, that is, whether it is sold on a regulated or unregulated market. Intrastate and interstate gas are not comparable in quality. They are conceptually and legally different. Also see note 38, infra.

28. Another case dealing with the meaning of the terms "at the well," used "off the premises," and dealing with costs chargable to the royalty interests, is Piney Woods School v. Shell Oil Co., 726 F.2d 225 (5th Cir.1984), rehearing denied 750 F.2d 69 (5th Cir. 1984), certiorari denied ___ U.S. ___, 105 S.Ct. 1868, 85 L.Ed.2d 161 (1985). The court stated:

"We conclude that the purpose is to distinguish between gas sold in the form in which it emerges from the well, and gas to which value is added by transportation away from the well or by processing after the gas is produced. The royalty compensates the lessor for the value of the gas at the well, that is, the value of the gas after the lessee fulfills its obligation under the lease to produce gas at the surface, but before the lessee adds to the value of this gas by processing or transporting it. When the gas is sold at the well the parties to the lease accept a good-faith sale price as the measure of value at the well. But when the gas is sold for a price that reflects value added to the gas after production, the sale price will not necessarily reflect the market value of the gas at the well. Accordingly, the lease bases royalty for this gas not on actual proceeds but on market value.

" 'At the well' therefore describes not only location but quality as well. Market value at the well means market value before processing and transportation, and gas is sold at the well if the price paid is consideration for the gas as produced but not for processing and transportation." * * * Based on the foregoing discussion, we conclude that the gas sold by Shell was not "sold at the well," within the meaning of the lease, even though the sale contracts provide that title to the gas passes on or near the leased premises.

"There is no need to question that, under the sale contract, title passed in the field. But the simple passage of title does not control whether the gas was 'sold at the well' within the meaning of the leases. In the leases, 'at the well' refers to both location and quality: gas is 'sold at the well' only if its value has not been increased before sale by transportation or processing. This is plainly not the case here."

38. In Matzen v. Cities Service Oil Co., 233 Kan. 846, 667 P.2d 337 (1983), certiorari dismissed ___ U.S. ___, 106 S.Ct. 20, 87 L.Ed.2d 698 (1985) the court held that evidence of regulated prices was competent to show value and that the highest federally regulated rate in the Hugoton field without regard to vintaging (old gas or new gas) should be used. The case contains a good discussion of cases. Also see note 25, supra.

(F) Expenses of Transportation and Preparation for Market

46. In Martin v. Glass, 571 F.Supp. 1406 (D.C.Tex.1983), affirmed 736 F.2d 1524 (5th Cir.1984) it was held that compression costs were properly charged against royalty and overriding royalty owners. The court stated that post-production costs are properly deductible from royalty and that the wellhead is the dividing point. Here compression was necessary to put gas into marketable condition. The case contains a good discussion of cases and alternative theories. The question of deduction of compression and transportation charges from royalty interests, where no mention of such charges is contained in the royalty clause of the lease, has become more frequently litigated as such charges and deductions are increasingly deducted from royalty interests. Also see discussion in footnote 24, supra.

§ 7.5 Division and Transfer Orders

(A) Nature of the Division Order

2. Shutts v. Phillips Petroleum Co., 235 Kan. 195, 679 P.2d 1159 (1984), affirmed in part, reversed in part ___ U.S. ___, 105 S.Ct. 2965, 86 L.Ed.2d 628 (1985), interest was payable on royalties suspended pending determination of lawful rates by FPC, as the funds remained in control and available for the use of the gas producer or purchaser. The division order clauses that royalties were payable "without interest" did not change the obligation of the lessee to pay interest, as can't change lease obligations by division order in Kansas. Also see Wortman v. Sun Oil Co., 236 Kan. 266, 690 P.2d 385 (1984) certiorari granted and judgment vacated ___ U.S. ___, 106 S.Ct. 40, 88 L.Ed.2d 33 (1985).

(B) Effect of the Division Order

17. The Kansas view is that lease provisions cannot be changed by the division order. See Maddox v. Gulf Oil Co. cited in main text, and Holmes v. Kewanee Oil Co., 233 Kan. 544, 664 P.2d 1335 (1983), certiorari denied ___ U.S. ___, 106 S.Ct. 322, 88 L.Ed.2d 305 (1985), where lease provided for payment of gas royalty of "gross proceeds at the prevailing market rate." Held that the division order could not change the current market value obligation of the lease clause, and that stripper well gas price could be considered. The court also held that receipt of a lesser amount of royalty by lessor did not constitute an estoppel and that prejudgment interest was not properly recoverable as action concerned an unliquidated amount.

Also see Schaffer v. Tenneco Oil Co., 278 Ark. 511, 647 S.W.2d 446 (1983), where the terms of the division order differed from the lease and royalty owner refused to sign division order. It was held that lease was not subject to cancellation for failure to pay royalty, however, lessee had obligation to pay royalty with accrued interest. The court did not discuss the issue, but the effect of the case is that the lessee has a duty to pay royalty even though lessor does not sign the division order or a stipulation of interest. The case is of some importance due to the fact that in some states like Texas, where it is held that the division order can change the lease provisions until revoked, a growing number of royalty owners are refusing to sign division orders changing the royalty provisions of the lease and also where they provide for transportation and other charges not provided for in the lease.

§ 7.7 Description and Mother-Hubbard Clause

6. Whithead v. Johnston, 467 So.2d 240 (Ala.1985).

13. Whithead v. Johnston, 467 So.2d 240 (Ala.1985) is a case of first impression in Alabama concerning the mother-hubbard clause. The clause read: "This lease also covers and includes, in addition to that above described, all land if any, contiguous or adjacent to or adjoining the land above described and (a) owned or claimed by Lessor by limitation, prescription, possession, reversion, or unrecorded instrument, or (b) as to which Lessor has a preference right of acquisition." The court held that the clause was valid and served to include a one-acre tract, acquired by adverse possession, adjacent to a five-acre tract. The text was cited by the dissent.

§ 7.11 The Force Majeure Clause

16. In Trinidad Petroleum Corp. v. Pioneer Natural Gas Co., 416 So.2d 290 (La.App.1982), writ denied 422 So.2d 154 (1982) it was held that the force majeure clause did not serve to protect the lessee where a well blew out, as the lessee could have drilled on other lease lands and saved the lease.

§ 7.12 The Free Gas Clause

16. Stapleton v. Columbia Gas Transmission Corp., 2 Ohio App.3d 15, 440 N.E.2d 575 (1981).

20. Anadarko Production Co. v. Taylor, 535 F.Supp. 103 (D.C.Kan.1982), reversed 726 F.2d 1474 (10th Cir.1984), limited to producing formations at time of agreement.

22. Accord: Stapleton v. Columbia Gas Transmission Corp., 2 Ohio App.3d 15, 440 N.E.2d 575 (1981), did not run to subdivided tracts where clause was to benefit "the mansion house on the premises."

23. Accord: Post v. Tenneco Co., 278 Ark. 527, 648 S.W.2d 42 (1983) where gas taken from lessor's land through unit well on non-lease tract, lessor could get gas for principal dwelling. Location of gas well was immaterial.

§ 7.13 Pooling and the Pooling Clause

(B) Basis and Authority of the Lessee to Pool

10. Where lessees formed leasehold unit from leases which had no pooling or unitization provisions and which lessors did not ratify, it was held that unit production from off lease unit tract, did not keep lease alive. Belden v. Tri-Star Producing Co., Inc., 106 Ill.App.3d 192, 62 Ill.Dec. 129, 435 N.E.2d 927 (1982).

14. Asberry v. Saint Joseph Petroleum Co., 653 S.W.2d 412 (Tenn.App. 1983).

15. Heath v. Fellows, 526 F.Supp. 723 (D.C.Okl.1981), pooling on last day of primary term not necessarily in bad faith.

24. Partial pooling is valid as to those in pool, where not all royalty owners joined. The court did not follow Guaranty National Bank case cited in main text. Heath v. Fellows, 526 F.Supp. 723 (D.C.Okl.1981).

25. In Brown v. Getty Resources Oil, Inc., 626 S.W.2d 810 (Tex.Civ.App.1981) it was held that owner of right to lease had no right to pool non-participating royalty interests. Where the royalty owners did not execute division order or demand royalty on a unit basis, royalty interest was not pooled.

28. In Shelton v. Andres, 122 Ill. App.3d 1089, 78 Ill.Dec. 430, 462 N.E.2d 549 (1984), affirmed 106 Ill.2d 153, 87 Ill.Dec. 954, 478 N.E.2d 311 (1985) owners of term mineral interest, together with other mineral and royalty owners entered into unit agreement for secondary recovery operations. The unit well was located off the tract in which the term mineral interest was located. Although owner of reversion under term grant did not enter into or ratify the unit, it was held that production maintained the term interest past the end of the term. The result is based partly on an Illinois statute and partly on the wording of the habendum clause of the term deed which read: "until when said production of oil on said described real estate ceases production."

(D) The Effect of Production and Operations Within the Unit Upon Acreage Within and Outside of the Unit

45. Accord: Jones v. Bronco Oil & Gas Co., 446 So.2d 611 (Ala.1984); Ego Oil Co. v. Garner, 115 Ill.App.3d 82, 70 Ill.Dec. 902, 450 N.E.2d 375 (1983), where unitized to "X" depth, unit production held part of lease outside of unit, i.e., below depth as well as above depth; Morgan v. Mobil Oil Corp., 556 F.Supp. 108 (D.C.Kan.1983); Asberry v. Saint Joseph Petroleum Co., 653 S.W.2d 412 (Tenn.App.1983) shut in gas royalty payment was constructive unit production and kept lease alive after end of primary term.

46. Contractual pugh clause does not apply to units formed by virtue of forced pooling statute, Bibler Bros. Timber Corp. v. Tojac Minerals, Inc., 281 Ark. 431, 664 S.W.2d 472 (1984).

CHAPTER 8

COVENANTS OF THE LESSEE TO PROTECT, DEVELOP, AND ADMINISTER THE LEASE

§ 8.3 Implied Covenants to Develop the Lease—After Production Is Acquired

(B) Reasonable Diligence of the Lessee

Read in connection with the first sentence in the full paragraph on page 419:

13.5 In Graefe & Graefe v. Beaver Mesa Exploration, 635 P.2d 900 (Colo. App.1981), appeal after remand 695 P.2d 767 (1984), lease lands outside of well cancelled absolutely. The court did not mention notice or speculation, but found that there existed no intent to develop outside lands, quoting the Sauder case.

19. Abandonment requires physical relinquishment of possession and intent to abandon, Olsen v. Schwartz, 345 N.W.2d 33 (N.D.1984), and also see, Sorum v. Schwartz, 344 N.W.2d 73 (N.D. 1984). Rook v. James Russell Petroleum, Inc., 235 Kan. 6, 679 P.2d 158 (1984), was an unusual case where storage rights under an oil and gas lease were severed from the producing function. It was held that the lease, except for storage rights, could be cancelled for abandonment where production ceased for 15 years and equipment and power source had been neglected or removed from the lease. Lessee had not entered upon the lease since 1972.

(C) Exploration and Development of Other Areas and Formations Where Profitability Cannot Be Shown

26. Meaher v. Getty Oil Company, 450 So.2d 443 (Ala.1984), mentions the implied covenant of further exploration and holding for speculative purposes; Byrd v. Bradham, 655 S.W.2d 366 (Ark. 1983), lease subject to outright cancellation where no acts for 28 years, court says in such circumstances it is not necessary to make demand where held for extended period, and also, not necessary to show lack of profitability; North York Land Association v. Byron Oil Industries, Inc., 695 P.2d 1188 (Colo. App.1985), citing Sauder, held that where lessee was holding the land for speculation, cancellation of the non-pooled area was proper without an alternative decree. The court here also found that a prudent operator would not explore or develop the leasehold now nor in the foreseeable future.

§ 8.7 Implied Covenant of Protection—Not to Depreciate the Lessor's Interest

1. Accord: Pinson v. Depco, Inc., 602 F.Supp. 27 (D.C.S.D.1985), citing text Section 8.7, follows Cook v. El Paso Natural Gas, cited in main text.

12. Accord: Seacat v. Mesa Petroleum Co., 561 F.Supp. 98 (D.C.Kan.1983).

§ 8.11 Remedies for Breach of Implied Covenants—Cancellation of Lease

3. Meaher v. Getty Oil Co., 450 So.2d 443 (Ala.1984); Slaughter v. Cities Service Oil Co., 660 S.W.2d 860 (Tex.Civ.App.1983).

CHAPTER 9

TRANSFERS BY THE LESSOR AND BY THE LESSEE

§ 9.1 Post-Lease Conveyances by the Lessor That Are Expressly "Subject to" an Outstanding Lease—Effect Upon the Quantum of Interests Conveyed

11. In Heyen v. Hartnett, 235 Kan. 117, 679 P.2d 1152 (1984), where the granting clause granted an undivided 1/16 mineral interest and the present lease clause granted 1/2 of royalties, the court found the deed to be ambiguous and allowed parole evidence to be considered, from this, together with the constructional preference favoring the grantee, the court held that the deed conveyed an undivided 1/2 mineral interest.

15. Alford v. Krum, 671 S.W.2d 870 (Tex.1984).

16. Cf. the later Texas Supreme Court case of Alford v. Krum, 671 S.W.2d 870 (Tex.1984), where the court discarded the Garrett v. Dils approach. In this case the granting clause granted an undivided 1/2 of 1/8 mineral interest. The present lease clause was consistent, granting 1/16 of royalty under any present lease. However, the future lease clause provided for a 1/2 mineral interest. The court found an irreconcilable conflict between the granting clause and the future lease clause and applied the granting clause. The court cites Sec. 9.1 from the text.

§ 9.5 The Entirety Clause

7. Brubaker v. Branine, 237 Kan. 488, 701 P.2d 929 (1985) indicates that in Kansas parties can include a provision for nonapportionment in a later deed and avoid apportionment under the entirety clause. In absence of the nonapportionment provision in the later deed, the entirety clause would be applied.

§ 9.8 Assignment of Oil and Gas Leases

Read following the last sentence in the first full paragraph on page 486:

4.5 It was held in Mai v. Youtsey, 231 Kan. 419, 646 P.2d 475 (1982) that where a lease was partially assigned as to separate tracts, each assignee had the right to use roads accross the entire lease. The assignment of the lease did not segregate the roads across the lease. However, where one assignee improved part of the road without benefit to other assignees, there existed no right to collect from the other non-improvers.

As to related problem of running a pipeline across unit lands to well tract, see Felmont Oil Corp. v. Cavanaugh, 300 Pa.Super. 520, 446 A.2d 1280 (1982).

§ 9.10 Divisibility of Covenants

2. Meaher v. Getty Oil Co., 450 So.2d 443 (Ala.1984), habendum clause is indivisible, absent a pugh clause.

(C) Divisibility of Implied Covenants

13. Kathe v. Jefferson, 109 Ill. App.3d 247, 64 Ill.Dec. 863, 440 N.E.2d 415 (1982), affirmed 97 Ill.2d 544, 74 Ill.Dec. 43, 455 N.E.2d 73 (1983), implied covenant to develop is indivisible, and compliance on any area bars cancellation as to the rest of non-developed lands. Cites § 9.10 from text.

§ 9.11 Relationship of Lessor, Lessee, and Owners of Non-Cost-Bearing Interests

(A) Creation of a Fiduciary Relationship

1. Three cases have been decided dealing with the nature of the relationship created by lessees execution of a joint operating agreement. Two of the cases held that the joint operating agreement, without more, creates a fiduciary relationship and that the duty of the operator to non-operators is not one of good faith and fair dealing, but of trust and confidence. See: Texas Oil and Gas Corp. v. Hawkins, 282 Ark. 268, 668 S.W.2d 16 (1984); and, Reserve Oil Co. v. Dixon, 711 F.2d 951 (C.A.10th 1983).

However, in Hamilton v. Texas Oil & Gas Corp., 648 S.W.2d 316 (Tex.1982) the court held mere execution of a joint operating agreement did not create a fiduciary relationship, that additional elements creating a joint venture must be present. See also Ayco Development Corp. v. G.E.T. Service Co., 616 S.W.2d 184 (Tex.1981). The view of the Texas court would seem to be the correct one.

5. Accord: Independent Gas & Oil Producers, Inc. v. Union Oil Co. of California, 669 F.2d 624 (C.A.10th 1982), also holding that modification clause did not violate the rule against perpetuities as old lease is extended, a new lease is not involved.

TABLE OF CASES

References are to Pages

Alford v. Krum, 24
Anadarko Production Co. v. Taylor, 21
Anderson v. Mayberry, 7
Andrus v. Kahao, 7
Asberry v. Saint Joseph Petroleum Co., 21
Ayco Development Corp. v. G.E.T. Service Co., 25
Bagby v. Bredthauer, 3
Barber v. Flynn, 10
Barby v. Cabot Corp., 6
Barby v. Singer, 15
Belden v. Tri-Star Producing Co., 21
Bibler Bros. Timber Corp. v. Tojac Minerals, Inc., 21
Blanton v. Bruce, 10
Brown v. Getty Resources Oil, Inc., 21
Browning v. Griggsby, 16
Brubaker v. Branine, 14, 24
Byrd v. Bradham, 22
Cali v. De Mattei, 4
Comanche Land & Cattle Co. v. Adams, 5, 6
Continental Group v. Allison, 3
Cook v. El Paso Natural Gas, 22
Cox v. Lasley, 10
Cross v. Lowrey, 13
Denney v. Teel, 6
Diamond Shamrock Corp. v. Cone, 7
Diamond Shamrock Corp. v. Harris, 18
Dixieland Distilling Co. v. Keil, 10
Dow Chemical Co. v. Warmack, 7
Earle v. International Paper Co., 3
Echolustee Oil Co. v. Johnson, 9
Ego Oil Co. v. Garner, 21
Estate of (see name of party)
Erwin v. Poole, 9
Federal Oil Co. v. Western Oil Co., 14
Felmont Oil Corp. v. Cavanaugh, 24
Fransen v. Eckhardt, 16
Friedman v. Texaco, 2
Gelfius v. Chapman, 2, 3
Gillespie v. Ohio Oil Co., 15
Gladys City Co. v. Amoco Production Co., 2, 3
Goin v. Eater, 9

Graefe & Graefe v. Beaver Mesa Exploration, 22
Gulf Coast Real Estate Auction Co. v. Chevron Industries, Inc., 12
Hamilton v. Texas Oil & Gas Corp., 25
Hathorn v. Amoco Production Co., 13
Heath v. Fellows, 21
Henry v. Ballard & Cordell Corp., 18
Herl v. Legleiter, 16
Heyen v. Hartnett, 24
Hill v. Gilliam, 10
Hillard v. Stephens, 18
HNG Fossil Fuels Co. v. Roach, 7
Holmes v. Kewanee Oil Co., 20
Hove v. Atchison, 15
Hunt Oil Co. v. Moore, 11
Hurst v. Rice, 11
Independent Gas & Oil Producers, Inc. v. Union Oil Co. of California, 25
J.M. Huber Corp. v. Square Enterprises, Inc., 6
Jackson v. Burlington Northern, Inc., 4
Jarrett v. Moore, 9
Jones v. Bronco Oil & Gas Co., 21
Kathe v. Jefferson, 25
Kincaid v. Gulf Oil Corporation, 15
Kirby v. Ashland Oil Inc., 7
Kothman v. Boley, 14
Latham v. Continental Oil Co., 14
Little v. Linder, 10
Lone Star Gas v. Stine, 18
McCoy v. Richards, 7
Maddox v. Gulf Oil Co., 20
Mai v. Youtsey, 24
Manges v. Guerra, 5, 6
Martin v. Glass, 19
Martin v. Kostner, 18
Martin v. Schneider, 2, 3
Matzen v. Cities Service Oil Co., 19
Mayers v. Sanchez-O'Brien Minerals, 16
Meaher v. Getty Oil Company, 22, 23, 24
Miami Oil Producers, Inc. v. Larson, 15
Michigan Wisconsin Pipeline Co. v. Michigan National Bank, 15
Morgan v. Mobil Oil Corp., 21

TABLE OF CASES

Morgan v. Roberts, 10
Moser v. United States Steel Co., 1, 2
Mueller v. Stangeland, 9
Murphy v. Amoco Production Company, 16
Mustang Producing Co. v. Texaco, 12
Nelson v. Christianson, 13
Nilson v. Tenneco Oil Co., 4
North York Land Association v. Byron Oil Industries, Inc., 22
Olsen v. Schwartz, 22
Peterson v. Simpson, 10
Pieszchalski v. Oslager, 15
Piney Woods School v. Shell Oil Co., 19
Pinson v. Depco, Inc., 22
Post v. Tenneco Co., 21
Pray v. Premium Petroleum Co., 15
Ratliff v. Beard, 12
Reidt v. Rock Island, 4
Reserve Oil Co. v. Dixon, 25
Richardson v. Citizens Gas & Coke Utility, 1
Riddleberger v. Chesapeake Western Ry., 7
Rook v. James Russell Petroleum, Inc., 22
Schaffer v. Tenneco Oil Co., 20
Seacat v. Mesa Petroleum Co., 22
Sellers, Estate of v. Home State Bank, 6
Sheffield v. Exxon Corporation, 16
Shell Oil Co. v. Williams, 19
Shelton v. Andres, 21
Shutts v. Phillips Petroleum Co., 20
Sibert v. Kubas, 10
Sidwell Oil and Gas Co. v. Lloyd, 14
Slaughter v. Cities Service Oil Co., 23
Son-Lin Farms, Inc. v. Dyco Petroleum Co., 16
Sorum v. Schwartz, 22
Spurlock v. Santa Fe Railroad Co., 2, 3
Stapleton v. Columbia Gas Transmission Corp., 21
Storm Assoc., Inc. v. Texaco, Inc., 2, 3
Stucki v. Parker, 4
T-Vestco Litt-Vada v. Lu-Cal One Oil Co., 4
Tar Heel Energy Corporation v. Menking, 14
TDC Engineering, Inc. v. Dunlap, 2
Texaco v. Short, 7
Texas Oil and Gas Corp. v. Hawkins, 25
Thibodeaux v. American Land & Exploration, Inc., 9
Thomason v. Mullinax, 11
Tiller v. Tiller, 6
Trinedad Petroleum Corp. v. Pioneer Natural Gas Co., 20
United States Steel Corp. v. Hoge, 2, 3
Utica National Bank & Trust Co. v. Marney, 14
Wagner v. Smith, 15
Wells v. Berry, 5
Westcott v. Bozarth, 9
Whithead v. Johnston, 20
Wilds v. Universal Resources Corporation, 17
Winn v. Nilsen, 12
Witt v. Sheffer, 10
Wortman v. Sun Oil Co., 20
Wrestler v. Colt, 15
Zehner v. Post Oak Oil Co., 12

†